50 states

89,000 localities

American diversity is reflected just as much in our governments as in our citizens. The key to understanding the similarities and differences across these governments lies in the comparative approach of *Governing States and Localities*.

A fresh, contemporary perspective on state and local politics, the fourth edition continues its coverage of the impact of the Great Recession, but with an eye toward the future. The economy is recovering, but budgets remain tight, the federal stimulus is ending, and the political climate is as polarized as ever. So what's next?

Find out in the pages of *Governing States and Localities*.

A blend of scholarship and news-style writing

- **Chapter-opening vignettes** pique student interest with headline-grabbing style through compelling stories that link to the broader themes of the chapter.

Finance

FILLING THE TILL AND PAYING THE BILLS

- What are the differences between progressive and regressive tax systems?
- Why are property taxes so important to communities?
- How does the federal government support state and local budgets?
- Are states' revenue and spending programs sustainable?

A combination of a poor economic conditions and bad fiscal decisions had been pushing Stockton, California, toward a financial cliff for years. On June 28, 2012, the city fell off the edge—right into the arms of Chapter 9 bankruptcy and the record books. It now has the dubious honor of being the largest city in U.S. history to go bust.

Stockton is far from being the only local government in the United States to find itself in financial straits in the past few years. The economy might have stabilized since the Great Recession, but it certainly has not fully recovered, and the coffers of some governments have simply not been able to support the wait for better economic times. Harrisburg, the capital of Pennsylvania, went into receivership in 2011. Montgomery County, the largest county in Alabama, filed for bankruptcy the same year. Central Falls, Rhode Island, became insolvent in 2010, and Detroit, Michigan, spent much of 2011 and 2012 barely one step ahead of its creditors.

Step up a level of government and the picture is just a little less alarming. No state has declared bankruptcy—at least not yet—and the budget situation in many states is actually improving compared to a few years ago. No one is popping champagne corks, though, because finances at the state level have only managed to advance from the catastrophic to

- **The Latest Research** boxes spotlight cutting-edge scholarship related to each chapter's discussion so students benefit from a deeper understanding of the social scientific study of states and localities.

The Latest Research

As discussed extensively in this chapter, the comparative method is an important tool used by scholars to understand how state-level differences translate into meaningful political and policy differences. A lot of these differences that make a difference are not static—indeed, some may be changing even as you read this textbook. Recently some of the most foundational state differences have been the subject of a series of studies that may change our understanding of those differences and their implications.

The "granddaddy" of all differences is political culture, a concept originated by Daniel Elazar that continues to be widely respected for its explanatory power. Yet, however powerful its explanatory capacities, Elazar's classification of state political cultures is not based on intensive statistical analysis; it is much more impressionistic. It is also static—in other words, the basic state classifications tackles one of the toughest questions in this area: of moralistic, traditionalistic, and individualistic have not changed since Elazar defined them nearly a half century ago. In the time that has elapsed since then, large shifts in demographics have taken place as the result of new waves of immigration, population and other relevant data have become more widely available, and sophisticated statistical analysis techniques have been developed and

broadly employed. All this gives state scholars the opportunity to undertake much more fine-grained analyses of regional value systems, how they translate into culture, how that culture might change, and what those changes might mean for state politics and policy.

Related to the renewed interest in studying and tracking cultural changes is a spate of new scholarship that focuses on measuring state-level political orientations and ideology, in effect capturing the political nuances of what makes a "red" state or a "blue" state or even a "happy" state. Several teams of scholars have been developing new measures of state-level policy attitudes and orientations, and these improved measures of political differences are proving themselves to useful for predicting important policy differences.

Below we summarize some of the cutting-edge research on the differences that make a difference.

- **Lieske, Joel.** 2010. "The Changing Regional Subcultures of the American States and the Utility of a New Cultural Measure." *Political Research Quarterly* 63: 538–552.

Joel Lieske, a political scientist at Cleveland State University, is the scholar most associated with the continuing study of state political cultures. Lieske's scholarship tackles one of the toughest questions in this area: How can we measure culture? This question is very useful but impressionistic, and efforts to quantify those classifications into "yardsticks" to measure degrees of cultural difference often amount to nothing more than putting numbers on Elazar's classifications. Lieske has long argued that immigration settlement patterns and degree of self-governance have nurtured the development of regional subcultures that may be more expansive than Elazar's threefold classification. Here he uses county-level data on racial origin, ethnic ancestry, religious affiliation, and various indicators of social structure to create a composite statistical measure of political culture. This is a much more sophisticated analysis than that employed by Elazar, and it results in not three primary subcultures but eleven. In Lieske's analysis, for example, moralistic cultures are actually made up of three related but distinct political subcultures—Nordic, Mormon, and Anglo-French, the labels representing the cultural elements of particular ethnic groups (especially Germans and Scandinavians) and different sects of dissenting Protestantism.

- **Lieske, Joel.** 2012. "American State Cultures: Testing a New Measure and Theory." *Publius: The Journal of Federalism* 42: 108–133.

In this article Lieske puts his new measure of state culture to the test. In a statistical contest, he pits his new measure against Elazar's typology and the most often used quantitative index of that typology (an index created in 1969 by political scientist Ira Sharkansky) to see which measure can better predict various indicators of state performance. Lieske's new measure of state cultural differences does the better job, suggesting that the new measure—which, unlike Elazar's, can at least theoretically be updated with new census data—better captures cultural differences.

- **Berry, William D., Richard C. Fording, Evan J. Ringquist, Russell L. Hanson, and Carl E. Klarner.** 2010. "Measuring Citizen and Government Ideology in the U.S. States: A Re-appraisal." *State Politics & Policy Quarterly* 10: 117–135.

One of the most important differences among states lies in the general political attitudes or orientations of the states' citizens. Scholars consider it critical to tap into those state-level attitudes for many reasons. For example, if we do not know the political orientations and attitudes of citizens, we have no means of assessing whether state lawmakers actually reflect and represent the wishes of their constituents. State-level measures of ideology are incredibly hard to construct. The central problem is that no comparable state-level scientific polls are done in all fifty states at the same time. One way to get around this problem is to infer state preferences by looking at the ideologies and policy preferences of the candidates who win congressional elections. This study employs these kinds of data to create a measure of state ideology that is found to do a good job of explaining differences in policies ranging from social welfare to incarceration rates.

- **Carsey, Thomas M., and Jeffrey J. Harden.** 2010. "New Measures of Partisanship, Ideology, and Policy Mood in the American States." *State Politics & Policy Quarterly* 10: 136–156.

This article takes an alternate approach to tackling the same measurement problem that Berry et al. address in the study cited above. Rather than inferring from lawmaker characteristics, however, Carsey and

(Continued)

- **How It Works** boxes take one state and one government process and dive into how, exactly, it works.

- **A marginal glossary** defines key concepts as they are introduced.

Powers Granted to Government. Perhaps the most important and surprising difference between the U.S. Constitution and state constitutions is the scope of the documents. The U.S. Constitution's original purpose was to organize a federal government with sharply limited powers. In contrast, state governments have what is called **plenary power,**

Natural Law, or Higher Law
A set of moral and political rules based on divine law and binding on all people.

Constitutional Amendments
Proposals to change a constitution, typically enacted by a supermajority of the legislature or through a statewide referendum.

Plenary Power
Power that is not limited or constrained.

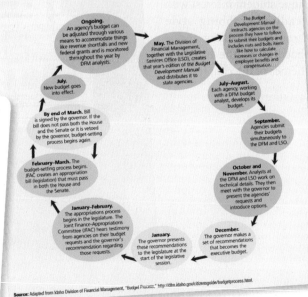

FIGURE 4-1

HOW IT WORKS

A Year in the Life of a State Budget: Idaho's Budgetary Process

Most folks first hear about state budget priorities through their governor's state of the state address, the forum in which most state budgetary news is presented. In reality, budget planning begins well in advance of this address and involves all three branches of government to some degree. In Idaho, each year in May (after the last of the potatoes have been planted), that state's Division of Financial Management (DFM) starts sowing its own seeds: overseeing the development of that state's budget for the coming fiscal year. This is the beginning of what is really an eighteen-month process: the planning for fiscal year 2014, for instance, will actually get under way about mid-year in 2012.

This chart shows how the process works in Idaho:

Ongoing. An agency's budget can be adjusted through various means to accommodate things like revenue shortfalls and new federal grants and is monitored throughout the year by DFM analysts.

May. The Division of Financial Management, together with the Legislative Services Office (LSO), creates that year's edition of the Budget Development Manual and distributes it to state agencies.

The Budget Development Manual instructs agencies on the process they have to follow to submit their budgets and includes nuts and bolts items like how to calculate increases or changes in employee benefits and compensation.

July–August. Each agency, working with a DFM budget analyst, develops its budget.

July. New budget goes into effect.

September. Agencies submit their budgets simultaneously to the DFM and LSO.

October and November. Analysts at the DFM and LSO work on technical details. They then meet with the governor to present the agencies' requests and introduce options.

By end of March. Bill is signed by the governor. If the bill does not pass both the House and the Senate or it is vetoed by the governor, budget-setting process begins again.

February–March. The budget-setting process begins. JFAC creates an appropriation bill (legislation) that must pass in both the House and the Senate.

January–February. The appropriations process begins in the legislature. The Joint Finance-Appropriations Committee (JFAC) hears testimony from agencies on their budget requests and the governor's recommendation regarding those requests.

January. The governor presents these recommendations to the legislature at the start of the legislative session.

December. The governor makes a set of recommendations that becomes the executive budget.

Source: Adapted from Idaho Division of Financial Management, "Budget Process." http://dfm.idaho.gov/citizensguide/budgetprocess.html.

- **Marginal state facts** present quick, complementary info on a U.S. state.

> **Texas is the country's fastest-growing state, with a 2.1 percent population increase in 2011. It narrowly beat out the previous population-growth champ, Utah, which came in second with an annual growth rate of 1.93 percent.**

Key features encourage comparison

- **Chapter-opening, comparative questions** encourage students to look systematically for answers using the comparative method.

- What are the advantages and disadvantages of federalism?
- What is the comparative method, and why is it a useful way to talk about state and local governments?
- What role do state and local politics play in determining how much certain services—such as a college education—cost?

- **A Difference That Makes a Difference** boxes provide clear examples of how variation among states and localities can be used to explain a wide range of political and policy phenomena.

A Difference That Makes A Difference

State Constitutions and the Right to Marry

"By the power vested in me, by the state of . . ." These words are repeated by wedding officials every day, in every state. States control who can marry and when. In Nebraska, teens younger than nineteen need their parents' permission to marry, while over the state line in Kansas, people can walk down the aisle at eighteen. A number of states prohibited interracial couples from marrying until 1967, when the U.S. Supreme Court declared Virginia's law unconstitutional in *Loving v. Virginia*. Today, debate rages around gay marriage. Just six states—Connecticut, Iowa, Massachusetts, New Hampshire, New York, and Vermont—have legalized the unions, while thirty states have amended their constitutions to prohibit them. Several additional states recognize domestic partnerships or civil unions, which grant couples some of the same state-level benefits of marriage. Washington, D.C., which is technically a federal city, not a state, allows gay marriage.

Legalization of gay marriage has been achieved through judicial review (in Connecticut, Iowa, and Massachusetts) and through legislation (New Hampshire, New York, and Vermont). Gay marriage has had a less fortunate time at the polls, where voters have rejected it time and time again—most recently in North Carolina in 2012. The most high-profile fight so far was waged in California in 2008 over Proposition 8, a ballot measure that sought to amend the state's constitution to define marriage as a union between one man and one woman—and to put a stop to the same-sex marriages that had begun there in June 2008, after the state supreme court ruled that the state's ban was unconstitutional. After both sides spent more than $55 million on their campaigns, voters narrowly approved Prop. 8. Approval of new same-sex marriages was halted, but the state continues to consider the more than 18,000 couples who wed legally as married.

The victory of Proposition 8 prompted further debate among proponents of gay marriage, some of whom wonder whether, given their continued defeats at the polls, they should wait to wage new legalization campaigns across the states. But the fight over Prop. 8 isn't finished—and it's not even limited to within the state's borders anymore. In April 2009, Theodore Olson, the former U.S. solicitor general, filed a brief in federal court challenging the amendment. In 2010, a federal district court ruled that Proposition 8 unconstitutionally violated the due process and equal protection clauses of the Fourteenth Amendment, a decision that was upheld in 2012 by a federal appeals court. As of this writing, the case has been appealed to the U.S. Supreme Court. If the Court accepts the case, the justices could make a ruling that will clarify whether or not same-sex couples have the same right to marry as heterosexual couples.

Sources: Christine Vestal, "Gay Marriage Legal in Six States," Stateline, June 4, 2009, www.stateline.org/live/details/story?contentId=347390; Ballotwatch, Initiative and Referendum Institute, "Same-Sex Marriage: Breaking the Firewall in California?," October 2008; Jo Becker, "A Conservative's Road to Same-Sex Marriage Advocacy," *New York Times*, August 18, 2009, www.nytimes.com/2009/08/19/us/19olson.html.

- **Local Focus** boxes spotlight how localities function independently of states and show how they are both constrained and empowered by intergovernmental ties.

Local Focus

The Federal City

Riddle me this. It is a city. It is sort of a state. It is ruled by Congress. What is it? It is the District of Columbia, otherwise known as Washington, D.C. It is also the nation's capital, and it is surely the most unusual local government in the country.

Technically, Washington, D.C., is a federal city. Article I, Section 8, Paragraph 17, of the U.S. Constitution gives Congress the power to rule over an area not to exceed ten square miles that constitutes the seat of national government. Yet it has never been quite clear what that means in terms of governance. Should Congress rule the city directly? Should the citizens of the city be given the right to elect a representative government? If they do this, should the government be subordinate to Congress or should it be counted as equivalent to a state and thus free to make any laws that do not violate the U.S. Constitution?

Throughout the city's history, these questions have been answered very differently. In the early 1800s, the district was a strange collection of cities and counties, each governed by different means. Washington City and Georgetown were municipalities run by a chief executive (a mayor) and a legislature (a council). Depending on the time period, however, the mayors were sometimes appointed by the federal government and sometimes elected. In addition to the two cities there were also two counties. Maryland laws governed Washington County; Virginia laws governed Alexandria County.

In the 1870s, Washington City, Georgetown, and Washington County were combined into a single governmental unit, a federal territory with a governor appointed by the president and a legislature elected by the territorial residents. This eventually became the District of Columbia, or Washington, D.C. For most of its history, commissioners appointed by the federal government governed the district. It was not until 1974 that the residents of Washington, D.C., gained home rule and the right to elect their own mayor and council.

This mayor-council arrangement, however, is unlike any other municipal government in the United States. The laws passed by the council have to be reviewed and approved by Congress. The laws that govern federal-state relationships treat the district as a state, even though it is not a state and cannot operate like one. The mayor is not considered the head of a federal agency, but he or she is expected to act like one when seeking appropriations from Congress.

This odd hybrid of local, state, and federal governments is reflected in the unique electoral status of Washington, D.C., voters. Voters in the district have a local vote, but only half of a federal vote. They can vote for the president but not for a member of Congress. They can vote for a mayor and council, but they have no voting representative in Congress. Yet Congress has the power to overturn laws passed by the council. The district now has three electoral votes. Prior to 1963, it had none and D.C. voters could not cast a ballot for president.

All this makes Washington, D.C., the nation's most unusual local government. It is the only municipality that is a creature of the United States rather than of a state constitution, and, as such, it is the only really national city in the country.

Source: Selected material from Council of the District of Columbia, "History of Self-Government in the District of Columbia," 1997, www.dccouncil.washington.dc.us.

Policy in Practice

Why Companies Avoid Overt Partisanship

Michael Jordan, the basketball legend, refused to engage publicly in partisan politics. The reason was simple, he explained: Republicans buy shoes, too, he said, and Jordan didn't want to antagonize any potential customers for Nike, whose products he endorsed. Major corporations tend to employ the same logic. They don't want to risk angering potential consumers who disagree with their politics.

Target, the big retailer, found itself the target of boycott campaigns in 2010 after it donated $150,000 to a super PAC that supported a gubernatorial candidate who opposed gay marriage. Perhaps more striking, however, was the defection of many major corporations from a previously obscure legislative group that had become the center of controversy in 2012.

The American Legislative Exchange Council, known as ALEC, had long championed conservative legislation. The group brought together state legislators and corporations to craft policy that was turned into model bills introduced in many states. Much of it had to do with fiscal matters, such as tax policy, or policies that had some direct benefit to the group's corporate members—including prison sentencing laws that helped bring business to ALEC's active private prison affiliates. Roughly a thousand bills based on ALEC language are introduced in an average year, with about 20 percent enacted into law.

With the GOP sweep in the 2010 elections, ALEC was poised to be more influential than ever. Legislation promoted by the group dominated discussion in many capitols around such issues as climate change, voter ID requirements, illegal immigration, and limits on public-sector pensions. Versions of ALEC's Freedom of Choice in Health Care Act, which was a direct challenge to the federal law championed by President Barack Obama, were introduced in more than forty states. "It's really no secret," said State Senator Jane Cunningham, the lead sponsor of Missouri's version. "I learned about the idea from ALEC and brought it back to Missouri."

For years, liberal advocacy groups decried ALEC's influence, but they were unable to alarm very many members of the public, since the group remained little known. That began to shift, however, in 2011, when 850 model bills generated by ALEC, along with other documents, were published on a Web site run by the liberal Center for Media and Democracy. That made it easier for journalists and the group's ideological opponents in individual states to compare proposed legislation with language crafted by ALEC. In addition, Common Cause, a group that supports campaign finance restrictions, called on the Internal Revenue Service to audit ALEC's books, claiming that the organization acted more like a full-fledged lobbying shop than a tax-exempt nonprofit.

ALEC was facing some public relations headaches, but its problems really began with the high-profile shooting of Trayvon Martin, an unarmed African American youth, in Florida in February 2012. The man who shot Martin, George Zimmerman, maintained that he was innocent of murder charges thanks to the state's "stand your ground" law, which allows people to use force when they feel they may be at risk.

That type of law had been promoted by ALEC. The group soon backed away from the issue, announcing two months after the shooting that it was disbanding the task force that dealt with public safety and elections issues. From now on, ALEC leaders said, they would stick purely to economic matters.

By then, it was too late for many of ALEC's corporate members. Several major companies, including Coca-Cola, Pepsi, McDonald's, and Kraft, had cut their ties with the group. Nearly three-dozen corporations and foundations would ultimately make the decision that being associated with ALEC, however effective the group had been in the past, had become bad for business.

That's why most of the major donors to super PACs during the 2012 election cycle were not big corporations. Rather, they were wealthy individuals or owners of privately held companies who didn't have to worry about what their shareholders would think about their politics.

Source: Adapted from Alan Greenblatt, "ALEC Enjoys a New Wave of Influence and Criticism," *Governing*, December 2011.

- **Policy in Practice** boxes demonstrate how different states and localities interpret and implement legislation.

States under Stress

Protest Movements Achieve Different Levels of Success

Two large-scale populist movements emerged during the first term of Barack Obama's presidency: the Tea Party movement and the Occupy movement. Participants in both were angry about the influence and power of large institutional forces in society. The two movements' platforms were diametrically opposed, however, and the approaches they took to trying to influence American politics were completely different.

The fast-growing Tea Party movement began in 2009, shortly after Obama became president. It was made up of individuals angry about the size of government—a backlash against the president's $800 billion stimulus program, a bank bailout plan that Congress had passed under President George W. Bush to the tune of $700 billion, and a deficit that in 2009 topped $1.4 trillion. "The Republicans for the last two decades have been a party whose litmus tests have been cultural issues, especially abortion," explained conservative columnist Michael Barone in 2010. "The tea partiers have helped to change their focus to issues of government overreach and spending."

Members of the movement also derided Obama's healthcare legislation, which they saw as obtrusive and a threat to individual liberty, since it mandated that most people buy health insurance. Not surprisingly, then, they aligned themselves largely with the Republican Party—even if many participants in the Tea Party movement insisted that they were independent.

The Tea Party movement, which derived its name from colonial-era protests against British taxation—quickly claimed more than one thousand different affiliate groups around the country. Tea Party–endorsed candidates prevailed in numerous GOP primaries in both 2010 and 2012. Republican strategists largely welcomed the burst of energy that Tea Partiers brought to their cause, which had been discouraged by widespread electoral losses in 2006 and 2008.

Some criticized the Tea Party for being too unyielding. Some of the candidates backed by Tea Party groups in primaries were unable to prevail in contests Republicans might have won had they nominated more "establishment" or mainstream candidates. And those Tea Party favorites who did win elections drew criticism once in office for refusing to compromise at all on budget matters, nearly forcing the country into default in 2011.

But while the Tea Party was influencing Republican politicians in Congress and the statehouses, those politicians were trying to co-opt the Tea Party, to harness its energy and enthusiasm without letting its agenda dominate the party's direction. "That's the secret to politics," GOP consultant Scott Reed said in 2011. "Trying to control a segment of people without those people recognizing that you're trying to control them."

Being co-opted in this way seemed to be the main thing the Occupy movement wanted to avoid. The movement began with a protest beginning in September 2011 in a park near Wall Street in Lower Manhattan; the demonstrators complained that too much wealth was concentrated in the hands of too few individuals.

The slogan "We are the 99 percent" went global, as did the idea of protesting by camping in place for twenty-four hours a day, which quickly spread to hundreds of cities. The issue of income inequality and the question of whether the wealthiest 1 percent held too much power soon became central concerns of the movement.

But Occupy was not able to translate its complaints into a policy agenda. It wasn't clear what the members of the movement wanted to have happen. The mere act of their camping out itself became problematic as winter set in and issues of sanitation and crowd control grew worse; in many cities, authorities ordered police to remove the protesters from public spaces.

- **States under Stress** boxes underscore how budgetary constraints are reshaping how state and local governments operate.

- **More than 80 tables, figures, and maps** provide an intuitively easy way for students to grasp the differences among states and localities, with up-to-date comparative data.

TABLE 2-3

Key U.S. Supreme Court Rulings Regarding Federalism, 1995–2012

Case	Decision
United States v. Lopez (1995)	Court strikes down a federal law prohibiting possession of firearms near public schools. State claim upheld.
Seminole Tribe of Florida v. Florida (1996)	Court rules Congress cannot allow citizens to sue states in a federal court except for civil rights violations. State claim upheld.
Printz v. United States (1997)	Court strikes down a federal law requiring mandatory background checks for firearms purchases. State claim upheld.
Alden v. Maine (1999)	Court rules that Congress does not have the power to authorize citizens to sue in state court on the basis of federal claims. State claim upheld.
United States v. Morrison (2000)	Court strikes down the federal Violence Against Women Act. State claim upheld.
Reno v. Condon (2000)	Court upholds a federal law preventing states from selling driver's license information. State claim overturned.
Bush v. Gore (2000)	Court overrules a Florida Supreme Court action allowing hand recounts of contested election ballots. State claim overturned.
Alabama v. Garrett (2001)	Court rules that state employees cannot sue their employers in federal court to recover monetary damages under the provisions of the Americans with Disabilities Act. State claim upheld.
Lorillard Tobacco Co. v. Reilly (2001)	Court strikes down Massachusetts laws regulating the advertising of tobacco products. State claim overturned.
Kelo v. City of New London (2005)	Court rules that government can seize private property for public purposes, including economic development. State claim upheld.
Gonzales v. Oregon (2006)	Court rules that the U.S. attorney general overstepped his authority by threatening to eliminate prescription-writing privileges for doctors who follow state law allowing physician-assisted suicide. State claim upheld.
Arizona v. United States (2012)	Court rules that states do not have the authority to enact and enforce immigration laws; however, it allows states to implement "show me your papers" regulations that require law enforcement officers to determine the immigration status of anyone they stop or detain.

FIGURE 6-2

State Party Fund-Raising over Time

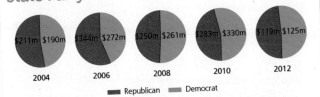

$211m $190m — 2004
$344m $272m — 2006
$250m $261m — 2008
$283m $330m — 2010
$119m $125m — 2012

■ Republican ■ Democrat

Source: Data compiled from the National Institute for Money in State Politics, "Industry Influence 2000–2012," http://followthemoney.org/database/IndustryTotals.phtml?f=P&s=0.

American Recovery and Reinvestment Act Funds Awarded by State, 2012

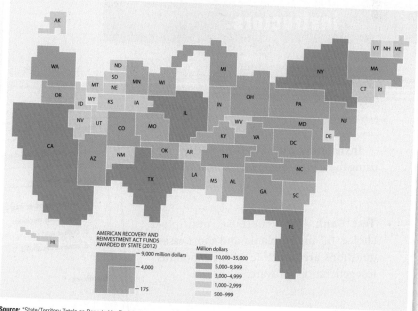

AMERICAN RECOVERY AND REINVESTMENT ACT FUNDS AWARDED BY STATE (2012)

— 9,000 million dollars
— 4,000
— 175

Million dollars
■ 10,000–35,000
■ 5,000–9,999
■ 3,000–4,999
■ 1,000–2,999
■ 500–999

Source: "State/Territory Totals as Reported by Recipients," Recovery.gov, reporting period February 7, 2009—March 31, 2012, www.recovery.gov/pages/textview.aspx?data=recipientHomeMap.

STATE STATS

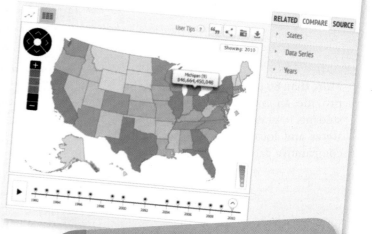

Local Government Total Expenditures

Category: Expenditures **Topic:** Government Finances: State and Local
National Total: $1,666,568,007,000 (2010)

A new data product from CQ Press, State Stats allows students to investigate reliable, easy-to-use data from more than 80 different sources, covering such areas as health care, crime, and education. Intuitive mapping and graphing tools allow students to compare states through data visualization.

Free with purchase of a new book, students use State Stats icons throughout the book, linking to exercises in each chapter that challenge students to apply the comparative method, exploring what they find interesting about a particular state.

STATE STATS
State Stats on Local Government

Explore and compare data on the states! Go to college.cqpress.com/sites/ govstateandlocal to do these exercises.

1. How has local government spending across the states changed between 2000 and 2010? Where has it changed the most and the least? What might account for some of the changes?

2. How has local government tax revenue changed in the states between 2000 and 2010? Where has it changed the most? The least? What might account for some of the changes?

3. Which state has the highest level of local government direct general expenditures? Which has the least? How does state population affect these expenditures? Why?

4. What is the homeownership rate in your state? How do changes in this rate affect the local governments' budgets?

5. What is the average value of new housing units in your state? How does this number affect local government budgets?

Support for instructors

www.cqpress.com/cs/ govstateandlocal/

Instructors can save time and effort by using these high-quality instructor resources:

- **Test Bank**—700 true/false, multiple-choice, fill-in-the-blank, and short essay questions are available with Respondus test generation software.

Preview Current Item

Appearance in Internet Explorer (other browsers may vary slightly).

OK

Most states require _____ for felony criminal cases.

- a. twelve-member juries
- b. unanimous decisions
- c. both a. and b.
- d. none of the above

Feedback

0.0% a.

0.0% b.

- **PowerPoint lecture slides**—key concepts and instructor notes enhance lectures.
- **Instructor's manual**—includes chapter summaries, lecture outlines, talking points for discussions and lectures, and sample syllabi.
- **Downloadable graphics**—every table, figure, and map from the book is available in PowerPoint and PDF.
- **Common course cartridge**—(which supports all major LMS including Blackboard, D2L, Angel, Moodle, and more) includes the entire test bank, PowerPoints, graphics from the book, useful content from the instructor's manual, quiz questions, and State Stats exercises from the student study site.

Comparative Method

- Studying the differences between two, or more, units of analysis to explain policy and/or structural variance
  - Texas performs many more executions than other states – Why?
  - Some localities provide curb-side recycling services while others don't – Why?
  - Is public education of the same quality in all states? What would explain the variance?

Support for students

www.cqpress.com/cs/govstateandlocal/

Students can increase understanding and get a better grade using the **open access student study site** which includes:

- **Study**—chapter summaries with review questions.

Study Quiz Flashcards Explore

Chapter 4. Finances: Filling the Till and Paying the Bills
Study
Chapter Summary

Dealing with finances is a highly politicized process for states and localities. Expenditures and the budgetary process in general provide clues to the political and policy priorities of a state's government and its local governments. State and local governments have six primary sources of revenue, including sales taxes, income taxes, excise taxes, and property taxes. Variation in state resources, geography, culture, history, and demographics has resulted in widespread variation in the use of such taxes among the states. For instance, states that forego income taxes rely heavily on property and sales taxes and are likely to have different tax rates to adjust to a different tax base. This variation among taxing mechanisms is reflected in variation in public policies.

The budget process among states and localities is defined primarily by the relationship between entitlement spending and discretionary spending. As entitlement spending (for example, Medicaid and welfare) increases, the ability of states to experiment with new policies and programs decreases. Meeting public expectations with regard to spending on education, healthcare services, highway infrastructure, and correctional institutions further limits the discretionary budgetary authority of states. Those states that adopted the referendum and initiative process also have had to deal with a strong "antitax" sentiment among their citizens, furthering limiting their ability to raise revenue. Such constraints have forced states and localities to be innovative. The resulting variation highlights the need for a comparative approach to studying finances in states and local governments.

Objectives

After reading this chapter, you should understand...

- the primary sources of revenue for states and localities
- the different types of taxes utilized by states and localities
- why tax capacity and tax effort vary among the states
- who controls the budget process
- how the state budget process differs from the federal budget process
- what the largest areas of expenditures are for state governments

- **Quiz**—multiple-choice questions with automatic feedback.

In a plural executive system, the governor:

A. Shares power with the state judiciary.

B. b. Is pretty much a first among equals. ✓

C. Must select nonpartisan cabinet members.

D. Is president of a least one legislative house.

Previous | Flip | Next

Term

Definition

Remove ✕

Shuffle ⤨

Reset ↻

Auto Play ◎

Total cards : 1

FISCAL FEDERALISM

Term 1 of 1

- **Flashcards**—viewable by definition or by word, with marking and reshuffling.

Study | Quiz | Flashcards | Explore

Chapter 12. Metropolitics: The Hole Government Problem
Explore

www.metroresearch.org/ — This Web site, sponsored by the Metropolitan Area Research Corporation, provides useful information on metropolitan areas.

The following are links to prominent councils of government:

· Denver Regional Council of Governments: www.drcog.org/
· Metropolitan Washington Council of Governments: www.mwcog.org/
· Portland, Oregon, Metro Government: www.metro-region.org/

The following are links to useful data released by the U.S. Census Bureau:

· Bureau of Labor Statistics Metropolitan Area Employment and Unemployment: www.bls.gov/news.release/metro.toc.htm
· Current Lists of Metropolitan and Micropolitan Statistical Areas: www.census.gov/population /www/estimates/metrodef.html
· U.S. Census Bureau Metropolitan Statistical Area Quick Facts: http://quickfacts.census.gov /qfd/meta/long_metro.htm

- **Explore**—annotated web resources.

Governing STATES and LOCALITIES

edition 4

New Hampshire

Vermont

Maine

Augusta ⊙

Montpelier ⊙

Concord ⊙

Massachusetts

Albany ⊙

Boston ⊙

Providence ⊙

New York

Hartford ⊙

Rhode Island

Connecticut

Pennsylvania

Trenton ⊙

Harrisburg ⊙

New Jersey

Annapolis ⊙

Dover ⊙

Delaware

Wisconsin

Madison ⊙

Michigan

Lansing ⊙

West
Virginia

Maryland

Iowa

⊙ines ⊙

Illinois

Indiana

Ohio

Columbus ⊙

Richmond ⊙

Indianapolis ⊙

Springfield ⊙

Charleston ⊙

Virginia

Frankfort ⊙

Jefferson City ⊙

Kentucky

Raleigh ⊙

Missouri

North Carolina

Nashville ⊙

Arkansas

Tennessee

South Carolina

Little Rock ⊙

Columbia ⊙

Atlanta ⊙

Alabama

Georgia

Mississippi

Montgomery ⊙

Louisiana

Jackson ⊙

Tallahassee ⊙

Baton Rouge ⊙

Florida

Admission to the Union

- Original Ratifiers*
  December 1787–June 21, 1788
- June 25, 1788–1799
- 1800–1848
- 1849–1899
- Entered Union after 1900

CQ Press, an imprint of SAGE, is the leading publisher of books, periodicals, and electronic products on American government and international affairs. CQ Press consistently ranks among the top commercial publishers in terms of quality, as evidenced by the numerous awards its products have won over the years. CQ Press owes its existence to Nelson Poynter, former publisher of the *St. Petersburg Times,* and his wife Henrietta, with whom he founded Congressional Quarterly in 1945. Poynter established CQ with the mission of promoting democracy through education and in 1975 founded the Modern Media Institute, renamed The Poynter Institute for Media Studies after his death. The Poynter Institute (*www.poynter.org*) is a nonprofit organization dedicated to training journalists and media leaders.

In 2008, CQ Press was acquired by SAGE, a leading international publisher of journals, books, and electronic media for academic, educational, and professional markets. Since 1965, SAGE has helped inform and educate a global community of scholars, practitioners, researchers, and students spanning a wide range of subject areas, including business, humanities, social sciences, and science, technology, and medicine. A privately owned corporation, SAGE has offices in Los Angeles, London, New Delhi, and Singapore, in addition to the Washington DC office of CQ Press.

Governing STATES and LOCALITIES

edition 4

KEVIN B. SMITH

University of Nebraska – Lincoln

ALAN GREENBLATT

NPR

SAGE | CQPRESS

Los Angeles | London | New Delhi
Singapore | Washington DC

Los Angeles | London | New Delhi
Singapore | Washington DC

FOR INFORMATION:

CQ Press
An Imprint of SAGE Publications, Inc.
2455 Teller Road
Thousand Oaks, California 91320
E-mail: order@sagepub.com

SAGE Publications Ltd.
1 Oliver's Yard
55 City Road
London EC1Y 1SP
United Kingdom

SAGE Publications India Pvt. Ltd.
B 1/I 1 Mohan Cooperative Industrial Area
Mathura Road, New Delhi 110 044
India

SAGE Publications Asia-Pacific Pte. Ltd.
3 Church Street
#10-04 Samsung Hub
Singapore 049483

Acquisitions Editor: Charisse Kiino
Development Editor: Nancy Matuszak
Editorial Assistant: Davia Grant
Production Editor: Laura Barrett
Copy Editor: Judy Selhorst
Typesetter: C&M Digitals (P) Ltd.
Proofreader: Joyce Li
Indexer: Maria Sosnowski
Cover Designer: Janet Kiesel
Marketing Manager: Erica DeLuca
Permissions Editor: Jennifer Barron

Printed in Canada

Library of Congress Cataloging-in-Publication Data

Smith, Kevin B., 1963-

Governing states and localities / Kevin B. Smith, University of Nebraska, Lincoln, Alan Greenblatt, NPR. — Fourth edition.

pages cm
Includes bibliographical references and index.

ISBN 978-1-4522-2633-0 (pbk. : alk. paper)

1. State governments—United States—Textbooks. 2. Local government—United States—Textbooks. 3. Comparative government—Textbooks. I. Greenblatt, Alan. II. Title.

JK2408.S57 2014
320.473—dc23   2013012543

This book is printed on acid-free paper.

13 14 15 16 17 10 9 8 7 6 5 4 3 2 1

Brief Contents

For my students, with thanks — KBS
For my wife, Megan — AG

Contents

Chapter 1   3

Introduction to State and Local Government: They Tax Dogs in West Virginia, Don't They?

Chapter 2   27

Federalism: The Power Plan

CONSTITUTION

Chapter 3   59

Constitutions: Operating Instructions

Chapter 4   87

Finance: Filling the Till and Paying the Bills

Chapter 5   115

Political Attitudes and Participation:
Venting and Voting

Chapter 6   151

Parties and Interest Groups: Elephants,
Donkeys, and Cash Cows

Chapter 13   409

Education: Reading, Writing, and Regulation

Chapter 14   439

Crime and Punishment

Chapter 15   471

Health and Welfare: State, Heal Thyself!

Tables, Figures, and Maps

Tables

Figures

Maps

Preface

The primary goal of this fourth edition of *Governing States and Localities* is to offer a comprehensive introduction to state and local governments and to do it with a difference. This book is a unique collaboration between academic and professional writers that rests on a foundation of academic scholarship, more than two decades of experience teaching undergraduates about state and local governments, and the insight and experience of a journalist who covers state and local politics.

Like its predecessors, this fourth edition aims to provide a fresh and contemporary perspective on state and local politics in terms of coverage and content as well as in the look and feel of the book. The text deliberately follows a newsmagazine's crisp newswriting style, and the book employs magazine-quality, full-color layout and design. Our intent is to deliver a text that meets the highest academic and pedagogical standards while remaining engaging and easily accessible to undergraduates.

This fourth edition contains a number of significant updates and revisions. New, full-color layout and design bring fresh life to the book's content and graphics and draw attention to its features. Among those features is the new "The Latest Research," designed to summarize the latest scholarship on key themes developed in each chapter and to provide students with an accessible introduction to cutting-edge academic research on state and local politics. "The Latest Research" concludes each chapter, where it can best put recent scholarship into the context of what students have just learned. In response to reviewer feedback, this new edition also features streamlined graphical presentations, offering illustrations that intuitively highlight key points in the text. Only the most useful data are presented, in the most effective displays, to encourage students' visual learning and data literacy.

Students can get more hands-on experience with data through this edition's new State Stats exercises, which appear at the end of each chapter. State Stats, a CQ Press database featuring data from more than eighty government and nongovernment sources, provides a tool to research key information and trends on the states. Students will be able to investigate reliable, easy-to-use data on areas such as health care, crime, and education, while intuitive mapping and graphing tools encourage them to compare data through visualization. The exercises can be carried out by accessing State Stats through the student companion site.

Perhaps most important, the text of the fourth edition has been revised to reflect a new overall theme of "What's next?" The Great Recession is technically over, but budgets remain tight and federal stimulus dollars are drying up. States and localities have cut budgets, reduced public-sector employment, consolidated agencies, and pushed back against federal policy priorities that are accompanied by mandates but not money. The stage is set for a resetting of intergovernmental relations, and although the specifics of this ongoing reshuffling of power and responsibilities are not always clear, we attempt to lay out the possible directions of this latest evolution of the federal system and its impact on all branches of state and local politics. All chapters have been revised substantially, with the content updated whenever possible to reflect the latest issues, trends, and political changes, including the following:

- Analysis of the results of the most recent legislative and gubernatorial elections
- Discussion of the most important state supreme court decisions and constitutional debates
- Exploration of key changes in campaign and elections regulations

- In-depth examination of recent events and issues that have had impacts on (and in some cases transformed) states and localities

Although these represent significant revisions, the current edition retains the pedagogical philosophy of the comparative method. This approach compares similar units of analysis to explain *why* differences exist. As scholars know well, state and local governments make excellent units of analysis for comparison because they operate within a single political system. The similarities and differences that mark their institutional structures, laws and regulations, political cultures, histories, demographics, economies, and geographies mean that they make exciting laboratories for asking and answering important questions about politics and government. Put simply, their differences make a difference.

The appeal of exploring state and local government through comparison is not just that it makes for good political science. It is also a great way to engage students because it gives undergraduates an accessible, practical, and systematic way to understand politics and policy in the real world. Students learn that even such seemingly personal concerns as why their tuition is so darned high are not just relevant to their particular situation and educational institution but also are fundamental to the interaction of that institution with its state's political culture, economy, history, and tax structure and even to the school's geographic and demographic position within the state and region. Using the comparative method, this book gives students the resources they need to ask and answer such questions themselves.

Key Features

This book includes a number of elements designed to showcase and promote its main themes. Sets of chapter-opening questions engage student interest and prompt students to look systematically for answers using the comparative method. The idea is not simply to spoon-feed the answers to students but, rather, to demonstrate how the comparative method can be used to explore and explain questions about politics and policy.

Following the comparative questions, each chapter moves on to an opening vignette modeled after a lead in a newsmagazine article—a compelling story that segues naturally into the broader themes of the chapter. Many of these vignettes (as well as many of the feature boxes) represent original reporting.

The feature boxes in each chapter also emphasize and reinforce the comparative theme:

- "A Difference That Makes a Difference" boxes provide clear examples of how variations among states and localities can be used to explain a wide range of political and policy phenomena. These pieces detail the ways in which the institutions, regulations, political culture, demographics, and other factors of a particular state shape its constitution, the way its political parties function, how its citizens tend to vote, how it allocates its financial resources, and why its courts are structured the way they are, to name a few.

- "Local Focus" boxes spotlight the ways localities function independent of the states and show how they are both constrained and empowered by intergovernmental ties. From battles to wrest control of their budgets from the state to constitutional restrictions on how they can tax and spend, the topics addressed in these boxes showcase the rich variety that exists in these nearly 87,000 substate entities.

- "Policy in Practice" boxes demonstrate how different states and localities have interpreted and implemented the legislation handed down from higher levels of government and the consequences of these decisions. Gubernatorial policy innovators, the surprising effects of new e-government tools, and the political and policy challenges involved in tuition hikes are just some of the issues addressed.

- "States under Stress" boxes demonstrate how the Great Recession is reshaping how state and local governments operate. The issues addressed in these boxes include power shifting toward the federal government, the scramble for federal stimulus dollars, and the weakened negotiating stand of public-sector labor unions.

Another key feature that serves the comparative theme is the design and use of graphics and tables. Nearly thirty full-color fifty-state maps, including four unique cartograms, provide a visual representation of and an intuitively easy way to grasp the differences among states and localities, whether these differences are the sizes of the state economies, the party affiliation requirements for voting in direct primaries, the methods of judicial selection, or state incarceration rates. Similarly, more than fifty tables and figures emphasize how states and localities differ and what these differences mean to politics and policy. State rankings of voter turnout rates, recent regional murder rates, and many other features support comparisons made in the text.

To help students assimilate content and review for tests, each chapter includes a set of highlighted key concepts. These terms are defined in the margins near the places where they are introduced and are compiled into a list at the end of each chapter with corresponding page numbers. A comprehensive glossary of key terms precedes the book's index.

Organization of the Book

The book is organized so that each chapter logically builds on previous chapters. The first chapter (subtitled "They Tax Dogs in West Virginia, Don't They?") is essentially a persuasive essay that lays the conceptual groundwork for the book. Its aim is to convince students that state and local politics are important to their day-to-day lives and to their futures as professionals and as citizens. That is, it makes the case for why students should care about state and local politics. Along the way, it introduces the advantages of the comparative method as a systematic way to explore this subject. In introducing the book's approach, the chapter provides the basic context for studying state and local governments, especially the differences in economics, culture, demographics, and geography that drive policy and politics at the regional level.

The next two chapters cover federalism and state constitutions. These chapters provide a basic understanding of what state and local governments are and what powers, responsibilities, and roles they have within the political system of the United States, as well as a sense of how they legally can make different political and policy choices.

Chapter 4 examines the finances of state and local governments. The key revenue streams for states and localities—income, sales, and property taxes—fell dramatically during the Great Recession and five years later have not fully recovered. Yet while revenues are still climbing back, the demand for state and local services continues to increase. This ongoing imbalance between revenues and expenditures continues to be a dominant driver of politics and policy at the state and local levels. This chapter gives students a fundamental sense of the revenues and expenditures of state and local governments and their central importance to virtually everything government does.

Chapter 5 examines political participation with an eye to helping students understand how citizens connect to the core policymaking institutions of government. Chapters 6–10 are separate treatments of those core institutions: parties and interest groups, legislatures, governors and executives, courts, and the bureaucracy. There is special emphasis in each chapter on how variations in the structure, powers, and responsibilities of these institutions have real-life implications for citizens of states and localities.

Chapters 11 and 12 focus on local government. Chapter 11 concentrates on laying out the basic structure, authority, and responsibilities of local government. Chapter 12 examines the relations among local governments from a regional perspective. The final four chapters are devoted to specific policy areas—education, crime and punishment, health and welfare, and the environment—that represent a selection of the most critical policy functions of state and local governments.

Ancillaries

We are pleased to offer an updated and expanded suite of high-quality, classroom-ready instructor and student ancillaries to accompany the book. Written by Jayme L. Nieman of University of Nebraska–Lincoln, the ancillaries are specifically tailored to the fourth edition of *Governing States and Localities*.

A set of downloadable instructor's resources is available free to adopters, including a comprehensive test bank of more than six hundred true/false, multiple-choice, fill-in-the-blank, and short-answer questions. Available in a number of formats, this test bank also can be used with *Respondus*—a flexible and easy-to-use test-generation software that allows professors to build, customize, and even integrate exams into course management platforms.

In addition, instructors will find more than two hundred PowerPoint lecture slides tailored to the text. These slides carefully detail the core concepts of each chapter, underscoring the book's comparative principles.

An instructor's manual with clear chapter summaries, downloadable lecture outlines, points for discussion, and sample syllabi for the course is included as well. Instructors have access to a full suite of .jpg and .ppt format files of all the tables, figures, and maps in the book, which they can use to create additional PowerPoint slides or transparency masters when covering comparative data in the classroom or in discussion groups. In addition, these visuals can be imported into exams.

A host of updated student resources can be found on the book's Web site at **http://college .cqpress.com/govstateandlocal**, including chapter summaries with clear chapter objectives and a set of self-testing study questions, nearly three hundred self-grading comprehensive quiz questions, a set of flash cards for review of key concepts, and a set of annotated links to important state and local Web sites. In addition, students can access State Stats through the book's Web site to complete the exercises that appear at the end of each chapter in the book, enabling them to get hands-on experience comparing data.

Students and instructors alike will find *Governing* magazine's Web site especially useful for further research and in-class discussion. To help them bring the latest word from the states and localities into their classrooms, adopters may receive a free semester-long subscription to *Governing* magazine.

Acknowledgments

A lot of effort and dedication go into the making of a textbook like this, only a fraction of which is contributed by those whose names end up on the cover. Jayme Nieman, a Ph.D. student at the University of Nebraska–Lincoln, deserves special recognition for her important contributions as a research assistant, as does Laura Wiedlocher at the University of Missouri–St. Louis. In addition, we thank Melissa Feinberg, the original author of the chapter on courts, for returning to revise that chapter, as well as Josh Goodman, of the Pew Center on the States, for his work on two key chapters.

To Nancy Matuszak, Charisse Kiino, Eric Garner, and Judy Selhorst, the editorial team at CQ Press and SAGE responsible for much of what happened from game plan to actualization, a single word: Thanks! The word is miserly compensation for their work, effort, and dedication, and in no way makes up for all the trouble we caused. Nonetheless, our thanks are most sincerely meant (again). We heartily thank our many reviewers, past and present, for their careful and detailed assistance with reading and commenting on the manuscript:

Sharon Alter, *William Rainey Harper Community College*

Jeff Ashley, *Eastern Illinois University*

Jenna Bednar, *University of Michigan*

Neil Berch, *West Virginia University*

Nathaniel Birkhead, *Kansas State University*

John Bohte, *University of Wisconsin–Milwaukee*

Shannon Bow O'Brien, *University of Texas–Austin*

William Cassie, *Appalachian State University*

Douglas Clouatre, *Mid Plains Community College*

Gary Crawley, *Ball State University*

Warren Dixon, *Texas A&M University*

Nelson Dometrius, *Texas Tech University*

Jaime Dominguez, *DePaul University*

Deborah Dougherty, *Illinois Central College*

Nicholas Easton, *Clark University*

Craig Emmert, *University of Texas–Permian Basin*

David H. Folz, *University of Tennessee*

Patricia Freeland, *University of Tennessee*

Michael E. Greenberg, *Shippensburg University*

Donald Haider-Markel, *University of Kansas*

George Hale, *Kutztown University*

William Hall, *Bradley University*

Susan Hansen, *University of Pittsburgh*

Dana Michael Harsell, *University of North Dakota*

Lisa Langenbach, *Middle Tennessee State University*

William Lester, *Jacksonville State University*

Madhavi McCall, *San Diego State University*

Bryan McQuide, *University of Idaho*

Gary Moncrief, *Boise State University*

Scott Moore, *Colorado State University*

Lawrence Overlan, *Bentley College*

David Peterson, *Iowa State University*

Lori Riverstone-Newe, *Illinois State University*

James Sheffield, *University of Oklahoma–Norman*

Kelly Sills, *Washington State University–Vancouver*

Lee Silvi, *Lakeland Community College*

Zachary Smith, *Northern Arizona University*

Kendra Stewart, *Eastern Kentucky University*

Charles Turner, *California State University–Chico*

John Woodcock, *Central Connecticut State University*

We hope and expect that each of them will be able to find traces of their numerous helpful suggestions throughout this final product.

Finally, in general, we express our appreciation to those political scientists and journalists who pay attention not only to Washington, D.C., but also to what is happening throughout the rest of the country.

About the Authors

Kevin B. Smith is professor of political science at the University of Nebraska–Lincoln. He is coauthor of *The Public Policy Theory Primer* and numerous scholarly articles on state politics and policy, and is the longtime editor of CQ Press's annual *State and Local Government* reader. He is also a former associate editor of *State Politics & Policy Quarterly.* Prior to becoming an academic, he covered state and local politics as a newspaper reporter.

Alan Greenblatt, a reporter at NPR, has been writing about politics and government in Washington, D.C., and the states for nearly two decades. As a reporter for *Congressional Quarterly,* he won the National Press Club's Sandy Hume award for political journalism. While on staff at *Governing* magazine, he covered many issues of concern to state and local governments, such as budgets, taxes, and higher education. Along the way, he has written about politics and culture for numerous other outlets, including the *New York Times* and the *Washington Post.*

Is government going to the dogs? State and local governments raise revenues in many different ways, including varying levels of income, sales, and property tax. They can tax virtually anything, including dogs. In some places man's best friend is not only a family pet but also a source of money for government.

Introduction to State and Local Government

THEY TAX DOGS IN WEST VIRGINIA, DON'T THEY?

- What are the advantages and disadvantages of federalism?
- What is the comparative method, and why is it a useful way to talk about state and local governments?
- What role do state and local politics play in determining how much certain services—such as a college education—cost?

Y ou could call Holden Thorp a pretty intelligent guy. He graduated from the University of North Carolina (UNC) with honors, got a Ph.D. from the California Institute of Technology, and then went on to Yale to do postgraduate work. He went back to UNC in 1993 and started rocketing through the ranks of one of the nation's premier research universities: from faculty member to department chair, from there to college dean, and not too long after that, at age forty-three, he became university chancellor. Along the way he cofounded a company that develops cancer-fighting drugs and wrote a widely respected book on entrepreneurship and innovation in universities. So you could call Holden Thorp pretty intelligent, but you'd be wrong. Holden Thorp is scary smart. That's a good thing for UNC, because it doesn't take a genius to figure out that his institution has a problem—a big problem that even the most engaged, active, and creative high-IQ types are struggling to resolve. You should be interested in this problem too, because if you are reading this book there's a reasonable chance it's your problem as well: figuring out how to fund a college education.

That problem is rooted not just in your bank balance but in a particular element of state politics, a combination of economic distress and fiscal conservatism that is pushing state legislatures to engage in a process of defunding public institutions of higher education. State colleges and universities, which is to say the vast majority of institutions of higher education, are products of state laws and regulations and are partially funded with state money. When states have less money, and most of them have less money these days, so does the entire nation's system of higher education. Good administrators such as Thorp are proactive and have tried to stay out in front of the economic tough times as much as possible—at UNC a stem-to-stern review designed to cut fat and make the institution more efficient is expected to cut $50 million in expenses. That will help, but it represents a fraction of the $230 million cut in state aid to the university in the past five years. This kind of thing is happening not just at UNC, but at pretty much all public colleges and universities. Adjusted for inflation, states are spending about 20 percent less on higher education than they were a decade ago. Twenty years ago, state appropriations covered about half of public university revenues; today that figure is about 30 percent and falling rapidly. Some of these cuts have been truly brutal—the California legislature cut all appropriations for higher education by $1.5 billion in a single year, the University of Wisconsin faced a similar quarter-billion haircut, and Florida cut its higher education spending by a quarter in four years.[1]

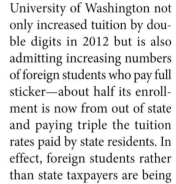

A number of public universities have already been effectively privatized—for example, the University of Colorado at Boulder and the University of Michigan at Ann Arbor now get only 6 or 7 percent of their revenues from their states. Yet at the same time state revenues have fallen off a cliff, demand for a college education has skyrocketed. Something has to give in such a situation, and it has. At UNC class sizes have expanded, 556 class sections have been whacked, salaries have been frozen for years, admissions to some programs have been reduced, and the university is finding it harder to compete for top faculty with more well-heeled (especially private) universities. Oh yes, and tuition has also increased. If you are enrolled at a public college or university, you can probably relate to this sort of thing—if anything, UNC is in better shape than most. But even annual tuition increases in the double digits are not enough to make up for shortfalls in state appropriations. Colleges are getting creative, figuring out how to tap into new revenue streams to keep their operations going. The University of Washington not only increased tuition by double digits in 2012 but is also admitting increasing numbers of foreign students who pay full sticker—about half its enrollment is now from out of state and paying triple the tuition rates paid by state residents. In effect, foreign students rather than state taxpayers are being asked to subsidize a state university. Perhaps the most radical approach to solving higher education's revenue problem has been given serious consideration at the University of California, Riverside: ditching tuition altogether and letting the university take a 5 percent share of students' salaries after they graduate.[2] Over the long term students will likely end up paying a lot more, but in the short term the idea of no tuition bills looks pretty attractive.

The bottom line is that if you are a student at a public institution of higher education, Holden Thorp's problem—figuring out how to fund such an operation—is your problem too. Actually, even if you are not a student at a public college, it's your problem. School revenues from states and localities come from taxes. If you get a paycheck, rent or own property, or buy anything, your state and local governments will take a cut and pass some on to good old State U whether you go there or not. How do you feel about having your taxes jacked northward to help college students take a course in, say, state and local politics? For many people struggling in a tough economy the answer to that question is emphatically negative and mostly not printable in a PG-rated textbook.

It is not even just about money. Some argue that publicly supported higher education is a mediocre deal for taxpayers even in economic good times and that its underlying business model needs to be rethought. This is especially the case for well-known conservatives, such as Pat Buchanan, who argue administrator salaries are too high, college professors don't work hard enough, and universities teach too much that is economically and socially pointless. The hard economy might have forced the hand of state legislatures, but some argue the time for higher education to be largely privatized and forced to the discipline of the market is overdue.

So whose problem is the current challenge of funding higher education? Well, administrators, staff, faculty, and students at the affected institutions must deal with the problem, of course, but so must anyone who pays taxes or has an opinion on the appropriate role of higher education in shaping economic and social opportunity. Holden Thorp's problem turns out to be *everybody's* problem. The takeaway point here is that this massive problem that involves everyone is ultimately a problem of state politics. It is just one example of the importance of state and local governments and how the politics surrounding those governments shapes the lives of all citizens of the United States.

One of the few positives of the Great Recession's impact on higher education is that it makes it a lot easier to convince college students that state and local politics is important and worthy of their attention. Holden Thorp's problem makes that point pretty stark and pretty clear. It is worth emphasizing this point, though, because it represents the first and fundamental goal of this book: everyone—not just college students—has a vested interest in knowing more about state and local government.

The Impact of State and Local Politics on Daily Life

Regardless of who you are and what you do or want to do, if you reside in the United States, state and local governments play a large role in your life. Regardless of what you are interested in—graduating, a career, relationships—state and local governments shape how, whether, and to what extent you are able to pursue these interests. To follow up on the example in the previous section, let's consider your college education. The vast majority of college students in the United States—about 70 percent—attend public institutions of higher education.[3] Public colleges and universities are created and supported by state governments. For many readers of this book, the opportunity to get a college education is possible only because each state government created a system of higher education. For example, California has three major higher education systems: the University of California, the California State University, and the California Community College System. State governments require that taxpayers subsidize the operation of these education systems; in other words, the systems were designed not just to provide educational opportunities but also to make those opportunities broadly accessible, with tuition covering only a portion of the actual costs of a student's education. Much of rest comes from the taxpayers' pockets via the state government. When that state subsidy falls, people like Holden Thorp get headaches and college students inevitably end up paying more in tuition. Yet even with state governments putting less into higher education these days, it is worth pointing out that they still are the single biggest revenue source for these institutions. Tuition and fees cover about 20 percent of public college revenues, compared to 30 percent from state appropriations (the rest comes from investments, foundations, local governments, the federal government, and other miscellaneous sources).[4]

Even if you attend a private college, the state government may still play a significant role in covering the costs of your education. A quarter

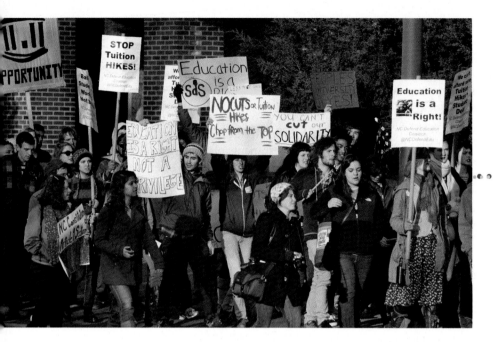

Many colleges and universities have raised tuition to offset declining appropriations from state legislatures, a move that critics argue is making higher education unaffordable for many. In February 2012, tuition hikes of 9 percent approved by the University of North Carolina Board of Governors prompted a student protest.

Local units of government operate most of these schools. Private grade schools also are subject to a wide variety of state and local government regulations, ranging from teacher certification and minimum curriculum requirements to basic health and safety standards. Whether you attended public or private school—or were homeschooled—at the end of the day you had no choice in the decision to get a basic grade school education. Although the minimum requirements vary, every state in the union requires that children receive at least a grade school education.

State and local governments do not exist simply to regulate large areas of your life, even if it sometimes seems that way. Their primary purpose is to provide services to their respective populations. In providing these services, state and local governments shape the social and economic lives of their citizens. Education is a good example of a public service that extends deep into the daily lives of Americans, but it is far from the only one. The roads you use to get to school are there because state and local authorities built them and maintain them. The electricity that runs your computer comes from a utility grid regulated by state government, local government, or both. State and local governments are responsible for the sewer and water systems that make the bathroom down the hall possible. They make sure that the water you drink is safe and that the burger, sushi, or salad you bought in your student union does not make you sick.[7] State governments determine the violations and punishments that constitute the criminal law. Local governments are responsible primarily for law enforcement and

of the students at private, nonprofit schools receive grants or other forms of financial aid directly funded by state governments. In fact, undergraduates at private colleges receive on average more than $2,500 in state grants or other financial aid from state or local government. Not including tuition, that amount of financial aid is several hundred dollars more than the average undergraduate at a public college receives from the state.[5]

State governments do not just determine what opportunities for higher education are available and what they cost. Some states have curriculum mandates. You may be taking a course on state and local politics—and reading this book—because your state government decided that it was a worthy investment of your time and money. In Texas, for example, a state politics course is not just a good idea—it's the law. According to Section 51.301 of the Texas Education Code, to receive a bachelor's degree from any publicly funded college in the state, a student must successfully complete a course on state politics.

Think that's a lot of regulation? The government's role in shaping your college education is actually pretty small. Compared to the heavy involvement of state and local governments in shaping K–12 education, colleges have free rein. Roughly 90 percent of students in grades 9–12 attend public high schools.[6]

fire protection. The services that state and local governments supply are such a part of our lives that in many cases we only notice their absence—when the water does not run, when the road is closed, or when the educational subsidy either declines or disappears.

The Comparative Method in Practice: Yes, They Really Do Tax Dogs in West Virginia

Recognizing the impacts of state and local government may be a reasonable way to spark an interest in the topic, but interest alone does not convey knowledge. A systematic approach to learning about state and local government is necessary to gain a coherent understanding of the many activities, responsibilities, and levels involved. In this book, that systematic approach is the **comparative method**, which uses similarities and differences as the basis for systematic explanation. Any two states or localities that you can think of will differ in a number of ways. For example, they really do tax dogs in West Virginia. The state authorizes each county government to assess a fee for every dog within that county's jurisdiction. This is not the case in, say, Nebraska, where dogs have to be licensed but are not taxed.[8] Another example: Texas has executed hundreds of criminals since the moratorium, or ban, on the death penalty was lifted in the 1970s; other states have executed none.

Or consider the electoral differences between states. In recent elections, Kansans and Nebraskans sent only Republicans to the U.S. House of Representatives (in 2012 all seven House members from these two states were Republicans). The people of Massachusetts sent just Democrats (all ten seats were held by Democrats in 2012). Differences between states and localities do not just involve such oddities as the tax status of the family pet or such big political questions as the balance of power in the House of Representatives.

Those of you who do something as ordinary as buying a soda after class may pay more than your peers in other states or cities. Some readers of this book are certainly paying more in tuition and fees than those in other colleges. Why?

The comparative method answers such questions by systematically looking for **variance**, or differences, between comparable units of analysis. For our purposes, states are one comparable unit of analysis. Local governments—governments below the state level, such as county boards of commissioners and city councils—are another. Governments at each of these levels, state or local, have basic similarities that make meaningful comparisons possible. One way to think of this is that the comparative method is based on the idea that you can learn more about apples by comparing them to other apples than you can by comparing them to oranges or bananas.

> Governments at each of these levels, state or local, have basic similarities that make meaningful comparisons possible. One way to think of this is that the comparative method is based on the idea that you can learn more about apples by comparing them to other apples than you can by comparing them to oranges or bananas.

For example, governmentally speaking, all fifty states have a lot in common. Their governmental structures are roughly the same. All have a basic division of powers among the executive, legislative, and judicial branches of government. All have to operate within the broad confines of

Comparative Method
A learning approach based on studying the differences and similarities among similar units of analysis (such as states).

Variance
The difference between units of analysis on a particular measure.

the single set of rules that is the U.S. Constitution. There's a bit more variety below the state level, with many different kinds and levels of local government (counties, municipalities, townships, and so forth), but broadly speaking all these governments share a basic set of responsibilities and all have to operate within the rules set down within their respective state constitutions. These similarities among states and among local governments make meaningful comparisons possible. Paradoxically, what makes such comparisons meaningful are not the similarities but the differences. This is because even though states share similar political structures and follow the same overall set of rules, they make very different choices. These differences have consequences. Take, for example, college tuition and fees. As noted earlier, there is a direct relationship between the size of a state government's contribution to higher education and a student's average tuition bill. Underlying this relationship is a set of differences that explains why your tuition bill is high (or low) compared to tuition charged by colleges in other states. Simply put, your tuition bill is comparatively higher (or lower) depending on the size of a state government's subsidy to higher education; this is a lesson hundreds of thousands of students have become all too painfully aware of in recent years. These sorts of meaningful differences extend far beyond how much you're paying for your college education. A similar difference explains why some of you will pay more for a soda after class than others. The sales tax on a can of soda ranges from 0 to 8 percent, depending on the city and state, hence the different prices in different locales.[9] These examples demonstrate the essence of the comparative method—from your tuition bills to the price of soda, differences between political jurisdictions make a difference in the daily lives of citizens.

Such differences can lend themselves to very sophisticated and very useful statistical analyses. For example, exactly how much is a tuition bill influenced by state support of public higher education? A professional policy analyst can use data on state higher education funding and tuition rates at state universities and colleges to provide a precise estimate of the relationship between the contributions from state government and your tuition bill. On average, for every appropriation of $1,000 per student by state government, tuition and fees at public four-year universities fall by a little more than $200.[10] Of course, the reverse is also true. For every reduction of $1,000 per student in state aid, tuition goes up by an average of $200.

This basic approach of looking for differences that make a difference can be used to answer a broad range of "why" questions. For example, we know that how much a state gives to higher education helps determine how much you pay in tuition. So why do some states provide more support to higher education than others? This is a question about one difference (variation in how much state governments spend on higher education) that can be answered by looking at other differences. What might these differences be? Well, they could range from partisan politics in a state's legislature to a state's traditions and history to a state's relative wealth. As a starting point for using the comparative approach to analyze such questions, consider the following basic differences among states and among localities.

Sociodemographics

The populations of states and localities vary enormously in size, age, and ethnicity. The particular mix of these characteristics, or **sociodemographics**, in a specific state or community has a profound impact on the state or community's politics. California is the most populous state in the nation, with more than 37 million residents. It is a racially and ethnically diverse population, with only 39.7 percent non-Hispanic whites and with many first-generation or second-generation immigrants. Roughly 13.7 percent of Californians live in poverty. Compare this with New Hampshire, which has about 1.3 million residents, 92.2 percent of whom are non-Hispanic whites and only about 7.8 percent of whom live below the poverty line.[11] These population characteristics present different challenges to the governments in these two states. Differences in

Sociodemographics
The characteristics of a population, including size, age, and ethnicity.

populations are likely to promote different attitudes about and policies on welfare, affirmative action, bilingual education programs, even the role and responsibilities of government in general.

And it gets better. All these population characteristics are dynamic. That is, they change. From 2000 to 2010, the population of McKinney, Texas, grew by more than 200 percent.[12] During roughly the same time period, the population of Parkersburg, West Virginia, shrank by more than 21 percent. Such population expansions and contractions create very different problems and policy priorities for local governments—the struggle to accommodate new growth in a fast-developing area versus the challenge of maintaining even basic services in a rural county in which there are ever fewer taxpayers to tax. Or consider the population of the entire state of Florida, which was still growing in 2010, but at the slowest annual rate seen in three decades. That gearing down of population growth is expected to influence everything from housing starts to job creation to state and local tax collections.[13]

How might sociodemographics be related to, say, your tuition bill? Consider the age distribution of a state's population, from young to old. There is less demand for college education among those older than sixty-five than there is among those in the traditional undergraduate demographic of eighteen to twenty-four. Given this, states with higher percentages of their populations in older age groups face a different set of education policy pressures than those with higher concentrations in younger groups. States with large aging populations are likely to face less demand for higher education spending and more demand for public programs that address the needs of the elderly, such as access to healthcare. Why do some states provide more support to higher education than others? At least a partial answer to this question is that different sociodemographics create different demands for higher education.

Study Map 1-1 for a moment. Believe it or not, you are actually looking at the United States. The reason the states look so strange is that this is a special kind of map called a cartogram. Instead of using actual geographical space to determine the size of a particular area represented in the map—the number of square miles in each state,

for instance—cartograms use other variables to determine how size is represented. This cartogram depicts the size of each state's population, another useful way to compare states. Notice that some states that are geographically actually pretty big, such as New Mexico at 122,000 square miles, are very small on this map because they have small populations. Other states that are geographically actually quite small, such as Connecticut (with only 5,000 square miles), look much bigger on this map because they have large populations. Some states, such as Virginia, don't look that different in size at all from their appearance on a traditional map.

Texas is the country's fastest-growing state, with a 2.1 percent population increase in 2011. It narrowly beat out the previous population-growth champ, Utah, which came in second with an annual growth rate of 1.93 percent.

Culture and History

States and localities have distinct "personalities" that are apparent in everything from the "bloody bucket" shoulder patch worn by the Pennsylvania National Guard to the drawl that distinguishes the speech of West Texas natives. Some states have been part of the Union for more than two hundred years and still project an Old World connection to Europe. Hawaii and Alaska became states within living memory and are more associated with the exoticism of the Pacific and the Old West. New York City prides itself on being a cosmopolitan center of Western civilization. The visitor's bureau of Lincoln, Nebraska, touts the city's small-town ambience and Middle American values. These differences are more than interesting variations in accent and local points of pride. They are visible symbols that represent distinct values and attitudes. Political scientists generally accept that these differences extend to government and that each state has a distinct **political culture**,

Political Culture
The attitudes and beliefs broadly shared in a polity about the role and responsibility of government.

MAP 1-1

Population by State

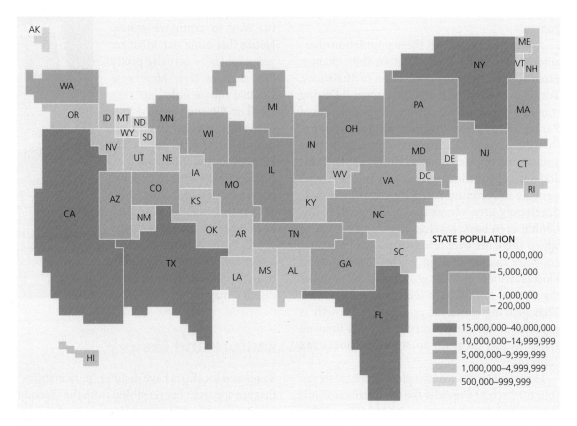

STATE POPULATION

- 10,000,000
- 5,000,000
- 1,000,000
- 200,000

- 15,000,000–40,000,000
- 10,000,000–14,999,999
- 5,000,000–9,999,999
- 1,000,000–4,999,999
- 500,000–999,999

Source: U.S. Department of Commerce, *Statistical Abstract of the United States, 2012* (Washington, DC: U.S. Census Bureau, 2012), "Table 16, Resident Population by Age and State: 2010," 21, www.census.gov/prod/2011pubs/12statab/pop.pdf.

identifiable general attitudes and beliefs about the role and responsibility of government.

Daniel Elazar's *American Federalism: A View from the States* is the classic study of political culture. In this book, first published more than forty years ago, Elazar not only describes different state cultures and creates a classification of state cultures still in use today but also explains why states have distinctly different political cultures. Elazar argues that political culture is a product of how the United States was settled. He says that people's religious and ethnic backgrounds played the dominant role in establishing political cultures. On this basis, there were three distinct types of settlers who fanned out across the United States in more or less straight lines from the East Coast to the West Coast. These distinct migration patterns created three different types of state political cultures: moralistic, individualistic, and traditionalistic.[14]

States with **moralistic cultures** are those in which politics is the means used to achieve a good and just society. Such states tend to be clustered in the northern parts of the country (New England, the upper Midwest, and the Pacific Northwest). Elazar argues that the Puritans who originally settled the Northeast came to the New World seeking religious freedom. Their political culture reflected a desire to use politics to construct the best possible society. This notion, that government and politics represent the means to the

Moralistic Culture
A political culture that views politics and government as the means to achieve the collective good.

Demographics and culture give each state and locality a unique "personality." Here teenagers celebrate the Chinese New Year by blowing confetti into the air in New York City's Chinatown.

greater good, creates a society that values involvement in politics and views government as a positive force for addressing social problems. This general orientation toward government and politics spread along the northern and middle parts of the country in successive waves of migration. Wisconsin, for example, is a classic moralistic state. First settled by Yankees and later by Scandinavians, Germans, and Eastern Europeans, the state has long had a reputation for high levels of participation in politics (for example, high levels of voter turnout), policy innovation, and scandal-free government.

States with individualistic cultures have a different view of government and politics. In individualistic cultures, people view government as an extension of the marketplace, something in which people participate for individual reasons and to achieve individual goals. Government should provide the services that people want, but it is not viewed as a vehicle to create a "good society" or to intervene in private activities. Politics in individualistic states is viewed like any other business. Officeholders expect to be paid like professionals, and political parties are, in essence, corporations that compete to provide goods and services to people. Unlike those in moralistic states, as long as the roads are paved and the trains run on time, folks in individualistic states tend to tolerate more corruption in government.

Why? In individualistic states, "Both politicians and citizens look upon political activity as

a specialized one," Elazar writes, "and no place for amateurs to play an active role."[15] The roots of this view of government, according to Elazar, come from the English, Scottish, Irish, and Germans who initially settled in states such as Maryland, New Jersey, and Pennsylvania. They came to the United States in search of individual opportunity, not to construct some idealized vision of the good society. This "every man for himself" attitude was reflected in politics, and the individualistic culture was carried by subsequent waves of migration into places such as Illinois and Missouri.

New Jersey is a good example of an individualistic state. The state, as political scientist Maureen Moakley puts it, "Has always been more of a polyglot than a melting pot."[16] Originally settled by waves of poor and uneducated immigrants in pursuit of the American Dream, in more recent times it has become home to more than a million foreign-born residents and large racial and ethnic minority populations. The result is a fragmented political culture in which many residents feel more connected to their local communities than to the state. Not surprisingly given all this, New Jersey has a long tradition of strong,

---

Individualistic Culture
A political culture that views politics and government as just another way to achieve individual goals.

A Difference
That Makes *A Difference*

Is It Better to Be a Woman in Vermont or a Gal in Mississippi?

According to the Institute for Women's Policy Research (IWPR), it is better to be a woman in Vermont than a gal in Mississippi.

Why? Well, in an analysis of the status of women in the states, the IWPR had several reasons for ranking Vermont as the best state for women and Mississippi as the worst. For example, in Vermont women had greater economic autonomy and enjoyed greater reproductive rights than women in Mississippi. This is only a partial answer to the question, however. To learn the rest of it, we must ask: *Why* would women have greater economic autonomy and more reproductive rights in Vermont than in Mississippi?

The comparative approach to answering this question involves looking for other differences between Vermont and Mississippi—differences that might explain the variance in the status of women. Some candidates for those explanatory differences are presented in Table 1-1. This table shows the top five and the bottom five states in the IWPR rankings, the dominant political culture in each state, and the percentage of state legislators in each state who were women in 2012. Notice any patterns?

You may have caught that all of the top five states have either moralistic or individualistic cultures. All of the bottom five states have traditionalistic cultures. Therefore, political culture might explain some of the difference in women's status. States in which the dominant political values stress the importance of everyone getting involved might offer more opportunities for women. So might states in which such values emphasize hard work as the predominant basis for getting ahead in life. States in which the dominant political values stress leaving the important decisions to established elites might offer fewer opportunities for women because, traditionally, elites have been male.

Also, take a look at the proportions of women in the state legislatures. On average, about one-third of state legislators in the top five states are women. In the bottom five states, that average is halved—only about 16 percent of state legislators are women. This is a difference that can have considerable impact. A number of studies show

TABLE 1-1

Politics and the Status of Women in the States: Some Variables

Five Best States for Women	Dominant Political Culture	Percentage of State Legislators Who Are Women
1. Vermont	Moralistic	38.9
2. Connecticut	Individualistic	29.9
3. Minnesota	Moralistic	32.8
4. Washington	Moralistic	32
5. Oregon	Moralistic	28.9
Five Worst States for Women	**Dominant Political Culture**	**Percentage of State Legislators Who Are Women**
46. Oklahoma	Traditionalistic	12.8
47. Arkansas	Traditionalistic	22.2
48. Kentucky	Traditionalistic	18.8
49. South Carolina	Traditionalistic	9.4
50. Mississippi	Traditionalistic	16.7

Sources: National Conference of State Legislatures, "Women in State Legislatures: 2012 Legislative Session," www.ncsl.org/legislatures-elections/wln/women-in-state-legislatures-2012.aspx; Institute for Women's Policy Research, *The Status of Women in the States,* 2004, www.iwpr.org/States2004/SWS2004/index.htm; Daniel J. Elazar, *American Federalism: A View from the States* (New York: Crowell, 1966).

that women legislators tend to support more progressive policies, are more likely to pay attention to women's issues, and are more likely to push these issues into law.[*]

Thus states that have more women in their legislatures are more likely to respond to issues such as reproductive rights, violence against women, child-support policies, and family-leave benefits. All these contribute to the IWPR's calculations. Why is Vermont a better state for women than Mississippi? A comparative answer to that question is that Vermont has a political culture that is more likely to encourage and support political participation by women and it also has a greater female presence in its state legislature.

---

[*]Michele Swers, "Understanding the Policy Impact of Electing Women: Evidence from Research on Congress and State Legislatures," *PS: Political Science & Politics* 34, no. 2 (2001): 217–220.

independent local government, with laws that give the state's nearly six hundred general-purpose local governments more power than localities in other states.

In **traditionalistic cultures**, politics is the province of elites, something that average citizens should not concern themselves with. Traditionalistic states are, as their name suggests, fundamentally conservative, in the sense that they are concerned with preserving a well-established society. Like moralistic states, traditionalistic states believe that government serves a positive role. But there is one big difference—traditionalistic states believe the larger purpose of government is to maintain the existing social order. Those at the top of the social structure are expected to play a dominant role in politics, and power is concentrated in the hands of these elites. Traditionalistic states tend to be rural states (at least historically) in which agriculture, rather than a broader mix of competing commercial activities, is the main economic driver.

Traditionalistic cultures tend to be concentrated in the Deep South, in states such as Georgia, Mississippi, and South Carolina. In these states, politics is significantly shaped by tradition and history. Like the settlers of individualistic states, those who settled the South sought personal opportunity. The preindustrial, agrarian economy of the South, however, led to a culture that was little more than a variation of the feudal order of the European Middle Ages. As far back as the 1830s, French aristocrat and writer Alexis de Tocqueville, writing about the United States, noted that "as one goes farther south . . . the population does not exercise such a direct influence on affairs. . . . The power of the elected officials is comparatively greater and that of the voter less."[17]

Few states today can be considered "pure" examples of any of these cultures. In other words, most states have elements of two of the cultures or of all three. For example, a number of traditionalistic states, such as Florida and Georgia, have seen huge influxes of people from northern states, people who often are not from traditionalistic cultures. The Deep South is also considerably more urban than it used to be. Such changes tend to add elements of the moralistic and individualistic cultures into the traditionalistic mix.

Even with such changes, however, for most states one of Elazar's three political cultures is likely to be dominant, as Map 1-2 shows. Numerous studies have found that the dominant

MAP 1-2

Dominant Political Culture by State

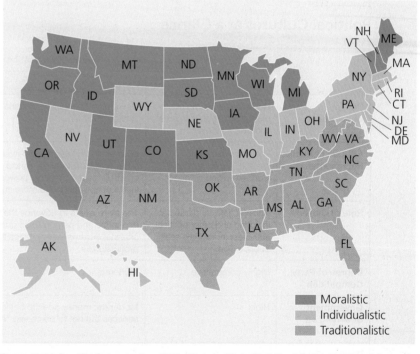

Source: Virginia Gray, "The Socioeconomic and Political Contexts of States," in *Politics in the American States: A Comparative Analysis,* 10th ed., ed. Virginia Gray and Russell Hanson (Washington, DC: CQ Press, 2013), 22.

Traditionalistic Culture
A political culture that views politics and government as the means of maintaining the existing social order.

political culture shapes politics and policy in important ways. Policy change and innovation, for example, are more likely in moralistic states.

Individualistic states are more likely to offer businesses tax breaks. Traditionalistic states tend to commit less public money to areas such as education.[18] Faced with similar problems, therefore, the Texas and Wisconsin state legislatures may propose radically different policy responses. These differences are at least partially products of the political cultures that still distinguish each state. In other words, culture and history matter.

These cultural differences certainly are apparent when it comes to supporting higher education. Moralistic states commit considerably more resources to higher education than do individualistic and traditionalistic states. They spend about 13 percent more per capita on colleges and universities than states with the other two cultures. Because moralistic states are those in which attitudes support higher levels of commitment to the public sector, these spending differences make sense in cultural terms. Why do some states provide more support to higher education than others? Apparently, another part of the answer is that some political cultures see higher education in more communal than individual terms.

Economy

The relative size and health of a state's economy has a huge impact on its capacity to govern and provide public services. The per capita gross domestic product—the state equivalent of the gross national product—varies from about $28,000 in Mississippi to $63,000 in Delaware[19] (see Map 1-3). This means government in Delaware has the ability to tap a greater amount of resources than government in Mississippi. The difference in wealth, in effect, means that if Delaware and Mississippi were to implement

TABLE 1-2

Political Cultures at a Glance

	Elazar Classification		
	Moralistic	**Individualistic**	**Traditionalistic**
Role of Government	Government should act to promote the public interest and policy innovation.	Government should be utilitarian, a service provider.	Government should help preserve the status quo.
Attitude of Public Representatives	Politicians can effect change; public service is worthwhile and an honor.	Businesslike. Politics is a career like any other, and individual politicians are oriented toward personal power. High levels of corruption are more common.	Politicians can effect change, but politics is the province of the elites.
Role of Citizens	Citizens actively participate in voting and other political activities; individuals seek public office.	The state exists to advance the economic and personal self-interest of citizens; citizens leave politics to the professionals.	Ordinary citizens are not expected to be politically involved.
Degree of Party Competition	Highly competitive	Moderate	Weak
Government Spending on Services	High	Moderate; money goes to basic services but not to perceived "extras."	Low
Political Culture	Strong	Fragmented	Strong
Most Common in . . .	Northeast, northern Midwest, Northwest	Middle parts of the country, such as the Mid-Atlantic; parts of the Midwest, such as Missouri and Illinois; parts of the West, such as Nevada	Southern states, rural areas

Source: Adapted from Daniel J. Elazar, *American Federalism: A View from the States,* 2nd ed. (New York: Crowell, 1972).

MAP 1-3

Economy by State

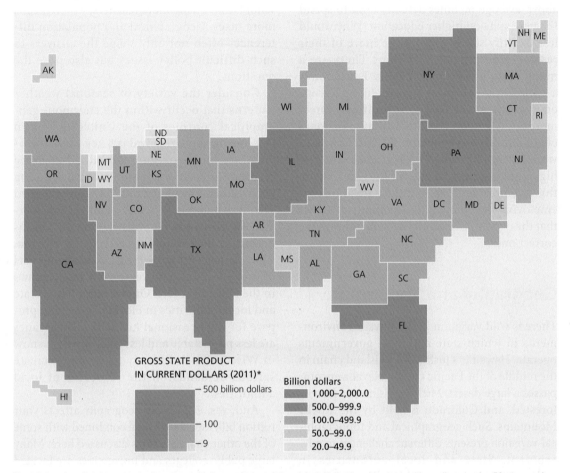

GROSS STATE PRODUCT
IN CURRENT DOLLARS (2011)*

— 500 billion dollars

— 100

— 9

Billion dollars

	1,000–2,000.0
	500.0–999.9
	100.0–499.9
	50.0–99.0
	20.0–49.9

The relative size of state economies is measured in terms of gross state product. Notice how big states with small economies (Montana and Alaska) compare to small states with big economies (New Jersey and Massachusetts).

Source: U.S. Bureau of Economic Analysis, "Gross Domestic Product by State (millions of current dollars)—All Industry Total, 2011," http://bea.gov/iTable/iTable.cfm?reqid=99&step=1.

identical and equivalent public services, Mississippi would have a considerably higher tax rate. This is because Mississippi would have to take a greater proportion of its smaller amount of resources than Delaware. These sorts of differences also are visible at the local level. Wealthy suburbs can enjoy lower tax rates and still spend more on public services than economically struggling urban or rural communities.

Regional economic differences do not just determine tax burdens and the level of public services. They also determine the relative priorities of particular policy and regulatory issues. Fishing, for example, is a sizable industry in coastal states in the Northeast and Northwest. States such as Maine and Washington have numerous laws, regulations, and enforcement responsibilities tied to the catching, processing, and transporting of fish. Regulating the economic exploitation of marine life occupies very little government attention and resources in places such as Kansas and Nevada, although agriculture in the former and gambling in the latter create just as many policy challenges and demands for government action.

Regardless of the basis of a state's economy, greater wealth does not always translate into more support for public programs. States with above-average incomes actually tend to spend *less* per capita on higher education. Why would less wealthy states concentrate more of their resources on higher education? There are a number of possible explanations. Education is a critical component of a postindustrial economy, so states that are less well-off may direct more of their resources into education in hopes of building a better economic future. Citizens in wealthy states may simply be better able to afford higher tuition costs. Whatever the explanation, this example suggests another advantage of employing the comparative method—it shows that the obvious assumptions are not always the correct ones.

Geography and Topography

There is wild variation in the physical environments in which state and local governments operate. Hawaii is a lush tropical island chain in the middle of the Pacific Ocean, Nevada encompasses a large desert, Michigan is mostly heavily forested, and Colorado is split by the Rocky Mountains. Such geographical and topographical variation presents different challenges to government. State and local authorities in California devote considerable time and resources to preparing for earthquakes. Their counterparts in Texas spend comparatively little time thinking about earthquakes, but they do concern themselves with tornadoes, grass fires, and hurricanes.

Combine geography with population characteristics and the challenges become even more complex. Montana is a large rural state in which the transportation logistics—simply getting students to school—can present something of a conundrum. Is it better to bus students long distances to large, centrally located schools, or should there be many smaller schools within easy commuting distance for relatively few students? The first is cheaper. Larger schools can offer academic and extracurricular activities that smaller schools cannot afford. But the busing

exacts a considerable cost on students and families. The second alternative eases transportation burdens, but it requires building more schools and hiring more teachers, which means more taxes. Geographical and population differences often not only shape the answers to such difficult policy issues but also pose the questions.

Consider the variety of seasonal weather patterns that occur within the enormous geographical confines of the United States. In Wisconsin, snow removal is a key service provided by local governments. Road-clearing crews are often at work around the clock during bad weather. The plows, the crews, and the road salt all cost money. They all require a considerable investment in administration and coordination to do the job effectively. In Florida, snow removal is low on local governments' lists of priorities, for good reason—it rarely snows in the Sunshine State. On the other hand, state and local authorities in Florida do need to prepare for the occasional hurricane. Hurricanes are less predictable and less common than snow in Wisconsin, and it only takes one to create serious demands on the resources of local authorities.

And, yes, even basic geography affects your tuition bill, especially when combined with some of the other characteristics discussed here. Many large public colleges and universities are located in urban centers because central geographical locations serve more people more efficiently. Delivering higher education in rural areas is a more expensive proposition simply because there are fewer people in the service area. States with below-average population densities tend to be larger and more sparsely populated. They also tend to spend more on higher education. Larger government subsidies are necessary to make tuition affordable.

Recognizing the Stakes

The variation across states and localities offers more than a way to help make sense of your tuition bill or to explain why some public school systems are better funded or to understand why taxes are lower in some states. These differences also serve to underline the central role of states and localities in the American political system. Compared to the federal government, state and local governments employ more people and buy more goods and services from the private sector. They have the primary responsibility for addressing many of the issues that people care about the most, including education, crime prevention, transportation, healthcare, and the environment. Public opinion polls often show that citizens place more trust in their state and local governments than in the federal government. These polls frequently express citizens' preference for having the former relieve the latter of a greater range of policy responsibilities.[20] With these responsibilities and expectations, it should be obvious that state and local politics are played for high stakes.

> Compared to the federal government, state and local governments employ more people and buy more goods and services from the private sector. They have the primary responsibility for addressing many of the issues that people care about the most, including education, crime prevention, transportation, healthcare, and the environment.

High stakes, yes, but it is somewhat ironic that state and local governments tend to get less attention in the media, in private conversation, and in curricula and classrooms than does their federal counterpart.[21] Ask most people to think about American government, and chances are they will think first about the president, Congress, Social Security, or some other feature of the national government. Yet most American governments are state or local. Only 535 elected legislators serve in the U.S. Congress. Thousands of legislators are elected at the state level, and tens of thousands more serve in the legislative branches of local government.

In terms of people, state and local governments dwarf the federal government. The combined civilian workforce of the federal government (about 3 million) is less than half the number of people working for a single category of local government—more than 6 million people work for public elementary and secondary schools alone.[22] Roughly 5 million state employees and more than 14 million local government employees punch the time clock every day (see Map 1-4). In terms of dollars, state and local governments combined represent about the same spending force as the federal government. In 2009, state and local government expenditures totaled approximately $3 trillion.[23]

The size of state and local government operations is commensurate with these governments' twenty-first-century role in the political system. After spending much of the twentieth century being drawn closer into the orbit and influence of the federal government, states and localities spent the century's last two decades, and much of the first decade of the twenty-first, aggressively asserting their independence. This maturing of nonfederal, or subnational, government made its leaders and its policies—not to mention its differences—among the most important characteristics of our political system. The Great Recession of 2008–2009 made that importance all too clear. As the economy went south and the budget gaps went north, state and local governments were forced into a painful process of cutting budgets. As pretty much any college student at a publicly supported college or university can attest, when state and local governments start hurting, the pain is felt by, well, everyone. What is at stake in state and local politics turns out to be not just what *you* are interested in, but just about anything that anyone is interested in. This is one of the reasons the federal government passed a massive economic

MAP 1-4

Number of Government Employees by State

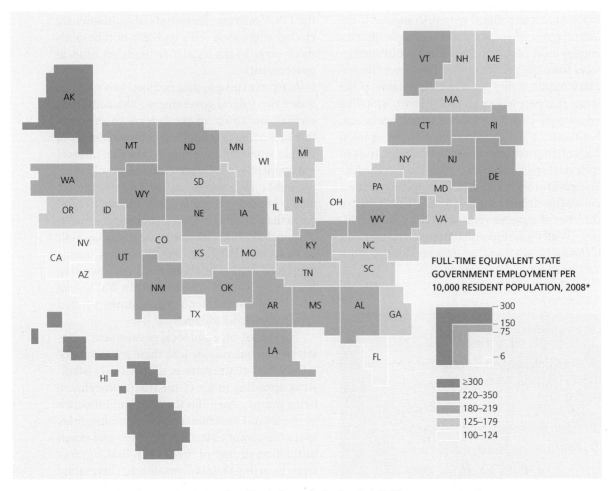

FULL-TIME EQUIVALENT STATE GOVERNMENT EMPLOYMENT PER 10,000 RESIDENT POPULATION, 2008*

- 300
- 150
- 75
- 6

- ≥300
- 220–350
- 180–219
- 125–179
- 100–124

Source: U.S. Census Bureau, "State Government Enrollment and Payroll Data by State and by Function: March 2011," www.census.gov/govs/apes.

stimulus package that sent billions of dollars pouring into state and local treasuries in 2010 and 2011. If you want a quick and direct way to reach the nation's economic, social, and political heart, then state and local governments are the obvious routes.

The context of the federal system of government, and the role of state and local governments within that system, is given more in-depth coverage in chapter 2. For now, it is important to recognize that governance in the United States is more of a network than a hierarchy. The policies and politics of any single level of government are

connected and intertwined with the policies and politics of the other levels of government in a complex web of interdependent relationships. The role of states and localities in these governance partnerships has changed considerably in the past few decades.

What states and localities do, and how they go about doing it, turns out to shape national life overall as well as the lives of individual citizens. Given what is at stake at the state and local levels, no citizen can fully comprehend the role and importance of government without understanding subnational politics.

Laboratories of Democracy: Devolution and the Limits of Government

U.S. Supreme Court Justice Louis Brandeis famously described the states as **laboratories of democracy**. This metaphor refers to the ability of states—and, to a lesser extent, localities—to experiment with policy. Successful experiments can be replicated by other states or adopted by the national government. For much of the past thirty years, state-federal relations have been characterized by **devolution**, or the process of taking power and responsibility away from the federal government and giving it to state and local governments. As a result, the states for a time aggressively promoted new ways to solve old problems in such high-profile policy areas as welfare, gun control, and education. That trend of increasing state policy autonomy came to a screeching halt with the severe economic contraction of 2008–2009; in the next few years states became critically dependent on federal money to stay solvent, and that meant they had to pay attention to federal policy priorities. Currently the federal government is in the process of drawing down its massive intergovernmental grants to state and local governments. Whether this will herald a reduction in federal influence and a resurgence of state policy independence remains to be seen—as we shall see in chapter 4, state budgetary conditions are far from rosy, and only the federal government has the power to print money.

We'll take a closer look at the details of inter-governmental relations in the next chapter, but it is important here to recognize that how state and local governments exercise their independent decision-making authority is dependent on a number of factors. Some of these factors are external. The U.S. Constitution, federal laws and regulations, nationwide recessions, and the like constrain what states and localities can and cannot do. Internal factors, such as the characteristics of a particular state, also play a critical role in setting limits on what the state decides to do.

The big three of these internal factors are wealth, the characteristics of the state's political system, and the relative presence of organized interest groups, those individuals who organize to support policy issues that concern them. Public programs cost money. Wealth sets the limits of possible government action. Simply speaking, wealthier states can afford to do more than poorer states. For most states, lack of funds is currently the biggest factor limiting independent policy action at the state and local levels. Simply put, many subnational governments do not have the money to launch expensive new policy initiatives. Indeed, in recent years many of these governments have not had the money to keep funding their existing programs and services (higher education, for example) at previous levels. While it is important, however, money is not the only factor that influences policy directions at the subnational level. Political system characteristics are the elements of the political environment that are specific to a state. States in which public opinion is relatively conservative are likely to pursue different policy avenues than states in which public opinion is more liberal. States in which Republicans dominate the government are likely to opt for different policy choices than states in which Democrats dominate. States with professional full-time legislatures are more likely to formulate and pursue sustained policy agendas than are states in which legislators are part-timers who meet only periodically. States in which the government perceives an electoral mandate to reform government are more likely to be innovative than are states in which the government perceives an electoral mandate to retain the status quo.[24] Organized interest group activity helps determine what sort of policy demands government responds to. Governments in states with powerful teachers' unions, for example, experience different education policy pressures than do governments in states in which teachers'

Laboratories of Democracy
A metaphor that emphasizes the states' ability to engage in different policy experiments without interference from the federal government.

Devolution
The process of taking power and responsibility away from the federal government and giving it to state and local governments.

It has a local government much like any other major municipality and electoral votes like a state, but it is ultimately ruled by Congress even though it has no representatives with full voting rights in the national legislature. Technically, Washington, D.C., is a federal city, the only political jurisdiction of its kind in the United States.

employment qualifications to maximum teacher-to-pupil ratios. Even within this range of tighter restrictions, however, local governments retain considerable leeway to act independently. School districts often decide to contract out cafeteria and janitorial services, cities and counties actively seek to foster economic development with tax abatements and loan guarantees, and police commissions experiment with community-based law enforcement. During the past two decades, many of the reforms enthusiastically pursued at all levels of government—reforms ranging from innovative management practices to the outright privatization of public services—have had their origins in local government.[25]

unions are politically weak. These three factors constitute the basic ingredients for policymaking in the states. Specifics vary enormously from state to state, and the potential combinations in this democratic laboratory are virtually infinite.

Localities face more policymaking constraints than states do because they typically are not sovereign governments. This means that, unlike states, local governments get their power from the level of government above them rather than directly from citizens. The states have much greater control over local governments than the federal government has over the states. Yet, even though local governments are much more subordinate to state government than state government is to the federal government, they do not simply take orders from the state capital. Many have independent taxing authority and broad discretion to act within their designated policy jurisdictions.

These policy jurisdictions, nevertheless, are frequently subject to formal limits. The authority of school districts, for example, extends only to funding and operating public schools. State government may place limits on districts' tax rates and set everything from minimal

> States and localities are not just safe places to engage in limited experimentation, they are the primary mechanisms connecting citizens to the actions of government.

What all this activity shows is that states and localities are not only the laboratories of democracy but also the engines of the American republic.

The Federal City

Riddle me this. It is a city. It is sort of a state. It is ruled by Congress. What is it? It is the District of Columbia, otherwise known as Washington, D.C. It is also the nation's capital, and it is surely the most unusual local government in the country.

Technically, Washington, D.C., is a federal city. Article I, Section 8, Paragraph 17, of the U.S. Constitution gives Congress the power to rule over an area not to exceed ten square miles that constitutes the seat of national government. Yet it has never been quite clear what that means in terms of governance. Should Congress rule the city directly? Should the citizens of the city be given the right to elect a representative government? If they do this, should the government be subordinate to Congress or should it be counted as equivalent to a state and thus free to make any laws that do not violate the U.S. Constitution?

Throughout the city's history, these questions have been answered very differently. In the early 1800s, the district was a strange collection of cities and counties, each governed by different means. Washington City and Georgetown were municipalities run by a chief executive (a mayor) and a legislature (a council). Depending on the time period, however, the mayors were sometimes appointed by the federal government and sometimes elected. In addition to the two cities there were also two counties. Maryland laws governed Washington County; Virginia laws governed Alexandria County.

In the 1870s, Washington City, Georgetown, and Washington County were combined into a single governmental unit, a federal territory with a governor appointed by the president and a legislature elected by the territorial residents. This eventually became the District of Columbia, or Washington, D.C. For most of its history, commissioners appointed by the federal government governed the district. It was not until 1974 that the residents of Washington, D.C., gained home rule and the right to elect their own mayor and council.

This mayor-council arrangement, however, is unlike any other municipal government in the United States. The laws passed by the council have to be reviewed and approved by Congress. The laws that govern federal-state relationships treat the district as a state, even though it is not a state and cannot operate like one. The mayor is not considered the head of a federal agency, but he or she is expected to act like one when seeking appropriations from Congress.

This odd hybrid of local, state, and federal governments is reflected in the unique electoral status of Washington, D.C., voters. Voters in the district have a local vote, but only half of a federal vote. They can vote for the president but not for a member of Congress. They can vote for a mayor and council, but they have no voting representative in Congress. Yet Congress has the power to overturn laws passed by the council. The district now has three electoral votes. Prior to 1963, it had none and D.C. voters could not cast a ballot for president.

All this makes Washington, D.C., the nation's most unusual local government. It is the only municipality that is a creature of the United States rather than of a state constitution, and, as such, it is the only really national city in the country.

Source: Selected material from Council of the District of Columbia, "History of Self-Government in the District of Columbia," 1997, www.dccouncil.washington.dc.us.

States and localities are not just safe places to engage in limited experimentation, they are the primary mechanisms connecting citizens to the actions of government. It is for exactly this reason that one of the central federal government responses to the economic crisis of 2008–2009 was to shore up local and state governments financially.

Conclusion

There are good reasons for developing a curiosity about state and local governments. State politics determines everything from how much you pay for college to whether your course in state and local governments is required or elective. Above and beyond understanding the impact of state and local governments on your own life and interests, studying such governments is important because of their critical role in the governance and life of the nation. Subnational, or nonfederal, governments employ more people than the federal government and spend as much money. Their responsibilities include everything from repairing potholes to regulating pot. It is difficult, if not impossible, to understand government in the United States and the rights, obligations, and benefits of citizenship without first understanding state and local governments.

This book fosters such an understanding through the comparative method. This approach involves looking for patterns in the differences among states and localities. Rather than advocating a particular perspective on state and local politics, the comparative method is predicated, or based, on a systematic way of asking and answering questions. Why is my tuition bill so high? Why does Massachusetts send mostly Democrats to the U.S. House of Representatives? Why are those convicted of capital crimes in Texas more likely to be executed than those convicted of comparable crimes in Connecticut? Why are sales taxes high in Alabama? Why is there no state income tax in South Dakota? We can answer each of these questions by comparing states and looking for systematic patterns in their differences. The essence of the comparative method is to use one difference to explain another.

This book's examination of state and local politics is organized into three distinct sections. The first section consists of five chapters designed to set the basic framework, or context, for studying state and local politics. Included here are chapters on federalism, state constitutions, budgets, political participation, and political parties and interest groups. The second section covers the institutions of state and local government: legislatures, executives, courts, and bureaucracy. Although elements of local government are discussed in all these, there are also two chapters in this section devoted solely to local politics and government. The final section covers a series of distinct policy areas: education, crime, healthcare and the environment. These chapters not only cover areas of substantive policy interests but also offer concrete examples of how a broad understanding of the context and institutions of state and local governments can be combined with the comparative method to promote a deeper understanding of the politics of states and localities.

The Latest Research

As discussed extensively in this chapter, the comparative method is an important tool used by scholars to understand how state-level differences translate into meaningful political and policy differences. A lot of these differences that make a difference are not static—indeed, some may be changing even as you read this textbook. Recently some of the most foundational state differences have been the subject of a series of studies that may change our understanding of those differences and their implications.

The "granddaddy" of all differences is political culture, a concept originated by Daniel Elazar that continues to be widely respected for its explanatory power. Yet, however powerful its explanatory capacities, Elazar's classification of state political cultures is not based on intensive statistical analysis; it is much more impressionistic. It is also static—in other words, the basic state classifications of moralistic, traditionalistic, and individualistic have not changed since Elazar defined them nearly a half century ago. In the time that has elapsed since then, large shifts in demographics have taken place as the result of new waves of immigration, population and other relevant data have become more widely available, and sophisticated statistical analysis techniques have been developed and broadly employed. All this gives state scholars the opportunity to undertake much more fine-grained analyses of regional value systems, how they translate into culture, how that culture might change, and what those changes might mean for state politics and policy.

Related to the renewed interest in studying and tracking cultural changes is a spate of new scholarship that focuses on measuring state-level political orientations and ideology, in effect capturing the political nuances of what makes a "red" state or a "blue" state or even a "happy" state. Several teams of scholars have been developing new measures of state-level policy attitudes and orientations, and these improved measures of political differences are proving themselves to useful for predicting important policy differences.

Below we summarize some of the cutting-edge research on the differences that make a difference.

• •

• **Lieske, Joel.** 2010. "The Changing Regional Sub-cultures of the American States and the Utility of a New Cultural Measure." *Political Research Quarterly* 63: 538–552.

Joel Lieske, a political scientist at Cleveland State University, is the scholar most associated with the continuing study of state political culture. Lieske's scholarship tackles one of the toughest questions in this area: How can we measure culture? Elazar's classifications are very useful but impressionistic, and efforts to quantify those classifications into "yardsticks" to measure degrees of cultural difference often amount to nothing more than putting numbers on Elazar's classifications. Lieske has long argued that immigration settlement patterns and degree of self-governance have nurtured the development of regional subcultures that may be more expansive than Elazar's threefold classification. Here he uses county-level data on racial origin, ethnic ancestry, religious affiliation, and various indicators of social structure to create a composite statistical measure of political culture. This is a much more sophisticated analysis than that employed by Elazar, and it results in not three primary subcultures but eleven. In Lieske's analysis, for example, moralistic cultures are actually made up of three related but distinct political subcultures—Nordic, Mormon, and Anglo-French, the labels representing the cultural elements of particular ethnic groups (especially Germans and Scandinavians) and different sects of dissenting Protestantism.

• **Lieske, Joel.** 2012. "American State Cultures: Testing a New Measure and Theory." *Publius: The Journal of Federalism* 42: 108–133.

In this article Lieske puts his new measure of state culture to the test. In a statistical contest, he pits his new measure against Elazar's typology and the most often used quantitative index of that typology (an index created in 1969 by political scientist Ira Sharkansky) to see which measure can better predict various indicators of state performance. Lieske's new measure of state cultural differences does the better job, suggesting that the new measure—which, unlike Elazar's, can at least theoretically be updated with new census data—better captures cultural differences.

• **Berry, William D., Richard C. Fording, Evan J. Ringquist, Russell L. Hanson, and Carl E. Klarner.** 2010. "Measuring Citizen and Government Ideology in the U.S. States: A Re-appraisal." *State Politics & Policy Quarterly* 10: 117–135.

One of the most important differences among states lies in the general political attitudes or orientations of the states' citizens. Scholars consider it critical to tap into those state-level attitudes for many reasons. For example, if we do not know the political orientations and attitudes of citizens, we have no means of assessing whether state lawmakers actually reflect and represent the wishes of their constituents. State-level measures of ideology are incredibly hard to construct. The central problem is that no comparable state-level scientific polls are done in all fifty states at the same time. One way to get around this problem is to infer state preferences by looking at the ideologies and policy preferences of the candidates who win congressional elections. This study employs these kinds of data to create a measure of state ideology that is found to do a good job of explaining differences in policies ranging from social welfare to incarceration rates.

• **Carsey, Thomas M., and Jeffrey J. Harden.** 2010. "New Measures of Partisanship, Ideology, and Policy Mood in the American States." *State Politics & Policy Quarterly* 10: 136–156.

This article takes an alternate approach to tackling the same measurement problem that Berry et al. address in the study cited above. Rather than inferring from lawmaker characteristics, however, Carsey and

(Continued)

(Continued)

Harden put together measures of state partisan identification, ideology, and policy mood using data from a series of polls taken in congressional election years from 2000 through 2006. The resulting measures are found to be good estimates of state-level differences on these dimensions.

- **Álvarez-Diaz, Ángel, Lucas González, and Benjamin Radcliff.** 2010. "The Politics of Happiness: On the Political Determinants of Quality of Life in the American States." *Journal of Politics* 72: 894–905.

This is a study of the differences that influence perhaps the most important difference, asking, What political differences influence the quality of life of citizens? The authors examine the ideology and partisanship of state governments and the policies these governments pursue, seeking to correlate these with measures of citizen satisfaction. Some may find the results surprising. States with more generous social welfare policies and more economic regulation—in other words, states that more closely resemble the social democratic countries of northern Europe—tend to have happier citizens who are more satisfied with their quality of life.

college.cqpress.com/
sites/govstateandlocal

Chapter Review

Key Concepts

- comparative method (p. 7)
- devolution (p. 19)
- individualistic culture (p. 11)
- laboratories of democracy (p. 19)
- moralistic culture (p. 10)
- political culture (p. 9)
- sociodemographics (p. 8)
- traditionalistic culture (p. 13)
- variance (p. 7)

Suggested Web Sites

- **http://academic.udayton.edu/sppq-TPR/index.htm.** Data archive Web site of *State Politics & Policy Quarterly,* an academic research journal devoted to the study of state-level questions.

- **http://library.cqpress.com/statestats.** A comprehensive and searchable database of state-level information (requires subscription).

- **http://quickfacts.census.gov/qfd.** U.S. Bureau of the Census Web site that lists state rankings on population, per capita income, employment, poverty, and other social and economic indexes.

- **www.csg.org/csg/default.** Web site of the Council of State Governments (CSG), an organization that represents elected and appointed officials in all three branches of state government. Publishes on a wide variety of topics and issues relevant to state politics and policy.

STATE STATS

State Stats on State and Local Government

Explore and compare data on the states! Go to college.cqpress.com/sites/ govstateandlocal to do these exercises.

1. How many state and local government employees are there in your state? Which state has the most? The least? How have these numbers changed in the past ten years? Why do you think these changes have occurred?

2. States with which political culture (individualistic, traditionalistic, or moralistic) spend the most, per capita, on higher education? Why might that be?

3. In your state, did the percentage of households headed by single mothers increase, decrease, or stay the same between 2006 and 2010? How might any changes in this percentage influence your state's budgeting decisions? How does this compare to states that neighbor yours?

4. What is the per capita state and local sales tax revenue in Delaware? What about in the states immediately surrounding Delaware? How are those states able to collect sales taxes? Why wouldn't neighboring citizens just drive to Delaware to do all of their shopping?

5. What is the per capita gross domestic product in your state? Is it above or below the national figure? Did your state's per capita GDP increase, decrease, or stay the same between 2010 and 2011? What differences between your state and others might explain why your state is above/ below the national average?

States and the federal government, like it or not, need each other. President Barack Obama and New Jersey governor Chris Christie may have different party loyalties and different policy preferences, but they set aside their differences to work together effectively to help New Jersey recover from the aftermath of a hurricane that devastated the state's coastal regions in fall 2012.

Federalism

THE POWER PLAN

- Why does the federal government seem to be gaining power while the states are losing it?
- What are the advantages and disadvantages of federalism?
- Why would some businesses prefer to be regulated by the federal government rather than by state governments?

In 1883 the poet Emma Lazarus was asked to pen a few words that might be donated to a charitable auction. The auction's purpose was to sell works of art and literature to raise money for a pedestal designed to hold a very big sculpture. You might have heard of the sculpture—the Statue of Liberty, which has raised high the torch of freedom over New York Harbor for more than a century and serves as one of the best-known and most iconic symbols of the United States. You might also know at least a few lines of "The New Colossus," the sonnet Lazarus composed for the cause—especially the bit that says, "Give me your tired, your poor, your huddled masses yearning to breathe free." The words express the idea of the United States as a nation of immigrants, founded not on race or religion but on a universal idea of individual liberty. *E pluribus unum* and all that. That sentiment of international roots and values, proudly engraved on a bronze plaque below Lady Liberty's tootsies, has been in pretty short supply in many states over the past couple of years. Indeed, state attitudes toward immigration have been less about welcoming the tired, poor, huddled masses than about telling them to get lost.

To be fair, the standoffish attitude of many states toward immigration these days is targeted specifically at illegal (or undocumented) immigration rather than at immigration in general. Immigration is an issue that sparks furious controversy. It is also an issue that highlights the often contentious and fractious relationship between state and federal governments. Historically and constitutionally, regulating immigration falls under the jurisdiction of the federal government. During the first decade of the twenty-first century, though, many states thought the federal government had punted on its responsibilities. By some estimates nearly 12 million people live in the United States in violation of federal residence laws, many of them from South American countries, seeking to emulate Europeans of an earlier century by immigrating in search of social and economic freedom and opportunity. For many state and local officials the rising rate of illegal immigration created a massive headache; it increased demand on public services and resulted in a sort of shadow society that posed challenges for everything from law enforcement to tax collections to accurate population estimates. States wanted the feds to do something—it was their job, after all. The feds did nothing. The states decided to take on the job themselves.

One of the most restrictive, and certainly the most famous, of the new state-level immigration laws is Arizona's Support Our Law Enforcement and Safe Neighborhoods Act (SB 1070), signed into law by Governor Jan Brewer in 2010. In a nutshell, SB 1070 made it a *state* crime to be in the United States illegally. Under its provisions immigrants had to carry paperwork proving their legal residence status and law enforcement officers were required to ask for that proof if they suspected someone of being in the state illegally. The law also made it illegal to hire, shelter, or transport those without proper documentation.

The bill, to put it mildly, was enormously controversial. Proponents saw it as an appropriate response to a problem Washington was ignoring. Critics saw it as barely veiled racism. Regardless, it put the state government into a direct confrontation with the federal government. When that happens—and it has happened a lot—the United States Supreme Court gets to serve as referee. In 2012 the Supreme Court struck down most, but not all, of SB 1070. The Court essentially ruled that the federal government immigration laws preempt state law, that under the Constitution's supremacy clause what the federal government wants takes precedence. And if the federal government wants to do nothing about illegal immigration, well, tough. Critically, though, the Court left intact SB 1070's requirement that immigrants carry documents proving they are legal residents of the United States, the "show me your papers" provision. As many other states had followed Arizona's lead and adopted immigration regulations,

some form of a "show me your papers" law is something many immigrants will now likely have to deal with whether they live in Arizona or not. This puts immigrants without those documents in a sensitive spot—any contact with law enforcement, even something as trivial as a speeding ticket, means they could be reported to federal authorities and, at least in theory, targeted for deportation. The feds might have supremacy in this area, but that does not mean the states will not play an important and high-profile role.

While it is too soon to assess the long-term impact of such state-level regulations, the whole immigration controversy is a good example of how subnational governments are, by design, assigned a central domestic policymaking role. States and localities, in short, enjoy a high degree of independence from the central government. This importance and independence are products of **federalism**,

> One of the most important questions in the American political system is: Who—the federal government or the state governments—has the power to do what?

a political system in which national and regional governments share powers and are considered independent equals. An understanding of this system of shared powers is critical to an understanding of the politics of states and localities and the central role they play in the U.S. political system. One of the most important questions in the American political system is: Who—the federal government or the state governments—has the power to do what? In the words of University of Chicago law professor Cass Sunstein, the debate over the distribution of powers between the state and federal levels holds "the ultimate fate of measures safeguarding the environment, protecting consumers, upholding civil rights, protecting violence against women, protecting endangered species, and defining criminal conduct

Federalism
Political system in which national and regional governments share powers and are considered independent equals.

in general and banning hate crimes in particular."[1]

Who gets the power to do what will affect the lives of virtually all citizens in the United States. This chapter provides a basic understanding of federalism, its history and evolution in the United States, and its implications for politics and governance in states and localities.

Systems of Power

We typically think of a nation as being ruled by a single sovereign government, that is, a government that depends on no other government for its political authority or power. This does not mean, however, that every nation has one government. Power and policy responsibility are distributed throughout any given political system in one of three ways, and all typically involve multiple levels of government. (See Figure 2-1.) The first option is to concentrate power in a single central government. Nations in which legal authority is held exclusively by a central government are known as **unitary systems**. Unitary systems typically do have regional and/or local governments, but these can exercise only the powers and responsibilities granted them by the central government. In other words, these governments are not sovereign; how much or how little power they are allowed to wield is up to the central government, not the citizens of the particular localities. The United Kingdom is a good example of a unitary system.

Unitary System
Political system in which power is concentrated in a central government.

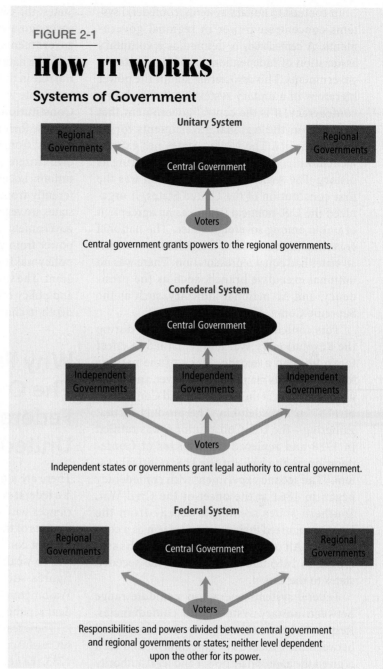

FIGURE 2-1

HOW IT WORKS
Systems of Government

Unitary System

Regional Governments

Central Government

Regional Governments

Voters

Central government grants powers to the regional governments.

Confederal System

Central Government

Independent Governments

Independent Governments

Independent Governments

Voters

Independent states or governments grant legal authority to central government.

Federal System

Regional Governments

Central Government

Regional Governments

Voters

Responsibilities and powers divided between central government and regional governments or states; neither level dependent upon the other for its power.

Although the United Kingdom has a strong tradition of local government and has set up regional legislatures in Scotland and Wales and (intermittently) in Northern Ireland, power is concentrated in the nation's Parliament. If it so chooses, Parliament can expand or contract the powers and responsibilities of these lower governments or even shut them down entirely (this has actually happened in Northern Ireland).

In contrast to unitary systems, confederal systems concentrate power in regional governments. A **confederacy** is defined as a voluntary association of independent, sovereign states or governments. This association stands the power hierarchy of a unitary system on its head. In a confederacy, it is the central government that depends on the regional governments for its legal authority. The United States has experimented with confederal systems twice during its history. The Articles of Confederation was the first constitution of the United States. It organized the U.S. political system as an agreement of union among sovereign states. The national government consisted of a legislature in which all states had equal representation. There was no national executive branch, such as the presidency, and no national judiciary, such as the Supreme Court.

This confederal system was adopted during the Revolutionary War and remained in effect for more than a decade. Many of the nation's founders saw its many flaws, however, and wrote its replacement at the Constitutional Convention of 1787 in Philadelphia. The product of that gathering—the U.S. Constitution—was ratified in 1788 and replaced the Articles of Confederation as the basis of the U.S. political system.[2] The second experiment with confederacy began in 1861 at the onset of the Civil War. Southern states seeking to secede from the Union organized their political system as a confederacy. All of this ended with the South's surrender in 1865 and the return of the seceded states to the Union.

Federal systems operate in a middle range between unitary systems and confederacies. Responsibilities in a federal system are divided between the two levels of government, and each is given the appropriate power and legal authority to fulfill those responsibilities. The system's defining feature is that neither level of government is dependent on the other for its power. Within its defined areas of responsibility, each is considered independent and autonomous. In the United States, the two levels of government considered sovereign are the federal government and state governments. States are legally equal partners with the national government and occupy a central role in the political system. Although required to operate within the rules laid down by the U.S. Constitution, states are considered sovereign because their power and legal authority are drawn not just from the U.S. Constitution but from their own citizens as codified in their own state constitutions. Local governments are treated very differently from states. Within their own borders, states are very much like unitary systems; substate governments such as cities and counties get their power from the state, and they exercise only the policymaking authority the state is willing to grant. The specifics of local governments' powers and policy responsibilities are discussed in more depth in chapter 11.

Why Federalism? The Origins of the Federal System in the United States

There are a number of reasons the United States is a federal system. Largely because of their experiences with the Articles of Confederation, the framers of the Constitution rejected the possibility of a confederacy. The national government was so weak under the Articles that prominent figures such as James Madison and George Washington feared it doomed the newly independent republic to failure.

These fears were not unfounded. Following the successful conclusion of the Revolutionary War in 1783, the new United States found itself in the grip of an economic recession, and the central government had little power to address the crisis. Indeed, it actually contributed to the problem by constantly threatening to default on its debts. Independence had brought political freedom, but it also meant American-made products now were in head-to-head competition with cheap, high-quality goods from Great Britain. This made consumers happy but threatened to cripple American

Confederacy
Political system in which power is concentrated in regional governments.

businesses. The economic difficulties pitted state against state, farmer against manufacturer, and debtor against banker. The weak central government really did not have the power to attempt a coordinated, nationwide response to the problem. It could do little but stand by and hope for the best.

As internal tensions mounted within the United States, European powers still active in the Americas threatened the nation's very sovereignty. Spain shut down shipping on the Mississippi River. The British refused to withdraw from some mil-

itary posts until the U.S. government paid off its debts to British creditors. George Washington believed the United States, having won the war, was in real danger of losing the peace. He said that something had to change in order "to avert the humiliating and contemptible figure we are about to make on the annals of mankind."[3]

For a loose coalition of the professional classes who called themselves Federalists, that "something" was obviously the central government. This group of lawyers, businessmen, and other individuals, drawn mostly from the upper social strata, sought to create a stronger and more powerful national government. Americans, however, were not particularly enthusiastic about handing more power to the central government, an attitude that is not so different from today. Most recognized that the Articles had numerous flaws, but few were ready to copy the example of the British and adopt a unitary system.

Two events in fall 1786 allowed the Federalists to overcome this resistance and achieve their goal of creating a more powerful national government. The first was the Annapolis Convention. This meeting in Maryland's capital convened to try to hammer out an interstate trade agreement. Few states sent delegates. Those who did show up had strong Federalist sympathies. They took advantage of the meeting and petitioned Congress to call for a commission to rewrite the Articles of Confederation.

The second event was Shays's Rebellion, named for its leader, Daniel Shays, a hero of the recently won Revolutionary War. The rebellion was an uprising of Massachusetts farmers who took up arms in protest of state efforts to take their property to pay off taxes and other debts. It was quickly crushed, but with further civil unrest threatening to boil over into civil war and with mounting pressure from powerful elites within the Federalist ranks, the Continental Congress was pushed to call for states to send delegates to Philadelphia in summer 1787. The purpose of the meeting, which came to be known as the Constitutional Convention, was the rewriting of the Articles of Confederation.

Once convened, the group quickly abandoned its mandate to modify the Articles and decided to write an entirely new constitution. In doing so, the Federalists who dominated the convention rejected confederacy as an adequate basis for the American political system. Their experience under the Articles had taught them that a central government subordinate to the states was not much of a government at all. What they wanted was a government capable of dealing effectively with national problems, and this meant a strong central government whose power was independent of the states.

Some Federalists, notably Alexander Hamilton, were attracted to the idea of a unitary government, but such a system was never seriously considered at the Constitutional Convention. Popular sentiment did not favor a unitary system, which was understandable given that Revolutionary War had been fought in no small part because of the perceived arrogance and abuse by a central government toward its regional subordinates (the states were originally colonies of the British Crown). Political realities also argued against pushing for a unitary system. To have any legal force the new constitution would have to be ratified by the states, and it was highly unlikely the states would voluntarily agree to give up all of their powers to a national government. Federalism was thus the only practical option.

Yet a federal system represented more than the political price that had to be paid to achieve a stronger national government. The founders were attempting to construct a new form of **representative government**, a form of government in which citizens exercise power indirectly, on the basis of a paradox. Convention delegates wanted a more powerful national government, but at the same time they did not want to concentrate power for fear that would lead to tyranny. Their solution to this problem was to create a system of separated powers and checks and balances. They divided their new and stronger national government into three branches—legislative, executive, and judicial—and made each branch partially reliant on the others to carry out its own responsibilities. This made it difficult for any single group to gain the upper hand in all three divisions of government and gave each branch the power to check the excesses of the other branches.

The delegates achieved a similar set of goals by making state and national governments coequal partners. By letting states remain independent decision makers in a wide range of policy arenas, they divided power between the national and subnational levels of government. The national government was made more powerful by the new constitution, but the independence of the states helped set clear limits on this power.

The Advantages and Disadvantages of Federalism

Federalism solved a political conundrum for the founders and helped achieve their philosophical aims of dispersing and separating power. Yet federalism is not necessarily better than a confederal or a unitary system, just different. In the United States, the pros and cons of federalism have benefited and bedeviled the American political system for more than two centuries.

There are four key advantages to the federal system. (See Table 2-1.) First, it keeps government closer to the people. Rather than the federal government's imposing a "one size fits all" policy, states have the freedom and authority to match government decisions to local preferences. This freedom also results in the local variance in laws, institutions, and traditions that characterizes the U.S. political system and provides the comparative method with its explanatory strength.

Second, federalism allows local differences to be reflected in state and local government policy and thereby reduces conflict. Massachusetts, for example, tends to be more liberal than, say, Alabama. California has a much more ethnically and culturally diverse population than Nebraska. Rather than having the various interests and preferences that spring from state-to-state differences engage in a winner-take-all policy struggle at the federal level, they can be accommodated at the state level. This reduces the friction among interests and lessens conflict.

Third, independent subnational governments allow for flexibility and experimentation. The states, as Supreme Court justice Louis Brandeis famously put it, are "the laboratories of democracy." Successful policy innovations in one state can be adopted by other states and copied by the federal government (see the box "Policy in Practice: Squeezing Lemons").

TABLE 2-1

Advantages and Disadvantages of Federalism

Advantages	Disadvantages
Allows for flexibility among state laws and institutions.	Increases complexity and confusion.
Reduces conflict because states can accommodate citizens' interests.	Sometimes increases conflict when jurisdictional lines are unclear.
Allows for experimentation at the state level.	Duplicates efforts and reduces accountability.
Enables the achievement of national goals.	Makes coordination difficult.
	Creates inequality in services and policy.

Representative Government
A form of government in which citizens exercise power indirectly by choosing representatives to legislate on their behalf.

Policy in Practice

Squeezing Lemons

Dan Brochu claimed that his new Oldsmobile Omega traveled well only when it was going up and down a repair lift. Maybe he wasn't exaggerating—inside a year the car went through four transmissions and a complete electrical system failure, and to add insult to injury, the paint started to peel. Thomas Ziemba could relate. His new Chevy Caprice had a skipping engine, a defroster that spewed steam, and a radio that seemed possessed—it would work only if he blew the horn first. Brochu and Ziemba had lemons, they knew it, and in 1982 they wanted the Connecticut state government to know it.

The state government not only got the message, it did something about the problem. The legislature passed Connecticut General Statute 743b, colloquially known as the "lemon law." When it was passed in the 1980s it was a new and innovative policy. The lemon law basically said that if a car was defective and its defects could not be repaired by reasonable effort (defined as four attempts or thirty days in the shop), it was legally a lemon and the consumer could sue the car's manufacturer. The basic upshot was that if someone could prove he or she had a lemon, the manufacturer had to cough up a refund or replace the car.

These days, this sort of law does not seem so innovative or unusual. There's a reason for that. After Connecticut passed its lemon law and it generally seemed to be effective in making manufacturers stand behind their products and warranty claims, other states, in so many words, said, "That's a good idea, let's get us a lemon law, too." And they did. Today all fifty states have some version of a lemon law.

The spread of lemon laws is a good example of one of the key advantages of federalism. By allowing states to experiment, federalism enables them to formulate effective policy innovations, which may then be adopted by other states. Effective policies will spread, while not-so-effective policies will not. While federalism clearly has some downsides, the laboratories of democracy, at least in this instance, were pretty good at whipping up some lemon-aid.

Sources: "Lemon Laws: Mixed Signals," *Newsweek,* May 31, 1982, 50; Better Business Bureau, "Standards of the Connecticut Lemon Law," www.bbb.org/us/Storage/16/Documents/BBBAutoLine/CT-LLsummary.pdf.

Fourth, the achievement of at least some national goals is made easier by the participation of independent subnational governments. For example, the federal government's 2010 Patient Protection and Affordable Care Act (popularly known as Obamacare) is the most sweeping reform of healthcare regulation in half a century. The primary goal of Obamacare is to reduce the number of people without health insurance, and one of the law's key provisions is the establishment of health insurance exchanges, basically centralized places where people can buy federally subsidized health insurance packages. As state governments constitute ready-made centralized regulatory bodies geographically distributed across the nation, it makes sense to have them set up and run these exchanges rather than have the federal government do it from scratch.

Along with its benefits, however, federalism confers a set of disadvantages. First, while allowing local differences does keep government closer to the people, it also creates complexity and confusion. For example, if you own a nationwide business, you have to deal with state *and* federal regulations—fifty-one sets of regulations in all. That means, among other things, fifty-one tax codes and fifty-one sets of licensing requirements. And many communities have their own restrictions and requirements that businesses must meet as well.

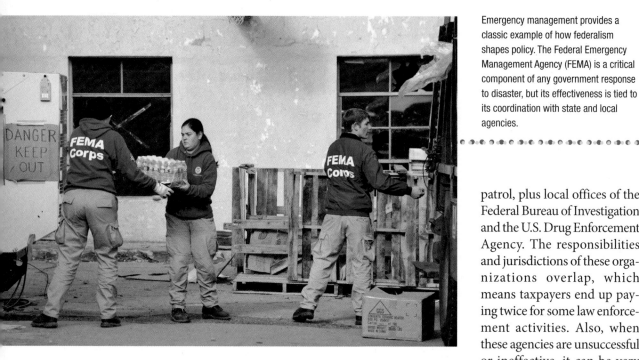

Emergency management provides a classic example of how federalism shapes policy. The Federal Emergency Management Agency (FEMA) is a critical component of any government response to disaster, but its effectiveness is tied to its coordination with state and local agencies.

Second, federalism can increase conflict as easily as reduce it. The Constitution is very vague on the exact division of powers between state and federal governments. This results in a constant struggle—and a lot of litigation—to resolve which level of government has the responsibility and legal authority to take the lead role in a given policy area. For example, who should challenge drug companies that make false or misleading claims about their products? In January 2007, thirty states settled with the Bayer Corporation for $8 million over safety concerns about a cholesterol-reducing drug that had since been pulled from the market. But just weeks earlier, the makers of four purported weight-loss drugs agreed to pay $25 million to settle allegations by the Federal Trade Commission that they had made unproven claims about the effectiveness of their products. Similar cases, but one was ruled on at the state level and the other at the national level.

Third, although federalism promotes flexibility and experimentation, it also promotes duplication and reduces accountability. For example, local, state, and national governments have all taken on law enforcement responsibilities. In some areas, this means there may be municipal police departments, a county sheriff's department, and the state patrol, plus local offices of the Federal Bureau of Investigation and the U.S. Drug Enforcement Agency. The responsibilities and jurisdictions of these organizations overlap, which means taxpayers end up paying twice for some law enforcement activities. Also, when these agencies are unsuccessful or ineffective, it can be very difficult to figure out which is responsible and what needs to change.

Fourth, the federal system can make it hard to coordinate policy efforts nationwide. For example, police and fire departments on opposite sides of a state border, or even within adjacent jurisdictions in the same state, may have different communication systems. It is hard to coordinate a response to a large-scale emergency if the relevant organizations cannot talk to each other, but the federal government cannot force state and local governments to standardize their radio equipment.

Finally, a federal system creates inequality in services and policies. The quality of public schools and welfare services, for example, depends heavily on the choices state and local governments make. This inevitably means that some states offer better educational opportunities and do more for the needy than others.

The Constitutional Basis of Federalism

The relationship between national and state governments is like a sibling rivalry. It is hard to imagine either level of government getting along without the other, yet because each is independent and focused on its own interests, conflict is common. The ink was barely dry on the newly ratified Constitution before the federal government and the states were squabbling over who had the power and authority in this or that policy area. In writing the Constitution, the founders recognized that the differences between states and the federal government were likely to be a central and lasting feature of the political system. Accordingly, they attempted to head off the worst of the disputes—or at least to provide a basis for resolving them—by making a basic division of powers between the national and state governments.

The Constitution grants the federal government both enumerated and implied powers. **Enumerated powers** are grants of authority explicitly given by the Constitution. Among the most important of these is the **national supremacy clause** contained in Article VI. This states that the Constitution "shall be the supreme law of the land; and the judges in every state shall be bound thereby." In other words, federal law takes precedence over all other laws. This allows the federal government to preempt, or override, areas regulated by state law. In recent decades, the federal government has aggressively used this power to extend its authority over states in a wide range of policy issues, so much so that **preemption** has been called "the gorilla that swallows state laws."[4]

Other enumerated powers are laid out in Article I, Section 8. This part of the Constitution details a set of **exclusive powers**—grants of authority that belong solely to the national government. These include the powers to regulate commerce, to declare war, and to raise and maintain an army and navy. Article I, Section 8, also confers a set of **concurrent powers** on the national government. Concurrent powers are those granted to the national government but not denied to the states. Both levels of government are free to exercise these prerogatives. Concurrent powers include the power to tax, borrow, and spend.

Finally, this same section of the Constitution gives the national government **implied powers**. The basic idea behind implied powers is that the authors of the Constitution realized they could not possibly list every specific power that the national government would require to meet the needs of a developing nation. Accordingly, they gave Congress the flexibility to meet unforeseen challenges by granting the federal government a set of broad and largely undefined powers. These include the **general welfare clause**, which gives the federal government the authority to provide for "the general welfare of the United States," and the **necessary and proper clause**, which authorizes Congress "to make all laws which shall be necessary and proper" to carry out its responsibilities as defined by the Constitution. (See Table 2-2 for explanations of these and other provisions.)

The Constitution says a good deal about the powers of the federal government but very little about the powers of the states. The original, unamended Constitution spent much more time specifying the obligations of the states than it did defining their power and authority. The obligations list includes Article IV, Section 2, better known as the **full faith and credit clause**. The clause

Enumerated Powers
Grants of authority explicitly given by the Constitution.

National Supremacy Clause
Constitutional clause that states that federal law takes precedence over all other laws.

Preemption
The process of the federal government overriding areas regulated by state law.

Exclusive Powers
Powers given by the Constitution solely to the federal government.

Concurrent Powers
Powers that both federal and state governments can exercise. These include the power to tax, borrow, and spend.

Implied Powers
Broad, but undefined, powers given to the federal government by the Constitution.

General Welfare Clause
Constitutional clause that gives Congress an implied power through the authority to provide for the "general welfare."

Necessary and Proper Clause
Constitutional clause that gives Congress an implied power through the right to pass all laws considered "necessary and proper" to carry out the federal government's responsibilities as defined by the Constitution.

Full Faith and Credit Clause
Constitutional clause that requires states to recognize each other's public records and acts as valid.

TABLE 2-2

The U.S. Constitution's Provisions for Federalism

What It Is . . .	What It Says . . .	What It Means . . .
Article I, Section 8 (commerce clause)	The Congress shall have Power . . . To regulate Commerce with foreign Nations, and among the several States, and with the Indian Tribes.	Gives Congress the right to regulate interstate commerce. This clause has been broadly interpreted to give Congress a number of implied powers.
Article I, Section 8 (necessary and proper clause)	The Congress shall have Power . . . To make all Laws which shall be necessary and proper for carrying into Execution the foregoing Powers, and all other Powers vested by this Constitution in the Government of the United States, or in any Department or Officer thereof.	An implied power giving Congress the right to pass all laws considered "necessary and proper" to carry out the federal government's responsibilities as defined by the Constitution.
Article IV, Section 3 (admission of new states)	New States may be admitted by the Congress into this Union; but no new State shall be formed or erected within the Jurisdiction of any other State; nor any State be formed by the Junction of two or more States, or Parts of States, without the Consent of the Legislatures of the States concerned as well as of the Congress.	Allows the U.S. Congress to admit new states to the union and guarantees each state sovereignty and jurisdiction over its territory.
Article IV, Section 4 (enforcement of republican form of government)	The United States shall guarantee to every State in this Union a Republican Form of Government, and shall protect each of them against Invasion; and on Application of the Legislature, or of the Executive (when the Legislature cannot be convened) against domestic Violence.	Ensures that a democratic government exists in each state and protects states against foreign invasion or insurrection.
Article VI (supremacy clause)	This Constitution, and the Laws of the United States which shall be made in Pursuance thereof; and all Treaties made, or which shall be made, under the Authority of the United States, shall be the supreme Law of the Land; and the Judges in every State shall be bound thereby, any Thing in the Constitution or Laws of any State to the Contrary notwithstanding.	States that federal law takes precedence over all other laws.
Tenth Amendment	The powers not delegated to the United States by the Constitution, nor prohibited by it to the States, are reserved to the States respectively, or to the people.	Guarantees a broad, but undefined, set of powers be reserved for the states and the people, as opposed to the federal government.
Fourteenth Amendment	All persons born or naturalized in the United States, and subject to the jurisdiction thereof, are citizens of the United States and of the state wherein they reside. No state shall make or enforce any law which shall abridge the privileges or immunities of citizens of the United States; nor shall any state deprive any person of life, liberty, or property, without due process of law; nor deny to any person within its jurisdiction the equal protection of the laws.	Prohibits any state from depriving individuals of the rights and privileges of citizenship and requires states to provide due process and equal protection guarantees to all citizens.
Sixteenth Amendment	The Congress shall have the power to lay and collect taxes on incomes, from whatever source derived, without apportionment among the several States, and without regard to any census or enumeration.	Enables the federal government to levy a national income tax, which helped further national policies and programs in subsequent years.
Seventeenth Amendment	The Senate of the United States shall be composed of two Senators from each State, elected by the people thereof, for six years; and each Senator shall have one vote. . . . When vacancies happen in the representation of any State in the Senate, the executive authority of each State shall issue writs of election to fill such vacancies: Provided that the legislature of any State may empower the executive thereof to make temporary appointments until the people fill the vacancies by election as the legislature may direct.	Provides for direct election of U.S. senators, rather than election by each state's legislature.

requires all states to grant "full faith and credit" to each other's public acts and records. This means that wills, contracts, and marriages that are valid under one state's laws are valid under all. Under the **privileges and immunities clause**, states are prohibited from discriminating against citizens from other states. The idea here was to prevent people traveling across state boundaries or temporarily residing in a state because of business or personal reasons from becoming the targets of discriminatory regulation or taxation.

The Constitution also sets out an often criticized system for electing the nation's president and vice president. The presidency goes not to the candidate who wins the most votes but, rather, to the one who wins the most states. Article II, Section 1, charges the states with appointing electors—one for each of a state's U.S. senators and representatives—who actually choose the president based on the winner of the state's popular vote. (If the Republican candidate gets the most votes in a state, the state's delegation to the electoral college is made up of Republican Party loyalists who vote for the Republican nominee.) A presidential candidate needs a majority in the electoral college, which requires the votes of at least 270 of the 538 state electors, to be named the winner.

Other than these responsibilities and explicitly granting the states the right to enter into compacts, or binding agreements, with each other on matters of regional concern, the Constitution is virtually silent on the powers of the states. This lopsided attention to the powers of the federal government was a contentious issue in the battle to ratify the Constitution. Opponents of the document, collectively known as Anti-Federalists, feared that states would become little more than puppets of the new central government. Supporters of the Constitution sought to calm these fears by arguing that states would remain sovereign and independent and that the powers not specifically granted to the federal government were reserved for the states. As James Madison put it, in writing the Constitution the Federalists were seeking "a middle ground which may at once support due supremacy of the national authority" but would also preserve a strong independent role for the states.[5]

Madison and his fellow Federalists offered to put these assurances in writing. In effect, they promised that if the Constitution were ratified, the first order of business for the new Congress would be to draft a set of amendments that would spell out the limits of central government power and specify the independence of the states. Although Anti-Federalist skepticism remained, the Federalists kept their promise. The First Congress formulated a series of changes that eventually became the first ten amendments to the Constitution and are collectively known as the **Bill of Rights**.

Most of these amendments set specific limits on government power. The aim was to guarantee certain individual rights and freedoms, and, at least initially, they were directed at the federal government rather than at state governments. The **Tenth Amendment**, however, finally addressed the power of the states. In full, the Tenth Amendment states: "The powers not delegated to the United States by the Constitution, nor prohibited by it to the states, are reserved to the states respectively, or to the people." This provided no enumerated, or specific, powers to the states, but those implied by the language of the amendment are considerable. The so-called reserved powers encompass all of the concurrent powers that allow the states to tax, borrow, and spend; to make laws and enforce them; to regulate trade within their borders; and to practice eminent domain, which is the power to take private property for public use. The reserved powers also have been traditionally understood to mean that states have the primary power to make laws that involve the health, safety, and morals of their citizens. Yet the powers reserved for the states are more implied than explicit, and they all rest in an uneasy tension with the national supremacy clause of Article VI.

Bill of Rights
The first ten amendments to the Constitution, which set limits on the power of the federal government and set out the rights of individuals and the states.

Privileges and Immunities Clause
Constitutional clause that prohibits states from discriminating against citizens of other states.

Tenth Amendment
Constitutional amendment guaranteeing a broad, but undefined, set of powers be reserved for the states and the people.

After the Tenth Amendment, the **Fourteenth Amendment** is the most important in terms of specifying state powers. Ratified in 1868, the Fourteenth Amendment is one of the so-called Civil War Amendments that came in the immediate wake of the bloody conflict between the North, or the Union, and the South, or the Confederacy. The Fourteenth Amendment prohibits any state from depriving individuals of the rights and privileges of citizenship and requires states to provide due process and equal protection guarantees to all citizens. The Supreme Court has used these guarantees to apply the Bill of Rights to state governments as well as to the federal government and to assert national power over state power in issues ranging from the desegregation of public education to the reapportioning of state legislatures.

The implied powers of the federal government, the limitations set on states by the Fourteenth Amendment, and the undefined "leftovers" given to the states by the Tenth Amendment mean that the scope and the authority of both levels of government are, in many cases, dependent on how the Constitution is interpreted. The Constitution, in other words, provides a basic framework for solving the sibling-rivalry squabbles between the states and the federal government. (See Figure 2-2.) It does not provide, however, an unambiguous guide to which level of government has the primary power, responsibility, and authority on a broad range of policy issues. This, as we will see, means that the U.S. Supreme Court is repeatedly thrust into the role of refereeing power disputes between national and state governments.

The Development of Federalism

Although clearly establishing a federal political system, the provisions of the U.S. Constitution leave considerable room for disagreement about

FIGURE 2-2

Powers of National and State Governments

National Government Powers	Concurrent Powers	State Government Powers
Coin money	Tax	Run elections
Regulate interstate and foreign commerce	Borrow money	Regulate intrastate commerce
Tax imports and exports	Charter banks and corporations	Establish republican forms of state and local government
Make treaties	Take property (eminent domain)	Protect public health, safety, and morals
Make all laws "necessary and proper" to fulfill responsibilities	Make and enforce laws and administer a judiciary	All powers not delegated to the national government or denied to the states by the Constitution
Make war		
Regulate postal system		**Powers Denied**
		Tax imports and exports
Powers Denied		Coin money
Tax state exports		Enter into treaties
Change state boundaries		Impair obligation of contracts
Impose religious tests		Enter compacts with other states without congressional consent
Pass laws in conflict with the Bill of Rights		

Source: Adapted from Samuel Kernell, Gary C. Jacobson, and Thad Kousser, *The Logic of American Politics,* 6th ed. (Washington, DC: CQ Press, 2013), Figure 3-2.

Fourteenth Amendment
Constitutional amendment that prohibits states from depriving individuals of the rights and privileges of citizenship and requires states to provide due process and equal protection guarantees.

which level of government—federal or state—has the power to do what. Disagreements about the scope and authority of the national government happened almost immediately when the First

Congress convened in 1789. The issue of a national bank was one of the most controversial of these early conflicts and the one with the most lasting implications. Alexander Hamilton, secretary of the treasury under President George Washington, believed a central bank was critical to stabilizing the national economy, but there was nothing in the Constitution that specifically granted the federal government the authority to create and regulate such an institution.

Lacking a clear enumerated power, Hamilton justified his proposal for a national bank by using an implied power. He argued that the necessary and proper clause implied the federal government's power to create a national bank because the bank would help the government manage its finances as it went about its expressly conferred authority to tax and spend. Essentially, Hamilton was interpreting *necessary* as "convenient" or "appropriate." Secretary of State Thomas Jefferson objected, arguing that if the Constitution was going to establish a government of truly limited powers, the federal government needed to stick to its enumerated powers and interpret its implied powers very narrowly. He thus argued that the *necessary* in the necessary and proper clause should properly be interpreted as "essential" or "indispensable." Hamilton eventually won the argument, and Congress approved the national bank. Still, the issue simmered as a controversial—and potentially unconstitutional—expansion of the national government's powers.

The issue was not fully resolved until 1819, when the Supreme Court decided the case of *McCulloch v. Maryland.* This case stemmed from the state of Maryland's attempts to shut down the national bank, which was taking business from state-chartered banks, by taxing its operations. The chief cashier of the national bank's Baltimore branch refused to pay the tax, and the parties went to court. The Supreme Court, in essence, backed Hamilton's interpretation of the Constitution over Jefferson's. This was important above and beyond the issue of a national bank. It suggested that the Constitution gave the national government a broad set of powers relative to the states. Key to this early affirmation of the federal government's power was U.S. Chief Justice John Marshall, whose backing of a broad

interpretation of implied powers laid the foundation for later expansions in the scope and authority of the federal government.

The full impact of *McCulloch v. Maryland,* however, would not be felt for some time. For the most part, the federal government began to feel its way into the gray areas of its constitutional powers pretty cautiously. Federalism went on to develop in four distinct stages—dual federalism, cooperative federalism, centralized federalism, and New Federalism—and the first of these stages leaned toward the more limited role of the federal government favored by Jefferson.

Dual Federalism (1789–1933)

Dual federalism is the idea that state and federal governments have separate jurisdictions and responsibilities. Within these separate spheres of authority, each level of government is sovereign and free to operate without interference from the other. It represents something of a middle ground in the initial interpretations of how the Constitution divided power. On one side of the debate were Federalists such as Hamilton, who championed a nation-centered view of federalism. They wanted to interpret the Constitution as broadly as possible to give the national government supremacy over the states.

On the other side were fierce **states' rights** advocates such as John Calhoun of South Carolina, who served as vice president in the administrations of John Quincy Adams and Andrew Jackson. Supporters of states' rights wanted the federal government's power limited to the greatest possible extent and saw any expansion of that power as an encroachment on the sovereignty of the states. In the 1820s and 1830s Calhoun formulated what became known as the **compact theory** of

---

Dual Federalism
The idea that state and federal governments have separate and distinct jurisdictions and responsibilities.

States' Rights
The belief that states should be free to make their own decisions with little interference from the federal government.

Compact Theory
The idea that the Constitution represents an agreement among sovereign states to form a common government.

federalism. The idea was that the Constitution represented an agreement among sovereign states to form a common government. It interpreted the Constitution as essentially an extension of the Articles of Confederation, a perspective that viewed the U.S. political system as more confederal than federal.

The compact theory argued that if sovereignty ultimately rested with the states, then the states rather than the Supreme Court had the final say in how the Constitution should be interpreted. The states also had the right to reject federal laws and make them invalid within their own borders. This process was known as **nullification**, and the compact theory took it to an extreme. Calhoun argued that states could reject the entire Constitution and choose to withdraw, or secede, from the Union. In the 1820s, national policies—especially a trade tariff—triggered an economic downturn in the southern states, which created wide support for nullification and **secession** arguments. These extreme states' rights views were not completely resolved until the Union victory in the Civil War ended them for good.

Dual federalism walked the line of moderation between the extremes of **nation-centered federalism** and **state-centered federalism**. Basically, dual federalism looks at the U.S. political system as a layered cake. The state and federal governments represent distinct and separate layers of this cake. To keep them separate, advocates of dual federalism sought to limit the federal government to exercising only a narrow interpretation of its enumerated powers. If the Constitution was to be interpreted broadly, that interpretation should favor the states rather than Congress. This became the central operating philosophy of the U.S. Supreme Court for much of the nineteenth century and is most closely associated with the tenure of Chief Justice Roger B. Taney, who served from 1836 to 1864. Compared with his immediate predecessor, John Marshall, Taney was much less sympathetic to arguments that interpreted the federal government's powers broadly.

The dual federalism doctrine gave rise to some infamous Supreme Court decisions on the powers and limitations of the federal government. Perhaps the best known is *Scott v. Sandford* (1857). This case dealt with Dred Scott, a slave taken by his master from Missouri, a slave state, to Illinois, a free state, and on into what was then called the Wisconsin Territory, where slavery had been outlawed by the Missouri Compromise of 1820. This federal law stipulated which new states and territories could and could not make slavery legal. After his master's death, Scott sued for his freedom, arguing that his residence in a free territory had legally ended his bondage. Scott's case was tied to the Missouri Compromise, which the Supreme Court subsequently ruled unconstitutional. The justices' justification was that Congress did not have the enumerated, or the implied, power to prohibit slavery in the territories. Thus Scott remained a slave, although his owners voluntarily gave him his freedom shortly after the Supreme Court decision. He died of tuberculosis in 1858, having spent only one of his nearly sixty years as a free man.

Cooperative Federalism (1933–1964)

In theory, dual federalism defines and maintains a clear division between state and national governments and sets a clear standard for doing so. If the federal government has the enumerated power to take the disputed action or make the disputed law, it has supremacy over the states in the particular case; if it does not have the enumerated power, then the Tenth Amendment reserves that power for the states, and state preferences take precedence.

Nullification
The process of a state's rejecting a federal law and making it invalid within state borders.

Secession
The process of a government or political jurisdiction withdrawing from a political system or alliance.

Nation-Centered Federalism
The belief that the nation is the basis of the federal system and that the federal government should take precedence over the states.

State-Centered Federalism
The belief that states are the basis of the federal system and that state governments should take precedence over the federal government.

The problem was that its clarity in theory rarely matched the complex realities of governance in practice. State and national governments share interests in a wide range of issues, from education to transportation. To divide these interests cleanly into separate spheres of influence was not only difficult, in many cases it was impractical and not desirable. Even at the height of the dual federalism era, state and federal governments were collaborating as much as they were fighting. The federal government, for example, owned vast tracts of land in the Midwest and West, and it made extensive grants of these lands to the states to help develop transportation and education systems. Many of the nation's best-known state universities got their start this way, as land-grant colleges.

In the nineteenth century, the federal government also gave out cash grants to support Civil War veterans housed in state institutions, gave money to the states to support agricultural research, and lent federal manpower—primarily U.S. Army engineers—to help state and local development projects.[6] Rather than a layered cake, some experts believe a more appropriate metaphor for federalism is a marble cake, with the different levels of government so thoroughly mixed with each other that they are impossible to separate. (See Figure 2-3.)

Certainly as the nation became increasingly industrialized and more urban, state and federal interests became increasingly intertwined. As the nineteenth century drew to a close and the twentieth century began, the federal government undertook a significant expansion of its policy responsibilities. In 1887, it began to regulate the railroads, a policy area with enormous significance for the economic development of states and

FIGURE 2-3

The Varieties of Federalism

Dual or "Layer Cake"
Federalism

Cooperative or "Marble Cake"
Federalism

Centralized or "Picket Fence" Federalism

localities. In economic and social terms, this was roughly equivalent to the federal government of today announcing its comprehensive regulation of the Internet and software manufacturers. By fits and starts, dual federalism gradually fell out of favor with the Supreme Court. The Court instead began to interpret the powers of the

> Even at the height of the dual federalism era, state and federal governments were collaborating as much as they were fighting.

federal government very broadly and to allow the jurisdictions of state and national governments to merge gradually.

Several events accelerated this trend. In 1913, the Sixteenth Amendment was ratified, giving the federal government the ability to levy a nationwide income tax. The new taxing and spending authority helped further national policies designed during the next decades.[7] World War I (1914–1918) resulted in a significant centralization of power in the federal government. During World War II (1939–1945) that power was centralized even further. The need to fight global conflicts pushed the federal government to assert the lead role on a wide range of economic and social issues. Even more important to the long-term relationship between state and national governments was the Great Depression of the 1930s, a social and economic catastrophe that swept aside any remaining vestiges of dual federalism.

The central catalyst for a fundamental change in the nature of state-federal relations was the election of Franklin Delano Roosevelt to the presidency in 1932. In an effort to combat economic and social malaise, Roosevelt aggressively pushed the federal government into taking a lead role in areas traditionally left to the states, and in the 1930s the federal government became deeply involved in regulating the labor market, creating and managing welfare programs, and providing significant amounts of direct aid to cities. The

general approach of Roosevelt's so-called New Deal agenda defined the central characteristics of **cooperative federalism**—using the federal government to identify a problem, set up the basic outline of a program to address the problem, and make money available to fund that program and then turning over much of the responsibility for implementing and running the program to the states and localities. This arrangement dominated state and federal relations for the next three decades.

Centralized Federalism (1964–1980)

Having all levels of government addressing problems simultaneously and cooperatively paid dividends. It combined the need to attack national problems with the flexibility of the decentralized federal system. Cooperative federalism, however, also signaled a significant shift in power away from the states and toward the federal government. The key to this power shift was money, specifically federal **grants-in-aid**, which are cash appropriations given by the federal government to the states. An ever-increasing proportion of state and local budgets came from federal coffers. At the beginning of the nineteenth century, federal grants constituted less than 1 percent of state and local government revenues. By the middle of the 1930s, federal grants accounted for close to 20 percent of state and local revenues.[8]

Cooperative Federalism
The notion that it is impossible for state and national governments to have separate and distinct jurisdictions and that both levels of government must work together.

Grants-in-Aid
Cash appropriations given by the federal government to the states.

○ ◗◗◖ ◗◖◗ ◖◗◖◗ ◖◗◗◖ ◗◗◖◗ ◖◗◖◗◖ ◗◖◗◖ ◗◖◖◗ ◗◖◗◖ ◗◖◗◖

The Sixteenth Amendment gave the federal government the power to levy an income tax. Some of the money collected by the federal government in income taxes is returned to the states in the form of grants to support a wide range of domestic policies and programs.

FIGURE 2-4

Key Dates in the History of American Federalism

Revolutionary War starts	1775	1776	Declaration of Independence adopted
Articles of Confederation ratified	1781	1783	Revolutionary War ends
Annapolis Convention	1786	1786	Shays's Rebellion
Constitutional Convention drafts new constitution	1787	1788	U.S. Constitution ratified
First Congress adopts Bill of Rights	1791		
McCulloch v. Maryland establishes that the federal government has a broad set of powers over the states	1819		
Roger Taney sworn in as chief justice; adopts dual federalism as model for federal-state relations	1836	1832	South Carolina attempts to nullify federal law
		1857	*Scott v. Sanford* demonstrates the limits of the federal government
Southern states experiment with confederacy as Civil War starts	1861	1860	South Carolina secedes from the Union in December; hostilities between North and South begin a month later
		1865	Civil War ends with Union victory; Thirteenth Amendment abolishes slavery
Fourteenth Amendment passes	1868		
		1887	Federal government regulates the railroads
Sixteenth Amendment passes	1913		
Great Depression	1930	1933	Franklin Delano Roosevelt takes office; Era of cooperation federalism begins
Era of centralized Federalism begins	1964		
		1972	Richard Nixon begins revenue sharing
Election of Ronald Reagan and emergence of New Federalism	1980		
Supreme Court decides *Bush v. Gore;* George W. Bush receives Florida's contested electoral votes and becomes president	2000	1986	William Rehnquist becomes chief justice; Supreme Court begins to look more favorably on states' rights arguments
		2008 –2009	Great Recession

For the next thirty years, the federal government continued to rely on grants to administer programs, including the 1950s construction of the federal highway system that Americans drive on today. The 1960s marked a shift, however. **Centralized federalism**, ushered in with Lyndon Baines Johnson's presidency, further increased the federal government's involvement in policy areas previously left to state and local governments. It is commonly associated with Johnson's Great Society program, which used state and local governments to help implement such national initiatives as the Civil Rights Act and the War on Poverty. Sometimes it is referred to as "picket-fence federalism" because of its many crosscutting regulations.

Those initiatives meant more money—and more regulations—for states and localities. The federal government aggressively began attaching strings to this money through **categorical grants**. Federal-state relations evolved into a rough embodiment of the Golden Rule of politics—he who has the gold gets to make the rules.

Richard Nixon's presidential administration took a slightly different tack. It cut some strings but continued to increase the number of grants doled out by the federal government.[9] In the late 1960s, the administration pioneered the idea of **general revenue sharing grants**, federal funds turned over to the states and localities with essentially no strings attached. Although popular with states and localities—from their perspective it was "free" money—this type of grant-in-aid had a short life span; it was killed by the Ronald Reagan administration in the early 1980s.

Federal grants, strings or no strings, do not sound so bad on the surface. Money is money, and a government can never have too much. The problem was that the grants were not distributed equitably to states and localities, and a central feature of cooperative federalism was the often fierce competition to control and access these revenues. The politics became complex. One form of conflict arose between the states and the federal government over what types of grants should be used for particular policies or programs. States and localities favored federal grants with fewer strings. Congress and the president often favored putting tight guidelines on federal money because this allowed them to take a greater share of the credit for the benefits of federal spending.

Perhaps the most important dimension of the politics of grants-in-aid, however, was the federal government's increasing desire to use its purse strings to pressure states and localities into adopting particular policies and laws. Beginning in the 1960s and 1970s, cooperative federalism began a new, more coercive era with the rise of ever more stringent grant conditions. These included **crosscutting requirements**, or strings that applied to all federal grants. For example, one requirement a state or locality must meet to receive virtually any federal government grant is an assessment of the environmental impact of the proposed program or policy. Accordingly, most state and local governments began writing—and defending—environmental impact statements for any construction project that involved federal funds.

The federal government also began applying **crossover sanctions**. Crossover sanctions are strings that require grant recipients to pass and enforce certain laws or policies as a condition of receiving funds. One example is the drinking age. The federal government requires states to set twenty-one as the minimum legal age for drinking alcohol as a condition of receiving federal highway funds.

Increasingly, the strings came even if there were no grants. State and local governments were issued direct orders, essentially were commanded, to adopt certain laws or rules, such as clean water standards and minimum wage laws.[10] These **unfunded mandates**

Centralized Federalism
The notion that the federal government should take the leading role in setting national policy, with state and local governments helping to implement the policies.

Categorical Grants
Federal grants-in-aid given for specific programs that leave states and localities with little discretion over how to spend the money.

General Revenue Sharing Grants
Federal grants-in-aid given with few constraints, leaving states and localities almost complete discretion over how to spend the money.

Crosscutting Requirements
Constraints that apply to all federal grants.

Crossover Sanctions
Federal requirements mandating that grant recipients pass and enforce certain laws or regulations as a condition of receiving funds.

Unfunded Mandates
Federal laws that direct state action but provide no financial support for that action.

became a particular irritant to state and local governments. Even when there was broad agreement on the substance of a mandate, subnational governments resented the federal government's taking all the credit while leaving the dirty work of finding funds and actually running the programs to the states and localities.

Congress eventually passed a law banning unfunded mandates in the mid-1990s, but it is full of loopholes. For example, the law does not apply to appropriations bills—the laws that actually authorize the government to spend money. The National Conference of State Legislatures has estimated that in a recent five-year period the federal government shifted $131 billion in costs to the states in unfunded mandates.[11] Congress, in other words, continues to pass laws that subnational governments must obey and to pass on the costs of implementing these laws to the states

New Federalism (1980–2002)

Centralized federalism's shift of power toward the national government always faced opposition from states' rights advocates, who viewed the growing influence of the national government with alarm. By the end of the 1970s, centralized federalism also was starting to face a practical crisis—the federal government's revenues could not keep up with the demand for grants. With the election of Ronald Reagan in 1980, the practical and ideological combined to create pressure for a fundamental shift in state and federal relations.

Reagan was not the first president to raise concerns about the centralization of power in the national government. A primary reason for Nixon's support of general revenue sharing, for example, was the attraction of giving states more flexibility by cutting the strings attached to federal grants. It was not until Reagan, however, that a sustained attempt was made to reverse the course of centralized federalism. Reagan believed the federal government had overreached its boundaries, and he wanted to return power and flexibility to the states. At the core of his vision of state-centered **New Federalism** was the desire to reduce federal grants-in-aid. In return, states would be given more policymaking leeway with the money they did get through **block grants**.

Reagan's drive to make this vision a reality had mixed success. The massive budget deficits of the 1980s made cutting grants-in-aid a practical necessity. We can see this in Figure 2-5, which shows federal government grants to state and local governments in billions of constant dollars from 1940 through 2011. There was a clear upward trend beginning in the 1960s that peaked in about 1978. After that, federal grants to states stayed relatively constant for about a decade—while the federal government was not really drastically cutting grants in the 1980s, in real terms it did not increase them either. At least for a while, the federal government managed to rein in the grant dollars flowing to states and localities. Reducing the federal government's influence over states and localities turned out to be another matter.

Reagan, like many conservatives, was a modern heir to a states' rights perspective that dated back to the Anti-Federalist movement. This means he believed that government should be as close to the voters as possible—in the city hall or the state capitol—rather than far away in Washington, D.C. Yet believing that government should be closer to the people in the abstract is far different from putting that belief into practice. Taking power from the federal government did advance a core philosophical belief of the Reagan administration, but it also created problems for Reagan supporters, who were not shy about voicing their displeasure.

Such core conservative constituencies as business and industry quickly realized that dealing with one government was much less of a headache than dealing with fifty governments. They almost immediately began to put counterpressure on the

New Federalism
The belief that states should receive more power and authority and less money from the federal government.

Block Grants
Federal grants-in-aid given for general policy areas that leave states and localities with wide discretion over how to spend the money within the designated policy area.

FIGURE 2-5

Federal Grants to States, 1940–2011 (in billions)

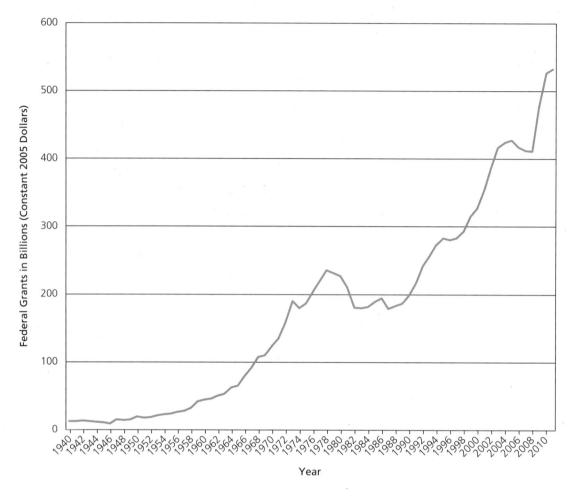

Source: U.S. Office of Management and Budget, *Budget of the United States,* Historical Tables, Table 431, "Federal Grants-in-Aid to State and Local Governments: 1990 to 2011," data released September 30, 2011.

movement toward expanded state policymaking authority. The result was something of a push-and-pull, with the Reagan administration trying to shove power onto the states with one set of legislative priorities and yank it back to the federal government with another. Ultimately, Reagan did succeed in cutting grants-in-aid. He consolidated fifty-seven categorical grants into nine new block grants. General revenue sharing and another sixty categorical grants were eliminated entirely. This reduced the amount of money sent to the states while increasing the states' ability to act independently.[12] Yet Reagan also engaged in a number of fairly aggressive preemption movements and backed a number of unfunded mandates. This reduced the

independence of states and forced them to fund programs they did not necessarily support.

The seeds of New Federalism had a hard time taking root at the national level, but its roots sank fast and sank deep at the state and local levels. States were caught between the proverbial rock of a cash-strapped federal government and the hard place of the demand for the programs traditionally supported by federal funds. They slowly and often painfully worked themselves out of this dilemma by becoming less reliant on the federal government. States began aggressively pursuing innovative policy approaches to a wide range of social and economic problems. By the 1990s, as one author puts it, there was "a developing agreement among state and national political elites that states should have greater authority and flexibility in operating public programs."[13]

The effort to take power away from the federal government and give it to the states was broadly supported by public opinion, as polls consistently showed that Americans placed more trust in state and local governments than they did in the federal government.[14] In the 1990s, the Clinton administration championed the idea of devolution, an extension of New Federalism that sought a systematic transition of power from the federal to the state level in certain policy areas.

Probably the best-known example of devolution is the Personal Responsibility and Work Opportunity Reconciliation Act of 1996, popularly known as the law that "ended welfare as we know it." The law, which Clinton signed under Republican pressure during the 1996 presidential campaign after vetoing it twice, ended Aid to Families with Dependent Children (AFDC) and replaced it with a block grant. In essence, the law embodied the deal between state and federal governments that embodied devolution—the federal government would provide less money, and the states would get more policymaking authority.

Like its parent, New Federalism, the devolution revolution faced strong resistance, often from an old enemy. Conservatives, at least rhetorically, still were the strongest states' rights advocates. Yet when states' rights conflicted with key portions of the conservative political agenda, conservative groups still fought tenaciously for federal supremacy over the states, just as they had during the 1980s. An example of this contradictory behavior is the 1996 Defense of Marriage Act. This federal law was proposed in the wake of movements in Hawaii and Vermont to legalize same-sex civil unions. Now, remember, the full faith and credit clause means that a contract made under the laws of one state is legally recognized and binding in all states. So, if one state made same-sex unions legal, it raised the possibility that the other forty-nine would have to recognize such civil unions as the legal equivalent of marriages. There was a strong push from many traditional states' rights advocates for the federal government to, in essence, grant states exceptions from their full faith and credit obligations. The Defense of Marriage Act did this. It also put the federal government into the business of defining what constitutes a marriage, an area traditionally left to the states.[15]

Ad Hoc Federalism . . . and a Return to Centralized Federalism? (2002–present)

The mixed commitment to New Federalism is perhaps best exemplified by the presidency of George W. Bush. Bush came to the White House from the Texas governor's mansion and, at least on the surface, was a strong supporter of the principles of New Federalism. The policy record of the Bush administration, though, was considerably at odds with New Federalism sentiments. For example, Bush's signature domestic policy was the No Child Left Behind Act, which asserted federal control over important aspects of public education, a policy area traditionally under the jurisdiction of state and local governments. Peter Harkness, editor of *Governing* magazine, summed up the Bush administration's record on federalism thus: "The administration has mandated more, preempted more and run roughshod over state initiatives that didn't conform to its own ideology."[16]

Michigan was the first state to plow its roads and to use the yellow dividing line on its highways.

Part of Bush's departure from the New Federalism philosophy was driven by recession and war. Throughout the history of the United States, during times of crisis power has become centralized in the national government—it simply is better equipped than the individual states to deal with national economic challenges or international conflict. The Bush administration found itself struggling with a soft economy at the beginning of its term and a disastrous slide into economic recession at the end of its term. In between, much of its focus was devoted to a global war on terrorism in response to the devastating attacks of September 11, 2001.

During the eight years of the Bush administration, the commitment to New Federalism dissolved more or less entirely. This did not necessarily mean that federal-state relations in the Bush era shifted from a commitment to devolution to a commitment to centralizing power in Washington, D.C. What it meant was that a principled guiding philosophy of state-federal relations—like dual federalism, cooperative federalism, or New Federalism—was abandoned. Instead a new, more partisan or ideologically based approach to state-federal relations came to fore, an approach described as **ad hoc federalism**.[17] Ad hoc federalism is the process of choosing a state-centered or nation-centered view of federalism on the basis of political or partisan convenience. In other words, the issue at hand, not a core philosophical commitment to a particular vision of federalism, determines a policymaker's commitment to state or federal supremacy.

This is not necessarily a bad thing for states or localities. For example, when the federal government failed to ratify the Kyoto Protocol, a treaty addressing climate change—an international agreement considered the province of the federal government—more than seven hundred generally liberal-leaning U.S. cities decided independently to adopt the treaty's provisions. In other words, based on the issue at hand, more liberal cities decided that treaties concerning global warming were within their jurisdiction. Similarly, as we have already seen, when the federal government would not pass an immigration law, more conservative states decided based on the issue at hand that this was within their jurisdiction. States such as Alabama, Arizona, Georgia, Indiana, South Carolina, and Utah, accordingly, passed immigration laws.[18] The big concern of ad hoc federalism is that it treats the key institutional feature of the American political system not as a consistent and stable basis for organizing policy and constitutional responsibilities, but as a more incoherent structure that is viewed differently depending on ideological convenience. Thus

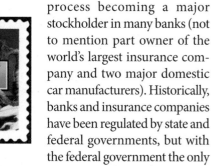

conservatives champion states' rights in arguing against the federal government's constitutional authority to mandate the purchase of a health insurance policy, but they conveniently forget states' rights when arguing for the federal government's authority to pass laws outlawing gay marriage. Similarly, while liberals traditionally have been more inclined to downplay states' rights arguments in favor of centralizing federal government power over a wide range of issues, they discover a commitment to states' rights when it suits them (on gay marriage, for example). Ad hoc federalism makes equal opportunity hypocrites of all.

The shift toward ad hoc federalism was, at least temporarily, slowed by the Great Recession of 2008–2009, which shook up state-federal relations and shifted power decisively toward the federal government. This was prompted in part by the nature of economic shock. For example, the financial industry was widely seen as helping to precipitate the economic downturn by making irresponsible loans and underestimating risk. To prop up the financial system, the federal government spent billions, in the process becoming a major stockholder in many banks (not to mention part owner of the world's largest insurance company and two major domestic car manufacturers). Historically, banks and insurance companies have been regulated by state and federal governments, but with the federal government the only entity with deep enough pockets to prevent an implosion on Wall Street, few doubt that the regulatory authority over these sectors of the economy will take a significant shift toward Washington, D.C., and away from the states

Those same deep pockets also paid for what amounted to a resurrection of centralized federalism, with the federal government setting policy priorities, deciding what to spend on those priorities, and delegating to the states the administration of the approved programs. This was not so much a premeditated attempt by the federal government to usurp the power of the states as it was a recognition that the empty coffers of states and localities needed to be filled, that only the federal government had the capacity provide that

---

Ad Hoc Federalism
The process of choosing a state-centered or nation-centered view of federalism on the basis of political or partisan convenience.

States under Stress

What Brand of Federalism Is Next?

A quarter century ago, John Herbers, a former national correspondent for the *New York Times,* wrote a cover story for *Governing* magazine heralding the advent of a largely unplanned, unpredicted new sort federalism. More responsibility and authority would be devolved down to the states and their localities as the Reagan administration reduced the federal imprint on American governance, and at the time states and localities seemed to be ready to accept a greater, more independent role.

State and local management capacity had improved substantially, mostly because during the era of cooperative and centralized federalism Washington had relied on state and local bureaucracies to manage federal money rather than expand its own. Also, states and localities were becoming more financially independent; they had raised as much in new taxes as the Reagan administration had cut. Most surprising from a contemporary perspective is not Herbers's assessment of subnational governments' mature management or revenue capacities but his description of the broad, bipartisan agreement on the direction federalism would take and what that would imply—devolution was the name of the game, and this would lead to less friction between states and the federal government.

In terms of the states being well positioned to handle the management and financial side of things, Herbers was spot-on. Indeed, coming out of the recession of 1980–1982, states in the subsequent four years grew their revenues by one-third, to $228 billion. And that didn't include mushrooming cash inflows from nontax sources such as lotteries, which had expanded into a majority of the states. Because the national economy was humming along quite nicely and the tax base had significantly expanded, state and local governments experienced what would be an almost three-decade run of solid increases in tax revenue—interrupted slightly by two mild recessions.

The political side of it, though, didn't go quite as Herbers had imagined. State-federal relations were sometimes rocky in the 1980s and 1990s, though there was agreement on a general direction of greater state independence. That general agreement disappeared and intergovernmental relations tipped into acrimony in the following decade. Somewhat surprisingly, this happened during the administration of George W. Bush. Though a conservative and an ex-governor, Bush showed little interest in following a traditional conservative, states' rights script as president and made a series of moves that yanked power back from the states and toward the federal government: the No Child Left Behind education law, the Real ID Act, and a wave of preemptions of state regulations and thinly disguised unfunded mandates (which supposedly had been banned). At the same time, Washington lobbyists pushed for more centralization, with the idea that their industries could cut a better deal at the federal level and avoid a patchwork of statutes and regulations. It was a time of what Don Borut, executive director of the National League of Cities, called "coercive federalism" or, when he was being more blunt, "shift-and-shaft federalism."

As relationships between the states and the federal government were souring, the Great Recession hit, weakening the financial and management capacities of the states. The Obama administration further centralized power, using a series of financial carrots and regulatory sticks to get states and localities to pay attention to federal policy priorities. Above all, intergovernmental relationships were influenced by a rising tide of partisanship and ideological rigidity that swamped both Washington and many of the states. That mixture has been pretty toxic for intergovernmental relations and has made it hard to replicate Herbers's crystal-ball gazing for the next twenty-five days, let alone the next twenty-five years.

So what brand of federalism will we see next? Will it be the kind John Herbers foresaw? Will federal and state governments share a broad understanding of the direction of intergovernmental relations and be willing to work across partisan and ideological lines to make it happen? Or will a mixture of crippling recession, massive cutbacks in discretionary federal spending, and continued political dysfunction at the national and state levels exacerbate the disadvantages of federalism and minimize its advantages? It is too early to tell.

Source: Adapted from Peter Harkness, "Potomac Chronicle: What Brand of Federalism Is Next?," *Governing,* January 2012.

much cash, and that the federal government was not going to give away that money without getting its policy priorities attended to. Accordingly, out of budgetary necessity states and localities found themselves orbiting the policy preferences of the federal government. As the economy returned to modest growth and the tide of federal grants-in-aid began to recede in the past few years, however, states and localities seemed increasingly eager to break the gravitational pull of the federal government. It is too soon to tell whether this heralds the resurrection of New Federalism or just the resumption of ad hoc federalism (see the box "States under Stress: What Brand of Federalism Is Next?").

The Supreme Court: The Umpire of Federalism

Article VI of the Constitution contains the national supremacy clause, which declares that the Constitution, laws passed by Congress, and national treaties are the "supreme law of the land." This does not mean that the states are always subordinate to the national government. Don't forget—the Tenth Amendment also counts as part of that supreme law. However, it does mean that federal courts often have to referee national-state conflicts. Because it has the final say in interpreting the Constitution, the Supreme Court is, in effect, the umpire of federalism. Its rulings ultimately decide the powers and limitations of the different levels of government.

The Rise of Nation-Centered Federalism on the Court

Throughout U.S. history, the Supreme Court has cycled through trends of state-centered and nation-centered philosophies of federalism. As we have already seen, the early Supreme Court under Chief Justice John Marshall pursued a fairly broad interpretation of the federal government's powers in such cases as *McCulloch v.*

Maryland. Marshall's successor, Roger Taney, took the Court in a more state-centered direction by establishing dual federalism as the Court's central operating philosophy. The shift from dual federalism to cooperative federalism required a return to a more nation-centered judicial philosophy. Although the Court initially took a more nation-centered direction in its rulings following the Civil War, it was not until the Great Depression and Roosevelt's New Deal that a decisive tilt in the Court's rulings cleared the way for the rise of cooperative federalism and the centralization of power in the national government.

The shift toward a liberal interpretation of the federal government's powers dominated the Supreme Court's operating philosophy for much of the next sixty years and is exemplified by its decision in *United States v. Darby Lumber Co.* (1941). The substantive issue at stake in this case was whether the federal government had the power to regulate wages. The Supreme Court said yes, but the decision is of more lasting interest because of the majority opinion's dismissive comment on the Tenth Amendment. Once considered the constitutional lockbox of state power, the amendment, according to the Court's ruling, now did little more than state "a truism that all is retained which has not been surrendered." In other words, the Tenth Amendment was simply a basket for the "leftover" powers the federal government had not sought or did not want.

During and after the New Deal era, the Supreme Court also accelerated a trend of broadly interpreting Congress's powers to regulate interstate commerce. It did this through its interpretation of the **interstate commerce clause**. In *Wickard v. Filburn* (1942), the Court ruled that the clause gave Congress the power to regulate what a farmer can feed his chickens. In *Heart of Atlanta Motel v. United States* (1964) and *Katzenbach v. McClung* (1964), the justices ruled that it gave

---

Interstate Commerce Clause
Constitutional clause that gives Congress the right to regulate interstate commerce. This clause has been broadly interpreted to give Congress a number of implied powers.

Congress the power to regulate private acts of racial discrimination.

A series of such decisions over the course of more than fifty years led some judicial scholars to conclude that the Supreme Court had essentially turned the concept of enumerated and reserved powers on its head. In effect, the assumption now seemed to be that the federal government had the power to do anything the Constitution did not specifically prohibit.[19] The states and localities were drawn ever closer into subordinate satellite roles in orbit around the federal government. This situation continued until just before the end of the twentieth century. At that point, the Court once again began siding with the states over the federal government.

A Tenth Amendment Renaissance or Ad Hoc Federalism?

By the mid-1990s, the Supreme Court was dominated by justices appointed by New Federalists. Reagan, who had campaigned on his intention to nominate federal judges who shared his conservative philosophy, appointed four. He also elevated a fifth, William Rehnquist—originally appointed as an associate justice by Nixon—to the position of chief justice. Reagan's vice president and presidential successor, George H. W. Bush, appointed two more justices. The end result was a mid-1990s Supreme Court chosen

TABLE 2-3

Key U.S. Supreme Court Rulings Regarding Federalism, 1995–2012

Case	Decision
United States v. Lopez (1995)	Court strikes down a federal law prohibiting possession of firearms near public schools. State claim upheld.
Seminole Tribe of Florida v. Florida (1996)	Court rules Congress cannot allow citizens to sue states in a federal court except for civil rights violations. State claim upheld.
Printz v. United States (1997)	Court strikes down a federal law requiring mandatory background checks for firearms purchases. State claim upheld.
Alden v. Maine (1999)	Court rules that Congress does not have the power to authorize citizens to sue in state court on the basis of federal claims. State claim upheld.
United States v. Morrison (2000)	Court strikes down the federal Violence Against Women Act. State claim upheld.
Reno v. Condon (2000)	Court upholds a federal law preventing states from selling driver's license information. State claim overturned.
Bush v. Gore (2000)	Court overrules a Florida Supreme Court action allowing hand recounts of contested election ballots. State claim overturned.
Alabama v. Garrett (2001)	Court rules that state employees cannot sue their employers in federal court to recover monetary damages under the provisions of the Americans with Disabilities Act. State claim upheld.
Lorillard Tobacco Co. v. Reilly (2001)	Court strikes down Massachusetts laws regulating the advertising of tobacco products. State claim overturned.
Kelo v. City of New London (2005)	Court rules that government can seize private property for public purposes, including economic development. State claim upheld.
Gonzales v. Oregon (2006)	Court rules that the U.S. attorney general overstepped his authority by threatening to eliminate prescription-writing privileges for doctors who follow state law allowing physician-assisted suicide. State claim upheld.
Arizona v. United States (2012)	Court rules that states do not have the authority to enact and enforce immigration laws; however, it allows states to implement "show me your papers" regulations that require law enforcement officers to determine the immigration status of anyone they stop or detain.

largely by conservative Republican presidents who wanted limits set on the federal government's powers and responsibilities. The justices obliged.

In a series of narrow—mostly 5–4—decisions in the 1990s, the Court began to back away from the nation-centered interpretation of the Constitution that had dominated its rulings during the era of cooperative federalism (see Table 2-3). *United States v. Lopez* (1995) was a significant victory for states' rights and a clear break from a half century of precedent. This case involved the Drug Free School Zone Act of 1990, which made it a federal crime to possess a firearm within one thousand feet of a school. Following a good deal of precedent, Congress justified its authority to regulate local law enforcement by using a very liberal interpretation of the interstate commerce clause. The Supreme Court disagreed and argued that the commerce clause granted no such authority.

Similar reasoning was used by the justices in *United States v. Morrison* (2000) to strike down the Violence Against Women Act (VAWA). Congress had passed this law in 1994 out of concern that the states, although having primary responsibility for criminal law, were not adequately dealing with the problem of violence against women. The key provision of the VAWA gave assault victims the right to sue their assailants in federal court. Congress argued that it was authorized to pass such a law because fear of violence prevented women from using public transportation or going out unescorted at night. Such fears, the reasoning went, placed limits on economic opportunities for women. This argument made the connection to commerce and Congress's constitutional authority. The Supreme Court again rejected this broad interpretation of the commerce clause.

At the same time that it was narrowly interpreting the Constitution to limit federal power, the Supreme Court after 1990 began to interpret the Constitution broadly to expand state power. Notably, the Court made a series of rulings that broadly interpreted the Eleventh Amendment's guarantee of **sovereign immunity** to the states. Sovereign immunity is essentially "the right of a government to be free from suits brought without its consent."[20] In cases such as *Seminole Tribe of Florida v. Florida* (1996) and *Alden v. Maine* (1999), the Supreme Court adopted an interpretation of the Eleventh Amendment that limited the right of citizens to sue states for violations of federal law. These rulings not only lessened the power of the federal government over the states but also arguably gave the states more power over their own citizens.

Although these and other rulings resurrected the Tenth Amendment and underlined the independent power of the states, there has been an element of inconsistency to Supreme Court decisions since 1990. In *Bush v. Gore* (2000), the Court abandoned its commitment to states' rights by overruling the Florida Supreme Court and ordering a halt to the contested recount of presidential ballots. Democratic presidential nominee Al Gore indisputably won the popular vote in 2000, but the outcome of the presidential election was decided by Florida's electoral votes. Gore and Bush ran neck and neck in this state, the decision so close that a series of controversial and hotly contested recounts were undertaken with the approval of the Florida courts. In effect, the U.S. Supreme Court overturned the state court's interpretation of state law—which allowed the recounts—and decided the presidency in favor of George W. Bush. Another decision that favored federal power over state power came in *Lorillard Tobacco Co. v. Reilly* (2001). Here, the Court overturned a Massachusetts law that regulated the advertising of tobacco products. The Court argued that federal law—specifically, the Federal Cigarette Labeling and Advertising Act—legitimately preempts state law on this issue.

The Court also trumped ten states that have legalized the use of marijuana for medical purposes. In *Gonzales v. Raich* (2005), the Court, led

---

Sovereign Immunity
The right of a government to not be sued without its consent.

by its more liberal justices, ruled that federal law enforcement officers, prosecutors, and judges can prosecute and punish anyone possessing marijuana. The ruling weakened the states' laws; however, it did not overturn them because state and local officials need not participate in any federal efforts to seize medical marijuana.[21] Just six months later, however, the Court upheld a state law related to serious illnesses when it ruled in *Gonzales v. Oregon* (2006) against the federal government's challenge of Oregon's law that allows physician-assisted suicide. In recent years, the Court has reviewed a number of preemptions of state law on everything from banking regulation to labor arbitration, and, for the most part, it has sided with federal authority.[22]

This was certainly the case in the Court's 2012 landmark ruling in *National Federal of Independent Business v. Sebelius,* which bitterly disappointed many conservatives. This case decided the federal government's power to enact the Patient Protection and Affordable Care Act ("Obamacare"), in particular the federal government's authority to require individuals to purchase health insurance. Chief Justice John Roberts, appointed by President George W. Bush and typically seen as a member of the Court's conservative bloc, surprised many by voting with the more liberal justices to affirm that power. Yet in another landmark case decided the same year, the Court put caveats on federal supremacy. In *Arizona v. United States* (2012), the case that decided Arizona's immigration law discussed in the opening section of this chapter, the Supreme Court essentially ruled that only the federal government has the power to set immigration policy but affirmed that states have the right to check the immigration status of people within their borders. In other words, the Court sort of split the difference between state and federal claims to power.

So over the past quarter century or so, the Supreme Court has sometimes zigged and sometimes zagged on state-federal relations. In the 1990s its rulings seemed to herald a resurrection of states' rights by conservative justices, but this commitment was never consistent, and something of that inconsistency is seen in the big landmark cases affecting state-federal of the past few years.

Some scholars argue that these sorts of inconsistencies have always been characteristic of the Supreme Court's federalism rulings. Ideology—not a firm commitment to a particular vision of state-national relations—is what ultimately decides how a justice rules in a particular case.[23] Therefore, a Court dominated by conservative appointees will occasionally depart from the state-centered notion of federalism if a nation-centered view is more ideologically pleasing, whereas a Court dominated by liberal appointees will do the opposite. The Supreme Court, like the president, finds it hard to resist the temptations of ad hoc federalism.

> Ideology—not a firm commitment to a particular vision of state-national relations—is what ultimately decides how a justice rules in a particular case.

Conclusion

The Constitution organizes the United States into a federal political system. This means that the states are powerful independent political actors that dominate important policy areas. Many of these policy areas are those with the most obvious and far-reaching roles in the day-to-day lives of citizens. Education, law enforcement, utility regulation, and road construction are but a handful of examples. The independence they are granted under the federal system allows states broad leeway to go their own way in these and many other policy areas.

The resulting variation has a number of advantages, such as making it easier to match local preferences with government action and allowing states and localities to experiment with innovative programs and policies. There are also a number of disadvantages. These include the complexity and difficulty in coordinating policy at the national level. The interests of state and national governments overlap in many areas. Because of this and because the Constitution does not clearly resolve the question of who has the power to do what in these arenas of shared interest, conflict is inevitable.

What is the future of federalism? In the past decade, the federal government's commitment to New Federalism all but collapsed, being replaced by a much more ad hoc approach to state-federal relations. Under the George W. Bush administration, the federal government veered away from the devolutionary trends of the 1990s and made numerous efforts to shift power to the national government. The economic shocks of 2008–2009 caused a significant retrenchment among subnational governments, which suddenly found themselves heavily reliant on the federal government as a major revenue source. As state budgets and an overextended federal government have slowed grants-in-aid, there are signs that states are looking to assert more independence. It is not at all clear, though, that New Federalism is back. If states' rights are championed only when they coincide with ideological or partisan preferences on given issues, what we are more likely to see is the resumption of ad hoc federalism. Regardless of what the future brings, there is no doubt that the federal system has evolved into a complex web of intergovernmental relationships that recognizes the practical necessity of cooperation among all levels of government. This creates a situation ripe for continued conflicts between state and federal governments, conflicts that in many cases will have to be resolved by the Supreme Court. The Court recently has exhibited some inconsistency in its own commitment to favoring states' rights in resolving state-federal conflicts. Yet, regardless of how these conflicts are ultimately resolved, the future undoubtedly will find states and localities continuing to play a central role in the U.S. political system, both as independent policymakers and as cooperative partners with the federal government.

The Latest Research

Federalism in the United States is dynamic. The roles and responsibilities of federal and state governments are constantly evolving based on political and economic context, policy demands and innovation, Supreme Court rulings, and the political philosophies and ideological preferences and partisan fortunes of lawmakers at both levels of government. Current scholars of federalism find themselves in a particularly interesting period in the development of intergovernmental relations. The worst of the recession is over, yet fiscal stresses remain. Federal, state, and local governments are trying to reset their relationships with each other to deal most effectively with what comes next—but no one is sure what comes next.

Below are summaries of some of the most recent research on federalism. Two constant themes emerge from this stream of scholarship: first, intergovernmental relations have undergone and are currently undergoing dramatic changes; and second, those changes have enormous implications not just for politics and policy but also for the day-to-day lives of citizens.

• •

- **Gamkhar, Shama, and J. Mitchell Pickerill.** 2012. "The State of American Federalism 2011–2012: A Fend for Yourself and Activist Form of Bottom-Up Federalism." *Publius: The Journal of Federalism* 42: 357–386.

   The scholarly journal *Publius* periodically publishes articles by scholars of state politics on the state of American federalism. This article is interesting because the authors conclude that we may be witnessing the emergence of what they call "bottom-up" federalism. They argue that political, economic, and judicial trends are pushing states and localities to become more independent, to figure out how to solve the financial and social challenges they face without being propped up by the federal government. Multiple causes are driving these trends. For example, as divided government and gridlock slow government action at the federal level on a wide array of policy issues, state and local governments are being forced to step up and take action on their own. As federal stimulus dollars disappear, states and localities increasingly have to figure out how to make the books balance on their own. The decreased reliance on federal dollars seems to be encouraging more assertive declarations of state sovereignty. For example, states have begun reasserting their independence by opting out of federal programs (e.g., health insurance exchanges, high-speerd rail initiatives) that provide financial aid.

- **Rivlin, Alice.** 2012. "Rethinking Federalism for More Effective Governance." *Publius: The Journal of Federalism* 42: 387–400.

In this article, a companion piece to the Gamkhar and Pickerill study described above, Rivlin argues that the realities of postrecession governance create a pressing need for a reconsideration of the relationship between state and federal governments. In particular, Rivlin pushes for two key reforms. First, she argues that state and federal governments should rethink their job responsibilities. Rather than taking on increasingly shared responsibilities in areas such as education, she suggests, one level of government should take primary responsibility. Who gets the job should depend on who is best positioned to do that job and who has traditionally had the legal authority to do it (in the case of education, this would be the states). This is essentially an argument that a good dose of dual federalism is not necessarily a bad thing. The second big reform that Rivlin endorses is a fundamental rethinking of how government funds itself. She argues that the existing federal tax system is poorly suited for the twenty-first

century and suggests the implementation of a kind of national sales tax, collected by the federal government but distributed to the states. This would allow states to recapture sales taxes lost to Internet sales as well as provide a more uniform and reliable revenue source for more distinct and defined policy responsibilities.

- **Robertson, David Brian.** 2012. *Federalism and the Making of America.* New York: Routledge.

The two articles described above are analyses of changes in intergovernmental relations more or less as they occur in real time. Robertson's book makes a good companion to these, placing such time-focused studies into perspective by offering a sweeping story of the historical development of federalism in America, from its birth at the founding of the Republic to the red-state–blue-state conflicts of the twenty-first century. The book is notable for its focus on federalism as the stage upon which most of the great policy battles in American history have been fought: racial relations, economic regulation, social welfare and regulation. All these issues and more have been critically shaped by America's system of intergovernmental relations.

- **Weissert, Carol S.** 2011. "Beyond Marble Cakes and Picket Fences: What U.S. Federalism Scholars Can Learn from Comparative Work." *Journal of Politics* 73: 965–979.

This article is Weissert's presidential address to the Southern Political Science Association, one of the more prestigious professional associations in the discipline. In it Weissert examines an issue critical to readers of this textbook: the comparative method. She argues that while there is no doubt that state scholars put the comparative method to good use, they have a particular blind spot—they fail to learn from scholars of other federal systems that employ the same method. If we want to learn what differences really make a difference—not just in the United States, but anywhere at any time—we need to pay attention to differences that make a difference in other federal systems, not just federalism in the United States.

Chapter Review

Key Concepts

college.cqpress.com/
sites/govstateandlocal

Suggested Web Sites

- **www.ncsl.org/statefed/statefed.htm.** Web site sponsored by the National Conference of State Legislatures and dedicated to state-federal issues.

- **www.nga.org.** Web site of the National Governors Association, which includes a section devoted to state-federal relations.

- **www.publius.oxfordjournals.org.** Web site of *Publius,* a scholarly journal dedicated to the study of federalism.

- **www.supremecourtus.gov.** Web site of the U.S. Supreme Court; includes text of the Court's opinions.

State Stats on Federalism

Explore and compare data on the states! Go to college.cqpress.com/sites/ govstateandlocal to do these exercises.

1. On average, the federal government contributes around 10 percent, the state government around 47 percent, and local governments around 44 percent to public K–12 schools. How much money, per pupil, does your state spend on elementary and secondary education? Is this an example of compact federalism, dual federalism, or cooperative federalism? Why?

2. What percentage of your state's population is enrolled in Medicaid? How does your state compare to the states around it? How might the Affordable Care Act change this number moving forward?

3. How many immigrants were admitted to New Mexico in 1997? How many were admitted to Arizona in the same year? How might this difference affect variations in policies regarding immigration?

4. What was the incarceration rate per 100,000 people in Utah in 2010? What was the rate in neighboring Idaho? Why might this difference be concerning?

5. What was the per capita net income that your state received from corporate taxes in 2011? What was the amount in a neighboring state? How might these differences affect a business that would like to have offices in both locations?

State constitutions differ from the U.S. Constitution in many ways. Some are older—the Massachusetts Constitution, shown here, was written about a decade before the U.S. Constitution was adopted. Most state constitutions are longer, more detailed, and much easier to change than their federal counterpart.

A

CONSTITUTION

OR

FRAME OF GOVERNMENT,

Agreed upon by the DELEGATES of the People of the State of MASSACHUSETTS-BAY,

IN

CONVENTION,

Begun and held at CAMBRIDGE on the First of *September*, 1779,

AND

Continued by Adjournments to the Second of MARCH, 1780.

[Revised and Corrected.]

BOSTON:
STATE OF MASSACHUSETTS-BAY.
Printed by BENJAMIN EDES & SONS, in State-Street.
M,DCC,LXXX.

Constitutions

OPERATING INSTRUCTIONS

- What impact do state constitutions have on our lives?
- Why do state constitutions differ?
- How do constitutions determine what state and local governments can and cannot do?

Y ou do not need a Ph.D. to help change the state constitution in Colorado. You just need to be a registered voter. Want to understand what you are being asked to change? Well, keep studying. For that, you really might need a Ph.D.

Like many states, Colorado has a process of **direct democracy**, in other words a system that allows citizens to make laws themselves rather than outsourcing the job to elected representatives. This includes the ability to vote on proposed amendments to the state constitution. Voting on amendments is one thing, though. Understanding them is quite another. For example, consider the following proposed amendment (fair warning—prepare to go cross-eyed):

> Concerning reform of the state civil service system, and in connection therewith, modifying the merit principle, exempting certain positions from the system, modifying the number of eligible applicants from which an appointment is to be made, modifying the residency requirement, expanding the duration of temporary employment, specifying the rulemaking authority of the state personnel board and the state personnel director, allowing the general assembly to reallocate the rulemaking

Direct Democracy
A system in which citizens make laws themselves rather than relying on elected representatives.

authority of the state personnel board and state personnel director, authorizing a modification to the veterans' preference, and making conforming amendments.[1]

Eh? Don't get it? Us neither—and one of us actually has a Ph.D. According to one study, the language of policy proposals put to voters in direct democratic processes is written at a seventeenth-grade level. That means these proposals are, on average, written for people who have at least a college degree. In Colorado, such proposals were written at a twenty-sixth-grade level—they are literally written so you need a Ph.D. to understand them (or not—it sure didn't help us make sense of the mouthful in the previous paragraph).[2]

This is important because, as we shall see, state constitutions have an enormous impact on state governments and policymaking—and on us. They affect the education we receive, the employment opportunities we enjoy, the political cultures of the states in which we live, and the rights we do (or don't) have. State constitutions and the rights and powers they provide also vary widely. Thus it would be nice if we could at least get a plain-English general gist of what these all-important sets of rules and laws mean and what they imply. Ballot initiatives written in dense legalese probably won't get you there, but hopefully we can help you understand the importance of state constitutions—no Ph.D. required.

This chapter explores how the role that state constitutions allow citizens to play significantly affects governing. For example, Colorado, as we have already seen, embraces the idea of direct democracy. In that state the constitution allows the **electorate**, or those individuals who can vote, to take policy matters into their own hands (even if the voters are not quite sure what they are holding). Ballot initiatives and referendums allow Colorado voters to amend the constitution or override the decisions of the state's elected officials—or even remove the officials entirely—with ease. In contrast, New York's constitution does not allow these things. New York politicians are famously insulated from voters' demands, and state-level decisions are made by a handful of senior elected officials.

So here's one difference that can make a big difference—some state constitutions allow direct democratic processes such as ballot initiatives and referendums and other states do not. That's far from the only difference, though. State constitutions include everything from rules about who can hold elective office (some states have term limits, others do not) to parking regulations for major municipalities. No two state constitutions are alike. What explains the tremendous variation among state constitutions? A state constitution reflects that state's particular historical experiences, its political culture, its geography, and its notions of what makes good government. Alabama's constitution, for instance, was drafted in 1901 by a small group of wealthy planters and reflects their fears that rapid industrial development would threaten the "best" form of government—that is, planter government. Although some resisted such ideas at the time, the state's generally traditional political culture made them broadly acceptable.[3] As time passes and a constitution becomes more entrenched, it begins to shape a state's culture and determine the range of political possibilities. Alabama remained a traditional state at least in part because its constitution thwarted industrialization and modernization; although the constitution has been amended more than eight hundred times, the state has resisted changing many of those features. And Alabama is far from alone in this regard. Many of the differences in subnational politics can be traced directly to state constitutions.

In recent years, state constitutions have become more important, not less. Since the 1990s, the U.S. Supreme Court has handed down a number of decisions that have strengthened state governments at the expense of the federal government as well as others that have trumped state law. The Court's insistence on determining the boundaries of federalism and evaluating state laws and regulations—a form of activism sometimes referred to as **judicial federalism**—even gained Chief Justice William Rehnquist the nickname "Governor Rehnquist."[4]

State supreme courts also are becoming more assertive. In 1977, Supreme Court justice William

---

Electorate
The population of individuals who can vote.

Judicial Federalism
The idea that the courts determine the boundaries of state-federal relations.

FIGURE 3-1

HOW IT WORKS

Alabama's State Constitution: The More Things Change, the More They Stay the Same

Since 1819, Alabama has adopted six different constitutions. The most recent was ratified in 1901 and consists of more than 360,000 words (that's about forty-five times longer than the U.S. Constitution). The bulk of this comes from the 835 (and counting) amendments that make it the world's longest operating constitution. It was the product of a constitutional delegation comprising 155 white males who, like convention president John Knox, were mostly large planters. They wished to hold back the industrialization that had left Alabama in great debt. Knox, however, described the constitution's primary purpose as "secur[ing] white supremacy." African American voters were stripped of voting rights, and interracial marriage was forbidden (as recently as 2012 the state's legislature was still working to strip racist language from the constitution). Civil rights advocate Booker T. Washington, among others, condemned the document.

Many of its original provisions are now defunct or have been retracted, but that doesn't mean there are not still big problems with the constitution. Some provisions allow the continuing disfranchisement of many citizens, delay of economic development, and denial of governing powers to localities. Critics have accused the constitution of encouraging unproductive government action; the state legislature spends more than half of its time debating issues that have only local relevance, and two-thirds of the constitutional amendments address issues specific to one town or county.

There have been numerous efforts to change Alabama's constitution—six different governors have tried to change the existing 1901 document. In each case, they were met with resistance from the legislature, the state supreme court, or powerful planters and industrialists. The latest attempt at reform involves a constitutional revision commission created in 2011 by the legislature. The job of this sixteen-member commission is to comb through the constitution and recommend changes. These are recommendations, though, not mandates. Recommendations by the commission can be rejected by the legislature and must be approved by voters before taking effect. So while Alabama's constitution is likely not set in stone forever, the prospects of a start-from-scratch do-over still seem slim.

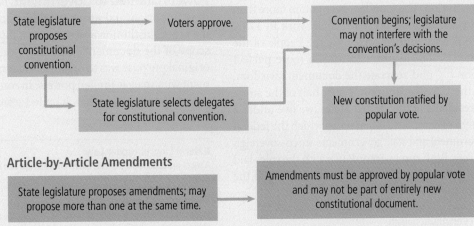

Constitutional Convention

State legislature proposes constitutional convention. → Voters approve. → Convention begins; legislature may not interfere with the convention's decisions. → New constitution ratified by popular vote.

State legislature selects delegates for constitutional convention.

Article-by-Article Amendments

State legislature proposes amendments; may propose more than one at the same time. → Amendments must be approved by popular vote and may not be part of entirely new constitutional document.

Source: Alabama Citizens for Constitutional Reform, www.constitutionalreform.org.

Brennan, a former justice of the New Jersey Supreme Court, wrote a now-famous article for the *Harvard Law Review* that noted that state constitutions afford their citizens another layer of rights above and beyond the rights protected in the U.S. Constitution. He urged state courts to pay more attention to these rights and to assert themselves more forcefully. They have. In the past decade, for example, state supreme courts in Connecticut, Iowa, Massachusetts, New Hampshire, New York, and Vermont have ruled that their constitutions guarantee equal marriage rights to same-sex couples. (See the box "A Difference That Makes a Difference: State Constitutions and the Right to Marry.") Ever more assertive courts, in other words, have found new rights in state constitutions. This means that the documents that reflect and determine what state and local governments can and cannot do have become even more important to an understanding of politics in the United States.

What State Constitutions Do: It's Probably Different from What You Think

Mention "the constitution," and chances are good that your listener will think instantly of the U.S. Constitution. The founders have gotten more than 225 years of good press for their work in 1787. Schoolchildren memorize "We the People of the United States, in order to form a more perfect Union . . ." and venerate the document's wisdom. Yet the U.S. Constitution is only half of the story. As residents of the United States, we live under a system of dual constitutionalism, in which the federal government and state governments are co-sovereign powers. Both run in accordance with the rules laid out in their respective constitutions. Despite the important role that state constitutions play in establishing our rights and organizing our local and state governments, most people know very little about them.

The U.S. Constitution and all state constitutions have some functions in common. They set forth the roles and responsibilities of the government, describe the basic institutional structure of the government, and establish procedures for the operation of these institutions. Most state constitutions reflect the influence of the U.S. Constitution. They create three primary branches of government (legislative, executive, and judicial) and provide a general governmental framework. Like the U.S. Constitution, they all contain something roughly equivalent to a bill of rights that spells out the rights of citizens and places specific limits on governmental powers. Most state constitutions place these rights firmly in the context of natural law, also known as higher law, a tradition that holds that these rights are not political creations but divine endowments. The constitutions and any subsequent constitutional amendments, or changes, are meant to ensure these rights for citizens.

Yet in many ways it is misleading to compare state constitutions with their better-known federal counterpart. Consider the important differences discussed below.

Powers Granted to Government. Perhaps the most important and surprising difference between the U.S. Constitution and state constitutions is the scope of the documents. The U.S. Constitution's original purpose was to organize a federal government with sharply limited powers. In contrast, state governments have what is called plenary power,

---

Dual Constitutionalism
A system of government in which people live under two sovereign powers. In the United States, these are the government of their state of residence and the federal government.

Natural Law, or Higher Law
A set of moral and political rules based on divine law and binding on all people.

Constitutional Amendments
Proposals to change a constitution, typically enacted by a supermajority of the legislature or through a statewide referendum.

Plenary Power
Power that is not limited or constrained.

which means their powers are not limited to those laid down in the U.S. Constitution or their own state constitutions. As the Tenth Amendment of the U.S. Constitution makes clear, *all* powers not expressly delegated or forbidden to the federal government are reserved for the states. In other words, this is not a limited grant of power in the sense of laying out the specifics of what states have the authority to do or not to do. It basically says that states can do whatever they want—they have complete or plenary power—as long as they do not contravene the U.S. Constitution.

That plenary power is vested in the lawmaking bodies of state government—that is, state legislatures. This does not meant that these legislatures can go around arbitrarily breaking the rules laid down by their own constitutions, which can be quite restrictive. What it means is they can act without express permission of the constitution—as long as their actions are not prohibited, they are good to go. Think of it like this: When passing a law, Congress must address the key question, "Is this allowed?" by the U.S. Constitution. For state legislatures the key question is, "Is this prohibited?" by the state constitution. That's the difference between limited and plenary powers in the federal system. State legislatures, through the U.S. Constitution and their own state constitutions, have these powers. The Congress does not. State constitutions, in short, do not establish limited governments in the same way the U.S. Constitution establishes a limited federal government.[5]

Permanence. The U.S. Constitution is widely seen as the document that created the United States—the embodiment of the founders' wisdom. As such, it is held in the highest regard by politicians and the public alike. It has lasted more than two centuries and has been formally changed only twenty-seven times. In contrast, state constitutions are amended and even replaced much more frequently. Most states have replaced their original constitutions at least once. California is currently on its second constitution. New York is on its fourth. Louisiana is on its eleventh. In fact, one political scientist has estimated that the average state constitution lasts for only about seventy years.[6]

Length. The federal constitution is a relatively short document. At about 7,400 words, it is shorter than most chapters in this book. In contrast, state constitutions tend to be much longer—about 26,000 words on average. Some are much, much longer. New York's constitution and California's ruling document are each roughly 50,000 words long. The longest state constitution, Alabama's, is more than forty-five times the length of the U.S. Constitution.[7]

Specificity. Why are state constitutions so much longer than the federal constitution and so much more likely to change? Part of the answer has to do with the different functions of the federal constitution versus those of state constitutions. The U.S. Constitution is primarily concerned with setting up the basic structures and procedures of government. State constitutions do these things too, but they often set forth procedures and address policies in much greater detail than the federal constitution. Whereas the federal constitution creates a framework for government, state constitutions often get into policy details. South Dakota, for instance, is one of several states that once sanctioned its state prison to produce twine and cordage. Oklahoma's constitution mandates that home economics be taught in school; Maryland's regulates off-street parking in Baltimore. Political scientist Christopher Hammonds has estimated that 39 percent of the total provisions in state constitutions are devoted to specific policy matters of this sort. In contrast, only 6 percent of the U.S. Constitution deals with such specific issues.[8]

> Whereas the federal constitution creates a framework for government, state constitutions often get into policy details. South Dakota, for instance, is one of several states that once sanctioned its state prison to produce twine and cordage.

State constitutions contain provisions on everything from free speech to parking fees, from how to organize government to how to build a pipe. Oklahoma's constitution, for example, requires schools to offer courses in the "domestic sciences." Unsurprisingly, state constitutions tend to be considerably longer than the U.S. Constitution.

Finances. Congress and the White House can run up as much national debt as they can persuade bond buyers to swallow. In contrast, thirty-two state constitutions require the legislative and executive branches to balance their budgets. Another seventeen states have statutes that mandate balanced budgets. Only Vermont can choose to run up debt like the feds. Even state constitutions that do not require a balanced budget take a much more proscriptive, or restrictive, view of budget matters than does the U.S. Constitution. California's constitution, for instance, mandates that almost 40 percent of the state budget go toward education, a requirement that has constrained legislators' options when the state has been faced with budget shortfalls.

Other state constitutions mandate a specific style and format for laws that allow the transfer of money to the executive branch. These are known as **appropriations bills**. During the 1990s, some states, including Arizona, Colorado, Nevada, Oklahoma, and South Dakota, amended their constitutions to require supermajorities—two-thirds or three-fifths of the electorate—instead of simple majorities of the legislature to increase revenues or taxes.[9] Sometimes constitutions get more specific still, prohibiting legislators from attaching "riders" to appropriations bills and requiring a single subject for each bill. (Riders are amendments or additions unrelated to the main

Embrace of Democracy. The U.S. Constitution creates a system of representative democracy; it purposefully rejects direct democracy as a basis for governance. The founders went to great pains to check "the whimsies of the majority" by designing a system of checks and balances that deliberately keeps policymaking at arm's length from the shifting winds of popular opinion. During the Progressive Era in the early 1900s, many states revamped their constitutions to do just the opposite. This was particularly true of the newer western and midwestern states, in which old-school politics was less entrenched and political cultures tended toward the moralistic or individualistic.

Progressive reformers believed old constitutional arrangements were outmoded and that citizens should have the opportunity to participate directly in making laws. Moreover, they worried that state legislatures had been captured by wealthy special interests. In other words, they thought that representative democracy was working for the benefit of a few rather than for the benefit of all. Their solution was to give the people the ability to amend their constitutions and pass laws directly through the use of referendums and ballot initiatives. Thus, in about half the states, state constitutions champion direct democracy in a way that the U.S. Constitution purposefully does not.

Appropriations Bills
Laws passed by legislatures authorizing the transfer of money to the executive branch.

bill.) Not surprisingly, state legislators sometimes try to evade these strict requirements. As a result, state judges tend to be much more involved in monitoring the government's budget process than their federal counterparts. In 2004, for instance, the Ohio Supreme Court reminded legislators that it would strike down any laws passed in violation of the state's single-subject rule.

The Evolution of State Constitutions

The first state constitutions were not technically constitutions at all. Rather, they were **colonial charters** awarded by the king of England. These charters typically were brief documents giving individuals or corporations the right to establish "plantations" over certain areas and govern the inhabitants therein. King James I of England granted the first charter in 1606. It created the Virginia Company of London, which in 1607 established the first English settlement in North America at Jamestown in what is now the state of Virginia.

As the colonies expanded, many of these charters were amended to give the colonists "the rights of Englishmen." Just what those rights were, however, was not entirely clear. Britain's constitution was not (and is not) a written document. It is a tradition based on the Magna Carta of 1215 and on a shared understanding of what government should and should not do. From the start, some colonies took an expansive view of their rights and privileges. The Massachusetts Bay Colony, like other English settlements in North America, was organized as a corporation and was controlled by a small group of stockholders. But whereas the charters of the other companies remained in England within easy reach of the British courts, Puritan leader John Winthrop took his colony's charter with him when he sailed for the New World in 1630. This made it difficult for the English government to seize and revoke the charter if the company misbehaved or operated illegally, which it

soon did. The Puritans excluded nonchurchgoers from local governments, punished people who violated their sense of morals, and generally behaved like an independent polity. This misbehavior eventually incurred the displeasure of King Charles II, who revoked the charter in 1691. Massachusetts then received a new royal charter that provided for a royal governor and a general assembly—a form of governance that lasted until the Revolutionary War, nearly a century later.[10]

When the colonies won their independence, it was clear that the colonial charters had to be replaced or at least modified. It was less clear what should replace them. Some colonial leaders believed that the Continental Congress should draft a model constitution that every state should adopt. Richard Henry Lee, a Virginia politician, explained the idea in a letter to John Adams in May 1776: "Would not a uniform plan of government, prepared for America by the Congress, and approved by the colonies, be a surer foundation of unceasing harmony to the whole?"[11]

Adams thought not. Although he liked the idea of uniform state constitutions in principle, he worried about what would happen in practice. He believed that effective government required a strong executive. The colonists' experience dealing with royal governors, however, had created an aversion to executive power. Adams feared that the Continental Congress would create governments dominated by powerful **unicameral legislatures** or even do away with governors altogether and create a special committee of legislators to handle the everyday business of governing. This would violate what he saw as the wise precautionary principle of the **separation of powers**.

Ultimately, despite being a unicameral body itself, the Continental Congress rejected that particular idea. Instead, it passed a resolution that urged the thirteen colonies to reorganize their authority solely "on the basis of the authority of

Colonial Charters
Legal documents drawn up by the British Crown that spelled out how the colonies were to be governed.

Unicameral Legislature
A legislature having only one chamber. Nebraska is currently the only U.S. state with a unicameral legislature.

Separation of Powers
The principle that government should be divided into separate legislative, executive, and judicial branches, each with its own powers and responsibilities.

the people."[12] This set the stage for the states to create their own varied blueprints for government.

After independence was declared and secured, the states convened special assemblies to draft new constitutions. Most adopted lightly modified versions of their old colonial charters. References to the king of England were deleted and bills of rights added. In most of the new states, power was concentrated in the legislative branch to diminish the possibility of tyrannical governors appearing in the political arena.

The First Generation of State Constitutions

This first generation of state constitutions created powerful **bicameral legislatures**—with a few exceptions. Georgia, Pennsylvania, and Vermont opted for unicameral legislatures. Governors and state judiciaries were clearly subordinate in most cases. In fact, legislatures often appointed both the governor and judges. No one envisioned that one day a state supreme court would have the power to overrule the acts of a legislature on the grounds that its laws were unconstitutional. Indeed, the states that did provide for a constitutional review entrusted that function to a special "council of revision" or to "councils of censor."

Nor did the early state constitutions embrace the now commonplace idea of "one person, one vote." Every early state constitution except Vermont's restricted voting access to white males who met certain minimum property requirements. Vermont gave the vote to every adult male. Supporters of a limited **franchise** defended these limitations as essential to the new republic. Without property qualifications, John Adams warned,

there will be no end to it. New claims will arise; women will demand a vote; lads from 12 to 21 will think their rights are not enough attended to; and every man who has not a farthing will demand an equal voice with any other, in all acts of the state. It tends to confound and destroy all distinctions, and prostrate all ranks to one common level.[13]

Indeed, Adams wanted to restrict the franchise even further by setting still higher property requirements.

In practice, the actual requirements necessary to achieve the right to vote varied widely. Some states, such as New Hampshire, let all white male taxpayers vote. This reflected the fact that New Hampshire was a state of small landowners with a fairly egalitarian political culture. However, even this fair state specified a higher threshold of property ownership that must be met should a man wish to hold office. In Virginia, a state with a more hierarchical political culture dominated by a small group of wealthy landowners and planters, the property qualifications were stiff. Only white males who owned at least twenty-five acres and a twelve-foot-by-twelve-foot house, or fifty acres unsettled, or a town lot with a twelve-foot-by-twelve-foot house could vote. It is not entirely clear how many people met these qualifications. Most scholars, however, believe that in the more democratic northern states 60–80 percent of white males could vote. Needless to say, women and nonwhites could not.

Over the course of the nineteenth century, the franchise was expanded gradually, although in a very uneven and often unjust fashion. A number of southern states, for example, rewrote their constitutions to allow minorities to vote only when such changes were forced on them as part of the price for their readmission to the Union after the Civil War. African American rights also were enshrined in the Fourteenth Amendment of the U.S. Constitution. Yet, despite these protections, gains for African Americans proved short-lived. In the last decade of the 1800s, African Americans' ability to vote and to participate in all aspects of society were harshly

---

Bicameral Legislature
A legislature made up of two chambers, typically a house of representatives, or assembly, and a senate.

Franchise
The right to vote.

A Difference That Makes A Difference

The Peculiar Constitution of Early Pennsylvania

The original American colonies were established for a wide variety of purposes. The Massachusetts Bay Colony, for example, started off as a haven for a persecuted religious sect. The Puritans were determined to create, in the words of Massachusetts's first governor, John Winthrop, "a city upon a hill" to serve as an example of a holy community for all people. Other colonies, such as Virginia, began as business ventures. Still others, including Pennsylvania, were both.

Pennsylvania's first colonial charter reflected the colony's dual purposes as a religious settlement and an investment. It illustrates how state charters were created to serve very particular goals—and how "rights" that Americans now take for granted, such as the right to self-governance, were by no means obvious to this country's founders.

The colony started out as a business venture. In 1681, William Penn received a proprietary interest—the controlling share—in what is now the state of Pennsylvania as repayment for a debt that England's King Charles II owed Penn's father. Penn was already deeply involved in land speculation in North America. He and eleven other investors already owned East Jersey (present-day New Jersey). Soon after buying into Pennsylvania, they acquired a lease on Delaware.

Penn, however, wasn't just a businessman. He was also a devout Quaker, a member of a peace-loving religious group that was often at odds with the official Church of England. Pennsylvania was to Penn "a holy experiment"—a unique chance to found a province dedicated to Quakerism's vision of equality and religious freedom.

William Markham, Penn's deputy, was sent in 1681 to establish a seat of government for Penn's new colony. Penn also instructed his representative to construct a "City of Brotherly Love"—Philadelphia. One year later,

Penn himself arrived in his fledgling colony. His first major action was to draw up a constitution, or charter, for his new colony, which he called "the Frame of Government." His second major act was to establish friendly relations with the American Indians in the area—an unusual action that reflected his pacific religious beliefs.

In many ways, the Frame of Government echoed Quakerism's progressive dogmas. Penn's constitution guaranteed religious freedom to everyone who believed in God. It also set forth a humane penal code and encouraged the emancipation of slaves. In contrast, the early settlers of Massachusetts were interested not in individual religious freedom but in establishing a just Puritan society. As a result, the functions of local churches and town governments were intertwined in early Massachusetts. Indeed, the colony was governed as a virtual theocracy for its first two hundred years.

However, the Pennsylvania model was not a uniform triumph of humane liberalism. Penn did use his charter to protect his business interests. The Frame of Government provided for an elected general assembly, but it also concentrated almost all power in the executive branch of government, which was controlled by Penn and the other proprietors.

It was not long before colonists began to chafe at some of the less progressive features of William Penn's early constitution. He was forced to return to Pennsylvania in 1701 and issue a new constitution, the Charter of Privileges, which granted more power to the provincial assembly. However, the conflict between proprietary and antiproprietary forces did not diminish until 1776. That year, noted revolutionary Benjamin Franklin led a convention to assemble and approve a new constitution for the state as it struggled for independence from Great Britain.

---

limited by the passage of **Jim Crow laws**. These laws provided for the systematic separation of races,

---

Jim Crow Laws
Legislative measures passed in the last decade of the nineteenth century that sought to systematically separate blacks and whites.

---

sharply restricted access to the franchise, and permitted the outright intimidation of African Americans.

Women fared only slightly better. Wyoming began to allow women the vote in 1869. By 1912, only thirteen states had followed suit. It took the

Nineteenth Amendment, ratified in 1920, to secure the right to vote, or suffrage, for all women nationwide. The limitations on the franchise imposed by many early state constitutions did little to promote good governance. State legislatures quickly developed an impressive record of corruption and fiscal extravagance because some of the men who had the legal right to vote also had money to influence politicians, an easy task in many states. But the era of unlimited legislative power did not last very long. New territories entering the Union, such as Indiana and Mississippi, opted for elected governors, as did older states that began to revise or replace their constitutions in the 1820s. The intention was to create more balance among the branches of government and allow all voters (not just the rich ones) more of a voice in deciding who would run a state. By 1860, South Carolina was the only state with a governor selected by the legislature.[14] In hindsight, the nineteenth century is seen as a period of tumultuous constitutional change.

Formal Constitutional Changes

More than 2,300 initiatives have been included on state ballots since 1904. Oregon leads the nation, with 355 initiatives presented by December 2010.

Every state constitution provides a method for making changes. Fourteen states actually require citizens to vote periodically on whether or not they want to convene a **constitutional convention**. Voters can decide if they want to amend or replace their state's constitution.[15]

In the early nineteenth century, suggesting such change could be an exciting—and dangerous—business. In 1841, a patrician attorney and renegade lawmaker by the name of Thomas Wilson Dorr convened an illegal constitutional convention. Its task was to replace Rhode Island's colonial charter with a more modern and progressive constitution.

The aged document still limited the franchise to voters owning land valued at $134 or more at a time when other states had long since abandoned such requirements. Dorr's supporters elected him "governor" the following year on a platform that proposed allowing all white males—even Catholic immigrants, a group viewed with great suspicion—to vote, which caused the sitting governor to order Dorr arrested and tried for treason. Thus began the Dorr War, or Dorr's Rebellion. Dorr's supporters then attempted to seize the arsenal in Providence but were repelled when their cannons failed to discharge. A month later, Dorr and his followers tried again. This time a force of militiamen and free blacks from Providence repelled them.[16] Still, Rhode Island's establishment got the hint. A new, more liberal constitution was quickly enacted.

The amendment process has since become a bit more routinized in most states. Amending or replacing a state constitution is typically a two-step process. First, a constitutional amendment or a new constitution must be proposed and meet a certain threshold of support. Then it must be ratified.

Changes to state constitutions are generally proposed in four primary ways: through legislative proposals, ballot initiatives or referendums, constitutional conventions, and constitutional commissions.

Legislative Proposals

Most attempts to change state constitutions begin with legislative proposals. Forty-nine state constitutions allow the state legislature to propose constitutional amendments to the electorate as a whole.[17] In seventeen states, a majority vote in both houses of the legislature suffices to send a constitutional amendment on for **ratification**. However, most states require a supermajority for a constitutional amendment to go into effect. Some states set the bar even higher. The constitutions of eleven states—Delaware, Indiana, Iowa, Massachusetts, Nevada, New York, Pennsylvania, South Carolina, Tennessee, Virginia, and Wisconsin—require the legislature to vote for a constitutional amendment in two consecutive sessions before it can be ratified.[18] In principle, some

---

Constitutional Convention
An assembly convened for the express purpose of amending or replacing a constitution.

Ratification
A vote of the entire electorate to approve a constitutional change, referendum, or ballot initiative.

MAP 3-1

Number of Constitutions per State

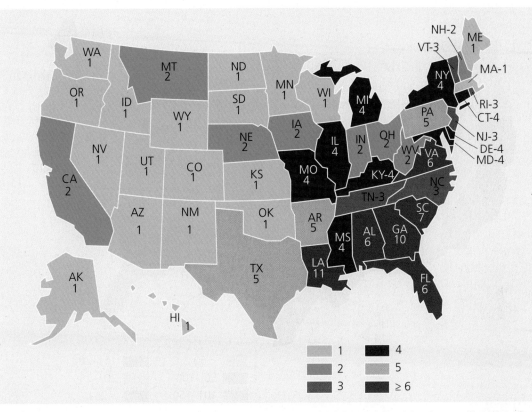

Source: Data from *The Book of the States 2012* (Lexington, KY: Council of State Governments, 2012), Table 1.1, http://knowledgecenter.csg.org/drupal/content/book-states-2012-chapter-1-state-constitutions.

state legislatures also can propose completely new constitutions to voters. However, no state legislature has successfully proposed a wholesale constitutional change since Georgia's did so in 1982.

Ballot Initiatives and Referendums

Twenty-four states give voters another way to propose constitutional amendments—through **ballot initiatives** or popular **referendums**. These ballot

---

Ballot Initiative
A process through which voters directly convey instructions to the legislature, approve a law, or amend the constitution.

Referendum
A procedure that allows the electorate to either accept or reject a law passed by the legislature.

measures offer citizens a way to amend the constitution or to enact new legislation without working through the legislature. South Dakota was the first state to provide voters with the option of ballot initiatives, in 1898, but it was only after Oregon embraced them in 1902 that the push for direct democracy really got under way. In the sixteen years that followed, nearly two dozen states followed Oregon's lead. The last state to approve ballot initiatives was Mississippi in 1992, some seventy years after its state supreme court tossed out its first ruling allowing initiatives.[19]

How ballot measures work in practice varies widely from state to state, although there are some common elements to the process. In most states, citizens must first provide the text of their proposal to an oversight body, usually the secretary of state's office or a legislative review committee. Then they need to gather enough signatures to

MAP 3-2

Number of Amendments Adopted per State

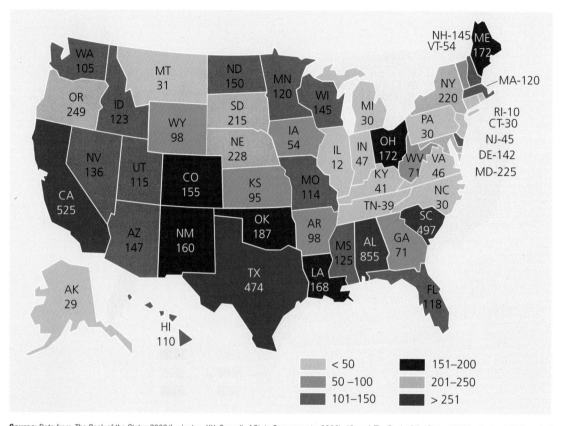

< 50	151–200
50 –100	201–250
101–150	> 251

Source: Data from *The Book of the States 2009* (Lexington, KY: Council of State Governments, 2009), 12; and *The Book of the States 2012* (Lexington, KY: Council of State Governments, 2012), Table 1.1, http://knowledgecenter.csg.org/drupal/content/book-states-2012-chapter-1-state-constitutions.

place the proposal on the ballot. This threshold varies widely among states, Wyoming sets the bar high, requiring a number of signatures equal to 15 percent of the votes cast for governor in the most recent election. The bar is lower in Colorado, where proponents need only gather signatures equal to 5 percent of the votes tallied for secretary of state in the previous election. The signatures are then verified, again by the secretary of state or the attorney general. Proposals that pass each test make it onto the ballot at the next election.

Ballot measures typically combine the proposal and ratification stages of the amendment process. Once a proposed amendment is on the ballot, it usually requires a simple majority to pass and become part of the constitution, although some state constitutions do require a supermajority.

The practical result is laws without lawmakers; the initiative is commonly employed to seek policy changes that, for whatever reason, are not being considered or undertaken by the legislature.

Constitutional Conventions

The most freewheeling approach to changing or replacing a state constitution is to convene a constitutional convention. Massachusetts, whose constitution was drafted in 1780 and is the nation's oldest, was the first state to adopt a constitution via a convention. Most other states quickly followed. Currently, the only states that make no provisions for changing their constitutions through the use of constitutional conventions are

Arkansas, Indiana, Mississippi, New Jersey, Pennsylvania, and Texas.

A constitutional convention typically begins when a state legislature passes a resolution that calls for a statewide referendum on whether a convention should be held. If a majority of the electorate votes in favor of the proposal, then the next step is to hold elections for convention delegates. In most states, a law is passed that provides for the election of convention members from local election districts. Of course, there are exceptions. The legislatures of Georgia, Louisiana, Maine, South Dakota, and Virginia can call a constitutional convention without the approval of the electorate. Iowa holds an automatic constitutional assembly every ten years, and Alaska's lieutenant governor can propose a constitutional convention through a ballot question if one has not occurred within the last decade.

Once delegates are selected, a constitutional convention can convene. The delegates are free to amend, revise, or even replace their state's constitution; a constitutional convention can change the existing document in any way it sees fit or write an entirely new constitution. Ultimately, its handiwork goes before the electorate as a whole to be voted in or cast out.

Or a constitutional convention can do nothing at all. In 1974, Texas convened a convention to rewrite its creaky 1876 constitution. The delegates spent several months drafting a new constitution, but when it came time to put it to a vote, a majority of the delegates unexpectedly came out against it. The next year, the state legislature voted to put the newly drafted constitution to the public anyway as a referendum. The voters turned it down.[20]

> State legislators tend to be wary of constitutional conventions and rarely convene them. The reason for this caution is that, once convened, a constitutional convention theoretically can examine any and all aspects of state and local government.

State legislators tend to be wary of constitutional conventions and rarely convene them. The reason for this caution is that, once convened, a constitutional convention theoretically can examine any and all aspects of state and local government. Lawmakers who approve a convention might end up initiating a process that leads to more far-reaching changes than they had expected. Increasingly, the average voter seems to share this skepticism. Voters in Alaska, Montana, and New Hampshire, among others, have rejected referendums that would have provided for constitutional conventions. In fact, the last U.S. state constitutional convention was held in 1986 in Rhode Island.[21] More recently, however, calls have been heard for a convention to reform California's constitution, which includes a series of contradictory provisions; for example, some mandate spending while others restrict taxation. The irony is, voters approved the amendments that made the document so at odds with itself—and now they may have a hand in forcing its overhaul.

Constitutional Revision Commissions

If constitutional conventions are for the bold and trusting, then **constitutional revision commissions** are often the cautious technocrat's preferred route to constitutional change. A constitutional revision commission typically consists of a panel of citizens appointed by the governor, by the state legislature, or by both. The commission suggests—but cannot mandate—changes to the state constitution. Between 1990 and 2000, seven states—Alaska, Arkansas, California, Florida, New York, Oklahoma, and Utah—convened constitutional revision commissions. Alabama's legislature created a constitutional revision commission in 2011 and charged it with a multiyear effort to recommend piecemeal changes to that state's bloated constitution (see Figure 3-1).

Constitutional Revision Commission
An expert committee formed to assess a constitution and suggest changes.

Two states go even further in their enthusiasm for constitutional commissions. Florida's constitution requires that a constitutional revision commission convene every twenty years. It also gives this commission a unique power—the right to present proposed changes directly to voters for their approval or rejection. Florida's last constitutional revision commission met in 1998. It recommended thirteen changes to the state constitution, including a provision that would allow local governments to expand their requirements for background checks and waiting periods for firearms purchases. That led the head of Florida's chapter of the National Rifle Association (NRA) to decry the proposal as a power grab and to issue a warning that gun owners might vote down all of the proposed constitutional changes, even changes with universal support, should the firearms provision be included.[22] The commission refused to back down. Six months later, more than 70 percent of voters supported the measure.

The other state with an unusual constitutional revision commission is Utah, the only state whose commission is permanent. Members of the Utah Constitutional Revision Commission are appointed by the governor, by the leaders of both houses of the legislature, and by sitting commission members. Unlike Florida's commission, Utah's commission can issue its recommendations only in the form of a public report to the governor. Although it is a permanent body, the Utah commission has not met much lately—it got into hot water for not supporting (or opposing) amendments favored by partisan interests in the state legislature. In response, the legislature passed a law mandating that the commission can meet only if it is specifically requested to do so by the governor or legislature, and neither has proven particularly eager to make such a request.

Ratification

Once an amendment has been proposed and found acceptable, it must be ratified before it can go into effect. In most states, this is a straightforward process. First, the proposed constitutional amendment or new constitution is put before the voting public in the next statewide election. Then, the electorate either approves or rejects it. Two states add a twist to this process. In South Carolina, a majority of both houses of the state legislature must vote to approve a constitutional amendment—after the successful popular referendum—before the amendment can go into effect. In Delaware, approval by a two-thirds vote in two successive general assemblies gets a constitutional amendment ratified. As already discussed, the ballot initiative essentially combines the proposal and ratification stages. Once a proposed amendment is qualified for the ballot, it usually requires only a simple majority to become part of the constitution.

Informal Methods for Changing Constitutions

In recent years, voters and legislators nationwide have generally resisted making major changes to their states' constitutions. However, many state constitutions have changed dramatically in informal ways. The most common route of informal constitutional change is via the state supreme courts. For instance, this is the case when a court interprets an existing constitution in a way that creates a new right, such as the right to an adequate or equitable education (discussed in chapter 13, on education).

Sometimes constitutional changes also come about from **judicial review**. In December 1999, the Vermont Supreme Court directed the state legislature to pass a law that would provide for civil unions. Its rationale? The court found that because the state constitution was "instituted for the common benefit, protection and security of the people," the state government could not refuse to provide the benefit of marriage to gay people. To those who objected that the state constitution, which was enacted in 1793 and at the time was a

---

Judicial Review
The power of courts to assess whether a law is in compliance with the constitution.

model of brevity at 8,200 words, said nothing about gay marriage, the court explained that its job was "to distill the essence, the motivating idea of the framers," not to be bound by eighteenth-century notions of jurisprudence.[23] In November 2003, the Massachusetts Supreme Court went further when it declared the state's ban on same-sex marriage unconstitutional, which prompted efforts to amend not just state constitutions but the U.S. Constitution as well to define marriage explicitly as a union between a man and a woman. While the attempt to amend the U.S. Constitution mostly fizzled, as of 2012 thirty states had amended their constitutions specifically to ban same-sex marriage.

State constitutions also can change when other branches of government successfully lay claim to broader powers. For example, Rhode Island's legislature has used its strong constitutional position—a clause in the state constitution says that the General Assembly "can exercise any power" unless the constitution explicitly forbids it—to take control of functions that most states delegate to governors. This means that in Rhode Island legislators not only sit on the boards and commissions that oversee a range of state agencies, but they also dominate the board that sets the salaries for high-ranking executive branch officials. Not surprisingly, this has given the legislature a great deal of power over executive branch decisions.

Procedures for Constitutional Amendment by Legislature

MAP 3-3

Legislative Vote Required for Proposal

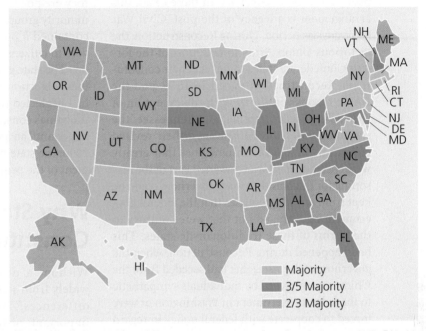

Majority
3/5 Majority
2/3 Majority

Source: Data from *The Book of the States 2012* (Lexington, KY: Council of State Governments, 2012), Table 1.1, http://knowledgecenter.csg.org/drupal/content/book-states-2012-chapter-1-state-constitutions.

MAP 3-4

Vote Required for Ratification

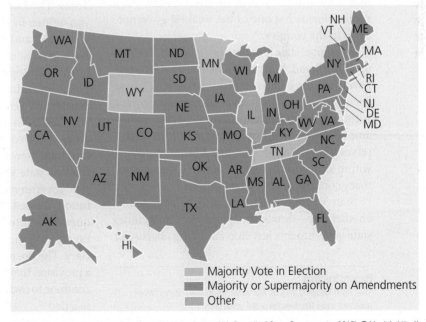

Majority Vote in Election
Majority or Supermajority on Amendments
Other

Source: Data from *The Book of the States 2012* (Lexington, KY: Council of State Governments, 2012), Table 1.1, http://knowledgecenter.csg.org/drupal/content/book-states-2012-chapter-1-state-constitutions.

In short, Rhode Island has just the type of government that John Adams feared.

Southern states such as Florida, Mississippi, and Texas also tend to have constitutions that provide for weak governors. In these cases, this arrangement is a legacy of the post–Civil War **Reconstruction** period. During Reconstruction, the victorious Union Army forced most of the former Confederate states to replace their constitutions. Reconstruction ended in 1876, and the Union troops withdrew. With the exception of Arkansas, North Carolina, and Tennessee, the southern states soon abandoned their revised constitutions in favor of new ones that greatly weakened gubernatorial powers.[24] Part of the reasoning for this was that weak governors could be kept from enacting policies that the federal government encouraged but that were contrary to the norms of these traditionalistic states. This had happened during Reconstruction, when the governors of the states that had seceded from the Union were replaced by individuals sympathetic to the federal government in Washington or were forced to cooperate with federal policy in regard to such issues as African American rights. For example, in 1885 Florida passed a constitution that took away the governor's right to appoint his own cabinet; members were elected instead. Although it has been amended many times since, that constitution is still in effect today. As a result, Florida has one of the weakest governorships in the country.[25]

Of course, state legislatures do not always gain the upper hand. In states whose constitutions give governors the edge, some chief executives have been very aggressive in expanding their powers. Although their techniques do not involve written amendments to the state constitutions themselves, they do affect the distribution of powers within state government—a function that is a primary concern of state constitutions.

State constitutions may also be changed in another way—through simple neglect. Sometimes state governments just stop enforcing obscure or repugnant sections of their state constitutions, effectively changing the constitutions in the process. No politician today would dare to argue for denying the vote to individuals simply because they are poor or do not own land or belong to a minority group, yet until 1999 Texas's constitution contained a provision that limited the right to vote to citizens who owned land and paid a poll tax. The state government had stopped enforcing these objectionable requirements long before but had neglected to actually repeal them. Likewise, Alabama's constitution outlawed interracial marriages until an amendment overturned the ban in 2000; the state had informally dropped enforcement of the provision years earlier.

Why State Constitutions Vary

Without a doubt, state constitutions vary widely from state to state. What explains these differences? Four factors seem particularly important: historical circumstances, political culture, geography, and changing notions of good government.

To understand how historical circumstances and culture can create a constitution—and then be shaped by that constitution—consider the case of Texas. The Lone Star State's current constitution was written in 1876, soon after federal troops had withdrawn and Reconstruction had ended. During Reconstruction, a strong Unionist governor backed by federal troops had governed the state, centralized police and education functions in state hands in Austin, and generally defied the white Democrats who had been in power before the Civil War. So Texas followed in the footsteps of other southern states and drew up a constitution designed to ensure that the state would never again have an activist state government. Toward that end, the new constitution allowed the legislature to meet only infrequently, limited the governor's power over the executive branch, and provided for an elected judiciary. The document's sole progressive feature was a provision that for the first time allowed women to continue to own their own property after they were married.[26]

Reconstruction
The period following the Civil War when the southern states were governed under the direction of the Union army.

A Difference That Makes A Difference

State Constitutions and the Right to Marry

"By the power vested in me, by the state of . . ." These words are repeated by wedding officials every day, in every state. States control who can marry and when. In Nebraska, teens younger than nineteen need their parents' permission to marry, while over the state line in Kansas, people can walk down the aisle at eighteen. A number of states prohibited interracial couples from marrying until 1967, when the U.S. Supreme Court declared Virginia's law unconstitutional in *Loving v. Virginia.* Today, debate rages around gay marriage. Just six states—Connecticut, Iowa, Massachusetts, New Hampshire, New York, and Vermont—have legalized the unions, while thirty states have amended their constitutions to prohibit them. Several additional states recognize domestic partnerships or civil unions, which grant couples some of the same state-level benefits of marriage. Washington, D.C., which is technically a federal city, not a state, allows gay marriage.

Legalization of gay marriage has been achieved through judicial review (in Connecticut, Iowa, and Massachusetts) and through legislation (New Hampshire, New York, and Vermont). Gay marriage has had a less fortunate time at the polls, where voters have rejected it time and time again—most recently in North Carolina in 2012. The most high-profile fight so far was waged in California in 2008 over Proposition 8, a ballot measure that sought to amend the state's constitution to define marriage as a union between one man and one woman—and to put a stop to the same-sex marriages that had begun there in June 2008, after the state supreme court ruled that the state's ban was unconstitutional. After both sides spent more than $55 million on their campaigns, voters narrowly approved Prop. 8. Approval of new same-sex marriages was halted, but the state continues to consider the more than 18,000 couples who wed legally as married.

The victory of Proposition 8 prompted further debate among proponents of gay marriage, some of whom wonder whether, given their continued defeats at the polls, they should wait to wage new legalization campaigns across the states. But the fight over Prop. 8 isn't finished—and it's not even limited to within the state's borders anymore. In April 2009, Theodore Olson, the former U.S. solicitor general, filed a brief in federal court challenging the amendment. In 2010, a federal district court ruled that Proposition 8 unconstitutionally violated the due process and equal protection clauses of the Fourteenth Amendment, a decision that was upheld in 2012 by a federal appeals court. As of this writing, the case has been appealed to the U.S. Supreme Court. If the Court accepts the case, the justices could make a ruling that will clarify whether or not same-sex couples have the same right to marry as heterosexual couples.

Sources: Christine Vestal, "Gay Marriage Legal in Six States," Stateline, June 4, 2009, www.stateline.org/live/details/story?contentId=347390; Ballotwatch, Initiative and Referendum Institute, "Same-Sex Marriage: Breaking the Firewall in California?," October 2008; Jo Becker, "A Conservative's Road to Same-Sex Marriage Advocacy," *New York Times,* August 18, 2009, www.nytimes.com/2009/08/19/us/19olson.html.

White Democrats' antipathy toward Reconstruction explains much of the content of Texas's 1876 constitution. The state's political culture explains why its constitution has endured to the present. Political scientist Daniel Elazar classifies Texas as a traditionalistic/individualistic state that, in his words, "places a premium on limiting community intervention" and "accepts a natural hierarchical society as part of the ordered nature of things."[27] Although Elazar's categories have blurred in recent years, state constitutions continue to bear them out. In short, Texas's constitution is well suited to the state's political culture—a culture that views strong activist government with suspicion.

In contrast, a constitution that allowed the legislature to meet only every other year would suit a moralistic state poorly. Not surprisingly, moralistic states such as Michigan, Minnesota, and Wisconsin allow their legislatures to meet far more frequently than does Texas. Because they envision fairly robust styles of governance, the constitutions in these states allow the legislatures to meet throughout the year, creating what are, for all intents and purposes, full-time professional legislatures.

New England's propensity for short, framework-oriented constitutions is a variation based noticeably on geography. One political scientist has hypothesized that such a variation may reflect the fact that New England states are small and relatively homogeneous and their citizens are thus less inclined to fight to include policies they support in their states' constitutions.[28]

Of course, history, political culture, and geography aren't the only factors that determine the kind of constitution a state will have. Another important factor is the changing sense of what works best. In the early nineteenth century, many states concluded that a system in which the legislature operates with unbridled power simply did not work well, so they changed their constitutions in ways that strengthened the chief executive. Eighty years ago, groups such as the National Municipal League argued that state constitutions should be more like the federal constitution; that is, they should be much shorter documents that provide a framework for governance rather than long documents that get into the details of policies. That argument gave rise to the **model constitution**, a kind of ideal that states interested in "improving" could adopt. During the 1960s and 1970s, many states did revise their constitutions in ways designed to make their governments more effective, although the last edition of the model constitution was written in 1968.

Model Constitution
An expert-approved generic or "ideal" constitution that states sometimes use as a yardstick against which they can measure their existing constitutions.

> Of course, history, political culture, and geography aren't the only factors that determine the kind of constitution a state will have. Another important factor is the changing sense of what works best.

Since the mid-twentieth century, however, some political scientists have questioned the assumptions behind the model constitution movement. To these revisionists, the fact that most state constitutions outside New England are long and policy rich is actually a good thing—a healthy sign of an engaged electorate. Revisionists argue that, although Americans have essentially left it to the U.S. Supreme Court to interpret and on occasion to change the federal constitution, citizens have defended their right to participate by shaping their state constitutions.[29]

How State Constitutions Differ

The most obvious ways in which state constitutions differ involve their length and ease of amendment. These differences are not simply cosmetic; they almost always reflect the different functions that state constitutions serve. Vermont has the shortest state constitution. Like the U.S. Constitution, its goal is primarily to establish a framework for effective government, not to regulate the details of specific policy matters. This is true to a lesser extent of other states in New England as well.

In contrast, constitutions in other regions of the country tend to be longer and more specific in their policy prescriptions. In most states, voters and interest groups that want to accomplish such goals as increased state spending on education will lobby the governor or the legislature. In California, a state with a long, policy-specific constitution that provides for a high degree of direct democracy, people often attempt to amend the constitution instead. Although the majority of political scientists wring their hands about this tendency, it is undeniable that Californians play a role in shaping their constitution that voters in New England cannot. Also note that these two differences—length and ease of amendment—not only reflect differences in goals and purposes but also directly influence each other. If a constitution is easier to amend, it makes sense that it is more likely to get amended—and that usually means it gets longer. Again, a difference makes a difference.

Operating Rules and Selection for Office

State constitutions create varying organizational structures and operating rules for the constituent elements of state government. They establish different methods and requirements for serving in state politics. Some of these differences reflect the historical differences among states as well as variations in political culture and geography. Other differences reflect differing notions of what makes good government. Sometimes these notions can be quite quirky. Consider the following, for example. To serve as the governor of Oklahoma, a state of 3.7 million people, you must be at least thirty-one years old. In contrast, to be the chief executive of California's population of 37 million, you need only be eighteen. You might be eligible to lead one of the nation's largest states, but don't plan on buying beer or wine, even at your own fund-raisers!

In addition, state constitutions differ widely in how many statewide elected positions they create and how those positions are filled. One of the most important of these differences has to do with the judiciary. At the federal level, judges are selected by the president and approved by the U.S. Senate. Things work very differently in the states. Some states elect their judges, some states appoint their judges, many states use a combination of appointment and election, and some states use different selection methods for different types of courts. The details of these various systems and their particular pros and cons are discussed in depth in chapter 9. What's important for our purposes here is that there are big differences from state to state in how judges end up on the bench,

and those differences are products of different constitutional approaches to structuring and staffing the judicial branch of government.

Even seemingly small institutional differences created by different constitutional approaches can have big impacts on how state governments work. For example, if a state's constitution gives the executive strong veto powers, the governor may have an easier time getting a recalcitrant legislature to consider his or her point of view on a particular piece of legislation than would a governor with weak veto powers. Similarly, some studies have shown that elected judges are more likely than those more insulated from the ballot box to uphold the death penalty in cases involving capital crimes.[30] In short, the different operating rules embedded in state constitutions lead to very different types of governance.

Virginia's executive mansion is the oldest continuously occupied governor's residence in the United States. It has been the home of Virginia's governors since 1813.

Distribution of Power

State constitutions make widely differing decisions about where power should reside. Although all state constitutions make at least a bow toward the principle of the separation of powers, in actuality many give one branch of government a preponderance of power. Under some state constitutions, the reins of government are clearly in the hands of the legislature or general assembly. Other states have amended their constitutions to give executives the upper hand.

Traditionally, state constitutions tended to create stronger legislatures and weaker executives. In recent decades, however, even though strong state legislatures are still the norm, constitutional changes in many states have bolstered governors' powers. More than forty state constitutions now give governors the important power of the **line-item veto**, the ability to veto certain portions of

---

Line-Item Veto
The power to reject a portion of a bill while leaving the rest intact.

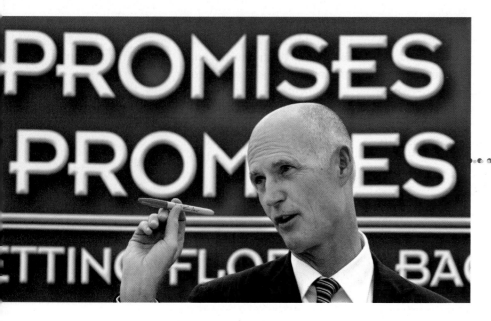

Rather than raise taxes to cover budget shortfalls, state policymakers have frequently turned to spending cuts. This was certainly the case for Florida governor Rick Scott, who promised to reduce spending and followed through by line-item vetoing more than $100 million out of the state's 2012–2013 budget.

appropriations bills while approving the rest. Exactly what counts as an item, and thus what is fair game for a governor's veto pen, is often unclear. As a result, line-item veto court cases have become a common part of the legal landscape.

Some states go even further. In Wisconsin, for example, the state constitution allows the governor the power to strike out an appropriation entirely and write in a lower figure.[31] During his term in office, Wisconsin governor Tommy Thompson pushed the power of the partial veto to strike passages and even individual words from bills that came to his desk. In some cases, Thompson would strike individual letters from bills to create entirely new words, changing the entire meaning of the legislation. Critics came to call Thompson's creative writing "the Vanna White veto." In one case, Thompson used the Vanna White veto and his Scrabble skills to transform a piece of legislation from a bill that set the maximum detention period for juvenile offenders at forty-eight hours into one that allowed for a ten-day detention period, a move that enraged the Democratic legislature.[32] Voters later amended the constitution to prohibit that particular veto maneuver. Yet, despite the controversies that surrounded such actions, during his record fourteen-year reign, none of Thompson's more than 1,900 budget vetoes was ever overturned by the legislature.[33]

The power structures set up by the constitutional systems of some states resist easy classification. Take Texas, for example. The fact that the legislature meets for only five or six months every other year might lead you to think that power in Texas resides primarily with the governor. Not so. In fact, the Texas constitution arguably makes the office of lieutenant governor the most powerful in the state. In Texas, the lieutenant governor presides over the Senate, appoints Senate committees and assigns bills, and chairs the powerful Texas Legislative Council, which is responsible for researching and drafting bills. Indeed, many observers attribute George W. Bush's two successful terms as governor to his close relationship with his lieutenant governor, Bob Bullock, a Democrat.

Rights Granted

State constitutions differ not only in the mechanisms of governance they create and the sets of constraints and powers they give to government but also in the rights they confer on citizens. For example, the U.S. Constitution does not explicitly mention a right to privacy, although the U.S. Supreme Court did define a limited right to privacy in *Griswold v. Connecticut* (1965). In contrast, Montana's constitution states that "the right to individual privacy is essential to the well-being of a free society and shall not be infringed without the showing of a compelling state interest."[34] As a result, courts in Montana—and in Kentucky and Tennessee—have interpreted the state constitution to protect adults' freedom to engage in consensual oral or anal sex, which until quite recently was illegal in many other states.[35]

Even rights that are directly addressed by the U.S. Constitution are often expanded, clarified, or given more specifics in state constitutions. For example, the Second Amendment says, "A well regulated Militia, being necessary to the security of a free State, the right of the people to keep and bear Arms, shall not be infringed." Legal scholars have been arguing over the meaning of this vaguely worded amendment for a long time—is the right purely an individual right? If so, the government has a narrow basis for regulating private ownership of firearms. Or is the right attached to the necessity of a "well regulated Militia"? If that's the case, it suggests a more expansive basis for government regulation of firearms. No such confusion is raised by Nebraska's state constitution, which says that "the right to keep and bear arms for security or defense of self, family, home, and others, and for lawful common defense, hunting, recreational use, and all other lawful purposes, and such rights shall not be denied or infringed."

Representative Government versus Direct Democracy

One of the most striking differences among state constitutions is the degree to which they have (or have not) embraced direct democracy. Most Americans celebrate the United States as a democracy, but the founders believed that they were establishing something somewhat different— a representative democracy. This is a form of government in which qualified representatives of the public make the decisions. Most of the founders viewed direct, or pure, democracy with suspicion. A "pure democracy, by which I mean a society consisting of a small number of citizens, who assemble and administer the government in person, can admit of no cure for the mischiefs of faction," warned James Madison, one of the primary authors of the U.S. Constitution, in his famous argument for the document in *Federalist* No. 10:

> A common passion or interest will, in almost every case, be felt by a majority of the whole . . . and there is nothing to check the inducements to sacrifice the weaker party or an obnoxious individual. Hence it is that such democracies have ever been spectacles of turbulence and contention; have ever been found incompatible with personal security or the rights of property; and have

in general been as short in their lives as they have been violent in their deaths.[36]

In other words, Madison believed that entrusting a simple majority with the power to carry out its will would lead to fickle and tyrannical behavior and to a government that would teeter between anarchy and autocracy.

The U.S. Constitution's solution to the problem of pure democracy was to create a representative government, or, as Madison saw it, government by a small group of elected officials "whose wisdom may best discern the true interest of their country."[37] In accordance with this belief, the U.S. Constitution created an upper chamber—the Senate—whose members would be selected by state legislatures from among their eminent men. The document also created an electoral college to elect the president. Both of these decisions were made to insulate the federal government from the whims of the majority. The Constitution makes no provision for direct democratic processes. There is not a single federal officeholder *directly* elected by the entire nation. Indeed, as we saw in 2000 with the election of George W. Bush, the electoral college system can result in a candidate's winning the presidency after losing the popular vote.

Whereas the creators of the federal government took great care to ensure it was insulated from direct democratic processes, many states decided to do just the opposite during the Progressive Era. By giving their citizens the chance to make laws and change their constitutions directly, the Progressives sought to circumvent legislatures and executives they viewed as being beholden to wealthy special interests. As Robert M. La Follette, a leader of the Progressive Party in Wisconsin and later a governor and senator from the state, put it:

> The forces of the special privileges are deeply entrenched. Their resources are inexhaustible. Their efforts are never lax. Their political methods are insidious. It is impossible for the people to maintain perfect organization in mass. They are often taken unaware and are liable to lose at one stroke the achievements of years of effort. In such a crisis, nothing but the united power of the people expressed directly through the ballot can overthrow the enemy.[38]

For politicians like La Follette, direct democratic mechanisms, such as the ballot initiative and the referendum, represented the general populace's best hope for breaking the power of political bosses and moneyed interests. From 1902 through 1918, direct democracy enjoyed a great vogue in the states. Sixteen states adopted the ballot initiative in that period. After World War I, ballot initiatives lost some of their luster as popular enthusiasm for Progressive ideas waned. Only five states—Alaska (1959), Florida (1968), Wyoming (1968), Illinois (1970), and Mississippi (1992)—have amended their constitutions to allow for ballot initiatives since the end of the Progressive Era.[39] What's more, note where these states are located. The majority of the states that allow direct democracy lie west of the Mississippi River, where the practice fits with much of the West's populist history.[40]

For much of their existence, initiatives and referendums were used sparingly. Then came Proposition 13 in California. In the 1970s, taxpayer activist Howard Jarvis and retired real estate salesman Paul Gann launched what at first seemed a foolishly impractical campaign to roll back California property taxes and cap the rate at which they could grow. Their campaign struck a chord with many Californians. The state's booming economy had sent property values skyrocketing. Higher property assessments led to higher real estate taxes, which created a huge revenue boom for the state and local governments. Indeed, at the time the state government had a $5 billion annual surplus. Yet despite the public outcry for relief from rising property costs, Governor Jerry Brown and the rest of the politicians in Sacramento could not agree on a tax reduction plan.

In 1978, California voters passed Proposition 13 and took the decision out of their hands. It directed the state to roll back real estate taxes to 1975 levels and decreed that property assessments could not increase by more than 2 percent a year, regardless of inflation. Most localities previously had reassessed real estate taxes every two years. Proposition 13 decreed that property could be reassessed only when it was sold. The legislation also cut property tax receipts in half and marked the beginning of a nationwide "taxpayer revolt." The revolt culminated in the election of former California governor Ronald Reagan to the presidency two years later.

California's political establishment viewed the passage of Proposition 13 with great trepidation. Politicians worried that it would cripple their ability to pay for the schools and infrastructure that had contributed so much to California's post–World War II successes. These fears proved well-founded. In the wake of Proposition 13, California went from having one of the nation's best-funded public school systems (in the top third in terms of per-pupil spending) to having one of the worst (in the bottom third). The proposition put such draconian limits on the ability of local governments to raise revenues that municipalities and counties became increasingly dependent on the state for their funding—so much so that ten years later, in 1988, California teachers' unions pushed through Proposition 98, which mandated that upward of 40 percent of California's general revenue go to education.[41]

In addition to complicating government finances and drastically reducing the flexibility of lawmakers in California, the success of Proposition 13 revived interest in ballot initiatives in the twenty-four other states in which they were permitted. In the three decades from 1940 through 1970, an average of nineteen initiatives appeared on ballots per two-year election cycle in the United States. In the 1980s, that number shot up to fifty initiatives in the average election cycle. In the 1990s, it hit seventy-six per election cycle.[42] Many of these initiatives were proposed constitutional amendments. Their sheer numbers indicate that states allowing ballot initiatives are now engaged in an almost continuous cycle of changing their constitutions. These changes are increasingly less about broad questions of good governance and more about pushing narrow agendas.

In the past two decades, the initiative process has been used to push through legislation on some of the most controversial political issues in the

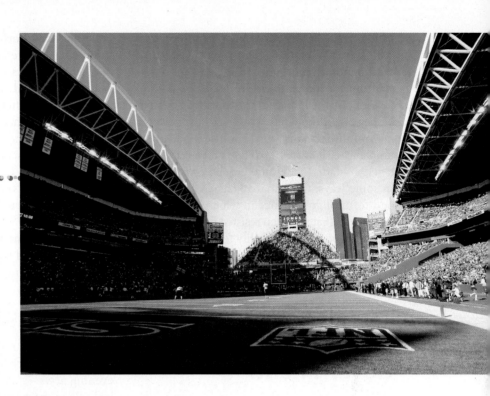

Qwest Field, home of the Seattle Seahawks, was made possible by a ballot initiative that provided $300 million in public financing for construction of the stadium. The team's owner, billionaire and Microsoft cofounder Paul Allen, financed the successful ballot initiative.

entire country. Oregon voters used a ballot initiative to narrowly (51–49 percent) approve physician-assisted suicide in 1994. In California, voters have used initiatives to impose some of the nation's strictest term limits on elected officials (Proposition 140), to end affirmative action (Propositions 209 and 96), to deny education and health benefits to families of illegal immigrants (Proposition 87), to spend $3 billion on stem-cell research (Proposition 71), and to recall a sitting governor and replace him with an action movie star.

The initiative process has become big business. In 2004, more than $200 million was spent in the battles waged over California's ballot measures alone.[43] Several companies are devoted to gathering the signatures needed to get issues placed on ballots for anyone who can afford their services. Signature gathering can be a pretty lucrative business—in 2010 and 2012 it cost, on average, more than a million dollars to collect enough signatures to get a proposal certified and on a state ballot.[44] Those who have used them successfully see ballot initiatives as tools for circumventing hostile legislatures and acting on the will of the majority. But most political scientists and close observers of state politics have a different viewpoint. They argue that the results of the use of ballot initiatives only reinforce the wisdom of the founders in their decision to keep direct democratic processes out of the U.S. Constitution. A number of those who have examined initiatives have concluded that the process has been hijacked by those with deep pockets and by individuals who use initiatives to further their own self-interests.

Veteran *Washington Post* political reporter David Broder describes ballot initiatives in scathing terms:

At the start of a new century—and millennium—a new form of government is spreading in the United States. It is alien to the spirit of the Constitution and its careful system of checks and balances. Though derived from a reform favored by Populists and Progressives as a cure for special-interest influence, this method of lawmaking has become the favored tool of millionaires and interest groups that use their wealth to achieve their own policy goals—a lucrative business for a new set of political entrepreneurs.[45]

Exploiting the public's disdain for politics and distrust of politicians, interest groups with deep pockets now have a mechanism through which they can literally rewrite state constitutions to advance their own agendas. For example, in 1997 Microsoft cofounder and Seattle Seahawks owner Paul Allen made an end run around a balky state legislature and spent $6 million on a ballot initiative that required the state of Washington to foot much of the cost for a new stadium for his team. It proved to be a good investment; the initiative passed with 51 percent of the vote. Although this was welcome news for many football fans, most political scientists probably see it as an illustration of the very problem that Madison identified in *Federalist* No. 10. In some ways, the initiative has created a very odd form of governance in which citizens live under laws that are often resisted by their elected governments. With its ability to make sweeping changes in state constitutions, the initiative process could radically change the American system of government in the next few decades.

Constitutions for Local Government?

For the most part, substate governments, such as school districts, counties, and many municipalities, are considered subordinate arms of the state. They may seem like autonomous political units, but they in fact operate under state constitutions and at the discretion of state governments. The courts generally have viewed only the federal government and the states as sovereign entities with the right to determine how their authority should be exercised. The authority and power of local governments is largely confined, if not outright dictated, by the states (these issues are discussed in more depth in chapter 11).

There are some exceptions to this rule. The **municipal charter** is a key example. In a rough sense, municipal charters are similar to the charters that served as the governing documents for the original colonies. Legally, most municipalities are corporations, and their charters describe the purposes of the municipalities and the processes for achieving these objectives. A charter is not a constitution; rather, it is a grant of authority derived from a constitution or from state law. Some states have **home rule**, which allows municipalities the right to draft and amend their own charters and to regulate local matters within their jurisdictions without interference from the state. Some states have municipal home rule provisions in their constitutions; others grant home rule to municipalities through legislation. Municipal home rule means that some local governments are operated by charters that "can take on many characteristics of a constitution."[46] Even in the most liberal home rule states, however, state constitutions and state law generally take precedence over municipal charters.

Conclusion

Even though you rarely read about them in the newspaper—much less hear about them on the evening news—state constitutions play *the* critical role in defining the possibilities of politics in most states. All state constitutions set the basic structure of government, apportion power and responsibilities to particular institutions and political actors, and determine the rights and privileges of citizenship. State constitutions reflect states' distinctive political cultures and, over time, reinforce or alter those traditions.

Beyond this common core of shared functions, however, state constitutions vary greatly. Some protect and extend the rights of the individual beyond the guarantees of the U.S. Constitution; others do not. Perhaps the single biggest difference among state constitutions is the degree to which they serve as a venue for policymaking. In western states, whose constitutions provide for a high degree of direct democracy, advocates and interest groups often attempt to enshrine their policy positions in the state constitutions. As a result, these states have long, detailed constitutions. In contrast, the constitutions of the eastern states, particularly in New England, more closely resemble the U.S. Constitution.

Municipal Charter
A document that establishes operating procedures for a local government.

Home Rule
A form of self-governance granted to towns and cities by the state.

State constitutions tend to have a bad reputation with political scientists, for understandable reasons. Although many function well, in more than a few instances they play an outright disruptive role. In states such as Alabama and Texas, antiquated state constitutions have made it difficult for state governments to promote economic development—a function that most people believe the state government should serve. In California and other states, interest groups have used state constitutions to ensure that the states' general revenues flow toward the programs they support. In the process, they have reduced—in some areas drastically— the flexibility of legislatures to make independent decisions, a set of constraints that amounts to putting limits on representative democracy.

But, as political scientist Christopher Hammonds has argued from another perspective, the fact that constitutions continue to be a contentious venue for politics in many states is not necessarily all bad. Although it is still theoretically possible to change the U.S. Constitution, for all practical purposes we as a society have given that right over to the U.S. Supreme Court. It takes an extraordinarily contentious issue, such as reproductive rights, to provoke talk about changing the federal constitution. In contrast, citizens continue to exercise their right to tamper with and tweak their state constitutions. Is that all bad?

The Latest Research

State constitutions are one of the most important and understudied aspects of subnational government. While it is not hard to find constitutional scholars in political science, the vast majority of these study the U.S. Constitution, not its state counterparts. There is more attention paid to state constitutions in the field of law, but even here scholars focusing on state constitutions regularly lament the relative lack of research available on these centrally important legal documents.

This lack of attention is surprising because, as the studies listed below amply demonstrate, state constitutions are important—not just as the bases for much of the criminal and civil law in the United States but also as documents that reflect deeper philosophical notions of what a government is, what it should do, and what rights citizens should or should not have. These are not just abstract theoretical arguments; your marriage rights, to take one prominent example, are almost wholly determined by the constitution and the laws it authorizes in the state in which you reside.

Below we summarize some of the more recent and prominent research on state constitutions. All of these studies reflect a constant theme: not just the central importance of state constitutions to the American political system but also how those constitutions are constantly changing and creating differences in state-level legal structure that have big, real-world impacts on the lives of state residents.

• •

- **Williams, Robert F.** 2009. *The Law of American State Constitutions*. New York: Oxford University Press.

Robert Williams is a one of the most widely recognized scholars of state constitutional law, and this book is one the most comprehensive and up-to-date scholarly analyses available of the nature and purpose of state constitutions. This work is notable not just for its overview of the historical development of state constitutions, their structure, and their legal implications, but for staking out a strong "positivist" position on these documents. Essentially, Williams argues that state constitutions should not be viewed as mini-versions of the U.S.

(Continued)

(Continued)

Constitution. Instead, each should be viewed as a unique text and interpreted—by scholars and judges—within that framework. This argument amounts to a strong rejection of the so-called common principles approach, which views and interprets state constitutions basically as a branch of common law—that is, a set of cases or precedents.

- **Dinan, John J.** 2006. *The American State Constitutional Tradition.* Lawrence: University Press of Kansas.

Many scholars have studied the U.S. Constitutional Convention of 1787 and debated the debates and negotiations among the delegates on the purposes of government, its appropriate structure and process, its proper limitations, and the rights it should or should not grant to citizens. Much less attention has been paid to the debates of state constitutional conventions, perhaps because there have been so many of them (more than one hundred, and for many of them we have much more detailed records than we have for the federal Constitutional Convention). Dinan sets out to rectify this, providing a sweeping study of the development of state constitutions. He finds that the delegates to state constitutional conventions have often very deliberately taken paths that differ from those taken by their federal counterparts. For example, whereas federal delegates rejected a direct role for citizens in government, state constitutional delegates have been much more willing to consider such a role. Federal constitutional delegates mostly had a negative concept of individual liberty; they worried about protecting citizens from the intrusions of government. State constitutional delegates have been much more willing to adopt a positive concept of liberty, seeing the government as a tool to enforce and maintain individual rights. These differences make a big difference to the substance and structure of state constitutions compared to the federal constitution.

- **Krislov, Marvin, and Daniel Katz.** 2008. "Taking State Constitutions Seriously." *Cornell Journal of Law and Public Policy* 71: 295–342.

This is a study of how state constitutions change. In comparison with the federal constitution, state constitutions generally have much less restrictive amendment processes, and even within individual states there may be multiple avenues to constitutional change. While noting the huge variation across states in these amendment processes, Krislov and Katz pay particular attention to direct democratic processes. Their analysis shows that such processes, in particular constitutional initiatives, have become a primary method of amending state constitutions. Yet even among states that allow ballot initiatives there is substantial variation in the rules and procedures for passage of a constitutional initiative. This study suggests that those differences create different sets of incentives for groups to pursue constitutional change and that the rapid shifts in state constitutional content create particular challenges for the process of state-level judicial review.

- **Lupia, Arthur, Yanna Krupnikov, Adam Seth Levine, Spencer Piston, Alexander Von Hagen-Jamar.** 2010. "Why State Constitutions Differ in Their Treatment of Same-Sex Marriage." *Journal of Politics* 72: 1222–1235.

This is an interesting companion study to the Krislov and Katz article. This team of researchers examines state-level variation in attitudes toward same-sex marriage and constitutional outcomes. One of the surprising findings of their study is that attitudes correlate fairly poorly with constitutional amendments on same-sex marriage. Public opinion regarding same-sex marriage does not differ greatly between states with constitutional amendments banning the practice and those without such amendments. The authors find that the differences that do exist are explained, at least in part, by the relative complexity of the rules and regulations associated with constitutional amendment. The fact that U.S. state constitutions differ in the legal status of same-sex marriage has less to do with attitudes on that topic in the states and much more to do with the institutional arrangements established by those constitutions to translate the will of the people into state law.

3

college.cqpress.com/
sites/govstateandlocal

Chapter Review

Key Concepts

- appropriations bills (p. 64)
- ballot initiative (p. 69)
- bicameral legislature (p. 66)
- colonial charters (p. 65)
- constitutional amendments (p. 62)
- constitutional convention (p. 68)
- constitutional revision commission (p. 71)
- direct democracy (p. 59)
- dual constitutionalism (p. 62)
- electorate (p. 60)
- franchise (p. 66)
- home rule (p. 82)
- Jim Crow laws (p. 67)
- judicial federalism (p. 60)
- judicial review (p. 72)
- line-item veto (p. 77)
- model constitution (p. 76)
- municipal charter (p. 82)
- natural law, or higher law (p. 62)
- plenary power (p. 62)
- ratification (p. 68)
- Reconstruction (p. 74)
- referendum (p. 69)
- separation of powers (p. 65)
- unicameral legislature (p. 65)

Suggested Web Sites

- **http://camlaw.rutgers.edu/statecon/statecon_1.html.** Web site for Rutgers University's Center for State Constitutional Studies.
- **www.iandrinstitute.org.** Web site for the Initiative and Referendum Institute at the University of Southern California, a clearinghouse for information about the initiative and referendum processes of the states.

STATE STATS

State Stats on Constitutions

Explore and compare data on the states! Go to college.cqpress.com/sites/ govstateandlocal to do these exercises.

1. Some scholars say that unicameral government works best when its citizens are a relatively small, homogenous group. Explore the demographic information about Nebraska. What about Nebraska's population makes it suited for unicameral government? Are there any states that are more homogenous than Nebraska? Why don't they have unicameral governments?

2. Vermont is the only state that does not have a balanced budget requirement. How does its outstanding government debt load compare to its neighboring states' debt load? Is this surprising? Why or why not?

3. Recall this chapter's example of a Colorado ballot initiative that is written at the post-graduate reading level. What is the percentage of the population in Colorado who are college graduates? Why might the ballot initiative, as written, be a problem for voters? Are there any states with lower college graduation rates? What are the implications of these numbers?

4. What percentage of the population in California is foreign-born? What about Montana? How might differences in the make-up of the electorate in these states impact their laws?

5. What was the percent change in Nevada's population of eighteen to twenty-four year olds from 1990 to 2000? How might this type of change influence (or not) the kind of policies that the citizens want? What does this kind of change generally do to voter turnout? Did this happen in Nevada?

State governments aren't the only ones that have had to deal with lingering revenue shortfalls as a result of recession. In the past few years, some local governments have been so financially stressed they've been forced into bankruptcy. In 2012, Stockton, California, became the largest municipality ever to go bust.

Finance

FILLING THE TILL AND PAYING THE BILLS

- What are the differences between progressive and regressive tax systems?
- Why are property taxes so important to communities?
- How does the federal government support state and local budgets?
- Are states' revenue and spending programs sustainable?

A combination of a poor economic conditions and bad fiscal decisions had been pushing Stockton, California, toward a financial cliff for years. On June 28, 2012, the city fell off the edge—right into the arms of Chapter 9 bankruptcy and the record books. It now has the dubious honor of being the largest city in U.S. history to go bust.

Stockton is far from being the only local government in the United States to find itself in financial straits in the past few years. The economy might have stabilized since the Great Recession, but it certainly has not fully recovered, and the coffers of some governments have simply not been able to support the wait for better economic times. Harrisburg, the capital of Pennsylvania, went into receivership in 2011. Montgomery County, the largest county in Alabama, filed for bankruptcy the same year. Central Falls, Rhode Island, became insolvent in 2010, and Detroit, Michigan, spent much of 2011 and 2012 barely one step ahead of its creditors.

Step up a level of government and the picture is just a little less alarming. No state has declared bankruptcy—at least not yet—and the budget situation in many states is actually improving compared to a few years ago. No one is popping champagne corks, though, because finances at the state level have only managed to advance from the catastrophic to the merely very bad. For fiscal year 2013 states faced a combined shortfall of $55 billion.[1] That's a whopping combined budgetary shortfall, but it is still a big improvement over a few years ago when a single state—California—was struggling to close a $50 billion hole in its budget. In other words, states are a long way from the let-the-good-times-roll numbers that policymakers would prefer to see in their balance sheets. Revenues still struggle to keep pace with obligations, and many states still face uncomfortable choices between cutting spending and raising taxes—or doing both.

Deficits are a bigger problem for state and local governments than for their national counterpart. For the federal government, a budget shortfall is an embarrassment, not a crisis. Virtually all the states (Vermont is the only exception) are required by law to balance their operating budgets every year, and most local governments are in the same boat. When the bills add up to more than what's coming in at the federal level, Congress is free to borrow to cover the gap. In other words, the federal government can run budget deficits as much as it likes. Not so for state and local governments. They can delay the inevitable by jiggering the books with some fancy accounting tricks and hoping for the best, but the sharpest of bean counters cannot shield them from the hard fact that the law requires their ledgers to be balanced. When income minus expenditure results in a negative number they cannot just borrow or print money and hope the future will somehow provide an easy way out; they have to figure out how to get more revenue and/or cut spending.

The Great Recession of 2008–2009 pushed many states toward a financial implosion because they simply could not manage that balancing act. The revenues that keep states functioning—especially income, sales, and property taxes—dropped precipitously,

and unemployment rates rose above 10 percent. In a single year's span, between June 2008 and June 2009, state income tax receipts plunged by more than a quarter.[2] At the same time consumer demand dried up, taking with it state sales tax revenues, and the housing crisis sent property values—and their resulting taxes—tumbling. That all happened just as demand for state services jumped; the demand for Medicaid, unemployment insurance, public colleges, and even libraries increases during a downturn.

States were rescued from this crisis by the American Recovery and Reinvestment Act (ARRA), a $787 billion package passed by Congress that was designed to stimulate the economy with targeted tax cuts, job creation, and government investments. Almost $300 billion of the stimulus was earmarked to help prop up state and local government programs, including $87 billion for state Medicaid programs and a $53.6 billion state fiscal stabilization fund, which most states used in 2009 and 2010 to stave off deep cuts to education and emergency services.[3] This massive financial injection made the federal government the single largest source of revenue for state and local governments for a year or two, but by 2012 the federal government was turning off the tap. This kept states and localities in a tough financial bind; their income sources were slowly starting to rise, but they were still struggling to approach prerecession levels, and the federal government was no longing shoveling cash their way. So state and local governments went right on looking for new revenue sources and spending cuts and resigned themselves to being less hopeful of finding a billion or two of extra federal aid between the couch cushions. The upshot is that these days there is less danger of a massive, widespread fiscal tsunami swamping all states and localities than there is of the odd government being unable to keep treading financial water and slipping under a sea of red ink.

Budget Deficit, or Shortfall
Cash shortage that results when the amount of money coming into the government falls below the the amount being spent.

Revenues
The money governments bring in, mainly from taxes.

American Recovery and Reinvestment Act (ARRA)
A $787 billion federal government package intended to stimulate economic growth during the recession of 2008–2009.

In 2009, residents of the United States paid approximately $4,160 in state and local taxes per person.[4] Along with **user fees**, those collections raised about $2.2 trillion.[5] State and local governments use these funds along with federal grant dollars to do everything from financing local schools and state universities to providing health insurance for low-income families and people with disabilities to building highways. The money also helps maintain correctional facilities that house more than 2 million people per year and provides police and fire protection to the remaining approximately 310 million of the population. In short, state and local taxes pay for the programs that Americans care most about and that most directly affect their daily lives.

There is a tendency to think of taxes and budgets as a bit of a yawn—isn't this topic dry, technical, and, boring? We'll be the first to admit that *The Fiscal Survey of States* is not exactly most people's idea of a rollicking good read, but this topic is actually among the most important and consequential in this book. Budgets are the subject of some of the most intense political struggles in state and local politics, and not just because people care about money. Budgets are extremely important because they are fundamentally about policy. Indeed, in many ways they are *the* central policy documents of government. They determine and reflect the policy orientations of elected leaders. If you want to know what your state or local government's priorities are, its budget will tell you.

> Budgets are extremely important because they are fundamentally about policy. Indeed, in many ways they are *the* central policy documents of government. They determine and reflect the policy orientations of elected leaders. If you want to know what your state or local government's priorities are, its budget will tell you.

This chapter discusses how state and local governments raise money, how they decide to spend it via the budget process, and what they spend it on. It examines why state and local governments make such different taxing and spending choices, and it explores the consequences of these varying choices. The chapter concludes with a discussion of how budgetary constraints and challenges are forcing many state and local governments to rethink how they pay for public services.

Show Me the Money: Where State Revenues Come From

More than half of the revenues of state and local governments in 2008 (the latest year for which comprehensive figures were available as this is written), or about $1.9 trillion, came from six primary taxes.[6] These were sales taxes, including **excise taxes,** often referred to as **sin taxes**, on tobacco and alcohol; property taxes; income taxes; motor vehicle taxes; **estate taxes**, also called death taxes; and **gift taxes**. As states struggled to balance their budgets in the last years of the decade, they increasingly turned to all of these taxes for help; they raised almost $24 billion in tax and fee increases in their 2010 budgets alone.[7]

Sales Taxes

In 2009, state and local governments took in $421 billion from **sales taxes**—about 34 percent of total state and local government tax revenues. About 81 percent of the money raised by sales taxes goes to state governments. In addition, most states

---

User Fees
Charges levied by governments in exchange for services. Such fees constitute a type of hidden tax.

Excise, or Sin, Taxes
Taxes on alcohol, tobacco, and other similar products that are designed to raise revenues and reduce use.

Estate Taxes
Taxes levied on a person's estate or total holdings after that person's death.

Gift Taxes
Taxes imposed on money transfers made during an individual's lifetime.

Sales Taxes
Taxes levied by state and local governments on purchases.

allow at least some counties and cities to levy additional sales taxes. Currently, about 7,500 localities do. Some states, such as California, return a small percentage of sales taxes to the areas in which the purchases were made. Overall, sales tax revenues account for nearly 16 percent of local government tax revenues nationwide.[8]

State governments and, to a much lesser extent, local governments also take in significant sums from gasoline taxes and sin taxes on tobacco and alcohol. Different states interpret these types of taxes very differently. Other factors often influence what gets taxed and for how much. North Carolina has a large tobacco-growing industry and a tax of only $0.45 on each pack of cigarettes. New York has no large-scale tobacco industry and levies a tax of $4.35 per pack of cigarettes sold.[9]

Politicians like sales taxes because they tend to be less visible to their constituents than an income tax. As such, they are less likely to cause voters to retaliate against them at the polls. Economists like sales taxes because they are **focused consumption taxes** that do not distort consumer behavior. That is, sales taxes, even relatively high ones, often do not cause consumers to buy less.

This does not mean that sales taxes do not receive their share of criticism. Many liberals and advocates for low-income people complain that these are **regressive taxes**. If Bill Gates buys a grande latte he pays about $0.28 in sales tax; a freshman at the University of Washington pays exactly the same. The tax is the same, but the student is paying a much higher percentage of his or her income to the government than Mr. Gates is. Put another way, if Bill Gates's income were even a mere $5 million a year and a typical student's income is $2,500 a year, guess how much Mr. Gates would have to pay in sales tax on that latte to face the same **tax burden** as a typical student. Give up? His grande latte would have to cost him a whopping but tax-proportionate

Focused Consumption Taxes
Taxes that do not alter spending habits or behavior patterns and therefore do not distort the distribution of resources.

Regressive Taxes
Taxes levied on all taxpayers, regardless of income or ability to pay; they tend to place proportionately more of a burden on those with lower incomes.

Tax Burden
A measurement of taxes paid as a proportion of income.

$566.20. Of course, as already noted, it doesn't really work that way. If and when Bill Gates goes to a coffee shop, he pays the same price and the same sales tax as anyone else.

States often do attempt to make their sales taxes less of a burden on low-income residents by exempting necessities such as food, clothing, and electric and gas utilities from taxation. In general, however, states that rely heavily on sales taxes tend to have more regressive tax systems than do other states.

Take, for example, Tennessee, a state that relies heavily on sales taxes rather than assessing personal income taxes. Rich and poor alike paid a 7 percent sales tax at the cash register in 2012. However, Memphis residents earning $25,000 a year or less paid an average of 12 percent of their incomes in state and local taxes. That is about $2,993 for a family of three. In contrast, those residents earning $150,000 or more a year paid only 6.5 percent, or $9,718, of their incomes in taxes.[10] So, whereas it *looks* like the $150,000 wage earners paid more, the low-income residents paid a higher percentage of their incomes in taxes than they might have if they lived in a state that relies more on income taxes. That makes Tennessee's tax system highly regressive.

Sales taxes have another problem—they simply are not bringing in as much revenue as they used to. In the words of James Hine, a finance expert at Clemson University, relying on the sales tax "is like riding a horse that is rapidly dying." What that basically means is that the sales tax base is slowly eroding. Two factors seem to account for this. First, services have become a much more important part of the economy. In 1960, 41 percent of U.S. consumer dollars was spent on services. By 2000, that percentage had risen to 58 percent. Yet most sales taxes are still skewed toward the purchase of products rather than the purchase of services. Buy a robotic massage chair at the Mall of America in Bloomington, Minnesota, and you'll pay $58.20 in sales tax on that $800 item.[11] Hire an acupuncturist for an hour from a holistic medical center in Bloomington, and you'll pay no sales tax at all.

Hawaii, New Mexico, South Dakota, and Wyoming have changed their tax codes so that sales taxes now apply to most professional and personal services.[12] However, most other states have been reluctant to follow suit because taxing services could put them at a competitive disadvantage. For instance, if Illinois were to place a sales tax on accounting services, there would probably be a sudden boom in business for CPAs in nearby Indiana.[13]

The second factor behind faltering sales tax revenues is the rise of the Internet and online shopping. In 1992, the U.S. Supreme Court ruled that states could not force companies to collect sales taxes for them in places where the companies had no physical presence. As a result, most online purchases are tax-free. A study by William F. Fox and Donald Bruce of the University of Tennessee, Knoxville, found that the overall losses of sales tax revenue from Internet sales were $8.6 billion in 2010, and the researchers predicted losses as high as $11.4 billion per year by 2012.[14] For states such as Texas and Tennessee that don't have income taxes and that rely heavily on sales tax revenue, this trend is a big problem. To make up for the kind of revenue loss that Fox and Bruce have predicted, Texas would have to raise its current statewide sales tax rate from 6.25 percent to 7.86 percent.[15]

The U.S. Congress has rejected states' pleas to stop exempting online retailers from collecting sales taxes, citing the difficulty the companies would have complying with the wide variety of state sales tax codes. In 2007, Congress extended the moratorium on online taxation until 2014. Absent federal intervention, states have banded together to collect taxes on online sales. Dozens of states have joined the Streamlined Sales Tax Project, agreeing to simplify their tax codes in exchange for the chance to convince retailers to collect the taxes voluntarily. The project went live in October 2005, with 150 retailers signing on in eighteen states.[16] By June 2011, more than 1,400 companies were

participating in twenty-four states.[17] Several states, led by New York, jumped ahead of the project by passing laws mandating that Amazon.com and other similar companies collect sales tax on purchases residents make from affiliates located in state. Amazon challenged the law, but the New York Superior Court upheld the state's law in 2009.[18] After years of controversy and legal battles, in 2012 California also managed to introduce a law requiring Amazon to collect local and state sales taxes. This was a big deal for the cash-strapped state government, which needed the revenue, but not such a good deal for California consumers—it added 7 to 10 percent to the cost of an Amazon purchase.[19]

Property Taxes

The second-largest source of tax revenue for state and local governments is property taxes. In 2009, property taxes raised approximately 33 percent, or $424 billion, of total state and local government tax revenues.[20] Most sales tax revenues go to state governments, but almost all property taxes go to local governments. As a result, property taxes are by far the most important source of revenue for local governments. Approximately 72 percent of local government tax revenues, but only a tiny fraction (2 percent) of state tax revenues, comes from property taxes.[21]

Just about every local government relies on property tax revenues, but property tax rates vary widely from community to community. Most Americans who own homes or condominiums face an effective tax rate

Will that be cash or charge? Either way, these shoppers at the Mall of America in Bloomington, Minnesota, got a break from sales tax on their clothing purchases. Minnesota is one of numerous states that consider clothing an essential item and, therefore, waive any sales taxes. Other states, such as New Hampshire, have no sales tax at all, which makes their malls and shopping outlets very popular with shoppers from neighboring states.

of about 1.39 percent.[22] The word *effective* simply acknowledges that some places have exemptions and adjustments that make the effective tax rate lower than the nominal tax rate. You can figure out the nominal tax rate by dividing the amount of tax paid by the amount of taxable income. You find the effective tax rate by dividing the amount of tax paid by the amount of total economic income.

In other words, if you own a condo worth $100,000, you probably pay about $1,390 a year in property taxes. In Manchester, New Hampshire, however, you'd pay $2,840 in property taxes on that same condo. That's because New Hampshire has an effective tax rate of 2.84 percent, which is one of the highest among cities across the country. Why are New Hampshire's property tax rates so high? Largely because the state has no income tax and no sales tax. That limits the state government's ability to raise funds. It also means that the state does not offer its towns the level of financial support that most state governments do. As a result, whereas most local governments receive 25 percent of their total revenues from property taxes, local governments in New Hampshire are forced to rely on property taxes for 53 percent of their total revenues.[23]

The Education Connection.
Property taxes are important for another reason: they pretty much finance public elementary and high school education. On average, school districts receive about 44 percent of their funding from local governments.[24] In most states, where you live determines how many education dollars your children receive. Wealthy communities with high housing values raise the most money from property taxes. School districts in these areas tend to have the most educational resources. Conversely, school districts in the poorest areas have the fewest resources. In recent years state and federal governments have stepped in to try to ease these funding gaps by providing more resources to poor schools that cannot compete resource-wise with schools that have strong property tax bases, but the gaps are persistent. For example, the federal government's main effort to reduce resource inequality comes through Title I of the Elementary and Secondary Education Act, which sends billions of dollars to schools that serve socioeconomically distressed students. One analysis of education spending in New York City found that schools in poorer communities make do with less per pupil revenue even with the help of Title I funds. Some schools serving the poorest communities do so with about 85 percent of the average per-pupil expenditure in New York.

The bottom line is that when schools are heavily dependent on property taxes, it is all but impossible to equalize resources. If states do nothing, schools in areas with high property values will have bigger budgets; if they try to equalize resources, they have to find the money (read: raise taxes), which is never popular and is especially resented if it is viewed as a tactic to divert money from local schools to nonlocal schools.

The Pros and Cons of Property Taxes.
Property owners generally pay their property taxes twice a year in large lump sums. As such, these taxes tend to be highly visible and extremely unpopular with the public. However, local officials like them because property tax receipts are historically less volatile and more predictable than other types of tax revenues. Local revenue departments assess the values of houses and businesses and then send the owners their tax bills, so the local government knows exactly how much revenue a property tax will yield.

In most instances, taxes seem worse when the economy is bad. Property taxes are the exception. They tend to rise most sharply when a town or city is experiencing an economic boom and housing prices are soaring. In these circumstances, an upsurge in property values can lead to a backlash.

The most famous of such backlashes occurred in California in 1978. In response to years of rising property values and related taxes, Californians passed Proposition 13. This piece of legislation capped the property tax rate at 1 percent of a property's purchase price and froze property assessments at their 1978 levels until the property is resold. Newcomers to a neighborhood have to pay property taxes based on the actual value of their houses.

To this day, Proposition 13 is hotly debated. Conservatives have long praised the movement that gave rise to it. They say that it was the harbinger of the conservative politics that former California governor Ronald Reagan would bring to Washington three years later. Most experts, however, believe that its effects have been devastating, especially to education. Prior to Proposition 13, California was one of the most generous contributors to public education among the U.S. states; in the years since, it has become one of the least generous.

Even the most liberal electorates can be goaded into atypical action by rising property tax rates. In 1980, Massachusetts voters passed Proposition 2½, which capped property tax increases at, you guessed it, 2½ percent. As a result, towns that want to increase spending by more than that, for such needs as increased funding for education, have to hold special override sessions. Towns also have come to rely on user fees (a phenomenon examined later in this chapter).

Many state and local governments have attempted to ease the burden of property taxes on senior citizens and, in some cases, on other low-income individuals. In about fifty Massachusetts towns, senior citizens can reduce their property taxes by performing volunteer work. Cook County, Illinois, limits property tax rate increases by tying them to the national rate of inflation.[25] Despite these efforts, tensions between retirees living on fixed incomes and parents eager to spend more on local schools are commonplace. These pressures can be particularly acute in areas with large numbers of retirees. Indeed, some "active-adult retirement communities" ban families with children altogether.

Another hidden cost of property taxes is worth noting. You might think that commercial and residential property owners are the only ones who pay, right? You're off the hook if you rent, right? Wrong! Most economists believe that landlords pass the cost of property tax increases on to renters in the form of rent increases.

Income Taxes

Personal **income taxes** account for 21 percent of all state and local tax revenues.[26] That makes income tax revenue the third most significant source of state and local government income. In some ways, however, this figure conceals more than it reveals. Almost all nonfederal income tax revenues go to state governments.[27] In many states, personal income taxes are assessed on a graduated scale, so higher wage earners pay a greater percentage of their income in taxes. This structure tends to make state tax systems that rely more heavily on the income tax than on the sales tax more **progressive**.

As with property taxes, states have different approaches to income taxes, with some using such taxes as a primary revenue source and others shunning them altogether. Alaska, Florida, Nevada, South Dakota, Texas, Washington, and Wyoming impose no income taxes at all, and New Hampshire and Tennessee impose taxes only on certain types of income. Your state's reliance (or lack of reliance) on income taxes influences not just how much you take home in your paycheck but also how much stuff costs. This is because states that do not collect income taxes usually rely heavily on sales tax revenues. States that have no sales tax tend to make up the loss by taking a bigger bite out of income. Oregon, for example, has no sales tax and is thus heavily reliant on income taxes (individual and corporate) as a primary revenue source. In 2009 Oregon's income tax provided 75 percent of the state's total tax revenues—the most of any state.[28] Voters in Oregon endorsed, and even increased, the state's reliance on its income tax in January 2010 by approving an increase in the tax rate on the highest-wage earners—the first time they have approved such an increase since 1930.

Two states, Alaska and New Hampshire, have neither income taxes nor sales taxes. How do they manage to function without two of the primary sources of revenue for most state governments? For Alaska, geology is the difference that makes a difference: the Prudhoe Bay oil fields bring in so much money that the state has little need for other revenue streams. The difference that makes a difference for New Hampshire is mostly the residents' hardheaded resistance to taxation. Unlike

---

Income Taxes
Taxes on wages and interest earned.

Progressive Tax System
A system of taxation in which the rate paid reflects ability to pay.

Alaska, New Hampshire has no big alternate revenue source—it just makes do. According to Donald Boyd of the Rockefeller Institute, New Hampshire's state government simply does less than most state governments. The state relies almost exclusively on local governments to finance elementary and secondary education rather than raising state revenue for this purpose. Unlike many other states, it also has managed to avoid court orders to spend dramatically more on secondary school education. It is able to do all this, in part, because the average New Hampshire resident has one of the highest levels of income in the country. The people of New Hampshire are able to pay for a lot of goods and services for themselves.

These states are the exceptions. On average, Americans pay about $767 a year in state income taxes.[29] However, residents of states with high tax rates, such as Maryland, Massachusetts, New York, and Oregon, pay significantly more in income taxes. (See Table 4-1.)

TABLE 4-1

State Individual Income Tax Collections per Capita, Fiscal Year 2010

State	Individual Income Tax Collections per Capita ($)	Rank	State	Individual Income Tax Collections per Capita ($)	Rank
Alabama	543	35	Nebraska	832	18
Alaska[a]	0	44	Nevada[a]	0	44
Arizona	379	41	New Hampshire[b]	63	42
Arkansas	719	29	New Jersey	1,176	7
California	1,229	5	New Mexico	466	38
Colorado	816	19	New York	1,796	1
Connecticut	1,616	2	North Carolina	961	13
Delaware	952	14	North Dakota	454	40
Florida[a]	0	44	Ohio	684	30
Georgia	726	26	Oklahoma	595	33
Hawaii	1,127	8	Oregon	1,293	4
Idaho	684	31	Pennsylvania	737	23
Illinois	736	24	Rhode Island	864	17
Indiana	597	32	South Carolina	473	37
Iowa	871	16	South Dakota[a]	0	44
Kansas	944	15	Tennessee[b]	27	43
Kentucky	728	25	Texas[a]	0	44
Louisiana	506	36	Utah	765	22
Maine	981	12	Vermont	782	20
Maryland	1,077	10	Virginia	1,086	9
Massachusetts	1,549	3	Washington[a]	0	44
Michigan	555	34	West Virginia	782	21
Minnesota	1,219	6	Wisconsin	1,020	11
Mississippi	456	39	Wyoming[a]	0	44
Missouri	724	28	United States (average)	767	—
Montana	724	27			

Source: Tax Foundation, "State Individual Income Tax Collections, 2010," http://taxfoundation.org/article/facts-figures-handbook-how-does-your-state-compare-0.

a. State does not tax wage income.

b. State does not tax wage income but does tax interest and dividend income.

Other Tax Revenue Sources: Cars, Oil, and Death

Car registrations, deaths, and oil and other natural resources also are major sources of state revenues. In 2008, car registration fees brought in almost $20 billion to state and local governments. Estate taxes, sometimes called death taxes, and gift taxes brought in another $5.3 billion.[30]

Thirty-two states levy **severance taxes** on natural resources that are removed, or severed, from the state. Some states are quite creative about devising severance taxes. Washington, for example, taxes oysters and salmon and other game fish caught in state. But despite some creative taxing, the only states that raise real money from severance taxes are states with significant coal, oil, and natural gas reserves, such as Wyoming and Alaska.

Other Sources of Income: Fees, Charges, and Uncle Sam

The total tax revenues discussed so far add up to a lot of money (nearly $2 trillion), but that only covers about two-thirds of the roughly $3 trillion in annual spending that state and local governments racked up in 2012. The rest of the money came from user fees and other charges, insurance trust money, and intergovernmental transfers.

These sources of revenue can be significant. In 2008, state and local governments raised $613 billion from "charges and miscellaneous fees." That is $165 billion more than they raised from sales taxes.[31] Government levies in the form of things such as university tuitions, public hospital charges, airport use fees, school lunch sales, and park permits obviously can make a big difference to the bottom line. Recently, states have increased fees to help close budget deficits and avoid more prominent tax increases. The pattern accelerated as tax revenues fell off in recent years: in 2010 state

budgets included $5.3 billion in fee increases.[32] In 2013 state budgets tacked on another $500 million in new fee increases. State and local governments earned another $144 million from utility fees and, yes, from liquor sales and licenses.[33]

Insurance Trust Funds

The amount of money shown on a pay stub before any deductions are taken out can be pretty impressive. The actual amount of the paycheck can be a bit disappointing. What many wage earners may not realize is that they are not the only ones paying the taxes and fees they see deducted from their paychecks. Their employers often have to match these payroll taxes and deductions. These **insurance trust funds** go to their state governments and to the federal government. Ultimately, the contributions are invested to support Social Security and retirement programs, workers' compensation and disability programs, and other related insurance programs that benefit employees.

Intergovernmental Transfers

The final portion of state and local government revenues comes from **intergovernmental transfers** of money. In the case of state governments, that means transfers from the federal government. In the case of local governments, it means transfers from state governments. In 2011, the federal government provided some $575 billion to state and

Thanks to unprecedented revenues from oil production, North Dakota is expected to have a $2 billion budget reserve at the end of fiscal year 2013. North Dakota recently surpassed Alaska to become the nation's second-biggest oil producer, following only Texas.

Severance Taxes
Taxes on natural resources removed from a state.

Insurance Trust Funds
Money collected from contributions, assessments, insurance premiums, and payroll taxes.

Intergovernmental Transfers
Funds provided by the federal government to state governments and by state governments to local governments.

A Difference That Makes A Difference

The Blessing and Curse of a Booming Economy

While the economic doldrums have left many states awash in red ink, North Dakota has found itself awash in cash. While most states struggle to deal with the lingering budgetary effects of a recession, North Dakota struggles to deal with the impact of a massive economic boom. While the cupboards are bare for many states, North Dakota's treasury is amply stocked.

How has North Dakota managed all this? Mostly by being the location of certain events predating the Great Recession—and we mean *way* predating the Great Recession. Like 417 million years ago. Somewhere around that time a large oil deposit formed under what is now the border between North Dakota and Canada. The first well sunk to try to tap that oil was drilled on land owned by a farmer named Henry Bakken; what is now known as the Bakken Formation is believed to hold a massive 4.3 billion barrels of oil.

While the Bakken Formation's potential had been known for a long time, it wasn't until relatively recently that the technology existed to allow anyone to tap that oil cost-effectively. Coincidentally, that technology came online and opened up the taps on the Bakken Formation pretty much at the same time the United States was hit by the worst financial crisis in five generations. Geology was thus a difference that made a big difference to this state. The happy coincidence that the sea of fossil fuel on which it sat was newly open to extraction meant that North Dakota pretty much missed the financial hard times of the Great Recession.

Taxes on oil and gas production netted the state $839 million in fiscal year 2011 and are expected to generate $1 billion a year to the state's bottom line for the foreseeable future. That's a big number for a small-population state like North Dakota. While other states have been cutting budgets, North Dakota has increased its biennial budget by 12 percent.

In these tough economic times, the oil boom makes North Dakota seem like some sort of alternate universe. While unemployment hovers around 8 percent nationally, and is much higher in some pockets, North Dakota has more jobs than people. In Williams County there are nine jobs for every person looking for work. The average oil and gas worker there earns $90,000 per year. Average household income in municipalities such as Stanley (population 1,458) has jumped 130 percent in a decade.

While the oil boom means that North Dakota does not have to worry much about budget deficits, the effects are not all positive. The state is undergoing a population boom that is straining public services and creating housing shortages. The impact of the oil and gas industry on the environment and on the largely rural, agricultural way of life that has defined generations of North Dakotans has raised worry and criticism in some quarters. And local governments do not benefit directly from taxes on oil and gas—these revenues flow mostly to the state.

Still, some states that are cutting services, raising taxes, and generally struggling make ends meet might be forgiven if they look at North Dakota's problems with envy. At least North Dakota has extra money to deal with its problems, which is more than many states can say.

Source: Ryan Holeywell, "North Dakota's Oil Boom Is a Blessing and a Curse," *Governing,* August 2011, www.governing.com/topics/energy-env/north-dakotas-oil-boom-blessing-curse.html.

local governments, making it the single largest source of revenues for these governments.[34] That situation is most likely to be temporary, however—a good portion of that money from the federal government came from the stimulus funds appropriated by the ARRA, as discussed in the introductory section of this chapter. Much of that money was disbursed to states and spent by 2012–2013.

MAP 4-1

American Recovery and Reinvestment Act Funds Awarded by State, 2012

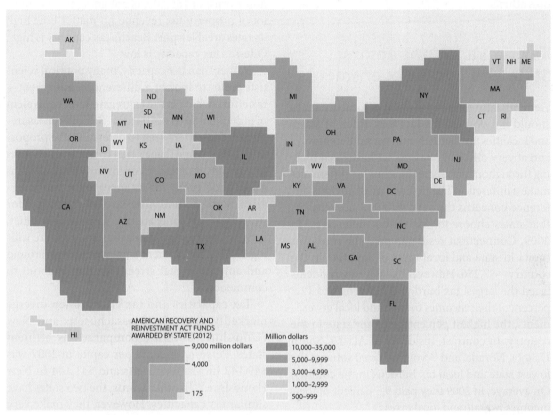

Source: "State/Territory Totals as Reported by Recipients," Recovery.gov, reporting period February 7, 2009—March 31, 2012, www.recovery.gov/pages/textview. aspx?data=recipientHomeMap.

Approximately 90 percent of federal funds go to specific state programs. Medicaid, the joint state-federal health insurance program for low-income people and people with disabilities, is by far the largest recipient. It receives about 64.6 percent of all federal funds that go to state governments.[35] Education (both K–12 and post–secondary school), transportation projects, and public welfare also receive significant federal funding. Most of these funds cannot be used on just anything—states must spend them on certain programs and often in a certain fashion.

During the 1960s, local governments and some neighborhood organizations also received substantial federal funding. Many of these programs have since ended or have been scaled back drastically. Aside from the stimulus bill, local governments get only about 4 percent of their total revenues from the federal government. Adding to the problem for localities is that states have reduced their support for local governments, too, as one tool to help balance their own budgets. Still, intergovernmental revenue transfers—mostly from state governments—account for about a third of local government spending.[36]

Localities generally have welcomed the money, but relationships between state governments and county and city governments have not always been easy. Over the course of the past decade, many city and county governments have found themselves stuck with unfunded mandates. These requirements have been imposed on them by federal or state legislation that forces them to perform certain tasks but fails to provide them with the money to carry out those tasks. Transfers of money and responsibilities, however, continue to be commonplace during economic downturns.[37]

Taxing Variations among State and Local Governments

Generalizations about state and local finances should not obscure the fact that different states and localities tax themselves in very different ways and at very different rates. As we have been hinting throughout our discussion thus far, differences make a difference. The first and most obvious difference concerns the very different tax burdens that states choose to impose on themselves. In 2009, Connecticut residents paid the most per capita in state and local taxes of any state in the country—$7,256. However, New Jersey residents faced the largest tax burden. They returned 12.2 percent of their incomes to state and local governments, the highest percentage of any state in the country. In contrast, residents of Alaska, South Dakota, Nevada, and Wyoming faced some of the lowest state and local tax burdens in the country. On average, in 2009 they paid 9.5 percent of their incomes in state and local taxes.[38]

State and local governments do not just choose to tax themselves at different rates. They also choose to tax themselves in different ways. Residents of many Tennessee counties pay sales taxes of almost 10 percent. New Hampshire relies on property taxes to generate 18 percent of its total state tax revenue. In contrast, property taxes do not contribute anything to state coffers in fourteen states, although localities rely heavily on them.[39]

In thinking about a state's tax burden, it is helpful to distinguish between its **tax capacity** and its **tax effort**. In Newport Beach, California, for example, many homes are worth more than $1 million—a far cry from the price tags of a few

years ago—but on that much value, even low property tax rates are going to bring in serious money. Conversely, Odessa, Texas, with a median home price of $66,700, is not going to generate a lot of property tax revenue no matter how high its rates are. Newport Beach's tax capacity is high; Odessa's tax capacity is low.

Rather than tax capacity, many political scientists prefer to look at a different measurement—tax effort, which is the aggregate-level equivalent of individual-level tax burden. Basically, measurements of tax effort seek to determine the proportion of its income that a given community chooses to pay out in taxes. A community's tax effort is also a good proxy for its appetite for public services. Some communities are willing to pay for street cleaning; some are not. Some communities, such as Cambridge, Massachusetts, even are willing to pay a government employee to drive around and announce that street cleaning is about to commence.

Tax capacities and tax efforts often diverge markedly. Consider Massachusetts and New Hampshire. Both are comparatively affluent states. Personal income per capita in 2007 was $49,142 in Massachusetts and $41,144 in New Hampshire.[40] In other words, the two states have similar tax capacities. However, they make very different tax efforts. New Hampshire has the second-lightest tax burden in the country. Its residents pay about $3,642 a year in state and local taxes. In contrast, residents of neighboring Massachusetts pay about $5,377.[41]

Explaining Tax Variations

What accounts for differences in tax capacity and effort such as those found between Massachusetts and New Hampshire? Political culture is one difference that helps explain the difference. New Hampshire prides itself on its rugged individualism. Its motto is "Live Free or Die." Residents tend to want the government to stay out of their way. In contrast, Massachusetts was founded as a commonwealth. The founding document of the Massachusetts Bay Colony describes a single "Body Politic" dedicated to the "general good" of the colony.[42] In this tradition, state and local governments are seen as

---

Tax Capacity
A measure of the ability to pay taxes.

Tax Effort
A measure of taxes paid relative to the ability to pay taxes.

effective ways of advancing that general good; thus higher taxes and larger governments are more acceptable.

Political culture, however, is not the only important variable that explains the very different tax efforts among states. Factors such as geography, geology, demographics, and history also influence the choices that state and local governments make.

Geography. One obvious, but easily overlooked, factor that influences state tax policies is geography. Some states use sales tax policy as a competitive edge. Delaware proudly recruits shoppers from nearby Mid-Atlantic states to its outlet malls with "no sales tax" advertisements. In contrast, Hawaii charges a 4.5 percent tax on nearly everything sold, including many services. How can it get away with the practice? Well, unless residents are willing to fly to the mainland for their sundries, they don't have much choice but to pay up.

Geology. As we have already seen, geology plays an important role in some state economies. This is most notably true in oil-rich and natural-gas-rich states such as Alaska, Wyoming, and North Dakota (see the box "A Difference That Makes a Difference: The Blessing and Curse of a Booming Economy"). Thanks in large part to Prudhoe Bay, state and local governments in Alaska are able to maintain high levels of spending with very low tax burdens. Alaska used its mineral riches to help establish the Alaska Permanent Fund, which is a sovereign wealth fund—basically a state-owned investment corporation. The fund's profits are partially redistributed to state citizens, so rather than the state taxing residents, the fund pays Alaskans for being Alaskans. The fund sends each eligible citizen a yearly **dividend** check; in 2012 the amount per person was about $878.

Dividend
A payment made to stockholders (or, in Alaska's case, residents) from the interest generated by an investment.

Demographics. Demographics also play an important role in determining the attitudes of state and local governments toward taxes. This is particularly true at the local level. Consider a city with a strong local economy and rising house prices. Such a city attracts a large number of young workers with children. These are people who might very well want to spend more money on local schools and are willing to deal with rising property tax revenues. However, as mentioned previously, for seniors living on fixed incomes, rising house prices and rising property taxes might spell disaster. During economic booms, conflicts between parents of school-age children and retirees are a common feature of local politics.

The Economic Cycle. Even when states make similar tax efforts and have similar cultures, their state and local finances can still vary widely because states (and even cities) can have very different economies. The national economic numbers that most people are familiar with— unemployment, productivity gains, income, and the like—are not necessarily accurate reflections of state economic conditions. Depending on the makeup of their economies, states can find themselves at very different points on an economic cycle at the same point in time. For example, industrial states such as Michigan and Indiana tend to experience economic downturns first. Texas historically has had a countercyclical economy. When rising oil prices threaten to push industrial states into recession, Texas tends to do well. The same is true of Wyoming, Alaska, and, most recently, North Dakota.

Demographics, geography, history, political culture, and the swings of the economic cycle are all important, but these variables do not explain all the financial choices that state and local governments make. Take Mississippi, for example. One of the most religious and politically conservative states in the country, Mississippi is the buckle of the Bible Belt. In 1990, however, Mississippi passed riverboat gambling legislation. This legislation allowed casino operators to build full-size casinos on barges moored permanently to the shoreline on the Mississippi River and the Gulf Coast. The goal was to turn the northwestern town of Tunica, which had gained a measure of renown after the television newsmagazine *60 Minutes* profiled it as the poorest city in America, into Las Vegas East.

What's important to keep in mind here is that Nevada and Mississippi have completely different political cultures. Political scientist Daniel Elazar describes Mississippi as a traditionalistic state and Nevada as an individualistic state. In short, Nevada has the kind of political culture that we might expect to produce, well, Las Vegas. Mississippi does not. Today, however, the hamlet of Tunica has more casino square footage than the East Coast gambling hot spot Atlantic City, in the individualistic state of New Jersey. Clearly, political culture isn't everything.

Debt

The final source of money for state and local governments is debt, generally issued in the form of **bonds**. These are financial instruments with which state and local governments promise to pay back borrowed money at a fixed rate of interest on a specified date. The interest rates paid by a government depend largely on the government's bond rating. Bond ratings are issued by three private companies—Moody's, Standard & Poor's, and Fitch—and are based on the governments' fiscal health; many states' bond ratings have fallen during the current recession. A rating of AAA is the best, and anything lower than BBB is considered "junk bond status" and would send a government's interest rates skyrocketing. No state has ever fallen below BBB rating.[43]

State and local governments, as well as quasi-governmental entities such as utility and water authorities, use bonds to finance **capital investments**, typically infrastructure upgrades such as new roads, new schools, and new airports. There are two types of bonds: **general obligation bonds**, which are secured by the taxing power of the jurisdiction that issues them, and **revenue bonds**, which are secured by the revenue from a given project, such as a new toll road. For state governments, capital investments are projects such as highway construction, power plant construction and pollution control, and even land conservation. Because the issuance of general obligation bonds must be approved by voters, state and local governments turn to revenue bonds more often.

Local governments use bonds to finance projects such as construction or improvement of schools, sewage and water lines, airports, and affordable housing. Investors like them too, in part because the earnings from most state bonds are exempt from state income taxes.

In 2012, state and local governments issued about $295 billion in bonds.[44] **Municipal bonds**, called munis, are generally safe and attractive investments, particularly for the rich. Municipal bondholders usually are exempted from paying federal or state taxes on income they receive from bonds. Sometimes, however, municipal finances go disastrously awry. In 2009, Jefferson County, Alabama, the largest county in the state, announced it would file for bankruptcy after defaulting on $3 billion in bonds to finance improvements to its sewer system.

Capital Investments
Investments in infrastructure, such as roads.

General Obligation Bonds
Investments secured by the taxing power of the jurisdiction that issues them.

Revenue Bonds
Investments secured by the revenue generated by a state or municipal project.

Municipal Bonds
Bonds issued by states, counties, cities, and towns to fund large projects as well as operating budgets. Income from such bonds is exempt from federal taxes and from state and local taxes for the investors who live in the state where they are issued.

Bonds
Certificates that are evidence of debts on which the issuer promises to pay the holders a specified amount of interest for a specified length of time and to repay the loans on their maturity.

Local Focus

Bonds and Broken Budgets

The story of how Jefferson County, Alabama, waded into budget and bond muck stretches back to 1993, when the Cahaba River Society, a group dedicated to preserving the river that flows through Birmingham, complained that the county's sewer system was discharging raw sewage into waterways. Federal officials issued a consent decree in which Jefferson County promised to upgrade the system.

The county paid for the upgrade by issuing $3 billion in bonds. As sewer service rates rose to meet those costs and Jefferson County struggled under its debt, county officials looked for a way to lessen the loan payments. In 2002 and 2003, they refinanced their bonds with variable-rate and auction-rate securities. (Auction-rate securities are bonds for which the interest rate is reset at auction every few weeks.)

Auction-rate securities were supposed to be safe, but the auction-rate market collapsed in February 2008. Then the bond insurance companies that were backing the county's debt suffered their own fiscal problems and their credit was downgraded. The result: Jefferson County's interest rates skyrocketed, much like the rates of homeowners whose subprime mortgages had just reset. The county's revenue from sewer fees could not cover the borrowing costs. On April Fool's Day 2008, Jefferson County failed to make its payment on its debt. Instead, it reached an agreement with its creditors to pay the interest and get an extension on the principal—an agreement that left the county of 660,000 teetering on the edge of bankruptcy.

County commissioners and other Alabama political players developed a variety of ideas to solve the sewer mess—to no avail. Without a solution in sight, the county made massive cutbacks: reducing department budgets by one-third, canceling road maintenance contracts, closing courthouses, and laying off hundreds of county workers. "We're having to downsize this government to the point that it may not be able to operate," County Commissioner Bettye Fine Collins said in 2009.

Collins's comments were prophetic. In December 2011 Jefferson Country filed for bankruptcy; by that time its debt had ballooned to more than $4 billion, a crushing burden the county simply could not manage.

As discussed in the opening section of this chapter, variations on the Jefferson County story have played out across the country as the recession significantly weakened local governments' financial footing.

Sources: Karen Pierog, "Default, Bankruptcy Fears Overhang U.S. Muni Market," Reuters, February 16, 2010; adapted from Josh Goodman, "Drained," *Governing,* August 2009.

The Budget Process

Once state and local governments have raised money from taxes, user fees, and bonds and have received money from intergovernmental transfers, they must decide how to spend it. These decisions are made during the **budget process**.

Most state and local governments budget for one **fiscal year**. Unfortunately for fans of simplicity in government, the fiscal year is not the same as the calendar year. The federal government's fiscal year runs from October 1 to September 30. Most state and local governments begin their fiscal year on July 1; Alabama, Michigan, New York, and Texas are exceptions. Thus, when legislatures debate the budget, they are almost always debating

---

Budget Process
The procedure by which state and local governments assess revenues and set budgets.

Fiscal Year
The annual accounting period used by a government.

MAP 4-2

Municipal Bankruptcies as of September 2012

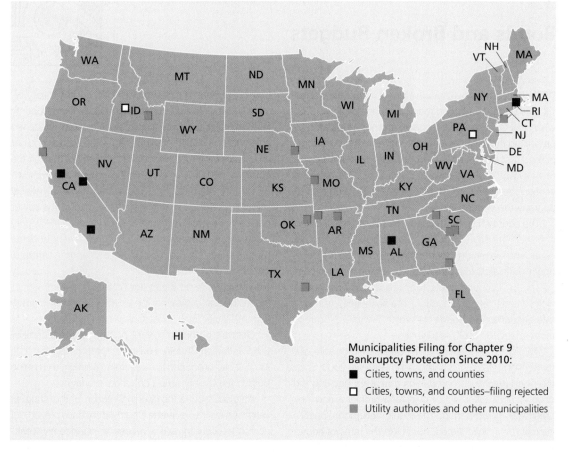

Source: "Bankrupt Cities, Municipalities List and Map," *Governing*, www.governing.com/gov-data/other/municipal-cities-counties-bankruptcies-and-defaults .html.

Note: Only about half of the U.S. states allow municipalities to file for Chapter 9 bankruptcy; laws in other states prohibit such filings. Not all bankruptcy filings were approved.

the budget for the coming fiscal year.[45] Nineteen states pass two-year budgets.[46]

Budget time lines do vary from state to state, but the budget process itself is quite similar across states. It begins with instructions from the governor's budget office. The executive branch agencies are told to draw up funding requests for the upcoming year. During the fall (assuming the typical fiscal year beginning on July 1), the budget office reviews the spending requests and helps the chief executive develop a unified budget for the executive branch.

Most chief executives unveil their budgets in state-of-the-state addresses in January. In forty-five states, governors and mayors are required by

law to submit a **balanced budget** to the legislature or city council. The legislative body reviews the budget, authorizes spending on certain programs, appropriates the necessary money, and presents its budget to the chief executive to sign into law.

As a guard against fiscal excess and abuse, forty-nine states have statutory or constitutional requirements that the state legislature must enact a balanced budget. Only Vermont is free to run up debt as it pleases.[47] All but five states also have laws that require lawmakers to save a certain portion of

Balanced Budget
A budget in which current expenditures are equal to or less than income.

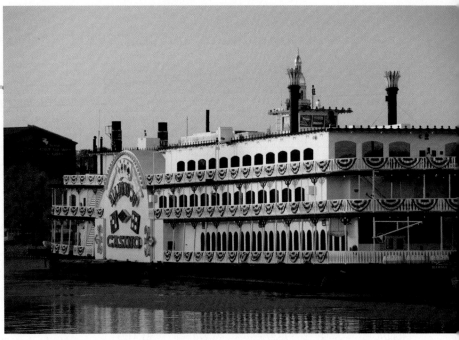

Despite some groups' moral objections to gambling, states have turned to casinos like this one floating on the Mississippi River in Dubuque, Iowa, to help raise much-needed revenues.

state revenues in so-called rainy day, or budget stabilization, funds. States can draw on these funds during times of recession, when revenues fall. Although rainy day funds rarely offset the revenue drops that occur during a recession, they do provide some cushion for the lawmakers who have to balance state budgets. In 2009 and 2010, for example, rainy day funds helped close more than $35 billion of states' budget gaps—funds that would have otherwise had to come from more severe program cuts or greater tax increases.[48] Many local governments face similar requirements because of state laws or their own municipal codes.

There are, of course, exceptions. In states such as Arkansas, Mississippi, and South Carolina, legislatures take the lead role in formulating the initial budget plan. Legislative bodies also take the lead in county and city governments with weak chief executives, such as Los Angeles, California. In many western states, citizens and special interests have become players in the budgeting process via ballot initiatives.

Expenditures, or Where the Money Goes

State and local governments spend a lot of money. In fiscal year 2010, state governments alone spent nearly $2 trillion. (See Table 4-2.) In 2012 state and local governments combined spent approximately $9,762.50 for every man, woman, and child in the country.[49] So, where did the money go?

Wages. Salaries are the single largest source of **expenditures** for state and local governments—roughly $800 billion in 2008. State and local

---

Expenditures
Money spent by government.

governments are the biggest employers in the United States. In 2008, state governments employed 5.1 million people nationwide. Local governments employed another 14.6 million people.[50]

Education. Education has long been the single largest functional spending category for state and local governments. In 2010 state governments alone spent $571 billion on education, the majority of it (about $316 billion) in the forms of transfers to schools and school districts.[51]

Despite the big financial commitment by states—they provide about half the funding—primary and secondary education traditionally has been the preserve of local governments. In most states, elected local school boards hire superintendents and principals, select curricula that align with state standards, and develop school budgets. Local governments typically devote about 38 percent of their budgets to education.[52]

State governments also devote a portion of their expenditures to higher education; in 2012 this amounted to a total of about $72.4 billion. That number has been steadily declining, however—in 2007 states spent more than $75 billion.[53] Funding for higher education has been cut largely because

TABLE 4-2

State Revenue, Expenditures, and Debt, 2010 (in millions of dollars)

Item	Total revenue	Total expenditure	Debt at end of fiscal year
UNITED STATES	2,035,700	1,942,822	1,113,355
ALABAMA	26,824	27,700	8,785
ALASKA	12,375	11,000	6,381
ARIZONA	32,842	33,016	13,956
ARKANSAS	19,595	17,354	4,261
CALIFORNIA	278,495	257,249	148,929
COLORADO	27,991	27,661	16,710
CONNECTICUT	26,840	27	30
DELAWARE	8	7,827	5,515
FLORIDA	91,653	81,629	40,403
GEORGIA	44,878	44,482	13,789
HAWAII	11,566	11,178	7,701
IDAHO	8,859	8,514	3,873
ILLINOIS	73,275	75,270	61,412
INDIANA	35,575	35,474	23,635
IOWA	21,265	19,109	5,140
KANSAS	16,546	16,584	6,478
KENTUCKY	26,993	29,098	14,393
LOUISIANA	32,188	33,616	17,443
MAINE	9,539	9,024	6,034
MARYLAND	37,394	37,488	24,475
MASSACHUSETTS	50,472	51,731	73,940
MICHIGAN	65,972	63,918	32,146
MINNESOTA	39,887	37,942	11,683
MISSISSIPPI	20,979	20,023	6,468
MISSOURI	33,916	30,772	20,421
MONTANA	7,141	7,052	4,374
NEBRASKA	10,063	9,585	2,330
NEVADA	14,053	12,935	4,436
NEW HAMPSHIRE	7,828	7,708	8,347
NEW JERSEY	66,740	67,971	60,958
NEW MEXICO	17,567	17,996	8,740
NEW YORK	195,460	174,308	129,530
NORTH CAROLINA	57,467	52,190	18,853
NORTH DAKOTA	6,119	5,134	2,198
OHIO	89,664	76,737	31,177
OKLAHOMA	23,692	22,640	9,963
OREGON	28,703	26,978	13,510
PENNSYLVANIA	83,287	87,285	44,738
RHODE ISLAND	8,809	8,211	9,498
SOUTH CAROLINA	28,869	28,927	15,771
SOUTH DAKOTA	4,493	4,429	3,483
TENNESSEE	29,720	29,675	5,835
TEXAS	120,390	119,605	42,034
UTAH	16,022	16,263	6,478
VERMONT	6,001	5,726	3,493
VIRGINIA	46,357	43,457	24,967
WASHINGTON	44,299	46,238	27,478
WEST VIRGINIA	13,564	12,343	7,144
WISCONSIN	48,088	38,590	22,319
WYOMING	7,411	5,757	1,514

Source: *State and Local Sourcebook,* online supplement to *Governing,* 2010, http://sourcebook.governing.com.

it comes out of general revenue funds; that is, it is part of what is known as **discretionary spending**. In tight economic times, discretionary spending is one of the first parts of a government budget to come under stress—when revenues shrink, legislatures have to reduce annual appropriations, and that means cutting discretionary spending. As publicly supported colleges and universities have ways to deal with spending cuts from state government (read: jack up your tuition and increase your class size), higher education funds have been particularly hard-hit by budget retrenchment.

Healthcare. Since the late 1990s, healthcare spending has surged dramatically. For state governments, spending on healthcare is now greater than spending for any other single item. Medicaid is the largest and most expensive state-run health program. When it was established in 1965, it was viewed as a limited safety net for the very poor and disabled. However, the numbers of low-income, uninsured Americans have grown, and medical care has become more expensive. The program has grown at an enormous rate as a result. In 1970, state governments spent $2 billion on Medicaid, and the federal government kicked in another $3 billion. By 2008, the states and the federal government

Discretionary Spending
Spending controlled in annual appropriations acts.

spent $311 billion on the program, up from $298 billion just a year earlier.[54] State Medicaid programs provide health insurance to more than 60 million people and account for 20.7 percent of total state spending.[55]

These numbers may be about to go up. In 2010 the federal government enacted the Patient Protection and Affordable Care Act—commonly known as Obamacare—which has the explicit aim of extending health insurance coverage to millions of uninsured people. The law is of central interest to the states because Medicaid is a program cooperatively run—and paid for—by both state and federal governments. As such, it is an example of **fiscal federalism,** a system of delivering public services that involves the federal government picking up most of the costs while states take responsibility for administering the services.

Obamacare was a contentious and controversial law opposed by some state officials, who viewed it as federal encroachment on state sovereignty. In 2012, however, the Supreme Court ruled its major provisions constitutional, so like it or not states have to learn to live with it. While a number of objections were raised against Obamacare, its potential budgetary impact was one of the biggest sources of concern for state officials. By some estimates Obamacare could add an extra 17 million people to the numbers covered by Medicaid, which is an **entitlement** program. This means states and the federal government are obligated by law to provide health insurance to low-income individuals who qualify for the program, regardless of the cost. If states have an unexpected surge of applicants and they have not set aside enough money for Medicaid, tough. The federal government has committed to covering many of the increased costs associated with Obamacare (which also has the overall goal of reining in the spiraling costs of healthcare), but at this point it is not certain how the program will affect the states' bottom lines. Some state officials have expressed concern that, at a minimum, they may be left in the lurch at some point in the future, stuck with the obligation of covering the costs of an entitlement program that the federal government is not fully funding. Until Obamacare has been fully implemented and operational for several years, however, it will be hard to assess whether or not it has increased state healthcare expenditures.

What is in no doubt is that Medicaid and other healthcare programs are expensive for both the states and the federal government. In 2010 total Medicaid costs were about $389 billion; states contributed about $126 billion, with the rest coming from the federal government.[56] The State Children's Health Insurance Program (CHIP) is another joint state-federal program that helps provide health insurance for children in poor families. In 2009, CHIP was a $10 billion program, with about $7 billion funded by the federal government and the rest provided by the states.

States do have some leeway in determining how generous they want to be with programs such as Medicaid and CHIP. Eligibility for these sorts of programs is typically determined by family or wage earner income relative to federally established poverty levels. While the federal government sets basic guidelines on those eligibility requirements, states can use more generous guidelines if they choose. For example, in Mississippi children under the age of five are eligible for Medicaid benefits in families earning up to 133 percent of the federal poverty level. In Wisconsin they are eligible if their families earn up to 300 percent of the federal poverty level.[57] In other words, whether someone is eligible for Medicaid benefits is dependent not just on how much his or her family earns but also on what state the family lives in.

Welfare. Welfare has been one of the most contentious issues in U.S. politics for a long time. Like Medicaid, welfare is an entitlement program; states have some leeway to determine eligibility, but they cannot deny or restrict benefits to qualified individuals. From 1965 to 1996, women with young children were eligible to receive monetary assistance through a welfare program known as Aid to Families with Dependent Children (AFDC).

In 1996, Republicans in Congress and President Bill Clinton joined forces to pass the Personal Responsibility and Work Reconciliation

---

Fiscal Federalism
The system by which federal grants are used to fund programs and services provided by state and local governments.

Entitlement
A service that government must provide, regardless of the cost.

FIGURE 4-1

HOW IT WORKS

A Year in the Life of a State Budget: Idaho's Budgetary Process

Most folks first hear about state budget priorities through their governor's state of the state address, the forum in which most state budgetary news is presented. In reality, budget planning begins well in advance of this address and involves all three branches of government to some degree. In Idaho, each year in May (after the last of the potatoes have been planted), that state's Division of Financial Management (DFM) starts sowing its own seeds: overseeing the development of that state's budget for the coming fiscal year. This is the beginning of what is really an eighteen-month process: the planning for fiscal year 2014, for instance, will actually get under way about mid-year in 2012.

This chart shows how the process works in Idaho:

Ongoing. An agency's budget can be adjusted through various means to accommodate things like revenue shortfalls and new federal grants and is monitored throughout the year by DFM analysts.

May. The Division of Financial Management, together with the Legislative Services Office (LSO), creates that year's edition of the *Budget Development Manual* and distributes it to state agencies.

The *Budget Development Manual* instructs agencies on the process they have to follow to submit their budgets and includes nuts and bolts items like how to calculate increases or changes in employee benefits and compensation.

July. New budget goes into effect.

By end of March. Bill is signed by the governor. If the bill does not pass both the House and the Senate or it is vetoed by the governor, budget-setting process begins again.

July–August. Each agency, working with a DFM budget analyst, develops its budget.

September. Agencies submit their budgets simultaneously to the DFM and LSO.

February–March. The budget-setting process begins. JFAC creates an appropriation bill (legislation) that must pass in both the House and the Senate.

October and November. Analysts at the DFM and LSO work on technical details. They then meet with the governor to present the agencies' requests and introduce options.

January–February. The appropriations process begins in the legislature. The Joint Finance-Appropriations Committee (JFAC) hears testimony from agencies on their budget requests and the governor's recommendation regarding those requests.

January. The governor presents these recommendations to the legislature at the start of the legislative session.

December. The governor makes a set of recommendations that becomes the executive budget.

Source: Adapted from Idaho Division of Financial Management, "Budget Process," http://dfm.idaho.gov/citizensguide/budgetprocess.html.

Act, which abolished AFDC and replaced it with the Temporary Assistance for Needy Families (TANF) program. TANF disbursed federal money to states in block grants and gave them considerable freedom in determining how they wanted to spend those funds. Many liberals predicted that such welfare "reform" would result in disaster. Instead, the number of people on welfare rolls declined dramatically. From 1994 to 1999 the welfare caseload declined by nearly 50 percent, from approximately 4 million people to 2 million people.[58]

Welfare continues to be a politically contentious issue even though, from a financial viewpoint, it is actually a pretty minor program. In 2011 states spent about $15 billion on TANF, with the federal government kicking in another $15 billion—that's no more than a percentage point or two of total state spending.[59]

Fire, Police, and Prisons. In 2008 state and local governments spent $129 billion on fire and police protection. They spent an additional $73 billion on prisons and correctional facilities.[60] State and local government spending on police protection and prisons varies widely. New York City, with a population of 8 million, employs a police force of 37,000. That works out to one police officer for every 216 people. In contrast, Los Angeles, a city of 3.8 million, employees only 10,000 police officers. That equals only one police officer for every 380 people.

States also have very different levels of enthusiasm for funding prisons. In fiscal year 2008 Florida devoted 4.8 percent of its state spending to prisons. That is a level of spending more than 1 percentage point higher than the national average and reflects Florida's incarceration rate, which is among the ten highest in the country. In contrast, West Virginia's state government spent only 1.1 percent of its state budget on corrections.[61]

Highways. In 2009 state and local governments spent about $120 billion on transportation, much of it devoted to highways and roads.[62] Most of this money came from dedicated revenue sources, such as the gasoline tax, but the federal government accounted for nearly a third of these funds.[63] The federal contribution to state transportation spending has been unusually high for several years

because of the ARRA, which channeled billions in federal stimulus money to the states in the form of highway funds.

Not surprisingly, states with wide-open spaces spend more money on highway construction and transportation. In 2008 Utah devoted 22.1 percent of total state expenditures to transportation. This was the highest percentage of any state in the country, followed by Montana at 13.4 percent and South Dakota at 12.7 percent. Nationwide, state governments spent 7.9 percent of total revenues on transportation in 2008.[64]

Restraints on State and Local Budgeteers

Politicians and journalists usually talk about "the budget" in the singular, as if elected officials meet every year or two to divvy up a single pot of money. That's misleading. State and local officials cannot actually lay their hands on all the revenues flowing into state and local coffers. Most of the money that comes from the federal government is earmarked for specific programs, such as Medicaid. Revenue streams from many state sources, such as the car registration tax, are likewise dedicated to specific purposes, such as highway construction. State and local officials develop their budgets under several additional restraints as well.

Governmental Accounting Standards Board. States conduct their accounting and financial reporting according to standards set by the Governmental Accounting Standards Board (GASB). In 2004, the organization issued GASB 45, a rule that mandated that states tally and disclose the cost of healthcare benefits pledged to current and retired state employees. As if that were not daunting enough, the states also had to find a way to begin saving enough to cover their pension liabilities, or they risked damaging their credit ratings. GASB 45 helped expose a massive gap between what states promised public-sector retirees and what they could actually pay for, a gap that was pushed wider by the revenue crunch of the Great Recession. The basic problem is that while state pension schemes have the funds to pay for promised retiree pensions and healthcare benefits in the short term, they do not have the money set aside to pay for the expected long-term increases in those costs. As of 2010 the gap between the assets of state pension funds and their financial obligation to cover promised pension and health-care benefits was $1.4 trillion (yes, that's trillion with a *t*).[65] States have taken some steps to try to close the gap by reducing benefits and increasing employee contributions to those benefits, but even with those reductions it is not clear that states will be able to cover their promises without resorting to getting more from taxpayers.

Unfunded Mandates. For years, state officials complained bitterly about the federal government's habit of mandating that states achieve a goal, such as an environmental cleanup, but then failing to provide any money to pay for it. State officials viewed such unfunded mandates as an affront to the notion of federalism itself. In 1995, Congress did something surprising. It passed legislation that curtailed dramatically the practice of imposing unfunded mandates on state governments. This measure alleviated some of the pressures on states, but it did not end the problem. Ironically, in the late 1990s, state governments increasingly imposed unfunded mandates on county and city governments. Evidently, many state governments were no more able to resist the temptation to set goals and make someone else pay for them than the federal government had long been.

As detailed in chapter 2, under federalism the state governments and the federal government are coequals, at least in theory. If the federal government encroaches too much on state prerogatives, the U.S. Supreme Court can step in and strike federal actions down. But states are not federations; indeed, within their own borders they are more accurately described as unitary systems. Local governments are not equal partners with state governments. In most cases, state governments are free to intervene in local arrangements as they please. Beginning in the late nineteenth century, many states did extend the sovereign powers of government to local governments by passing legislation that provided for home rule. Communities could enact charters and ordinances, change their names, and annex their neighbors without the permission of the legislature. They also controlled their own budgets and property taxes.

At the time, California was one of the strongest home rule states. In recent years, however, that has changed. California cities now control less than half of their discretionary spending. The state tells them what they must do with the rest. The situation is even worse for California's counties. They have the final say over less than one-third of the money they spend.[66]

Ballot Initiatives and the Budget Process. California's experience illustrates one of the most significant trends in state finances—the growing use of ballot initiatives to shape and restrain state tax systems. According to Bill Piper of the Initiative and Referendum Institute, voters put 130 tax initiatives on ballots nationwide from 1978 through 1999. Roughly two-thirds were antitax initiatives that cut, limited, or eliminated taxes in some way. Of these, 41 passed. In fact, a whopping 67 percent of all anti-tax initiatives that came up for a vote from 1996 through 1999 passed.[67] The net effect of all those initiatives was to create a massive headache for California's budget makers in the twenty-first century—in simple terms, they got to control less and less of the state's financial affairs, which were increasingly constrained or just put on automatic pilot.

The big problem with using direct democracy to make far-reaching budgetary decisions is that while citizens generally prefer low taxes, they also tend to favor fairly high levels of spending on a wide range of government programs and services. The end result is that state and local governments are required to do a lot of expensive things even as they are being legally required to limit their revenues. These same constraints also made it hard for some states to respond effectively to the fast-moving economic hits brought on by the Great Recession. California is just one of a number of ballot initiative states that are choking on tax and spending policies put in place by voters.

At their worst, antitax budget initiatives can paralyze state legislatures and local governments. At least fifteen states have passed initiatives or referendums that require tax decisions to gain supermajorities in a legislature in order to be approved. Assembling those supermajorities—typically two-thirds or three-quarters of the legislature—is an enormous challenge. In Montana, for example, the required supermajority is three-quarters of the legislature. State Senator Roy Brown once commented on the slim chances of changing tax policy with that obstacle in place: "We can't even get a three-fourths majority vote to go to the bathroom."[68]

Conclusion

State and local governments rely on six major types of taxes to fund the operations of government: property taxes; income taxes; sales taxes; sin, or excise, taxes; user fees; and gift taxes. Each of these taxes has distinct pros and cons. Local governments like property taxes because they set the rates and thus control exactly how much revenue is raised. However, when property taxes rise, seniors and people on fixed incomes often suffer. Income taxes tend to be more progressive; sales taxes are more regressive. The exact configuration of taxes in any given state reflects that state's history and political culture. Tax revenues, in turn, support the budget process by which state and local governments set their spending priorities. Increasingly, governments are relying on user fees—collected in relatively small amounts, but frequently—to supply key revenues.

State and local government finances can be difficult to unravel. However, this is an area that citizens are well-advised to watch. Not only do the budget decisions of state and local governments determine the services that individuals enjoy and how much they pay in taxes, but this also is often the arena in which the priorities of public life are sorted out. Is it fair or unfair to ask wealthy citizens to pay a higher percentage of their income in taxes? States such as Texas and Florida, which have no income taxes, have in a sense decided that it is unfair. States such as California, which has an income tax, have reached a different conclusion. Should everyone pay more in taxes to extend healthcare to low-income citizens? Massachusetts's tax policies suggest that its answer is yes. Many states in the Deep South have reached different conclusions. In short, the consequences of budget decisions are very real.

There is another reason to pay close attention to state and local finances. Over the past few years, the recovery from the most severe recession since World War II has been sluggish, and states' revenue systems are not set up to make the most of today's evolving economy. To get consistently back in the black, state financial structures almost certainly will need to change. States such as Tennessee that rely heavily on sales tax revenues face particularly serious long-term challenges. As Internet sales and dollars spent on untaxed services continue to grow, sales tax revenues in particular will most likely continue to falter. This will create a need for new revenue-raising measures. Yet states with ballot initiatives may well find new approaches blocked by antitax sentiments at the voting booth.

The Latest Research

The running theme of this chapter is that state and local budgets are all important. The process of how subnational governments get their money, spend their money and keep revenue and expenditures in a legally mandated balance is ground zero for the most important current policy debates in state and local politics.

Academic research typically lags behind current events by several years, so the latest research on taxing and spending is mostly not based on data from the past fiscal year or two. Nevertheless, the latest research has plenty of lessons for states and localities facing tough fiscal decisions and for voters who want to hold policymakers accountable for those decisions. The research discussed below reflects two central themes: (1) the real-life impact of state-level economic conditions and who does or does not get held responsible for those conditions, and (2) the efforts of states to deal with the effects of taxing and spending limitations.

• •

(Continued)

(Continued)

- **Brown, Adam R.** 2010. "Are Governors Responsible for the State Economy? Partisanship, Blame, and Divided Federalism." *Journal of Politics* 72: 605–615.

One of the long-standing debates in state politics scholarship is who gets held accountable for economic performance: the president, governors, or a combination of both. This is a particularly interesting time to revisit this question, as governors are pursuing different approaches to addressing state-level fiscal problems and President Barack Obama was recently reelected to a second term despite sluggish economic growth and unemployment rates flirting with double digits. Brown's study is interesting because it shows that voters assign blame or credit for economic fortunes not on state or national economic conditions or the policies of policymakers, but on the partisanship of who holds high executive office. Essentially, if the economy is doing poorly, voters who share their governor's partisanship will give the governor a pass—and blame the president if he is from the opposite party. If the economy is doing well, voters who identify with the governor's party will give that official the credit. This has the interesting implication that objective economic conditions are not as important to voters' judgment of the performance of a chief executive's taxing and spending policies as one might think.

- **Bifuloco, Robert, Beverly Bunch, William Duncombe, Mark Robbins, and William Simonsen.** 2012. "Debt and Deception: How States Avoid Making Hard Fiscal Decisions." *Public Administration Review* 72: 659–667.

The vast majority of state governments, as noted in this chapter, are legally required to have balanced budgets. This seems simple enough; doesn't it just mean that revenue has to equal expenditure? Well, sort of. Over the past few years, states have tried all sorts of accounting gimmicks to satisfy the letter if not the spirit of balanced budget mandates. Some of those gimmicks can obscure the real health of state government balance sheets. Bifuloco and his colleagues examine how several states borrow to finance current operating expenditures—something that seems mighty close to the deficit spending that state governments are supposedly prevented from doing. To make their financial statements look balanced, states underfund long-term obligations, defer payments, restructure debt, and borrow money from designated funds to cover general fund deficits. These moves are largely designed to get

state governments cash in the short term while piling up debt obligations in the long term. This study reveals the extent to which this sort of deficit financing in all but name goes on and raises questions about the transparency of state financial statements.

- **Bae, Suho, Seong-gin Moon, and Changhoon Jung.** 2012. "Economic Effects of State-Level Tax and Expenditure Limitations." *Public Administration Review* 72: 649–658.

More than thirty states have tax and expenditure limitations, or TELs. TELs are designed to place limits on how much state governments can tax and, at least according to their advocates, to help boost economic growth by keeping government smaller. This study, however, uses the comparative method to show that the theory does not work in practice. It looks at state economic data over a twenty-year period, comparing economic performance between states and the particular types of TEL mechanisms the states do or do not employ. The authors conclude that TELs have no impact on per capita income in states and have a negative effect on employment. Rather than boosting private-sector economic activity, TELs are more likely to simply reduce the production of public goods and services. The results of this study impart a cautionary—and controversial—lesson for states that are balancing budgets by cutting spending and avoiding tax hikes.

- **Kelly, Nathan, and Christopher Witko.** 2012. "Federalism and American Inequality." *Journal of Politics* 74: 414–426.

One of the most contentious issues in current American politics is income inequality. Do the haves get too much and the have-nots too little? If so, should government do anything to balance things out? In an era of tight budgets and bruising arguments over who, if anyone, should be taxed more and how that money should or should not be spent, answers to these questions are contested and controversial. This debate has played out primarily on a national stage, but this study uses the comparative method to show that state-level factors contribute greatly to income inequality. Kelly and Witko look at more than three decades' worth of state-level data and find that things such as a state's demographics, the degree of unionization in its labor pool, and the partisan makeup of its government are differences that make a difference to income inequality.

4

college.cqpress.com/
sites/govstateandlocal

Chapter Review

Key Concepts

- American Recovery and Reinvestment Act (ARRA) (p. 88)
- balanced budget (p. 102)
- bonds (p. 100)
- budget deficit, or shortfall (p. 88)
- budget process (p. 101)
- capital investments (p. 100)
- discretionary spending (p. 104)
- dividend (p. 99)
- entitlement (p. 105)
- estate taxes (p. 89)
- excise, or sin, taxes (p. 89)
- expenditures (p. 103)
- fiscal federalism (p. 105)
- fiscal year (p. 101)
- focused consumption taxes (p. 90)
- general obligation bonds (p. 100)
- gift taxes (p. 89)
- income taxes (p. 93)
- insurance trust funds (p. 95)
- intergovernmental transfers (p. 95)
- municipal bonds (p. 100)
- progressive tax system (p. 93)
- regressive taxes (p. 90)
- revenue bonds (p. 100)
- revenues (p. 88)
- sales taxes (p. 89)
- severance taxes (p. 95)
- tax burden (p. 90)
- tax capacity (p. 98)
- tax effort (p. 98)
- user fees (p. 89)

Suggested Web Sites

- **www.cbpp.org.** Web site of the Center on Budget and Policy Priorities. Founded in 1981, the center studies fiscal policy and public programs at the federal and state levels that affect low-income and moderate-income families and individuals. An excellent source of information on state budget issues.

- **www.census.gov/compendia/statab.** The U.S. Census Bureau provides an online version of the *Statistical Abstract of the United States.* Section 8, "State and Local Government Finances and Employment," provides a wealth of information on state and local government revenue and spending. The Census Bureau has announced that it is ceasing publication of the *Abstract* after 2012 as a budget-cutting measure. The 2013 version is to be published by a private company, ProQuest.

- **www.gao.gov.** Home page of the Government Accountability Office, which is tracking the use of ARRA stimulus funds in sixteen of the largest states.

- **www.nasbo.org.** Web site of the National Association of State Budget Officers.

- **www.ncsl.org.** Web site of the National Conference of State Legislatures. NCSL's fiscal program produces periodic state budget and tax updates and tracks state actions to close budget gaps.

- **www.recovery.gov.** The federal government's Web page dedicated to tracking ARRA.

STATE STATS

State Stats on Finance

Explore and compare data on the states! Go to college.cqpress.com/sites/govstateandlocal to do these exercises.

1. In 2011 the national per capita federal economic stimulus fund amount was $855. How does your state compare to this average? What might account for some of the variation? Is this the same trend as usual when it comes to your state receiving money from the federal government?

2. Does your state collect income tax? Sales tax? Which source of revenue does your state most heavily rely on? Do you think that this is a good thing? How does it compare with neighboring states?

3. Mississippi collects a relatively high amount of sales tax revenue per capita. Considering its population, why might some people have a problem with this taxation system? Explain why you agree or disagree. Now, look next door at Alabama. Why might these two neighboring states be so different in terms of sales tax revenue?

4. How much outstanding debt does your state have? If your state mandates a balanced budget, where did this debt come from? How does your state's debt load compare to the states around it?

5. Which state has the most local government direct general expenditures? Which state has the least? Why do you think that there is so much variation? Do these expenditures translate into jobs and services in these states?

Long lines were the order of the day for many voters on election day 2012, even though turnout was not at record levels. Many states have passed controversial laws in recent years that require individuals to present identification before they can vote.

Political Attitudes and Participation

VENTING AND VOTING

- What causes some states or localities to change party preferences?
- How do state regulations affect voting?
- How do politicians tune in to what citizens are thinking?

There was something striking about Republican presidential nominee Mitt Romney's pick of Wisconsin congressman Paul Ryan as his running mate in August 2012. Ryan is Catholic, while Romney, the former governor of Massachusetts, is Mormon. The pick showed how few white, Anglo-Saxon Protestants—both derided and celebrated as "WASPs"—are still in place at the top of the U.S. government structure.

Barack Obama, of course, is the nation's first African American president. Joe Biden, his vice president, is Catholic—as are John Boehner, Speaker of the House, and Nancy Pelosi, House minority leader. Every member of the U.S. Supreme Court is either Jewish or Catholic, and Harry Reid, the Senate Democratic leader, is Mormon. Only Mitch McConnell, the Republican leader in the Senate, is a WASP. "The no-Protestant ticket is a reminder: the top male WASP in government is the Senate minority leader—who's married to an Asian American," John J. Pitney Jr., a professor of government at Claremont McKenna College, tweeted the day of the Ryan pick.[1]

While there are still a lot of white males in that bunch, the complete political dominance of WASPs with a Y chromosome is increasingly a thing of the past. Women and racial, ethnic, and religious minorities are becoming a greater presence at the peak of government power, and not just federal government power. When Romney picked Ryan as his running mate, across the fifty states there were six women governors, two Hispanic governors, one African American governor, and two governors of Indian descent. This all reflects demographic changes taking place in the country at large. William H. Frey, a demographer at the Brookings Institution, has suggested that the electorate that propelled Obama to power in 2008 offered a possible glimpse into the future of American politics. It is both "post-ethnic" (candidates can appeal to upper-income whites as well as racial minorities) and "post-boomer" (candidates can appeal across age groups). Frey cautioned that the political future hasn't yet fully arrived, but the long-term trends point in that direction—even more so after Obama's reelection victory over the Romney-Ryan ticket, which was driven largely by his support among African Americans, Hispanics, Asian Americans, young people, college-educated voters and women.[2] Political professionals are paying close attention to those trends. As long ago as the release of the 2000 census figures, some Republican strategists recognized that their party was facing a serious long-term demographic challenge. Rich Bond, a former Republican National Committee chairman, told the *Washington Post,* "We've taken white guys about as far as that group can go. We are in need of diversity, women, Latino, African-American, Asian."[3]

Consider that during the 1950s, whites made up more than 90 percent of the electorate (95 percent in 1952).[4] During the decades since, African Americans have secured their place in the voting booth through the passage of civil rights laws, and the Latino share of the population has skyrocketed. In 2012, whites made up 72 percent of the electorate, their lowest share ever. African Americans made up 13 percent of the electorate, and Hispanics constituted 10 percent, according to exit polls. Generally speaking, voting participation has increased among ethnic minorities since 2004, while among eligible whites voting has declined.

Despite the continuing shift toward demographics traditionally associated with Democratic voters, Republicans have won plenty of elections. In 2010 many groups were not happy with their government and expressed that dissatisfaction by hammering Democrats and rewarding Republicans.

All this demonstrates two things. First, demographics are not destiny. Although many groups show a propensity for voting for one party or the other—for example, African Americans for Democrats, regular churchgoers for the GOP—no group votes entirely as a bloc. Second, even groups that give overwhelming support to one party's candidates at a particular time do not do so forever.

The same lessons generally apply to states. During the presidency of George W. Bush, pundits routinely characterized states as either "Republican red" or "Democratic blue" (based on the colors that broadcast and cable television networks used to show how states voted on election nights). But that was never entirely accurate. Some states have tended to vote one way for president but the opposite for governor or other important offices. Localities such as counties increasingly tend to vote for one party over the other— that's one reason there are so few competitive U.S. House or state legislative seats. Still, even in the bluest of blue or reddest of red communities there are always exceptions. This is why political pros are increasingly borrowing technology and demographic breakdowns from consumer marketers. Political data mining has evolved far beyond the old idea that you can guess a voter's partisan leanings by looking at the types of magazines he or she subscribes to. Now, campaigns access all manner of consumer databases, gleaning such near-complete portraits of individuals' habits and inclinations as to threaten the sanctity of the secret ballot, according to Chris Evans, managing editor of the *Minnesota Journal of Law, Science & Technology.* "The goal of these 'digital dossiers' is to profile likely voters and identify traits that predict voting habits," Evans wrote in 2012. "Political data-mining has proven to be a winning election tactic, but the resulting erosion of voter privacy has gone unabated."[5]

The reason for this micro-level attention to voters, of course, is that it is difficult to predict how people will vote based just on where they live. It is a safer bet to examine the issues they care about and the interest groups they belong to. Interest groups, as discussed at greater length in chapter 6, are organizations that attempt to influence policymakers. Although most people will rarely, if ever, call or write to their members of Congress or state officials, many of them will belong to groups that make the case for particular positions on given issues.

Interest groups can bring resources to a campaign in return for attention to their issues by candidates. But all voters do not belong to interest groups—or think of themselves as being part of any—and politicians know that their careers depend on more than financial contributions from these organized interests. Come election time, they need the support of the vast majority of people who do not belong to such groups and who do not pay close attention to politics on a regular basis.

Given all this, how do politicians figure out what the voters back home are thinking when it seems that the only people they hear from at the capitol or city hall are part of some organized group? How can they pay attention to the needs and desires of the majority of constituents who do not speak out and do not subscribe to *Guns & Ammo,* much less to their local newspaper?

This chapter answers those questions, and also looks at how voters maintain or change the political cultures and preferences of their states and districts over time. Some of the mechanisms for change discussed include elections and the avenues for direct democracy, such as ballot initiatives and referendums. Public opinion—and how and whether politicians respond to it—is another factor that influences political outcomes.

Elections

Unquestionably, we have created an odd paradox as a nation. We like elections—we hold more of them than any other country on earth—yet we consistently score one of the lowest voter turnout rates of any democracy in the world.

State political cultures are reflected and sustained through elections, when a majority or **plurality** of voters elects officials who more or less reflect the political beliefs of the majority or plurality. The use of elections to select the holders of public office is the fundamental process of representative democracies. More bluntly, elections are the main way that the will of the people connects to and influences the actions of government. Election laws are set and controlled by the states, and each state must determine what constitutes a valid vote. There has long been a great deal of variation among states regarding how easy or how hard it is for citizens to vote. Some of the differences have been smoothed away in recent years by federal laws and court decisions, but many remain, and they largely reflect the types of political cultures that Elazar describes (and that are outlined in the preceding chapters).

These differences, in turn, affect national politics. The way that people vote in their own states—the type of access they have to the ballot—helps determine the success or failure of presidential candidates and the makeup of Congress. With numerous states in recent years enacting voter identification requirements and other restrictions that make it harder for people to register and vote, voting rights have reemerged as one of the most salient issues in American politics.

But differences in election laws are not the only reason one state may tend to vote differently than its neighbors, in partisan terms. For about one hundred years after the Civil War, for example, Republicans were not a true national party. They had next to no presence in the South, which still resented Republican intrusions during the Civil War and Reconstruction in support of abolition, suffrage, and equal opportunity for African Americans. That is one reason Democrats held the region for decades. In fact, the Republican Party of the nineteenth century bore a closer resemblance in some ways to the Democratic Party of today than to its twenty-first-century GOP descendant. Times and political parties change, however. These days, the South is one of the pillars of Republican strength. The region's continuing conservatism now fits well within the GOP.

Southern states and the less populous, heavily rural states of the Mountain West, such as Idaho, Wyoming, and Montana, tilt toward Republican interests and form a bloc that helps elect presidents through its disproportionate share of the electoral college. Each state's electoral college

---

Plurality
The highest number of votes garnered by any of the candidates for a particular office but short of an outright majority.

votes are equal to the size of its congressional delegation. Because each state is guaranteed at least two U.S. senators and one U.S. representative, the electoral college gives a minimum of three votes to each state, regardless of population. This means that the voting power of smaller states in the electoral college is disproportionately larger than the states' population, whereas the voting power of bigger states is disproportionately lower.

For example, in 2012 California had fifty-five electoral votes to represent a population of nearly 37.7 million. In that presidential election, then, each of California's electoral college votes represented about 685,000 people. Contrast that with Wyoming, which had the minimum of three electoral college votes but had a population of only about 568,000. Each of Wyoming's electoral college votes, in other words, represented nearly 190,000 people. Political analyst Steven Hill, director of the political reform program at the New America Foundation, calls this "affirmative action for low-population states."[6] This is one reason George W. Bush was able to win the presidency in 2000 despite losing the popular vote. This imbalance in the representation of electoral college votes leads to periodic efforts by groups that want to make sure no one ends up in the White House with fewer popular votes than the opponent—an incredibly tough reform to pull off without amending the constitution. In recent years, for example, states such as Maryland, Massachusetts, and California have enacted laws that will require them to award their electoral votes according to national popular vote percentages, but those measures won't take effect until a preponderance of states are on board with the idea. In states where the GOP controls the legislature but voters have tended to prefer Democratic presidential candidates, such as Pennsylvania and Virginia, legislators have talked about awarding electoral votes by congressional district rather than sticking with the traditional winner-take-all system. But those efforts have yet to meet with success.

The Mountain West, meanwhile, may also be shifting in terms of partisan leanings. No state within the region supported a Democrat for president between 1968 and 1998, but in 2008 Barack Obama carried Colorado, Nevada, and New Mexico. He won all three states again in 2012, and Democrats have their eye on Arizona for the future. The region retains its traditional libertarian response to government in that it wants to be left alone by a federal government that owns the vast majority of the land in many western states. But the region's demographics have changed, and this shift has changed its politics to some extent. There have been dramatic increases in the minority share of the population as well as large influxes of other new citizens from outside the region, with the bulk of folks now living in metropolitan areas.[7]

Similar resistance in the suburbs to conservative stances on social issues has helped Democrats in recent elections. In St. Louis County, Missouri, for instance, Democrat Jeanne Kirkton won a state House seat in 2008 that had been Republican as long as anyone could remember; it had been filled for the previous thirty-two years by Republican women who were fiscally conservative but who all supported abortion rights and were liberal on other social issues. That year, Republican primary voters rejected a moderate female candidate in favor of a man who took a hard line against abortion and favored school vouchers. Kirkton won on a platform of support for gun control and stem-cell research, while Jay Nixon carried the county in winning back the governorship for the Democrats.

In Missouri, as the Democratic core vote continued to extend outward from the central city of St. Louis, Republicans were left with less room with which to work. They dominate Missouri's legislature and congressional delegation, but in statewide races they need to turn out voters en masse in dozens of sparsely populated rural and exurban counties to offset not just the big cities but also their recent losses in the suburbs. In 2012, Republicans gained a supermajority in both legislative chambers, but Democrats won every statewide race but one. "Running statewide for a Republican is a harder challenge," said Mike Gibbons, a former GOP state senator from St. Louis County who lost in his 2008 bid for state attorney general. "You have to gain a substantial margin in the smaller counties. That means you have to travel all over the state, and you also have to compete in suburban areas to hold them close."[8]

A similar dynamic has played out in suburban parts of California, Virginia, New York, and numerous other states in recent years, as suburbs have become more dense and diverse, with more immigrants settling outside the central cities that had long been most attractive to newcomers. "The so-called inner-ring suburbs are now almost as dense and almost as politically Democratic as the central cities," says Lawrence Levy, director of the Center for Suburban Studies, at Long Island's Hofstra University.[9]

A Voice for the Public

Elections may be how citizens can speak out for their beliefs, and they may give states a voice in national politics, but you wouldn't know it from the interest they generate among the general public. The franchise appears to be diminishing, with the act of voting on the decline. People do not feel well connected to government. Some hate it. Less than half the voting-age population cast ballots in presidential elections. In elections in which congressional or statewide offices are at the top of the ticket, the percentage drops to less than 40 percent. For municipal elections, turnout rates are generally less than 20 percent.

Voting does tend to pick up for competitive races, when voters feel like they have a genuine choice and might make a real difference. The major political parties, however, have reconciled themselves to the reality that millions of people feel their votes don't count. (Sometimes the parties are even accused of suppressing turnout by using negative ads and other means to sour people who might vote for the other side.)

Upset that an estimated 4 million evangelical Christians did not vote in 2000, Karl Rove, President George W. Bush's lead political adviser, designed a reelection campaign in 2004 to motivate these voters through the use of such issues as limitations on stem-cell research and bans on gay marriage. The campaign did use other issues to appeal to other blocs of voters, but it was designed primarily to motivate Bush's base voters rather than to reach across the political spectrum and

appeal more broadly. The strategy worked, at least in the short run. Conversely, in the run-up to his reelection bid in 2012, Obama sought to appeal to various Democratic constituencies; for example, he courted Latinos and gays, respectively, by halting federal efforts to deport many younger illegal immigrants and by coming out in favor of same-sex marriage, and he tried to cut into Republican rival Mitt Romney's support among working-class voters by accusing him of having sent jobs overseas during his business career.

> The idea that voters are most easily motivated by appeals to a few core issues is also related to the growing use of ballot initiatives as a means of promoting turnout. For instance, the numbers of conservative Ohio voters who turned out to cast their ballots in favor of a constitutional ban on gay marriage in 2004 are said to have helped Bush carry that year's most contested state.

The idea that voters are most easily motivated by appeals to a few core issues is also related to the growing use of ballot initiatives as a means of promoting turnout. For instance, the numbers of conservative Ohio voters who turned out to cast their ballots in favor of a constitutional ban on gay marriage in 2004 are said to have helped Bush carry that year's most contested state. Two years later, liberals, looking for weapons of their own, ran initiatives for minimum wage increases on half a dozen state ballots. Some political scientists have found evidence that controversial ballot initiatives do increase turnout, particularly in nonpresidential election years.[10]

But the idea that most voters are motivated by a single issue, or a handful of issues, oversimplifies things in much the same way that the red-state/blue-state divide flattens our perception of actual electoral behavior. It is true that the majority of voters remain loyal to one party over the other throughout most of their voting lives. They can be convinced to cast their votes—or even to change their votes—by any number of factors. The state of the economy, the health of a state's budget, corruption scandals, or the course of a military conflict may change minds and voting habits. "Each election forces one to revisit such topics as to what's effective in voter mobilization or who you aim at," says independent political analyst Rhodes Cook.[11]

After 2008, the story seemed to be young voters. Turnout rates have traditionally been abysmal for college students and other young people. Young voters turned out in record numbers for Obama in 2008 but returned to their usual habits of apathy in the congressional and state elections of 2010. Despite widespread media predictions that young voters would stay home in 2012, voters under thirty again gave heavy support to Obama and made up a slightly larger share of the electorate than they had four years earlier.

State Supervision of Elections

It seems obvious to say, but elections are fundamental to democracy. They are the source of authority for governmental decisions and power. On these occasions, a majority of eligible citizens presumably give their blessing to office-holders who will determine the course of policy. Elections are the main conduit through which citizens express their pleasure or displeasure with governmental decisions. If voters are unhappy with the decisions that their elected officials have made, they can turn them out of office at the next election. For all the system's faults, politicians and parties have to win approval from voters at regularly scheduled intervals if they are to remain in power.

The U.S. Constitution gives states the authority to determine "the times, places and manner of holding elections." In nearly every state, the secretary of state has the practical duty of running elections: setting dates, qualifying candidates, and printing and counting the ballots. In a few states, the lieutenant governor or a state election board oversees these chores. The states, in turn, rely on the counties or, in some cases, cities to run the polls themselves. The localities draw precinct boundaries and set up and supervise polling places. In many cases, they have the main responsibility for registering voters. Following an election, county officials count up the ballots and report the results to the appropriate individual, such as the secretary of state, who then tabulates and certifies the totals.

The styles of the ballots used vary from state to state. California currently uses a random alphabet system to decide the order in which candidate names appear, rotating the starting letter of that alphabet in each state assembly district. The **office group ballot**, also known as the **Massachusetts ballot**, lists candidates' names, followed by their party designations, under the title of the office they are seeking (governor, state representative, and so on). The other major type of ballot is the **party column ballot**, or the **Indiana ballot**, which "arranges the candidates for each office in columns according to their party designation."[12] Fifteen states make it even easier for citizens to vote for party nominees—voters can cast a **straight ticket** vote for all of one party's candidates with one computer click or pull of the lever. This is a practice in decline, however; several states have abolished it, most recently Wisconsin in 2011.[13]

Each state's election code determines the specific details about ballots and, perhaps most important, the order in which offices and candidates will appear. This varies considerably among the states. By 1992, about 80 percent of the states had replaced paper ballots with punch cards, machines in which voters pull a lever next to the names of the candidates of their choice, or optical-scan voting machines.[14] Voters in most states now use electronic systems resembling automated teller machines (ATMs), but many

---

Office Group (Massachusetts) Ballot
A ballot in which candidates are listed by name under the title of the office they are seeking.

Party Column (Indiana) Ballot
A ballot in which the names of candidates are divided into columns arranged according to political party.

Straight Ticket
Originally, a type of ballot that allowed voters to pick all of one party's candidates at once; today, voting a straight ticket refers to voting for all of one party's candidates for various offices—for instance, voting for all Democrats or all Republicans.

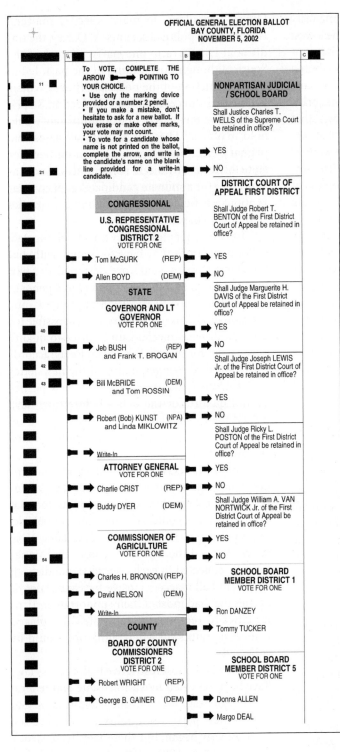

OFFICIAL GENERAL ELECTION BALLOT
BAY COUNTY, FLORIDA
NOVEMBER 5, 2002

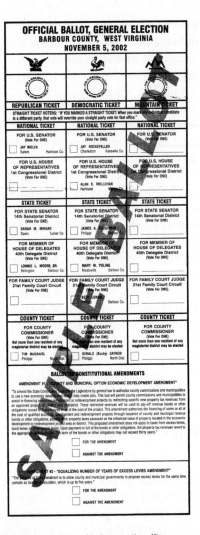

OFFICIAL BALLOT, GENERAL ELECTION
BARBOUR COUNTY, WEST VIRGINIA
NOVEMBER 5, 2002

The two main types of ballots are the office group ballot and the party column ballot. These sample ballots from elections in Florida and West Virginia show the differences between the two basic approaches to ballot design. The West Virginia ballot exemplifies the party column ballot, which lists the candidates in columns that indicate their party designations. The Florida ballot, on the other hand, emphasizes office rather than party. This is the key feature of the office group ballot, which lists candidates by name and party under the title of the office they are running for.

states require a paper trail to allow for verification of the electronic results. All but a handful of states tabulate votes for write-in candidates, although victories or even significant showings by such candidates are few and far between.

A few cities, including Minneapolis and San Francisco, use instant-runoff voting (IRV) for municipal elections. Rather than picking one candidate, voters rank all the choices. If one candidate receives more than 50 percent of the first-choice vote, he or she wins. If no one receives a majority of first-choice votes, the candidate with the lowest number of votes is disqualified and his or her supporters' second-place choices are redistributed among the remaining candidates. This process continues until someone emerges with a majority. The benefit of such a system, supporters say, is that a candidate who is acceptable to a majority of voters will win, as opposed to the outcome in a winner-take-all election in which a candidate with only, say, 30–40 percent of the vote comes out on top of a large split field. Both the Heisman Trophy winner and the winner of the Academy Award for Best Picture are now determined by an IRV or preferential voting system. But instant-runoff voting has its critics, who say it can result in victories for candidates who were the first choice of few. Jean Quan, for instance, was elected mayor of Oakland, California, in 2010 after being picked as the first choice of just 24 percent of voters. Burlington, Vermont, and Aspen, Colorado, have abandoned the IRV method after complaints that it left voters confused.[15]

Regulating the Parties

A state's authority to print ballots or purchase voting software gives it enormous control over which parties and candidates are presented to the voters. Until the late nineteenth century, parties themselves printed the ballots, a system that obviously encouraged voters to select a straight ticket of their chosen party's nominees. The advent of the **secret ballot**, also known as the **Australian ballot**, led the states to print their own ballots and, therefore, to determine which parties should appear on ballots. "From there," writes Kay Lawson, a retired San Francisco State University political scientist, "it seemed but a short step to requiring that parties show a minimum level of support to qualify."[16]

The Republican and Democratic parties are themselves regulated at the state level by a bewildering array of varying state laws. Some states provide detailed regulations for party organization, activities, and nominating procedures.

Secret (Australian) Ballot
A ballot printed by a state that allows voters to pick and choose among different candidates and party preferences in private.

Others are silent on many specific matters. According to political scientist V. O. Key, the traditional Democratic one-party control of the South, although now a thing of the past, led to the introduction of the political primary. Voters had no real choice in the general election, so primaries gave them a say in who ultimately would hold an office.[17] These days, nearly all states hold primary elections to pick party nominees for state offices, although some states, such as Virginia, still nominate candidates at party conventions. (A fuller discussion of political parties is found in chapter 6.)

The two major parties may not like all the state ballot regulations they have to comply with, but the rules in many states are designed to favor them over new or minor parties and independent candidates. Prior to the 1968 Supreme Court decision in *Williams v. Rhodes,* it was possible for states to have no mechanism in place to qualify new parties for their ballots. Even today, according to Richard Winger, editor of the newsletter *Ballot Access News,* in eleven states new parties cannot qualify for the ballot before they have picked their candidates, who must be listed on their ballot access petition, the collection of voters' signatures.[18]

The Court's decision meant that a state no longer could require that a certain percentage of signatures be collected in each county. But that did not mean states could not erect new roadblocks to keep out aspiring parties or candidates. Nine states changed their laws to require that signatures be collected in each congressional district. This kept ballot access elusive for candidates or parties that had most of their support in particular cities or regions. Fifteen states also placed time constraints on when signatures could be collected.

Some of the most restrictive ballot access laws have been repealed by various state and federal courts. For example, Ohio and California used to require new parties to qualify even before the election year began, but these laws were struck down in 2006 and 2012, respectively. Virginia formerly blocked petitioners from gathering signatures outside their home congressional districts, but that law was also struck down in 2012. In West Virginia the law used to require petition

Policy in Practice

Vote Counts More Accurate—but Still Not Perfect

Perhaps nothing demonstrates more clearly how much better states and counties have gotten at counting votes than a look at how other entities do it.

Republican presidential caucuses in 2012 were plagued with problems. Several states were embarrassed by snafus following their caucuses, which are run by political parties rather than by public officials.

In Iowa, an eight-vote election-night win for Mitt Romney was later converted into a thirty-four-vote victory for Rick Santorum, with party officials admitting that they didn't, in fact, know the actual number. (The state party chair resigned.) Counting of caucus votes was slow enough in Nevada to raise doubts during the delay, while in Maine, the GOP decided to declare Romney the statewide winner even before some counties had held their caucuses. "It's been stunning to watch," said Cathy Cox, a former Georgia secretary of state. "Caucus voting looks like the Wild West of voting."

Election experts agree that vote counting has generally gotten quicker and more accurate since presidential election results in Florida were disputed all the way up to the U.S. Supreme Court in 2000. After that controversy, the federal government devoted billions of dollars to help states modernize their voting machinery, leading to widespread adoption of electronic, touch-screen voting.

But voting in the United States is a highly decentralized process. Every state has its own rules, which are then generally implemented separately by individual counties. State and county election officials continue to suffer embarrassing moments, as when New York City found nearly 200,000 uncounted votes a month after the general election in 2010, an oversight Mayor Michael Bloomberg called "a royal screw-up."

Despite concerns raised from the start about electronic voting, such screw-ups are generally caused by human error. Most New York State jurisdictions download the votes cast on voting machines onto flash drives that are taken to a central computer for counting. The problems in New York City were the result of a system of counting votes by hand, with district poll workers writing results out on tally sheets that get delivered (one hopes) by hand to a central counting house.

Those kinds of problems might recur in other places. With federal dollars from the Help America Vote Act (HAVA) of 2002 pretty much having run dry, many jurisdictions are strapped when it comes time to buy new machines. And some don't want to. After being pressed by activists nervous about the lack of paper trails from electronic machines and the risks of vote tampering through hacking, the Virginia General Assembly in 2007 banned local governments from buying new touch-screen voting machines when the current electronic models wear out. Voters instead will be using a scanning system that requires them to mark paper ballots and then scan them into a machine.

Problems caused by the improper reading of paper ballots are what spurred innovations in voting machines over the past decade. And concerns remain about electronic voting machines. In at least some polling places in sixteen states, machines don't produce any paper trail that can be used as a backup in case of a recount or dispute. And about half the states have systems that are vulnerable to hacking, especially when it comes to military personnel voting overseas, according to a 2012 study by researchers at Rutgers Law School. That means the job of counting votes remains more complicated than it looks—as GOP caucus organizers have found. "If you can't produce pretty instantaneous results, people are going to lose confidence in the results and you're going to open up the floodgates to opportunities for fraud," says Cox, the former Georgia official.

Source: Adapted from Alan Greenblatt, "Caucus System Cracks Revealed during 2012 GOP Primary Season," *Governing,* May 2012.

circulators who were trying to collect signatures to tell everyone they approached, "If you sign my petition, you can't vote in the primary." That happened to not be true—but it was the law, until a court struck it down in 2004. Why make a law requiring circulators to fib to voters? Well, such a fib benefits the major parties by keeping out the competition, and the major parties write the laws.

These sorts of laws benefiting political parties, if not the democratic process, remain on the books in various places. In Texas, voters who participate in major-party primaries are not allowed to sign petitions to get new parties on the ballot; the state also requires citizens to know their voter registration numbers and to affix those numbers next to their signatures on petitions. Quick— what's your voter registration number? In its 1971 decision in *Jenness v. Fortson,* the Supreme Court upheld a Georgia law that requires minor parties or independent candidates to collect signatures that represent 5 percent of registered voters. In 1986, the Georgia legislature lowered that threshold to 1 percent, but that still means more than 50,000 signatures, a bar no one has been able to meet since 2000. "This is a very, very major organizational undertaking," Larry Jacobs, a political scientist at the University of Minnesota, said about minor-party ballot access. "It's like building an army from scratch."[19]

For third-party and independent candidates, then, it can be a real challenge to gain access to the ballot. Of course, how hard or easy it is for these political outsiders to get on the ballot varies from state to state. As with everything else, there are differences that make a difference. Given what we know about Elazar's theory regarding southern, or traditionalistic, states and their hierarchical attitude toward politics, it should not surprise us that states such as Alabama, North Carolina, and Oklahoma have the most restrictive ballot access laws. That does not mean that hundreds of minor party and independent candidates have not overcome all these hurdles and more to win spots on statewide ballots. A few of them have even won election as governor— for instance, in Minnesota in 1998, Maine in 1994 and 1998, and Rhode Island in 2010 (though note that all three of these examples involve moralistic or

individualistic states). Their place on a ballot one year, however, is no guarantee that members of their parties will qualify the next time around. Alabama requires that a minor party poll at least 20 percent of the vote for governor to win an automatic qualification for the next ballot. New Jersey, Oklahoma, and Virginia require at least 10 percent, and Pennsylvania requires 15 percent, or more than 1 million votes. Given all the restrictions, Lawson concludes, "The laws have been effective in keeping minor parties off the ballot in election after election."[20]

Minor-party candidates are concerned about ballot access in more progressive states as well. Since 2008, Washington State has used a top-two or **blanket primary** system, in which the top two finishers proceed to the general election, regardless of party. California voters adopted the same system in 2010. The blanket primary presents a big obstacle to minor parties and independent candidates; primary elections tend to be low-turnout affairs dominated by voters who are major-party partisans. As a result, independents and minor-party candidates rarely have the chance to appear on general election ballots. "It's the biggest threat to independent and third parties in the last 50 years," complained Christina Tobin, a Libertarian Party candidate for California secretary of state in 2010.[21]

Why all the restrictions? Keeping minor parties off the ballot naturally helps the two major parties. Those who are in power control the rules that keep them in power. "VA's D legislature thought the rules up, knowing they would benefit themselves & friends," tweeted Larry Sabato, director of the University of Virginia's Center for Politics, in 2011. "Then Rs, once in power, liked restrictions too."[22]

Restricting Voters

States do not just regulate the access of parties to the ballot; they also regulate the interaction of

---

Blanket Primary
An initial round of voting in which candidates from all parties appear on the same ballot, with the top two vote-getters proceeding on to the general election.

citizens with that ballot. They determine who can register to vote and how they can register. Changes in federal law over the years have removed many of the barriers that states had once imposed to restrict voting rights, those based on property ownership, literacy, race, sex, and age. But there are still differences among states in how easy or difficult it is for citizens to register to vote—a necessary step toward having the chance to vote in every state except North Dakota, which does not require voter registration. Those differences have become more pronounced in recent years, with seventeen states passing new laws to tighten registration or voting requirements in 2011 and 2012 alone.

In the early years of the nation, most eastern states required citizens to own property in order to be eligible to vote. Those requirements diminished over time, in large part because the western frontier states lacked the type of class structure that reinforced them. The eastern states, however, soon came up with the idea of imposing literacy tests. Before they could vote, new immigrants had to demonstrate knowledge of the state constitution or other complex issues to the satisfaction of the local election official.[23] Native whites who were illiterate often were exempted from this requirement. Southern states took up literacy testing as a means of keeping African Americans from voting, as African Americans generally received an inadequate education in schools segregated by race. Literacy tests remained a part of the southern legal landscape until the federal Voting Rights Act of 1965 barred them. Southern states also sometimes imposed poll taxes as a means of disenfranchising African Americans and some poor whites until the Supreme Court found them unconstitutional in 1966. (See the box "A Difference That Makes a Difference: How Some States Discourage Voters.")

Several amendments to the U.S. Constitution expanded voting rights to include minorities and women. The Fifteenth Amendment, passed following the Civil War, was meant to end discrimination against black men seeking to vote. Until the civil rights movement of the 1960s, however, southern states effectively bypassed the provisions of the amendment for a century through literacy tests, intimidation, and other means.

The Voting Rights Act of 1965 gave the federal government the authority to review state requirements for registration and voting. In 1964, the Twenty-Fourth Amendment banned the use of poll taxes meant to keep African Americans and other poor people from voting. Women received the right to vote with the ratification of the Nineteenth Amendment in 1920. The voting age was lowered to eighteen by the Twenty-Sixth Amendment in 1971. In 1993, Congress passed what became known as the "motor voter" law, which requires states to allow citizens to register to vote when they take tests to receive their driver's licenses.

Why all the effort to get people registered to vote? The purpose of registering voters is to prevent fraud. Registration is intended to stop people from voting more than once or outside their home jurisdictions. This makes sense, but throughout the nation's history, many states have used registration laws as a means of making voting inaccessible to some.

Voter fraud has become a contentious topic in recent years, with opinion largely split along partisan lines. Republicans say such measures as requiring each voter to show a form of photo identification are necessary to guard against fraud, while Democrats argue that the GOP is simply trying to block access by poor people and members of minority groups, who are least likely to have such identification—and most likely to vote Democratic. In 2008, the Supreme Court upheld a 2005 Indiana law requiring that anyone seeking to vote produce a government-used photo ID at the polls, such as a passport or driver's license. "This notion that somehow voter fraud is a dirty word, I don't understand it, because you're talking about people stealing votes, canceling out legitimate votes," Attorney General Alberto Gonzales testified in 2007.[24]

Political scientist Andrew Hacker wrote after the decision that the justices failed to take into account the hardships that requiring a "license to vote"

About 18 percent of the total number of registered voters in Minnesota—542,257—registered to vote on election day in 2008. Minnesota is one of just six states to allow same-day registration.

would impose on the 15 percent of Indiana's voting-age population who have no driver's license or other photo identification. Hacker noted that in Milwaukee County, Wisconsin, 53 percent of African Americans lacked a driver's license, compared with 15 percent of the adult white population statewide. "Requiring a driver's license to vote has a disparate racial impact, a finding that once commanded judicial notice," Hacker wrote.[25]

Voter Turnout

Even as some states are tightening requirements for voter registration, with some now requiring individuals to provide proof of citizenship, others are seeking to make the mechanics of registering easier. In August 2012, Maryland became the tenth state to allow citizens to register to vote online. That same month, Washington State unveiled an app that allows citizens to register using personal data through Facebook. "In this age of social media and more people going online for services, this is a natural way to introduce people to online registration and leverage the power of friends on Facebook to get more people registered," said Shane Hamlin, Washington's co-director of elections.[26]

But efforts to ease registration do not always lead to higher voter turnout. The motor voter law produced an initial spike in registration, but it had little or no effect on the number of people voting. According to Curtis Gans of the Committee for the Study of the American Electorate at American University, **voter turnout** rates have declined by about 25 percent over the past forty years.[27] Turnout did spike for the hotly contested 2004 presidential race, but it dropped again in 2006. A record 131 million Americans cast votes in 2008, but that number dropped by about 5 million four years later. There are countless reasons voter turnout has decreased, including a general disaffection with politics and government, a measurable decline in civic education and newspaper reading, a weakening of such civic-minded institutions as student government and unions, and the changing role of political parties away from engaging and educating voters and toward raising money and providing services to candidates.

Turnout rates are in decline, but they are not declining uniformly across the states. There are many reasons some states have turnout rates 20 percentage points higher than others, most of which are related to political culture, demographics, and party competition.

In general, the closer you live to Canada, the more likely you are to vote. The states with turnout rates of more than 70 percent for the 2008 presidential election, including New Hampshire, Iowa, and Wisconsin, were mostly in the northern tier of the country. The states with lower turnout rates, including Arkansas, Hawaii, Tennessee, and Utah, are in the South or far West. (See Table 5-1.) What explains the difference? Culture, for one thing. Elazar's theory about moralistic states appears to hold up, at least as far as voter turnout goes. "You're talking about states with fairly vigorous political parties, communications media that do cover politics and an educational system more geared toward citizen engagement than other parts of the country," says Gans. A big state such as California has a mix of cultures—individualistic and moralistic—according to Elazar.

It is not just political culture that makes a difference. Demographics also matter, and moralistic states tend to be more likely to have demographic profiles favorable to turnout. People are more likely to vote if they are better educated, if they are elderly, and if they are white. "In states with high percentage of minorities, you're going to have low turnout," says Steven Hill of the New America Foundation. "States with higher voter turnout, such as Minnesota and Maine, tend to be fairly white states."[28] Such moralistic states historically also have bred strong two-party competition. This tends to increase turnout. Citizens in states or districts dominated by one party tend not to vote as eagerly. Their candidate of choice is certain to win—or to lose if they are "orphaned" voters whose party is weak in their home state or district. What we see here are differences that interact with other differences to produce variation in turnout.

Voter Turnout
The percentage of voting-eligible citizens who register to vote and do vote.

TABLE 5-1

Percentage of the Voting-Age Population Casting Ballots in the 2012 Presidential Election

Rank	State	Percentage of Total Voting-Age Population	Elazar Classification	Rank	State	Percentage of Total Voting-Age Population	Elazar Classification
1	Minnesota	71.3	Moralistic	27	District of Columbia	56.8	
2	Wisconsin	69.4	Moralistic	28	Connecticut	55.6	Individualistic
3	New Hampshire	67.8	Moralistic	29	Idaho	55.5	Moralistic
4	Iowa	67.1	Moralistic	30	Florida	55.2	Traditionalistic
5	Maine	66.9	Moralistic	31	Alaska	55.1	Individualistic
6	Colorado	68.1	Moralistic	32	South Carolina	53.8	Traditionalistic
7	Ohio	65.2	Individualistic	33	Kansas	53.5	Moralistic
8	Michigan	62.0	Moralistic	34	Rhode Island	53.4	Individualistic
9	Montana	61.6	Moralistic	35	Illinois	53.3	Individualistic
10	Virginia	60.8	Traditionalistic	36	New Jersey	53.3	Individualistic
11	Massachusetts	60.4	Individualistic	37	Kentucky	53.2	Traditionalistic
12	North Carolina	60.2	Traditionalistic	38	Indiana	56.0	Individualistic
13	Maryland	59.6	Individualistic	39	Georgia	52.2	Traditionalistic
14	Missouri	59.5	Individualistic	40	Utah	51.4	Moralistic
15	North Dakota	59.4	Moralistic	41	New Mexico	49.5	Traditionalistic
16	Vermont	59.3	Moralistic	42	Tennessee	49.4	Traditionalistic
17	Oregon	58.6	Moralistic	43	Nevada	48.7	Individualistic
18	Washington	58.3	Moralistic	44	Arkansas	47.5	Traditionalistic
19	Delaware	58.0	Individualistic	45	Arizona	46.5	Traditionalistic
20	South Dakota	57.7	Moralistic	46	New York	46.2	Individualistic
21	Mississippi	57.3	Traditionalistic	47	Oklahoma	46.2	Traditionalistic
22	Louisiana	57.1	Traditionalistic	48	West Virginia	45.5	Traditionalistic
23	Pennsylvania	57.1	Individualistic	49	California	45.1	Moralistic
24	Nebraska	56.8	Individualistic	50	Texas	41.7	Traditionalistic
25	Wyoming	56.8	Individualistic	51	Hawaii	40.0	Individualistic
26	Alabama	56.0	Traditionalistic				

Source: United States Election Project, "2012 General Election Turnout Rates," http://elections.gmu.edu/Turnout_2012G.html.

Voter turnout rates actually have increased in the South, where many of the historical impediments to registration and voting have declined and the major parties have become more competitive than had been the case for more than one hundred years. But the region has merely stabilized at a turnout rate that is slightly lower than that in the rest of the country. Its high proportion of African Americans and its historical legacy of suppressing their votes and the votes of some whites keep the South's turnout rates sluggish even though African Americans do tend to vote in greater numbers than do other minorities, such as Hispanics.

> Hispanics have long been considered the "sleeping giant" of American politics because of their failure to vote in numbers commensurate with their share of the population. They cast just 6 percent of the ballots in the United States in 2004, barely half as many as African Americans, even though they constitute a larger portion of the national population.

Hispanics have long been considered the "sleeping giant" of American politics because of their failure to vote in numbers commensurate with their share of the population. They cast just 6 percent of the ballots in the United States in 2004, barely half as many as African Americans, even though they constitute a larger portion of the national population. Their numbers ticked upward in 2008 but still trailed well behind those of African Americans, who turned out in high numbers in support of Obama. A record number of Hispanics voted in 2010, with their share of the electorate ticking up to nearly 7 percent; still, less than a third of eligible Hispanics cast ballots that year.[29] By 2012, it appeared that the sleeping giant had awakened. Hispanics made up 10 percent of voters that year, and their share of the electorate—and their influence—is considered certain to grow.

But growth in the Latino electorate is still lagging well behind the rate of growth of the Hispanic population as a while. The standard explanation is that Hispanics simply lack the well-established political organizations needed to encourage registration and turnout. But other factors are involved as well. More than 20 percent of voting-age Hispanics are noncitizens, and thus not eligible to vote. As Ruy Teixeira, a Democratic polling expert, says, "People who look at the overall size of the Hispanic population and look at the vote think, 'Oh my God, what if these people ever get mobilized?' . . . But so many of these people can't vote anyway."[30]

Then there's age. The median age of Hispanics in the United States is just twenty-seven, compared with forty-two for non-Hispanic whites. A much higher percentage of Hispanics do not vote because they are simply too young. That will change. About 50,000 Hispanics will turn eighteen every month for the next fifteen years. This could mean that Hispanic voting rolls will swell enormously—or it could mean that young Hispanics, just like young Americans of every race, will fail to exercise their right to vote in great numbers. Hispanics, in other words, already behave pretty much like everybody else.

As previously mentioned, many other factors also determine rates of voter turnout. Elderly people tend to vote in high numbers—which is one reason Social Security and Medicare are always important political issues. Young people, by contrast, vote in lower numbers, in percentage terms. People who are wealthy tend to vote more than the poor, and people with higher levels of education vote much more regularly than do people with limited education. These are some of the reasons a high-income state with an educated population, such as Connecticut, has much higher turnout rates than a low-income state where the population is poorly educated on the whole, such as Hawaii.

A competitive election will draw a crowd even in a state that normally has low voter turnout. When people feel like they have a real choice, they are more likely to make the effort to vote. A close three-way race for governor, such as took place in Minnesota in 1998, will produce record turnout, whereas a yawner between a popular incumbent and a no-name opponent will make people sit on their hands. Some states tend to have consistently competitive elections because the two major parties are matched fairly evenly, each getting a roughly equal share of support from the electorate. Other states are one-party states, with Republicans or Democrats dominant. One-party states rarely have competitive elections—but when they do, voter turnout is certain to go up.

In his best-selling 2000 book *Bowling Alone*, Robert Putnam notes that moralistic states such as Minnesota and the Dakotas have much higher rates of volunteering, attendance at public meetings, and "social trust," as measured by polls, than do traditionalistic states.[31] In other words, voter turnout is just one indication of the overall sense of civic engagement in a place. States with strong "socializing institutions"—anything from membership organizations to news media that still cover politics—are more likely to be places where people are engaged enough to vote.

What Elections Are Used For

Forty-nine states elect a governor and two sets of state legislators: state senators and members of a state house of representatives, delegates, or assemblymen. Nebraska, the only exception, elects a governor and a one-chamber legislature. Beyond that, there is quite a bit of variation among the states in what they allow people to vote for. Some states allow voters to pick a number of statewide officeholders, such as attorney general and secretary of state, whereas in a few places these are appointed positions. Judges are elected at the voting booth in most places but not in about a dozen states. Roughly half the states allow voters to make policy decisions directly through ballot initiatives and referendums.

A look at state elections shows that states have quite different rules about who gets to vote for whom. That, in turn, can affect how a state makes policy. A governor who can appoint his or her entire cabinet is likely to have better success at pushing through policies than is a governor who has to contend with a group of elected officials, each with his or her own agenda.

All this is putting aside local elections, which also vary considerably. Most large cities, such as Chicago and San Francisco, allow voters to elect a mayor directly. Many smaller cities have what is called a council-mayor format, in which the city council picks one of its own members to serve as mayor, while the city is administered by a city manager, who is not elected. The same holds true for counties. In some places a county commission picks its own leader, whereas in others voters pick a county executive on their own. Local elections are, for the most part, nonpartisan—that is, candidates do not run under a party label. But, again, there are exceptions, such as the highly partisan elections for mayor of New York City.

Electing the Executive Branch

Until recently, New Jersey voters elected only their governor out of all statewide officeholders. This system helped to create one of the most powerful governorships in the country. It wasn't always so. For centuries, New Jersey governors were much weaker players than the state's legislatures. They were limited to a single term and had weak veto and appointment powers. County officials in the state also were quite powerful, at the expense of state officials. That all changed, however, beginning with the new state constitution of 1947. The constitution was pushed through by reformers of the moralistic strain that had always been present, although usually not dominant, in New Jersey politics. The reformers got new powers for the state's governors, including the ability to succeed themselves, authority to appoint not just cabinet officials but also about five hundred board and commission members, and broad authority to reject legislation. New Jersey's governors now can veto all or part of many bills and can issue conditional vetoes, meaning a governor can reject portions of a bill while suggesting new language for it.[32]

Compare all that influence with the limited powers of the governor of Texas. In Texas, the governor is only one of twenty-five elected statewide officials—and he or she is not even generally considered the most powerful one among them. That distinction belongs to the lieutenant governor. In most states, the lieutenant governor holds a purely symbolic office, with little to do but wait around for something crippling to befall the governor. (New Jersey for many years did not even

---

Nonpartisan Election
An election in which the candidates do not have to declare party affiliation or receive a party's nomination; local offices and elections are often nonpartisan.

A Difference That Makes A Difference

How Some States Discourage Voters

The notion of equal access to the ballot for all—one person, one vote—is a cornerstone of American democracy. But how do you determine whether the person seeking to vote has the right to vote?

That question is at the center of one of the major debates in U.S. politics in recent years. Numerous states have put in place greater safeguards to protect against voter fraud, demanding evidence of identification such as driver's licenses at polling places and sometimes requiring that those wishing to register to vote produce documents such as birth certificates.

These laws were given the green light by the U.S. Supreme Court in 2008, when it upheld a 2005 Indiana law requiring that voters produce government-issued photo ID at the polls. Kris Kobach, the Republican secretary of state in Kansas and sponsor of his state's 2011 voter ID law, says that requiring voters to show a photo ID is no burden at a time when they have to do the same to board an airplane, enter a federal building, or even "buy the kind of Sudafed that works."

Such arguments have been persuasive, at least with the general public. Polling in 2012 showed that about three-quarters of Americans supported voter ID laws.

Still, critics of the laws—mostly Democrats—complain that they amount to attempts at voter suppression. The people least likely to be able to produce government-issued IDs are minorities and the young and the old, all groups expected to favor Democratic candidates in general. "He's doing a better job as Republican state chair as secretary of state than he did when he was the Republican state chair," Kansas state representative Ann Mah, a Democrat, said of Kobach.

Voter ID laws are a solution in search of a problem, the argument goes. The 41 incidents of improper voting or registration activity for 2010 that Kobach's office cited are mostly accounted for by honest mistakes, Mah argued, such as snowbirds accidentally seeking to vote in two states or felons being allowed to vote although they were ineligible. There was no evidence that Kansas was seeing large numbers of illegal aliens voting, or that there was a conspiracy on the part of any party or group to affect the outcomes of elections, said Chris Biggs, Kobach's Democratic predecessor as secretary of state.

Those findings track those of national studies. An analysis of 2,068 reported fraud cases dating back to 2000 by a Carnegie-Knight investigative reporting project in 2012 found that there had been just 10 cases of alleged in-person voter impersonation since 2000. "With 146 million registered voters in the United States, those represent about one for every 15 million prospective voters," reported the *Washington Post*.[a]

During the 2012 election year, media reports appeared frequently about senior citizens who had voted for decades but had been turned away from the polls when they were unable to produce long-lost documents that were suddenly the key to the franchise. Matt Barreto, a University of Washington political scientist, conducted a survey in 2012 that found that, while most Pennsylvanians believed they had proper ID, 13 percent of registered voters lacked the kind of identification required by the state's new law.[b]

Eric Holder, President Obama's attorney general, likened voter ID requirements to "poll taxes," a long-discredited and abandoned tool meant to disenfranchise

Voter identification laws became controversial in 2012. Democrats argued that Republicans were seeking to suppress Democratic supporters, their fears fueled by remarks from Pennsylvania House GOP leader Mike Turzai that a new voter ID law would "allow" Republican presidential nominee Mitt Romney to win the state.

Herman Fredrick, a resident of Norristown, Pennsylvania, had to show photo identification to vote in a primary election in April 2012. Pennsylvania was among a number of states that had controversial voter ID requirements in place for that year's presidential election.

African American voters. Despite the Supreme Court ruling, the U.S. Justice Department and other entities challenged numerous voter ID laws in court.

Pennsylvania lawmakers were chagrined when their own attorneys had to concede in court that the state had no awareness "of in-person voter fraud in Pennsylvania and do not have direct personal knowledge of in-person voter fraud elsewhere." They were even more embarrassed when Mike Turzai, the Pennsylvania House Republican leader, seemed to verify critics' complaints that the state had passed the law for partisan purposes, saying at a June 2012 rally, "Voter ID . . . is going to allow Governor [Mitt] Romney to win the state of Pennsylvania."

Much of the debate ultimately swirled around competing visions of election regulation—whether the goal should be to ensure that access to the ballot is strictly enforced to protect against abuse, or whether chances for fraud are too slim to justify denying eligible voters their right to vote simply because they lack certain forms of documentation. Both political debate and court cases turned not only on voter ID requirements but also on efforts to purge voter rolls and limit the numbers of hours polling places would be open.

Most people—and certainly most Republican lawmakers—seemed to feel that protecting the ballot box and insisting that citizens make the extra effort to obtain proper identification was the way to go. During debate over Florida's voter ID law in 2011, Republican senator Mike Bennett said, "I don't have a problem making [voting] harder. I want people in Florida to want to vote as bad as that person in Africa who walks 200 miles across the desert. This should be something you do with a passion."

Still, plenty of people believed this view of the matter was too harsh, that too many Americans had to endure long lines on election day or, worse, were at risk of being unfairly turned away for lack of knowledge about the new laws and difficulty in acquiring the right kinds of ID.

In May 2012, a federal judge threw out a portion of a Florida law that made it more difficult for independent groups such as the League of Women Voters to register voters. With such groups shying away from the state, voter registration by that point was down significantly from 2008 levels. "If the goal is to discourage voter registration drives and thus also to make it harder for new voters to register, this may work," Judge Robert L. Hinkle wrote. "Otherwise, there is little reason for such a requirement."

But a month later, Hinkle blocked a Justice Department request to stop the state from purging its voter rolls of noncitizens and other people ineligible to vote, saying that leaving such persons on the rolls could do "irreparable harm" to legitimate voters.[c]

[a]Katasha Khan and Corbin Carson, "Election Day Impersonation, an Impetus for Voter ID Laws, a Rarity, Data Show," *Washington Post*, August 11, 2012, www.washingtonpost.com/politics/election-day-impersonation-an-impetus-for-voter-id-laws-a-rarity-data-show/2012/08/11/7002911e-df20–11e1-a19c-fcfa365396c8_story.html.

[b]Angela Couloumbis, "Numbers Behind Pa. Voter-ID Law Debated in Court," *Philadelphia Inquirer*, July 27, 2012, http://articles.philly.com/2012-07-27/news/32870331_1_voter-law-form-of-photo-identification-thousands-of-inactive-voters.

[c]Lizette Alvarez, "Judge Sides with Florida on Purging Voter Rolls," *New York Times*, June 28, 2012, A14.

bother with the office of lieutenant governor, but following a string of gubernatorial vacancies, voters created the position in 2005; the change took effect following the 2009 elections.) In Texas, the lieutenant governor is the president of the state Senate and therefore wields tremendous influence over the course of legislation.

In contrast, the governor of Texas can recommend a budget, but he or she has no authority to make the legislature grapple with it seriously. Compare that to Maryland, where legislators can only accept or defeat the governor's spending proposals; they can make no fresh additions of their own. The Texas governor appoints the secretary of state and members of many boards and commissions, but many of the latter serve staggered terms. This means that the governor might have to work with people who were appointed by his or her predecessor.

Bills have been put forward to provide the governor of Texas with more power. Generally, they have gone nowhere, although versions of an ambitious bill passed both the state House and Senate in 2003. The state's **plural executive system** illustrates the desires of the framers of the 1876 state constitution to keep any one person or institution from having too much power. They believed in a separation of powers not just between branches of government but also within the executive branch.[33] The weakened powers of the governor are a reflection of the distrust that Texans had for strong government, in keeping with their constitution's many restrictions on raising taxes.

A couple of other southern and traditionalistic states, such as Alabama and Georgia, also divide power within the executive branch. In 1999, Alabama Democrats in the state Senate sought to strip control of their chamber along with other powers from Lieutenant Governor Steve Windom, a Republican. And they could have done it if only

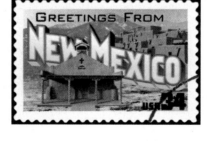

he had left the Senate floor, but Windom refused. To stay present in and to keep control of the chamber for that day, and thus for the rest of his term, he did what was necessary, even urinating into a plastic jug in the chamber.[34]

Other states chart more of a middle-of-the-road course, electing a handful of statewide officials. In most states, in addition to a governor, voters elect a lieutenant governor, treasurer, secretary of state, and attorney general. A few states elect other officers as well, such as an insurance commissioner. Some observers believe that appointed officials are removed from political concerns and can make decisions without regard to partisan interests. Others believe that having to answer directly to the public makes individual officeholders more responsive to the public's needs and desires. Regardless of which side is correct, the fact that many statewide officeholders run for office independent of the governor gives them a power base of their own.

Attorneys general, treasurers, and other statewide officials often have aspirations of becoming governor themselves one day. This often leads to conflict with the sitting governor. Some of these fights occur along partisan lines. New Mexico attorney general Gary King, a Democrat, complained in 2012 that Republican legislators were trying to examine his office e-mails in retaliation for his office investigating the state Department of Public Education to determine whether resources were being used for political gain. "This is not the first time that the Republican Party has done such a thing where there are allegations made at Governor [Susana] Martinez for some sort of wrongdoing and just days after, the Republican Party filed a complaint or something that appeared to be designed to at a minimum take up the time of the attorney general's office," King said.[35] Such rancor isn't always partisan. Today in Texas, every statewide officeholder is Republican, but that has not put an end to squabbling within the executive branch. Carole Keeton Strayhorn, the state comptroller, has frequently provoked the governor and lieutenant governor, accusing them of using dishonest budget numbers and raising fees

---

Plural Executive System

A state government system in which the governor is not the dominant figure in the executive branch but, instead, is more of a first among equals, serving alongside numerous other officials who are elected to their offices rather than appointed by the governor.

Current new Mexico governor and former district attorney Susana Martinez is considered a rising star in Republican circles.

excessively. "Sounds like the primary started early this year," Lieutenant Governor David Dewhurst said in 2003.[36] Strayhorn ran unsuccessfully for governor as an independent in 2006.

Legal Offices

Voters pay comparatively little attention to candidates running for some state executive branch offices. Races for, say, state treasurer or secretary of state are, for the most part, just not seen as all that exciting. Most often, the party that wins the governorship takes the lion's share of the secondary executive branch offices anyway, so there is not much ticket splitting. These are offices often pursued by legislators or other politicians looking to move up the political ladder. They hope these second-tier positions will firm up their résumés for their future bids for prominent offices such as governor.

One office for which the majority-party-takes-all dynamic no longer holds is that of attorney general, the chief law enforcement officer in the state. For many years, Democrats completely dominated the office in most states, but that began to change in the late 1990s. For one thing, the job came to be seen as a more important stepping-stone to the governorship than in the past; in 2012, eight former state attorneys general were serving as governors. Attorneys general in ten other states, including Michigan, Pennsylvania, and California, ran for governor in 2010. Republicans, understandably, became increasingly unwilling to concede this important gateway to the chief executive's office.

Moreover, state attorneys general, who traditionally had concentrated on law enforcement and consumer protection disputes within their states, had joined in a series of multistate settlements that represented important challenges to corporate interests. They forced a series of settlements in 1998, for instance, that pushed the major tobacco companies to change their marketing strategies and to pay states an estimated $246 billion over twenty-five years. Some Republicans believed that these activist attorneys general were

engaging in "government lawsuit abuse"—not targeting criminal behavior but, instead, going after companies to achieve changes in policy and regulation that could not be accomplished in the legislative arena. They founded the Republican Attorneys General Association (RAGA) as a campaign wing to elect members of their party to the office and funneled contributions from businesses and conservative interest groups that were threatened by the new activism to their candidates. "Historically . . . attorney general races were off most business people's radar screens," according to Bob LaBrant of the Michigan Chamber of Commerce. In the new environment, he says, "there's greater incentive to get involved in an attorney general race because of the increased involvement of attorneys general across the country in litigation against the business community."[37]

Such interest group money and influence do make a difference. In 2002, the Law Enforcement Alliance of America, an arm of the gun lobby, ran an estimated $1.5 million late-season ad campaign that helped keep the Texas attorney general's office in Republican hands. This was an expanded version of the U.S. Chamber of Commerce's effort in Indiana in 2000, when a $200,000 ad campaign was widely viewed as a leading factor in driving an incumbent Democrat attorney general out of office.[38] Such numbers, once eye-popping, have become routine. All told, Republicans improved their numbers after

RAGA's founding from just twelve attorneys general in 1999 to twenty in 2003 to twenty-six by 2012. Both parties now believe that campaigns for attorney general will remain more expensive and competitive than they had been historically.

A related phenomenon is affecting judicial elections, which traditionally had been sleepy affairs. All but eleven states hold some type of elections for judicial posts. These are either direct elections by voters or retention elections used by voters to grant additional terms to justices appointed by the governor or the state legislature. Until the mid-1990s, judicial campaigns were cheap and fairly ho-hum. What campaign contributions candidates did receive came mainly from trial lawyers, along with contributions from unions and other constituencies allied with the Democratic Party. All of that began to change, however, when Republicans and their business allies grew weary of seeing their legislative victories in areas such as tort law and workers' compensation overturned by the high courts. In 2000, candidates in supreme court races in twenty states raised a total of $45.5 million, a 61 percent increase over the previous record. The average cost of winning a judicial election jumped 45 percent between 2002 and 2004, while individual races also kept breaking records, with one Illinois contest nearing the $10 million mark in 2004.[39] Elections for individual lower-level judgeships have broken through the million-dollar barrier also. In 2007 and 2008, judicial candidates raised $62 million, with more than $18 million of that coming from lawyers, lobbyists, and their firms, according to the National Institute on Money in State Politics.

The issue of fund-raising by judicial candidates drew attention with the 2008 publication of best-selling mystery writer John Grisham's novel *The Appeal*. Its plot turns on a rigged Mississippi Supreme Court election. The following year, the U.S. Supreme Court ruled in *Caperton v. Massey* that a West Virginia Supreme Court justice who had benefited from a $3 million campaign orchestrated by a coal-mining company that had a large case before the court had a conflict of interest. But Chief Justice John Roberts, writing in dissent, noted that the majority had not drawn a clear line in terms of what constitutes the appearance of corruption, and this will lead to further confusion.

Direct Democracy

In addition to electing officials to state and local offices, voters can participate in certain forms of direct democracy. As discussed in chapter 3, in about half the states, voters can pass legislation on their own through ballot initiatives or referendums, which also are available in hundreds of municipalities across the country. In twenty-four states, citizens can petition to place a piece of legislation or a constitutional amendment on the ballot for approval or rejection by voters. Also in twenty-four states—mostly the same states—citizens can petition to review a law passed by the legislature and the governor, which they then can accept or reject. (See Table 5-2.)

TABLE 5-2

Avenues for Direct Democracy

State	Popular Referendum	Ballot Initiative	Constitutional Amendment by Initiative	Recall of State Officials
Alabama	No	No	No	No
Alaska	Yes	Yes	No	Yes
Arizona	Yes	Yes	Yes	Yes
Arkansas	Yes	Yes	Yes	No
California	Yes	Yes	Yes	Yes
Colorado	Yes	Yes	Yes	Yes
Connecticut	No	No	No	No
Delaware	No	No	No	No
Florida	No	Yes	Yes	No

State	Popular Referendum	Ballot Initiative	Constitutional Amendment by Initiative	Recall of State Officials
Georgia	No	No	No	Yes
Hawaii	No	No	No	No
Idaho	Yes	Yes	Yes	Yes
Illinois	Yes	Yes	No	No
Indiana	No	No	No	No
Iowa	No	No	No	No
Kansas	No	No	No	Yes
Kentucky	Yes	No	No	No
Louisiana	No	No	No	Yes
Maine	Yes	Yes	No	No
Maryland	Yes	No	No	No
Massachusetts	Yes	Yes	Yes	No
Michigan	Yes	Yes	Yes	Yes
Minnesota	No	No	No	Yes
Mississippi	No	Yes	Yes	No
Missouri	Yes	Yes	Yes	No
Montana	Yes	Yes	Yes	Yes
Nebraska	Yes	Yes	Yes	No
Nevada	Yes	Yes	Yes	Yes
New Hampshire	No	No	No	No
New Jersey	No	No	No	Yes
New Mexico	Yes	No	No	No
New York	No	No	No	No
North Carolina	No	No	No	No
North Dakota	Yes	Yes	Yes	Yes
Ohio	Yes	Yes	Yes	No
Oklahoma	Yes	Yes	Yes	No
Oregon	Yes	Yes	Yes	Yes
Pennsylvania	No	No	No	No
Rhode Island	No	No	No	Yes
South Carolina	No	No	No	No
South Dakota	Yes	Yes	Yes	No
Tennessee	No	No	No	No
Texas	No	No	No	No
Utah	Yes	Yes	No	No
Vermont	No	No	No	No
Virginia	No	No	No	No
Washington	Yes	Yes	No	Yes
West Virginia	No	No	No	No
Wisconsin	No	No	No	Yes
Wyoming	Yes	Yes	No	No
Total number of states with	25	24	18	18

Source: Data compiled from the Initiative and Referendum Institute at the University of Southern California, www.iandrinstitute.org/statewide_i&r.htm; and the National Conference of State Legislatures, www.ncsl.org/LegislaturesElections/ElectionsCampaigns/RecallofStateOfficials/tabid/16581/Default.aspx.

States under Stress

Protest Movements Achieve Different Levels of Success

Two large-scale populist movements emerged during the first term of Barack Obama's presidency: the Tea Party movement and the Occupy movement. Participants in both were angry about the influence and power of large institutional forces in society. The two movements' platforms were diametrically opposed, however, and the approaches they took to trying to influence American politics were completely different.

The fast-growing Tea Party movement began in 2009, shortly after Obama became president. It was made up of individuals angry about the size of government—a backlash against the president's $800 billion stimulus program, a bank bailout plan that Congress had passed under President George W. Bush to the tune of $700 billion, and a deficit that in 2009 topped $1.4 trillion. "The Republicans for the last two decades have been a party whose litmus tests have been cultural issues, especially abortion," explained conservative columnist Michael Barone in 2010. "The tea partiers have helped to change their focus to issues of government overreach and spending."[a]

Members of the movement also derided Obama's healthcare legislation, which they saw as obtrusive and a threat to individual liberty, since it mandated that most people buy health insurance. Not surprisingly, then, they aligned themselves largely with the Republican Party— even if many participants in the Tea Party movement insisted that they were independent.

The Tea Party movement, which derived its name from colonial-era protests against British taxation— quickly claimed more than one thousand different affiliate groups around the country.[b] Tea Party–endorsed candidates prevailed in numerous GOP primaries in both 2010 and 2012. Republican strategists largely welcomed the burst of energy that Tea Partiers brought to their cause, which had been discouraged by widespread electoral losses in 2006 and 2008.

Some criticized the Tea Party for being too unyielding. Some of the candidates backed by Tea Party groups in primaries were unable to prevail in contests Republicans might have won had they nominated more "establishment" or mainstream candidates. And those Tea Party favorites who did win elections drew criticism once in office for refusing to compromise at all on budget matters, nearly forcing the country into default in 2011.

But while the Tea Party was influencing Republican politicians in Congress and the statehouses, those politicians were trying to co-opt the Tea Party, to harness its energy and enthusiasm without letting its agenda dominate the party's direction. "That's the secret to politics," GOP consultant Scott Reed said in 2011. "Trying to control a segment of people without those people recognizing that you're trying to control them."[c]

Being co-opted in this way seemed to be the main thing the Occupy movement wanted to avoid. The movement began with a protest beginning in September 2011 in a park near Wall Street in Lower Manhattan; the demonstrators complained that too much wealth was concentrated in the hands of too few individuals.

The slogan "We are the 99 percent" went global, as did the idea of protesting by camping in place for twenty-four hours a day, which quickly spread to hundreds of cities. The issue of income inequality and the question of whether the wealthiest 1 percent held too much power soon became central concerns of the movement.

But Occupy was not able to translate its complaints into a policy agenda. It wasn't clear what the members of the movement wanted to have happen. The mere act of their camping out itself became problematic as winter set in and issues of sanitation and crowd control grew worse; in many cities, authorities ordered police to remove the protesters from public spaces.

When citizens or groups other than elected officials put a measure on the ballot to become a law, this is called a popular initiative. When citizens put a measure on the ballot to affirm or reject an action of the legislature or other political actor, this is called a popular referendum. When the legislature places a measure on the ballot to win voter approval (such as a constitutional amendment or bond issue), it is called a legislative referendum. Some referendums are nonbinding—expressing the will

As Rosemary Feurer, a historian at Northern Illinois University, has noted, protest movements typically don't start out with set lists of goals that they want politicians to achieve. The populist movements of the nineteenth century and early labor union activity began in ways similar to the beginnings of the Occupy movement: an encampment of people came together, found they shared a sense of dissatisfaction with the status quo, and worked to change it. As Feurer has observed, "What starts these movements is a list of grievances. You don't start with a list of goals, but with a sense of what's wrong."[d]

Occupy gatherings sought to run by consensus, with those gathered expressing approval or disapproval of simple items, such as the order of speakers, through hand gestures. The movement, by its nature, was suspicious of leaders. "Don't lose sight of the bigger message of this movement being driven from the bottom up by consensus and not affiliation or deference to any group that's out there," said Ed Needham, a media spokesman for Occupy Wall Street.[e]

As such, Occupy had a hard time finding allegiance even with politicians who might have been sympathetic. This was exemplified when John Lewis, a Democratic congressman from Georgia and hero of the civil rights movement, showed up at the Occupy Atlanta site. Protesters there praised Lewis but refused to let him speak right away, as that would have disrupted the scheduled agenda.

Lewis, who had other obligations, decided to leave, although he said he took no offense. Recalling his own days as head of the Student Nonviolent Coordinating Committee during the 1960s, he said civil rights groups sometimes reached consensus slowly and refused to be deferential to more established leaders. "It is growing, it is maturing, it will work out," Lewis told reporters, speaking about the Occupy movement at the Atlanta site. "It will come of age."

Just a few months after the protests began, however, it didn't appear that Occupy would have continuing relevance. What were highly visible encampments had already given way to sporadic, sparsely attended marches. "Occupy does not have a traditional leadership structure, making it difficult for the movement to engage in conventional political organizing in support of state legislators and members of Congress, like the Tea Party has," the New York Times reported in April 2012. "And some activists, angry at politicians across the board, do not see electoral politics as the best avenue for the movement, complicating efforts to chart its direction."[f]

Source: Original piece written for this book by Alan Greenblatt.

[a]Michael Barone, "Tea Party Brings Energy, Change and Tumult to GOP," Washington Examiner, March 14, 2010, http://townhall.com/columnists/michaelbarone/2010/03/15/tea_party_brings_energy,_change_and_tumult_to_gop/page/full.

[b]Peter Katel, "Tea Party Movement," CQ Researcher, May 19, 2010.

[c]Quoted in Matt Bai, "'You're Nuts!,'" New York Times Magazine, October 16, 2001, 44.

[d]Quoted in Alan Greenblatt, "For Wall Street Protests, What Constitutes Success?," NPR.org, October 14, 2011, www.npr.org/2011/10/14/141347126/for-wall-street-protests-what-constitutes-success.

[e]Phone interview with Ed Needham, October 12, 2011.

[f]Michael S. Schmidt, "For Occupy Movement, a Challenge to Recapture Momentum," New York Times, April 1, 2012, A21.

of the people but not becoming law—but most are binding and do have the force of law once passed.

In all fifty states, the legislature or other government agencies have the power of legislative referendum. In the decades following independence, citizens in several northeastern states ratified new constitutions; Congress subsequently made legislative referendums for constitutional amendments mandatory for all new states entering the union after 1857.[40]

As discussed in chapter 3, the notion of popular referendums and initiatives really took root because of the efforts of reformers from the Populist and Progressive movements. These individuals sought to give citizens more influence over state political systems that they saw as dominated by moneyed interests such as banks, railroads, and mining companies. A majority of the states that have adopted the popular initiative process (under which citizens can collect a certain number of signatures to place issues directly on the ballot) did so in the late 1800s and early 1900s. Most of these states are in the West and the upper Midwest, which had political cultures that welcomed the idea of populist control. Much of the opposition in the southern and eastern states grew out of racist concerns that giving people direct authority to make laws would give too much power to African Americans or to new immigrants such as the Irish.

Recent ballot initiatives and referendums have covered a wide range of topics, from banning or allowing gay marriage and legalizing marijuana to making sure that pregnant pigs are housed in large-enough pens (an amendment to the Florida constitution approved by voters in 2002). Many initiatives have to do with tax and spending issues. Sometimes voters send contradictory signals. For instance, in Washington State, voters in recent years have approved limitations on property and other taxes while at the same time approving such expensive programs as teacher pay increases and school class size limitations.

Those who favor the initiative process say that it gives voters a chance to control government directly. Voters know that they are voting for an environmental safety program or a campaign finance law, as opposed to voting for candidates who say that they favor these things but who may act differently once in office. Initiative states do tend to have lower state spending per capita, but that gap generally is bridged by local spending, which tends to run higher in initiative states.[41]

Critics of the initiative process say that it creates more problems than it solves. Because voters are presented with a straight yes-or-no choice about spending more on, say, elementary and secondary education, they do not take into account other competing state priorities, such as transportation or colleges, the way legislators must. Voters can say, as those in Washington have, that they want both lower taxes and more services but leave legislators and governors few tools for balancing the budget or responding to economic recessions.

Those opposed to initiatives also say that the idea that they express the popular will better than elected representatives sounds good in theory but is flawed in practice. In many states—particularly California—initiatives have become big business. They are not necessarily the expressions of grassroots ideals anymore; instead, they are proposed and paid for by wealthy individuals or interest groups, such as teachers' unions or the owners of gambling casinos.

Far and away the most famous and influential modern ballot initiative was Proposition 13, approved by California voters in 1978, which limited property tax rates and made other changes to the state's tax and spending laws (see chapter 3). The initiative was copied successfully in Michigan and Massachusetts, and most states soon placed limitations on their own property tax rates. The success of Proposition 13 fueled the modern initiative movement. Only eighty-seven statewide initiatives were proposed during the entire decade of the 1960s. Since 1978, however, about three hundred initiatives have been proposed per decade. Ninety-three statewide initiatives were placed on ballots in 1996 alone. That appears to have been the peak year, with supporters of the initiative process complaining since then that state legislatures have placed new restrictions on ballot access and signature collection. But following a long decline, the numbers of initiatives started going up again in 2012 and are likely to continue to climb, according to Jennie Bowser, a senior fellow with the National Conference of State Legislatures, because there is "an industry" that relies on an active initiative process.[42]

The power of initiatives can be seen in the establishment of legislative term limits, which exist in nearly every state that allows ballot initiatives but in only a couple of states that do not. Term limits have been imposed in virtually every case by voters through ballot measures, not by legislators themselves. In addition, congressional term limits were a popular idea during the early 1990s and were approved in a number of states; however, the U.S. Supreme Court ruled in 1995 that states cannot unilaterally alter the constitutional requirements for holding federal office. State legislators are subject to term limits in fifteen states, but the defeat of a term limits initiative in Oregon in 2006 seems to have signaled the end of the movement.

Rather than looking to expand term limits, legislators and many others concerned with the effects of term limits on good governance have been seeking to expand the length of time legislators may serve. Term limits are still too popular to repeal, but some people believe that allowing legislators ten to twelve years in a chamber, as opposed to six to eight, will make them more expert in grappling with the complex policies they must address. Even these efforts, however, have proven to be tough sells.

Ballots have become regular battlegrounds for a number of other issues as well. Limitations on reproductive rights, such as parental notification requirements for minors seeking to obtain abortions, have been debated by voters in many states, as have smoking bans and property rights protections. Although many ballot measures involve putting restraints on government, by limiting state spending, for instance, or by holding judges more accountable for their decisions, voters in recent cycles have rejected these ideas. Public officials have been able to make the case that the sometimes rigid restrictions proposed would tie their hands even in emergency situations. Perhaps surprisingly, their arguments have been echoed in many states by organized business groups that, although fiscally conservative, have been concerned that artificial limits on government might affect their own priorities, such as improvements in education and transportation projects.

Since 2004, perhaps the most prominent measures on many ballots have sought to place a ban on gay marriage. Many states already had defined marriage as the union of a man and a woman, but following a Massachusetts court decision that found gays had a right to marry, thirty states have changed their constitutions to ban same-sex marriage. In May 2012, North Carolina voters approved such a ban, but the next day, President Obama said that he was now in favor of legalizing same-sex marriage (while stressing it was a policy best handled by the states). Supporters of gay marriage enjoyed their first successes at the ballot box in November 2012. Minnesota voters rejected a ban on same-sex marriage, while voters in Maine and Washington granted marriage rights to same-sex couples and Maryland voters approved the legislature's decision to allow gay marriage.

As noted earlier, some political scientists have suggested that high-profile initiatives do lead more people to vote. Given the attention a proposed gay marriage ban received in Ohio in 2004, when that state's electoral votes ultimately decided the presidency, there was much coverage in the media that looked at the question of whether the initiative helped President Bush by encouraging social conservatives to vote. "I'd be naïve if I didn't say it helped," Robert T. Bennett, chair of the Ohio Republican Party, told the *New York Times*. "And it helped most in what we refer to as the Bible Belt area of southeastern and southwestern Ohio, where we had the largest percentage increase in support for the president."[43]

Not surprisingly, liberals decided to jump on this particular bandwagon, finding causes, such as minimum wage increases and stem-cell research support, to place on ballots in hopes that more progressive voters would turn out as well. But there is a school of thought that argues that they need not have bothered. Simon Jackman, a statistician at Stanford University, has shown that same-sex marriage initiatives boosted turnout by about 3 percent in the eleven states that had them on the ballot in 2004. On examining data from all of Ohio's counties, however, he concluded that that state's initiative did not boost support for Bush.[44]

Others have noted that it is not an accident that high-profile initiatives tend to appear in closely contested states. "The list of [presidential]

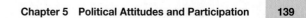

battleground states almost exactly matches up with the list of controversial ballot measures this year," said Bowser, who tracks initiatives for the National Conference of State Legislatures, in 2004.[45]

Beyond initiatives and referendums is perhaps the ultimate expression of popular dissatisfaction—the **recall**. Recalls of local officials are allowed in thirty-six states and 61 percent of U.S. municipalities—more local governments than allow initiatives or referendums. Like ballot initiatives, recall laws are mainly by-products of the intention of early twentieth-century reformers to make state governments more responsive to average citizens. Recalls of state officials are allowed in eighteen states. No governor had faced a recall since the 1920s when, in 2003, California Democrat Gray Davis was recalled and replaced by Republican Arnold Schwarzenegger. In 2012, Wisconsin governor Scott Walker, a Republican, survived a recall attempt in what became one of the most expensive elections in U.S. history. These high-profile recalls helped promote growth in recalls at the local level, with everyone from county commissioners to school board members being shown the door. In 2011, at least fifty-seven mayors faced recall attempts—up from twenty-three in 2009. Not all of these recall attempts succeeded, but in recent years, serious recall attempts have been launched against mayors in cities such as Omaha, Kansas City, and Portland, Oregon. The overwhelming recall election loss of Carlos Alvarez, mayor of Miami-Dade County, Florida, in 2011 makes him perhaps the most prominent victim of the recall trend at the local level.[46]

Still, over the past one hundred years, fewer than two dozen recall elections have involved state officials, including legislators (although Wisconsin Democrats, who failed to recall Walker, did manage in the same election to recall several members of the Republican state Senate and regain control

of that chamber).[47] The only governor to be recalled before Davis in California was Lynn Frazier of North Dakota in 1921. Frazier, the state attorney general, and the agricultural commissioner all lost their offices after a grassroots movement swelled against scandals in Frazier's government. The only other governor who has ever faced a scheduled recall election was Evan Mecham of Arizona; the legislature saved voters the trouble by removing him from office in 1987.

California makes the recall process relatively easy, requiring the gathering of proportionately fewer signatures than are necessary in other states to place the recall before the voters. California requires a number of signatures equal to only 12 percent of the number of people who voted in the last election for the office, whereas most states require 25 percent and Kansas requires 40 percent. Gray Davis was unpopular, having won reelection the year before by a small plurality. He also had come to be blamed for the state's $38 billion deficit and electricity crisis.

Public Opinion

Randall Gnant, the former president of the Arizona Senate, says that there is quite a contrast between the politics of today and those of the 1800s. Back then, he says, "it seemed that everybody took part in the political process—there were torchlight parades, party-run newspapers for and against candidates." Today, "we're into sort of a reverse kind of period. Now, almost nobody participates in the electoral process—voter turnout rates are abysmally low." But that does not mean that citizens are not paying any attention to the political process. Given the importance of Web sites, Twitter, and other media that quickly spread public opinion—or at least a share of it—the old idea that voters agree to a sort of contract with politicians whom they elect to two- or four-year terms is rapidly becoming dated. Voters are more than willing to express their displeasure about a given policy well before the next scheduled election day. "Try to get somebody interested in electing a candidate and they just don't want to get involved,"

Recall

A way for voters to oust an incumbent politician prior to the next regularly scheduled election; they collect signatures to qualify the recall proposal for the ballot and then vote on the ouster of the politician.

Gnant points out. "But they are perfectly willing to get involved if somebody does something they don't want them to do."[48]

Citizen opinion usually does not register loudly enough to result in a recall or other formal protest. On most issues that come before policymakers at the state level, citizen opinion hardly seems to exist or be formulated at all. After all, how many citizens are going to take the time to follow—let alone express an opinion about—an obscure regulatory issue concerning overnight transactions between banks and insurance companies?

This lack of interest, or, at the very least, this lack of time, begs an important question. If citizens do not or cannot make their feelings known on every issue addressed in the hundreds of bills that wend through the average state legislature each year, how can legislators know that their votes will reflect the will of their constituents? After all, as V. O. Key writes, "Unless mass views have some place in the shaping of policy, all the talk about democracy is nonsense."[49]

Responding to Opinion

Doug Duncan served for a dozen years as county executive of Montgomery County, Maryland, before giving up the job in 2006. Like many veteran officeholders, he found that one of the biggest changes in his job came in the area of communications. "Doing it is half the job," he says, "and the other half is telling people about it so they know how you're spending their money."[50] The old outlets for government officials making announcements or responding to criticism—local daily newspapers and evening TV news broadcasts—have declined in audience or even gone away completely in some cases. Nevertheless, with the growth of the Internet, more information sources are available now than ever before. "The information's there," Duncan says. "It's just a question of how you make it available."

E-mail, Twitter, and Web sites devoted to neighborhood concerns or services such as libraries have made it easier for public officials to know what their constituents are thinking—at least, those constituents who are motivated enough to make their opinions known on a given issue. And elected officials have become fairly quick to adopt new platforms, such as Facebook and Twitter. But let's be realistic—state officials, in particular, cannot know what the

majority opinions are in their districts on every issue they confront. Mike Haridopolos, the GOP president of the Florida Senate, cautions officials against reading too much into what they hear through social media. "I tell my members, just because you get a tweet or an e-mail doesn't mean your whole district is concerned about something," he says.[51] And even multiple e-mails might be the work of just one or two individuals using multiple aliases.

On most issues, legislators do not hear from any constituents at all. A few high-profile concerns, such as tax increases or the legalization of casino gambling, may lead a newspaper or an interested party to conduct a statewide poll, but even on the rare occasions when polls are conducted on state issues, the resulting data are not broken down by legislative district. Given their lack of specific information about how constituents view particular areas, public officials have to rely on a series of clues.

Some political scientists have taken data from various nationwide polls, broken them down by state, and analyzed how well elected officials have reflected the general ideologies and desires of the public in their states.[52] What they have found is that average state opinion does seem to be reflected in the policy decisions made in individual states. What does *average state opinion* mean? It encompasses the types of things we discussed earlier in regard to Daniel Elazar's classifications of the states. Some states tend to be more liberal overall, whereas others are more conservative. The average citizen's desires—whether in a conservative state such as Texas or a more progressive one such as Vermont—tend to be pretty well reflected by state laws on

> For one thing, elected officials devote an enormous amount of time to trying to gauge how opinion is running in their districts. They may not hear from constituents on every issue, but they pay close attention to those concerns that are registered through letters and phone calls.

A Difference
That Makes A Difference

Town Hall, Version 2.0

Governments can't think of everything. That's why Vivek Kundra, who served as chief technology officer of Washington, D.C., before becoming chief information officer for the Obama White House, went to "outsiders" to ask for ideas on how to enhance D.C. services through computer applications. He announced the "Apps for Democracy" contest in October 2008. The general public was invited to take data—yes, dry digital data from D.C. files—and turn them into useful and absorbing information for residents, visitors, and government employees.

When the closing bell rang on the thirty-day contest in mid-November, Kundra's office had received forty-seven submissions. The government's cost: $50,000—nearly half of it for prize money. That's cheap for dozens of new and usable applications. If the government had had to develop all of them on its own, it would have taken more than a year and, Kundra estimates, $2.6 million.

Five of the entries were quickly put to use. "That's the power of democratizing data," Kundra says.[a] It fosters the design of quick and nimble applications, allowing citizens to be "co-creators of government." Using the wisdom of crowds is a huge philosophical shift from how government usually runs, Kundra adds.

The whole business of citizens trying to contact governments and of governments wanting to relay good information to citizens has always been a creaky process. New tools such as blogs, wikis, and public comment software are smoothing things out a little and allowing governments to enhance some of the traditional ways in which they have communicated with the public.

Carole Brown, then board chair of the Chicago Transit Authority (CTA), started a blog in 2005 after feeling frustrated by negative newspaper reports on what was happening at the CTA. When Brown read letters to the editor of the newspaper, she realized that readers who were angry at the CTA didn't understand the complexities behind public transportation funding. So Brown blogged away, offering details that riders weren't getting from the press. The blog, Ask Carole, served many purposes, from straightening out misconceptions that riders were getting from other sources to allowing the agency to communicate early and often with transit riders. "My blog is an incredible tool," said Brown. "We're using it to focus on issues most important to our riders, and they have no problem telling us what those are." (The blog was discontinued in 2009, when Brown left the CTA.)

A 2011 study by DCI Group found that every governor's office had a Twitter account, while legislators in every state had Facebook page—more than 2,500 state lawmakers in all.[b] Numerous state officials were making frequent use of YouTube or holding Twitter town halls. At some electronic town hall meetings, city officials bring people together in groups of eight or ten, placing each group at a table with one laptop computer and a trained facilitator. As the citizens give their opinions on issues, someone types them up and forwards them to a team of people who gather and distill the ideas by theme. Concepts that crop up over and over are then flashed on large overhead screens. Eventually those are whittled down to a handful of top priorities by the participants, who vote on them by keypad.

Such a distillation was helpful to San Francisco mayor Gavin Newsom at his first electronic town hall meeting. He already had plenty of information about what lobbyists and professional advocates wanted. What the mayor hoped to find out was what the rest of the city wanted. The virtual town hall was a novel, and helpful, way for him to do that. "The average resident is not typically asked to come or doesn't have time or an entrée to attend a three-hour meeting with the mayor to offer opinions," said Jennifer Petrucione, the mayor's spokeswoman.

Source: Adapted from Ellen Perlman, "The Missing Link," *Governing,* March 2006.

[a]Ellen Perlman, "The Wisdom of Crowds," *Governing,* February 2009, 46.

[b]Julie Barko, "Digital America Project Looks at How State Legislators Use Social Media," GovLoop, March 9, 2011, www.govloop.com/profiles/blogs/digital-america-project-looks.

Elected officials do not just have to address the issues they campaigned on, respond to views expressed at the ballot box, deal with the demands of special interest groups, and be attentive to the expectations of political parties. They also have to be prepared to deal with the unexpected. Hurricane Katrina was a dramatic example of this, but other kinds of emergencies, natural and otherwise, happen all the time. Here, Nebraska governor Dave Heineman (right, in blue) and state senator Deb Fischer survey the damage done by a wildfire that destroyed homes in the city of Valentine. State and local emergency agencies were required to control the fire, and other agencies helped deal with the aftermath.

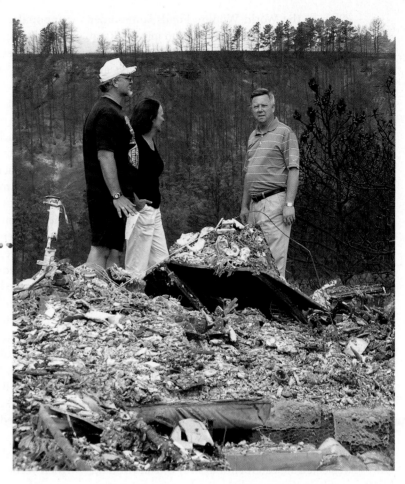

issues that range from restrictions on abortion services to welfare spending, the death penalty, environmental protections, and gay rights.[53]

How does this happen? For one thing, elected officials devote an enormous amount of time to trying to gauge how opinion is running in their districts. They may not hear from constituents on every issue, but they pay close attention to those concerns that are registered through letters and phone calls. They go out and seek opinions by attending religious services and civic events where they can hear the concerns of constituents directly. They use surrogates—such as newspaper articles and interest groups—as ways of determining what is on their constituents' minds. Susan Herbst, executive vice chancellor and chief academic officer for the University System of Georgia, spent some time earlier in her career hanging out with legislators in Springfield, Illinois. She found that the media were important in shaping public opinion by giving a voice to average people in their stories. The media also shaped the terms of debate. Herbst noted that people in the capital thought that lobbyists often provided good indicators of how people felt about an issue: "Staffers seem to think that the nuances and intensity of public opinion are best captured in the communications of interest groups."[54] More recently, political scientists at the University of Minnesota have found that media coverage of debates among political elites—those most directly engaged in actual legislative debates, such as trade associations—does help to shape mass public opinion on issues.[55]

This is not to say that using interest groups as surrogates can't be misleading sometimes. The National Rifle Association, for example, may call on its state members to send letters to legislators in numbers that dwarf those mustered by gun control advocates—even in places where a majority favors gun control. "Intense minorities can come off potentially sounding like majorities when in fact they're not," says Illinois Wesleyan University political scientist Greg Shaw.[56] Legislators like to think that they have a pretty good sense of whether a mail-writing campaign has sprung up spontaneously or shows signs of having been organized—multiple participants signing their names to the same form letter, for example—but sometimes this is easier said than done.

Formal interest groups do not represent every constituent. Some people may favor environmental protection but not give money to the Sierra

Club or the World Wildlife Fund. Some older people actually resist invitations to join AARP at cheap rates. Still, legislators do gain some sense of how active such groups are in their states and whether they seem to have favorable support at home. A lot of this is inexact, but legislators learn from talking to people whether their constituents are most upset about crime or transportation problems. They are convinced that if they vote for things that voters broadly support, such as mandatory sentencing guidelines for drug offenders or limits on welfare benefits, they will be rewarded politically.

Conversely, a legislator's major fear is of being punished politically. Failure to get reelected can be the death knell of a political career. It is important to note, however, that if legislators or governors did not broadly reflect the wishes of the populace that elected them, they would never have won their positions in the first place. In this age of computer-assisted **redistricting**, legislative districts in particular are shaped according to the local political culture, which tends to lean in one ideological direction. Ninety times out of a hundred, a liberal is not going to get elected to a conservative district.

Once elected, legislators who want to get reelected are careful not to stray too far from the public opinion in their districts, as best as they can perceive it. They cannot know what the public opinion is about the specifics of every bill, but the fact that not every individual is paying close attention to state politics does not mean that legislators can do whatever they want. Political officials recognize that lobbyists and other interested parties are watching their voting records carefully and can use such information against them, if necessary. "Legislators aren't worried about what their constituents know—they are worried about what an opponent might do with their record in the next election," says Paul Brace, a Rice University political scientist. They act, therefore, as if there is someone or some group out there who has a chance of using a potentially unpopular record against them. "Legislation is written in minutiae, but you know if you vote for it, you'll get an opponent who can dumb it down and use it against you in the next election, and you won't do it."[57]

Some states offer less opportunity for using a politician's record against him or her. In a moralistic state such as Minnesota, there are more daily newspapers paying close attention to state policy matters than in, say, individualistic Wyoming. There are more public interest groups and state-level think tanks closely monitoring St. Paul than there are monitoring Cheyenne. Citizens in states with higher levels of civic engagement are more likely to keep their politicians "honest"—reflecting voters' overall policy desires—than are citizens in less engaged states.

In a state such as Idaho or Maryland, one party so completely dominates state politics that only rarely are politicians voted out of office because their records do not reflect public opinion. But even Idaho Republicans or Maryland Democrats can lose—if only in the party primary—if voters sour on their records. Every state capital has engendered enough of an echo chamber that examines and discusses the work of legislators and other elected officials that an overall sense of their records—conservative or liberal, sellout or crusading—is known to people who care enough about politics to vote. If those records do not reflect local opinion, the jobs will go to other candidates in the next election.

Conclusion

This is a highly partisan era, with little civility or cooperation, it seems, between Republicans and Democrats. But the war between the red and the blue will never be as heated as the war between the blue and the gray—the North and the South during the Civil War. Although voters today are divided, they are not as deeply divided as they have been at other moments in the country's past, such as during the Civil War or at the time of the Watergate scandal.

This fact is reflected in the recent series of contentious but ultimately narrowly won presidential contests, and on down through other levels of government. As with Congress and the electoral

---

Redistricting
The drawing of new boundaries for congressional and state legislative districts, usually following a decennial census.

college, state legislatures have been closely divided, with the two main parties switching leads in total number of seats nationwide throughout the early twenty-first century. The lead among governorships has switched around, too, with Democrats currently up.

The outcomes of recent elections reflect the divided public mood. State and local officials have less ability to control who participates in the political process because of the many changes in voting laws passed at the federal level. They do still maintain a lot of control over whom citizens can vote for through their regulation of political parties and their ability to decide who deserves to get their names on the ballot.

Which state officials citizens get to vote for differs depending on where the citizens live. In most states, citizens vote for several statewide officials such as governor, attorney general, and secretary of state. In others, they might vote only for the governor. Similarly, in some localities citizens elect the mayor directly, whereas in others the mayor is chosen by the city council from among its own membership. Some states allow people to vote directly for judges, while in other states judges are appointed to office. Some localities allow residents to vote for school board members; in others, these positions are appointed.

In general, citizens vote for enough officeholders with the authority to control policies that the majority's will becomes law. However, because polling is done far more often at the national level than it is at the local or even the state level, officeholders sometimes have only an anecdotal sense of what their constituents are thinking. They do pay close attention to the clues they are given and monitor opinion as closely as they can. They are well aware that if they do not create the types of policies that most people want, they are not going to stay in office for long.

The Latest Research

This chapter has explained in some depth the role of state and local governments in structuring elections. As discussed above, what citizens need to do in order to register to vote, where they vote, when they vote, and the mechanics of how they vote are largely decisions made by state and local governments. States have differences on all these matters, and it should come as no surprise after reading this chapter that these are differences that make a difference. Tougher registration requirements, for example, tend to result in lower voter turnout.

The studies discussed below represent some of the latest research on how the basic mechanics of elections—for example, deciding what type of ballot to use or where to set up polling stations—can have big impacts on electoral participation. The common theme here is that how states decide to regulate elections is one of the most important, and often overlooked, influences on political participation in local, state, and federal elections.

• •

- **Herrnson, Paul, Michael Hanmer, and Richard Niemi.** 2012. "The Impact of Ballot Type on Voter Errors." *American Journal of Political Science* 56: 716–730.

  This study examines how ballot format and type of voting system (paper or electronic) influence voter error. Specifically, the researchers examined two types of error: (1) wrong-candidate error, which happens when a voter mistakenly casts a ballot for the wrong candidate; and (2) unintentional undervoting, which happens when a voter plans to cast a ballot for a

(Continued)

(Continued)

particular elective office but does not. They found that there was not much difference in these sorts of errors across voting systems (paper ballots had a slightly higher error rate); however, there was a big difference between standard office group (Massachusetts) ballots and ballots that offered the option of voting a straight ticket. The straight ticket option led to significantly more errors. For example, voters in elections using ballots with this option were more likely not to vote in nonpartisan races they had intended to vote in (such races would not be included in a straight ticket option) and, more disturbingly, they were more likely to vote unintentionally for the wrong candidate. The error rate was small, generally less than 5 percent, but it was still enough to make a difference in an election, at least in theory.

- **Brady, Henry, and John McNulty.** 2011. "Turning Out to Vote: The Costs of Finding and Getting to the Polling Place." *American Political Science Review* 105: 115–134.

One of the most important aspects of voting controlled by state and local governments is the determination of where voters can cast their ballots. This study shows that locations of polling places can make a big difference in turnout. Los Angeles County consolidated its voting districts during the 2003 gubernatorial recall election, thus changing the polling places of large numbers of voters. Did these changes in polling stations make a difference? This study suggests that they did: the consolidation was associated with a reduction in polling place turnout by a bit more than three percentage points. One of the implications of this finding is that changing polling places can make a big enough difference in turnout to theoretically make a difference in a close election.

- **Hood, M. V., III, and Charles Bullock III.** 2012. "Much Ado about Nothing? An Empirical Assessment of the Georgia Voter Identification Statute." *State Politics & Policy Quarterly* 12: 393–414.

As discussed above, among the more controversial reforms of voting regulations in recent years has been the decision by some states to require voters to provide proof of identification before casting ballots. Opponents of these laws worry that they will suppress turnout, especially among certain disadvantaged (especially racial minority) groups who are less likely to have typical government approved IDs such as driver's licenses. This study examines the impact of Georgia's decision to implement a voter ID law beginning in 2007. The researchers did not find that the new law suppressed turnout in any particular racial demographic. However, they did find that the law reduced voter turnout, although not by much. The new regulation was associated with a decrease in turnout of less than one-half of a percentage point.

- **Davidson, Chandler.** 2009. "The Historical Context of Voter Photo-ID Laws." *PS: Political Science & Politics* 42: 93–96.

This essay argues that regardless of the empirical impact of voter ID laws, their adoption raises some disturbing questions about their intent given the history in numerous states of attempting to suppress minority voting. The author notes that proponents in Indiana argued that a voter ID law was needed to reduce the possibility of one particular type of voter fraud: somebody impersonating someone else in order to vote at a polling place. They could produce little evidence, however, that this sort of fraud was ever a problem in that state. While the historical record reveals almost no significant amount of voter impersonation, the author points out, attempts to suppress minority voting have a deep and extensive history. Thus it seems less likely that these laws are designed to prevent a type of fraud that is not happening than they are to suppress turnout among targeted groups. What this essay highlights is that empirical findings such as those reported in the Hood and Bullock study discussed above are not likely to end the voter ID controversy. The debate is fueled not just by the impact of the laws but by the underlying intent motivating them.

Chapter Review

Key Concepts

- blanket primary (p. 124)
- nonpartisan election (p. 129)
- office group (Massachusetts) ballot (p. 120)
- party column (Indiana) ballot (p. 120)
- plural executive system (p. 132)

- plurality (p. 117)
- recall (p. 140)
- redistricting (p. 144)
- secret (Australian) ballot (p. 122)
- straight ticket (p. 120)
- voter turnout (p. 126)

Suggested Web Sites

- **http://fairvote.org.** Web site of the Center for Voting and Democracy, which promotes voting and advocates instant-runoff voting and the abolition of the electoral college.

- **http://pewresearch.org.** Web site of the Pew Research Center for the People & the Press, which conducts surveys and publishes studies that look at the demographic trends affecting politics.

- **www.lwv.org.** Web site of the League of Women Voters. Provides a wealth of voter education information.

- **www.nass.org.** Web site of the National Association of Secretaries of State. Secretaries of state typically serve as chief election officials, and their offices have primary responsibility for recording official election outcomes.

STATE STATS
State Stats on Political Attitudes and Participation

Explore and compare data on the states! Go to college.cqpress.com/sites/govstateandlocal to do these exercises.

1. Considering the historical support of African Americans for one political party over the other, if you were running for president as a Democrat, would you be more likely to win in Michigan or West Virginia? Why?

2. If voters in lower income brackets are less likely to vote than their richer counterparts, would you expect to see higher voter turnout in Texas or Utah? Why?

3. What is Nebraska's per capita expenditure on welfare programs? What is Maine's? What political variables might account for such a big difference between the two states?

4. The chapter notes that government leadership is not nearly as white and Protestant as it used to be. How has the percentage of the population in your state that is white changed between 2000 and 2010? What (if anything) does this mean for politics?

5. Which states have the largest percentage of the population who are marijuana users? How does this correlate with the results of the recent election that legalized marijuana for recreational use in two states? If this trend continued, which states might we expect to see legalize marijuana next? Why?

Once seen as a fringe cause, legalization of marijuana use won voter approval in two states in 2012. But demonstrators such as Joe Tremolada in Oakland, California, are still protesling federal enforcement of drug laws.

Parties and Interest Groups

ELEPHANTS, DONKEYS, AND CASH COWS

- Why are political parties weaker than they used to be?
- Why are political parties stronger in some states than in others?
- How do interest groups influence policymakers?

How did Thomas Massie get elected as a Republican congressman from Kentucky? Many people think it had a lot to do with a twenty-one-year-old college student from Texas.

Massie was considered an underdog in a western Kentucky congressional district where the incumbent, Republican representative Geoff Davis, was retiring in 2012. Davis and Senator Jim Bunning had both given their blessing to a state representative named Alecia Webb-Edgington, and Massie headed into the May Republican primary as an underdog.

But Massie won the support of several outside interest groups—as well as James Ramsey, a college student who had inherited a fortune from his grandfather. Ramsey started his own campaign committee, known as a **super PAC**, which devoted some $500,000 to the race— roughly double what Massie or Webb-Edgington were able to raise in support of their

---

Super Pac
A political action committee that can spend unlimited funds on behalf of a political candidate but cannot directly coordinate its plans with that candidate.

campaigns. Just before the vote, Massie said he had never met Ramsey, but admitted he was likely to send him a Christmas card. Because the district votes so reliably Republican, Massie's primary win was tantamount to his election to Congress. "It shows the role you can play in congressional districts, where you don't have to have that much money," said Trey Grayson, director of the Harvard University Institute of Politics. "Essentially one person, a college kid who inherited a lot of money, created a super PAC that swung the race dramatically in Massie's direction."[1]

Massie's victory showcases three important trends in contemporary American politics. For one thing, the district he was running in, by being so reliably Republican, demonstrates the extent of **polarization** in U.S. politics. Voters increasingly live in districts—both congressional and legislative—that tend to favor one party or the other. There is little ideological overlap between the parties and less bipartisan cooperation in Congress or statehouses than there used to be. As a result, the key electoral contests in many cases have become the **primary elections** in which party nominees are decided.

Massie's ability to prevail over a candidate who had the backing of top elected officials from her party also illustrates the shifting dynamics in U.S. politics. So-called **establishment** candidates, who typically would have been expected to garner most nominations in the past, now often struggle against opponents who may have lighter political résumés but can win over voters by portraying themselves as insurgents who will challenge the status quo. In large part, that's because such insurgents have new organizing and fund-raising tools at hand. Social media help, but, crucially, these candidates also are able to raise campaign funds independent of the prevailing party structure. Thanks to recent court decisions, money is able to flow more freely into campaigns than has been the case for the past hundred years. Sometimes insurgent candidates are able to raise funds themselves, but often, as in Massie's case, dollars finds their way into their races through independent **political action committees (PACs)**, including super PACs.

Super PACs are not allowed to coordinate their messages directly with candidates, but sometimes these organizations are run by close allies of candidates, such as former aides. Other times, they have no connection to candidates at all—which leads some observers to worry that such groups could end up dominating the political conversation. With the rise of super PACs, "candidates, those on the ballots, will be much more of an afterthought than they ever were before," said Wisconsin state senator Jon Erpenbach, a Democrat. "In some cases, candidates don't even matter."[2]

In any event, the changing financial landscape is having one certain effect: the line between **political parties** and **interest groups**—individuals, corporations, or associations that seek to influence the actions of elected and appointed public officials on behalf of specific companies or causes—is becoming more blurred. Historically, political parties have helped select, groom, and promote candidates, who were then largely aligned with their parties' platforms. Today, candidates at both the state and federal level may end up relying more heavily, for financial support at least, on outside interest groups. Such a group may have a broad political agenda that closely mirrors that of

---

Polarization
A split among elected officials or an electorate along strictly partisan lines.

Primary Election
An election that determines a party's nominees for offices in a general election against other parties' nominees.

Establishment
The nexus of people holding power over an extended period of time, including top elected officials, lobbyists, and party strategists

Political Action Committee
A group formed for the purpose of raising money to elect or defeat political candidates. PACs traditionally represent business, union, or ideological interests.

Political Parties
Organizations that nominate and support candidates for elected offices.

Interest Groups
Individuals, corporations, or associations that seek to influence the actions of elected and appointed public officials on behalf of specific companies or causes.

a party—helping to support and elect more Republicans, for instance—or it may be more concerned with a single issue, such as protecting the environment or keeping taxes low.

In either event, political parties—and candidates themselves—have less control over the political agenda than they did even a few years ago, simply because campaign finance is now structured in such a way as to make interest groups more influential. And interest groups are acting more like parties did in the past, helping to recruit candidates as well as supporting them financially once they decide to run.

Still, parties have an important role to play—arguably a more important one than was the case a generation ago. This chapter explores the roles political parties play and how those vary by state, as well as the influence that interest groups have, not only on elections but also on governance.

A Primer on Political Parties

Political parties are not as dominant in American life as they once were. From roughly the 1820s until the 1940s, political parties constituted a leading organizing force in this country. They not only provided citizens with political identities but also were major sources of social activity and entertainment—and, in many cases, jobs. Today, parties are not as effective as they used to be at getting people out to vote or even at organizing them around an issue. However, they do remain important to candidates, giving them a kind of "brand" identification and acting as fund-raisers.

Although there are two major national parties, the party organizations play larger roles at the state level than they do as national forces. Their respective strength varies widely from state to state and is affected by such factors as the different ways states regulate parties, the differences in the historical roles that parties have played within each state, and the amount of competition between the major parties within a given state. In general, the more closely balanced the two main parties are in a state, the more likely that they will have well-funded and well-organized state-level party organizations.

Political parties recruit candidates for offices and provide them with support for their campaigns. They give candidates money or help them to raise it and offer logistical and strategic assistance. Just as important, they help coordinate the candidates' messages with those of other candidates running for other offices under the party's banner.

Since the 1850s, the vast majority of candidates for political office in the United States have run as members of either the Democratic or the Republican Party. The Democratic Party as we know it today evolved from **factional splits** in the earliest days of the American republic. The country started without a two-party system, but factions soon developed. The Federalists, led by Alexander Hamilton, favored a strong central government with power rooted in the industrial North. The Democratic-Republicans, led by Thomas Jefferson, emerged as the party opposing the Federalists. They argued for states' rights against a "monarchical" rule by the aristocracy and declared that farmers, craftspeople, and shopkeepers should control their own interests without interference from the capitol.

Jefferson's party, which eventually morphed into the Democratic Party, dominated politics throughout the first half of the nineteenth century. That same period saw the creation of numerous parties: Whigs, Know-Nothings, Barnburners, Softshells, Hunkers, and Free Soilers. They all had some success, but the Democratic Party of Jefferson and Andrew Jackson dominated so completely that, as the main source of political power, the party split into factions, with northern and southern Democrats arguing over the expansion of slavery. That argument created an opening for a new major party.

The Republican Party was formed in 1854 in opposition to slavery. It soon replaced the Whig Party, which had been formed in 1834 to protest the spoils-system politics of Andrew Jackson. The Republican Party, also known as the Grand Old Party (GOP), quickly enjoyed congressional success. Following the election of Abraham Lincoln in 1860, Republicans dominated the presidency for decades to come. Their antislavery stance, however, guaranteed that the party remained practically nonexistent in the South until the civil rights

---

Factional Splits, or Factions
Groups that struggle to control the message within a party; for example, a party may be split into competing regional factions.

era of the 1950s and 1960s. Democrats reemerged as the nation's dominant party in the 1930s, when Republicans were took the blame for the Great Depression. The Democrats' New Deal coalition of southerners, union workers, African Americans, the poor, and the elderly drove American politics well into the 1960s but fragmented after that, resulting in a loss of political control.

Long-standing Democratic majorities at the congressional and state levels eroded. Republicans dominated presidential elections from 1968 through 1988, winning five out of the six contests. Since then, however, Democrats have met with more success, carrying the popular vote five of six times. But national elections are still highly competitive. In 2004, Republican George W. Bush became the first presidential candidate since 1988 to win a majority—51 percent—of the popular vote. (He had prevailed in the electoral college four years earlier, despite trailing in the national popular vote count by 500,000 votes.) In 2012, Democrat Barack Obama won reelection with 51 percent of the vote—down from 53 percent in 2008, making him just the third president in U.S. history to have been reelected with a smaller share of the vote than he received during his initial election. (The other two were Franklin D. Roosevelt, whose winning percentage ticked down in both 1940 and 1944, and Andrew Jackson, who took less of the popular vote in 1832.) The narrow margins of presidential victories suggest that, at least at the national level, the two major political parties have spent a decade at roughly equal strength. At the congressional level, Democrats were able to gain a majority in the House of Representatives in 2006 but lost it four years later. Similarly, the Democratic edge in state legislative seats was wiped out by the Republican wave in 2010, when the GOP gained the most seats at that level since the 1920s.

It is no secret that contemporary politics is highly competitive. Neither side enjoys a consistent advantage nationally. Candidates from either party are capable of winning statewide offices in nearly every state. Overall support for the parties is, however, split along regional lines. Democrats enjoy more support along the West Coast and in the Northeast, whereas Republicans are dominant in the South and the Plains states. The upper Midwest and parts of the Mountain West such as Colorado have become the most competitive regions.

Although most Americans are familiar with the Republican and Democratic parties, many may not realize that political parties technically take many different shapes. When people refer to Democrats or Republicans, they are really referring to officials belonging to two umbrella groups that cover a wide variety of parties. Each of the national parties is in reality a consortium of state parties. Party chairs and other representatives from the state parties dominate the national party committees. State parties, in turn, are consortia of local parties. In some states local parties are defined by counties, whereas in others they are defined by congressional districts. Although both the Democratic and Republican parties are active in every state, some state and local parties are more active than others. Parties in densely populated states such as Florida and California are well-funded, professionally run organizations. In less populated states such as Montana and Idaho, the parties have very small full-time staffs and take on more personnel just during the few months leading up to an election.

A given state may have a particularly dominant political party, but overall, the political parties in most of the world's other Western-style democracies are much stronger than those in the United States. For example, in the United States, party leaders are not able to nominate candidates of their own choosing. Most candidates are now chosen directly by the voting public through primaries. In fact, even a party's top nominee—its presidential candidate—may not have been the first choice of party leaders. This is much different from the way party politics operates in, say, Great Britain. There, political parties are much more centralized. Leadership within a party translates more cleanly into leadership in government. The parties, not voters, select the parties' nominees for the office of prime minister.

In the United States, the national Republican and Democratic Parties essentially are made up of state parties. The Republican and Democratic National Committees are made up almost exclusively of state party chairs and one male and one female representative from each state. Representatives from the territories—Puerto Rico, Guam, and the U.S. Virgin Islands, among others—form the rest of the body for each party. U.S. political parties tend to be regulated at the state level. The ways in which they raise and spend money, their organizational structures, and the rules they follow to nominate candidates and place them on ballots all are subject to differing state regulations. How much power the national parties have in relation to the state parties shifts over time, as we will see.

> For many people, partisanship represents a psychological attachment to a political party—a sort of brand loyalty—rather than a rational assessment of personal beliefs and party stance.

That is not to say that parties are not collections of interests. They are conglomerations of people who share some overlapping ideology, or set of political, economic, and social beliefs. These days, Democrats are supported by pro-choice groups and gun control advocates. Environmentalists, trial lawyers, labor union members, Hispanics, Asian Americans, and African Americans also tend to be Democrats. Republicans gain support from corporate and small businesses and social conservatives. Party members tend to advocate respect for limited government, private property, and protection of rights for gun owners. Republicans are also more likely than Democrats to attend church regularly. These differences, however, are far from absolute. For many people, partisanship represents a psychological attachment to a political party—a sort of brand loyalty—rather than a rational assessment of personal beliefs and party stance.

After Ronald Reagan and other Republicans chipped into Democratic support among certain groups in the New Deal coalition, the Democrats became a famously argumentative group, with various factions within the party finding it hard to find common cause with one another. As recently as 2006, a Democratic strategist wrote about "the Democratic Party's well-deserved reputation for being a fractious coalition of infighting special interests."[3] But following their poor showing in that year's elections, Republicans began to argue more loudly among themselves about which ideas should prevail within the party—a fractious debate that continued through and after the party's losing presidential campaigns in 2008 and 2012. Conservative, populist, so-called Tea Party groups began holding large rallies in 2009 to decry big government, President Obama's administration, and their more moderate counterparts within the Republican Party. But by 2013, major Republican donors had formed a super PAC in the hope of nominating more "electable" candidates for offices such as U.S. Senate, rather than the more ideologically pure nominees favored by the Tea Party wing. "There is clearly a war going on in the Republican Party," Bob Smith, a Republican and former U.S. senator from New Hampshire, said. "The sooner the party's leadership recognizes that, the better off they'll be."[4] Other groups are made up of so-called **swing voters**—that is, voters who might support candidates of either major party. Swing voters include farmers, suburbanites, and the elderly. Neither party can take their votes for granted, so they are highly sought after. Young people have tended not to vote much at all, or at least not in proportion to their share of the population, which is why their concerns have often been ignored, but they have emerged more recently as a key source of Democratic support. Pulling together as wide an assortment of interests as they can, political parties help voters and groups connect with the government while furthering their own ideals.

Swing Voters
Individuals who are not consistently loyal to candidates of any one party. They are true independents whose allegiance is fought for in every election.

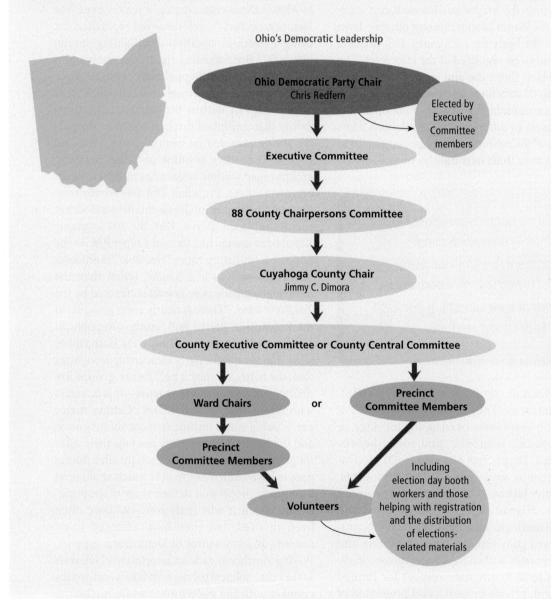

FIGURE 6-1

HOW IT WORKS

Democratic and Republican Party Organization in Ohio and Cuyahoga County

Ohio's Democratic Leadership

Ohio Democratic Party Chair
Chris Redfern

Elected by Executive Committee members

Executive Committee

88 County Chairpersons Committee

Cuyahoga County Chair
Jimmy C. Dimora

County Executive Committee or County Central Committee

Ward Chairs or **Precinct Committee Members**

Precinct Committee Members

Volunteers

Including election day booth workers and those helping with registration and the distribution of elections-related materials

Political parties, however, remain different from other groups that participate in the political process, including interest groups. As already noted, a political candidate runs under a single party label, such as Republican, Democratic, or Green. The candidate campaigns for office and is nominated as a member of that party. In contrast to political parties, an interest group may support a candidate, but that person's candidacy is not based on affiliation with the group. The interest

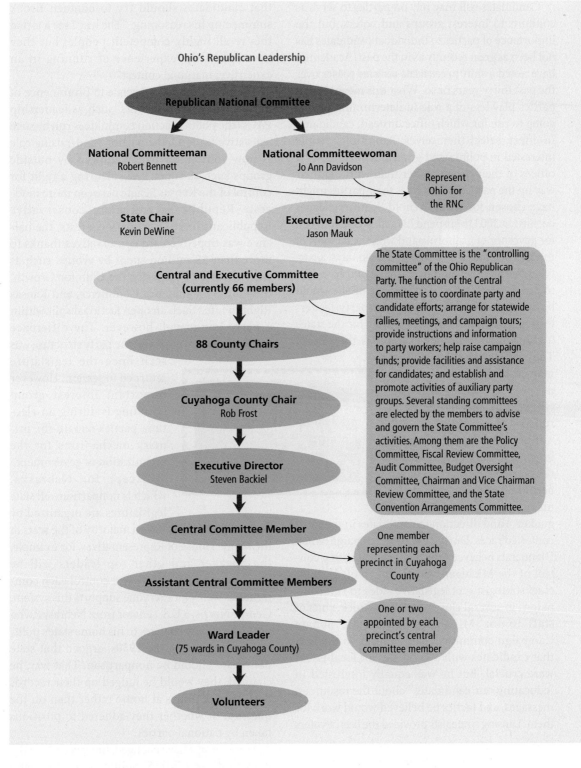

Ohio's Republican Leadership

Republican National Committee

National Committeeman
Robert Bennett

National Committeewoman
Jo Ann Davidson

Represent Ohio for the RNC

State Chair
Kevin DeWine

Executive Director
Jason Mauk

Central and Executive Committee
(currently 66 members)

The State Committee is the "controlling committee" of the Ohio Republican Party. The function of the Central Committee is to coordinate party and candidate efforts; arrange for statewide rallies, meetings, and campaign tours; provide instructions and information to party workers; help raise campaign funds; provide facilities and assistance for candidates; and establish and promote activities of auxiliary party groups. Several standing committees are elected by the members to advise and govern the State Committee's activities. Among them are the Policy Committee, Fiscal Review Committee, Audit Committee, Budget Oversight Committee, Chairman and Vice Chairman Review Committee, and the State Convention Arrangements Committee.

88 County Chairs

Cuyahoga County Chair
Rob Frost

Executive Director
Steven Backiel

Central Committee Member

One member representing each precinct in Cuyahoga County

Assistant Central Committee Members

One or two appointed by each precinct's central committee member

Ward Leader
(75 wards in Cuyahoga County)

Volunteers

group did not recruit the candidate and does not support him or her to run in its name. The interest group, in fact, might be supporting candidates from several parties. Increasingly, however, politically engaged interest groups tend to be associated with one party or another.

Candidates still may rely on parties to serve as conduits to interest groups and voters, but the importance of parties to individual candidates has not been as great recently as in the past. Academics have noted a shift to **candidate-centered politics** over the past thirty years or so. What this means is that parties play less of a role in determining who is going to run for which office. Instead, candidates, in effect, select themselves. Ambitious people interested in politics and government run for the offices of their choice rather than working their way up the party ranks in roles their parties might have chosen for them. Arnold Schwarzenegger decided in 2003 to suspend his acting career to run for governor of California and won the support of the state's Republican Party. In the old days, a party's gubernatorial candidate first would have had to put in years in lower offices. He or she would have had to earn the support of party leaders throughout the state before running for the state's highest office. Another example is the case of Thomas Massie, the congressman from Kentucky, who did not need the blessing of his party's elders to make his successful run for office in 2012.

But political parties remain important. They have started to reassert themselves, again becoming lead fund-raisers for many campaigns and providing guidance and direction to candidates in the most contested races. During the 2006 campaign, when Democrats believed they had a shot at taking control of the Michigan Senate (they failed), their chief strategist sent legislative aides to run campaigns in several close races. Ken Brock, chief of staff to the Michigan Democratic Senate Campaign committee, paid homage to the idea that candidates with a good feel for local issues were crucial. But he was equally interested in "educating our candidates" about the resources, messages, and tactics he believed would work for them. Lansing strategists provided the lists of voters that candidates should try to contact. Brock summed up his reasoning: "The way I see it is that they're all highly competent people, but they haven't had the experience of running in an expensive, marginal contest."[5]

Even with the reemergence to prominence of parties and their offshoots, such as leadership PACs (the political action committees run by state legislative leaders), the parties' fund-raising role is now sometimes overshadowed by outside groups such as super PACs. During a fight for control of the Kansas Senate between more moderate Republicans and more conservative Republicans in 2012 primary contests, the balance was tipped toward conservatives thanks to more than $8 million spent by groups such as Americans for Prosperity, the Club for Growth, the Kansas Chamber of Commerce, and Kansas Right to Life.[6] Such an open factional split within a party is unusual, however. The difference between these groups and the party structure was seen once the legislature returned to session. However important interest group spending is during an election, parties remain the primary mechanisms for the organization of government.

Except for Nebraska, which is nonpartisan, all state legislatures are organized by party. If Democrats have a majority of the seats in the Maine House of Representatives, for example, the Speaker and other top leaders will be Democrats and the party will control each committee as well. Not everyone supports this system. George Norris, a U.S. senator from Nebraska who promoted many changes to his home state's political system during the 1930s, argued that state politicians should be nonpartisan. That way, he claimed, they would be judged on their records dealing with issues at home rather than on the question of whether they adhered to positions taken by national parties.

Some things have changed, however. Once the dominant force in U.S. politics—deciding who would run for which office and with how much support—political parties have become such

Candidate-Centered Politics
Politics in which candidates promote themselves and their own campaigns rather than relying on party organizations.

loose conglomerations of differing interests that they might be best described as marketing organizations. They are brand names that individual candidates choose to apply as a shortcut to identification in the marketplace. For example, to say that you are a Democratic candidate provides voters with a fairly reliable indication that you are for abortion rights legislation. Republicans—those who run for office, if not all rank-and-file party members—nearly always feel the opposite. These days, there is little overlap between the parties on a whole host of issues, including tax policy, gun ownership rights, and environmental protections.

Given the overall decline of strong **voter identification** with either major party, today's politics generally centers more on individual candidates than on party politics. Parties have found a new role as support organs. They offer consulting and fund-raising services to self-selected aspirants. They have become "basically what you might call holding companies," says Walter Dean Burnham, a former political science professor at the University of Texas. "They organize cash and spread it around."[7] But now parties are being forced to adapt to legal restrictions on those functions as well. A federal campaign finance law passed by Congress in 2002 and upheld by the Supreme Court in 2003 makes it more complicated for parties to spend money on activities designed to register voters or encourage them to vote. (The Supreme Court reaffirmed the law's constitutionality in 2007 and, as pertains to party fund-raising limits, again in 2010.) Thanks to subsequent court decisions, such roles are now often played by super PACs and other groups that are at least technically separated from political parties and their candidates.

This does not mean political parties have become irrelevant to state and local politics. What they do and how they do it have changed considerably, but democratic politics—and this certainly includes politics in states and localities—is virtually unthinkable without political parties. As a theoretical ideal, or baseline, political scientists use the **responsible party model** as a way to measure and assess political parties. The responsible party model holds that political parties should present clear policy options to voters, that voters will cast ballots based on the options they favor the most, that while in office parties try to create and implement the programs they promise, and that in the next election the parties will be judged by their performance in delivering these programs. In short, this model views political parties as connecting the wishes of citizens to government programs and policies, organizing the government to deliver on those wishes, and acting as the agents used to hold government accountable for delivering on what it promises. These are all highly valuable services to democratic politics, and despite all their changes, political parties have always served and continue to serve these roles.

Of course, how well parties serve these functions varies from state to state. To have some semblance of a responsible party model, you need at least two competitive political parties offering voters clear choices on policies and programs. You also need parties that actually try to deliver on these policies and programs once they secure a controlling influence in government. Finally, you need voters who pay attention to what the party in power is doing and vote accordingly. States where only one party is competitive at the polls or where there is consistently low voter turnout are less likely to fulfill the promises of the responsible party model.

What Parties Were Like

In their early years, political parties in the United States were a lot more than just brand identifiers and fund-raisers. Many of the social services now provided by local governments, such as food assistance and job placement services, were the

---

Voter Identification
When a voter identifies strongly with one of the major parties, he or she is considered a Democrat or a Republican; many voters, however, are considered weakly aligned with either major party.

Responsible Party Model
The theory that political parties offer clear policy choices to voters, try to deliver on those policies when they take office, and are held accountable by voters for the success or failure of those policies.

province of political parties throughout much of the nineteenth century. For all of the contemporary complaints about the "liberal media," one-sided bloggers, and the domination of talk radio by conservative hosts, today's nonpartisan "mainstream" media are a far cry from the newspapers of the late nineteenth century, which were often openly affiliated with particular parties. The pro-Republican *Chicago Tribune,* on learning that a Democrat had won the 1876 presidential election, ran a headline that read, "Lost. The Country Given over to Democratic Greed and Plunder."[8] Such an openly partisan statement is unimaginable in the mainstream media of today (although not nearly as unlikely in a blog post or on Twitter).

People's party loyalties were so strong in this period because many of their livelihoods revolved around party interests. Party machines doled out jobs, government contracts, and other benefits to their workers and supporters. The idea was that "offices exist not as a necessary means of administering government but for the support of party leaders at public expense," as one political scientist writes of nineteenth-century party cliques in New York State.[9]

Politics in many cities and some states was totally dominated by these usually indigenous party machines. In Rhode Island, the Democratic Party was dominant through much of the twentieth century, and party leaders brooked little dissent. Only a handful of free-agent candidates were able to pry nominations away from those who had been endorsed by the party. In Providence, the state capital and largest city, only three individuals held the office of mayor from 1941 until 1974. Two of those men were state Democratic Party leaders. Over the same thirty-year period, only two chairs headed the Providence Democratic Party. Both of them doubled as head of the city's Department of Public Works. Party leaders controlled 2,800 jobs, doling them out roughly equally among the various wards, or political districts, within the city.[10]

The close links connecting control of jobs, government spending, and party activity were hardly

---

Political Machines

Political organizations controlled by small numbers of people and run for partisan ends. In the nineteenth and twentieth centuries these organizations controlled party nominations for public office and rewarded supporters with government jobs and contracts.

unique to Rhode Island. Chicago, Nassau County on Long Island, New York, and Pennsylvania were all home to legendary **political or party machines**. A long-standing joke about Chicago politics held that as many dead people voted as living ones (because the names of those who died were not removed from the election rolls and were used to cast extra votes for favored candidates). In Oklahoma, the state gave control of most government jobs—the decision-making power over hiring and firing workers—to individual officeholders. These individuals were not afraid to exploit such control for their own benefit. "I have 85 employees—garage men, road workers, janitors, elevator operators—and they work for me when I need them," said a county commissioner. "These people care if I stay in office."[11]

> "I have 85 employees—garage men, road workers, janitors, elevator operators—and they work for me when I need them," said a county commissioner. "These people care if I stay in office."

The machine system was self-perpetuating, with control of jobs and power and offices feeding off one another. "Each succeeding election was viewed not as a separate contest involving new issues or new personalities," writes political scientist Joel Sibley, "but as yet another opportunity to vote for, and reaffirm, an individual's support for his or her party and what it represented."[12] Party machines and rival factions ran "slates," or specific lists, of endorsed candidates for offices and lent their backing to the favored candidates. Sometimes this support came at a price. For instance, contenders for the West Virginia General Assembly once had to pay between $250 and $400 each for the honor of being listed on one of the various slates in Kanawha County, in which the state capital of Charleston is located.

Given party contacts and contracts with private-sector entities, party control of jobs often extended well beyond the borders of government. Sometimes—as was the case in Jersey City, New Jersey—the

"To the victor belong the spoils." President Andrew Jackson popularized a system of patronage, insisting that public offices should be filled by supporters of the party in power.

machines would charge an automatic kickback, demanding, say, 3 percent of public employee salaries. Such trimmings were not always enough to satisfy machine leaders. The exposure of clear cases of corruption, such as evidence that a party was extorting union funds, running gambling operations, and taking kickbacks on government contracts, often led to the election of reform candidates for mayor and other city and state offices.

There were other backlashes against such obvious corruption. In New Orleans, a Democratic Party political machine called the Old Regulars ruled the city from the 1890s until the mid-1930s. By then, they were the only political force left in Louisiana outside the control of the Populist governor, Huey Long. In 1934 and 1935, Long concentrated all of his powers on changing the machine's management. He limited local control over jobs and triggered a police investigation. He even sent the National Guard into New Orleans. In the end, the machine had no choice but to accept a new city leader and get on board the Long bandwagon.[13]

Breaking up the machines usually took less extreme effort. For one thing, in many states, such as Alabama, Florida, and Michigan, elected officials and party leaders had little opportunity to practice **patronage**—that is, to hand out jobs to their friends and supporters rather than hiring people based on qualifications. Therefore, there was little motivation to build up a machine. In some places, such as Texas, nineteenth-century political parties were weak. They helped administer the election code and tried to remain acceptable to all candidates. In other places, disgust over corruption in politics led to antimachine statutes,

CIVIL SERVICE REFORM.
Office-Seeker. "St. Jackson, can't you save us? Can't *you* give us something?"

such as the imposition of civil service requirements for many government jobs and tougher anticorruption laws. The widespread use of **nonpartisan ballots** for municipal offices was the direct result of reforms imposed in reaction to political machines. These ballots, which do not list candidates by political party, are designed to separate city government from party voting.

California may be the best example of a state that had such a progressive reaction against the machines. The state was hostile toward parties, lacked any type of patronage system, and held nonpartisan elections. Precinct and ward organizations were weak, whereas individual candidates were assertive.[14] Party organizations were once banned from endorsing candidates in primary contests. The law also limited state party

---

Patronage
The practice of elected officials or party leaders handing out jobs to their friends and supporters rather than hiring people based on merit.

Nonpartisan Ballot
A ballot that does not list candidates by political party; this type of ballot is still often used in local elections.

chairs to two-year terms and required the rotation of chairs on a geographical basis every two years. In 1989, the U.S. Supreme Court threw out the statute and declared it unconstitutional.[15]

But California was the exception to the rule. Throughout the 1800s, most states essentially treated parties as private associations and chose not to regulate them. This remains the position of many other countries today. But, during the twentieth century, that all changed in the United States. States began to regulate parties as though they were public utilities. Such state regulation of political parties is examined later in this chapter.

Parties in the Twentieth Century

At the dawn of the twentieth century, political machines were generally locally based, and local parties were much more important political actors than state parties in states where there were powerful big-city machines. Elsewhere, state parties often were funded and controlled by corporate interests—in many cases by just one interest, such as the DuPont Corporation in Delaware or the Anaconda Copper Company in Montana. Following the Progressive Era reforms in states such as California, state parties became little more than empty shells. As late as the 1970s, many state parties lacked permanent headquarters and were run out of their chairs' homes.[16]

State parties lost much of their influence because of the rise of primary elections. In primary elections, voters select the candidates who will represent the parties in general elections, the contests between party nominees that decide which candidates will actually win political office. Before primary elections became common, parties picked their nominees through party conventions, meetings of a few hundred party officials or supporters. At conventions, party leaders closely controlled most votes and thus had enormous influence over who would or would not become the party's official nominee in the general election. This influence is lost in a primary election; in a primary, members of the general public have the chance to cast secret

ballots. This gives party officials less direct control over the nominating process. Some states, such as Virginia, still allow for the option of nominating candidates by party conventions, but every state now has a system in place to nominate candidates through primaries. Every party holds statewide conventions, and many hold conventions at the local or district level as well. Nowadays, practically anyone who cares to attend a state or local party convention can do so, but it still takes some effort or connections to attend a national party convention, especially as a voting delegate.

Direct primaries allow rank-and-file voters to choose nominees for public office through means of a direct ballot. This contrasts with the convention system, in which the role of voters is indirect—voters choose delegates to a convention, and the delegates choose the nominee. At the state level, there are three basic types of direct primaries. In a **closed primary**, only registered members of the party holding the primary are allowed to vote, meaning that an individual must be a registered Democrat to vote for the Democratic nominee for office or a registered Republican to vote for the Republican nominee. This type of primary prevents **crossover voting**, in which a member of one party votes in another party's primary (a Democrat voting in a Republican primary, for instance). This practice is not allowed in all states. In an **open primary**, independents—and in some cases members of both parties—can vote in the primary of any party they choose. In a blanket primary—a type of primary invalidated in 2000 in the U.S. Supreme Court case *California Democratic Party v. Jones*—all candidates from all parties are listed on a single ballot and voters are allowed, in effect, to mix and match the primaries they participate in. That is, a voter could vote in one party's primary for a particular office, then switch

Party Convention
A meeting of party delegates called to nominate candidates for office and establish party agendas.

Closed Primary
A nominating election in which only voters belonging to that party may participate. Only registered Democrats can vote in a closed Democratic primary, for example.

Crossover Voting
Members of one party voting in another party's primary. This practice is not allowed in all states.

Open Primary
A nominating election that is open to all registered voters regardless of their party affiliations.

General Election
A decisive election in which all registered voters cast ballots for their preferred candidates for a political office.

to another party's primary for another office. Louisiana holds what is essentially a nonpartisan blanket primary—sometimes called a jungle primary—in which all candidates run in the same primary regardless of party. If no candidate wins an outright majority in the primary, the two top vote-getters—regardless of party—go on to a general election face-off. A **runoff primary** sometimes occurs in some states if no candidate receives a majority of the vote in an initial primary. In that case, the top two candidates face off. Washington State and California voters in recent years have established similar "top-two" primary systems, in which candidates from all parties appear together on a single primary ballot, and the top two finishers, regardless of party, proceed to the general election. Map 6-1 shows a state-by-state breakdown of the main types of primaries.

The opposite of the relative openness of primaries is the "smoke-filled room"—a historic term referring to an area at a convention closed off to the public, in which party barons, some puffing on big cigars, chose a candidate of their liking. It is one of the classic images in American politics. Examples of such cronyism abound. At the 1912 Republican national convention, President William Howard Taft had to stave off a challenge from his predecessor, Theodore Roosevelt. Roosevelt had been able to demonstrate his popularity among the party's rank and file by winning every primary that year, save the Massachusetts primary. At the time, however, only a dozen states even held primaries. Taft retained the support of the national party machinery and dominated delegate selection in the nonprimary states. Ultimately, he controlled the convention. Taft was renominated, but he was not reelected. Roosevelt bolted the party, angrily maintaining that Taft's nomination thwarted the will of the "honestly elected majority" of GOP delegates, and ran on a third-party ticket. The split within Republican ranks was enough to allow the

election of Woodrow Wilson, only the second Democrat to win the White House since the Civil War.[17]

As late as 1968, party officials selected about 600 of the 2,600 delegates to the Democratic Party's national convention—almost 25 percent—two to four years ahead of the convention. Senator Eugene McCarthy, D-Minn., had made such a surprisingly strong showing in the New Hampshire primary that he drove President Lyndon Johnson from the race. But Johnson's backing was still significant enough to help his vice president, Hubert H. Humphrey, win the support of delegates controlled by party officials. McCarthy believed he had been cheated by the party rules, so he proposed that all delegates to the nominating convention be chosen through "procedures open to public participation" in the same year in which the convention was to take place.[18]

Humphrey recognized that McCarthy and Senator Robert F. Kennedy, D-N.Y., both of whom had campaigned on anti-Vietnam platforms, had taken 69 percent of the primary vote. Respectful of what that number meant, he wanted to reward their followers with a consolation prize. So Humphrey coupled McCarthy's changes with one proposed by Senator George McGovern, D-S.D. McGovern wanted to see delegations demographically match—or at least reflect—the compositions of the states they represented. More and more states threw up their figurative hands as they tried to meet each of these new requirements. Taking the path of least resistance, they decided that the easiest thing to do was to hold popular-vote primaries. Democratic primaries were held in only fifteen states in 1968, but by 1980 the number had risen to thirty-five. Conventions were reduced to little more than coronation ceremonies.[19]

How State Parties Recovered: Campaign Reform in the Late Twentieth Century

There aren't many smoke-filled rooms at party conventions anymore—and not just because of

---

Runoff Primary
An election held if no candidate receives a majority of the vote during the regular primary. The two top finishers face off again in a runoff to determine the nominee for the general election. Such elections are held only in some states, primarily in the South.

MAP 6-1

Party Affiliation Requirements for Voting in Direct Primaries

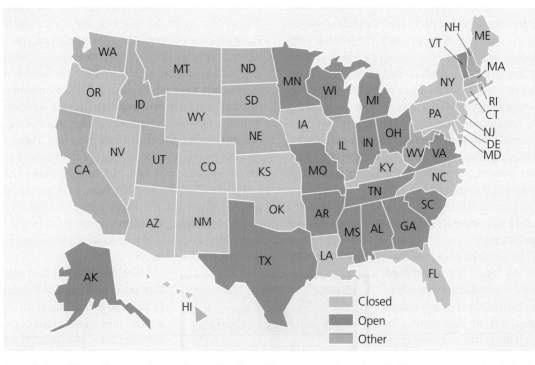

Source: Center for Voting and Democracy, "Primaries: Open and Closed," www.fairvote.org/congressional-and-presidential-primaries-open-closed-semi-closed-and-top-two#.UNt5xXfNmSq.

Notes:

Alaska: Closed caucuses for both parties, but voters may change party affiliation at polls or caucus.

California: In 2010, California approved a system in which all candidates compete on the same primary ballot, with the two top finishers, regardless of party, proceeding to the general election.

Idaho: Democrats have an open caucus in Idaho, while the Republicans have an open primary.

Illinois: Must vote in primary of same party as last primary the voter participated in. Loosely enforced. Voters may change party affiliation at polls or caucus.

Iowa: Closed caucuses, but voters may change registration at polls.

Kansas: In the Democratic caucus, independent voters can register as Democrats on caucus day. For Republicans it is a closed caucus.

Louisiana: Primaries are closed for presidential elections. For congressional elections, they are effectively open, because Louisiana currently uses a top-two runoff system. The state switched to a closed primary for congressional races after 2006.

Maryland: Parties can choose to open primaries but both Democrats and Republicans have chosen not to. If a voter does not choose a party, he or she will be recorded as "unaffiliated" and is permitted to vote in any nonpartisan primary in his or her local jurisdiction.

Massachusetts: Registered Democrats and Republicans can vote only for their own party in the primary, but independent voters may decide which party they would like to vote for.

Montana: Republicans have a closed caucus, while Democrats have an open primary.

New Hampshire: Registered Democrats and Republicans can vote only for their own party in the primary, but independent voters may decide which party they would like to vote for. Unregistered voters can register on election day.

New Jersey: Registered Democrats and Republicans can vote only for their own party in the primary. Any New Jersey voter who has never on a previous occasion voted in a New Jersey primary election may declare a party affiliation at the polling place. Independents may also decide which party to vote for.

North Carolina: A person registered with a party must vote in that party's primary. Unaffiliated voters may choose a party on the day of the primary election.

North Dakota: North Dakota has no voter registration. Voters must only prove that they have been a resident for at least thirty days.

Ohio: A voter must vote in the primary of the same party he or she participated in at the last primary election.

Rhode Island: If voters are registered as "unaffiliated" they may vote in the primary of any party they choose. Once they vote in a primary, however, they are considered a member of that party until and unless they "disaffiliate."

Utah: Currently only Republicans close their primary. Democrats and independents can vote in the Democratic primary. Conventions are held by the political parties prior to the primary.

Virginia: Parties may choose to nominate by convention rather than by primary election.

Washington: The state in 2004 moved to an open, "top-two" primary system, which the Supreme Court upheld in 2008.

West Virginia: Republicans have a closed convention, while Democrats hold a primary in which unaffiliated voters and independents may participate.

health concerns. By the time the conventions are held, candidates have already been selected by voters through primary elections. Yet the conventions are still important networking occasions for officeholders and activists; they also provide occasions for parties to change their internal rules. The action for candidates now is in the primary and general election seasons. This is when they have the chance to woo voters directly, if not personally. Candidates no longer need hierarchical machines to reach voters. The decline of party machines was followed in time by the advent of televised campaign commercials as the dominant mode for trying to persuade citizens to vote.

The increasing reliance on campaign ads, ironically, led to restored strength for state and national political parties and spelled the decline of local party strength in federal elections. The move from greeting potential voters in person at party dinners and county fairs to airing TV ads meant that politicians had to run more professional campaigns. They now hire pollsters to figure out which issues will resonate best in their ads. Consultants help shape their message on these issues, and media gurus produce the ads and place them during favorable time slots. Once more changing with the times, state parties became important clearinghouses, connecting candidates with consultants. Eventually, they evolved into important consulting organizations themselves.

Every Democratic and Republican state party now has a full-time chair or executive director. Most have other professional staffers as well, who handle fund-raising, communications, field operations, and campaigns.[20] In general, Republican state parties tend to be better funded and, therefore, better run than their Democratic counterparts. Democratic state parties, however, often gain support from their allied groups, such as labor unions.

With their massive computer databases, maintained and updated from year to year, political parties help candidates target and reach voters who are sympathetic to their messages. It's common now for candidates to carry iPads and smartphones loaded with the latest voter registration data instead of the old-fashioned clipboards full of paper printouts on which they could scribble notes.

Parties also play an important role in helping interested groups and potential contributors determine which of their candidates have a realistic shot at winning. The major parties are not the voter organizers they were in the machine days, when individuals were encouraged to vote "early and often," but they do still contact up to 25 percent of the electorate in any election cycle. Individuals contacted by parties have a much higher tendency to vote than do people who are not contacted, possibly because they feel like they were called because their parties think their votes matter, or maybe just because of the helpful reminder. While the national parties typically play a greater role in polling and developing issues, "local and state parties [are] particularly important for registering voters and conducting get out the vote campaigns."[21]

One state chair in the 1950s exemplified the move that parties made toward professionalized consulting services. Ray Bliss took over the Ohio Republican Party after it suffered an electoral drubbing in 1948. He immediately began to identify and recruit better candidates. He also looked at ways to encourage citizens to vote, noting that, in 1948, 140,000 rural Republicans did not vote and 150,000 potential Republican voters in urban areas were not even registered. Following Bliss's registration and get-out-the-vote drives, Ohio Republicans in 1950 reelected a U.S. senator, won three statewide offices, and regained control of the state legislature.[22]

For years, Republicans were so dominant in Ohio that they controlled every statewide office and both chambers of the state legislature. The Democratic candidate for state attorney general in 2002 tried to turn this hegemony into a campaign issue, complaining, "What has happened in Ohio is that in many ways we have turned government over to the business community with this one-party rule."[23] That kind of complaint became more salient in 2006, when a series of scandals involving GOP officials and their cronies led to the election of a Democratic governor for the first time in twenty years. But the Republicans quickly managed to bounce back, unseating that Democrat in 2010.

Minority-party members enviously keep close tabs on the governing party, and they alert the public and the press to every perceived misstep and abuse. It also is important for minority parties to avoid being demoralized and to continue to offer voters alternatives, so that candidates from their parties will be in place once the public is ready for a change. For instance, conservative Republicans dominated the Arizona Senate during the late 1990s. It seemed certain that Arizona Speaker of the House Jeff Groscost would join their ranks in 2000 because he was running in a Senate district that heavily favored the GOP. Late in the campaign season, however, Groscost was implicated in a scandal surrounding a massive tax break that aided sports utility vehicle (SUV) owners—including a Groscost friend who sold the vehicles—and cost the state hundreds of millions of dollars. Groscost was defeated by his previously unknown Democratic challenger, and the Senate ended up operating under divided control between the parties.

Today, the two parties remain so closely competitive nationally that political scientists refer to a period of **dealignment**, meaning that neither party is dominant. In earlier periods of American history, one party or another generally had dominated politics, holding most of the important offices. The two major examples are Republican dominance from the time of the Civil War into the 1920s and the Democratic New Deal coalition, which held power from the presidential election of 1932 into the 1960s. The 1932 election of Franklin D. Roosevelt is the best example of a **realignment**, the switching of popular support from one party to another. Neither party has pulled off a similarly lasting realignment since then, in that voters seem about equally supportive of both major parties. Indeed, Republican hopes of creating a "permanent majority" following George W. Bush's 2004 win were dashed quickly when Democrats took control of the U.S. Congress in the 2006 midterm elections, followed by Barack Obama's win in the 2008 presidential election. Conversely, Democrats took a shellacking in 2010, although they were able to recover to some extent by 2012 with Obama's reelection.

Dealignment
The lack of nationwide dominance by any one political party.

Realignment
The switching of popular support from one party to another.

State Party Regulation and Finance

It is important to note that the parties do not dry up and blow away once an election is over, although they are obviously most active during campaign seasons. Not only must they plan for the next election—and the one after that and the one after that, in perpetuity—but they also play an important role in actual government operations. Granted, parties no longer are able to run government strictly to perpetuate their own power, as was true to a certain extent in the machine era, but they still help their most important supporters maintain access to officeholders and other officials.

The Nebraska state legislature is organized on a nonpartisan basis (as are most municipal governments), but every other state legislature is organized by party. In other words, if the Republican Party holds a majority of the seats in a state's house of representatives, Republicans not only control the leadership, schedule, and agenda of the house, but they chair the house committees as well. There are exceptions and examples of shared power, particularly when partisan control of a legislature is tied, but these are rare. The more normal state of affairs is for the majority party to rule.

State Party Regulation

Remember that states did not regulate political parties until the beginning of the twentieth century, when the progressive backlash against machine abuse led states to intervene. Political scientists now refer to parties as equivalent to public utilities, such as water and electricity, in which the public has a sufficient interest to justify state regulation.[24] Political parties, after all, are the main conduits through which elections are contested and government is organized. The legal justifications that states have used to regulate parties revolve around registration requirements—twenty-nine states and Washington, D.C., register voters by party[25]—because party names are printed alongside the names of candidates on ballots.

Thirty-eight states regulate aspects of the structure of their state and local parties, often in explicit detail, to prevent antidemocratic, machine-boss control.[26] Some states determine, for instance, how the members of state parties' central committees should be selected and how often those committees will meet. A state might specify which party organization can name a substitute candidate if a nominee dies or withdraws prior to an election. Such regulation is practiced whether in regard to a state party in Minnesota or a local party in Pennsylvania.

A relatively limited number of state parties have challenged the laws regulating parties in the wake of the 1989 Supreme Court decision, mentioned previously, in which the Court ruled that the state of California did not have the authority to dictate how political parties are organized. The major parties in New Jersey did adopt a number of changes in party structure, but for the most part the parties seem satisfied with the way things are being run under the systems imposed on them by the states.

The decision in 1989 was neither the first time nor the last time the U.S. Supreme Court weighed in on concerns related to political parties. The nation's highest court has issued a number of other decisions in recent years to clarify the legal rights of parties. In a series of cases emanating from Illinois during the 1970s and 1980s, the Court made it clear that "party affiliations and support" are unconstitutional bases for the granting of a majority of government or public jobs, except at the highest levels.[27] In 1986, it ruled that the state of Connecticut could not prevent independents from voting in Republican Party primaries if the GOP welcomed them.[28] This precedent, which allowed the parties rather than the state to determine who could participate in the parties' primaries, was later followed in several other states. The parties have not always gotten their way, however. In 1999, the Court determined that states have the constitutional right to regulate elections and prevent manipulation. The ruling blocked a new party in Minnesota from "fusing" with the state's Democratic Party by nominating candidates for election that the Democrats already had nominated.[29]

Campaign Finance

In 1996, the U.S. Supreme Court lifted federal limits on how much parties could spend. Under the new rules, a party could spend as much as it liked to support a candidate, as long as the candidate did not approve the party's strategy or ads or have any say over what the party was doing. The Court decided that no one had the right to restrict **independent expenditures**—that is, funds spent on activities or advertising without the candidate's knowledge or approval. "We do not see how a Constitution that grants to individuals, candidates, and ordinary political committees the right to make unlimited independent expenditures could deny the same right to political parties," wrote Justice Stephen G. Breyer.[30] A decade later, the Court tossed out a Vermont law that sought to limit fund-raising and the amounts that candidates could spend on state campaigns.

In addition to this legal windfall, state parties already had been exempted from a number of federal campaign finance limits. In 1974 and 1976, Congress enacted laws that limited the amount of money candidates could collect from individuals and political action committees. Congress revised the law in 1979 after complaints from party leaders that the new laws almost completely eliminated state and local party organizations from participating in presidential campaigns. The old law, party leaders contended, put too many restrictions on how parties could spend money during a presidential election year. The revised law lifted all limits on what state and local parties could raise or spend for "party-building" activities. These included purchasing campaign materials, such as buttons, bumper stickers, and yard signs, and conducting voter registration and get-out-the-vote drives.[31]

It quickly became clear that the more lax restrictions were broad enough to allow for the purchase of TV ads and the funding of other campaign-related activities with so-called **soft money**

A total of $8,713,918 was contributed to Hawaii's Democratic and Republican candidates and committees in 2012, with $7,414,853 of that going to Democrats.

Independent Expenditures
Funds spent on ad campaigns or other political activities that are run by a party or an outside group without the direct knowledge or approval of a particular candidate for office.

Soft Money
Money not subject to federal regulation that can be raised and spent by state political parties. A 2002 law banned the use of soft money in federal elections.

Policy in Practice

Does It Make Sense to Limit Campaign Finance?

Politicians seem to have no trouble raising money these days. Presidential contests have become billion-dollar affairs, the cost of gubernatorial contests in some states has approached or even exceeded $100 million, and million-dollar state legislative races are not uncommon.

Nevertheless, many candidates are being outgunned by super PACs and other outside groups with nearly unlimited funds at their disposal. With billionaires dashing off multimillion-dollar checks to super PACs, political scientists and some politicians themselves are worried that candidates have become mere bystanders in their own campaigns.

This situation has triggered a debate about whether it makes sense to have a system in which campaign finance limits apply mainly to political parties and candidates. Opinion on how best to fix the problem remains split roughly along party lines.

An increasing number of Republicans want to close what they consider the opposite of a loophole, saying it makes no sense to handcuff candidates when money is otherwise flowing so freely. "The problem is the limits," Tennessee GOP senator Lamar Alexander said at a committee hearing in 2012. "These new super PACs exist because of the contribution limits we've placed upon parties and candidates. Get rid of the limits on contributions, and super PACs will go away."

Abolishing those limits, however, would only open the door to outright influence peddling, according to Democrats and others who advocate keeping the rules in place for candidates and parties. "To suggest that the solution to the problem is for candidates to raise the money themselves would just double down the possibilities for corruption," says Josh Orton, political director of Progressives United, a Wisconsin-based group that favors campaign finance limits. "Can you imagine the kind of conversations that could happen if we lifted the restrictions on corporations giving to candidates themselves?"

Individuals are limited to donations of $2,500 per federal candidate per election, which means they can contribute that amount for both primary and general election campaigns. Limits on gifts to parties are higher; for instance, an individual may give a national party $30,800 per year and a state party $10,000. About half the states banned corporations from spending money directly on campaigns, but such strictures were struck down by the Supreme Court in 2012.

Other limits on what outside groups can spend on campaigns have largely been eroded since the Supreme Court's *Citizens United* ruling in 2010. That decision has been hailed—and derided—for ushering in a new era of campaign finance law. But it was an earlier Supreme Court decision, in *Buckley v. Valeo,* that made it hard to make

donations, which were nominally meant to support party building. Restrictions on how parties spent soft money, which was raised in increments of $100,000 and more from corporations, unions, and wealthy individuals, were nearly meaningless—as long as the parties did not coordinate directly with candidates in spending the money. Parties violated the spirit, although not the letter, of the law, with state parties acting as virtual soft money–laundering machines for the national parties and for each other. In 2002, Congress revisited the issue and enacted the McCain-Feingold campaign finance law, which blocked the national parties from collecting soft money donations.[32]

Meanwhile, the state parties themselves are no slouches at raising money, as Figure 6-2 shows. Democrats and Republicans at the state level raised more than $500 million during the 2008 election cycle—a slight dip because of the loss of federal party transfers under McCain-Feingold.[33] But no matter what limitations are placed on campaign finance, money finds its way into the system because the U.S. Supreme Court has held that political expenditures are equivalent to free speech. In January 2010, in *Citizens United v. Federal Election Commission,* the Court ruled that political spending by corporations in candidate elections cannot be restricted. That finding was at at odds with long precedent and the campaign

campaign finance restrictions stick. That case found that money in politics is protected as equivalent to free speech. Ever since the 1976 *Buckley* decision, money has been like water, finding its way into the political system through new means, regardless of what restrictions have been enacted. "Right now, you have the worst of all worlds—unlimited contributions to third-party entities, with some, but certainly not instant, disclosure," says Trey Grayson, a former Republican secretary of state from Kentucky who now directs the Harvard University Institute of Politics.

Grayson says he'd rather see money put in the hands of candidates and parties, who are more accountable to voters than campaign committees that may disappear after the election. Currently, messages from candidates themselves in a contested race are likely to make up only a "small sliver" of total campaign advertising, says Ed Goeas, a Republican consultant who favors lifting limits while requiring disclosure of donors. "Money is now at the end that's furthest away from the candidates and furthest away from the parties," Goeas says. "The money is with these other groups that are having more impact on the campaign than the campaign itself."

Super PACs are not supposed to coordinate their messages or strategies with candidates, but many political observers agree that the line often gets blurry, with former aides to candidates sometimes running super PACs that support their campaigns. Still, erasing the line entirely would do great damage to the political system, argue the proponents of maintaining campaign finance limits. Having politicians directly receive large or unlimited funds from entities they might regulate would be a sure-fire recipe for corruption. "We're in pretty bad shape right now, but there are still some lines," says Meredith McGehee, policy director for the Campaign Legal Center. "By funneling large amounts of money to politicians, what you would actually have is just more candidates elected who are beholden to a small elite."

Supporters of such limits point to possible models to stem the tide of money. Public financing systems in Maine and Arizona, for example, give politicians incentive to raise small amounts of money from constituents.

But even those who would seek to level the playing field by allowing candidates and parties to raise more money directly believe that the genie may already be out of the bottle. Many rich donors have come to like super PACs, which allow them to control their own messages through advertising, without relying on politicians to have to deliver them.

Source: Original piece written for this book by Alan Greenblatt.

finance laws of at least two dozen states, but in a 2012 ruling, the Court made clear that states cannot ban direct political spending by corporations. Says University of Virginia government professor Larry J. Sabato:

> There is no way to stop the flow of interested money and there will always be constitutional ways around the restrictions enacted into law. What is so fundamental is that politics and government determine the allocation of goods and values in society. Those goods and values are critical to the success or failure of hundreds of interest groups and millions of individuals.

Those groups and individuals are going to spend the money to defend their interests, period.[34]

FIGURE 6-2

State Party Fund-Raising over Time

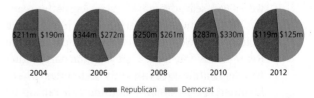

$211m $190m | $344m $272m | $250m $261m | $283m $330m | $119m $125m
2004 | 2006 | 2008 | 2010 | 2012

■ Republican ■ Democrat

Source: Data compiled from the National Institute for Money in State Politics, "Industry Influence 2000–2012," http://followthemoney.org/database/IndustryTotals.phtml?f=P&s=0.

Party Competition: Why Some States Are More Competitive than Others

The Republican Party came out of the 2002 elections with control over many of the nation's political institutions. Republicans held the White House and the U.S. House of Representatives, and they regained control of the Senate. They defied predictions and held on to a majority of governorships. For the first time since 1952, the party came out ahead in the total number of state legislative seats. Yet their victories did not represent political breakthroughs that they could necessarily bank on. All the Republican majorities were quite narrow, reflecting the level of parity between the two major parties that has kept both of them from achieving firm political dominance for a decade.

Just how narrow were some of the margins? Republicans had only two more governorships than the Democrats. Both congressional chambers were nearly tied; following the 2002 elections, Republicans held 49.6 percent of the nation's 7,400 legislative seats, whereas Democrats trailed just slightly with 49.4 percent of the seats. Republicans held a slight edge in the number of state chambers and legislatures they controlled, but the margins often were slim. In fact, a vacancy in any of a dozen legislative chambers could have resulted in a change of party control.[35] Things got even tighter after the 2004 elections, when the two parties ended up essentially tied in the total number of seats they controlled nationwide.

In 2006, the Democratic Party not only regained control of Congress but made impressive gains at the state level as well. Following that year's elections, Democrats held twenty-eight of the fifty state governorships—their first majority in a dozen years. In addition, Democrats emerged with a 660-seat advantage in state legislative seats. By 2008, Democrats controlled both legislative chambers in twenty-seven states, compared to the Republicans' fourteen. That year, the party didn't win legislative races in only the states where Democrats traditionally dominate; it ran up its margins in states where Republicans only recently had controlled at least one house, such as Minnesota and Oregon.[36]

These gains were wiped out, however, in the strong Republican year of 2010. The GOP made a net gain of 63 seats in the U.S. House—enough to win back control of that chamber—and six seats in the U.S. Senate. Republicans made a net gain of six governorships and nearly 700 seats in state legislatures—giving them their best showing at that level since 1928. Once again, however, the tide soon shifted back, if only slightly. Democrats in 2012 took control of about 200 additional state legislative seats, while picking up a net gain of eight seats in the U.S. House and two in the U.S. Senate.

Historically, most state political cultures have heavily favored one party or the other, as shown in Map 6-2. A well-known example of this is the old Democratic "Solid South." For more than a century, most southern voters were "yellow-dog Democrats," meaning they would sooner vote for a yellow dog than for a Republican. From 1880 to 1944, all eleven states of the old Confederacy voted for Democrats in every presidential election—with a couple of exceptions in 1920 and 1928. These states elected only Democrats and a few independents governor, and they elected only Democrats to the U.S. Senate after popular voting for senators began in 1916.[37] The Democratic hegemony in the South began to break up with the civil rights era that began, roughly, with the elections of 1948.

Today, both parties start out with a fair chance of winning statewide elections in just about every state. That is actually a big change. Republicans are now about even—or dominant—politically in the South, but they have lost their edge in the Northeast, which is now one of the more Democratic sections of the country. Republicans hold the advantage in many states of the Mountain West, but Democrats are stronger along the Pacific Coast. All this was perhaps most noticeable in the 2002 gubernatorial elections, when old party strangleholds finally broke. Georgia elected a Republican governor for the first time since 1868, ending the longest drought for either party in any state before or since. The GOP also took the governor's mansion in other states that had traditionally gone Democratic. These states included Maryland, which elected a Republican for the first time since 1966, and Hawaii, which

MAP 6-2

Interparty Competition, 2007–2011

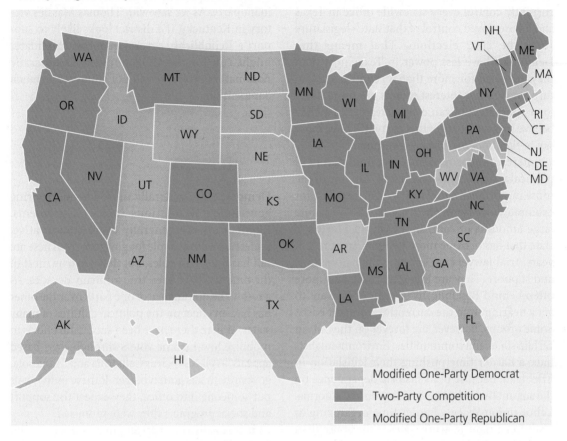

Modified One-Party Democrat

Two-Party Competition

Modified One-Party Republican

Source: Data compiled from Thomas Holbrook and Raymond La Raja, "Parties and Elections," in *Politics in the American States: A Comparative Analysis,* 10th ed., ed. Virginia Gray and Russell L. Hanson (Washington, DC: CQ Press, 2013), 88.

chose the GOP for the first time since 1959. Democrats, meanwhile, won in Illinois, Maine, Michigan, and Wisconsin for the first time in well over a decade, and they seated governors in Arizona, Kansas, Oklahoma, and Wyoming— states that had been supporting mostly Republicans in recent years.[38] Of the twenty-four new governors elected in 2002, twenty wrested control from a governor of another party. Why the decline of one-party dominance in nearly every state? One factor is the increased mobility of the American population. In the past people put down roots and perpetuated the political cultures of their families, but today the country's population is constantly shifting. The many northeasterners who have moved into the South, for example, do not hold the same cultural memory of the Civil War that kept many conservatives from supporting

Republicans. Immigrants to California have made the state more Democratic—Republicans politically misplayed their hand with California Hispanics by pushing an anti-immigrant ballot initiative during the 1990s (a pattern that may have been repeated at the national level in 2006, when House Republicans supported a bill to deport illegal aliens). But the departure of many conservative voters who moved to other western states, such as Nevada and Utah, has made the Golden State more Democratic as well.

All of that said, there are still plenty of places that are dominated by a single party. In fact, one of the striking results of the 2012 elections was that, at the legislative level, Republican "red" states got redder, while "blue" states elected more Democrats. The result was supermajority control in about half the legislative chambers. Once a party loses power, it is at a disadvantage in recovering power. Its traditional allies also have a harder time pushing their agendas. Republicans currently control every statewide office in Texas and have enjoyed control of that state's legislature since the 2002 elections. That means that Democrats have less power in Texas now than they have had for more than a century. This, in turn, means that interest groups are more likely to support Republican candidates because they believe that members of that party will have more say in the function of state government.

Interest groups recognize the fluid nature of political power. Trial lawyers make up one of the most important Democratic constituencies, for example, because of their ability to contribute large amounts of campaign cash. In Florida, a state that has become more Republican in recent years, trial lawyers are splitting their donations and support. They are lining up more and more often behind Republicans because they want to get a hearing from the currently dominant party. Some groups, however, are forever on the outs in certain states and communities. Environmentalists have a harder time pushing their legislation in Michigan, because of its historic dependence on the automotive industry, than they do in California. Labor unions have a harder time organizing in traditional right-to-work states in the South than they do in the Northeast or Midwest, but even there, unions—particularly those representing public-sector workers—have come under attack in recent years.

Also important to remember is that even though plenty of state legislative chambers are politically competitive, most of the seats within them are not. Legislative districts are redrawn following each decennial census. Given computerization and other tools, political leaders are able to predict the likely voting patterns of people on a block-by-block or sometimes house-by-house basis. Following the 2010 census, nearly every district in the country was redrawn in such a way that it became reasonably safe for a candidate of one party over the other. In other words, there are now many safe Democratic districts and safe Republican districts, and there are not a lot of districts that are competitive. This means that most of the competition for any given seat will take place in the primary race of the dominant party. As we saw with Thomas Massie's victory in Kentucky, if a district looks likely to support a Republican, several qualified candidates might run for the GOP nod; the Democratic nomination probably will not stimulate as much competition.

The Effect of Parties on Political Culture

Democrats are generally more liberal, favoring governmental solutions to social problems. Republicans are generally more conservative, preferring a limited role for government. These are not hard-and-fast rules, but they are true most of the time and have been true for many decades. As a result, the dominance of one party over the other has had an effect on the political cultures of many states. Where there have been successful efforts to mobilize low-income voters through class-based appeals, in places such as California and Minnesota, government has gotten bigger. If these individuals put someone into office, they expect the support and social programs they were promised.

It is equally unsurprising that politicians who have come to power promising not to raise taxes have kept government growth in check. In New Hampshire, William Loeb, the editor of the *Manchester Union Leader* newspaper, came up with the idea of challenging political candidates to sign a no-tax pledge. The pledge became embedded in the state's political culture and has since spread nationwide among federal GOP candidates through the efforts of a group called Americans for Tax Reform. Within thirty years of Loeb's innovation, New Hampshire was transformed from a relatively high-revenue state, one that could depend on gaining adequate moneys from taxes to fund public programs, to a low-revenue state.[39]

What may be surprising is the fact that when the parties *really* held real sway—when the machines were more important than any individual officeholder—they were not very interested in expanding government either. Machine politicians wanted to maintain their grip on the government jobs and contracts they already had. This would seem to make sense for a conservative machine such as that run by Senator Harry Byrd Sr., D-Va., from the 1920s to the 1960s. After all, Byrd and his acolytes shared a respect for balanced budgets and a small public sector. But party machines in general, even progressive ones, usually were not expansionistic. In the machine era, party officials squabbled more over who got control of which government jobs than about changing the number or nature of those jobs. They certainly did not present new government-based solutions to problems. Keeping jobs tied to political loyalties discouraged the creation of a professionalized bureaucracy.

In the meantime, the public did not want corrupt machine politicians to control any more of their money than necessary. Interest groups, such as unions, that might have wanted an expansion of government programs did not hold enough influence to promote them.[40] As the parties and political machines weakened, however, candidates, party activists, and interest groups became free agents, free to promote all manner of new programs and government expansion.

Party Factions and Activists

Parties are no longer able to reward their followers directly with jobs or other payoffs. Decisions handed down by the U.S. Supreme Court have made it clear that party affiliation is not a constitutional basis on which to decide government hires. Kentucky governor Ernie Fletcher learned that the hard way in 2006 when he and several other top state officials were indicted for hiring supporters. Fletcher had been the first Republican elected to run the state in more than thirty years, and members of his administration were apparently too eager to hire party loyalists for government positions, disregarding the state's merit-hiring law in some instances.

With party leaders prevented from dispensing prizes such as jobs, party activism and various party tasks are now largely carried out by volunteers. And because people seldom work for free unless they believe in something very strongly, political volunteers have become more ideological. People work for candidates and parties because they believe in specific causes, such as handgun control legislation or protections for small business owners.

Just because jobs are no longer the parties' golden eggs does not mean that politicians and parties do not seek to pluck favors from their constituents through policies or promises. Both major parties court the elderly with assurances of healthcare benefits, such as Medicare, because senior citizens vote and thus are worth courting. Young people, by contrast, have historically tended not to vote. Only 24 percent of Americans thirty years of age and younger voted in 2006, which was the best midterm showing for the young in twenty years.[41] The young voter turnout increased in the 2004 and 2008 presidential elections—51 percent of the population between the ages of eighteen and twenty-nine cast ballots in 2008—but the group's participation continued to trail that of older voters by almost 15 percentage points.[42] In 2012, the number of people between the ages of eighteen and twenty-nine stayed about the same as in 2008—about 23 million—but because of a decline in voter participation overall, their share of the total electorate ticked up by one percentage point to 19 percent.

Each party has its main constituent groups, but that does not preclude both parties from trying to poach supporters from the other side. Democrats have been at pains in recent years to present a friendly face to business interests, while Republican president George W. Bush courted the Teamsters and building trade unions. Remember, however, that each party is a kaleidoscope of interest groups and can only appeal so much to any one group before it risks alienating support among other groups. Republican support for abortion and contraceptive restrictions or outright bans has helped solidify the party's dominance among evangelicals and other social conservatives, for instance, but at the cost of alienating many women voters, particularly single women.

It is obvious that one person cannot simultaneously support higher pay for teachers and cutting educational budgets. That is why politicians must perform the neat trick of motivating the true believers within party ranks to support their candidacies during primary elections without pinning themselves down so much that they do not appeal to members of the other party and independents during the general election. Often, the more contentious the issue, the more a party will try to blur its differences with the other party. Candidates do not want to promise so much to their core supporters—known as the base—that they cannot then reach other voters. By promising a lot of money for public transportation, for instance, a candidate might gain support in the city but lose it in the suburbs.

Both major parties try to appeal to as much of the populace as possible, but their supporters sometimes care more about promoting particular issues than they do about winning elections. Interest groups now raise their own funds and use them freely to promote their issues in campaigns. We discuss how interest groups lobby governments a little later in this chapter, but for now it is worth examining quickly the type of role these groups can play in contemporary politics.

A 2009 special election for a vacant congressional seat based in Watertown, New York, demonstrates the difficulty the parties have in maintaining discipline in message and candidate selection. The state GOP nominated Dede Scozzafava, a pro-choice, pro–gay marriage state assemblywoman. Notable figures within the national Republican Party, including former vice presidential nominee Sarah Palin and Minnesota governor Tim Pawlenty, were opposed to Scozzafava's candidacy and publicly backed the Conservative Party candidate instead. Scozzafava dropped out of the race three days before the election and threw her support to Bill Owens, the Democratic candidate and eventual winner.[43]

Numerous interests took an active role in that particular general election campaign that fall, including pro–term limits groups, antiabortion and pro-choice advocates, labor unions, environmental organizations, and antitax groups. In fact, the amount of money the candidates spent on their own campaigns was dwarfed by the amount spent by these and other outside groups. Such situations have become more the rule and less the exception in recent years. In Wisconsin, political

races have been dominated for years by issue ads run by the Wisconsin Manufacturers and Commerce and the Wisconsin Education Association Council. Because these two groups care so much about taxes and education, respectively, these issues dominate many races. Politicians and parties have no control over such ads, so they cannot control the agenda. Anything else the candidates might want to emphasize is likely to be drowned out. Nobody disputes that taxes and schools are important, but making them the only subjects in an election detracts from other issues.[44]

Now those groups sometimes find themselves outgunned as well, with numerous organizations from inside and outside the state making their opinions known. This dynamic was heightened with the recall elections that dominated the state's politics in 2009 and 2010. Jennifer Shilling, a Democratic state representative, decided to challenge Republican senator Dan Kapanke in one of several recall contests that took place in 2009 after GOP leaders had slashed budgets and eliminated collective bargaining rights for most public-sector employees. Shilling raised $400,000 for the race, against Kapanke's $1.6 million. But both candidates' treasuries were dwarfed by the millions spent by outside groups that ran independent expenditure campaigns. Shilling won, but, she said, "It was just numbing to look at my financial report, knowing what we needed to be competitive and get our messages out."[45]

During the 1980s, it appeared that candidates were fairly free agents. They were rid of the old party machine apparatus and able to set their own agendas and spread their own messages, largely through broadcast ads. Twenty years later, times changed again. Yes, candidates are now more independent, presenting themselves for party nomination and spending sums they have raised to get into the public eye. The campaigns, however, have become such big business that the candidates' funds and self-motivation often are not enough. Plus, candidates need votes, and to get these votes, they must join ranks with party officials and interest groups that tend to take the ball and run away with it. Candidates become mere pawns in campaigns that have been overtaken by deep-pocketed interest groups. They stand on the sidelines and watch as the parties or other groups run the greater volume of ads, redefining their campaigns for them.

It is easy to become confused about which is the most powerful—candidates, interest groups, or political parties—and in which situations they hold that power. What is important to remember is that all three are vital parts of the political process and that their relative importance varies depending on the time and place. It is impossible to illustrate every variation, but none of them is ever either nothing or everything. Their roles are entwined.

Pragmatism versus Idealism

Interest groups, just like parties, are most likely to play a prominent role in races that are closely contested or that can tip the partisan balance in a legislature. Redistricting at both the federal and state legislative levels, however, has grown so sophisticated—with so much emphasis placed on making districts safe for incumbents—that relatively few of these races are closely contested. Much of the action takes place in primary contests. But in true swing districts, where either party has a shot at winning, both major parties and all their allies will spend as much money as they can muster to win.

In these cases, party leaders grow frustrated when interest groups trumpet issues that do not appeal to a wider public. The main goal of parties is to win elections, so they are much more interested in fielding candidates who fit the profile of the office in contention than they are in promoting a specific ideology. The Republican National Committee, for example, defeated an attempt in 1998 to pass a party resolution that would have blocked the party from giving any money to candidates opposed to a ban on late-term abortions. Social conservatives were angry that the national committee had spent $760,000 supporting the reelection effort of New Jersey governor Christine Todd Whitman, who had vetoed a state ban on the procedure. "I'm about as pro-life as anybody," said Bob Hiler, Indiana's member of the national committee, "but I just cannot accept a situation in the Republican Party where there is a litmus test if you want to join or be a candidate. I respect the decisions of our national party

leaders to place money where it needs to go to ensure that we win that seat."[46]

With just two broad-based national parties, neither can afford to preach an unyielding gospel on any single issue. The people most interested in politics may be motivated by their investment in particular issues, but if they hang around long enough, they come to realize that no one can win all the time. Perversely, the parties that are best able to keep their troops in line and satisfied with less-than-perfect ideological purity are the parties currently out of power. In other words, the desire to get back into the White House or to hold majority control of a legislature is often strong enough to convince all the quarreling factions to back someone who looks like a winner—even if that candidate is not "perfect" on all of the issues.

But the fact that both parties spend a good deal of time blurring their positions on the most important issues of the day to try to appeal to the most people while alienating the fewest number has made a lot of voters sour on them. Many Americans believe that politicians do not stand for anything and are more interested in preserving their power than in doing the right thing. That is a major reason increasing numbers of voters have declared themselves independent in recent decades and have refused to give lifelong allegiance to one party over the other in the same way that their grandparents did. "It probably would have been better for the parties if the public had become more negative rather than more neutral toward them," writes political scientist Martin Wattenberg. "Negative attitudes can easily be turned into positive attitudes by better performance or a change in policies. To induce people to care about political parties once again may well be more difficult."[47]

Third Parties and Independents

If millions of people are disenchanted with the Republican and Democratic parties, for a variety of reasons, why isn't there more of a movement toward establishing a viable third, or minor, party as an alternative? Every election cycle seems to find more people dissatisfied with the major parties and more willing to identify themselves as independent. In 2008, a greater share of the electorate—39 percent—identified itself as independent rather than as either Democratic (34 percent) or Republican (26 percent); that was the fifth straight election year in which independents were a plurality.[48] In 2012, slightly more people identified themselves as Democrats than as independents.

Still, in 2012 there was nothing resembling a strong third-party movement in the presidential race. If anything, the opposite was true. An organization known as Americans Elect sought to create a place for a strong third-party candidacy, spending $35 million on marketing, social media and other technology tools, and ballot access, securing a spot on the ballots of twenty-eight states by May 2012. But it shut down its crusade that month, having been unable to persuade a viable candidate to run under its banner.[49]

In most other democracies numerous parties exist, each with strong support. In countries such as Israel and Italy, the leading party typically does not have enough seats in parliament to construct a government on its own and has to enter into a coalition with other parties.

That has never been the case in the United States for a number of reasons. Democrats and Republicans, as we have been exploring, have established wide networks of contacts and supporters—individuals and groups that have long loyalties to one party or the other. They have officeholders at all levels who can help with strategy and fund-raising.

The major parties also have many other institutional advantages. For one thing, the United States favors a winner-take-all system in which the person receiving the most votes in a district wins. In some countries, seats in the legislature are distributed on a percentage basis, so that if a party gets 5 percent of the vote it receives about 5 percent of the total seats available. But if a party took only 5 percent of the vote across the United States, it probably would not win a seat anywhere. In 1992, Texas computer billionaire Ross Perot, the most successful third-party presidential candidate in decades, took 19 percent of the vote but did not carry a single state.

For the 1996 presidential race, Perot established the Reform Party, which he called his gift to the American people. Perot used that gift himself, running for a second time but not doing nearly so well. He had a hard time getting on the ballot in some states—rules regarding ballot access differ across states and are often complicated. In the state of New York, for instance, a candidate must collect a certain number of signatures from each of the congressional districts to get on the ballot. Many candidates with more modest financial means than Perot have had difficulty gaining access to ballots. Perot himself was excluded from the presidential debates. The commission running the debates—composed of officials from the Democratic and Republican parties—decided he was not showing enough strength in the polls to warrant being included.

Excluded though he was, Perot nevertheless took 8 percent of the vote in 1996. This was enough to guarantee the Reform nominee in 2000 a spot on all fifty state ballots, as well as $12 million in federal campaign funds. With Perot out of the running, however, the Reform nomination dissolved into chaos. Two separate conventions nominated two different candidates. The states were left having to decide which candidate deserved the spot on the ballot. "There are no statutes to guide us," said Mike Cooney, Montana's former secretary of state, in 2000. "The Reform Party needed to resolve this issue before it got to this point. It's an internal party problem that has been foisted upon the states and put us all in a bad situation."[50] The eventual Reform nominee proved not to be as much of a factor in the race as did Green Party nominee Ralph Nader. The Reform Party seemed to have self-destructed. Several of the old minor parties that had taken up its banner, such as Minnesota's Independence Party, soon returned to their original names.

Difficulties of Building Support

Many Democrats blamed Nader for the defeat of their candidate in 2000, Al Gore. Gore won more popular votes than Republican George W. Bush but was defeated in the electoral college. Some people believe that a third-party candidate will never be anything more than a "spoiler" who deprives major-party candidates of needed votes. Others believe that third parties help present a real and needed alternative to the Democrats and Republicans. Unless the major parties are challenged, the thinking goes, they will never change.

> The major parties, however, have proven quite adept at co-opting the most popular ideas presented by third-party candidates. Both Democratic and Republican candidates in the 1990s took the idea of a balanced federal budget more seriously because Perot had raised the issue.

The major parties, however, have proven quite adept at co-opting the most popular ideas presented by third-party candidates. Both Democratic and Republican candidates in the 1990s took the idea of a balanced federal budget more seriously because Perot had raised the issue. During the 1930s, Franklin D. Roosevelt lifted many of the ideas of Socialist candidate Norman Thomas. When faced with the rare strong minor-party challenge, a major-party candidate can argue that he or she offers the best vehicle for presenting any shared ideals—and stands a better chance of beating the other major-party candidate. Perot's 1992 showing was the best by a third-party candidate since Theodore Roosevelt's in 1912—and neither one of them came close to winning.

Minor-party candidates have enjoyed more success running for lower offices, but not much. Within a state or a legislative district, there is a better chance that an individual will enjoy enough personal popularity to equalize the playing field against Democrats and Republicans, who typically are better funded and connected. Still, only a half dozen governors elected during the past fifty years have been neither Democrats nor Republicans.

Three of those six—Walter Hickel of Alaska, Lowell Weicker of Connecticut, and Lincoln Chafee of Rhode Island—had earlier won statewide office as Republicans. Another two were elected in Maine, a state noted for the independent-mindedness of its electorate. The fifth, Jesse Ventura of Minnesota, served only one term, and the would-be successor from his Independence Party finished a distant third in 2002.

At the legislative level, things are just as grim for third-party candidates. Following the 2012 elections, there were only twenty-nine third-party or independent state legislators in the United States (not counting nonpartisan Nebraska), out of a total of 7,400. Each of these candidates had dedicated followers. But from a pragmatic perspective—say, that of a voter interested in seeing his or her agenda become law—it probably makes better sense to support a Democrat or Republican who has a chance of serving in the majority party than it does to pull for a person who will hold just one vote.

A few minor parties have enjoyed periods of success in certain states, such as the Progressive Party during the 1920s in Wisconsin and the Farmer-Labor Party during the 1930s in Minnesota. Over time, however, these parties have been unable to survive the loss of early popular leaders or have been absorbed by one of the major parties. For example, the official name of Minnesota's Democratic Party is still the Democratic Farmer-Labor Party, in reference to its merger with the defunct minor party. The Liberal Party of New York boasted a New York City mayor in the 1960s named John Lindsay. New York is one of the few states that allow candidates to be listed multiple times on a ballot, as the nominee of, for instance, both the Liberal and the Republican parties. In 1980, U.S. senator Jacob Javits was denied the nomination of the state's Republican Party and ran as the Liberal candidate. He succeeded only in splitting the votes of liberals, moderates, and Democrats and helped to elect a more conservative Republican. The Liberal Party disbanded in 2003 after failing to garner enough votes in the previous year's gubernatorial contest to maintain its guaranteed spot on state ballots. "Parties, I suppose, have a life span," said Dan Cantor, executive director of the Working Families Party. "They had their heyday in the [19]50s and [19]60s. It looks like they have come to a full stop."[51]

Ultimately, it is the states that publish the ballots and have the authority to decide which parties' nominees are going to be listed on them. It is the states that grant ballot access to parties based on their having won a minimum percentage of the vote in a previous statewide general election. The threshold varies from 1 percent in Wisconsin to as much as 20 percent in Georgia. Such high institutional barriers make minor parties' complaints about two-party dominance of American politics about as fruitless as trying to hold back the tide.

Major-Party Support

One other reason minor parties have trouble gaining traction is that people are not, in the main, terribly unhappy with the major parties. The major parties, after all, do devote themselves to appealing to as broad a range of citizens as possible. That said, voter identification with the parties has declined. Some states once allowed voters to vote a straight ticket, meaning they could pull one lever to vote for all the Democratic or Republican candidates on the ballot. Such procedures are now considered quaint. Voters are more and more willing to divide their ballots, a practice called **ticket splitting**. One voter joked, "I vote for the man for president, and give him a Congress he can't work with."

In 1960, the Gallup Organization found that 47 percent of respondents identified themselves as Democrats, 30 percent as Republicans, and just 23 percent as independents or members of other parties. By the 1990s, those numbers had converged. Polling by the Pew Research Center for the People & the Press over a fifty-four-month period in the mid-1990s found that an average of 33 percent of the respondents called themselves Democrats, 29 percent identified as Republicans, and 33 percent said they were independents, with a handful naming other specific parties.[52] A poll released by the Pew Research Center in 2009 found that as the proportion of Republicans continued to shrink, Democrats picked up strength,

but self-described independents had become the largest of the three groups, with 39 percent of respondents choosing the label—the highest such proportion in seventy years.[53]

As subsequent polling by Pew and other groups has found, however, most self-identified independents are not true independents, however. Their preferences generally do lean toward one of the major parties. "Partisan loyalties in the American populace have rebounded significantly since the mid-1970s, especially among those who actually turn out to vote," concluded political scientist Larry M. Bartels in 2000.[54] The proportion of pure independents, those who do not lean toward either party, peaked at 16 percent in 1976. Twenty years later, true independents were just 9 percent of the populace.[55]

Many people may not choose to identify themselves with either major party, but they mostly tend to vote one way or the other, a team of political scientists concluded in the 1992 book *The Myth of the Independent Voter*.[56] "Independents have a great pride factor—'I vote for the person, not the party,'" said Jane Jech, a Republican candidate for the Iowa Senate in 2012. "But in truth, they lean one way or the other."[57]

The Republicans and Democrats have dominated American politics for 150 years. They have met every challenge—both ideological and structural—and found a way to preserve their near-total control. As political scientist Jeff Fishel puts it:

> If there's any lesson of history about the two major parties in American politics, it is that they're incredible adaptive survivors. They lost the monopoly they had, particularly on candidate recruitment and finance. That certainly does not mean that they're going out of business, just that they have to compete with other groups.[58]

Interest Groups and Lobbies

If many citizens are cynical about political parties, they're even more put off by interest groups. It's true that lobbyists representing big companies, unions, and other organizations often push for legislation to promote or protect their own

---

Ticket Splitting
Voters' or districts' voting for different parties' nominees for different offices—for instance, supporting a Republican for president while supporting a Democrat for Congress.

narrow interests. But lobbying is how citizens and private companies make their views known to policymakers between election seasons. Sometimes people even lobby for altruistic reasons rather than self-interest.

College students of this generation will be familiar with Invisible Children, a group that sought to influence U.S. policy in Africa. The group called for people—primarily teenagers and young people—to pressure politicians, celebrities, and adults of their acquaintance to bring Central African warlord Joseph Kony to justice for murder, child abduction, and rape. Invisible Children, which had shown films about Kony to countless school groups, released a video on the Web known as *Kony 2012* that became one of the greatest Internet sensations in history. It drew more than 100 million views on YouTube and Vimeo within days of being posted in March 2012, as the word spread through Twitter and other social media.

Invisible Children had already enjoyed some success influencing policymakers, helping to convince Congress to pass a law that led to the United States sending one hundred military advisers to Uganda. *Kony 2012* called on young people to "cover the night" on April 20, putting up posters wherever they lived, to sear Kony into the nation's consciousness. But almost as soon as the video reached mass attention, a backlash set in. Invisible Children was criticized for simplifying the issues involved and for how it spent its funds. By the time April 20 rolled around, it appeared that most students had moved on. "Just a few weeks ago, students were ready to participate in fund-raising efforts or the Cover the Night event," said Alison Decker, a nineteen-year-old sophomore at Northwestern University. "Unfortunately, most of the fervor has seemed to change to apathy or eye rolls about the legitimacy of Invisible Children."[59]

It's not just that some of the group's claims and strategies drew criticism. Ten days after the release of *Kony 2012,* Jason Russell, a cofounder of Invisible Children and leading character in the video, was hospitalized by police in San Diego after he had stood naked and screaming on a street corner. He was the apparent victim of exhaustion and dehydration, but a video of his breakdown—which was itself widely disseminated and viewed—undermined his group's credibility. Part of the power of *Kony 2012* was the way Russell was able to personalize the cause, showing how he and his young son had come to understand the menace and impact of Kony and his group, the Lord's Resistance Army. But Russell's having made himself central to the film's message created a public relations crisis when he was caught acting out on tape, said Marcus Messner, a communications professor at Virginia Commonwealth University. The incident was parodied in an episode of *South Park* that showed a character named Stan stripping his clothes off in San Diego after an antibullying video he directed had become a huge success that was then roundly reviled. "What was really a turnoff, particularly for young people, was the amateur video showing the [Invisible Children] organizer dancing naked on a street corner," Messner said. "While most people did not personally hear the criticism of the [*Kony 2012*] video, they did see the video of the breakdown." The VCU chapter of Invisible Children broke its ties with the group, changed its name, and decided to donate funds directly to children's programs in Uganda.[60]

Other student-led campaigns in recent years—such as attempts to pressure universities to divest from companies that supply arms to the government in Sudan—have been more successful. In 2012, a seventy-seven-year-old probation officer named Will Cavanaugh convinced more than two thousand people to sign an online petition calling on Idaho governor Butch Otter to approve a Medicaid expansion that was part of the new federal healthcare law.[61]

But such cause campaigns are different in kind than the average work done by interest groups, which tend to have long-standing interests in issues or regulations that affect the groups or their members directly. As should be apparent by now, interest groups have always been important resources for candidates, providing volunteers and other services as well as money. They have taken on even greater importance in the current era of high-stakes fund-raising and super PACs. They are the organizations that take a direct interest in political activity—both in terms of supporting candidates during an election season and in terms of lobbying elected and appointed government officials regarding policy and spending matters. Still, they differ from parties in that politics and elections are not their whole reason for being. As political scientist Frank J. Sorauf notes, "The American Medical Association devotes only part of its energies to protecting its interests through political action. Not so the political party. It arises and exists solely as a response to the problems of organizing the political process."[62] In other words, the American Medical Association (AMA) may spend millions of dollars annually trying to affect elections and legislation, but it devotes more of its energy and resources to educating its members, promoting good healthcare techniques, and other private activities. This difference in focus illustrates a fundamental and obvious trait that separates political parties from special interest groups—political parties run candidates for office under their own labels, whereas special interest groups do not.

Interest groups basically come in five flavors. One is the membership group, such as the AMA or the Sierra Club, made up of individual members with a common interest. A second type is the trade association, which represents individuals or organizations in a particular industry or field, such as the National Restaurant Association or the Alliance of Automobile Manufacturers. The third type of interest group is that consisting of an individual institution; many large organizations, such as Microsoft and General Motors, have lobbyists on staff or devote a significant portion of their executives' time to lobbying. The fourth type is that consisting of government lobbyists (sometimes called legislative liaisons), those who represent the interests of one branch of government to another. Executive branch officials have aides designated to lobby Congress or a legislature on their behalf, and cities, counties, and states hire lobbyists to make their cases in Washington. The fifth, and smallest, category is the interest group made up of private individuals who lobby

on their own behalf for a pet project or against a policy that they find reprehensible.[63]

People and organizations have a constitutional right to petition the government for redress of grievances. That means that they have the right to complain to lawmakers and regulators about their disagreements with laws and how they are enforced. That is what lobbying is. It is worth noting that the government runs some of the most active lobbies. The White House maintains a lobbying shop to try to persuade Congress of the wisdom of its policies. Municipal governments hire lobbyists and associations to protect their interests in their state capitals. Currently about 40,000 lobbyists are working in state capitals, and the number of associations and related groups has quintupled over the last fifty years. Lobbying in the states is now a billion-dollar business every year.[64]

The Internet has made it easy to track which interest groups are active in which states. Open up a search engine and type in the name of a state and "lobbying registration," and you'll quickly find the Web site of an ethics commission or other state board with which all lobbyists must register. The National Institute on Money in State Politics (www.followthemoney.org) and the Center for Public Integrity (www.publicintegrity.org) also offer detailed information about campaign finance and lobbying activity in the states, as well as studies about overall trends.

The raw numbers—who is spending what where—tell only part of the story, however. It is often difficult to find out which group has influenced the outcome of a specific piece of legislation. Some interest groups, such as Invisible Children, play a very public game, but others are more secretive, playing an insider game in which influence is a matter of quiet access to legislators.

That is why many interest groups hire **contract lobbyists,** usually lawyers or former government staffers or elected officials who are valued for possessing insider knowledge and contacts within particular state capitals. Contract lobbyists generally have a number of clients, as lawyers

---

Contract Lobbyist
A lobbyist who works for different causes for different clients in the same way that a lawyer represents more than one client.

do. About 20 percent of lobbyists registered to ply their trade in a given capital are contract.[65] They use their relationships and contacts to convince legislators that they should or should not pass particular bills. And although lobbyists ignore the executive branch at their peril, given that spending decisions and regulatory action are carried out there, more lobbying activity happens in the legislative arena. "You don't change their minds," said a California lobbyist. "You find ways of making them think they agreed with you all along."[66]

Alan Autry, who was an actor on the television show *Dukes of Hazzard* in the early 1980s and who later served as mayor of Fresno, California, arrived in Washington one day in 2003 to ask for money for his city. He met with members of Congress and a senator who represented his area—who nevertheless needed reminding about Fresno's need for funds for law enforcement and an industrial park. Autry was thrilled when Senator Barbara Boxer looked him in the eye and pledged her support for a $500,000 study that was the first step toward a major mass transit system in the San Joaquin Valley. "When you sit face to face to get a commitment, that's huge," he said.[67]

But, although Autry saw the value of traveling to Washington to "beg" in person, he recognized that most of his time would be spent back in Fresno, running the city day to day. That's why he hired Len Simon, a lobbyist for cities, to keep track of his projects and build support—for a fee of $24,000 a year. Many other city leaders have done the same. For them, Simon walks the corridors of the capitol, reiterating the same points to the same members of Congress, staff members, and executive branch bureaucrats, because it is an article of faith in any capital that legislators respond to repetition—if an interest group keeps asking about a project, it must really want that project. That kind of pricey persistence pays off. The city of Sandy, Utah, spent almost $200,000 on contract lobbyists in 2007 and claimed more than $1 million in federal earmarks—which a city spokeswoman called a "return on investment."[68]

Legislators often rely on lobbyists to provide them with information, whether simply data about an industry's economic outlook or their opinions about whether a bill would cost jobs in the legislators' districts. Legislators are always grappling with many issues at once: the state budget, education, the environment, and so on. It is up to lobbyists to keep legislators and their staffs apprised of who favors a particular bill and who would benefit from or be hurt by it. Lobbyists build up relationships with legislators over time, and legislators come to trust some of them for reliable information, even if they hold differing positions on particular issues. Often, members of trade associations and other groups will seek to inform legislators about their views without necessarily knowing whether the politicians they're meeting with agree with them or not; this is "lobbying as primarily engaged in providing information about constituency views, with groups pressing lawmakers to enact particular policies based on how constituents will respond," as one academic wrote after spending time working on Capitol Hill.[69]

Standing in contrast to a contract lobbyist such as Simon is a **cause lobbyist**, someone who promotes a single-issue agenda, such as medical marijuana or campaign finance reform. A cause lobbyist often plays an outsider's game, using the media to sway public opinion and pressure public officials. Groups that do not have an economic interest in legislative outcomes are able to get away with this tactic because their ideological position is clear for all to see. Major industries also occasionally play outside games as they seek to pressure politicians by stirring up interest through issue advertising.[70] People such as Len Simon, by contrast, engage in **direct lobbying**, dealing

Cause Lobbyist
A person who works for an organization that tracks and promotes an issue, for example, environmental issues for the Sierra Club or gun ownership rights for the National Rifle Association.

Direct Lobbying
A form of lobbying in which lobbyists deal directly with legislators to gain their support.

Policy in Practice

Why Companies Avoid Overt Partisanship

Michael Jordan, the basketball legend, refused to engage publicly in partisan politics. The reason was simple, he explained: Republicans buy shoes, too, he said, and Jordan didn't want to antagonize any potential customers for Nike, whose products he endorsed. Major corporations tend to employ the same logic. They don't want to risk angering potential consumers who disagree with their politics.

Target, the big retailer, found itself the target of boycott campaigns in 2010 after it donated $150,000 to a super PAC that supported a gubernatorial candidate who opposed gay marriage. Perhaps more striking, however, was the defection of many major corporations from a previously obscure legislative group that had become the center of controversy in 2012.

The American Legislative Exchange Council, known as ALEC, had long championed conservative legislation. The group brought together state legislators and corporations to craft policy that was turned into model bills introduced in many states. Much of it had to do with fiscal matters, such as tax policy, or policies that had some direct benefit to the group's corporate members—including prison sentencing laws that helped bring business to ALEC's active private prison affiliates. Roughly a thousand bills based on ALEC language are introduced in an average year, with about 20 percent enacted into law.

With the GOP sweep in the 2010 elections, ALEC was poised to be more influential than ever. Legislation promoted by the group dominated discussion in many capitols around such issues as climate change, voter ID requirements, illegal immigration, and limits on public-sector pensions. Versions of ALEC's Freedom of Choice in Health Care Act, which was a direct challenge to the federal law championed by President Barack Obama, were introduced in more than forty states. "It's really no secret," said State Senator Jane Cunningham, the lead sponsor of Missouri's version. "I learned about the idea from ALEC and brought it back to Missouri."

For years, liberal advocacy groups decried ALEC's influence, but they were unable to alarm very many members of the public, since the group remained little known. That began to shift, however, in 2011, when 850 model bills generated by ALEC, along with other documents, were published on a Web site run by the liberal Center for Media and Democracy. That made it easier for journalists and the group's ideological opponents in individual states to compare proposed legislation with language crafted by ALEC. In addition, Common Cause, a group that supports campaign finance restrictions, called on the Internal Revenue Service to audit ALEC's books, claiming that the organization acted more like a full-fledged lobbying shop than a tax-exempt nonprofit.

ALEC was facing some public relations headaches, but its problems really began with the high-profile shooting of Trayvon Martin, an unarmed African American youth, in Florida in February 2012. The man who shot Martin, George Zimmerman, maintained that he was innocent of murder charges thanks to the state's "stand your ground" law, which allows people to use force when they feel they may be at risk.

That type of law had been promoted by ALEC. The group soon backed away from the issue, announcing two months after the shooting that it was disbanding the task force that dealt with public safety and elections issues. From now on, ALEC leaders said, they would stick purely to economic matters.

By then, it was too late for many of ALEC's corporate members. Several major companies, including Coca-Cola, Pepsi, McDonald's, and Kraft, had cut their ties with the group. Nearly three-dozen corporations and foundations would ultimately make the decision that being associated with ALEC, however effective the group had been in the past, had become bad for business.

That's why most of the major donors to super PACs during the 2012 election cycle were not big corporations. Rather, they were wealthy individuals or owners of privately held companies who didn't have to worry about what their shareholders would think about their politics.

Source: Adapted from Alan Greenblatt, "ALEC Enjoys a New Wave of Influence and Criticism," *Governing,* December 2011.

This super PAC–sponsored ad targeted Texas solicitor general Ted Cruz with an allegation of corruption. Cruz ran for—and won—an open seat in the Texas Senate, but like many candidates for office in the 2012 election, he faced an increase in opposition ads from interest groups, which are now allowed to organize into super PACs and dig into deeper spending pockets.

directly with legislators in hopes of persuading them. The students trying to get public officials to divest from Sudan were taking part in **indirect lobbying**, building support for their cause through the media, through rallies, and through other ways of influencing public opinion, hoping that legislators would be swayed by the resulting buzz.

Using the media effectively can be trickier for private corporations and other entities directly affected by legislation. The media nearly always portray this third type of lobbyist in a negative light. If a politician sponsors a bill favoring a particular industry and individuals in that industry have made substantial donations to his or her campaign treasury, news stories are bound to be written about that money trail. Numerous states, including Kentucky, Massachusetts, and Minnesota, have passed ethics laws in recent years that preclude lobbyists, who used to wine and dine legislators, from giving legislators anything of value, even a cup of coffee.[71]

Today, many interest groups try to combine the direct and indirect approaches, hitting up legislators for favors in private meetings while also running public relations campaigns through the media. Groups also are likely to join together in coalitions, hoping that a united front will not only present a more coherent and persuasive message but also prevent any individual group

from looking like it is pleading from narrow self-interest. Interest groups often look for surprising allies who will plead their case. For instance, groups wanting to increase funding for after-school programs will enlist law enforcement agencies to argue that the programs help cut crime by giving young people something constructive to do.

As mentioned earlier, some interest groups, particularly those with ideological agendas, tend to be loyal to one party over the other. Interest groups as a whole, however, do not give most of their support to candidates of a particular party. Rather, they give most of their support to the *incumbents* of either party. One reason for this is that incumbents are reelected the vast majority of the time, so betting on their victory is pretty safe. It makes more sense, pragmatically speaking, to curry favor with someone who possesses power than with someone who does not. Even if the incumbent does not subscribe to an interest group's entire program, the group may find it is able to work with the individual on an issue or two.

Interest groups also favor incumbents because the campaign contributions such groups make are based more on rewarding public officials for positions they already have taken than on trying to persuade them to take new

---

Indirect Lobbying

A form of lobbying in which lobbyists build support for their cause through the media, rallies, and other ways of influencing public opinion, with the ultimate goal of swaying legislators to support their cause.

MAP 6-3

State Corruption Report Card

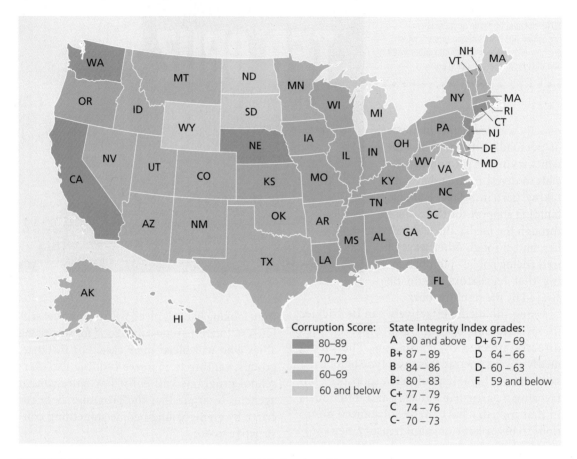

Corruption Score:
- 80–89
- 70–79
- 60–69
- 60 and below

State Integrity Index grades:

Grade	Range	Grade	Range
A	90 and above	D+	67 – 69
B+	87 – 89	D	64 – 66
B	84 – 86	D-	60 – 63
B-	80 – 83	F	59 and below
C+	77 – 79		
C	74 – 76		
C-	70 – 73		

Source: State Integrity Investigation, Center for Public Integrity, www.stateintegrity.org/your_state.

positions altogether. In other words, if a legislator already has demonstrated support for gun owners' rights, the NRA will be inclined to support him or her. The group does not give donations to gun control advocates in the hope of changing their minds. The money follows the vote, in most cases, rather than the other way around. "Someone isn't going to vote one way or the other on gun control based on whether or not they received a contribution from the NRA," says John Weingart, associate director of the Eagleton Institute of Politics at Rutgers University. "But the example we always use here is that if there's a fight between ophthalmologists and opticians about what the regulations should be, a campaign contribution might make a difference because most people don't care."[72]

The adoption of bans on gifts and other ethical restraints has not stopped the lobbying industry or deterred interest groups. Too much is at stake in too many state capitals for corporations, unions, or cause activists not to play an active role. At the beginning of the twentieth century, one or two powerful home-state companies dominated many state political cultures. State capitals remained old boys' clubs, where just a few powerful interests typically held sway, until about World War II. Since then, states have come to rival Washington in terms of the buzz of activity among competing interests.

About 1,100 different occupations are regulated by states today, and, as Weingart suggests, fighting among those industries is never-ending. Art therapists, for instance, want their

TABLE 6-1

Top Ten Most Influential Interests in the States, 2007

Ranking	Organization
1	General business organizations
2	Schoolteacher organizations (National Education Association and American Federation of Teachers)
3	Utility companies and associations (electric, gas, water, telephone/telecommunications)
4	Manufacturers (companies and associations)
5	Hospital/nursing home associations
6	Insurance: general and medical (companies and associations)
7	Physicians/state medical associations
8	Contractors, builders, developers
9	General local government organizations (municipal leagues, county associations, elected officials)
10	Lawyers (predominantly trial lawyers, state bar associations)

Sources: Data compiled from Anthony J. Nownes, Clive S. Thomas, and Ronald J. Hrebenar, "Interest Groups in the States," in *Politics in the American States: A Comparative Analysis,* 9th ed., ed. Virginia Gray and Russell L. Hanson (Washington, DC: CQ Press, 2008), 117.

profession recognized by more state legislatures so that they will be guaranteed reimbursement from insurance companies. Mental health counselors, on the other hand, do not want the added competition and oppose such recognition. Orthopedic surgeons and podiatrists face off over who gets to treat ankle injuries and force legislators to debate whether the ankle is part of the foot. (The Colorado legislature decided it was, opening up the field to podiatrists.) Dog groomers fight veterinarians for the right to brush canine teeth.[73]

While states got into the professional licensing business in a big way to protect public health and safety, they are also pushed to enforce regulations by groups that want to set a bar high enough to discourage competition. Consider the case of Jestina Clayton, who moved at age twenty-two from a village in the West African nation of Sierra Leone to a town called Centerville in Utah. She started a business offering traditional African hair braiding, but soon enough she was warned that in order to practice her trade she needed a cosmetology license, which would require two years of schooling costing approximately $16,000 in tuition. She appealed to the state governing body—the Barber, Cosmetology/Barber, Esthetics, Electrology and Nail Technology Licensing Board—for an exemption. The board, made up mainly of licensed barbers and cosmetologists, shot her down. Clayton then enlisted the help of a sympathetic state representative, but his bill to exempt hair braiding from the licensing law was blocked by full-force lobbying by the Professional Beauty Association, which favored regulation that would keep hair care the exclusive province of its professionals. Such scenarios are not uncommon, said Morris Kleiner, a University of Minnesota economist who coauthored a proposal at the federal level to abolish state licensing rules that do more harm than good. Approving such a proposal is good policy but "political suicide," Kleiner said. "When you talk about reductions in licensing, you have every occupation from the plumbers to the CPA's to the electricians lining up to argue why regulation should not be reduced."[74]

Beer is regulated at the state level, which is why Anheuser-Busch InBev, the maker of Budweiser, hires lobbyists in all fifty states. Insurance also is regulated at the state level. Many more industries, in fact, are turning their attention to the states because that is where the federal government and the courts have sent increasing amounts of power. The states have assumed authority over issues such as securities regulation and have taken the lead on issues that have not progressed in Congress. The federal government has failed in recent years to regulate health maintenance organizations, but over the past decade more than forty states have passed bills addressing the topic.

The active role of the states in regulating economic and social activities has induced some business interests, such as the pharmaceutical industry, to maintain lobbies that are just as powerful in the states as they are in Washington. Others, such as the oil industry, have a major presence at the federal level but are weaker players in most states because state politics largely don't affect them. National companies that are not based in particular states are likely to hire local contract lobbyists to work in those states to lend clout to their causes. The consumer products company Johnson & Johnson has its own lobbyists but also maintains memberships in organizations in its home state, such as the New Jersey Chamber of Commerce, the state's Business and Industry Association, and the New Jersey Health Products Company Group. It also belongs to industry associations in California, Illinois, Massachusetts, and elsewhere. At the national level, Johnson & Johnson belongs to the Pharmaceutical Research and Manufacturers of America, the Health Care Industry Manufacturers' Association, and still other groups.[75]

When an industry has relatively little credibility, it often will turn to allies to represent the public face of its cause. Tobacco companies favor hiring lobbyists who have earned the respect of state legislators as former colleagues or by working for other, less controversial clients. They also seek other groups to take the lead on a lot of their fights. When a state considers legislation that will regulate smoking in public places, for example, the most public opponents are more likely to be restaurant groups rather than the tobacco industry. "We're going to participate in a very upfront way," said a spokesman for the Philip Morris tobacco company. "But like any other industry, we're going to look to people who share that point of view on any given issue" to take a role as well.[76]

As in the case of tobacco companies fighting smoking bans, lobbyists spend the majority of their time playing defense, trying to kill bills they believe would harm their companies or clients. Still, interest groups and their desires stir up much of the activity in state capitals. "Frankly, the legislature in New Jersey exists for the lobbyist," said one lobbyist there.[77] What he was suggesting is that the governor may want five or six bills passed during a session, while individual legislators may want one or two of their own passed as well. The remaining 99 percent of the thousands of bills introduced in a given year are a wish list of the wants and needs of the lobbyists and the interests they represent.

> When an industry has relatively little credibility, it often will turn to allies to represent the public face of its cause. Tobacco companies favor hiring lobbyists who have earned the respect of state legislators as former colleagues or by working for other, less controversial clients. They also seek other groups to take the lead on a lot of their fights.

That is why interest groups are an important part of the political landscape in every state. Certain groups play a disproportionate role in particular states—for example, gambling in Nevada or the poultry industry in Arkansas[78]—but the full range of interest groups has crucial influence over the workings of every state. Clive S. Thomas and Ronald J. Hrebenar, two political scientists who have been studying interest group activity in the states for decades, rank the states according to which have policies that are most influenced by interest groups. In no state are interest groups subordinate to—that is, consistently outgunned by—other policy players, such as governors or political parties.

Those players are stronger in some states than in others. The relative weakness of political parties led Thomas and Hrebenar to argue that interest groups are most powerful in a few states in the South and West, such as Alabama, Nevada, and West Virginia.[79] Certain interest groups may hold greater sway at specific times. The importance of environmental issues, in particular, seems to ebb and flow. But Thomas and Hrebenar note that in the majority of states, the influence of interest groups as a whole remains fairly constant—and fairly strong.

The influence of interest groups is difficult to measure, but it is nonetheless quite apparent, part of the very air that policymakers breathe. Some groups may score a victory here and there: dentists looking for a regulatory change or animal rights activists looking to ban cockfighting. Other groups have become a permanent part of

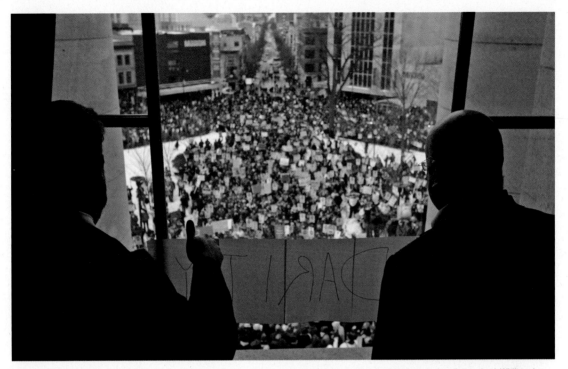

Politicians in the past have worked hard to gain the support of unions, many of which are strong, outspoken, and well organized. While union support may still be sought after in many states, in others the tide has turned. Wisconsin union supporters staged mammoth protests in 2011 when Governor Scott Walker proposed ending collective bargaining rights for public employees.

the landscape, such as business lobbies concerned with taxes, transportation, and education.

There are some interest groups that are powerful everywhere because their members are everywhere. Groups such as teachers' unions and associations of car dealers, restaurant owners, and real estate agents hold particular sway because they have members in every legislative district, and legislators are more likely to be persuaded by individuals or employers from their home districts. Most lobbying by the National Association of Realtors, for example, is handled by volunteer members and state association staff rather than by hired contract lobbyists because Realtors tend to be well connected in their communities. They also make it a point to have particular members of their professional community get to know individual legislators from their districts and keep them up to date about their issues of concern. Realtors, like members of other professions affected at the state policy level, also seek office themselves in part-time legislatures. During the 2005–2006 session, no fewer than twenty-two

people who made their livings in real estate also served as members of the Utah legislature—including the president of the National Association of Realtors.[80]

Taken together, interest groups are the means through which individual citizens and private companies, as well as governmental bodies, influence the policy decisions that affect their lives or ways of doing business. "I don't believe there are some states where interest groups are stronger and others where they're weaker," says Alan Rosenthal, an expert on state politics at Rutgers University. "In every state, interest groups are important. That's the way interests are represented, through groups."[81]

Conclusion

The essential job of political parties is to nominate candidates for public office. The parties no longer control many government jobs, but despite changes in campaign finance laws, they have maintained their positions as crucial fund-raising organizations. They also perform many other functions in American democracy. They aggregate and articulate political interests and create and maintain majorities within the electorate and within government. They are not the dominant organizing forces they once were, in part because voters and candidates—and nonparty fund-raising organizations such as super PACs—have become more independent than they were decades ago. Parties, however, do still play important roles in recruiting political candidates, supporting them financially and logistically, and helping them market themselves to like-minded voters.

For the past 150 years, two major parties—the Democrats and the Republicans—have dominated politics in the United States. Few candidates not belonging to either of these parties have won office at any level of government, and in most cases, the victories of those few have been based on personal appeal rather than support for the third party they represented. The Republican and Democratic parties have been able to adapt to changing times and tastes in ways that have kept them in power, if not always in perfect favor.

With states regulating increasing numbers of industries, interest groups have proliferated so that there are now far more lobbyists than elected officials. Interest groups help push agendas subscribed to by individuals or corporations. Other interest groups push back. Their primary mission is to win as many political offices as possible, so the parties, with varying success, collate and mute the ideological agendas of their interest group allies. Parties cannot afford to have any one group's ideas play such a prominent role that other groups or voters are alienated. It is a difficult balancing act to try to appeal to the majority of voters at any given time while also standing for principles that are clear enough that most people are willing to support them.

The Latest Research

This chapter makes clear that political parties have critically important roles to play in democratic governance. How they go about fulfilling those roles has an enormous impact on politics and policy, in effect setting the boundaries of what will or can be done by the government. One aspect of how parties are executing those responsibilities has evolved into one of the dominant issues in contemporary American politics: the increasing polarization of the two major parties. Much of the evidence for and discussion of the increasing partisanship of Democrats and Republicans, however, is concentrated on the federal level, especially on Congress, where bipartisanship has faded with the shrinking numbers of moderates from both sides of the aisle. Yet scholars of state politics are also intensely interested in the development and direction of political parties and their associated interest groups, and by employing the comparative method they have uncovered some fascinating insights about the polarized stances of political parties.

Indeed, the research discussed below suggests that if we want to know why political parties and interest groups are the way they are, polarized or not, we need a deeper understanding of what is happening outside government, especially at the local level. It is increasingly what happens there—especially in terms of interest group activity—that ultimately determines not just levels of partisanship but the very definition of what a political party is.

• •

- **Masket, Seth.** 2011. *No Middle Ground: How Informal Party Organizations Control Nominations and Polarize Legislatures.* Ann Arbor: University of Michigan Press. In this provocative book Seth Masket, a political scientist at the University of Denver, takes a sustained look at what political parties are and what has caused the increasing partisanship in

American politics. Traditionally, political scientists have viewed political parties as products of politicians. The basic argument is that political elites create formal organizations (that is, political parties) to help them gain office, run government, and pursue particular sets of policies. Masket turns conventional wisdom on its head. Rather than centralized and hierarchical organizations, he argues, political parties, at least in the contemporary world, are characterized by what he terms informal party organizations (IPOs). These organizations, loose affiliations of individuals and interest groups, have enormous influence over primary elections. If elected officials—be they state legislators or members of Congress—want to keep their jobs, they need the support of these IPOs. This is because IPOs have the resources to mobilize enough voters to decide who wins in low-turnout primaries. This ends up distorting democratic representation. IPOs often have more extremely partisan viewpoints than do members of the general electorate, but an elected official who moderates his or her views once in office runs the risk of not making it through the next primary. Thus politicians end up being creatures of (informal) political parties, rather than the other way around.

- **Bawn, Kathleen, Martin Cohen, David Karol, Seth Masket, Hans Noel, and John Zaller.** 2012. "A Theory of Political Parties: Groups, Policy Demands, and Nominations in American Politics." *Perspectives on Politics* 10: 571–597.

This article picks up on and develops a number of the ideas expressed in Masket's *No Middle Ground.* The central argument is that interest groups and activists are now the key actors in shaping political parties. Rather than political parties being tools of elected officials to help them win and keep office, parties are now dominated by interest groups and activists—essentially the IPOs described in Masket's book—who are less interested in the preferences of voters than in their own narrow agendas. These groups focus their efforts on controlling the nomination process—that is, primary elections. This control provides them the whip they need to keep elected officials focused on narrow rather than general interests.

- **Kroger, Gregory, Seth Masket, and Hans Noel.** 2010. "Cooperative Party Factions in American Politics." *American Politics Research* 38: 33–53.

This study takes a closer look at the interest groups and factions that are driving party politics. The authors examine how parties, candidates, and interest groups share information and money-raising resources and find that lying underneath the two political parties are two distinct networks. They find separate "teams" of interest groups and media outlets working with one political party but not the other. Furthermore, these teams appear to be fairly cohesive, at least internally. The various members of the two big partisan networks cooperate with each other, but not with players on the other team. Again, we see evidence of political parties being influenced by powerful nongovernmental actors.

- **Shor, Boris, and Nolan McCarty.** 2011. "The Ideological Mapping of American Legislatures." *American Political Science Review* 105: 502–551.

Political scientists have extensively mapped the growing partisan divide in Congress. While scholars have done similar studies at the state level, data-collection challenges have prevented large-scale studies employing the comparative method. This study goes a long way to filling that gap. Boris and McCarty combine roll-call data from all states since the mid-1990s with surveys of state legislatures to examine how partisanship compares across state legislatures, as well as between state legislatures and Congress. This reveals some clear differences across states and equally clear differences between state and federal legislatures. Notably, in Congress it is well established that the most liberal Republicans are still to the right of the most conservative Democrats, and vice versa. This ideological gap is seen as one of the primary reasons that the bipartisan compromise crucial to action on pressing issues has proven so elusive for recent Congresses. At the state level, however, there are still some legislatures in which the most liberal Republicans are to the left of the most conservative Democrats, and vice versa. This makes finding that all-important bipartisan compromise more likely.

Chapter Review

Key Concepts

- candidate-centered politics (p. 158)
- cause lobbyist (p. 181)
- closed primary (p. 162)
- contract lobbyist (p. 180)
- crossover voting (p. 162)
- dealignment (p. 166)
- direct lobbying (p. 181)
- establishment (p. 152)
- factional splits, or factions (p. 153)
- general election (p. 162)
- independent expenditures (p. 167)
- indirect lobbying (p. 183)
- interest groups (p. 152)
- nonpartisan ballot (p. 161)
- open primary (p. 162)

- party convention (p. 162)
- patronage (p. 161)
- polarization (p. 152)
- political action committee (p. 152)
- political machines (p. 160)
- political parties (p. 152)
- primary election (p. 152)
- realignment (p. 166)
- responsible party model (p. 159)
- runoff primary (p. 163)
- soft money (p. 167)
- super PAC (p. 151)
- swing voters (p. 155)
- ticket splitting (p. 178)
- voter identification (p. 159)

college.cqpress.com/
sites/govstateandlocal

Suggested Web Sites

- **http://ballotpedia.org.** A wiki providing information on candidates and ballot measures in all the states.
- **http://fivethirtyeight.blogs.nytimes.com.** Nate Silver's blog, now hosted by the *New York Times,* covering electoral polling and politics at the national and state levels.
- **http://influenceexplorer.com.** Web site run by the Sunlight Foundation provides data on campaign finance and lobbying expenditures
- **http://moneyline.cq.com.** CQ-Roll Call's Political MoneyLine Web site, which provides information on campaign finance, lobbying and lobbyists, and parties and candidates.
- **www.dnc.org.** Web site of the Democratic National Committee.
- **www.followthemoney.org.** Web site of the National Institute on Money in State Politics, which tracks political donations and lobbying in all fifty states.
- **www.gop.com.** Web site of the Republican National Committee.
- **www.irs.gov/Charities-&-Non-Profits/Political-Organizations/Political-Organization-Filing-and-Disclosure.** The Internal Revenue Service's Political Organization Filing and Disclosure Web site.
- **www.ncsl.org.** Web site of the National Conference of State Legislatures.
- **www.opensecrets.org.** Web site of the Center for Responsive Politics, a nonpartisan organization tracking money in politics.
- **www.publicintegrity.org.** Web site of the Center for Public Integrity, which produces, among other investigative journalism reports, pieces on campaign finance and lobbying activity in the states and Washington, D.C.

**STATE
STATS**

State Stats on Parties and Interest Groups

*Explore and compare data on the states! Go to college.cqpress.com/sites/
govstateandlocal to do these exercises.*

1. If you were a lobbyist for the oil industry, would you devote your time
   working in North Dakota or in Louisiana? Why? Would your answer have
   been different ten years ago? Why?

2. What is the percentage of the population in Mississippi enrolled in
   Medicaid? Based on this information alone, would you expect Mississippi
   to favor Democratic or Republican candidates for office? Is your
   expectation correct? Why or why not? Now, what percentage of the
   population in Wisconsin is enrolled in Medicaid? Why might Mississippi
   and Wisconsin have different political leanings considering this
   information?

3. How does the per capita state government tax revenue in New
   Hampshire compare to neighboring Vermont's? What the state's history
   and politics led to this disparity? What are some of the possible
   implications?

4. How has the percentage of Hispanic residents in Colorado changed
   since 1995? What do you expect that this has done for Colorado's
   political leanings and why?

5. In the 1950s, Ray Bliss identified pockets of rural Americans who were
   not mobilizing to vote. Which states have the highest percentages of rural
   residents now? Which have the least? How do those states tend to lean
   politically? Why?

Every state capitol attracts school groups, protesters, lobbyists, and people only casually interested in getting a glimpse of their government in action.

Legislatures

THE ART OF HERDING CATS

- Why do so many citizens think that legislatures accomplish so little—or accomplish the wrong things altogether?
- What constraints do legislatures face in making effective laws?
- Why are some legislators more powerful than others?

State legislatures operate in complex ways, especially when it comes to how members negotiate with their colleagues as they attempt to make laws. The basic dynamics of legislatures, however, are fairly similar to how you and your friends decide what pizza to order.

Let's say you're really jonesing for some pizza. The cafeteria is closed and for the sake of argument let's say you have $5 in cash and your credit cards are maxed out—and the pizza place's minimum charge for delivery is $10. To get pizza, you need friends. If friends go in on the order, however, you're pretty sure that you won't get your ideal pizza—hamburger with onions and red peppers—because your friends have all made it clear they think that's a disgusting combination. You need to make a deal, and that will involve compromise.

You go around your dorm and pretty quickly find four other people willing to go in on a delivery. Of the five people ordering, two of you want some kind of meat, but three of you are vegetarians. If all votes are counted as equal, you're going meatless. Similarly, if Republicans hold sixty seats in the Indiana House of Representatives and Democrats have only forty, most of the time the Republicans are going to get their way. This is called **majority rule**.

But bills do not always pass according to predictable partisan majorities. Let's change our pizza-ordering scenario. Now it is just you (a young man), your roommate

---

Majority Rule
The process in which the decision of a numerical majority is made binding on a group.

(also a man), and your girlfriend. Your roommate doesn't want hamburger or sausage or pepperoni—and your girlfriend, instead of siding with you, agrees with him! Something similar happens regularly in legislatures, when some members abandon their fellow Democrats or Republicans to vote with the opposing party. For instance, most Democrats might want to pass stricter gun control laws, but some of their rural, more conservative Democratic colleagues might block them by joining with the GOP. This is called **coalition building**.

Although your girlfriend voted initially with your roommate, she actually finds the idea of splurging and enjoying some pepperoni pretty enticing. She also knows that it is not smart policy to favor your roommate's taste over yours. In her heart, she would rather stay vegetarian, but she knows she is better off in the long run if she agrees with you on this. She might even get you to watch that romantic comedy you've been avoiding if she supports your order. In much the same way, legislators often vote for bills that they do not particularly like in order to win support for other priorities. They might want to curry favor with their party leaders, or they might simply want to earn a colleague's help in the future by voting for the colleague's pet bill now. This is called trading votes, or **logrolling**.

Or maybe you have learned that you cannot count on your girlfriend to stick up for you when it's time to call the pizza parlor. So you go around to all your pals in the dorm and plant the idea that what would really be fun tonight would be getting a pizza. You ask only guys you are pretty sure will be good with pepperoni. Just to make sure, you ask Cecilia, who is known to eat more meat than any of the guys. Legislators—and other people concerned with what legislators are up to—do this all time. They try to solicit support from people who are going to vote long before a vote actually takes place so that the result will come out the way they want. This is called lobbying and is similar to the kind of lobbying that interest groups do, as we have seen in chapters 5 and 6.

But let's say that while you are busy polling your friends, one of them unexpectedly says that he hates pepperoni worse than poison and that he refuses even to think about sausage. And surely you would run into opposition if you dared to ask for anchovies. This sort of thing often happens in legislatures. If there is a bill to increase state spending for abortion clinics, for instance, you can bet that one or more legislators will do everything in their power to block that spending.

An adamant opponent can stop a hated piece of legislation's progress through a chamber in many ways, including by mounting a **filibuster**, a kind of endless debate sometimes used in the U.S. Senate. Another way is to attach unwanted amendments, or **riders**, to a bill. The road to a bill's passage into law is twisty and sometimes full of unexpected hurdles. John Dingell, D-Mich., the longest-serving member of the U.S. House of Representatives, perhaps best described the strange relationship between the actual substance of a bill and how it moves through the House when he said in 1984, "If you let me write procedure and I let you write substance, I'll screw you every time."[1]

All these complicated dynamics are why legislative leadership has sometimes been compared to the job of herding cats. "You come into the Senate every day with a wheelbarrow of 33 cats," writes William Bulger, a former president of the Massachusetts Senate. "Your job is to get the wheelbarrow with 17 of those cats to the other side of the chamber."[2]

Coalition Building
The assembling of an alliance of groups to pursue a common goal or interest.

Logrolling
The practice in which a legislator gives a colleague a vote on a particular bill in return for that colleague's vote on another bill to be considered later.

Filibuster
A debate that under U.S. Senate rules can drag on, blocking final action on the bill under consideration and preventing other bills from being debated.

Rider
An amendment to a bill that is not central to the bill's intent.

In all fairness, legislatures were not designed to be simple. The congressional system was designed to be difficult enough to prevent new laws that have not been properly thought through and debated from bothering everybody. "The injury which may possibly be done by defeating a few good laws will be amply compensated by the advantage of preventing a number of bad ones," wrote Alexander Hamilton in *Federalist* No. 73.[3] Most state legislatures share the basic structure of the U.S. Congress, with a house chamber and a senate chamber, each of which must approve a bill before it can go to the governor to be signed into law. That means that even if a bill makes its way through all the circuitous steps of getting passed by the house, including **committee** fights and winning a majority in the chamber, it can easily die if the senate refuses to sign off on an identical version. "If we passed the Lord's Prayer, we'd send it to the Senate and they'd amend it and send it back," said Bob Bergren, Speaker of the Montana House.[4] Getting the 150 or so legislators who serve in a state to agree on anything is one of the toughest tricks in politics.

> Legislators work hard. They address thousands of bills and constituent complaints every year, but the institutional structures of the legislatures make it difficult for them to respond quickly to the issues of the day.

The consequence of this complexity is a grave misperception by the general public about how well legislatures work and how competent individual legislators are. Legislators work hard. They address thousands of bills and constituent complaints every year, but the institutional structures of the legislatures make it difficult for them to respond quickly to the issues of the day. In states where the electorate is split politically, it is especially difficult for legislators to reach agreements that please everyone.

The fact is that today's legislators are mostly working harder to address more complicated problems than did their counterparts in the past. But the public's perception is that they are not getting the job done. Recent studies show that the average person is not in touch with what his or her legislature is up to, considers the legislature to be unnecessarily contentious, and thinks legislators are guilty of talking when they should be acting. Many people believe that legislators are too cozy with the interest groups that provide them with campaign contributions and perhaps other favors. Voters wonder why their representatives do not simply vote the "right" way and go home.

The problem is that there is no one "right" way. Many crosscurrents run through every legislature. Some legislators represent liberal **districts**; others represent conservative areas. Some represent cities; others represent farmlands grappling with entirely different, nonurban issues. Legislators acting in good faith will come to different conclusions about what is the right approach to take on any number of issues, from education and transportation to job creation and taxes. All sides get to present their most convincing arguments, but only rarely can a majority of members of a legislature come to an agreement that pleases them all. In their disagreement, they reflect the different opinions of their **constituents**, the citizens back home—which is precisely the way the system is supposed to work.

Let's say that you and your friends are still arguing over pepperoni and the vegetarian combo. Only this time, each choice has the same number of fans. In the end, you decide that you will just go with cheese. Nobody is thrilled about this—none of you gets the toppings you were hoping for—but everyone can live with the choice.

Committee
A group of legislators who have the formal task of considering and writing bills in a particular issue area.

District
The geographical area represented by a member of a legislature.

Constituents
Residents of a district.

This is called **compromise**, and it is the kind of agreement legislators make more than any other. The purpose of this chapter is to give you a sense of how legislators come to their decisions, who they are, what they do, and how they organize themselves in their institutions. Localities—city and county governments—typically have some form of legislature as well; these are covered in chapter 11.

The Job of Legislatures

On June 24, 2011, the New York state legislature voted to make the state the sixth, and by far the largest, to legalize gay marriage. The decision came as a significant surprise. Just two years earlier, when Democrats had the majority in the New York Senate, a bill to legalize gay marriage had failed on a lopsided vote. In the 2010 elections, Republicans won the edge in the New York Senate. As in most places, in New York Democrats are more likely than Republicans to favor gay marriage, yet, even with Republicans in charge, the legislation passed in the Senate because four Republicans joined with all but one of the chamber's Democrats in voting in favor.

The four Republicans had several reasons to break with their party. Polling showed that a strong majority of New Yorkers thought same-sex nuptials should be legal, so senators risked voter anger if they said no. Legalizing gay marriage was a top priority of the state's popular Democratic governor, Andrew Cuomo, and senators needed to stay in the governor's good graces to enact their own priorities. Still, the senators said that they had merely done what they thought was right. "I apologize for those who feel offended," said Mark Grisanti, one of the four Republicans. "I cannot deny a person, a human being, a taxpayer, a worker, the people of my district and across this state, the State of New York, and those people who make this the great state that it is the same rights that I have with my wife."[5]

Not surprisingly, some were offended. Social conservatives who oppose gay marriage play a key role in the Republican Party's coalition. "Marriage

---

Compromise
The result when there is no consensus on a policy change or spending amount but legislators find a central point on which a majority can agree.

has always been, is now and always will be the union of one man and one woman in lifelong, life-giving union," the New York State Catholic Conference said in a statement. "Government does not have the authority to change this most basic of truths."[6] In 2012, the next time they were up for reelection, all four of the Republicans who had voted yes faced serious primary opposition from fellow Republicans, with foes spending hundreds of thousands of dollars to oust them. But gay marriage supporters also kicked in large amounts of campaign cash in their defense. One decided to retire rather than run again. Another lost in the Republican primary. A third lost to a Democratic opponent in the November election. As a result, when the legislature reconvened in 2013, Grisanti was the only one of the four left in the Senate.

The story of the four New York Republican senators demonstrates several key points about how legislatures operate today. Everyone understands that it is the job of the legislature to set policy for the state, in consultation with the governor—or sometimes despite the governor's wishes, if there are sufficient votes to override his or her veto. Nevertheless, the decisions that legislators make are, by their nature, political. It's difficult to please everybody, and often legislators have to balance competing interests. In this case, they had to choose between the desires of their party on one hand and the majority view of the state on the other. They had to choose which of two opposing interest groups they would offend, knowing that either choice would likely put their political careers at risk. And they had to consult their consciences too.

Many state legislatures are not as polarized as Congress, where the members of the two political parties barely speak to one another and the two sides seem to castigate each other as being made up of treacherous enemies as often as they collaborate. But the party caucuses in the state legislatures have grown further apart in recent years, with less agreement across party lines. The case of the New York gay marriage vote, in which just a few legislators broke with their party, is typical. For example, in Virginia in 2012, the legislature was weeks late completing its most basic job, writing a new state budget, because the Virginia Senate was evenly split between Democrats and Republicans—twenty members on each side—and not a single member was willing to cross over and vote with the rival party.

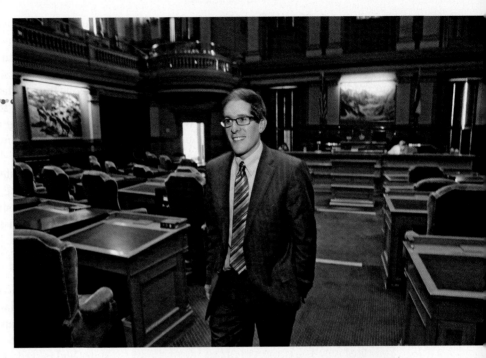

Denver Democratic representative Mark Ferrandino is the first openly gay lawmaker in Colorado to hold the title of House Speaker. He became Speaker in January 2013.

Such deep disagreements make the job of finding the right compromise—getting to an agreed-on set of pizza toppings—that much more difficult. But they also give voters a clear choice between candidates of the two parties.

What Legislatures Do

All state legislatures share four basic interrelated and often overlapping functions:

- *A lawmaking function:* They pass laws and create policy for their states.
- *A representative function:* They provide a means for various groups and individuals to have their interests represented in state policymaking.
- *A constituent service function:* They offer personalized constituent service to help residents sort out their problems with the state government.
- *An oversight function:* They oversee the activities of the governor and the executive branch and some private businesses through public hearings, budget reviews, and formal investigations.

Although state legislatures all address similar issues, including taxes, budgets, and a broad range of other matters (such as regulating office safety and requiring sex offenders to register their places of residence with police), differences in timing, state history, and political culture may cause one state's laws on a topic to differ widely from those of other states. Occasionally, legislatures are pressured to pass uniform laws, as when the federal government, through the National Minimum Drinking Age Act of 1984, insisted that the states raise their legal drinking ages to twenty-one or lose highway funding. Louisiana resisted the longest, adopting a minimum drinking age of twenty-one in 1987.

More often than not, laws are adapted to the local scene and are not easily molded to match other states' versions. Large insurance companies are regulated at the state level. They would love to have their agents qualified to sell in every state rather than having to take fifty different qualifying exams. "I'm still not sure what happens if Michigan says you can be an insurance agent if you can sign your name with your eyes shut, and New York says you've got to take a three-year course," said Alexander Grannis, chair of the insurance committee in the New York Assembly. "What happens if someone screws up—if we cancel a Michigan guy's license to practice here for malpractice, does that mean Michigan can retaliate and cancel a New Yorker's right to practice there?"[7]

Within a given state, the media and the public manage to register many failures of a legislature while not giving the institution enough credit for its successes in balancing all the competing interests within the state. Ethics scandals generally receive greater coverage than do substantial debates, yet legislators debate and pass laws that cover everything from levels of Medicaid health insurance funding to clean water protections to aid for local governments to workers' compensation payments to the price of milk. In most legislatures, 90 percent of the bills receive almost no media attention and are of interest only to those they directly affect. The news media—and the voting public—pay attention only when issues that affect the broadest range of people are considered, such as increases (or cuts) in property tax rates. Legislators do not have the luxury of tuning out when complex and boring but important issues crop up.

> State senators and representatives fight their biggest fights over budgets. Most of their power is derived from the fact that with the approval of the governor they can set fiscal policy, including tax rates.

One of the arguments against term limits is that legislators have to cope with many complicated issues, getting quickly up to speed on such topics as water rights and regional transportation plans. If they can serve for only limited terms, there is the potential that legislatures will end up reopening fights that had been settled through painful negotiations years earlier, because no one is around who remembers what the earlier lawmakers went through.

State senators and representatives fight their biggest fights over budgets. Most of their power is derived from the fact that with the approval of the governor they can set fiscal policy, including tax rates. Dealing with how much money the state devotes to each of its programs is a way of revisiting all the problems that never go away. How much is enough to spend on education? How much of that education tab should the state pick up? Although public schools traditionally were funded by local property taxes, most states now pick up one-third of the bill or more. How much money should be spent on healthcare? How long

should prison terms be for all manner of crimes, and what should be done to reintegrate offenders into society once they've served their time? How big an investment should the state make in roads or public transportation? How much can be spent overall before the state is taxing individuals and businesses too highly? Practically every state has a legal requirement to balance its budget every year, so legislators debate how to make spending match what the state takes in through taxes—or at least how to make the numbers look like they match on paper. State legislatures annually address hundreds of such issues, large and small.

Lawmaking

Legislatures tend to be reactive institutions. Early in 2005, Jessica Marie Lunsford, a nine-year-old Florida girl, was raped and buried alive by a convicted sex offender. By the end of 2006, half the states had passed a version of Jessica's Law, which required longer sentences for sex offenders and electronic tracking of their whereabouts following their release from prison. Jessica's Law was just one among hundreds of laws passed by states in recent years in reaction to high-profile sex crimes against children and the attention they received from programs such as Bill O'Reilly's show on Fox News Channel and *To Catch a Predator* on NBC.

Most issues attract far less attention. The Texas state legislature grappled with more than ten thousand bills in 2011, while even much mellower Montana took up more than a thousand that year.[8] Despite this amount of activity—or perhaps because of it—legislators generally do not go looking for issues to address. The typical bill is introduced for one of several reasons: it is a bill that has to be considered, such as the annual state budget; it is a bill dealing with a common problem modeled on another state's legislation; or it is something that an individual or a group outside the legislature—such as constituents, the governor, or lobbyists—wants considered.

It may not always seem like it, but constituents can have a lot of influence in government. In Massachusetts, for instance, legislators are obliged to consider petitions to introduce bills on any topic that a state resident wants. During the state's debate over same-sex marriages in 2004, for instance, various groups petitioned the legislature with the approaches they favored. In effect, they filed their own amendments.

Governors and the executive branch are also powerful players in the legislative process, promoting ideas they want legislators to work on. Some of these bills are designed to address immediate problems quickly. For example, when the National Football League's Minnesota Vikings threatened to leave the state unless the team received financial help to build a new stadium, Governor Mark Dayton made the stadium bill a top priority. In 2012, he succeeded in persuading the legislature to commit $348 million in state funds to the project.

In other cases, governors struggle for years to persuade legislatures to make big changes. Soon after he was elected governor of South Carolina in 2002, Mark Sanford asked legislators to vote to restructure the state's government. Many of South Carolina's government functions, such as budgeting, hiring, procurement, and information technology, are overseen by a five-member Budget and Control Board that includes representatives from both the legislative and executive branches. Sanford argued that this setup lacked accountability—if five different people were in charge, then no one was really in charge—and asked legislators to instead create a Department of Administration to oversee many basic functions, with a single director to be appointed by the governor. Legislators realized, however, that giving more power to the governor's office meant giving more power to Sanford—and they didn't like Sanford. Legislators clashed with him regularly. In one famous incident in 2004, Sanford brought squealing, defecating pigs in his arms to the state capitol to highlight what he saw as wasteful spending. The issue came up again and again during Sanford's tenure as governor, but the legislators would not create a Department of Administration.[9] When a new governor, Nikki Haley, was elected in 2010, she also promoted the concept. But relations between Haley and the legislature quickly soured too. In 2012, the state Senate voted unanimously in favor of a preliminary bill to create a Department of Administration, only to fail to vote on a final version.

Finally, lobbyists representing a client such as a beer company or auto manufacturer often will promote draft legislation in the hope that a member of the legislature or general assembly—as the legislatures are known in Colorado, Georgia, Pennsylvania, and several other states—will sponsor it as a bill. True.com, an online dating service, convinced legislators in several states in 2006 to introduce legislation requiring such Web sites to conduct background checks of all their users. "I was shocked when I found out that dating services, which market themselves as finding someone's true soulmate, don't provide any kind of even cursory background checks," said Illinois state representative John Bradley, whose bill passed the state House that year. But, even though True.com's founder said he was motivated by an online meeting that ended in murder, his competitors were able to convince legislators that the bill was only a "PR stunt" designed to make True.com's services, which included background checks, look more enticing. They said there was no way of checking on customers, who everyone knew to be fibbers. "There's sort of a joke in the industry that the average person lies by 10 pounds and 10 years," said Eric Straus of Cupid.com.[10]

Although lobbyists promote bills, they also devote an enormous amount of energy to trying to kill bills. Part of the job of the legislative process is to act as a sort of referee among a lot of competing interests. Any proposed change in state law that someone views as a positive step is likely to adversely affect—or at least frighten—someone else. In 2011, the Kentucky Medical Association and the Kentucky Academy of Eye Physicians fought to kill a bill that would allow optometrists to perform laser eye surgeries. The groups argued that optometrists lack the right training to perform the surgery, but they were also defending their turf—they represent ophthalmologists, not optometrists. Their adversary, the Kentucky Optometric Association, proved to be too strong, however. The optometrists had hired eighteen lobbyists to advocate for the legislation and had contributed campaign cash to all but one of the legislature's 138 members over the previous two years.[11] The bill passed. In Kentucky and elsewhere, disputes like this are common: doctors battle with nurse practitioners or dentists disagree with dental hygienists. When a bill comes up for a vote, state legislators are forced to pick a side.

Legislators react most strongly to bills in which they have a personal stake or that they know will affect their constituents directly. Let's say that environmentalists are concerned about a river's water quality and want to require new water filters at a paper mill. The mill's owners, concerned that the cost of the filters will be exorbitant, warn that they will have to lay off three hundred employees if the bill goes through. A legislator from that area will have to worry about whether creating a healthier environment is worth being accused of costing people their jobs. Legislators who live clear across the state from the river and its mill, however, will hold the deciding votes. The people directly affected—the company, the workers, and the downstream residents worried about pollution—will all try to portray themselves as standing for the greater good. If no side is clearly right and favoring one side over the other can do political damage, the bill easily could die. Legislators could then be accused of doing nothing when in reality they are merely reflecting the lack of statewide consensus about how to solve the problem.[12]

Representation

The bulk of the work legislators do involves formulating the law and trying to keep an eye on the executive branch, but legislators' primary responsibility is to provide **representation** for their constituents. Basically, they ensure that the interests of those for whom they speak are properly considered as part of decision making at the state level. For example, in 2012 California state representative Roger Dickinson introduced a bill to create a Public Employees Bill of Rights in the state. The legislation set out a host of new rules to help government workers, such as mandating that they could not be required to work extra when their colleagues were fired unless they were paid extra

---

Representation
Individual legislators acting as the voices of their constituencies within the house of representatives or senate.

for their time. Some critics mocked the concept. California has some of the worst budget problems of any state. Why, the critics wondered, would the state offer new protections to government workers when it is already struggling to pay the salaries and benefits of its workforce and to maintain funding for basic services such as education and healthcare? "There is hardly a workplace in recession-battered America that has not been hit with layoffs," the *Modesto Bee* newspaper said in an editorial. "Private-sector workers regularly shoulder additional responsibilities along with pay cuts. It's how many deal with a drastically altered economic reality. Despite the valuable work that many of them do, government workers should not be shielded from such realities."[13] Dickinson, though, was just looking out for his constituents. His district is in Sacramento, California's capital, where state agencies are headquartered. The city is home to more public workers than any other in the state.[14]

If a problem is real and persistent enough, a state's legislature will address it eventually. Sometimes there is a general recognition that a long-festering problem just needs to be fixed once and for all. That does not mean the fix is going to be easy. Some states, including Kansas, Ohio, and Pennsylvania, have had to tweak their school funding formulas continually in response to state supreme court decisions that found their education systems inadequate. And numerous states, including Oklahoma, Pennsylvania, and Tennessee, have changed their tort laws, laws that cover damages to individuals, in the past few years. They have done this to help their doctors and trauma centers afford medical malpractice insurance. Addressing medical malpractice issues is difficult in part because trial lawyers object to any limitations on the punitive damages that people can receive from lawsuits after suffering as a result of medical negligence.

The political reason that this objection by trial lawyers is important is that trial lawyers are influential constituencies in Democratic politics. This is especially true in the Deep South, which has long had a reputation for hefty jury verdicts. States such as Alabama and Mississippi traditionally have been hostile to trade unions, having "right to work" laws that have made it difficult for the unions to organize. Elsewhere, in the Midwest and Northeast, where unions are active, they are important donors to Democratic candidates. But where unions are

Local Focus

Taking on the Law in the Land of the Free . . . and the Home of the Silly

Rich Smith, a British journalism student, spent one Christmas Day playing board games. He came across a reference to an obscure law in Florida that made it illegal for divorced women to go parachuting on Sundays. Enchanted by this and a treasure trove of other dumb American laws, he decided to spend the summer after graduation driving all across the United States and breaking every outdated or just plain absurd law he could find. "Tying giraffes to lampposts seemed a funnier way in which to become a felon" than arson or murder, Smith writes in his book about the spree, *You Can Get Arrested for That.*[a]

Smith and a friend attempted to break two dozen laws in all, succeeding in most cases. Many of the laws concerned personal behavior. Traveling east from San Francisco, Smith carried out his first successful crime by peeling an orange in a hotel room, an action illegal throughout California.

He then drove to Globe, Arizona, where it is illegal to play cards on the street against an American Indian, and did just that. He made sure to order plenty of garlic bread along with his pizza in Indianapolis because in that city it is illegal to enter a theater within three hours of eating

garlic. He also broke the law by eating watermelon in a cemetery in Spartanburg, South Carolina, and by sleeping on top of a refrigerator in Pennsylvania.

The fashion police have made it illegal to wear a goatee in Massachusetts, so Smith grew one in plenty of time for his visit to that state. He also broke several laws concerning fishing, including his attempt to hunt down marine mammals in a lake in Utah and, of course, his blatant disregard for Chicago's ban on fishing while wearing pajamas. But he lacked sufficient skill to violate Tennessee's stricture against catching a fish with a lasso.

Although Smith managed to break numerous laws, several others defeated him. He failed to find a bathtub to carry illegally across the village green in Longmeadow, Massachusetts, and he couldn't persuade a woman in Iowa to kiss him for longer than five minutes (or at all).

Several of his crimes were witnessed by police or private security guards, but perhaps it's in the nature of "dumb" laws that they aren't rigorously enforced. The only time Smith and his buddy got into serious trouble was when they drove at ninety-seven miles per hour in a seventy-five-mile-per-hour zone in Wyoming. That time, they got nailed.

[a]Published by Three Rivers Press, New York, 2006.

---

weak, trial lawyers have become the major source of funding for Democrats. (The roles of such interest groups are discussed in chapter 6.)

Legislatures often finish their work on an issue not because of outside pressure but because of internal changes. New leaders in the Arizona Senate in 2001 brought with them solutions to long-standing issues that included understaffing in the state's highway patrol, underfunding of the state's mental health system, and provisioning for water through new contracts. Legislators even managed to repeal antiquated sex laws that made it a crime for unmarried couples to live together.[15] More recently, in 2008, Republicans won control of both legislative chambers in Tennessee for the first time since the Civil War. They quickly began

pushing long-sought legislation in areas such as the regulation of guns, charter schools, and abortion. "I think every bad bill I've seen in my 10 years got resurrected this year and had a chance of passing," complained Mike Turner, chair of the House Democratic Caucus.[16] Two years later, the Republicans won even bigger legislative majorities and one of their own, Bill Haslam, was elected governor. They quickly enacted an ambitious agenda that included many party priorities, phasing out the inheritance tax, weakening teacher tenure, enacting tort reform, and overhauling civil service rules.

Not surprisingly, states with stagnant leadership or long-term control by one party or the other may have a harder time making breakthroughs.

Changes in partisan control bring in new leaders and, with them, new agendas that reflect new priorities and different constituencies. After all, before a bill can even get far enough to be debated, the idea for it must be developed. To get ideas for bills, legislators turn to each other, to staff, to colleagues in other states, and to outside sources such as companies with causes of their own or think tanks interested in pushing change. As Alan Rosenthal, a leading expert on state legislatures at Rutgers University, points out, "Legislation is becoming a national phenomenon."[17] National associations of legislatures, such as the National Conference of State Legislatures and the American Legislative Exchange Council, promulgate ideas that quickly spread from state to state, as do bills pushed by national corporations and interest groups. And states may be addressing new issues that crop up on a similar time frame. In 2009, prompted by the story of a middle school student who suffered a severe brain injury after returning to a football game with a concussion, Washington became the first state to pass a law setting standards for when youth athletes can return to games after head injuries. Around that time, new research began to show that multiple concussions could cause severe ailments such as Alzheimer's disease and dementia. By 2012, thirty-eight states had enacted laws similar to Washington's.[18]

Fire-safe cigarettes, as their name suggests, do a lot to prevent accidental fires. They go out when a smoker stops puffing, and they have extra rings of paper that prevent them from burning on their own if a smoker falls asleep or drops a lit cigarette. But tobacco companies always oppose fire-safe cigarettes on the grounds that they cost more to produce. As a Democratic member of Congress from Massachusetts in the 1980s, Jim Shannon fought to require that all cigarettes have these safety features, but his legislation went nowhere because Big Tobacco was able to lobby successfully against it.

Things began to change in 2004, however, when New York became the first state to mandate fire-safe cigarettes. "Maybe what we need to do is forget about beating our heads against the wall in Congress," Shannon recalls thinking.[19] By that time, Shannon was president of the National Fire Protection Association. This group, which spends most of its time writing safety codes for equipment such as building sprinklers and smoke alarms, wasn't the usual sort of public health advocacy group that cigarette manufacturers were used to fighting; it was able to recruit firefighters and marshals to help make its case in more state capitals. Between 2006 and 2009, the group helped persuade the legislatures of forty-four states to enact laws requiring self-extinguishing mechanisms in cigarettes, leaving Wyoming as the only state without such a mandate.

By the end of 2009, the lone holdout hardly mattered. Fire-safe cigarettes had become, de facto, the law of the entire land—especially since the tobacco lobby had given up the fight against them. Instead, tobacco companies worked hard to ensure that no state diverged from the model New York had created. It's one thing to have to meet the specific manufacturing requirements imposed by one state; it would be far more difficult for a national company to have to meet different standards in each state. "If the standards were reasonable and consistent, we could live with them," said Frank Lester, a spokesman for R. J. Reynolds Tobacco Company.[20]

Sometimes private companies are able, like the firefighters, to go "venue shopping," finding sympathetic legislators in a state who will pass a law that may become a model for other states. But most ideas are still homegrown. Minnesota has an unusually fertile landscape when it comes to ideas for the legislature. More than 750 foundations are active in the state's public life. During the mid-1990s, 30 of them matched funds with the legislature to help nonprofit groups plan for federal budget cuts and changes in welfare law.[21] In addition, the state capital of St. Paul has the now-unusual benefit of being able to mine two major metropolitan daily newspapers—the *Pioneer Press* and the *Star Tribune,* which serves the capital's "twin city" of Minneapolis. Once upon a time, numerous communities were served by two or more competing newspapers. Today, consolidations and foldings have forced most areas to make do

Texas legislators approved a bill that would allow for random drug testing of thousands of high school athletes in an effort to stamp out steroid use.

with one, if that. Fortunately for Minnesota's legislators, both of the Twin Cities' papers actively cover public policy. Perhaps as a result, the state was the first to ban smoking in restaurants, the first to allow schoolchildren to choose among public schools, the first to allow charter schools, and the first to enact requirements that people holding comparable jobs receive comparable pay. Such engagement from the media—and, by extension, interest from the public—has become fairly rare. We discuss how the media cover state legislatures a little later on in this chapter.

Constituent Service

Aside from debating and passing laws, and ensuring that the interests of various groups are represented in decision making, legislators devote a good deal of time and energy to **constituent service**. They help clear up problems that citizens are having with public agencies or even private companies. They also act as liaisons between their constituents and unelected parts of the government in the executive branch, the bureaucracy that everyone knows and loves to hate.

Legislators and their staffs spend incredible amounts of their time dealing with constituent service requests, also known as **casework**.[22] Residents of a state may experience all manner of frustration coping with state laws or may merely want assistance in sorting through regulatory requirements. One of the advantages of being an **incumbent** is having the ability to dole out this kind of personalized help. While a recount battle dragged on in Minnesota for more than six months following the 2008 election, U.S. senator Amy Klobuchar, D-Minn., and her staff had to do the work of two senators—handling double the usual caseload of sorting through issues, from helping military veterans in the state navigate the federal bureaucracy "to adoptions that have been stalled out in Guatemala," she told MSNBC.[23]

Constituent Service
The work done by legislators to help residents in their voting districts.

Casework
The work undertaken by legislators and their staffs in response to requests for help from constituents.

Incumbent
A person holding office.

At the state level, some legislators have staff members devoted solely to helping constituents. This is particularly true in their district offices—offices located in the area back home that they represent, as opposed to their capitol offices. Typical issues include tracking down deadbeat dads for child support, figuring out how constituents can receive proper health coverage under Medicaid programs, and determining which federal agency to contact with questions about military matters.

In one humorous case, Jim Townsend received a call from a constituent complaining that the grass in the median strip of a state road near his house had become overgrown. Townsend was not only a legislator but also the majority leader of the Oklahoma House. When he called the highway department, he expected action. He was promised prompt service, but the same constituent called him back two weeks later to report that nothing had been done. Townsend took matters into his own hands, putting his own riding mower in the back of his pickup truck and doing the mowing himself.[24] "I spend a tremendous amount of time on constituent service," said Tennessee senator Rosalind Kurita, D-Clarksville. "When we are in session, I probably make five or six calls a day and easily [write] that many e-mails and letters. To me, that is one of the most important things we do."[25]

No one objects to a senator like Kurita helping a seven-year-old boy who has outgrown his wheelchair figure out how to receive a new one through the state's health insurance program. The problem is that attempts to help individuals sometimes morph into policy decisions. That is, a legislator might not only write a letter to help a particular person but also write a bill that changes the way the state approaches a program, such as health insurance. Helping an individual may be all well and good, but changing the system based on the personal story of one constituent is not necessarily the best way to change policies that will affect thousands.

Undoubtedly, it is important for legislators to hear about the real-world experiences of their constituents. Because they cannot meet with everybody, however, they need to rely on reports and studies to get a complete picture. They otherwise might be swayed too greatly by personal interactions. The danger of politicians' having to raise significant campaign finance treasuries is

FIGURE 7-1

HOW IT WORKS

A One-Eyed Frog's View of the Legislative Process, or How a Bill Really Became a Law in Minnesota

The mechanisms by which a bill becomes a law at the state level are similar to the mechanisms at work at the federal level. And we've all seen the flowcharts that outline the ins and outs: a bill goes in one side, gets debated, marked up, and reported out, and then comes out the other side as a real-life law to be implemented, or it gets returned to the legislature for an override, or it gets "killed." You'd be forgiven for thinking that beneath that abstraction lies a more complex and interesting process.

You'd be right. Below is a different flowchart, this one fleshing out what actually happened when a group of Minnesota teens brought to light the fact that the frog population in their area was turning up with extra limbs and missing eyes. About eight months and $151,000 later, the frogs were in much better shape.

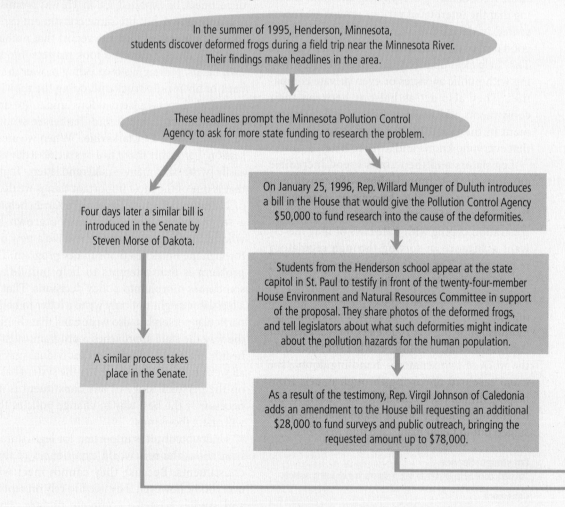

In the summer of 1995, Henderson, Minnesota, students discover deformed frogs during a field trip near the Minnesota River. Their findings make headlines in the area.

These headlines prompt the Minnesota Pollution Control Agency to ask for more state funding to research the problem.

Four days later a similar bill is introduced in the Senate by Steven Morse of Dakota.

On January 25, 1996, Rep. Willard Munger of Duluth introduces a bill in the House that would give the Pollution Control Agency $50,000 to fund research into the cause of the deformities.

Students from the Henderson school appear at the state capitol in St. Paul to testify in front of the twenty-four-member House Environment and Natural Resources Committee in support of the proposal. They share photos of the deformed frogs, and tell legislators about what such deformities might indicate about the pollution hazards for the human population.

A similar process takes place in the Senate.

As a result of the testimony, Rep. Virgil Johnson of Caledonia adds an amendment to the House bill requesting an additional $28,000 to fund surveys and public outreach, bringing the requested amount up to $78,000.

Source: Minnesota House of Representatives Public Information Office, "Capitol Steps: How Six Bills Became Law," www.house.leg.state.mn.us/hinfo/How6bil.pdf.

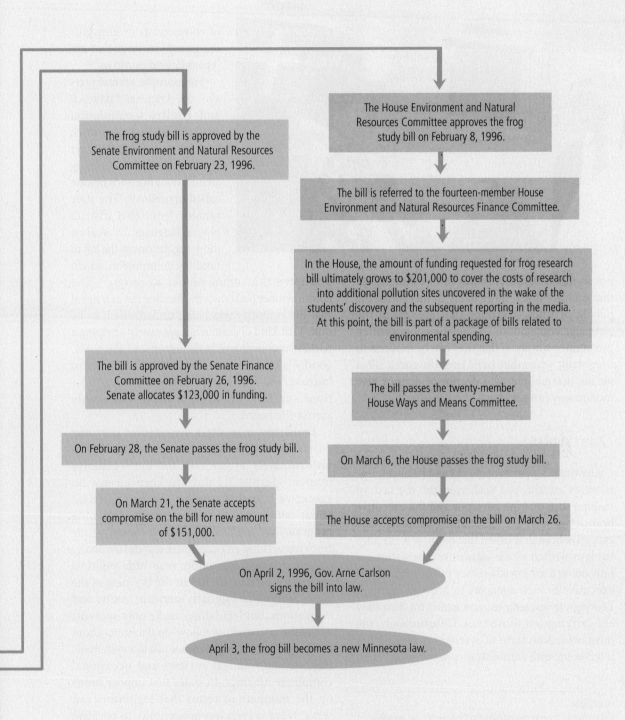

The frog study bill is approved by the Senate Environment and Natural Resources Committee on February 23, 1996.

The House Environment and Natural Resources Committee approves the frog study bill on February 8, 1996.

The bill is referred to the fourteen-member House Environment and Natural Resources Finance Committee.

In the House, the amount of funding requested for frog research bill ultimately grows to $201,000 to cover the costs of research into additional pollution sites uncovered in the wake of the students' discovery and the subsequent reporting in the media. At this point, the bill is part of a package of bills related to environmental spending.

The bill is approved by the Senate Finance Committee on February 26, 1996. Senate allocates $123,000 in funding.

The bill passes the twenty-member House Ways and Means Committee.

On February 28, the Senate passes the frog study bill.

On March 6, the House passes the frog study bill.

On March 21, the Senate accepts compromise on the bill for new amount of $151,000.

The House accepts compromise on the bill on March 26.

On April 2, 1996, Gov. Arne Carlson signs the bill into law.

April 3, the frog bill becomes a new Minnesota law.

Being mayor means constantly meeting with constituents, as Tom Barrett (in tie and gray hair) does here outside a Milwaukee post office.

of constituents or constituent groups in ways that are "episodic and punitive."[26]

For example, several years ago, the Arkansas Livestock and Poultry Commission filed suit against a livestock sales barn for failure to meet state regulations concerning an infectious livestock disease called brucellosis. The state senator from that district placed language to weaken those regulations in the bill to fund the commission, which prompted the commissioner to resign.[27] The commissioner had taken the funding cut as a signal that his authority was being undermined, so he quit. That kind of scattershot approach—helping a particular constituent at the expense of the public good—is by its nature inequitable. The point of bureaucratic norms is to make sure that regulations and laws are applied fairly and evenly across the board.

Legislators may attack agencies for pursuing policies that hurt their constituents, but it's unfortunately pretty rare for the legislative branch—despite its duty to keep an eye on executive branch functions—to be consistent about taking a hard look at whether ongoing programs are functioning as they should. Aside from unearthing an occasional scandal involving misspent funds, legislators reap little political reward for poking around in the business of the state. Staff aides regularly perform audits and evaluations, but legislatures make only sporadic use of them in making follow-up decisions about funding. Most oversight comes in a less systematic way, through budget reviews and occasional committee hearings. In states that impose limits on the numbers of terms that legislators can serve, there is even less opportunity to perform oversight. Members have less time to become

not so much that their votes can be bought but that they are much more likely to meet with the people or interest groups that give them the campaign contributions. Campaign donors often give money simply so that they can have access to a legislator when they hand over the check. That means that people who do not or cannot give money may not get heard.

Oversight

Under the U.S. system of checks and balances, legislatures are charged with **oversight**, the task of making sure that the governor and the executive branch agencies are functioning properly. The executive branch is called that because it executes the laws written by the legislature. Legislators are only doing their job when they call governors and executive branch agencies to account through hearings, investigations, and audits for how they are carrying out those laws. Unfortunately, the most ubiquitous form of oversight is a legislator's intervening with administrative agencies on behalf

---

Oversight
The legislature's role in making sure that the governor and executive branch agencies are properly implementing the laws.

Local Focus

Constituent Service: Going the Extra Mile

When John Medinger was a member of the Wisconsin State Assembly, he worked backbreaking hours to do his job—and to make sure that his constituents knew he was doing his job. He needed to let people know how seriously committed he was to representing them and their interests because Medinger is a Democrat who represented a Republican district.

He drove the 137 miles to the capitol in Madison and the 137 miles back home to La Crosse three times a week, even when the legislature was not meeting. When he was in La Crosse, he was in perpetual motion. "If I don't have anything to do at home," he said, "I go sit in a coffee shop and shoot the breeze. I might be home two nights a week to tuck my kids in. I go to every pancake breakfast and every rummage sale. I am always looking for something to do. If there's nothing else, I go to a basketball game and mingle with the crowd."

All that work paid off politically. One year, Medinger got a perfect 100 rating from the American Federation of Labor and Congress of Industrial Organizations (AFL-CIO) but was rated at 29 by the Wisconsin Association of Manufacturers. The La Crosse chamber of commerce endorsed him for reelection anyway. As Medinger once said, "There are some Republicans in my district who could run against me and make my life miserable. . . . But the Republicans can't come up with

candidates who will put in 100-hour weeks. So they don't make it."[a] The fact is, no one who interacts with legislators doubts that they work hard. They work long hours meeting with colleagues, constituents, lobbyists seeking favors for their clients, and business leaders from their districts and across the state.

For all of the clear evidence that politicians work hard, some people still question whether all the meeting and studying and debating those legislators do actually accomplishes anything. "A politician's day is long," says satirist P. J. O'Rourke. "He gets into the office early, reads newspaper clippings with his name highlighted, submits to a radio interview with Howard Stern, goes to a prayer breakfast and an ACLU [American Civil Liberties Union] lunch, checks opinion polls, meets with an NRA delegation, makes a friendly call to Al Sharpton, sits in the Inland Waterways Committee hearing room drawing pictures of sailboats and seagulls on a notepad, proposes National Dried Plum Week, votes 'yea' (or is it 'nay'?) on something or other (consult staff), exercises with the president, recovers from a faked charley horse after being lapped on the White House jogging track, watches the signature machine sign letters to constituents, returns a corporate campaign contribution to WorldCom, speaks at a dinner supporting campaign-finance reform, goes home, gets on the phone, and fundraises until all hours."[b]

[a]Quoted in Alan Ehrenhalt, *The United States of Ambition* (New York: Times Books/Random House, 1991), 133.

[b]P. J. O'Rourke, "No Apparent Motive," *Atlantic Monthly*, November 2002, 34.

expert in any particular area, and so they often rely heavily on expert testimony from the very executive branch they are meant to oversee.

And for each program, it seems, there are not only agency officials but also program beneficiaries and lobbyists who will question the motives of legislators or staffers who seek to audit the program's work. In other words, there's often not much reward for a legislator in taking the job of oversight seriously. For example, in 2007, the

North Carolina legislature created the Program Evaluation Division, which was charged with compiling a scorecard to show how state agencies were performing, in much the same way information about the performance of private companies might be compiled for investors. John Turcotte, the division's founding director, said his goal was to "target programs for evaluation that are important to the General Assembly and also look at all state government programs collectively to avoid legislative oversight gaps."[28] Turcotte's first report looked at agricultural research stations. North Carolina had the most of any state in the country—twenty-one, compared with only eleven in the much larger state of California—and Turcotte's group concluded that there was no economic or strategic justification for the state to support so many. "That report was like setting off a nuclear weapon in the area of Raleigh," he said. "Any time you question the necessity of an institution or a major component of a program, you will create massive opposition."[29]

Organization and Operation of Legislatures

The U.S. system of representative democracy was designed to be messy. In their 2003 book *Republic on Trial,* Alan Rosenthal and his coauthors argue that the institutions of democracy should be more popular because they work pretty well, but they concede, "The American political system was not designed for people to understand."[30] Legislatures were created because, even in colonial days, this country was too large and its problems too complex to be addressed by its vast numbers of individual citizens. We elect legislatures in our republican form of government to argue out our problems at appointed times and in a single space, in sessions at the capitol. The ranks of the legislatures have become far more diverse over the past thirty years. Although the average state legislator is still a white male, there are nearly four times as many African Americans and nearly six times as many women serving in legislatures today as there were in 1970. Also over the past thirty years or so, legislatures have become better equipped to do their job by hiring more and better professionally trained staffers. None of these changes, however, have made state legislatures any more popular with the public.

Bicameralism

Legislatures are not, of course, random groups of people hanging around a dorm and picking pizza toppings. Every state has a constitution that describes a body that can pass state laws. In every state but Nebraska, which has a unicameral (or one-house) legislature, the legislature is bicameral (or divided into two houses), pretty much like the U.S. Congress. As mentioned earlier in this chapter, one chamber is normally called either the house of representatives or the assembly and the other is called the senate. The Tenth Amendment of the U.S. Constitution reserves to the states all powers not given to the federal government, and state legislatures can write any state law that does not interfere with federal laws.

The house, or assembly, is considered more of a "people's house," with its members representing fewer people for shorter terms than their colleagues in the senate. The house always has more members, known as state representatives, than the senate. There are 163 representatives in the Missouri General Assembly, for example, but only 34 senators. There are some exceptions, but generally senators serve four-year terms, whereas house members have to be reelected every two years. The two chambers operate independently, with separate leaders, committees, and agendas, although both chambers have to pass the same version of a bill before it can be sent to the governor to be signed into law or vetoed. Nebraska, with its unicameral legislature, is the one exception.

Legislative Leadership

Most state legislatures have essentially the same leadership structure, at least for their top positions. At the beginning of a session, each house votes in its Speaker. This is generally someone picked beforehand by a **caucus**, or meeting, of members of the majority party. The majority leader and the minority leader rank just below the Speaker of the house. *Majority* and *minority* here refer to the respective strengths of the major parties. Either the Democratic or the Republican Party may hold the majority of seats in a chamber. (In 2012, fewer than ten legislators—out of more than seven

---

Caucus
All the members of a party—Republican or Democrat—within a legislative chamber. Also refers to meetings of members of a political party in a chamber.

TABLE 7-1

Total Number of State Legislators (House and Senate), 2012

State	Senate Members	House Members	Total Members
Alabama	35	105	140
Alaska	20	40	60
Arizona	30	60	90
Arkansas	35	100	135
California	40	80	120
Colorado	35	65	100
Connecticut	36	151	187
Delaware	21	41	62
Florida	40	120	160
Georgia	56	180	236
Hawaii	25	51	76
Idaho	35	70	105
Illinois	59	118	177
Indiana	50	100	150
Iowa	50	100	150
Kansas	40	125	165
Kentucky	38	100	138
Louisiana	39	105	144
Maine	35	151	186
Maryland	47	141	188
Massachusetts	40	160	200
Michigan	38	110	148
Minnesota	67	134	201
Mississippi	52	122	174
Missouri	34	163	197
Montana	50	100	150

State	Senate Members	House Members	Total Members
Nebraska	49	n/a	49
Nevada	21	42	63
New Hampshire	24	400	424
New Jersey	40	80	120
New Mexico	42	70	112
New York	62[a]	150	212
North Carolina	50	120	170
North Dakota	47	94	141
Ohio	33	99	132
Oklahoma	48	101	149
Oregon	30	60	90
Pennsylvania	50	203	253
Rhode Island	38	75	113
South Carolina	46	124	170
South Dakota	35	70	105
Tennessee	33	99	132
Texas	31	150	181
Utah	29	75	104
Vermont	30	150	180
Virginia	40	100	140
Washington	49	98	147
West Virginia	34	100	134
Wisconsin	33	99	132
Wyoming	30	60	90
Total	**1,971**	**5,411**	**7,382**

Source: National Conference of State Legislatures, "2012 State and Legislative Partisan Composition," www.ncsl.org/documents/statevote/2012_Legis_and_State.pdf.

a. New York added a Senate district with the 2012 election, which increased the number of senators to 63.

MAP 7-1

Partisan Control of State Government, 1954

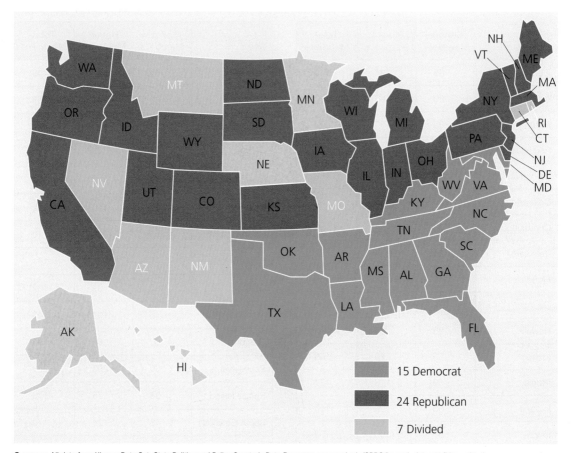

Source: All data from Klarner Data Set, State Politics and Policy Quarterly Data Resource, www.unl.edu/SPPQ/journal_datasets/klarner.html.

thousand nationwide—were independents or members of third parties.) In the senate, the top leader is known as the president, president pro tempore (often shortened to president pro tem), or majority leader.

Certain aspects of the leadership positions remain constant across all the states. For example, a Speaker will typically preside over daily sessions of the house or assembly, refer bills to the appropriate committees, and sign legislation as it makes its way over to the senate or the governor's desk. Leaders appoint committee chairs (in some states, all the members of committees), set or change committee jurisdictions, and offer staff or legislative help to rank-and-file members. They also often help with campaigns, including providing financial support.

The amount of power invested in the office of Speaker or senate president does vary by state, however. In the Texas Senate, leadership powers

are invested in the office of lieutenant governor. Lieutenant governors normally do not possess much formal power, but in Texas, they appoint the members of committees and committee chairs in the thirty-one-member body and decide which bills are considered and when. In some older legislatures, such as those in New Jersey and Massachusetts, the Senate president performs all of those functions, presides over debates, counts votes, and ensures member attendance. In California, those powers rest with the Senate president pro tem. But regardless of how the formal duties are divided up, usually there is one individual who emerges as holding the most power and speaking for the chamber in negotiating with the other chamber and the governor.

With the exception of Nebraska, where parties are actually banned from the nonpartisan

MAP 7-2

Partisan Control of State Government, 2012

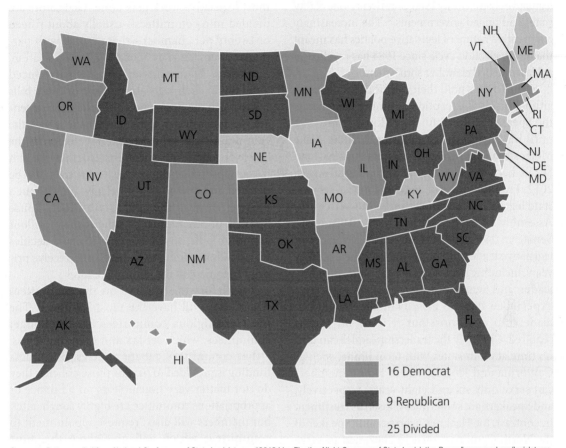

16 Democrat

9 Republican

25 Divided

Source: Data compiled from National Conference of State Legislatures, "2012 Live Election Night Coverage of State Legislative Races," www.ncsl.org/legislatures-elections/elections/statevote-2012-election-night-results-map.aspx; and National Conference of State Legislatures, "Live 2012 Election Night Results: Governors," www.ncsl.org/legislatures-elections/elections/statevote-election-night-governor-map.aspx.

unicameral legislature, legislatures are divided along party lines (and even in Nebraska, the Democratic and Republican parties endorse candidates for the legislature, so it's well-known which lawmakers affiliate with which party). Not only does the majority party get to pick the top leader, but it gets to fill virtually all of the important committee chairs as well. A party majority is worth much more than the comfort of knowing that your fellow Democrats or Republicans will help you outvote the opposition on most bills. Holding the leadership and chair positions means that the majority party gets to set the agenda—deciding which bills will be heard for a vote. From the 1950s into the early 1990s, Democrats held a two-to-one edge in the number of legislative seats and controlled many more chambers than their Republican counterparts. Much of the Democratic Party's dominance came from the South, where many of the Democrats were conservatives who had little in common with the national party. At the start of this century, Republicans pulled into near ties both in terms of raw numbers of legislators and in how many chambers they controlled. Democrats regained a slight but significant advantage back in the election cycles of 2006 and 2008, but, just as they did at the congressional level, Republicans won historic victories in state legislatures in 2010. Afterward, the Republican Party held the most legislative seats it had controlled since 1928 and approximately sixty of the nation's ninety-nine legislative chambers.[31] Democrats made medium-sized gains in the 2012 elections, but Republicans maintained an overall edge.

At the end of World War II, all but seven of the forty-eight states had united governments, meaning one party controlled the governorship and both legislative chambers. By 1986, only twenty-one of fifty states had united governments.[32] The increasingly competitive nature of legislative politics has meant that every election cycle since 1984 has resulted in at least one tied chamber somewhere.[33]

Some leaders hold their positions for decades, although this is exceptional. Jimmy Naifeh was the Speaker of the Tennessee House from 1991 until his party lost its majority in 2009. Mike Miller started his run as president of the Maryland Senate back in 1987 and was still going strong in 2012. Fred Risser is the nation's longest-serving state legislator; he was elected to the Wisconsin Assembly in 1956 and then to the Wisconsin Senate in 1962 and has served in a variety of legislative leadership positions over the past fifty years, including stints as majority leader, minority leader, and Senate president. Lots of legislative experience can be an advantage in getting leadership positions, but it is by no means required. Climbing the leadership ladder can take no time at all in states with term limits, such as California and Florida, where House members can serve only six and eight years, respectively, and Speakers are sometimes chosen as freshmen. In contrast, Joe Hackney, who became Speaker of the North Carolina House in 2007, had to serve more than a quarter century before attaining that post. "When I came to the legislature, I more or less regarded it as a long-term thing," he says. "It wasn't my plan to be there two or four or six years and quit. It was my plan to make a contribution, and I saw that those who make a contribution built up seniority and experience."[34] Hackney held the position of Speaker for four years, before Republican victories in 2010 forced him from power.

Voters unhappy with the status quo often will unseat top leaders in symbolic decapitations. That happened in 2006 to Bob Garton, who had led the Indiana Senate for twenty-six years but lost his seat when voters grew unhappy about a health insurance perk for senators. That same year, Robert Jubelirer, a twenty-five-year leader in the Pennsylvania Senate, was one of seventeen incumbents ousted in primaries by voters angry about a legislative pay raise.

Committees

Regardless of party control, committees are where most legislative work gets done. Legislators are divided into committees—usually about fifteen or twenty per chamber—that grapple with particular issues, such as education, transportation, and taxes. Thousands of bills are introduced annually in each legislature. Most of these bills never reach the floor where the full house or senate meets. Basically, they never make it past the committee stage to be debated or voted on by the house or senate as a whole. Instead, they are sent to the appropriate committee, where they may be debated and amended but usually die without a hearing. Just as the senate president, house Speaker, or other leader sets the agenda for floor action on bills, so the committee chair decides which bills are going to be heard and receive priority treatment at the committee level.

Legislators try to serve on the committees where they will have the most influence. The most prestigious committees are the budget committees, which set tax and spending levels. Other committees debate policies, but unless funding is provided to pay for those policies, they do not matter very much. Seats on a finance or appropriations committee are highly sought after, but members will also "request appointment to committees which will give them the most visibility and interest in their districts."[35] Thus a senator from a rural district may want to serve on an agriculture committee. A representative who previously served on a city council may want a seat on the local government committee.

While any member can introduce legislation on any topic, members of the education committee, for example, are more likely to introduce and influence bills that affect schools. When an education bill is being debated in the full house or senate, other members, who have other specialties, will turn to members of the education committee for guidance about what the bill would do and how they should vote. The same holds true for other issues, such as transportation and healthcare.

Rank-and-File Members

Not every legislator, of course, can be a leader. The majority of legislators—those who provide leaders with their votes—are known as **rank-and-file members** of the legislature. And no legislator—leader or rank-and-file member—can be fully versed on the details of all of the dozens of bills that confront him or her every day during a session. Legislators turn to many sources for information on how to vote. There is a classic notion, posited by political philosopher and statesman Edmund Burke, that divides legislators into **delegates**, who vote according to the wishes of their districts, and **trustees**, who vote according to their own consciences.[36] Given the proliferation of legislation, however, members never hear from a single constituent on probably 90 percent of the bills that they must consider. Instead, they rely for guidance on staffers, other legislators, interest groups and lobbyists, executive branch officials, foundations, think tanks, and other sources.

The fact that legislators cannot rely solely on their own judgment to vote is the source of many people's sense that legislators' votes can be bought—or at least rented. This is ironic, considering that political scientists note that most of the time most legislators are extremely attentive to their districts and vote according to

their sense of their constituents' desires. Their primary goal, after all, is to win reelection. In addition, most states have made it tougher for lobbyists to get lawmakers' attention. It is difficult under the new ethics rules for a lobbyist to spring for a legislator's cup of coffee, much less treat him or her to lunch. In Kentucky, for example, there are fewer of the nightly receptions that once kept Frankfort well fed, and lobbyists are prohibited from making any personal contributions to candidates for the legislature. "A lot of the principal lobbyists are still here, so folks have had to learn to adapt," says Bobby Sherman, head of the Kentucky legislature's nonpartisan research staff. "It's more work for them. They have to build relationships in a different way, and information delivery is much more important."[37]

All of this is necessary because, as with most things, times have changed. It used to be that rank-and-file members voted pretty much the way they were instructed by their party leaders. In Connecticut, the legislature of the early 1960s was an assemblage of party hacks—members beholden to the party chair for patronage. This meant that most of the legislature's important decisions were made in small meetings to which the public—or even most rank-and-file members—were not invited.

Examples do still exist of members caving in to party or leadership pressure. In his book *Experiencing Politics,* former state representative John McDonough, a Democrat, recounts one afternoon in fall 1995 when he was sitting on the floor of the Massachusetts House of Representatives. The chamber was preparing to vote on a huge tax break for Raytheon, a locally based defense contractor. McDonough thought the tax break was a terrible idea. He considered it a form of corporate blackmail. So he pushed the little red button on his desk and voted against it. Then the majority whip—the party's head vote counter—came over to see him. "The Speaker wants a green [light] from you on this," the whip said. That did not make any sense to McDonough. The tax break was passing easily. His vote was not needed. The whip did not answer his question as to why the Speaker needed his vote. "He just does," she said. So, McDonough tells us, he caved. A few months down the road, he had his own favorite bill coming up, and he wanted the Speaker's help. He did not want to take any chances. He walked right back to his desk and switched his vote. It was a classic example of trading votes. "Was my switch," he asks, "an example of naked, opportunistic self-interest or of a hard trade-off necessary to achieve a higher good? Anyone can characterize my action either way. The most honest answer is that both perspectives contain some degree of truth."[38]

Such practical decisions are made all the time. Nevertheless, the wishes of leaders today carry

---

Rank-and-File Members
Legislators who do not hold leadership positions or senior committee posts.

Delegates
Legislators who primarily see their role as voting according to their constituents' beliefs as they understand them.

Trustees
Legislators who believe they were elected to exercise their own judgment and to approach issues accordingly.

much less weight with members than they did even a generation ago. Leaders these days are no stronger than members want them to be; they often lead by listening. They have to pay attention to customer service, and their main customers are rank-and-file legislators. Leaders help other legislators intervene with the governor or the rest of the executive branch and help green-light bills in order to build up political chits. "As long as it wasn't against the law, didn't require that I go to confession, or wouldn't break up my marriage, I did it," recalled Ralph Wright, a one-time Speaker of the Vermont House.[39]

Consider two examples from some years ago. Connecticut House Speaker Irving Stolberg was considered a brilliant legislator, but he was heavy-handed as a leader. When he met with his lieutenants, it was not to consult them on strategy but, rather, to tell them what the strategy would be. Many of the Democrats under him thought he abused his power, so they coupled their votes in 1989 with House Republicans and drove him out.[40] Compare this to a story from across the country the following year. In May 1990, months of work on a workers' compensation reform package threatened to go to waste during a meeting in the office of Oregon House Speaker Vera Katz. Bob Shiprack, chair of the labor committee, grew impatient as the conversation got stuck on the topic of how chiropractors would be treated under the law, so he stormed out. Katz, rather than ordering him to get back to work, ran after him and mothered him, soothed him, and sympathized with his exhaustion. "It disarmed me," Shiprack said. "Vera loves to disarm." Katz's tactic worked, and the workers' compensation package went though.[41]

Leaders cannot bully their way through as they did a generation ago, for two reasons. Leadership offices control direct fund-raising efforts designed to build or maintain majorities, but the leadership efforts are mainly directed at the relatively few contests that will make or break a majority. Dick Saslaw, the Democratic Senate president in Virginia, for example, spent about $1.5 million in campaign cash in 2011 trying to defend his party's narrow majority, funneling money to incumbents and challengers in the most competitive races.[42] Most rank-and-file members today raise their own money and have greater access to expert advice for hire and separate sources of money,

whether from political action committees run by industries or labor unions or elsewhere. The politician who spent the most on Virginia's 2011 legislative elections wasn't a member of the legislature at all. It was Bob McDonnell, the state's Republican governor, who contributed $3.7 million to candidates through a PAC he controls.[43]

We have already touched on the other factor—members do not have to rely on leaders as much as they once did for information about bills or for help in writing legislation. The proliferation of lobbyists and the **professionalization** of legislatures have meant that members have their own resources to draw on.[44]

Apportionment

One more issue that profoundly affects all legislators is **apportionment**. Following the nationwide census that occurs every ten years, each state draws new lines for its legislative districts. In states with more than one member of Congress, congressional districts are redrawn as well. The **redistricting** process is the most naked exercise of political power in the states. Within the legal limits that exist—Supreme Court rulings in the 1960s set the requirement that districts be roughly even in population—the incumbent party will do everything it can to preserve its hold or, preferably, increase its numbers. Each party will seek to draw the maximum number of districts possible that are likely to elect members of its own party. The two major parties will fight each other as best they can to make certain that the other side does not gain the upper hand. "Just like there are no atheists in foxholes, there are no nonpartisans in redistricting," says Paul Green, director of the School of Policy Studies at Roosevelt University in Chicago. "You use whatever leverage you can."[45]

Professionalization
The process of providing legislators with the resources they need to make politics their main career, such as making their positions full-time or providing them with full-time staff.

Apportionment
The allotting of districts according to population shifts. The number of congressional districts that a state has may be reapportioned every ten years, following the national census.

Redistricting
The drawing of new boundaries for congressional and state legislative districts, usually following a decennial census.

MAP 7-3

The Upside-Down Elephant District

Texas's Thirty-Fifth Congressional District drew attention for its odd shape, the result of what many viewed as a partisan effort to redraw the district's lines.

Source: Texas Legislative Council.

Travis County, Texas, where Austin is located, is one of the most Democratic jurisdictions in the state. President Obama won almost 64 percent of the vote in Travis County in 2008. In 2011 the Republican-controlled Texas legislature sliced and diced Travis County so that four of the five congressional districts that include parts of the county lean toward Republicans. They did that by packing Democrats into a single district that includes both parts of Austin and parts of San Antonio, three counties away—with the two halves connected only by a narrow strip of land. The district outline looked so strange on a map that the *Washington Post* held a contest to describe it: the winning entry was "Upside-down elephant (spraying water)."[46] Travis County's government, among other groups, challenged the redistricting in court, but judges allowed the five-way split to go into effect for the 2012 elections.[47]

Gerrymanders
Districts clearly drawn with the intent of pressing partisan advantage at the expense of other considerations.

Malapportionment
A situation in which the principle of equal representation is violated.

Political district boundaries that link disparate communities or have odd shapes that resemble earmuffs or moose antlers are known as **gerrymanders**, a term derived from the name of Elbridge Gerry, an early nineteenth-century governor of Massachusetts. **Malapportionment** occurs when districts violate the principle of equal representation. In the past, some state legislative districts could have many times the numbers of constituents in other districts. Votes in the smaller districts, in effect, counted for more. Relatively few people in, say, a sparsely populated rural district would have the same amount of representative clout in the legislature as many more people in a densely populated urban district.

As Texas's experience shows, the party in control of redistricting really does matter. Likewise, in 2006 in Ohio, Democrats won 60 percent of the vote in state Senate elections but only gained a single formerly Republican-held seat. Afterward, Republicans still had twenty-one members in the chamber, to the Democrats' twelve. One big reason the Democratic votes didn't translate into more Democratic victories is that the GOP in Ohio had controlled the line-drawing process after the 2000 census. The Republicans had crafted Senate districts to give their party an edge.[48] Democrats typically do the same thing when they are in charge. In 2011 in Illinois, Democrats drew a new congressional map that imperiled more than half the state's Republican incumbents.

Legislatures define district boundaries in most states, but there are exceptions. Since the 1980s, Iowa's political maps have been created by the nonpartisan Legislative Services Agency. The agency uses computer software to draw one hundred House districts and fifty Senate districts according to rules that keep population as equal as possible from district to district, avoid splitting counties, and keep the districts compact. In contrast to legislature-drawn maps, those drawn by the agency do not take into account party registration, voting patterns, or the political territory of incumbents. Largely as a result, partisan control of the Iowa legislature has flipped just about every ten years since the agency was created.

While Iowa's system is unique, reformers elsewhere regularly try to find ways to prevent redistricting from flagrantly favoring one party over the other. Lately, the reformers have won

Thom Tillis, House speaker in the North Carolina state legislature, represents a few of the trends evident in state legislatures in the past couple of years: he is a relatively junior member who has become speaker, he is among the Republicans who have taken control since 2010, and he is part of the new generation, in that half the states' legislative chambers in 2011 had new leaders.

some important victories. In Florida in 2010 voters approved a constitutional amendment that mandated rules for redistricting, including forbidding the drawing of lines for the purpose of favoring incumbent officeholders or political parties. When the Republican-controlled Florida legislature nonetheless approved a new state Senate map that was seen as benefiting the GOP, the Florida Supreme Court rejected it on the grounds that it violated the 2010 amendment. Meanwhile, California approved a pair of citizen initiatives in 2008 and 2010 that took redistricting out of the hands of state legislators and entrusted it to an independent commission.

Independent commissions in some states, such as Washington, have succeeded in making redistricting somewhat less overtly partisan, but they have almost never taken politics entirely out of the process. California went to extremes to bar anyone with strong political motivations from serving on the new redistricting commission after the 2010 census. The law rejects from serving on the commission anyone who in the past ten years has run for state or federal office; anyone who has been a registered lobbyist; anyone who has worked for a political candidate, campaign, or party; and even anyone who has made large political contributions. Plus, the law specifies a complicated screening process for the selection of commission members, and the membership must be

politically balanced: five Democrats, five Republicans, and four others. Despite that, once the commission was established, before it even drew a map it was accused of a political bias based on the consultants the members had hired to assist them. Those accusations gained some weight when an investigation by ProPublica journalists pointed to places where the commission had adopted district lines promoted by supposed "good government" groups that actually were run by Democratic operatives.[49] "It wasn't so much that the Democrats tried," says Douglas Johnson, a fellow at the Rose Institute of State and Local Government and one of the consultants the commission passed over. "Of course they tried. The surprise is that it worked."[50] Still, independent observers agreed that the new maps would allow for much more competitive elections than the incumbent-protection plan lawmakers had enacted ten years earlier.

Partisanship is the primary concern of redistricting, but it is not the only one. Issues of representation also play a big part. African Americans are overwhelmingly Democratic, but some joined with Republicans following the 1980 and 1990 censuses to create black majority districts, especially in the South. For African Americans, their deal with the GOP offered the advantage of creating districts in which African American candidates were likely to be elected. It wasn't that

Majority-Minority District
A district in which members of a minority group, such as African Americans or Hispanics, make up a majority of the population or electorate.

they joined the Republican Party, of course. They simply allied themselves with the GOP to draw **majority-minority districts**, which guaranteed the election of more African Americans but also made the neighboring "bleached" districts more likely to elect Republicans. Following the Voting Rights Act of 1982, the federal Justice Department encouraged state legislators to create majority-minority districts whenever possible, until a series of U.S. Supreme Court decisions during the 1990s limited the practice. In a confusing and often contradictory series of rulings, the Court ruled that race could not be the "predominant" factor in redistricting.[51]

Redistricting also changes representation in ways that go beyond black and white. With each new round of redistricting, power shifts to places that are growing quickly and away from ones that are not. One of the major themes of the 2010 round of redistricting was a shift in power away from rural areas and to suburbs and exurbs that experienced far stronger population growth in the previous ten years.[52] Alaska legislators were so concerned about having fewer lawmakers representing rural areas—and about the remaining rural districts becoming even more massive—that they submitted a constitutional amendment to voters in 2010 to add more seats to the legislature. One of the lawmakers supporting to change was State Senator Albert Kookesh, who represented the largest state legislative district in the country. From its southeastern corner, Kookesh's district extended 1,185 miles west, about the same distance as that from Jacksonville, Florida, to Minneapolis, Minnesota, and about 1,000 miles north, about the same as the distance from Phoenix, Arizona, to Portland, Oregon.[53] Getting around an area of that size cannot be done efficiently in a car; it's hard enough to do it by plane. "In order for me to get to one of my villages, Lime Village, I would have to go from Angoon to Juneau, Juneau to Anchorage, Anchorage to Fairbanks, Fairbanks to Aniak, and Aniak to Lime Village," Kookesh said.[54] Alaska voters rejected the plan to add legislative seats.

State Legislators

If you were to make a composite drawing of the average state legislator, he—and it would be a he— would be white and in his fifties or maybe sixties. He would have had at least some college education, have an income topping $50,000, describe himself as moderate or conservative, and have lived in the community he is representing for at least ten years.[55] There are many, many exceptions to all the aspects of this composite. The type of person who runs for state legislative office has changed a good deal over the past thirty years—for example, there are far more women and African Americans in office and fewer lawyers—but nonetheless, the type of middle- to upper-middle-class American male described here still predominates.

The nation's 7,383 state legislators come from all backgrounds, particularly in the states where the house and senate meet for only part of the year. In states with full-time legislatures, such as California and Pennsylvania, the legislators tend, not surprisingly, to be career politicians who have served in local or other elected offices or perhaps as members of legislative staffs. In states with part-time legislatures, such as Arkansas and Indiana, members come from many different walks of life, devoting perhaps one-third of their working hours to politics while earning their livings through some other means.

Professional Background

Some employers encourage the political hopes of their employees because they know legislative service can be good for business. This holds true especially for professions most directly affected by state lawmaking, such as big business. Buddy Dyer kept up his law practice while serving in the Florida Senate and in 2002 had to respond to complaints that the bills he proposed would have protected his industrial company clients from fines and lawsuits. His defense? "Probably not a bill that goes through the Legislature" that did not affect one of his firm's clients.[56]

Other groups enjoy considerable representation within legislative bodies. In 2006, Al Mansell stepped down from his leadership role as president of the Utah Senate to become president of the National Association of Realtors. He stayed in the Senate, however, sponsoring legislation that helped members of his profession. He was one of twenty-two people who worked in real estate who were serving in the Utah legislature at that time. "I've got people who are on county commissions, mayors, state senators," said Chris Kyler, CEO of the Utah Association of Realtors. "Our lieutenant governor was president of our state association about 20 years ago. Our people are involved in the parties, too. We've got precinct chairs and vice chairs and county delegates throughout the state."[57]

Consider public education. Teachers' unions are usually among the most active lobbying groups in any state, but schools do not necessarily have to rely on outsiders to influence the legislature. Teachers themselves are often members of legislatures, and employees of other institutions of higher learning also serve. In Maine, state law requires that teachers be granted leave from their jobs if they want to run for office. Maine's legislature meets for only six months every other year. But even that chunk of time is enough to play havoc with a person's work schedule, and there's a good deal of concern in the state that retirees are coming to dominate the legislative chamber.

The reality is that retired people account for only about 12 percent of state legislators nationwide. About 15 percent of legislators are lawyers—a big decline from past decades. In New York, 60 percent of the assembly and 70 percent of the Senate used to be made up of lawyers.[58] Nowadays, the dominant group in legislatures nationwide comprises people with business backgrounds. They make up about 30 percent of today's legislators. The remaining half or so come from education, healthcare, real estate, insurance, and agriculture.

Demographic Diversity

The numbers of women legislators have risen dramatically since the "second wave" feminist era of the late 1960s and early 1970s, but they still do not reflect the female share of the overall population. In 1970, women held just 4 percent of all state legislative seats.[59] Their numbers doubled quickly, to 8 percent of all legislators by 1975, and they climbed to 18 percent by 1991. The ranks of women legislators held steady at just over 20 percent for about a dozen years before spiking to 23.5 percent after the 2006 elections. The figure ticked up to just above 24 percent following the 2008 campaigns. Only six states—Arizona, Colorado, Maryland, Minnesota, New Hampshire, and Vermont—could brag in 2007 that one-third or

more of their legislators were women.[60] But, in 2009, the New Hampshire Senate became the first legislative chamber in the nation to have a majority of women members. Women served as its president and majority leader, and another woman served as Speaker of the New Hampshire House.[61] Republican victories in the 2010 elections dropped the national number back below 24 percent—about 60 percent of the women in state legislatures are Democrats.[62]

The numbers of women entering state legislatures may not be growing exponentially, but the types of women holding house and senate seats have changed. In the old days of the 1970s—years before most readers of this book were born—most women running for office came to politics later in life than did their male counterparts. They had not been tapped to run by party professionals or other "queenmakers." Instead, they jump-started their own careers, drawn into the policy realm out of concerns about their children's schools or their local communities. Men may know from the time they are in school that they want to run for office, says Barbara Lee, who runs a foundation dedicated to helping women run for office, but women often find out later in life that it is important to enter the game because of their specific concerns and experiences.[63] This dynamic has changed to some extent. Women now enter politics at ages comparable to men. Many still tend to care about particular issues (education, healthcare, and the environment) that are noticeably different from the top priorities of men (taxes and budgets), but sometimes they focus on such issues because they still find it harder than men to gain seats on the more powerful finance committees in representative numbers.

Back in the 1970s, when the first relatively large numbers of women legislators entered the capitols, they tended to be less politically ambitious than the men they served with, and thus less likely to enter the ranks of legislative leadership. They devoted more attention to constituent service matters and tended to serve on education, health, and welfare committees. They also tended to have less education than their male counterparts, and to come from jobs that were not as prestigious or well paying as those held by the men. During the 1980s, the average socioeconomic status of women legislators improved, and women served on a broader range

A Difference That Makes A Difference

Life in the Minority: Stall Tactics and "Sacred Sperm"

After Republicans won historic victories in the 2010 elections, they quickly used their new power to pursue an ambitious conservative agenda across a broad range of cultural, economic, and fiscal issues. Every Republican cause, from tax cuts to private school vouchers to gun rights expansions, suddenly had a better chance of passing in many states. Democrats were left reeling—and searching for any tactic to slow the Republicans down. For example, many legislative chambers have rules that a certain number of legislators, a "quorum," must be present for bills to advance. When Republicans in Wisconsin and Indiana began to move bills to weaken labor unions, a key Democratic Party constituency, Democrats in those states fled the legislative chambers—and the states entirely—as a way to prevent the Republicans from reaching the quorum they needed to act. Dozens of Indiana Democrats, for example, holed up at the Comfort Inn and Suites in Urbana, Illinois, in February 2011. These tactics succeeded in bringing national attention to the disagreements, but they didn't ultimately stop the legislation from passing.

When Republicans pushed forward new restrictions on women's access to abortion and birth control—eighty such bills were enacted in 2011 alone—Democratic women legislators found a different way to fight back. They introduced bills using language meant to sound equally intrusive when it came to men and their bodies. Their legislation was also intended to make male legislators squirm. An Ohio bill would have required Viagra-seeking men to undergo psychological counseling and to produce a notarized affidavit from a sex partner attesting to recent erectile dysfunction before being allowed to purchase the drug. A Georgia bill would have banned vasectomies except when needed to avoid death or "impairment of a major bodily function." And in Oklahoma, an "every sperm is sacred" amendment to a "personhood" bill would have defined life as beginning at ejaculation and made it clear that depositing semen anywhere but in a woman's vagina is a crime against the unborn. "It wasn't until I got graphic that people finally heard what I was saying," says Oklahoma senator Constance Johnson, sponsor of the ejaculation bill.

These graphic bills indeed received a lot of media attention. Not surprisingly, pro-life legislators and advocacy groups were ticked off by the tactic. "On acts that are meant to mock or parody something that is seen as a very serious issue by the caucus, the life or pro-life issues, it's about gravitas," said David Atkins, the spokesman for Oklahoma Senate leader Brian Bingman. "At the end of the day you would hope that elected officials would recognize that and they would treat the issue seriously."

The women legislators argued that their amendments were no less serious—or at least no less demeaning—than the abortion and birth control legislation coasting through so many capitols. Democratic women in many red states know that they are fighting at best a rearguard action. Putting in legislation that holds up an unflattering mirror to the majority party's agenda may be the best minority legislators can do.

And, at least in a few instances, their efforts have done more than that. In response to a bill in Virginia that originally would have required a woman seeking an abortion to undergo a transvaginal ultrasound exam with what *Doonesbury* called a "10-inch shaming wand," Democratic senator Janet Howell put forward an amendment that would have required men to undergo rectal exams and counseling before they could receive Viagra or other erectile dysfunction drugs. The amendment fueled national media exposure, including bits on both *The Daily Show* and *Saturday Night Live*. That bright spotlight forced the bill's sponsors to back down some before the bill was signed into law. Women seeking abortions in Virginia now do have to undergo ultrasounds, but not transvaginal ones.

Source: Original piece written for this book by Alan Greenblatt.

of committees, but they mostly still focused on issues of women, family, and children. By the 1990s, women legislators held about 15 percent of all legislative leadership positions but were still unlikely to serve on tax committees.[64] Their backgrounds had become more varied, and they had also become more conservative, although they still were more liberal than men—and significantly more likely than their male colleagues to initiate legislation.[65] Women also became more likely than men to get their priority bills through the legislative process successfully.[66]

Women legislators, however, do not alter the fundamental political dynamics in legislatures, perhaps because they remain a fairly small minority in most states. For example, women legislators are more likely than their male counterparts to favor reproductive rights, but they do not have an especially powerful impact on a given state's policy regarding this issue. Whether a state devotes much funding toward abortion programs or places a number of restrictions on such programs, including requiring parental notification in the case of minors seeking abortions, depends more on whether the state's overall political culture is liberal or conservative than on whether women make up a large minority of legislative caucuses.[67] Still, gender composition of a state legislature is a difference that makes a difference: women legislators do tend to bring up issues and concerns that would not be raised by an all-male legislature.

This tendency is even truer of issues of concern to minorities. African Americans have made gains similar to those of women in legislatures over the past forty years, growing from a microscopic minority to a larger minority, albeit one that still does not reflect their overall share of the population. The numbers of African American legislators have nearly quadrupled, to about 625—less than 10 percent of all the legislators nationwide.

Although it can be both dangerous and wrong to generalize about any group, it has been observed that the interests of African Americans as a whole have long been fairly stable and predictable. "On

questions of public policy, ideology, and candidate choice," writes Kerry L. Haynie in his 2001 book on black state legislators, "African Americans have been the most cohesive and consistent policy subgroup in United States politics."[68] In short, the racial composition of state legislatures is also a difference that makes a difference. This is especially the case as state influence over issues important to African American legislators increased just as their numbers were increasing. Since the 1970s, decisions about many issues of importance to African Americans, including Medicaid, student aid, school lunch programs, community development, welfare, and environmental protection, have devolved from the federal level to the states.[69] In his study of how representatives in Arkansas, Illinois, Mississippi, New Jersey, and North Carolina acted in three different sessions, Haynie found that 55–82 percent of African American legislators introduced bills that addressed issues of particular interest to blacks. White legislators, by contrast, almost never introduced such legislation. In only one of the three years that Haynie studied (1969, 1979, and 1989) did more than one-quarter of nonblack legislators introduce even one bill of interest to African Americans.[70] It may sound obvious, but so-called black issues are much more likely to be addressed when African Americans are serving in state legislatures.

Black legislators, of course, do not focus solely or even mostly on issues that are specific to their racial group. One reflection of this is that in recent years African American legislators have been voted into leadership roles by their colleagues in states with relatively few black voters. At the start of the 2009 legislative sessions, in the same month President Obama first took the oath of office, Colorado became the first state with a black Senate president and a black House Speaker simultaneously. Malcolm Smith was elected New York's first African American Senate president, and Steve Horsford became Nevada's first African American Senate majority leader that same year.

The fact that there are more African American legislators does not mean that voting trends change, however. Voting remains polarized along racial lines. Whites will support African American incumbents but are often reluctant to vote for black newcomers. The main reason for the growth in the number of black legislators, therefore, has been the creation of majority-black districts.[71]

Professional versus Citizen Legislators

As discussed above, legislatures, strictly white male playgrounds in the past, have become more inclusive of women and minorities and more attentive to their concerns. But even bigger changes in legislatures over the past thirty-five years have come in the very ways that they do business. Whereas once legislatures were sleepy backwaters where not much got done—and even less got done ethically—now many chambers are highly professional operations. Most legislatures used to meet for short periods every other year. These days all but a handful meet every year and, in a few cases, nearly year-round. "No single factor has a greater effect on the legislative environment than the constitutional restriction on length of session," two leading legislative scholars wrote long ago.[72]

The most pronounced differences among the states are between "professional" legislatures that meet full-time, pay members high salaries, and employ large staffs and "amateur," or "citizen," legislatures that meet part-time, have members who usually hold other jobs, and have smaller staffs. To some extent, all legislatures have become more professional. Even "amateur" legislators devote a third of their time to legislative work. In the early 1940s, the legislatures of only four states—New Jersey, New York, Rhode Island, and South Carolina—met in annual sessions, but the number meeting yearly has climbed continuously.[73] Today, only four states do not meet in regular annual sessions. Expenditures per legislator have increased above the rate of inflation in nearly every state, and today, the most professional legislatures have resources that rival those of the U.S. Congress.[74] Lately, however, that trend has slowed. The number of legislative staffers nationwide actually dropped from 1996 to 2009 after decades of increases.[75]

There are many variations among states as to how professional their legislatures are, and level of professionalism has profound impacts on legislatures' effectiveness, how much institutional strength they have compared to governors, and how popular they are with the public. Some disagreement still exists about whether professional legislators really do a better job than their citizen-legislator cousins. Typically, however, the more professional a legislature, the more effective it is at the essential jobs of drafting and passing laws and overseeing the governor and the executive branch. With the exception of Texas, the more populous states have highly professional legislatures. Such legislatures are able to provide more resources to their chambers, which allows these chambers to keep up with the wider variety of issues that arise in densely populated states in comparison with most of their less populous neighbors. Legislatures in some states, such as Pennsylvania and California, meet essentially year-round; in contrast, Montana's part-time legislature meets for only ninety days only in odd-numbered years.

More populous states have the money to invest in the full-time legislatures that are necessary for their governments to keep on top of issues facing these states' more complicated and developed economies and diverse populations. The reason that Texas, with a population second only to California's, has a part-time legislature lies in the state's distrust of government in general. Texas is one of only nine states that do not impose an income tax, and a legislature that meets only part-time every other year is in keeping with this general low-tax, low-service point of view. Other states have traditions of embracing more expansive government. States with strong progressive traditions, such as Michigan and Wisconsin, have long used full-time, professional legislators with substantial staffs at their command.

As distrust of government has spread to more state capitols, there have been some moves to reverse the trend toward better-staffed, more expensive, more professionalized legislatures. It was a sure sign of unhappiness with the Michigan legislature amid its struggles to pass budgets in a difficult economic time that serious, although ultimately unsuccessful, petition drives were launched in 2008, including one by a local area chamber of commerce, to turn it into a part-time body. In Pennsylvania, efforts to scale back the legislature's spending on itself grew out of a double-digit pay increase legislators approved for themselves at 2:00 A.M. on July 7, 2005. Since then,

TABLE 7-2

State House Demographic Diversity: Total Numbers and Percentages of Legislators Who Are Women, African American, and Hispanic, 2012

State	Total Number of Legislative Seats	Women State Legislators		African American State Legislators		Hispanic State Legislators	
		Total	Percentage of Total Seats	Total	Percentage of Total Seats	Total	Percentage of Total Seats
Alabama	140	19	14	34	24	0	0
Alaska	60	15	25	1	2	0	0
Arizona	90	30	33	2	2	17	19
Arkansas	135	30	22	15	11	0	0
California	120	34	28	9	8	28	23
Colorado	100	40	40	3	3	5	5
Connecticut	187	56	30	19	10	6	3
Delaware	62	16	26	5	8	1	2
Florida	160	41	26	25	16	17	11
Georgia	236	56	24	56	24	3	1
Hawaii	76	27	36	0	0	1	1
Idaho	105	29	28	0	0	1	1
Illinois	177	54	31	29	16	11	6
Indiana	150	31	21	13	9	1	1
Iowa	150	32	21	3	2	0	0
Kansas	165	45	27	6	4	4	2
Kentucky	138	26	19	7	5	0	0
Louisiana	144	16	11	29	20	0	0
Maine	186	55	30	0	0	0	0
Maryland	188	58	31	42	22	4	2
Massachusetts	200	49	25	8	4	5	3
Michigan	148	31	21	19	13	3	2
Minnesota	201	66	33	1	> 1	3	1
Mississippi	174	29	17	42	24	0	0
Missouri	197	47	24	12	6	1	1
Montana	150	36	24	0	0	1	1
Nebraska	49	11	22	1	2	1	2
Nevada	63	16	25	7	11	3	5

State	Total Number of Legislative Seats	Women State Legislators		African American State Legislators		Hispanic State Legislators	
		Total	Percentage of Total Seats	Total	Percentage of Total Seats	Total	Percentage of Total Seats
New Hampshire	424	103	24	1	> 1	2	< 1
New Jersey	120	35	29	10	8	5	4
New Mexico	112	31	28	2	2	44	39
New York	212	47	22	43	20	17	8
North Carolina	170	40	24	26	15	2	1
North Dakota	141	21	15	0	0	0	0
Ohio	132	31	24	16	12	0	0
Oklahoma	149	19	13	6	4	0	0
Oregon	90	26	29	3	3	1	1
Pennsylvania	253	43	17	21	8	1	< 1
Rhode Island	113	29	26	1	1	3	3
South Carolina	170	17	10	28	17	1	1
South Dakota	105	21	20	0	0	0	0
Tennessee	132	24	18	12	9	1	1
Texas	181	37	20	14	8	36	20
Utah	104	17	16	0	0	2	2
Vermont	180	70	39	1	1	0	0
Virginia	140	24	18	17	12	1	1
Washington	147	47	32	3	2	3	2
West Virginia	134	24	17	0	0	0	0
Wisconsin	132	32	24	8	6	1	1
Wyoming	90	13	14	0	0	2	2
Total	7,382	1,746	24	600	6	238	4

Sources: National Conference of State Legislatures, "Women in State Legislatures: 2012 Legislative Session," www.ncsl.org/legislatures-elections/wln/women-in-state-legislatures-2012.aspx; National Conference of State Legislatures, "Number of African American Legislators 2009," www.ncsl.org/default.aspx?tabid=14781; National Conference of State Legislatures, "2009 Latino Legislators," www.ncsl.org/Default.aspx?TabId=14766.

Note: Percentages are rounded to the nearest whole number. Numbers are latest available; those for women legislators are from 2012, those for African American and Hispanic legislators are from 2007.

one perennial idea promoted by some in the state has been to save money by having fewer legislators. No one could accuse Pennsylvania's House members of serving their own career interests when they voted in 2012 for a constitutional amendment that would have cut the House from 203 to 153 members.[76] The Senate, which the amendment would have shrunk from 50 members to 38, did not act on the proposal.

The northeastern states have maintained their traditional interest in hands-on government, which grew out of their old practices of self-government, including town hall meetings. These states boast some of the largest legislatures. The New Hampshire House is the most extreme example, with 400 members—one for every 3,300 or so state residents. California's legislature is one of the best equipped and most professional in the

States under Stress

Minnesota Goes Dark

In the first three weeks of July 2011, Minnesota's state parks closed, road repairs were halted, and the state stopped issuing new driver's licenses. The state lost money because it stopped selling lottery tickets and collecting tolls, but it didn't know how much money because the state workers who would have made such calculations were out of work, along with 22,000 of their colleagues. All this happened because a mix of partisan disagreements and serious financial problems led the legislature and the governor to fail in their most basic responsibility: agreeing to a new state budget. The result was a prolonged government shutdown, a rarity in state government.

In 2011 Minnesota, like many states, was continuing to feel the effects of the recession that began in December 2007. Tax revenue was well short of prerecession levels, demand for state services was high, and federal help from the stimulus package Congress enacted in 2009 was drying up. Minnesota budgets on a two-year cycle, and the new cycle began July 1, 2011, so the legislature needed to pass and the governor needed to sign a new budget by that date to keep government funded. Projections in the spring, however, showed the state was billions of dollars short of the revenue it needed to pay for its existing level of services.

The Republican-controlled legislature's answer was to cut spending. When the GOP won majorities in both houses of the legislature in 2010, many Republican lawmakers had made promises not to raise taxes. They had no interest in breaking those pledges. Yet Minnesotans had also elected a Democrat, Mark Dayton, as the state's new governor in 2010. Dayton's solution was a large income tax on the wealthy. He offered some cuts, but he refused to shrink government as far as the Republicans wanted. Through the spring and early summer neither side budged, until July 1 arrived.

Some states are notorious for passing their budgets after the start of the new fiscal year. When New York approved an on-time budget in 2005, it was the first time the state had done so in twenty-one years. Pennsylvania's budget was consistently late in the 2000s. In California, the practice of passing the budget late is so common that banks in Sacramento, the state capital, regularly offer interest-free loans to legislative staffers when they miss out on paychecks because of late budgets.

What many states do in such a situation is pass a short-term budget to keep government running until a full budget is approved. Dayton and the Minnesota legislature, though, couldn't even agree on a stopgap measure, and the result was the shutdown. That didn't mean that Minnesota prisons were left unguarded or that nursing homes were left without money to pay their bills. A judge made decisions about which services were essential and allowed those to continue. Still, the effects were deeply disruptive to the lives of many Minnesotans.

By the time the situation was finally resolved twenty days later, the shutdown had become the longest any state had experienced in decades. The compromise the legislature and Dayton reached involved delaying payments to school districts. That balanced the budget on paper by pushing off the expenses into future years. But the state will have to pay the bill eventually—which could put it at greater risk of more budget crises in future years.

Sources: Rachel Weiner, "In Minnesota Shutdown, Workers Who Calculate the Cost Are Laid Off," *Washington Post*, The Fix blog, July 6, 2011, www.washingtonpost.com/business/economy/in-minnesota-shutdown-workers-who-calculate-the-cost-are-laid-off/2011/07/06/glQA7nnJ1H_story.html; Josh Goodman, "Mischief after Midnight," *Governing*, June 2009, 40, www.governing.com/topics/finance/Mischief-After-Midnight.html; Josh Goodman, "Budget Gimmicks Explained: Five Ways States Hide Deficits," Stateline, June 23, 2011, www.pewstates.org/projects/stateline/headlines/budget-gimmicks-explained-five-ways-states-hide-deficits-85899375319.

country. It has to be, considering that each member of the assembly has more than 450,000 constituents.

Some states impose severe restrictions on the meeting times of their legislatures. In Colorado, the state constitution limits the House and the Senate to no more than 120 days per year. Sometimes such limits are honored mostly in the breach. The governor may insist that the legislature meet in special session to address a budget crisis or other issue that cannot wait until the next regular session. Or the legislature may simply carve out a little more time for itself, as happened in 2002 in North Carolina. House rules require that the chamber be shut down by 9:00 P.M., so members stopped the clock one night at 8:50, essentially "freezing time," so they could continue debate until 3:35 A.M. and finish a session that had run for months longer than expected.[77]

Just like most of us, legislators feel intensely the pressure to get their work done on time. The fact that they have deadlines—for passing budgets or for adjournment—usually keeps them focused in much the same way that a final exam will make college students finally hit the books or do their serious Googling at term's end. Newspapers, however, routinely report on legislatures missing their budget deadlines and often publish commentary critical of the

MAP 7-4

Full-Time, Hybrid, and Part-Time Legislatures

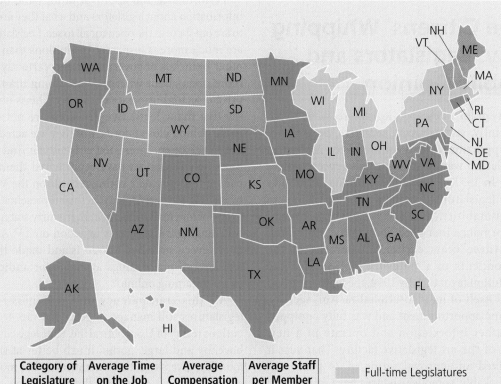

Category of Legislature	Average Time on the Job	Average Compensation	Average Staff per Member
Full-time	80%	$68,599	8.9
Hybrid	70%	$35,326	3.1
Part-time	54%	$15,984	1.2

- Full-time Legislatures
- Hybrid Legislatures
- Part-time Legislatures

Source: Data compiled from the National Conference of State Legislatures, www.ncsl.org/programs/legman/about/partfulllegis.htm.

practice. The reality is that a legislature is pretty cheap to operate—in no state does it cost much more than 0.5 percent of the state budget—but elected officials know that their overtime does not play well with voters.[78]

Mississippi's largest paper, the *Clarion Ledger,* for instance, ran a typical editorial condemning legislators for wasting money in a special session in 2008, even though the extra time cost the state only $59,895 for the first day and $39,420 a day for each one after that. At that rate, the session would have had to drag on for weeks to add just 1 percent to the $90 million budget deficit the state faced the next year.[79] Such media coverage is one reason legislatures, even as they get more professional and better at their jobs, remain unpopular with the public. Map 7-4 shows the breakdown of full-time, hybrid, and part-time legislatures among the states.

The Citizens' Whipping Boy: Legislators and Public Opinion

Thirty or forty years ago, legislatures were, to put it bluntly, sexist, racist, secretive, boss ruled, malapportioned, and uninformed. Alabama's legislature was an extreme but representative case. In 1971, it ranked fiftieth out of the fifty state legislatures in independence, fiftieth in accountability, and forty-eighth in overall performance in a Ford Foundation study. Yet, just three years earlier, 65 percent of the respondents in a statewide poll judged the institution favorably. By 1990, the legislature had freed itself of its institutional racism, secrecy, and malapportionment and was fully equipped to gather information and operate in a new state-of-the-art legislative facility. That year it received an approval rating of 24 percent.[80] Remarkably, some legislatures have fallen even further than that in recent years. During a leadership crisis in 2009, just 11 percent of New Yorkers said the state Senate was doing an excellent or good job.[81] The California legislature's approval rating fell to 10 percent in the fall of 2010 and never exceeded 23 percent from September 2008 to February 2012.[82]

> Performance and approval ratings and other information about legislators and what they are up to are out there in the open for all to see. Legislatures are much more transparent institutions than the other branches of government and certainly are more open about what they are doing than are private-sector businesses or unions.

Performance and approval ratings and other information about legislators and what they are up to are out there in the open for all to see. Legislatures are much more transparent institutions than the other branches of government and certainly are more open about what they are doing than are private-sector businesses or unions. This is not to say that many legislative decisions are not still made behind closed doors, but they are acted on out in the open. Interested citizens can find out how their legislators have represented them by paging through their voting records on the Web, by reading the newsletters that their representatives and senators mail to them, and, in thirty states, by watching their legislatures in action on TV. As of 2012, every state but Rhode Island made their legislatures' proceedings available for audio or video streaming online.[83]

All this transparency and openness—yet legislatures still manage to get a bad rap. It is a curious reality of U.S. political life. State legislatures have, by and large, gotten much better at their jobs. The diversity of their membership has moved steadily toward reflecting the population as a whole. Legislatures have reformed themselves and have become more honest, ethical, and competent in the process. The average person, however, still views them as out-of-control institutions that would do less harm by meeting as little as possible.

"The legislature is an ideal whipping boy (or girl)," writes Alan Rosenthal in his book *Engines of Democracy*. It is an institution, after all. Although it is made up of individuals, a legislature as a whole is not a flesh-and-blood person, like a governor. Everyone can easily complain about something the legislature has done recently—including legislators, many of whom campaign by promising to be the ones who will bring sanity and righteousness back to the capitol. Average citizens are disturbed by the influence that interest groups wield, but members of interest groups themselves are often unhappy because things don't always break their way. Finally, as Rosenthal writes, "people generalize from the worst cases, not the best cases." They do not assume that most legislators are like their own representative or senator, whom they tend to like; rather, they think most are like "the relative few who are convicted or indicted in a court of law, reprimanded by a state ethics commission, or are accused . . . in the media."[84]

By now, however, it should be evident that legislatures, just like books, cannot be judged by the average person's perception of their covers. State legislatures have become more efficient and effective units of government over the past thirty years. At the federal level, Congress has punted on many of the major domestic issues of the past several years, but state legislatures have picked up those balls and run with them. After Democrats took over the U.S. House of Representatives in 2007, they proudly touted a group of priority bills that they were able to pass. Yet many of their signature initiatives, including a minimum wage increase and funding for stem-cell research, already had been approved in numerous states. And the reason that states were pressing hard that year for expanded healthcare coverage programs was that Congress had failed to act in this area and the Bush administration publicly had suggested that states should take the lead on the issue. This dynamic began to change following the election of President Obama in 2008. He quickly took an aggressive approach in areas of policy that states had pretty much had to themselves. Still, some of Obama's signature initiatives, in areas such as healthcare and education, borrowed heavily from concepts that already had been implemented at the state level.

For all of this, legislatures are as unpopular as they have ever been. Following the terrorist attacks of September 11, 2001, polls indicated that the public's faith in government had been restored. Firefighters and cops became popular figures, but elected representatives did not bask in the same sort of glow for very long. If anything, legislators have become more unpopular than they were a generation ago. The increases in staff, in salaries, and in other professional tools that legislators have acquired in recent decades probably have made them better at their jobs. But as they have become more professional, legislatures also have become larger targets of disdain for a public that believes it has little or no use for professional or career politicians. Amateur legislatures hold a stronger appeal to deeply rooted American desires for limited government and limited governmental power.

To a large extent, the general public does not view large staffs and good salaries as ways of ensuring that legislators do their jobs in a professional manner. Instead, these increases in legislative resources are seen as yet more proof that politicians want to exploit their offices for personal gain. Rather than reacting strongly to policy issues, the public is quick to anger over such ethical questions as legislative pay raises and other perks for elected officials. "The public does not want the same thing out of a legislature that you think they might want," says John Hibbing, a University of Nebraska political scientist who has written about the unpopularity of legislatures. "The public wants a legislature whose members are not in a position to feather their own nests."[85]

Legislators have done a poor job of selling the idea that what they do is important and necessary in a democracy. "It's our fault" that the legislature is viewed as "dysfunctional," "sheep," and "not independent," says Richard Brodsky, a member of the New York Assembly. "We have never gotten the message out in a coherent way of what we do well and right."[86]

For their part, the media are more concerned with dramatizing conflicts than with explaining what are sometimes awfully dry policy matters; therefore, they have not helped legislators to make their case. A primary job of the media in a democracy is to report on what the government is up to, but less and less media attention is devoted to legislatures. Books about such media failings are even more tiresome, if you can believe

Alabama State Senator Bill Holtzclaw

Follow Bill on Facebook and Twitter

Home   Newsletter   Bill's Blog   Contact Bill   Meet Bill

Busy, Busy Day in Montgomery
03/06/2013

I started the morning with an Education Policy committee meeting at 8:30, followed by the General Fund Committee Meeting at 9:30, followed by the Education Trust Fund Committee meeting at 10:30. As luck would have it, all of these meetings were held in the same committee room...making for a long morning!

Highlights of the committee meetings include the Common Core bill being carried over, allowing all parities to continue working toward a common solution, the Tim Tebow bill and the 2014 General Fund Budget being voted out of committee, and the School Calendar "Opt-Out bill being debated in committee with the amendment discussed in last night's blog being offered. The bill is schedule for a vote next week – this could get interesting and I believe will fall along geographical lines vs. party lines as reported here.

The afternoon included several back-to-back-to-back meetings in my office concerning a wide range of topics: midwifery, dental insurance plans, common core standards, and CPR standards. Just a sampling of my compartmentalized world!

I finished up the afternoon visiting with 40+ members of Huntsville Leadership along with Madison County area legislators. It is always great to visit with community leaders from back home. I enjoyed listening to their

Author

Bill Holtzclaw is the Senator for the Alabama 2nd District representing Limestone and Madison Counties in North Alabama.

RSS Feed

Many state legislators attempt to keep their constituents informed about their doings through social media. On his blog, Alabama Republican Sen. Bill Holtzclaw runs through his day, describing meetings and including links to legislation occupying his time.

the press sometimes loses sight of is that the vast majority of legislators are law-abiding citizens who mostly try to do their best as public servants.

Reporters may be too cynical about what legislators are up to, but a bigger problem might be that there are so few reporters watching them. An *American Journalism Review* survey in 2009 found that there were only 355 full-time newspaper reporters covering the state capitols—a drop of 32 percent since 2003 and only about one-thirteenth the number of journalists who covered the Super Bowl that year. (Although, given the parlous state of journalism, even the number reporting on that event has come down in recent years.)[89] That is an average of seven reporters per state, but Georgia, for instance, had only five full-time statehouse reporters. The number of capitol reporters in some other states, such as Michigan, had dropped by nearly half in the previous decade or so. Several states had seen formerly competing papers, such as the *St. Petersburg Times* and the *Miami Herald,* combine forces and share reporters and coverage. The numbers are even weaker for television coverage.[90]

Fewer reporters translate into fewer stories about what legislators are doing to earn their taxpayer-financed livings. The more populous states, such as New York and California, still boast relatively sizable, if diminished, capitol press corps, but even in these states the legislatures lose out because their stories get lost in the clutter of other news. The South Dakota legislature, when it is in session, is a major source of news in that underpopulated state, whereas the Illinois General Assembly loses out to coverage of other activities in Chicago and the surrounding area.[91] As a result of diminished coverage, says Gary Moncrief, a political scientist at

it, than books about state and local government—but a few points are worth making here.

First, ever since Watergate, the scandal that forced President Richard Nixon to resign in 1974, the press has taken an adversarial position toward the government. People in government, including legislators, are not very good in the first place at getting out the good news about what they are doing or publicizing their successes. And reporters, who are by their nature skeptics, are good at covering scandals and mistakes. "Skepticism is not just a personality quirk of journalists," says one reporter. "It's a core value, the wellspring of all our best work."[87] The media have made boo-boo coverage practically the mainstay of government reporting. This is not true in 100 percent of cases, of course, but the press's general attitude toward government was summed up well a few years ago by a reporter in Pennsylvania who told a public official, "Your job is to manage the public business and mine is to report when you do it wrong."[88] To be fair, legislators do it wrong sometimes. Two former Speakers of the Pennsylvania House began sharing a jail cell in 2012 after they were convicted in separate corruption scandals. A year doesn't go by without several legislators being charged with crimes. In covering these scandals, though, what

Policy in Practice

Outwit, Outlast, Outplay: Who Really Got the Best Deal with Term Limits?

The biggest change to hit state legislatures over the past quarter century has been the advent of term limits. In the fifteen states with term limit laws—which were almost all approved through ballot initiatives by voters sick of career politicians—legislators are limited to serving no more than six, eight, or twelve years in either the house or the senate. Although that may sound like a long time, it turns out not to be enough for most legislators to master all the complexities of understanding and formulating a wide range of policy.

Term limits have failed the public's goal of bringing in more "citizen legislators." Instead, legislators are constantly seeking their next political jobs rather than carving out decades-long careers in one chamber. Term limits also have failed to bring the anticipated and hoped-for substantial numbers of women and minorities into the legislative ranks. The total number of women legislators is up nationwide, but their ranks have actually been slower to grow in states that impose term limits.[a]

But if they haven't fulfilled all their promises, term limits have not been quite the disaster their opponents predicted either. One of the most common predictions—that with members serving so briefly, lobbyists hoarding institutional and policy knowledge would accrue all the power—appears to have missed the mark. Term limits pretty much have been a mixed bag for lobbyists, who must introduce themselves to a new, skeptical set of legislators every couple of years rather than relying on cozy relations with a few key committee chairs. "I don't know one lobbyist who thinks it's a good thing," said Rick Farmer, who wrote about term limits as an academic before going to work for the Oklahoma House. "If term limits are such a good thing for lobbyists, why do so many lobbyists hate them?"

It does seem clear, however, that legislators in term-limited states have lost power to the executive branch—the governors and their staff who actually know how to operate the machinery of government. "Agency heads can outwait and outlast anyone and everyone on the playing field and they have consolidated their power," said one southern legislator-turned-lobbyist.

Academic studies in term limit states, including California, Colorado, and Maine, have found that legislators make far fewer changes to governors' budgets than they used to, representing many billions of dollars in legislative discretion that is no longer exercised. "The crumbling of legislative power is clear across states," said Thad Kousser, a political scientist at the University of California, San Diego, and author of a book about term limits. "There's no more clear finding in the research than a shift in power where the legislature is becoming a less than equal branch of government."

For all that, it's become common to hear governors and other executive branch officials complain about term limits because the laws mean they lack negotiating partners whose knowledge and expertise they can count on. It seems that no one who works in a state capitol—or in the law and lobbying shops that surround any capitol—likes term limits.

But there is one group that still finds them attractive—the voting public. Polls suggest that as much as 75 percent of the public favors them. "With new people in office, you have people with real world experience," says Stacie Rumenap, president of U.S. Term Limits, a group that advocates limits. "Under term limits, you might have a schoolteacher sitting on the education committee."[b]

That sort of suggestion often is made about term limits—you get rid of the professional politicians and get people who know what the real problems are because they themselves are real. And while Idaho and Utah have repealed their limits, efforts to extend or weaken term limits have been rejected several times since 2002 by voters in Arkansas, Maine, California, Florida, Montana, and South Dakota. California voters did relax the state's term limits slightly in 2012.

The main effects of term limits, after all, are procedural. It's difficult to make a convincing case that term limits have made any one particular policy worse, let alone imperiled the quality of life in any state that observes them. The underlying complaint of term limits opponents, that they make legislators less powerful, is one reason many people supported them to begin with.

Source: Adapted from Alan Greenblatt, "The Truth about Term Limits," *Governing,* January 2006, 24.

[a]Peter Slevin, "After Adopting Term Limits, States Lose Female Legislators," *Washington Post,* April 22, 2007, A4.

[b]Interview with Stacie Rumenap, October 4, 2002.

Boise State University, "I'm not sure the American public is very attuned to the inner workings of legislatures and the fact that they probably do work better today than thirty or forty years ago."[92]

Some of the slack has been taken up by new online-only publications, from blogs written by single activists or political junkies to nonprofit outlets with something closer to traditional newsrooms and staffs. Many of the nonprofits, such as MinnPost, the Texas Tribune, the Connecticut Mirror, and California Watch, have gone quickly from start-ups to leading sources of news for state government officials, lobbyists, and fellow reporters. They've broken big stories, such as California Watch's investigation of the earthquake risk of state schools. As newspapers can attest, however, good statehouse reporting does not guarantee a viable business model. These publications are counting on continued donations, ad revenue, and other more unconventional sources of funding to survive. "There's no question in my mind that with the right team of journalists and leadership, you can do consistent and high-quality journalism," says Robert Rosenthal, a former *New York Times* reporter and *Philadelphia Inquirer* editor who is now executive director of California's Center for Investigative Reporting. "How you keep that going financially, though, is still a huge question mark."[93]

While fewer reporters are covering statehouses, legislators have found ways to cut out the middleman. Through social media sites such as Facebook, YouTube, and Twitter, legislators are able to communicate directly with their constituents and the wider world more easily than ever before. In a typical example, New Jersey senator Jim Whelan held a town hall meeting in July 2012 during which he answered questions from a radio host on the Senate Democrats' Ustream channel while simultaneously accepting tweeted questions from the public via his own Twitter feed. Afterward, the chat was posted on the Democrats' Ustream channel, their YouTube page, and Whelan's own YouTube page.[94]

Twitter has had a particularly profound effect on state capitols, allowing breaking news, policy

arguments, and snarky comments to spread instantaneously. The direct interactions with the public that Twitter makes possible, however, have been a mixed blessing for legislators. Feuds that once would have been private—or wouldn't have had a venue in which to happen at all—are now public. For example, after New York Senate majority leader Dean Skelos criticized actor Alec Baldwin for supporting an income tax increase on the wealthy, the *30 Rock* star fired back on Twitter. "His partisanship doesn't bother me," Baldwin tweeted, using hashtags such as #nooneslieslikedeanskelos. "It's that he's so dumb." Skelos didn't back down from the fight, tweeting back, "Hypocritical @AlecBaldwin rages against corporate greed yet is a paid spokesperson for corporate giant (Capital One Bank)."[95]

Many political figures have learned the hard way that some inside knowledge and some thoughts are best left untweeted. In 2009, when Democrats held an edge of only two seats in the Virginia Senate (twenty-one to the Republicans' nineteen), Republicans nearly persuaded one Democratic senator, Ralph Northam, to leave his party's caucus. If Northam had switched sides, the Democrats' majority would have been gone. But before the move was a done deal, Jeff Frederick, the chairman of the Virginia Republican Party, tweeted, "Big news coming out of Senate: apparently one dem is either switching or leaving the dem caucus. Negotiations for power sharing underway." Democrats sprang into action, calling in Governor Tim Kaine to help persuade Northam to stick with the party. Ultimately, Northam agreed to stay with the Democrats. Some observers believed it was Frederick's premature tweet that alerted the Democrats and prevented them from closing the deal.[96] A couple of months later, Frederick was removed as party chairman.

The decline of general coverage and the rise of often partisan commentary and news sites on the Web are among the reasons that amateur legislatures are much more popular with their constituents than are more professional chambers. The urge to return legislatures to their more humble but lovable position as citizen institutions has been the main driver behind the term limits movement. Limits on the number of terms an individual may serve in the house or senate have been approved in most of the states that allow ballot initiatives. As of 2009, there were fifteen states with term limits. The limits range from a low of six years of service per legislative chamber in states such as Arkansas and Michigan to twelve years of service in Nevada, Oklahoma, and Louisiana.

Term limits are especially strict in states where the public thinks there has not been enough turnover in the legislature. "The lower the existing turnover rate in the legislature," a pair of political scientists concluded in 1996, "the harsher the term limits they tend to adopt."[97] In California, for example, Assemblyman Willie Brown became the poster child for a term limits initiative because of his fourteen years as Assembly Speaker. In 1990, California voters sent a strong message. When they limited terms, they also cut the legislature's budget and staffing levels by 40 percent—the third cut in six years. The same year, Colorado voters imposed eight-year term limits on legislators and limited sessions to no more than 120 days a year.

In keeping with the public disdain for professional or full-time legislatures, policy competence in legislators is often viewed as a negative. The idea is that if they are too distracted by details and special interest wishes, they will never shut up and actually do something to serve the common good.[98] Political nominees are eager to appeal to this public sentiment. "I just want to get things done," one candidate said in 2002 in a typical statement. "Hewing to the party line—any party's line—does not interest me."[99]

Lately, power in Washington, D.C., and the states has alternated back and forth between the parties, with Republicans winning big victories in 2002 and 2010 and Democrats enjoying their own victories in 2006 and 2008. The American electorate clearly remains divided, and even in states in which one party is clearly dominant there still can be plenty of disagreement. To cite one example, although the GOP controlled both of Kansas's legislative chambers in 2012, relations deteriorated so far between the conservative House and the more moderate Senate—the sides disagreed on tax cuts and a host of social issues—that one House Republican tried to secretly record a conversation with a Senate colleague about contentious healthcare changes.[100] The

Senate moderates were routed by conservatives in Republican primaries that year, and many of the challengers were House members.

If there is no agreement in your dorm room about whether to get pepperoni on the pizza or leave it off, why should anyone in a society as diverse as ours expect easy agreement among legislators about tax rates, budgets, healthcare, guns, or the environment? Legislators simply reflect the messiness of public opinion. No matter which way they decide an issue—even if it is only to decide to maintain the law as it stands—they are bound to make some people angry. People prefer decisions to be neat and simple and harmonious. Maybe that is why no one likes legislatures.

Conclusion

Legislatures have one of the toughest jobs in the political system. It's hard enough trying to get a group of friends to agree on pizza toppings. Imagine trying to get a hundred or more people—many of whom flat-out oppose your preferred choice—to sign off on something as controversial as, say, a welfare bill. Now imagine trying to do that over and over again—researching; negotiating; meeting; balancing partisan interests, special interests, and constituent interests; and, finally, hammering out an agreement that no one is fully satisfied with and everyone is willing to criticize. That gives you some idea of the reality of a legislator's job.

Historically speaking, legislators today do their jobs more effectively and more fairly than at any previous time. For this achievement, they are mistrusted and disliked. Why? Ultimately, this is perhaps because a legislature can never give all the people everything they want. Democracy is simply not set up to do this because people want very different things. Legislatures do not really create conflict; they simply reflect the disagreements that exist in the electorate. Or at least they do if the legislators are reasonably effective at representing the preferences of their constituencies. What democracy promises, and what state legislatures largely deliver, is not what everyone wants—on most issues no such option exists—but reasonable compromises that most people can live with. Like a group with differing tastes in pizza, legislatures are successful when they can agree on second best.

The Latest Research

This chapter has noted at various points the impact of term limits, which constitute arguably the biggest institutional reform of state legislatures in the past quarter century. As discussed in some detail above, roughly one-third of all states limit in some fashion how long state legislators can serve. Although term limits are popular with the public, academic analyses give them a much more mixed review.

The impacts of term limits are still not fully understood. Only a limited number of election cycles have occurred in which term limits have forced big turnovers in legislative membership, and the impact of filling statehouses with rookies can take some time to assess. Still, term limits provide a golden opportunity for researchers to put the comparative method into action. We now have states that have term limits and states that do not. Is this a difference that makes a difference, and, if so, a difference in what? Below we summarize some of the latest research seeking answers to this question. As you will see, those answers are not what term limit advocates or opponents expected.

• •

- **Cummins, Jeff.** 2012. "The Effects of Legislative Term Limits on State Fiscal Conditions." *American Politics Research* 20: 1–26.

One of themes running throughout this entire book, not just this chapter, is how battered state finances continue to be a major influence on policy and politics. This study analyzes state budgets between 1983 and 2008 and finds that as legislative turnover increases, budgets are more likely to head toward the red. This happens for several reasons. More experienced legislators may be better equipped to handle fiscal crises, in the same fashion a veteran pilot is better prepared for in-air emergencies. Legislators who have short time horizons are less likely to take into account the long-term implications of policy. The findings of this study have particular resonance given that term limits were increasing legislative turnover during and after the Great Recession.

- **Susan Miller, Jill Nicholson-Crotty, and Sean Nicholson-Crotty.** 2011. "Reexamining the Institutional Effects of Term Limits in U.S. State Legislatures." *Legislative Studies Quarterly* 36: 71–97.

By now a number of studies have documented that term limits tend to pull power away from legislatures and toward other political actors, such as governors and interest groups. Based on an extensive series of statistical analyses, this study provides a more nuanced picture of these shifts in power. It turns out that a governor or interest groups do not automatically gain more influence once a legislature is term limited. The legislature's decrease in power is contingent on a number of factors. Upper chambers (state senates), for example, tend not to lose much at all. As legislatures and legislative leaders tend to have different levels of influence in different states, term limits might leave a legislature less powerful than it was—but still more powerful than its counterparts in other states.

- **Masket, Seth, and Jeffrey Lewis.** 2007. "A Return to Normalcy? Revisiting the Effects of Term Limits on Competitiveness and Spending in California Assembly Elections." *State Politics & Policy Quarterly* 7: 20–38.

Some of the positive impacts uncovered by some early studies of term limits were that they led to more electoral competition and drove down campaign spending. This study reassesses these findings to see if they hold up over time. The research focuses on differences in elections for the California Assembly between the periods 1976–1990 (before term limits) and 1992–2004 (after term limits). The findings suggest that the impact of term limits over time is fairly insignificant. In the term limits era, incumbents were more likely to be involved in close races but were slightly less likely to lose them. In other words, term limits have not done much to reduce the electoral advantage of incumbents. Campaign spending is as high in the term limits era as it was in the pre–term limits era. In short, the positive effects of term limits found by earlier studies, at least in California, were found to be fairly short-lived.

- **Wright, Gerald.** 2007. "Do Term Limits Affect Legislative Roll Call Voting? Representation, Polarization, and Participation." *State Politics & Policy Quarterly* 7: 256–280.

One of the more startling findings of early research on the impact of term limits was that term-limited legislators became less representative of their constituents. This raised worries that term limits might cut the electoral connection—in other words, result in a reduction in legislator concern about constituent interests. After all, why worry about representing the interests of your district if you are going to be booted from office regardless of how good a job you do? Wright's findings suggest that some of those concerns were exaggerated. This comparative study of roll-call voting in state legislatures found that term-limited legislators are just as representative as legislators who are not term limited.

Chapter Review

Key Concepts

- apportionment (p. 214)
- casework (p. 203)
- caucus (p. 208)
- coalition building (p. 194)
- committee (p. 195)
- compromise (p. 196)
- constituents (p. 195)
- constituent service (p. 203)
- delegates (p. 213)
- district (p. 195)
- filibuster (p. 194)
- gerrymanders (p. 215)
- incumbent (p. 203)
- logrolling (p. 194)
- majority-minority district (p. 216)
- majority rule (p. 193)
- malapportionment (p. 215)
- oversight (p. 206)
- professionalization (p. 214)
- rank-and-file members (p. 213)
- redistricting (p. 214)
- representation (p. 200)
- rider (p. 194)
- trustees (p. 213)

Suggested Web Sites

- **http://ncsl.typepad.com/the_thicket.** The National Conference of State Legislatures Web site offers coverage of state issues in its blog The Thicket.

- **http://stateline.org.** A foundation-sponsored news service that provides daily news about state government.

- **www.alec.org.** Web site for the American Legislative Exchange Council, an influential conservative organization that drafts model legislation. Both legislators and private-sector interests are members.

- **www.csg.org.** Web site for the Council of State Governments, which provides training and information to state government officials.

- **www.ncsl.org.** Web site of the National Conference of State Legislatures; provides a wealth of information about legislative structures and procedures as well as the major issues faced by legislators.

State Stats on Legislatures

Explore and compare data on the states! Go to college.cqpress.com/sites/ govstateandlocal to do these exercises.

1. According to the ballots, in 2010, 54.3 percent of the eligible population turned out to vote in Washington state. What percentage of the eligible population *reported* voting? Why might there be a discrepancy here?

2. In 2012, the Virginia legislature was late in passing its state budget. What was its budget in 2010? Was this higher or lower than the national average? What is the problem with comparing the total budget amounts between states?

3. Utah has a very Republican state legislature, while Vermont has a very Democratic one. What is the difference in the state and local tax burden of these states? How might the partisan makeup of the state legislatures influence this?

4. State legislatures determine most of the budgetary allocations in their states, including spending on health programs like Medicaid. Which state spends the largest percentage of its budget on healthcare? Which spends the least? What might account for the differences?

5. How has the crime rate in your state changed since 2000? Is this what you expected? Why or why not?

Louisiana governor Bobby Jindal used his executive power to order major spending cuts in the summer of 2012 to deal with the state's large budget shortfall. Although Louisiana's part-time legislators had gone home for the year, many objected to being cut out of the process, but they were wary of crossing the governor, who has the power to appoint top legislative leaders.

Governors and Executives

THERE IS NO SUCH THING AS ABSOLUTE POWER

- How did governors get to be such powerful players, when for much of American history their offices were weak?
- Why do some states still give their governors more pomp than power?

Bobby Jindal, the Republican governor of Louisiana, faced a big budget shortfall in the summer of 2012. The state's part-time legislature had gone home for the year, so Jindal decided to take care of the problem himself. He ordered nearly $1 billion in spending cuts, slashing some programs by 34.5 percent (reductions of 35 percent or more would have required legislative approval). He shut down major state-run facilities, including a prison and a mental hospital, in some cases giving local legislators less than an hour's notice before publicly announcing the shutdowns.

Needless to say, many legislators were unhappy. Some called for a special session to address the cuts. "I think legislators ought to be involved," said Dee Richard, a state representative. "Most of the cuts might be right, but we have no input."[1] Richard gained no traction with his call to bring the legislature back into session, however. Not only is Louisiana's legislature dominated by Republicans largely sympathetic to Jindal's desires, but the governor in that state gets to appoint top legislative leaders, including the House speaker and committee chairs. Legislators in Louisiana think carefully before crossing the governor. Even in states where the governors hold fewer cards than Jindal, legislators hesitate to go up against them. "If you're a legislator and you look at the governor, he's calling the shots, whoever he is," Rutgers University political scientist Alan Rosenthal said—at the annual meeting of the National Conference of State Legislatures, no less.[2]

Governors are the prime political actors in virtually all states. The governor sets the agenda, largely determining which policy issues will be pursued and how the state budget will look. Governors are unique among state-level politicians in terms of the media attention they can attract. This helps them promote their causes, but they must rely on other institutional players if they are going to accomplish more than making speeches.

Recently, governors have become a lot better equipped to control the rest of the executive branch, and they are running states in fact as well as in theory. For more than one hundred years after the founding of the American republic, governors were strong in title only, with little real power. Throughout the last decades of the twentieth century, however, governors were given more and more formal control over the machinery of government at the same time that the federal government was shifting greater control of many programs, including welfare, to the states. Governors have longer terms than they once did and enjoy greater authority to appoint the top officials in virtually all government agencies. (Only New Hampshire and Vermont still have two-year gubernatorial terms. The rest of the states have four-year terms. Only Virginia limits its chief executive to a single consecutive term—although two-term limits are common among the states.) These changes were the results of changes in laws in many states that were specifically designed to strengthen the office of governor in the hope of creating greater accountability and coherence in government. Governors are now, with few exceptions, not just the most famous politicians in their states but also the most powerful. "The weakest governor has a built-in advantage over the strongest legislature," said Rosenthal, who is the author of a recent book on governors titled *The Best Job in Politics.*

> Governors are like mini-presidents in their states. Like a president, the governor commands the lion's share of political attention in a state, is generally seen as setting the agenda for the legislative branch, and is basically the lead political actor—the figure most likely to appear on television on a regular basis. Also like a president, the governor tends to receive the blame or enjoy the credit for the performance of the economy.

Governors are like mini-presidents in their states. Like the president, the governor commands the lion's share of political attention in a state, is generally seen as setting the agenda for the legislative branch, and is basically the lead political actor—the figure most likely to appear on television on a regular basis. Also like the president, the governor tends to receive the blame or enjoy the credit for the performance of the economy.

And, again like the president, the governor shares responsibility for running the government—implementing laws, issuing regulations, and doing the work of building the roads, maintaining the parks, and performing other public functions—with the help of a cabinet. Presidents appoint their cabinet officials to run the Departments of Defense and Agriculture and the like. Governors have help in running state-level departments of agriculture, finance, environmental protection, and so on. In most cases, the governor appoints officials to head these departments, but some other statewide officials, such as attorneys general, often are elected on their own and may even represent another party. We explore the roles of these other executive branch officials later in this chapter.

This chapter also answers these questions: How did governors get to be such powerful players, when for much of U.S. history their offices were weak? Why is this so? Why do some states still give their governors more pomp than power? We look at how the office of governor has changed over the years. We examine the types of powers governors can command by virtue of the office and which powers they must create out of the force of personality. We also look at what sorts of people get elected governor and how they get elected. Finally, we survey some of the other important statewide offices, such as lieutenant governor and attorney general.

The Job of Governor

Following the American Revolution, governors had very little power for one simple reason—distrust. Colonial governors, appointed by the British, had imposed unpopular taxes and exploited their positions to make themselves rich. Americans did not want to invest too much power in individuals who might turn into mini-dictators. There was no national president, after all, under the original Articles of Confederation. In the states, most of the power was disbursed among many individuals holding office in legislatures and on state boards and commissions. Governors in all but three of the original states were limited to one-year terms. While in office, they were not given control over state departments and agencies. Separately elected individuals, boards, or commissions ran these instead. After his state's constitutional convention, one North Carolina delegate said that the governor had been given just enough power "to sign the receipt for his salary."[3]

The number of agencies grew as government became more complex toward the end of the nineteenth century. Lack of central control over these agencies, however, meant that states had difficulty functioning coherently. Governors lacked the authority to perform in ways that the public expected of them, given their position at the top of the political pyramid. This problem persisted well into the twentieth century.

Lynn Muchmore, a political scientist, sums up the sort of frustrations governors had as late as the 1980s in terms of getting various parts of government to act as they wished. Muchmore lays out a theoretical case of a governor elected on a platform of promoting growth in the state's rural areas and documents the difficulties he had in making good on those promises. In this scenario, the new governor found that the highway department, which was run by a separate commission, had decided a decade ago to complete urban segments of the state's road system. This decision siphoned money away from plans to develop better roads in rural areas. The board that oversaw the public colleges and universities had a policy of phasing out satellite campuses in favor of investing in three urban campuses. The state's department of commerce would not work in any county that did not have a local economic development corporation. Many rural counties lacked such corporations because they did not have the population or tax base to support them. And the state legislature had passed restrictions that denied new businesses breaks on rural utility rates.[4] Despite his promises, the governor's battle to help rural areas was an uphill one.

Not every scenario is so extreme, but it is often the case that state agencies not headed by people appointed by the governor—and therefore not answering to him or her—have their own constituencies and concerns. They do not have in mind the big picture of how the different parts of state government can best work together to promote the general good. Only the governor sees the whole field in that way.

In recent decades, governors have been granted greater powers, including much more power over appointments than they once had. This means that they are able to put their own teams in place to carry out their policies. They have become important symbols of their states, not only at home but also in other states and abroad as ambassadors who promote their states to businesses that they hope to attract. YouTube is littered with clips of governors laying out their cases for why their states are the best.

Terry Sanford, a former governor of North Carolina, sums up the job of the contemporary governor well:

> The governor by his very office embodies his state. He must . . . energize his administration, search out the experts, formulate the programs, mobilize the support, and carry new ideas into action. . . . Few major undertakings ever get off the ground without his support and

leadership. The governor sets the agenda for public debate; frames the issues; decides on the timing; and can blanket the state with good ideas by using his access to the mass media. . . . The governor is the most potent political power in the state.[5]

Governors must be multitaskers. They propose legislation, which has to win approval from the legislature. They can implement regulations that help clear up how those laws actually are applied to individuals, businesses, and other groups. Increasingly in recent years, governors have become the strongest advocates and public relations people for their states, traveling to promote tourism and help close deals with out-of-state trading partners that might locate offices or operations in their states. Below, we explore all these roles in some detail.

Chief Legislator

Things were starting to go sour for Arkansas governor Mike Beebe. In 2009, both chambers of the state legislature passed a new three-cent tax on milk and dairy products to raise money to prop up the state's beleaguered farmers. This move ran directly counter to one of Beebe's signal accomplishments—a two-thirds reduction in grocery taxes that he had achieved since taking office in 2007. "It was a little inconsistent," he admitted. It was not just inconsistent but also highly unpopular. Over the course of just a few days, the owner of a small chain of Arkansas pizza parlors had persuaded more than seven hundred of his customers to call Beebe's office and complain about the new tax. Because the plan already had passed the legislature, bigger milk purchasers also targeted the governor directly, running a full-page color ad in the *Arkansas Democrat-Gazette* that featured a little girl in pigtails pleading with Beebe not to tax her milk money.

It looked as if Beebe was in a box. He knew that vetoing the milk tax would mean little, because its sponsors had more than enough votes to override him. Instead, he scrubbed the budget and found several million dollars sitting in an obscure agriculture biodiesel fund that could, without too

much sleight of hand, be shifted over to help the dairy farmers. Just like that, Beebe's problem was solved. With the money in hand, the new milk tax was withdrawn. The governor called his solution "kind of a lucky brainstorm,"[6] but in a way it was vintage Beebe, taking advantage of his extensive knowledge of state government, based on twenty years in the state Senate and four years as attorney general, to solve a political problem.

Just as the president does not serve in Congress, governors do not sit as members of state legislatures. Like the president, however, they have enormous influence over the work legislatures do. Governors outline their broad proposals in inaugural and annual state of the state addresses. They and their staffs then work with individual legislators and committees to translate these proposals into bills.

Some governors are better than others at getting what they want from legislatures. Why? Part of it is personal charm, but a lot of it has to do with the powers granted to a governor in a given state. In Texas, for instance, most of the influence that the executive branch holds over legislation is given to the lieutenant governor, not the governor. Governors vary in terms of how much authority they have in blocking bills they do not like through use of the **veto,** or rejection, of the bills. Those variations in authority help to determine how much clout a governor has in the legislature.

Governors never get everything they want from state legislatures, but they do have a great deal of impact on which bills become laws. There are a number of reasons for this. Bills almost never become law without the governor's signature, and governors have veto power. Legislators can get around a veto, but that often means that they have to pass the bill again by a **supermajority vote.** Supermajority votes are usually votes of two-thirds

---

Veto
The power to reject a proposed law.

Supermajority Vote
A legislative vote of much more than a simple majority, for instance, a vote by two-thirds of a legislative chamber to override a governor's veto.

Maryland governor Martin O'Malley uses a farm tour to tout his new budget, which includes funds to help farmers promote environmentally friendly practices. While most governors exercise considerable influence over budgets, the Maryland governor has more power than most. A number of legal restrictions make it difficult for the Maryland legislature to make major changes to the budget proposed by the governor.

or more. That means a governor needs the support of only one-third plus one vote in either chamber to sustain a veto. Because it is hard enough to get both legislative houses to agree on a bill in the first place, such a large vote against most governors rarely happens. If you can't pass a law without the governor's approval, it stands to reason that you will want to work with him or her to create a version of the bill that will win such approval.

Another factor that makes governors enormously influential in the legislative process is their command of state budgets. In nearly every state, the main responsibility for creating a state budget rests in the office of the governor. The governor proposes a budget that details the amounts of money that will go to every state agency, welfare program, highway department, and school district. There are often restrictions on how a state must spend much of its money from year to year, whether because of old laws or federal requirements. But the governor gets first crack at deciding how most of the state's money is going to be spent. "As far as legislators are concerned," one political scientist writes, "the ability to create the budget is so powerful that it becomes *the* major tool for a governor in achieving his legislative programs."[7]

While the legislature might set the overall dollar amount that goes to the transportation department, the governor might get to decide, for instance, whether bridges are going to be built in particular districts. To get those bridges—or any other goodies they might want—legislators often have to give the governor what he or she wants in terms of passing major initiatives. "Any legislator who says he needs nothing from the governor's office is either lying or stupid," according to one observer of the Alabama political scene.[8]

Head of State Agencies

Governors at one time had very little control over who ran their states' departments. This meant that people with other agendas could set policy on taxes or healthcare or other issues. Only about half of the governors chose their own cabinet officials in 1969, but nearly all of them do today.[9] (From 1965 to 1979, twenty-one states embarked on comprehensive reorganizations of their executive branches.)[10] "Reformers had long advocated strengthening the governor's office by lengthening the governor's term of office, allowing consecutive succession in office, broadening the veto power, increasing appointment and removal power, and increasing budgetary authority," noted a trio of political scientists in 2010. "States have generally responded by adopting many of the reformers' propositions, and by late in the twentieth century, most governors enjoyed significantly enhanced formal powers."[11]

The power to appoint people to run state departments offers obvious benefits for governors. They can pick their own people, who they know will pursue their policy preferences. If those people fail, they can be fired. Arguing for expanding the appointment power of New Hampshire governors, former legislator Marjorie Smith wrote in 2012: "With the possible exception of Texas, New Hampshire's governor has power more limited than that of any other state's governor. We elect a governor with the expectation that she will shape the policy over the course of her term, but do not give her the power to name department heads who will carry out that policy."[12]

Just like any other boss, a governor may be disappointed in the performance of the people working for him or her. The ability to hire and fire people, however, as well as the ability to determine how much money the state's departments are going to get, means that the governor is truly the leader of the executive branch of government.

Chief Spokesperson for the State

Mississippi governor Haley Barbour was the first to credit the countless government workers who helped southern Mississippi cope with Hurricane Katrina, which devastated the Gulf Coast in 2005. But a major crisis such as Katrina also demands a strong leader who can communicate calm to the public and provide "a central decision-making point for when things get balled up or go sideways, which they do," as Barbour says. He excelled at both. Barbour was straight with the facts about the utter devastation in the area, but his own demeanor in public appearances suggested that the state would summon the will to rebuild.[13] No governor wishes for disaster, of course, but a strong response to such a challenge can enhance a governor's image, as Oklahoma governor Frank Keating found after the federal building in Oklahoma City was bombed in 1995, killing 168 people. "The public had a view of me as a crisis manager," Keating said.[14]

A governor acts as the chief spokesperson and public face of a state's government in good times as well as bad. Governors didn't always think it was part of their job description to attract jobs and industry to their states, but they do now. The template was set for them by Luther Hodges, who served as governor of North Carolina from 1954 to 1961, before becoming U.S. secretary of commerce. Hodges created a business development corporation in his state to supply capital to businesses, changed the state's corporate income tax rates, and employed the expertise of nearby University of North Carolina, North Carolina State University, and Duke University in the creation of the 5,000-acre Research Triangle industrial park, which in turn led to the development of the state's high-tech infrastructure. "My administration was considered by many to be 'industry hungry,'" Hodges once said. "It was!"[15]

Governors regularly send out press releases about their role in helping to land new jobs and companies through tax incentives, the creation of cooperative business ventures, and other economic development activities. The day after his election in 2002, New Mexico governor Bill Richardson got on a plane to talk to executives in California's Silicon Valley in the hope of persuading them to set up operations in New Mexico. Once in office, Richardson proudly boasted that he calls CEOs on a daily basis and "sucks up to them big time."[16]

Governors are also important lobbyists in Washington, seeking more federal money for their states. They are just about the only people who lobby in the nation's capital who can be sure that members of Congress and cabinet officials will meet with them directly rather than having them meet with staff.

Party Chief

Governors are also the leading figures in their parties within their states. U.S. senators arguably might be more influential figures, but governors are more important politically at home. Governors command more foot soldiers. A governor may be able to call on thousands of state workers, whereas a senator's staff numbers in the dozens at most. Not all of a governor's workers are loyal members of the same party—in fact, changes in patronage laws and the creation of a civil service system mean that governors appoint far fewer state employees than they did some decades ago. Governors, however, have more people whose jobs depend on them than do any other elected officials.

Governors often pick state party chairs of their liking. They help to recruit and raise money for candidates for other statewide offices and the legislature. They use the media attention they attract to campaign for those they support. They are still the titular heads of their parties in their states, and no modern politician (who isn't already rich) can avoid the duties of raising campaign contributions.

Commander in Chief of the National Guard

Even in this country's earliest days, when governors had few powers, each governor's military position was strong, "with all states designating him as commander-in-chief."[17] Southern governors perhaps most famously used their power to control the National Guard in resisting desegregation during the 1950s and 1960s. The National Guard in each state is a state agency, but the president has the power to federalize it, calling up units to perform federal service. That happened in the civil rights era, when the Guard was ordered to work for the feds against governors who were resisting integration. Those serving in today's National Guard are more likely to fight alongside federal soldiers in such places as Iraq.

Governors do not use the Guard as their private armies, however. Instead, they can call out units to respond to natural disasters or riots. Milton Shapp, governor of Pennsylvania during the 1970s, remembered his years in office in terms of emergency responses to floods, a pair of hurricanes, droughts, ice storms, fires, and a gypsy moth infestation rather than in terms of lawmaking and policy agenda setting.[18]

Still, the question of who controls the National Guard has become a politically potent one in recent years. The federal government pays for troop training and many of the Guard's operations, and the Supreme Court has found that the feds—not governors—have the final say over where units are deployed.[19] In 2006 Congress passed a law that made it easier for the White House, rather than the statehouse, to take command of the Guard during times of disaster. All fifty governors signed a letter protesting an earlier version of the law.

The Powers of Governors

Anyone who follows sports understands that natural ability does not necessarily translate into success. Some players look great on paper—they're strong, they can run fast, they have whatever skills should help them dominate their sport. But, for whatever reason, these players sometimes squander their talents and are shown up by athletes who are weaker but who nevertheless have a greater understanding of the game, work harder, or simply find a way to win.

It is the same with governors. Some of them look incredibly strong on paper, and their states' constitutions give them powers that their neighbors can only envy. Nevertheless, states that have set up the governor's office to be strong sometimes end up with weak governors. Conversely, states in which the governor's **formal powers** are weak sometimes can have individuals in that office who completely dominate their states' politics. They are able to exploit the **informal powers** of their office—they manage to create personal powers, as opposed to relying on relatively weak institutional powers.

Below we outline the different types of powers that governors actually do have, both the formal ones, those that come as part of the necessary equipment of the office, and the informal ones that these individuals create for themselves by using the office as a platform.

More than 2,100 National Guard troops were called on to support relief efforts in New Jersey after Superstorm Sandy ravaged the state's coastline in 2012.

Formal Powers

Most governors have a wide variety of formal powers granted to them by state constitutions or other laws. Among the most important of these are the power to appoint officials to run state agencies, the power to veto legislation, the power to craft budgets, the power to grant pardons, and

---

Formal Powers
The powers explicitly granted to a governor according to state law, such as being able to veto legislation and to appoint heads of state agencies.

Informal Powers
The things a governor is able to do, such as command media attention and persuade party members, based on personality or position, not on formal authority.

the power to call legislatures into session. We examine each of these aspects of a governor's job description in this section.

The Power to Appoint. The first governors lacked **appointment powers.** They could not pick their own people to run state agencies, which made those agencies more independent. Nowadays, governors can pick their own teams, giving them greater authority to set policy. When John Engler served as governor of Michigan during the 1990s, for example, he put in place a series of appointees with a strong ideological commitment to limited government. These appointees helped him carry out his desire to shrink the state's government. Engler's contemporary, Ann Richards of Texas, set out to change the face of state government by changing the faces of the people within it, appointing women, African Americans, and Hispanics to replace the white men who had always run things in Austin.

Having loyal foot soldiers on your team rather than free agents is important for governors who want things done their way. This is not the only benefit the power of appointment carries with it, however. Governors get to appoint dozens and sometimes thousands of people to full-time government jobs and to commissions and boards. For instance, if you are attending a public college, chances are that the governor appointed the board of governors of your school or university system. These are considered plum jobs, and giving them out is a way for a governor not only to influence policy but also to reward campaign contributors and other political allies.

Of course, there is a downside to the power of appointment, which is the risk of picking the wrong people. Earlier, we mentioned former Pennsylvania governor Milton Shapp, who remembered his administration mainly as a time of dealing with natural disasters. It is little wonder he prefers to remember his time in office that way

---

Appointment Powers
A governor's ability to pick individuals to run state government, such as cabinet secretaries.

because many of his appointments turned into disasters of his own making. His secretary of property and supplies was sent to prison for contracting irregularities. The same fate befell a member of his turnpike authority. Other members of his administration came under ethical shadows as well. Even though Shapp himself was never touched by scandal, subsequent candidates—including the man who succeeded him as governor—ran campaigns against corruption. They won office by pledging to clean up Harrisburg.[20]

Power to Prepare State Budgets. The most powerful tool governors have may be their ability to shape their states' budgets. As we noted earlier in our discussion of Bobby Jindal's unilateral decision to cut $1 billion in spending, the power over the budget gives governors enormous influence in their dealings with the legislature. The same is true of their ability to maintain control over state agencies. In most states, agencies and departments submit their budget proposals to a central budget office that works as part of the governor's team. The governor's ability to deny them funds or shift money among departments helps make sure that agencies remain focused, at least to some extent, on the governor's priorities.

A governor can use the budget process to override old agency decisions, for example, to make sure that the transportation department fully funds bike trails that previously had been ignored. Even when an agency has some independence about how it spends its money, a governor can persuade officials to fund other priorities—such as a new law school at a state university—by threatening to withhold some percentage of their agency's overall budget.

Power to Veto. In talking about the governor as chief legislator, we touched on the governor's ability to veto legislation in every state. (North Carolina's governor was the last to win this power, in 1997.) Legislators can override vetoes, but that rarely happens because of supermajority vote requirements. Members of the governor's own party usually are reluctant to vote to override a veto. That means that if the governor's party holds just one-third of the seats in a legislative chamber, plus one, a veto is likely to be sustained—meaning the governor wins.

Legislators, therefore, try to work with the governor or the governor's staff to craft a version of a bill that the governor will sign. There is little point in passing a bill if you know it is going to be rejected by the governor. Of course, legislatures sometimes pass a bill just to get it vetoed, to make the governor's opposition official and public. That happened often when Gary Johnson was governor of New Mexico during the 1990s. "During his eight years as New Mexico's governor, Gary Johnson competed in the Ironman Triathlon World Championship, won the America's Challenge Gas Balloon Race, played guitar with Van Halen's Sammy Hagar, and helped save a house when massive wildfires struck Los Alamos," political scientists Thad Kousser and Justin H. Phillips write in their 2012 book *The Power of American Governors*.[21] Yet, they note, he never succeeded in persuading legislators to enact items on his legislative agenda.

That didn't mean Johnson was irrelevant. Johnson, who ran as the Libertarian Party candidate for president in 2012, did not support any bill that increased the size of government, and so he ended up vetoing more than seven hundred bills. Legislators sent him bills that would increase funding for popular programs, such as education, in the hope that his vetoes would make him look bad. Whether that happened or not, Johnson almost always won the procedural battle. Not only was the legislature unable to override his vetoes except in one instance, but he also was reelected to a second term. All but six governors—those in Indiana, Nevada, New Hampshire, North Carolina, Rhode Island, and Vermont—have a power known as the line-item veto; that is, they can reject just a portion of a bill. If there is a bill funding education, for example, the governor can accept all of it except for an increase in funding for a school in the district of a legislator who is a political enemy. Governors can use the line-item veto to try to cut spending, as when New York governor George Pataki eliminated spending for more than one thousand items from the state budget in 1998. The governor's ability to cut legislators' pet projects out of the budget forces most of them to support that governor's major initiatives. Congress tried to give the president line-item veto authority, but the U.S. Supreme Court ruled the practice unconstitutional in 1998.

When Tommy Thompson was governor of Wisconsin during the 1990s, he used the line-item veto to an unusual degree. Some governors can strike not only projects from bills, but individual words and letters as well. Thompson became notorious for vetoing just enough letters in a bill's wording to alter the meaning of the bill (see chapter 3). The courts upheld his right to do so, but that power was soon curbed. Nevertheless, in 2005, Jim Doyle, the state's Democratic governor, was able to strike 752 words from a budget bill in order to cobble together a new 20-word sentence that shifted $427 million from transportation to education.[22]

Texas governor Rick Perry (left) is introduced by Texas lieutenant governor David Dewhurst. Although technically the second-ranking executive in the Texas state government, Dewhurst actually may wield more power than the governor, who has very few formal powers. The lieutenant governor presides over the state Senate, sets the agenda, and appoints senators to the committees. This makes Dewhurst the executive with the most direct influence over the Texas legislature.

States under Stress

Arizona Governor Pays Price for Revenue Fall

Jan Brewer was Arizona's popular secretary of state when her political career took a turn for the worse—she became governor.

With Democrat Janet Napolitano departing the state in 2009 to serve in President Obama's cabinet, Brewer, who is a Republican, stepped in as her replacement. The timing was awful. From 2007 to 2010, Arizona's revenues dropped by one-third, brought down by the housing bust. When Brewer took office, she faced a $3.4 billion shortfall for fiscal year 2010, out of an overall budget of less than $10 billion.

It wasn't that Brewer was unwilling to cut spending. In 2010, she signed a budget package that made Arizona the first state to eliminate funding for its Children's Health Insurance Program and included cuts in Medicaid deep enough to threaten coverage for 300,000 adults.

But, throughout 2009, Brewer surprised many in Arizona by advocating for a penny increase in the sales tax. Brewer had a long-standing reputation as an opponent of higher taxes, but soon after taking office she proposed a public referendum on a sales tax increase to help balance the budget. Her fellow Republicans, who controlled both houses of the legislature, recoiled. Brewer tried to strike a deal by coupling the sales tax vote with future tax cuts, including a move to a flat income tax beginning in 2012.

Democrats rejected that bargain—and Brewer still didn't get the Republican support she needed.

The inability to reach an agreement led to a stalemate lasting many months. In September 2009, Brewer signed some budget bills that, without the sales tax increase, still left the state's finances $1.5 billion out of balance, a shortfall that continued to grow into 2010.

Finally, legislators decided that she was right, that voters deserved the chance to decide for themselves whether they were willing to pay more in taxes. A referendum was put on the ballot in May 2010, and the voters approved the sales tax increase. But that is hardly likely to be the end of the political battling. Opponents of the plan termed it, correctly, the largest tax increase in Arizona history.

Further, the issue made Brewer's path to winning a full term of her own much steeper. She drew three opponents in the GOP primary, but she managed to win reelection in 2010 nonetheless. Raising taxes might have been an ironic turn of events for Brewer, who was seen as an aggressive Republican unlikely to buck her party on tax policy. Soon after winning reelection, she called the legislature into special session to cut several taxes on businesses. In 2012, Arizona voters rejected a permanent extension of her earlier sales tax increase.

Source: Adapted from Josh Goodman, "Lonely at the Top," *Governing,* November 2009, 17.

Prompted by Doyle's move—and by near-daily editorials in the *Wisconsin State Journal* newspaper and on the paper's Web site—the legislature in 2008 further restricted the governor's veto authority. The governor of Wisconsin can no longer stitch together words from different parts of a bill, but he or she can still delete words from individual sentences or change numbers—quickly converting $100 million to $10 million, for instance. "It seems like each governor gets more creative in their use of the partial veto, and this was clearly an abuse," said state senator Sheila Harsdorf, a sponsor of the successful anti-Frankenstein referendum. "When people saw that veto, it was pretty hard to justify."[23]

Power to Grant Pardons. One clichéd motif of old movies and television dramas was the depiction of a prisoner about to be put to death only to be spared by a last-minute pardon from the governor. Governors, like the president, can forgive crimes or commute (change) sentences if

TABLE 8-1

The Governors: Powers

State or Other Jurisdiction	Budget-Making Power		Item Veto Power			Item Veto—2/3 Legislators Present or 3/5 Elected to Override	Item Veto—Majority Legislators Elected to Override	Authorization for Reorganization through Executive Order
	Full Responsibility	Shares Responsibility	Governor Has Item Veto Power on All Bills	Governor Has Item Veto Power on Appropriations Only	Governor Has No Item Veto Power			
Alabama	*(a)	...	*	...	...	...	*	...
Alaska	*	...	...	*	...	*	...	*
Arizona	*(a)	...	...	*	...	*	(b)	...
Arkansas	...	*	...	*	...	...	*	*
California	*(a)	...	...	*	...	*	...	*(c)
Colorado	...	*	...	*	...	*	...	*
Connecticut	...	*	...	*	...	*	...	...
Delaware	*(a)	...	*	...	...	*	...	*
Florida	...	*	...	*	...	*	...	*
Georgia	*	...	...	*	...	(b)	...	*
Hawaii	...	*	*	...	...	*	...	*
Idaho	(d)	(d)	...	*	...	*	...	*
Illinois	...	*	*	...	...	*	...	*
Indiana	*	...	...	...	*	...	...	*
Iowa	...	*	...	*	...	*	...	*
Kansas	*	...	...	*	...	*	...	*
Kentucky	*(a)	...	...	*(e)	...	*	*	*
Louisiana	...	*	...	*	...	...	*(f)	*(g)
Maine	...	*	...	*	...	...	*	...
Maryland	*	...	*	...	...	*	...	*
Massachusetts	*	...	*	...	...	...	*(f)	*(c)
Michigan	*(h)	...	...	*(e)	...	...	*(f)	*
Minnesota	...	*	...	*	...	...	*(f)	*(i)
Mississippi	...	*(j)	*	...	...	*	...	*
Missouri	*(a)	...	...	*	...	*	...	*
Montana	*	...	...	*	...	*(k)	...	*(l)
Nebraska	...	*	...	*	...	*(m)	...	...
Nevada	*	...	...	...	*	...	...	...
New Hampshire	*(a)	...	...	...	*	...	...	...
New Jersey	*(a)	...	...	*	...	...	*(f)	*(n)
New Mexico	*	...	...	*	...	*	...	...
New York	...	*	*	...	...	*	...	...
North Carolina	...	*	...	...	*	...	...	*(o)
North Dakota	*	...	...	*	...	*	...	*
Ohio	*	...	...	*	...	*	...	...
Oklahoma	...	*	...	*	...	...	*(f)	...
Oregon	...	*	...	*	...	*	...	*
Pennsylvania	*	...	...	*	...	*	...	...

(Continued)

TABLE 8-1 (Continued)

State or Other Jurisdiction	Budget-Making Power		Item Veto Power					Authorization for Reorganization through Executive Order
	Full Responsibility	Shares Responsibility	Governor Has Item Veto Power on All Bills	Governor Has Item Veto Power on Appropriations Only	Governor Has No Item Veto Power	Item Veto—2/3 Legislators Present or 3/5 Elected to Override	Item Veto—Majority Legislators Elected to Override	
Rhode Island	...	*	...	...	*	...	...	...
South Carolina	...	*	...	*	...	*	...	...
South Dakota	*	...	...	*	...	*(p)	...	*
Tennessee	...	*	...	*	...	...	*	*
Texas	...	*	...	*	...	*	...	*
Utah	...	*	...	*	...	*	...	*
Vermont	*	...	...	...	*	...	...	*
Virginia	*	...	...	*	...	*(p)	...	*
Washington	*	...	*(q)	...	...	*	...	...
West Virginia	*	...	...	*	....	*	...	...
Wisconsin	*(a)	...	...	*(r)	...	*	...	...
Wyoming	...	*	*	...	...	*	...	...
American Samoa	...	*	...	...	...	...	...	*
Guam	*	...	*	...	...	*	...	*
No. Mariana Islands	...	*	...	*	...	*	...	*
Puerto Rico	...	*	...	*	...	*	...	*(s)
U.S. Virgin Islands	*	...	...	*	...	*	...	*

Source: The Council of State Governments' survey of governor's offices, December 2011. Reproduced by permission of The Council of State Governments.

Key:

*—Yes; provision for.

. . .—No; not applicable.

(a) Full responsibility to propose; legislature adopts or revises and governor signs or vetoes.

(b) Two-thirds of members to which each house is entitled required to override veto.

(c) Authorization for reorganization provided for in state constitution.

(d) Legislature has full responsibility with regard to setting the state's budget.

(e) Governor may veto any distinct item or items appropriating money in any appropriations bill.

(f) Two-thirds of elected legislators of each house to override.

(g) Only for agencies and offices within the governor's office.

(h) Governor has sole authority to propose annual budget. No money may be paid out of state treasury except in pursuance of appropriations made by law.

(i) Statute provides for reorganization by the commissioner of administration with the approval of the governor.

(j) Governor has the responsibility of presenting a balanced budget. The budget is based on revenue estimated by the governor's office and the Legislative Budget Committee.

(k) If the legislature is not in session when the governor vetoes a bill, the secretary of state must poll the legislature as to the question of an override, but only if the bill had passed by a vote of two-thirds of the members present.

(l) The office of the governor shall continuously study and evaluate the organizational structure, management practices, and functions of the executive branch and each agency.

The governor shall, by executive order or other means within his authority, take action to improve the manageability of the executive branch. The governor may not, however, create an agency of state government by administrative action, except that the governor may establish advisory councils and must approve the internal organizational structures of departments.

(m) Three-fifths majority required to override line-item veto.

(n) Executive reorganization plans can be disapproved by majority vote in both houses of the legislature.

(o) Executive order must be approved by the legislature if changes affect existing law.

(p) Requires two-thirds of legislators present to override.

(q) Governor has veto power of selections for nonappropriations and item veto in appropriations.

(r) In Wisconsin, governor has "partial" veto over appropriation bills. The partial veto is broader than item veto.

(s) Only if it is not prohibited by law.

they feel that particular persons have been convicted unfairly. They sometimes act on the recommendations of pardon boards, but the decision to pardon is theirs alone and not reversible.

A famous example of the use of pardon power happened in Illinois in 2003. During his last week in office, Governor George Ryan pardoned 4 prisoners condemned to death and commuted the sentences of the other 167 death-row prisoners to life in prison. Ryan had grown concerned that the number of capital cases that were being overturned because of new evidence, such as

DNA lab work, indicated that the death penalty was being unfairly and inequitably applied. He appointed a commission to study the application of the death sentence and became convinced that the state could not impose the death penalty with such absolute certainty that innocent people would not be put to death. The move gained Ryan international celebrity among death penalty opponents but was criticized by prosecutors and others at home.

Not all governors use their pardon powers in such a high-minded way. In Tennessee in 1979, Lamar Alexander was sworn in as governor three days early to prevent outgoing governor Ray Blanton from commuting the sentences of any more prisoners. Blanton already had granted fifty-two last-minute pardons, and the Federal Bureau of Investigation (FBI) had arrested members of his staff for extorting money to sell pardons, paroles, and commutations. More recently, outgoing governor Haley Barbour of Mississippi drew national condemnation by pardoning some two hundred people during his final days in office in 2012, including five who were still in prison and five others who had worked in the governor's mansion. Despite a challenge from Mississippi's attorney general, the state Supreme Court quickly ruled that Barbour's actions had been perfectly in keeping with his power. In part because they fear political backlash if pardoned criminals should reoffend, the practice of pardoning has become increasingly rare among governors since the 1960s, with some governors currently in office never having pardoned anyone at all.[24]

The Power to Call Special Sessions. Many legislatures meet only part-time and generally have fixed session schedules. When necessary or desired, however, every governor has the power to call legislatures into special session. Nearly half the nation's governors have the ability to set the agenda of a special session. This means that in such a session legislators can deal only with those issues that the governor wants addressed.

Special sessions can be useful for governors who want to deal with particular issues right away. In recent years, many governors have called special sessions when their states' revenues have fallen short so that the legislatures can help them cut spending. Sometimes a special session allows legislators to focus on a complex issue, such as changing medical malpractice liability laws. Such issues might get lost in the shuffle of a regular session, when most attention is devoted to passing a budget.

Although governors can call special sessions, they typically will not enjoy success unless they can work out deals on their pet bills in advance. "If a governor calls a special session without knowing what the outcome's going to be," said former Mississippi House Speaker Tim Ford, "it's chaos for everybody."[25] Without a deal already in place, legislators who have been called into session will sit around reading newspapers and eating snacks while their leaders try to hammer out an agreement with the governor. They are likely to resent having to give up time from their regular jobs to sit idly in the capitol.

In 2011, the South Carolina legislature persuaded the state Supreme Court that governor Nikki Haley didn't have the power to call the legislature into special session to take up bills she was insisting get consideration—bills that would have expanded her office's control over government operations. "She has to be mindful and respectful of the separation of powers," complained Glenn McConnell, the president of the state Senate. "She is not respectful of that."[26]

Even though governors are able to call legislators into special session, they cannot necessarily make them do anything. In Iowa in 2002, Governor Tom Vilsack called the legislature back into session in the hope that it would increase funding for education and health, but the legislators adjourned after a single day without debating any bill. "We just came in and went home," said House majority leader Christopher Rants. Vilsack then signed a package of budget cuts he had accepted in meetings with legislators and went on to call a second special session later in the month.[27]

Informal Powers

The powers just outlined are spelled out in state constitutions and statutes. Governors either have line-item veto authority or they do not. Much of the outcome of a governor's program, however, depends on the governor's individual ability to

FIGURE 8-1

HOW IT WORKS

Merging Formal and Informal Gubernatorial Powers: Florida's Governor Crist Takes on Category 5 Insurance Problems

As powerful as they are, there are some things governors may not be able to control. The weather is one. The insurance industry may be another. Florida's Republican governor Charlie Crist tackled both in his first term as he worked behind the scenes and in front of the cameras to pass legislation to stem rising insurance costs in the state.

THE PROBLEM. The disastrous 2004 and 2005 hurricane seasons left many of Florida's homeowners with more than just flattened roofs: it landed them with crushing insurance bills. The cost of insuring a home more than doubled in 2006, and many residents considered leaving the state altogether. Joining a chorus of voices advocating for a host of insurance reforms, Governor Crist urged Floridians to stay put and promised to work with lawmakers to help bring down insurance rates.

That's no small feat. Insuring property in a state that saw nearly $36 billion in storm damages in one year alone is an expensive business—and regulating that industry is the state's responsibility. Even the industry's harshest critics understand that the premiums homeowners pay on a regular basis to insure their homes must keep pace with the amounts that agencies anticipate will be paid out in future claims. That's basic math. But, critics say, insurers' profits have soared in recent years. Some agencies have adopted such misleading or unfair practices as creating differently named subsidiary companies that offer different rates than their parent agencies. Others offer restricted insurance plans to Floridians (for example, they offer auto but not homeowners insurance). Still others refused to offer policies in that state, leaving many without coverage.

In their wake stands Citizens Property Insurance, a state-run agency created in 2002 by the Florida legislature as an insurance "safety net." Under its original rules, homeowners were allowed to switch to Citizens only if they had been denied coverage by a national company or if their premiums were quoted at more than 25 percent higher than Citizens's rates. By 2006, however, Citizens was set to become the insurer for more than half of all of Florida's homeowners—about 1.3 million policyholders—making it the state's largest insurance company rather than the agency of last resort.

With so many homeowners forced to pay exorbitant rates or cut loose from national policies altogether and Citizens stepping in to fill the gap, Governor Crist and Florida's lawmakers were made to reconsider the role that Citizens should (or could) play in wholesale insurance reform.

THE PROCESS. In January 2007 Crist called a weeklong special legislative session to try to hammer out a plan. Crist himself brought several aggressive measures to the table, including recommendations to lower threshold requirements for homeowners to get coverage through Citizens, to cap the agency's ability to raise rates, and to crackdown on subsidiaries. He also asked for the power to appoint the company's director. But the hallmark of his plan was to make Citizens more competitive with private insurers. After the special session, the legislature continued the reform debate during its regular session.

Early predictions of Crist's likelihood of success were not good. The insurance lobby came on strong, as did a handful of legislators from his own party, who warned the public that increasing the role of the state-sponsored Citizens was tantamount to socialism and potentially could bankrupt the state. But having once been a state legislator himself, Crist knew how to work the ropes. His main advantage was his stratospheric popularity: he had plenty of political capital, and he wasn't shy about spending it.

To promote his plan, Crist put in rare appearances before several House and Senate committees and stumped to persuade homeowners that the promised rate relief wasn't an illusion. He also traveled to Washington, D.C., to help Florida lawmakers appeal for a national disaster relief fund to help defray costs to that state's homeowners.

Crist and his staff continued to work behind the scenes, too, with the governor's staff "buttonholing" legislators. State senator J. D. Alexander reported that "there had been some political arm-twisting," adding, "You don't go against a governor with a 77-percent approval rating."[a]

Both the House and Senate took up bills that included a number of Crist's original proposals; by the end of their regular session, they'd reached resolutions.

THE OUTCOMES. Crist got a lot of what he wanted. Legislators agreed to freeze Citizens's rates at 2006 levels through 2009. Policyholders will be allowed to choose coverage through Citizens if they receive quotes from national insurers that are more than 15 percent higher than Citizens's annual premiums. Other provisions also are in place to allow the agency to be more competitive with private insurers.

"You put the nail in the coffin this afternoon on the industry that was hurting our people. That's right and just fair and important, and you did it, and God bless you for fighting for the people of Florida," Crist told legislators. "I hear some groans from insurance lobbyists? Tough. That's right. We work for the people, not them."[b]

But Crist didn't get everything he asked for. Legislators killed an amendment giving him the power to appoint Citizens's director. Also rejected was a proposal that would have allowed the agency to write policies for auto, theft, and fire insurance that would have made it better able to amass greater financial reserves and offer lower premiums.

[a] Paige St. John, "Crist Still Pushing for Property-insurance Legislation," *Tallahassee Democrat.* www.tallahassee.com/apps/pbcs.dll/article?AID=2007705030346.

[b] S. V. Date, "Sessions End More Like Recess Than Finale," Palm Beach Post.com. www.palmbeachpost.com/state/content/state/epaper/2007/05/05/m1a_XGR_session_0505.html.

wield informal powers—the ability to leverage the power and prestige of the office into real influence in a way that may not be replicated by successors. Governors may be personally popular, have a special gift for working with legislators, or have some other skills that help them do their jobs well but that are not based on any authority granted by the state. They can "exert leadership," as onetime South Carolina governor Richard Riley put it, using informal powers "such as negotiations, public relations and strategizing."[28]

Popular Support. One thing that will always help a governor is popular support. A governor who wins with 51 percent of the vote has all of the same formal powers as a governor who wins with 73 percent, but the more popular governor is clearly going to have an edge. Legislators and other officials will accept more readily the need to go along with a popular governor's program because they believe that program is what most voters in the state want. This is especially true if the governor had strong support for election in their districts. "I think if a governor has strong popularity ratings, he's got a bigger **bully pulpit,**" said former Ohio governor Bob Taft. "If a governor is strong and popular, whether or not he's going to use the electoral power that gives him, legislators still think that he might use that either for or against them in their reelection."[29]

It is a long time between gubernatorial elections—four years in most cases—so to maintain and build on their popularity governors do all sorts of public relations work. They never fail to alert the press to all their good deeds, they constantly travel their states to appear in any number of forums—TV shows, groundbreakings, dedications, state fairs, church socials—where they can impress the public, and they propose legislation that they believe will be popular. The fortunes of governors rise and fall with the health of the economy of their states, but individual governors can make themselves more or less popular depending on how well they appear to address the problems of the day.

Bully Pulpit

The platform from which a high-profile public official, such as governor or president, commands considerable public and media attention by virtue of holding office.

Party Support in the Legislature. Having members of their own party dominate the legislature certainly helps governors get their agendas passed. Governors can be successful if the other party controls the legislature, but it is a lot tougher. The reasons are fairly obvious. Republican legislators want to see a Republican governor succeed, and the same holds true, obviously, for Democratic legislators serving under Democratic governors. Voters perceive politicians who belong to the same party as being part of the same team. Therefore, the political fortunes of these politicians will be tied together during the next election. Members of the same party are likely to hold similar positions on such issues as taxes, levels of social service spending, and the environment.

Governors are more likely to grant favors to legislators of their own party or raise money for them. This, in turn, makes those legislators more likely to support the governors' programs. Some governors curry favor with legislators because they used to be legislators themselves and still have friends in the house or senate. One-time Tennessee governor Ned McWherter, for example, was a longtime legislator before taking the top office. As governor, he concentrated his attention on a few pet initiatives, such as a major overhaul of the state Medicaid system, and went along with whatever his pals in the legislature were thinking on most other matters.

More typically, "each party attempts to strengthen the institution it commands and to weaken the institution controlled by the opposition," notes one political scientist.[30] In other words, a Republican holding the governorship will try to make that office more powerful at the expense of a Democratic legislature and vice versa. When power is shared under divided government, however, the two parties cannot just attack each other's programs. If they share power, they also share responsibility in the eyes of the voters, and so they have to work together to forge compromises on central issues such as the budget. Following the elections in 2012, however, fewer states had divided government. Power in both legislative chambers and the governorship was held by the same party in all but a dozen states.

Ability to Communicate. We have already touched on the advantage governors have over

TABLE 8-2

Ranking of the Institutional Powers of Governors, 2010

State	Separately Elected Executive Branch Officials	Tenure Potential	Appointment Powers	Budgetary Powers	Veto Powers	Party Control	Total Score	Rank
Massachusetts	4	5	3	5	4	5	26	1
Alaska	2.5	4	3.5	5	2.5	3.5	21	2
Maryland	4	4	3	5	4	5	25	2
New Jersey	5	4	4	4	5	2	24	2
New York	4	5	3	2	5	3	22	2
West Virginia	2	4	3	5	2.5	4	20.5	2
Utah	4	5	3	2	2.5	5	21.5	7
Colorado	4	4	3	2	2.5	3	18.5	8
North Dakota	3	5	3.5	5	2.5	4	23	8
Illinois	4	5	3.5	2	5	4	23.5	10
Iowa	3	5	3.5	2	2.5	3	19	10
Nebraska	4	4	3	2	2.5	3	18.5	10
Pennsylvania	4	4	3	5	2.5	2	20.5	10
Tennessee	2	4	4.5	2	2	4	16.5	10
New Mexico	4	4	3.5	5	2.5	2	21	15
Arkansas	2	4	2	2	2	4	16	16
Connecticut	4	5	3	2	2.5	4	20.5	16
Florida	3	4	3	2	2.5	4	18.5	16
Maine	5	4	3	2	2	3.5	20	16
Michigan	4	4	3	4	4	4	23	16
Minnesota	4	5	3.5	2	2	4	20.5	16
Missouri	2	4	2.5	4	2.5	2	17	16
Ohio	4	4	3	5	2.5	4	22.5	16
Washington	1	5	4	5	5	4	24	16
Delaware	2	4	3	4	5	4	22	25
Montana	3	4	3	5	2.5	2	19.5	25
Oregon	1.5	4	2	2	2.5	3	15	25
Wisconsin	3	5	1.5	4	2.5	4	20	25
Arizona	2	4	2.5	4	2.5	4	20	29
Hawaii	5	4	2.5	2	5	5	23.5	29
Louisiana	2	4	4	2	2	3	17	29
California	1	4	2	4	2.5	4	17.5	32
Georgia	1	4	1.5	5	2.5	4	18	32

(Continued)

TABLE 8-2 (Continued)

State	Separately Elected Executive Branch Officials	Tenure Potential	Appointment Powers	Budgetary Powers	Veto Powers	Party Control	Total Score	Rank
Idaho	1	5	2	1	2.5	5	16.5	32
Kansas	3	4	2.5	5	2.5	4	21	32
Kentucky	2.5	4	3	4	2.5	3	19	32
New Hampshire	5	2	2.5	4	0	3	16.5	32
Texas	2	5	1.5	2	2.5	4	17	32
Virginia	2.5	3	3.5	5	3	3	20	32
Wyoming	2	4	3	2	5	5	21	40
Nevada	2.5	4	2.5	5	0	4	18	41
South Carolina	1	4	2.5	2	2.5	4	16	41
South Dakota	3	4	3	5	3	4.5	22.5	41
Indiana	3	4	3.5	5	0	4	19.5	44
Mississippi	3	4	2	5	5	3	22	44
North Carolina	3	4	2.5	2	1.5	2	15	44
Alabama	1.5	4	2.5	4	4	4	20	47
Oklahoma	1	4	1.5	2	2	4	14.5	47
Rhode Island	4	4	3	2	0	1	14	49
Vermont	2	2	2.5	5	0	4	15.5	50

Source: Thad Beyle and Margaret Ferguson, "Governors and the Executive Branch," in *Politics in the American States*, 10th edition, eds. Virginia Gray and Russell L. Hanson. (Washington, D.C.: CQ Press, 2012).

Separately Elected Executive Branch Officials: 5 = only governor or governor/lieutenant governor team elected; 4.5 = governor or governor/lieutenant governor team, with one other elected official; 4 = governor/lieutenant governor team with some process officials (attorney general, secretary of state, treasurer, auditor) elected; 3 = governor/lieutenant governor team with process officials, and some major and minor policy officials elected; 2.5 = governor (no team) with six or fewer officials elected, but none are major policy officials; 2 = governor (no team) with six or fewer officials elected, including one major policy official; 1.5 = governor (no team) with six or fewer officials elected, but two are major policy officials; 1 = governor (no team) with seven or more process and several major policy officials elected. **Source:** *The Book of the States 2007* (Lexington, KY: Council of State Governments, 2007).

Tenure Potential: 5 = 4-year term, no restraint on reelection; 4. 5 = 4-year term, only three terms permitted; 4 = 4-year term, only two terms permitted; 3 = 4-year term, no consecutive election permitted; 2 = 2-year term, no restraint on reelection; 1 = 2-year term, only two terms permitted. **Source:** *The Book of the States 2007* (Lexington, KY: Council of State Governments, 2007).

Appointment Powers: In six major functional areas, including corrections, K–12 education, health, highways/transportation, public utilities regulation, and welfare. The six individual office scores are totaled and then averaged and rounded to the nearest 0.5 for the state score. 5 = governor appoints, no other approval needed; 4 = governor appoints, a board, council, or legislature approves; 3 = someone else appoints, governor approves or shares appointment; 2 = someone else appoints, governor and others approve;

1 = someone else appoints, no approval or confirmation needed. **Source:** *The Book of the States 2007* (Lexington, KY: Council of State Governments, 2007).

Budgetary Power: 5 = governor has full responsibility, legislature may not increase executive budget; 4 = governor has full responsibility, legislature can increase by special majority vote or subject to item veto; 3 = governor has full responsibility, legislature has unlimited power to change executive budget; 2 = governor shares responsibility, legislature has unlimited power to change executive budget; 1 = governor shares responsibility with other elected official, legislature has unlimited power to change executive budget. **Sources:** *The Book of the States 2007* (Lexington, KY: Council of State Governments, 2007); National Conference of State Legislatures, "Limits on Authority of Legislature to Change Budget" (1998).

Veto Power: 5 = governor has item veto and a special majority vote of the legislature is needed to override a veto (three-fifths of legislators elected or two-thirds of legislators present); 4 = has item veto with a majority of the legislators elected needed to override; 3 = has item veto with only a majority of the legislators present needed to override; 2 = no item veto, with a special legislative majority needed to override a regular veto; 1 = no item veto, only a simple legislative majority needed to override a regular veto. **Source:** *The Book of the States 2007* (Lexington, KY: Council of State Governments, 2007).

Party Control: The governor's party—5 = has a substantial majority (75% or more) in both houses of the legislature; 4 = has a simple majority in both houses (under 75%), or a substantial majority in one house and a simple majority in the other; 3 = split control in the legislature or a nonpartisan legislature; 2 = has a simple minority (25% or more) in both houses, or a simple minority in one and a substantial minority (under 25%) in the other; 1 = has a substantial minority in both houses. **Source:** National Conference of State Legislatures Web site.

Score: Total divided by six to keep 5-point scale.

legislators in regard to media exposure. There is no law that says newspapers and TV stations have to pay more attention to pronouncements from the governor—but that is what happens anyway. Pretty much anything legislators say and do takes a backseat. The governor is a single, well-known individual who is important to every voter in the state. A legislator, by contrast, even a powerful one, is just an individual legislator among 120 or 150 legislators and represents a district that makes up only a fraction of the state. Whereas a governor speaks clearly with one voice, Rosenthal notes, a legislature speaks with many—not just because it is made up of many individuals, but also because there are differing points of view between the chambers and between the majority and minority parties.[31] "In any squabble, the governor had a distinct edge over what amounted to a gang of unknowns in the legislature," writes former Vermont House Speaker Ralph Wright.[32]

Governors have to play both an inside game and an outside game. They have to appeal to capital insiders as well as to the public at large. A governor who makes every move based on the ability to turn it into a press release or who appeals to the public by bashing the "corruption" in the capital may score points with the media and the public but soon will have few friends in the legislature. In Illinois, Rod Blagojevich was elected governor thanks to his railing against the corruption of state government, and he did not change his theme song once he took office. He refused even to establish a permanent residence in the state capital of Springfield, instead commuting from his home in Chicago. "We're going to keep fighting to reform and change the system and give the people a government that stops spending their money like a bunch of drunken sailors," he said toward the end of his first year in office.[33] Needless to say, the legislators whom Blagojevich had likened to drunken sailors were not eager to cooperate with him any more than they had to—even though his own party had a majority in both chambers. They continued to feud with him throughout his tenure—one publicly called the governor "insane"

in 2007[34]—and did not hesitate to impeach him in 2009 after federal investigators revealed tapes of phone conversations in which Blagojevich was caught trying to sell President Obama's U.S. Senate seat, which the governor had the power to fill following Obama's ascension to the White House.

Many governors have bashed their state legislatures. What they have found is that, although this made them popular with the public, it did not help them get their agendas passed. That was the lesson Arnold Schwarzenegger learned. When he was first elected governor of California in 2003, Schwarzenegger continually threatened to take his agenda directly to the people through ballot initiatives and referendums if the legislature refused to go along for his ride. Yet even the Man Who Was the Terminator could not convince voters about items he could not get passed in the legislature.

Schwarzenegger, a Republican, was elected in an unusual recall election at the end of 2003. During his first year in office, he showed himself to be a savvy negotiator. He outmaneuvered the Democrats who dominated the legislature, making unusual alliances with various groups to get his way on such major issues as an overhaul of the state workers' compensation insurance law and a series of budget packages. He knew how to use his celebrity to focus attention on a problem, win a victory, and then carry that momentum forward into the next fight.

That was his first year—during his second year, he lost his way. He took to calling Democrats "girlie men" for not supporting his priorities and vowed to take his proposals directly to the public in the form of ballot initiatives. He then ended up doing just that. Schwarzenegger called a special election in 2005 to determine the fate of his proposals to limit state spending and weaken his opponents through changes in redistricting and campaign spending. How did his gamble pay off? Every one of his proposals went down to defeat, and his own approval rating slipped to 38 percent. Early polling in 2006 suggested Schwarzenegger would lose his bid for reelection.

Instead, he staged an amazing comeback. He began cooperating with legislators rather than calling them names. Together, they passed some $40 billion worth of infrastructure projects and a landmark bill to address global warming. Schwarzenegger won a decisive reelection victory. What the actor-turned-politician had learned was that, although as governor he called the tune, he needed other players to join his band if he was going to accomplish anything. "Where he has gotten so much of his recent star power is in his ability to work compromises with the legislature," Mark Baldassare, director of research for the Public Policy Institute of California, said early in 2007. "His popularity is derived from working both sides of the aisle to come to a compromise. That's what he's going to have to do, or he will see his star power diminish."[35]

But governors often enjoy the upper hand in their relations with the legislature. Roy Barnes, who served one term as governor of Georgia from 1999 until 2003, had said during his days in the state legislature, "When you are called down to the governor's office, it is a very impressive office, you're talking to the governor, and you know that he controls things that could be good or ill for your district. He controls grants, he controls roads, and other things."[36] In other words, the formal powers of the governor (the ability to control projects) merge with informal powers (the mystique of the office) to influence legislators and other supplicants.

Becoming Governor and Staying Governor

We have described governors as the most powerful and important political actors in their states. It should come as little surprise, then, given the history of politics in this country, that middle-age white males have dominated the job. Women are being elected to governorships with greater frequency—only three women were elected governor during the nation's first two centuries—but plenty of states have yet to elect a woman for the top job.[37] In 2007, nine women served as governor, the highest number ever to serve at one time. (Their ranks have since been slightly depleted by retirements and presidential

appointments; just five women governors were in office following the 2012 elections.) In 1873, P. B. S. Pinchback, the black lieutenant governor of Louisiana, was elevated to the post of acting governor for forty-three days, but only two African Americans have ever been elected as governor of any state:[38] Douglas Wilder of Virginia held the job during the first half of the 1990s, and Deval Patrick was elected to the office in Massachusetts in 2006. David A. Paterson, who is African American and legally blind, became governor of New York following Eliot Spitzer's 2008 resignation due to a sex scandal. There have been a handful of Hispanic and Asian American governors, including Brian Sandoval of Nevada and Susana Martinez of New Mexico. In 2007, Bobby Jindal of Louisiana became the first Indian American to be elected governor; he was joined by Nikki Haley of South Carolina in 2010.

Many nonpoliticians have been elected governor, including Arnold Schwarzenegger, former wrestler Jesse Ventura of Minnesota, and business executives Mark Warner of Virginia and John Lynch of New Hampshire. Most governors, however, have had a good deal of previous government experience. They have served in the U.S. Congress, the state legislature, or other statewide positions such as lieutenant governor, attorney general, or even state supreme court justice. Throughout the twentieth century, in fact, only about 10 percent of governors had no prior elective experience.[39] Only a handful of independent or third-party candidates have been elected governor in recent years, including Lincoln Chafee of Rhode Island, who had served in the U.S. Senate as a Republican.

One qualification for modern governors is quite clear—they must have the ability to raise money. Gubernatorial campaigns have become multimillion-dollar affairs, particularly in heavily populated states, where television ads are expensive to run because the media markets are competitive and costly. The total cost of the campaigns for the thirty-seven governors' races in 2010 was $1.1 billion—the first time gubernatorial campaign costs exceeded $1 billion. Contributing mightily to that total were two self-funding candidates, both Republicans: Meg Whitman, the former head of eBay, who lost the California governorship despite spending $140 million of her own money; and hospital executive Rick Scott, who became governor of Florida thanks in part to his ability to devote $78 million in personal funds to his own campaign.

Factors Driving Gubernatorial Elections

Like the Winter Olympics, gubernatorial elections in most states have been moved to the second year of the presidential term in what are called off-year elections. Thirty-four states now hold their gubernatorial elections in the off year. Another five states—Virginia, New Jersey, Kentucky, Mississippi, and Louisiana—hold their elections in odd-numbered years. Nine states—Delaware, Indiana, Missouri, Montana, New Hampshire, North Carolina, North Dakota, Utah, and Vermont—hold their elections at the same time as the presidential contest. In addition, New Hampshire and Vermont, the only states that have clung to the old tradition of two-year terms, hold elections for governor every even-numbered year.

The majority of governors are elected in even-numbered off years because states wanted to insulate the contests from getting mixed up in national issues. Many states from the 1960s to the 1980s moved their gubernatorial elections to the presidential midterm because they hoped this would allow voters to concentrate on matters of importance to the states, without having their attention diverted to federal issues brought up in presidential campaigns. This was the desire and the intent, but the plan has not been a 100 percent success. In gubernatorial elections the office of governor is often the biggest thing on the ballot, so voters use these races as a way of expressing their opinions about who is *not* on the ballot. "There is simply no question that the primary motivation was to reduce presidential coattails on the election for governor and to increase the voters' attention on state rather than national issues," says Larry J. Sabato, director of the University of Virginia's Center for Politics. "What changed? Party polarization increased. It is easier to link the president and governor (and Congress and state legislatures) because almost all Democrats now are liberal and almost all Republicans are conservative, at least on critical social, tax, and spending issues."[40]

In 2002 and 2003, when Republican president George W. Bush was generally popular, Republicans did better than had been expected in gubernatorial contests. But as Bush's popularity sank, so did the ranks of Republican governors. Democrats in 2006 regained the majority of governorships for the first time since 1994, holding twenty-eight states, compared with the GOP's twenty-two. Democratic gubernatorial candidates paid the price for Obama's midterm ebb in popularity in 2010, with the GOP that year gaining six governorships. The only governorship to change hands in 2012 was North Carolina's—Republican Pat McCrory won election to succeed an unpopular Democrat. McCrory had

TABLE 8-3

Who's Who among U.S. Governors, 2012

State	Governor	Party	Education (highest degree obtained)	First Elected in[a]	Previous Political Life
Alabama	Robert Bentley	Republican	University of Alabama	2010	Member, Alabama State House of Representatives
Alaska	Sean Parnell	Republican	Seattle University (JD)	—	Lieutenant governor
Arizona	Jan Brewer	Republican	Radiology technician	—	Elected Arizona secretary of state
Arkansas	Mike Beebe	Democrat	University of Arkansas (JD)	2006	State attorney general
California	Jerry Brown	Democrat	Yale University (JD)	1974	California attorney general

(Continued)

TABLE 8-3 (Continued)

State	Governor	Party	Education (highest degree obtained)	First Elected in[a]	Previous Political Life
Colorado	John Hickenlooper	Democrat	Wesleyan University	2010	Mayor of Denver
Connecticut	Dan Malloy	Democrat	Boston College (JD)	2010	Mayor of Stamford
Delaware	Jack Markell	Democrat	University of Chicago (MBA)	2008	State treasurer
Florida	Rick Scott	Republican	Southern Methodist University (JD)	2010	Started at the top as governor; previously a businessman
Georgia	Nathan Deal	Republican	Walter F. George School of Law (JD)	2010	Member, U.S. House of Representatives
Hawaii	Neil Abercrombie	Democrat	University of Hawaii, Mamoa	2010	Member, U.S. House of Representatives
Idaho	C. L. "Butch" Otter	Republican	College of Idaho	2006	Member, U.S. House of Representatives
Illinois	Pat Quinn	Democrat	Northwestern University (JD)	—	Lieutenant governor
Indiana	Mitch Daniels	Republican	Georgetown University (JD)	2004	Chief of staff, Richard Lugar
Iowa	Terry Branstad	Republican	University of Iowa	1982	Member, Iowa House of Representatives
Kansas	Sam Brownback	Republican	Kansas State University	2010	Member, U.S. Senate
Kentucky	Steve Beshear	Democrat	University of Kentucky (JD)	2007	Lieutenant governor
Louisiana	Bobby Jindal	Republican	Brown University (also Rhodes scholar at Oxford University)	2007	Member, U.S. House of Representatives
Maine	Paul LePage	Republican	University of Maine	2010	Mayor of Waterville
Maryland	Martin O'Malley	Democrat	University of Maryland (JD)	2006	State field director for Barbara Mikulski's 1986 campaign
Massachusetts	Deval Patrick	Democrat	Harvard University (JD)	2006	Appointed assistant attorney general for civil rights by Bill Clinton
Michigan	Rick Snyder	Republican	University of Michigan (JD)	2010	Chair of the Michigan Economic Corporation
Minnesota	Mark Dayton	Democrat	Yale University	2010	Member, U.S. Senate
Mississippi	Phil Bryant	Republican	Mississippi College	2011	Lieutenant governor
Missouri	Jay Nixon	Democrat	University of Missouri (JD)	2008	Missouri attorney general
Montana	Brian Schweitzer	Democrat	Montana State University (MS)	2004	Appointed to the USDA Farm Service Agency Committee
Nebraska	Dave Heineman	Republican	U.S. Military Academy	2005	Lieutenant governor
Nevada	Brian Sandoval	Republican	Ohio State University	2010	District judge for the District of Nevada

State	Governor	Party	Education (highest degree obtained)	First Elected in[a]	Previous Political Life
New Hampshire	John Lynch	Democrat	Georgetown University (JD); Harvard University (MBA)	2004	Appointed to the New Hampshire University System Board of Trustees, then chair
New Jersey	Chris Christie	Republican	Seton Hall University (JD)	2009	U.S. attorney for New Jersey
New Mexico	Susana Martinez	Republican	University of Oklahoma (JD)	2010	Elected district attorney
New York	Andrew Cuomo	Democrat	Albany Law School (JD)	2010	New York attorney general
North Carolina	Bev Perdue	Democrat	University of Florida (EdD)	2008	Lieutenant governor
North Dakota	Jack Dalrymple	Republican	Yale University	—	Lieutenant governor
Ohio	John Kasich	Republican	Ohio State University	2010	Member, U.S. House of Representatives
Oklahoma	Mary Fallin	Republican	University of Oklahoma	2010	Member, U.S. House of Representatives
Oregon	John Kitzhaber	Democrat	University of Oregon Medical School	1994	President, Oregon State Senate
Pennsylvania	Tom Corbett	Republican	St. Mary's University School of Law (JD)	2010	Pennsylvania attorney general
Rhode Island	Lincoln Chafee	Independent	Brown University	2010	Member, U.S. Senate
South Carolina	Nikki Haley	Republican	Clemson University	2010	Member, South Carolina House of Representative
South Dakota	Dennis Daugaard	Republican	Northwestern University (JD)	2010	Lieutenant governor
Tennessee	Bill Haslam	Republican	Emory University	2010	Mayor of Knoxville
Texas	Rick Perry	Republican	Texas A&M University	2000	Member, Texas House of Representatives
Utah	Gary Herbert	Republican	Brigham Young University (no degree)	—	Lieutenant governor
Vermont	Peter Shumlin	Democrat	Wesleyan University	2010	Member, Vermont House of Representatives
Virginia	Bob McDonnell	Republican	Regent University (JD)	2009	State attorney general
Washington	Chris Gregoire	Democrat	Gonzaga University (JD)	2004	Elected state attorney general
West Virginia	Earl Ray Tomblin	Democrat	University of Charleston	—	President, West Virginia Senate
Wisconsin	Scott Walker	Republican	Marquette University	2010	County executive of Milwaukee
Wyoming	Matthew Mead	Republican	University of Wyoming College of Law (JD)	2010	U.S. attorney for Wyoming

Source: National Governors Association, "Governors of the American States, Commonwealths and Territories, 2012," www.nga.org/files/live/sites/NGA/home/governors/current-governors/col2-content/list---governors-links/book-of-governors-biographies%40/BIOBOOK.PDF.

a. Those individuals with no dates shown in this column (—) were not elected to the governorship when they first took that office; rather, each was elevated to the position after the elected governor left office for some reason.

lost his bid for the office four years earlier and had jokingly blamed his loss on Obama to the president's face during a White House meeting in 2009, attributing his narrow loss to the Democrats' voter turnout efforts.

Overall, however, gubernatorial races are still less prone to following national trends than, say, elections for the U.S. Senate. The reason? Voters understand that the governor's position is important in and of itself. They consider state-level issues carefully when choosing a governor. The dominant concern in most gubernatorial contests is the state economy. Even the most powerful politicians have only limited control over the economy at best, but voters tend to reward or punish the incumbent party based on the state's economic performance. If a state is faring poorly or doing considerably worse than its neighbors, the incumbent party is likely to struggle.

Voters more often use party as a guide in lower-profile contests, such as state legislative races, but are better informed about individual gubernatorial candidates. One reason is the greater news coverage of the races. Another important factor is the amount of money that candidates for governor spend to publicize themselves. Candidates create extensive organizations that promote their campaigns and use all the modern techniques of political consultants, polling, and media buys. Voters are far more likely, even in less populous states, to get to know the candidates through TV ads and brochures than through speeches or other personal appearances. As noted above, gubernatorial elections are now a billion-dollar business, with individual races sometimes costing in excess of $100 million. Candidates and outside groups spent more than $80 million in the unsuccessful recall election of Wisconsin Republican Scott Walker in 2012 (roughly $14 for every man, woman, and child in Wisconsin.), more than doubling the previous gubernatorial record in that state.[41]

Keeping and Leaving Office

Despite all of the potential for upsets, the office of governor is a pretty stable one these days. States used to change governors just about every chance they got, but that is no longer the case. According to political scientist Thad Beyle, states changed governors on average more than two times each during the 1950s. By the 1980s, however, turnover occurred on average just over once a decade. During the 1990s, the rate climbed back up a bit, so that the average state changed governors 1.4 times.

It is not unusual to see governors get reelected by vote margins that top 70 percent. Not only are governors in charge of setting policy, but they also actually get things done. They educate children, build roads, and respond with help when miners get trapped. They also are much less likely than legislators to concern themselves directly with

contentious social issues, such as gun owners' rights and gay marriage. In reviewing two years' worth of state of the state addresses, in which governors typically lay out their priorities for the year, political scientists Thad Kousser and Justin H. Phillips found that governors talked a lot about education and the economy but barely mentioned social issues—making just 15 proposals on such issues out of a total of 1,088.[42]

Translation? Governors generally are viewed more favorably than legislators. From a constituent's standpoint, what do legislators do, after all, except vote?—and their votes tend to be highly partisan. Governors, on the other hand, have to compromise because of the number of people they must deal with. Of course, there are governors who are polarizing figures, but in the main governors are less contentious figures than state legislators or members of Congress.

Governors are rarely booted out of office prematurely. In June 2004, Connecticut governor John Rowland resigned after being investigated by the legislature for accepting gifts from a contractor with business before the state. Faced with possible **impeachment** and a federal criminal investigation, Rowland, one of the nation's longest-serving governors at the time, chose to step down. Rod

---

Impeachment
A process by which the legislature can remove executive branch officials, such as the governor, or judges from office for corruption or other reasons.

Blagojevich, the disgraced Illinois governor caught by the FBI on tape plotting to sell the appointment to President Obama's old Senate seat, continued to insist on his innocence even after he was impeached in 2009, but he was convicted in 2011 and sentenced to fourteen years in prison. In 2003, Gray Davis of California was the first governor forced to leave office by a **recall election** since Lynn Frazier of North Dakota was booted out more than eighty years earlier on charges of corruption. Voters felt that Davis had dug the state into such a deep hole financially that it would take years to recover. His liberal views on such issues as gay marriage also had stirred up controversy. Arnold Schwarzenegger won the special election held on the same day as Davis's recall.

Wisconsin's Scott Walker in 2012 became the first governor to survive a recall election. He had angered labor unions and Democrats by pushing through legislation a year earlier that eliminated collective bargaining rights for most public-sector workers. The unions and their allies had no difficulty gathering more than a million signatures calling for his recall, which in Wisconsin amounts to a "do-over" election—Walker had to run for office again in midterm. He was able to beat back a repeat challenge by his 2010 opponent, Milwaukee mayor Tom Barrett, in part because he was able to amass enormous sums for the campaign and in part because even some Democrats felt it would be wrong to remove a governor in the middle of his term over a policy dispute, as opposed to a personal failing such as corruption or gross incompetence.

Arizona governor Evan Mecham was impeached and convicted in 1987 for impeding an investigation and lending state money to a car dealership that he owned. The most recent previous conviction dates back to 1929, when Henry Johnston of Oklahoma was removed for general incompetence by a legislature with possible political motives. A few governors, including Fife Symington of Arizona (1997), Jim Guy Tucker of Arkansas (1996), and Guy Hunt of Alabama (1993), have resigned following criminal convictions. More recently, two governors have resigned amid sex scandals: Eliot Spitzer of New York (2008) and Jim McGreevey of New Jersey (2004).

A more common threat to gubernatorial staying power is term limits. Governors in thirty-six states are limited to either two terms or two consecutive terms in office. The governor of Utah can spend no more than three terms in office. The only two states that have two-year terms instead of four-year terms—Vermont and New Hampshire—place no limits on the number of terms a governor may serve. Howard Dean served five full terms as governor of Vermont before running for president in 2004.

> A more common threat to gubernatorial staying power is term limits. Governors in thirty-six states are limited to two terms or two consecutive terms in office.

So what do governors do once they leave office? Several of them, like Dean, run for higher offices, such as the presidency or a Senate seat. Four out of the last five presidents prior to Barack Obama, in fact, were governors before winning the White House (see the box "A Difference That Makes a Difference: From State House to White House: Translating a Governorship into a Presidency"). Governors also regularly run for the U.S. Senate. A dozen senators and one representative serving in 2010 previously had been governors.

Entering the Senate or serving as a cabinet official generally is considered a step up the professional ladder from being a governor. Many politicians, however, find that being governor—able to make and implement decisions, with a large staff and all the machinery of state government at their disposal—is the best job they'll ever have. Dirk Kempthorne, who gave up a Senate seat to run for governor of Idaho in 1998, said that many of his colleagues regretted having to give up governorships to come to Washington and be just one more legislative voice among many. "They all said that being governor is the best job in the world," Kempthorne said on taking office. "I'm ready to find out."[43]

Recall Election
A special election allowing voters to remove an elected official from office before the end of his or her term.

TABLE 8-4

Recall Rules

State	Grounds for Recall	Specific Signature Requirement	Petition Circulation Time	Election for Successor
Alaska	Yes	25%	Not specified	Successor appointed
Arizona	No	25%	120 days	Simultaneous (5)
California	No	12%	160 days	Simultaneous (6)
Colorado	No	25%	60 days	Simultaneous (6)
Georgia	Yes	15% (1)	90 days	Separate special
Idaho	No	20% (1)	60 days	Successor appointed
Kansas	Yes	40%	90 days	Successor appointed
Louisiana	No	33.3% (1)	180 days	Separate special
Michigan	No	25%	90 days	Separate special
Minnesota	Yes	25%	90 days	Separate special
Montana	Yes	10% (1)	3 months	Separate special
Nevada	No	25%	60 days	Simultaneous (5)
New Jersey	No	25% (2)	320 days (4)	Separate special
North Dakota	No	25%	Not specified	Simultaneous (5)
Oregon	No	15% (3)	90 days	Separate special
Rhode Island	Yes	15%	90 days	Separate special
Washington	Yes	25%	270 days	Successor appointed
Wisconsin	No	25%	60 days	Simultaneous (5)

Source: Adapted from the National Conference of State Legislatures and Alan Greenblatt, "Recall Rules," in "Total Recall," *Governing*, September 2003, 26.

Note: Signature requirement is percentage of votes cast in last election for official being recalled. Exceptions: (1) percentage of eligible voters at time of last election; (2) percentage of registered voters in electoral district of official sought to be recalled; (3) percentage of total votes cast in officer's district for all candidates for governor in last election; (4) applies to governor or U.S. senator; all others 160 days; (5) recall ballot consists of a list of candidates for the office held by the person against whom the recall petition was filed; the name of the officer against whom the recall was filed may appear on the list; and (6) recall ballot consists of two parts: the first asks whether the officer against whom the recall petition was filed should be recalled, and the second lists candidates who have qualified for the election; the name of the officer against whom the recall was filed may not appear on this list.

Many former governors in other positions complain that they never had it so good as back when they were running their states. "My worst day as governor was better than my best day as a United States senator," Thomas Carper, D-Del., said in 2009.[44] Wisconsin's Tommy Thompson openly lamented the second-guessing to which he was subjected as President George W. Bush's secretary of health and human services during a 2006 appearance before the National Governors Association, an organization he had once chaired. "When you're a Governor, you can wake up in the morning and you can have an idea and you can have somebody working on it by 11 o'clock in the morning," Thompson said. "When you go to Washington . . . I get up, get the same idea, go in. Then you have to vet it with 67,000 people who all believe sincerely they're smarter than you."[45]

An unusual number of governors sought to win back their old jobs in 2010, including Terry Branstad, who had previously served four terms as governor of Iowa during the 1980s and 1990s. He won, as did two other comeback governors on the West Coast, Jerry Brown of California and John Kitzhaber of Oregon. But Maryland's Bob Ehrlich and Georgia's Roy Barnes both lost their return runs that year.

Other Executive Offices

Only the president is elected to the executive branch of the federal government. The vice president is the president's running mate and is elected as part of a package deal. The heads of all the cabinet departments—Defense, Transportation, Energy, Agriculture, and so on—are appointed by the president, subject to Senate approval. Voters do not get to say who gets in and who stays out.

Things work differently at the state level. The governor is the only statewide official elected in every state. Most states, however, also have several other statewide officials elected in their own right. This is a holdover from earlier times when the governor was not invested with much power and authority was distributed among a number of officeholders. Texas still has two dozen officials who are elected statewide, whereas New Jersey for many years elected only the governor. (That changed in 2009, when Garden State voters elected a lieutenant governor for the first time.) Most states have handfuls of officials elected statewide; we outline the responsibilities of a few of them below.

Lieutenant Governor

The office of lieutenant governor traditionally has been seen as something of a joke. Lieutenant governors, it's been said, have nothing to do but wait for their governors to resign or die so that they can accrue some real power. That situation has changed in just the past few years. Some states, such as Georgia and Virginia, responded to budget shortfalls of recent years by slashing the budgets and limiting the powers of their lieutenant governors' offices. More states, however, have expanded the purview of the office,

recognizing that the security demands created by the terrorist attacks of 2001 mean that there is plenty of work to go around and the skills of the second in command should be used more fully.

In Nebraska, for example, Governor Mike Johanns appointed Lieutenant Governor Dave Heineman to head all of the state's homeland security efforts immediately after the September 11, 2001, terrorist attacks. Minnesota lieutenant governor Carol Molnau was given charge of the state's department of transportation after her election in 2002 and saved the state the $108,000-a-year expense of hiring a separate transportation secretary. Similarly, right after the 2003 election, Kentucky's new lieutenant governor, Stephen Pence, was named secretary of the department of justice, which put him in charge of public safety, corrections and law enforcement, the state police, and vehicle enforcement. Today, "it's rare that the lieutenant governor doesn't have some specific duties," says Julia Hurst, director of the National Lieutenant Governors Association.[46]

In each of the cases just cited, power was granted to the lieutenant governor because of the desire of the governor. The next person to hold the office may have very different responsibilities or nothing to do at all. In many states, however, the lieutenant governor's responsibilities are laid out by law. In Indiana, for example, the lieutenant governor's portfolio includes the departments of commerce and agriculture. In half the states, the lieutenant governor presides over the state senate, having varying degrees of authority in that chamber from state to state. In Texas and Mississippi, lieutenant governors play much more than a ceremonial role. Not only do they preside over the senate, but they also set the agenda and appoint senators to committees. In both states, the lieutenant governor often is referred to as the most powerful figure in the state, with authority in both the executive and legislative branches.

Twenty-five states elect their governors and lieutenant governors as part of the same ticket. (New Jersey opted for this model after two recent governors left office prematurely. As noted above, the state elected its first lieutenant governor in 2009.) In eighteen other states, the two are elected

A Difference
That Makes A Difference

From State House to White House: Translating a Governorship into a Presidency

How big of an advantage is it to run for the presidency as a sitting governor as opposed to holding some other position? For more than a quarter century prior to Barack Obama's election in 2008, it looked like it was about as big as they come.

Four of the previous five presidents had been governors: Jimmy Carter, Ronald Reagan, Bill Clinton, and George W. Bush. The one exception was George W. Bush's father, George H. W. Bush, who came to the Oval Office after serving as Reagan's vice president. Seventeen presidents in all had served earlier as governors.

Lately, though, governors have had bad luck. Former Massachusetts governor Mitt Romney lost to Obama in 2012, after having beaten Texas governor Rick Perry and former Minnesota governor Tim Pawlenty, among other opponents, in the GOP primaries.

Obama's first race had been dominated by senators, including John McCain, Hillary Rodham Clinton, and Obama himself. (Obama had served four years in the U.S. Senate when he was first elected, after having spent eight years in the Illinois Senate.) They outpolled a large number of gubernatorial contenders that included Romney, Bill Richardson of New Mexico, Mike Huckabee of Arkansas, and Mark Warner of Virginia. Sarah Palin was serving as governor of Alaska when McCain picked her as his running mate (she resigned her post in Juneau the following year).

But if their recent track record isn't so great, compare governors to holders of other offices. No sitting U.S. senator before Obama had been elected president since John F. Kennedy in 1960. No member of the U.S. House has been elected since James Garfield, all the way back in 1880.

What makes governors such attractive candidates for the nation's most powerful office? And what makes legislators usually so *un*attractive?

For one thing, governors are the only politicians aside from presidents who have run governments that are anywhere near as complicated as the federal government. True, governors do not formulate foreign policy, but they do have to become experts in running departments that cover everything from taxes and education to public health and public safety. Governors have to run things. Members of Congress just vote. "Because the presidency is no place to begin to develop executive talents, the executive careerist clearly is preferable to the legislator," writes political scientist Larry J. Sabato.[a]

Furthermore, a legislator has to vote yes or no on thousands of issues, leaving a long paper trail. This trail

---

separately. The other six states—Arizona, Maine, New Hampshire, Oregon, Tennessee, and Wyoming—don't elect lieutenant governors, although in Tennessee the Speaker of the Senate is given the title. Electing the governor and lieutenant governor separately can be a source of mischief, especially if the people elected are not from the same party. The lieutenant governor often assumes the powers of the governor when the boss is out of the state. During the 1970s, Republican Mike Curb of California had a lot of fun appointing judges and issuing **executive orders** while Democratic governor Jerry Brown was busy out of the state doing, among other things, his own presidential campaigning.

Attorney General

Perhaps the statewide office that has undergone the greatest transformation in recent years is

---

Executive Orders
Rules or regulations with the force of law that governors can create directly under the statutory authority given them.

is bound to contain more controversial elements than any governor's list of bridges built and budgets balanced. Opponents often distort legislators' records in smear campaigns that make use of attack ads and mudslinging. A vote for a $300 billion bill can become defined by one tiny provision it contained.

Also, Congress is a major part of "official" Washington, and senators and representatives can hardly say they have no connection with what occurs there. Conversely, governors running for the White House can always claim they are Washington "outsiders" who are going to sweep in and clean up the town. Former governor-turned-president Bill Clinton reportedly advised then senator Joseph Biden, D-Del., that senators had to overcome big handicaps to run for president. Not only did they have their records to explain, but they also had forgotten how to speak the language of the average person. "When you get to Washington, the only people you talk to are the elites: elites in the press, elites among the lobbyists, elites that you hire on your own staff," Clinton told Biden. "You're not regularly talking to ordinary, everyday people."[b] Biden didn't listen to Clinton, launching his second bid for the presidency in 2008 and ultimately being elected at Obama's side as vice president. But, then, neither did Clinton's wife, who served as Obama's first secretary of state after losing to him in the 2008 primaries.

Still, the out-of-touch image of Congress and Washington in the public mind hampers members of Congress who seek national office. "It could probably be shown by facts and figures that there is no distinctly native American criminal class except Congress," Mark Twain wrote in his 1897 book *Following the Equator*. Governors running for national office invariably present themselves as fresh alternatives to the tired habits of Washington, promising to change the culture and tone of the nation's capital.

That they fail to do so is almost a given. That opens up the field for the next fresh face from the state of California or Arkansas or Texas. Within hours of Obama's reelection, attention turned to governors as potential candidates in 2016—among Republicans and Democrats alike.

---

[a]Larry J. Sabato, *Goodbye to Good-Time Charlie: The American Governorship Transformed*, 2nd ed. (Washington, DC: CQ Press, 1983), 33.

[b]Quoted in E. J. Dionne Jr., "Govs 4, Senators 0. Tough Odds," *Washington Post*, January 4, 2004, E4.

that of attorney general. Always referred to as the top law enforcement officer in the state, the attorney general sometimes has had duties that have been quite minimal because most criminal prosecutions are taken care of at the county level. But attorneys general have become major political players, finding new power by banding together in multistate consumer protection cases against Microsoft, financial firms, toy manufacturers, drug companies, and the shoe manufacturers Reebok and Keds, among many other examples.

The granddaddy of all such cases was the series of lawsuits filed against the tobacco companies during the mid-1990s. The attorneys general argued that the cigarette makers had engaged in fraud and caused a great deal of sickness and health conditions that the states had ended up paying to treat through Medicaid and other programs. An initial agreement reached between the states and the industry was not ratified by Congress. Instead, in 1998 the attorneys general settled their lawsuits with the companies on their own. The

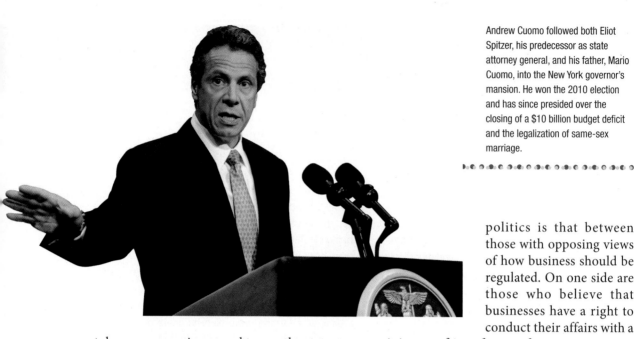

Andrew Cuomo followed both Eliot Spitzer, his predecessor as state attorney general, and his father, Mario Cuomo, into the New York governor's mansion. He won the 2010 election and has since presided over the closing of a $10 billion budget deficit and the legalization of same-sex marriage.

tobacco companies agreed to pay the states an estimated $246 billion over twenty-five years. More recently, state attorneys general in 2012 reached a $25 billion settlement with home mortgage servicers—the largest joint federal-state settlement in history. Beginning in 2007, New York State attorney general Andrew Cuomo won $13 million in settlements from lenders and universities that had violated state laws with their student loan policies. One of the first things Cuomo did after taking office as governor in 2011 was to use the money to set up a national student loan center that would offer "unbiased" financial advice to students and their parents.

Not surprisingly, there has been a backlash against these newly powerful officials. In part, this has been based on the fact that for many attorneys general the job has been a successful launching pad toward the governorship. In 2010, nine former attorneys general were serving as governors, with about as many seeking the office in elections that year. "It seems to be considered the second most prominent and important position to governor," said veteran Arkansas newspaper columnist John Brummett. "The other statewide offices are mostly clerical and pointless."[47]

But the fight over control of the office of attorney general has largely been ideological. One of the great philosophical divides in U.S. politics is that between those with opposing views of how business should be regulated. On one side are those who believe that businesses have a right to conduct their affairs with a minimum of interference from state governments, which can only hinder their productivity and profits. On the other are those who believe just as strongly that conducting business in a state is a privilege that comes with a number of responsibilities that the state has the duty to enforce. The majority of state attorneys general over the past few years have acted as if they were members of the "privilege" camp, and that has fueled the rise of groups designed to combat what the business sector sees as excessive regulatory activism.

Attorneys general have traditionally been Democrats, their campaigns funded by trial lawyers. In recent years, the U.S. Chamber of Commerce and many other business groups have spent millions trying to defeat "activist" attorney general candidates. "Historically . . . attorney general races were off most business people's radar screens," says Bob LaBrant of the Michigan Chamber of Commerce. Today, "there's greater incentive to get involved in an attorney general race because of the increased involvement of attorneys general across the country in litigation against the business community."[48] The Republican Attorneys General Association was founded in 1999 to elect candidates who believe that their colleagues have gone too far in pursuit of business regulations and the revenues such cases can generate. Their strategy

TABLE 8-5

The Powers of the Offices

In Many States, Lieutenant Governors . . .	Secretaries of State . . .	Attorneys General . . .
Preside over the senate	File and/or archive state records and regulations, other corporate documents	Institute civil suits
Appoint committees	Administer uniform commercial code provisions	Represent state agencies and defend and/or challenge the constitutionality of legislative or administrative actions
Break roll-call ties	Publish state manual or directory, session laws, state constitution, statutes, and/or administrative rules and regulations	Enforce open meetings and records laws
Assign bills	Open legislative sessions	Revoke corporate charters
May be assigned special duties by governors	Enroll and/or retain copies of bills	Enforce antitrust prohibitions against monopolistic enterprises
Serve as cabinet members or members of advisory bodies	Register lobbyists	Enforce air pollution, water pollution, and hazardous waste laws in a majority of states
Serve as acting governors when the governors are out of state		Handle criminal appeals and serious statewide criminal prosecutions • Intervene in public utility rate cases • Enforce the provisions of charitable trusts

Sources: Compiled from the National Lieutenant Governors Association, www.nlga.us/Members.htm; *The Book of the States 2003* (Lexington, KY: Council of State Governments, 2003), 215, 221, and 224; and the National Association of Attorneys General, www.naag.org/ag/duties.php.

appears to have worked—the number of GOP attorneys general climbed from twelve in 1999 to twenty by 2003; as of 2012, the two major parties each could boast of twenty-five attorneys general.

When any institution of government extends its power, there is the likelihood of a counterreaction by some other part of government or by the media or other private-sector forces—and the main battleground is always the ballot box. Voters elect those candidates they feel will get the most done for them and for the state.

Other Offices

Every state elects its governor, and most states elect a lieutenant governor and attorney general. In terms of which other offices are held by

elected officials—as opposed to officials appointed by the governor or by boards and commissions—the states vary widely. The theory behind electing many officials directly is that it gives the public a greater voice in shaping a variety of state programs, instead of just selecting a governor and leaving it all up to him or her.

In 2003, New Mexico governor Bill Richardson convinced voters to approve a referendum that gave him the power to name the state's top education official directly. Richardson knew he would receive the credit or blame for running the schools anyway, so he wanted to have the power to shape policy in that office by being the boss of the person who ran it.

Only a few states, including Georgia, Montana, and Oregon, elect a state superintendent of education. In Nebraska, a state board of education is elected and the board in turn selects a superintendent. Several states, mostly in the South, directly elect a secretary of agriculture. An increasing number of states allow citizens to vote for an insurance commissioner. Most states elect a secretary of state who, in turn, regulates elections in those states. Overall, many states structure their executive branches similarly—if there isn't an elected agriculture secretary, there is certain to be an appointed one.

Some believe, however, that electing separate department heads makes too much of government political. A state treasurer who has to worry about getting reelected might not make politically unpopular but fiscally necessary decisions to make sure that the state's books are balanced. The other trouble with electing officials is that the departments they head will squabble over money and power instead of working together as part of a team to promote the greater good.

Election officials themselves have become controversial in some cases. Secretaries of state often oversee elections, and some have been accused of partisan bias in this role. Colorado secretary of state Scott Gessler came to his job after a career as one of the GOP's top campaign lawyers in the state. He was accused by Democrats of retaining a partisan bias in office, notably in participating in a fund-raiser to pay off a campaign fine levied by his office. He was sued no fewer than eight times during his first year in office.[49] Similarly, Democrats in other states complained that GOP secretaries of state favored their parties by making changes to early-voting rules and implementing voter identification laws that they claimed were meant to suppress voting by those likely to vote Democratic. Kris Kobach had served as chair of the Kansas Republican Party before becoming secretary of state and sponsoring that state's voter ID law. "He's doing a better job as Republican state chair as secretary of state than he did when he was the Republican state chair," complained Democratic state representative Ann Mah.[50]

Secretaries of state are the top election officers in thirty-seven states, and many of them are therefore cautious about the dangers of appearing too partisan. In 2012, only a dozen among the thirty-seven endorsed a candidate for president. Ben Cannatti, a political consultant who advises Republican candidates for secretary of state, said concerns about potential bias among partisan officials in recounts or election enforcement are overblown. "The dozen secretaries of state who have endorsed either the president or Gov. Romney are doing so as political leaders in their states," Cannatti said in 2012. "It's neither surprising nor alarming. That's what politicians do. As public officials, they've taken an oath to uphold the law and run elections fairly in their states. To do anything else is politically and legally disastrous."[51]

Conclusion

How did governors become the most important political figures in their states? Over the years, their offices have become the centers of state power, with more and more authority given to them. The power of governors now matches, in most cases, the prestige they have always enjoyed. States have been involved in the difficult balancing act of trying to weigh the interests of direct citizen selection of leaders against the need to have professional people appointed to pursue a coherent policy promulgated by a single accountable leader. In recent decades the pendulum has mostly swung in favor of investing more power in the office of the governor.

Once weak, unable to set policy or budgets, governors have now become unquestioned leaders. They are able to select cabinets that run most of the state agencies according to the governors' priorities. Sometimes their staff picks prove to be embarrassments, but they are also able to fire such people in the hope of seeing their agendas pushed forward by more eager replacements. Many positions are designed with staggered terms, so that governors cannot appoint their own people to every position. Strong governors, however, are able to combine their appointment powers with their ability to command attention from the mass media to set the terms of political issues and the direction these issues take in their states. That clout extends to the judicial branch, with many governors able to appoint most state judges.

Their control of budgets and veto authority provide governors with enormous sway over the legislative branch as well. Although they never get everything they want from their legislatures, they almost always get more of what they want than do any individual legislators.

The unrivaled power of governors and their ability to command attention from the media and political donors make them the leading political actors at the state level. Their ability to put people to work in shaping policy and campaigns, as well as their ability to raise money, makes them players in political races ranging from local and legislative contests all the way, in many instances, to the presidency.

Governors, in short, are the top dogs in the states. "As far as policy leadership goes," concludes Alan Rosenthal, "there may be big winners but there are no big losers among the nation's contemporary governors."[52]

The Latest Research

Understanding the evolving power and policy influence of governors through the comparative method has been a particular focus of political science for at least two decades. Much of this focus traces to Thad Beyle, a professor at the University of North Carolina at Chapel Hill, who in the mid-1990s began developing and publishing quantitative measures of gubernatorial powers (see Table 8-2). Ever since, researchers have used these indexes to examine how gubernatorial power, and what types of power, translate into political and policy influence.

Gubernatorial powers, however, are constantly shifting. Institutional reforms—such as increases in staff and expansion of appointment powers—may change formal power. Informal power, of course, shifts every time a new governor is elected and brings his or her own personal characteristics to the job. How do these changes shape the ability of chief executives to get their agendas enacted into law? Are these powers enough to give governors the tools they need to meet the increasingly heavy expectations voters place on them? Are those expectations—especially of the economic variety—realistic given that even the most powerful governor leads a state that is open to economic forces beyond his or her control? Political scientists search for systematic answers through the comparative method, examining differences in power and expectations to see whether they predict differences in political influence and policy success. Below we summarize some of the most recent research on the powers and expectations of governors.

• •

- **Crew, Robert E., Jr., and Christopher Lewis.** 2011. "Verbal Style, Gubernatorial Strategies, and Legislative Success." *Political Psychology* 32: 623–642.

As discussed above, one of the more interesting findings emerging from the study of executive power is that informal powers are at least as important as formal powers. This study takes an in-depth look at a particular dimension of the informal powers of Florida governors: verbal style. The central premise of the study is that speech making—the delivery of speeches such as the state of the state address—is an important governance tool. Speeches represent attempts at persuasion, opportunities to get important constituencies to buy into the governor's agenda. Communications scholars have developed a number of ways to measure how people use

(Continued)

(Continued)

language persuasively, and this study appropriates one of these indexes to look at four dimensions of the verbal styles of governors: activity (language implying action), optimism (language reflecting praise or inspiration), certainty (language reflecting inflexibility), and realism (language reflecting tangible and immediate issues). The research finds that language and verbal style matter to policy. Governors with more optimistic and action-based verbal styles tend to have greater legislative success than do those whose verbal style is based more in certainty.

- **Krupnikov, Yanna, and Charles Shipan.** 2012. "Measuring Gubernatorial Budgetary Power: A New Approach." *State Politics & Policy Quarterly* 12: 438–455.

The standard measure of formal gubernatorial powers used by political scientists is, as discussed above, that developed by Thad Beyle. This index has undergone a number of changes and updates as Beyle and others have sought to provide an ever more accurate indicator of the comparative power of governors. This study takes this development a step further: the authors argue that the standard power index suffers from some important measurement errors, and they propose an alternative. The specific focus is on measuring governors' budgetary powers. The authors' central criticism of Beyle's index is that as typically constructed its measures of budgetary power are comparable across states, but not across time. This is because as part of its evolution and refinement Beyle's index changed how budgetary powers were measured. This is potentially a problem for scholars using the comparative method because they often do not look at differences that make a difference in one year, but at differences that make a difference over multiple years. The authors of this study develop what they argue to be an index that is comparable from year to year as well as from state to state.

- **Bowman, Ann O'M., Neal D. Woods, and Milton R. Stark II.** 2010. "Governors Turn Pro: Separation of Powers and the Institutionalization of the American Governorship." *Political Research Quarterly* 63: 304–461.

There are two ways to think about state chief executives. The first is by looking at the person—that is, who

occupies the office. The second is by looking at the office—that is, the institution of governor. The institution is where formal powers are concentrated, and the institution of governor has been expanding in many states. This research examines the growth of these institutions by using a straightforward comparative analysis; the authors look at differences in gubernatorial staffing and expenditures across states during a two-decade period and examine what other differences predict these changes. What their analysis reveals is that governors' offices get bigger and command more resources as government responsibilities increase, when the governor's party controls the legislature, and, notably, to keep pace with institutional growth in the legislature. Increases in legislative sessions and legislative staff support tend to trigger countervailing increases in the executive branch.

- **Brown, Adam.** 2010. "Are Governors Responsible for the State Economy? Partisanship, Blame, and Divided Federalism." *Journal of Politics* 72: 605–615.

Unlike the other research summarized in this section, this study is more about the expectations placed on governors than it is about the powers they have to meet those expectations. A number of studies have examined whether voters hold governors (or, more broadly, state government) responsible for local economic conditions or place credit/blame for the local economy on national political actors. This study is an interesting addition to that body of research because it shows that people tend to assign policy responsibility for the economy based on partisanship. Imagine a scenario where a state's governor is Democratic and the president is Republican. If the economy is doing well, Republican voters will give the president the credit and Democratic voters will give the governor the credit. If the economy is doing poorly, Republicans will blame the governor and Democrats will blame the president. In other words, regardless of how much power a governor does or does not have, and regardless of how he or she employs that power to make policy, on at least one critical policy issue judgments of the governor's job performance are always going to be heavily influenced by the partisanship of the individual doing the judging.

college.cqpress.com/
sites/govstateandlocal

Chapter Review

Key Concepts

- appointment powers (p. 244)
- bully pulpit (p. 252)
- executive orders (p. 264)
- formal powers (p. 243)

- impeachment (p. 260)
- informal powers (p. 243)
- recall election (p. 261)
- supermajority vote (p. 240)
- veto (p. 240)

Suggested Web Sites

- **http://library.cqpress.com.** The CQ Press Electronic Library, which features an online voting and elections collection with a component for gubernatorial elections.

- **www.csg.org.** Web site of the Council of State Governments, a forum for state officials to swap information on issues of common concern, such as drugs, water, and other policy matters.

- **www.naag.org.** Web site of the National Association of Attorneys General, which has become increasingly prominent as state attorneys general have banded together on a number of high-profile cases.

- **www.nga.org.** Web site of the National Governors Association, which shares information among governors and also lobbies the federal government on their behalf.

- **www.stateside.com.** Web site of Stateside Associates, a lobbying firm that keeps close tabs on policies and actions in the states.

STATE STATS

State Stats on Governors and Executives

Explore and compare data on the states! Go to college.cqpress.com/sites/ govstateandlocal to do these exercises.

1. In 2003 the governor of Illinois commuted the death penalty for 167 prisoners and pardoned 4 more. How many death sentences have been overturned or commuted in the United States since 1973? Which state has had the most? The least? Might there been political or cultural explanations for these numbers?

2. In 2010 Arizona citizens voted to increase the sales tax rate by a penny. How has the per capita sales tax revenue in Arizona changed between 2005 and 2011? Does this make sense? What is a possible explanation?

3. The governor in most states can direct transportation funding toward specific projects, such as repairing deficient bridges. How many deficient bridges are there in your state? How does this compare to the national average? Do you think that this is something that should be prioritized in the budget?

4. The authors refer to governors as mini-presidents. Considering the population in some of the larger states, is this the case? How do the budgets of these larger states compare to those in the smaller states? What are the implications of these differences?

5. The governor of Maryland has more control over the state budget than any other governor. Has this power made Maryland's per capita outstanding debt better, worse, or similar to the surrounding states?

Judges have increasingly found themselves in the crosshairs of bitter partisan battles as they rule on cases related to important legislative issues such as voter identification. Some judicial decisions have raised accusations that "activist judges" are legislating from the bench. Judges often rule on cases concerning issues near and dear to legislators and the public, from gun rights to education, and their rulings will never please everyone.

Courts

TURNING LAW INTO POLITICS

- Why are some states' judges elected and some appointed?
- Why are some states' courts more likely than those in other states to impose the death penalty?
- What effects do state campaign finance rules have on judges and on the decisions they make?

Judges who make decisions in high-profile, politically charged cases can find themselves under pressure from all sides. In 2012, Pennsylvania commonwealth court judge Robert Simpson found himself in the middle of a bitter partisan split over voter rights when he rejected arguments that a Republican-backed law requiring voters to show identification at the polls would disenfranchise voters—in particular minorities, college students, and the elderly. As Pennsylvania is a key swing state, some said that Simpson's decision could affect who ended up in the White House.

Simpson is not the only judge to get an earful in recent years. Angry political rhetoric and personal attacks have intruded on the once quiet hallways of state courts in a big way. "Activist judge!" has become a rallying cry for politicians when judges do not immediately rubber-stamp their political and legislative goals. Organizations decry "runaway courts" and judges "run amok" or "subverting the laws." While campaigning for the 2012 Republican presidential nomination, former House Speaker Newt Gingrich suggested sending capitol police or U.S. marshals to haul activist judges before Congress to explain their decisions, and Representative Michele Bachmann derided judges in Iowa as "black robed masters." From the other side of the political spectrum, *New York Times* columnist Maureen

Activist Judge
A judge who is said to act as an independent policymaker by creatively interpreting a constitution or statute.

Dowd, incorrectly assuming that the U.S. Supreme Court was poised to strike down President Obama's Patient Protection and Affordable Care Act, called the Court "hacks dressed up in black robes." When Justice Roberts instead surprised conservatives by upholding the act, radio host Glenn Beck sold T-shirts with Roberts's face and the word "COWARD" boldly printed in yellow.

Of course, railing against judges is nothing new. In 1954, when the U.S. Supreme Court, under Chief Justice Earl Warren, ordered an end to the practice of segregating schools by race, "Impeach Earl Warren" signs popped up along roadsides in many states. But, as former Supreme Court justice Sandra Day O'Connor has written, the "breadth of rage currently being leveled at the judiciary may be unmatched in American history."[1] In fact, attacks against judges by politicians have moved beyond name-calling. According to the National Center for State Courts, judges faced more impeachment attempts in 2011 than in any previous year in history. In all but two instances, "the sole accusation was that the judges in question issued opinions that displeased members of the legislature."[2] In 2006, a handful of western states voted on ballot initiatives that were designed to rein in "out of control" judges. The most extreme was in South Dakota, where a group called JAIL 4 Judges advocated a state constitutional amendment to create special grand juries to punish judges for unpopular decisions. None of these initiatives passed, but they reflected a frustration felt by many regarding unpopular state court decisions.

Judges are often in the position of deciding cases that involve sensitive and polarizing issues, such as abortion, gun control, criminal sentencing, zoning laws, and school vouchers. The losing side, whether liberal or conservative, increasingly blames the outcome on "activist judges" creating new laws to fit their personal political beliefs. Judges can face criticism for "legislating from the bench"—that is, substituting their judgment for that of a democratically elected state legislature—if they overturn a piece of legislation important to a particularly vocal constituency. Because this criticism can come from either end of the political spectrum, it is not always clear what—if anything—is meant by it beyond the

critics' not being happy with the outcome of a case. As Lee Epstein, a law and political science professor at Washington University, has suggested to her students, "Maybe the best definition of a judicial activist is a judge you don't like."[3] Judges also face criticism when they impose mandates so specific that they look a lot like legislation; for instance, a series of New Jersey Supreme Court cases imposed elaborate school financing formulas and required the creation of preschools in certain school districts.

Case in point: The polarizing issue of gay marriage has caused considerable frustration among social conservatives, who fear that no matter what laws are passed the final say will come from state courts interpreting state constitutions. When, in 2003, Massachusetts became the first state to legalize gay marriage, it wasn't because the legislature passed a law; instead, the Massachusetts Supreme Judicial Court ruled that the Massachusetts constitution required it. The years immediately following this ruling brought a period of losses for gay marriage advocates. Thirty-one states amended their state constitutions expressly to ban gay marriage, thus taking the issue out of the purview of state judges entirely. Many others passed statutory bans on gay marriages, which are still subject to being held unconstitutional by state judges. Currently nine states and the District of Columbia have legalized gay marriage, with New York being the largest state to do so. In 2012, Maryland, Washington, and Maine became the first states to approve gay marriage by voter referendum, thus bypassing the state courts and the state legislatures. The status of California's law banning gay marriage is headed for the U.S. Supreme Court, presenting the Court with the opportunity to decide whether state bans on gay marriage violate the fundamental right to marry protected by the federal Constitution.

Of the states with current marriage equality laws, only one joined Massachusetts to arrive there solely through the action of its state supreme court. In 2009, the Iowa Supreme Court, in a unanimous decision, legalized same-sex marriage in Iowa. The next year, three of the seven justices were up for a retention election, usually a quiet up or down vote on a judge's qualifications. Not this time. Well-financed national organizations, including the

National Organization for Marriage and the American Family Association, spent record sums opposing them, urging voters to unseat the justices with television ads accusing them of, among other things, "becom[ing] political and ignoring the will of the voters." The justices, as had been traditional in these kinds of races in the past, did not actively raise campaign money and made few public appearances in the period leading up to the election. They were all recalled. Another of Iowa's state justices, David Wiggins, faced the voters in 2012. Despite Iowa's tradition of nonpartisan elections, the chairman of the Republican Party in Iowa, A. J. Spiker, issued a statement calling on voters to remove Wiggins from the court as punishment for his part in the decision that legalized marriage for same-sex couples in Iowa. The *New York Times* quoted Justice Wiggins's response to the campaign against him: "Our system is built on checks and balances between independent branches of government. Two of those branches are designed to be political. It is unfortunate that Mr. Spiker apparently thinks that all three branches should be political."[4] This time the results were different; 55 percent of Iowans voted to retain Wiggins on the supreme court despite his steadfast refusal to campaign for his job.

Just as angry rhetoric toward judges has increased, vast sums of money have been flooding into state judicial elections. The U.S. Supreme Court's decision in *Citizens United v. Federal Election Commission* (2010), which invalidated laws placing limits on independent corporate and union campaign spending, did not specifically involve judicial elections, but concerns voiced by Justice John P. Stevens in his dissent have proved prophetic:

> The consequences of today's holding will not be limited to the legislative or executive context. The majority of the States select their judges through popular elections. At a time when concerns about the conduct of judicial elections have reached a fever pitch . . . the Court today unleashes the floodgates of corporate and union general treasury spending in these races.[5]

Dramatic increases in campaign spending had already been seen in the thirty-nine states that elect state court judges, more than doubling the amount spent in the previous decade. *Citizens United* heightened concerns about judicial spending by making it easier for unaffiliated groups to spend unlimited sums to elect judges. In 2012, the first judicial super PAC was created to support an incumbent state supreme court justice in a hotly contested race in North Carolina. Such money translates into more of the mud-slinging attack ads of the type we are more used to seeing from politicians and from special interest groups that support political candidates but are not strictly affiliated with them. The increasing political rhetoric and money invested in judicial elections put pressure on judges to pay more attention to the potential political fallout of their decisions. And interest groups are increasingly seeing the benefit of funding high-cost judicial campaigns. After all, what is the point of getting legislation passed if a judge is going to throw it out as unconstitutional?

In a closely divided political climate, courts increasingly find themselves in the middle of the most overtly political decisions possible—deciding who won particular elections. Most notably, in 2000 the U.S. Supreme Court decision on Florida's recounting of ballots pretty much handed the presidential election to George W. Bush, then the Texas governor, over then vice president Al Gore. Less visibly, decisions of the same type are made in political contests across the country. In Montana, the court intervened in a close 2004 election to give a state House seat to Democrat Jeanne Windham and thus decided control of that chamber. In

> In a closely divided political climate, courts increasingly find themselves in the middle of the most overtly political decisions possible— deciding who won particular elections. Most notably, in 2000 the U.S. Supreme Court decision on Florida's recounting of ballots pretty much handed the presidential election to George W. Bush, then the Texas governor, over then vice president Al Gore.

2009, the West Virginia Supreme Court upheld a lower court's ruling in favor of Scott Edwards, mayor of Hurricane, West Virginia, in his race against contender Sam Cole.

Increasingly, judges themselves are objecting to being used as political punching bags and are arguing for the importance of an independent judicial branch. They emphasize that a judge's job is to provide a check on the other two branches of government and to protect minority rights, not to uphold the political sentiments of the day. Judges' actions in both of these vital roles will at times anger a majority of people, and judges cannot fulfill these roles if they are in fear for either their jobs or their lives, whether figuratively or literally. Again, former U.S. Supreme Court justice Sandra Day O'Connor, who has spoken out about the importance of judicial independence, has framed the significance of the issue: "It takes a lot of degeneration before a country falls into dictatorship, "but we should avoid these ends by avoiding these beginnings."[6] Those angriest with judges' decisions tend to frame the issues in terms of accountability and democratic values rather than independence. They are outraged when judges interfere with what they regard as the political arena.

Ironically, at the same time that money is flooding into state court judicial elections, the state courts themselves are being starved of funds. Economic conditions across the country have led to plunging local tax revenues, and nearly all states have cut judicial branch funding. In many localities, budget cuts to local court systems have been so steep that they have placed, in the words of Georgia chief justice Carol Hunstein, "some court systems on the edge of an abyss."[7] While the judiciary is a separate and coequal branch of government, the courts depend on the political branches for funding. Dramatic budget cuts have led to closed courts, furloughed court workers, and a growing backlog of cases and delays, particularly for civil cases, which often are put on a back burner so the courts can deal with urgent criminal matters. The same economic conditions that have led to these budget shortfalls have led to an increase in recession-related lawsuits. New York left 4.7 million cases unresolved

at the close of 2009, the most ever. Many of these claims involved debt defaults and contract disputes linked to lost jobs and foreclosures.[8]

Despite these multiple challenges, the work of the state courts continues. There is no single "right way" in which judges, justices, and courts operate. Each of the fifty states, the District of Columbia, and Puerto Rico has its own unique court system. Sometimes it seems as if every county in every state has its own way of doing things. From judicial selection to sentencing reform, states have organized their justice systems to meet the needs of the states' own unique political pressures and social dynamics.

All this is of the utmost importance because it may affect public confidence in the state courts, institutions with a tremendous amount of power. This chapter provides an introduction to state court systems. First, we examine the types of courts and the different ways these courts are structured. Then the focus turns to the different ways state court judges are chosen and retained and the controversies that these processes create. Many issues surround the various players in state justice systems, from prosecutors and defenders to victims and jurors; we explore these before turning to a discussion of some possible areas of reform.

The Role and Structure of State Courts

When people complained on old TV shows about how they felt abused or ripped off by their friends, those friends would often say, "Don't make a federal case out of it." In the real world of crime and legal conflict in the United States, there are actually relatively few federal cases, because such cases must involve violations of federal law, federal constitutional rights, or lawsuits that cross state borders. With the exception of celebrity trials such as the Casey Anthony murder case, state courts operate largely below the public's radar.

Yet they are enormously important institutions. The federal U.S. district courts hear several hundred thousand cases a year. By comparison, close to 100 million cases are filed in the lowest

At the apex of most state court systems is a supreme court. State supreme court justices, such as Mississippi Supreme Court justices Jess Dickinson (left) and Michael Randolph (right), typically have the final say on appeals from lower courts.

state courts every year. These courts have the awesome responsibility of resolving the vast majority of the nation's disputes. If you crash your car or your landlord evicts you, if you get divorced and fight for child custody, if your neighbor's tree lands in your yard, or if your employer won't pay you, any legal remedy you seek will be decided in a state court. State courts are also where virtually all criminal cases are tried, from drunk driving to murder, from misdemeanors to capital offenses. If you contest a traffic ticket, you will find yourself in a state court.

There are two basic kinds of court cases: criminal and civil. **Criminal cases** involve violations of the law, with the government prosecuting the alleged perpetrators, or criminals. Those found guilty usually go to jail. By contrast, **civil cases** involve disputes between two private parties, such

as a dry cleaner and a customer with badly stained pants. In civil cases, individuals sue each other, usually for financial judgments. Both types of cases start out in **trial court**. If the parties in a case cannot reach agreement through a **settlement** or a **plea bargain**, they go to trial.

Every trial has a winner and a loser. The losing side, if unhappy with the trial's outcome, can file an **appeal**. Most states have two levels of courts that hear appeals from trial court judgments. The appeal first goes to an **intermediate appellate court**, which reviews the original trial's record to see if any errors were made. After the appellate court has ruled, a party who still is not satisfied can attempt to appeal to the highest state court of appeals, usually called the **state supreme court**. In most states, this court does not automatically have to take an appeal; rather, it can pick and choose among cases. Typically, a state supreme court will choose to hear only those cases whose resolutions will require novel interpretation of the state constitution or clarification of the law. Such resolutions could set

Criminal Case
A legal case brought by the state intending to punish a violation of the law.

Civil Case
A legal case that involves a dispute between private parties.

Trial Court
The first level of the court system.

Settlement
A mutual agreement between parties to end a civil case before going to trial.

Plea Bargain
An agreement in which the accused in a criminal case admits guilt, usually in exchange for a promise that a particular sentence will be imposed.

Appeal
A request to have a lower court's decision in a case reviewed by a higher court.

Intermediate Appellate Court
A court that reviews court cases to find possible errors in their proceedings.

State Supreme Court
The highest level of appeals court in a state.

precedent that will have consequences well beyond the specifics of the case being appealed.

The state supreme court is the highest legal body in the state court system. This gives it the ultimate power to interpret the state constitution, and its decisions are almost always final. Only the U.S. Supreme Court outranks the highest state courts. Even the nine justices in Washington, D.C., however, cannot review—that is, come up with a new decision for—a state supreme court judgment unless that judgment conflicts with the U.S. Constitution or federal law.

When such federal issues are involved, there is no question that state courts must follow the rulings of the federal courts. The chief justice of the Alabama Supreme Court, Roy S. Moore, learned this lesson in 2003 after he oversaw the installation of a two-and-a-half-ton monument to the Ten Commandments in the rotunda of the state supreme court building. Federal judges ruled that such a display violated the First Amendment's separation of church and state and ordered Moore to have the monument removed. He refused and ultimately was expelled from office by a state ethics panel for having tried to place himself above the law. In 2006, Justice Tom Parker, a former colleague of Moore's on the court, expressed anger at other Alabama Supreme Court justices for following the U.S. Supreme Court precedent that prohibits the use of the death penalty for crimes committed by minors. Justice Parker unsuccessfully urged his colleagues not to follow Supreme Court opinions "simply because they are precedents."[9]

Trial Courts

More than 100 million cases were filed in state courts in 2009, about one case for every three citizens. These numbers have stayed relatively constant over the past ten years, although they have edged up recently. More than half the cases involved traffic offenses. The number of civil and criminal cases was roughly equal—19.5 and 20.7 million cases, respectively—and there were 7.8 million domestic and juvenile cases.[10] The vast majority of these millions of cases were resolved through plea bargains or settlements. Only a small minority ever went to trial.

When parties do go to trial, they appear before a state court judge in what is often referred to as a **court of first instance**. In this court, nothing has been determined and nothing is a "given." The trial is a blank canvas on which the parties can introduce documentary and physical evidence, such as fingerprints or DNA. Witnesses can testify as to what they saw or heard, and experts can try to help explain complex evidence.

The judge presides over the introduction of evidence; rules on objections, which occur when either of the parties thinks that the other party has said or done something improper, and issues of admissibility, that is, whether or not it is all right for specific evidence or facts to be included in the trial; and instructs the jury as to the relevant laws. The judge further instructs the jury members that they must apply the laws as stated to the facts as they find them. It is the jury, however, that must decide what the facts are. (In a **bench trial**, there is no jury and fact-finding is done by the judge.) The jury (or the judge in a bench trial) must decide who and what to believe and what happened. Unless the jury's final decision is based on a legal mistake, such as improper evidence, hearsay testimony (testimony based on rumor), or a misleading statement of the relevant law, the result typically will be upheld on appeal. The business of the trial court is to examine the facts to resolve the dispute. Subsequent appellate courts review the trial court's application of the law to those facts.

A key distinction among state courts is between **general jurisdiction trial courts** and **limited, or special jurisdiction, trial courts**. A general jurisdiction trial court hears any case not sent to a special court, whether it is civil or criminal. The kinds of cases

---

Precedent
In law, the use of the past to determine current interpretation and decision making.

Court of First Instance
The court in which a case is introduced and nothing has been determined yet.

Bench Trial
A trial in which no jury is present and the judge decides the facts as well as the law.

General Jurisdiction Trial Court
A court that hears any civil or criminal cases that have not been assigned to a special court.

Limited, or Special Jurisdiction, Trial Court
A court that hears cases that are statutorily limited by either the degree of seriousness or the types of parties involved.

A Difference
That Makes *A Difference*

The New Judicial Federalism

A century ago, state supreme courts were described as being so quiet that "you could hear the justices' arteries clog."[a] No one says this today, and the new judicial federalism is one big reason that is so.

This no longer so "new" doctrine describes a newfound reliance on state constitutions to protect those rights not covered by the U.S. Constitution. Under the principles of federalism, each state has its own justice system—distinct from those of its neighbors and from the federal system—and its own constitution. The U.S. Constitution is the supreme law of the land, and no state court can interpret its own state's constitution in a way that limits rights secured by the federal charter. States are free, however, to interpret their own constitutions any way they like, except for that single proviso.

For most of the country's history, state constitutions were overlooked. Rarely did the courts rely on them to overturn state laws, especially on the basis of civil rights. But starting in the early 1970s state supreme courts increasingly began to use state constitutions as independent sources of rights. By 1986, U.S. Supreme Court justice William J. Brennan characterized the "rediscovery by state supreme courts of the broader protections afforded their own citizens by their state constitutions [as] . . . probably the most important development in constitutional jurisprudence in our time."[b]

In many legal areas, the actual impact of judicial federalism on civil liberties has not been all that sweeping. It is still true that most state court judges continue to interpret state constitutions in lockstep with interpretations of the U.S. Constitution. One scholar found, however, that in approximately one out of every three constitutional decisions, state courts extended rights beyond federal levels.[c] In some areas, such as the interpretation of the right to exercise religion freely and in search-and-seizure rulings, state courts, relying on their own constitutions, have continued to grant rights after the U.S. Supreme Court's interpretation of the Constitution took a more conservative and restrictive turn.

In other cases, state courts rely on unique constitutional provisions. For instance, state constitutions, unlike the federal document, often commit state governments to the achievement of particular policy ends. The New Jersey constitution requires a "thorough and efficient system of free public schools," the Illinois constitution requires the state to "provide and maintain a healthful environment for the benefit of this and future generations," and the New Mexico constitution requires the state to provide bilingual education. Relying on explicit provisions such as these, state supreme courts have ordered legislatures to restructure the way they finance public education when inequalities are so extreme they rise to the level of a state constitutional violation.

Today, the new judicial federalism is well established, with more and more cases raising state constitutional issues and sparking a renewed interest in these once-overlooked documents. State supreme court justices are more likely now to take a fresh look at their own constitutions than to slavishly follow the interpretations of the U.S. Supreme Court. Activists also have focused more attention on state constitutions, mounting campaigns to amend them to either extend or curtail rights.

[a]G. Alan Tarr, "The New Judicial Federalism in Perspective," *Notre Dame Law Review* 72 (1997): 1097.

[b]William J. Brennan, "State Constitutional Law," special section of *National Law Journal* 9 (September 29, 1986): S-1.

[c]James N. G. Cauthen, "Expanding Rights under State Constitutions: A Quantitative Appraisal," *Albany Law Review* 63 (2000): 1183, 1202.

that can be tried in special jurisdiction courts are statutorily limited. Some are limited to cases of less seriousness, such as misdemeanors or civil cases that involve small amounts of money. Others are limited in regard to the types of parties involved, such as juvenile offenders or drug abusers.

Not all states make this distinction between types of trial courts. Illinois has no limited

FIGURE 9-1

HOW IT WORKS

State Court Structure in Illinois and New York

At a glance, it's easy to see why New York state's court system has been called Byzantine—just compare it to Illinois's (left). Although it encompasses 23 circuits with more than 850 justices, Illinois's single trial court system (its general jurisdiction courts) looks like a model of clarity and simplicity compared to New York's 10 different trial courts (the courts of general and limited jurisdiction). But the differences run deeper than what a simple organizational chart can reveal. New York's three-hundred-year-old town and village justice court system, in particular, has been subject to loud and persistent criticism for cronyism, corruption, fiscal mismanagement, and plain old inefficiency. According to *New York Times* reporter William Glaberson, "the [town and village justice] courts have survived in part because the justices—most of them not even lawyers—have longstanding and deep ties to the upstate political system, and because of the substantial cost of replacing them with more professional courts."[a] With 2,300 justices involved at that level, this would indeed be a tall order.

What can be done? In 2006, New York's former chief judge Judith S. Kaye, the state's top advocate for court reform, recommended changes "across four broad areas: court operations and administration; auditing and financial control; education and training; and facility security and public protection."[b] A few of these proposed changes could be implemented right away, including requiring word-for-word records of court proceedings—a bona fide court transcript—to ensure fairness and the purchasing of recording equipment to make that possible.

Other changes would require more sweeping institutional modifications. Judge Kaye called for state funds to help support the town and village justice courts, which are currently funded and operated locally. This change would require legislative approval. Her most aggressive recommendation—to simplify the trial court structure itself into a more common two-tiered organization—would require an amendment to the state's constitution. Legislators received the proposals coolly. A commission on state court reform backed some of Kaye's ideas in 2008 with its suggestion that the state eliminate as many as five hundred of the justice courts, but New York had not instituted the changes by early 2010.[c]

Illinois's State Court Structure

Court of last resort	**Supreme Court** 7 justices en banc
Intermediate appellate court	**Appellate Court** 5 districts 54 authorized judges and 12 circuit court judges
Court of general jurisdiction	**Circuit Court** 23 circuits 517 authorized circuit judges and 389 associate judges

jurisdiction courts. In contrast, New York, the state with the largest number of judges, is also the state that relies most heavily on limited jurisdiction courts. More than 3,000 of the state's 3,645 judges sit on limited jurisdiction courts.[11] (See Figure 9-1.) The majority of these limited jurisdiction courts are "town and village courts" or "justice courts." In states that do not rely on limited jurisdiction courts, appeals go directly to appellate courts. In states that make the distinction, some issues can be appealed from limited jurisdiction courts to general jurisdiction courts.

Appeals Courts: Intermediate Appeals and Courts of Last Resort

When one of the parties in a trial is dissatisfied with the outcome, that party can challenge the result by filing an appeal. As a general rule, an appeal cannot be based on mere dissatisfaction

New York State's Court Structure

Court of last resort	**Court of Appeals** — 7 judges en banc
Intermediate appellate court	**Appellate divisions of Supreme Court** — 56 justices / **Appellate terms of Supreme Court** — 14 justices
Court of general jurisdiction	**Supreme Court** — 12 districts, 326 supreme court judges / **County Court** — 57 counties outside New York City, 129 county court judges
Court of limited jurisdiction	**Court of Claims** — 1 court / 86 judges; **Surrogate's Court** — 62 counties / 30 surrogates; **Family Court** — 62 counties / 127 judges; **District Court** — 2 counties / 50 judges; **City Court** — 79 courts, 158 judges; **Criminal Court of the City of New York** — 1 court / 107 judges; **Civil Court of the City of New York** — 1 court / 120 judges; **Town and Village Justice Court** — 1,487 courts / 2,300 justices

[a] William Glaberson, "Justice in Small Towns to Be Upgraded," *New York Times,* November 22, 2006, A1.

[b] Judith S. Kaye and Jonathan Lippman, "Action Plan for the Justice," November 2006, available at www.state.ny.us/publications/pdfs/ActionPlan-Justice.pdf.

[c] Joel Stashenko, "Study Supports Elimination of Hundreds of Justice Courts," *New York Law Journal* 240, no. 56 (2008): 2.

with the trial's result. An appellant does not get a free second chance to try his or her whole case. Appellate courts do not decide issues of guilt or innocence or ensure that trials were conducted perfectly. Instead, an appeal must be based on a claim that there were legal errors in the original trial. Further, it is not enough to show that an error occurred; the error had to have been **prejudicial**—

Prejudicial Error
An error that affects the outcome of a case.

that is, it had to have affected the outcome of the case. The appellant has to argue that there was a good chance the result would have been different if the error had not been made. This often is a very challenging argument to make.

To cite just one example, in 2006 the defense attorney representing the convicted murderer of an Indiana University freshman asked that the sentence should be thrown out, arguing that the jurors may have been drinking during legal proceedings, given that some of the male jurors in the trial had painted their toenails and raced down a hotel hallway in a bailiff's backless high heels. "Two men with heels on, painting their toenails, it is not a normal activity unless they are intoxicated," the attorney said. The judge ruled against him, saying there was no indication of drunkenness in court or during the actual deliberations.[12]

There is no one way in which all the state appellate courts decide how to hear appeals from the trial courts. States have made different decisions about how many levels of review to grant an appeal, how the courts must choose which cases can be appealed, and how many judges will hear an appeal. These decisions combine to form the different appellate court structures.

For example, not all states have both an intermediate appellate court and a supreme court. Back in 1957, only thirteen states had intermediate appellate courts. Today, only eleven states and the District of Columbia still resolve all their appeals with only one level of review. These states, which include Delaware, Montana, North Dakota, Rhode Island, South Dakota, Vermont, and Wyoming, have relatively small populations—seven have fewer than 1 million residents—and thus tend to have fewer cases to resolve than do more populous states. Smaller populations generally give rise to more manageable court caseloads.

In the majority of states, the sheer volume of appeals makes it impossible for one appellate court to hear and resolve every appeal. To deal with burgeoning caseloads, almost all states have created another tier of review. In these states, appeals go first to an intermediate appellate court. Only after they have been reviewed at this level can they move on to the court of last resort, usually the state supreme court. The intermediate court makes it possible for the state judicial system to hear many more appeals and creates the possibility of a second level of appeal.

Intermediate appellate courts range in size from 3 judges (in Alaska) to 105 judges (in California). States with many judges at the intermediate appellate level usually divide the judges' jurisdictions into specific regions. California, for example, has six appellate divisions. By contrast,

New Jersey, with 32 appellate judges, has the largest appellate court that is not divided into judicial regions.[13] Regional divisions help the courts to operate smoothly, but they also create a danger. All these different courts may come up with different rulings on the same or similar issues. This has the potential to set different, possibly conflicting, precedents for future litigation.

State appellate courts also vary in whether they have **discretionary jurisdiction** or **mandatory jurisdiction**. In other words, in some states the courts have a right to pick and choose which cases they hear. In other states, judges must consider every case, the principle being that everyone has the right to an appeal. It is widely accepted that a loser in a single-judge court ought to have the right to at least one appeal to a court with multiple judges. This one appeal, however, is generally considered sufficient to correct any prejudicial errors made in the trial courts. Even in states in which the court of last resort has discretionary jurisdiction, appeals may be mandatory in capital punishment cases.

Two tiers of appellate courts allow petitioners the right to one appeal to the intermediate appellate court, followed by the possibility of a further appeal to the court of last resort. Such a structure allows the supreme court or other court of last resort to choose whether to hear cases that might have relevance beyond the parties in the cases, allowing the court to make the law clear to others.

One more variable in the state court system structure involves the number of judges at each level who hear a particular appeal. At the level of either the appellate court or the court of last resort, judges may hear an appeal **en banc**, or all together, or they may sit in smaller **panels**, typically of three

Discretionary Jurisdiction
The power of a court to decide whether or not to grant review of a case.

Mandatory Jurisdiction
The requirement that a court hear every case presented before it.

En Banc
Appeals court sessions in which all the judges hear a case together.

Panel
A group of (usually) three judges who sit to hear cases in a state court of appeals.

judges. Sitting in panels may be more convenient because appellate courts sit simultaneously in different locations. This allows more appeals to be heard and makes the courts more convenient to the parties. However, as with regional divisions, this may also lead to problems of unifying doctrine created by various courts at the same level.

States that use panels have a variety of techniques to limit the divergence of opinions among panels. These include conferencing drafts of opinions en banc. This means that each panel's draft opinions are circulated among all the judges, even those not on that panel. Two states, Texas and Oklahoma, have created systems in which there are two supreme courts with different subject-matter jurisdictions rather than one supreme court sitting in panels. In these states, one supreme court has largely civil jurisdiction and one supreme court hears only criminal appeals; each of these courts sits en banc. In Texas, the intermediate appellate court

has both civil and criminal jurisdiction. In Oklahoma, the intermediate appellate court has only civil jurisdiction—all criminal appeals go directly to the court of last resort for criminal cases. A few states have created systems that have intermediate appellate courts with differing subject-matter jurisdictions and then a single court of last resort.

States have mixed and matched all these variables to come up with different ways to organize the appellate court review process. The most common pattern, adhered to by half the states, involves an intermediate appellate court, sitting in panels, that must consider all appeals. The decisions of these panels are then subject to review by a court of last resort, such as a supreme court, sitting en banc. Usually, this highest court hears just the cases it sees fit to hear. In states without an intermediate court of appeals, often the courts of last resort must hear all the cases that are sent to them. One such state, West Virginia, eliminated discretionary review for its supreme court in a historic change in 2010. In the next year, the number of appeals heard by the state's highest court tripled. In the District of Columbia, all appeals are heard by a court of appeals with nine justices who often sit in panels

of three and have mandatory jurisdiction over most cases.

In other words, no matter what state you are in, if you lose your case in court, you will have at least one chance—and sometimes more than one chance—to get your appeal heard. There is tremendous variation among states in courts and panels and rules; luckily, you need to know only the rules of the state where you file your case.

Selecting Judges

How judges are selected is a significant political decision. Historically, such decisions have generated tremendous controversy, and the controversy continues today. Why is there no clear consensus on this important issue? Controversy is perhaps inevitable. The judiciary is one of the pillars of the U.S. political system, but at the same time, we want to believe that judges are above politics. We like to think that they are independent and will rule only as justice requires, based on the specific facts presented and the applicable law. But, of course, judges are only human. That's why we want them held accountable for their decisions. These competing values—independence and accountability—tug judicial selection procedures in different directions. If independence is seen as more important than accountability, it makes sense to appoint judges for lifetime tenures. This is done in the federal system. If accountability is seen as more important than independence, it makes sense to elect judges. Elections are a key element of judicial selection at the state level. Yet they are not the only component; states have formulated a variety of selection systems in an effort to balance the competing values of independence and accountability. These specifics matter. How a state structures its courts and chooses its judiciary may affect the types of decisions made by individual judges and the confidence citizens have in their courts to provide fair trials.

Almost no two states select judges in the exact same way, although the states can be roughly divided into two camps of almost equal size. The first group includes states that choose judges through popular elections, either partisan or

The merit selection of judges, widely adopted by states across the country to fill some or all judicial vacancies, originated in Missouri from a power struggle between Governor Lloyd Stark, pictured here, and powerful political boss Tom Pendergast.

How states choose their judges has been historically volatile. Movements to change the methods for judicial selection rise up, gain popularity, and then, eventually, are supplanted by the next big reform movement. How a state originally chose its judges had much to do with which reform was in vogue at the time the state entered the Union and ratified its constitution. No single judicial reform has ever succeeded in completely replacing earlier methods, however, and so there is tremendous variation among the states in the way they select judges.

Under the U.S. Constitution, the president, with the advice and consent of the Senate, appoints all federal judges. Similarly, the original thirteen states chose to appoint judges, giving the appointment power to one or both houses of the legislature or, less commonly, to the governor, either alone or with the consent of the legislature.[14]

Then, in the mid-1800s, during the presidency of Andrew Jackson—a period marked by distrust of government and a movement toward increased popular sovereignty—the appointive system came under attack. Every state that entered the Union between 1846 and 1912 provided for some form of judicial elections.[15] At the dawn of the twentieth century, concern that judges were being selected and controlled by political machines led to a movement for nonpartisan elections. By 1927, twelve states employed this practice.[16]

During the second half of the twentieth century, judicial reformers focused on persuading states to adopt a new method of choosing judges, referred to as merit selection. The variations of merit selection systems are discussed in detail in the following section on appointment. Basically, a merit system is a hybrid of appointment and election. It typically involves a bipartisan judicial nominating commission whose job is to create a list of highly qualified candidates for the bench. The governor appoints judges from this list, who must then face a **retention**

nonpartisan. In partisan elections, judicial candidates first run in party primaries, and then the winning candidates are listed on the general election ballot along with designations of their political parties. The names of candidates in nonpartisan elections appear on the ballot without any party labels. The second group consists of states that have appointed, rather than elected, judges. Under the appointment model, the governor or the legislature may appoint judges. In some states, only persons selected by a nominating committee are eligible for judicial appointments.

To make matters even more confusing, many states use different methods to choose judges at different levels of their judiciaries. A state might, for example, choose trial judges by popular election but appoint supreme court justices. What's more, regions within a given state often employ different methods. In Arizona, for example, trial courts in counties with populations greater than 250,000 choose judges through merit selection; less populous districts rely on nonpartisan elections. Indiana holds partisan elections in a portion of its judicial districts and nonpartisan elections in others. Finally, some states that generally elect their judges fill midterm judicial vacancies by appointment.

Retention Election

An election in which a judge runs uncontested and voters are asked to vote yes or no on the question of whether they wish to retain the judge in office for another term.

election. The retention election for a newly appointed judge, which is usually set to coincide with the next general election, provides voters with a simple choice: to keep or not to keep the judge on the bench. If the vote is for retention, the judge stays on the bench. If the vote is against retention (this is rare), the commission goes back to work to come up with another list of candidates for the post.

Under some merit systems, all judges (not just newly appointed ones) must face periodic retention elections, although the length of term and other specifics vary from state to state. Missouri became the first state to adopt such a judicial selection method in 1940, which is why judicial merit selection is sometimes referred to as "the Missouri Plan." The movement enjoyed considerable success from the 1960s to the 1980s. The number of states that embraced merit selection for choosing supreme court justices grew from three in 1960 (Alaska, Kansas, and Missouri) to eighteen by 1980.[17]

Recently, however, this movement appears to have lost momentum. Approximately half the states still rely on merit selection to choose some or all of their judges, and no merit selection state has returned to selection through elections. However, since 1990, most states that have considered adopting merit selection, whether for trial courts or appellate-level courts, have rejected it. In Nevada, for example, the legislature sponsored a bipartisan ballot question in the 2010 election asking whether the Nevada constitution should be amended to adopt the Missouri Plan. It was rejected by 58 percent of the voters.[18] A poll taken in early 2007 showed that an overwhelming majority of Pennsylvanians opposed changing the method of selecting judges from election to appointment.[19] In recent years, several states have debated doing away with merit selection altogether, including Missouri, where it began. In the sections that follow, we discuss at length each method for selecting judges and the issues it raises. (Map 9-1 shows the system of selection for each state.)

Popular Elections

Why do some states elect judges? Elections allow greater popular control over the judiciary and more public accountability for judges. Proponents argue that such elections are compatible with this country's democratic traditions and that voters can be trusted to make choices for judges that are as good as those that legislators or mayors would make. To these supporters, the appointment of judges smacks of elitism and raises worries about old-boy networks—that is, they fear that judges will get appointed because they are the cronies or political allies of elected officials.

Some argue that electing judges can increase the representation of women and minorities on the bench, but studies have found negligible differences between selection methods and judicial diversity.[20] Regardless of system, state judiciaries have grown slightly more diverse over time, but the percentages of minority and women judges continue to trail their numbers in the population at large. Nationwide, as of 2010, 43 (12 percent) state supreme court justices were members of minority groups and 111 (33 percent) were women.[21]

Those on the other side of the argument are critical of judicial elections in general, whether partisan or nonpartisan, asserting that such elections often become referendums on political issues rather than serve as forums that allow the public to evaluate the temperaments, backgrounds, and experience of the candidates. Opponents of judicial elections focus on what they see as the threat to the independence of the judiciary posed by the introduction of politics into the selection process and the danger that the need to solicit campaign contributions makes judges vulnerable to improper influence by donors. Further, opponents note that the tone of judicial elections has deteriorated substantially and in a manner that could damage the image of the judiciary. Given this, qualified candidates for office could choose not to run.

This is a debate about more than academic ideas, however. How a state chooses its judges has very real political impacts, with consequences for judicial impartiality, campaign fund-raising, the role of interest groups, and the character of judicial campaigning. Some point to these problems as reasons to move away from selecting judges through judicial elections and toward a merit selection system. Others argue that there is no need to abandon elections altogether; rather, any problems can be addressed through targeted changes. Die-hard supporters of judicial election see the increased politicization of the process as a positive thing; they assert that greater competitiveness translates into more meaningful choices for voters.

MAP 9-1

Initial Judicial Selection, by Type of Court

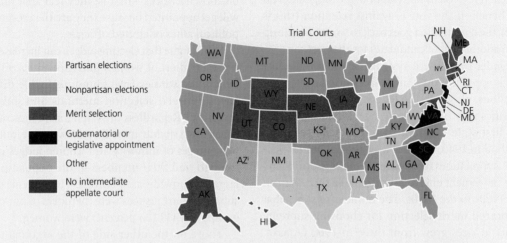

Trial Courts

Legend

- Partisan elections
- Nonpartisan elections
- Merit selection
- Gubernatorial or legislative appointment
- Other
- No intermediate appellate court

Source: American Judicature Society, "Methods of Judicial Selection." www.judicialselection.us/judicial_selection/methods/selection_of_judges.cfm?state=.

Notes:
iThe Arizona Constitution provides for merit selection and retention of judges in counties with populations of 250,000 or greater. Counties whose populations are less than 250,000 may adopt merit selection through ballot initiative.

iiJudges are selected by merit selection in 17 districts and by partisan election in 14 districts.

iiiJudges in Kansas City, Springfield, and St. Louis are selected by merit selection; all others are elected by partisan election.

ivThe chief justice of the supreme court assigns superior court judges to the appellate court division.

vChosen from among active and retired district judges, retired supreme court justices, and attorneys

viCandidates who want to challenge incumbent justices must be nominated at party conventions. Candidates appear without party affiliation on the general election ballot.

Intermediate Appellate Courts

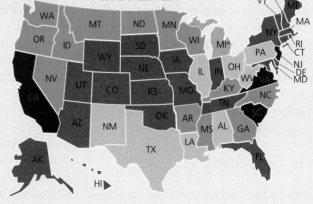

Courts of Last Resort

Source: American Judicature Society, "Methods of Judicial Selection," www.judicialselection.us/judicial_selection/methods/selection_of_judges.cfm?state=.

Before we jump into a discussion of the consequences of judicial elections, we should note that it is important to remember that elections for state court judges, when they are held, can be either partisan or nonpartisan. Most or all of the judges in eight states (Alabama, Illinois, Louisiana, Michigan, Ohio, Pennsylvania, Texas, and West Virginia) are selected through partisan elections. Another five states (Indiana, Kansas, Missouri, New York, and Tennessee) select some of their judges this way.[22] Nonpartisan elections are held to select most or all judges in thirteen states (Arkansas, Georgia, Idaho, Kentucky, Minnesota, Mississippi, Montana, Nevada, North Carolina, North Dakota, Oregon, Washington, and Wisconsin) and some judges in another seven states (Arizona, California, Florida, Indiana, Michigan, Oklahoma, and South Dakota).[23] In some cases, labeling a popular election partisan or nonpartisan may be a distinction without a difference. All Ohio judges and Michigan Supreme Court justices run without party labels on the ballots, but the candidates are chosen through party primaries or conventions, and the parties are heavily involved in judicial campaigns.

The legislative and executive branches are clearly political. Representatives of the people are chosen and held accountable through elections. Why shouldn't judges be elected in the same manner as other powerful players in the political system? Because the role of judges is designed to be different. Judges decide specific cases and controversies based on the evidence. They are supposed to rely only on statutes, case precedent, constitutional law, and the unique facts presented by each case. They are not supposed to rule based on the wishes of those who elect them or with the next election in mind.

A lot rides on the public's belief that judges are neutral and impartial. That belief underpins the willingness to bring disputes to the courts and to abide by the results—the keys to both economic and political stability. Judges cannot, as political candidates do, make campaign promises about future decisions; to do so would be to undermine respect for the impartiality and independence of the judiciary. For the same reasons, judges cannot represent specific interest groups or constituents or even the will of the majority. There are times when all judges, when doing their jobs properly,

are compelled by the law to make unpopular judgments or to protect the rights of those without political power.

In 1999, U.S. Supreme Court justice Anthony Kennedy pointed out in an interview that there are times for every judge when the law requires the release of a criminal whether the judge likes it or not. Characterizing the judge in such a case as "soft on crime" betrays a misunderstanding of the judicial process and the constitution.[24] In the same television interview, Justice Stephen Breyer also expressed concerns about the way judicial elections require judges to court public opinion. He asked, "Suppose I were on trial. Suppose somebody accused me. Would I want to be judged by whether I was popular? Wouldn't I want to be judged on what was true as opposed to what was popular? . . . We have a different system. And our system is based upon . . . neutrality and independence."[25]

> Why are some courts more likely than others to impose the death penalty? Some research indicates that state supreme court justices facing reelection in states in which capital punishment is particularly popular are reluctant to cast dissenting votes in death penalty cases.

Is this how it really works? Or is it only how it is *supposed* to work? The highly charged issue of capital punishment makes a useful test case. Why are some courts more likely than others to impose the death penalty? Some research indicates that state supreme court justices facing reelection in states in which capital punishment is particularly popular are reluctant to cast dissenting votes in death penalty cases. Researchers Paul Brace and Melinda Gann Hall found that, among politically comparable states, rulings to uphold death sentences are more likely in states with elected judges.[26] Not only that, but the closer supreme court justices are to reelection, the more likely they are to support capital punishment.[27]

Texas and Florida have at least one thing in common—hundreds of inmates on death row with a high volume of death penalty appeals. But the similarity stops there. Texas justices are elected in partisan elections, and they almost never reverse a death sentence. In Florida, however, supreme court justices are merit selected, and the court has one of the nation's highest reversal rates.[28] It is not misguided for a judge facing reelection to fear reversing a death sentence. There are numerous examples of state supreme court justices who were voted off the bench after they were labeled as soft for opposing the imposition of capital punishment in particular cases. This occurs even when the unpopular opinions are later held to be correct by the U.S. Supreme Court.[29]

The effects of judicial selection ripple out beyond those cases that tackle politically volatile issues such as capital punishment and raise issues of improper influence on the judiciary. Law professor Stephen Ware reviewed all arbitration decisions made by the Alabama Supreme Court from 1995 to 1999. Justices there are selected through partisan elections, and this period encompassed a shift in the court majority from Democrats to Republicans. In virtually all cases—even those that involved bland issues of law that appeared ideologically neutral—Ware found a direct correlation between voting and campaign contributions.[30] The Democrats, funded mostly by lawyers who worked for the plaintiffs, opposed arbitration. The Republicans, financed primarily by business interests, favored it. In 2006, the *New York Times* published the results of an examination of campaign financing over twelve years in regard to the Ohio Supreme Court. The investigators found that justices routinely sat on cases after receiving campaign contributions from the parties involved or from groups that filed supporting briefs and that justices, on average, voted in favor of contributors 70 percent of the time, with one particular justice voting for his contributor 91 percent of the time.[31]

A 2012 report published by the Center for American Progress collects illustrations from six states with particularly expensive judicial elections: Alabama, Illinois, Michigan, Ohio, Pennsylvania, and Texas. The high courts in these states, the report notes, "are much more likely to rule in favor of big business and against individuals who have been injured, scammed or subjected to discrimination."[32] In one example, the Ohio legislature had passed three laws curtailing the right to sue an employer for on-the-job injuries. The first two laws were held unconstitutional. The insurance industry donated to judicial campaigns, and the winning justices upheld the law on its third try.[33]

Okay, so this all sounds shady, but candidates running for judicial office must raise money. Frequently, this money comes from the very people who have vested interests in the outcomes of cases that are or will be before a judge. Describing judicial fund-raising, Justice Paul E. Pfeifer, a Republican member of the Ohio Supreme Court, said, "I never felt so much like a hooker down by the bus station in any race I've ever been in as I did in a judicial race."[34] But the need to find dollars to run for a seat cannot supersede good judgment. In *Caperton v. Massey* (2009), the U.S. Supreme Court ruled that Justice Brent Benjamin of the West Virginia Supreme Court of Appeals should have recused himself from a case in which the chief executive officer of the lead defendant, after losing a $50 million verdict in the trial court, raised $3 million to elect Benjamin to the court that was hearing the case's appeal. Benjamin was the deciding vote in favor of the defendants. Chastising Justice Benjamin for not sitting out this appeal, the U.S. Supreme Court stated, "Just as no man is allowed to be a judge in his own cause, similar fears of bias can arise when . . . a man chooses the judge in his own cause." In Benjamin's case, the $3 million from the CEO of A. T. Massey Coal Co. represented about 60 percent of his electoral war chest[35]—another piece of evidence that the funds required to run a campaign have been skyrocketing, particularly in state supreme court races. From 2000 to 2009, candidates for state supreme court seats raised more than $200 million, more than double the $83 million they raised in the previous decade.[36] Much of the money raised by judicial candidates comes from lawyers, litigants, and other groups with interests in the outcomes of litigation.

In the wake of *Citizens United* (2010), which invalidated laws placing limits on corporate campaign contributions, the spending has continued to increase, with the majority of the spending coming from corporations. Why do these groups contribute so much money to judicial elections? As with any other political donation, there is at least some truth to the cynic's sense that campaign contributions are a good investment. The president of the Ohio state bar concluded, "The people with money to spend who are affected by court decisions have reached the conclusion that it's a lot cheaper to buy a judge than a governor or an entire legislature, and he can probably do a lot more for you."[37] When the judicial reform organization Justice at Stake surveyed 2,428 state court judges, one-quarter said that campaign contributions influenced their decisions.

Even if justices do not allow campaign contributions to affect their decisions, the appearance of conflict already has been created. A 2009 USA Today/Gallup Poll found that 89 percent of voters believe campaign contributions to judges influence decisions.[38] This appearance of bias, whether actual bias exists or not, affects the confidence of citizens in the courts' ability to administer justice impartially. Single-issue interest groups may target a judge for a specific ruling on a topic such as capital punishment, abortion, or same-sex marriage. Groups may criticize or praise the judge, taking the case completely out of its legal context, transforming an election into a referendum on a political cause. Such groups have joined together in coalitions similar to those formed in other partisan political contests. Given the power of interest groups, Santa Clara University law professor Gerald Uelmen has observed that judicial independence is most endangered in states with growing death-row populations and rare executions, states with laws requiring parental consent for abortions by minors, and states that allow statutory enactments or constitutional amendments by initiative.[39] In two states, Ohio and Kentucky, these

three judicial land mines have come together. Both states elect supreme court justices in highly partisan and expensive races on a recurring basis.

Prior to 2002, judges' campaigns generally were subject to codes of judicial conduct that placed tight restrictions on campaigning to prevent judges from discussing topics that might later come before them on the bench. In *Republican Party of Minnesota v. White* (2002), however, the U.S. Supreme Court struck down such restrictions as violations of judges' free speech rights. Since then, interest groups such as the Christian Coalition of Georgia have asked judicial candidates to complete questionnaires, pressuring them to reveal their views on hot-button issues. The groups then target specific "bad" judges for removal. Some candidates themselves have run outspoken campaigns, stating their opinions on issues, such as school funding, that will clearly appear before the court.

Campaigns increasingly rely on thirty-second TV spots, which can do little more than offer simplistic sound bites about complicated issues. According to Justice at Stake, in 2002 only one in ten of these TV ads was negative; that number had risen to more than one in five by 2004. In 2010, judicial candidates themselves paid for only a quarter of the negative ads, with three out of every four attack ads being purchased by noncandidate groups, including special interests and political parties.[40] One notorious attack ad run by the Michigan Democratic Party in 2008 featured a "dramatization" portraying the Michigan chief justice as sleeping on the bench, an allegation that was never proven.[41] In 2010, a coalition of groups seeking to oust a sitting Illinois supreme court justice aired a radio ad with actors purporting to be some of the state's worst criminals, recounting their crimes in grisly detail and portraying the judge as taking their side.[42] These kinds of ads do seem to make a difference. In 2004, thirty-four judicial elections featured some form of television advertising, and in twenty-nine of them, the candidate with the most ad expenditures won.[43]

Added to this mix of expensive campaigns and thirty-second TV spots is the fact that ordinary citizens have very little information with which to make informed choices about judicial races. Voters commonly vote only for candidates at the top of the ticket, such as governors or senators, and leave the part of the ballot listing judicial candidates incomplete. A 2007 poll conducted by the Colorado League of Women Voters found that 52 percent of those who did vote in judicial elections admitted to being uninformed about the candidates. When these uninformed voters were asked to describe their voting strategies, the results were roughly evenly split between those who said they always voted to keep judges, always voted to remove them, or made random choices.[44] Both lack of voter participation and uninformed voting undermine the public's ability to keep the judiciary accountable and make judges more vulnerable to targeting by single-issue groups.

In partisan elections, an additional danger is that the political parties may expect favors from the candidates they put forward. In 1976, the Michigan Supreme Court decided a redistricting case in a way that favored Republicans. In the next election, the Democratic Party refused to renominate the court's Democratic chief justice.[45] Thomas Phillips, onetime chief justice of the Texas Supreme Court, has asked:

> When judges are labeled as Democrats or Republicans, how can you convince the public that the law is a judge's only constituency? And when a winning litigant has contributed thousands of dollars to the judge's campaign, how do you ever persuade the losing party that only the facts of the case were considered?[46]

Appointment

The systems used by states in which judges are appointed rather than elected can be divided into two general categories: **pure appointive systems** and merit selection systems that rely on nominating committees. Federal judges have always been selected through a pure appointive system. The president appoints judges who, if they are confirmed by the Senate, "shall hold their Offices

---

Pure Appointive System
A judicial selection system in which the governor appoints judges alone, without preselection of candidates by a nominating commission.

during good Behavior." No state, however, employs precisely this method of judicial selection.

In four states—California, Maine, New Hampshire, and New Jersey—the governor appoints state court judges without a nominating commission. That is, these governors are not limited in their selections to a list of names provided by someone else.[47] Judges' nominations still require some kind of second opinion, however. In Maine, the governor appoints judges subject to confirmation by a legislative committee, the decision of which may be reviewed by the Senate. In New Jersey, the state Senate must confirm the governor's appointees, who then serve an initial seven-year term, after which the governor may reappoint them. A special five-member elected council confirms judicial appointees in New Hampshire. California's governor appoints judges after submitting names to a state bar committee for evaluation, but the governor is not bound by the committee's recommendation.[48]

Virginia is the only state in which the legislature appoints all state judges without a nominating committee. A majority vote of both houses of the Virginia General Assembly is required to appoint any judge.

Merit selection, initially endorsed by the American Bar Association in 1937, was conceived as a way to limit the intrusion of politics into judge selection and strike a balance between partisan election and lifetime appointment.[49] Under such a system, after an appointed judge serves an initial term, he or she must stand for a retention election. In this election, the judge runs unopposed. Voters may indicate only either yes or no on the question of whether the judge should be retained.

Most states that currently appoint judges rely on a method of merit selection through nominating committees. Twenty-four states and the District of Columbia rely on a merit selection plan for the initial selection of some or all judges. Another ten states use such plans to fill midterm vacancies at some or all levels of the courts.[50]

What puts the *merit* into merit selection? It is misleading to describe merit selection as if it were a single method for selecting judges, because the details vary considerably from state to state. At its core, it requires that the state assemble a nonpartisan nominating committee. This committee forwards a list of names from which either the governor or the legislature chooses a judge. How a partisan, distrustful legislature solves the problem of creating a nonpartisan committee differs in almost every state. Some states require parity of political party affiliation for the commission members. Others have adopted extremely complex methods to ensure the impartiality of nominating commissions. While the details of how a nominating committee is chosen may seem innocuous and dry, they have significant impact on just how successful a merit selection plan can be in minimizing the politicization of the judiciary. In 2012 three merit selection states—Missouri, Florida, and Arizona—held referendums on the issue of increasing the power of governors and legislatures in the selection of judges. These efforts mostly focused on giving executives or legislatures more power to influence merit system selection committees. While retaining the basic framework of a merit system, giving partisan actors a greater role in selection com-

mittee appointments nudges a merit system toward giving greater weight to political concerns than to judicial qualifications. For example, Missouri has had several failed attempts in recent years to revoke merit selection entirely and replace it with partisan elections. Opponents have since shifted tactics, focusing on an effort to give the governor the power to appoint a majority of the members of the judicial selection committee. The Missouri referendum did not pass, but such a move would have drastically increased the governor's power over who ends up sitting on the bench.

Even after the composition of a nominating commission has been determined, states have varying ways of choosing who will fill the most influential position, that of commission chair. In some states, including Maryland, New Hampshire, and Utah, the governor can exert considerable control over the commission through the ability to appoint its chair.[51] Other states, such as Alaska, Arizona, Colorado, and Utah, designate the chief justice of the state supreme court as chair. Some states allow the commission to choose its own chair. New Mexico's constitution designates the dean of the University of New Mexico Law School as the chair of the state's judicial nominating commission.[52]

Usually, the governor chooses judicial appointees from a list forwarded by the nominating commission. In South Carolina and Connecticut, the nominating committee forwards a list of names to the legislature, which then meets in joint session to appoint judges by a majority vote.[53]

The ways in which judges are retained after they are appointed also vary by state. In most states, judges appointed through merit selection serve relatively short initial terms, usually one or two years. After that, they participate in retention elections. These special elections were conceived as a means to provide some public participation in the selection of judges while avoiding the intrusion of politics. This worked relatively well for some time, as retention elections appeared immune to the kind of big-money politics seen in partisan elections. But this all changed in the elections of 2009–2010, when incumbent justices in some states, notably Illinois, Iowa, Alaska, and Colorado, faced unprecedented and highly financed opposition in races as fiercely partisan as popular elections.

Some merit selection states have dispensed with elections altogether. For instance, in Connecticut, Delaware, and Hawaii, judges are reevaluated and reappointed by the judicial selection commission. In Vermont, after an initial appointment through merit selection, a judge receives an additional term as long as the General Assembly does not vote against it.[54]

Terms of Office

The length of a judge's tenure is another element in the balance between judicial independence and judicial accountability. In the federal court system, judges serve life terms "during good behavior"—that is, judges can be removed only through an impeachment process for cause. This life tenure is considered an important element, perhaps the most important element, in ensuring the independence of the federal judiciary.[55] There has never been a conviction of an impeached federal judge based solely on an unpopular judicial decision in the federal system.[56]

With only a few exceptions, state court judges serve fixed terms of office and must therefore seek reappointment or reelection. The rare exceptions are judges in Rhode Island, who serve life terms, and judges in Massachusetts and New Hampshire, who hold their positions until the age of seventy. Judges in states with fixed terms typically serve for less than ten years. New York trial court judges serve the longest terms in the states—fourteen years—and are required to retire at age seventy.[57]

Shorter tenures bring with them the increased danger that political interests and pressures will intrude on judicial decision making. Longer terms allow for judges to be evaluated on more complete records; any particular controversial decisions may have weaker effects when there are long periods between elections. To look at this another way, research indicates that judges with longer terms of office are more willing to manifest partisanship than are judges with shorter terms. For example, researchers Paul Brace and Melinda Gann Hall found that, out of all the judges they studied, Democrats with long terms were least likely to support capital punishment, whereas Republicans with long terms were most likely to support it. This led them to conclude that "term length influences the willingness of individual justices to express their partisanship."[58]

Judicial Compensation

In addition to selection and tenure, compensation is one of the bellwethers for assessing independence of the judiciary. How a state determines the salaries of its judges and whether those salaries can be reduced makes a difference. The U.S. Constitution forbids reducing federal judicial salaries as a protection for judges who make unpopular decisions. In 2012, Governor Chris Christie of New Jersey ran headlong into a similar state constitutional prohibition on lowering judicial pay. In his signature attempt to lower state expenditures, he sought to mandate increased pension and health benefit contributions from all state employees. Not so fast, said the state supreme court when it ruled in favor of the 375 state court judges who sued.[59] However, not all state constitutions include this proscription. In Florida, for instance, the constitution does not prevent the legislature from amending state laws to reduce salaries to discipline judges for unpopular decisions.[60]

According to the National Center for State Courts, at least twenty states have created independent judicial compensation commissions to advise their legislatures on judicial salary levels. The goal of these commissions is to determine the amount necessary to retain and recruit qualified judges and to eliminate the need for judges to lobby for their own salaries. States without such commissions rely on a variety of methods to eliminate partisan bickering over judicial salaries. The District of Columbia links its judges' salary increases to those of federal judges. Judges' salaries

TABLE 9-1

Associate Justices' Salaries, by Rank, 2010 (dollars)

Courts of Last Resort		Intermediate Appellate Courts		Trial Courts	
Top Five		**Top Five**		**Top Five**	
California	218,237	California	204,599	California	178,789
Illinois	201,819	Illinois	189,949	Illinois	174,303
Pennsylvania	186,450	Alabama	178,878	Alaska	170,976
Delaware	185,050	Pennsylvania	175,923	Delaware	168,850
Alaska	184,908	Alaska	174,696	New Jersey	165,000
Bottom Five		**Bottom Five**		**Bottom Five**	
Mississippi	112,530	Mississippi	105,050	Mississippi	104,170
Montana	113,964	New Mexico	117,506	Montana	106,870
South Dakota	118,173	Idaho	118,506	South Dakota	110,377
Maine	119,476	Oregon	122,820	New Mexico	111,631
Idaho	119,506	Missouri	128,207	Maine	111,969

Source: Data compiled from the National Center for State Courts, "National Rankings by Position (Most Current)," January 1, 2010, www.ncsconline.org/d_kis/salary_survey/national_rank.asp.

in South Dakota are linked to annual increases of the salaries of other state employees. In Pennsylvania, judicial salary increases are tied to increases in the Consumer Price Index.[61] (See Table 9-1.)

Prosecution and Defense of Cases in State Courts

Criminal cases at the state court level most often involve a face-off between two state or county employees. The **prosecutor** pursues the case on behalf of the people and usually seeks the incarceration of the accused. Little difference exists among the states in the selection of the chief prosecutor; an elected county official almost always fills the position. The individual often is politically ambitious and views the job of chief prosecutor as a stepping-stone to higher elected office. For this reason, the policies of prosecutors tend to reflect the specific wishes of the county voters.

Private attorneys defend those individuals who can afford their services. In many cases, however, a **public defender**, an attorney also on the public payroll, represents the accused. Public defenders fulfill the state's constitutional requirement to provide indigent defense services—that is, defense services for those who are poor. There is much more variety in how states organize their systems of indigent defense than in their systems of prosecution. Some are organized into statewide systems of public defenders. Others states have established statewide commissions that set guidelines for local jurisdictions, sometimes distributing limited state funds to local programs that follow specific standards. Still others delegate the responsibility of deciding how to provide and fund indigent defense entirely to the counties.

The competing values of state oversight and local control play out differently depending on the cultural and political realities of each state as well as any practical concerns involved. Even some states with statewide public defenders' offices exclude rural areas where the case volume would make supporting such offices impracticable. In the current climate of runaway costs, increased caseloads, and widespread litigation-challenging programs, the trend has been toward more state oversight.

The Prosecutor

Commentators have gone so far as to say that the prosecutor has become the "most powerful office in the criminal justice system."[62] The prosecutor's office is run by an attorney referred to, depending on the state, as the chief prosecutor, district attorney, county attorney, commonwealth attorney, or state's attorney. Whatever the title, this lawyer represents the public in criminal and other cases. Most prosecutors are elected and typically serve four-year terms. It is a daunting job, particularly in major metropolitan districts, where the top prosecutor manages hundreds of lawyers and support staffers, deals with horrific crimes, and balances the need to serve justice with the "unavoidable scrutiny of won-lost statistics that become a factor in re-election campaigns."[63] This focus on statistics may, according to one commentator, undergird some prosecutors' resistance to the use of postconviction DNA testing to determine conclusively if the correct person was incarcerated for a crime.[64]

The authority to prosecute comes from the state, but prosecutors' offices are essentially local. A prosecutor's authority is over a specific jurisdiction, usually a county. County governments fund these offices, although close to half of them also receive some portion of their budgets from state funds.[65] Nationwide, there are more than 2,000 state court prosecutors' offices, employing approximately 78,000 attorneys, investigators, and support staffers.[66] They handle more than 2 million felonies and 7 million misdemeanors a year.

Most chief prosecutors serve jurisdictions with fewer than 100,000 people. About one-third of chief prosecutors' offices have a total staff of four or fewer.[67] The top 5 percent of prosecutors' offices, however, serve districts with populations of 500,000 or more. They represent almost half the entire U.S. population.[68] In 2001, these large offices handled approximately 66 percent of the nation's serious crimes and had a median budget

---

Prosecutor
A government official and lawyer who conducts criminal cases on behalf of the people.

Public Defender
A government lawyer who provides free legal services to persons accused of crimes who cannot afford to hire lawyers.

of more than $14 million.[69] The Los Angeles County district attorney's office has the largest staff, consisting of more than 2,200 people, including more than 1,000 attorneys.[70] The types of cases handled by these offices have grown increasingly complex as prosecutors' offices encounter high-tech crimes, including identity theft and credit card fraud, and as they take on homeland security responsibilities.

A state's chief prosecutors have enormous discretion in the conduct of most of their responsibilities. The prosecutor makes all decisions as to whether or not to prosecute, whom to prosecute, and with what cause of action to prosecute. Discretion in charging is, in the words of one scholar, "virtually unchecked by formal constraints or regulatory mechanisms, making it one of the broadest discretionary powers in criminal administration."[71] Charging decisions are enormously important, particularly in states where statutory guidelines set minimum sentences or where the same act can be subject to a number of different charges.

Several reasons exist for giving prosecutors such broad powers. One is the trend toward **legislative overcriminalization**, the tendency of legislatures to make crimes out of everything that people find objectionable.[72] By creating a large number of broadly defined crimes, legislatures have made it impossible for states to enforce all of their criminal statutes, even as they have made it possible for prosecutors to charge a single act under multiple, overlapping provisions.[73] This ability to charge the same act in multiple ways gives a prosecutor tremendous leverage over a defendant. It is a powerful tool to coerce a guilty plea to a lesser charge through the process of plea bargaining.

A second reason prosecutors are given broad discretion is the need to individualize justice. Each case involves a unique set of facts and issues and requires careful weighing of the evidence. To determine how best to spend limited resources, a prosecutor must balance the severity of the crime against the

probability of sustaining a conviction. Prosecutors have been reluctant to publish general guidelines regarding their charging decisions. A Florida prosecutor stated that his office declines to prosecute cases of cocaine possession when the amount of cocaine involved is deemed too small. But he refused to say just how much is too small. Understandably, he worried that drug smugglers would package their shipments in smaller batches than this arbitrary limit and thus escape prosecution.[74]

There are some limits to prosecutorial authority, for instance, in regard to the trial process itself. In many jurisdictions, before proceeding to trial the government first must obtain an **indictment**, a formal criminal charge, from a **grand jury**. The U.S. Supreme Court has noted that the grand jury historically has been regarded as the primary protection for the innocent. However, only prosecutors and their witnesses appear before a grand jury; no members of the defense are present. Prosecutors are able to offer their interpretation of the evidence and the law and have no obligation to inform the grand jury of evidence of a defendant's innocence. Grand juries hear only one side of any given case and thus almost always indict. For this reason, no discussion of grand juries is complete without mention of the immortal quip by former New York state judge Sol Wachtler that a grand jury could "indict a ham sandwich." It is also part of the reason that many states have abolished the grand jury and now rely instead on a preliminary hearing in which a judge decides if enough evidence exists to warrant a trial.

At trial, a criminal jury must determine guilt beyond a reasonable doubt. The possibility of **jury nullification** exists if the jury does not believe a case

---

Legislative Overcriminalization
The tendency of government to make a crime out of anything the public does not like.

Indictment
A formal criminal charge.

Grand Jury
A group of between sixteen and twenty-three citizens who decide if a case should go to trial; if the grand jury decides that it should, an indictment is issued.

Jury Nullification
A jury's returning a verdict of "not guilty" even though jurists believe the defendant is guilty. By doing so, the jury cancels out the effect of a law that the jurors believe is immoral or was wrongly applied to the defendant.

should have been brought to court. Trials, however, rarely come into play as a check on the discretion of prosecutors—few cases actually end up going to trial. Most are resolved through plea bargaining. Plea bargaining is another area in which prosecutors have broad discretion. Judges rarely question or second-guess plea bargains reached between prosecutors and defendants. Prosecutors ultimately have to answer to the voters, because chief prosecutors are elected in everywhere other than Alaska, Connecticut, New Jersey, and Washington, D.C.[75]

There are positive and negative aspects to subjecting the prosecution of local crimes to the political process. On the positive side, the person deciding which laws to enforce and how to enforce them is answerable to the people of that district. More worrying is that political pressures—rather than the facts of a case—may guide the exercise of prosecutorial discretion. Prosecutors, for example, may choose not to charge politically connected friends. Some attributed the multibillion-dollar savings and loan scandal of the 1980s and 1990s to the reluctance of prosecutors to subject their friends and political allies to criminal indictment.[76] Discretion also can be misused when race enters the equation. Studies have shown that when the victim is white and the defendant is black, prosecutors are much more likely to seek the greatest possible punishment.[77]

Defense Attorneys

Anyone with even a casual acquaintance with TV crime dramas knows that after the police make an arrest they must inform the suspect of certain rights. One is that "you have the right to an attorney. If you cannot afford one, one will be appointed for you." This right derives from the Sixth Amendment of the U.S. Constitution: "In all criminal prosecutions, the accused shall enjoy the right . . . to have the assistance of counsel for his defense." In 1963, the U.S. Supreme Court found in *Gideon v. Wainwright* that this right to counsel is so fundamental and essential to a fair trial that the Constitution requires the state to provide a poor defendant with a lawyer at state expense. Nine years after *Gideon,* the Court extended this right to counsel to all criminal prosecutions, state or federal, **felony** or **misdemeanor**, that carry a possible sentence of imprisonment. The Court also has made it clear that the Sixth Amendment guarantees "the right to the *effective* assistance of counsel." If an attorney is unprepared, drunk, or sleeping during a trial, that can be grounds for appeal.

No money came along with the constitutional mandate for counsel, and its scope is tremendous because most criminal defendants in the United States cannot afford to pay for legal services. In 1991, about three-quarters of state prison inmates reported that they had been represented by a court-appointed lawyer.[78] In thirty states, a public defender system is the primary method used to provide indigent criminal defendants with lawyers.[79] In 2007, 957 public defenders' offices across the country received almost 6 million cases, at a cost of $2.3 billion. Twenty-two states' public defenders' offices are funded almost exclusively by state sources, eleven use a combination of state and county funds, and sixteen use only county funds.[80]

Not only did the mandate come with no funding, but it also lacked any specifications as to how indigent services must be provided. States and localities, as a consequence, have devised differing systems, with the quality of service provided varying tremendously. Three primary models have emerged throughout the nation, with most states employing public defender programs, **assigned counsel**, **contract attorneys**, or some combination of these. The method chosen may vary from county to county within a state, or a state may rely primarily on one type and use either of the other types for casework overload or the inevitable cases involving conflict of interest. Among the nation's one hundred most populous counties in 1999 (the latest figures available), public defender programs were operating in ninety counties, assigned counsel programs in eighty-nine counties, and contract programs in forty-two counties.[81] Public

---

Felony
A serious crime, such as murder or arson.

Misdemeanor
A less serious crime, such as shoplifting.

Assigned Counsel
Private lawyers selected by the courts to handle particular cases and paid from public funds.

Contract Attorney
A private attorney who enters into an agreement with a state, county, or judicial district to work on a fixed-fee basis per case or for a specific length of time.

A 2005 survey of 2,485 Anchorage residents found that only 6.4 percent of respondents felt defense attorneys were excellent at treating people fairly. Prosecutors and judges fared little better, at 8 and 13.3 percent, respectively.

defenders usually serve metropolitan areas, and assigned counsel programs and contract programs serve less populous regions.

Public defenders' offices draw on salaried staffs of attorneys. They provide criminal legal defense services either as employees paid directly by the government or through public or private nonprofit organizations. Large public defenders' offices generally employ attorneys who are trained and supervised and who are supported by investigative, paralegal, and clerical staffers. The American Bar Association has observed, "When adequately funded and staffed, defender organizations employing full-time personnel are capable of providing excellent defense services."[82] The challenge is to fund and staff these offices adequately. In 2009, the Michigan Court of Appeals ruled in favor of criminal defendants who charged that three counties' public defense systems were so underfunded that they failed to provide adequate representation. Put simply, the defendants contended that the system was unconstitutional due to lack of funding—and the court agreed, sparking debate statewide about potential reforms.[83] In Washington, the state supreme court recently entered this debate by setting explicit limits on acceptable public defender workloads. The court set these limits after overturning convictions in a number of cases because of inadequate defenses provided by overburdened public defenders. In one such case, for instance, a twelve-year-old boy convicted of sexually molesting a neighbor child was represented by a public defender who handled about five hundred cases a year. The defender failed to investigate the case and only spoke with the boy to urge him to plead guilty. After the high court granted the boy a new trial, he was completely exonerated.[84]

Another type of system uses assigned counsel; here private attorneys are chosen and appointed to handle particular cases, either on a systematic or an ad hoc basis, and are paid from public funds. Depending on the state, individual judges, assigned counsel program offices, or the court clerk's office may make the appointments. In the oldest type of assigned counsel program, judges make ad hoc assignments of counsel. Sometimes the only basis for these decisions is whoever is in the courtroom at the time. These arrangements frequently are criticized for fostering patronage (the granting of jobs to political allies), particularly in counties with small populations.

Most states using assigned counsel appoint lawyers from a roster of attorneys available for assigned cases. These rosters are compiled in various ways. Generally, defense attorneys need do no more than put their names on a list to be appointed to cases. No review of their experience, qualifications, or competence is conducted. Some states, particularly those with organized plans administered by independent managers, may require that attorneys receive specific training before they can be included on the roster. Assigned counsel are generally paid either a flat fee or an hourly rate, in some cases subject to an overall fee cap. Many are paid at very low rates, such that only recent law school graduates or those who have been unsuccessful in the business of law will agree to take assignments.[85]

Contract attorney programs are another way in which states provide defense services. A state, county, or judicial district will enter into a contract for the provision of indigent representation. Such a contract may be awarded to a solo attorney, to a law firm that handles both indigent and private cases, to a nonprofit organization, or to a group of lawyers who have joined together to provide services under the contract. The contractor may agree to accept cases on a fixed-fee per case basis or to provide representation for a particular period of time for a fixed fee.

Fixed-fee contracts specify the total amount of compensation the lawyer will receive for work on all cases taken during a specified period of time. The contractor must accept all cases that come up during the duration of the contract. For this reason, some view the use of fixed-fee contracts as a quick fix that allows the funding body to limit costs and accurately project expenses for the coming year. However, such contracts have been criticized severely by the courts and by national organizations such as the American Bar Association, because to make a profit, the contracting attorney has to spend as little time as possible on each case.

Few states rely on contract attorneys to provide representation for all or even a majority of their indigent defense cases. More commonly, they use such attorneys to handle periods of public defender overload or when conflicts of interest arise. Sometimes, public defenders' offices will contract out specific categories of cases, such as juvenile or traffic offenses. Of the total amount spent on indigent criminal defense in the nation's one hundred largest counties in 1999, only 6 percent was spent on contract programs.[86]

Regardless of the model used by a county or state, all public defender systems depend on adequate funding to successfully provide "effective assistance of counsel." Inadequate funding leads to lawyers' carrying impossible caseloads. Overburdened lawyers make crucial decisions based on too little investigation of the facts and inevitably pressure clients to plead guilty. Many indigent defense systems are plagued by lack of funding and resources, high attorney workloads, and little or no oversight of the quality of services—problems that can and do result in the conviction of innocent people. "Providing genuinely adequate counsel for poor defendants would require a substantial infusion of money and indigent defense is the last thing the populace will voluntarily direct its tax dollars to fund," writes attorney David Cole. "Achieving solutions to this problem through the political process is a pipe dream."[87]

How secure would you feel if you were facing more than twenty years in jail for a felony you didn't commit in Virginia, where your appointed lawyer could be paid a maximum of $1,235 to defend you?[88] If you don't plead guilty quickly, your lawyer will lose money on your case. Recently, a wave of successful lawsuits against underfunded and overburdened public defenders, assigned counsel programs, and contract attorneys by groups such as the American Civil Liberties Union have led legislators to enact reforms that "even the most skeptical observers admit have the potential to bring important changes to the process of criminal justice."[89] Some of these have led to successful injunctions or settlements, increased funding for indigent defense, and improved administration of such programs. Furthermore, the defense community and organizations such as the American Bar Association have been focusing on the need for standards for indigent criminal representation. The goal is to educate those policymakers who design the systems through which these legal services are delivered.

Juries

If you vote, pay a utility bill, or have a driver's license, you may be called to jury duty at some point in your life. You may be asked to decide whether a defendant in a capital case lives or dies; whether someone spends the rest of his or her life in prison; whether a civil plaintiff, injured and unable to work, should be able to collect damages; or whether a civil defendant must be bankrupted by the large amount of damages ordered to be paid. Service on a jury may require spending days or weeks listening to intricate scientific evidence and expert testimony, some of it conflicting, and deciding who is credible and who is not to be believed. Or you may spend one day in a large room with other potential jurors, break for lunch, and go home at the end of that day without ever hearing a single case.

The right to a jury trial in state criminal proceedings is granted by the Sixth Amendment. Not all criminal prosecutions trigger the right to a jury trial—minor offenses involving potential sentences of less than six months do not require juries. Neither do juvenile proceedings, probation revocation proceedings, or military trials.

The jury's role in a trial is that of fact-finder. The judge has to ensure a fair and orderly trial, but it is the jurors who must determine the facts of the case. In some instances, parties may agree to forgo a jury trial and, instead, choose a bench

> Stereotypes might lead you to think that juries are less capable than judges of separating emotion from reason or that juries decide cases more generously for injured plaintiffs or that grisly evidence in criminal cases may motivate juries to base their decisions on passion or prejudice. Not so.

Local Focus

Maricopa County's Flat Fees and the Death Penalty

You know you're in trouble when you're facing the death penalty and your lawyer would rather go to jail himself than work on your case. In the late 1990s, Phoenix attorney Mike Terribile represented convicted murderer Richard Rivas, but as the case entered the sentencing phase, he refused to do any more work. The reason? Terribile said the flat fee he had received from Maricopa County to handle the case as a contract attorney was not enough to cover his costs. He appealed the payment contract to a judge, saying he would refuse to prepare Rivas's defense if he was turned down, even if that meant being held in contempt and jailed.

As in many jurisdictions, the public defenders' office in Maricopa County simply can't handle all the indigent cases it receives—more than 50,000 each year. To alleviate the problem, the county contracts with private attorneys to handle the overflow. The county generally pays about $64,000 for a set of eight cases. Maricopa County administrator David Smith says that's plenty. "If a case settles with just a few hours' work, they [still] get the $8,000," Smith points out. He says that there is a

provision in the contract that allows for extra compensation if a case gets complicated, but he notes that 97 percent of the cases in the county are plea-bargained out. "We expect that it will all even out." Contract attorneys handling capital cases were paid more—$10,000 at the start and an additional $10,000 if the case went to trial—but those cases demand many more than just a few hours' work.

After years of battle, the county stepped up payments for capital cases to at least $50,000, with the possibility for more based on the number of hours spent on a case. Contract attorneys welcomed the additional money but soon recognized another problem—there were too few of them to staff the county's death penalty cases. Inadequate defense is a major reason the American Bar Association has called for a death penalty moratorium. "You go to any death penalty state and start asking questions about counsel in those cases and, with very few exceptions, there are substantial problems," says Tye Hunter, former executive director of North Carolina's Indigent Defense Services Commission.

Source: Adapted from Alan Greenblatt, "Flat Fees and Death Penalties," *Governing,* March 2001, www.governing.com/archive/archive/2001/mar/glimpses.txt; Michael Terribile, "And So It Goes" and "We Won, and No One Told Us," Arizona Attorneys for Criminal Justice, July 28, 2007, and January 25, 2006, www.aacj.org/news-indigent-defense.php.

trial, in which the judge serves as both judge and jury. In a criminal bench trial, the judge alone decides guilt or innocence.

Differences and similarities in how judges and juries rule have been the subject of much research and review. Stereotypes might lead you to think that juries are less capable than judges of separating emotion from reason or that juries decide cases more generously for injured plaintiffs or that grisly evidence in criminal cases may motivate juries to base their decisions on passion or prejudice. Not

so. For instance, research shows that civil plaintiffs in product liability and medical malpractice cases have more success before judges in bench trials.[90]

Historically, juries in the United States have been composed of twelve people who must come to a unanimous verdict. Since 1970, however, a series of U.S. Supreme Court decisions has allowed states to move away from this standard.[91] In state jury trials, whether unanimity is required depends on the size of the jury. A conviction by a twelve-member jury may be less than unanimous, whereas a six-member jury must have unanimity. A majority of states continue to require twelve-member juries to make unanimous rulings in

Liability
A legal obligation or responsibility.

felony criminal cases, but seven states use six-member or eight-member juries for noncapital felonies. Two states, Louisiana and Oregon, do not require unanimous verdicts in such cases.[92] Most states provide for civil juries of six members or eight members. Those that still require twelve members typically allow the parties to civil cases to agree to smaller juries. Unanimity is not required in most civil trials; instead, most states provide for verdicts based on a supermajority of either five-sixths or two-thirds.

States develop and maintain master lists from which they identify potential jurors. Their sources include driver's licenses, motor vehicle registrations, telephone directories, tax rolls, utility customer lists, voter registration rolls, and lists of actual voters. It is very hard to avoid ever being called in for jury duty. Jurors must be residents of the county in which the court sits and must generally be eighteen years old, although in Alabama and Nebraska the minimum age is nineteen and in Mississippi and Missouri it is twenty-one. States also usually have some sort of requirement regarding literacy and the ability to understand or communicate in English, or both. South Carolina requires that jurors have at least a sixth-grade education, and Tennessee explicitly excludes those of "unsound mind" and "habitual drunkards." Most states also require that jurors not be convicted felons.

The provisions for selecting jurors typically are the same for all the trial courts within a state, although some make distinctions between limited and general jurisdiction courts. The formal process of jury selection begins with a **voir dire** examination. This is the process by which prospective jurors are interviewed and examined by the attorneys for both sides in a case. Some may be excused following challenges by the attorneys. The primary purpose of this process is to impanel, or select, an impartial jury. If it appears during the questioning that a juror is biased or has a particular view of the case, either attorney may ask that the juror be excused for cause. There is no limit on the number of **for cause challenges** a party can make. In addition, each party receives a certain number of **peremptory challenges**, which allow the lawyers to kick individuals off the jury for any reason other than race or gender.

Defendants' Rights versus Victims' Rights

A crime typically involves at least two actors: a perpetrator and a victim. Traditionally, the criminal justice system in the United States interposes the ideal of public prosecution between the two. That is, all crimes are crimes against the state. The prosecutor, representing the public and not any particular individual, sees that justice is done objectively and fairly. The public's interest, under this system, is distinct from the victim's interest in retribution.

Numerous provisions in the Bill of Rights balance the rights of criminal defendants against the powers of the state. These defendants' rights include the following:

- The right to be presumed innocent until proven guilty
- The right to be safe from arrest or searches and seizures unless the government has made a showing of probable cause
- The right to a lawyer
- The right to a jury trial
- The right to confront witnesses
- The rights to due process and the equal protection of laws
- If proven guilty, the right to punishment that is not cruel and unusual

In spelling out these rights, the framers sought to prevent the overreach of government power. They worried that innocent people otherwise might be railroaded into jail on charges they never had a chance to defend themselves against adequately. The Bill of Rights makes no mention of the rights of crime victims.

In the past three decades, the balance between defendants' rights and victims' rights has undergone

Voir Dire
The interviewing and examination of potential jurors by the attorneys for both sides of a case.

For Cause Challenge
A lawyer's asking the judge to excuse a potential juror because the individual appears to be biased or unable to be fair.

Peremptory Challenge
A lawyer's dismissal of a potential juror for any reason except race or gender.

a radical transformation. Defendants still have all of the rights listed, but now state courts are increasingly balancing them against a new class of victims' rights. The movement advocating an increasing role in the courts for the victims of crime has become a formidable force and has achieved tremendous success in enacting legislation in all the states. The momentum started in 1982, when a president's task force on victims of crime described the U.S. justice system as "appallingly out of balance." That is not to say that victims were helpless—the number of state laws addressing victims' rights was already in the hundreds. By 1998, however, the number of crime victim–related statutes had soared to more than 27,000. Twenty-nine states had passed victims' rights constitutional amendments.[93]

Today, every state has either a constitutional amendment or a statutory scheme that protects victims' rights. Some predict that the next amendment to the U.S. Constitution will be a victims' rights amendment. Supporters of victims' rights frequently argue that the justice system favors defendants over victims and that, without modification, the system itself constitutes a second victimization. On the other hand, civil rights organizations fear that some victims' rights laws upset the system of checks and balances in the nation's criminal justice system and undercut the basic due process protections designed to keep innocent people out of prison.

The specifics of victims' rights laws vary among the states. A variety of statutes and amendments guarantee that crime victims receive monetary compensation, notice of procedural developments in their cases, protection from offender harm, and more attentive treatment from the justice system. The more controversial of such laws are directed toward providing victims with significantly greater involvement in actual prosecutions. This includes providing victims the right to confer with the prosecutor at all stages, including plea bargains; the right to attend all stages of the case, even if the victim will be called as a witness; and the right to introduce victim-impact statements at the sentencing phase of the trial.

Perhaps the most controversial and interesting of the victims' rights laws concern victim-impact evidence. This may be particularly true in capital cases, in which impact statements have been described as

highly emotional, frequently tearful testimony coming directly from the hearts and mouths of the survivors left behind by killings. And it arrives at the precise time when the balance is at its most delicate and the stakes are highest—when jurors are poised to make the visceral decision of whether the offender lives or dies.[94]

In 1991, the U.S. Supreme Court reversed itself and ruled that impact statements that detailed the particular qualities of the victim and the harm caused to the victim's family could be admissible in capital sentencing hearings.[95] Today, all states allow victim-impact evidence at the sentencing phase of a trial. Most of the states with the death penalty allow it in capital trials.

Sentencing

The total U.S. prison population has ballooned in the past thirty years, rising from less than 320,000 in 1980 to a high of 2.3 million in 2008.[96] The trend might be reversing, as 2009 and 2010 marked the first declines in total prison population in four decades.[97] Corrections has been one of the fastest-growing items in state budgets, and, although it slowed considerably owing to widespread revenue shortfalls and limited state resources after 2008, it still averaged 31 percent of total state spending and 7.3 percent of state general fund budgets in 2010.[98]

In most states, after a jury finds a defendant guilty, the judge holds a separate sentencing hearing. In capital cases, the U.S. Supreme Court has held that only a unanimous jury, and not the judge, can sentence a defendant to death.[99] In many states, capital juries are instructed that a sentence of life in prison without the possibility of parole is an option. In noncapital cases, by contrast, it is almost always the judge who sets sentence. Only in Arkansas, Kentucky, Missouri, Oklahoma, Texas, and Virginia do juries choose the sentences of those they find guilty. In most of these states, the judge is free to reduce but not to increase the jury's sentence, except to comply with mandatory sentencing laws. Most of these states choose their judges through popular election, so having juries decide on sentences allows trial judges to evade political heat for sentencing.

Sentencing policy involves the balancing of value judgments, such as the perceived severity of the crime and the perceived severity of different punishments, with the relevance of mitigating circumstances. It must include consideration of the costs to the taxpayers and to society of incarceration. Surveys indicate that attitudes toward sentencing follow regional patterns, "with residents of New England demonstrating the greatest tendency to be lenient and residents of central southern states displaying the least leniency."[100] It is not surprising, then, that state sentencing laws vary and that the punishment a convict faces depends not just on what that person did but also on where the crime was committed. Voters in California and Oklahoma, for instance, view drug offenses differently. In California state courts, a cocaine dealer is subject to a two- to four-year prison term. The same offense in Oklahoma brings a minimum of five years and a maximum of life imprisonment.[101]

The amount of discretion given to judges also varies from state to state. Depending on the type of crime and where the defendant is charged, the sentence can be a matter of "do the crime, do the time" or whatever the judge or parole board thinks is best.

A few decades ago, it was possible to talk of a predominant American approach to criminal sentencing. At all levels of the nation's criminal justice system, a concern for rehabilitation and deterrence led states to embrace **indeterminate sentencing**. Legislatures set very wide statutory sentencing margins within which judges had the discretion to impose sentences for imprisonment with little fear of appellate review. The sentencing was indeterminate because the parole board, not the judge, had ultimate control over the actual release date. Under this system, judges and parole boards had to apply their discretion to tailor punishments to the specific rehabilitative needs of individual defendants. This practice led to wide discrepancies in the sentences imposed on different persons convicted of the same crimes.

Indeterminate sentencing came under attack from several angles during the 1970s. The lack of guidance for judges led to the potential for discrimination in sentencing based on such factors as race, ethnic group, social status, and gender. There was also criticism of the ability of parole boards to determine successfully whether inmates had or had not been rehabilitated. Finally, rehabilitation lost favor as the country entered an era of tough-on-crime rhetoric and a "just deserts" theory of criminal sentencing.[102] Reformers sought to replace indeterminate sentencing with **determinate sentencing**. This led to the adoption of federal sentencing guidelines, a structured system of binding sentencing rules that greatly limited judicial discretion in sentencing in the federal courts.

In contrast to the federal court system, there has been no single sweeping sentencing reform across all fifty states. Some states have made wholesale changes to determinate sentencing laws, but most continue to use indeterminate sentencing.

Indeterminate sentencing does not necessarily mean more lenient sentencing. It just means that the actual amount of time served may vary depending on the judge or the findings of a parole board. For instance, before the charges were dropped, Los Angeles Lakers star Kobe Bryant was charged with felony sexual assault in Colorado. The sex offense statutes there are considered among the harshest in the country. Any sentence on a sex assault charge can mean the possibility of life imprisonment. The severity of the sentence depends in part on the results of a battery of tests administered to the convicted defendant. The judge uses these results in sentencing, and the parole board uses them to determine whether the prisoner is a continued threat. The tests include a plethysmograph test, which involves placing an electric band around the penis in an attempt to measure deviant thoughts as the

---

Indeterminate Sentencing
The sentencing of an offender, by a judge, to a minimum and a maximum amount of time in prison, with a parole board deciding how long the offender actually remains in prison.

Determinate Sentencing
The sentencing of an offender, by a judge, to a specific amount of time in prison depending on the crime.

person is shown images of abusive behaviors. Although the tests have been described as "very Clockwork Orangish" by Don Recht, former head of the Colorado Defense Bar, the results are studied carefully nonetheless. Under Colorado's indeterminate sentencing law, convicted sex offenders are released only when parole boards deem them safe to reenter society.

Most states still rely on indeterminate sentencing, but all states have adopted at least some features of determinate sentencing, although in greatly differing degrees. When it comes to sentencing reform, "the states have served as hothouses of experimentation during the last thirty years, with so much activity that the diversity of provisions among the states has become exceedingly complex."[103] Some of the major reforms adopted include sentencing guidelines (either presumptive, meaning the judge can deviate with a good reason, or purely voluntary), **mandatory minimum sentences** that are imposed for conviction of specified crimes, **habitual offender laws**, and **truth-in-sentencing laws**. With the implementation of these reforms, the time served in prison by those convicted has been increasing as a percentage of the sentence imposed. In 1993, the percentage of a sentence that an offender spent in prison was 31.8 percent; that figure had increased to 46.7 percent by 2009.[104] The average length of an incarceration increased as well; offenders who were released from state prisons in 2009 served an average of almost three years behind bars, nine months longer than those released in 1990.[105]

All fifty states and the District of Columbia have enacted some form of mandatory minimum prison sentencing laws.[106] These laws limit judicial discretion by requiring that individuals found guilty of specific crimes be incarcerated for no less than specified lengths of time. Such crimes may include drug possession or trafficking, drunk driving, and sexual offenses. The mandatory sentencing laws also may include "bump ups" that take effect if certain acts enhanced the severity of the underlying crime, for instance, if weapons were involved or if the crime occurred near a school. If a crime involved the use of a deadly weapon, New Mexico requires an additional year for the first offense and three additional years for a second offense. The use of a firearm in the commission of a crime in Nevada requires a doubling of the sentence for the underlying crime. In Ohio, the use of a deadly weapon requires an additional term of three to six years.[107]

Habitual offender laws also are common among the states. These statutes impose more severe sentences for offenders who previously have been sentenced for crimes. California's "three strikes" law was a prototype of this kind of legislation. The law states that if a defendant convicted of a felony has one prior conviction for a "serious" or "violent" felony, the sentence is doubled. Defendants convicted of a felony with two prior convictions for "serious" or "violent" felonies receive a life sentence without possibility of parole. The law has been severely criticized for its "unbending harshness," but it has withstood constitutional challenges.[108] As written, according to Michael Romano, director of the Three Strikes Project, the law has sentenced people to life in prison for relatively small crimes such as drug possession or petty theft. In 2004 a ballot proposition to revise the law to impose a life term only if the third felony conviction is for a "serious or violent offense" failed. Supporters reintroduced the proposal for the 2012 elections, and this time it passed by a wide margin. Twenty-four states have enacted some form of "two or three strikes" legislation. One such state is Michigan, where the sentence is one-and-a-half times the maximum sentence for the second conviction and twice the maximum sentence for a third conviction.[109]

Another sentencing reform movement began in the 1990s as a reaction to the sometimes jarring disparity between the sentence handed down by a judge and the actual amount of time served in prison. These "truth-in-sentencing" laws reduce the amount of discretion parole boards have to shorten sentences for good behavior. They do this by specifying the proportions of sentences that offenders

---

Mandatory Minimum Sentence
The shortest sentence that an offender may receive upon conviction for a certain offense. The court has no authority to impose a shorter sentence.

Habitual Offender Laws
Statutes imposing harsher sentences on offenders who previously have been sentenced for crimes.

Truth-in-Sentencing Laws
Laws that give parole boards less authority to shorten sentences for good behavior by specifying the proportion of a sentence an offender must serve before becoming eligible for parole.

must serve before they may be considered for parole. The federal government encourages truth-in-sentencing laws by conditioning the states' receipt of federal prison construction funds on the requirement that certain violent offenders serve at least 85 percent of their sentences. With this carrot, almost all states and the District of Columbia have adopted some form of truth-in-sentencing laws. Most, however, still have parole boards with some discretionary release authority and systems in which incarcerated felons can accumulate "good time" under specified formulas. Arkansas, Louisiana, Vermont, and Wyoming are among the many states that provide for a day of "good time" for each day—or less—served. North Dakota grants five days of "good time" for every month served.

These formulas also can be complicated by the accumulation of work or education credits. Some states, such as Illinois, have cut through the confusion by eliminating "good time" credits for certain serious offenses. Others have eliminated such credits altogether. Michigan eliminated "good time" for all felony offenses committed after December 2000, and the District of Columbia has not offered it since 1994.[110]

As states reduce judges' discretion and increase the amount of time that offenders spend in prison, a considerable burden has been placed on the facilities and personnel of the state prison systems. In California, atrocious conditions caused by prison overcrowding have become such a problem that the U.S. Supreme Court held in *Brown v. Plata* (2011) that California prisons violate the Eighth Amendment ban on cruel and unusual punishment. The Court ordered the release over the next several years of tens of thousands of prisoners to reduce overcrowding to 137.5 percent of capacity. For this reason, many nonviolent offenders find their prison terms greatly reduced. In November 2011, actress Lindsay Lohan served only four hours on a three-day sentence for probation violations before being released to reduce overcrowding.

While few question that putting more people in prison for longer terms has played a role in the drop in crime rates since the 1990s, longer sentences have also been the primary drivers of increasing prison costs. In a 2012 report, the Pew Center on the States put the financial impact of longer prison stays at $10 billion for offenders released in 2009 alone; the report further suggested that a significant portion of nonviolent offenders could have served shorter stays with no adverse impact on public safety.[111] In response to such research findings and increasingly tight state budgets, some states are starting to take a step back on mandatory minimum sentencing. New York, for instance, has eliminated mandatory minimums for first- and second-time nonviolent drug offenses. In 2002 Michigan repealed most of its mandatory minimums for nonviolent drug offenders, a move that has saved the state $41 million a year.

In addition, most states are exploring sentencing options for their less serious offenders that are less severe than imprisonment but more serious than ordinary probation. One such option is house arrest. Offenders under house arrest are required to remain in their residences for the duration of their sentences. They often must wear electronic wrist or ankle bracelets that send continuous radio signals to verify their locations.

Many states rely on "intensive probation." This form of probation involves much closer supervision by parole officers with smaller caseloads than the norm. In such a program a parolee is typically required to hold a job, submit to urinalysis, pay restitution to victims, and perform community service. To alleviate prison overcrowding, some states release prisoners to "halfway houses" that assist with their reintegration into the community. Young first-time offenders may be sentenced for short periods to "boot camps," where they are subjected to strict military-style discipline. Nonviolent offenders may be offered work release; weekend sentencing; alcohol, drug, or mental health treatment; or release subject to appearance at daily reporting centers.

Problems from the Lack of Sentencing Uniformity

Since the 1970s, sentencing reform movements have concerned themselves more and more with the sentencing disparities that occur when judges and parole boards have broad discretion in the sentencing of criminal offenders. Many states have felt pressure to reform sentencing, but how they have responded has varied substantially. State sentencing guidelines, adopted by a minority of states, are not as rigid as the latest federal guidelines. State judges also tend to have more discretion than do federal judges.

A parallel trend in criminal law involves the increased federalization of crimes that were once the sole domain of the states. Many street crimes, such as low-level gun and drug offenses, are now federal offenses. Law enforcement officials have the choice of sending such cases to federal or state prosecutors and courts, and the cases are subject to the differing sets of sentencing guidelines. The trend away from discretion in sentencing has led to some uniformity nationwide in sentencing in federal courts. Ironically, however, the federal sentencing guidelines and the increased federalization of local crimes have increased the sense of randomness in sentencing within communities.

Whether an offender is charged in a state court or a federal court can make a huge difference in the sentence he or she receives. Nationwide, drug and weapons violations result in sentences that are, on average, three times longer in federal courts than in state courts.[112] In some cases, the essentially random decision to charge an individual in federal court can lead to a death penalty, even where local voters have twice rejected capital punishment, as in the District of Columbia. In some areas, prosecutors have been suspected of "shopping" for either a state or federal trial depending on the race of the offender. In one region of Massachusetts in the late 1990s, white crack cocaine dealers were tried exclusively in state courts, whereas many black dealers were tried in federal courts.[113] When two members of the same community who do the exact same thing are subjected to drastically different treatment, public confidence that justice is being done is undermined. This was one of the concerns that led to the passage of sentencing reforms in the first place.

The Case for Court Reform

How state courts are organized is not static or carved in stone. States constantly evaluate the practices and procedures of their criminal justice systems as they attempt to adapt to changing demographic, economic, and political conditions. This section discusses some reforms being adopted or at least being discussed in most states. Specialized courts to handle drug offenses or family matters are currently in vogue as ways to accommodate increasing caseloads and lower costs, as are attempts to streamline and speed up court dockets. Given the controversy surrounding judicial elections, particularly post–*Citizens United* (the Supreme Court decision that opened the door for unlimited campaign spending by super PACs), many states have not waited for major reforms to merit selection; instead, they have focused on modifying judicial elections to minimize the problems posed by the need for campaign contributions. Finally, this section addresses some of the pressures for court reform that stem from the lack of uniformity across the country and within individual states.

The Problem of Increasing Caseloads

Nationwide, violent crime rates are down. State courts, nonetheless, have found themselves on the front lines dealing with the results of societal problems such as substance abuse and family violence since the 1980s. From 1984 to 1999, the U.S. population grew by only 12 percent, but the number of juvenile criminal cases grew by 68 percent, and the number of domestic relations cases grew by 74 percent. Criminal cases, mostly misdemeanors, grew by 47 percent.[114]

In reaction to such growth, many states have created "problem-solving courts." These include community courts, domestic violence courts, mental health courts, and drug treatment courts. Their purpose is to deal decisively with low-level nonviolent crimes while reducing congestion in the general jurisdiction courts. The solutions often involve closely monitored treatment plans meant to stop the revolving door of **recidivism**, or relapse into criminal behavior. Drug courts, with their focus on judicially supervised treatment for

---

Recidivism
A return to, or relapse into, criminal behavior.

nonviolent drug-addicted offenders, have been shown to contribute to the decline in violent crime and to save local and state governments millions of dollars annually from reduced incarceration rates. While it is difficult to determine the cost-effectiveness of drug courts, a definitive evaluation of a Portland, Oregon, court estimated that total savings from drug court participation were more than $5,000 per participant. With an annual caseload of three hundred participants, the program saved the state more than $1.5 million per year.[115]

States also have been experimenting with integrated family courts. These courts, referred to as "one family/one judge" courts, adopt a holistic approach to all the issues that affect a single family in a single court system. Such integrated courts can address these issues more efficiently than can multiple courts, especially in cases in which delays can leave children in foster care limbo. Many individuals who appear in such family courts traditionally would have been forced, instead, to face multiple proceedings in different courts: assault charges in county court, custody disputes in family court, and divorce issues in yet another court. The current trend is to put all of a family's problems before a single, informed judge to eliminate conflicting orders and multiple appearances. New York has estimated that its integrated domestic violence courts slashed the number of family court cases from more than three thousand to fewer than nine hundred in its first two years while reducing delay and duplication and increasing cost-effective case management.[116]

This increased focus on court administration and case management has not been confined to the criminal side of the court calendar. Until just a few years ago, crowded civil dockets and multiyear waiting periods were relatively common in many states. "Back in the 1980s, there was no incentive for an insurance company to settle a case for the first year," said Bill Sieben, who was then president of the Minnesota Trial Lawyers Association. "They knew the case wasn't even going to be nearing a trial for several years."[117] This is becoming less true as states focus on clearing their overcrowded and overly cumbersome

civil dockets. Tom Phillips, former chief justice of the Texas Supreme Court, has attributed faster-clearing caseloads primarily to the rise of the managerial judge.[118] Most trial judges today may insist on strong case management systems, but a generation ago, when caseloads were smaller and more manageable, not many of them did.

In recent years, not content with merely handing down verdicts, forceful judges have seized control of their courts and made it clear that things will run according to their schedules, not at the convenience of lawyers who never seem quite ready to go to trial. "A very strong component of civil cases is, just set a trial date and the case will go away," said Kevin Burke, formerly the chief judge of the Hennepin County Court in Minnesota. "Left to their own devices, lawyers aren't necessarily going to manage it to a speedy resolution."[119]

State initiatives to speed up dockets, or court case schedules, have included an increased reliance on **alternative dispute resolution**. In certain types of cases, such resolution is now mandated, and lawyers are required to inform their clients about alternatives to standard court fights. These alternatives usually involve hashing things out in front of an expert mediator. Some courts have been creative in finding appropriately authoritative experts. Hennepin County courts, for instance, refer disputes involving dry cleaning—complaints about stained pants, torn dresses, and busted buttons—to a retired owner of a dry cleaning business for speedy resolution. An accountant may serve as mediator in the resolution of a financial dispute. These innovations increase the efficiency of the court system and free up trial judges for more complex cases.

Several states are experimenting with the **rocket docket**, patterned after an innovation in a Virginia federal court. In essence, this fast-tracked docket

---

Alternative Dispute Resolution
A way to end a disagreement by means other than litigation. It usually involves the appointment of a mediator to preside over a meeting between the parties.

Rocket Docket
Fast-tracked cases that often have limited, specific deadlines for specific court procedures.

imposes tight, unbending deadlines on lawyers for the handling of pretrial motions and briefs. In the Vermont Supreme Court, the rocket docket applies to cases that present no novel issue likely to add to the body of case law. Rather than all five justices sitting en banc to hear these cases, each month they split and rotate through a smaller and less cumbersome panel of three that is able to reach consensus more quickly. The panel releases its decisions on 99 percent of rocket docket cases within twenty-four hours.

Rocket dockets are not always a panacea, however. Florida implemented the approach as thousands of home foreclosures began clogging the courts in late 2006. The foreclosure courts could clear 250 cases a day, each in a matter of minutes. But, although it represented a success for the state, attorneys found fault with the system. The few homeowners who attended the hearings had little time to be heard, and one review of 180 cases in Sarasota found that only one in four had complete paperwork. By late 2009, one judge found a way to slow the rapid-fire process, at least a bit—he gave any homeowners who showed up at the courthouse an additional three months to work to save their homes or to move.[120]

In Colorado, rapid population growth has led to mounting lawsuits, and courts increasingly have turned to **magistrates** to resolve less important cases. Often local officials or attorneys hired on contract, these magistrates have helped the state to stay on top of an 85 percent increase in case filings despite only a 12 percent increase in the number of judges. A magistrate issues a preliminary decision that must then be upheld by a judge, but this is a formality in most cases. This modification is credited with enabling the state court system to handle routine cases efficiently and allowing more time for more complex cases, but some have complained to the Colorado Bar Association that this reliance on contract attorneys to serve as magistrates decreases the accountability of judges and does not yield sufficiently clear precedents to provide guidance to the attorneys who must practice before them.[121] Given these concerns, a task force on civil justice

---

Magistrate
A local official or attorney granted limited judicial powers.

reform convened by then governor Bill Ritter recommended that the state create additional district and county court judgeships to alleviate the caseload strain on the system.[122] A 2007 act created forty-three new positions for judges across Colorado; however, in light of state revenue shortfalls, funding was provided for only twenty-eight.

The Reform of Judicial Selection

Nationally, 87 percent of all state judges face partisan, nonpartisan, or retention elections or some mix of these.[123] As discussed earlier, the trend in recent years has been for these elections to become more and more like the elections for legislative and gubernatorial offices: loud, nasty, and expensive. Some fear that this will lead to a blurring of the distinction between the judicial and political branches of government and throw into question the independent decision making of the judiciary.

Indeed, two recent decisions from the U.S. Supreme Court may have brought politics closer than ever to the judicial election process. First, in *Republican Party v. White* (2002), a 5–4 majority ruled that the First Amendment does not allow the government "to prohibit candidates from communicating relevant information to voters during an election." This includes judicial candidates who wish to speak publicly about disputed legal matters. At the same time, the Court acknowledged the core responsibility of judges to "be willing to consider views that oppose [their] preconceptions, and remain open to persuasion when the issues arise in a pending case." Today, states that hold elections for judicial offices, such as Ohio, Pennsylvania, and Wisconsin, feature public debates among judicial candidates similar to those held for candidates for legislative office.

Then, in 2010, the Supreme Court ruled in the controversial *Citizens United v. Federal Election Commission* that laws placing limits on campaign spending by outside groups such as corporations and unions are unconstitutional. At the time, twenty-four states had laws banning independent expenditures in judicial elections; all were rendered moot by the holding in *Citizens United.*

States under Stress

This Court Will Not Come to Order

In Birmingham, Alabama, domestic relations judge Suzanne Childers keeps a .38-caliber Smith & Wesson revolver under her bench. That, and a can of pepper spray, have served as protection for her courtroom since budget cuts eliminated two deputies' positions. Childers's story is extreme, but hers is not the only courtroom that has been left less safe as a result of the state and local fiscal crisis. In Massachusetts, open court officer positions were not filled between the end of 2008 and early 2010, and in Maine, metal detectors in courthouses go unstaffed. "It's a question of do you want to close courthouses and run [fewer] courthouses with full security? Or do you want to keep all your courthouses open and compromise on security?" said Mary Ann Lynch, a spokeswoman for Maine's court system.[a]

In many states, courts are opening later in the day, closing earlier, and shutting their doors entirely for several days per month. Kansas and Oregon have begun closing courts on Fridays, and one court in Georgia has stopped hearing civil matters altogether to focus time on critical criminal matters. In some parts of North Carolina and Ohio, cases have ground to a halt because the courts could not afford to buy more paper. With states facing severe budget shortfalls, almost every state court system is trying to get by with less. A survey conducted by the National Center for State Courts (NCSC) in 2011 estimated that at least forty-two state court systems were facing cutbacks in their 2012 budgets, leading most courts to shrink staff and reduce hours.[b] Iowa, for instance, now has fewer employees in the judicial branch than it had twenty-four years ago, even though case filings in the state increased by 54 percent in the same period.[c]

NCSC reported that the cuts would lead to increased backlogs in civil, criminal, and family court cases. Such backlogs lead inevitably to delays; in San Francisco, it can now "take up to a year from the time you first get a [traffic] ticket until you get a trial date," says Ann Donian, communications director for San Francisco Superior Court.[d]

Making matters worse, states expected that the very programs they had implemented to help alleviate backlogs—alternative dispute resolution and problem-solving courts—would themselves end up on the chopping block.

When budget cuts eliminated courtroom security guards, Jefferson County, Alabama, domestic court judge Suzanne Childers resorted to keeping a .38-caliber pistol under her desk during session for protection.

---

[a]Quoted in Denise Lavoie, "Budget Cuts Force Tough Choices on Court Security," *Seattle Times*, January 10, 2010, http://seattletimes.nwsource.com/html/businesstechnology/2010758141_apuscourthousesecuritycuts.html.

[b]National Center for State Courts, "State Budget Cuts Threaten Public's Access to Courts," November 29, 2011, www.ncsc.org/Newsroom/Backgrounder/2011/Court-Budget-Cuts.aspx.

[c]Alan Greenblatt, "Sue Me? Not a Chance This Year," NPR, April 12, 2012, www.npr.org/2012/04/12/1504294441/sue-me-not-a-chance-this-year.

[d]Quoted in ibid.

This ruling magnified the already growing debate about the impact of increased spending in judicial elections and the best method of judicial selection.

The major reform movement of the latter half of the twentieth century was the merit selection of judges, described previously. This movement initially was very successful, but, after roughly half the states adopted merit selection systems, it has stalled in recent years. Since 1990, all the legislatures that have considered merit selection have rejected it. In the wake of *Citizens United,* a dozen state legislatures proposed changing away from selecting judges through popular elections, but none was successful. States seeking to adopt merit selection are confronted with both cultural and political obstacles. They face an ingrained cultural belief that elections are a critical part of our democracy that are not to be sacrificed without a fight. Combined with this is the political reality that in most states a change to merit selection would require the legislative supermajority and public approval necessary for a constitutional change.

Recognizing these barriers to the adoption of merit selection, reformers are focusing on improving popular judicial elections to minimize the threat they pose to judicial independence and impartiality. A fifty-state survey commissioned by the California legislature reviewed state trends in the wake of *Citizens United* and the unprecedented level of interest group activity in judicial elections.[124] In one trend, more than half the states have proposed more stringent reporting and disclosure of campaign contributions to increase the information available to voters. Iowa, for instance, passed a law requiring all political ads to run "paid for by" disclosures. Other states have focused on **recusal** and disqualification rules, which until recently have been very lenient, allowing judges to decide on their own whether they should recuse themselves from particular cases. Two kinds of recusal requirements have been proposed. Some require recusal if a case involves a contributor who has donated more than a specific cutoff amount to the judge's campaign, and other plans require that any recusal motion be heard by someone other than the

challenged judge. Other states have focused on limiting permissible contributions to a judicial campaign. Minnesota, for instance, now limits contributions to $2,000 in election years. Some states have focused instead on limiting donations from certain donors. Florida proposed barring direct contributions by corporations, although, of course, *Citizens United* prevents the state from barring independent expenditures by corporations. New Mexico considered a flat ban on contributions and endorsements from lawyers.

Some states have focused their reform efforts on the dangers inherent in campaign financing and have experimented with public financing of judicial campaigns. They hope that this will reduce the potential of campaign contributions' influencing or creating the appearance of influencing outcomes. In 2002, North Carolina became the first state to provide full public financing of elections for appeals court and supreme court candidates who accept spending limits. All North Carolina's judicial candidates participated in the plan in 2010, and Judge Wanda Bryant stated, "I've run in two elections, one with the campaign finance reform and one without. I'll take 'with' any day, anytime, anywhere."[125] In 2009, Wisconsin passed the Impartial Justice Act, which enabled the public funding of the campaigns of state supreme court candidates through a one-dollar state tax return checkoff. However, the Wisconsin reform demonstrates one of the weaknesses of public financing of judicial elections: it leaves the independence of the judiciary dependent on continuing support from lawmakers, particularly if it relies on tax dollars, and Governor Scott Walker's budget has proposed gutting the funding from his state's campaign finance law.

Conclusion

State and local courts play a profound role in state governments. They resolve civil disputes and hand out justice in criminal cases. They also protect the citizens of their states from unconstitutional behavior by the political branches of government. Despite the importance of this role, or perhaps because of it, judicial systems differ tremendously from state to state. There are organizational differences from initial trial to final appeal. Judges

Recusal
The disqualification of a judge because of an actual or perceived bias or conflict of interest calling the judge's impartiality into question.

in some states are elected by voters and in others are appointed by the governor. Such differences reflect each state's unique orientation toward the values of politics, law, judicial independence, and accountability.

The focus in this chapter has been on the players involved as a case works its way through the judicial system. In a criminal case, the elected prosecutor has tremendous freedom to decide which charges to bring against an accused criminal. Anyone charged with a crime has the right to an attorney, and the state must provide attorneys to those unable to afford their own. Usually the accused is represented by a public defender. If a plea bargain is not reached, the case goes to trial, and the fate of the accused rests in the hands of a panel of ordinary citizens who have been called to jury duty. Potential jurors are selected from a pool of individuals who may have done something as simple as paying a utility bill. This does not mean, however, that there is anything simple about a jury's task. Often, this group holds the future of another individual in its hands.

If an accused person is found guilty and sentenced to incarceration, the length of time the offender actually spends in jail depends a lot on how the values of rehabilitation, deterrence, and retribution have played out in a particular state's political system. Differences here can have an enormous impact. One state may try a nonviolent drug offender in a special drug court that focuses on treatment; another may try the same offense in a general trial court in which the judge has no choice under rigid minimum sentencing guidelines but to apply a sentence of lengthy incarceration.

None of the choices that states make in structuring their courts is fixed and unchanging. States are always responding to altered societal or political realities, experimenting with what works, and adapting to political movements. Some of the areas of reform and change examined in this chapter were triggered by the political rise of victims' rights movements, by the realities of changing caseloads, or by a perception that the selection of judges has become increasingly political.

 # The Latest Research

State courts, like state constitutions, are one of the aspects of government that remain relatively understudied by political scientists. Although there is a long record of court studies, especially by law scholars, truly systematic research using the comparative method dates back only a few decades and is considerably less common than research examining state legislatures and executives. This is unfortunate because, as this chapter has explained in detail, state courts shoulder enormous responsibility for the administration of criminal and civil justice, and their decisions have far-reaching policy implications.

As this chapter makes clear, one of the perennial controversies in this branch revolves around how states can best select judges. Above we have given a flavor of the increasing politicization of the bench. Some champion this development as increasing democratic accountability, whereas others lament it as the courts losing their independence. Ultimately, which of these values is best

to emphasize in selecting judges? Below we summarize some of the latest research on state courts. All of these studies focus on the running theme of the impact of judicial elections, which are at the center of controversies regarding judicial selection.

• **Bonneau, Chris, and Melinda Gann Hall.** 2009. *In Defense of Judicial Elections.* New York: Routledge.

An extended comparative examination of state supreme court elections, this book makes an empirical case that judicial elections have a number of benefits. The authors argue that judicial reforms aimed at depoliticizing the courts have had a number of potentially negative impacts. When states started moving toward Missouri Plan–type systems, judges' names were still

(Continued)

(Continued)

showing up on ballots, but without opponents or partisan labels. The net result was that voters knew virtually nothing about judicial candidates; the courts became so low profile, accountability was lost. This, however, did not make the judicial branch any less political. The authors point to the justices of the U.S. Supreme Court as examples of judges who are appointed for life but clearly take on big political issues and decide them along roughly partisan lines. But at least the U.S. Supreme Court is high profile, and candidates for the Court are scrutinized closely in a relatively open process. There is little of this in a typical Missouri Plan setup. The authors find that competitive, partisan state supreme court elections do not just serve as accountability mechanisms, they confer more democratic legitimacy on the courts—voters trust the judges more because they know them and are more directly linked to them through the normal process of representative democracy.

- **Streb, Matthew, and Brian Frederick.** 2011. "When Money Cannot Encourage Participation: Campaign Spending and Rolloff in Low Visibility Judicial Elections." *Political Behavior* 33: 665–684.

One known way to increase voter turnout in legislative elections is to make those races partisan. Party labels give voters important information and a stake in the outcome of elections. Another known way to increase turnout in legislative races is to have competitive elections; competing candidates tend to spend more money and mobilize more voters. Do these same factors also increase turnout in judicial elections? This study takes a look at 172 appellate court elections between 2000 and 2008 and arrives at two key findings. First is a confirmation of the impact of partisan labels—if candidates for judicial office run on a party label, people are more likely to vote in that election. Second, and somewhat surprisingly, the authors find that campaign spending does nothing to boost turnout significantly. In these low-visibility elections, even well-resourced candidates seem to struggle to get enough information to voters to make them confident in casting their ballots. The simplest and most basic piece of political information, partisanship, seems to be the important factor for increasing participation in judicial elections.

- **Gibson, James, Jeffrey Gottfried, Michael DelliCarpini, and Kathleen Hall Jamieson.** 2010. "The Effects of Judicial Campaign Activity on the Legitimacy of the Courts: A Survey-Based Experiment." *Political Research Quarterly* 64: 545–558.

This study examines how citizens feel about the legitimacy of the Pennsylvania courts. Its key contribution is a creative experiment in which different sets of people were randomly assigned to watch different kinds of campaign ads for judicial candidates, ranging from a straightforward candidate endorsement by an interest group to negative attack ads. Overall, the authors find that elections have a positive impact—voters confer more legitimacy on the courts when judges periodically have to be approved by the voters. In contrast, some of the usual components of elections—that is, campaign ads—tend to decrease support for the courts. The positive overall impact of elections is larger than the negative impact of campaign ads, but one of the inferences that can be taken from this study is that while voters like the idea of judges being elected, they are less enthusiastic about judges actually acting like candidates for electoral office.

- **Gibson, James.** 2008. "Challenges to the Impartiality of State Supreme Courts: Legitimacy Theory and 'New-Style' Judicial Campaigns." *American Political Science Review* 102: 59–75.

Opponents of judicial elections argue that at least three components of electoral contests serve to undercut trust in and support of the courts: campaign contributions (which undermine trust by creating the perception that groups may "buy" judges), attack ads (which undermine trust in judges as individuals), and policy pronouncements (which make judges look less impartial and more partisan). This study, using a creative experiment embedded in a survey, found that the first two, contributions and attack ads, affect attitudes toward courts in pretty much the same way they affect attitudes toward legislatures. In short, they lead to less support and trust in the institution. The third component, taking particular policy positions, does not have the same impact. When judges promise to make certain decisions or to make decisions in certain ways, this does not chip away at the legitimacy of courts in the same fashion as judges' accepting contributions or launching attack ads.

college.cqpress.com/
sites/govstateandlocal

Chapter Review

Key Concepts

- activist judge (p. 275)
- alternative dispute resolution (p. 307)
- appeal (p. 279)
- assigned counsel (p. 297)
- bench trial (p. 280)
- civil case (p. 279)
- contract attorney (p. 297)
- court of first instance (p. 280)
- criminal case (p. 279)
- determinate sentencing (p. 303)
- discretionary jurisdiction (p. 284)
- en banc (p. 284)
- felony (p. 297)
- for cause challenge (p. 301)
- general jurisdiction trial court (p. 280)
- grand jury (p. 296)
- habitual offender laws (p. 304)
- indeterminate sentencing (p. 303)
- indictment (p. 296)
- intermediate appellate court (p. 279)
- jury nullification (p. 296)
- legislative overcriminalization (p. 296)
- liability (p. 300)
- limited, or special jurisdiction, trial court (p. 280)
- magistrate (p. 308)
- mandatory jurisdiction (p. 284)
- mandatory minimum sentence (p. 304)
- misdemeanor (p. 297)
- panel (p. 284)
- peremptory challenge (p. 301)
- plea bargain (p. 279)
- precedent (p. 280)
- prejudicial error (p. 283)
- prosecutor (p. 295)
- public defender (p. 295)
- pure appointive system (p. 292)
- recidivism (p. 306)
- recusal (p. 310)
- retention election (p. 286)
- rocket docket (p. 307)
- settlement (p. 279)
- state supreme court (p. 279)
- trial court (p. 279)
- truth-in-sentencing laws (p. 304)
- voir dire (p. 301)

Suggested Web Sites

- **www.abanet.org.** Web site of the American Bar Association, the largest voluntary professional association in the world, with a membership of more than 400,000.

- **www.ajs.org.** Web site of the American Judicature Society, a nonpartisan organization with a national membership that works to maintain the independence and integrity of the courts and increase public understanding of the justice system.

- **www.brennancenter.org.** Web site of the Brennan Center for Justice, a nonpartisan center at New York University that conducts research and advocates on a range of judicial topics, including state court reform and campaign financing.

- **www.justiceatstake.org.** Web site of the Justice at Stake Campaign, a nonpartisan effort working to keep courts fair and impartial.

- **www.ncsconline.org.** Web site of the National Center for State Courts, an independent nonprofit organization that assists court officials to better serve the public.

- **www.ojp.usdoj.gov/bjs.** Web site for the Bureau of Justice Statistics, which provides statistics and other information on a variety of justice system–related areas, including courts, sentencing, crimes, and victims.

State Stats on Courts

Explore and compare data on the states! Go to college.cqpress.com/ sites/govstateandlocal to do these exercises.

1. What is the per capita state and local government expenditure on corrections in your state? How does this compare to the national average? Do you think that this amount is too little, too much, or just about right? Why?

2. Which state had the most authorized wiretaps in 2010? Which had the least? What factors may have contributed to this?

3. How many prisoners have been sentenced to death since 1973 versus how many have been executed in Texas? What about in Massachusetts? Why is there such a discrepancy?

4. Which state spends the most per capita on state-supported alcohol and drug prevention programs? Which state spends the least? What are the implications of these numbers for drug and alcohol-related arrests?

5. How much do supreme court justices make in your state? Do you think that it is a fair salary considering the scope of the job? Would you raise or lower this amount? Are there some states where you think it is reasonable that justices would make more money? Why?

A swimming pool is not what usually springs to mind when you mention bureaucracy. Public agencies, however, come in many shapes and forms, including parks and recreation departments that are responsible for maintaining swimming pools. Publicly run pools, believe it or not, fit right into the formal definition of a bureaucracy.

Bureaucracy

WHAT NOBODY WANTS BUT EVERYBODY NEEDS

- Why do we have so much bureaucracy?
- How good—or bad—a job does bureaucracy really do?
- How does technology enable more efficient and effective bureaucracy?

For a group of civic-minded kids the 2011 U.S. Open golf tournament seemed a great opportunity to squeeze gold from lemons. They set up a lemonade stand near the Congressional Country Club in Bethesda, Maryland, with the dual aim of quenching the thirst of parched spectators and raising some cash for a nonprofit foundation dedicated to helping families of children with cancer. Entrepreneurial kids putting their energy into supporting a good cause—well, who could oppose that sort of operation? We'll save you the suspense—Montgomery County officials could and did oppose that operation.

County officials slapped the kids with a citation for operating a business without a permit, which meant their parents were liable for a court date and a $500 fine. The parents were not amused and neither were a lot of other people. The story got picked up by the national media and was universally held up as an example of bureaucracy run amok.[1] No wonder business interests complain about regulatory overload if even the all-American lemonade stand can be shut down by petty officialdom. This is just one more example, as if we needed it, of everything that's wrong with government bureaucracy, right? Bureaucracy is overbearing, interfering, and a needless complication in citizens' lives, right?

Wrong. In this instance, bureaucracy was not quite the ogre it was made out to be in the press. The problem for the county was that vendors on Persimmon Tree Road (a major traffic artery into and out of the country club where the U.S. Open was being held) created traffic and safety problems, so they were intent on keeping the thoroughfare clear. They asked the kids to move the stand around the corner to a less heavily used road and rescinded the citation. They even drummed up business for the stand; people attending the Open were so outraged when they heard that bureaucrats were being mean to kids, they made a point of doing their cold-beverage business at the stand and even kicked in extra donations.

The permits and regulations underlying the whole fuss are actually pretty reasonable rules. They are not designed to shut down lemonade stands run by kids raising money for charity, but to ensure public safety and to control temporary vendors such as hot dog stands. Left unregulated, the latter could operate anywhere at any time, creating the potential for traffic problems, neighborhood nuisances, and unscrupulous business practices. What the red-tape showdown at the lemonade stand highlights is not bureaucracy's inherent silliness or uselessness, but its paradoxical nature. On one hand, bureaucracy inevitably does mean rules and regulations that can be inconvenient at best and at worst can defy common sense. Yet bureaucracy does not produce or enforce these rules just for kicks. Like it or not, there are good reasons for the rules, and someone wants the bureaucracy to enforce them.

Bureaucracy represents what is perhaps the political system's greatest contradiction. We do not particularly like it, yet we seem unable to live without it. Like a trip to the dentist, bureaucracy often is inconvenient, involves too much paperwork, and can result in a certain amount of pain. Ultimately, however, it turns out to be good for us.

This chapter explores this workhorse of the U.S. political system—the state and local bureaucracies that implement and manage most public programs and services. We discuss what bureaucracy is and why it plays such an important role. Most important, we use the comparative method to arrive at some explanations for why the American political system has so much bureaucracy when many citizens seem to value it so little.

What Is Bureaucracy?

For our purposes, **bureaucracy** consists of the public agencies and the public programs and services that these agencies implement and manage. Thus **bureaucrats** are simply the employees of the public agencies. Most of these agencies—generically known as government bureaucracies—are located in the executive branches of state and local governments. Although these agencies vary greatly in terms of the programs and services they manage and deliver, the vast majority of them are organizationally very similar. There is a specific set of organizational characteristics associated with bureaucracy:

- *Division of labor.* Labor is divided according to task and function. Most large bureaucracies, for example, have separate technical, personnel, and financial specialists.
- *Hierarchy.* There is a clear vertical chain of command. Authority is concentrated at the top and flows down from superiors to subordinates.
- *Formal rules.* Bureaucracies are impartial rather than impulsive. They operate on the basis of rationally formulated guidelines and standardized operating procedures.
- *Maintenance of files and records.* Bureaucracies record their actions.
- *Professionalization.* Employees of bureaucratic agencies earn their jobs based on qualifications and merit.[2]

Virtually all large, complex organizations have these characteristics, not just government agencies. Wal-Mart and IBM have these characteristics and can thus be considered bureaucratic organizations, even though they are private companies. What separates a public bureaucracy

---

Bureaucracy
Public agencies and the programs and services that they implement and manage.

Bureaucrats
Employees of public agencies.

such as a state department of motor vehicles or the local school district from a private bureaucracy such as IBM is a difference in goals. In the end, what separates public bureaucracies from private bureaucracies is not what they are, but what they do.

What Does Bureaucracy Do?

Public bureaucracies play two fundamental roles in state and local political systems. First, they are the key administrators in the democratic process. They are charged with carrying out the decisions and instructions of elected public officials. This is the central focus of the academic discipline of public administration. Their second role is more controversial. Bureaucracies not only carry out the decisions of the democratic process, but, as it turns out, they also have a fairly important say in what those decisions are.

Bureaucracy as Policy Implementer

The first job of bureaucracy is to be the active manifestation of the will of the state. This is just a fancy way of saying that bureaucracy does what the government wants or needs done.[3] The whole process is known as **policy implementation**. Agencies implement policy by issuing grants and contracts, by enforcing laws and regulations, and by undertaking and managing programs directly. For example, when elected officials decide to build a new road, they do not adjourn the legislature to go survey land, drive bulldozers, and lay asphalt. It is a public agency that negotiates to buy and survey the land. It is the agency that either issues the contracts to build the road or takes on the job of construction using its own employees and equipment. This is what makes private and public bureaucracy different: IBM and Wal-Mart exist to make money, whereas public agencies exist to serve the public interest by turning the decisions of elected officials into concrete reality.

Policy Implementation
The process of translating the express wishes of government into action.

The job of the bureaucracy is staggering in its scope and complexity. Citizens ask government for a lot: roads, education, health benefits, safe drinking water, parks, reliable power grids—the list is virtually endless. Governments respond by passing laws that create programs or policies, which then must be put into action and then managed or enforced. Governments respond, in other words, with bureaucracy. State and local bureaucracies manage not only state and local programs but federal programs as well. The federal government relies on state and local agencies to implement the vast majority of its welfare, education, and highway programs.[4]

> Citizens ask government for a lot: roads, education, health benefits, safe drinking water, parks, reliable power grids—the list is virtually endless. Governments respond by passing laws that create programs or policies, which then must be put into action and then managed or enforced.

In their roles as implementers, managers, and enforcers, state and local government bureaucracies shape the day-to-day lives of citizens more than does any other part of government.[5] The single largest form of bureaucracy in the United States is a fundamental part of virtually every community: public schools. Employing more than 3 million teachers, public schools serve almost 50 million students and have a combined budget of $519 billion.[6]

Other public agencies regulate and set the licensing requirements for professions ranging from lawyers to bartenders. Think of the need to ensure that professionals are qualified to deliver the services they sell. Look around at all the public libraries, swimming pools, and parks that offer recreational and educational opportunities at little or no cost. Think of programs for garbage removal, law enforcement, and fire protection. From the barber who is licensed to cut our hair to the street sweeper who is hired to clean the paths we walk, bureaucracy literally covers us from our heads to our toes.

Bureaucracy as Policymaker

The second fundamental role of the bureaucracy is more controversial than its job as the government's agent of implementation. Public bureaucracies not only help translate the will of a government into action, but in many instances they also actually determine the will of the government. Put bluntly, bureaucracies do not just do policy; they also make it.[7] They do this in at least three ways.

The first way is through what has been called the power of the **street-level bureaucrat**. Street-level bureaucrats are the lower-level public employees who actually take the actions that represent government law or policy. In many cases, street-level bureaucrats have the discretion, or ability, to make choices about what actions they do or do not take. In making these choices, they are essentially making policy. For example, the street-level bureaucrat associated with speed limits is the traffic cop. This public employee is actually on the highway with a radar gun making certain that motorists abide by the speed limits specified by state or local law. The legislature may have passed a law setting a maximum highway speed of 65 miles per hour, but if the traffic cop decides to go after only those motorists doing 75 miles per hour or faster, what really is the speed limit that motorists must obey? And who has set that limit? Arguably, it is not the legislature but, rather, the street-level bureaucrat.[8]

This is not to suggest that street-level bureaucrats are power-hungry tyrants. In many cases, they have no choice but to make choices. On a road on which speeding is common, it may be impossible to stop

every leadfoot. Doesn't it make more sense to concentrate on the most flagrant offenders who pose the most risks? Street-level bureaucrats have to balance the goals, laws, and regulations relevant to their agencies with the practical demands of the day-to-day situations they deal with. That often means making, not just implementing, policy.

The second way in which bureaucracies make policy is through rulemaking. **Rulemaking** is the process by which laws or mandates approved by legislatures are turned into detailed written instructions on what public agencies will or will not do.[9] Rules are necessary because most laws passed by legislatures express intention, but they do not specify the details of how to make that intention a reality. For example, the Nebraska state legislature created the Nebraska Games and Parks Commission to enforce a number of laws related to hunting, fishing, wildlife preservation, and boating. The details of enforcing those laws—such as setting permit fees, determining bag limits for particular types of fish, and designating no-wake zones on lakes—are rules established by the commission rather than laws passed by the legislature. This makes sense. The legislature would quickly become bogged down if it had to delve into the myriad details that must be addressed to put a public program into action. These details are left to individual agencies.

Once a rule is approved, it typically becomes part of the state's administrative code, which is the bureaucratic equivalent of state statutes. These rules have the force of law—violate them and you could face fines. Just ask anyone who has ever been caught fishing without a license. Given this, rules are not left to the discretion of the street-level bureaucrat. Most state agencies have to follow a well-defined process for making rules. This process includes seeking input from agency experts, holding public hearings, and, perhaps, listening to special interests. The Nebraska Games and Parks Commission is required to give public notice of any intention to create a rule and must hold a public hearing to allow interested parties to have their say. If this sounds a lot like the process of making laws in a legislature, it is. Rulemaking is probably

Inside Erie County, New York, there are three cities, twenty-five towns, fifteen villages, and almost one thousand special fire, sewer, and lighting districts.

Street-Level Bureaucrat
A lower-level public agency employee who actually takes the actions that represent law or policy.

Rulemaking
The process of translating laws into written instructions on what public agencies will or will not do.

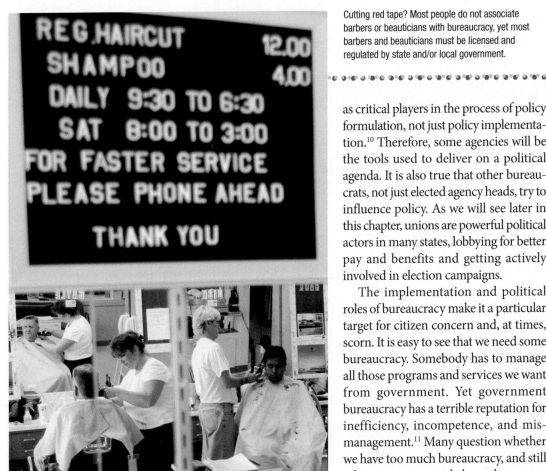

Cutting red tape? Most people do not associate barbers or beauticians with bureaucracy, yet most barbers and beauticians must be licensed and regulated by state and/or local government.

as critical players in the process of policy formulation, not just policy implementation.[10] Therefore, some agencies will be the tools used to deliver on a political agenda. It is also true that other bureaucrats, not just elected agency heads, try to influence policy. As we will see later in this chapter, unions are powerful political actors in many states, lobbying for better pay and benefits and getting actively involved in election campaigns.

The implementation and political roles of bureaucracy make it a particular target for citizen concern and, at times, scorn. It is easy to see that we need some bureaucracy. Somebody has to manage all those programs and services we want from government. Yet government bureaucracy has a terrible reputation for inefficiency, incompetence, and mismanagement.[11] Many question whether we have too much bureaucracy, and still others are concerned about the powerful political role of what are mostly unelected officials. Why do we have so much bureaucracy? How good a job does it really do? Could we get by with less of it? Is there a better way to run public programs and services? Is there too much bureaucracy and too little democracy in state and local government? These are reasonable questions that the comparative method can help answer.

the most important political activity of bureaucracy. In effect, it is a large lawmaking operation that most citizens do not even know exists.

Finally, bureaucracies also contribute to policymaking directly by pursuing political agendas. Street-level discretion and rulemaking are *passive* policymaking in the sense that they involve bureaucrats' responding or not responding to something such as a speeding car or a newly signed bill. Yet bureaucracies and bureaucrats also take *active* roles in politics. They do this in a number of ways. At the state and local levels, the heads of many public agencies are elected. Such positions include everything from county sheriff to state attorney general. As elected officials, these agency heads often make campaign promises, and, once in office, they try to get their agencies to deliver on those promises.

The visibility and importance of these elected state and local agency heads increased with the rise of New Federalism. They now are widely recognized

What Is "Enough" Bureaucracy?

Most people believe that, whatever the merits of bureaucracy, there is too much bureaucracy in government and in our lives. Undeniably, state and local governments have a lot of bureaucracy. How much? Some insight into the size and scope of state and local agencies can be gleaned from Table 10-1, which lists the numbers of employees on state and local government payrolls by function. Combined,

TABLE 10-1

State and Local Government Employment by Function

Function	Total Individuals (in thousands)	State Government (in thousands)	Local Government (in thousands)
Elementary and secondary education	8,037	67	7,970
Higher education	3,093	2,487	606
Hospitals	1,090	446	644
Police protection	1,017	107	909
Corrections	763	489	274
Streets and highways	560	240	320
Public welfare	549	247	303
Other government administration	429	62	366
Electric power and gas supply	94	4	90
Judicial and legal	456	183	273
Financial administration	432	173	258
Fire protection	429	0	429
Natural resources	208	159	49
Social insurance	83	83	0
State liquor stores	10	10	0
Other	514	201	313
All functions	19,809	5,329	14,480

Source: U.S. Department of Commerce, *Statistical Abstract of the United States, 2012* (Washington, DC: U.S. Census Bureau, 2012).

state and local governments have more than 19 million full-time and part-time employees. Most of these—approximately 14 million—are employees of local rather than state governments.[12] Whether at the local or state level, the vast majority of these individuals work in what we would recognize as a bureaucracy.

The numbers contained in Table 10-1 confirm that there are a lot of state and local bureaucrats, but numbers alone give little insight into whether there is too much or too little bureaucracy. In reality, the size of the bureaucracy and the extent of its role in the day-to-day life of any given individual vary from state to state and locality to locality for two main reasons. First, in each locality, citizens make different kinds of demands on each state and local government agency. Some localities need more of one particular resource, whereas others need less. In Eden Prairie, Minnesota, the public demands more

cross-country ski trails, and in Yuma, Arizona, the citizens need more public swimming pools. As a result, the size and role of the public sector can vary significantly from place to place—more demand equals more bureaucracy.

Second, there is no universally agreed on yardstick for measuring what constitutes a "reasonably" sized bureaucracy. Where one person sees a bloated public sector overregulating citizens' lives, a second sees the same set of agencies providing important public goods and services. At the very least, to compare the size of bureaucracy across states and localities we need to explore not just the total number of public employees but also the size of a specific public sector relative to the size of the public it serves. Table 10-2 shows one way to do this. It lists the states with the five largest and the five smallest bureaucracies as measured by the

TABLE 10-2

States with the Most and the Least Bureaucracy by Number of Employees

State	State Employees (per 10,000 citizens)
Top Five	
Hawaii	602
North Dakota	374
Alaska	372
Delaware	362
New Mexico	314
Bottom Five	
Florida	119
Illinois	122
Pennsylvania	131
California	138
New York	139

Source: U.S. Bureau of Labor Statistics data for 2008, as reprinted in *State and Local Sourcebook,* online supplement to *Governing* magazine, 2009.

number of government employees per every 10,000 citizens.

By this measure, the mostly large, urban, and populous states have the *smallest* bureaucracies. More rural, less populous states, conversely, have the *largest* bureaucracies. How can this be? Why would North Dakota have more bureaucracy than California? The answer is actually pretty simple. Fewer people do not necessarily mean less demand on the government. Even the most rural state still needs an educational system, roads, and law enforcement. These are all labor-intensive propositions. Indeed, they may be even more labor-intensive in rural states. For example, to serve a widely dispersed population, an educational system either has to build lots of small schools or figure out a way to transport lots of students over considerable distances to a smaller number of large schools. More urban, densely populated states can take advantage of the economies of scale that come with centralized locations. Basically, less bureaucracy is needed where the citizens being served are

close by. Increasingly, however, cash-strapped governments are saving money by relying on technology to bridge the distances between their offices and those they serve—resulting in a need for fewer employees and thus less bureaucracy.

The same tale is told when we use expenditures—in this case, the amount of money states spent for services—to measure the size of bureaucracy. Alaska is among the five states with the largest bureaucracies as measured by both number of employees and per capita expenditure. (See Table 10-3.) Not coincidentally, it is also one of only two noncontiguous states—Canada separates Alaska from other U.S. states, and Hawaii is an island chain in the Pacific. Geographical isolation requires that these states do more for themselves, which means more bureaucracy.

Expenditures and employees tell us something about the size of the bureaucracy, but they do not tell us much about its influence or power over the daily lives of citizens. An undermanned bureaucracy with a small budget still can have considerable impact on the interests of an individual. If you have ever spent time in a university

TABLE 10-3

States with the Most and the Least Bureaucracy by Expenditures

State	State and Local Expenditures (dollars per capita)
Top Five	
Alaska	15,924
New York	12,499
Wyoming	11,647
California	10,100
Massachusetts	9,622
Bottom Five	
Idaho	6,373
Arkansas	6,587
South Dakota	6,608
Oklahoma	6,699
Missouri	6,775

Source: U.S. Census Bureau data, as reprinted in *State and Local Sourcebook,* online supplement to *Governing* magazine, 2009.

financial aid office, you probably already understand the point here—when people complain about bureaucracy being too big, they often mean the red tape and rules that come with it, not its budget or payroll. For the number of forms you fill out at the financial aid office, you may feel that the bureaucracy owes you a free meal, but there is only so much money in the pot. It is very easy to recognize this sort of thing as a central part of bureaucracy. It is very hard to measure it objectively. The lack of good measures of "red tape" or "rules" makes drawing comparisons difficult. If there are no comparative measures, it is harder to use the comparative method to help show why some bureaucracies have more influence than others.

Despite this, there is little doubt that public bureaucracies play a more powerful role in the day-to-day lives of citizens in large urban areas than they do in less populous rural areas. Why? It is not because bureaucracy is more power hungry in cities but, rather, because more concentrated populations require more rules. Building codes are more critical in urban areas because of the associated fire-safety and health risks—a problem with one building can pose risks for those working or living in the surrounding buildings. Building regulations thus tend to be more detailed, and the enforcement of these rules tends to be a higher priority, in urban than in rural areas. In this sense, urban areas do have more bureaucracy than rural areas.

Measuring Bureaucratic Effectiveness: It Does a Better Job than You Think

So far, our application of the comparative method has given us a sense of how big bureaucracy is and why it is so big—because characteristics such as urbanization and geography result in different demands being placed on government. These different demands translate into public agencies of different sizes and with varying levels of involvement in our day-to-day lives. What the comparative method has not told us is how good (or bad) a job public agencies do. The widespread belief is that such agencies are, at best, mediocre managers of public programs and services.[13] Although this negative stereotype is held by many, for the most part it is wrong. Public agencies, as it turns out, are very good at what they do.

How good? Well, in many cases, they are at least as good as, if not better than, their private sector counterparts. The assumption is that the private sector is more efficient and more effective than the public sector, but numerous studies have found that this assumption is based more on stereotypes than on facts.[14] For example, **contracting out** is a term used to describe having private or nonprofit organizations rather than government agencies deliver public services. The basic idea is that rather than using an expensive and inefficient bureaucracy to provide a public good or service, the job is awarded to an outside organization through a competitive bidding process. The bidder that can do the best job with the least charge to the taxpayer gets the

business, and government reaps the efficiency benefits of the market. At least, that's the theory. The record of contracting out in practice is much more mixed. While it certainly works well in some circumstances, it is far from a panacea.

For example, faced with rising healthcare costs and a reluctance to increase student fees on top of rising tuition bills, a number of colleges and universities have experimented with contracting out student healthcare services. The University of Northern Colorado outsourced its student health center in 2003, but the large healthcare provider that took over the operation asked to be released from its contract a few years later when it found it couldn't make a profit. Auburn University outsourced its student health center in 1999, but one of the private companies that won the contract went bust in 2001. These teething problems, though, were overcome, and

Contracting Out
Government hiring of private or nonprofit organizations to deliver public goods or services.

Policy in Practice

Privatizing an Entire City

Sandy Springs, Georgia, is a suburb of Atlanta and ground zero of an intriguing experiment in local government. Basically, Sandy Springs is set up to answer the question: What if there were no public bureaucracy?

To say Sandy Springs has minimal government is an understatement. It is a municipality with 94,000 residents and seven employees at city hall. Actually, that's not quite true. It doesn't have a city hall; the government of Sandy Springs operates out of an office complex in an industrial park. Sandy Springs has contracted out—effectively privatized—just about every public service, program, and facility possible, and that includes its center of operations.

You name the program or service—business licensing, building permits, trash collection—and it's handled not by a public bureaucracy but by a private company hired to do the job. Even the municipal court is not exempt. The court's administrative staff all work for a private company, and the judge is a private practice attorney who temps for the city as a judge for a hundred bucks an hour.

Sandy Springs does have two relatively old-fashioned public agencies—a police department and a fire department. It only has those, though, because contracting out law enforcement and firefighting services would leave the city facing some prohibitively high insurance rates. Even when it comes to emergency management services the city contracts out where it can: its 911 dispatch center, for example, is run by a private company.

Privatizing big chunks of the public sector means Sandy Springs escapes some big traditional costs associated with old-fashioned bureaucracies. The city has no pension obligations, for example, and it doesn't have to bother with building or maintaining facilities to house its nonexistent bureaucrats. While other municipalities are struggling financially, Sandy Springs seems just fine.

While effectively turning over the running of a city to set of corporations seems to have worked in Sandy Springs, it is not without controversy. Sandy Springs is a relatively affluent and white area within Fulton County, which tends to be poorer and has a high minority population. When Sandy Springs incorporated in 2005, some saw the town as basically seceding from Fulton County with an eye to keeping its tax revenues local and preventing them from being spent in more needy areas. Other parts of the county cannot repeat Sandy Springs' success, in other words, because they don't have the money or the tax base to support that level of services. Because the incorporation of Sandy Springs has cost Fulton County revenues, the traditional public agencies that do serve those areas may have to do so with fewer resources.

Source: David Segal, "A Georgia Town Takes the People's Business Private," *New York Times*, June 23, 2012.

---

the health center privatization is generally reckoned a success at Auburn. Not so at the University of Denver, where an experiment with privatization was largely a failure. The healthcare company that took over the university's student healthcare services seemed to focus too much on its bottom line and too little on the outreach services central to the original health center's mission. The university brought its health center back in-house and funded it with student fees.[15]

Some of the problems associated with contracting out often include a loss of accountability and transparency, difficulty in specifying contracts to cover all possible contingencies (for example, who bears the costs if bad weather delays road construction), and a clash of public service versus make-a-profit value systems. All this can create conflict between private contractors and governments, conflict that can be messy, litigious, and expensive. After experimenting with contracting out, some governments—like the University of Denver—end up deciding it causes more headaches than it's worth. This is a pretty common experience; local governments that contract out services frequently bring those services back in-house after a year or two.[16] A public bureaucracy might be old-fashioned, but it generally can be counted on not just to get the job done, but also to be responsive to its elected bosses rather than its profit-loss statement.

Although popularly viewed as inferior to their private-sector counterparts, public agencies actually come out equal to or better than the private sector on a wide range of employee characteristics used to identify effective organizations. Public- and private-sector employees are roughly equal in terms of their job motivation, their work habits, and their overall competence. Compared to private-sector employees, however, public-sector employees tend to have higher levels of education, express a greater commitment to civic duty and public service, abide by more stringent codes of ethical behavior, and be more committed to helping other people.[17] Various studies have shown that over the past thirty years state and local agencies have become more productive and more professional, and they have done so during an era when they have shouldered an increasing share of the burden for delivering programs and services from the federal government.[18]

There *is* wide variation between and within the states when it comes to how well public bureaucracies are managed. Good management has an enormous impact on the capacities and effectiveness of programs and agencies. States that engage in prudent, long-range fiscal planning are better positioned to deal with economic downturns, and they generally can deliver programs more efficiently. States that do a better job of attracting qualified employees with a strong commitment to public service almost certainly are going to be rewarded with more effective public agencies. States that make training their employees a priority are likely to enjoy similar benefits. The bottom line is that well-managed public agencies lower costs and improve results, whereas the reverse is true for badly managed agencies.[19]

So how can we tell if agencies are being well managed or not? Many states are using performance measurement programs that attempt to bring at least some objectivity to performance evaluations of public-sector bureaucracies. These efforts, however, are not comprehensive and not comparative—in other words, they focus on agencies in one state. One performance program that was truly comprehensive was the Government Performance Project (GPP), one of the most massive long-term studies of public agency management ever conducted. The basic idea behind the GPP was to hold state governments publicly accountable for the quality of management within their jurisdictions.[20] Starting in 1999, the GPP did this by researching management practices and performance in four areas (money, people, infrastructure, and information) and issuing states grades for performance in each area. The most recent GPP was in 2008, and the grades issued showed most states getting Bs and Cs for overall performance; there were no Fs and only one D (New Hampshire). In other words, most state agencies seem to be doing at least reasonably well.

Still, there were plenty of differences in the GPP. For instance, why did California get a C while Virginia got an A-minus? What accounts for that sort of difference in public-sector performance? The answers are generally not found in the bureaucracy but, rather, in the broader political environment of the states. Ultimately, legislatures and governors are responsible for bureaucratic performance. This is true not only because they set the laws that control personnel, management, and training practices; their decisions on a wide range of policy issues have tremendous consequences even for smoothly running agencies. The most obvious example is budgets. States have gone through boom-and-bust cycles during the past fifteen years, with the economic good times of the 1990s followed by a fiscal crisis shortly after the turn of the century; a few years of prosperity returned before the nation plunged into the worst recession since World War II. Through it all, some states practiced good fiscal management, with legislatures that resisted the temptation to spend excessively and enact large tax cuts. As the economy soured, these states also acted quickly to stabilize revenues.

Other states—such as California—did the opposite. These states increased spending during the economic good times, tried to put off the day of reckoning with creative accounting practices, and ultimately left their agencies facing disaster as the Great Recession took hold. In these states the fiscal crisis rocked the public sector, leaving it underfunded, understaffed, and a little shell-shocked—not exactly the ingredients for smoothly running public programs. Generally speaking, the comparative method shows us that it was the states that avoided big tax cuts in the 1990s, the states with divided governments (that is, in which the governor was from one party and the legislature was controlled by another), and the states with powerful governors that spent less, had better financial management, and had public agencies with higher grades in the GPP.[21]

Many of the faults attributed to public bureaucracies actually can be traced to legislatures, which give agencies conflicting and confusing missions and often do not provide them with adequate resources to fulfill these missions. It is the legislatures that demand what is politically expedient, not what is effective or efficient, and then roundly and repeatedly criticize the bureaucracies for not performing well. The real surprise is not that some bureaucracies are ineffective or poorly run but that the vast majority of them, most of the time, manage to more or less serve the public interest. And they do so in spite of democratic institutions rather than because of them. At least one professional student of bureaucracy has suggested that any objective view of the joint performance of bureaucracy and representative democracy would lead to the conclusion that what we need is more bureaucracy and less democracy![22]

That sentiment has taken real shape in some states in the form of increased performance auditing designed to improve the efficiency and effectiveness of government programs. "That's where you find out if money is being spent the way it is supposed to, or whether you're getting the most bang for the buck," says former Colorado state representative Brad Young.[23]

Past perceptions of auditors pegged them as glorified bean counters, but in some states, the independent reports of auditors carry significant weight. California's nonpartisan Legislative Analyst's Office has served as a model for other states,[24] and strong legislative support kept Florida's Office of Program Policy Analysis and Government Accountability operating even when the governor wanted to downsize it.[25] In Washington State, even the citizens see the benefits of performance audits; voters there approved a 2005 ballot initiative that increased the state auditor's authority to study state and local agency performance.

Is There a Better Way to Run Public Programs and Services?

Looking at bureaucracy comparatively, we learn how big it really is, why it is so big, and how well it performs. But is a traditional bureaucracy really the best way to run public programs and services? Do we really need less democracy and more bureaucracy? Do we really need 19 million people on the state and local government payrolls? The short answer is no. As we have already discussed, public services and programs could be contracted out and delivered through a competitive bidding process by the private sector. Public agencies could be staffed and run by political party loyalists or special interest supporters. Things could be done differently. Before we abandon the traditional public bureaucracy, however, it is worth considering why public agencies are so, well, bureaucratic.

Remember the key characteristics of bureaucratic organizations listed earlier? These turn out to be important advantages when it comes to running public programs and services. For one thing, bureaucracies tend to be impartial because they operate using formal rules, not partisan preference, bribes, or arbitrary judgment. If you need some form of license or permit, if your shop is subject to some form of environmental or business regulation, or if you are trying to receive benefits from a public program, it

FIGURE 10-1

HOW IT WORKS

Virginia's Bureaucracy—for This, You Get an A–

The Commonwealth of Virginia receives gold stars for its bureaucracy—it was one of the three top-ranked states (Utah and Washington were the others) in the most recent ratings conducted by the Government Performance Project. Part of what puts Virginia at the top of the class is the state's practice of holding the more than one hundred cabinet members and agency heads accountable to formal "executive agreements." These are reviewed by the governor and outline clear measurable goals for each agency against which its performance is appraised. Yearly public assessments of each agency are available online.

These scorecards evaluate performance in human resource management, government procurement, financial management, technology, and emergency preparedness. In effect, this is an assessment of those agencies' leaders and their subordinates. The table here shows only a portion of the scorecard for Virginia's executive agencies for 2009 and includes ratings for agencies in the Offices of Administration, Commerce and Trade, Education, Finance, Health and Human Services, and Public Safety. Overall, ten of the fifty-three rated agencies met expectations in every category. The remaining forty-three were rated as needing to make progress in at least one area, including five that were rated as below expectations in at least one area.

Virginia's Executive Branch Agencies 2009 Scorecard

Legend:

M = Meets Expectations   P = Progress toward Expectations   B = Below Expectations   U = Results Unavailable

Agency	Secretariat	Emergency Preparedness	Financial Management	Government Procurement	Human Resources	Information Technology
Compensation Board	Administration	M	M	M	M	P
Department of General Services	Administration	M	M	M	M	P
Department of Human Resource Management	Administration	P	M	M	M	M
Department of Minority Business Enterprise	Administration	M	P	P	M	B
State Board of Elections	Administration	U	P	M	U	U
Department of Business Assistance	Commerce and Trade	B	P	M	M	M
Department of Housing & Community Development	Commerce and Trade	M	M	M	P	P
Department of Labor & Industry	Commerce and Trade	M	M	M	M	M
Department of Mines, Minerals & Energy	Commerce and Trade	M	M	M	M	M
Department of Professional & Occupational Regulation	Commerce and Trade	P	M	M	M	P

Agency	Secretariat	Emergency Preparedness	Financial Management	Government Procurement	Human Resources	Information Technology
Virginia Employment Commission	Commerce and Trade	M	M	M	M	M
Virginia Racing Commission	Commerce and Trade	M	M	M	M	M
Department of Education	Education	M	M	M	M	P
State Council of Higher Education for Virginia	Education	U	M	P	M	P
The Library of Virginia	Education	M	M	P	P	M
Virginia Commission for the Arts	Education	M	M	P	M	M
Virginia Museum of Fine Arts	Education	P	M	M	M	M
Department of Accounts	Finance	P	M	M	M	M
Department of Taxation	Finance	M	M	M	M	P
Department of the Treasury	Finance	P	P	M	M	P
Comprehensive Services for At-Risk Youth and Families	Health & Human Resources	P	M	M	M	P
Department of Behavioral Health and Developmental Services	Health & Human Resources	P	P	M	P	P
Department for the Blind & Vision Impaired	Health & Human Resources	P	M	P	M	P
Department of Health	Health & Human Resources	M	P	P	M	M
Department of Medical Assistance Services	Health & Human Resources	M	M	M	M	M
Department of Rehabilitative Services	Health & Human Resources	P	M	M	M	P
Department of Social Services	Health & Human Resources	P	M	M	M	P

Sources: Commonwealth of Virginia, "Organization of State Government," www.commonwealth.virginia.gov/StateGovernment/StateOrgChart/OrgChart2006–2007.pdf; "Virginia Performs: Administrative Measures, 2009," www.vaperforms.virginia.gov/agencylevel/src/ScoreCardResults.cfm.

does not matter to the bureaucracy if you are rich or poor, liberal or conservative, an influential high-roller or an average citizen. What matters to the bureaucracy are the rules that define the application process, eligibility, and delivery of the necessary service or program. Following bureaucratic rules can be maddening, but these rules do help ensure that public agencies are more or less impartial.

The bureaucratic characteristics of hierarchy and record keeping help hold public agencies accountable. Public agencies are expected to be answerable for their actions. They have to justify why they do what they do to legislatures, executives, the courts, and citizens.[26] An action at a lower level of bureaucracy almost always can be appealed to a higher level. Students at most colleges and universities, for example, can appeal their grades. In such appeals, the bureaucrat responsible for issuing the grade—the instructor—is expected to justify to the appeals board and the dean why the grade represents a fair and reasonable application of the rules of the class and the grading policies of the university. Setting rules, requiring records, and setting up a clear chain of authority help ensure that bureaucrats and bureaucracies do not exceed their authority or act unfairly. If they do, these same factors provide a means for holding the bureaucrat or bureaucracy accountable.

Professionalization is another bureaucratic characteristic that is desirable in public agencies because it promotes competence and expertise. To get a job in most state and local bureaucracies, what you know is more important than who you know. Getting a job as a professor at a state university requires a specific set of professional qualifications. The same is true for an elementary school teacher, an accountant at the Department of Revenue, or a subway operator. Of course, setting and enforcing such qualifications as the basis for employment and promotion means another set of rules and regulations. These qualifications also help ensure that merit—rather than partisan loyalty, family connections, or political influence—is the basis for an individual's gaining public-sector employment.

Professionalization
The rewarding of jobs in a bureaucratic agency based on applicants' specific qualifications and merit.

The great irony of public bureaucracy is that the very characteristics that help ensure neutrality, fairness, and accountability also produce the things that people dislike about bureaucracy: red tape and inefficiency. Formal rules help guarantee equity and fairness, but—as anyone who has spent time filling out forms and waiting in line can attest—they can be a pain. Enforcing rules, or "going by the book," may mean bureaucracy is fair, but it is not particularly flexible. Treating everyone the same is an advantage from an equity standpoint, but the fact is that not everyone *is* the same. Surely there are ways to make bureaucracy more responsive to the individual? Well, yes, there are. But the history of bureaucratic reform in the United States suggests that the cures are often worse than the problem. Although going through this history is not a particularly comparative exercise, it is a necessary step toward understanding why bureaucracy is the way it is.

State Bureaucracy: From Patronage to Professionalism

Public agencies have undergone a remarkably radical transformation during the past century. They have become more professionalized, more organized, and more able to shoulder a large share of the political system's responsibilities.

For much of the early history of the United States, there was little in the way of state and local bureaucracy. State and local government functions that we now take for granted, such as public schools, libraries, and fire protection, were left largely to the private sector. In most cases, this meant they did not exist at all or were available only to those who could afford them. Public education is the single largest public program undertaken by state and local governments. Yet public education in the contemporary sense did not exist until the last half of the nineteenth century, roughly one hundred years after the nation's founding. As the nation grew, however, so did the demands on government. The country needed to build roads, regulate commerce, clean the streets, and curtail crime. And taxes had to be collected to make all this happen. There was no centralized plan to expand public bureaucracy—it evolved in fits and starts as governments took on the jobs citizens wanted done.

Political machines were powerful organizations that dominated many state and local governments for parts of the nineteenth and twentieth centuries. Their power was based on their ability to control government jobs, awarding these positions to supporters or, as this cartoon suggests, to the highest bidder.

At the federal level, staffing the bureaucracy was initially a job for which only the educated elite were considered qualified. This example often was followed at the state and local levels. Public service was seen as an obligation of the aristocratic class of a community or state. This "gentlemen's" system of administration was swept away following the election of Andrew Jackson to the presidency in 1828.

Jackson believed in the **spoils system**, that is, the right of an electoral winner to control who worked for the government. The intent was to democratize government and make it more accountable by having regular citizens who supported the electoral winners run the government agencies. This process of giving government jobs to partisan loyalists is called **patronage**.

Instead of producing a more democratic bureaucracy, the spoils system and patronage invited corruption. Following Jackson's example, electoral winners used positions in the administrative arms of many state and local governments as ways to pay off political favors or to reward partisan loyalty. Perhaps the most famous examples are the big-city political machines that flourished well into the twentieth century and produced some of the most colorful characters ever to wield power in state and local politics. As discussed in chapter 6, political machines, or party machines, were organizations headed by party committees or party bosses. A committee or boss led a subset of ward or precinct leaders whose job it was to make sure voters in their districts supported the machine-endorsed candidates. Supporters of the machine were, in turn, rewarded with government jobs and contracts. They also were often expected to contribute a set percentage of their salaries to the machine.[27] This created a well-regulated cycle, or machine—votes in one end, power and patronage out the other.

Political machines dominated politics in many urban areas and even whole states in the nineteenth and early twentieth centuries. They produced some of the most fascinating characters in U.S. political history: Boss Tweed of New York, Tom Pendergast of Kansas City, and Gene Talmadge of Georgia, to name just a few. These men wielded enormous power, aided in no small part by their ability to dole out government jobs and contracts. Some machines survived well into the twentieth century. Mayor Richard Daley of Chicago ran what many recognize as a political machine well into the 1960s.

While the machines made for lively politics and brought almost unlimited power to their leaders, they were often corrupt. Machine politics meant that getting a government job was based on whom you knew rather than on what you knew. Job security lasted only as long as you kept in your political patron's good graces or until the next election. Understandably, then, there was a tremendous incentive to make the most of a government position. Kickbacks and bribery inevitably made their way into many state and local agencies.

Spoils System
A system under which an electoral winner has the right to decide who works for public agencies.

Patronage
The process of giving government jobs to partisan loyalists.

The founders of the modern conception of government bureaucracy were the progressive reformers of the late nineteenth and early twentieth centuries. They wanted a lasting solution to the gross dishonesty and inefficiency they saw in public administration. Toward this end, these reformers created a new philosophy. At its center was the idea that the administrative side of government needed to be more insulated from the political arena.[28] Reformers promoted **neutral competence**, the idea that public agencies should be the impartial implementers of democratic decisions, not partisan extensions of whoever happened to win the election.

To achieve these ends, progressive reformers began to push for public agencies to adopt the formal characteristics of bureaucratic organizations. This was accomplished in no small part through lobbying for the merit system as an alternative to the spoils system. In a **merit system**, jobs and promotions are awarded on the basis of technical qualifications and demonstrated ability instead of given out as rewards for political loyalty. A merit system also makes it harder for public employees to be dismissed without due cause. But this does not mean a guaranteed job. The idea is to create a system within which public employees can be fired only for failing to do their jobs and not because they missed a payment to a political boss. The overall goal was to make government bureaucracies less political and more professional.

The federal government shifted from the spoils system to the merit system in 1883 with the passage of the Pendleton Act. The main features of this merit system were (1) competitive examination requirements for federal jobs, (2) security from political dismissals (that is, people could not be fired simply because they belonged to the "wrong" party or supported the "wrong" candidate), and (3) protection from being coerced into political activities (so that workers were no longer expected or required to contribute a portion of their salaries to a political party or candidate). The basic principles of merit systems have since been expanded to include equal pay for equal work; recruitment, hiring, and promotion without regard to race, creed, national origin, religion, marital status, age, or disability; and protection from reprisals for lawful disclosure of lawbreaking, mismanagement, abuse of authority, or practices that endanger public health—called whistle-blower laws.

States and localities once again followed the example of the federal government and began shifting from spoils systems to merit systems. New York State was the first to do so, adopting a merit system in the same year that the Pendleton Act became law. In 1935, the federal Social Security Act made merit systems a requirement for related state agencies if they wished to receive federal grants. This stimulated another wave of merit-based reforms of state and local bureaucracies. By 1949, nearly half the states had created merit-based civil service systems. Fifty years later, virtually all states and many municipalities had adopted merit systems. All of this helped professionalize state and local bureaucracies and turned what had been sinkholes of patronage and corruption or marginally competent old-boy networks into effective instruments of democratic policymaking.

Politics and the Merit System

Although using merit as the basis for public bureaucracy has effectively created agencies that are competent and professional, it has its drawbacks. Remember the two key roles of the bureaucracy, policy implementation and policymaking? Merit systems have positive and negative implications for both.

In some ways, merit-based bureaucracy is a victim of its own success. The whole idea of shifting to a merit system was to insulate public agencies and their employees from undue political influence. We want bureaucrats to work for the public interest, not for the interests of party bosses. We want bureaucrats to apply rules neutrally, not to interpret them through the lens of partisan prejudices. To a remarkable extent, merit

---

Neutral Competence
The idea that public agencies should be the impartial implementers of democratic decisions.

Merit System
A system used in public agencies in which employment and promotion are based on qualifications and demonstrated ability; such a system blends very well with the organizational characteristics of bureaucracy.

systems have had exactly that effect. Rules are rules, and bureaucracies more or less competently and impartially enforce them regardless of which party controls the legislature or who sits in the governor's mansion. The merit system has undoubtedly been an enormous positive for the policy implementation role of bureaucracy.

The impact of merit systems on the policymaking, or political, role of bureaucracy is more open for debate. Merit systems did not eliminate the political role of the bureaucracy; they merely changed it. Under the spoils system, bureaucracy was an agent of a particular boss, party, or political agenda, and it favored the supporters of electoral winners. The merit system cut the connection between the ballot box and the bureaucracy. Distancing bureaucracy from elections, however, arguably makes it less accountable to the democratic process—a big concern if bureaucracy is policymaker as well as policy implementer.

Once distanced from the ballot box, public agencies and public employees discovered their own political interests and began to pursue them with vigor. Organized interests outside the bureaucracy also began to realize that being able to influence lawmaking and, especially, rulemaking offered enormous political opportunities. All you have to do is get your favored policy written into the rules, and bureaucracy will enforce it well beyond the next election. These sorts of developments raise serious questions about the drawbacks of the merit system. As examples of how these concerns play out in state and local agencies, let us consider two issues: public labor unions and affirmative action.

Public Labor Unions

Public-sector labor unions are a relatively new political force. Unions were almost exclusively a private-sector phenomenon until the 1960s. This changed in 1962 when President John F. Kennedy issued an executive order that recognized the right of federal employees to join unions and required federal agencies to recognize those unions. The 1960s and 1970s saw a considerable expansion in the number of state and local employees joining unions. Today, roughly three to four times as many public-sector as private-sector workers belong to unions.[29]

The reasons for the expansion in public-sector union membership are not hard to fathom. For much of their history, public employees received lower wages than their private-sector counterparts. Public employees also had limited input with regard to personnel decisions. Despite the merit system, many still saw favoritism and old-boy networks as having too much influence in pay and promotion decisions. Public-sector labor unions pushed for the right to engage in **collective bargaining**, a process in which representatives of labor and management meet to negotiate pay and benefits, job responsibilities, and working conditions. The vast majority of states allow at least some public unions to bargain collectively.

What should not be missed here is that the outcomes of collective bargaining are important policy decisions. They are decisions in which the voter—and sometimes the legislator—has little say. Negotiations about pay and benefits for public employees are, in a very real sense, negotiations about taxes. A raise won by a public employee represents a claim on the taxpayer's pocketbook. And it is a claim that is worked out not in an open democratic process but often in closed-door negotiations.

And it is not just money. Collective bargaining agreements can result in fairly complex rules about what public employees are and are not expected to do. Such rules reduce both the flexibility of agency managers, who are constrained from redirecting personnel from their assigned jobs, and the responsiveness of bureaucracy to legislatures and elected executives.

Labor unions have given public employees more than just collective bargaining muscle; they also have started to do some heavy lifting in electoral politics. Unions that are able to deliver their members' votes can have a powerful say in who

---

Collective Bargaining
A process in which representatives of labor and management meet to negotiate pay and benefits, job responsibilities, and working conditions.

holds office. Understandably, people seeking public office pay attention to the policy preferences of public-sector unions. By raising money, mobilizing voters, even running independent campaigns, unions exercise considerable political clout. Consider the Wisconsin Education Association Council (WEAC). This teachers' union, long recognized as an important political actor in the state, has a well-thought-out set of legislative goals and supports candidates accordingly.[30] It also spends its money strategically. In the 2010 election cycle, WEAC spent roughly $1.5 million on state political campaigns.[31] That made the union the biggest-spending political action committee in state politics.

The boots-on-the-ground political organization combined with big bucks translates into considerable political clout for public labor unions, enough to shape how the merit system actually works. A basic principle of the merit system is that competence is supposed to be rewarded. Expertise and job performance are supposed to be the bases of promotion and pay increases. In contrast, unions tend to advocate seniority—the length of time spent in a position—as the basis for promotions and pay increases. Public employees with more experience may—and often do— deserve such rewards, but it is not always the most senior employee who is the most productive or who contributes the most to an agency's success. Even in the absence of unions, seniority plays a considerable role in the pay and benefits of public employees. This is much to the chagrin of critics, who view civil service protections as failing the public interest. For example, some critics view tenure at colleges and universities as a system that rewards laziness and allows "deadwood"—unproductive faculty members—to collect healthy paychecks.[32]

In recent years there have been several efforts to curtail the power of public unions, especially their rights to collective bargaining. The two most high-profile efforts to take on public unions were spearheaded by Scott Walker and John Kasich, the governors of Wisconsin and Ohio, respectively.

Walker and Kasich were both elected in the so-called Republican Red Tide of 2010, and both came to office promising to shrink government and curb its power. In Wisconsin, Walker backed enormously controversial legislation that sought to roll back the hard-won collective bargaining rights of public employee unions. The plan bitterly divided the legislature along party lines—at one point Democratic legislators blocked the proposed legislation by fleeing the state to deprive the state Senate of a quorum. As many as a 100,000 demonstrators descended on the state capitol to protest the plan, and when the legislature passed the proposal it triggered a recall effort aimed at Walker and several Republican legislators who backed the legislation. Walker survived the recall, but the collective bargaining restrictions were also attacked in court. In 2012, rulings by both federal and state judges chipped away at the restrictive provisions on collective bargaining rights; supporters of the law vowed to appeal these rulings. In Ohio, Kasich backed a similar measure to restrict the collective bargaining rights of public unions. Among other things, the Ohio law would have prevented public employees from striking and would have restricted their right to bargain collectively for wages and benefits. Opponents spearheaded a drive to overturn the law, which culminated in a statewide referendum in which the legislation was decisively defeated (the vote was 61 percent in favor of overturning the law).

While Walker and Kasich presented their efforts as attempts to help control government spending in tight economic times, they were perceived by many as thinly disguised attempts at union busting. As events in Wisconsin and Ohio amply demonstrate, if you want to take on public unions, you had better be ready for a fight. Government downsizing may have thinned their membership rolls and raised big questions about the future of the public-sector workforce (see discussion below), but for now public unions remain a potent political force.

There is a simple reason for this. Despite efforts by their opponents to paint them otherwise, unions are far from all bad—they have

---

Seniority
The length of time a worker has spent in a position.

fought successfully for reasonable compensation packages and safer work environments for people who perform some of society's toughest, dirtiest, and most thankless jobs. The people who make up public-sector unions—police officers, firefighters, teachers, social workers, and the like—are appreciated at least as much as they are resented by voters. Nor are unions as stubbornly devoted to inefficiency as their critics suggest. In most instances, unions support the merit system as long as it also protects seniority. Unions are also far from incompatible with effectiveness and productivity. For example, comparative studies of student performance and the strength of teachers' unions have found that states with the strongest teachers' unions also tend to have the highest student achievement scores.

While the pros and cons of unions can be debated, the experiences of Wisconsin and Ohio leave no doubt that public unions have helped politicize the bureaucracy. It is a different sort of politics than the favoritism and outright corruption that marked the spoils system, but it is politics nonetheless.

Affirmative Action

Public unions show how a political role for bureaucracy can be generated internally—public employees get organized and pursue their interests in the political arena. Yet bureaucracies can be politicized from the outside as well. Consider **affirmative action**, the set of policies used to get government to make a special effort to recruit and retain certain categories of workers who historically have been underrepresented, in order to achieve better and fairer representation. It is illegal for government agencies to have employment, evaluation, or promotion practices that discriminate on the basis of race, age, color, creed, gender, physical disability, or other characteristics not related to the job or job performance. Yet, even though such discrimination has been banned outright, public bureaucracies are not particularly diverse in a number of these factors, especially race and gender.

About 54 percent of state and local government employees are males and about 68 percent are white. Males hold roughly 62 percent of the top management jobs in public agencies, and more than 80 percent of the individuals—male or female—in these positions are white. In contrast, racial and ethnic minorities tend to be much more concentrated in lower-ranking positions. They constitute about 19 percent of the top management jobs in state and local government but more than 46 percent of the service and maintenance positions.[33] Consider the New York Police Department (NYPD), which in 2005 had approximately 680 officers at the rank of captain or above. Of these, approximately 10 percent were minorities.[34] That proportion clearly did not reflect the overall population of New York City, which was more than 50 percent minority.

The lack of diversity in the management ranks of the NYPD is probably not the result of the outright racism of individuals. A bigger problem is that the nondiscriminatory hiring practices that form the foundation of the merit system are passive; they ensure access to hiring opportunities but make no guarantees about jobs or promotions. In choosing who should be hired or promoted, the merit system looks at such things as experience and qualifications. It does not account for gender, race, or ethnicity. The problem here is that minorities historically have had fewer educational opportunities. Less education means fewer qualifications. This translates into a tougher time gaining access to jobs. The end result is that, even if race is not an explicit factor in hiring and promoting, whites tend to have more education and better connections in bureaucratic hierarchies.[35] This strikes many as unfair.

One of the remedies offered to address this unfairness is affirmative action, a set of policies that, in essence, constitute proactive attempts to increase diversity. Such policies are highly controversial—are they necessary to remove institutionalized racism from the merit system, or are they simply a way for certain groups to profit from a double standard that makes a mockery of the merit system? Defenders argue that such policies are necessary because of the political role of the bureaucracy.

There is more than the desire for multiracial balance behind this argument. A fairly long-standing

---

Affirmative Action
A set of policies designed to help organizations recruit and promote employees who are members of disadvantaged groups.

Federal government programs and policies directly affect state and local bureaucracies. Federal policymakers are well aware of this; the three most recent U.S. presidents all served time in state office as either governors or legislators.

theory in the field of public administration suggests that more diverse bureaucracies actually may be more effective bureaucracies. According to the theory of **representative bureaucracy**, public agencies that reflect the diversity of the communities they serve are more likely to account for the interests of all groups when managing programs and delivering services.[36] To serve a diverse and democratic society well, a bureaucracy should include affirmative action as an important part of its hiring and promoting practices. Remember our street-level bureaucrat, the traffic cop deciding which speeders to stop? What if all the traffic cops were white and most of the speeders stopped were black—or vice versa? Regardless of who was going how fast, this sort of situation is likely to create friction. Some may view the agency as unfair, which can make the bureaucracy's job harder. If traffic cops are ethnically diverse, it is less likely

that the bureaucracy is going to be seen as playing favorites, and it is better able to focus on its job.

Opponents of affirmative action reject such arguments. Males and whites often resent establishing preferential recruitment and promotion policies for women and for racial and ethnic minorities. Some see the policies as little more than reverse discrimination. From this perspective, affirmative action represents the success of special interests in getting their favored agendas written into the law and the rules that run bureaucracies. In a merit system, technical qualifications and job performance—not race or gender—are supposed to drive personnel decisions in the ideal bureaucracy. Opponents of affirmative action argue that it produces quotas and favoritism for certain groups. In effect, affirmative action has bureaucracy wage politics on behalf of the favored groups. Speeders should be stopped, and the race or gender of the driver and of whoever issues the ticket should be irrelevant.

Which of these viewpoints is correct is a matter of fierce debate. Whatever the underlying pros and cons, the fight comes down to what is

Representative Bureaucracy
The idea that public agencies that reflect the diversity of the communities they serve will be more effective.

the best way to recruit and promote public employees, and who—if anyone—should be given preferential treatment. This is ultimately a political fight about who gets government jobs. That fight took center stage in June 2009, when the U.S. Supreme Court ruled that the city of New Haven, Connecticut, discriminated against nineteen white and Hispanic firefighters when it threw out their scores on an exam that would have qualified them for promotions, fearing a lawsuit from minority employees. But despite the case's high profile—U.S. Supreme Court justice Sonia Sotomayor had ruled on the case as an appellate court judge—the ruling left this area of employment law as gray as ever, ensuring the fight will go on.[37]

If Not Merit . . . Then What?

Traditional bureaucracy and the merit system have some clear advantages: equity, competence, and something approaching neutrality. They also have disadvantages: a measure of red tape and inefficiency, a lack of flexibility and accountability, and a political role that makes many uncomfortable. No clear answer exists on whether the pros outweigh the cons or vice versa, but this has not stopped the nearly constant search for a better way to do things. Bureaucratic reform is a perennial issue in American politics.

Many of the reform efforts are variations on a single theme that reflects a popular belief that government would be better if it were run more like a business. In practice, this means introducing competition into the delivery of public programs and services, making the organizations that deliver these goods and services less hierarchical, and making greater use of the private sector to deliver public services.[38] The idea is to introduce the benefits of the market into the public sector, which in theory could lead to more efficiency through lower costs while increasing responsiveness, because competition means paying attention to your customers or going out of business. The great difficulty facing reformers is how to get these benefits without

leaving behind the advantages of the traditional, tried-and-true merit-based bureaucracy.

Over the past two decades reformers have made a sustained effort to try to change the entire philosophy of delivering public programs and services from the use of a traditional bureaucracy to the use of a more business-based model. Although these reforms come in many different packages, collectively they often are described as new public management (NPM). NPM has six core characteristics that have been widely pursued and adopted by state and local governments:

1. A focus on productivity that emphasizes "doing more with less," that is, providing public services with fewer resources.

2. A market orientation that looks increasingly to the private sector to deliver public services. This typically is done through a process of competitive bidding, during which private companies vie to gain a government contract to run a public program.

3. A drive to improve customer satisfaction with public services.

4. A decentralization of decision-making power, an effort to push policymaking choices as close as possible to the people who are going to be affected by them.

5. A movement to improve the government's capacity to make, implement, and manage public policy and public programs.

6. An effort to maintain accountability, that is, to make the government deliver on its service promises.[39]

These characteristics all sound fairly positive when presented as a simple list. In practice, however, they have proven to be a mixed bag. The basic problem with trying to run government more like a business is that government is not a business. For the most part, we as citizens do not like rules and red tape—until there is a problem or a scandal. Then we want to know what went wrong and who is to blame. We want government agencies to act more like a business until bureaucracy takes a calculated risk—as businesses do routinely—and loses taxpayer money. We want bureaucrats to be given the freedom to be flexible and make choices—until those choices result in favoritism or program failure. We like the idea of competition and the profit motive; we like it until a private company contracted to provide public services puts profit above the public interest.

> The basic problem with trying to run government more like a business is that government is not a business.

Although most efforts to make government bureaucracy more market-like have produced very mixed results, they have done little to reduce the widespread belief that government is best run as a business. This belief has spawned a veritable alphabet soup of business-oriented reform movements. Reinventing government (REGO) stresses making public agencies entrepreneurial. Total quality management (TQM) emphasizes having public programs and services designed and shaped by the clients who actually consume those services and focuses on preventing problems rather than reacting to them. Management by objectives (MBO) and performance-based management (PBM) are approaches that focus on setting goals and achieving them. There are many other such movements. All originated in private-sector management trends that do not fully account for the unique problems of the public sector. Support and enthusiasm for making government more like a business tend to fade when these systems are put into practice and it becomes apparent that there are good reasons government is not run like the typical 9-to-5 corporation.

As the problems with these proffered replacements for traditional bureaucracy become apparent, public agencies gravitate back to their tried-and-true bureaucratic ways of doing things, at least until they get swept up in the next big reform movement.

Some of these movements are counterproductive from the beginning because they spread more confusion than efficiency and leave public managers with vague or complicated sets of guidelines that are difficult to implement and are based on concepts that are hard to understand.

Another big drawback to trying to replace the traditional merit-based bureaucracy is that the advantages of such a bureaucracy get overlooked until they are no longer there. Many of the attempts to radically reform the bureaucracy by either making agencies more like businesses or eliminating the merit system end up doing little more than returning public programs and services to the spoils system.[40]

This is not to say that is impossible to implement long-lasting changes in public bureaucracies. Indeed, the Great Recession brought about some of the biggest and potentially most long-lasting changes to public agencies in at least a generation. One of the most obvious of these changes is that, personnel-wise, public agencies have been shrinking. Cash-strapped state and local governments started shedding jobs shortly after the financial crunch hit in 2008, and as of 2013 they were still handing out pink slips at a fairly steady clip. If citizens really want smaller government, then over the past few years they've gotten it. Flint, Michigan, cut twenty-three of its eighty-eight firefighters and closed two fire stations. Dallas, Texas, laid off 4 percent of its workforce (500 people) as a money-saving measure; especially hard-hit were the city's libraries. San Jose, California, cut employee compensation by 10 percent, fired thirty managers, and shut twenty-two community centers. Hundreds of these sorts of actions have been taken by state and local governments over the past few years, and taken together they add up to some big numbers.[41] In 2011 alone, almost a quarter million state and local employees lost their jobs; from 2008 to 2011, the overall state and local workforce dropped from 65 employees per 1,000 population to 61 employees per 1,000 population. In other words, the size of state and local bureaucracy shrank by a little more than 6 percent in a three-year span.[42]

The impacts of the shrinking public-sector workforce show up in different ways. Some governors have used the financial crisis as leverage to

FIGURE 10-2

Monthly Changes in State and Local Government Employment, 2009–2012

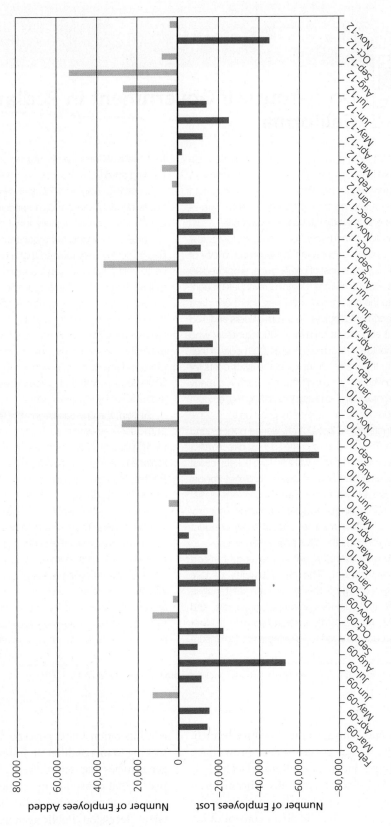

Source: "State and Local Government Employment: Monthly Data," *Governing,* www.governing.com/gov-data/monthly-government-employment-changes-totals.html.

Local Focus

Do-It-Yourself Government in Redlands, California

While most local governments are preparing to do less with less, officials in Redlands, California, are taking a different approach: They are trying to maintain current levels of service through other means. One of these options is increasing the use of volunteers.

Take the police department, for example. Just a few years ago the police department in Redlands, a city of 71,000 about sixty miles east of Los Angeles, employed 98 sworn officers and 208 civilians. Declining revenues brought budget cuts to the department, however, and these days the police department employs 75 sworn officers and 138 civilians, but it also draws on nearly 300 volunteers who annually contribute a total of more than 31,000 hours of their time to the city. If you start to figure out the labor costs for 30,000 person-hours, you don't have to push too many buttons on your calculator to realize that getting that amount of human resources for free is a pretty good deal.

These volunteers are not just answering phones and making coffee. They cordon off crime scenes, direct traffic, patrol the city's fourteen parks, write parking tickets, assist with animal control, and provide crowd control at special events. They are also trained to check in parolees, assist with records processing, and take reports on property crimes. Two volunteer reserve officers even conduct investigations alongside the city's police detectives.

Such extensive use of volunteers extends beyond the police department. The city's Quality of Life Department is in charge of things such as maintenance of streets and traffic lights, the municipal airport, and city parks. As the department struggled with budget cuts of 10 percent, it turned to volunteers to help ensure that the level of services stayed the same even as its funding shrank.

Does this really work? Can volunteers really put in the hours needed and perform sensitive and highly skilled jobs? Well, sort of. Initially local agencies were using volunteers to fill gaps, but organizations such as the police department quickly realized that a better approach would be to shift a series of routine tasks to volunteers. These tasks—things like directing traffic, taking reports, and providing crime scene control—often constituted a big part of an officer's workday. Also, some highly specialized jobs were suited to being handled by volunteers. For example, the Redlands Police Department dropped its plans to lease a helicopter from the county at a cost of $500,000 a month and instead uses a 1967 Cessna 172 that is flown by volunteer pilots.

All told, the city has been able to maintain its level of public services even though city personnel have been cut by 16 percent. Still, there are limits—volunteers cannot replace professional, sworn police officers, for instance. Further, if a volunteer wants to stop volunteering, he or she is free to do so, and there's no guarantee another volunteer will be available to take on that person's responsibilities. There may also be an ironic downside to the creative approach Redlands has taken to maintaining top-notch services. With revenues continuing to decline and the city struggling to keep up levels of service even with its creative approach, in 2010 Redlands asked its citizens to approve a half-cent sales tax. The citizens turned it down. There was no visible sign of declining public services, so why pay more taxes for them?

Source: Adapted from John Buntin, "Does Government Work Require Government Employees?," *Governing*, April 2011.

consolidate and centralize the executive branch. For example, Kansas governor Sam Brownback folded the largely independent Kansas Health Policy Authority (which historically administered Medicaid) into the state health department, the latter being more under the direct control of his administration. Other governors have been actively seeking to merge different bureaucracies into bigger agencies that report directly to the chief executive.[43] That consolidation of power will last long after the economy has fully recovered from the Great Recession. Public agencies facing big losses in human resources are also experimenting with volunteers and other ways to maintain their previous levels of services. The biggest impact, however, may be in who will work in the public sector in the future. As a result of structural changes brought on by the fiscal crisis—things such as limits on collective bargaining rights and generally lower levels of public service provision—it seems clear that going forward there will be fewer public workers, and they will likely be paid less and have less job security than did such workers in the past. Further, they will not have the generous pensions and benefits that historically have helped motivate people to seek careers in public service. Some scholars suggest the end result may be a public sector that has not just less compensated but also less qualified employees and greater employee turnover.[44]

Conclusion

Although bureaucracy is often despised and disparaged, it is clear that the effectiveness of government bureaucracy is underestimated, and bureaucratic agencies do not get the credit they actually deserve. A wide range of state and local agencies support and deliver the programs and services that make up social and economic life as we know it. The comparative method shows us that bureaucracy is big—but only as big as we want it to be. If we want less bureaucracy, we can choose to make fewer demands on government. The comparative method also shows that, for the most part, bureaucracies do their

jobs remarkably well. In contrast to the popular stereotype, most public agencies tackle difficult jobs that are unlikely to be done better by any other alternative. Perhaps the most astonishing thing about bureaucracy is how much we take it for granted. Public schools, safe drinking water, working utility grids, and roads are simply there. We rarely contemplate what astounding administrative and logistical feats are required to make these aspects of everyday life appear so mundane.

Indeed, perhaps the one thing that makes us pay attention to the upside of bureaucracy is when that bureaucracy is not there. The financial toll of the Great Recession has led to fewer police, fewer teachers, fewer librarians, and big difficulties in maintaining prerecession levels of public goods and services. The high cost of those services has prompted an ongoing debate about what government should do and may result in a shift of more of what was traditionally considered public administration toward the private sector.

Bureaucratic reform movements, at least in some ways, should be viewed with skepticism. Criticizing the bureaucracy is a traditional sport in American politics, and a lot of reforms turn out to be little more than fads that quickly fade when the pleasing rhetoric meets the real-life challenge of delivering the goods. Some reforms, such as the rise of the merit system, can radically reshape what bureaucracy is and what it does. One thing, however, will almost certainly remain constant: whatever the government is, and whatever it does, it will rely on bureaucracy to get it done.

The Latest Research

As discussed above, the Great Recession had an enormous and potentially long-lasting impact on public agencies. Most obviously, public-sector payrolls shrank as states and localities shed hundreds of thousands of employees in an attempt to keep the books balanced. By 2013 that exodus was tapering off, but it was clear

things were not just going to return to the way they were. The big question, of course, was what was going to happen? Would agencies stay lean and try to keep doing with less? Would they engage in more contracting out? Would the shattered traditional notion of a secure government-sector job make it more difficult for agencies to

(Continued)

(Continued)

recruit the best and the brightest into careers in public service? What about representation—did the massive disruption in employment leave bureaucracies more or less representative of the constituencies they serve? These are big questions that social scientists have been busily studying, and the research reviewed below offers some perspective on what the answers might be.

• •

• **Levine, Heliss, and Eric Scorsone.** 2011. "The Great Recession's Institutional Change in the Public Employment Relationship: Implications for State and Local Governments." *State and Local Government Review* 43: 208–214.

The Great Recession made the pay and benefits of public employees a white-hot political issue. Rightly or wrongly, government employees were sometimes accused of being more insulated from economic problems than their counterparts in the private sector. This chapter discussed the bitter fights that broke out in Wisconsin and Ohio over labor relations in the public sector, fights that were repeated on a less heated scale in many states and localities. Does all this mean that the public labor sector is undergoing a dramatic and long-term shift? If so, what does it imply? Levine and Scorsone take a crack at answering these questions. They conclude that the Great Recession has brought about one of the biggest changes in public employment in fifty years. The fallout of that change is probably lower pay and fewer benefits for government employees. As a result, public agencies of the future may struggle to attract a high-quality labor pool, which may in turn have implications for the quality if not the cost of public goods and services.

• **Joaquin, M. Ernita, and Thomas J. Greitens.** 2012. "Contract Management Capacity Breakdown? An Analysis of U.S. Local Governments." *Public Administration Review* 72: 807–816.

At least in theory, contracting out allows governments to leverage the power of the marketplace to deliver goods and services more efficiently. In practice, as the discussion of university health services in this chapter made clear, contracting out has a mixed track record. Sometimes it works, sometimes it doesn't. This study tries to figure out what some of the underlying causes of this variation might be. Specifically, the authors look at "capacity," essentially the ability of local governments to effectively manage these contracts, which are often made with the private sector. Disturbingly, they conclude that there has been a long-term trend toward the diminishment of this capacity. This may be a result of a combination of decreasing competition and the highly complex and demanding nature of the contracts. Contracting out seems to have increased the need for public officials to undertake often very demanding evaluation responsibilities, even as their capacity to fulfill those responsibilities has shrunk. Given the huge toll the Great Recession took on the public sector, it seems that such capacity is unlikely to begin increasing in the foreseeable future.

• **Nicholson-Crotty, Jill, Jason Grissom, and Sean Nicholson-Crotty.** 2011. "Bureaucratic Representation, Distributional Equity, and Democratic Values in the Administration of Public Programs." *Journal of Politics* 73: 582–596.

One of the key concepts discussed in this chapter is that of representative bureaucracy, or the idea that bureaucracies that sociodemographically mirror the constituencies they serve will do a better job of representing constituents' interests in the provision of public goods and services. Needless to say, this has been a controversial theory given its potential implications of a merit/diversity trade-off. While there is considerable research suggesting that increasing minority representation in bureaucracy leads to better service and outcomes to the same minorities in the community served by that bureaucracy, virtually no research has examined the potential trade-offs of such outcomes. Goods and services can be limited and divisible—in other words, there's only so much of something, and if one person gets it, then another person does not. This is a comparative study—the unit of analysis is a national sample of elementary schools—that looks at the racial and ethnic breakdown of gifted and talented (G&T) students. There are only so many G&T seats to go around. Does more white teachers mean more white G&T students and fewer black and Hispanic students? Does more black teachers mean more black students and fewer white and Hispanic? Through careful research, the authors found that increasing minority representation does not necessarily lead to such predictable winners and losers. What it generally results in is more distributional equity—in other words, the G&T seats are spread out more proportionally relative to race. This suggests that a more diverse bureaucracy may be a fairer bureaucracy.

college.cqpress.com/
sites/govstateandlocal

Chapter Review

Key Concepts

- affirmative action (p. 335)
- bureaucracy (p. 318)
- bureaucrats (p. 318)
- collective bargaining (p. 333)
- contracting out (p. 324)
- merit system (p. 332)
- neutral competence (p. 332)
- patronage (p. 331)
- policy implementation (p. 319)
- professionalization (p. 330)
- representative bureaucracy (p. 336)
- rulemaking (p. 320)
- seniority (p. 334)
- spoils system (p. 331)
- street-level bureaucrat (p. 320)

Suggested Web Sites

- **www.aspanet.org.** Web site of the American Society for Public Administration, the largest professional association for those who work for or study public agencies.

- **www.governing.com.** Web version of *Governing* magazine, which is dedicated to covering state and local issues. Includes numerous stories and other resources on agency leaders and performance, e-government, and more.

- **www.pewstates.org.** State and Consumer Initiatives section of the Web site of the Pew Charitable Trusts is home to a number of analyses of government effectiveness and efficiency, including the Government Performance Project.

State Stats on Bureaucracy

Explore and compare data on the states! Go to college.cqpress.com/sites/govstateandlocal to do these exercises.

1. What is the average salary for a full-time government worker in California? Why might a state like California have to have relatively high wages for government workers?

2. How many government employees are there in your state? If, for example, budget cuts forced a 5 percent reduction in the government workforce, how many people would lose their jobs?

3. Which state has the most number of law enforcement agencies? Why might they have so many, even though they may not have the highest population?

4. How does your state compare to the average in terms of per capita state and local government expenditures on welfare programs? How do you think that this would translate into the workforce that is necessary to administer these programs?

5. How many K–12 public school teachers are there in your state? Do you normally think of teachers as part of the bureaucracy? Why or why not?

The ancient Greeks pledged allegiance to their cities, not to any nation-state. There are plenty of people who still make formal commitments to serve local government, including police officers and firefighters. Pictured here is the graduation ceremony of the 36th Alaska Law Enforcement Training class; these individuals will go on to work as municipal police officers and fire marshals and in other law enforcement posts in towns and cities across Alaska.

Local Government

FUNCTION FOLLOWS FORM

- Why do local governments vary so much within and between states?
- How and why have local governments changed over the years?
- What are the positive and negative aspects of Dillon's Rule?
- How has the Great Recession affected local governments?

The ancient Greeks did not pledge allegiance to ancient Greece. At that time and place, the nation-state as we know it didn't really exist. Instead of the nation-state, the Greeks devoted their patriotic loyalty and civic duty to city-states, such as Athens and Sparta. And, boy, did the Greeks take their civic duty seriously.

The Athenian Oath, recited by the citizens of Athens more than two thousand years ago, is still cited as a model code for civic responsibility. Citizens who took this oath pledged: "We will never bring disgrace on this our City by an act of dishonesty or cowardice. . . . We will revere and obey the City's laws, and will do our best to incite a like reverence and respect in those above us who are prone to annul them or set them at naught."[1]

Americans don't quite reach that level of civic commitment to their cities, but attitudes toward local government in the twenty-first century are not as far from the ancient Greek ideal as you might imagine. The United States has a long tradition of strong local government, which is unsurprising given the political system's founding principles of division and decentralization of power. Woven tightly into the country's political fabric is a mistrust of centralized power, and Americans generally prefer to keep government as close as possible to citizens, where they can keep an eye on it.

Government does not get any closer than local government—the cities, counties, and other political jurisdictions that exist at the substate level. It is this level of government that Americans tend to trust the most, and it is this level of government that citizens generally want to have more rather than less power. In 2012, only about one-third of Americans had favorable opinions of the federal government. Nearly twice as many had favorable opinions of local government (about half had favorable opinions about state government).[2] What accounts for these differences? One element is clearly the perceived poor performance of the federal government in dealing with important issues. Maybe more important is the general notion that local governments not only do a good job but also are less profligate spenders of the taxpayers' money. In bang-for-buck assessments, local governments are seen as doing more with less in comparison to state and federal governments, which suggests that Americans, as a general rule, prefer, value, and trust government down at the grassroots level.[3] Given those attitudes, it is somewhat paradoxical that local government is, technically speaking, the weakest level of government. The federal government and state governments are sovereign powers, equal partners in the federal system that draw their powers from their citizens. Pull a state out of the federal system and view it independently, however, and what you find is not a federal system but a unitary system. (See Figure 11-1.) Hierarchically speaking, as discussed in some depth in this chapter, states are superior to local governments. Local governments are not sovereign; they can exercise only the powers granted to them from the central authority of the states.

An individual state, however, is a strange sort of unitary system. Whereas a state government is clearly the seat of power, below the state are an astonishing number and variety of political jurisdictions, many of them piled on top of one another and related to one another in no clear organizational fashion. Many of them operate independent of each other even when they occupy the same geographical space and provide services to the same citizens. For example, a city and a school district may overlap each other entirely but have different governance structures, different

leaders, and different purposes. One of these governments is not the boss of the other; the city cannot tell the school district what its tax rate should be any more than the school district can tell the city to build another library.

It is down here in the crazy quilt of local governments that much of the grunt work of the political system takes place. Local governments provide law enforcement, roads, health services, parks, libraries, and schools; they are mostly responsible for regulating (or even providing) utilities, such as sewer and water; they run airports, public transportation systems, mosquito control programs, and community recreation centers. The list goes on. And on. Collectively, these are the public services we encounter most in our daily lives, generally take for granted, and almost certainly could not get along without. No wonder citizens tend to think that local governments give them good value for the money (well, at least compared to what they get from state and federal governments).

Local governments, however, go well beyond just providing services. They must make political and philosophical decisions that affect their residents' quality of life and reinforce values. Many citizens believe local governments have an obligation to provide a safety net for the poor, strike a balance between the need for sufficient revenues and public resistance to high taxation, and referee disputes over land-use planning that pit, say, developers against environmentalists or middle-income homeowners against low-income renters.

In short, local governments are worth getting to know. This chapter examines the powers, responsibilities, and specific forms of local government; how and why these forms evolved; how they differ by state and region; and how the political

FIGURE 11-1

Substate "Unitary" System

State-Level Unitary System

Local Governments ← State Government → Local Governments

At the state level, state government grants power to local governments.

Strong attachments to localities are not unusual. Detroit has faced its fair share of troubles in recent years, dealing with everything from fiscal stress to underperforming sports teams. Being the center of America's iconic automobile industry gives Detroiters a strong identity and a rallying point for community pride.

process works within the astonishing number and variety of substate governments.

The Many Faces of Local Government

The importance of local governments to the American political system is evident, on one level, from their sheer numbers. According to the U.S. Census Bureau, at last count in 2012 more than 89,000 local governments were operating in the United States. (See Table 11-1.) That works out to roughly one local government for every 3,450 people.[4]

The forms these local governments take, the responsibilities and powers they exercise, and the numbers of particular kinds that exist in given geographical or demographic areas vary wildly from state to state. The number of local governments within a state's boundaries, for example, depends on the state's history, culture, and administrative approach to service delivery. New England states have a tradition of active civic participation and social spending that accommodates a large number of local governing units. By contrast, the South has much less of a tradition of civic engagement in local government, and even today a relatively small number of powerful county leaders dominate such services as school governance.

In terms of differences, local governments make state governments look like they were all stamped from the same cookie cutter. Take the average of 3,450 people for each local government. That number can be misleading because local governments are not evenly spread out demographically. Hawaii has relatively few local governments. It has no incorporated **municipalities**, just four

counties, and the consolidated city-county government of Honolulu. Georgia, on the other hand, has 153 counties, and all of them are vested with municipal-like powers. The city of New York is the largest city in the United States, with a resident population of more than 8 million. The city of Hove Mobile Park, North Dakota, has a population of one. No, that's not a typo. Hove Mobile is an incorporated municipality whose entire population consists of an elderly woman living in a trailer park.[5]

Local governments are not evenly spread out geographically, either. They range from villages covering less than a square mile to counties that cover nearly 125,000 square miles. Within or adjacent to their borders may be mountains, deserts, beaches, urban centers, or vast stretches of nothingness.

Municipalities
Political jurisdictions, such as cities, villages, or towns, incorporated under state law to provide governance to defined geographical areas; more compact and more densely populated than counties.

Counties
Geographical subdivisions of state government.

TABLE 11-1

Number of Government Units, Ranked by State and Type

State	All Government	County	Municipal	Township	School Districts	All Special Districts
Illinois	6,968	102	1,298	1,431	905	3,232
Pennsylvania	4,905	66	1,015	1,546	514	1,764
Texas	4,856	254	1,214	—	1,079	2,309
California	4,350	57	482	—	1,025	2,786
Kansas	3,806	103	626	1,268	306	1,503
Missouri	3,752	114	955	312	534	1,837
Ohio	3,702	88	938	1,308	668	700
Minnesota	3,633	87	854	1,785	338	569
New York	3,454	57	617	929	679	1,172
Wisconsin	3,123	72	595	1,255	440	761
Michigan	2,877	83	533	1,240	576	445
Colorado	2,818	62	271	—	180	2,305
Indiana	2,694	91	569	1,006	291	737
North Dakota	2,666	53	357	1,314	183	759
Nebraska	2,581	93	530	419	272	1,267
South Dakota	1,979	66	311	907	152	543
Iowa	1,939	99	947	—	366	527
Oklahoma	1,854	77	590	—	550	637
Washington	1,831	39	281	—	295	1,216
Florida	1,554	66	410	—	95	1,983
Arkansas	1,543	75	502	—	239	727
Oregon	1,509	36	241	—	230	1,002
Georgia	1,365	153	535	—	180	497
Kentucky	1,314	118	418	—	174	604
New Jersey	1,344	21	324	242	523	234
Montana	1,240	54	129	—	321	736
Alabama	1,208	67	461	—	132	548
Idaho	1,161	44	200	—	118	799
Mississippi	991	82	297	—	164	448
North Carolina	964	100	553	—	—	311
Tennessee	920	92	345	—	14	469
New Mexico	854	33	103	—	96	622
Massachusetts	852	5	53	298	84	412
Maine	841	16	22	466	99	238
Wyoming	795	23	99	—	55	618
Vermont	728	14	43	237	291	143
South Carolina	681	46	269	—	83	283
Arizona	659	15	91	—	244	309
West Virginia	658	55	232	—	55	316
Utah	613	29	245	—	41	298
Connecticut	644	—	30	149	17	448
New Hampshire	542	10	13	221	166	132

State	All Government	County	Municipal	Township	School Districts	All Special Districts
Louisiana	530	60	304	—	69	97
Virginia	497	95	229	—	1	172
Maryland	347	23	157	—	167	—
Delaware	338	3	57	—	19	259
Nevada	190	16	19	—	17	138
Alaska	177	14	148	—	—	15
Rhode Island	134	—	8	31	4	91
Hawaii	21	3	1	—	17	—

Source: U.S. Census Bureau, "2012 Census of Governments," www.census.gov/govs/cog2012/#tml.

These differences help explain why some local governments are interested in maintaining subways and others worry about maintaining clean beaches.

Political and cultural traditions also vary at the local level. For instance, the degree of loyalty that citizens display toward a local governing entity often depends on whether they personally identify with the area or whether they ignore their membership and regard the area as an artificial construct. Put another way, a Manhattanite probably feels more community pride than, say, a user of the Buncombe County, North Carolina, Metropolitan Sewer District.

All these differences provide multiple opportunities to put the comparative method into practice, but they also can be confusing. Local authority, for example, overlaps—school districts sprawl across municipalities, which, in turn, are covered by counties. A couple may plan on getting married in the city of Chapel Hill, North Carolina, but their marriage certificate will carry the insignia of Orange County, North Carolina. That is because in most states the power to grant marriage licenses is vested in counties, not in cities. Adding to the confusion, the units of government at the substate level vary in their duties and obligations from state to state. Depending on where you live, you may rely on a different set of authorities to get a pothole filled on your street, arrange for a stop sign to be installed at a dangerous intersection, or register your opinion on a bond issue for a new high school.

Despite all these differences, however, there are only three general forms of local government in the United States: counties, municipalities, and special districts. Counties traditionally are viewed as geographical and administrative subdivisions of states. The exact definition of a municipality varies from state to state, although municipalities generally are political units that are distinguished geographically from counties by being more compact and distinguished legally by being independent corporations rather than "branch offices" of the state government. Special districts cover a huge range of local governments. Typically, special districts are single-purpose governments. Unlike counties and cities, which are general purpose governments, special districts usually are created to provide a specific public service rather than a range of services. School districts are a good example. These are geographically defined local units of government created to provide educational services. Other special districts include water management and sewage treatment districts.

The Organization and Responsibilities of Local Governments

Even within each of the three basic categories of local government, there is considerable variation in organizational structure, autonomy, and responsibilities. These categories are distinct enough, however, to wrangle those more than 89,000 local governments in the United States into a general understanding of what local governments are and why they take on the forms they do.

Between the County Lines

To learn what county government is all about, you would find it instructive to take a trip to your local

Illinois has 6,968 local governments—the most of any state.

county courthouse. There you are likely to find signs pointing you toward a variety of self-explanatory government offices: district attorney, coroner, sheriff, treasurer, and the like. You also may find signs for offices whose purposes are not quite so self-evident. President Harry Truman once walked into the courthouse in Allegheny, Pennsylvania, and was taken aback by one of the signs he saw. "What the hell is a prothonotary?" he famously asked. Well, a prothonotary, Mr. President, is the chief record keeper of a civil court. Truman's bewilderment over this obscure county office encapsulates some of the confusion over what county government is and what it does. People might be asked to vote on a prothonotary come election time, but chances are only a small minority knows what the heck a prothonotary is or why the position is necessary.[6]

In your particular courthouse the prothonotary might travel under a less mysterious title, such as clerk of the civil court. Regardless, however, the office of prothonotary points out what county government is often about: the unglamorous, but undoubtedly necessary, administration of central (that is, state) government functions. Civil courts and criminal courts for the most part function under the framework of state rather than county authority. Yet at the county courthouse the court's record keeper, prosecutor, and judge are typically county-level elective offices. It is the county government that represents the local face of the central government.

The unglamorous utilitarian governing unit known as the county grew out of a thousand-year-old tradition brought over from England, where it was known as the shire. (Many English county names still carry this suffix; one of the authors of this book was born in the county of Oxfordshire.) In the United States, counties "are nothing more than certain portions of the territory into which the state is divided for the more convenient exercise of the powers of government," wrote U.S. Supreme Court chief justice Roger B. Taney in *Maryland ex. rel. Washington County v. Baltimore & Ohio Railroad Co.* (1845).[7]

Centralizing day-to-day governance for an entire state in the state capital simply was, and largely still is, impractical. Thus states divided themselves into smaller geographical units—counties—and created a governance structure within each to provide a local "branch office" of the state government.

Called parishes in Louisiana and boroughs in Alaska, more than three thousand counties are drawn on the maps of the remaining forty-eight states. How many county governments reside within a state varies wildly. Rhode Island and Connecticut are the only states that have no county governments (as geographically compact states, they have no need for such administrative subunits of state government). Some states have just a handful. Delaware, for example, has only three counties. Supporting the claim that everything is bigger in Texas, the state has 254 counties, the most in the nation.

Geographically speaking, counties are typically the largest local governments, although, like their numbers, their sizes can vary enormously. Arlington County, Virginia, covers 42 square miles, which is on the smallish side. North Slope Borough, Alaska, encompasses 142,224 (mostly uninhabited) square miles. Measured by population, counties range from 9.8 million in Los Angeles County, California, to forty-two people in Loving County, Texas.[8] (See Tables 11-2 and 11-3.)

Because, among substate governments, counties generally cover the largest amounts of geographical territory, they bear much of the burden of providing services widely, if not lavishly. The majority of the million citizens in California's Sacramento County, for example, live in unincorporated territory. This means that their property is not part of any city, town, or township that can provide municipal services. Hence the burden falls on the county to provide these residents with such services as law enforcement, parks and recreation, and storm water management.

The autonomy and authority of county governments also vary considerably from state to state. There are some regional patterns to such differences. For example, in the Northeast, local government traditionally is centered in towns and villages. These are the units of government that attract the most participation, make the most high-profile decisions, and are the focus of most attention. County governments in this region are historically viewed as just the local offices of state government, representing a form of government and governance more remote than the village board.

In the South, counties are also technically creatures of state government in that they were

TABLE 11-2

Twenty-Five Largest U.S. Counties by Population, 2010

Rank	Geographic Area	Population Estimates
1	Los Angeles County, Calif.	9,818,605
2	Cook County, Ill.	5,194,675
3	Harris County, Tex.	4,092,459
4	Maricopa County, Ariz.	3,817,117
5	San Diego County, Calif.	3,095,313
6	Orange County, Calif.	3,010,232
7	Kings County, N.Y.	2,504,700
8	Miami-Dade County, Fla.	2,496,435
9	Dallas County, Tex.	2,368,139
10	Queens County, N.Y.	2,230,722
11	Riverside County, Calif.	2,189,641
12	San Bernardino County, Calif.	2,035,210
13	Clark County, Nev.	1,951,269
14	King County, Wash.	1,951,269
15	Wayne County, Mich.	1,820,584
16	Tarrant County, Tex.	1,809,034
17	Santa Clara County, Calif.	1,781,642
18	Broward County, Fla.	1,748,066
19	Bexar County, Tex.	1,714,773
20	New York County, N.Y.	1,585,873
21	Philadelphia County, Pa.	1,526,006
22	Alameda County, Calif.	1,510,271
23	Middlesex County, Mass.	1,503,085
24	Suffolk County, N.Y.	1,493,350
25	Sacramento County, Calif.	1,418,788

Source: U.S. Census Bureau, "Total Population 2010 Census Summary File," http://factfinder2.census.gov/faces/tableservices/jsf/pages/productview.xhtml?pid=DEC_10_SF1_P1&prodType=table.

TABLE 11-3

Twenty-Five Smallest U.S. Counties by Population, 2010

County, State	Population	Rank
Loving, Tex.	82	1
Kalawao, Hawaii	90	2
King, Tex.	286	3
Kenedy, Tex.	416	4
Arthur, Neb.	460	5
Blaine, Neb.	478	6
Petroleum, Mont.	494	7
McPherson, Neb.	539	8
Grant, Neb.	614	9
Loup, Neb.	632	10
Borden, Tex.	641	11
Thomas, Neb.	647	12
Yakutat City and Borough, Ala.	662	13
Banner, Neb.	690	14
Harding, N.M.	695	15
San Juan, Colo.	699	16
McMullen, Tex.	707	17
Mineral, Colo.	712	18
Treasure, Mont.	718	19
Slope, N.D.	727	20
Hooker, Neb.	736	21
Logan, Neb.	763	22
Billings, N.D.	783	23
Esmeralda, Nev.	783	24
Kent, Tex.	808	25

Source: U.S. Census Bureau, "Total Population 2010 Census Summary File," http://factfinder2.census.gov/faces/tableservices/jsf/pages/productview.xhtml?pid=DEC_10_SF1_P1&prodType=table.

formed and granted their authority by state legislatures, yet county governments are much more likely than they are in other regions to be a central focus of local government. County government tends to be the form of local government that wields the most political power and policy influence, and thus it tends to be the focus of local political elites. The reason for these differences primarily has to do with the more urban nature of the Northeast compared to the historically more rural South. Rural areas by definition lack substantial urban centers, which means they lack large and powerful city or village governments. County governments thus occupy the center of local government, and the county seat—the place where county government is physically located—becomes the locus of local politics.

Counties are distinct from municipalities (which are discussed in depth later), although the distinctions have blurred. County governments are historically rural governments that help conduct state government business. The quintessential county government is a keeper of public records (such as property deeds, birth and death certificates, and mortgages) and an administrator of property taxes, local road maintenance, election results certification, criminal courts, and jails run by county sheriffs. The typical U.S. municipality, on the other hand, performs such day-to-day functions as police and fire protection, sewage disposal, sanitation, and the maintenance of public parks and other infrastructure facilities, including stadiums, airports, and convention centers.

In the messy real world, however, such clear distinctions often disappear. Many modern county governments—particularly urban ones—have their official fingers in these classic city functions as well. In many regions there is substantial overlap between county and city functions, and county and city governments operate cheek by jowl. For example, in Phoenix, Arizona, the city hall is directly across the street from the Maricopa County administration building.

As a general rule, however, counties tend to be kept on a tighter leash by state governments than are municipalities (especially large urban cities). In New Hampshire, for example, state legislators still approve county budgets. In Texas, each county is required by the state to appoint a county judge-at-large and four commissioners, regardless of whether the county's population numbers in the hundreds or the millions. Counties, in other words, are still in theory and often in practice the administrative subunits of state government.

County governments, like all other subnational governments, became more dependent on federal grants after the economic woes of 2008 and 2009, but they have always had independent sources of revenue. The primary funding source controlled by county governments is the property tax, which historically accounts for about 30 percent of county government income. Like everything else about local government, however, there is considerable variation in where county governments get their money and what they spend it on. In 2012, real estate taxes accounted for about 60 percent of revenues in Fairfax County, Virginia, with another 16 percent of the county's revenue coming from personal property taxes. Orange County, California, in contrast, got only about 14 percent of its revenue from sales and property taxes combined; its biggest source of income was intergovernmental transfers—that is, money from the state and federal governments.[9]

Just as there are huge variations among counties in terms of revenue, there are similar variations in spending priorities. Where county governments focus their spending depends on geography, politics, and relations with neighboring jurisdictions. A significant chunk of county spending goes to basic social services; public welfare, hospitals, and other healthcare programs account for about 60 percent of county government expenditures. Other categories of expenditure range from roads to sewers to schools to general administration.[10]

The Structure of County Government. There are three basic forms of county government: commission, council-executive, and commission-administrator. What differentiates the three forms is the degree of separation between legislative and executive powers and who is responsible for the day-to-day administration of the executive side of government.

The most common form is the county commission system, which concentrates legislative and executive functions and powers into an elected board of commissioners. For example, the commission exercises legislative powers by passing county ordinances and approving the budget. Further, it wields executive powers, as it is responsible for a broad range of hiring and firing decisions and exercises considerable control over many administrative offices.

Depending on the state and the county, members of these county-level legislatures may be called county commissioners, supervisors, selectmen, county board members, or judges. In Louisiana, these locally elected legislators are called parish jurors. In New Jersey, the county legislatures are called boards of chosen freeholders. Whatever their official titles, commissioners are typically members of small groups elected to serve staggered two- or four-year terms.

The most significant reform of county government since its inception has been the separation of executive and legislative powers through the creation of an independent county-level executive office. A county government using a council-executive system typically has an independently elected officer who serves as the county-level equivalent of a governor. County executives frequently have the power to veto ordinances passed by the board of commissioners and the authority to appoint key department heads. Thus the main difference between the commission and council-executive forms of county government is the approach to separation of powers. (See Figure 11-2.)

County Commission System
A form of county governance in which executive, legislative, and administrative powers are vested in elected commissioners.

Council-Executive System
A form of county governance in which legislative powers are vested in a county commission and executive powers are vested in an independently elected executive.

Commission-Administrator System
A form of county governance in which executive and legislative powers reside with an elected commission, which hires a professional executive to manage the day-to-day operations of government.

The commission-administrator system of county government stands somewhere between the commission and council-executive forms. In this form of government, an elected commission retains most legislative and executive powers but appoints a professional administrator to actually run the government. County administrators usually serve at the pleasure of the commissioners—that is, they can be hired and fired as the county commissioners see fit. In practice, commissioners typically delegate considerable powers to administrators, including the powers to hire and fire department heads and to prepare a budget for the commission's approval.

Commission-administrator and, to an even greater extent, council-executive structures have been popular reforms to the traditional commission form of county government. Diffuse and ineffective decision making and outright corruption were the primary reasons for the shift away from commissions in the twentieth century. Reformers were concerned that under the commission approach power was so diffuse that county governments tended to drift in the absence of clear leadership; also, commissioners too often appointed their friends to important positions. As a result, an increasing number of counties, as many as 15 percent, now are run by elected county executives who exert firm leadership on policy and hiring. This reduces the role of the commissioners to something closer to an advisory level. Another 12 percent of counties are led by appointed administrators. State policymakers have contributed to this trend—Arkansas, Kentucky, and Tennessee now mandate that their counties be headed by elected executives.

Although such reforms have reduced entrenched corruption, even today there are examples of county governments going very badly astray. When this happens, states have been known to step in and, in effect, put these county governments out of business. For example, in 1997, the Massachusetts House of Representatives voted to abolish the government of Middlesex County, which it believed had become a corrupt, debt-ridden, and expensive administrative burden. The state retained a handful of county-based positions (for example, the sheriff, district attorney, and register of deeds) as independently elected offices, but it simply absorbed much of the rest of the county government. Still today, the most populous county in the state of Massachusetts

FIGURE 11-2

HOW IT WORKS

The Structure of County Government

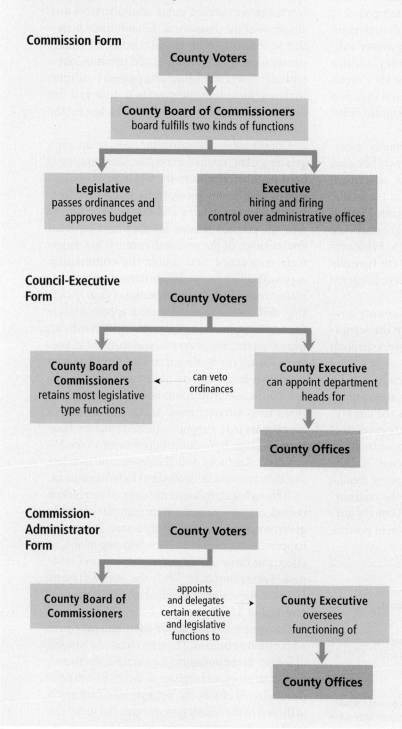

Commission Form

County Voters

↓

County Board of Commissioners
board fulfills two kinds of functions

Legislative
passes ordinances and
approves budget

Executive
hiring and firing
control over administrative offices

Council-Executive Form

County Voters

County Board of Commissioners
retains most legislative
type functions

← can veto ordinances

County Executive
can appoint department
heads for

↓

County Offices

Commission-Administrator Form

County Voters

County Board of Commissioners

appoints
and delegates
certain executive
and legislative
functions to →

County Executive
oversees
functioning of

↓

County Offices

The three basic forms of county government differ in the division of powers and in who is responsible for day-to-day administration of county government. In the commission form, voters elect county commissioners who exercise legislative and executive powers and exercise considerable authority over day-to-day administration. In the council-executive form, voters elect commissioners who exercise legislative powers and independently elect a county executive who wields executive powers and serves as the chief administrator. In the commission-administrator form, voters elect commissioners who retain most legislative and executive powers. However, they hire a professional manager to handle day-to-day administration of county government.

(roughly 1.5 million residents) does not have a county government.

Most counties, however, continue to have representative forms of government that include elected heads of a broad range of administrative and executive offices. These typically include a district attorney, a sheriff, a treasurer, a clerk of records, and, yes, sometimes even a prothonotary.

Municipalities

A municipality is a political jurisdiction formed by an association of citizens to provide self-governance within a clearly defined geographical area. Municipalities encompass two basic forms of government: townships and cities. **Cities** are corporations. In other words, they are legal entities incorporated under state law for the purpose of self-government at the local level. This is a central difference between counties and cities. Counties were created by the state from the top down; states mandated these political jurisdictions and delegated to them certain powers and functions. Cities are bottom-up creations. A local community seeks the authority of self-governance by incorporating itself as a legal entity with certain powers and responsibilities under state law. Such corporate municipal governments also may be called villages, towns, or boroughs (although, somewhat confusingly, *towns* and *boroughs* in some states can also refer to nonincorporated governments).

Townships constitute an interesting category of local government that all but defies general description. In some states, townships are shells of government, little more than geographical subdivisions of counties vested with little in the way of responsibility or power. In other states, townships are vested with a considerable range of responsibilities and essentially function as mini-county governments. They typically are run by boards of commissioners or township supervisors—a county commission form of government in miniature. These more active townships typically are responsible for such functions as snowplowing rural roads.

In still other states, townships (or towns) exercise as much power as cities do, if not more. This is particularly true in the New England states, where the township is the traditional form of local governance. These kinds of townships function as municipalities. Like cities, they are bottom-up institutions, political entities formed by groups of local citizens for the purpose of self-governance. Many are incorporated, like cities, and some of them have been working units of government longer than the United States has been in existence. The Maine town of Dover-Foxcroft, for example, was incorporated in 1769, seven years before the Declaration of Independence was approved.[11] Townships, in other words, can be viewed as being like counties, like cities, or like large geographical spaces with little in the way of governance structure within them. Which of these descriptions is accurate depends on state law and the traditions of local governance.

What distinguishes cities and city-like townships from counties and county-like townships is that they are formed by associations of citizens rather than brought to life as designated subunits of states. Municipalities are general-purpose governments that provide a range of public services and address a variety of political issues at the local level. They are brought into existence because groups of citizens, usually those concentrated in compact urban areas, want to exercise a degree of political self-determination over their community. Accordingly, they incorporate, bringing to life a legal entity—a municipality—that grants them the right to a broad degree of self-governance.

Governance arrangements vary even more at the municipal level than at the county level. In municipalities, there is variation in the powers of the executive, or **mayor**, and the legislature,

---

Cities
Incorporated political jurisdictions formed to provide self-governance to particular localities.

Townships
Local governments whose powers, governance structure, and legal status vary considerably from state to state. In some states, townships function as general-purpose municipalities; in others, they are geographical subdivisions of counties with few responsibilities and little power.

Mayor
The elected chief executive of a municipality.

typically a **city council**. A strong role often is played by an appointed administrator, or **city manager**, who is given the day-to-day responsibility for running municipal operations. Municipal governance systems can be divided into four basic types: the mayor-council system, the city manager system, the commission system, and the town meeting system.

Mayor-Council Systems

One of the most common forms of municipal governance is the **mayor-council system**. It is distinguished by a separation of executive and legislative powers. According to the International City/County Management Association (ICMA), approximately 43 percent of U.S. cities use this system. Executive power is vested in a separately elected mayor, although the powers that a mayor actually is allowed to exercise vary considerably.

Mayor-council systems can be broken down into **strong mayor** and **weak mayor systems**. In discussions of city governance, these terms have less to do with a politician's personality than with the powers that a given mayor enjoys when stacked up against the powers of the city council and the bureaucracy. Under the strong mayor system, the executive is roughly the municipal-level equivalent of a governor. Strong mayors exercise a great deal of power, and typically they have the authority to make appointments to key city offices, to veto council decisions, to prepare budgets, and to run the day-to-day operations of municipal government in general.

City Council
A municipality's legislature.

City Manager
An official appointed to be the chief administrator of a municipality.

Mayor-Council System
A form of municipal governance in which there is an elected executive and an elected legislature.

Strong Mayor System
A municipal government in which the mayor has the power to perform the executive functions of government.

Weak Mayor System
A municipal government in which the mayor lacks true executive powers, such as the ability to veto council decisions or appoint department heads.

The strong mayor system is most common in the Northeast and the Midwest. One example of a strong mayor in action is Carleton S. Finkbeiner, who was elected mayor of Toledo, Ohio, in 1994. Early in his tenure, he overrode resistance from school authorities and placed uniformed police officers in every junior high school and high school as a way to reduce violence. The policy took some cops off the streets, but it also created trust between police and students. Further, this preventive approach reduced drug and gang problems by providing mentors and role models for students. The U.S. Conference of Mayors cited the program as an example of best practice in 2000.[12] What Finkbeiner demonstrated was the ability of a strong mayor to make important policy decisions independently. Making such decisions can often be controversial, although it doesn't seem to have hurt Finkbeiner. With one term limit–enforced break to host a TV show on public affairs, he served three full terms as mayor between 1994 and 2010.

A weak mayor system retains the elected executive, but this is more of a ceremonial than a real policymaking office. In a weak mayor system, the executive, as well as legislative, power is wielded by the council. Executives in weak mayor systems still can exercise considerable influence, but they have to do this by using their powers of persuasion rather than the authority vested in their office. In many cities where mayors have limited powers, individuals with strong personalities are nevertheless able to exert huge influence. They do this by fostering cooperative relationships with their powerful city managers. Examples are Pete Wilson, the mayor of San Diego in the 1970s, and Henry Cisneros, the mayor of San Antonio in the 1980s.

In both strong and weak mayor systems, the council serves as the municipal-level legislature and can wield extensive policymaking power. No major policy or program can get far in a city without massaging from the city council. Councils average six members, but in many large jurisdictions twelve to fourteen members are elected. Los Angeles, for example, has fifteen. Chicago has a whopping fifty council members, and New York City has fifty-one. These individuals exert a major influence over a city's livability. They steer policies on such vital issues as zoning and urban renewal, as well as the provision of a wide range of public services—everything from law enforcement and fire protection to libraries and parks.

> Like legislatures at the state and the federal levels, however, councils are subject to conflict, gridlock, and disagreement with the executive branch. While some councils are exemplars of good democratic governance, others are notorious for their levels of self-interest and corruption.

Like legislatures at the state and the federal levels, however, councils are subject to conflict, gridlock, and disagreement with the executive branch. While some councils are exemplars of good democratic governance, others are notorious for their levels of self-interest and corruption. Illinois politics has long had a reputation for high levels of corruption—two recent Illinois governors are currently serving prison terms for various forms of malfeasance—and the Chicago city council has played its part in that reputation. The council consists of fifty aldermen, each elected from a neighborhood **ward**. Between the late 1970s and 2009, thirty Chicago aldermen were convicted of federal crimes ranging from extortion to income tax evasion.[13] While few other councils can rival that level of criminal activity, council members in many cities report that they are frustrated with the more typical legislative issues of gridlock and conflict, which are exacerbated by interest group pressure and media coverage.[14] In some cases all it takes is just one or two individuals to hold up their hands or raise objections in council chambers, and entire city operations can grind to a halt.

Council-Manager Systems

Rather than separating executive and legislative functions, the **council-manager system** is based on the principle of separating the political and administrative functions of government. In such a system, a council makes policy decisions but places the implementation of those decisions in the hands of a professional administrator, usually called a city manager, hired by the council. (See Figure 11-5.)

The origins of this system are in the Progressive reform movement that swept through government at all levels beginning at the end of the nineteenth century. As discussed elsewhere in the context of state-level party politics, a century ago political machines ran the typical large city in the United States. Places like Boston, Chicago, and New York were governed by charismatic politicians who took advantage of their ties to ethnic minorities, such as the Irish or the Italians. Patronage jobs were given out to their personal friends, whose chief qualification was that they were campaign supporters. Elections were fraught with partisanship, which produced high incumbent reelection rates. Many machine insiders got themselves elected as city commissioners and were given authority to run individual departments, including police, fire, and sanitation services. This resulted in politically powerful, but often corrupt and incompetent, municipal governments.

During the first half of the twentieth century, reform groups began pressuring city governments to become more professionalized and less politicized. The National Municipal League (now the National League of Cities), which focused on small to medium-size cities, was one such group. The U.S. Conference of Mayors, whose members head larger cities, and the ICMA were two others. In the belief that the top vote-getters in a given city may not be the best managers, the National Municipal League

---

Wards
Divisions of municipalities, usually representing electoral districts of the city council.

Council-Manager System
A form of municipal governance in which the day-to-day administration of government is carried out by a professional administrator.

FIGURE 11-3

Strong Mayor–Council Form of Government

Source: John P. Pelissero, "The Political Environment of Cities in the Twenty-First Century," in *Cities, Politics, and Policy: A Comparative Analysis,* ed. John P. Pelissero (Washington, DC: CQ Press, 2003), 15.

FIGURE 11-4

Weak Mayor–Council Form of Government

Source: John P. Pelissero, "The Political Environment of Cities in the Twenty-First Century," in *Cities, Politics, and Policy: A Comparative Analysis,* ed. John P. Pelissero (Washington, DC: CQ Press, 2003), 15.

glad-handing voters and trolling for campaign cash.

This reform movement by no means eliminated the urban political machines or the power wielded by strong executives. For example, Richard J. Daley, mayor of Chicago from 1955 to 1976, continued to run the city with unequaled influence, even though Chicago had a supposedly independent city council. He swayed his city council members, the national Democratic Party, and the Chicago-area delegation to the U.S. Congress. Even today there are a handful of mayors with political influence that extends far beyond municipal borders. For example, Rahm Emanuel, Daley's modern-day successor, continues the tradition of high-profile and powerful Chicago mayors. Prior to being elected mayor in 2011, Emanuel was President Barack Obama's chief of staff, and before that he was a member of the House of Representatives and chair of the Democratic Caucus in that chamber. While Emanuel does not have Daley's political machine, his political résumé and national-level political network, and the clout that these imply, make him a formidable mayor.

Worries about mayors or city councils wielding political power for their own interests rather than the public interest were at least part of the motivation behind the notion of a city manager. This is an individual who is appointed, not elected, and who, at least in theory, can counter the powers of commissioners or city council members with nonpartisan technical administrative expertise. In some cities, this manager is paired with a mayor. In such cases, the mayor acts as more of a ceremonial figurehead and seldom blocks anything that the manager or the council members want. Supported by a legislative body that is elected by popular vote and that meets about every two weeks to deal with policy issues, the manager is empowered to hire and fire all city employees, set pay scales, prepare an annual budget that is approved by elected officials and implemented by staff, and make policy recommendations.

drafted a model charter that laid out the powers of mayors, city councils, and administrators.

In 1913 Dayton, Ohio, became the first major U.S. city to create a position for a strong manager, largely in response to suburbanization (the establishment of residential communities on the outskirts of the city) and the rise of an educated middle class. The idea was that a government run by a professional city manager would be less prone to corruption and partisan favoritism than one led by the classic big-city mayor. Such managers are generally more interested in implementing organizational systems than they are in

FIGURE 11-5

Council-Manager Form of Government

City Voters

City Council ← Mayor is member — Mayor
← Mayor presides —

Mayor is member
Mayor presides

appoints

City Manager

City Departments

Police   Fire   Clerk   Public Works   Streets   Sanitation   Parks   Planning

Source: John P. Pelissero, "The Political Environment of Cities in the Twenty-First Century," in *Cities, Politics, and Policy: A Comparative Analysis*, ed. John P. Pelissero (Washington, DC: CQ Press, 2003), 16.

Today, the council-manager system of city government is seen in more than 3,000 cities, or 49 percent of communities with populations of more than 2,500. (See Table 11-4.) It is most popular in medium-size cities, primarily in the South and the West. The reason council-manager systems tend to be concentrated in cities of medium size is that smaller cities cannot afford to pay a full-time manager's salary and big cities tend to want a more partisan mayor. However, there are exceptions to this rule. Large cities that use a manager-council system include Dallas, Texas, and San Diego and San Jose, California.[15]

And the trend toward professionalization continues. A survey conducted by the ICMA showed that the proportion of city managers with advanced degrees rose from 27 percent in 1971 to 73 percent in 1995. Managers are also less likely to use volunteer committees to farm out work and more likely to use professional staffs. They supervise the systems that provide detailed financial controls and report transparency. For example, in Phoenix, Arizona, the city manager issues a monthly report detailing performance measures for every municipal department, ranging from fire service response times to the public housing occupancy rate to hits on the public library's Web site.[16]

Commission Systems

Similar to their county-level counterparts, municipal **commission systems** concentrate executive and legislative powers into a single elected body. These bodies make key policy decisions in the same way a legislature does. Yet each commissioner is also the head of an executive department. Commissioners run for office not as representatives in a legislative body but as the heads of particular city departments: commissioner for public safety, commissioner for public works, and so on. Most commission systems also have a mayor, but this is not an independent executive office. The position usually is held by a commissioner chosen to preside over commission meetings; it is not an independent executive office but more of ceremonial position.

As a form of municipal (as opposed to county) governance, the commission system originated in

TABLE 11-4

Most Common Forms of City Government in the United States, 2007*

Form	Number (percentage)
Council-manager	3,511 (49 percent)
Mayor-council	3,116 (43.5 percent)
Commission	143 (2.0 percent)
Town meeting	339 (4.7 percent)
Representative town meeting	62 (0.9 percent)

Source: International City/County Management Association, www.icma.org/upload/library/2007-04/{F55E2557-92E4-4791-9DFC-FB9D282E3DF1}.doc.

*Represents only those cities with populations of 2,500 or greater.

City Commission System
A form of municipal governance in which executive, legislative, and administrative powers are vested in elected city commissioners.

Galveston, Texas, in the early 1900s. Galveston had suffered a devastating hurricane that killed thousands and left the city in ruins. The existing city government proved ineffective in dealing with the aftermath of this disaster. In response, the Texas legislature approved a completely new form of municipal government—the commission system—to try to deal with the huge task of rebuilding the city. It proved successful; Galveston was rebuilt and put back on the civic track.

This success led other municipalities to follow Galveston's lead and adopt the commission form of governance. The commission system's success, however, has been limited, and only a relative handful of cities currently operate under it. Its main drawbacks are two. First, the merging of elected and administrative positions leads to commissioners' becoming the entrenched advocates of their departments. Second, winning an election and administering a large bureaucracy are very different skills. Good politicians, in other words, do not always make good department heads.

Only about 2 percent of municipalities with populations greater than 2,500 use the commission form of government.[17] The drawbacks of commission governments are much the same as the drawbacks of commission systems at the county level—executive authority is so diffuse it tends to produce a government with no real direction. Because commissioners serve as the heads of their own departments, with no real central authority above their positions, commission systems at the municipal level function as legislatures consisting of elected executives. This can make coordinating departments difficult and providing a strong sense of direction for the government overall even harder.

Town Meetings

The **town meeting form of government** is largely unique to the United States and is mostly found in towns in New England states (in New England, towns are basically municipalities, although they may also

Town Meeting Form of Government
A form of governance in which legislative powers are held by the local citizens.

have some of the functions traditionally associated with county government in other states). Although not a particularly widespread form of local governance, it is probably the oldest, and it is certainly the most democratic. Its origins are rooted in the religious communities that made up early colonial settlements in New England. A high premium was put on consensus in these communities, and the town meeting evolved as a means to reach such widespread agreement. Town meetings allowed citizens to have a direct role in deciding which laws they would pass and who would be responsible for implementing and enforcing these laws. In many cases, the politics were worked out before the actual meetings took place, with neighbors talking to neighbors across their fences and in taverns. The grassroots agreements hashed out in these informal discussions then were expressed as community consensus in the town meeting.[18]

What all this boils down to is that the legislative functions are concentrated in the citizens themselves. A town meeting is convened through a warrant, or an announcement of the date, time, and place of the meeting and the items to be discussed. It is open to all community citizens, and all have an equal vote in matters of town policy. Such legislative power often is exercised directly; for example, budgets are approved by town meetings. Some authority, however, may be delegated to a representative board, whose members are called selectmen. The board of selectmen exercises whatever authority is granted to it and is responsible for seeing that policies enacted in the town meeting are carried out.

Towns also have incorporated some elements of the council-manager system by voting to hire professional managers to handle the administrative side of government. The manager system seems to work well with this type of government; for example, roughly 30 percent of the towns in Maine—most of them small communities with fewer than 2,500 residents—have managers but hold town meetings as well.[19]

The town meeting is probably the most idealized form of government that has ever existed in the United States. Thomas Jefferson, for example, saw this grassroots democratic approach to

The town meeting form of government is largely unique to the United States, and even in the United States is mostly confined to the Northeast. In this form of local governance, legislative powers are vested in citizens, who exercise those powers during town meetings of local residents. Here, residents in Strafford, Vermont, are meeting to discuss local issues and elect town clerks.

self-governance as "the wisest invention ever devised by man."[20] Alexis de Tocqueville, the nineteenth-century French aristocrat who wrote one of the most celebrated analyses of the American political system, referred to towns as the "fertile germ" of democracy.[21] For even modestly large communities, however, this approach simply isn't practical. A gathering of citizens that runs into the thousands would be too unwieldy, and the likelihood of getting broad agreement from such a large group on any number of policy issues is pretty low. This goes a long way toward explaining why this approach is largely confined to smaller communities in New England.

Special Districts

Special districts, for the most part, are fundamentally different from the other forms of local government

Special District
A local governmental unit created for a single purpose, such as water distribution.

already discussed. Counties and municipalities are general-purpose governments that provide a broad range of public services within their given jurisdictions. Special districts, on the other hand, are mostly single-purpose governments. They are created to provide specific services that are not being provided by a general-purpose government.

With few exceptions, special districts exist outside the consciousness of the average citizen. More than 50,000 special districts have been created across the country—and often across borders of other units of government—to administer single programs or services. Still, most people know very little about these governments. The single biggest exception to this general rule of special district anonymity is the school district; there are more than 12,000 independent school districts in the United States. Public schools are often one of the best-known and most widely used local public institutions. Few might know a lot about a school district's politics, but a lot of people will know teachers, students, and administrators, how the school sports teams are doing, and which schools have good or poor reputations for academic performance. That level of knowledge and intimacy drops off quickly for other types of special districts. Among the most numerous forms of special districts are sewer and water system districts, which account for about one-third of special districts nationwide. Few people know much at all about these sorts of districts—many may be completely unaware of their existence.

Other types of special districts administer fire and housing services, public transportation, soil conservation, mosquito control, and even libraries. Commuters may not know it, but hundreds of thousands of them use some pretty well-known special districts every day. The Port Authority of New York and New Jersey, Boston's Massachusetts Bay Transportation Authority, and the Washington Metropolitan Area Transportation Authority of the District of Columbia collectively cover hundreds of square miles and cross dozens of government borders.

Why use special districts to provide single programs or services? Why not just have the county or municipality add those services to its governing portfolio? Well, in certain situations, single-purpose governments can seem attractive solutions to political and practical problems. For example, special districts sometimes are implemented as a way of heading off threats of political annexation of one local government by another. They also are used as a tool for community and business improvement. Freed of local tax authority, administrators of special districts often can get infrastructure items built and services provided without dipping into any one locality's funds. For example, farmers in special water districts, particularly in the West, are eligible for discounted federal loans to help them with irrigation. In addition, special districts can use private-sector business techniques in management, such as paying market rates instead of government rates to contractors.

Oklahoma was one of five territories to gain statehood in the twentieth century. At one point, American Indians initiated efforts to create a state from land in the Indian and Oklahoma territories. Today, the state is home to the most members of recognized tribes in the country, and, like other native groups in the United States, many of these have their own government and judicial systems.

Working within Limits: The Powers and Constraints of Local Government

Local governments, regardless of their particular form, differ from state and federal governments in a fundamentally important way—they are not sovereign. This means that local governments draw their power not from the citizens they serve but from the government immediately above them—the state government (this is why states considered in isolation are referred to as unitary governments in the introduction to this chapter).

This is not to say that local governments are powerless. Far from it. Local governments are charged with the primary responsibility for delivering a broad range of public services (such as education, law enforcement, roads, and utilities), and they have broad authority to levy taxes and pass regulations and ordinances (an ordinance is a law passed by a nonsovereign government). Local governments can also exercise the power of eminent domain. Yet, despite all their responsibilities and powers (not to mention their sheer numbers), not all forms of local governments are, at least technically, equal partners in government. They are subordinate to the state governments from which they are granted their power.

Why is this the case? The short answer is the Tenth Amendment to the U.S. Constitution. Local governments are not mentioned anywhere in the U.S. Constitution, which divides power between the federal and state governments. Despite the long-standing cultural practice of having strong local governments, legally these governments fall under the purview of the Tenth Amendment's guarantee of state sovereignty. This means the power to determine the scope of authority of local governments is among the powers "reserved to the States respectively, or to the people." In other words, states get to say what localities can and cannot do. They set the limits and define the terms.

Dillon's Rule

The legal doctrine that defines the division of power between state and local governments is known as **Dillon's Rule**, named for Iowa Supreme Court justice John F. Dillon. In addition to having a fine legal mind, Dillon was a highly respected and well-read scholar of local government. An argument he formulated in 1868 has served ever since as the basis for understanding and justifying the power—or, more accurately, the lack of power—of local government. Dillon's Rule is built on the legal principle of *ultra vires,* which means "outside one's powers." In a nutshell, it states that local governments are limited to the powers expressly granted to them by their state and to those powers indispensable to the stated objectives and purposes of each local government.

> Dillon's Rule is built on the legal principle of *ultra vires,* which means "outside one's powers." In a nutshell, it states that local governments are limited to the powers expressly granted to them by their state and to those powers indispensable to the stated objectives and purposes of each local government.

What Dillon essentially did was build a legal argument that the Tenth Amendment secures power for the states but not for local governments. As Dillon himself put it in his famous 1868 ruling in *City of Clinton v. Cedar Rapids and Missouri Railroad,* local governments are "mere tenants at the will of their respective state legislatures." The rule has structured legal thinking on the power of local governments ever since, although it has always had its critics and opponents. It was challenged as early as the 1870s, when Missouri legislators rewrote the state constitution specifically to allow municipalities a degree of independence from the constraints of state government.[22]

For the most part, however, Dillon's Rule holds. In a nutshell, state power trumps local government power, which means that state legislatures invariably win power struggles with local governments. In Virginia, for example, anti-tax lawmakers continually prevent localities from restructuring their tax systems to raise revenue. It should come as no surprise that ambitious state legislators hoard power over their county and city counterparts. States have the authority to limit even traditionally exercised local government powers, such as eminent domain (see the box "Policy in Practice: Eminent Domain and Local Power").

Yet, although Dillon's Rule says state governments can grant powers to local governments and retract those powers as they see fit, Dillon himself felt that it would be a bad idea for state governments to take full advantage of this legal authority. The bottom line is that the division of labor between local and state governments, broadly speaking, works. It makes sense, Dillon argued, for states to respect local government autonomy because of cultural tradition and sheer practicality. Accordingly, the independence and powers that state governments grant to localities vary considerably. Some state governments are more willing than others to let local governments make their own decisions. Many of these differences can be explained by state culture and degree of citizen participation. Idaho and West Virginia reserve the most local powers to the state; Oregon and Maine give localities the most freedom.[23]

The powers granted to substate political jurisdictions, in other words, reflect the cultural traditions, politics, and practicalities of governance unique to each state. This variation is a difference that can make a difference. For example, it can make a difference in taxes. What local governments can or cannot tax, and by how much, is structured by state law. For example, Virginia allows cities with populations greater than five

Dillon's Rule
The legal principle that says local governments can exercise only the powers granted to them by state government.

Policy in Practice

Eminent Domain and Local Power

Local governments are not sovereign, but this does not mean they are powerless. Many local governments, for example, have the power of eminent domain, or the right to take private property without the owner's consent.

The Fifth Amendment to the U.S. Constitution compels any government exercising such powers to offer the owner just compensation for the property taken. That, however, often does little to mollify people who have their lives or communities uprooted to make way for a new road or a new development.

In 2005 the U.S. Supreme Court significantly expanded the scope of local government powers of eminent domain. In *Kelo v. New London* (2005), the Court ruled that homeowners could be forced to sell not just to a city but to private developers who would add to the city's tax base. The Court reasoned that local governments have a central role in planning and that economic development cannot be halted simply because some property owner objects. In short, a city could force a property owner to sell to a developer even when the property owner wanted to do no such thing.

This significant boost to the power and reach of local governments was quickly limited, however. Indeed, the years since the *Kelo* ruling have provided an instructive lesson in Dillon's Rule. Prior to *Kelo* only seven states had laws specifically limiting local government powers of eminent domain. As of 2012, forty-four states had passed such laws, with almost all of this legislation being driven by reaction to the Supreme Court decision. The bottom line is that eminent domain is a power exercised by local governments, which, according to Dillon's Rule, means it is also a power that can be regulated by the states. And regulate it they have. The expanded powers the Supreme Court gave local governments in *Kelo* have been limited or taken back entirely by state governments. Even though the ruling specifically expanded local government powers, *Kelo* actually ended up underlining the limits of local government authority. Unlike state governments, local governments are not fully sovereign, and when they are given power—even if that power is given by the Supreme Court—the states can take it back.

Source: Adapted from Alan Greenblatt, "Land Law," *Governing,* August 2005.

---

thousand to operate independent of the counties of which they are a part. It also gives these communities the right to impose sales taxes on meals, lodging, and cigarettes. On the other hand, counties in Virginia rely heavily on a single revenue source—property taxes—to pay their bills.[24] This can pose a serious dilemma for county leaders. When the housing market is booming, many homeowners watch their property assessments, and hence their annual taxes, rise relentlessly. In many cases, the property taxes rise faster than their incomes. These homeowners, subsequently, take their annoyance at the tax increases out on county leaders come election time.

And taxes are not the only issue. State governments can, and sometimes do, place regulatory limits on local government in areas ranging from taxes to titles, from personnel to pensions. For example, the city of Buffalo, New York, is prevented from controlling the salaries and pensions of its uniformed workers because of New York state labor laws. The state limits the pool of candidates the city can consider when hiring managers. And state requirements for thorough hearings in cases of alleged disciplinary infractions by city employees make it tough for a city official to speedily fire an unsuitable staffer.

The lack of local government sovereignty embodied in Dillon's Rule has added to the financial struggles of many substate governments. In addition to limiting the revenues of local governments by limiting their taxing authority, states can require these governments to provide programs or services. Such unfunded mandates can put a severe squeeze on city and county governments. For example, in 2011 the New York State Association of Counties estimated that its members had spent more than $11 billion to implement or manage policies or programs imposed on them by the state.[25] In effect, what this means is the state is creating programs and forcing counties to deliver and pay for them. As these counties are heavily reliant on property taxes as a primary revenue source, they are put in the tough position of increasing very unpopular levies to pay for programs over which they have relatively little control.

Financial challenges created by economic recession, unfunded mandates, poor decisions, and collapsing property values have in recent years provided blunt examples of the difference in sovereignty between state and local governments. In some cases states have pushed aside financially struggling local government authorities and taken over their governance responsibilities. More than half of the states have laws allowing them to exercise some degree of direct supervision over financially stressed localities. Harrisburg, Pennsylvania; Central Falls, Rhode Island; and Nassau County, New York—all went bankrupt in the past few years and ended up with state-appointed rather than locally elected leaders calling the shots on a range of important decisions. In Michigan a number of struggling cities have been effectively taken over by the state, with state-appointed administrators assuming virtually all the powers typically vested in local officials (see the box "States under Stress: "Emergency Financial Managers in Michigan").

Home Rule

Dillon's Rule establishes a clear legal hierarchy between state and local governments. Unlike federal and state governments, which are coequal partners, local governments are unquestionably subordinate to state governments. Yet states, if they so choose, can grant considerable autonomy to local governments. Many states make such grants of autonomy formal by giving local governments home rule, or the freedom to make local decisions without interference from state government. Home rule typically is enshrined in a charter, which spells out the powers and purposes of the local government. In effect, a charter is the municipal equivalent of a constitution.

The movement for such charters started in the nineteenth century and peaked in the early 1970s. Charters can be adopted only after voters approve a council-approved or citizen-written petition. Thirty-six of the forty-eight states that use a county form of government allow charters or some form of home rule, according to the National Association of Counties. This can free these communities from both state and county obligations. Even under home rule, however, the state may place some strict limits on local governmental autonomy. And even those who might be thought of as natural advocates of home rule support keeping a measure of state control. For instance, city or county employees may prefer state protections to giving the local mayor or city manager too much authority. Antitax groups often fear that independent cities free of state regulation will raise new taxes.

Home rule can be granted in two basic forms. Legislatures may approve home rule in general act charters, which apply to all cities, or in special act charters, each of which affects only one community.

Home Rule
The right of a locality to self-government, usually granted through a charter.

Charter
A document that outlines the powers, organization, and responsibilities of a local government.

General Act Charter
A charter that grants powers, such as home rule, to all municipal governments within a state.

Special Act Charter
A charter that grants powers, such as home rule, to a single municipal government.

States under Stress

Emergency Financial Managers in Michigan

A visitor to Pontiac, Michigan, in 2012 might have felt a bit like Alice when she got her first glance at Wonderland. Everything seemed upside down. The city council would meet for hours, although it had nothing on its agenda. There was a mayor, but he had no power. The workers in city hall were not employed by the city. The guy in charge was a charming seventy-four-year-old named Lou Schimmel. He had almost unilateral power to run the city government, even though no one had voted for him.

Schimmel was an emergency manager, an official appointed by the state government to take over the fiscally stressed city and try to get its books balanced. He hired and fired employees, forced major changes to labor contracts, set the budget, sold city property, and created ordinances. So great was his power that the legislation authorizing his takeover was referred to by critics as "the dictator law."

The so-called dictator law is Public Act 4, championed by Republican governor Rick Snyder and passed by the Michigan legislature in 2011. Basically what this legislation does is allow the state to appoint people to swoop into a financially struggling local government, make an independent assessment of the fiscal mess, and then take whatever measures they deem necessary to fix it. The argument for the law is not simply that the state has sovereign power over local authorities, à la Dillon's Rule. Rather, it is that if a local government goes bust, state taxpayers can be stuck with paying the bill. As the state is potentially on the hook for cleaning up a local government's financial mess, the reasoning goes that when a locality heads up the financial creek without a paddle, the state gets to take over as captain.

The upshot of the law is that nowhere in the United States do local officials have less control—and state appointees more—than in financially distressed communities in Michigan. While some support the tough approach, others are appalled that it not only runs roughshod over traditions of local governance but also replaces democratically elected leaders with appointees who are beholden to no local constituency. This last point is particularly controversial in a place like Pontiac—Schimmel is white, and the majority of the city's residents are black. While supporters of the law argue it was born solely of financial necessity, the fact that white appointees took over a mostly black city created a perception of racial bias and added a divisive element to the process.

The big question, of course, is whether an emergency fiscal manager such as Schimmel can make a difference. Ideally, a manager will turn a struggling city's financial situation around and then leave. Schimmel has said that he'd like to work himself out of his job as quickly as possible. And, as of fiscal year 2013, Pontiac's finances did seem to be heading toward the black. Still, fixing Pontiac is not something that can be done quickly. The underlying factors that created the financial mess in the first place are hard to turn around—high levels of unemployment tied to a shrinking manufacturing sector and property vacancy rates as high as 20 percent. Schimmel candidly says that his primary mission is not economic development, but it's hard to see how the city can be put on a long-term path to financial viability without more in the way of business investment and urban renewal.

What everyone seems to agree on is that Pontiac has serious problems. Whether an emergency manager can provide some long-term solutions remains to be seen.

Source: Adapted from Ryan Holeywell, "Emergency Financial Managers: Michigan's Unwelcome Savior," *Governing,* May 2012.

Either type can be initiated by state legislators, local councils, or citizens' groups. In cases of citizen initiatives, advocates gather the requisite number of signatures on petitions, which are then converted into legislation or language for a ballot referendum that is put before voters.

For example, in 2000, a ballot question for the city of Signal Hill, California, asked voters whether the city should become a locally governed charter city, as opposed to a general-law city that would be governed by all statewide laws. The question explained that the charter would serve as the city's constitution, giving it full control over its municipal affairs.

The ballot text specified that municipal affairs included the "regulation of municipal utilities; procedures for bidding and contracting; regulation of parks, libraries, and other facilities; salaries of officers and employees; parking regulations; franchise and other fees; taxation; and zoning and election procedures." It also noted that the charter could exempt the city from some state sales taxes.

The city would remain subject to state law on "matters of statewide importance," however. This basically meant environmental regulations, General Plan requirements, open-meeting laws, public records, and redevelopment. Despite the complexity of the issue and the uncertainty about the fiscal impact of home rule, the charter city ballot question passed with 86 percent of the vote.[26] The lopsided vote highlights that, at least in principle, American voters are supportive of local government autonomy even though with such autonomy come new responsibilities.

Although voters generally support the notion of local government autonomy and generally oppose state or federal governments' making decisions on behalf of local communities, there are benefits to state or federal oversight. What is lost in local control can be offset by the deeper pockets of the larger, sovereign governments. Much of what local leaders wish to accomplish requires infusions of funds from Washington and state capitals. Those intergovernmental sources of revenue are especially critical during hard economic times, when the traditional local government sources of funding, such as property and sales taxes, tend to take a hit. With oversight, at least local governments also get some cold, hard cash. The superior capacity of state governments and the federal government to raise revenues is another limit on the powers of localities.

The important point here is that there are trade-offs that go along with greater local government autonomy. County officials, for example, are responsible for the building and maintenance of extensive road systems, as well as for enforcing traffic and safety laws on those roads. That's an expensive proposition, and counties generally welcome state and federal money to support these critical public services. Yet the Golden Rule—he who has the gold makes the rules—means those funds inevitably come with strings. The obligations that come with the money, in the form of state or federal mandates, are not nearly as popular as the cash. This sets up a love-hate relationship between local authorities and the state and federal governments above them. In addition, state and federal governments cause frustration by restricting the decision-making freedom of local authorities. Restrictions and conditions, however, are often the price of the intergovernmental grants that underwrite important local government functions.

Participation in Local Government

Local governments are distinguished from state and federal governments not only by their power (or lack thereof) but also by their politics. Comparatively speaking, state and federal politics are dominated by political parties, which contest elections, mobilize voters, and organize government. Things are different down at the local level, where more than two-thirds of governments are nonpartisan. Since the decline of the big-city political machines of the early twentieth century, candidates for county boards and city councils run on their personal competence for the most part rather than on ideology or past affiliation. Only 17 percent of city councils hold partisan elections, according to the ICMA. Yet in some cities, party labels that have been abolished officially continue to play a role unofficially. This has occurred in Chicago, where city government has been officially nonpartisan since the 1930s, but Democrats continue to dominate the heavily African American city.

Council members usually run in **ward, or district, elections**. The advantage of organizing such elections on the basis of defined geographical areas is that they assure each neighborhood of having a local on the city council who knows the streets and residents by name. This is especially important for minorities, who may be grouped together by housing patterns. Very large cities, however, have to balance the desire to have districts small enough so that council members really know the neighborhood concerns with the practical matter of having a municipal legislature that has a reasonable number of members. In some places, the populations of council districts are themselves the equivalent of midsize cities. Los Angeles, for examples, is split into fifteen city council districts. Given the city's population of roughly 3.8 million, that means each district has something like a quarter million constituents.

Other jurisdictions permit candidates to run in **at-large elections**. This means that they can hail from any part of the jurisdiction. The advantage of having candidates run at-large, and the reason most cities opt for it, is that it makes room for the largest possible pool of highly qualified and talented people who, presumably, look at the interests of the city as a whole rather than just the parochial interests of their own wards or neighborhoods. Some city charters require a combination of ward representatives and at-large members. But the use of at-large elections can get controversial. In 1991 in Dallas, court-ordered redistricting required a switch from an at-large system to one in which fourteen city council members were chosen by

districts. The result was that more Hispanics and African Americans won seats.

There is perhaps no better example of the unique nature of local politics than the town meetings that define local governance in New England. Usually held twice a year when the elected council or clerk issues a warrant, or agenda, these gatherings epitomize direct democracy in action. Citizens can do everything from passing a budget to opposing a developer's plan for a new golf course. There simply is no equivalent to this comprehensive citizen legislature at the state or federal level, nor, as a practical matter, could there be.

One of the paradoxes of local government is that, although it is the level of government that citizens support the most, it is also the level of government in which they participate the least. The voter turnout in local elections is often half the national turnout average of 55 percent in a presidential election. This reflects a general indifference among many citizens toward the prosaic affairs of local government. Neighborhood volunteer and community development organizations, although generally run by articulate and dedicated activists, often involve as little as 3–12 percent of the local population.[27]

Yet the absence of popular fervor over local issues does not mean that local offices are not important. Indeed, politics at this level can have implications for state and even national politics. For example, local government offices often serve as proving grounds for up-and-coming politicians who go on to higher office at the state or national level. New immigrants, particularly Asians and Latinos, increasingly are working their way into public office on this level. By the end of the twentieth century, one-third of all cities with more than 200,000 residents had elected either a Hispanic or an African American mayor.[28] In 2007, there were more than 5,000 elected Hispanic or Latino officials, with the majority holding local offices and with many of those in state and federal

Ward, or District, Election
An election in which voters in a municipal ward vote for a candidate to represent them on a council or commission.

At-Large Election
An election in which city or county voters vote for council or commission members from any part of the jurisdiction.

offices coming from local government backgrounds. Representative Nydia Velázquez, D-N.Y., for example, was the first Puerto Rican American woman elected to Congress and served as the chair of the influential Congressional Hispanic Caucus. She began her career as a member of the New York city council.

The increase in black local officials during the final third of the twentieth century was dramatic. According to the Washington-based Joint Center for Political and Economic Studies, from 1970 to 2001 the number of black mayors rose from 48 to 454, the number of black city council members rose from 552 to 3,538, and the number of black county commissioners rose from 64 to 820.

Women also have made great gains in local government, although they remain far from matching their proportion as half the total population. According to the Center for

American Women and Politics in Washington, D.C., in January 2012, 1,248 mayors of cities with populations of more than 30,000 were women. These included the mayors of Baltimore, Maryland; Fresno, California; and Las Vegas, Nevada. Added to their number in December 2009 was Annise Parker, who won a runoff race to become mayor of Houston, Texas, the fourth-largest city in the United States.

Where partisan affiliations are allowed at the local level, there have been some historically important divisions among voters. For example, Democratic candidates have tended to draw votes from minority groups, Catholics, and the liberal intelligentsia. Republicans have tended to draw votes from WASPs (white Anglo-Saxon Protestants), big business, and law-and-order enthusiasts. This is changing, however. In New York City in 2001, billionaire Michael Bloomberg, who had switched from

Although their ranks in high office are far below the roughly 50 percent of the population they represent, women hold some of the most important leadership positions in local government. Here, U.S. district judge Vanessa Gilmore swears in Annise Parker (center) as mayor of Houston, the nation's fourth-largest city. In addition to being only the second female mayor of Houston, Parker is the first openly gay mayor of a city with more than 1 million residents. Accompanying Parker is her partner Kathy Hubbard (right).

the Democratic Party to the Republican Party, spent millions of dollars of his own money to win an upset victory over Democratic public advocate Mark Green. One reason for Bloomberg's success was that he was able to attract Hispanic voters.[29]

The payoff for winning local office is more likely to come in the form of visibility and personal satisfaction than in cold, hard cash. Mayors, many of whom work part-time, earn an average of less than $10,000 per year. New York mayor Michael Bloomberg shelled out more than $100 million to win a third term in 2009, but he declines to take a salary; he works for a token $1 per year. Typically, mayors of big cities get considerably more than that. Los Angeles mayor Antonio Villaraigosa's annual salary was more than a quarter million dollars, although, like many city employees, he was actually paid less than his official wage in his last few years in office (his second term ended in June 2013). This was because of his administration's policy of mandating furloughs, or unpaid leaves of absence, for city workers as a budget-balancing measure. Like other city employees, the mayor did not get paid on furlough days. Council members generally earn less than mayors. In most small and medium-size cities, being a member of the city council is more of a public service than a part-time job. Even in large mayor-council cities—where being a member of the city council is a full-time job—compensation can be less than $40,000 per year.[30]

On the other hand, the job of professional city or county manager tends to be a fairly well-compensated, white-collar position. According to payscale.com (a Web site devoted to compensation analysis), city managers across a number of states averaged about $100,000 per year in 2012 (check out the compensation numbers yourself at www.payscale.com/research/US/Job=City_Manager/Salary/by_State). The weekly average workload for council members in small, medium, and large cities is twenty, twenty-five, and forty-two hours, respectively. The typical proportion of their time that council members spend doing services for constituents has risen to 35 percent. In larger cities with mayor-council systems, more

than 90 percent of elected officials have staffs at their disposal, compared to only 50 percent in smaller cities, according to the National League of Cities.[31]

> Many citizens oppose large salaries for their local officials, particularly at the school board level, because they feel the nominal fees the officials receive are not an hourly wage but, rather, a stipend that honors public spiritedness.

Given the low pay and relatively high workloads, it is not surprising that 66 percent of city council members surveyed by the National League of Cities said they wanted a raise. Many citizens oppose large salaries for their local officials, particularly at the school board level, because they feel the nominal fees the officials receive are not an hourly wage but, rather, a stipend that honors public spiritedness.

The Road Ahead

The forms and functions of local governments have evolved through myriad permutations, nearly all of them designed to produce leaders and practices that maximize both efficiency and responsiveness to voters. Yet few local governments can go it alone. In the first five years of the twenty-first century, local governments suffered considerably as recession squeezed their budgets. By 2006, most local governments had significantly improved their fiscal outlooks, helped by a hot real estate market that improved property tax revenues. The real estate market, however, began to cool in 2006, signaling that market forces were about to put downward pressure on the growth of property tax revenues. That pressure became an overwhelming force in 2008 and 2009 as the national housing bubble burst, the country slid into the deepest economic recession since the Great Depression, and local governments faced a fiscal crisis.

In response to plunging sales and property taxes, local governments were forced to take some drastic actions. A 2010 survey by the Center for State & Local Government Excellence reported that nearly 70 percent of state and local governments had enacted hiring freezes, more than 40 percent had laid off workers, and roughly one-third had instituted furloughs and reformed employee benefits packages to reduce costs.[32] A similar survey by the ICMA highlighted the sweeping changes that the Great Recession brought specifically to local government. More than 80 percent of those responding to the ICMA survey said the financial crisis had affected their local governments' operations and that in response city and county managers were making hard choices about deferring capital projects and maintenance, increasing fees, and cutting some services altogether. Tellingly, the overwhelming majority of respondents (67 percent) reported that the changes forced by the Great Recession were not temporary; local government management professionals saw the wrenching contractions as a new "business norm" for the foreseeable future. As Jason

Gage, city manager of Salina, Kansas, put it: "Some of the changes we've implemented will continue once the recession ends. We will continue to emphasize performance, explore ways to restrict staffing, and this has been a wake up call to pay close attention to our daily expenditures."[33]

ICMA director Robert O'Neill Jr. says that there is a silver lining to the Great Recession's brutal impact on local governments: the possibility of creative destruction. O'Neill argues that the fiscal crisis has forced local governments to become more efficient, more adaptable, and more focused on seeking out new and creative ways to address long-standing problems. Although local governments may be smaller in the postrecession era, they are likely to be tougher and better equipped to address bigger problems with fewer people, less cash, and more creativity. Experiencing a fiscal crisis of historic proportions is forcing localities to question everything about their way of doing business, and, O'Neill argues, that's not necessarily a bad thing for the long term.[34]

Despite the rough ride over the past few years, the long-term durability of governments at the town, city, county, and special district levels continues to be seen in the variety of ways each responds to its own unique circumstances, not just economic trends but the full array of particular traits and challenges unique to every locality. There is no shortage of candidates willing to pay the price in time, sweat, and sacrificed income that it takes to make a go of it in the modern world of local elected offices. These small-scale leaders continue to debate and organize to provide valued services using a process consistent with a loftier vision of democracy. Tocqueville noted nearly two hundred years ago that democracy in America is practiced unusually effectively at the local level, where "inhabitants with the same interests" manage to provide "all the elements of a good administration."[35] At least in this way, recession or not, local government hasn't changed much at all.

Conclusion

Alexis de Tocqueville viewed local governments in the United States as sort of mini-republics. He saw them as civic entities in which citizens were closest to government and in which government reflected accurately what citizens desired. In many ways, that perspective is still valid. Local governments wield actual power, and they are responsible for important programs and services. They come in a bewildering variety of types, many of which reflect state or regional history, culture, and preferences. Taken as a whole, all these differences can seem confusing. Yet in any single place—your hometown or local county—the government and what it does or does not do probably seem perfectly reasonable and natural.

Local government certainly remains the most common form of government in the United States, and it is still the form of government the average citizen is most likely to come into contact with on a day-to-day basis. Counties, municipalities, and special districts build and maintain roads, police those roads, run schools, manage libraries, and provide other programs and services too numerous to list. And they do all of this while employing very different approaches to government. Some are run by powerful executives, others are run by more egalitarian councils or commissions, and still others are mostly run by professional managers.

Yet local government is far from ideal. These mini-republics are constrained by Dillon's Rule.

They tend to have relatively low voter turnout for elections. The idiosyncrasies of local government structure can mean that someone with no real administrative experience may be elected to run a complicated bureaucracy with a multimillion-dollar budget.

Local governments today face significant challenges, most notably an uncertain fiscal future. Part of the fallout of the Great Recession seems to be a "new normal" characterized by relatively stagnant property and sales tax revenues. Yet while revenue is stubbornly slow to grow, demand for local government services remains high. The conflicting pressures of restrained revenues and high demand for services are forcing local governments to take a hard look at doing things differently or not doing them at all. That makes tough choices unavoidable. Just because the politics is local does not mean it is less difficult.

The Latest Research

Despite their numbers and importance to the day-to-day lives of citizens, local governments are surprisingly understudied by political scientists. Certainly, systematic comparative studies on local governance are few and far between in the discipline's major journals. Part of the reason for this may be the astonishing variety of local governments and their sometimes bewildering numbers of responsibilities. It is hard to say something generalizable about local governments because, unlike state governments, they are not necessarily comparable units. A county, a school district, and a municipality not only have different responsibilities, but they may also be organized and run very differently. Yet one thing common to all governments is the need for accountability. Local governments exist to provide certain goods and services, and some do a better job of it than others. Given the myriad forms of governance and responsibilities, who holds these governments accountable for doing a decent job, and how? All of the studies

described below examine this general question. Given the numbers and variety, it is not surprising to find that accountability in local government comes in many different forms.

• •

• **Arnold, R. Douglas, and Nicholas Carnes.** 2012. "Holding Mayors Accountable: New York's Executives from Koch to Bloomberg." *American Journal of Political Science* 56: 949–963.

This study seeks to answer a simple question: How do citizens evaluate the performance of municipal executives? This question is important—one of the things we have learned from our study of state executives is that popular support is a key component of informal power, which is arguably the most important tool governors have for making policy and influencing the public agenda. Although such questions seem basic and have been the subject of intense study at the level of state executives, we have no comparable basis of knowledge at the local level. We are not even sure if citizens hold mayors accountable for the quality of municipal services or city life in general. Arnold and Carnes seek to fill that gap by doing the first-ever study to track mayoral approval across time, analyzing how approval ratings change in response to local conditions and whether that level of public opinion has electoral implications. They do this by examining responses on 150 public opinion surveys, taken over a twenty-five-year period, that included questions on mayoral approval in New York City. They find that New Yorkers hold the mayor accountable for levels of crime and economic conditions—when crime rates go up and economic conditions worsen, mayoral approval dips. Those approval ratings translate into votes. What this study suggests is that citizens treat local executives the same way they treat state executives. Even if the relevant conditions are clearly beyond a mayor's control—a weakening national economy, for example—citizens hold the mayor accountable and punish him or her at the polls if conditions do not improve.

- **Tekniepe, Robert, and Christopher Stream.** 2012. "You're Fired! County Manager Turnover in Large American Counties." *American Review of Public Administration* 42: 715–729.

While the Arnold and Carnes study noted above examines how citizens hold elected executives accountable, Tekniepe and Stream examine how elected officials hold hired bureaucrats accountable. As discussed in this chapter, county-manager systems are common forms of government at the county level. County managers are hired to run the day-to-day operations of county government, which makes them responsible for delivering the same sorts of public services that elected executives (such as mayors) are held accountable for. As the Arnold and Carnes study shows, if crime rates go up or local economic conditions take a turn for the worse, voters are more likely to vote to fire the executive in the next election. But what about county managers, technocrats who take on many of the day-to-day responsibilities of

executive office but are hired by elected officials, not by the voters—do county managers get pushed out for the same sorts of reasons? This study suggests the answer is no. Unlike mayors, county managers do not generally lose their positions because of local economic conditions. County manager turnover seems to have less to do with local quality-of-life considerations and much more to do with local political conditions. Tekniepe and Stream found that the best predictor of involuntary departure by a county manager was turnover in the county board or a shift in county board leadership. They conclude that political volatility seems to be the biggest threat to county manager job security.

- **Martell, Christine, and Robert Kravchuck.** 2012. "The Liquidity Crisis: The 2007–2009 Market Impacts on Municipal Securities." *Public Administration Review* 72: 668–677.

Markets, like elections and county boards, are also instruments of accountability. Investors will reward or punish bond issuers depending on their financial management history, their fiscal condition, and how they intend to use the funds raised by bonds. This study makes an interesting comparison study to the two just described because it looks at how local governments were punished by the securities market following the Great Recession. This happened even though local governments didn't necessarily do anything wrong. The bursting of a housing market bubble froze credit markets, making it difficult for local governments to raise cash from those markets and making it harder for them to finance public projects such as building sewers or roads. This problem was exacerbated by a big drop in property values. As we've learned, local governments depend heavily on property taxes as a primary source of revenue. As that revenue source contracted, municipal bonds became riskier investments and made it even harder for local governments to get projects financed. The upshot is that financial managers at the local level have had to reexamine how they do business. As access to credit gets harder, retaining the confidence of investors through prudent fiscal management becomes more important.

college.cqpress.com/
sites/govstateandlocal

Chapter Review

Key Concepts

- at-large election (p. 370)
- charter (p. 367)
- cities (p. 357)
- city commission system (p. 361)
- city council (p. 358)
- city manager (p. 358)
- commission-administrator system (p. 355)
- council-executive system (p. 355)
- council-manager system (p. 359)
- counties (p. 349)
- county commission system (p. 355)
- Dillon's Rule (p. 365)
- general act charter (p. 367)
- home rule (p. 367)
- mayor (p. 357)
- mayor-council system (p. 358)
- municipalities (p. 349)
- special act charter (p. 367)
- special districts (p. 363)
- strong mayor system (p. 358)
- town meeting form of government (p. 362)
- townships (p. 357)
- ward, or district, election (p. 370)
- wards (p. 359)
- weak mayor system (p. 358)

Suggested Web Sites

- **www.brookings.edu.** Web site of the Brookings Institution, one of Washington, D.C.'s oldest think tanks, which pursues independent, nonpartisan research in such areas as metropolitan policy and governance.

- **www2.icma.org/main/sc.asp.** Web site of the International City/County Management Association, whose mission is to create excellence in local government by developing and fostering professional local government management worldwide.

- **www.naco.org.** Web site of the National Association of Counties, the only national organization that represents county governments in the United States.

- **www.natat.org.** Web site of the National Association of Towns and Townships, which seeks to strengthen the effectiveness of town and township governments by exploring flexible and alternative approaches to federal policies to ensure that smaller communities can meet federal requirements.

- **www.nlc.org.** Web site of the National League of Cities, the oldest and largest national organization representing municipal governments in the United States.

- **www.usmayors.org.** Web site of the U.S. Conference of Mayors, which is the official nonpartisan organization of the 1,183 U.S. cities with populations of 30,000 or more.

State Stats on Local Government

Explore and compare data on the states! Go to college.cqpress.com/sites/ govstateandlocal to do these exercises.

1. How has local government spending across the states changed between 2000 and 2010? Where has it changed the most and the least? What might account for some of the changes?

2. How has local government tax revenue changed in the states between 2000 and 2010? Where has it changed the most? The least? What might account for some of the changes?

3. Which state has the highest level of local government direct general expenditures? Which has the least? How does state population affect these expenditures? Why?

4. What is the homeownership rate in your state? How do changes in this rate affect the local governments' budgets?

5. What is the average value of new housing units in your state? How does this number affect local government budgets?

Critics of urban governance argue that there is a hole in local government. Not a hole quite as literal as this one, but rather the general absence of meaningful regional government. While many issues—such as transportation and highway maintenance—are essentially regional in nature, there is a notable lack of regional political jurisdictions.

Metropolitics

THE HOLE PROBLEM OF GOVERNMENT

- What is the "hole" in government?
- Why do the decisions of one local government affect the decisions of other local governments?
- Why do patterns of growth create pressure for new forms of local government?

A llegheny County, Pennsylvania, has a lot of governments. There is the county government, of course. You've probably also heard of the county seat, Pittsburgh, a city famed for football (the Steelers are six-time Super Bowl champs), ketchup (the headquarters of the H. J. Heinz Company), and steel (in the early twentieth century, Pittsburgh accounted for half of the nation's steel manufacturing). Pittsburgh is a major metropolitan city, with a general-purpose government organized under a mayor-council system.

Chances are, however, that you can't name even a tiny fraction of all the governments in Allegheny County, even if you live there. If you can, you have a remarkably good memory. Shoehorned into this single county are 128 municipalities, 101 special districts, and 44 school districts. That's 273 governments—everything from the city of Pittsburgh to the West Mifflin Sanitary Sewer Municipal Authority to the Allegheny County Hospital Development Authority. Allegheny County is one of the densest concentrations of local governments in the United States.[1]

In Allegheny County there is, on average, 1 government for every 2.56 square miles, or 1 government for every 4,494 residents.[2] All those political jurisdictions add up to a lot of differences, and, you guessed it, those differences make a difference. Hundreds of police and fire departments operate within the county.[3] No one has actually managed a full tally of all the different public works departments, library systems, purchasing operations, and the like, but there's no doubt that there are a bunch of them. You get the point. There are a lot of differences. And how do they make a difference? Well, in taxes for one thing.

Municipal property taxes, for example, vary wildly across the county. In 2012 someone owning property valued at $100,000 in Pine Township, on the county's northern edge, paid $120 in annual municipal property taxes. A similarly valued property in the city of Pittsburgh cost its owner $1,080 in municipal property taxes.[4] In other words, the property tax burden can vary by a factor of nearly ten, depending on where the property is located within the county's borders. Of course, not everybody pays taxes for the same public services. What public services are available, and the quality of those services, also vary from place to place.

Keeping up with all this variation can cause a headache. So can trying to make rational sense of it. The problem with large urban areas such as Pittsburgh and its immediate surrounding areas is that their fragmented political systems are not really designed to deal with the realities of governing. In Allegheny County, a lot of governments are engaged in providing the same services, and each has its own political leaders, governance structure, and bureaucracy. Some say this is a bad thing. Splitting the responsibilities of local government into literally hundreds of small slices adds up to a lot of redundant inefficiency.

It also makes it incredibly difficult to coordinate an effective response to a wide range of problems that have multijurisdictional causes and consequences. Consider traffic. Authorizing, say, the construction of a new industrial park means there will be a lot of new commuters. Chances are that many of these commuters will live in other communities, which they will drive through on their way to work. Those communities will face increased pressure on their transportation infrastructures and will have to deal with the expensive consequences of a more heavily used transportation system. In other words, a decision by one local government can have important implications for

other local governments. This not only makes coordination difficult, but it can also lead to a lot of hard feelings and conflict.

Other individuals, however, say, "*Vive la différence.*" Pittsburgh and Allegheny County are like most other major metropolitan areas in that for a lot of people they are pretty terrific places to work, live, go to school, and raise a family. So what if there are a lot of local governments? The positive side to having a lot of different municipalities, townships, and counties, with their different tax rates and levels of public services, is choice, and lots of it. All those differences mean people can choose to live in a place that has the right mix of taxes and public services to suit their individual preferences. Of course, this assumes they actually have the resources and the knowledge to make such choices, an assumption that more than one political scientist has questioned. Consider that in the larger Pittsburgh metropolitan area, which extends beyond Allegheny County, there are nearly a thousand local governments.[5] So if you are considering a move to the Pittsburgh area and want to comprehensively comparison shop taxes and public services among that lot, good luck— we hope you have a lot of spare time and access to a supercomputer.

This chapter explores the consequences of differences in local governments and what they mean for everything from effective environmental policies to dealing with racial segregation, poverty, crime, political inequality, and traffic congestion. Addressing such problems in places like Allegheny County is hard because it demands that not just one or two governments do something but that dozens—or even hundreds—of governments do something. And whatever that something is, it needs to be effectively coordinated if it is going to provide a reasonable solution to the problem. And there's the rub. According to some, the organization and structure of government at the local level not only makes it hard to forge solutions to certain problems, but it also makes finding those solutions more difficult.

Chapter 11 discussed the different forms of local government and different ways of organizing local government. This chapter focuses more on the importance and difficulty of coordinating all those different localities. Most Americans live in urban areas like Allegheny County, areas where local governments are cheek by jowl and piled on top of one another. The central economic and social problems that governments must address in these areas are regional rather than local in nature. Yet the United States has no tradition, and few examples, of regional government. It has a lot of local governments with limited abilities and limited incentives to act regionally. How to fashion coherent responses to regional problems is the central challenge of local governance in urban areas. This problem has become particularly acute in the wake of the Great Recession. The federal government is increasingly recognizing that local economies are defined by metro regions rather than by the sometimes arbitrary geographical lines of states or localities. Boosting the economy means targeting these metro areas for grants and other programs, which can be difficult when there is little or no governance infrastructure specifically designed to tie the polyglot mix of local governments into a coherent policy agenda. It raises questions about how governments below the state level are organized, as well as fundamental questions of political power, especially questions that deal with who has the authority to make policy and who has to pay for it.

It is not just densely populated places such as Allegheny County that are dealing with these sorts of problems. Rural areas are facing the same governance challenges, although for different reasons. Rural areas are being forced to grapple with regional-level coordination issues because shrinking populations cannot provide the tax base needed to support general-purpose governments in small communities. Thus local governments in rural areas, like local governments in urban areas, are feeling their way toward more cooperative arrangements, sharing the burden of providing public services, and even considering mergers. So, urban or rural, the biggest challenge for all is dealing with a world in which the problems are regional but the governments are local.

The Missing Level of Government

You might not have noticed, but according to some scholars there is a hole in the organizational structure of the federal system. The basic organization of the federal government and the powers and responsibilities of state and federal governments are covered by the U.S. Constitution. The organization of the state governments and the powers and responsibilities of state and local governments are covered by individual state constitutions. The hole is at the regional level. There is nothing in the U.S. Constitution, and virtually nothing in state constitutions, that addresses even the notion of regional government, let alone its organization or powers and responsibilities.

In some ways this is understandable. The federal arrangement set up by the Constitution is the bedrock of the U.S. political system and is deeply woven into the fabric of society. No one seriously proposes to fundamentally alter this arrangement. Even though it stands on less legal authority—local governments, remember, are not sovereign—there is a strong tradition of local government. People tend to be oriented toward their local communities and tend to place more faith in city hall than in the state or national capitol. In contrast, there are no strong legal foundations for regional governments and no strong tradition of regional government either. Regional government is the poor relation of the U.S. political system: little thought of and, outside the community of urban scholars and a handful of officials, not much loved.

Yet the majority of local governments in the United States are, like the 273 governments of Allegheny County, embedded in larger metropolitan regions. These regions have similar policy challenges and problems that have common sources and call for common solutions. This absence of some sort of regional umbrella government has been called a "fundamental flaw in America's governance structure." Why? Because "metropolitan regions have become the most important functional units of economic and social life in almost all modern societies."[6] Labor and jobs, for example, rarely are concentrated in a single local political jurisdiction. The bottom line is that localities are intertwined economically and socially but are governed as if such matters can be isolated within the preexisting geographical boundaries of political jurisdictions.

The basic problem, then, is that political geography no longer lines up with economic and social geography. The center of economic and

MAP 12-1

Pittsburgh Metropolitan Statistical Area and Surrounding MSAs

Source: U.S. Census Bureau, Population Division.

(and 8 more in Puerto Rico). More than 80 percent of U.S. residents live in such metropolitan areas, with 30 percent living in central cities.[8] These metros are where some of the most important policy challenges of the twenty-first century are not just concentrated but irretrievably interconnected. Consider traffic congestion. According to metro scholar Bruce Katz, roughly 60 percent of all the vehicular miles logged in the United States occur in the top one hundred metropolitan areas. This reflects not just the population concentration of those areas or just the challenges of traffic congestion and maintaining transportation infrastructure, but the effects of such concentration on global warming (that much traffic produces a lot of greenhouse gases) as well as on global trade, shipping, and freight.[9]

Local governments in these metros, like it or not, simply cannot confine their problems or their ambitions to within their own borders, any more than they can independently control global trade or air pollution. In metros, the cities, their suburbs, and the counties in which they are geographically located all blend together into a dense urban concentration. The vast majority of Americans live, work, and play in such urban areas, more often than not crossing local government jurisdictions as they go from one of these activities to another. But there are even bigger units to consider. These dense metropolitan areas often bump into each other, forming an even larger urban geographical area referred to as a **megaregion**. A megaregion is an urban area made up of several large cities and their

social life in the United States is increasingly less a city or a county than a larger metropolitan area. The U.S. Office of Management and Budget defines a **metropolitan area** as a region with "a large population nucleus, together with adjacent communities having a high degree of social and economic integration with that core." It is important to note that this definition goes on to specify that a metropolitan area comprises "one or more entire counties."[7]

For data-gathering and reporting purposes, the federal government formally defines metropolitan areas using the concept of the **metropolitan statistical area (MSA)**, an area made up of a city of 50,000 or more people together with adjacent urban communities that have strong ties to the central city. As of 2010, there were 374 MSAs in the United States

---

Metropolitan Area

A populous region typically comprising a city and surrounding communities that have a high degree of social and economic integration.

Metropolitan Statistical Area (MSA)

An area with a city of 50,000 or more people together with adjacent urban communities that have strong ties to the central city.

Megaregion

An urban area made up of several large cities and their surrounding urban areas that creates an interlocking economic and social system.

TABLE 12-1

Metropolitan Statistical Areas at a Glance

Ten Largest MSAs by Population, 2010	Rank
New York–Northern New Jersey–Long Island, N.Y.–N.J.–Pa.	1
Los Angeles–Long Beach–Santa Ana, Calif.	2
Chicago–Joliet–Naperville, Ill.–Ind.–Wisc.	3
Dallas–Fort Worth–Arlington, Tex.	4
Houston–Sugar Land–Baytown, Tex.	5
Philadelphia–Camden–Wilmington, Pa.–N.J.–Del.–Md.	6
Washington–Arlington–Alexandria, D.C.–Va.–Md.–W.V.	7
Miami–Fort Lauderdale–Miami Beach, Fla.	8
Atlanta–Sandy Springs–Marietta, Ga.	9
Boston–Cambridge–Quincy, Mass.–N.H.	10

Ten Smallest MSAs by Population, 2010	Rank
Ames, Iowa	356
Elmira, N.Y.	357
Corvallis, Ore.	358
Great Falls, Mont.	359
Danville, Ill.	360
Hinesville–Fort Stewart, Ga.	361
Columbus, Ind.	362
Sandusky, Ohio	363
Casper, Wyo.	364
Lewiston, Idaho–Wash.	365
Carson City, Nev.	366

Top Ten MSAs by Percentage Change, 2000–2010	Rank
Palm Coast, Fla.	1
St. George, Utah	2
Las Vegas–Paradise, Nev.	3
Raleigh–Cary, N.C.	4
Cape Coral–Fort Myers, Fla.	5
Provo–Orem, Utah	6
Greeley, Colo.	7
Austin–Round Rock–San Marcos, Tex.	8
Myrtle Beach–North Myrtle Beach–Conway, S.C.	9
Bend, Ore.	10

Source: U.S. Census Bureau, "Population Estimates," www.census.gov/popest/data/metro/totals/2011/index.html; U.S. Census Bureau, "Population Distribution and Change 2000 to 2010," www.census.gov/prod/cen2010/briefs/c2010br-01.pdf.

surrounding urban areas—in effect, a string of MSAs. Megaregions represent a new type of urban geography, a merging of metropolitan areas into a massive interlocking economic and social system. Megaregions may spill across multiple counties or even multiple states, but there is typically no overarching institution at this level with anything like the powers of a municipal, let alone a state, government. Instead, within megaregions are dozens and dozens of governments trying to balance local and regional interests, with mixed success. All of these different governments share a set of common interests because a decision by any one jurisdiction in a megaregion has implications for other jurisdictions. This interdependence fuels an increasing recognition of the need for local governments to coordinate with one another in policy and decision making on everything from transportation infrastructure to economic development to public housing.

Achieving that sort of coordination is incredibly difficult in the United States because of the relative lack of regional government. Because these metropolitan areas span not just county but also state and even national borders, exercising any form of centralized planning over their growth and operation is incredibly difficult. As in Allegheny County, in megaregions literally hundreds of governments are making thousands of decisions, often with little coordination or thought to their regional effects. Not only does this fragmentation of political authority make it hard to address regional problems, but it is arguably the cause of some of those problems.

Take, for example, the rise of so-called **edgeless cities**. These are sprawling, unplanned office and retail complexes that are not pedestrian-friendly and often become ghost towns at night. They do have obvious economic attractions—they mean jobs, sales taxes (people who work in them buy stuff, even if it is just gas and incidentals at a convenience store), and also property taxes (office complexes are valuable properties).

Yet, whatever local benefits they produce, they also export a set of costs to the larger region. Most of the people who work in edgeless cities commute home to greener residential areas. This means such developments segregate and put considerable geographical distance between where people live and where they work. The end results—traffic congestion and smog—affect all communities in the region, but individually there is not much any local government can do about such problems.

Sprawl: How Metropolitan Regions Grow

The fragmented nature of governance in metropolitan areas creates an interconnected set of problems that are difficult to address in a systematic and coordinated fashion. To understand the causes and consequences of these problems, as well as the challenges involved in effectively addressing them, it helps to have a little historical background on the roots of metropolitan growth.

Metropolitan areas (and certainly megaregions) are a relatively new concept. As recently as the 1920s, scholars recognized that the growth of suburbs, rapid and easily accessible transportation, and new forms of communication were transforming urban areas into a new social and economic phenomenon. They also recognized that existing forms of local government were ill equipped to deal with this new urban reality, and some even went so far as to call for a new form of metropolitan government to address the gap between state and local political jurisdictions.[10]

It was not until after World War II, however, that the country really saw the explosive growth of metropolitan areas and the broad-scale governance problems that accompanied this growth. In some ways, this growth was inevitable. A population boom created enormous pressure for new development, and that development typically took place on the peripheries of large cities or urban areas in the form of low-density suburban housing and commercial developments. This created an interrelated set of problems that can be traced to the catchall phenomenon of **sprawl**. Although the term *sprawl* is often used generically to refer to the rapid growth of any metropolitan area, most urban scholars consider sprawl to be a particular type of growth. There is no universal definition of sprawl, but this type of growth does have a set of specific characteristics: single-use zoning, low-density development, leapfrog development, car-dependent living, and fragmentation of land-use powers. We discuss each in turn below.

Single-use zoning. One of the central political powers of local government is control over land use. This power is typically exercised through **zoning laws**. These laws can allow land to be used for a mix of commercial, recreational, and residential development or for single uses, when land is used for single-purpose developments. Local governments in metropolitan areas have tended to favor the latter approach. The end result has been the geographical separation of the places where people work, live, and play.

Low-density development. The growth of metropolitan areas has been defined not only by single-use development but also by low-density development. In effect, local governments have exercised their powers over land use to dictate that the growth in metropolitan areas will be out rather than up. Rather than multifamily developments

---

Edgeless Cities
Office and retail complexes without clear boundaries.

Sprawl
The rapid growth of a metropolitan area, typically as a result of specific types of zoning and development.

Zoning Laws
Regulations that control how land can be used.

Low-Density Development
Development practices that spread (rather than concentrate) populations across the land.

such as high-rise condominiums and apartments, suburbs and other urban municipalities have favored single-family developments. These developments make for lower population densities, but obviously they also require more land. For example, the population of the Milwaukee, Wisconsin, metropolitan area increased roughly 3 percent between 1970 and 1990, but geographically the metro area increased by 38 percent. Los Angeles is a classic case of how low-density development can consume vast stretches of land. Population-wise, Los Angeles grew about 45 percent between 1970 and 1990; land-wise, it grew by 300 percent.[11]

Leapfrog development. Leapfrog developments jump—or leapfrog—over established developments, leaving undeveloped or underdeveloped land between developed areas. This puts a particular strain on infrastructure—not just on roads but also on water and sewer facilities. When new development bypasses undeveloped land, utilities have to be stretched out further to serve the newly developed areas.

Leapfrog development is partially driven by the economic incentives of developers. Most established municipalities like to create uniform requirements for developments within their own jurisdictions, for example, by enforcing specific building codes. They may even impose what are sometimes called impact fees. Municipalities charge builders of new housing or commercial developments impact fees to help offset the costs of extending services such as parks, schools, law enforcement, and fire protection services to these developments. A new housing development, for instance, may require the building of a new fire station, and impact fees can help offset that cost. It is not hard to see, then, why developers often favor

building in unincorporated areas, typically on land with geographical separation from municipal borders that is still close enough to make for an easy commute to the urban center. The land in unincorporated areas tends to be cheaper, and there are fewer regulations to deal with.

Car-dependent living. Developing metropolitan areas through single-use, low-density developments means that citizens have to be highly mobile. Getting from a suburban home to a job in a commercial office development and from home to the kids' soccer game on the weekend pretty much requires an automobile. In low-density housing developments, it is often impossible—or at least impractical—to do something like "run to the corner store." Getting a six-pack to watch the game or a bag of sugar to bake cookies, or even arranging a play date for the kids, requires transportation. Because public transportation systems are, for the most part, not set up for convenient and efficient transportation across large, multijurisdictional geographical areas, having a car becomes a necessity for anyone living in a metropolitan area.

Between 1950 and 1990 the population of the United States increased by about 40 percent, but the number of miles traveled in cars increased 140 percent. The imbalance between population growth and the growth in automobile use is a direct consequence of how land has been developed in metropolitan areas. The rise of car-dependent living exacts an environmental toll. Governments have done a reasonably good job of controlling "point" sources of pollution (concentrated sources of pollutants that tend to be limited in number, such as factories and power plants) over the past three decades or so. However, nonpoint sources of pollution are harder to identify and control because they consist of many sources, each putting out a relatively small amount of pollutants but collectively having a large-scale impact on the environment. Cars are a classic example of a nonpoint

---

Leapfrog Development
Development practices in which new developments jump—or leapfrog—over established developments, leaving undeveloped or underdeveloped land between developed areas.

Impact Fees
Fees that municipalities charge builders of new housing or commercial developments to help offset the costs of extending services.

Car-Dependent Living
A situation in which owning a car for transportation is a necessity; an outcome of low-density development.

One of the consequences of urban development patterns is traffic congestion. Because people tend to live in one place and work in another, commuting by car is a daily ritual for millions of Americans.

contributed to, and in some cases is a primary cause of, problems such as traffic congestion and smog. According to many academics who study urban politics and growth, these same development patterns produce a wide range of other problems as well. These problems include the concentration of poverty and crime into certain neighborhoods, segregation by race and class, and inequality in public services, fiscal resources, and political power.

source of pollution and are a major cause of air-quality problems in metropolitan areas.[12]

Fragmentation of land-use powers. A key characteristic of sprawl is the division of powers among local political jurisdictions, in particular the power over land use. Local governments frequently have strong incentives to use these powers in a way that provides benefits for those within the particular local jurisdiction but creates costs for neighboring communities.

The basic characteristics described above have defined the growth and development of many major metropolitan areas in the United States during the past half century or so. The result has been largely unplanned growth (growth with no systematic coordination to balance local benefits with regional costs) spread out across ever-larger geographical regions, gobbling up previously rural areas and replacing them with low-density, single-use developments.

As new low-density housing developments began popping up around core cities after World War II, the middle and upper classes began moving from the cities to the suburbs. There were "push" and "pull" reasons for the migration of the better-off classes to the suburbs. One reason was the lure of the lifestyle—the home with the white picket fence on a leafy suburban lane—that "pulled" people out of the city. Another was the racial desegregation of public schools in the 1960s and 1970s; increasing numbers of less well-off nonwhites began to make up an ever greater proportion of urban schools, acting as an incentive for whites to move, "pushing" them out to the suburbs.

The racial—and perhaps racist—undertones of this demographic shift have been repeatedly noted by academics.[13] Because the middle and upper classes were largely white, this demographic phenomenon became known as **white flight**. As whites left the dense, multiuse neighborhoods of cities for the lure of single-family homes on large lots in suburbia, minorities became concentrated in the core urban areas. Because racial minorities also were much more likely to be less socioeconomically well-off than whites, this meant that inner-city neighborhoods became poorer.

The Cons of Metropolitan Growth

By now it should be fairly obvious that the characteristic sprawl-like growth of metropolitan areas over the past fifty or sixty years has

White Flight
A demographic trend in which the middle and upper classes leave central cities for predominantly white suburbs.

As the city neighborhoods became poorer, the remaining middle-class residents felt more pressure to decamp to the suburbs, and a self-reinforcing trend set in; the poor and ethnic minorities became increasingly concentrated in core city neighborhoods. In the past couple of decades, this trend has started to occur in the suburbs themselves. Minorities who managed to get far enough up the socioeconomic ladder to move to an inner-ring suburb have triggered another round of white flight; as these comparatively less white, less well-off people move into the inner-ring suburbs, the better-off move farther out. The end result is the increasingly racial and socioeconomic homogeneity of particular political jurisdictions.

Some local political jurisdictions are well-off and tend to have property values that support high-quality public services. Middle- and upper-class suburbs, for example, tend to have high-quality public schools. So do **exurbs**, or municipalities in more rural settings that serve as bedroom communities, with residents commuting to jobs in the cities or suburbs during the day and returning to their homes after work. This tends to be in stark contrast to some inner-city neighborhoods and inner-ring suburbs in which poverty is concentrated. Property values are low in such neighborhoods, which means that they cannot support high-quality public services.

It is important to note that the end result is economic *and* racial segregation based on housing patterns. This trend is made apparent by school districts. In some urban areas, for example, African Americans make up less than 3 percent of the total population but constitute 70 percent of the enrollment in school districts.[14] These are invariably schools that serve poor communities, where crime and other social problems place enormous strains not just on public education but also on social and economic opportunities in general. While people can, and do, experience challenge and struggle out in the suburbs, suburban communities are much more likely to have the fiscal capacity to support such public services as good school systems. And because good schools play an important role in determining where the

> Place matters because wealth is segregated by communities across metropolitan regions, communities that are themselves concentrated in different political jurisdictions. As one well-known study of metropolitan politics and policy concludes, where you live in a given metropolitan area both affects your quality of life and shapes your social and economic opportunities.

middle class wants to live, again this becomes a self-reinforcing trend.

In other words, here is a difference that makes a big difference to the quality of life of millions of people. Place matters because wealth is segregated by communities across metropolitan regions, communities that are themselves concentrated in different political jurisdictions. As one well-known study of metropolitan politics and policy concludes, where you live in a given metropolitan area both affects your quality of life and shapes your social and economic opportunities. Place affects access to jobs, public services, level of personal security (crime tends to be higher in some socio-economically stressed neighborhoods), availability of medical services, and even the quality of the air we breathe (the people commuting in from the exurbs contribute to urban smog but escape to the cleaner rural air after the workday is done).[15]

Take the issue of jobs. Two-thirds of all new jobs are created in suburbs (think of the big-box stores, such as Wal-Mart and Home Depot, that dot suburban landscapes—even in the hard economic times of recent years, they still represent a lot of jobs). The people who most desperately need some of those jobs, and the social and economic opportunities they represent, are concentrated in poorer inner-city neighborhoods. Three-quarters of all welfare recipients live either in the central cities or in poorer rural areas.[16]

Exurbs
Municipalities in rural areas that ring suburbs. They typically serve as bedroom communities for the prosperous, providing rural homes with easy access to urban areas.

These people cannot move to the suburbs, where the jobs are, because they cannot afford the expensive homes that typify low-density, single-use housing developments. Buying and operating a car also are expensive propositions that can levy a harsh financial toll on those less well-off. That leaves public transportation, which is often an inefficient way to cover the huge geographical spaces that separate inner-city homes from suburban workplaces.

Critics of the consequences of sprawl argue that the end result will be metropolitan areas that continue to promote and reinforce economic and racial segregation and create disparities in tax bases that lead to huge differences in the quality of public services among local political jurisdictions. On top of that, from a regional perspective, the patterns of metropolitan growth are economically inefficient (jobs and the labor market are disconnected) and environmentally dangerous (all those cars pump out a lot of toxic emissions).[17]

Government Reform in Metropolitan Areas

Racial and economic segregation, inequities in tax bases and public services, and, above all, political fragmentation that creates difficulty in coordinating rational and effective responses to regional challenges—the problems of governance in metropolitan areas are well-known. But what can be done about them?

A number of strategies have been developed for rationalizing government in metropolitan areas, all of which have been either implemented or considered to various degrees in virtually all major urban areas. The reform perspective pushes for such rationalization and begins with the assumption that the key problems and challenges of governance in metropolitan areas are regional in nature and, as such, should be addressed regionally. Proponents also tend to argue that many of the problems have been created by political fragmentation in the first place, in that there are lots of smaller governments making decisions

---

Reform Perspective
An approach to filling gaps in service and reducing redundancies in local governments that calls for regional-level solutions.

that may produce local benefits but export the costs to other jurisdictions. If the root cause of these problems is political fragmentation, government consolidation is the obvious solution. In other words, new regional governing structures should be created to fill the hole in the federal system, governments that are better positioned to respond effectively to the interconnected problems of large metropolitan areas.[18]

There is no universal response to filling that hole, however. Instead, there are a number of different strategies that range from creating new pan-regional governments to eliminating long-standing local jurisdictions.

Regional Governments

Adherents of the reform perspective are strong advocates of creating regional authorities to address regional problems. This can be done in a couple of ways. First, new government structures can be created to sit above existing political jurisdictions and be given the authority to oversee regional land-use planning. This sort of approach has been popular with a number of civic activists from the reform tradition. Former Albuquerque mayor David Rusk, former Minnesota state representative Myron Orfield, and syndicated columnist Neal Pierce have all been popular champions of pan-regional planning authorities.

A couple of well-known examples of such regional planning authorities are frequently cited by advocates as examples of the benefits of taking a top-down approach to land-use regulation. One of the best known of these is the Metropolitan Service District in Portland, Oregon, known simply as Metro. Metro is a true regional government that covers Clackamas, Multnomah, and Washington Counties and the twenty-five municipalities in the Portland metropolitan area; all told, its jurisdiction extends over approximately 1.5 million people, or about 40 percent of Oregon residents. It is governed by an elected legislature (a six-member council) and an elected executive (the council president).[19] Metro exercises real regulatory authority in areas such as land-use planning, regional transportation, recycling and garbage disposal, and a host of other policy areas that are regional rather than local in nature.

A number of academic observers have concluded that the Portland top-down approach to regional planning has reaped considerable benefits not seen in metropolitan areas that have no comparable regional governance. For example, white flight has been markedly lower in Portland than in other cities. In contrast to the pattern seen in many other major cities, in Portland the middle class—especially young, highly educated individuals—tend to settle in the central city rather than in the suburbs or nonmetropolitan areas.[20]

One of the notable characteristics of the Portland Metro is the presence of an **urban growth boundary (UGB)**. A UGB controls the density and type of development by establishing a boundary around a given urban area. Land inside the UGB is slated for high-density development; land outside the UGB is slated for lower-density, rural sorts of development. In effect, this type of planning regulation forces cities to grow vertically rather than horizontally and, thus, sets limits on sprawl and the problems it generates.

Critics of UGBs argue that they have a significant downside. By limiting the land available for development, UGBs drive up prices for land in particular and real estate in general. The end results are high property values and limited supplies of affordable housing. This does not seem to have happened in Portland, however, at least to any extreme. In fact, property values there are considered reasonable compared with the rest of the West Coast. Reformers have pointed to the success of the UGB in Portland to promote the adoption of similar policies in other urban areas. Three states—Oregon, Tennessee, and Washington— now mandate cities to establish UGBs.

Regional Councils

Although Metro is a true regional government, it is also a very rare example—the vast majority of metropolitan areas in the United States lack any form of regional government with comparable authority and policymaking power. There are, however, a large number of regional planning authorities that provide at least a rudimentary form of coordination among the local governments packed into their metropolitan areas.

Probably the most common attempt to rationalize local policymaking across multi-jurisdictional metropolitan areas is the formation of regional councils. A **regional council** is "a multi-service entity with state and locally-defined boundaries that delivers a variety of federal, state and local programs while continuing its function as a planning organization, technical assistance provider and 'visionary' to its member local governments."[21]

Regional councils are made up of member governments, such as municipalities and school districts, although other nonprofit, civic, private, or academic organizations also may be included. They originated in the 1960s and 1970s as vehicles for delivering state and federal programs to regional areas. Since then, they have grown to become an important means of making and coordinating region-wide policy and planning in such areas as land use, transportation, economic development, housing, and social services. Regional councils are a way to recognize that decisions made in one community can trigger domino effects in neighboring communities and that it therefore makes sense to address some problems regionally rather than locally. There are 516 such bodies in the United States, and of the roughly 39,000 general-purpose local governments in the country (which include counties, cities, municipalities, villages, boroughs, towns, and townships), about 35,000 are served by regional councils.[22]

A related form of regional authority is the **metropolitan planning organization (MPO)**. MPOs are

---

Urban Growth Boundary (UGB)
A border established around urban areas that is intended to control the density and type of development.

Regional Council
A planning and advisory organization whose members include multiple local governments. Regional councils often are used to administer state and federal programs that target regions.

Metropolitan Planning Organization (MPO)
A regional organization that decides how federal transportation funds are allocated within that regional area.

regional organizations that decide how federal transportation funds are allocated within their regional areas. MPOs are interesting because they represent a specific recognition by federal law that regions—as opposed to localities—are central functional policy units. The Intermodal Surface Transportation Efficiency Act of 1991 (ISTEA) mandated that every metropolitan region had to identify an institution (an MPO) to serve as the central coordinating authority for federal transportation funds in that area. These MPOs have the responsibility of developing transportation plans and programs for their metropolitan regions. Every transportation project involving federal money—which is to say virtually every major transportation project—has to be approved by an MPO. Some MPOs administer billions of dollars in federal transportation grants, and control over such large amounts of money, coupled with the MPOs' authority over critical transportation programs, translates into major political clout.[23] There is even a nascent effort to coordinate the decision making of MPOs within megaregions, which would extend their influence on transportation infrastructure policy across even wider geographic areas.

Regional councils and MPOs, however, should not be confused or equated with Portland's Metro. They are different in the sense that they are more a vehicle for intergovernmental cooperation than an actual form of government with executive and legislative authority independent of local government interests. Formal organizations of local governments in metropolitan areas have existed in some form or another for decades; regional councils and MPOs are just the more common and better-known examples. Hashing out roles and responsibilities, not to mention making decisions, involves a complicated—and often contentious—give-and-take among the local governments that constitute the membership of these regional bodies.

For example, most formal organizations of local governments, in metropolitan areas at least, began by allowing every member to have an equal voice in the organization. What this meant was that a small rural township had exactly the same

influence on regional issues as a core city, even though it had a fraction of the population. Figuring out more representational, equitable, and democratic decision making in these regional bodies has been, to put it mildly, a challenge. Smaller jurisdictions are, understandably, loath to give up their influence to bigger neighbors for fear of having their interests take a backseat. The bigger neighbors, in turn, resent having their interests yoked to the interests of much smaller communities.

Intergovernmental institutions such as regional councils are, at best, confederal sorts of regional governments that are creatures of the often conflicting interests of their members. This complicates decision making and makes it harder for these bodies to exert firm regulatory authority over critical areas such as land use. Still, in most parts of the country they come the closest to filling the hole in the organizational structure of the federal system. A move in this direction has been growing support for regional planning efforts that emphasize **smart growth**, development practices that emphasize more efficient infrastructure and less dependence on automobiles. Smart growth is reflected in regional, or even single-jurisdiction, policies that promote mixed-use developments that are pedestrian- and bicycle-friendly, emphasize building community rather than just buildings of bricks and mortar, and consciously account for development's impact on the environment.

The bottom line on regional councils and MPOs is that, for the most part, there is a considerable mismatch between their governance capacities and the need for effective and coordinated responses to regional issues. As one study of regional councils concludes, "Despite the efforts of progressive reformers to push strategies encouraging . . . strong, centralized regional government institutions, most regional institutions find it difficult to address issues affecting the quality of life in a metropolitan area."[24]

Smart Growth
Environmentally friendly development practices, particularly those that emphasize more efficient infrastructure and less dependence on automobiles.

> One of the lessons to emerge from the massive economic stimulus effort initiated by the federal government in response to the Great Recession was that the existing mechanisms of disbursement—state and local governments—do not effectively connect federal dollars with their intended policy targets. Part of this disconnect is clearly due to the lack of effective regional governance.

Despite their obvious limitations, these councils are currently the only politically viable regional governance mechanisms that "most local jurisdictions can use to address multiple and cross-cutting issues."[25] And the power and role of regional councils and MPOs may be increasing because of a shift in philosophy at the federal level. One of the lessons to emerge from the massive economic stimulus effort initiated by the federal government in response to the Great Recession was that the existing mechanisms of disbursement—state and local governments—sometimes do not effectively connect federal dollars with their intended policy targets. Part of this disconnect is clearly due to the lack of effective regional governance. The overarching intent of the federal government in providing the stimulus money was to stimulate the economy, and that meant targeting metro areas, where much of the nation's economic activity takes place. Yet for the most part there were no effective, general-purpose regional governments available to implement that sort of region-wide policy goal. Because of the "hole" in government, most of the stimulus dollars went to states and localities that were scrambling to get their individual shares of the federal pie. Powerful metro-level governments with the ability to address key issues across political jurisdictions effectively got less stimulus money for the simple reason that they largely do not exist. In response, the federal government began an effort to tie federal grants to increased regional cooperation, which puts regional councils and MPOs in a good position to increase their governance capacities in the future. (See the the box "States under Stress: "Tying Federal Funding to Regional Cooperation").

Many local governments also engage in looser, informal cooperative arrangements rather than creating formal institutions such as regional councils or MPOs. This sort of cooperation is known as an **interjurisdictional agreement (IJA)**, an increasingly common form of intergovernmental cooperation. An IJA may take the form of a binding agreement. For example, a town may contract with the county for law enforcement services or for dispatch services. Other IJAs may be much more informal and rest on nothing more than good-faith agreements between two or more local governments to provide a service jointly or to work together on planning or management issues. No one really knows how many IJAs there are or how effective they are in promoting effective integrated responses to regional problems. Given the shortcomings of more formal institutions such as regional councils and MPOs, however, IJAs often represent one of the few viable alternatives for multijurisdictional governance.[26]

Government Consolidation

One way to regularize or rationalize governance in a metropolitan region is to create a pan-regional institution. As already discussed, such an institution can take the form of a new level of government (such as Portland's Metro) or a formal institution of intergovernmental cooperation, such as a regional council. A second approach is to reduce the number of

---

Interjurisdictional Agreement (IJA)
A formal or informal agreement between two or more local governments to cooperate on a program or policy.

States under Stress

Tying Federal Funding to Regional Cooperation

How the federal government interacts with states and localities across a wide range of policy areas is evolving, and part of that change will reshape the entire structure and process of dispensing federal funds and steering federal policy.

During the early years of the Obama administration, the White House embraced a concept, advanced largely by the Brookings Institution's Metropolitan Policy Program, that stresses the primacy of the nation's metro regions—cities or clusters of cities, plus their inner and outer suburbs and some rural areas that are linked to them economically. The Brookings mantra is that these regions are the economic drivers of the country; they do, after all, contain three-quarters of the American population and generate most of the nation's economic activity. So, the idea is for Washington to start approaching the governments below its own level not as separate states, cities, and counties but as metros.

Soon after it took office, the administration started pushing its domestic agencies to find a more regional approach to dealing with all subgovernments. Federal departments in charge of housing, transportation, energy, the environment, labor, and small businesses are trying to coordinate hundreds of programs addressing a wide range of activities. And the expectation is that the efforts they will be funding—clusters of governments acting collaboratively—must be similarly integrated. If they are, great. If not, no dough.

The federal stimulus money disbursed in an effort to blunt the effects of the Great Recession was mostly subject to the old rules because Washington wanted to pump it out as fast as possible and didn't have time to write new rules. A New York Times analysis of more than 5,000 transportation projects in the first few months under Obama showed that "the 100 largest metropolitan areas are getting less than half the money from the biggest pot of transportation stimulus money. In many cases, they have lost a tug of war with state lawmakers that urban advocates say could hurt the nation's economic engines."

That prompted a a rethinking of how and to whom the federal government should send its dollars. Top managers in all the relevant agencies seem serious about forcing metropolitan collaboration, particularly when it involves more than one area of domestic policy. Bruce Katz of the Brookings Institution predicts optimistically that the growing recognition of the importance of metro areas "will stimulate a new generation of political and policy organizing at the metro scale." He believes this will include reinvigorating and funding long-dormant MPOs that were resuscitated sixteen years ago when Congress passed a landmark transportation bill, only to be largely ignored in more recent years.

Of course, there are problems with this strategy, both practical and political. As columnist Mary Newsom of the *Charlotte Observer* points out, far too many MPOs still seem to believe that "'transportation' means only highways" and that regional organizations are little more than instruments for the protection of local turf. The Charlotte metropolitan region, Newsom notes, "is home to four separate MPOs, or five, depending on how you count. So transportation planning here is completely fragmented—and Charlotte gets shorted when dollars are divvied."

That's true in a lot of places because governors and legislatures like to spread the funds around their states rather than concentrating them in metros. And they may not be too interested in changing the process or the rules. But that is exactly what the Obama administration is pressuring them to do.

Federalism scholar Paul Posner of George Mason University has some doubts about how successful the initiative to invigorate MPOs will be, not only because states and locals have the political clout to avoid ceding too much authority but also because "the feds have a track record of good intentions over the past 50 years" that have ultimately amounted to very little.

But Posner concedes that some incremental progress is taking place. "The lesson learned," he says, "might be that the only way the federal government will succeed in institutionalizing regionalism is if it follows and supports demand from the bottom of our system, rather than seeking to create and impose demand from the top. Where the demand exists and the regional institutions are strong, there is promise. But where they are not, then progress will be much slower."

Source: Adapted from Peter Harkness, "Tying Federal Funding to Regional Cooperation," *Governing,* September 2009.

governments through merger or consolidation. This is typically done through the merging of a city with a county.

On the face of it, this makes a good deal of sense. Cities and urban counties share the same geographical space and provide similar services. A classic example is law enforcement services. Think of an urban county sitting on top of a large city. The county will have a sheriff's office; the city will have a police department. Each can have its own jails, dispatch centers, training facilities, and purchasing departments. It strikes many that there is a lot redundancy and inefficiency in duplicating these services in such close quarters. Why not consolidate at least some of these functions? That is exactly what Des Moines, Iowa, and Polk County did with their city and county jails. The county and city jails sat on opposite sides of the Des Moines River—directly across from each other—and consolidating facilities and operations just seemed to make sense.

If consolidating operations can reduce redundancy and improve efficiency, why not go whole hog and merge municipal and county governments into a single government? Cities and counties often duplicate bureaucracies and paperwork, so there seems to be an obvious logic to city-county consolidation. With as many as 75 percent of all major urban areas in the United States contained within single counties, it would seem to make sense that such mergers would be common and easy. But they aren't, and it doesn't.

According to the National Association of Counties, of the nation's more than three thousand counties only about forty (roughly 1 percent) have consolidated with cities. Since 1990, there have been only about forty-five formal proposals to consolidate city and county governments, and only about a dozen have actually passed.[27] Unsuccessful efforts include the attempts to merge Gainesville, Florida, with Alachua County and Spokane, Washington, with Spokane County.

Despite the glacial pace of city-county consolidation, it is an idea that has been around for a long time. The earliest consolidation dates back to 1805, when the city of New Orleans was consolidated with New Orleans Parish (remember, in Louisiana counties are called parishes). The practice even enjoyed an era of popularity in the 1960s and 1970s.

Proposals for consolidation often come in response to state initiatives or regional challenges. For example, the citizens of Jacksonville, Florida, in Duval County, were experiencing industrial waste in their river, underachieving high schools, and clashes between city and county officials during the 1960s. Local business leaders lobbied the state legislature for help. The legislature created a commission that proposed a consolidation plan. The plan was approved in 1967 by the legislature and, subsequently, by the voters in a referendum.

For the most part, this merger has worked for the two governments involved. But even after the merger, there were municipalities in Duval County (Atlantic Beach, Baldwin, Jacksonville Beach, and Neptune Beach) but outside Jacksonville city limits that continued as independent local governments. These communities periodically have considered splitting off from Jacksonville/Duval and forming a new county (Ocean County) as a means to recover a county government less tied to the city of Jacksonville. Thus far, however, these efforts have not progressed beyond the discussion stage, and all these municipalities remain a part of Duval County.

Still, only a few dozen mergers in two hundred years leaves a lot of cities and counties sitting right on top of each other duplicating services. Why haven't city-county consolidations happened more often? The answer in part has to do with who supports and who opposes the mergers when they are proposed.

Consolidation typically is favored by business groups and others who favor efficiency in government spending and regulation over local control of government. These individuals seek a reorganization of government to reduce bureaucratic redundancy and to allow communities to speak "with one voice." The politics of consolidations, however, are tricky. Middle-class

---

City-County Consolidation
The merger of separate local governments in an effort to reduce bureaucratic redundancy and service inefficiencies.

TABLE 12-2

Consolidated City-County Governments

City-Counties Operating Primarily as Cities		Metropolitan Governments Operating Primarily as Cities		Areas with County-like Offices in Other Governments (city, township, special district, state)	
Alaska	City and borough of Anchorage	Tennessee	Hartsville and Trousdale County	Florida	County of Duval (City of Jacksonville)
	City and borough of Juneau		Lynchburg and Moore County	Georgia	County of Clarke (City of Athens) County of Echols (City of Statenville) County of Greley (City of Tribune)
	City and borough of Sitka		Nashville and Davidson County		County of Muscogee (City of Columbus)
	City and borough of Yakutat				County of Richmond (City of Augusta) County of Quitman (City of Georgetown) County of Webster (City of Preston)
California	City and county of San Francisco			Hawaii	County of Kalawao (State of Hawaii)
Colorado	City and county of Broomfield			Indiana	County of Marion (City of Indianapolis)
	City and county of Denver			Kentucky	Lexington-Fayette Urban County
Hawaii	City and county of Honolulu			Louisiana	Parish of East Baton Rouge (City of Baton Rouge)
Kansas	Unified Government of Wyandotte County and City of Kansas City				Parish of Lafayette (City of Lafayette)
Montana	Anaconda–Deer Lodge County				Parish of Orleans (City of New Orleans)
	Butte–Silver Bow County				Terrebonne Parish Consolidated Government
				Massachusetts	County of Nantucket (Town of Nantucket)
					County of Suffolk (City of Boston)
				New York	Counties of Bronx, Kings, New York, Queens, and Richmond (all part of the City of New York)
				Pennsylvania	County of Philadelphia (City of Philadelphia)

Source: National League of Cities, "List of Consolidated City-County Governments," www.nlc.org/build-skills-and-networks/resources/cities-101/city-structures/list-of-consolidated-city-county-governments.

suburbanites may be concerned that mergers will benefit mostly downtown residents while raising taxes in the suburbs; inner-city minorities may fear their voting power will be diluted. Elected officials reflect these concerns and perhaps add some of their own. Consolidated governments mean fewer elected politicians and, most likely, fewer public employees. This creates internal pressure to resist merger movements.

Policy in Practice

Is Merging Worth It?

Wouldn't it make sense to combine some of the more than 90,000 local governments in the United States? Wouldn't this reduce duplication of services and gain economies of scale? Wouldn't the new governments be better able to deal with the realities of the twenty-first century than cities and counties whose boundaries were drawn when it took a daylong buggy ride to get from one to the other? Maybe.

The evidence on the benefits of consolidating city and county governments is mixed, at least when it comes to reducing government expenditures. Although efficiency is often touted as one of the big payoffs of consolidation, the numbers contradict that claim as much as they support it, according to Kurt Thurmaier, director of the Division of Public Administration at Northern Illinois University. Sometimes, for example, only the major cities within the county are included, and when employee salaries and benefits within the combining jurisdictions are brought in line with each other, the rounding tends to be up, not down.

Things have worked out better for Kansas City, Kansas, and Wyandotte County, according to Dennis Hays, who has been administrator of that unified government since it was created seventeen years ago (and who before that was the city's administrator for three years). Before the consolidation, he says, "we were slipping into the deep abyss, and if we hadn't done consolidation when we did, who knows where we'd be?" Since then, according to Hays, the quality of services has improved, thanks to economies achieved when duplicative departments were merged. Taxes have been cut by 15 percent, and the combined workforce has been reduced by 20 percent. But in Hays's view, having a single policymaking body willing to take on the tough decisions has made the biggest difference, resulting in real improvements to the local quality of life. "We are an older blue-collar community, and now we are seeing young people wanting to move into Wyandotte for the first time in decades."

Nashville, Tennessee, is in the process of celebrating fifty years of consolidation with Davidson County.

Mayor Karl Dean, the combined government's sixth mayor since consolidation, believes that the overwhelming majority of his constituents see the merger as a key component of the success the city has had, including not experiencing the population exodus that a lot of cities have. In addition to efficient service delivery, Dean says, the consolidation has allowed Nashville to deal with issues such as economic development and securing sports teams without involving a lot of small political jurisdictions. And consolidation has provided a larger tax base, something that's critically important in efforts to improve services while holding down costs. As another bit of evidence of the success of consolidation, Dean notes that once or twice a year someone from another city asks Nashville how to do it.

The answer, of course, is that consolidations are politically very difficult to pull off. Somebody has to give up power, and consolidations usually require a vote of the electorate in each of the combining jurisdictions. So it shouldn't be surprising that there have been many more defeats than victories. From 1921 to 1996, there were 132 formal consolidation attempts with only twenty-two successes, according to a history of consolidations by Pat Hardy of the University of Tennessee's Municipal Technical Advisory Service. In the 1990s alone, there were thirteen unsuccessful referendums on consolidation.

Little wonder that many pundits keep declaring the idea dead. Yet it keeps coming up. Since 1805, when New Orleans combined with Orleans Parish, there have been thirty-three city-county consolidations, according to Hardy's research, with about two per decade since World War II and four in the 1990s. The most recent consolidation was that of Louisville, Kentucky, and Jefferson County in 2003.

Consolidation is not a panacea, but in the end structure does matter. Where would New York City be today if it were still five separately governed boroughs? Marrying political sovereigns is hard, but no consolidated government has ever divorced.

Source: Mark Funkhouser, "Cities, Counties and the Urge to Merge," *Governing,* October 2012.

There is also plain, old-fashioned community loyalty. The point has been made before about the strong tradition of local government in the United States. People identify with their local governments and tend to trust them (at least compared to state and federal governments). There is no tradition of regional government, and citizens and public officials treat these new and unknown entities with a degree of mistrust.

All this combines to make city-county consolidations a tough political undertaking, even when most objective observers agree they make a good deal of sense. Allegheny County and the city of Pittsburgh, for example, have been flirting with the issue of consolidation for more than a decade. A series of blue-ribbon panels, committees, and commissions have studied the pros and cons of an Allegheny-Pittsburgh consolidation, and they have mostly come to the same conclusion. "There's no question you could save money and provide much better service," states David O'Laughlin, who served on one such panel.[28]

There has been some progress. The city and county have managed to consolidate some operations, including 911 call centers, fingerprinting duties, and some court functions. But a full-scale merger, despite its apparent advantages, still seems a long way off. In 2006, yet another panel was formed to study city-county consolidation, and in 2008, it recommended that a merger take place. As of 2013, there was still no merger. Allegheny County and the hundreds of governments within its borders sometimes cooperate and sometimes feud, but they retain their local political independence. The bottom line is that local governments as a general rule do not want to share customers and definitely do not want to put themselves out of business.[29]

Like a good marriage, the consolidation of a city and a county depends critically on partners that trust each other and can make equal contributions to the merger. For example, Phoenix, Arizona, has won awards for its state-of-the-art management innovations. Surrounding Maricopa County, in contrast, has a reputation for management inefficiency. Good luck getting those two governments down the aisle.[30]

Despite the inherent difficulties, in the past few years there has been a renewed interest in consolidation, especially by state governments. A good deal of this interest has been driven by economic pressures stemming from the Great Recession. In Michigan, for example, there are nearly two thousand municipalities, more than a thousand fire departments, more than six hundred police departments, and a similar number of school districts. Michigan is a state that was particularly hard hit by the recession; as discussed in chapter 11, a number of its local governments fell into such precarious financial positions they were effectively taken over by the state. The massive bureaucratic duplication at the local level did not make a whole lot of sense to Governor Rick Snyder when he took office in 2011. Snyder, whose background is primarily as a business executive and venture capitalist, saw all that government as inefficient and made attempts to trim it down. While the governor cannot force local governments to merge, he can create incentives to do exactly that. He made hundreds of millions of dollars in state aid for cities contingent on the elimination of duplication in areas such as fire departments and trash collection.[31]

Similar proposals were floated around the country in the past few years as elected officials sought ways to make government cheaper and more efficient in an era of scarcity. These proposals, however, generally have met the same fate as Snyder's—they have run into strong opposition at the local level. People are all in favor of smaller government, it appears, as long as it is not their government. People are loath to give up local control and tradition and, besides, the evidence for the promised efficiencies of consolidation seem mixed (see the box "Policy in Practice: Is Merging Worth It?").

Annexation

Rather than forming new governments like Portland's Metro or merging old ones, another option for dealing with the problems of sprawl,

---

Annexation
The legal incorporation of one jurisdiction or territory into another.

traffic congestion, and uneven economic development is to make the existing political jurisdictions bigger. **Annexation** is the legal incorporation of one jurisdiction or territory into another. Usually, the jurisdiction that does the annexing is the more politically powerful, whereas the "annexee" is weaker and may not be enthusiastic about becoming the latest addition to a larger municipal neighbor. This approach is relatively common in the South and West, regions where there are large tracts of unincorporated land adjacent to major cities. Cities such as El Paso, Houston, and Phoenix have annexed hundreds of square miles and, in doing so, have turned themselves into regional governments by sheer geographical size. Oklahoma City, for example, has more than 600 square miles within its city limits, with much of that added over the years through annexations.[32]

Annexation is principally a tool used by municipalities that want to control development along their peripheries and engage in planned expansions of their tax bases. Remember that cities like to place uniform requirements on area developers, leading developers to favor unincorporated areas where land is cheaper and there are fewer regulations. One way cities can put a stop to developers avoiding regulation and impose a more coherent and orderly plan on metropolitan growth is simply to annex that unincorporated land.

A city government that wishes to annex a tract of land must organize the citizens of the unincorporated area to sign a petition. Some communities seek to expand by annexing prospectively, working to incorporate still-undeveloped parcels of land farther out from suburban parcels already being transformed from woods or farmland into subdivisions. This, in turn, may alienate rural landowners, including farmers, who value their traditional identity as separate from that of the city.[33] Annexation, in short, can create a lot of conflict, with some residents of unincorporated areas seeing it as a land grab that threatens to develop their rural communities out of existence.

Given this sort of conflict, it should not be too surprising to find that states make it tough for cities to annex new land. For example, in 1963 the California legislature created fifty-eight local agency formation commissions (LAFCOs) as boundary watchdogs to discourage annexation. Among other things, LAFCOs are supposed to discourage urban sprawl. However, because urban sprawl pretty much describes metropolitan growth in the past four decades in large parts of the state, many Californians believe that these commissions are too weak to deal with rapid suburbanization.

Annexation can make sense from a big-picture perspective in that it can help impose the orderly expansion of urban municipalities, but there is no getting around the fact that it creates losers as well as winners. And the losers often are not interested in losing at all. For example, in Ohio, townships and counties are pushing for more say over annexations, deliberately trying to limit the ability of municipalities to gobble up unincorporated land in the name of development.[34]

Annexation also has natural limits—there has to be land available to annex. Although municipalities tend to have the upper hand over sparsely populated, unincorporated territories, if they bump up against another city, it's a different story. Unlike cities in the South and West, cities in the North and East are more likely to be ringed by incorporated suburbs; in effect, core cities are fenced in by other cities, with no real option to expand. Pittsburgh, for example, covers about 58 square miles—a fraction of Oklahoma City's 600-plus square miles. Outside of a merger with Allegheny County, it is unlikely that Pittsburgh is going to grow to anywhere near the geographical size of Oklahoma City.

The Case against Reform: Public Choice and the Tiebout Model

Although metropolitan areas undoubtedly have problems, not everyone agrees that these problems require stronger regional governments. Indeed, some argue that some of the underlying problems have been exaggerated, or at least not balanced adequately against the benefits of metropolitan growth.

Backing this argument is the fact that cities are, for the most part, pretty decent places to live. Core cities have not been swirling down into a uniform death spiral of relentless flight to the suburbs, leaving poverty, racial segregation, and crime. In many MSAs, the core cities remain the economic and social hubs of their regions. Scholars and musicians, business leaders and actors—people

In June 2006, Anaheim, California, became the first major U.S. city to go wireless. Residents can subscribe to the service on a monthly basis, and visitors can purchase temporary usage capabilities.

in a wide range of fields are still more likely to be attracted to the city to pursue their opportunities and dreams than to an exurb or single-use housing tract. Core cities remain exciting places, centers of innovation and culture, shopping and business activity.

So, despite the undeniable downsides to growth patterns in metropolitan areas, there are also some positives, at least for some people. First and foremost are the quality-of-life benefits. That house in the suburbs can be a pretty darn nice house, in a pretty darn nice neighborhood. Good-quality schools are not hard to find in the suburbs, and neither are relatively crime-free developments with nice parks and maybe even a golf course nearby. This looks pretty attractive to those who have the means to take advantage of such opportunities. The same developments that often are castigated by academic critics of urban planning (or the lack thereof) can be job-generating machines.

For example, many consider Levittown in Nassau County, New York, to be the original "cookie-cutter" modern suburban housing development. Eventually totaling more than 17,000 homes, Levittown was built in an unincorporated area in the late 1940s and early 1950s. It was, literally, a community built from the ground up. First came the housing development; then public services (schools and parks) followed. Levittown served as a model for suburban growth across the United States, and what is notable about it for present purposes is that it was designed as an affordable housing development. The houses were nothing fancy—brand-new they cost less than $8,000, which even by the standards of the early 1950s was a good price for a single-family home. What they offered was not economic segregation for the moneyed class but, instead, the American Dream of homeownership for a generation of World War II veterans.[35]

And the middle and upper classes have not abandoned every neighborhood in every city. Indeed, some decaying urban areas have undergone a renaissance, with old warehouses being turned into upscale condos and downtown neighborhoods becoming the focus of thriving cultural scenes. This process of physical rehabilitation of urban areas, which attracts investment from developers and drives up property values, is known as **gentrification**. Gentrified neighborhoods do present something of a double-edged sword, however. Although gentrification clearly can resuscitate decaying areas, the rise in property values means that poorer people (the original residents) can no longer afford to live there. In essence, gentrification creates pockets of middle-class wealth within cities. These pockets may be growing. Long commutes and the falling values of suburban properties brought on by the Great Recession have made city living more attractive to younger, middle-class people. This is the demographic that started heading to the suburbs fifty or sixty years ago. We may be seeing the beginning of that demographic's return to a more urban lifestyle.

In short, there is a glass half-full perspective that sees in the cities innovation and vitality, high standards of living, and social and economic opportunities; this contrasts with a glass half-empty perspective that focuses on segregation, smog, and economic inequality. There are also strong theoretical arguments against any large-scale movement to replace multiple local jurisdictions with larger regional governance structures.

> In short, there is a glass half-full perspective that sees in the cities innovation and vitality, high standards of living, and social and economic opportunities; this contrasts with a glass half-empty perspective that focuses on segregation, smog, and economic inequality.

Gentrification
The physical rehabilitation of urban areas, which attracts investment from developers and drives up property values.

Public choice is a model of politics that views governments and public services in market terms. In the public choice model, governments are seen as producers of public services and citizens are seen as consumers. As in most markets, competition among producers is seen as a good thing. With lots of local jurisdictions, citizens can choose their favored "producers" by moving to the cities or towns that have the mixes of taxes and public services that suit them best. If local governments fail to satisfy individual citizen consumers—in other words, if their taxes go too high or their public services drop too low—the citizens can vote with their feet and move to other jurisdictions with more attractive tax–public service packages.

Multiple jurisdictions mean multiple producers, a set of competing "products" in the form of different mixes of taxes and public services. That competition keeps governments responsive to their constituents and puts pressure on the governments to be efficient and to keep the quality of public services as high as possible and taxes as low as possible. If local governments are inefficient—that is, their taxes are high and their public services are poor—they risk having their constituents move to other jurisdictions that offer better deals.

From a public choice perspective, concentrating local governments into regional governments, either through formal or informal mechanisms, risks a considerable downside. Government consolidation basically represents the creation of monopoly service providers and brings with it all the problems of monopolies that are well understood from private markets: lack of response to consumers, high costs, and indifferent quality.

This perspective on local government was most famously articulated by Charles Tiebout in the 1950s. The **Tiebout model** of local government calls for a metro area made up of a series

of micropolitical jurisdictions. If each jurisdiction can control its tax-service package, fully mobile citizens will respond to the available packages by gravitating to the one that suits them best. Or, as Tiebout put it, the mobility of citizens will provide "the local public goods counterpart to the private market's shopping trip."[36]

In addition to highly mobile citizens, the Tiebout model requires informed citizens. If people do not know what different governments are offering in the way of alternative tax-service packages they are not going to be very good local government "shoppers," and local governments may be able to take advantage of that ignorance by becoming lazy and inefficient producers of public goods and services.

If the mobility and information requirements are met, the Tiebout model makes a strong theoretical case for political fragmentation in metropolitan areas, obviously arguing against the reform perspective of pushing for government consolidation. From the Tiebout model perspective, a regional government or a merged city and county government represents a big monopoly, which is likely to produce a large, inefficient bureaucracy that is unresponsive to citizens and has little incentive to keep quality high and costs low.

The "if" on the mobility and information requirements, however, is a big one. A number of scholars have argued that citizens are neither fully mobile nor fully informed. The constraints on mobility are fairly obvious: where you can live is determined by how much money you can earn. This means the well-off, if they so choose, can be fairly mobile. The less well-off, on the other hand, are more likely to find their mobility limited by their pocketbooks. They simply cannot afford to move to better neighborhoods, even if they want to, because property prices are too high. There are some important implications here. The Tiebout model, remember, makes a good case that local governments will be responsive to people who have a real exit option, in other words, people who can pack up and move if they do not like what the local government is doing. If those people are defined by wealth, it means governments in metropolitan areas are likely to be

---

Public Choice Model
A model of politics that views governments and public services in market terms; governments are seen as producers of public services and citizens are seen as consumers.

Tiebout Model
A model of local government based on market principles wherein a metro area is made up of a series of micropolitical jurisdictions that, on the basis of their services and costs, attract or repel certain citizens.

more responsive to the concerns of the well-off than to those of the poor.

The requirement that citizens be informed also turns out to be a fairly restrictive burden on using the Tiebout model as a practical template for metropolitan governance. As it turns out, most people have only a vague notion of the details of the tax-service package offered by their own local government, let alone what the tax-service packages of neighboring local governments offer. Three political scientists, William Lyons, David Lowery, and Ruth Hoogland DeHoog, undertook one of the more comprehensive field tests of the Tiebout model in the early 1990s. They surveyed citizens who lived in what they termed "monocentric" metropolitan areas (areas where there was a consolidated city-county government) and "polycentric" metropolitan areas (places defined by a range of smaller political jurisdictions). They found there was no difference in citizens' reported satisfaction with public services in the two types of metropolitan settings, that mobility was extremely low in both settings (the probability of moving was 2.66 percent in polycentric areas and 1.32 percent in monocentric settings), and that citizens were better informed in monocentric than in polycentric settings.[37] These findings raise considerable questions about whether the Tiebout model can serve as a practical guide to governance in metropolitan areas.

In the 1990s, the Tiebout model was reworked by a group of political scientists who argued that the central idea did not require that *all* citizens be mobile and highly informed. It just required that *enough* citizens have these characteristics to force government to be responsive to their interests. The question, of course, became what sort of citizens would be motivated enough to inform themselves about local government and be willing to use that knowledge to form the basis of buying property.

The logical test case for this argument seemed to be school districts. Schools are an important consideration in real estate purchases, and if anyone was going to have the motivation to bone up on local government, it would be parents moving into a new school district. A survey of people who recently had bought homes in Suffolk County, New York,

revealed that these recent movers were more informed than longtime residents. If wealthy movers tend to be highly informed, this suggests there might be a subgroup of citizens who resemble those in the Tiebout model.[38] Whether this small subgroup is enough to create market-like pressures for efficiency on local governments, however, remains a point of contention.[39]

Regardless, the Tiebout model demonstrates that there is a theoretical case to be made for political fragmentation in metropolitan areas. Coupled with high suburban standards of living and gentrification in the core cities, there is a reasonable counterargument to the calls for more centralized government in metropolitan areas.

Rural Metropolitics

Rural governments frequently face a different set of challenges from those that confront the urban areas discussed thus far. For example, some rural counties are dealing with shrinking and aging populations, as younger people shift from rural agricultural areas to more metropolitan areas in search of educational, social, and economic opportunities.

Consider that nationwide there are roughly three hundred counties with populations under 25,000 that lost at least 10 percent of their population between 2000 and 2010.[40] At least in part, this reflects a population exodus that tracks a massive consolidation in agriculture as family farms give way to vast corporate operations. Fewer farms means fewer agricultural jobs, which means that younger people move to the cities, where the jobs are, leaving smaller rural communities with fewer shoppers, fewer schools, and fewer businesses. That is a recipe for decline that can be hard to reverse.

Rather than white flight, rural states with agriculture-based economies such as Iowa, Kansas, and Nebraska face **rural flight**, the movement of the young and the middle class to more

---

Rural Flight
The movement of youth and the middle class from rural areas to more urban areas.

urban areas. Although the underlying cause is different, the end result can be pressure for a solution that sounds familiar to any veteran of the political battles over urban growth—regional government. Iowa, for example, is a mostly rural state. It has a population of roughly 3 million and more than a thousand general-purpose governments. If special districts (schools and the like) are included, Iowa has something like one government per 1,600 residents. Most counties in Iowa do not have a lot of people; what they have is a lot of government. (See Map 12-2 for county-by-county population changes in Iowa.)

That makes government tremendously inefficient; in rural areas, there are redundant layers of government sitting on stagnant tax bases. That puts upward pressure on property taxes, and it also creates incentives to make government more efficient. Consolidating governments is one way to do this, and it is an option that increasingly is being considered in rural states. Schools are typically among the first sets of merger candidates. As student populations decrease in a rural community, it is harder to fund a comprehensive K–12 school system. If there is another community within busing distance, it can make a good deal of financial sense for the two communities to split educational services—for example, to have elementary schools in both communities, the junior high in one town, and the high school in the other.

These sorts of pressures have made for a steady stream of school district consolidations in rural states. As recently as the mid-1980s, for

MAP 12-2

Population Changes by County, Iowa, 2000–2010

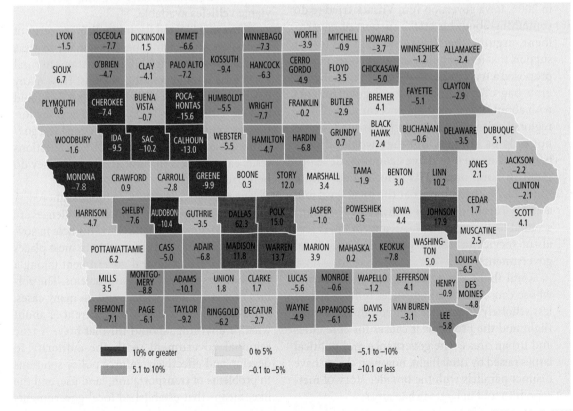

Source: U.S. Census Bureau, Population Division, Table 1, "Annual Estimates of the Resident Population for Counties of Iowa: April 1, 2000 to July 1, 2008" (CO-EST2008-01-19), release date March 19, 2009.

example, Nebraska had more than a 1,000 public school districts. As of 2012, it had 249; in a thirty-year span three-quarters of school districts in Nebraska consolidated or went out of business.[41] It is not hard to fathom the economics behind this massive contraction of governments. School consolidations make financial sense from the standpoint of the statewide taxpayer; larger districts can take advantage of economies of scale, rationalize class sizes, and lower per pupil spending. From a community perspective, however, school consolidations are less about dollars and cents than about identity, or even survival. A rural community that loses its school loses a central social and cultural institution, and the loss of teachers also means losing a significant chunk of a town's middle class. Many see the loss of a school, especially a high school, as a devastating blow to a rural community.

When economics come up against strong loyalties to local governments, the local loyalties often win, but those victories mean higher property taxes and fewer public services. Back in 2005, Iowa governor Tom Vilsack tried to do something about his state's surplus of government, arguing that Iowans simply could not support that level of public infrastructure. Vilsack proposed a truly radical solution—replacing the grab bag of hundreds of local governments with about fifteen regional governments. These regional governments, Vilsack reasoned, would not only be cheaper, but they would also be better positioned to drive economic development in rural areas. His plan landed with a thud; it got little support at the local level and a chilly reception in the legislature.[42] Iowans seemed to prefer higher taxes and/or lower levels of service to losing their traditional local governments.

Rural flight is a demographic phenomenon whose causes and consequences tend to attract less scholarly and media attention than do white flight and the problems it causes for core cities and urban areas. The governance and political issues raised by rural flight, however, clearly have distinct parallels with the broader story of metropolitics told in larger urban areas.

Conclusion

The central issue of metropolitics—and its rural equivalent—boils down to the gap that exists between local and state governments. Local governments were founded and organized in a horse-and-buggy era, and those organizational structures do not always make for a rational fit with twenty-first-century realities. This gap became particularly noticeable during the Great Recession. Dense urban concentrations, or metros, are where most economic activity in the United States is located, and this activity is integrated and interconnected across a region rather than confined within a single local government's borders. It was natural for the federal government to focus its stimulus efforts on these regional economic engines, but the relative lack of effective governance institutions at this level meant it had no local partners to work with. States and local governments, which vary wildly in their ability and willingness to integrate policy functions across jurisdictions, were the only politically viable vehicles available.

Above and beyond the immediate concerns of a recession, political fragmentation in urban areas and dispersed and shrinking populations in rural areas raise a tough set of questions: How many governments are too many? What exactly should they have the power to do? Should new institutions be created to fill the hole between local governments and state government? These questions resist easy answers in rural areas just as they do in metropolitan ones.

The questions, however, cannot be ignored. A broad array of social and economic challenges are essentially regional in nature, and the hole in government organization means that in most places there is no strong central government taking a regional perspective on these problems. The politics of metropolitan areas—and, in many cases, rural areas—boils down to differences about what, if anything, should fill that hole. A true regional government, with the authority to develop and effectively enforce policy solutions to problems of transportation, land use, and the like, means that established local governments must cede their power to this new government. In the case of consolidation, they have to, in effect, put themselves out of business. The politics involved can be contentious.

Despite the difficulties, however, the realities on the ground are pushing local governments toward regional perspectives through cooperative agreements and joint action. The social and economic challenges that are regional in nature demand that the hole in government be filled. The unanswered question is how.

The Latest Research

Local government in the United States is organized for a nineteenth-century social and economic environment, not for its twenty-first-century equivalent. As this chapter has made crystal clear, we have many local governments, often crammed into the same metropolitan area, all making decisions that affect each other and the broader region with varying levels of cooperation and coordination. While there is more or less universal agreement on these points, there is less agreement on what a twenty-first-century model of local governance should look like. Should it involve more city-county consolidation and a move to true regional governments, like Portland's Metro? Or do we want less centralization and more fragmentation, a concentrated effort to create a flexible and efficient market for public services along the lines of the Tiebout model? As the studies described below suggest, the latest research on these questions gives conflicting answers.

• •

- **Faulk, Dagney, and Georg Grassmueck.** 2012. "City-County Consolidation and Local Government Expenditures." *State and Local Government Review* 44: 196–205.

One of the central arguments for reducing the number of local governments is efficiency. Supporters say consolidation can make government more efficient and less costly by eliminating duplication of services and increasing economies of scale. This argument has taken on particular resonance during the past half decade, as cash-strapped local governments have begun dusting off old consolidation proposals and debating whether they might offer an obvious means to do more with less. Yet evidence for the promised cost savings of consolidation is pretty mixed. This study is worth noting because of its powerful comparative method research design. Faulk and Grassmueck examine two groups of cities and counties: one group consolidated, and the other considered but ultimately rejected consolidation. This allows them to make an apples-to-apples comparison of local government expenditures. The key finding of this study is actually a nonfinding: there was no difference in per capita expenditures between the consolidated and the unconsolidated groups. The authors conclude that consolidated governments might be able to produce better public services, but consolidation does not make those services any cheaper.

- **Hendrick, Rebecca, Benedict Jimenez, and Kamna Lal.** 2011. "Does Local Government Fragmentation Reduce Local Spending?" *Urban Affairs Review* 47: 467–510.

This makes for an interesting companion piece to the study just reviewed. The research team looks at local government spending in 126 metropolitan regions covering 538 counties. The key research question is

(Continued)

(Continued)

whether greater fragmentation in these regions leads to higher spending. The answer is yes . . . and no. One of the key findings is that geographical areas with more single-purpose governments have higher levels of local government spending. This seems to support the argument for consolidation; the obvious implication is that merging the responsibilities of those single governments into fewer general-purpose governments will reduce spending. Yet another key finding of this study is that areas with more centralized governments also have higher spending. The takeaway story here is that the costs and benefits of fragmentation versus centralization are not clear-cut. Neither the many governments along the lines of the Tiebout model nor the fewer governments recommended by metro advocates are one-size-fits-all solutions. The pros and cons of more versus fewer governments depend on what sorts of governments (e.g., single-purpose versus general-purpose) are involved, as well as on the political, economic, and social context.

- **Heiney, Joseph.** 2012. "Can State and Local Government Consolidation Really Save Money?" *Journal of Business and Economics Research* 10: 539–546.

    This study takes a slightly different approach to the question of whether consolidation results in more efficient government. At the heart of this research is an analysis of teacher salaries in public schools. Schools are a good target for comparative research on the pros and cons of reducing the number of governments. Many states, especially rural states, have eliminated hundreds—perhaps thousands—of small school districts in recent decades in an effort to rationalize education services. The basic argument is that it makes little economic sense for small communities to support full-service school districts that serve small and decreasing student populations. Bigger, more centralized districts, the argument goes, can do the job more efficiently for less money. This research adds a wrinkle, however, by showing that teacher salaries tend to be higher in larger

districts than in small districts. This doesn't necessarily contradict the argument for efficiency—one better-paid teacher can still be cheaper than two lower-paid teachers if they teach the same number of students. Still, as a huge proportion of education costs are wrapped up in salaries and benefits, this study suggests that any upward pressure on labor costs brought on by school consolidation needs to be accounted for in consolidation debates.

- **Bowman, Ann O'M., and Richard Kearney.** 2012. "Are U.S. Cities Losing Power and Authority? Perceptions of Local Government Actors." *Urban Affairs Review* 48: 528–546.

    This is not a study of the pros and cons of consolidation versus fragmentation, but a study of the distribution of power. As we learned from the discussion of Dillon's Rule in chapter 11, local governments are not sovereign—they wield only those powers that states allow them to have. This raises an interesting question given the focus and theme of this chapter. If there really is no functioning level of regional government between states and localities, will states take on the job themselves? Especially given the social, economic, and political stakes (all discussed above), will states leave local governments to keep going their own way, or will they start to exercise their sovereign authority and start to lessen the power of local authorities? Bowman and Kearney get at this question by surveying state and local government officials to get their perspectives on the evolution of state-local relationships. Their findings show that state officials generally see a reasonable distribution of power, with local officials given a more or less appropriate balance of authority and discretion. The authors report that the view from local officials is decidedly different: "From the perspective of city managers . . . the past decade has been one of loss of power and discretionary authority accompanied by encumbering (state) mandates in numerous policy areas." Lacking meaningful regional government structures, perhaps states are taking on that job themselves.

Chapter Review

college.cqpress.com/
sites/govstateandlocal

Key Concepts

- annexation (p. 396)
- car-dependent living (p. 385)
- city-county consolidation (p. 393)
- edgeless cities (p. 384)
- exurbs (p. 387)
- gentrification (p. 398)
- impact fees (p. 385)
- interjurisdictional agreement (IJA) (p. 391)
- leapfrog development (p. 385)
- low-density development (p. 384)
- megaregion (p. 382)
- metropolitan area (p. 382)
- metropolitan planning organization (MPO) (p. 389)
- metropolitan statistical area (MSA) (p. 382)
- public choice model (p. 399)
- reform perspective (p. 388)
- regional council (p. 389)
- rural flight (p. 400)
- smart growth (p. 390)
- sprawl (p. 384)
- Tiebout model (p. 399)
- urban growth boundary (UGB) (p. 389)
- white flight (p. 386)
- zoning laws (p. 384)

Suggested Web Sites

- **www.ampo.org.** Web site of the Association of Metropolitan Planning Organizations, the national organization for MPOs. AMPO is mainly oriented toward transportation issues, but the site includes downloadable studies and publications on a range of issues facing metropolitan areas.

- **www.metro-region.org.** Web site of Portland, Oregon's Metro, a rare example of a true regional government in the United States; includes the history of Metro's formation and information on a range of its activities.

- **www.narc.org.** Web site of the National Association of Regional Councils, an organization of metropolitan planning organizations that seeks to promote cooperation between governments; covers urban, suburban, and rural governments.

STATE STATS | State Stats on Metropolitics

Explore and compare data on the states! Go to college.cqpress.com/sites/ govstateandlocal to do these exercises.

1. This chapter discusses the large number of local governments in Allegheny County, Pennsylvania. How does Pennsylvania stack up against the rest of the country in terms of the number of elected officials? Is this surprising? Why or why not?

2. Kansas City is unique in that it is actually made up of two cities, Kansas City, Missouri, and Kansas City, Kansas. Say you live in Kansas City, Kansas, and work in Kansas City, Missouri. Should you gas up your car close to home or close to work? Why? What are the implications of this?

3. How has the number of public high schools in Nebraska changed between 2001 and 2011? Why has this change occurred?

4. New York, northern New Jersey, and portions of Pennsylvania make up the largest metropolitan statistical area in the United States. What is the average household income in these states? What might this tell us about the relationship between these states? Do we have enough information here to make this analysis?

5. One of the drawbacks of metropolitan growth is the dependence on cars that it creates. Which states have the most cars per driver? Which have the least? Why is there such a large difference?

K–12 education is one of the single largest categories of expenditure for state and local governments. That means when budgets get tight, schools suffer. The Texas legislature's plans to cut millions in school aid drew protesters young and old to the state capitol.

Education

READING, WRITING, AND REGULATION

- Why are some school systems so much stronger than others?
- Why do curricula vary so much from state to state?
- Why are there so many different brands of school reform?
- Why has the federal government increased its involvement in education, traditionally a function of local and state governments?

President Lyndon B. Johnson once called education "the answer to all our national problems."[1] There's nothing too shocking about expressing this sentiment—faith in education's power to cure a wide variety of social and economic ills has long been broadly shared by American citizens. What is notable is who was saying it: the president of the United States. Notable because, historically speaking, the federal government—let alone the president—had no role in the governance of public schools. That responsibility was almost exclusively the province of states and localities. Yet if education is going to be considered the cure for *national* problems, it is inevitably going to attract the attention—some might say the meddling—of the federal government. And it has. Johnson's administration led some of the first major federal forays into regulating public education, and successors have expanded those expeditions into this most traditional of state and local policy jurisdictions. As a result, public education has evolved into a classic example of the push and pull of federalism. Although public education systems are legally under the jurisdiction of states (all state constitutions in some fashion legally authorize these systems' existence), federal policy interests and the dollars and mandates that come with them have given the national government an ever-increasing role in governing neighborhood schools.

This increasing federal role has dismayed a number of state officials, who over the past decade or so have fought vigorously to limit the federal government's growing role in public education. Nowhere is this made clearer than in the

controversial history of the **No Child Left Behind Act (NCLB)**, a federal law that has been at the center of education policy reform debates for more than a decade. Passed in 2002 with broad bipartisan support, NCLB was the signature domestic policy program of President George W. Bush. The central goals motivating the legislation—to improve academic achievement, to eliminate gaps in educational achievement and opportunity between white and minority students, and to hold schools more accountable for student achievement—were broadly shared. The means used to achieve those goals, however, put different levels of government on a collision course. NCLB relied heavily on a mandated regime of standardized tests, set minimum standards of proficiency for passing those tests, and required schools to have all demographic groups reach that proficiency standard or risk being branded as "failing." This required states to implement expensive new curriculum and testing systems that were not always welcomed, especially when the federal government failed to live up to its promises to help cover the costs. In addition to funding squabbles and disagreements about the educational merits of "teaching to the test," a battery of critics argued that the standards set by NCLB were unrealistic and impossible to meet. Effectively, NCLB told states that all their public school students had to be above average by 2014 or the states' schools would be punished.

As that federally mandated deadline got closer, states started pushing back. In 2011 Montana superintendent of public instruction Denise Juneau said her state was fed up with NCLB and was not going to impose unrealistic and possibly harmful performance targets on its school system.

"We're not asking for permission," said Juneau. "We're just telling them we won't raise our annual objectives."[2] Idaho, South Dakota, and Utah soon followed suit. Rather than punish states for backing away from NCLB mandates, the administration of President Barack Obama began granting them waivers, essentially freeing them from NCLB requirements as long as they had plans to improve education performance. Given the criticism and the growing state-level backlash against NCLB, as of 2013 there was a general recognition that Congress needed to fix, fund, or forget the law altogether. Yet even if the last of these options is ultimately taken (which seems unlikely), it is probably impossible for states to put the federal education genie back in its bottle. States and localities will retain primacy over public education for the foreseeable future, but they will do so with the federal government as an important partner, whether they like it or not.

The NCLB controversy and the interest and involvement of all levels of government reflects the broad acceptance of President Johnson's claim that all the nation's social and economic problems have a solution in education. It wasn't always this way. Up until the twentieth century, there wasn't much of a public education system for anyone to be interested or involved in. Luckily, one intensely interested and involved person was Horace Mann, a nineteenth-century Massachusetts education chief who is widely recognized as the father of the American **common school,** which remains the basis of the American system of public education. At a time when schooling was reserved mostly for children whose families were able to afford tutors or boarding schools, Mann's common school concept represented radical reform. The one-room schoolhouses that Mann inspected as the first secretary of Massachusetts's **state board of education** were crude and ill equipped. Many of the teachers

---

No Child Left Behind Act (NCLB)
Federal law enacted in January 2002 that introduced new accountability measures for elementary and secondary schools in all states receiving federal education aid.

Common School
In a democratic society, a school in which children of all income levels attend at taxpayer expense.

State Board of Education
Top policymaking body for education in each of the fifty states, usually consisting of appointees selected by the governor.

were poorly paid and lacked training, and regular attendance by students was not required by law. Through personal advocacy and his widely circulated writings, Mann did much to build up state government as the primary actor in the fledgling experiment of public education in the United States. Mann's ideas evolved from radical reform to public education as we know it today, a system of taxpayer-funded schools governed and regulated primarily through state law.

States being states, there are big differences across education systems, in everything from funding to curricular requirements to investment in infrastructure. Yep, you guessed it—these differences make a difference. The physical state of a classroom, the salary and qualifications of the teacher running that classroom, and—despite NCLB—what a student has to do to pass that class can vary widely from state to state. There are some constants, however. All states have laws requiring all taxpayers, not just families with school-age children, to support society's bid for an educated citizenry. All states also have to live with the burden of expectations that comes with the sentiments expressed by President Johnson. Education is seen not just as a solution to all national problems but as the basis for individual social and economic opportunity. Education is thus an area of governance that brings out panic in some parents who feel that their children's entire futures are at stake with every report card. It is an area that allows ambitious political candidates to make names for themselves by vowing to hold schools more accountable and promising to get better results in the classroom from taxpayer dollars. Politicians get involved in education policymaking despite occasional resistance by professional educators, who value their autonomy and resent burdensome regulation.

The high political stakes surrounding education are not unique to the twenty-first century or to NCLB. For decades, state and federal lawmakers have been expressing concern that public education in the United States is underperforming, and that this underperformance hinders the nation's social and especially economic fortunes. In 1983 the administration of President Ronald Reagan commissioned a study of education in the United States; the resulting report, titled *A Nation at Risk,* created a firestorm with its declaration

that the mediocrity of public schools invited the defeat of the United States by a foreign power. NCLB is just one example of a near-continuous education reform effort that was sparked by that report and generally focuses on themes such as **back to basics**, new curriculum **standards**, and **high-stakes standardized testing**.

In this chapter we take an in-depth look at education policy. This perennial obsession of parents, reformers, and lawmakers, held up by presidents as the answer to all our problems, is the focus of much friction in the federalist system and is one of the primary policy responsibilities of state and local governments.

Organization and Leadership: Schools Have Many Bosses

The United States is one of the few industrialized countries with no national ministry of education. The federal government does have a cabinet-level education agency—the U.S. Department of Education—but its regulatory and funding authority is limited. The agency was created in 1978 as the fulfillment of a campaign promise by President Jimmy Carter, and its existence has been controversial ever since. Many critics, especially conservatives and Republicans, argue that education is not the federal government's policy concern and that Washington has no business sticking its large bureaucratic nose into a primary concern of the states. In 1980 Ronald Reagan campaigned on an explicit promise to abolish the Department of Education, and in 2012 Republican presidential nominee Mitt Romney campaigned on a promise to shrink the agency drastically if not kill it outright. While the department has proven remarkably

---

Back to Basics
A movement against modern education "fads" advocating a return to an emphasis on traditional core subjects such as reading, writing, and arithmetic.

Standards
In education, fixed criteria for learning that students are expected to reach in specific subjects by specific grade years.

High-Stakes Standardized Testing
Testing of elementary and secondary students in which poor results can mean either that students fail to be promoted or that the school loses its accreditation.

resistant to such plans, its survival and expansion over the past three decades has not centralized governance over education at the federal level. The primary authority for running schools remains with the fifty states. The reason education is controlled by states rather than the federal government is the Tenth Amendment, which dictates that the powers not delegated by the Constitution to the federal government are reserved to the states. In effect, that means regulatory authority over education ultimately rests with the states. The big exception to this is the District of Columbia, which technically is a federal city and not a state; its board of education derives its funds from the city's appropriation from Congress.

In contrast to the Johnny-come-lately federal government, states have been taking on the task of schooling their citizens for a very long time. For example, in 1857, Minnesota's constitution proclaimed that because the "stability of a Republican form of government depends upon the intelligence of the people, it is the duty of the legislature to establish a general and uniform system of public schools."[3] In other words, the consensus was that creating a well-educated population not only helps individual citizens prosper but also helps to entrench the democratic process. Indeed, most state constitutions justify their provisions for taxpayer-supported education systems and compulsory school attendance laws not by citing economic reasons but by arguing that democracy needs an educated citizenry to function.[4]

> Legend has it that a national education chief in Europe can look at a clock on any given weekday and know precisely which lesson is being taught in classrooms across the country at that moment.

Fifty varying traditions make for a lot of bosses in a democratic approach to education. A system that permits local innovations and variations is a far cry from the systems in use in other countries. Legend has it that a national education chief in Europe

can look at a clock on any given weekday and know precisely which lesson is being taught in classrooms across the country at that moment. This is not the case in the United States, where education systems can be very different from state to state.

Generally speaking, it is state legislatures working with state **departments of education** that are the major players dealing with state education policy questions and large-scale resource issues. A state legislature can raise teacher salaries statewide, equalize funding among districts, and set up health benefits and retirement plans for the state's pool of teachers. It can borrow money by floating state bonds to provide schools with construction funds, which commits taxpayers to long-term debts. The states are also the main players in determining **teacher licensure procedures**. For example, they determine whether or not teacher candidates must take standardized tests and how schools are awarded **accreditation**. States also set curricular standards and graduation requirements.

The more complex state decisions are proposed and implemented by an experienced educator who is the chief state school officer. Such an official may be appointed by the governor, as in Iowa, Maine, and New Jersey, or by a state board of education, as in Louisiana, Utah, and Vermont. In some states, the top school official is elected, whether on a partisan ballot, as in North Carolina and Oklahoma, or on a nonpartisan ballot, as in North Dakota and Oregon. This official works closely with the state board of education, the members of which are also appointed or elected, depending on the state. The members of a state's board usually represent all the regions of the state.

While regulatory authority over education is concentrated at the state level, the actual administration of schools is widely decentralized. Most public schools are not run directly by the state but

---

Department of Education
A state-level agency responsible for overseeing public education.

Teacher Licensure Procedures
The processes states use to qualify teacher candidates to work in school districts; requirements for licensing typically include attainment of certain academic degrees, work experience, and adequate performance on adult standardized tests.

Accreditation
A certification process in which outside experts visit a school or college to evaluate whether it is meeting minimum quality standards.

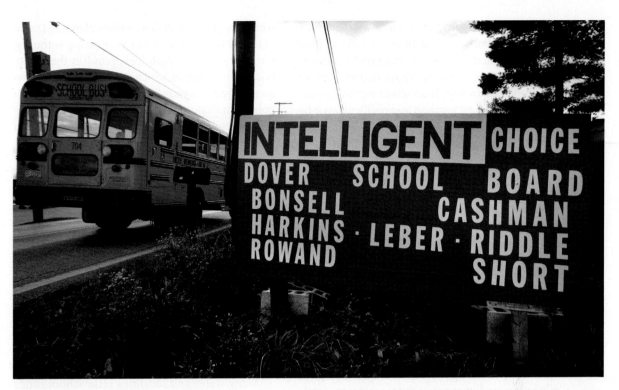

Special interests frequently target school board elections. A few years ago, the Dover (Pennsylvania) Area School Board elections were contested by one slate of candidates pledging to remove intelligent design from the curriculum and one slate of candidates pledging to keep intelligent design as a part of science classes.

by **local education agencies (LEAs)**, which have been formed in nearly 15,000 **school districts** scattered over cities, counties, and townships. School districts are staffed with full-time professionals, but they carry out policies set by **school boards** or other locally elected officials.

The extent of policymaking authority enjoyed by each LEA or district is determined by the state's legislature, and this is a difference that can make a difference. In Horace Mann's region of New England, local control is strong. In contrast, the population of states in the Deep South traditionally has been poor and rural. Many southern citizens are suspicious of government and untutored in its workings. As a result, the legislatures of these states have retained a more centralized role.

Even within states there are huge differences in economies, traditions, and demographics. Think of rural, mountainous Northern California versus densely populated, arid Southern California. Also, Northern Virginia, an affluent suburban area of Washington, D.C., that tends to favor active government, is very different from Virginia's rural areas, in which folks tend to favor limited government.

The degree of flexibility in education that states can give to localities depends greatly on scale. It also depends on how passionate local citizens are about participating in school governance. The nation's school districts are a patchwork quilt, the parts of which evolved as individually as the states themselves. Texas, for example, contains more than one thousand school districts. These vary widely, from the liberal college town of Austin to the conservative business center of Dallas. In contrast, Hawaii has one school district covering the whole state.

Local Education Agency (LEA)
A school district, which may encompass a city, a county, or a subset thereof.

School District
A local administrative jurisdiction that hires staff and reports to a school board on the management of area public schools.

School Board
An elected or appointed body that determines major policies and budgets for a school district.

School boards are quintessentially U.S. democratic institutions that got their start in the Progressive Era at the end of the nineteenth century. These citizen boards were envisioned as a way to end the spoils system. Individuals would no longer be able to show partisan and political favor by awarding school jobs to their followers. This would make way for the shared pursuit of effective public education.

Looking back now, that promise seems quaint; various groups have long targeted school board elections to further special interests rather than the public interest. In Virginia, school board elections were actually abolished in the early 1950s because southern white traditionalists feared that too many candidates were sympathetic to the then growing school desegregation movement. It was not until 1992 that elected members once again replaced appointed members. More recently, conservative Christian political activists have zeroed in on school board elections as battlegrounds for their agenda of promoting school prayer, eliminating sex education, and promoting the teaching of "intelligent design" as a curricular counterweight to science classes that teach evolution.

Some critics say school boards actually produce fewer school improvements than they do campaign bumper stickers. That is one reason they were curbed by city governments during the 1990s in Boston, Chicago, Cleveland, and Detroit, and a little later in New York.[5] Faced with stagnating test scores and an exodus of families to private or parochial schools, urban leaders argued that emergency action to arrest the decline of the schools was more important than the democracy of a thousand voices.

The idea is that a centralized authority figure, such as a mayor or school chief, is more visible and thus more accountable than low-profile school board members, who are often more worried about getting reelected than about making difficult decisions. Members appointed by an elected mayor are more likely to take decisive action and worry less about glad-handing, returning campaign favors, and seeking reelection. The jury is still out on such propositions, and proposals to abolish elected school boards tend to appear only in districts that are in dire straits.

To be fair, most school boards are genuinely focused on their responsibilities, but they often face formidable challenges. Keep in mind that by law a public school must accept all students who live within its jurisdiction. This makes planning tricky. Many school boards do not have taxing authority, but most prepare budgets for approval by the county board or city council, which must balance education spending against spending on police and fire protection and transportation. It is the board that hires the superintendent, who hires the principals, who, in turn, hire the teachers who taught you to read.

Money Matters

Public education is funded almost exclusively by state and local governments; indeed, public education is by far the largest single category of spending for these governments. Approximately 28 cents of every dollar spent by state and local governments goes to primary (K–12) education.[6] On average, states funded 46.7 percent of school budgets in 2008–2009, with 43.7 percent coming from local jurisdictions and just 9.6 percent from the federal government.[7]

Many states and localities raise school funds from income taxes and sales taxes. Twenty-seven states earmark lottery funds for education, although the budgetary impact of this often controversial revenue source is debatable. While there is no doubt lotteries can provide funds to support public schools, those moneys tend to be a modest fraction of overall education budgets. The lottery in California, for example, covers about 1 percent of that state's education spending.[8] While education is funded by a diverse revenue stream, the biggest and often most controversial source of school funds is local property taxes. These taxes are paid by homeowners and businesses based on the assessed value of their homes and businesses, usually a percentage of each $100 in assessed value.

There is logic to using property values as a basis for education funding. All taxpayers in a given community are believed to benefit from a high-quality school system—it helps maintain attractive real estate values and helps create an educated workforce. And property taxes are progressive, meaning that homeowners whose property is worth more pay more in nominal amounts, although all pay the same percentage. Most mortgage companies inconspicuously collect these tax funds for homeowners. The money is then kept in the homeowners' personal escrow accounts until the taxes are due.

The downside of property taxes is that, as property values gain in value, the assessment and corresponding property taxes also rise—irrespective of whether a homeowner's income is rising along with it. This vicious circle is what fueled passage of California's famous Proposition 13 in 1978. This statewide ballot measure capped property taxes and ignited a tax revolt in other states.

An even deeper problem with funding schools through property taxes is the fact that wealthier districts are able to keep theirs at an attractively low percentage rate and still produce enough revenue dollars to support good schools. For example, in affluent Beverly Hills, California, property was—and still is—very expensive. Yet the tax rate cited in *Serrano v. Priest* (1971), a famous school funding equity case, was only $2.38 per $100 in assessed value. Place this up against the $5.48 per $100 in the low-income Baldwin Park area. There the schools were demonstrably inferior, and the community was able to spend only half the amount that was spent in Beverly Hills. The California Supreme Court agreed that families in Baldwin Park were being denied a "fundamental right" to good-quality schools.[9] The court ordered the legislature to find a way to make school funding more equitable.

A slightly different principle was spelled out by the U.S. Supreme Court in the 1973 ruling in *San Antonio Independent School District v. Rodriguez.* In this case, attorneys for a largely Mexican American population found that their clients were paying a tax rate 25 percent higher than that paid by people in nearby affluent school districts. These less affluent districts, however, were able or willing to fund

MAP 13-1

Spending per Student, 2009–2010

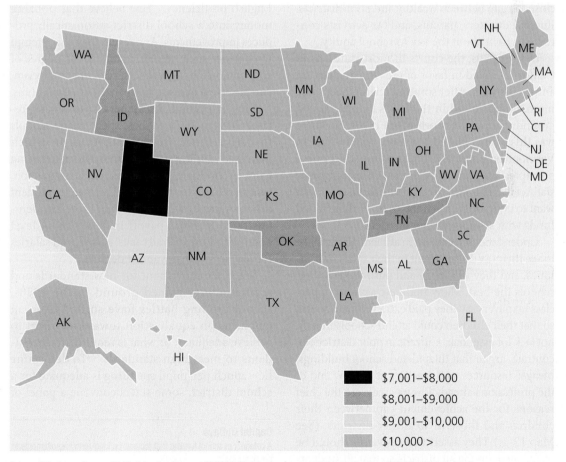

■	$7,001–$8,000
■	$8,001–$9,000
■	$9,001–$10,000
■	$10,000 >

Source: U.S. Census Bureau, "Public Education Finances: 2010," Table 11, www.census.gov/newsroom/releases/pdf/cb12-113_table11.pdf.

Wyoming has the fewest enrolled public school students (88,000 in 2008–2009). California has the most (6,177,000).

schools with only 60 percent of the amount enjoyed by wealthy San Antonio neighborhoods. Here the Supreme Court acknowledged the disparities but ruled that equal school funding is not a federal constitutional right: "The Equal Protection Clause does not require absolute equality or precisely equal advantages," the justices wrote. Despite this ruling, the precedent was set. State courts began to see themselves as protectors of poor and rural students, and the movement for school funding equity at the state level gathered more steam.

These two cases launched a decades-long period of constitutional litigation on school funding that has spread to nearly every state. It pits the principle of local control against pressures to close the gap between wealthy and poor districts. Jurists, educators, parents, and tax activists continue to fight about the key to school equity.

In the 1970s, the courts in most states, as in California, ruled in favor of greater equalization among districts. After some judicial setbacks, the momentum slowed in the 1980s before gaining ground again in the courts of the 1990s. Nowhere was this drama played out more visibly than in Vermont, where a 1997 state supreme court ruling prompted the legislature to enact the controversial Act 60. This law forces wealthier districts that want to upgrade their schools to share their added funds with schools in poor districts.

Understandably, citizens in affluent districts like to see their tax dollars spent in their own communities, and they will lobby and push to keep their schools the best. Many middle-class and upper-class taxpayers say they paid extra for their homes so that their children could attend schools that do not lack for essentials. Citizens in poor districts, by contrast, argue that dilapidated school buildings, meager resources, and teachers at the low end of the profession's already low pay scale are the chief reasons for the achievement gap between their children and those in wealthier districts. (See Map 13-1.) They assert that resources should be distributed among all districts so that all students

receive an essentially equitable level of education. Should individuals from less affluent areas be denied access to a good education? Must funneling more resources into disadvantaged communities require "penalizing" affluent communities?

Responses among state legislatures to court orders on school funding have varied. The issue has not always broken down easily along conservative-liberal lines. Indeed, the percentage of per-pupil expenditures has risen most steeply during periods of conservative ascendancy, such as the 1920s and 1950s.[10] This demonstrates the degree to which creating quality schools is a near-universal value.

Researchers examining the role that money plays in learning have created models that attempt to factor in such variables as a school's percentage of student dropouts, graduation rates, teacher salaries, and enrollment. These models also look at the percentage of children living in poverty and those in female-headed households, how many students have disabilities and how many of these have severe disabilities, and how many students possess limited English proficiency.[11] Few believe that pouring money into a school district automatically produces improvements. As a result, they also attempt to consider such human factors as the degree of cooperation among teachers, rates of absenteeism, and the extent of disruptive behavior in classrooms.

Most important, researchers try to isolate precisely how moneys are best spent inside schools to derive the most benefit. Areas in which increased funding translates into student learning gains, according to one study, include instruction, central office administration, and teacher/student ratios. Areas in which spending more has demonstrated less of a payoff include school-level administration, overall **capital outlays**, and salaries for teachers with advanced degrees.[12]

Since the movement for new standards and accountability gained ground in the 1990s, school funding battles have shifted from an emphasis on equalization toward an effort to achieve adequacy, or what is required to get students to meet high standards.[13] To determine how much per-pupil spending is adequate for a school district, some states convene a panel of

---

Capital Outlays
A category of school funding that focuses on long-term improvements to physical assets.

Policy in Practice

California's Misguided Effort to Equalize School Funding

Policymakers often look at different types of taxes and see interchangeable ways to raise revenue. Sometimes, however, the way policymakers decide to fund a program can have a dramatic impact on how the program itself works—or on whether it works at all.

One example of a well-intentioned reform gone awry is California's effort to provide equal educational funding for all students in kindergarten through twelfth grade. In 1971, the California Supreme Court ruled in *Serrano v. Priest* that the state's existing education financing scheme was unconstitutional.

The system relied on local property taxes to support local schools. There was only one problem: relying on property taxes meant that children in "property-rich" communities often attended lavishly financed schools, while children in "property-poor" communities had to make do with facilities and instruction that were often completely inadequate.

In 1977, after years of such litigation, the California legislature responded. It voted to funnel money from the state's large budget surplus to local schools. However, the legislation didn't stop there. The state also required communities that wanted to boost school spending by raising local property taxes to share the additional funds they brought in with other school districts.

In hindsight, this "district power equalization" was ill conceived. Californians no longer had any incentive to raise local property taxes to pay for education. In fact, the incentive was now to do just the opposite. Under the new system, each district received a base level of support regardless of its local tax revenue and tax rate. As a result, every district had an incentive to set its local property tax rate as low as possible. In other words, instead of raising education spending to a new higher level for most students, equalization actually may have lowered the average amount spent on education.

Some economists believe that by breaking the link between local property taxes and local school spending, the 1971 *Serrano* decision laid the groundwork for Proposition 13, which capped property taxes and banned reassessment of a house's value as long as the owner stayed in it. The result was less money for everyone.[a]

New Mexico, South Dakota, and Utah—other states that tried to equalize school funding by confiscating "extra" revenues raised by local school districts—also ended up driving school funding down rather than up. According to Harvard economist Caroline Hoxby, "It appears that some students from poor households would actually have better funded schools if their states had not attempted such complete equalization."[b]

---

[a]William Fischel, "How Judges Are Making Public Schools Worse," *City Journal,* summer 1998.

[b]Caroline Hoxby, "All School Finance Equalizations Are Not Created Equal," *Quarterly Journal of Economics* 116, no. 4 (2001): 1228.

---

experts who use their professional judgment to pick the resources needed by schools, determine the costs of acquiring these resources, and then adjust their recommendations in favor of the needier districts. Examples of such states are Maine, Oregon, and Wyoming. Other states use the **successful schools model**, wherein groups of schools whose students have done well according to state standards are examined for their average per-pupil costs, which are then applied across the state. Examples of these states are Illinois, Mississippi, and Ohio.[14]

The funding appropriated by state legislatures depends on the input expected of localities. In New York State, for example, disparities in per-pupil spending between affluent and less affluent districts can amount to thousands of dollars.[15] The amounts also vary by regional costs of living and by states' philosophies on the proper reach of government.

Successful Schools Model
An education model that uses observed spending levels in the highest-performing schools as the basis from which to calculate necessary spending in other, lower-performing schools.

MAP 13-2

Student Enrollment in Public Schools by State, 2008–2009

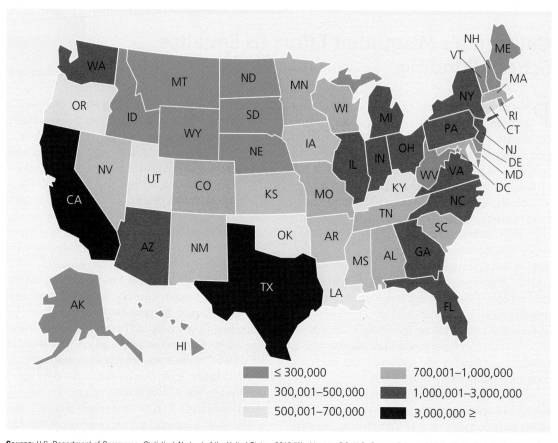

Legend	
≤ 300,000	700,001–1,000,000
300,001–500,000	1,000,001–3,000,000
500,001–700,000	3,000,000 ≥

Source: U.S. Department of Commerce, *Statistical Abstract of the United States, 2012* (Washington, DC: U.S. Census Bureau, 2012), "Table 244, Public Elementary and Secondary Schools and Enrollment—States: 2008 to 2009," www.census.gov/compendia/statab/2012/tables/12s0244.pdf.

Furthermore, affluent suburban communities often differ from their urban counterparts in funding priorities. Parents in downtown Detroit or Cleveland, for example, may want extra moneys for crime prevention and building upgrades, whereas suburbanites in places such as Bloomfield Hills, Michigan, and Shaker Heights, Ohio, want more money spent on computer technology and extracurricular programs.

Rural districts in states such as South Dakota or Wyoming have their own problems. They may have trouble raising teacher salaries, for example, if this means pushing those salaries out of line with comparable local salaries in other professions.

Looking strictly at per-pupil spending, the state offering the least in 2008–2009 (the most recent year for which comprehensive statistics are available) was Utah at $6,612. The state spending the most was New York at $17,746. The District of Columbia's total per-pupil expenditures were even higher at $19,698. School funding suffered considerably as a result of the tough economic times ushered in by the Great Recession. It is estimated that in the 2012–2013 school year, thirty-five states were spending less per student than they did in 2008. Seventeen of those states saw per-pupil expenditures drop by at least 10 percent, and three states (Arizona, Alabama, and Oklahoma) cut education spending by more than 20 percent. In contrast, only two states (Iowa and North Dakota) have increased per-pupil expenditures by more than

10 percent. Even though the recession was technically long over by 2012, revenue growth was still so stagnant in some states that they were forced to keep cutting. Even states recovered enough by 2012 to start increasing education spending could not make up for past cuts. Florida, for example, increased per-pupil spending by $273 in the 2012–2013 school year, but that wasn't even half of the $569 slashed in per-pupil spending during the previous four years.[16]

The postrecession squeeze on education spending is not just a function of flat revenue growth at the state level but also a product of federal stimulus dollars drying up (these funds were often used to shore up spending in the short term) and the reluctance of local governments to increase property taxes. This half-decade spiral in education funding has had big consequences. For example, more than 300,000 teachers have lost their jobs. The cuts have been so big for so long that some experts are now openly arguing for higher taxes to stem the losses (see the box "States under Stress: Cutting Spending versus Raising Revenue in Education").

The Pressure to Perform

Except in the minds of some nostalgists, it is doubtful there ever was a halcyon era of consensus among education's disparate stakeholders. There are far too many views about the nation's public schools for all parties ever to agree that they at some point achieved a satisfactory level of quality. Today's charge that schools are going to the proverbial hell in a handbasket also was heard throughout the 1940s and 1950s.

This charge intensified in 1957 after the Soviet Union launched its *Sputnik* satellite. Americans feared that U.S. students had fallen behind the country's Cold War rivals in science and math. Traditionalists who hearken back to the classic education taught in the early twentieth century sometimes forget that in 1900, only 6 percent of children in the United States finished high school. Back then, the best that most could count on was a solid job in, say, manufacturing. For many, college wasn't an option.[17]

> Traditionalists who hearken back to the classic education taught in the early twentieth century sometimes forget that in 1900, only 6 percent of children in the United States finished high school. Back then, the best that most could count on was a solid job in, say, manufacturing. For many, college wasn't an option.

The current crisis over performance was set in motion during the early 1980s by the Reagan administration. Education secretary Dr. Terrell Bell lit a fire under sometimes resentful educators in 1983 by publishing *A Nation at Risk*. This report ranked states by school achievement data. Today, there are continuing laments that test scores are plummeting, kids don't know U.S. history, and graduates arrive in college or in the workplace unable to write a declarative sentence.

It is true that school test scores have been stagnant for many years. It is hard to argue that a yawning achievement gap has not persisted between the preponderance of African American and Hispanic students at the lower end of the achievement scale and the frequently more affluent whites and Asian Americans near the top. Yet test scores are not locked into a downward spiral. Those who choose to see the school performance glass as half full point to the nation's ever-replenishing supply of successful entrepreneurs. Look at the country's proliferation of Nobel Prize winners, they say. Step back and admire how American corporations continue to dominate the world economy. If public education plays a foundational role in supporting the economy and promoting new knowledge, clearly America's schools are doing something right.

Yes, a large majority of respondents to the annual Gallup Poll for *Phi Delta Kappan* magazine give the nation's overall school system a grade of less than A or B. But far more assign those same grades to the

States under Stress

Cutting Spending versus Raising Revenue in Education

Since 2008 nearly three-quarters of a million public employees have lost their jobs, and more than a third of them were teachers. Under normal circumstances, the number of teachers increases each year to keep pace with an expanding student population. The past half decade has seen anything but normal circumstances; primary education has not been protected from defunding as in previous recessions. Education spending has been cut and cut again to keep state and local budgets balanced.

When the recession first hit and state revenues began their downward spiral, the federal government's stimulus package helped make up at least some of the shortfall. That ended in 2011, and the feds have been cutting back on the help they offer states ever since, with the predictable negative impact on education spending. This puts pressure not just on state governments but also on local governments, the latter being where the rubber really meets the road in education. States foot 44 percent of education spending bills, but the ultimate funders are local governments. Unfortunately, their revenues are in even deeper trouble than those of state or federal systems, largely due to their dependency on property taxes, which generated less revenue in 2012 than in 2011 thanks to falling property prices.

In the wake of a devastating burst housing bubble, it's hard to imagine any local government relishing the prospect of asking people to pay more taxes on properties that are losing value. But there is no reason sources of revenue other than property taxes cannot be tapped to support education, and there is at least some evidence that citizens might be willing to shell out more in taxes if those taxes are dedicated to education. For example, one CBS-New York Times Poll showed that a huge majority of Americans—74 percent—would not trade lower-quality schools for lower taxes.

Given that sentiment, some people, such as Yale economist Robert Schiller, have suggested it's worth asking whether states and localities might successfully pursue new revenues for education rather than reflexively focusing on cuts to balance distressed budgets. If a proposed tax increase were to be targeted specifically to hiring teachers—or, even more specifically, to preventing the kindergarten or high school English teacher who lives down the road from being let go—might taxpayers be receptive?

The general hypothesis was recently put to a test in Arizona. Of all U.S. states, Arizona recorded the single biggest reduction in education spending between 2008 and 2013—a precipitous drop of about 22 percent. In 2012 Arizona voters were asked to renew a one-cent sales tax dedicated to education funding. The initiative was overwhelmingly defeated, with 65 percent casting a no vote. However painful education cuts might be, people seem to prefer them to tax hikes.

Sources: Adapted from Penelope Lemov, "Raising Money for Education," *Governing,* September 2012.

performance of their own local schools.[18] Is it fair to blame a school for its students' performance, defenders ask, without considering each child's opportunity to learn? What about the income disparities that subject poorer kids to inferior schools—schools that, however well-intentioned their staffs, present less rigorous curricula, underqualified teachers, low expectations, insufficient resources, and disruptive climates? These students also tend to suffer from performance anxiety, negative peer influences, racial discrimination, sketchy preschool attendance, and homes in which the value of learning is not emphasized. Back and forth—the debate roars on.

Teaching to the Test

Although increasingly controversial, the main performance indicator for schools remains not grades, not responses to satisfaction surveys, not performance on oral exams, but scoring on standardized tests, an indicator that has taken on new significance in the era of NCLB. Critics bemoan the trend of "teaching to the test," which skews classroom time toward the subjects covered on the tests, often at the expense of classes such as art and music.[19]

A thriving commercial testing industry has grown up to supply schools with inexpensive, mass-produced tests for quick computerized scoring of large numbers of students from kindergarten to twelfth grade. Familiar giants in this multibillion-dollar industry include the Comprehensive Test of Basic Skills, the Iowa Test of Basic Skills, and the Stanford Achievement Test (SAT; note that this is not the SAT formerly known as the Scholastic Assessment Test, which many of you took when applying to colleges).

Each publisher has developed procedures to continually rotate questions, keep the tests statistically valid and as free as possible from cultural bias, and minimize scorekeeping errors. And all for good reason. When things go awry, the result can be lawsuits. Some of these tests are **criterion-referenced tests**, intended to measure mastery of a given subject as defined by state standards. Most, however, are **norm-referenced tests**, meaning that students are graded on how well they approach the mean student score on that same test administered across the country.[20]

A large number of states developed their own tests, and these continue to be permitted under NCLB, largely because advocates of local control mounted strong resistance to proposals made in the 1990s for a national student test. Florida has its Florida Comprehensive Assessment Test (FCAT), Virginia has its Standards of Learning, and New York has its Regents Exam. Critics still question whether these tests are properly aligned with given districts' or states' curricula and whether such tests are comparable to those used in other states.

In an effort to provide some uniformity and continuity in testing, the federal government has administered its own test since 1969—the **National Assessment of Educational Progress (NAEP)**. Nicknamed "the nation's report card," it is administered in volunteer sample districts to students in grades four and eight. Over the years, NAEP scores have remained essentially flat, with subgroups' scores rising and falling. Since the early 1990s, fourth and eighth graders have shown improvement in math but little change in reading ability. The federal government used to track twelfth graders' scores as well, but it has not released the information in recent years because fewer high schools have agreed to participate in the testing.[21]

Another key performance indicator coordinated by the U.S. Department of Education is the **Trends in International Mathematics and Science Study (TIMSS)**. Designed to compare the academic achievement of students in forty-eight countries, the 2007 TIMSS (the latest for which data are available) found, for example, that the scores for U.S. fourth and eighth graders exceeded the TIMSS averages for both math and science. Students in the United States beat out those in Italy and Australia in math but trailed students in Japan and Singapore in science. And although U.S. school reform advocates frequently point out the superior academic performance of students in many other countries as a sign of the urgent need for the United States to introduce more resources and more accountability measures, the 2007 TIMSS results showed that American students had made progress in math between 1995 and 2007. (Science scores held about constant in the same time frame.)[22]

Many of the countries that participate in TIMSS run schools that have established rigid tracks, one for college-bound elite students and one for the remainder, who normally attend vocational schools. In the United States, all students have an equal opportunity to advance, at least in theory. Most students applying to college

---

Criterion-Referenced Test
A standardized test designed to gauge a student's level of mastery of a given set of materials.

Norm-Referenced Test
A standardized test designed to measure how a student's mastery of a set of materials compares with that of a specially designed sampling of students determined to be the national "norm" for that age group.

National Assessment of Educational Progress (NAEP)
The only regularly conducted, independent survey of what a nationally representative sample of students in grades four, eight, and twelve know and can do in various subjects; known as "the nation's report card."

Trends In International Mathematics and Science Study (TIMSS)
A regularly updated study launched by the United States in 1995 that compares the performance in science and mathematics of students in forty-six countries.

endure the stomach-churning tests known as the SAT and the less widely used ACT (which is used primarily in the Midwest). Designed by the private nonprofit Educational Testing Service and run by the private nonprofit College Board, the SAT is designed to be a predictor of college achievement. The test has been renamed and recalibrated on several occasions. What began as the Scholastic Aptitude Test became the Scholastic Assessment Test and now is known simply as the SAT. Thirty years of annual scores from this test have prompted much anguish.

In the early 1980s, a study found that the average SAT scores had fallen by 81 points from 1963 to 1977—from 478 down to 429 on the verbal test and from 502 to 470 on the math test. During the 1990s and early part of the twenty-first century, however, the College Board had reason to be upbeat; in an August 2003 report, the board reported the highest level of math scores in thirty-five years. Then the College Board revised the test once again, adding a writing section and including higher-level math. In 2012, average scores on the revised test were 496 in critical reading, 514 in mathematics, and 488 in writing. Those scores had remained essentially flat since 2008.[23]

Standardized tests are not the only benchmark used to measure the performance of the education system; high school graduation rates are also widely used. Graduation rates, however, have some inherent drawbacks as a comparative measure. Historically, the states have applied a patchwork of methods for figuring these rates, and at the district or school level experts have long pointed out the temptation to calculate rates by simply subtracting the number of dropouts from the number collecting a diploma. That approach can result in misleading figures because some dropouts transfer to other schools in a **general equivalency diploma (GED) program**, get their GEDs on their own, or are incarcerated.

It is often difficult to account for these missing students because they can be hard to track down. Furthermore, states and districts have little

incentive to invest scarce resources to rectify such gaps in their accounting because the poor performance of these students can contribute to the perception of "failure" on the part of school or district. Unsurprisingly, few states spend the money required to perform longitudinal studies of the fates of such students. Some districts have even deliberately ignored these students in an effort to make their graduation rates look higher than they really are. Most famously, in 2003 city high schools in Houston, Texas, were found to be spectacularly underreporting dropout rates to appear to be performing better under the state's accountability plan. The officially reported citywide dropout rate was 1.5 percent, when in reality the rate was somewhere between 25 and 50 percent.[24]

For these reasons and others, graduation rates are not fully reliable. In 2005, the governors of all fifty states signed on to a formula proposed by the National Governors Association: divide the number of students receiving diplomas in a given year by the number of students entering ninth grade for the first time that same year. However, few states implemented the change, leading U.S. Secretary of Education Margaret Spellings to issue a regulation in October 2008 mandating that a single dropout rate formula be used across the country; despite this regulation, states continue to employ different definitions.[25] One long-used measure of the dropout rate nationally is the percentage of 16- through 24-year-olds who are not enrolled in school and have not earned a high school diploma, a GED, or an equivalent certificate. Using that definition, the dropout rate in the United States was 7.4 percent in 2010, although the rate varied considerably across demographic groups. For example, the rate among Asian Americans was 4.2 percent while that for Hispanics was 15.1 percent.[26]

Many Brands on the School Reform Shelf

It is one thing to theorize about how to improve schools and quite another to implement real-world programs that get results. Decades of promising techniques—and sometimes utopian

---

General Equivalency Diploma (GED) Program
A program offering a series of tests that an individual can take to qualify for a high school equivalency certificate or diploma.

promises—have rotated through solutions that span everything from site-based management to early-reading programs to smaller class sizes, to name just a few. No consensus has materialized, only more debate. Still, the main schools of thought on school reform can be boiled down to those addressed in the sections below.

Standards and Accountability

The standards movement first drew attention at a 1989 education summit in Charlottesville, Virginia. Attended by President George H. W. Bush and state governors, including future president Bill Clinton, the summit created a national panel to set and monitor education targets that would become Goals 2000, or the Educate America Act. That same year, the Kentucky Supreme Court struck down that state's entire education system, which prompted the enactment of the Kentucky Education Reform Act the following year. This paved the way for the standards movement nationwide.

The premise was simple. The establishment of standards requires laying out in advance what students should be able to do at each grade in each subject, aligning tests to that content, and then evaluating who reaches the standards. Without question, determining what students should know in each subject area was a task for professional associations. The National Council of Teachers of Mathematics produced the earliest standards. As momentum built in the early 1990s, the Clinton administration worked to give the movement a national framework in its reauthorization of the Elementary and Secondary Education Act, originally passed in 1965.

Site-Based Management
A movement to increase freedom for building administrators such as school principals to determine how district funds are spent at individual schools.

Standards Movement
An effort to create benchmarks of adequate learning in each subject for each grade level so that students and teachers can be evaluated on the mastery of this predetermined material.

Goals 2000
The Educate America Act, signed into law in March 1994, which provided resources to states and communities to ensure that all students could reach their full potential.

Kentucky Education Reform Act
The 1990 law passed in response to court findings of unacceptable disparities among schools in Kentucky; considered the most comprehensive state school reform act to date.

Prodding from governors and the business community produced considerable progress on the integration of a standards-based approach. Fully forty-nine states laid out standards. Iowa—the lone holdout—proudly leaves standards to local school districts. By summer 2002, forty-seven states were issuing "report cards" on student achievement. Not quite half were breaking the data down by racial subgroups, level of income, and/or limited English proficiency. Among teachers, according to an *Education Week* survey, eight in ten reported that their curricula were now more demanding. Six out of ten said their students were writing more.

The standards movement reached something of a threshold in 2009 with the beginning of a coordinated effort by states to formulate a uniform, national set of academic standards. This effort, known as the Common Core State Standards (CCSS), was backed by the National Governors Association and the Chief Council of State School Officers. The basic idea is to develop a consistent, rigorous set of standards aligned with the academic skill sets students need to get good jobs or pursue higher education opportunities.[27] The hope is that the CCSS will provide a consistent and uniform framework that will replace the often idiosyncratic academic standards and testing programs currently used by states. By 2013, forty-five states and the District of Columbia had committed to the CCSS, and standardized testing on the common core standards is set to begin in 2014–2015. Although this is a state-based and -led initiative, the effort reflects an increasing push to impose a more centralized and uniform set of achievement expectations on schools nationwide.[28]

While the standards movement has clearly matured into a force that is substantively reshaping education, it is not without its critics. The heavy focus on standardized testing that is a central component of the standards movement has been particularly controversial. There is no consensus that standardized tests truly measure learning, given that some children who perform well in written and oral and problem-solving situations do not test well, perhaps due to pressure. Plus,

---

Elementary and Secondary Education Act
Federal law passed in 1965 as part of President Johnson's Great Society initiative; steered federal funds to improve local schools, particularly those attended primarily by low-income and minority students.

many who test well forget what they memorized soon after.[29]

It is not just students who face pressure from these tests. Schools and teachers are increasingly judged on the basis of the test scores of their charges, and the pressure to keep those test scores rising or at least above set standards can be intense. There have been a number of scandals associated with teachers, schools, and school districts who have cheated to keep their numbers looking good. In 2011, a ten-month investigation by Georgia authorities revealed widespread cheating on state standardized tests in the Atlanta public schools. The report detailed a school district under intense pressure to keep test scores rising, and that pressure apparently led teachers and administrators to cheat by giving students test answers or changing responses after the tests had been handed in. Dozens of educators throughout the district admitted to such cheating.[30] Critics argue that this sort of thing is just an extreme example of a general problem that arises when too much emphasis is placed on standardized testing—it creates a set of incentives that have less to do with teaching and education and more to do with manipulating the numbers.

Recruiting Good Teachers

Research has demonstrated that the single most important factor in student learning, more important than curriculum, family income, student health, or parental involvement, is good teaching.[31] Economists have even quantified the effect, estimating that the best teachers give their students an extra year's worth of learning and perhaps increase their standardized test scores by fifty points.[32] Such gains are seen particularly with minority students, many of whom enter school socially or economically disadvantaged.

While the importance of teachers is recognized, finding qualified teachers and holding on to them can be a problem for schools. This problem is particularly pronounced in high-poverty schools, which tend to suffer from heavy staff turnover. More generally, there are notable shortages of teachers in certain subject areas, including special

education, mathematics, science, bilingual education, and technology.[33] This is in part due to the fact that teacher salaries often are too low to attract candidates who can earn more at high-tech firms and corporations. School districts must make do, then, with whomever they have to teach the necessary courses. The use of teachers by school districts, however reluctantly, to instruct in areas in which they do not hold degrees affects between 4 and 16 percent of high school students in the liberal arts, according to the Department of Education.[34]

One piece of NCLB aims at improving this record. It originally called for all teachers of core subjects to be "fully qualified," defined broadly as holding a teaching license and showing command of the subjects they teach, by the 2005–2006 school year. When the U.S. Department of Education realized that most states were unlikely to meet this deadline, it declared them compliant if they could demonstrate "good faith and effort" toward meeting the goal. All but seven passed that test.[35] A survey of states and school districts revealed, however, that few believe the NCLB requirement has significantly improved teacher quality.[36]

Colleges and universities that have schools of education are working to improve the quality of their graduates and to provide aspiring educators with more substantive knowledge and less jargon and abstract pedagogy. Many current researchers believe that teachers with the most content knowledge in their fields are most effective in raising student achievement. This suggests that the techniques of working with young people and diagnosing student impediments are best acquired on the job.[37]

Alternative licensure programs that provide appropriate training, mentoring, and testing to interested individuals now are permitted in twenty-four states and the District of Columbia. Examples of such programs include Troops to Teachers, which opens up classroom jobs to former military personnel, and Teach for America, which involves recent college graduates who want to fight poverty. Thousands of teachers enter the profession through these programs each year.

Perhaps the biggest obstacle to recruiting good, qualified teachers has already been discussed earlier in the chapter—stressed education budgets

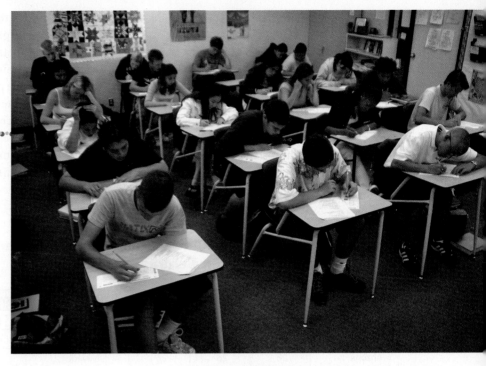

School reform efforts have brought a new focus on test scores as proof of student improvement and achievement. Standardized tests have become common nationwide, and students increasingly must pass exams to advance in grade or to graduate.

mean that tens of thousands of teachers have lost their jobs over the past few years. The benefits of hiring new well-qualified teachers are unlikely to be realized if schools do not have the money to keep the teachers they already have.

Many Schools, Few Resources

Teach for America places its newly minted teachers in urban and rural schools, a boon to districts that have difficulty recruiting and retaining high-quality instructors. On average, the salaries of teachers in rural school districts are 88 percent of the salaries of their nonrural counterparts. While rural schools do have lower crime and dropout rates than urban schools, teachers in rural districts—home to 19 percent of public school students—must also contend with the perpetual challenges of few opportunities for professional development, limited curricula, and threats of school and district consolidation.[38]

The consolidation of small rural schools has been controversial since it began back in the days of Horace Mann and his one-room schoolhouse. The practice, often pursued by states and districts in search of cost savings, picked up steam throughout the twentieth century. According to the National Center for Education Statistics (NCES; part of the U.S. Department of Education), the nation's 117,108 school districts in the 1937–1938 school year had been cut back to 13,924 by 2007–2008. During that same period, enrollment grew from 25.5 million students to 49.2 million.[39] States continue to propose consolidation plans, despite conflicting evidence of the strategy's success.[40] West Virginia closed more than three hundred schools between 1990 and 2005, and Iowa consolidated 14 percent of its districts during the same period.[41] And proposals for consolidations increased later in the decade as municipal and state budgets plunged steeply downward. Through its consolidation law, Maine has cut seventy-five school districts, resulting in hundreds of thousands of dollars in savings. Other states are eyeing yet more drastic measures. Mississippi governor Haley Barbour asked a blue-ribbon committee to develop a plan for cutting districts by one-third, and in 2009, Pennsylvania governor Edward G. Rendell recommended reducing the state's school districts from five hundred to one hundred, although his plan failed to gain traction among legislators.[42]

Backlash against further consolidation, accompanied by the continuing realization that cost savings need to be made, has some districts and states rethinking their strategies and turning, yet again, to technology. Distance learning is more than just correspondence courses; it encompasses videoconferencing and online learning modules and can vastly expand learning opportunities for both students and teachers.[43] This is not to say that computers are a panacea for all of the ills plaguing rural school districts—after all, they still have to come up with the money to invest in the technology—but proponents argue that distance learning is a strong alternative to closing schoolhouse doors.

Choosing Wisely: Alternatives to Public Schools

The issue of school choice, always guaranteed to stir up emotions, has been brought to the forefront of the education debate by NCLB. Under NCLB, schools that fail to make adequate yearly progress for two consecutive years (see Table 13-1) are deemed "in need of improvement," giving parents the right to transfer their children to another public school. NCLB has not led to a high volume of student transfers; polls show the public would rather reform the public school system from within. Alternatives such as charter schools and voucher programs excite varying levels of support.[44] Nevertheless, reformers continue to promote school choice, and increasing numbers of parents are taking

TABLE 13-1

Percentage of Schools Failing to Make Adequate Yearly Progress as Required by No Child Left Behind

State	2006–2007	2007–2008	2008–2009
Alabama	16	17	13
Alaska	34	41	43
Arizona	28	26	26
Arkansas	39	28	53
California	33	48	57
Colorado	25	40	n/a
Connecticut	32	40	41
Delaware	30	30	35
Florida	67	76	77
Georgia	18	31	14
Hawaii	35	60	64
Idaho	73	44	34
Illinois	24	31	40
Indiana	46	n/a	n/a
Iowa	9	9	**n/a**
Kansas	11	10	12
Kentucky	21	29	44
Louisiana	n/a	n/a	17
Maine	26	38	18
Maryland	23	16	n/a
Massachusetts	37	50	59
Michigan	17	20	14
Minnesota	38	49	46
Mississippi	17	14	51
Missouri	30	60	63

State	2006–2007	2007–2008	2008–2009
Montana	10	28	27
Nebraska	n/a	n/a	n/a
Nevada	31	38	41
New Hampshire	41	59	53
New Jersey	28	n/a	36
New Mexico	55	68	68
New York	n/a	n/a	n/a
North Carolina	n/a	n/a	29
North Dakota	9	36	25
Ohio	38	36	42
Oklahoma	n/a	n/a	n/a
Oregon	21	35	29
Pennsylvania	23	28	22
Rhode Island	20	26	19
South Carolina	61	82	50
South Dakota	17	n/a	19
Tennessee	16	15	22
Texas	10	14	4
Utah	25	20	13
Vermont	12	38	29
Virginia	26	26	28
Washington	35	n/a	57
West Virginia	19	20	23
Wisconsin	4	7	7
Wyoming	6	25	n/a

Source: National School Boards Association, *An Analysis of State AYP Results for 2007–08* (Alexandria, VA: National School Boards Association, 2008); National Center for Education Statistics, "State Education Reforms," http://nces.ed.gov/programs/statereform/tab1_2.asp.

Note: n/a = not applicable.

advantage of the options available. The percentage of students attending their assigned public schools fell from 80 percent in 1993 to 73 percent in 2007.[45]

Charter Schools

Entrepreneurs who want to launch their own schools with public money have been applying to run **charter schools** since the early 1990s. These schools reflect less an educational philosophy than a variation on school governance. Charter schools range in theme from Montessori to the fact-based niche curriculum called Core Knowledge to ranching to online (distance) learning. Sponsors have included former public and private school principals, parent groups, universities, social service agencies, and nonprofits such as the YMCA. By 2010, nearly five thousand charter schools had sprung up in the forty states that have enacted charter laws, with more than 1.6 million students enrolled.[46] The approach is poised for greater adoption because President Obama has made public school alternatives a cornerstone of his education reform proposals.

In principle, students who attend charter schools are given the same per-pupil expenditure as students in mainstream schools, although the founders often must scrounge to find facilities. The willingness of a state to encourage the establishment of charter schools depends on the condition of its public schools and the energies of would-be charter school founders. Some states set up special chartering boards, whereas others allow local school boards to approve the applications.

State charter laws vary widely. Arizona's loose regulations provide start-up funds, a fifteen-year authorization, and the freedom for existing private schools to convert to charter status. Kansas's strict charter law, in contrast, provides no start-up funds, allows only a three-year term before a charter school must seek a renewal, and caps the number of schools permitted.[47]

Charter Schools
Public schools, often with unique themes, managed by teachers, principals, social workers, or nonprofit groups. The charter school movement was launched in the early 1990s.

Backers see charter schools as laboratories of innovation that bypass staid bureaucracies and satisfy the parental desire for choice. Evidence of the academic achievement of charter schools is modestly favorable but not spectacular. Some have been forced to close due to corruption, such as embezzlement by administrators, or because they have failed to attract enough students or to maintain physical facilities. In one high-profile case, California's largest charter school operator announced in August 2004 that it would be closing at least sixty campuses amid an investigation into its academic and financial practices, leaving 10,000 students stranded just weeks before the start of the school year.[48] In addition, critics worry that charter schools will balkanize public education and that states may exploit them as a way to avoid dealing with unionized teachers. Some observers also fear that these schools may present administrative headaches to those school superintendents charged with monitoring them to prevent abuses of funds.

To determine whether particular charter school models should be scaled up and duplicated throughout the country, researchers do not just want to know whether a charter's own students' test scores improve. They also want to know if the schools these children's families chose to leave are using the departures as an incentive to do better.[49] To that end, studies have been carried out. Advocates of charter schools, including the George W. Bush administration, suffered a blow in August 2006 when a long-awaited study of test scores by the U.S. Department of Education revealed that fourth graders in charter schools scored significantly lower than their peers in traditional public schools.[50] (See Table 13-2.)

But there are also plenty of individual charter school success stories. Especially in some larger urban areas, charters schools have become a common and desirable alternative to traditional public schools. In 2010, 99 of the 181 public schools in Washington, D.C., were charter schools, and students in D.C.'s charter schools have scored comparatively well on standardized tests.[51]

Some studies suggest that tracking students over time might provide additional favorable findings. Tom Loveless, director of the Brown Center on Education Policy at the Brookings Institution, conducted a two-year study of 569 charter schools

TABLE 13-2

Charter School Scores

| | Percentage of Fourth Graders at or above Basic Level in . . . | | | |
| | Math | | Reading | |
	Charter Schools	Other Public Schools	Charter Schools	Other Public Schools
Gender				
Male	69	77	55	58
Female	68	75	60	65
Race				
White	84	87	73	74
Black	51	54	37	39
Hispanic	58	62	45	43
Income				
Eligible for public lunch	53	62	39	45
Not eligible	81	88	72	76
Location				
Central city	58	67	50	51
Non–central city	79	80	66	66

Source: U.S. Department of Education, Institute of Education Sciences, National Center for Education Statistics, National Assessment of Educational Progress (NAEP), 2003 Reading Charter School Pilot Study, December 2004.

in ten states. He found that, although charter school students do score lower on state tests, over time they progress faster than students in traditional public schools. Other proponents believe that students in charter schools also score lower initially, in part, because they were further behind to begin with in their previous, traditional schools.[52] A comparison study by Stanford University researchers of charter and traditional public schools in fifteen states and Washington, D.C., found that charter school students in poverty and English-language learners earned higher scores than their traditional school counterparts. Across all students, however, 37 percent of charter schools fared worse than the traditional schools.[53]

Vouchers

Considered a more radical reform than charter schools, school vouchers have been proposed in some form since the 1950s. The idea of school voucher programs is to mimic government grants used in higher education by giving interested families set amounts of public money that they can use to enroll their children at any accredited school: public, private, or parochial (religious). Voucher enthusiasts emphasize that voucher programs provide parents with more choice and serve to break up the "monopoly" of the public education bureaucracy to boost competition. More recently, many have advanced the argument that vouchers serve a civil rights function in that they can rescue low-income black families from failing schools in low-income neighborhoods.

Opponents worry that vouchers spell the beginning of the end of society-wide efforts to maintain and improve universal public education. They note that private schools can be selective about which students they accept. In addition, the proposed amounts for vouchers are often less than half of actual tuition charges at many schools. In some communities, the number of available slots at area private schools is insufficient for the number of interested applicants. Voucher proponents aren't without counterarguments, however. They assert that the programs create competition that forces public schools to improve and that they give lower-income students opportunities they might not otherwise have.[54]

Critics also object to the widespread participation of religious schools in voucher programs. Many are uncomfortable with the idea that through vouchers taxpayer funds go to institutions that support the inculcation of particular sets of religious beliefs. Despite these concerns, in June 2002, the U.S. Supreme Court ruled that vouchers can go to a religious school as long as the school's chief purpose is education—in other words, a school that offers a comprehensive secular curriculum, albeit with religious rituals and instructors, as opposed to a Sunday school or Bible study school.

Despite the Supreme Court ruling that vouchers can be used to fund parochial school tuitions, concerns about taxpayer money being funneled to religious institutions is likely a central reason for the failure of voucher programs to gain much traction on state ballot initiatives. Such proposals

---

School Voucher Movement
Movement dating to the 1950s to allow taxpayer dollars to be given to families to use at whatever public, private, or parochial schools they choose.

Charter schools have grown across the country as alternatives to traditional public schools. President Barack Obama has made school competition, including the encouragement of charter schools, a hallmark of his proposals to reform the No Child Left Behind Act and the nation's education system.

were defeated in Michigan and California in 2000 and in Utah in 2007.[55] Opponents of a 2012 Florida initiative to repeal that state's ban on using public dollars to purchase services from religious service providers argued that the initiative was paving the way for a private school voucher system. That amendment also failed. And while the U.S. Supreme Court has ruled that voucher programs do not necessarily violate the U.S. Constitution, that does not mean such programs are allowable under all state constitutions. In 2006, the Florida Supreme Court struck down the state's voucher program, a key part of then governor Jeb Bush's education plan, as unconstitutional. Efforts to reinstate part of the program at the ballot box in 2008 failed when the court rejected the questions due to technicalities.[56]

Despite mixed political support, some voucher programs have been in place for decades. Probably the two best known are programs that, at least initially, were aimed at long-troubled and racially isolated schools in Cleveland, Ohio, and Milwaukee, Wisconsin. Cleveland's voucher program, which served 5,800 students during the 2005–2006 school year, was folded into Ohio EdChoice. This statewide voucher program offers up to 60,000 renewable scholarships to students attending schools considered in "academic emergency" or on "academic watch," the state's two lowest rankings for school performance.[57]

Milwaukee's program offers vouchers worth up to $6,500 to low-income families, who may send their children to any of 112 participating private schools. The program included only secular schools when it started, but in 1995 it expanded to include parochial schools, a measure protected by the 2002 Supreme Court ruling. By 2006, religiously affiliated schools constituted about 70 percent of the participating schools. In 2006, Wisconsin governor Jim Doyle signed a bill to raise the number of vouchers issued annually from 15,000 to 22,500 in exchange for increased accountability on the part of schools accepting vouchers, including standardized testing and accreditation.[58]

Whether students who use vouchers experience achievement gains is a matter of fairly intense debate. Dozens—likely hundreds—of studies have produced mixed evidence. Studies backed by advocacy groups, unsurprisingly, have found significant gains for voucher students.[59] More academic studies have a much more mixed record, with some showing significant gains and other showing no impact. A recent study of the Milwaukee school choice program, for example, shows voucher students have slightly higher reading test scores than comparable nonvoucher students, but no differences in math test scores are found between these groups.[60] More generally, studies by the U.S. Department of Education and by University of Illinois researchers have found that public and private school students perform similarly when test scores are adjusted for race and other factors, and a congressionally requested study by the U.S. General Accounting Office (GAO; now the Government Accountability Office) of the Milwaukee and Cleveland experiments "found little or no difference in voucher and public school students' performance" in the schools of those two cities.[61]

Homeschooling

A major school reform movement gaining popularity is **homeschooling**. In 1999, according to a survey by the U.S. Department of Education, an estimated 850,000 students were being taught at home. By 2007, that number had jumped by 29 percent, to more than 1.5 million, according to the NCES.[62]

Homeschooling champions have organized a legal defense network and a lobbying effort. As the movement has grown, homeschooling parents have organized sports leagues, field trips, proms, and graduation ceremonies. And there are plenty of homeschooling success stories, including Harvard acceptances and solid scores on standardized tests.

Homeschooling advocates are a diverse group, but the two main strands are fundamentalist Christians and "free-school" advocates who favor more student choice of subject matter. Parents who can make the time to homeschool like the security and personal imprint they can leave on their youngsters. An NCES study found that 30 percent of homeschooling parents surveyed wanted the flexibility to teach their children moral or religious lessons. Another 31 percent cited concerns about the environment of traditional schools.[63]

Of course, throughout the history of this country, there always have been those who have chosen to teach their children at home. The modern homeschooling movement, however, really started taking off in the 1980s. State governments have accommodated homeschoolers to varying degrees. Some require a parent to have a bachelor's degree to homeschool. Others require parents to submit their curricula for approval, and still others give parents the choice of giving their children standardized tests selected by the school district or hiring their own qualified evaluators.

Michael Farris, cofounder of the Home School Legal Defense Association, based in Purcellville, Virginia, has been at the forefront of the national movement. His organization ranks states based on how tightly or loosely they regulate homeschooling. States with no requirements for homeschoolers to notify state authorities include Idaho, Michigan, and Texas. States with low regulation include Alabama, Kentucky, and Mississippi. Most other states in the Southeast moderately regulate homeschooling, whereas most states in New England regulate more intensively.[64]

Critics fear that homeschooled students miss important opportunities for social development and that many parents are not qualified to teach. They also worry that some homeschooling parents isolate their children and instill in them religious prejudice. Some state and local officials consider homeschooling an inconvenience. It forces them to come up with policies on home visits, gauge assessments that may be out of sync with conventional report-card grades, and wrestle with dilemmas such as whether a homeschooled student can play in the public high school band.

Can't Tell the Players without a Program: Groups That Influence Public Education

When the Texas Supreme Court struck down school funding disparities in *Edgewood Independent School District v. Kirby* (1989), it declined to specify a precise solution to the problem. Instead,

---

Homeschooling
The education of children in the home; a movement to grant waivers from state truancy laws to permit parents to teach their own children.

it opted to launch a dialogue with legislators and education officials. In Kentucky, the state supreme court was even more an activist—it declared the state's school system unconstitutional and not adequate as "an efficient system of public schools." The court went on to lay out a set of goals and ability standards to be pursued.[65]

In both cases, the courts knew that no legal ruling on the subject of education would hold sway without public support and buy-in from key stakeholders. That meant going far beyond a small elite of education officials. In Texas, for example, the Mexican American Legal Defense and Educational Fund (MALDEF) played an influential role in developing and supporting the state's new education reforms.

In Kentucky, the legislation and landmark school reform program that resulted from the state court's ruling gained ground largely because of support from such players as newspaper editorialists and a group of education and business leaders called the Prichard Committee for Academic Excellence. Such groups as these are common participants in the educational debate and are part of the following roster of familiar players in the education dramas that unfold across the country.

Teachers' Unions

For decades, the major **teachers' unions** have been the National Education Association (NEA), which boasts 3.2 million members, and the American Federation of Teachers (AFT), which reported more than 1.5 million members as of 2012.[66] These groups organize employees from the preschool level to the K–12 level to the university level to form state and local affiliates. They engage in collective bargaining, lobby for resources, and seek to upgrade teacher professionalism through training and publications.

For years these two unions, both headquartered in Washington, D.C., have flirted with a merger, but style differences always intervene. The AFT

was quicker than the NEA to join the school reform parade, for example, by participating in the creation of standards and charter schools. By the late 1990s, however, both had turned sour on the school choice movement, which they consider a threat to public education and their members' livelihoods. They have been critical, too, of NCLB, with the NEA leading the charge in lawsuits challenging the federal government's administration of the law. Both unions align themselves with the Democratic Party, one reason most Republicans blame them for obstructing school reform.

Parents' Groups

The **National PTA**, with 5 million members, bills itself as the "largest volunteer child advocacy organization in the United States."[67] For decades, this umbrella group for local parent-teacher associations and organizations was stereotyped as a klatch of moms putting on bake sales. Today, however, the PTA has school-based state and national organizations that combine to form a sophisticated lobbying and policy force. For the most part, the organization works to boost parent involvement and to encourage parent-teacher cooperation.

The National PTA has strict rules about remaining nonpartisan. Despite this, local PTAs' occasional endorsements of state legislative candidates based on school funding commitments have gotten some in hot water. Other parent groups have emerged over the years to focus on narrower school-related issues, such as the school desegregation efforts of the Mississippi-based Parents for Public Schools.

National Political Parties

For much of the latter part of the twentieth century, education was Democratic Party turf, mostly because of the Great Society legislation pushed through in the mid-1960s. The Democrats traditionally wanted to expand government spending to close the gap between affluent and low-income

---

Teachers' Unions
Public-sector unions that organize employees at all educational levels to form state and local affiliates. In the United States, the two major teachers' unions are the National Education Association and the American Federation of Teachers, both headquartered in Washington, D.C.

National PTA
Umbrella organization founded in 1897 consisting of state-based and school-based parent-teacher associations of volunteers who work to improve and support schools.

schools. Republicans, on the other hand, emphasized local control and social issues, such as efforts to overturn the ban on school prayer. During the Reagan administration, Republicans vowed to abolish the federal Department of Education set up by President Jimmy Carter. Many of them opposed proposals made during the mid-1990s to introduce a national standardized test. They based their protests on the need to preserve local control of schools.

By 2000, however, Texas governor George W. Bush moved the Republicans dramatically to the center of the education debate while campaigning for the Oval Office. His eventual victory in enacting NCLB, which is modeled in part on the system used since the early 1990s in Texas and borrows its name from the liberal Children's Defense Fund, was attributable to support from key Democratic lawmakers. President Bush's brother, former Florida governor Jeb Bush, is another Republican who has spearheaded important education reforms that have become part of the national debate about public schooling. Jeb Bush has championed grading schools on the basis of student performance on standardized tests, establishing mandatory grade standards, instituting merit pay for teachers, and pushing alternatives to traditional public schools, not just charters and vouchers but also online "virtual" schools.[68]

> Republicans' efforts to woo Democrats to their side on the more controversial proposals for school vouchers have been less successful, due to the strong support that Democrats depend on from antivoucher teachers' unions and the Democrats' general skepticism about market-based alternatives to government programs.

While Republicans' efforts in some areas have resulted in bipartisan agreement, their efforts to woo Democrats to their side on the more controversial proposals for school vouchers have been less successful, due to the strong support that Democrats depend on from antivoucher teachers' unions and the Democrats' general skepticism about market-based alternatives to government programs.

Business Groups

Corporations and small businesses have been among the most vocal in pushing for school reform. They cite what they perceive as a decline in the writing and math skills of young job applicants as industry has become more complex technologically. Business leaders, such as former Intel chairman Craig Barrett, have joined with business groups, such as the Business Roundtable and the National Alliance of Business, to meet with governors, educators, and school reform activists to press for higher standards for students and teachers. The Business Coalition for Student Achievement, led by the Business Roundtable and the U.S. Chamber of Commerce, has issued recommendations to improve NCLB, including a call to improve teacher quality, to focus on college and workplace readiness, and to strengthen science, math, and technology curricula.[69] Through his foundation, Microsoft chairman Bill Gates has been active in promoting a wide range of education reforms, including supporting the Common Core State Standards projects.

Professional and Advocacy Groups

Within the education "establishment," each of the managerial groups—administrators, principals at the elementary and secondary levels, and school boards—has its own association. The official decision makers in these groups usually win their jobs through a prerequisite set of academic credentials, years of experience in the classroom, and dues paid on the front lines of management.

Also influencing public education are research groups such as the Education Trust, which is based in Washington, D.C., and performs research to encourage those in higher education to help with elementary and secondary school reforms. And there are the advocacy groups, such as the Center for Education Reform, which promotes school choice, and the Public Education Network, which organizes local funds to improve public engagement in school reform.

Conclusion

Although each state has its own internal time line for success, NCLB, as envisioned and enacted under the Bush administration, required that all schools bring every single student to proficiency by the 2013–2014 school year. That bold, bipartisan vision is unlikely to be realized. While most shared the goal of educational improvement, there were always mixed opinions at the state level, not just about the realism and feasibility of NCLB but also about the expanded role of the federal government in this most traditional of state policy arenas. President Barack Obama has started granting waivers to states to release them from the mandates of NCLB, but it is a safe bet that those debating school performance, accountability, and funding, as well as teacher quality, will continue to invoke, with passion, lofty themes of democracy and civic ideals. Efforts to strengthen the federal role in public education will continue to run up against the centuries-old tradition of local control. Advocates of increased funding targeting the poor will still lock horns with those who stress reforms in pedagogy and new incentives.

If Horace Mann is watching from school reformers' heaven, he probably isn't surprised that the ancient debates over school reforms remain unsettled. The governance of the U.S. public education system is rooted in local control and wide variations in state and community traditions. This guarantees that it always will be characterized by diverse approaches and active political maneuvering. The quest for the ideal school continues to be more art than science. The results? They are as glorious—and as messy—as democracy itself.

The Latest Research

Education is such a sprawling, perennially high-profile topic that it should come as no surprise that a very large research industry is devoted to examining its every dimension and nuance. Many political scientists, economists, and sociologists study education issues, as do many more researchers from exclusively education-based disciplines such as educational psychology, and this is not to mention the large number of scholars in university teaching colleges and departments who not only train educators but also conduct studies on everything from curricular development to best practices in educational administration. Entire academic journals are devoted to research in education (e.g., *American Journal of Education, American Educational Research Journal*). Given this, it is all but impossible for us to summarize here anything but a narrow slice of the latest education research.

That said, one of the more interesting developments in the latest research is the current direction of debates over the effectiveness of the market-based reforms that have provided much of the intellectual firepower behind the standards and accountability movement discussed in this chapter. These reforms—most of which are discussed above—include such things as the strong focus on standardized testing and the introduction of competition through charters schools and vouchers. For more than twenty years, dueling studies have claimed to provide evidence to support or contradict the efficacy of such reforms. While a lot of that continues, over the past half decade or so scholars have been increasingly

(Continued)

(Continued)

paying attention to what the mixed messages of all this research mean. Does the inconsistent message on the efficacy of these reforms, or the lack thereof, mean that the evidence on the impacts is not clear, even though some of the reforms have been in place for decades? Does it mean that the studies are, consciously or unconsciously, being conducted to serve political agendas rather than to get at objective assessments of what works and what does not? Are the studies' results simply being cherry-picked by key players in the reform debate who ignore contradicting evidence and the often careful caveats that study authors place on the interpretation of their findings? Given the high stakes involved for state governments, which have often invested heavily in these reforms, these are important questions. Below we discuss some representative research looking hard for answers, especially in trying to understand the actual payoffs of charter schools, which have been touted in many states and on both sides of the aisle in the federal government as effective alternatives to traditional public schools.

• •

- **Ravitch, Diane.** *The Death and Life of the Great American School System.* New York: Basic Books, 2010.

   Any discussion of the hard questions being asked about the market-based reform movement and the research that supports it has to include this book. Ravitch is an education historian and policy scholar at New York University and a former assistant U.S. secretary of education. She was initially a supporter of many of the reforms championed by charter and voucher advocates and an early backer of NCLB. However, she has come to question the evidence supporting the effectiveness of such reforms, and this book lays out her case. Long respected by all sides of the reform debate, Ravitch shocked many with this book, which presents strong criticisms of the reforms she once championed.

- **Henig, Jeffrey.** *Spin Cycle: How Research Is Used in Policy Debates, the Case of Charter Schools.* New York: Russell Sage Foundation/Century Foundation, 2009.

Henig is one of the most widely known political scientists studying education policy. This book, which won the American Educational Research Association's Outstanding Book Award, is an in-depth examination of how social science research is used in the often contentious debates surrounding school choice. Henig argues that although research is often used as partisan ammunition for one side or the other, the people who actually do this research tend to have much less entrenched viewpoints and recognize the significance of findings contrary to their own. In the case of charter schools, Henig suggests that the research actually points toward consensus on some key issues: charter schools do not significantly boost achievement, and they do not help create a competitive educational marketplace, but, on the other hand, they do not promote racial segregation and they do seem to increase levels of school satisfaction among parents and students.

- **Betts, Julian R., and Richard C. Atkinson.** 2012. "Better Research Needed on the Impact of Charter Schools." *Science* 335: 171–172.

   This article, published in one of the premier academic research journals, is coauthored by an economist and a former director of the National Science Foundation. Betts and Atkinson argue that although the past two presidential administrations have been enthusiastic supporters of charter schools, the evidence backing that advocacy is thin. They suggest that most studies of charter schools suffer from a range of methodological and sampling problems that make it hard to generalize the results, let alone use those results to reach a consensus on the efficacy of such schools. Betts and Atkinson argue that more randomized field trials—studies in which students are essentially assigned to traditional public or charter schools by lottery—are needed to produce better scientific evidence on the pros and cons of charter schools. They also call on states to make it easier for researchers to access student-level data on test scores. Without access to good data, they argue, researchers cannot arrive at valid and reliable estimates of reform impacts.

- **Imberman, Scott.** 2011. "Achievement and Behavior in Charter Schools: Drawing a More Complete Picture." *Review of Economics and Statistics* 93: 416–435.

  This article reports on a study of the impact of charter schools that is notable for the particularly rich data set employed. It compares student outcome measures from charter and noncharter schools not just on academics—math, reading, and language—but also on a long list of behavioral outcomes, such as attendance rates, substance abuse, and disciplinary infractions. Imberman examined data on dozens of schools from 1994 to 2007, as well as hundreds of thousands of observations from individual students—a very strong foundation for empirical analysis. Imberman's findings? Charter schools do not seem to improve test scores much, but they do seem to have a positive behavioral impact, promoting increased attendance and better student discipline.

college.cqpress.com/
sites/govstateandlocal

Chapter Review

Key Concepts

- accreditation (p. 412)
- back to basics (p. 411)
- capital outlays (p. 416)
- charter schools (p. 427)
- common school (p. 410)
- criterion-referenced test (p. 421)
- department of education (p. 412)
- Elementary and Secondary Education Act (p. 423)
- general equivalency diploma (GED) program (p. 422)
- Goals 2000 (p. 423)
- high-stakes standardized testing (p. 411)
- homeschooling (p. 430)
- Kentucky Education Reform Act (p. 423)
- local education agency (LEA) (p. 413)

- National Assessment of Educational Progress (NAEP) (p. 421)
- National PTA (p. 431)
- No Child Left Behind Act (NCLB) (p. 410)
- norm-referenced test (p. 421)
- school board (p. 413)
- school district (p. 413)
- school voucher movement (p. 428)
- site-based management (p. 423)
- standards (p. 411)
- standards movement (p. 423)
- state board of education (p. 410)
- successful schools model (p. 417)
- teacher licensure procedures (p. 412)
- teachers' unions (p. 431)
- Trends in International Mathematics and Science Study (TIMSS) (p. 421)

Suggested Web Sites

- **http://nationsreportcard.gov**. Web site of the National Assessment of Educational Progress, the program that administers standardized tests to all fourth and eighth graders across the United States.

- **www.aasa.org.** Web site of the American Association of School Administrators. Founded in 1865, AASA has more than 13,000 members worldwide. Its mission is to support and develop individuals dedicated to the highest-quality public education for all children.

- **www.aft.org.** Web site of the American Federation of Teachers, which represents the economic, social, and professional interests of classroom teachers. The AFT has more than 3,000 local affiliates nationwide, 43 state affiliates, and more than 1.3 million members.

- **www.cep-dc.org.** Web site of the Center on Education Policy, a national independent advocate for more effective public schools.

- **www.ed.gov.** Web site of the U.S. Department of Education, which oversees the federal government's contributions to public education.

- **www.edexcellence.net.** Web site of the Thomas B. Fordham Foundation, whose mission is to advance the understanding and acceptance of effective reform strategies in primary and secondary education.

- **www.edreform.com.** Web site of the Center for Education Reform, a national organization dedicated to the promotion of more choices in education and more rigorous education programs.

- **www.edweek.org.** Web site of *Education Week,* a weekly publication devoted to primary and secondary education and funded by Editorial Projects in Education. *Education Week* publishes *Quality Counts,* an annual evaluation of K–12 education in all fifty states.

- **www.nea.org.** Web site of the National Education Association, which is dedicated to advancing public education. The organization has 2.8 million members at every level of education, from preschool to university graduate programs, and affiliates in every state, as well as in more than 13,000 local communities across the United States.

- **www.nsba.org.** Web site of the National School Boards Association, a not-for-profit federation of state associations of school boards across the United States.

State Stats on Education

Explore and compare data on the states! Go to college.cqpress.com/sites/govstateandlocal to do these exercises.

1. How has the per capita amount of revenue that states receive from the federal government changed from 2000 to 2010? What accounts for this change?

2. How did the average public school eighth grade math scores change in Montana from 2005 to 2007? What about from 2007 to 2011? Do you think that the state's exemption from NCLB will change this trend?

3. In 2001, which state had the highest average SAT score? Which had the lowest? What are some of the variables that might cause this difference?

4. For the most recent year available, which state has the largest percent of their schools operating as charter schools? Which has the smallest? Why is there such a difference?

5. In 2000, what was the national average salary for a public elementary or secondary school teacher straight out of college? How does your state compare? Is this enough? Why or why not?

Three strikes and you're . . . in. Mandatory sentencing laws and other reforms designed to stem crime have led to increased prison populations. In California, prison costs have contributed to billions of dollars in budget shortfalls, and the state has been ordered by the courts to reduce overcrowding in its facilities, such as California State Prison in Los Angeles.

ch. 14

Crime and Punishment

- Why did different types of policing develop in the United States?
- Why has creative problem solving become so important to law enforcement?
- How does political culture affect law enforcement in the different states and localities?

It has been one of the biggest public policy successes of the past generation—but no one is exactly sure why. Violent crime has plunged since the frightening rates of twenty years ago, but the reasons for this success are still unclear. State and local governments have tried all manner of ways to fight crime, including tougher and longer sentencing, putting more cops on the beat, and changing the way members of the police and sheriffs' departments go about their daily business. But it's not clear which of these changes—in combination with broader demographic shifts—is most responsible for the drop in crime.

Contrary to some expectations, crime hasn't ticked back up in recent years, despite recession and serious budget and personnel cuts in many law enforcement agencies. There were only 414 homicides in New York City in 2012—still a substantial number, but nearly 20 percent lower than the figure reached in the previous year, lower than the number of suicides in the city, and the lowest number since 1963. In the early 1990s, annual murder totals of more than 2,000 were common in the city. The number of crimes overall in the city was up slightly in 2012, but that increase was wholly attributable to 3,890 incidents of theft of iPhones and other Apple products.[1]

New York is now considered one of the safest big cities in the world, but its success in curbing the murder rate is not unique. In 1990 alone, 23,438 people were murdered in the United States. By 2008, that number had fallen to 16,272—and this after a period in which the population of the country as a whole grew by 55 million people.[2] Crime in general dropped in 2012 for the country as a whole for the fifth consecutive year. The last time the rates of serious crimes—murder, rape, robbery, and assault—were at such low levels, 50 years earlier, gasoline cost 29 cents a gallon and the average working American earned $5,807 a year.[3]

At the same time that crime is dropping, however, prisons are overflowing. Double- and triple-bunking has gotten so bad in some state prisons that courts have ordered the states to release prisoners simply to reduce overcrowding. Some states now spend more on corrections than they do on higher education. As a result, many state legislators, motivated not only by humanitarian concerns but also by concerns about costs, have for the first time in a generation put serious thought and significant dollars into **reentry programs**. These programs are designed to help ex-felons stay out of prison following release by providing them with help such as drug treatment and job training. Some 95 percent of prisoners, after all, will return to their home communities at some point after their incarceration ends.

Some are appalled that one out of every 100 American adults is in prison, and that prison populations include disproportionately high numbers of African Americans and Hispanics. But many criminologists credit the nation's high incarceration rate with the reduction of the crime rate, along with numerous other factors, such as the changing nature of the drug market, the aging of the U.S. population, and even improved trauma procedures in hospital emergency rooms and legalized abortion.[4] In other words, the police don't deserve all or perhaps even much of the credit. "The bottom line is that one can't really give a lot of credence to the strong statement about the police having a huge *independent* role in reducing crime, particularly homicide," according to University of Cincinnati criminologist John Eck.[5]

Other researchers, however, do credit the crime reduction to a revolution in policing. There have been enormous changes over the past dozen years in the technologies, methods, and priorities applied in policing. Many criminologists believe that further reductions in crime are possible as more and more police departments adopt new methods, which are continuing to evolve. And, given that the vast majority of law enforcement officers work not for the FBI but for municipal police departments, county sheriffs' offices, and state law enforcement agencies, it's possible to credit state and local governments with the improvements that have been made in public safety.

This chapter is about the U.S. criminal justice system, which for most Americans translates to their local police departments and their state prison systems. It explores not just how the system works but also whether it works. Can police reduce crime? Do tougher penalties and longer jail terms deter criminals? Do Americans as a society have or want to have a penal system that emphasizes punishment? Or do we want a system that stresses rehabilitation?

Gangs, guns, murder, drugs, and hard time are just some of what this chapter examines. This exploration of the criminal justice system also offers an opportunity to investigate our society's most basic values. After all, crime is about the transgression of a society's ethical norms, and punishment is about the enforced adherence to them. Understanding how a society disciplines itself and punishes people also provides insights into the nature and limits of state power, into the society's conception of justice, and, ultimately, into the nature of democracy itself.

Private Wrongs, Public Justice

Americans are fascinated with crime. Books about private eyes, criminals, and the courts regularly

---

Reentry Program
A program designed to ease released prisoners' return to society and thus prevent recidivism.

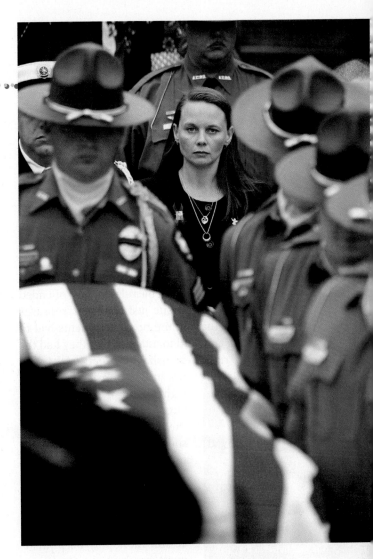

Melissa Christian mourns at a memorial service for her husband, Elmer "Buddy" Christian, a senior police officer who was slain in Athens, Georgia. Another officer was shot and seriously wounded in the same incident in 2011.

top the best-seller lists. Television shows about cops, drug dealers, and even serial killers are staples. In fact, anyone who watches TV has a pretty good idea of how the criminal justice system in the United States works: The police enforce the law and make arrests, but they do not have the power to punish—that authority rests with the state. District attorneys initiate prosecutions. Elected at the county level—except in Alaska, Connecticut, and New Jersey, where they are appointed by the governor—these individuals represent the state's interests in criminal cases. As discussed in chapter 9, defendants are represented by defense attorneys, often public defenders, and most of the time they agree to plea bargains without ever going to trial.

If a case does go to trial, a jury decides the guilt or innocence of the accused. If the accused is found guilty—and most defendants are—then a circuit judge metes out a penalty in accordance with relevant law. Judges may be appointed or elected, depending on the state, but their responsibilities are the same in this situation. A defendant who believes he or she received an unfair trial may file an appeal request with an appeals court or even with the state supreme court.

That is the U.S. criminal justice system, as seen on *CSI* or *Law & Order*. It's a pretty accurate picture, as far as it goes. The problem is, it doesn't go far enough. In fact, Americans' seeming familiarity with the system obscures some basic facts about it. Take, for instance, the fact that punishment is a public function.

One of the most (pardon the pun) arresting features of the U.S. criminal justice system is that the state initiates and dispenses punishment for such crimes as homicide, assault, robbery, and burglary. To Americans, this seems entirely natural. Crime is thought of as an offense not just against an individual but against society itself. As a result, the state initiates the punishment—and the punishment can be severe. It can take the form of imprisonment or **probation**. Punishment deemed to be cruel and unusual, such as torture, is not allowed under the U.S. Constitution, but for homicide, the death penalty is still an option.

People in the United States are aware of the differences between civil and criminal affairs. Civil disputes are private. Your neighbor knocks down your fence and then refuses to put it back up or pay to repair it. You've never much liked that neighbor, so you decide to sue. The state offers a forum for the dispute—the court—and sees that any penalty is carried out, but the dispute is between two private individuals and their lawyers. You don't expect

Probation
Supervised punishment in the community.

the county district attorney to initiate criminal proceedings against your neighbor over a broken fence. No matter how precious your fence or how guilty your neighbor, the state will not lock your neighbor away. In short, a civil offense is an offense only against an individual.

A look at the historical record reveals something interesting: the distinctions that Americans see as natural are, in fact, not at all universal. For most of human history, from ancient Greece to monarchical Europe, private prosecution was the norm.[6] In medieval Britain, the attorney general initiated cases only for the king. Justices of the peace began prosecutions only when there was no private individual to initiate punishment.

Until relatively recently, the governments of most nations simply set the rules for how offended parties should pursue justice. Their role was essentially that of umpire. Governments had to fight long and hard to establish that they had the *exclusive* right to punish wrongdoers.[7] A key figure in this transference of the right of retaliation from the wronged party to the state was the public prosecutor. For reasons that historians still do not fully understand, public prosecutors first appeared in North America—in Great Britain's Atlantic colonies.

On the whole, the state's successful monopoly on punishment has brought enormous benefit to the United States. Conflicts such as the famous one between the Hatfields and McCoys notwithstanding, the nation is essentially free of ongoing feuds or vendettas.

The feud between the Hatfields of West Virginia and the McCoys of Kentucky came to involve the U.S. Supreme Court and the National Guard before the families agreed to end the conflict in 1891.

Common Law, Sovereign Power

The criminal justice system in the United States is rooted in the tradition of English **common law**.

Common Law
Law composed of judges' legal opinions that reflects community practices and evolves over time.

The common law is made up of legal opinions written by judges that recognize commonly accepted community practices and evolves gradually over time as a community's ideas change. Forty-nine states operate within this common-law tradition. (The exception is Louisiana. As a former French colony, the state instead operates under the Napoleonic Code, which Emperor Napoleon I put forth in the early nineteenth century.) Common law makes the U.S. system quite unlike the legal systems of most other countries. In most of the world, law is enacted by a single sovereign power: a legislature, a monarch, or some combination.

> Americans are governed by a mixture of formal (statutory) law and case (or common) law. The common law is made up of legal opinions written by judges that recognize commonly accepted community practices and evolves gradually over time as a community's ideas and mores change.

This is partially true in the United States as well, of course. The nation is a federation in which the federal government and the state governments are both sovereign. Congress and the state legislatures each make laws—as do county and city governments at the discretion of the states. Citizens must obey these laws or risk punishment. However, lawmakers are not the only source of laws. Americans are governed by a mixture of formal (statutory) law and case (or common) law.

One of American society's most important inheritances from the common-law tradition is the institution of the jury. Serving on a jury is *the* defining act of citizenship. It is just about the only thing every citizen must do. (Men between the ages of eighteen and twenty-five must also register with the Selective Service in the event that the government needs to reinstitute a military draft.) In most states, ignoring a jury summons is a crime. Failing to appear for jury duty without being properly exempted constitutes contempt of court and may present a somewhat less appealing opportunity to experience the criminal justice system, such as fines or even imprisonment. Unless you commit a crime or have the misfortune of being one of the roughly 5 million people who fall victim to a crime every year, serving on a jury probably will be your primary interaction with the criminal justice system.[8]

As discussed in chapter 9, there are two types of juries. In most states east of the Mississippi River, a grand jury determines whether there is sufficient evidence for the state to prosecute someone for a crime. In states west of the Mississippi, the district attorney usually has the authority to indict someone and take that person to trial. Presented with a less clear instance of wrongdoing, a prosecutor also may impanel an investigative grand jury to study the evidence and determine exactly who should be targeted for prosecution. Once a grand jury or the district attorney has indicted an individual, another trial begins and another jury is formed to hear the case.

So what is the role of a juror? Most jurors are given clear instructions by the presiding judge. The word **verdict** comes from the Latin phrase *vera dicere,* "to speak the truth." Jurors usually are told that their role is to determine exactly what the truth of a case is. They are to apply the law, regardless of whether they personally agree with it or not. As a result, the role of the juror often is that of a cog—albeit a very important one—in the criminal justice machine.

The jury system is not the only inheritance left to the United States by the British legal system. Many of the other institutions that characterize the U.S. criminal justice system have their roots in the English system as well. County sheriffs are the most notable example. More than one thousand years old, the office of sheriff is the oldest law enforcement office within the common-law system. The king of England appointed a representative called a reeve to act on behalf of the king in each shire or county. The *shire reeve,* or king's representative, became the *sheriff* as the English language changed. These days, the sheriff remains the primary law enforcement official in most communities.

Together with state law enforcement agencies such as the highway patrol, county sheriffs make up the vast bulk of the law enforcement capacity in the United States. In most states, each law enforcement agency focuses on maintaining order in a specific geographical area, although agencies frequently do cooperate.

The Texas Rangers are the nation's oldest law enforcement agency, unofficially organized in 1823 and formally created in 1835.

The Purpose of Punishment

The criminal justice system of nearly every state comes from the same English common-law tradition. As a result, most states share an idea of what is permitted and what is a crime. Even Minnesota and Mississippi more or less agree on what constitutes a crime these days.

This is much less true of punishment, however. Here the differences among the states become more evident. States in the Deep South, for instance, imprison people at much higher rates than do states in other parts of the country. (See Map 14-1.) As discussed previously, different states and localities do have very different political cultures, so it should come as no shock that they define some crimes differently and punish them differently.

Still, efforts to understand this dynamic better have produced some interesting findings. Studies have shown that the percentage of African American residents in a state's population correlates closely with the severity of penalties meted out in its criminal justice system. The more black residents a state has, the tougher its laws tend to be.[9] Social scientists question the degree to which what is supposed to be an objective, color-blind criminal justice system—one that is administered largely by whites—systematically disadvantages blacks.[10]

The severity of punishment also is tied closely to the preferences of the political parties. States with more Democratic legislators tend to have less severe

---

Verdict
A jury's finding in a trial.

MAP 14-1

Incarceration Rates per 100,000 Population, 2011

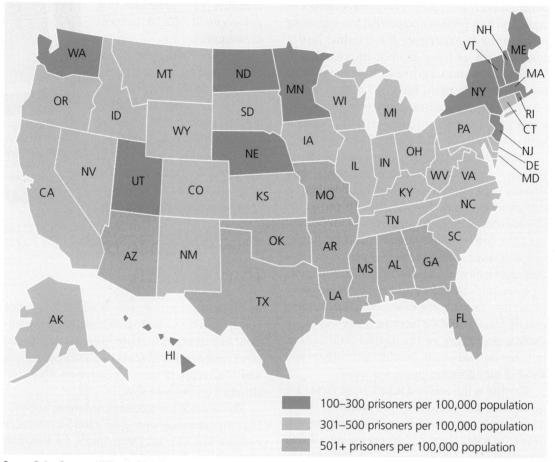

	100–300 prisoners per 100,000 population
	301–500 prisoners per 100,000 population
	501+ prisoners per 100,000 population

Source: E. Ann Carson and William J. Sabol, *Prisoners in 2011,* Bureau of Justice Statistics Bulletin NCJ 239808 (Washington, DC: U.S. Department of Justice, December 2012), Table 3, http://bjs.ojp.usdoj.gov/content/pub/pdf/p11.pdf.

penalties than do states with more Republican legislators. Not surprisingly, election years tend to produce calls for tough new penalties as well.[11] The fairness and effectiveness of these penalties are hotly debated issues (see discussion later in this chapter).

Cultural differences cannot be dismissed in any examination of criminal justice at the state and local levels. They play an important role in explaining why states approach crime differently. New England, with its Puritan heritage, is a region that has always taken a strong interest in saving souls, whether the people involved wanted their souls saved or not. During the nineteenth century, it was the center of the national abolitionist movement. The region exported missionaries, built universities, and fostered the temperance movement. It also sent hundreds of thousands of emigrants west, where they settled much of the Upper Midwest and Pacific Northwest. As a result, these regions share many cultural similarities. To use the typology of the political scientist Daniel Elazar, they all have a strong moralistic streak.[12]

Given this cultural background, it should be evident why New Englanders and their descendants and other moralistic groups, such as Quakers, view punishment as they do. By the early nineteenth century, a growing number of people in the Northeast were turning against the view that painful punishments deter crime and are the fitting "just deserts" of those who participate in criminal activity. Instead, they embraced a new idea—protecting society while rehabilitating criminals.

Examples of a new kind of institution—the penitentiary—soon spread across the landscape.

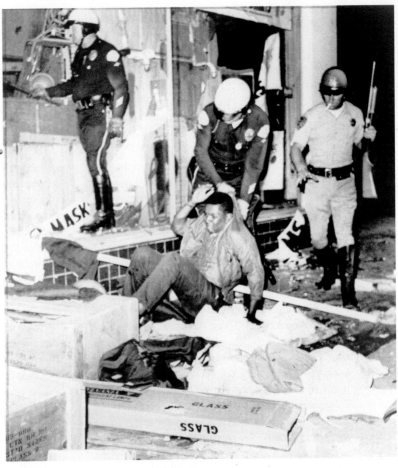

The riots that swept the Watts neighborhood of Los Angeles in August 1965 confirmed the beliefs of many nationwide that the law enforcement system needed an overhaul. In a spiral of violence, a police action started a retaliatory backlash from African Americans that caused further violence on the part of law enforcement. Nearly four thousand people, like the young man in this picture, were arrested for looting and destruction of property.

Unlike prisons, penitentiaries were designed for correction, not for punishment. The most famous penitentiary in early America was located in Philadelphia. Eastern State Penitentiary was designed to force criminals to face their consciences. It operated under a system of maximum solitary confinement. The facility went to extremes to achieve its goal. For example, until 1903, inmates were required to wear face masks when they left their cells. An unfortunate side effect of this "reform" was that many inmates, confronted with such extreme isolation, suffered mental breakdowns.[13] This was not the last well-intentioned but ultimately unsuccessful criminological reform.

Of course, correction and penance are not the only purposes that a criminal justice system serves. Deterrence of crime, incapacitation of offenders, and even vengeance are also goals of such systems. The debate over the proper purpose of punishment is very old. Different societies have addressed it in different ways at different times. Three centuries before the birth of Christ, in ancient Athens, public punishment was administered to salve the wounds and ease the anger of the injured party. The philosopher Socrates was the first Athenian to argue that public punishment should aim at correcting the deficiencies of the criminal and not just at revenge. For his efforts, Socrates eventually was tried and sentenced to die by drinking an infusion poisoned with hemlock for "corrupting youths" and for heresy.

Here in the United States, punishments also have changed to reflect the evolving political cultures. To Pennsylvania Quakers, accustomed to silent contemplation, forcing inmates to confront their misdeeds in silent isolation was a natural idea. In the traditionalistic Deep South, governments chose another model of correction. Facilities such as Parchman Farms in Mississippi and Angola Prison in Louisiana were organized as working plantations until well into the twentieth century. For their overwhelmingly African American inmate populations, the similarities to antebellum slavery were unmistakable.[14] Different histories and cultures produced very different institutions. Nonetheless, reformers believed that correction, not punishment, was the future. Then came the 1960s.

New Freedoms, New Fears

The 1960s was a decade of extremes. Its early years saw the birth of arguably the two most significant social movements of recent times: the civil rights movement and the modern feminist movement.

A Difference That Makes A Difference

Jury Power: What the Courts Don't Want You to Know

The origins of the modern jury go back to the early 1200s, when the English Crown enlisted the most notable men in local communities across England into administrative divisions called "hundreds." Twice a year, the king's circuit court judges would meet with these hundreds of notable individuals and ask them to identify all the miscreants in each village who had violated the king's peace. Fines and other forms of punishment were allotted accordingly.

By the fourteenth century, it had become clear that this approach was subject to abuse. As a result, it was decided that jury verdicts had to be unanimous. The presiding judge could punish juries that could not come to an agreement. Despite this strong-arming, the right to issue a verdict remained firmly in the hands of the local juries.[a]

In the mid-sixteenth century, the criminal justice system took a big step toward law and order as it is known today when Queen Mary decreed that henceforth justices of the peace had the power to investigate accusations, take statements from the accused and the accuser, and indict potential criminals. Justices of the peace were then to present their findings to a jury. They even could instruct the jury on how to proceed. In short, the state was asserting ever more control over the way the criminal justice system worked.

But, sometimes, juries refused to play along. This was particularly true when it came to enforcing laws about religion. In 1670, William Penn, a Quaker, was brought to trial for illegally preaching to the public. Under English law, only state-sanctioned Anglican priests could preach in public. Penn admitted that he had broken the law, but he argued that the law itself was illegal. He asked the jury to acquit him. It did, despite instructions from the presiding judge to enforce the law.

The Crown was profoundly displeased because, in a sense, the jury's challenge raised a very fundamental issue: Who really held sovereign power? When a jury could set aside laws made by the queen in Parliament, the clear implication was that the jury, not the government, was the ultimate power in society. To demonstrate where power really lay, the Crown fined all twelve jury members.

Juryman Bushel, however, refused to pay. His appeal went to the court of Chief Justice Robert Vaughan, who ruled in favor of the stubborn juror. Vaughan rejected the practice of penalizing jurors for ruling in defiance of the law, and his opinion established something remarkable. Juries truly became the final authority in the English justice system. This had been rather vague until that moment, and so Vaughan's ruling marked a turning point in judicial history. Today, the practice whereby juries set aside laws or penalties that they disagree with is known as jury nullification. In the United States, the right to a trial by jury is one of a citizen's basic constitutional rights, enshrined in the Sixth Amendment of the U.S. Constitution.

Despite these accomplishments, the decade ended in a social inferno. A wave of race-related riots nearly snuffed the life out of several inner-city neighborhoods, jump-started "white flight" migration out to the suburbs, and ushered in a new era focused largely on public safety issues.

The first such urban disturbance occurred in summer 1964 in the historically African American neighborhood of Harlem in New York City. The event that triggered it all was the police shooting of a fifteen-year-old African American boy. The shooting confirmed a widespread belief that law enforcement in minority neighborhoods was arbitrary, ineffective, and sometimes brutal. One year later, a police stop in the Los Angeles neighborhood of Watts set off riots that lasted six days, cost thirty-nine people their lives, and caused hundreds of millions of dollars in damages. In summer 1967, large swaths of Newark, New Jersey, and Detroit, Michigan, went up in flames.

Then, on April 4, 1968, civil rights leader Martin Luther King Jr. was assassinated in

William Penn went on to establish the colony of Pennsylvania in North America. Like him, jury nullification also jumped across the Atlantic. In the tumultuous years leading up to the Revolutionary War, American juries repeatedly refused to convict John Hancock and other agitators who were brought to trial on charges of smuggling because they viewed the defendants' activities as principled acts of defiance rather than as crimes. During the 1850s, juries in the North regularly refused to enforce the Fugitive Slave Act, which had been passed at the insistence of the South in 1850 and made it illegal for anyone to assist a runaway slave.[b] Southern anger at northern "lawlessness" and northern anger at southern "overreach" became major issues of contention in the years leading up to the Civil War.

The practice of jury nullification and the spirit of civil disobedience that inspired it also inspired other, less savory actions. For instance, in the 1950s and 1960s, many white juries in the South would not convict white citizens who assaulted and sometimes killed civil rights workers. The federal government responded by enacting new guidelines for jury selection that made juries more representative of the community as a whole. Women, minorities, and poor whites began to sit on juries after centuries of exclusion.

Despite the important role that jury nullification has played in U.S. history, no government in the country is keen on letting folks know about it. Many states bar defense lawyers and judges from even mentioning that jurors may set aside a law. State constitutions in Georgia, Oregon, Indiana, and Maryland include provisions guaranteeing the right of jurors to "judge" or "determine" the law in "all criminal cases." Courts in those states have held that a jury has the power—but not the right—to acquit a guilty person, but jurors should not be told that they may ignore or nullify the law. As in the days of Juryman Bushel, the state remains uneasy about the discretion that juries enjoy.

Does the fact that jurors can find whatever they want mean that they should? Not necessarily. Chief Justice Vaughan upheld the right of an English jury to reject laws promulgated by a thoroughly undemocratic monarchical government. In contrast, the United States today is a democracy in which nearly every adult citizen has the right to vote. Today, jury nullification can be seen as a profoundly undemocratic act. After all, laws are passed by democratically elected bodies. However, it is also a right that jurors continue to enjoy. It may be a secret, but under the U.S. system of law, the jury is still sovereign.

---

[a]Danielle S. Allen, *The World of Prometheus: The Politics of Punishing in Democratic Athens* (Princeton, NJ: Princeton University Press, 1999), 7.
[b]Ibid., 5–6.

Memphis, Tennessee. Within days of King's death, Washington, D.C., Chicago, and many other cities were torn apart by riots. By one estimate, 329 "important" racial disturbances took place in 257 cities between 1965 and 1968, resulting in nearly 300 deaths, 8,000 injuries, 60,000 arrests, and hundreds of millions of dollars in property losses.[15] The decade-long increase in crime showed no sign of stopping.

Crime continued to rise throughout the 1970s. (See Figure 14-1.) In many U.S. cities, residents believed that authority was collapsing and anarchy was at hand. Nowhere was this sense of imminent disaster more apparent than in New York. On the evening of July 13, 1977, lightning strikes, coupled with a Con Edison repair mistake, caused a blackout that plunged the city into darkness. In many neighborhoods, riots and looting broke out. Thousands of fires were set. Although the police ultimately arrested more than three thousand people, much of the city experienced what *Time*

FIGURE 14-1

The Rise and Fall of Crime Rates: Aggravated Assault, Robbery, and Homicide Rates per 100,000 Residents, 1960–2011

Rate per 100,000 population

Source: "Estimated Number and Rate (per 100,000 inhabitants) of Offenses Known to Police, 1960–2011," *Sourcebook of Criminal Justice Statistics Online*, www.albany.edu/sourcebook/pdf/t31062011.pdf.

magazine described as "a night of terror."[16] The country was entering a world of fear that would last for years, and popular-culture imagery showed cities as dystopian nightmares, as in the 1981 film *Escape from New York,* which portrayed Manhattan as a giant maximum-security prison.

The War on Drugs

The riots were dramatic and unsettling, but one ongoing problem in particular stood out—illegal drugs. By 1978, one-third of all kids ages twelve to seventeen admitted to having tried an illegal drug.[17] In the country's inner cities, heroin use was a particular problem. Many government officials first viewed the upsurge in drug use as a public health issue. However, as a strong link between illegal drug use and crime became clear, most turned to the criminal justice system for solutions.

Faced with a seemingly unstoppable rise in violence, more and more states responded by increasing the penalties for dealing and possessing drugs. Nelson Rockefeller, the liberal Republican governor of New York State, led the way. In 1973, Rockefeller and the state legislature agreed to impose new drug laws that were among the toughest in the nation. Anyone found in possession of four or more ounces of

a narcotic such as heroin or cocaine faced the likelihood of a mandatory fifteen-year prison sentence. Selling as little as two ounces of the same narcotic could result in a similar penalty. The hope was that such harsh penalties would drive up drug prices and deter potential users. New York's strategy was an application of **deterrence theory**, the belief that if the punishment is severe enough, it will keep people from committing the crime. Other states and many cities quickly followed suit. State legislatures upped the penalties for the possession of illegal narcotics, and local and county law enforcement officers focused their resources on catching dealers.[18]

In the state of Arkansas, possession of more than an ounce of marijuana can open you up to prosecution on felony charges. Penalties can range from four to ten years in prison. In Montana, a first-time offender can face a life sentence for selling 1 pound of marijuana. But in New Mexico, the maximum penalty for selling 10,000 pounds of marijuana is three years.[19] In 2012, voters in Colorado and Washington State voted to decriminalize the possession of marijuana for recreational use, and nearly twenty states have done the same for medical marijuana. Why is there such a wide variation in penalties? At least part of the answer can be traced back to the differing political cultures of these states.

All in all, the tough new penalties directed against drug users had a minor effect at best on drug use. What they did succeed in doing was putting a lot more people in jail. In 1973, New York State incarcerated approximately 10,000 people. By 1980, that number had reached 20,000. To many, it seemed that things could hardly get worse—but by the mid-1980s, they did.

Deterrence Theory
A theory advanced by criminologists that harsh penalties will deter people from committing crimes.

Policy in Practice

Is It Time to Admit Defeat in the War on Drugs?

Listen to the nightly news or read the daily paper and it's easy to conclude that the "war on drugs" has been something of a disaster. Billions of dollars spent and tens of thousands of Americans in prison, and yet drug use remains constant. The price of drugs actually has gone down. So, is it time to raise the white flag and do something different?

"The global war on drugs has failed, with devastating consequences for individuals and societies around the world." So concluded the Global Commission on Drug Policy in 2011. The commission, which included ex-presidents and prime ministers and a former U.S. secretary of state and Federal Reserve Board chairman, called for decriminalization of drug use and legal regulation of the sale of drugs, starting with marijuana. "I really believe we should treat marijuana the way we treat beverage alcohol," Pat Robertson, a prominent evangelist and former GOP presidential aspirant, told the *New York Times* in 2012.

Some states have been moving in that direction, allowing the use of marijuana for medical purposes and even, in the cases of Washington State and Colorado, for recreational use. Many argue that marijuana can stop costing states and localities so much in enforcement costs and start bringing in serious revenue if it is regulated and taxed. The movement to legal pot, for years a fringe cause, has clearly gone mainstream.

This is not a development that everyone welcomes. In recent years, drug use has gone up. Drug policy experts say this reflects changes in the perceived risks of taking drugs—both of being caught and of suffering societal disapproval. "There is such a push on the part of the marijuana lobby to soften up the public," said Eric Voth, a physician who chairs the Institute on Global Drug Policy, an antidrug alliance of physicians, scientists, and attorneys. "The perception of harm has dropped. You saw this increase in pot first and now you're seeing this increase in ecstasy and meth." A disproportionately high number of young people are among today's users of illicit drugs. Even if the use of these drugs were legalized, society would not want these young people using drugs, just as it currently does not want teenagers to smoke cigarettes.

Caught by surprise by the passage of ballot initiatives allowing medical marijuana use, states at first did little to regulate pot cultivation and sales. That has changed, and much greater oversight is now in place. Ten states and Washington, D.C., have set up systems of authorized dispensaries, and sixteen states have outlined specific conditions for which medical marijuana can be used.

Even if most narcotics were legalized, say, for people twenty-one years old and older, it is likely there would still be a serious illegal drug problem. This leads University of California, Los Angeles, criminologist Mark Kleiman to this opinion about legalizing marijuana:

> My view is that the risks [related to cannabis use] are substantially greater than most of my well-educated boomer friends believe. Taking the entire population of people who have used cannabis at least five times, the risk in that group of becoming a heavy daily cannabis user for a period of at least months is something like one in nine.

The federal government's stance aligns with Kleiman's opinion. It hasn't moved toward legalization; instead, it uses the Office of National Drug Control Policy to aggressively market an antidrug message through print advertising and television and radio spots. President Obama says that federal prosecution of drug laws in states that allow marijuana use should not be a "top priority," but his administration at various times has shifted its position, or at least the amount of effort it is willing to devote to cracking down on marijuana sales.

Sources: Mark Kleiman, "Revenge of the Killer Weed," September 8, 2002, available at www.markkleiman.com; Lloyd D. Johnston, Patrick M. O'Malley, Jerald G. Bachman, and John E. Schulenberg, "Teen Marijuana Use Tilts Up, While Some Drugs Decline in Use," University of Michigan News Service, December 14, 2009, available at www.monitoringthefuture.org; Jesse McKinley, "Latest Legal-Marijuana Push Is All about the Tax Revenue," New York Times, March 26, 2010, A1.

Crack Cocaine

In the early 1980s, intrepid drug dealers discovered that they could add baking soda and water to high-quality powder cocaine and bake up the resulting solution to create small rocks. These rocks could be smoked in homemade pipes. Nicknamed "crack," for the crackling sound the rocks made when broken, the drug could be bagged in small portions that could be sold for as little as five dollars each. Before, cocaine had been a yuppie drug, available only to those with the right connections and the right amount of cash. Now a teenager could buy it for less than a week's allowance.

Crack delivered a potent high at a bargain price. As a result, it quickly found users—with devastating results. Highly concentrated, it created a craving in most users that was so intense they would do almost anything to get more. Some crack addicts abandoned their children. Some began engaging in prostitution to get money to support their habits. Crack addicts broke into condemned buildings and stripped them of their contents, even of their plumbing pipes, just to make more money to buy crack.

To serve this new market, open-air drug markets sprang up on street corners across urban America. In drug-infested neighborhoods, teenagers often occupied the perfect dealing niche. Many were juveniles and thus were hard to arrest or at least to prosecute. But dealing drugs on a street corner could be a violent business. Because these open-air drug markets were profitable, the street-level dealers became popular robbery targets. So they started carrying handguns. Neighborhood fistfights and gang brawls turned into running gun battles. Homicide rates, which had been rising slowly for years, skyrocketed.

Harsher Punishments and Penalties: Prison Nation

State and local government officials responded to this frightening surge in violence and crime in much the same way that legislators had responded to drug use concerns a decade earlier: they imposed tough new penalties for the use and possession of crack. Many states also made fundamental changes to their sentencing practices. For most of the post–World War II era, courts across the United States had enjoyed considerable leeway in determining the severity of the punishments they delivered. In academic-speak, this was known as indeterminate sentencing (see chapter 9).

By the 1980s, however, the public's rising fears led to more strident demands to get tough on crime. Most judges obliged, if only to placate voters. Federal judges are nominated by the president and approved by the Senate for life service. However, most states rely at least in part on elections to select judges—even state supreme court justices.[20]

Stories of judges releasing hardened criminals with little more than a slap on the wrist resulted in a growing number of states' moving toward determinate sentencing. "Truth in sentencing" laws were passed. These restricted judges' ability to set penalties and curtailed parole boards' freedom to release prisoners early. Some states went even further. Fourteen states abolished discretionary parole and parole boards altogether. In 1994, California voters approved a "three strikes" law, under which individuals arrested and convicted of three felony crimes were to be imprisoned for a minimum of twenty-five years, if not for the rest of their lives. In 2004, the U.S. Supreme Court further constrained judges' sentencing flexibility but also set the stage for potentially shorter sentences when it ruled that only juries, not judges, can increase sentences beyond the maximums suggested by sentencing laws.

The increased reliance on incarceration had a big effect on state budgets. In 1978, state governments spent about $5 billion on maintaining prisons and jails. By 2007, prison spending had risen to $44 billion, or 10 percent of state expenditures. More than one in every one hundred U.S. adults were under lock and key.[21] Spending has since ticked down a bit, but states still spend an average of 7 percent of total general revenue funds—$1 out of every $14—on prisons.[22]

Not everyone felt the weight of determinate sentencing equally. By 2006, 5 percent of all black males in the United States were serving time either in a state prison or in a city or county jail. That stood in sharp contrast to the 1 percent of white males jailed during the same period.[23] Nearly one-third of all black males ages twenty to twenty-nine were either in prison or under some form of supervision, such as probation or **parole**. One study estimated that in 1997 black males had a 32 percent chance of going to prison at some point in their lives. In contrast, Hispanic males had a 17 percent chance of being imprisoned, and white males had a 5.9 percent chance.[24]

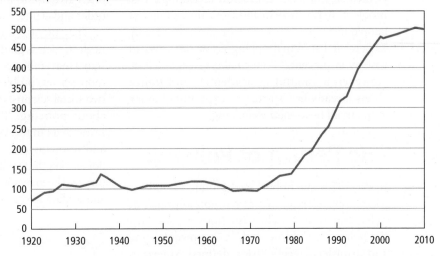

FIGURE 14-2

U.S. Incarceration Rate, 1920–2010

Prisoners per 100,000 population

Source: M. W. Cahalan, *Historical Corrections Statistics in the United States, 1850–1984* (Washington, DC: U.S. Department of Justice, 1986); Bureau of Justice Bulletins, *Prisons in 2008, Prisons in 2011.*

Statistics like these eventually prompted policymakers to take a closer look at mandatory minimum sentences, such as those established in the late 1980s for crack and powder cocaine. An offender who possessed 5 grams of crack was subject to the same minimum sentence in federal prison as an offender who had 500 grams of powder cocaine. African Americans make up 80 percent of the offenders in prison for crack, and they have been sentenced to much longer prison terms than they would have received if they had been caught with the equivalent amount of powder cocaine. In 2007, the U.S. Sentencing Commission recommended equalizing the sentences for possession and use of crack and powder cocaine, and a federal law to ameliorate the disparity was enacted in 2010.[25]

Many incarcerated individuals have a good chance of repeating their time, too. For too many, prison now functions as a kind of criminal finishing school, an educational facility whose graduates usually return to a life of crime. Roughly two-thirds of the people who leave prison after serving time for felonies return within three years.

The high incarceration rate for black males has meant that many no longer can vote. Forty-eight states—Maine and Vermont being the exceptions—have laws that prohibit prisoners from voting. Felons on probation or out on parole are barred from voting in thirty states. Florida, Iowa, Kentucky, and Virginia deny convicted felons the right to vote *ever* again unless the governor or clemency board restores the right; these decisions are made on a case-by-case basis, following a waiting period. A number of states have repealed or amended their felon disenfranchisement laws. Still, 5 million voting-age Americans could not vote in 2012. This means that nearly 8 percent of all black men cannot vote.[26] In Kentucky, Virginia, and Florida, more than 20 percent of potential African American voters are disenfranchised.[27]

States recently have embraced the restoration of voting rights for convicted criminals. Most of the impetus for this effort has come from civil rights organizations, which argue that state laws that deny felons the right to vote penalize African American males disproportionately. Between 1997 and 2007, seventeen states responded to these concerns by removing

Parole
Supervised early release from prison.

or scaling back their voting restrictions on former convicts.[28]

Longer prison terms undoubtedly kept some violent offenders off the streets, but they had little immediate impact on the rapidly escalating crime problem. Between 1985 and 1992, the number of people incarcerated in the United States rose by 79 percent. Far from dropping, crime rates instead rose by 17 percent.[29] Policymakers were at a loss. However, a handful of academics and police chiefs already had started to experiment anew with an old idea—better policing.

The Return of Policing

In the 1820s, Sir Robert Peel founded London's Metropolitan Police, the first recognizably modern police department. "The basic mission for which the police exist," wrote Peel, "is to prevent crime and disorder."[30] Peel's vision defined American policing until the 1960s. Race riots and rising drug abuse then convinced criminologists and many police departments that there was little they could do to reduce crime in the face of shifting demographic trends.[31] By the 1970s, however, a handful of people began to rethink the role that law enforcement agencies should play. In time, these ideas would revolutionize the practice of policing.

The first big idea came in the late 1970s. Put forward by Herman Goldstein, a professor at the University of Wisconsin Law School in Madison, the idea was that the proper role of the police was not to enforce the law but to solve problems. Goldstein's work encouraged police chiefs in cities such as Madison, Wisconsin, and Newport News, Virginia, to think in more creative ways about how to deal with such issues as street-level drug problems. Goldstein urged local officials to search for ways to solve underlying societal problems. This philosophy came to be known as problem-oriented policing. Although it was more than a decade before Goldstein's theory began to take root in police departments, the idea that police ought to function as creative problem solvers eventually transformed the way in which many departments thought about policing.

The second breakthrough came in the early 1980s. Political scientist James Q. Wilson and criminologist George Kelling hatched an idea that changed the future of policing in the United States.

Arguably, it changed the future of urban America. Their basic premise, which became known as the "broken windows" theory, was simple: minor kinds of disorder, such as shoplifting and vandalism, often give rise to much more serious types of disorder and crime, such as robbery and arson.

They theorized that seemingly minor signs of neglect, such as graffiti, trash, and broken windows, signal that authority is absent and give rise to much more serious problems, such as violent crime. The two social scientists went on to make a larger point about policing. Those police officers whom researchers in the 1950s observed walking around and resolving disputes actually might have been doing something important. By their very presence, they had been maintaining order. It was time, Wilson and Kelling wrote, to go back to the past.[32]

Community Policing versus the Professional Model

Wilson and Kelling argued for a dramatic break from the **professional model of policing**. This approach to fighting crime emphasizes squad cars and quick response times; police departments across the country embraced it during the 1970s. The reason for this was an important new innovation—the 911 emergency number. Cops who had once walked the beat and played the role of friendly neighborhood supervisor now were put into squad cars. Response time—how quickly the police responded to a call for assistance—became the criterion by which departments were judged as successes or failures. It was an all-or-nothing situation because there simply were not enough police officers available to both monitor neighborhoods *and* answer emergency calls.

The professional model originated on the fast-growing West Coast. Long before the advent of 911 calls, many West Coast police departments emphasized technology. They prided themselves on their small, highly mobile forces. The influence of the Los Angeles Police Department

---

Professional Model of Policing
An approach to policing that emphasizes professional relations with citizens, police independence, police in cars, and rapid responses to calls for service.

(LAPD) in particular on police technique nation-wide cannot be overstated. For many years, the LAPD was seen as the prototype for effective police departments. Its cool professionalism ("Just the facts, ma'am") was captured in the TV show *Dragnet*. The department was the first to buy helicopters; it also pioneered the use of the now ubiquitous special weapons and tactics (SWAT) teams.

West Coast police departments were convinced that they had a better way. Good tactics and high-tech equipment would prevail. And, for a while, departments such as the LAPD did maintain order, although at a cost. Their smaller forces used aggressive tactics—sometimes in a very arbitrary fashion. Senseless stops by the police became an all-too-familiar experience for residents of many predominantly minority areas. Consequently, a considerable number of African Americans and Hispanics in Los Angeles came to distrust the police department.

This state of affairs was dramatically underscored by the violence that broke out following the 1992 acquittal of police officers involved in the beating of Rodney King.[33] The previous year, a bystander had videotaped LAPD officers violently subduing King, a black motorist who had led them on a high-speed chase and then resisted arrest.[34] When an all-white jury found the officers not guilty, riots erupted throughout the city. For six days, the police force, caught unprepared in part because of political maneuvering at its top levels, struggled to regain control.

A Return to Community Policing

By the early 1990s, it was obvious that a different model was needed. That model was **community policing**. In a sense, this represented a return to one of Sir Robert Peel's earliest ideas—that police officers should walk beats and get to know their neighborhoods. Community policing emphasizes the importance of good relations between police officers and the residents of local neighborhoods and the need for residents and police officers to solve problems jointly. Isolated experiments with community policing began to appear in a handful of police departments, including San Francisco's, as early as the late 1960s.

Momentum for this change did not begin to build, however, until the late 1980s and early 1990s. Police departments such as those in Madison, Wisconsin, and Houston, Texas, embraced and developed the model during this period.[35] Then the Rodney King riots spotlighted the problems of the professional model, pushing other departments toward the community policing model. The most significant variation on community policing appeared in New York. During the early 1990s, Mayor David Dinkins introduced the precepts of this model of policing into the nation's largest police department, the New York Police Department.

At the same time that the NYPD was experimenting with community policing, the city's transit police were attempting to test Wilson and Kelling's belief that disorder left unattended breeds crime. **Broken windows policing**, which emphasizes the maintenance of public order, was instituted. The result was immediate and dramatic. The transit police discovered that many of the vandals and turnstile jumpers they arrested were ex-felons who also were carrying guns or skipping out on warrants. By getting to these people early, the police were, in effect, disarming them. After crime in the subways had increased by 48 percent from 1988 to 1990, the transit police, under the leadership of Chief Bill Bratton, managed to bring robberies down by 40 percent in 1990–1991.[36]

Bratton's successes caught the attention of an ambitious U.S. attorney, Rudolph Giuliani. Two years later, Giuliani won a close race against

The first police car went on patrol in Akron, Ohio, in 1899. It was electric powered and could reach a speed of sixteen miles per hour.

Community Policing
An approach that emphasizes police officers' forming relationships with neighborhood residents and engaging with them in collaborative problem solving.

Broken Windows Policing
Policing that emphasizes maintaining public order, based on the theory that disorder unattended breeds crime.

As part of his rounds, Evansville, Indiana, police officer Nick Sandullo informs resident Alonzo Briscoe about recent vandalism in the city's arts district. "It's nice to see them making an effort to connect with the community and an effort to improve the neighborhoods," Briscoe said. "I think it shows that the police are getting more involved and it's appreciated."

It was an unprecedented and—in the eyes of most criminologists—outlandish commitment. Most experts believed that other factors, such as demographics, were far more important than any type of policing in explaining crime rates. And the demographics were bad. The problem was young people. People between the ages of eighteen and twenty-five commit crimes at a disproportionate rate—they are responsible for more than five times the amount of crimes committed by people ages thirty-five and older. (See Figures 14-3a and 14-3b.) During the 1990s, the proportion of young people in the population as a whole was growing fast. Demographers saw this trend as an echo of the post–World War II baby boom in that a large number of the children of

Dinkins to become mayor of New York City. Reducing crime was one of his major priorities. The young chief who had done so much with the transit police immediately went to the top of Giuliani's list to head the NYPD. What secured the job offer for Bratton was his promise to Giuliani that, if he got the job, he would deliver a 40 percent crime reduction for the whole of New York City within three years.

FIGURE 14-3a

Violent Crime, Arrests by Age, 1995–2011

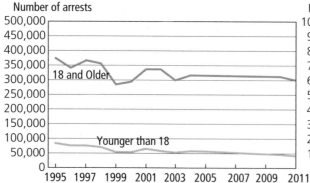

Number of arrests

Source: Federal Bureau of Investigation, *Crime in the United States 1993–2011*, Table 32, www.fbi.gov/about-us/cjis/ucr/crime-in-the-u.s/2011/crime-in-the-u.s.-2011/tables/table-32.

FIGURE 14-3b

Homicide, Arrests by Age and Weapon, 1976–2005

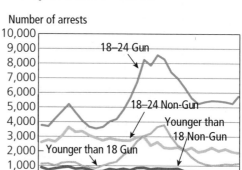

Number of arrests

Source: Federal Bureau of Investigation, *Crime in the United States 1993–2011*, Table 32, www.fbi.gov/about-us/cjis/ucr/crime-in-the-u.s/2011/crime-in-the-u.s.-2011/tables/table-32.

CapStat

Departmental Performance Indicators: Citywide Crime

During Q4 2009, the Washington, D.C., Metropolitan Police Department recorded a total of 7,627 crimes committed—a 13 percent decrease from Q4 2008. By late March 2010, crimes committed in D.C. were down even more—by 26 percent compared to 2009.

Of the total crimes committed in Q4, 5,817 (76 percent) were nonviolent crimes and 1,810 (24 percent) were violent crimes. Nonviolent crimes include burglary, larceny, and auto theft. Violent crimes are murder, rape, robbery, and aggravated assault. The city experienced increases in burglary and assault with a gun only. By mid-March 2010, even those were down.

Crime Type	Q4 2008	Q4 2009	Change (%)	January 1– March 21, 2009	January 1– March 21, 2010	Change (%)
Homicide	45	43	−4	25	17	−32
Sex abuse	91	82	−10	77	54	−30
Robbery (excluding gun)	730	636	−13	562	435	−23
Robbery (with gun)	447	438	−2	328	210	−36
Assault with deadly weapon (excluding gun)	444	441	−1	351	374	+7
Assault with deadly weapon (with gun)	169	170	+1	118	95	−19
Total violent crime	**1,926**	**1,810**	**−6**	**1,461**	**1,185**	**−19**
Burglary	837	936	+12	671	633	−6
Theft	2,335	1,959	−16	1,898	1,322	−30
Theft from auto	2,340	1,846	−21	1,732	1,087	−37
Stolen auto	1,264	1,062	−16	902	686	−24
Arson	15	14	−1	14	7	−50
Total property crime	**6,791**	**5,817**	**−14**	**5,217**	**3,735**	**−28**
Total crimes	**8,717**	**7,627**	**−13**	**6,678**	**4,920**	**−26**

Like CompStat, CapStat is a computer-based mapping system that provides up-to-date citywide information, including which crimes are being committed and where they are being committed. This allows police departments to identify trends quickly and target law enforcement efforts to the hot spots of criminal activity.

people born between 1946 and 1964 were reaching their teen years. Criminologists saw it in different terms—they predicted the coming, much hyped by the media, of juvenile **superpredators**.

Fortunately for New York City, Mayor Giuliani was not much interested in criminology's conventional wisdom. Bratton's bold offer and the promise that broken windows policing had shown underground in the subway system appealed to the new mayor. Bratton got the nod. By the time he resigned two years later, homicides in New York had fallen by 39 percent.

So what happened? Officials in the NYPD say the answer is simple—better policing. The key innovation was a new computerized crime-mapping system known as CompStat. This system allowed the police

---

Superpredators
Ultraviolent youth who experts at one time predicted would further drive up the nation's crime rate.

Chapter 14 Crime and Punishment 455

to map crime in virtual real time, identify patterns or problems, and then shift resources and devise solutions accordingly. Before the creation of Comp-Stat, the NYPD compiled crime statistics every quarter. CompStat provided fresh numbers every week and allowed police commanders to look for crime patterns and "hot spots." It also encouraged officers to try new tactics and introduced an element of accountability into policing.[37] Today, nearly 70 percent of large police departments in the United States use some version of this system. An increase in the numbers of police officers and a focus on broken windows, or quality-of-life offenses, rounded off the prescription for success.

However, another dynamic soon became evident that caught public officials off guard. Many cities that had done nothing to improve their police departments were also enjoying dramatically falling crime rates. (See Figure 14-4.) Los Angeles was a case in point. Once one of the most admired police forces in the country, the LAPD had fallen on hard times by the early 1990s. In the years that followed the Rodney King riots, the department quickly went through two chiefs and struggled with sagging officer morale. Yet, despite

all this, homicides in Los Angeles fell from 983 in 1990 to 425 in 1999.

As crime rates fell almost everywhere, regardless of policing techniques, questions about Bratton's accomplishment in New York and his philosophy of crime reduction reappeared. Criminologists began to look for factors other than improvements in policing. They explored such areas as changes in the structure of urban drug markets, demographics, the economic boom of the 1990s, and the high rates of incarceration during the 1980s and 1990s.[38] The debate between those who give the police most of the credit for the crime reduction of the 1990s and those who do not continues.

Crime, Punishment, and the Essence of Modern America

At the beginning of this chapter, we stated that the way a society chooses to define crime and mete out punishment offers fundamental insights into the nature of that society. When the young French nobleman Alexis de Tocqueville decided in the early 1830s to visit and investigate the fledgling democracy of the United States, his first stop was the prisons. When British author Charles Dickens visited in 1842, he too sought out the prisons and asylums.

Today, many Europeans view punishments such as the death penalty as evidence of American cruelty and racism. They use the death penalty to argue against American "justice" in much the same way that critics of U.S. actions in the Middle East seized on the abuses at Abu Ghraib prison to criticize the U.S. occupation of Iraq. Most U.S. citizens these days are shielded from the reality of the nation's criminal justice system. It operates largely out of sight. Only a small percentage of Americans see what modern punishment looks like in this country. A tour of state

FIGURE 14-4

Homicides in Large U.S. Cities, 1995, 2000, 2005, 2010

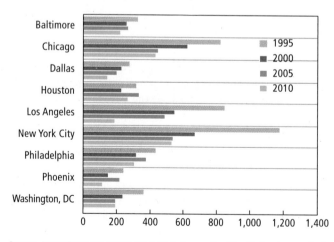

Source: Jeremy Travis and Michelle Waul, "Reflections on the Crime Decline: Lessons for the Future?," Urban Institute, 2002, www.urban.org/uploadedpdf/410546_crimedecline.pdf; Federal Bureau of Investigation, *Crime in the United States 2010*, Table 8, www.fbi.gov/about-us/cjis/ucr/crime-in-the-u.s/2010/crime-in-the-u.s.-2010/tables/10tbl08.xls/view.

prisons and county and city jails may prove enlightening.

First, the system is rife with violence. According to a Justice Department survey of former inmates released in 2012, nearly 10 percent of prisoners suffer sexual abuse while incarcerated in state prisons, local jails, or postrelease treatment centers. Nearly 4 percent said they were forced to have nonconsensual sex with another prisoner, while more than 5 percent reported incidents involving facility staff. For many of these prisoners, rape may be just the beginning. Male prisoners who are passive or effeminate may end up as slaves, forced to do menial jobs and sometimes "rented out" to other inmates to be used sexually.[39]

> An estimated 56 percent of state prisoners and 64 percent of local jail inmates suffer from mental health disorders, including serious conditions such as schizophrenia, bipolar disorder, and depression. That's more than a million mentally ill prisoners and inmates—far more than there are patients in mental hospitals.

Second, the prison population is a sick population. In the 1960s, most states disbanded the psychiatric hospitals that held many of society's mentally ill. At the time, the goal was to replace the old, often cruel networks of state mental hospitals with more humane, community-based clinics, but the states did away with the hospitals without building the clinics. An estimated 56 percent of state prisoners and 64 percent of local jail inmates suffer from mental health disorders, including serious conditions such as schizophrenia, bipolar disorder, and depression. That's more than a million mentally ill prisoners and inmates—far more than there are patients in mental hospitals. What's more, about three-quarters of those inmates with mental illnesses also are addicted to drugs or alcohol.[40]

Once in prison, do people with mental illnesses receive adequate treatment? Although more than a quarter of state prisoners report having taken medications prescribed to treat mental illnesses since entering prison, for the most part, the answer is no. Many prison mental health services are woefully deficient, crippled by understaffing, insufficient facilities, and limited programs. All too often, seriously ill prisoners receive little or no meaningful treatment. They are neglected, accused of malingering, and treated as disciplinary problems.[41] All this has led to lawsuits in numerous states, including Ohio, Michigan, and California. But some healthcare experts point out that even the most basic prison healthcare is better than the low quality—or total lack—of mental and physical healthcare available in the low-income communities many prisoners came from. "It's sad to say, but if a jail has a decent mental-health system, people are getting better treatment than they do in the community," says Jeffrey L. Metzner, a psychiatrist and clinical professor at the University of Colorado School of Medicine. "Correctional people almost always want to do the right thing" by mentally ill prisoners, he says, "but unless they're in a very rich or liberal state, they have a hard time making the case" to legislators and the public.[42]

A century and a half ago, many visitors to the United States praised the nation's prisons and asylums. Today, they do not. A 2009 study by the human rights group Amnesty International stated: "There were reports of ill-treatment by police and prison officers . . . often involving cruel use of restraints, or electro-shock weapons. . . . Thousands of prisoners continued to be confined in long-term isolation in high security units where conditions sometimes amounted to cruel, inhuman or degrading treatment."[43]

The organization found that more than 20,000 prisoners continued to be held in conditions of extreme isolation in **supermax security prisons**. In addition, from 1976 through 2009, 1,188 people were executed in the United States. Of those executed in this period, roughly 35 percent were African American.[44]

Supermax Security Prison
A high-security prison designed to house violent criminals.

What most shocks the rest of the developed world about the American criminal justice system, however, is its treatment of children. According to Amnesty International, the United States is in violation of international law—and treaties it has ratified—when it sentences defendants who were under eighteen at the time of their crimes to life without the possibility of parole.[45] In 2012, the U.S. Supreme Court found that "mandatory life without parole for those under the age of 18 at the time of their crimes violates the Eighth Amendment's prohibition on 'cruel and unusual punishments'" and that a "judge or jury must have the opportunity to consider mitigating circumstances before imposing the harshest possible penalty for juveniles."

Amnesty International estimates that from 1995 through 2003 the United States executed roughly two-thirds of the total children ages seventeen and under who were put to death worldwide. Until the Supreme Court ruled the practice unconstitutional in 2005, the United States was the only developed country that made child execution a regular part of its criminal justice system.[46] The nation also leads the world in the execution of people with mental impairments.

Not Just Tough on Crime

For years, politicians competed to show who was the most "tough on crime," passing laws that made sentences mandatory and long and promoting policies that gave little thought to rehabilitating prisoners. (As a memorable political ad put it, one candidate's suggestion for how prisoners should spend their time was to "introduce them to the joys of busting rocks.")

But responses to crime and levels of punishment have always gone in cycles. After years of trying to get tough, states have recently begun addressing what they see as the worst excesses of recent decades. In California, voters in 2012 modified the state's influential "three strikes" law, ending the practice of sending petty thieves and shoplifters to prison for life by limiting the punishment called for by the law to serious or violent offenders. A month later, a judge in North Carolina resentenced three death-row inmates, two African Americans and one Lumbee Indian, to life without parole after finding that there was "powerful evidence" that prosecutors had violated the state's 2009 Racial Justice Act in their trials, which were tainted by racial bias. "Innocence projects" have sprung up around the country, with law students and even district attorneys examining old cases and finding evidence, often through the examination of DNA samples, that has exonerated some prisoners, many of whom are minorities.

Perhaps the biggest policy change at the moment is the newfound attention being paid to rehabilitation, or what is now called reentry. Reentry programs are designed to help prisoners and former prisoners navigate the range of demands and needs they face once they get out—from finding a job and a place to live to dealing with drug or alcohol habits or psychological problems connected with past crimes. "We've got an unprecedented volume of people coming out of prison and jail," says Michael Thompson, director of the Council of State Governments Justice Center, which has been working with state governments on the issue since 2001. At the same time, "Policy makers are looking at very high failure rates of people coming out of prison. That's obviously a public-safety problem. And states don't have the money to keep growing the prison and jail population. Suddenly you've got more momentum for improving reentry success rates than ever before."[47]

For years, the political incentives all ran against states' spending money on reentry. Why spend money "coddling" prisoners the public preferred to see punished—especially when a fair percentage of them are bound to commit new crimes once they get out? But as corrections expenditures kept rising, the calculus changed—even in states known for harsh criminal penalties, such as Texas. That state's prison population roughly doubled between 1993 and 2007, so when Department of Criminal Justice officials came to the legislature looking for more than $500 million to buy three new prisons, lawmakers realized the time had come for a different strategy. The legislature decided to spend about half that amount on various reentry programs, with the result that by 2010 the Texas prison population had declined rather than risen by 15,000 inmates, as had been projected, and probation recidivism had fallen by nearly a quarter.[48]

Issues to Watch

Making accurate predictions about the direction of crime rates is difficult. Radical improvement is still the goal in many cities even as they struggle against budget and staffing cutbacks. Today, Detroit has one of the country's highest rates of violent crime and underwent an 18 percent cut in its 2012–2013 law enforcement budget—a loss of 380 positions.[49] The city's population has shrunk over the years while its violent crime has climbed, with 344 murders in 2011, an 11 percent increase from the previous year. Despite these daunting numbers, Detroit's police department is striving to make up for the gap in funding and decrease in human resources by using "virtual precincts" through which citizens can report nonemergency crimes to free up more officers to respond to 911 calls.[50] Whether the virtual precincts will help balance the scales toward safer streets in Detroit remains to be seen, but some important trends already are evident nationwide.

Policing

Experts predict that the retreat from the professional model of policing will continue. The belief that the professional model was a misguided reform is now conventional wisdom. Even the West Coast, the one-time citadel of the professional model, now is trying to revamp its departments. Still, even now, residents of East Coast cities continue to enjoy far larger police forces than do residents of West Coast cities. To police a city of nearly 4 million people, the LAPD relies on approximately 10,000 officers. In contrast, New York City has a population of 8 million and 37,000 police officers. That is more than twice the number of police officers per capita for New York than for Los Angeles. Granted, Los Angeles and New York are extreme examples of (comparatively) small and large police forces, but such differences are visible among other cities as well. Cities in the upper Midwest—including Chicago, Illinois; Milwaukee, Wisconsin; and Detroit, Michigan—tend to have larger police departments, in line with the size of East Coast forces. Cities in the Southwest and the Southeast—such as Dallas and El Paso, Texas; Phoenix, Arizona; Charlotte, North Carolina; and Memphis, Tennessee—often have smaller departments, comparable to West Coast cities like Los Angeles.[51]

But even in New York, which was a pioneer in community policing, the pendulum may be starting to swing the other way. At the start of this chapter, we noted that the city's murder rate is now at its lowest ebb in fifty years. In announcing this information, city officials put relatively little emphasis on good police relations with residents, instead crediting the NYPD policy of "stop, question, and frisk," which allows police to stop and question people on the street without probable cause. The policy is not only controversial but also led a federal judge in 2012 to conclude that many of the stops (85 percent of which involve blacks and Hispanics) do not meet constitutional standards for searches.

The End of Federal Support

This chapter has discussed crime and punishment as almost an entirely local matter. According to the Bureau of Justice Statistics, there are roughly 732,000 state and local law enforcement officers nationwide and only 105,000 federal law enforcement officers. This does not mean that the federal contribution to law enforcement is insignificant. Federal agencies take the lead in responding to crimes that cross state boundaries. They also are in charge of investigating certain categories of crime, including counterfeiting and, to a lesser extent, gun trafficking. Sometimes the division of responsibilities between federal law enforcement agencies, such as the Drug Enforcement Agency and the FBI, and state and local agencies can be quite unclear.

The most significant federal contribution to state and local law enforcement, however, has

---

Recidivism
The tendency of criminals to relapse into criminal behavior and be returned to prison.

been financial. During the late 1960s, the federal government created the Law Enforcement Assistance Administration. This agency funneled hundreds of millions of dollars to local law enforcement agencies before its elimination in 1982. In the mid-1990s, President Bill Clinton and Republicans in Congress enacted legislation that provided nearly $20 billion to states and localities to build more prisons and helped localities add about 70,000 police officers to their forces.

More recently, the Great Recession has drained state and local police department budgets. The federal stimulus law made $1 billion in grants available to these agencies in 2009, helping them create or preserve about 5,000 law enforcement positions for three years.[52] Additional state budget stabilization funds in the stimulus package helped cities fill gaps in their police budgets. But that money has since dried up. Concerns not only about budgets but also about pension obligations have led many cities and counties to cut back on law enforcement personnel. For example, continued cuts dropped the overall size of law enforcement in Michigan from 22,488 officers in 2001 to 18,849 a dozen years later, with cuts expected to continue into 2013.[53]

The New Criminal Frontier

There is a sense that the locus of crime is shifting. During the 1960s, 1970s, and 1980s, the notion of the city as a dangerous place established a powerful hold on the American mind. Today, New York is one of the safest cities, not just in the country but also in the world. Although gun crimes are still much, much rarer in European cities, London residents are more than twice as likely as New Yorkers to be the victims of crime. That's why today New York is more likely to be seen as a yuppie playground in TV shows such as *How I Met Your Mother* and *Don't Trust the B---- in Apartment 23* and romantic comedies like *New Year's Eve* and *Friends with Benefits* than as an out-of-control cesspool, which was its image in 1970s movies such as *Escape from New York* and *Fort Apache, The Bronx.*

In fact, a new dynamic is now at play in cities that reduced their rates of violent crime dramatically

during the 1990s. These communities have exported much of their crime to their surrounding suburbs. Guns, gangs, and drug problems are no longer limited to large cities. In 2011, more than a quarter of all violent crime occurred in suburban areas.[54]

The countryside is not as quiet as the stereotype portrays it, either. Police departments in small towns increasingly fight the same battles against drugs and gangs as their urban neighbors. However, those departments lack many of the resources of their city counterparts. A survey conducted for the National Institute of Justice found that fewer than a quarter of small and rural police departments had the capability to use computers to aid their criminal investigations and that they underutilized other technologies, such as digital fingerprint imaging and global positioning systems.[55]

Many rural areas connect a rise in crime to the rise in the use of methamphetamine, a drug often made at home using ingredients found in cold medicine. Meth's popularity exploded in such states as Montana, Nebraska, and Oklahoma in the late 1990s. Surveys by the National Association of Counties consistently rank meth as counties' top drug problem— higher than cocaine and marijuana combined— leading the association to develop the Meth Action Clearinghouse for its members.[56] By 2005, states across the country had attempted to curtail the drug's availability by moving over-the-counter medicines containing pseudoephedrine, meth's main ingredient, behind the pharmacy counter. In October 2005, Oregon passed a law requiring a prescription for these previously over-the-counter drugs. The states were ahead of the federal government, which passed a law limiting the distribution and sales of pseudoephedrine in March 2006.

There is some evidence that these laws have helped reduce the number of meth labs. In Oregon, the number of labs dropped from 192 found in 2005 to just 10 in 2009, and monthly meth lab seizures are down 96 percent statewide.[57] But hard-core meth addicts may now be looking elsewhere for their fix, with the increase in imports of "ice," a meth product from labs in Mexico and Southern California. "Ice" is vastly more expensive than homemade meth, leading to an increase in crimes committed by addicts, who need money to pay for the drug.[58]

The Uncertain Future of the Death Penalty

In 1972, the U.S. Supreme Court found that the application of the death penalty in many states had been cruel, arbitrary, and unconstitutional. A moratorium, or indefinite delay, was placed on all executions. Four years later, the Court lifted the moratorium. By then, the states had passed sentencing guidelines that addressed the Court's concern that the death penalty was being applied in an arbitrary fashion. Today, the statutes of thirty-three states allow prosecutors to request the death penalty. (The federal death penalty, of course, can apply anywhere in the country.) More than 1,300 prisoners have been executed since capital punishment was reinstated, and another 3,152 people were on death row in October 2012, according to the Death Penalty Information Center.

The fact that most states sanction capital punishment does not mean that they use it in similar ways. Some counties and states are much more enthusiastic in its use than others. For example, suburban counties tend to apply the death penalty with more zeal than do urban counties. In 2009, San Mateo County, a suburb of San Francisco, had seventeen people on California's death row; by contrast, San Francisco itself, a larger city with twice as many murders, had sentenced only four people to death. Richard Willing and Gary Fields found in 1999 that "fifteen counties account for nearly a third of all prisoners sentenced to death but only one-ninth of the population of the states with capital punishment."[59] One reason for this may be the rising crime rates in suburban areas and a "fight back" reflex felt by residents who have seen their safe communities become danger zones.

During the 1990s, the scientific breakthrough of DNA testing shook up the capital punishment systems of most states. In state after state, lawyers and public interest groups convinced courts and prosecutors to reexamine forensic evidence. What they found was that many people had been convicted of crimes they had not committed. By December 2012, postconviction DNA testing had cleared 301 Americans, according to the Innocence Project at the Cardozo School of Law at Yeshiva University. Eighteen of these people had been sentenced to death; 70 percent of the total were persons of color. The impact of this new research has been felt. In January 2000, Illinois governor George Ryan, a Republican and an avowed supporter of capital punishment, became the first governor in the nation to halt executions in his state.

> During the 1990s, the scientific breakthrough of DNA testing shook up the capital punishment systems of most states. In state after state, lawyers and public interest groups convinced courts and prosecutors to reexamine forensic evidence.

Other states began examining the most widely used method of execution—lethal injection—after the U.S. Supreme Court ruled in June 2006 that lower courts must consider the possibility that the process can be cruel and painful, a finding that would make the procedure unconstitutional. Several states proposed adding an anesthesiologist to monitor executions and confirm that the three-drug process, intended to sedate, paralyze, and finally kill the prisoner, was working properly. There was just one problem—anesthesiologists balked at presiding over executions because that would go against their Hippocratic Oath to "do no harm." When California could not find a workable solution, the death penalty went on trial. In December 2006, a federal judge found California's method of lethal injection unconstitutional but said the system could be fixed.[60] Even as they were voting to soften the "three strikes" law in November 2012, however, California voters turned down a measure to repeal the death penalty.

In 2007, New Jersey became the first state in forty years to repeal capital punishment, and all states participated in a seven-month national death penalty moratorium, until the U.S. Supreme Court in April 2008 upheld Kentucky's lethal injection

Policy in Practice

Does Gun Control Work?

A few days before Christmas in 2012, the nation was plunged into grief by a tragedy in Newtown, Connecticut. A gunman killed twenty children—first graders, ages six and seven—along with six adults at Sandy Hook Elementary School, before killing himself. It was not the first mass shooting the nation had witnessed that year, but the death of young children in their neighborhood school revived the gun control debate in a way that nothing had in years.

Not all politicians responded in the same way, however. President Obama pledged to do everything in his power to prevent future tragedies of this sort. Democrats in the U.S. Senate pledged to bring up bans on assault-style weapons and large-capacity magazines such as the shooter had used in Connecticut. Lawmakers in states such as California pledged to respond with similar measures, while localities such as San Diego rushed to expand gun buyback programs.

But not everyone embraced these traditional types of restrictions on firearms or newer ideas for tagging or taxing ammunition. The National Rifle Association responded to the shooting by calling for armed personnel and police to be put in every school—an idea that legislators in some states, such as Missouri and Tennessee, had already talked about. "It's magnified in the moment, but I expect red states will vote to expand gun rights and the blue states will seek to enact gun control legislation," Scott Melzer, an expert on gun politics at Albion College in Michigan, said in the days following the shooting.

Would tougher gun control laws save lives? For some people, the answer is obvious. In 2011, the United States suffered 11,000 gun-related homicides. Countries with strict gun control laws, such as Great Britain and Japan, had well under 50 apiece.

For others, the very suggestion of outlawing handguns is outrageous. Many gun owners view individual firearms ownership as a basic constitutional right—a point of view the Supreme Court has upheld twice in the last few years. The Second Amendment proclaims, "A well-regulated militia being necessary for the security of a free state, the right to keep and bear arms shall not be infringed." Some have argued that allowing citizens to carry concealed weapons would improve overall public safety. They claim that the country would be safer if more Americans carried guns. The massacre of thirty-two people at Virginia Tech in 2007 led some states to make it easier to carry concealed weapons on college campuses.

In general, the courts have not agreed with this more expansive interpretation of the Constitution. As a result, the extent of your right to bear arms depends very much on where you live. Thirty-five states essentially require law enforcement agencies to provide concealed weapon licenses to any law-abiding citizens who apply. Ten states give law enforcement agencies the discretion to issue or deny concealed weapons licenses based on a variety of factors. Illinois was the last state that banned concealed weapons altogether, but its law was struck down in 2012.

process. Many states have since resumed executions, although at least a half dozen states have continued to suspend their systems while they review their administration of lethal injection,[61] and New Mexico followed New Jersey's repeal with its own in 2009. (The most recent state to repeal capital punishment was Connecticut, in 2012.) Other states continue to struggle with their systems, including Ohio, where at least three executions were delayed when the

needles necessary for the lethal injections could not be placed correctly. In light of these challenges, some experts are calling for a return to other execution methods, including the electric chair and the firing squad. "We've known for a long time that there are better methods, but states don't want to look bad and horrifying," says Deborah Denno, a law professor at Fordham University who has written about the death penalty.[62]

In Alaska, Arizona, Vermont, and Wyoming, no permit is needed to carry a concealed weapon.

Both sides of the gun debate believe that they argue for actions that will increase public safety. The advocates of gun ownership point out that localities with strict gun control laws often have very high crime rates and that all bans on handguns do is ensure that only criminals have guns. The advocates of gun control acknowledge the problems but counter that the real problem is that borders are porous and other surrounding jurisdictions often have very weak gun control laws. In fact, according to criminologist Garen Wintemute at the University of California, Davis, a dispassionate look at the evidence seems to support the key claims of both sides. Studies have shown that certain types of gun restrictions— waiting periods, background checks, and some level of screening for gun buyers—work. In Wintemute's words, "They reduce rates of criminal activity involving guns and violence among people who are screened out and denied purchase of a gun—about 25 percent to 30 percent of those who are screened." Other types of restrictions, such as gun "buybacks," do not. Buybacks often encourage people to turn in only old, sometimes inoperable guns.

Some measures, such as requiring gun manufacturers to install trigger locks on new handguns, are still too new to allow researchers to evaluate the effects. However, the argument for treating gun violence as a public health problem is a strong one. Gun wounds, most of which are accidental, are among the leading causes of death in the United States.[a] At the same time, there is no evidence to suggest that gun control laws reduce violent crime. This raises an intriguing question: How can gun control laws work and yet not work at the same time?[b] One possible reason it's hard to say: "The NRA has blocked most efforts at serious gun research, going so far as to restrict access to the highly informative data available from Justice Department traces of guns used in crimes," according to the *New York Times.*[c]

Source: Original piece written for this book by Alan Greenblatt.

[a]For a discussion of the public health approach to gun violence, see David Hemenway, *Private Guns, Public Health* (Ann Arbor: University of Michigan Press, 2004). For statistics related to injuries and fatalities by year, see the U.S. Centers for Disease Control and Prevention's National Center for Injury Prevention and Control, www.cdc.gov/ncipc.

[b]Wintemute's answer: "The resolution of that apparent paradox is that under current criteria so few people are denied the purchase of a firearm under Brady and its state-level analogs relative to the number of people who purchase guns every year that an impact on that select group is too small at the population level to be noticed." Quoted in Jeremy Travis and Michelle Waul, "Reflections on the Crime Decline: Lessons for the Future?," Urban Institute, 2002, 16, www.urban.org/uploadedpdf/410546_crimedecline .pdf.

[c]Gary Gutting, "The N.R.A.'s Science Ban," *New York Times,* December 23, 2012, SR3.

A New Interest in Alternative Punishments

An end to executions seems unlikely, but other changes to state criminal justice systems are becoming evident. Cost pressures are driving some of the changes, as states search for savings amid their worst fiscal crisis since World War II. For instance, even during the less severe 2001–2002 economic recession, many states concluded that they could no longer afford to warehouse ever-growing numbers of prisoners. Some states, notably Oregon and Alabama, responded with a simple but perhaps shortsighted solution— they released inmates early. Given high recidivism rates, law enforcement officials may soon place many of these individuals back behind bars for other crimes.

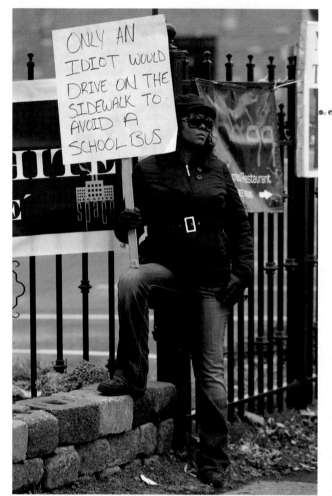

A Cleveland woman fulfills her sentence for driving on a sidewalk to avoid a school bus. The sign she carries is part of her court-ordered sentence, intended to draw public attention and shame her. Similar "shaming sentences" have been levied across the country for offenses ranging from damaging a Nativity scene to drunk driving.

that eat 11 percent of the annual statewide budget, is cutting its prison population by 6,500. Along with additional changes to its parole policies, California is looking to save $100 million per year.[64] Over the years, states have tried a number of alternative approaches, some more successful than others. During the late 1980s and early 1990s, states such as Arizona and Georgia pioneered the use of military-style boot camps for juvenile offenders, but this tactic seemed to have no impact on future criminal activities. The recidivism rates for juveniles who had gone through the boot camps were no lower than recidivism among juveniles who had not. The number of juvenile boot camps declined precipitously after the mid-1990s.[65]

Another alternative strategy has demonstrated greater success. **Drug courts**, special tribunals that offer nonviolent drug offenders a chance at reduced or dismissed charges in exchange for undergoing treatment or other rehabilitation, are an initiative that got under way during the Clinton administration. As of December 2011, more than 2,600 drug courts were operating across all fifty states. National Institute of Justice researchers found evidence that the programs are successful in both reducing recidivism and lowering long-term costs. The researchers report that enrolling a participant in a drug court program saves more than $12,000 in criminal justice and victimization costs.[66]

Drug courts are closely connected to the **community, or restorative, justice movement**. This

Since then, a number of other states have approached early release in a more methodical way, by revising their sentencing and corrections policies with the goal of returning to society those prisoners less likely to reoffend. Mississippi, for example, tweaked its "truth in sentencing" law in 2008 to make nonviolent offenders eligible for parole after serving just one-quarter—not the previous 85 percent—of their sentences. That change resulted in more than 3,000 inmates being released an average of thirteen months earlier than they otherwise would have been and contributed to a decrease in Mississippi's prison population of 5.4 percent between the end of 2008 and early 2010. What's more, just 0.2 percent of those released early reoffended during their first postrelease year, a far cry from the national average of 10.4 percent.[63] California officials hope to have similar results to report in coming years. The state, under court order to reduce overcrowding in its prison system and stressed by prison system costs

Drug Court

A special tribunal that offers nonviolent drug offenders a chance at reduced or dismissed charges in exchange for their undergoing treatment or other rehabilitation; an alternative forum for sentencing nonviolent drug offenders.

Community, or Restorative, Justice Movement

A movement that emphasizes nontraditional punishment, such as community service.

movement's basic goal is to give neighborhoods a voice in determining which kinds of criminals prosecutors should pursue. Sometimes restorative justice involves sentences that are tailored to fit both the crime and the perpetrator. A woman convicted of stealing from a nursing home patient may have to fill vases with potpourri for a senior center, for instance, or an artist convicted of drunk driving may have to paint a picture for the organization whose lawn she drove over. Although such sentences are sometimes belittled as not just soft but mushy on crime, some communities have found that they are more effective than traditional probation in leading perpetrators to commit fewer offenses in the future. In practice, community justice initiatives range from the modest (placing prosecutors in local police stations, where they can see the neighborhood needs firsthand) to the ambitious (alternative courts that may require juvenile offenders to apologize to the people they have harmed and perform community service in an attempt to rectify the harm done by the crime committed).

Conclusion

Crime is one of the most complex—and most contentious—issues in public policy. Its causes are not well understood, and the fairness of the criminal justice system and the best strategies for responding to crime are hotly debated. Nevertheless, the past twenty years have brought remarkable progress. Such innovations as community policing, broken windows policing, and CompStat have given law enforcement agencies new tools and a new sense of purpose. Contrary to some alarmist predictions, crime rates have fallen sharply and youth violence also has declined. However, serious issues, notably the high incarceration and victimization rates of African American men, remain. Will new innovations continue to push crime down, or is the crime decline over? So far, at least, the news has been mostly good.

The Latest Research

This chapter has examined the reasons violent crime rates have dropped dramatically over the past twenty years, pointing out that there is little agreement about which factors have been most important in bringing this change about. Without understanding which models of policing were most effective, it is hard to replicate success in areas where, for instance, the murder rate remains high.

Recent scholarship in this area reflects the lack of consensus regarding the best recipe for success, or even the relative importance of different ingredients, such as law enforcement techniques, demographics, and other factors such as the economy. But researchers are paying attention to this issue, as well as exploring relatively recent phenomena such as the reemergence of reentry programs for ex-offenders.

● ●

● **Benson, Michael L., Leanne Fiftal Alarid, Velmer S. Burton, and Francis Cullen.** 2011. "Reintegration or Stigmatization? Offenders' Expectations of Community Re-entry." *Journal of Criminal Justice* 39: 385–393.

A survey of 1,031 adult males convicted in Texas confounds expectations about whether ex-prisoners will feel stigmatized after serving their sentences. Although prior researchers had found that offenders experience the criminal justice system as degrading and stigmatizing, this survey found that most of the men surveyed expected to be accepted and helped by friends and family upon their release. Some worried about finding employment, but even in an era of mass incarceration, most were optimistic about their prospects, regardless of race. The findings suggest that young adult offenders in particular are good prospects

(Continued)

(Continued)

for reentry and restorative justice programs that take advantage of their willingness to accept responsibility for lawbreaking and building relationships that will move them away from crime.

- **Blumstein, Alfred.** 2006. "The Crime Drop in America: An Exploration of Some Recent Crime Trends." *Journal of Scandinavian Studies in Criminology and Crime Prevention* 7: 17–35.

From 1993 to 2000, violent crime rates in the United States dropped by more than 40 percent. Many factors were in play, including changes in policing and demographic shifts. Two factors appear to have been most important, however. One was a significant drop in demand for crack cocaine among new users, which meant fewer young people were drawn into the drug-selling trade. (Most of the growth in rates of violence in the preceding years had been among young offenders.) The other was a reduction in violence by people thirty years old and older, mainly due to incarceration, as the per capita prison population grew to seven times the size it had been throughout much of the twentieth century.

- **Nunley, John M., Richard Alan Seals, and Joachim Zietz.** 2011. "Demographic Change, Macroeconomic Conditions, and the Murder Rate: The Case of the United States, 1934–2006." *Journal of Socio-Economics* 40: 942–948.

Demographics—particularly the share of the population that is young—have been considered a prime driver of variations in crime rates. During the 1980s, the murder rate dropped even though there was a dramatic drop in the percentage of those ages fifteen to twenty-four. Looking over a longer time span, the authors conclude that the size of the youth population is still the biggest indicator that murder rates will rise, with some fluctuations explained primarily by the "misery index"—the combination of inflation and unemployment rates.

- **Stewart, Daniel M., and Robert G. Morris.** 2009. "A New Era of Policing?" *Criminal Justice Policy Review* 20: 290–309.

Following the terrorist attacks of September 11, 2001, there was a widely shared assumption that homeland security—preventing terrorism and responding to major emergencies—would become perhaps the central mission of law enforcement in the United States. That expectation has seeped in even among police chiefs, most of whom believe homeland security is a central part of the overall law enforcement mission. However, while many local police departments have launched homeland security initiatives, few of them say that homeland security is a major strategic concern within their own departments. The assumption that others must be making it a priority points to the fragmented nature of law enforcement in the United States and suggests, Stewart and Morris conclude, that relations between federal and local law enforcement agencies still could use improvement.

college.cqpress.com/
sites/govstateandlocal

Chapter Review

Key Concepts

- broken windows policing (p. 453)
- common law (p. 442)
- community, or restorative, justice movement (p. 464)
- community policing (p. 453)
- deterrence theory (p. 448)
- drug court (p. 464)
- parole (p. 451)
- probation (p. 441)
- professional model of policing (p. 452)
- recidivism (p. 459)
- reentry program (p. 440)
- supermax security prison (p. 457)
- superpredators (p. 455)
- verdict (p. 443)

Suggested Web Sites

- **www.amnesty.org.** Web site of Amnesty International gives a sense of how the rest of the world views the U.S. criminal justice system through recent and archived material.

- **www.fbi.gov.** Web site of the Federal Bureau of Investigation offers information on national and international criminal activities as well as crime prevention tips.

- **www.manhattan-institute.org.** Web site of the Manhattan Institute includes archived articles from the institute's *City Journal,* which addresses such issues as the effects of racism.

- **www.ncjrs.gov.** Web site of the National Criminal Justice Reference Service provides statistics on a variety of topics involving crime.

- **www.nij.gov.** Web site of the National Institute of Justice, the research, development, and evaluation agency of the U.S. Department of Justice; the agency researches crime control and justice issues, particularly at the state and local levels.

- **www.sentencingproject.org.** Web site of the Sentencing Project offers data and information about racial disparities in the U.S. criminal justice system.

- **www.vera.org.** Web site of the Vera Institute of Justice, a nonprofit organization that conducts research, demonstration projects, and technical assistance to improve the justice system.

State Stats on Crime and Punishment

Explore and compare data on the states! Go to college.cqpress.com/sites/ govstateandlocal to do these exercises.

1. In 2009, what percentage of the population in Washington were marijuana users? What was the percentage in Colorado? How do you think these numbers influenced the recent passage of recreational marijuana use laws?

2. It costs around $90,000 more per year, per prisoner to keep someone on death row in California rather than in regular confinement. In 2010, how many death row prisoners did California have? How much per year would California save by commuting these sentences to life in prison?

3. What is the reported crime rate at colleges and universities in your state? Do you think that this is an accurate number? Why or why not?

4. In 2001, what was the average, national, annual operating cost of correctional facilities per state prisoner? How does your state compare? Does this seem like a reasonable amount to you? Why or why not?

5. How many drug laboratories were seized in your state during 1999? How did this change by 2006? What might account for this change?

Undeniably, the patients aren't the only ones who are sick in the U.S. healthcare system. The system itself needs more than an aspirin and an apple a day to heal itself, and it remains to be seen whether the federal healthcare reform package will provide that solution. Meanwhile, states and localities continue to pick up the slack. Here, Dr. Gwen Wurm, a pediatrician with the University of Miami Health System, checks five-year-old Christina Brownlee's ears in October 2007.

Health and Welfare

STATE, HEAL THYSELF!

- Why does access to healthcare vary so widely across the country?
- How will federal healthcare reform affect states, cities, and counties?
- What roles do state and local governments play in maintaining public health?

Just after 10:00 A.M. (EST) on June 28, 2012, John Roberts surprised most of the political and health policy world. The conservative chief justice of the U.S. Supreme Court joined with the Court's four liberal members to uphold the Patient Protection and Affordable Care Act, better known as the Affordable Care Act, Obamacare, or the federal healthcare reform law. In particular, Roberts and his colleagues had upheld the "individual mandate"—the requirement in the law that virtually every American possess health insurance or pay a fine. Many conservatives were shocked and dismayed that Roberts, an appointee of George W. Bush, would side with President Obama and against the law's critics on the right. Those critics included a large group of Republican governors and state attorneys general: Twenty-six states had joined the litigation against the law.

Yet it soon became clear that at the same time they had rebuffed the Affordable Care Act's critics at the state level, Roberts and his colleagues had empowered them too. The central goal of the law is to provide health insurance to more of the millions of Americans (48.6 million as of 2011) who lack it. One of the central ways the law attempts to do that is by expanding **Medicaid**, a program that has traditionally provided health insurance to poor children, their parents, and people with disabilities. Medicaid is administered by states and funded with a

---

Medicaid
A joint state and federal health insurance program that serves low-income mothers and children, the elderly, and people with disabilities.

combination of state and federal dollars. Under the new federal healthcare law, states had the choice to offer Medicaid to anyone with income up to 133 percent of the federal poverty line. The federal government promised to pay most of this cost, but, starting in 2017, states had to kick in money too. The Congressional Budget Office estimated that 13 million Americans would gain health insurance because of the Medicaid expansion. It was something close to an offer states couldn't refuse. If a state didn't expand, it would lose every federal Medicaid dollar it received. For most states, that would mean missing out on billions of dollars.

What Roberts and the Supreme Court ruled is that for the federal government to coerce states in this way was unconstitutional. The portion of the law that said states would lose their existing Medicaid dollars if they did not expand eligibility was struck down, but the federal government was still allowed to tie new dollars to whether states expanded. That decision means states have a big choice. They can expand Medicaid and receive billions of federal dollars to provide health insurance to millions of people who currently lack it, in which case they will also be forced to kick in large amounts of state money from their already fragile budgets, or they can say no. One reason many Republicans objected to the Affordable Care Act is that they felt it made states subservient to the federal government in an area where the states traditionally had held considerable sway. With the Court's ruling, however, states will have a critical role in determining how the most ambitious, consequential American healthcare law in nearly fifty years plays out.

But it doesn't take an act of Congress for government to play a central role in the health of the American people. One of the most important functions of government is protecting **public health**. Public health is the area of medicine that deals with the protection and improvement of citizen health and hygiene through government agencies. Since the earliest days of the United States, state and local governments have met public health needs. This is especially true in regard to the poorest and to the disabled members of society.

State and local governments also have taken the lead in responding to public health crises. In practice, this includes responses as simple as making sure an ambulance or fire truck responds to a 911 call and responses as complex as managing an epidemic. A century ago, the latter might have involved yellow fever, cholera, or influenza. In 1918, it involved a flu **pandemic** that killed an estimated 600,000 Americans and 100 million people worldwide.[1] Such diseases pose continued threats. As a result, state and local governments spend an increasing amount of time planning for such crises and carrying out drills intended to simulate public health emergencies.

Just how active state and local governments should be on these issues is often a source of heated debate. Terrorism experts warn that the United States has far too few hospital beds to provide the care that would be needed in the event of a real emergency.[2] Many communities cannot even keep an adequate blood supply available to healthcare facilities when things are quiet and uneventful. Despite the dangers posed by illnesses such as swine flu, most counties maintain only skeletal public health departments.

Pandemic flu, anthrax, and the specter of bioterrorism are frightening new developments in the field of public health, but they are not the only threats to the public. Sometimes the public is its own worst enemy. The impact of recent "outside" health threats pales beside more longstanding public health concerns. According to the U.S. Centers for Disease Control and Prevention (CDC), smoking tobacco causes more than 400,000 deaths a year in the United States.[3]

In addition, a growing percentage of Americans are overweight or suffer from **obesity**. Some state and local officials have made combating obesity a

---

Public Health
Area of medicine that addresses the protection and improvement of citizen health and hygiene through the work of government agencies.

Pandemic
An outbreak of a disease that spreads across a large geographical area and affects a high proportion of the population.

Obesity
The medical condition of being excessively overweight; defined as having a body mass index (BMI) of more than 25.

major priority. They have pushed for educational programs for parents, and for children they have restored physical education classes in and removed soft drink machines from schools. Others resist the idea that obesity is a problem that should be addressed through government policy.

The scope of public health programs varies from state to state. Some states are generous providers of assistance to their low-income citizens to cover the expenses associated with illness and hospitalization. Other states are much more restrictive. The explanations for these differences are explored in this chapter.

For all the variation among state and local governments, it is clear that over the course of the past two decades many of these governments have become much more assertive concerning public health. During the economic boom of the mid- and late 1990s, the states worked with the federal government to find new ways to extend health insurance to low-income parents and children. When the economy slipped into recession, states led the effort to find ways to reduce the cost of medical care and to improve the quality of care.

Forty years ago, most states were minor players in the nation's healthcare system. The proponents of expanded health coverage and healthcare reform looked to the federal government for solutions. A decade of inaction and partisan division in Washington in the 1990s shifted some of the most important—and most difficult—healthcare issues to the state and local governments. Since then, the lawmakers tackling tough issues such as the rising rate of obesity, rising prescription drug costs, the need to provide long-term care, the spread of the human immunodeficiency virus (HIV) and other sexually transmitted diseases, and the problem of illicit drug use have been more likely to be sitting in the state capitols than under the Capitol dome in Washington, D.C. When the federal government acted on decades of debate over healthcare reform in early 2010 to pass the Affordable Care Act, the center of power might reasonably have been expected to shift back to Washington.

Increasingly, however, there are signs that states will continue to play a central role even under the federal healthcare reform regime. One sign is the Supreme Court's ruling that leaves the decision on whether to expand Medicaid in the hands of states. Even before that decision, however, the law had left some important powers with the states. Aside from the Medicaid expansion, one key way the law attempts to expand health insurance is by creating state health insurance exchanges, online marketplaces where consumers can choose among different health insurance plans. The exchanges represent an alternative to employer-provided insurance. For low-income and middle-income people, the cost of insurance purchased through the exchanges is subsidized by federal tax credits. In following the exchange model, the Affordable Care Act borrowed from ideas that had already been tried at the state level. Massachusetts established a health insurance exchange in a law enacted under Governor Mitt Romney in 2006 to expand access to health insurance.

Under the federal law, states themselves can run the exchanges if they choose to. States that administer the exchanges themselves will get to make important choices, such as whether to allow every health insurance plan that meets basic criteria into the exchange or to provide more structure to consumers' options.[4] As of February 2013, seventeen states and Washington, D.C., had committed to creating their own health insurance exchanges under the law, either by passing legislation or through a governor's executive order. Twenty-six states (mostly states with Republicans in charge) had decided not to. In addition to the exchanges, the Obama administration announced in December 2011, states will have broad discretion to make another key decision under the law: what level of coverage a health insurance plan must, at a minimum, meet to count as health insurance under the law.[5]

In addition, states have taken the lead in rethinking such safety net programs as welfare, which provides cash payments to needy families. In 1996, Congress abolished the existing **Aid to Families with Dependent Children (AFDC)**, or welfare,

---

Aid to Families with Dependent Children (AFDC)
The original federal assistance program for women and their children, started under Roosevelt's New Deal.

program and replaced it with a system of block grants to the states, called **Temporary Assistance to Needy Families (TANF)**. These grants gave state governments the leeway to design their own personalized, work-oriented, time-limited welfare programs. The result has been a profusion of sometimes very different welfare-to-work programs.

For instance, starting in 2000, Governor Frank Keating launched the Oklahoma Marriage Initiative using TANF funds. The state helped pay to train government workers and religious volunteers to administer a program developed by the U.S. military and designed to strengthen the marriages of people moving from welfare to work. More than a decade later, the state was still requiring that TANF recipients participate in marriage workshops. In contrast, other states, including New York, have downplayed such so-called family formation policies. Part of this difference in emphasis reflects states' different political cultures; however, the structure of the state government also plays an important role. New York's welfare system is decentralized; the state relies on the county governments to administer programs.[6]

The Influence of Culture

How state governments define public health has a lot to do with the distinctive political cultures of their regions. All public health officials would agree that certain issues, such as terrorism and acquired immunodeficiency syndrome (AIDS), are important public health issues. No one would argue that a flu epidemic or the contamination of a major watershed would not also qualify.

Other topics are not so easily categorized. Is gun violence a public health issue? Researchers at the CDC think so. They point out that gun-related deaths, most of which are accidental, are the country's second leading cause of death. The American Medical Association now advises doctors to talk with patients about the proper handling and storage of any guns they may own.

Many gun owners, however, vehemently reject the idea that guns are a public health issue.

On other health fronts, some cities have attempted to reduce the transmission of dangerous blood-borne illnesses, such as HIV and hepatitis C, by providing drug addicts with clean needles. Others have rejected these needle exchange programs, charging that they give rise to disorder and crime and that they send the message that intravenous drug use is okay.

Then there is the always controversial question of sexual health and education. Should parents, educators, and other adult role models emphasize **abstinence** to teenagers or teach them to use condoms? Or is instruction in a variety of options that include both abstinence and birth control the answer? What role should government play in providing access to contraception?

As these examples demonstrate, state and local governments are being asked to respond to a variety of public health challenges, and they are doing so in very different ways. As we have seen before, often these different positions reflect very different political cultures. Oregon has granted terminally ill patients the right to physician-assisted suicide. Most other states continue to classify such an action as a felony, even if it is rarely prosecuted. Arizona passed legislation to ban abortions at twenty weeks of pregnancy, and even though the law almost immediately landed in court, the Arizona legislature had made its preferences known.

Different states have very different notions about the roles state governments should fill. Wisconsin's innovative early attempts at welfare reform in the late 1980s and early 1990s laid the groundwork for the federal decision to junk AFDC altogether in 1996 and return most welfare responsibilities to the states. States such as Massachusetts and Maine sought to expand healthcare coverage to nearly every resident in advance of the passage of federal healthcare reform in 2010, whereas other states have shown no great enthusiasm for providing healthcare to low-income citizens.

Yet even states that have shown little interest in taking on new responsibilities have found that healthcare is *the* unavoidable issue. This is due largely to Medicaid, the joint state-federal health insurance

---

Temporary Assistance to Needy Families (TANF)
The next-generation welfare program (passed in 1996) that provides federal assistance in the form of block grants to states, which have great flexibility in designing their programs.

Abstinence
Refraining from sexual activity, usually intercourse.

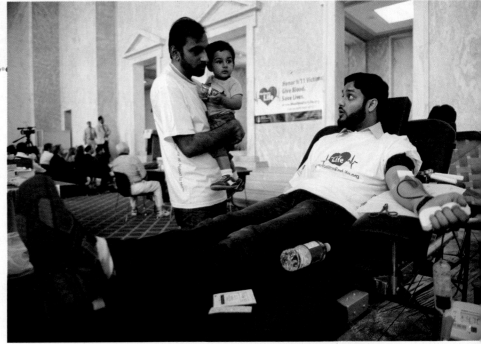

program for low-income mothers and children, the elderly, and people with disabilities. When Congress created it in 1965, it was supposed to be a modest program that served only a small number of extremely poor people. But it didn't work out that way.

As soon as it was created, Medicaid expenditures started growing quickly—and never stopped. As of June 2011, Medicaid provided health insurance and services to more than 52 million Americans—an all-time high. This included more than 30 million children and more than 15 million seniors and people with disabilities (including 4 million disabled children).[7] States now devote an average of about 16 percent of their general revenue funds to Medicaid.[8]

The continuing growth of Medicaid has huge implications for the future of state governments, which, even five years after the recession began, had not fully recovered. Temporary stimulus funding helped buoy state Medicaid programs in 2009 and 2010, but it was just that—temporary. That means that as healthcare costs grow, states will either have to raise taxes or cut funding for other state priorities such as education, transportation, and criminal justice.

Some states are already confronting these sorts of choices. With their state's stimulus funds used up, Alabama lawmakers considered spending the least money on the general fund budget since 2004—even though state budgets in normal circumstances regularly increase because of inflation and population growth. One option was cutting Medicaid, but Alabama already has one of the least generous Medicaid programs in the country and one that is heavily dependent on help from Washington (the federal government pays for a greater share of Medicaid costs in poor states such as Alabama than it does in richer ones). The federal government

sets minimum standards for who must be covered under Medicaid and what types of healthcare services must be provided. During the budget debate, Donald Williamson, state health officer, warned that it would be very difficult for the state to cut Medicaid deeply without causing cascading negative consequences and without falling out of compliance with state and federal law.

The state could cut prescription drug benefits, Williamson said, but that would drive patients to seek more costly care in hospitals. It could cut payments to doctors and healthcare facilities serving Medicaid patients, but doctors might leave the state, and hospitals and nursing homes might close. Nearly 70 percent of Alabama's nursing home patients are on Medicaid. Every dollar the state cut from Medicaid would cost it roughly two dollars in federal funds. "I think it very quickly becomes a house of cards that would on the funding side come crashing down," Williamson said. "You'll just begin to see the system of care slowly but surely unravel."

Cutting Medicaid would be hard, but the state's other options weren't good either. The head of the state's corrections department warned that potential cuts would mean thousands of prisoners would go free, work-release programs would end, and multiple prisons would close. The state could have raised taxes, but doing so might well have earned the wrath of Alabama's conservative voters. In the

States under Stress

Arizona's Transplant Debate

While many states have cut Medicaid coverage for services that the federal government deems to be optional in recent years, no state has stirred as much emotion on the subject as Arizona. Arizona was one of the states that suffered the most in the housing bust, and its budget felt the pain too. Against that backdrop, the state eliminated a host of optional Medicaid services in 2010, from speech therapy to emergency dental work. But the move that drew the most attention by far was the state's decision to eliminate Medicaid coverage for certain types heart, liver, lung, and bone marrow transplants—true matters of life and death.

In explaining their decision, Arizona officials argued that the state's budget problems, combined with looming costs under the federal healthcare law, forced their hand. "This spending cut was made literally as a last resort," Paul Senseman, a spokesman for Arizona governor Jan Brewer, told the Associated Press. Lawmakers who supported the cutbacks also argued that data showed that many patients who received transplants died quickly anyway. Others disputed those figures. Diane Rowland, director of the Kaiser Commission on Medicaid and the Uninsured, told the *New York Times* that Arizona's cutbacks to transplants were "a classic example of making decisions based not on medical need but based on a budget."

In November 2010, a man died after being denied a bone marrow transplant to treat his leukemia. In December a second person, who hospital officials said might have lived with a transplant, died. Political pressure quickly mounted on Brewer and the Arizona legislature to reverse the cuts. Democrats, who had been stung by the claim that the Affordable Care Act included provisions for "death panels," now argued that it was Arizona Republicans who were denying lifesaving care. By the following spring, lawmakers had restored the transplant coverage. At the same time, however, they made new deep cuts in funding for schools, social services, and Medicaid.

Sources: Paul Davenport, "Arizona Medicaid Cuts Include Transplant Funding," Associated Press, October 1, 2010, www.washingtonpost.com/wp-dyn/content/article/2010/10/01/AR2010100106287.html; Kevin Sack, "Arizona Medicaid Cuts Seen as a Sign of the Times," *New York Times,* December 4, 2010, www.nytimes.com/2010/12/05/us/05transplant.html?_r=0; Paul Davenport, "Ariz. Restores Transplant Coverage with New Budget," Associated Press, April 8, 2011, www.businessweek.com/ap/financialnews/D9MFFFM01.htm.

end, Alabama's lawmakers found a way to delay the moment of crisis. To help balance the budget, they asked voters for permission to remove money over the next three years from a trust fund—a savings account, in effect—consisting of taxes the state had collected from offshore oil and gas drilling. Scared by the possibility of draconian budget cuts, Alabama's normally tightfisted voters overwhelmingly agreed in the September 2012 vote. But that was only a temporary solution. The savings account won't last forever, especially given that offshore drilling is declining in Alabama waters. Alabama faces major budget challenges in the years ahead—and Medicaid is a big reason why.[9]

While Alabama's problems are worse than those of many other states, a number of others have in fact cut Medicaid in one way or another in recent years. The Affordable Care Act largely forbids states to reduce the number of people who are eligible for Medicaid, but it doesn't stop them from scaling back coverage in certain ways. In 2012, for example, Florida cut the number of days most Medicaid patients could spend in hospitals from forty-five to twenty-three, and Maine eliminated coverage for podiatry, optometry, and dental care.[10] In 2011, California tried to end a well-regarded adult day-care program for Medicaid patients that had succeeded in keeping seniors and people with disabilities out of nursing homes. Lawmakers were tempted by the possibility of saving $145 million immediately, even though having more people in nursing homes would likely have cost the state more money in the long term.[11] After opponents of the cuts sued, the state agreed to maintain a more modest program.

As these examples illustrate, the states and the federal government have been tugging Medicaid in opposite directions since 2010. Through the Affordable Care Act, the federal government is attempting to expand health insurance to tens of millions of additional Americans. Yet many states' inclination has been to cut back to save money. That tension helps explain why some states are reluctant to agree to expand their Medicaid programs under the Affordable Care Act—a decision the Supreme Court's 2012 ruling left in the hands of states.

In one sense, the Medicaid expansion is a tremendous deal for states. Under the Affordable Care Act, the federal government will pay the full cost of the expansion through 2016, then taper its share back to 90 percent by 2020. Taking the deal doesn't just mean more people will have health coverage—it also means billions of dollars will be pumped into states' economies via their healthcare systems. In certain ways, states are likely to save money: if fewer people are uninsured, fewer will seek treatment in hospital emergency rooms and stick the state with the bill. On the other hand, the Medicaid expansion is so large that even the remaining 10 percent could mean hundreds of millions of dollars a year for many states. Given the precarious condition of many states' budgets, adding any new costs is a difficult sell.[12]

There is a political dimension to the debate over the Medicaid expansion, too. In Republican-controlled states, many political leaders are generally philosophically opposed to raising taxes to pay for more generous government services. Many of those leaders have been opposed to the federal healthcare law from the start. Immediately after the Court's ruling, a group of Republican governors came out against expanding Medicaid.

Although Medicaid is states' biggest immediate healthcare expense, it is hardly their only one. States provide health insurance to their own employees and, in many cases, to their former employees after they retire. As with employee pension costs, paying for retired state employees'

healthcare costs has emerged over the last decade as one of states' leading long-term budget challenges. Traditionally, states have paid for the retiree healthcare bill that shows up each year, rather than setting aside money in advance. The looming bill is so large in coming decades, though—as of 2010, states had promised $627 billion more in retiree healthcare than they had assets set aside—that many states are starting to rethink that strategy.[13] In 2012, West Virginia, which has a long-term bill of $10 billion, became the first state to dedicate a specific amount of tax money for retiree healthcare, committing $30 million per year. West Virginia also did what many other states have done: it made retiree healthcare benefits less generous for future retirees. State and local employees have gone along with the changes reluctantly. "Does it give me heartburn?" Josh Sword, political director of the American Federation of Teachers–West Virginia, asked. "Sure. But at the end of the day, the state cannot continue to afford this level of benefit."[14]

States are also responsible for providing healthcare for inmates in state prisons. No state has struggled more with inmate healthcare than California, where state prisons have long been massively overcrowded. In 2006, a federal judge said that one inmate a week was dying unnecessarily because of the low quality of care, a violation of the U.S. Constitution's prohibition of cruel and unusual punishment. The judge took control of the prisoner healthcare system away from the state and placed it in the hands of an independent receiver. Since then, the state has made some gradual improvements—improvements that have come at a cost. The state spends well above $10,000 per prisoner each year for medical care, far more than most other states.[15] Still, the changes have not been enough to convince federal courts that the problems are solved. In 2011, the U.S. Supreme Court upheld an order that California cut its prison population of 142,000 by more than 30,000 as a way to improve care, although it allowed the state two years to implement the order and indicated that more time could be requested.[16]

County and city governments spend significant amounts on healthcare as well. In many parts of the country, hospitals and clinics funded by counties and cities continue to function as a critical social safety net for people without health insurance. These are people who earn too much to qualify for Medicaid but too little to be able to pay for private health insurance. Cities and counties also run the facilities that were tested during the 2009 H1N1 influenza pandemic, and if the United States ever experiences a large-scale biological attack, such facilities will determine how well this society survives.

How Government Got into the Healthcare Biz

If Texas chooses not to expand Medicaid under the federal healthcare law, it will miss out on $65.6 billion in federal funds over the next decade.

Any serious discussion of healthcare soon arrives at a basic question: Who should pay for what? Over the past two decades, answers to this question have varied widely. During the early 1990s, the solution offered by many Democrats was that the federal government should provide health insurance to everyone who does not have it. By the early twenty-first century, however, a lot of those same Democrats were arguing that the state governments, not the federal government, should lead the way. Universal—or nearly universal—coverage, they stated, should be created through the gradual extension of existing health insurance programs, notably Medicaid. Such programs should be expanded to encompass various populations not currently eligible for them. In contrast, some Republicans argued that health insurance should be extended through federal tax credits. How much health insurance should be provided has been another hotly contested topic. When President Obama entered office with a Democratic-majority Congress in 2009, his party once again saw the federal government as the best venue for action, leading to the Affordable Care Act.

It wasn't always so complicated. For most of the nation's history, elected officials believed that the government should serve as the health and welfare provider of last resort for society's poorest and sickest members. The level of government that officials had in mind, however, was not the federal government and not even state governments. It was local government.

The role of local governments in health and welfare goes back to the very beginning of U.S. history. In colonial America, local communities maintained almshouses to feed and clothe people who could not care for themselves and who had no families to care for them. Back then, few distinctions were made among the sick, the mentally ill, and people without means of support. As sociologist Paul Starr has noted, almshouses "received dependent persons of all kinds, mixing together promiscuously the aged, the orphaned, the insane, the ill, the debilitated."[17] Those with infectious diseases, such as typhoid fever and cholera, were sent into quarantine in pesthouses to survive as best they could.

That began to change in the nineteenth century. By the middle of the century, elected officials, social reformers, and physicians—who were just beginning to establish medicine as a respectable profession—came to believe that mixing juveniles, beggars, the mentally ill, widows, and others in almshouses was no longer the best course of action. In effect, physicians and public officials began to distinguish between the sick and the destitute. A new institution was needed—the hospital.

From the early to mid-1800s, cities such as Philadelphia and New York transformed some of their almshouses into hospitals.[18] Privately organized charitable hospitals, many run by religious groups, appeared in many cities too. Even state governments made modest forays into healthcare. By 1860, most states had established mental hospitals and homes for the blind and the deaf.

Like almshouses, the first hospitals were institutions for unfortunates without money or family. For people with family or money, a house call from the doctor was the preferred form of medical care. According to Starr, "Almost no one who had a choice sought hospital care."[19] Hospitals were regarded with dread, and rightly so. They were dangerous places, in part because of the medical and hygienic practices of the time. Sick people were safer at home. The few who became hospital patients did so because of special circumstances. They might be seamen in strange ports, travelers, the homeless, or the solitary aged, individuals who, whether traveling or destitute, were unlucky enough to fall sick without family, friends, or servants to care for them.[20]

Hospitals and physicians made a spirited effort to improve their image. Hospitals moved their sickest residents—as well as patients who were dissolute or morally objectionable—to other institutions. In 1847, for instance, Bellevue Hospital in New York decided to move the penitentiary and almshouse off its grounds and concentrate on medical care.[21] The hospital was beginning to emerge as a distinct institution.

The Idea of a Social Safety Net

The arrangement described above continued in the United States until well into the twentieth century. The duty of providing healthcare and welfare remained firmly in the hands of local governments. States assisted those with mental illnesses and people with disabilities. The federal government ran a compulsory health insurance system for the merchant marine, so that sick sailors could get care in any port, and provided pensions and healthcare to military veterans.

By the end of the nineteenth century, a new idea was percolating in progressive circles. Many social reformers came to believe that the federal government should take a much larger role in securing healthcare and pensions for the working class.

The idea first arose in Germany. In 1883, the conservative government of German chancellor Otto von Bismarck created the world's first compulsory sickness and unemployment insurance fund, which required employees and employers to set aside money to cover the costs of medical treatment for workers. Bismarck later created a compulsory retirement program, the cost of which was divided among employees, employers, and the national government, in much the same way that the Social Security system operates in the United States today. These innovations were momentous in the development of the state. Before Bismarck, most talk of healthcare, unemployment insurance,

and pensions had come from socialists and communists. He showed that conservative capitalist countries could enact such programs too. Indeed, they could take the lead in developing a generous social safety net. Over the course of the next thirty years, other European countries followed Germany's lead.

The United States, however, did not. During the heyday of the Progressive movement in the early twentieth century, discussions about national health insurance were widespread. Eventually, opposition from physicians and from the country's largest labor union, the American Federation of Labor (the forerunner of today's AFL-CIO), fearful of government control of the healthcare system, effectively derailed the idea. During the 1920s, many states took the first small steps toward creating a social safety net by setting up workers' compensation funds for injured workers. However, amid the affluence of the times, there was little support for a more ambitious social safety net.[22] That changed with the start of the Great Depression.

The Birth of the American Safety Net

On Thursday, October 24, 1929, the stock market in New York City collapsed in what the *New York Times* called "the most disastrous trading day in the stock market's history."[23] By spring 1933, it was clear that the United States had entered an unprecedented economic slump—the Great Depression.

In response to this economic disaster, the federal government for the first time took on some of the social safety net functions that European governments had pioneered decades earlier.[24] In 1935, President Franklin Delano Roosevelt and Congress teamed up to pass the Social Security Act. This act established two social safety net programs. The first was a joint federal-state program of unemployment compensation. The second was a federally run program of retirement benefits for senior citizens, which soon would be known simply as Social Security.

The federal government also created AFDC, the purpose of which was to provide monetary assistance to widowed women with children, women who had been abandoned by their husbands, and

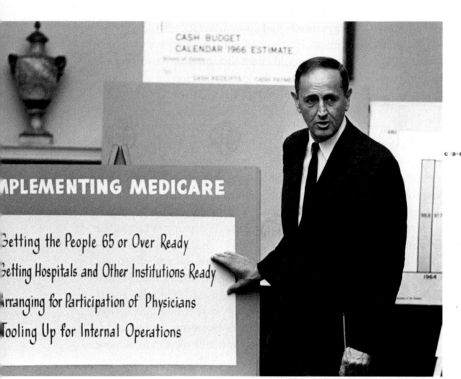

CASH BUDGET
CALENDAR 1966 ESTIMATE

IMPLEMENTING MEDICARE

Getting the People 65 or Over Ready

Getting Hospitals and Other Institutions Ready

Arranging for Participation of Physicians

Tooling Up for Internal Operations

With the strong backing of President Lyndon Johnson, Congress created Medicare in 1965. The federal health insurance program for the elderly has proven to be wildly popular. Pictured here is John Gardner, Johnson's secretary of health, education, and welfare. His outline for implementing Medicare notably says nothing about who is covering the costs.

were determined to pass legislation that would cover hospital costs for senior citizens. Congressional Republicans, however, had a different proposal in mind. They supported a voluntary health insurance program that would cover the cost of physician visits for seniors. In 1965, the two parties decided to compromise in classic Washington fashion—by doing both. The result was **Medicare**, the federal health insurance program for the elderly.

But Congress didn't stop there. While it was on a roll, it also created Medicaid. Despite their similar names, Medicare and Medicaid are very different programs. Medicare is run and paid for entirely by the federal government. As with Social Security, every senior who worked for ten years and paid taxes—or whose spouse worked for ten years and paid taxes—is eligible to participate, as are people with certain types of disabilities. The program is financed in part by a small payroll tax. Most retirees, however, take far more out of Medicare than they contributed during their working years.[26] Understandably, Medicare almost immediately became a popular program.

Medicaid, on the other hand, is a joint state-federal program that is paid for in part by the general revenue funds of state and local governments. The federal government does pick up most of the cost, however. On average, it covers nearly 60 percent of Medicaid expenditures; for poorer areas, the percentage is higher. Arkansas, Idaho,

women who were in some way incapacitated. Funded by the federal government, the program was administered by the states.

The Roosevelt administration briefly considered adding a compulsory health insurance program to the Social Security Act. However, given the medical industry's continued vehement opposition to such a program due to fear of too much government control, the proposal was eventually dropped as too controversial. Instead, the Social Security Act provided federal grants to help states pay for programs for the disabled and the aged and to provide child welfare services, public health services, and vocational rehabilitation.[25] As a result, responsibility for providing a healthcare safety net remained in the hands of state and local governments.

A Multibillion-Dollar Afterthought

State governments became major participants in the U.S. safety net system almost by accident. After the assassination of President John F. Kennedy in 1963, Lyndon B. Johnson ascended to the Oval Office. Johnson and congressional Democrats

Medicare
The federal health insurance program for elderly citizens.

Kentucky, Mississippi, South Carolina, and West Virginia all receive more than 70 percent of their Medicaid expenditures from the federal government.[27] Wealthier states split the cost 50-50. The federal government's share will rise for states that take the Medicaid expansion under the Affordable Care Act. States do not have to participate in Medicaid; however, since 1982—when Arizona finally signed on—all states do.

Therefore, Medicaid is not an unfunded mandate; the federal government does not force states to participate in it. It is, however, an **entitlement program**; that is, it does create legally enforceable rights. In fact, it is a double entitlement program. First, states have a right to a certain amount of federal money for Medicaid every year; and second, individuals who meet eligibility thresholds are entitled to Medicaid services, regardless of the cost. States are required to provide coverage to certain populations, including children in families with income below the **poverty line, or poverty threshold**, and parents who qualify for TANF.[28]

Beyond these basics, the states enjoy considerable leeway when setting those eligibility standards. (See Table 15-1.) They have created healthcare safety nets with very different levels of generosity. As of July 2012, Arkansas was the least generous state in the country. It allowed only those earning less than 17 percent of the federal poverty level—the threshold set by the U.S. Bureau of the Census to measure poverty—to receive Medicaid. That means that a working parent with two children who earned more than $270 a month—slightly more than $3,200 a year—earned too much to qualify. Few states want to be stingy when it comes to health coverage, but they need to balance their budgets, and paring back eligibility levels is one way to make the numbers work, especially when Medicaid expenditures increase by double-digit percentages every year.

Entitlement Program
A government-run program that guarantees unlimited assistance to those who meet its eligibility requirements, no matter how high the cost.

Poverty Line, or Poverty Threshold
An annual income level, set by the federal government, below which families cannot afford basic necessities.

The most generous state was Minnesota. It allowed families earning up to 215 percent of the federal poverty level to receive Medicaid benefits. In other words, a working parent with two children could earn up to $3,420 a month—more than $41,000 a year—and still qualify for Medicaid.[29] Even controlling for the fact that most parts of Arkansas have considerably lower costs of living than Minnesota, that is a dramatic difference. The United States may have one safety net for seniors, but for everyone else, it is a country with fifty-one safety nets.

In 2011 Medicaid expenditures accounted for 7 percent of Wyoming's total budget but 36.3 percent of Missouri's.

Oops! The Unexpected Cost of Health Insurance

Medicare and Medicaid were structured very differently, but the two programs soon revealed a common trait. They both quickly proved to be fantastically expensive. From 1965 to 1970, the annual rate of increase in state and federal health expenditures was 20.8 percent.[30] By fiscal year 2011, the federal government and state governments spent nearly $400 billion annually on Medicaid alone.[31]

As Medicaid spending soared, another disturbing trend was becoming evident. The number of women with children receiving financial assistance under AFDC was soaring too. After two decades of slow growth, the number of AFDC beneficiaries took off in the late 1960s, rising from slightly more than 2 million recipients in 1960 to more than 10 million recipients by 1972.

The composition of AFDC recipients also was changing. The widows of the 1940s were being replaced by divorced and separated women with children as well as single mothers who had never been married. By 1979, single mothers made up nearly 80 percent of all AFDC recipients.[32]

TABLE 15-1

Amount a Working Parent with Two Children Applying for Publicly Funded Coverage May Earn and Still Be Eligible for Medicaid (as of July 2012)

State	Monthly Income-Eligibility Threshold (dollars)	Annual Income-Eligibility Threshold (dollars)	Percentage of 2012 Federal Poverty Line
Alabama	382	4,582	24
Alaska	1,611	19,335	81
Arizona	1,686	20,235	106
Arkansas	270	3,245	17
California	1,686	20,235	106
Colorado	1,686	20,235	106
Connecticut	3,038	36,462	191
Delaware	1,893	22,717	119
District of Columbia	3,277	39,325	206
Florida	923	11,072	58
Georgia	780	9,354	49
Hawaii	1,830	21,960	100
Idaho	620	7,445	39
Illinois	3,038	36,462	191
Indiana	382	4,582	24
Iowa	1,304	15,654	82
Kansas	509	6,109	32
Kentucky	939	11,263	59
Louisiana	398	4,773	25
Maine	3,182	38,180	200
Maryland	1,845	22,144	116
Massachusetts	2,116	25,390	133
Michigan	1,002	12,027	63
Minnesota	3,420	41,044	215
Mississippi	700	8,400	44
Missouri	573	6,872	36
Montana	875	10,500	55
Nebraska	907	10,881	57
Nevada	1,384	16,608	87
New Hampshire	780	9,354	49
New Jersey	3,182	38,180	200
New Mexico	1,352	16,227	85
New York	2,386	28,635	150
North Carolina	780	9,354	49
North Dakota	939	11,263	59
Ohio	1,432	17,181	90

State	Monthly Income-Eligibility Threshold (dollars)	Annual Income-Eligibility Threshold (dollars)	Percentage of 2012 Federal Poverty Line
Oklahoma	843	10,118	53
Oregon	636	7,636	40
Pennsylvania	732	8,781	46
Rhode Island	2,879	34,553	181
South Carolina	1,448	17,372	91
South Dakota	827	9,927	52
Tennessee	2,004	24,053	126
Texas	414	4,963	26
Utah	700	8,400	44
Vermont	2,943	35,317	185
Virginia	493	5,918	31
Washington	1,161	13,936	73
West Virginia	509	6,109	32
Wisconsin	3,182	38,180	200
Wyoming	811	9,736	51

Source: Adapted from Kaiser Family Foundation, "Where Are States Today? Medicaid and CHIP Eligibility Levels for Children and Non-disabled Adults," July 2012, www.kff.org/medicaid/upload/7993-02.pdf.

Note: The federal poverty level for a family of three was $19,090 for the forty-eight contiguous states and Washington, D.C.; $21,960 for Hawaii; and $23,870 for Alaska. Monthly and annual income thresholds are rounded to the nearest dollar.

As the group benefiting from welfare changed, the program became increasingly unpopular with the public. During the late 1970s and early 1980s, Ronald Reagan and other conservative politicians railed against what they saw as the excesses of the welfare state. They evoked images of "welfare queens" who drove Cadillacs and paid for steak dinners with fat rolls of food stamps.[33] Reagan's welfare queen proved to be more myth than reality, but it was arguably true that the United States had created a set of permanent dependents of the sort that Roosevelt had warned against when he called government relief "a narcotic, a subtle destroyer of the human spirit."[34]

The Devolution Revolution

The supporters of Ronald Reagan weren't the only people who were fed up. State and local officials were too. Many were frustrated by the high-handed way the federal government administered welfare and Medicaid. Medicaid was theoretically a joint state-federal program, but the federal government always held the whip over state governments. The Centers for Medicare and Medicaid Services (CMS) is the federal agency responsible for administering both Medicare and Medicaid. Formerly called the Health Care Financing Administration, this agency monitors state governments in much the same way that a reform school principal might monitor juvenile offenders.

Of course, the federal government sometimes had reason to be suspicious. Many states, most notably Louisiana, have long sought to shift as many Medicaid expenses to the federal side of the ledger as possible. Despite sometimes questionable actions on the part of states, even federal officials began to come around during the 1980s to the idea that perhaps the states should be given greater freedom to experiment with their welfare and Medicaid programs. In the late 1980s, the U.S. Department of Health and Human Services, the parent organization of the CMS, began to grant states demonstration waivers that allowed them to experiment with how they provided welfare and healthcare. By 2006, every state had received at least one waiver for a portion of its Medicaid program. States were able to extend or augment health insurance to more than 7 million individuals who otherwise would not have been eligible to receive it.[35] Recently, with the Affordable Care Act, the federal government has taken the lead role in offering health insurance to more people. States, however, are at the forefront of a different type of innovation. They have experimented with new ways to coordinate care in the hope of improving patients' health outcomes and saving money simultaneously. (See the box "A Difference That Makes a Difference: North Carolina's Medical Home Model.")

Welfare Reform

One of the first states to take advantage of federal flexibility was Wisconsin. In 1987, Tommy Thompson entered the governor's office, and one of his first acts was to bring together about a dozen people for lunch at the state executive mansion to discuss one of the most contentious topics in American politics—welfare reform. Thompson's first lunch underscored that he was eager to think outside the box and achieve real reform. Unlike most governors, Thompson didn't invite policy wonks or advocates, either pro or con. Instead, he invited welfare mothers so that he could hear firsthand about the obstacles that made it difficult for them to get and keep jobs.[36]

Thompson took the answers he got that day and, during his subsequent yearly lunches, set out to radically reorient welfare in Wisconsin. In doing so, he managed to avoid the dead ends that previous reformers had encountered. In the past, most states had attempted to move welfare recipients into the job market by providing training and education opportunities. All these programs were expensive, and only some were successful. Thompson decided to focus on getting welfare recipients job—any jobs. Virtually all welfare recipients were required to work. If a recipient was unable to find a job, then a subsidized one or one in community service was made available. In addition, if a welfare recipient needed child care during the workday or transportation to get to work, the state provided it.

Essentially, Thompson subverted one of the major arguments for ending welfare—namely, that welfare recipients were free-riding on the tax-paying public. In doing so, he actually increased funding for child care, healthcare, and transportation. Once recipients were working, they were provided with one-on-one job counseling, education, training, and other support services.[37]

Not all of Thompson's actions to reform welfare were as touchy-feely as his yearly lunches or as supportive as providing child care and transportation, however. Some of them were downright coercive. For example, funds were cut off to the parents of truant children. Also, marriage incentives were created for teenage parents.

By forcing welfare recipients to get jobs *in addition to* offering them the support they realistically needed to enter the job market, Thompson disarmed both conservative and liberal critics and pointed the way to workable reforms to the system. Other states soon followed suit. Work requirements were strengthened and time limits on benefits were imposed. New assistance with child care and transportation was offered. By summer 1996, more than forty states had received statewide waivers that allowed them to vary the work requirements for AFDC recipients.[38]

Thompson's reforms, coercive or otherwise, were remarkably effective. Providing services such as child care and transportation increased per capita welfare costs in the short run, but in the long run it paid off. State welfare costs fell by about 65 percent over the course of the decade. The state saved more than $1 billion. Such successes later earned Thompson the position of secretary of health and human services under President George W. Bush.

In 1996, Congress and President Bill Clinton formally embraced the reforms that the states had initiated and replaced AFDC with TANF. As part of this new program, the Personal Responsibility and Work Opportunity Reconciliation Act put a five-year cap on federal payments to welfare recipients. It also required states to put a large portion of welfare recipients to work.

The new legislation was most notable, however, for what it did not require. Gone were most of the requirements that the federal government sign off on the state plans. TANF gave states the freedom to set benefit levels, eligibility requirements, and financial incentives and penalties as they saw fit.

MAP 15-1

TANF Income Eligibility Thresholds, 2010

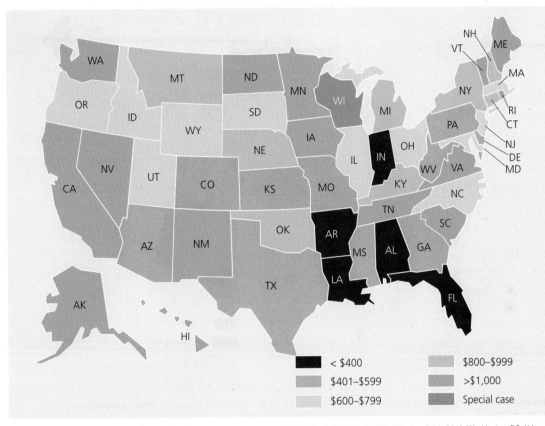

■ < $400	■ $800–$999
■ $401–$599	■ >$1,000
■ $600–$799	■ Special case

Source: David Kassabian, Tracey Vericker, David Searle, and Mary Murphy, Welfare Rules Databook: State TANF Policies as of July 2010 (Washington, DC: Urban Institute, August 2011), 72–73, www.urban.org/UploadedPDF/412381-Welfare-Rules-Databook.pdf.

TANF also converted welfare from an entitlement program to a block grant program. In the past, people who met eligibility guidelines had been legally entitled to welfare, no matter the cost. Now, the federal government would provide only a finite amount of money to the states. At first, the federal payout was quite generous. The intent was to give states plenty of funds to devise and implement the support programs of their choice. Over time, however, the federal contribution grew smaller and smaller.

The number of welfare recipients declined sharply, from approximately 6 million in 1996 to less than 4 million by 2008. Poverty rates for single-parent households also fell during this period. By and large, the alarming outcomes predicted by opponents of the welfare reform bill failed to materialize, although caseloads began creeping northward through 2009 as national unemployment topped 10 percent.[39] Still, even as the economy remained weak in 2012, fewer people were receiving TANF benefits than in 2005. That stands in contrast to entitlement programs such as food stamps, which grew rapidly during the recession and its aftermath.[40]

The Feds Falter

When Bill Clinton took office in 1993, he and his administration were prepared to let states take the lead on welfare reform. After all, the president's previous job had been governor of Arkansas. However, the president and his wife, Hillary Rodham Clinton, did see the problem of the uninsured as primarily a federal one. In early 1994, Clinton introduced the Health Security Act. This was legislation that would

MAP 15-2

Rates of Uninsurance among Nonelderly, 2011

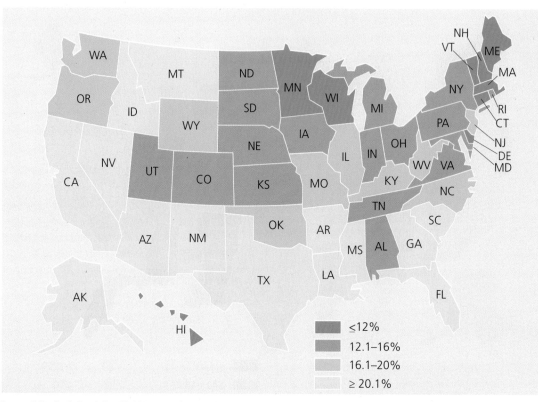

■	≤12%
■	12.1–16%
□	16.1–20%
□	≥ 20.1%

Source: Kaiser Family Foundation, "Health Insurance Coverage of Nonelderly 0–64, States, U.S. (2011)," www.statehealthfacts.org/comparetable .jsp?ind=126&cat=3.

have provided universal health insurance to all Americans.

Senate Republicans initially countered with a proposal that would have extended health insurance coverage dramatically but would still have fallen short of universal health insurance. Clinton rejected this counterproposal, vowing to veto any measure that failed to provide 100 percent coverage.[41] Politics being politics, the two major parties were unable to find common ground. Nine months later, the Clinton health insurance proposal went down in defeat.[42]

Fast-forward more than fifteen years. In 2010, the year Congress approved the Affordable Care Act, 50 million Americans lacked health insurance—fully 16 percent of the population.[43] (See Map 15-2.) The Kaiser Commission on Medicaid and the Uninsured has estimated that some 20 percent of uninsured residents are non-citizens, who often work in low-wage jobs that do not include health coverage.[44]

The Rise of the Healthcare State

The collapse of healthcare reform efforts in the 1990s at the federal level left states in a tricky position. They were being squeezed between the pincers of the rising costs of state Medicaid programs and the rising demands for assistance from citizens struggling with prescription drug costs and a lack of health insurance. Finally, in the mid-1990s, states found what looked like a good way to both contain costs and expand coverage—**managed care**.

Proponents of managed care originally saw health maintenance organizations (HMOs) as a way to improve the quality of care that patients

Managed Care
An arrangement for the provision of healthcare whereby an agency acts as an intermediary between consumers and healthcare providers.

received. Most medical care that patients receive in the United States is poorly coordinated. Different doctors often cannot easily share a patient's medical records. In addition, physicians have little incentive to offer preventive services because they get paid for dealing with sickness. Paul Ellwood, the physician who coined the phrase *health maintenance organization* in the early 1970s, believed that HMOs would rationalize and coordinate the medical care that patients received. This would improve the quality of the healthcare for members of an HMO; moreover, HMOs would reduce costs by emphasizing preventive healthcare.

Under managed care, instead of paying doctors a fee for each service provided, states typically paid an HMO a flat fee for each Medicaid patient enrolled in a plan. The fees that states offered HMOs were designed to be lower than the expenses the states would have incurred if patients had remained in a traditional fee-for-service Medicaid program. HMOs agreed to these lower rates because they believed that, even with lower reimbursement rates, they would still be able to squeeze inefficiencies out of the system and turn a profit.

Medicaid recipients benefited too. They were able to join health plans that gave them access to physicians and services that often had been unavailable under the old program. Traditional fee-for-service Medicaid reimbursement rates are so low that many physicians simply refuse to see Medicaid beneficiaries. Ultimately, the states saved money, at least theoretically.

A Promising Beginning

For a while, the HMO approach seemed to work. By 1998, approximately half of all Medicaid recipients nationwide were in managed care programs.[45] As enrollment increased, health costs slowed. From 1995 to 1999, Medicaid expenditures grew at the relatively modest rate of 4.3 percent annually. This was dramatically lower than the unprecedented 27 percent growth of the early 1990s.[46] In addition, as the economic expansion that began in the early 1990s gained momentum and swelled state coffers, a growing number of state officials and healthcare advocates began to think about addressing other problems of the uninsured. Advocates set their sights on a new state-federal partnership. The first goal: to extend health insurance to uninsured children in families that earned too much to qualify for Medicaid but too little to pay for healthcare on their own.

In August 1997, Congress created the **State Children's Health Insurance Program (CHIP)** at the behest of President Clinton. CHIP was designed to provide health insurance to roughly 6.5 million children in low-income families without health insurance.[47] As with Medicaid, CHIP would be designed and administered by the states and paid for primarily by the federal government. The federal government would spring for about 80 percent of total costs.

The states were given considerable flexibility in designing their child health programs. They were free to fold CHIP into their Medicaid programs or create stand-alone CHIP programs. As with Medicaid, they determined the eligibility levels. They also could cap CHIP enrollments and force recipients to pay some of the costs for the health insurance they received.[48]

Not surprisingly, states have taken advantage of this flexibility. About fifteen states allow children living in families earning up to 200 percent of the federal poverty level to qualify for CHIP. More than twenty states cover children in families with even higher incomes—sometimes significantly higher. The highest is New York at 400 percent—or nearly $80,000 a year for a family with one adult and two children. Just two states, Idaho and North Dakota, cap coverage at less than 200 percent of the poverty level.[49]

Congress reauthorized the program in 2009 with an additional $33 billion in federal funds, and the Affordable Care Act further bolstered CHIP by extending program funding through 2015 and establishing the program itself until at least 2019.

State Children's Health Insurance Program (CHIP)
A joint federal-state program designed to expand healthcare coverage to children whose parents earned income above the poverty line but still were too poor to afford insurance.

There's just one catch: the legislation mandates that states maintain their CHIP eligibility standards as they existed on March 23, 2010. The rule came just a week after Arizona policymakers had agreed to eliminate the state's CHIP, which covers 38,000 children, as part of its budget-balancing moves. Because the Arizona program was not due to end until June 2010, the state was forced to find the funds to reinstate it.[50] The federal government did, however, give Arizona permission to freeze CHIP for new applicants.

Does It Work?

By the late 1990s, many health policy experts and advocates had come to see the gradual expansion of Medicaid and CHIP and of the state-federal partnership as the best way to address the widespread lack of health insurance in the United States. The Robert Wood Johnson Foundation reported in 2006 that the number of uninsured children had dropped by 20 percent since CHIP's introduction.[51]

That is clearly a significant accomplishment. Unfortunately, the CHIP approach has not reached everyone it is supposed to reach. The Urban Institute estimated that in 2002 more than a quarter of all poor children—those whose families had incomes below 100 percent of the federal poverty level—continued to lack insurance.[52] Indeed, data from 2011 show that 10 percent of children in the United States are not covered by insurance.[53] Among poor children—who make up about one-fifth of all children—that figure is significantly higher. This is despite the fact that almost all of this population qualifies for CHIP.[54] In the early 2000s, officials saw promise in CHIP as a vehicle for covering adults as well as children. But as Medicaid spending accelerated and state revenues shriveled in 2002 and 2003, states retreated from plans to expand their CHIP programs and shifted their emphasis to containing costs as best they could. Caught in the budgetary crossfire were federal waivers allowing states to use CHIP to cover adults who didn't qualify for Medicaid. Federal officials had expected the program to cover 2.7 million uninsured adults, but states simply couldn't afford to expand the coverage. By 2009, programs under the waivers covered only about 270,000 adults.[55]

The Safety Net Widens

What effects do these different policies have on the residents of these states? Researchers have found a strong correlation between having health insurance and access to and use of healthcare services.[56] In addition, giving more people more access to public healthcare is one direct way to increase their healthcare use. Some research shows that expanding Medicaid results in lower death rates and that Medicaid participants report being in better health.[57] But expanding eligibility for health insurance does not necessarily guarantee that a state will have a lower number of uninsured. Massachusetts and Vermont are two states that have made major efforts to expand eligibility for public health insurance; consequently, they have lower numbers of uninsured children than do other states, such as Idaho and Montana. However, that is not universally the case. As of 2011, 10 percent of children were uninsured in "generous" New Jersey, while only 8 percent were uninsured in "stingy" North Dakota.[58] Such a paradox can be caused by a combination of factors: the availability of jobs offering health insurance, parents' awareness of programs for which their children qualify, and the cost of insurance for those just beyond the eligibility thresholds.

Not having health insurance does not necessarily translate into no healthcare. Government-supported community health centers provide healthcare to more than 20 million uninsured Americans in thousands of communities across the country every year. These clinics treat people regardless of their ability or inability to pay.[59] In addition, hospitals are required to provide treatment to people who come into their emergency rooms whether these people can pay or not.

Along with community health centers, public hospitals have long assumed a particularly important role in providing services to the uninsured.

For many low-income individuals, the emergency room of a public hospital is their first and only way to access medical care. Many public hospitals border high-crime neighborhoods and provide essential advanced emergency and trauma services, as well as outpatient clinics for these same communities. These are critically important functions. They are not, however, very profitable ones. The Urban Institute estimates that uncompensated care—medical care provided to the uninsured that they do not pay for themselves—costs the medical system $64 billion annually.[60] In 2008, 16 percent of public hospitals' costs were uncompensated, compared to 5.8 percent for hospitals nationwide, according to the National Association of Public Hospitals and Health Systems.[61]

> Many public hospitals border high-crime neighborhoods and provide essential advanced emergency and trauma services, as well as outpatient clinics for these same communities. These are critically important functions. They are not, however, very profitable ones.

The result is that public hospitals have a tough time staying open. Between 1996 and 2002, the number of public hospitals in the nation's one hundred largest cities fell from 730 to 645.[62] The recent recession crunched them even further; public hospital systems across the country cut back on programs, including mental health services, pharmacies, and oncology clinics. New York cut four hundred positions from its public hospitals in 2009.[63]

Lack of access to care is not an issue limited to cities and suburbs. Rural areas long have been plagued by fragmented healthcare systems and shortages of doctors and nurses. Even worse, rural residents tend to be older and poorer than their urban and suburban counterparts, factors that often translate into a greater need for healthcare services.[64] It's not a formula for a healthy population.

The problem has not gone unnoticed. In partnership with the federal government, all fifty states have established offices of rural health. One way doctors reach more patients in rural areas is through "telemedicine." While doctors can't remove a gallbladder remotely, they can often discuss a patient's symptoms just as easily over a TV screen as in a doctor's office. For patients in isolated rural areas, telemedicine can improve access to healthcare. The technology for doing so has existed for years now, but states are still sorting through the regulatory issues. Doctors practicing telemedicine need to be compliant with the laws and regulations of the state in which the patient is located. A doctor in Virginia, for example, wouldn't have a problem using telemedicine for an in-state patient, but medical facilities could encounter some legal issues if a patient lives in North Carolina, West Virginia, or Maryland. Further, a doctor is required to establish a physician-patient relationship in order to prescribe medications. As of 2012, only twelve states allowed an electronic examination to meet the requirements of a face-to-face examination.[65] Some states are working to overcome these regulatory barriers. The New Mexico Medical Board, for example, will issue a telemedicine license to any healthcare provider outside the state who is licensed in any other state or territory in the United States.[66]

Beyond Managed Care

After their initial surge of success mentioned earlier, many HMOs failed to meet the high hopes of their boosters. Consumers were dismayed by the ways in which HMOs limited their choices of doctors to small groups of physicians who had agreed to lower reimbursement rates. In some cases, the programs demanded that doctors receive preapproval before performing certain procedures. By the late 1990s, many consumers had turned against HMOs.

Eager to separate themselves from the HMOs they had initially supported, state legislators acted on their constituents' desires. Many states passed "patients' bill of rights" legislation. These laws made it easier for patients to sue HMOs and generally made it more difficult for managed care plans to restrict healthcare. Such acts may

A Difference That Makes A Difference

North Carolina's Medical Home Model

Dr. Jugta Kahai had a problem. One of her patients, a nine-month-old boy with asthma, kept showing up in the emergency room. He was struggling for breath. His mother was distraught. And Dr. Kahai was puzzled. During office visits, she had talked at length with the mother about the importance of keeping the home clean and free of environmental factors that might trigger an asthma attack. The mother seemed to understand the doctor's suggestions. And yet the child was still arriving in the emergency room in extreme distress.

Fortunately, the baby's physician had access to a resource most doctors only dream of—a local case manager, funded by the state, who could assist her in caring for patients with chronic illnesses. What the case manager found when she went to see the baby and his mother in their home was surprising. The family's mobile home was in a rough part of town, but it was spotless—too spotless. The mother proudly explained that she cleaned the house every three days using half a gallon of bleach. And that, it turned out, was the problem. The fumes from the bleach were triggering asthma attacks in the child.

The bleach cleaning stopped. Soon after, so did the emergency room visits. And North Carolina's Medicaid program was spared tens of thousands of dollars in unnecessary expenses.

This wasn't a random good catch. Over the course of the past fifteen years, North Carolina's Community Care program has made major strides toward achieving one of the most-discussed goals in health reform: a patient-centered form of care that replaces episodic treatment based on individual illnesses with a long-term coordinated approach—what health experts sometimes refer to as the "medical home."

North Carolina's Community Care program isn't traditional case management, where a nurse or outside vendor calls and visits patients, independent of their physician, in an effort to get the patients to take their medications or otherwise comply with the doctor's instructions. Instead, it's an integrated, team-based approach. Primary care physicians and case managers, guided by claims data and chart audits, work together to improve care and coordinate treatment.

As of 2012, 4,500 doctors and 600 case managers were participating in the program. Primary care doctors are paid a small fee to participate and also receive money for each patient they oversee to hire case managers and other staff to provide a network of care. This model helps doctors know what is going on with their patients. "Every patient, every enrollee who went to the emergency room or who was admitted to the hospital, they know that [information] within 24 hours," says Tork Wade, the executive director of the Community Care program. "It's real-time data that the networks then can act on, have their care manager follow up and visit the patient in the hospital. Many of our care managers are now embedded in hospitals to be able to reach the patient as early as possible, making sure they get their medications, and that they get connected back to their primary care practice as quickly as possible."

In North Carolina, coordinating care hasn't just helped doctors treat patients—it has also saved money. By one estimate, the state avoided $1.5 billion in healthcare costs from 2007 to 2009. As a result, North Carolina has come closer than most other states to achieving the holy grail in health policy: to lower costs and improve health outcomes at the same time.

Sources: Adapted from John Buntin, "Health Care Comes Home," *Governing*, February 28, 2009, www.governing.com/topics/health-human-services/Health-Care-Comes-Home.html. See also John Buntin (interview with Tork Wade, executive director, Community Care of North Carolina), "Managing Care without Managed Care," *Governing*, January 24, 2012, www.governing.com/topics/health-human-services/gov-col-managing-care-without-managed-care.html.

have curbed some of the HMOs' more egregious practices, but they also came with a cost of their own. By making it harder for HMOs to limit care and access to physicians, lawmakers also deprived HMOs of negotiating leverage and reduced their ability to hold down costs. Costs were again on the rise by the late 1990s.

Nonetheless, the use of managed care in Medicaid programs was alive and well. As of 2010, 71 percent of Medicaid patients were enrolled in managed care plans.[67] The trend has been for states to shift ever more patients into managed care, with Florida, Illinois, and South Carolina all deciding in 2011 to virtually end traditional fee-for-service in Medicaid. Yet, more and more, states are deciding that managed care on its own isn't enough.

The accountable care organization (ACO) is one possible successor to the HMO. ACOs are partnerships of healthcare providers—including primary care doctors, specialists, and sometimes hospitals—that agree to a set budget for serving all of the health and long-term care needs of a defined group of patients. In other words, ACOs are a lot like HMOs, except that healthcare providers themselves, rather than third-party entities, manage the care they provide. Under the ACO model, the healthcare providers have a financial incentive to work together to keep patients healthy, to treat those who are sick efficiently, and to help patients who have chronic illnesses control the effects of their diseases. If costs fall below a set budget, the ACO shares in the profits. If costs exceed the budget, some ACOs share in the losses. Budgets are set based on the overall health of the population to be served, and payments are tied to quality measurements.[68]

The ACO concept is still in its infancy. So far, it has been used more commonly in Medicare than in Medicaid. Some skeptics view it as little more than managed care with a different name. Nonetheless, some states are very interested. Borrowing heavily from the ACO model, in 2011 Oregon approved a law to move close to a million people—including Medicaid enrollees, but also teachers and other government employees—into coordinated care organizations.[69] "We have the opportunity to do something that no other state has done, and something that has eluded our nation for decades," Oregon governor John Kitzhaber said at the time. "That is creating a system that actually improves the health of the population at a cost we can afford."[70]

Time for Reform

After the initial success of HMOs, healthcare costs were on the rise again by the early 2000s. In fiscal year 2000, Medicaid expenditure grew by 9 percent. By 2002, it was growing at 12.8 percent. What was behind this surge in healthcare spending? Several factors stand out: jumps in prescription drug costs; increasing unemployment, which left more Americans relying on the healthcare safety net; and the growth of the elderly population, which left greater numbers of people in need of long-term care, whether in their homes or in settings such as nursing homes and assisted living facilities. The budget pressures were enough to push states toward ever more creative experiments to control costs while expanding coverage.

> What was behind this surge in healthcare spending? Several factors stand out: jumps in prescription drug costs; increasing unemployment, which left more Americans relying on the healthcare safety net; and the growth of the elderly population, which left greater numbers of people in need of long-term care, whether in their homes or in settings such as nursing homes and assisted living facilities.

Lofty Goals

The defeat of federal healthcare reform in the 1990s left the states in charge of efforts to expand health insurance coverage. Maine and Massachusetts unveiled universal (or near-universal) healthcare plans that served as precursors to the federal healthcare reform bill passed in 2010.

When Dirigo Health, Maine's plan, began in 2004, 14 percent of the state's residents lacked health insurance, and 80 percent of the uninsured worked for small businesses that could not afford to provide coverage. Private insurers agreed to provide coverage, which the state would administer and, for the first year, subsidize. In the first phase of enrollment, geared toward small businesses and self-employed workers, 250 businesses and 1,000 individuals signed up.[71] By late 2006, however, researchers found that, even though the program had enrolled more than 16,000 Mainers, it had reduced the state's uninsured population by less than 10 percent. They also reported that the state had raised insufficient funds to support Dirigo.[72] The plan ultimately ran into financial problems and capped enrollment well below its original goal.[73] "The time has passed for states to go it alone; DirigoChoice helps prove that," Maine representative Sharon Anglin Treat, chair of the state's Joint Standing Committee on Insurance and Financial Services, wrote in a letter to the editor of the *Wall Street Journal* in 2009.[74]

Maine's experience did not stop Massachusetts from launching an even more ambitious plan of its own. The plan required every resident of the state to have health insurance by July 2007 or face tax penalties. Under the law, every resident below the federal poverty line can receive insurance fully subsidized by the state; subsidies are extended on a sliding scale to those earning between 100 and 300 percent over the established federal poverty line. Businesses that do not provide health insurance are required to pay the state $295 per employee per year; this money is used to fund the coverage subsidies. However, calling the Massachusetts plan "universal healthcare" isn't exactly accurate. State officials estimated the law would extend health insurance coverage to as much as 95 percent of the state's population. They expected that the remaining residents would accept the tax penalties rather than pay for insurance that may still be too expensive, despite the government subsidies.[75]

By 2008, just 6.1 percent of the state's population was uninsured, the lowest rate in the nation. But Massachusetts was beginning to suffer under the strains of the initiative's expense. The Massachusetts Taxpayers Foundation estimated that the program added more than $700 million per year in annual costs, which the state splits 50-50 with the federal government. The state cut its payments to hospitals for uncompensated care and raised its cigarette tax by $1 a pack, but, coupled with declining revenues, its efforts weren't sufficient to close the gap.[76] In response, Massachusetts adopted an ambitious, multifaceted new plan in 2012 designed to limit the state's expenses. Among other things, the plan now limits by law how fast the state's healthcare costs are allowed to rise and redirects more patients into managed care, accountable care organizations, and other arrangements that are designed to spend less by improving coordination.[77]

Shortly after taking office, President Barack Obama declared that the federal government would, once again, take on healthcare reform. Members of Congress invoked the Massachusetts program often during their debates; those in favor of reform pointed to its success in reducing the uninsured population, while those opposed singled out its costs. Ultimately, after nearly a year of hearings and speeches, President Obama signed the Affordable Care Act into law on March 23, 2010. Federal healthcare reform had finally been accomplished, but the debate was far from over. "It'll probably be 10 years before it all shakes out," said Chris Whatley, Washington director of the Council of State Governments. "This will push the fabric of the state-federal relationship in new directions, and we don't know how it will all come out."[78]

Issues to Watch

Passing federal healthcare reform legislation was just the first step. States will continue to grapple

Obamacare supporters and opponents gather in front of the U.S. Supreme Court in Washington, D.C., on June 28, 2012, to find out the ruling on the Affordable Care Act. The Court upheld the act but made the Medicaid expansion optional for states, giving them vastly more power to determine how the law is implemented.

with the law's effects inside their borders, and they must continue to address a number of other burgeoning challenges, including those discussed below.

Health Information Technology

In an age when laptops and smartphones are ubiquitous, anyone who has had to fill out identical paperwork for multiple doctors has probably wondered why those documents couldn't be saved electronically and shared. The federal government and states are working with private healthcare providers to enable them to do just that, through a number of health information technology (IT) initiatives. These initiatives seek to integrate electronic medical records, prescription ordering, and other critical patient documents and facilitate the sharing of files among doctors and hospitals. A 2005 study by the RAND Corporation found that health IT could save the country as much as $77 billion annually in efficiencies.[79] Most of the technology that the initiatives need already exists, but the states and the federal government must still convince private practitioners to participate, identify national standards to match technologies across state lines, address patient privacy concerns, and find a way to pay for it all.[80]

The 2009 federal stimulus bill included nearly $26 billion for health IT for Medicare, Medicaid, and the general population. A small fraction of that money—about $560 million—was made available in competitive grants to states to help them pay for the development of health information exchanges, the backbone of the nationwide network. The stimulus funding produced some quick results. By November 2011, 34 percent of doctors had access to basic electronic health records, up from 22 percent two years earlier. By May 2011, every state had a coordinator in charge of health IT.[81]

While the stimulus funds provided some seed money to states, they were temporary. That means states need an ongoing revenue stream to keep their health information exchanges operational. Starting in 2008, Vermont began generating its funds through a fee the state charges insurance companies. Within a year, the fee had pumped enough money into the state to pay for an electronic medical records system for physicians who are not affiliated with hospitals (independent practitioners often cannot afford the average $44,000 start-up cost).[82] Tennessee is an example of a state that has been less successful in finding a financially viable way to sustain its health information exchanges. Beginning in 2005, a regional health information organization began serving eastern Tennessee. At one point, 1,500 doctors had signed up. Yet the organization couldn't persuade enough local healthcare providers to pay fees to join in order to make the financing work—area hospitals chose not to participate. The organization shut down in 2011.[83] The federal government has described regional health information organizations like the one that failed in Tennessee as the building blocks to a national health information network. The organizations are being built, however, to work with industry within a state, not necessarily outside it. Such designs could make a national linkup problematic.

Long-Term Care

Unlike private-sector health insurance plans, state Medicaid programs have an additional responsibility. Medicaid provides long-term care to the elderly and other services to people with disabilities. These services can range from providing nursing home care for low-income Medicaid recipients to developing rehabilitation plans for people with disabilities. All these services are extremely expensive. Although the elderly and disabled make up only about 25 percent of the people enrolled in Medicaid, they account for two-thirds of total Medicaid spending.[84] More than 10 million Americans now use some form of long-term care.[85]

Moreover, the cost of long-term care is growing fast. According to the Congressional Budget Office, caring for elderly and disabled Medicaid beneficiaries accounted for more than 72 percent of the program's cost increases between 1975 and 2002. States' long-term care bills hit $147 billion in 2009 and may reach as much as $346 billion by 2040.[86]

Demographics are largely driving those cost increases. According to the Census Bureau, the number of people eighty-five years of age and older will grow by 40 percent by 2020. By 2040, that population is expected to grow by more than 250 percent, to 15.4 million people.[87] As it does, the number of people with serious disabilities will almost certainly increase. Many of these people will be unable—or unwilling—to pay for long-term care on their own.

Some states, such as Oregon, have kept costs down by shifting the elderly away from expensive care in nursing homes and toward less expensive at-home care and assisted living centers. Seniors overwhelmingly prefer such alternatives to nursing homes. The federal government has encouraged states' efforts in this direction despite opposition from the strong nursing home lobby. The percentage of Medicaid long-term care spending that went to noninstitutional care more than tripled from between 1995 and 2010, rising to 45 percent.[88] The Affordable Care Act will use financial incentives to move states more aggressively toward the provision of home-based services.

Despite the expense to states, the long-term care coverage provided under Medicaid comes with a big drawback. To qualify, a patient must have almost nothing in assets. Examples abound of long-term care patients spending down hundreds of thousands of dollars in life savings before they qualify for Medicaid.[89] The Affordable Care Act attempted to find a new model. It created the first national long-term care insurance plan, a voluntary program to be financed through payroll deductions.[90] During the debate over the law, however, Republicans who were concerned about the potential cost of the program succeeded in convincing Congress to include a provision requiring the federal government to design the program in a way that it would pay for itself over the course of seventy-five years. In October

2011, the Obama administration conceded that making the program financially solvent wasn't possible and abandoned it.

The Return of Public Health

The states have become major players in the field of healthcare. However, local governments at both the county and city levels continue to play important roles as well. In many parts of the country, local governments, unlike state governments, are direct healthcare providers.

In the wake of the terrorist attacks of September 11, 2001, many government officials have come to view the public health system in a new light. Individuals in this field now are seen as the first responders to possible biological terrorism, pandemics, and natural disasters such as Hurricane Katrina. "Any community that fails to prepare and expects the federal government will come to the rescue is tragically wrong. It's not because we don't care, don't want to, or don't have the money, but because it's logistically impossible," Mike Leavitt, the U.S. secretary of health and human services under President George W. Bush, told state and local officials in 2006.[91] Some experts now believe that, instead of downsizing public hospitals, governments should look for ways to keep them available in case a crisis generates a high number of casualties.[92]

State and local governments had begun drawing up emergency response plans before swine flu emerged in 2009. The National Association of City and County Health Officials, anticipating as much as one-third of the population falling ill in such an epidemic, issued a guide to planning for local governments. Overall, experts thought the systems worked reasonably well during the height of the H1N1 pandemic. "Capacities were stretched but not broken by this pandemic," said William Schaffner, chair of the Department of Preventive Medicine at the Vanderbilt University School of Medicine.[93] Another test may come when, as experts expect, H1N1 returns for another round.

Another controversial issue in many communities involves sexual health and education. One in nine girls between the ages of sixteen and nineteen becomes pregnant outside of marriage, yet a considerable number of parents remain opposed to their children learning about sexuality in the classroom. These parents helped to resurrect abstinence-only sex education programs, which have received $1 billion in federal funding since 1998, when only 2 percent of schools offered such programs. By 2002, the proportion of schools teaching abstinence as the only way to avoid sexually transmitted diseases and pregnancy had risen to 23 percent.[94] Congressional Democrats allowed the program to expire in June 2009, but it was partially revived as part of a federal healthcare reform compromise. The bill will provide $250 million over five years for abstinence education—if states can provide 75 percent matching funds. It also allocates $375 million for comprehensive sex education.[95]

Evaluations of abstinence-only programs report conflicting findings that are often used by both proponents and opponents to advance their positions. One recent study conducted by a Pennsylvania State University researcher found that, compared with counterparts who had taken comprehensive sex education classes, fewer middle school students who were enrolled in an abstinence-only education program engaged in sexual activity within two years. Further, more students in both groups remained sexually inactive in comparison with students who had no sex education at all.[96] Regardless of the teaching method, the statistics seem headed in the right direction: in 2010, the rate of births to teenage mothers fell to the lowest level since the 1940s.[97]

The states are also the battlegrounds in the debate over access to contraception. At least twenty-six states have passed laws that require insurers that cover prescription drugs to include coverage of contraceptives. Twenty-one of the states, however, allow exemptions for employers who oppose such coverage for religious reasons.[98] In this way, the states foreshadowed a debate that would take place in early 2012 at the federal level. The Affordable Care Act requires health insurance to cover contraceptives. Initially, the Obama administration said that even religious groups with objections to contraception coverage would be required to provide it to their employees. But, facing a backlash even from some of its allies, the administration decided on a compromise instead. Religious organizations themselves wouldn't be required to provide contraception, but employees of the religious groups would still be offered the coverage directly from their health insurance companies. This deal borrowed directly from the states: it was called the "Hawaii rule" because it mimicked a policy in that state.[99] Many religious conservatives weren't satisfied with the deal, however, including some in state capitols. Arizona approved a law in May 2012 to permit religious employers not to cover contraception and, in so doing, directly challenged the federal mandate.[100]

What Is Good Health Anyway?

As if these issues were not enough, local health officials are increasingly wrestling with another question we have not yet touched on in this chapter: What exactly constitutes a health issue anyway?

> The latest figures show that more than two-thirds of all adults in the United States are overweight or obese; in 2011, at least 20 percent of the population was classified as obese in every state.

Consider obesity. Media attention has turned to this issue more and more as an ever-growing list of health studies proclaim just how out of shape Americans are. The films *Super Size Me* (2004) and *Fast Food Nation* (2006) address people's obsession with fast food. The latest figures show that more than two-thirds of all adults in the United States are overweight or obese; in 2011, Colorado had the nation's lowest adult obesity rate at just over 20 percent.[101] (See Map 15-3.) Kids are getting heavier too. In the past two decades, the number of overweight and obese children has nearly tripled. Today, according to the CDC, roughly 18 percent of children between the ages of six and eleven are overweight—up from just 4 percent in the early 1970s. The number is 18 percent for adolescents between the ages of twelve and nineteen too; that is also a significant change from the early 1970s, when just 6 percent of teens weighed too much.[102]

Obesity contributes to a variety of ailments, among them heart disease, certain types of cancer, diabetes, stroke, arthritis, breathing problems, and psychological disorders such as depression. Overweight individuals suffer from these and other related conditions at much higher rates than do people who are not overweight. Indeed, researchers attribute about 112,000 deaths each year to obesity in the United States alone.[103] In 2003, obesity in the United States cost about $92.6 billion in medical spending.[104] Researchers at Emory University have estimated that if the United States could curb the rate of increase of obesity, the nation could save $821 per adult by 2018.[105]

In 2006, New York City reignited the debate over government's role in promoting healthy eating habits when it banned the use of trans fats (some of the most dangerous fats) in city restaurants. Soon after, other cities and states began to consider similar legislation. Parent groups and health organizations demanded better, healthier fast-food options, and the fast-food restaurants quickly took notice. McDonald's, the world's largest fast-food chain, received such a negative rap for its unhealthy products that it was under strong pressure to take immediate action. It began expanding its "healthy" meal options with great fanfare, began shooting commercials showing Ronald McDonald rollerblading and exercising with children instead of sitting in the restaurant eating, and began posting fact sheets on its Web site announcing how much healthy food it had sold worldwide. Wendy's, KFC, Chili's, and other restaurant chains began using oils free of trans fats for frying.

One of New York City's next public health initiatives was to require chain restaurants to post calorie counts on their menus, based on the theory that if diners eating fast food knew how many calories were in their meals, they would eat less. Some research showed that the calorie labels didn't succeed in encouraging consumers to eat less, at least initially.[106] Nonetheless, the Affordable Care Act nationalized the concept, requiring all chain restaurants with at least twenty locations to post calorie counts. Even before the rule went into effect, McDonald's announced that it was updating its menus at its 14,000 locations nationwide to include calorie labels.

Not all efforts by states and localities to discourage the consumption of fast food and junk food have

MAP 15-3

Obesity Trends among U.S. Adults: 2000 and 2011

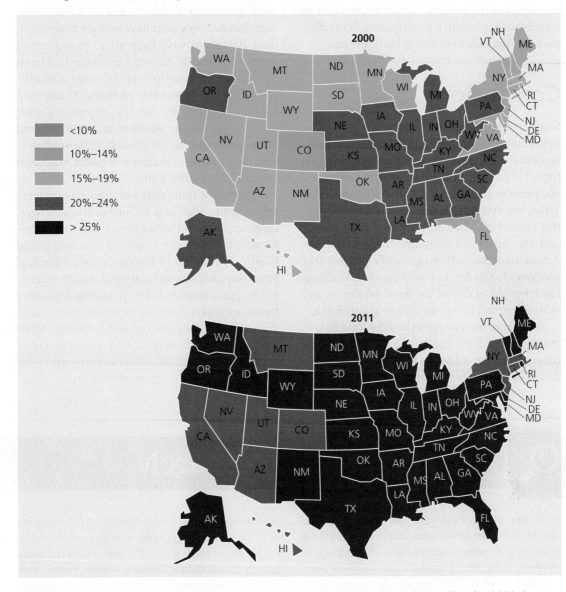

2000

- <10%
- 10%–14%
- 15%–19%
- 20%–24%
- > 25%

2011

Source: Data compiled from U.S. Centers for Disease Control and Prevention, "U.S. Obesity Trends, 1985 to 2011," www.cdc.gov/obesity/data/adult.html.

Note: Body mass index (BMI) equal to or greater than 25 is considered overweight for a woman whose height is 5 feet, 4 inches.

gone so smoothly. In 2010, several states, including New York, California, Washington, Kansas, and Rhode Island, engaged in spirited debates about new taxes on soft drinks. Every state has a cigarette tax, and research shows that these taxes have succeeded in helping to discourage young people from starting smoking. The idea behind the proposed soda taxes was that they would have the same effect—reducing consumption of unhealthy sugary beverages while raising money for states. Yet most of the states didn't end up enacting soda taxes. Washington did approve such a tax, only to have voters repeal it in November 2010. The soda industry fought back against the efforts to tax its products by portraying the efforts as examples of overly intrusive government. "It's government digging into the grocery cart of people," said Chris Gindlesperger, director of communications at the American Beverage Association.[107] Once again, New York City wasn't willing to let the issue rest. In September 2012, the city's board of health banned the sale of many sugary beverages by restaurants, movie theaters, and other vendors in containers larger than sixteen ounces. Soon after, the beverage industry sued to block the rule.

Conclusion

State and local governments have played an important role in providing healthcare and assistance to the poorest members of society for a long time. They also have the responsibility to protect and promote public health. Things changed in the 1960s, however, when Congress passed legislation that created the Medicare program for the elderly and the Medicaid program for low-income Americans. This set into motion a process that continues to this day. In recent decades, Medicaid has emerged as one of the most expensive and most important functions of state government.

States have been forced to look for ways to save money on one hand and extend health insurance coverage on the other. Despite the difficulty in reconciling these tasks, some state governments have achieved notable successes. The State Children's Health Insurance Program, known as CHIP, has made health insurance available to most American children, and in some cases, experimental programs have brought coverage to their parents as well. Even after the passage of federal healthcare reform legislation in March 2010, states continue to be at the center of healthcare expansion in the United States. Thanks to a June 2012 ruling by the U.S. Supreme Court, states get to decide whether or not to expand Medicaid under the law. At stake in those choices are many billions of dollars and health insurance for millions of Americans.

At the same time, state and local governments are grappling with new public health challenges. Illnesses such as influenza show that local governments still have a role to play in guarding public health. The threat of biological and chemical terrorism also presents local public health officials with a grave responsibility. In addition, governments' expenses continue to mount for treating diseases caused by obesity and smoking. All of this means that healthcare will almost certainly continue to be a major concern of state and local governments for the foreseeable future.

The Latest Research

As we have seen in this chapter, the federal Affordable Care Act is an attempt to provide health insurance to tens of millions of Americans—an attempt in which, willingly or unwillingly, states will be intimately involved. It will be years before anyone will be able to say with confidence whether the law has succeeded or failed. Even so, before the law's major provisions were to kick in on January 1, 2014, academics began making educated guesses about whether the law could achieve its ambitious goals.

States have more than a passing interest in these predictions. As a result of the Supreme Court's ruling in 2012, states get to decide whether or not to expand their Medicaid programs under the law. The Medicaid expansion is one of the central ways the act attempts to expand health insurance coverage to nearly every American, but for many state officials, whether or not to pursue it has proved to be a difficult choice. While states are wondering what the law's consequences—intended or otherwise—will be, the research shows that they will not be merely passive observers once the law is in effect. Instead, how well the law works may well hinge on states' own actions.

● ●

• **Leininger, Lindsey Jeanne, Donna Friedsam, Laura Dague, Shannon Mok, Emma Hynes, Alison Bergum, Milda Aksamitauskas, Thomas Oliver, and Thomas DeLeire.** 2011. "Wisconsin's BadgerCare Plus Reform: Impact on Low-Income Families' Enrollment and Retention in Public Coverage." *Health Care Research Services* 46: 336–347.

One of the crucial questions states are asking right now is what exactly will happen if they expand Medicaid under the Affordable Care Act. This article provides clues to the answer by examining Wisconsin's own expansion of Medicaid in 2008. One key conclusion from the article is that if you offer it, they will come. In Wisconsin, Medicaid enrollment for both children and adults increased substantially. Interestingly, however, many of the new Medicaid enrollees were people who were already eligible before the expansion but hadn't signed up. At the same time it was offering Medicaid to a larger group of people, Wisconsin also made it easier to enroll and marketed the program more heavily—steps that brought in more of the previously eligible population. In making this point, the authors show that merely offering coverage is not enough. Clear communications to the public will be essential for the healthcare law's Medicaid expansion to reach its goals.

- **Baicker, Katherine, and Amy Finkelstein.** 2011. "The Effects of Medicaid Coverage: Learning from the Oregon Experiment." *New England Journal of Medicine* 365: 683–685.

Like Leininger et al., Baicker and Finkelstein use a previous state Medicaid expansion to study what will happen under the Affordable Care Act. As states weigh whether to expand Medicaid, some officials are asking whether their residents will really be better off with the coverage. The answer isn't quite as obvious as it seems: Medicaid is relatively low-quality health insurance, and people who are uninsured still receive some care from clinics and emergency rooms. But the authors find that in Oregon, participants in the state's Medicaid expansion reported being both in better health and in better shape financially. Participants in Oregon's Medicaid expansion were selected by a lottery, so the authors were able to compare two groups of people who were alike in every way other than whether they were in Medicaid—making their findings much more definitive. Medicaid, this study shows, can make a positive difference in beneficiaries' lives.

- **Sommers, Benjamin D., and Arnold M. Epstein.** 2011. "Why States Are So Miffed about Medicaid: Economics, Politics, and the 'Woodwork Effect.'" *New England Journal of Medicine* 365:100–102.

While the Medicaid expansion could offer substantial benefits to newly insured people, those benefits come with a cost. Sommers and Epstein show that the cost to states is much greater than just the portion they have to pay for the population that is newly eligible for the program. They predict that many of the approximately 9 million people who already were eligible for Medicaid but had not signed up will "come out of the woodwork" and enroll once the Affordable Care Act kicks in. The law's promise of near-universal coverage will make more people realize Medicaid is available to them—even people who would have been eligible all along. While the federal government has promised to pay 90 percent of the cost of the newly eligible population under the law, states will bear a larger share for new enrollees who were eligible all along. By identifying this effect, Sommers and Epstein help explain why some governors and legislators are worried the Medicaid expansion will cost more than their states can afford.

- **Sommers, Benjamin D., and Sara Rosenbaum.** 2011. "Issues In Health Reform: How Changes in Eligibility May Move Millions Back and Forth between Medicaid and Insurance Exchanges." *Health Affairs* 30: 228–236.

Under the Affordable Care Act, whether someone receives coverage through Medicaid or through subsidized private health insurance depends on that individual's income. Sommers and Rosenbaum identify a potential problem with that: a person's income changes over time. If people are bouncing back and forth between Medicaid and private insurance, they may become confused or frustrated or face disruptions in coverage—disruptions that could put their health at risk. By studying individuals' historical income data over time, Sommers and Rosenbaum show that many millions of people are likely to be bouncing back and forth. Aside from posing an administrative challenge for patients, this "churning" could pose administrative challenges for states, since states run Medicaid and many states will run the health insurance exchanges where individuals will buy subsidized coverage. How well the new healthcare law works will depend in part on whether states can meet this administrative challenge. In making this point, Sommers and Rosenbaum offer an important lesson: to a substantial extent, healthcare reform will end up being what states make of it.

Chapter Review

Key Concepts

- abstinence (p. 474)
- Aid to Families with Dependent Children (AFDC) (p. 473)
- entitlement program (p. 481)
- managed care (p. 486)
- Medicaid (p. 471)
- Medicare (p. 480)
- obesity (p. 472)
- pandemic (p. 472)
- poverty line, or poverty threshold (p. 481)
- public health (p. 472)
- State Children's Health Insurance Program (CHIP) (p. 487)
- Temporary Assistance to Needy Families (TANF) (p. 474)

Suggested Web Sites

- **www.americashealthrankings.org.** Web site of America's Health Rankings, a twenty-year project tracking health indicators at the state level.

- **www.astho.org.** Web site of the Association of State and Territorial Health Officials.

- **www.familiesusa.org.** Web site of FamiliesUSA, a liberal advocacy group that promotes a more activist government policy.

- **www.healthyamericans.org.** Web site of Trust for America's Health, a nonprofit organization dedicated to protecting public health.

- **www.kaiserhealthnews.org.** Web site of Kaiser Health News, a nonprofit news organization covering state and federal healthcare issues, funded by the Kaiser Family Foundation.

- **www.kff.org.** Web site of the Henry J. Kaiser Family Foundation offers a wealth of detail on state healthcare initiatives in general and Medicaid in particular.

- **www.naccho.org.** Web site of the National Association of County and City Health Officials.

- **www.statehealthfacts.kff.org.** A Kaiser Family Foundation Web site that provides detailed information on state healthcare policies.

STATE STATS

State Stats on Health and Welfare

Explore and compare data on the states! Go to college.cqpress.com/sites/ govstateandlocal to do these exercises.

1. Which state spent the largest percentage of its budget on health programs in 2009? Which state spent the least? Why do some states spend more than others?

2. How did healthcare spending in your state change between 2000 and 2009? What might account for this change?

3. In 2011, which states had the largest percentages of their population aged 85 or older? What are the implications for these states' healthcare spending?

4. How has the population over 65 years of age changed in Delaware between 1997 and 2011? How might this affect healthcare spending?

5. What was the national average Medicaid expenditure per enrollee in 2002? How does your state compare with others? Why might there be so much variation between states?

California state senator Fran Pavley announces that the Obama administration will reconsider the state's request to mandate strict environmental standards on vehicles, which the Bush administration had turned down. Governor Arnold Schwarzenegger looks on at the January 26, 2009, news conference. The Obama administration later went on to establish stricter standards.

Environment and Climate Change

THINKING GLOBALLY, ACTING LOCALLY

- How did states become important voices on a global problem?
- Why has climate change become a partisan issue?

Fran Pavley's journey to the White House took seven years. In 2002, Pavley, who was then a freshman state legislator in California, wrote a landmark law to regulate the tailpipe emissions of vehicles to cut down on greenhouse gases. Although the law was soon emulated by thirteen other states, it was tied up for years by court challenges and never received the federal sign-off necessary for it to take effect.

A few months into his presidency, however, President Barack Obama fulfilled a campaign promise by supporting Pavley's initiative. In May 2009, Obama summoned Pavley and other political leaders from California to a White House Rose Garden ceremony, where he announced that the federal government would regulate carbon emissions from vehicles, proposing standards that closely mirrored the Pavley bill's requirements. The federal government would also speed up rules to require higher gas mileage. "There were a lot of high fives and hugs," Pavley said of the ceremony. "It was a seven-year journey. I equated it to a cat with nine lives. We went through a [U.S.] Supreme Court decision, several federal court decisions, two presidents, and a recalled governor."[1]

It was a moment of vindication for Pavley personally, but a few years down the road it's looking like a high-water mark for the environmental movement. Despite years of skepticism—sixteen states passed legislation rejecting the Kyoto Protocol, the 1997 international treaty that sought to limit the emissions of carbon and other gases that contribute to global warming, even as California was enacting Pavley's bill—states found the political will to address climate change. During the years Obama has been in office, however, what looked like a groundswell of interest in the states that was likely to force federal action has become much less pressing.

That may change once again. "Extreme weather" conditions, such as severe droughts in Texas and the Midwest, along with a proliferation of powerful storms, had politicians talking about climate change in urgent tones just as Obama was winning his second term in 2012. In fact, just days before that election, Superstorm Sandy caused billions of dollars in damage along the Eastern Seaboard, leading to calls for populated areas to fortify themselves against rising sea levels. "There has been a series of extreme weather incidents," New York governor Andrew Cuomo told reporters after a seawater surge caused by Sandy flooded subways in Lower Manhattan. "That is not a political statement, that is a factual statement. Anyone who says there is not a dramatic change in weather patterns is denying reality."[2]

Across the United States, 2012 proved to be the hottest year on record. But climate change had become a political issue, with Republicans generally having grown much more skeptical in recent years about whether human activity and energy use affect climate. Just a few years ago, Republican governors were among those calling most loudly for concerted efforts against climate change. Some of those individuals have passed from the political scene—or have changed their minds. And even as climate change becomes more of a partisan issue than it once was, the regional divides among states remain in force, with many in the South and the industrial Midwest much more resistant to climate change efforts than those on the West Coast or in the Northeast.

Roughly half the states have taken little to no action related to climate change, either because they are concerned that the price of addressing the issue, through limiting energy use, is simply too high, or because their leaders and political cultures remain skeptical that global warming is anthropogenic (that is, caused largely by human activity). In general, states have lately come to concentrate less on limiting energy consumption than on promoting the development of energy resources. Numerous states have been undergoing booms in oil and natural gas production in recent years.

Many states, however, have put in place new measures meant to limit reliance on fossil fuels. In 2006, Pavley was a sponsor of another California law, one aiming to reduce industrial carbon dioxide emissions by 25 percent by 2020, that represented the first imposition of statewide enforceable limits

on greenhouse gas emissions that included penalties for non-compliance. (The law was challenged by a ballot initiative in 2010 that would have kept it from taking effect until unemployment dropped to 5.5 percent, but the measure was defeated.) More than half the states have adopted renewable energy portfolio standards requiring utilities to rely on renewable sources such as wind and solar energy to generate a significant share of their electricity (25 percent in most states) in future years. And groups of states in the Northeast, upper Midwest, and interior West have formed regional compacts to create cap-and-trade systems to reduce industrial emissions. "They're committed to moving forward on various measures that they've already started in the absence of federal action," says Jessica Shipley, a fellow at the Center for Climate and Energy Solutions. "Definitely, states are still working hard on climate, in conjunction with federal action."[3]

This represents an important new role for states, which traditionally have taken a backseat to federal efforts when it comes to environmental issues. The major environmental laws of the early 1970s, such as the Clean Air and Clean Water Acts, set out strict federal guidelines that states had to follow. In contrast to this "command and control" model, in which the federal government called all the shots, in the area of climate change the American states are leading, influencing not only federal policy under Obama but also efforts in many other countries through state partnerships with regions and provinces in other nations.

Approaches to climate change, then, have become a particularly interesting exercise in federalism. States have sought to fill the vacuum left by the absence of federal leadership on an issue that state leaders themselves realize calls for a national—indeed, international—set of solutions. "States have been tripping all over themselves to show national leadership on this issue," says Barry G. Rabe, a professor of public policy at the University of Michigan. "California, I would argue, has made as heavy an investment in time and treasury into climate change as any government on Earth, including the European Union."[4]

In short, inaction by the federal government and differences across states and localities have resulted in significant obstacles to a coordinated response to environmental problems, especially problems associated with global warming. Climate change is certain to remain an important issue among states and localities, but whether a subset of the subnational governmental units of the United States can make a significant impact on greenhouse gas emissions in the absence of further action at the national and international levels remains very much in question.

In this chapter, we consider some of the specific environmental policy challenges facing states and localities. These include substantive policy topics such as regulating tailpipe emissions and promoting renewable energy, but they also include the problems that the federal system itself poses to comprehensive action on climate change, as well as the widening partisan divide that further fragments state and local government action on the environment.

States Get Serious about the Environment

Unlike education, crime, taxes, and budgets, the environment is a relatively modern policy concern for state and local governments. Indeed, it is a relatively recent policy concern for the federal government. The modern environmental movement can be traced to the 1960s, which in turn led

to a concerted federal response in the early 1970s. This included the passage of landmark laws regarding air and water quality and the creation of the U.S. Environmental Protection Agency (EPA). Enforcing and expanding those responsibilities has made environmental policy one of the central responsibilities of the federal and, increasingly, state and local governments. "Today, after nearly four decades, environmental protection is the most heavily funded regulatory responsibility in the United States," writes Marc Allen Eisner, a political scientist at Wesleyan University.[5]

New Jersey has 116 Superfund sites—the most of any state.

At the heart of contemporary environmental debates is climate change, which has become a hot issue not just among national (and international) policymakers but also for state and local officials. It's worth remembering, however, that policymakers at all levels have taken this issue seriously for a relatively short time. "We're still very much at the embryonic stage of dealing with climate change in this country," says John Cahill, who worked on environmental legislation as an aide to former New York governor George Pataki.[6]

The federal government has, to put it mildly, a mixed record in dealing with the climate change challenge. Environmentalists derided President George W. Bush for not seriously addressing global warming, but Bush's predecessor's record was not notably stronger. Congress rejected President Bill Clinton's 1993 proposal to impose a tax on energy, and the Senate passed a unanimous resolution in 1997 that it would reject U.S. participation in the Kyoto Protocol if it harmed the U.S. economy.

At least initially, states followed the skeptical approach of the federal government. It soon

---

U.S. Environmental Protection Agency (EPA)
The federal agency charged with protecting the environment.

Climate Change
A shift in global temperatures.

Global Warming
Rising average temperatures worldwide.

Kyoto Protocol
A 1997 international treaty that sought to reduce emissions of greenhouse gases.

became clear, however, that many states were eager to address the problem of global warming, particularly after Bush's formal rejection of the Kyoto Protocol in 2001. "Ironically . . . American states may be emerging as international leaders at the very time the national government continues to be portrayed as an international laggard on global climate change," Rabe wrote in 2004.[7]

Most of these initial state-level efforts were largely symbolic, lacking specific mandates or resources. Unlike the federal government, however, some states actually put teeth into their efforts. As early as 1989, New Jersey governor Thomas Kean, a Republican, signed an executive order instructing all state agencies to take the lead in reducing **greenhouse gases**. In 2001, Massachusetts governor Jane Swift, also a Republican, issued a rule limiting a variety of pollutants from six major power plants, including the nation's first **carbon dioxide** standards. "The new, tough standards will help ensure older power plants in Massachusetts do not contribute to regional air pollution, acid rain and global warming," Swift said.[8] Her action was soon copied in New Hampshire.

Indeed, it was actually a state government—California's—rather than the federal government that emerged as the leader in addressing climate change–related policies. California stepped into this policy arena not simply because of its green-leaning political constituencies or its large economy or its role as a national cultural trendsetter, although all these factors certainly played their roles. As the only state allowed to set air pollution controls stricter than those mandated by federal law (thanks to a provision in the **Clean Air Act**), California occupies a unique policymaking niche in the federal system. That law—written at a time during the early 1970s when Southern California was notorious for its **smog**—gives California the authority to regulate any such pollutant as long as the state can get a waiver from the EPA. Other states are then allowed to follow California's rules. There was strong pressure from environmentalist forces within California to move on the issue of greenhouse gases following the 1998 elections, with both the legislature and the governor's mansion in Democratic hands for the first time in two decades. Thus, on a series of important environmental issues, California began to act. Other states, following California's lead, began experimenting with innovative environmental policies. One of the biggest obstacles that the states faced in these efforts was the federal government.

Regulating Vehicles

In 2002, California lawmakers enacted Pavley's measure to regulate **tailpipe emissions**, or greenhouse gases released from vehicles, which in 1999 accounted for 37 percent of carbon dioxide emissions in the state.[9] The idea came from Bluewater Network, a San Francisco environmental group that has since become part of Friends of the Earth, a global organization. The group found its sponsor in Pavley, a Democratic freshman state representative willing to take on the fight when more prominent legislators were avoiding it. "We were happy at that point to find any progressive author, because we knew it would be a difficult bill," said Bluewater executive director Russell Long.[10]

The legislation survived a committee challenge and was ready to reach the floor by the middle of 2001, but Pavley held off on a vote until 2002 so she could broaden her backing. Carmakers and oil companies spent an estimated $5 million attempting to sink it, and she was ardently attacked by talk-radio hosts for impinging on the freedom of Californians to drive SUVs and other large vehicles.

Pavley responded with polls demonstrating overwhelming popular support for the bill, even among SUV owners. She also got help from water-quality districts, religious leaders, technology

---

Greenhouse Gases
Emissions—primarily carbon dioxide but also other gases such as methane—that are believed to contribute to global warming.

Carbon dioxide
A naturally occurring gas, the prevalence of which is increased by the burning of fossil fuels.

Clean Air Act
The law, initially enacted in 1970, that provides authority for federal regulation of air pollution.

Smog
A type of air pollution; the word comes from the combination of *smoke* and *fog*.

Tailpipe Emissions
Greenhouse gases released by cars and other vehicles.

Seattle mayor Greg Nickels fills a car with a blend of biodiesel fuel at a west Seattle Safeway gas station in 2007. The station was the first of Safeway's nearly three hundred fuel stations to offer biodiesel products.

executives from Silicon Valley, and celebrities such as Paul Newman, Tom Hanks, and former president Bill Clinton, who made calls to wavering lawmakers.

Her bill's progress was also helped immeasurably by legislative leaders, who showed the former civics teacher some parliamentary tricks to ensure its passage. One was to put language into the bill all in capital letters highlighting the fact that the California Air Resources Board would not have the power to ban SUVs or other specific types of vehicles, as bill opponents were warning would be the case in their advertisements. One of Pavley's colleagues called these the "We Really Mean It" amendments. The substance of the bill was not changed, but the amendments were "put in to clarify it for the public," Pavley said. "Admittedly, in all the years I taught 'how a bill becomes law,' we didn't talk about that possibility."[11]

But her law did require the Air Resources Board to adopt "cost-effective" and "reasonable" restrictions on carbon dioxide emissions from cars and light trucks by 2005, with automakers having until 2009 to comply. Not surprisingly, carmakers fought the law through numerous court challenges.

More than a dozen other states enacted laws saying they would abide by California's rules once they were approved, and several others pledged to do so, but the Bush administration refused to grant California the necessary waiver. "All we asked for was permission to enforce, because the rules were all in place," California Air Resources Board spokesman Stanley Young said in a 2008 interview. "We've been ready for two years on Pavley. The rules were fully fleshed out. They were formally adopted back in 2005, and we're ready to move on them as soon as we get the green light."[12]

Challenging the Environmental Protection Agency

In the face of federal reluctance to regulate greenhouse gas emissions, several environmentalist groups as early as 1999 had petitioned the EPA to use its authority under the Clean Air Act to regulate the gases. The agency denied it had such authority and also argued that the link between greenhouse gases and climate change was not firmly established.

Massachusetts and eleven other states appealed the EPA's denial. In April 2007, the Supreme Court ruled 5–4 in the states' favor, noting that they had standing to bring such a case due to the "risk of catastrophic harm" they faced as sovereign entities. Justice John Paul Stevens wrote that the EPA had provided "no reasonable explanation for its refusal to decide whether greenhouse gases cause or contribute to climate change." In his dissent, Chief Justice John G. Roberts Jr. argued that it was an issue better decided by Congress and the executive branch.[13] But the Court's majority had determined that carbon dioxide was indeed an air pollutant under the federal Clean Air Act.

The 2007 Supreme Court decision set the political stage for Congress to set a new mileage standard for cars and light trucks. In December 2007, President Bush signed into law requirements that a car manufacturer's entire fleet average thirty-five miles per gallon by 2020.

Just hours after that bill was signed, however, EPA administrator Stephen L. Johnson dashed hopes that the *Massachusetts v. EPA* decision would lead the agency to approve California's waiver application for enforcement of the Pavley bill. "The Bush administration is moving forward with a clear national solution, not a confusing patchwork of state rules, to reduce America's climate footprint from vehicles," Johnson said in a statement.[14]

California had been granted more than fifty waivers under the Clean Air Act, which allowed it to develop such innovations as the catalytic converter, which reduces tailpipe emissions; tighter fuel caps to reduce gasoline evaporation; and computerized detectors to warn when a car's smog controls are not working. California's standards have often been adopted by other states and, thus, by carmakers. "If not for California's leadership, I think it's fair to say that cars wouldn't be as clean as they are today," said Ron Burke, Midwest climate change director for the Union of Concerned Scientists. "We would have suffered through more bad air days over the last thirty years."[15]

The *Los Angeles Times* reported that EPA staff had urged Johnson to grant the waiver. "California met every criteria . . . on the merits. The same criteria we have used for the last forty years on all the other waivers," one EPA staffer told the *Times*. "We told him [Johnson] that."[16] Technical and legal staff of the EPA also reportedly advised Johnson he would likely lose a legal challenge. The *St. Petersburg Times* reported that during the late summer and fall, Secretary of Transportation Mary Peters had quietly urged members of Congress and some governors to let the EPA know her department opposed the waiver request.[17]

As noted earlier, the waiver had to wait until President Obama granted it—representing the federal government's first step toward regulating greenhouse gases. Under rules finalized in April 2010 by the EPA and the Department of Transportation, emission and mileage standards for new vehicles would require an average performance of 35.5 miles per gallon by 2016. "The rules are expected to cut emissions of carbon dioxide and other heat-trapping gases about 30 percent from 2012 to 2016," the *New York Times* reported.[18] The Obama administration estimated that the new standards would add $985 to the price of a car but would save the consumer $4,000 in fuel costs over the life of the vehicle.

Canada adopted identical standards the same day. The federal rules were largely based on the California law, but they also reflected an agreement hammered out with carmakers.

Cap and Trade

Cars are not the only source of greenhouse gas emissions. In 2006, Fran Pavley and other California lawmakers were promoting a piece of legislation, known as AB 32, that sought to address the stationary sources of pollution, such as power plants, oil refineries, and cement plants. The law aimed to reduce industrial carbon dioxide emissions by 25 percent by 2020. AB 32 represented the first imposition of statewide enforceable limits on greenhouse gas emissions that includes penalties for noncompliance. The legislation was the first in the nation to require a cap-and-trade system to address greenhouse gases.

Cap and trade puts an overall limit—or cap—on the emission of a pollutant, such as carbon dioxide. Once the limit is set, polluters are given or sold some number of emissions allowances, in essence, permits to pollute. The amount of pollution they can release—say, 1,000 tons of carbon dioxide at a power plant—is slowly reduced over time. If they come in below their limits, they can sell or trade their excess permits; if not, they have to pay fines or buy extra permits from other polluters. That's the trade part. Late in 2012, California held its first auction of 23.1 million carbon emission permits, which sold for $10.09 a piece. When the law took effect at the beginning of 2013, California became the world's second-largest carbon market, after the European Union.[19]

Cap-and-trade systems have been used by the federal government and by other states to address environmental concerns. Congress created such a system to address acid rain in the 1990 Clean Air Act. (Acid rain is rain that contains a high concentration of sulfur dioxide; it is blamed for polluting lakes and streams.)

Ten states in the Northeast and Mid-Atlantic—Connecticut, Delaware, Maine, Maryland, Massachusetts, New Hampshire, New Jersey, New York, Rhode Island, and Vermont—signed on to a cooperative effort known as the Regional Greenhouse Gas Initiative (RGGI), which uses cap and trade. (New Jersey dropped out in 2011.) These states have capped carbon dioxide emissions from their power sectors, requiring gradual reductions that will bring emissions down 10 percent by 2018.

Governors from seven states began RGGI negotiations in 2003, reached a formal agreement in 2006 (with the last three states, Maryland, Massachusetts, and Rhode Island, signing on the following year), and began auctioning pollution permits to power companies in 2009. The history of RGGI includes many touch-and-go moments when states dropped out of or rejoined the program. But the effort stayed afloat based on the hope that, once carbon emissions carry a price, utilities will burn less coal, oil, and natural gas because it's in their economic interest, making carbon-free alternatives comparatively more attractive.

With its 2007 Next Generation Energy Act, the Minnesota state legislature adopted the strategic goal of reducing the state's greenhouse gas emissions by at least 80 percent of 2005 levels by 2050.

The early auctions were considered a success, but not everyone is convinced that the most optimistic scenarios about reducing emissions will play out as intended. The region-by-region approach has left open plenty of opportunities for undermining the system.

In the Northeast, for example, it would be easy enough for a big industrial customer in New York, which is part of RGGI, to look for cheaper power generated by coal-fired plants in Pennsylvania or Ohio, which are not part of the initiative. If that occurs, said Kenneth Pokalsky, a regulatory analyst for the Business Council of New York State, "we'll have the worst of both worlds: higher energy costs in New York to implement a program that has no discernible impact on worldwide greenhouse gas emissions."[20]

The other regional initiatives have not been as productive as RGGI. The midwestern regional initiative outlined a cap-and-trade system, with an advisory group releasing its final recommendations and model rules in May 2010, but the states involved then failed to follow through on their greenhouse gas reduction goals through the accord. The Western Climate Initiative (WCI), originally comprising seven states and four Canadian provinces, appeared bolder in its approach than RGGI, targeting not just carbon dioxide but other greenhouse gases as well, but every U.S. member state, save California, had dropped out of the WCI by 2012. The three regional initiatives joined forces in 2012 with the creation of North America 2050: A Partnership for Progress, a group of sixteen states and four Canadian provinces

---

Cap and Trade

A system for limiting pollution by assigning allowances to polluters, which can sell their excess permits if they succeed in reducing their emissions.

designed to share ideas and techniques for moving toward a low-carbon economy.

A cap-and-trade proposal was central to the approach taken by the 2009 bill passed by the U.S. House, but the concept itself became highly charged over the course of congressional debate. Critics derided the idea, calling it "cap and tax" and claiming that it would add billions to the nation's energy costs.

As White House counsel under President George H. W. Bush, C. Boyden Gray was an architect of the 1990 Clean Air Act cap-and-trade program designed to address acid rain. Nevertheless, he added his voice to the chorus of complaints about the cap-and-trade model proposed by federal climate change legislation. "The proponents always say they're copying the highly successful cap-and-trade program of the Clean Air Act and they're most decidedly not, because they've thrown in this auction function," Gray said. "It's purely a revenue function, and that becomes a tax. You pull $2 or $3 trillion out of the economy and that's what people are objecting to."[21]

In March 2010, in a move seen largely as a response to complaints that a cap-and-trade bill would hurt the economy by raising energy prices, Obama outlined a plan to open up much of the East Coast to offshore oil drilling. His proposal would have ended a long-time moratorium on offshore oil exploration. The West Coast would remain closed to drilling and exploration, as would the East Coast from New Jersey northward. But opening up oil exploration from Delaware down to the central coast of Florida covered 167 million acres of ocean.[22] Obama's move, which included more environmental protections than a similar idea previously floated by President George W. Bush, was mainly cheered by oil companies and supporters of increased domestic energy production—as well as by state officials, who welcomed the chance to share in oil-extraction tax revenues.

But within three weeks, an offshore oil rig exploded forty miles off the Louisiana coast. (This occurred in the Gulf of Mexico, an area that had long been open to oil drilling, not in the newly designated area.) The resulting catastrophic oil spill effectively ended any chance for an expansion of offshore drilling for a time, but in 2011, the Obama administration announced a proposal for a new five-year plan. It opened up new areas in the Gulf of Mexico and Alaska to oil drilling, but barred development along the East and West Coasts. Overall, domestic oil production during Obama's first term grew by more than 10 percent.

Promoting Renewable Energy

Meanwhile, all but a dozen states are pushing forward on another front intended to reduce greenhouse gas emissions and reduce U.S. dependence on fossil fuels. Most states outside the South and the Great Plains regions now require utilities to rely on **renewable energy** sources, such as wind, solar, biofuels, and geothermal power, to generate a significant share of electricity—usually up to 25 percent in future years. That's nearly three times as many states as had renewable portfolio standards in place in 2004. "It's an important step in the process of weaning ourselves from foreign oil," said Rhode Island state senator David E. Bates, who helped push through legislation in 2004 that requires a 20 percent renewable energy portfolio in his state by 2020. "We provided incentives for companies to produce renewable energy. We also took great pains to make it a workable formula. You can't tell a national grid to produce green energy in twenty years without making sure the energy is available."[23]

Meeting the required targets remains quite a challenge, however, especially in coal-dependent regions such as the South and the Midwest. Coal is used to generate about half the nation's electricity. As governor of West Virginia, Joe Manchin touted wind energy but noted in 2008 that his state's coal production is the key source of electrical power for the entire Eastern Seaboard. "Economists and scientists . . . will tell you that coal is

Renewable Energy
Power generated using natural sources that can be replenished, such as wind and solar energy, as opposed to nonrenewable fossil fuels.

MAP 16-1

Renewable and Alternative Energy Portfolio Standards

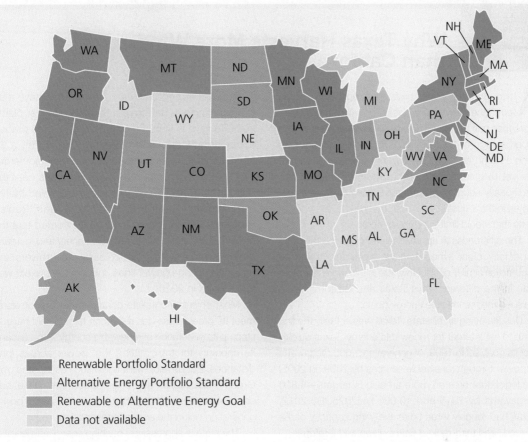

Legend:
- Renewable Portfolio Standard
- Alternative Energy Portfolio Standard
- Renewable or Alternative Energy Goal
- Data not available

Source: Center for Climate and Energy Solutions, "Renewable & Alternative Energy Portfolio Standards," October 25, 2012, www.c2es.org/us-states-regions/policy-maps/renewable-energy-standards.

going to be the primary factor that's going to power this nation and most of the world for the next thirty to fifty years."[24]

According to the U.S. Department of Energy, wind energy capacity has been growing rapidly, with wind turbines installed capable of generating more than 50,000 megawatts of additional electricity. That's up from 17,000 megawatts of capacity as recently as 2007. Investment in geothermal energy grew 26 percent in 2009, thanks largely to public investment. A total of 188 projects in fifteen states could produce as much as 7,875 megawatts, according to the Geothermal Energy Association, which attributed the growth to a combination of state renewable energy portfolio standards, federal investment tax credits, and spending from the 2009 federal stimulus package.[25] By 2012, the association noted that

> Critics charge that an emphasis on renewable energy sources is not a panacea. Despite heavy public investment and tax breaks, renewable energy production remains more expensive than energy produced using coal. It also remains less reliable.

4,500 megawatts' worth of projects were under development in Nevada, Oregon, and California alone.

A Difference
That Makes A Difference

Why Texas Harvests More Wind than California

Although many states have taken aggressive steps to reduce greenhouse gases, not all of them have. More than half the states now require utilities to generate a percentage of their power from renewable sources such as wind and solar energy, but this is an idea that has yet to gain traction in the Southeast, which has traditionally sought weaker environmental protections. States in the industrial Midwest, meanwhile, are wary of ideas that would limit their use of coal.

The differences in approaches among the states are especially clear when two or more are trying to accomplish similar goals. Nowhere is this more apparent than in the different ways Texas and California have pursued their renewable energy goals.

Despite being an oil state, Texas was actually the first state to set a target for renewable energy. Texas quickly met its goal, set in 1999, of generating 2,000 megawatts of power through renewable sources by 2009. In 2005, the legislature created more ambitious targets—8,800 megawatts by 2015 and 10,000 by 2025. By 2012, Texas had roughly three times the wind capacity of the second- and third-ranked states, Iowa and California.

Lots of states are home to plenty of wind and land. But Texas had one additional advantage—lack of regulation. Texas developers have minimal dealings with the state and are able to cut the development deals they need with local officials.

California, by contrast, has built few big wind farms since the 1980s because of the costs and delays caused by the need to comply with environmental regulations, including concerns about the fact that wind turbines often kill birds.

Regulation and environmental worries have also slowed efforts in California to build large solar plants in the Mojave Desert. Environmentalists were divided about the construction of Green Path North, a $2 billion transmission line intended to convey geothermal and solar energy from remote desert areas near the Salton Sea to the 5 million customers served by the Los Angeles Department of Water and Power. Residents in San Bernardino County worried that the project would defile some natural scenery and increase the risk of forest fires with colossal steel towers and ugly high-voltage power lines. Indeed, the project was abandoned in 2010.

Most environmentalists concede that California, to meet its greenhouse gas reduction targets, will have to step up its generation of renewable energy—and expand its capacity for transmitting that power across long distances. But development fights such as the one over Green Path North are one reason the state has concentrated many of its efforts not in the area of power generation but in the area of conservation.

The state is aggressively pushing energy efficiency. A 2008 law allows local governments to create assessment districts to provide low-cost, long-term financing for homeowners who install solar panels or upgrade their heating and air-conditioning units. "Strict building codes and energy-saving requirements for home appliances and light bulbs—measures that have been largely ignored by Texas—make an excellent fit for California, where residents are used to being regulated," reports the *New York Times*.[a]

Source: Original piece written for this book by Alan Greenblatt.

[a]Kate Galbraith, "California and Texas: Renewable Energy's Odd Couple," *New York Times*, October 18, 2009, 3.

But critics charge that an emphasis on renewable energy sources is not a panacea. Despite heavy public investment and tax breaks, renewable energy production remains more expensive than energy produced using coal. It also remains less reliable. "Over the past fifteen years, I've participated in or seen many of the analyses of the economic impact of reducing greenhouse gases," said Margo Thorning, senior vice president of the American Council for Capital Formation, a Washington think tank. "In every case there is a slower economy and less overall employment, even though new green jobs are created. The reason that happens is that renewables are more expensive."[26]

Some of the states' requirements are not realistic anyway, according to Rabe. He notes that California set a renewable energy standard for utilities of 20 percent by 2010, which the state could not meet. (It was at 11 percent at the end of 2009.) Legislators in 2010 debated raising the standard to 33 percent by 2020, which Republican governor Arnold Schwarzenegger also sought by executive order. Rabe called it "hubris" for states to create ever-tougher but elusive standards for the future.[27] But Schwarzenegger's successor, Democrat Jerry Brown, signed a bill in 2011 codifying the 33 percent target for 2020.

Terry Tamminen, who served as an energy and environmental adviser to Schwarzenegger, argues that ambitious targets have helped move things in the right direction. "Everyone forgets that the original law set the target at 2017, so by accelerating the date we've moved it up by at least five years," he said in a 2009 interview.[28]

Cutting Back on Coal

At the same time that states are promoting generation of energy from renewable sources, they are also simply clamping down on coal. Construction was canceled on nearly one hundred coal-fired power plants in 2008 and 2009 because of environmental concerns. The Texas energy giant TXU Corporation shelved eight out of eleven planned coal plants, investing heavily in wind energy instead. Only three of ten plants that were once planned for southern Illinois remained active.[29]

Nowadays, wherever a coal-fired plant is proposed, the Sierra Club or an allied group steps forward with a lawsuit to block it.[30] Environmentalists believe that delays, and their concomitant costs, can only serve to move power generation away from coal. "Each time you step back and reassess the politics and economics of coal," said Bob Eye, a Sierra Club attorney and former counsel to the Kansas Department of Health and Environment (KDHE), "things are more difficult for the coal plant proponents."[31]

In 2007, Rod Bremby, KDHE secretary, blocked a pair of massive coal-fired power plants. Citing that year's *Massachusetts v. EPA* Supreme Court decision (which sought to force the EPA to regulate greenhouse gases), Bremby overruled his own staff and rejected Sunflower Electric Power Corporation's application to build a $3.6 billion power plant project outside Holcomb. Bremby was the first regulator to block a power plant strictly out of concern for climate change and without getting specific statutory cover from the legislature. "To approve the permit didn't seem a reasonable option, given that carbon dioxide is a pollutant and we're talking about 11 million tons of carbon," he said.[32] Since Bremby's original decision, more than 120 power plants have been retired or new projects seen their permits denied, delayed, or withdrawn for reasons similar to the ones he cited.

A lot of this had to do with environmentalists' complaints and regulation, but another factor was at work as well. Thanks to a boom in **fracking**, natural gas prices dropped in 2012 below $3 per million British thermal units (BTUs), down from about $8 in 2008, and some gas-fueled plants were able to generate electricity for about two cents per kilowatt, or less than half what it costs to run many coal-fired operations. That year, "natural gas pulled even with coal as a fuel source for power plants," according to the *Washington Post,* with coal usage down 17 percent and natural gas up 27 percent.[33] The trend of electric companies shutting down coal-fired plant capacity was set to continue at least through 2016.

Limiting Land Use

In addition to addressing the consumption of energy directly, states are looking at ways to cut back on individuals' use of fuel. Many environmentalists blame **sprawl**—the growth of suburban and exurban communities far from central cities and existing transit and transportation infrastructure—for contributing to the greater consumption of natural resources.

Tom Adams, president of the California League of Conservation Voters, argues that his state must cut down on sprawl to meet its long-term environmental goals. In 2008, the state took a big step in the direction that Adams favored by enacting a major new land-use law.

Fracking
A process in which water, sand, and chemicals are pumped into the ground to enable the extraction of natural gas and oil.

Sprawl
The rapid growth of a metropolitan area, typically as a result of specific types of zoning and development.

A Difference That Makes A Difference

Boom in Energy Production Sparks Environmental Fears

While most states were slow to recover from the Great Recession and its aftermath, North Dakota was booming. The reason was oil. New technologies have made it possible to extract oil from rock as thick as concrete through horizontal drilling and hydraulic fracturing, or fracking. As a result, North Dakota has experienced an oil boom. The high price tag of those extraction techniques means they're only economically feasible now that the price of a barrel of crude oil at times hovers around $100. Oil companies are rushing to tap the ground before the cheap preboom leases they signed with mineral rights owners expire, and North Dakota is reaping the benefits. By the end of 2010, the state had more than 6,000 wells capable of producing oil and gas, and an additional 20,000 wells could be drilled within the next ten or twenty years, followed by more than thirty years of pumping oil. "This boom is just wild and crazy," said Ward Koeser, mayor of Williston, the largest city in the center of the oil activity. "It's more than you can fathom."

For the past hundred years, the number of people in North Dakota has remained virtually stagnant. It's the only state in the country that had more residents in 1930 than it does today. Now the population is booming in the western part of the state, where some parts of oil country saw their populations increase an estimated 13 percent from 2009 to 2010. "We had dying small towns that had resigned themselves to the fact that the mayor would eventually turn the light switch off when he left town," said Vicky Steiner, a state representative who leads the North Dakota Association of Oil and Gas Producing Counties.

Today, she says, "some of our communities that were dying are now flourishing."

North Dakota isn't the only state to use fracking for its economic rewards. Fracking is the process of pumping a mixture of water, sand, and chemicals into the ground to extract natural gas and oil. Early forms of fracking have been around since 1947, but the vast increase in its use in recent years has made fracking perhaps the top environmental concern facing states, and they differ in how they balance the risks and rewards.

The benefits of fracking are readily apparently. According to the Heritage Foundation, the process has been used to retrieve more than 7 billion barrels of oil and more than 600 trillion cubic feet of natural gas. Each trillion cubic feet of natural gas is enough to heat 15 million homes for one year. Fracking has made it possible to tap the Marcellus Shale in the Mid-Atlantic region, one of the richest natural gas deposits in the world. This rock formation lies more than a mile beneath the earth's surface, and until fracking came along there was no economical way to extract the gas. Ohio Republican governor John Kasich has referred to the formation as "a gift from heaven."

All of this exploration has helped to lower energy prices and create jobs. But along with its benefits, fracking presents many potential environmental hazards. Industry officials insist that their processes are safe, but environmentalists are worried that the chemicals released in fracking pollute both air and groundwater. Some are even worried just about the amount of water that fracking requires. Each well can use up to 5 million gallons of water per year—in some parts of the country,

---

Typically, land-use policies are decided at the local level, with cities or counties passing **zoning laws,** or ordinances, that, for instance, keep industrial sites separate from residential areas or require that no more than one house be built on each quarter acre of land. Some areas impose only loose zoning restrictions—or none at all, as in Houston. But state governments often do influence land-use policy, if only through their transportation programs. Numerous states, led by Maryland, have enacted policies in recent years

Zoning Laws
Regulations that control how land can be used.

even more. In Carroll County, Ohio, alone, the state has issued permits to drill 161 wells. Across the state, as many as 2,250 wells could be drilled to get at the Utica Shale by 2015.

In addition to concerns about water consumption and pollution, activists who say "no fracking way" point to the increase in seismic activity in states such as Colorado and Texas where fracking has been employed. The problem seems to be the wastewater—the water that has been used in fracking and then retrieved and injected into waste wells. The waste wells can be thousands of feet deep, under high pressure that can build up for months or years, eventually causing earthquakes. From 2010 through 2012, Oklahoma residents felt more than 250 temblors, quite startling when earthquakes had only rarely been strong enough to be felt in the previous decades. The largest earthquake in the state's history, a 5.7 magnitude quake in 2011 that damaged about two hundred buildings, was "likely caused by fluid injection," according to scientists from the University of Oklahoma, Columbia University, and the U.S. Geological Survey.

Scientists say that the earthquake risk caused by fracking could be reduced by regulations demanding more careful placement and construction of wells. Following a series of earthquakes in 2011, Ohio instituted a moratorium on new wastewater injection permits. It resumed issuing the permits the following year, after putting more safeguards in place.

In general, the fracking boom has been so rapid that it has seen comparatively little regulation. A study released in 2012 by OMB Watch, a research and advocacy group, found that only thirteen of the thirty states engaged in natural gas drilling had passed legislation related to fracking. Hundreds of other bills were under consideration in other states.

Some government officials, however, have demanded further study before allowing fracking to proceed. Even as neighboring states such as Pennsylvania were going full steam ahead with fracking, Maryland governor Martin O'Malley, a Democrat, placed a de facto moratorium on the practice in 2011, pending completion in 2014 of a $1.5 million study by the state Department of the Environment. (Permits can be issued before the study's completion if drilling is otherwise determined to be safe.)

Another Democrat, New York governor Andrew Cuomo, had appeared to be ready to give fracking the green light, but after four years of study, he decided to put off lifting the state's moratorium, pending still more review. Antifracking protesters had been stalking Cuomo for months—not just at speaking engagements, but at his home and office—while celebrities including Lady Gaga lined up to express their disapproval of fracking.

Fracking will remain controversial, but given the resources at stake, it's still likely to continue its rapid growth in most places for some time to come.

Source: Original piece written for this book by Alan Greenblatt.

aimed at cutting down on sprawl—saying that the state will not build infrastructure outside approved development areas, for instance. Most such laws have proved to be largely toothless.

California's 2008 law, known as SB 375, goes further than most. SB 375 directs the California Air Resources Board to come up with targets for reducing emissions from cars and trucks. Regional planning boards will then rewrite their master growth plans in ways that seek to meet those targets—for instance, by planning more housing near existing mass transit lines. The regions that come closest to the goals will be rewarded with extra federal and state transportation dollars.

It's no surprise that SB 375 was backed by environmentalists, but it also had the support of California's home builders, who liked the prospect of greater predictability in the zoning process. One of the main goals of the bill is to induce localities to coordinate their major planning tasks: transportation, land use, and housing. Few had been doing that. In addition, SB 375 provides relief from certain air-quality standards that had, perversely, discouraged developers from undertaking infill projects. "Builders thrive on certainty, knowing what the rules are," says Tim Coyle of the California Building Industry Association.[34] Local governments also supported the law; it provides incentives and creates a policymaking framework, but it doesn't create specific mandates for any individual region. "It's really a very important piece of legislation," says Peter Kasabach of New Jersey Future, a smart-growth group. "How we develop our land is going to impact our greenhouse gas targets. A lot of folks think that if we drive hybrids or change our lightbulbs, we'll be okay. But a significant amount of our greenhouse gas targets will be met by how we get around and reduce vehicle miles traveled."[35]

But various regions of California have struggled to meet requirements under the law. For instance, a judge ruled in 2012 that a transportation plan put forward by the San Diego Association of Governments relied too much on temporary measures such as telecommuting to meet specific emission reduction targets, with the pace of reductions achieved slipping over time (from 14 percent per capita in 2020 to 9 percent by 2050). In addition, Tea Party activists and other conservatives have come to oppose such zoning restrictions, seeing them as a challenge to private property rights. One particular document that has drawn their ire is Agenda 21, a sustainability program adopted by the United Nations back in 1992. Police have been called out to quell protests against the plan even in such pro-zoning jurisdictions as Maryland and California. In 2012, the Republican Party made opposition to Agenda 21 part of its official platform.

Still, the notion that sprawl is bad both for the environment and for the health of communities has become fashionable over the past decade—perhaps nowhere more so than in Miami. That's surprising because, when it comes to building and construction, Miami had always been a wide-open town, home to endless rows of towering condo buildings. In late 2009, the city council approved a new zoning code that is likely to have a profound effect on development. Ardently promoted by Miami mayor Manny Diaz but drafted in large part by architect Elizabeth Plater-Zyberk, the code embraces the **New Urbanist** principles that made Plater-Zyberk and Andrés Duany (her husband and professional partner) famous.

The new code, known as Miami 21, seeks to encourage street-level pedestrian activity and reduce automobile dependence. The hope is that neighborhoods will fit within a comfortable scale, with plenty of shops out front and buildings that conform to fixed height limits with upper-story setbacks from the street. At the same time, the goal is to create corridors with enough density that public transit will be viable. But the most important idea may be the decision to focus on entire neighborhoods rather than on individual projects.

New Urbanist codes have been adopted in various places around the country for new projects in previously unbuilt areas (greenfields) and for specific areas undergoing redevelopment, such as riverfronts. But Miami became the first city of any size to attempt to apply these principles throughout its borders.

Advocates of the approach are making grand claims about its potential to transform much of the landscape and have explicitly promised that it will make Miami far more environmentally friendly as well. "A whole city is changing its strategy consistent with this idea of preventing climate change," says Armando Carbonell, chair of the Department of Planning and Urban Form at the Lincoln Institute of Land Policy.[36]

Miami was horrendously overbuilt during the overheated housing market that collapsed in 2007. It is home to thousands of foreclosed condos. "Our economic condition stinks down here," Truly Burton, a lobbyist for the Builders Association of

---

New Urbanism
A design movement that seeks to promote walkable communities through transit-oriented, mixed-use development.

Manny Diaz (right), attends a green certification ceremony. As Miami mayor, Diaz promoted Miami 21, a redevelopment plan intended to manage growth and sustainability for the city in the twenty-first century. It was approved by the City Commission in 2009 after much debate.

South Florida, said bluntly after the code had passed.[37] Developers, looking for a hedge against the next downturn, over the past couple of years have taken advantage of Miami 21's mixed-use provisions to help convert all-condo buildings into combined live-work spaces, which has succeeded in increasing residency in areas such as the city's downtown and Wynwood arts district.

Green Building

Some states and localities have tried to change not only the way buildings are laid out in relation to one another but their interior efficiency as well. In 2008, Chicago mayor Richard Daley unveiled what the *New York Times* described as "perhaps the most aggressive plan of any major American city to reduce heat-trapping gases."[38] The plan, which aimed to cut Chicago's carbon output by 25 percent by 2020, focuses on tougher building codes.

"Green" building codes have drawn significant attention among local governments seeking to cut back on carbon emissions. Buildings account for 40 to 50 percent of a city's energy demands. They use 25 percent of the drinking water and produce 35 percent of the solid waste, mostly in the form of construction materials. And buildings produce anywhere from 30 to 70 percent of municipal carbon emissions, according to the American Institute of Architects (AIA). Many cities have received grants from former president Bill Clinton's foundation to rewrite their codes, but far more are pursuing such strategies on their own. In 2012,

Building Codes
Rules regarding the standards for structures; they mainly have to do with safety issues but sometimes also include requirements for things such as exterior pedestrian walkways.

nearly 25,000 local officials attended the Greenbuild conference in San Francisco sponsored by the U.S. Green Building Council.

The trend has exploded in recent years. From 2003 to 2009, the number of cities with green building programs grew by more than 600 percent, from 22 to 138, according to the AIA. By 2009, 20 percent of municipalities with populations of more than fifty thousand had adopted such programs.

By and large, cities' green building programs are based on the standards of the council's rating system, known as LEED (Leader in Energy and Environmental Design). To encourage developers to build green, cities are offering tax incentives, reductions in permit fees, and access to grants for projects that meet certain environmental benchmarks. Some cities offer bonus density allowances; a green building project might be exempt from height restrictions, for example. But the most popular incentive by far is expedited permitting for green projects. This policy has proven extremely attractive to cities, because they can implement it at virtually no cost to themselves.

Some cities are going further and actually requiring energy-efficient construction through their building codes. In 2006, Washington, D.C., became the first major U.S. city to mandate green construction for all private buildings of at least fifty thousand square feet, beginning in 2012. And in 2007, Boston became the first city actually to implement a green requirement for private construction and renovation projects.

Since then, a handful of other cities have adopted similar mandates. In 2009, the New York City Council began requiring the owners of the city's largest buildings to perform energy audits and upgrade lighting, and the council is considering more rules regarding the heating and insulation of individual apartments. In 2008, San Francisco adopted the strictest codes of any U.S. city so far, requiring green standards for any residential building taller than seventy-five feet and commercial buildings of more than five thousand square feet. That same year, California became the first state to include green environmental standards, such as requirements to recycle construction waste, reduce the use of polluting materials, and improve energy efficiency in new structures, in its statewide building code; these rules took effect in 2010.

Builders routinely have said that they support the goals of such regulations, but they have often also complained that they are too costly. Nevertheless, increased energy efficiency of new and existing structures has become a primary goal for all levels of government. In 2007, in response to requests from the U.S. Conference of Mayors and other groups, Congress authorized up to $2 billion annually in block grants for state and local programs designed to save energy. That authorization went unfunded until the 2009 enactment of the American Recovery and Reinvestment Act (ARRA), the federal stimulus bill. ARRA included $3.2 billion for energy efficiency block grants for states and localities and an additional $5 billion in funding for Department of Energy **weatherization** efforts, much of which also amounted to grants for the states.

Weatherization, at least for the first year after ARRA passed, became a case study in the difficulties of quickly ramping up an entirely new program within the federal system. Neither the states nor the federal government had ever devoted much money to weatherization, and suddenly both were spending billions. In addition, because the work relied on great numbers of local providers—such as nonprofit groups and individual contractors—many states were slow to get projects under way.

For example, Washington State fell badly behind schedule during the first year of its stepped-up weatherization efforts. By summer's end, local agencies had weatherized just 10 percent of the units the state had planned. The problem drew the attention of Democratic governor Christine Gregoire's office, which helped untangle some of the regulatory and labor law problems that were hampering efforts. By the end of 2009, the state had exceeded its targeted goals.

In general, however, the boom in green building codes hasn't exactly triggered a green building boom. In 2009, Seattle employed incentives to encourage twelve developers to build projects that would generate all their own electricity and use only water that fell on-site. Three years later, just one such project was under construction, and only two more were in the planning stages.

Green Jobs

Another area where environmentalists and others have made grand promises—which, at least initially, look overblown—is the notion of **green jobs**. Just what a green job is has been hard to define. Clearly, making wind turbines would qualify. But most of the jobs that are labeled "green" are positions that already exist and bear only tangential relationships to the environment. A study done for the state of Colorado counted some Wal-Mart employees as green because a percentage of the products that the retailer sells are certified by Energy Star, the federal

> However you define green jobs, generating them—another central goal of ARRA—has been slower than some promised. Many people still are counting on green-collar jobs not only to revive the economy but also to restore the manufacturing sector in places where it has long been in decline.

Weatherization
The practice of protecting buildings from the elements (for example, by installing insulation) both to improve their habitability and to cut down on energy use.

Green Jobs
Occupations that contribute to environmental sustainability.

Environmentalists hope that the conversion to cleaner energy technologies such as wind power will not only curb carbon emissions but also provide a new source of jobs. Here, Cerro Coso Community College instructor Mike Servantes explains safety procedures to students about to make their first climbs on a wind turbine in Tehachapi, California. His students enrolled in the technical course after being laid off from auto or construction work.

government's program to rate the efficiency of appliances. Cashiers, janitors, accountants, secretaries, lawyers, and even government officials—all can be categorized as "green" workers if their work touches energy efficiency in almost any way.[39]

However you define green jobs, generating them—another central goal of ARRA—has been slower than some promised. Many people still are counting on green-collar jobs not only to revive the economy but also to restore the manufacturing sector in places where it has long been in decline. "American cities have suffered more than anyone from the loss of manufacturing jobs," said Minneapolis mayor R. T. Rybak. "Cities have become the green incubators for America."[40]

Plenty of studies have suggested that there will be an explosion of investment and job creation in the green sector. The Apollo Alliance, a coalition of business, labor, and environmental groups, estimates that a $300 billion investment over ten years would create 3.3 million jobs in renewable energy, hybrid cars, and infrastructure replacement.[41] The U.S. Conference of Mayors forecasts there will be 4.2 million green jobs by 2038 and suggests that cities and towns prepare to compete for them.[42]

According to Fran Pavley, the California state senator, $3.3 billion, or about 60 percent of the venture capital devoted to clean technology in the country, was invested in her state in 2009.[43] "Everything that is good for global warming is good for jobs," Van Jones, who served briefly as a White House adviser and wrote the 2008 book *The Green Collar Economy,* said in a 2008 conference

call with reporters. "Buildings do not weatherize themselves, wind turbines do not construct themselves, solar panels do not install themselves. Real people are going to have to get up in the morning and do these things."

However, despite all its apparent promise, the interest in green technology has not yet translated into either mass employment or a huge economic windfall. "People are talking about this in the future, but it's not happening today," said Eric Crawford, president of Greenman Alliance, a Milwaukee-based recruiting firm. "Everyone wants a green job," but the demand for such jobs totally outstrips the supply.[44] The Bureau of Labor Statistics released a definition of "green jobs" in 2010; two years later, it found that just under 2 million people were employed by companies engaged in "green goods and services." (See Map 16-2.)

And government investment in clean technology has not always reaped large dividends. Under New Jersey's energy master plan, solar power should account for more than 2 percent of the Garden State's electricity by 2020. But by mid-2008, solar systems were generating only 0.07 percent of current energy needs, despite the fact that the state had already handed out more than $170 million in rebates to encourage their installation. The state revised its goals for solar power

MAP 16-2

Green Goods and Services Jobs as a Percentage of Total Employment in a State

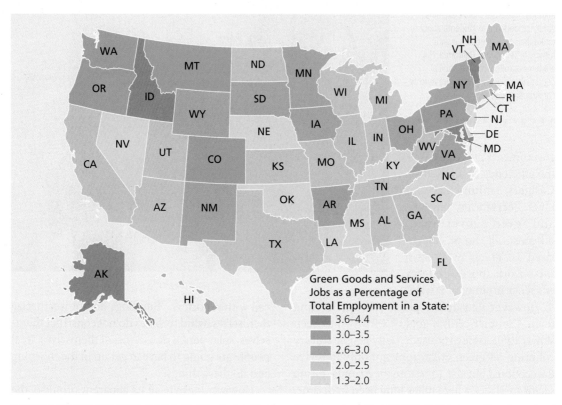

Green Goods and Services Jobs as a Percentage of Total Employment in a State:

- 3.6–4.4
- 3.0–3.5
- 2.6–3.0
- 2.0–2.5
- 1.3–2.0

Source: U.S. Bureau of Labor Statistics, "Employment in Green Goods and Services—2010," news release, March 22, 2012, 16, Table 4, www.bls.gov/news.release/pdf/ggqcew.pdf.

Note: The GGS scope consists of industries that may produce green goods and services within one or more of the following five groups: (1) energy from renewable sources; (2) energy efficiency equipment, appliances, buildings and vehicles, and goods and services that improve the energy efficiency of buildings and the efficiency of energy storage and distribution; (3) pollution reduction and removal, greenhouse gas reduction, and recycling and reuse goods and services; (4) organic agriculture, sustainable forestry, and soil, water, and wildlife conservation; and (5) governmental and regulatory administration and education, training, and advocacy goods and services.

in 2010. "We need to do things differently because ratepayers can't keep paying for rebates indefinitely," said Jeanne M. Fox, president of New Jersey's Board of Public Utilities.[45]

"This idea that we're going to have a massive environmental WPA—it's not going to help the economy, it's going to hurt the economy," said Myron Ebell, director of energy and global warming policy at the Competitive Enterprise Institute. (WPA, the Works Progress Administration, was a Depression-era jobs program.) Putting government money into green energy would not create great economic returns, Ebell suggested, because—at least so far—renewable energy is more expensive than dirty fuels such as coal; it also means directing dollars away from other fields entirely. "I believe just on a very simple analysis that there is no question it will take net jobs out of the economy and it will be a net economic harm," Ebell said.[46]

A 2010 study from the McKinsey Global Institute suggests that clean energy will ultimately have less in common with manufacturing sectors than with the semiconductor industry, which once promised to generate millions of high-tech jobs but, instead, mainly employs robots. Green jobs employ only 0.6 percent of the U.S. workforce—a number the McKinsey report suggests won't grow by much. "The bottom line is that these 'clean' industries are too small to create the millions of jobs that are needed right away," said James Manyika, a McKinsey director.[47]

But even if the critics are correct, the goal of green investment is not only to stimulate the economy but also to help clean up the environment. In a column published in the *New York Times* just after the November 2008 election, former vice president Al Gore called for large governmental investments in clean energy as the optimum way to address climate change—a shift from his traditional focus on increased regulation of carbon pollution.[48] "With his op-ed, Gore has reversed the longstanding green-lobby prioritization of regulation first and investment second," wrote Michael Shellenberger and Ted Nordhaus for the *New Republic* Online.[49]

Adaptation

In 2006, the U.S. Army Corps of Engineers proposed a plan to help protect Long Beach, home to 33,000 people on a barrier island just off of Long Island, New York. The plan involved the erection of sand dunes and the elevation of beaches along more than six miles of coast to protect the island. But the project would have cost $98 million, and the city would have had to chip in a $7 million share. And people just didn't like the idea of having their ocean views obscured and giving up their nice, wide, flat beaches. So the city council voted unanimously to block the project.

It was a decision Long Beach came to regret. In 2012, the storm known as Sandy did some $200 million worth of property damage to the town. Neighboring communities on the barrier island had approved construction of 15-foot-high dunes and were able to avoid suffering catastrophic losses in the storm.[50]

The effects of Superstorm Sandy in 2012 and other high-impact weather events turned the attention of some policymakers away from the question of how to prevent climate change to planning for coping with its effects. If climate change is already having real impacts—and will continue to do so, even if efforts to reduce greenhouse gas emissions succeed—state and local governments have little choice but to deal with these effects. So how should state and local governments begin to adapt to the resulting problems, such as flooding, coastal erosion, and species loss? Should they, for example, build higher seawalls to offset rising sea levels? Many officials in areas affected by Sandy became

believers, but facing price tags potentially reaching into the hundreds of billions of dollars, some remained skeptical. "I don't think there's any practical way to build barriers in the oceans," New York City mayor Michael Bloomberg said in November 2012. "Even if you spent a fortune, it's not clear to me that you would get much value for it."[51]

Up until 2007 or so, most environmentalists dismissed talk about **adaptation** to climate change. Their concern seemed to be that shifting the policy debate away from efforts to prevent climate change by cutting down on carbon emissions amounted to conceding to conservatives' denials that human activity causes global warming. They also felt that planning for the effects brought about by climate change was defeatist. "It was seen as a potential smokescreen behind which high-emission countries could hide so they wouldn't have to make binding agreements to reduce," said Nathan Hultman, a professor of science, technology, and international affairs at Georgetown University.[52]

Some advocates still argue that discussion about how to adapt to climate shifts amounts to a distraction from the larger project of reducing emissions. "There are people out there working on adaptation, but I have to say the overwhelming effort is to try to reduce our emissions," said Tom Adams, president of the California League of Conservation Voters. "At this point, some fairly significant climate impacts are inevitable, but a lot of us feel that this is a genuine planetary emergency, and it's imperative that we cut emissions."[53] But the notion that talking about adaptation is just a smokescreen to conceal the lack of effort to reduce greenhouse gases seems to be fading away. There's a growing recognition among those concerned about global warming that even if carbon emissions were reduced to zero tomorrow—which clearly isn't going to happen—there is already enough carbon

On January 1, 2010, stores selling food or beverages in the District of Columbia began charging a five-cent user fee on every paper or plastic bag. The money collected goes to cleaning the Anacostia River, and the law is meant to encourage shoppers to provide their own reusable bags.

Adaptation
Taking steps to prepare for and deal with the effects of climate change.

dioxide in the air to guarantee more changes to come. The Intergovernmental Panel on Climate Change, which shared the 2007 Nobel Peace Prize with former vice president Al Gore, has stressed the importance of adaptation in its recent reports, and in 2007 a group of scientists published an article in the journal *Nature* titled "Lifting the Taboo on Adaptation."[54]

As a practical matter, policymakers are increasingly concerned about how to plan for the climate-related changes their communities are facing. Not surprisingly, the issue has drawn the most attention in areas along coastlines, such as in Maryland and Oregon. In 2011, the city of Boston released a climate action plan to prepare for sea levels rising by two to six feet by the end of the century, depending on the rate of polar ice melt. Added to a hurricane storm surge, some models show parts of Boston under ten feet of water. Researchers have warned city officials that by midcentury such storms could happen every two to three years.

But because climate change will manifest itself differently in different locales, adaptation questions are drawing attention all over. For instance, government officials in Vermont been working with the state university to begin crafting plans to help the forestry and farming industries cope with the local effects of climate change.

In parts of the nearby Cascade Range in Washington State, snowpack has declined by as much as 60 percent. In response, King County, which includes Seattle, has begun planning backward from 2050, formulating plans to adapt to the climate change effects that are seen as likely to occur even if carbon emissions are cut significantly between now and then. For example, officials

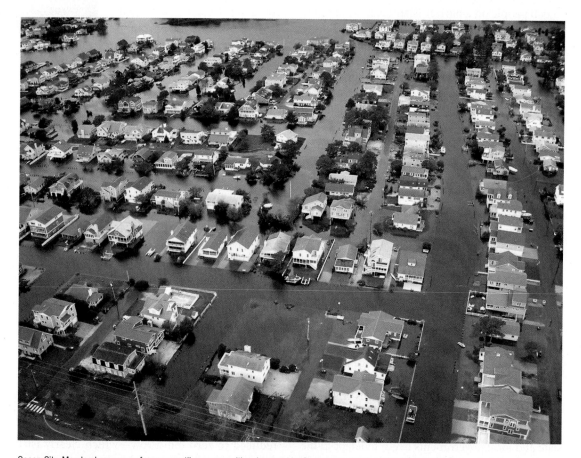

Ocean City, Maryland, was one of many coastline communities damaged by Superstorm Sandy in October 2012. The storm's destruction ran up the East Coast, prompted several declarations of states of emergency, and cost billions of dollars in cleanup. Discussion in the wake of the storm included the possibility of similar storms in the future and their risk to a coast made increasingly vulnerable by Sandy's foray in from the sea.

expect coastal erosion problems associated with rising sea levels, health effects such as new infectious diseases and heat stroke, increasing numbers of forest fires, and ecological issues affecting salmon. In 2007 the county council agreed to a tax inspired by such looming dangers, part of county executive Ron Sims's $335 million plan to bolster river levees and reduce flood risks. The county is now building climate change risks into all its long-term planning and policy development. "We're learning to define ourselves not in 2009 terms but in 2050 terms," said Sims, who went on to serve with the federal Department of Housing and Urban Development. "We're making decisions based on something that has not occurred yet."[55]

Like most environmentalists, Ron Burke, the Midwest climate change director for the Union of Concerned Scientists, says that both responses to climate change—reduction of carbon emissions, or mitigation, and adaptation—are important. Still, he says, "If you had to argue one versus the other, which I don't think is really helpful, I think mitigation is a higher priority given the urgency with which we need to create these reductions. You see that reflected in how most cities and states are going about their planning. They're definitely doing the mitigation piece first and then moving onto adaptation."[56]

One of the world's biggest adaptation efforts is taking place in the Netherlands. The Dutch are spending billions to create "floating communities" that can rise with floodwaters and to otherwise reengineer their long coastline. They expect to spend $100 per year per person on climate-proofing over the next century, according to the *Washington Post*. Although some say their efforts are excessive, according to the *Post,* U.S. officials have consulted with the Dutch about how to protect New Orleans and other low-lying coastal areas.[57]

Relatively few jurisdictions in the United States have turned their full attention to adaptation and planning questions. Even normally proactive California has barely paid attention to adaptation issues and is unprepared for the flooding, coastal erosion, and loss of wildlife habitat predicted to occur in coming decades as the results of higher

Mitigation
Reduction of emissions of greenhouse gases and other steps taken to curb the forces that cause climate change.

temperatures.[58] Only in 2008 did Governor Arnold Schwarzenegger issue an executive order directing state agencies to identify the state's biggest vulnerabilities to rising sea levels and draft an "adaptation strategy."[59] That strategy, formally adopted in 2009, was revised in 2012. The California Coastal Commission may require all waterfront communities to include forecasts for extreme flooding and sea-level rise in their plans; those that don't comply risk losing some state funds. In 2012, the San Francisco Bay Conservation and Development Commission amended its San Francisco Bay Plan to make sure projected sea-level rise is accounted for by new projects, such as a planned $1.5 billion development on Treasure Island, which rests in the bay midway between San Francisco and Oakland.

> States and local governments face a practical challenge when it comes to crafting adaptation plans. Much of the science in this area has been, not surprisingly, global in scope. Thus, planning for climate change's local impacts will require experts to downscale the large-scale data to make them applicable to and useful for communities.

States and local governments face a practical challenge when it comes to crafting adaptation plans. Much of the science in this area has been, not surprisingly, global in scope. Thus, planning for climate change's local impacts will require experts to downscale the large-scale data to make them applicable to and useful for communities. According to Sims, it is imperative for states, cities, and counties to accept the need to make decisions based on scientific modeling rather than historical experience. "With all the discussion we've had on global warming, I am stunned that people haven't realized that it's actually going to occur," he said in 2007. "The ice caps are melting now. They're not going to refreeze next year because we reduce our emissions. We're going to live in that world. So plan for it."[60]

Issues to Watch

Growing Partisanship and Skepticism

Of course, not everyone believes we are going to be living in a world forever altered by climate change. In 2012, James Lawrence Powell, executive director of the National Physical Science Consortium, searched 13,950 peer-reviewed articles on climate change dating back to 1991. He found that only 24 rejected the idea of human-caused global warming.[61] Nevertheless, public opinion polls in recent years have shown that Americans are increasingly skeptical about the alarm bells that have been sounding about climate change. A Gallup Poll in March 2012 found that 55 percent of Americans worried about global warming "a great deal" or "a fair amount"—up slightly from the year before, but well below the peak of 72 percent in 2000.[62] Polling by Gallup and other groups has consistently found that the public does not consider global warming in particular and the environment in general nearly as important as other issues, such as the economy.

A series of small controversies helped shift opinions on climate change in recent years, including a mistake about glacier loss in the Himalayas in a report by the Intergovernmental Panel on Climate Change and a scandal involving European climate scientists whose e-mails, suggesting they had withheld contradictory data, were hacked into and released. Official inquiries subsequently cleared the scientists of any serious wrongdoing, but the damage was done.[63]

Just as a series of mild winters in the Northern Hemisphere and a batch of devastating hurricanes had contributed to fears about global warming in earlier years, an unusually cold and snowy winter in 2010 eased such concerns for some. Senator Jim DeMint, R-S.C., an opponent of climate change legislation, tweeted in the midst of a series of large snowfalls in the Washington, D.C., region, "It's going to keep snowing until Al Gore cries 'uncle.'"[64] Those concerned about global warming tended to make the opposite point during the heat of summer.

Media attention devoted to the climate change issue turned largely into disquisitions about whether all these points raised by skeptics had been blown out of proportion and why climate scientists, who appeared to have won the argument about whether global warming was real, now appeared to be on the defensive on the public relations front.

But advocates for measures addressing climate change were losing ground in Congress, as well. A cap-and-trade system that was the centerpiece of the climate change bill passed by the U.S. House in June 2009 appeared dead even before the major Senate climate change bill was introduced in April 2010. Interior Secretary Ken Salazar said during a March 2010 CNBC interview, "I think the term 'cap and trade' is not in the lexicon anymore."[65]

At the state level in 2010, a number of legislatures debated legislation that highlighted the skepticism about global warming—notably a resolution adopted in South Dakota urging schools to offer "balanced teaching" about global warming, saying that it "is a scientific theory rather than a proven fact." In 2012, conservative groups led by the American Legislative Exchange Council and the Heartland Institute attempted to persuade legislators to roll back renewable energy requirements, which they claimed would come at a cost to consumers.

What is most striking for political scientists, as opposed to climate scientists, is not only how much the ground has shifted on this issue but also how partisan it has become. As climate change began to emerge as an issue of pressing concern a few years ago, it was associated with Democrats such as Al Gore, and many of the leading doubters were Republicans, such as James Inhofe of Oklahoma, who chaired the Senate Environment and Public Works Committee when the GOP held the majority.

Yet many of the voices calling loudest for a policy response were Republicans. Senator John McCain, R-Ariz., the GOP presidential nominee in 2008, had sponsored cap-and-trade legislation.

Some of the most prominent governors cheerleading for action on the issue were Republicans, including Arnold Schwarzenegger of California, George E. Pataki of New York, Charlie Crist of Florida, Jon Huntsman Jr. of Utah, and Tim Pawlenty of Minnesota. It was still easier to muster support for climate change legislation among Democrats than among Republicans at all levels of government, but the issue was far less partisan in nature than, say, healthcare or taxes.

By the 2010 midterm election season, however, it was hard to find a Republican who was raising climate change as an issue—unless it was to denounce it. Some Republicans who had advocated tough environmental measures are leaving the scene, such as Schwarzenegger, who signed a landmark California law capping carbon emissions in 2006 but was term-limited out of office as governor in 2010. Others have switched their position, now advocating more of a market response and shying away from strict governmental controls. That's especially true of Republicans reaching for higher office—including the presidency. Insisting on caps on energy use has become something of a nonstarter for GOP candidates. The March 2012 Gallup Poll showed that only half as many Republicans as Democrats were worried about global warming.

"You see growing sentiment that climate change has been exaggerated," said Karlyn Bowman, a polling expert at the American Enterprise Institute, a conservative think tank. Still, she added, she is struck by the growing partisan divide on the issue: "The Republican-Democrat and conservative-liberal differences are quite large."[66]

Opposition to cap-and-trade legislation nearly became official Republican Party dogma. It was one of ten items on a list that some members of the Republican National Committee wanted candidates to be required to take a stand on; candidates would receive party backing only if they agreed to at least eight. The committee ultimately rejected the idea of such a "purity test," but party candidates have needed no such official sanction to express their disapproval of cap and trade. Sarah Palin had always expressed skepticism that climate change was human-made, but when she was governor of

Alaska she thought her state should prepare for its effects. In late 2010, however, she tweeted that climate science was "bogus."[67]

In 2008 Republican governor Pawlenty of Minnesota appeared with Janet Napolitano, then the Democratic governor of Arizona, in a nationwide radio advertisement criticizing Congress for not addressing climate change. But appearing on NBC's *Meet the Press* in February 2010, Pawlenty, who was briefly a candidate for the presidential nomination in 2012, said, "Cap and trade . . . would be a disaster." "With Tim Pawlenty, I guess he sees that there's a need to talk about climate change in a more skeptical frame to make himself more appealing in a Republican primary," said Jim DiPeso, vice president for policy and communications at Republicans for Environmental Protection.[68]

Other GOP politicians also seem to have experienced their own changes of heart. As a state senator, Scott Brown voted in 2008 in support of Massachusetts's participation in the Regional Greenhouse Gas Initiative. During his successful campaign in a special U.S. Senate election in 2010, however, Brown expressed doubts about the science underpinning global warming theories. He explained his new position by saying that RGGI hadn't worked.

Similarly, Marco Rubio, as Speaker of the Florida House, declared in 2007 that "this nation—and ultimately the world—is headed toward emission caps."[69] He backed the idea of creating a state cap-and-trade program the following year. In his 2010 campaign for the U.S. Senate, however, Rubio blasted Crist, his primary opponent, for having pushed the cap-and-trade idea. Rubio said that he doesn't believe the scientific evidence for human-influenced climate change.

It's true that Senator Lindsey Graham, R-S.C., worked on drafting the main Senate climate change bill in 2010 with John Kerry, D-Mass., and Joseph Lieberman, I-Conn. But Graham attracted no other Republicans to the effort and was widely castigated back home in South Carolina for his work. The Charleston County GOP passed a resolution condemning Graham for undermining "Republican leadership and party solidarity for

Local Focus

On a Global Issue, Acting Locally

In 2008, Seattle mayor Greg Nickels recalled his concern as he looked out over the Cascade Mountains during the winter of 2005. The snowpack that his city relies on for both drinking water and hydroelectric power had almost failed to materialize.

"At that point, it was sort of an 'Aha' moment," he says. "Climate change went from being an esoteric issue affecting someone else in the near future to hitting us here, now."

Nickels went on to spearhead an effort among local officials to abide by the Kyoto Protocol, even though it hasn't been ratified by the U.S. Senate. More than one thousand mayors have signed on from cities that are home to a total of more than 81 million Americans, according to the U.S. Conference of Mayors. "We as mayors recognize the threat of hurricanes, drought and the lack of snowpacks" that have been linked to global warming, says Nickels, who lost his reelection bid in 2009. "It's our obligation to take action."

But there are limits on what local officials can do. They lack the authority to regulate the dominant sources of greenhouse gas emissions—power plants and vehicles. The mayors' efforts, as a result, have mostly been small-scale affairs. Many local officials lack the ability even to measure their cities' total emission levels, let alone reduce them.

In many instances, their actions appear more symbolic than substantive. Critics say that it's going to take more than the door-to-door promotion of new lightbulbs (to cite one Minneapolis initiative) or the replacement of inefficient streetlights to prevent global warming. "Virtually all of the actions that have been taken at the local level are symbolic," said Myron Ebell, director of energy and global warming policy at the Competitive Enterprise Institute, a business-backed advocacy group. "They are meant to gain immediate public approval for the current incumbent and put all the responsibility for achieving those future goals on some future officeholder."

Even some environmentalists concede that the mayors' efforts, although obviously well-intentioned, aren't enough to put a serious dent in carbon emissions. "It's a mixed bag," said Teri Shore, a campaign director with Friends of the Earth, an environmental group in San Francisco. "You've got a lot of cities and counties that have signed up and set goals, but the harder part comes with actually implementing those goals."

Barry G. Rabe, a University of Michigan political scientist, notes that, because of the lack of standardized emissions reporting, it's hard to know which efforts have been successful and which haven't. For example, it was only in 2008 that Chicago put forward models of the first city-specific climate change projections. At that time, Chicago mayor Richard M. Daley announced a plan to reduce the city's greenhouse gas emissions by 25 percent in 2020, compared to 1990 levels, through tougher building codes, improved transportation, reduced industrial pollution, and use of clean and renewable energy sources. "We can't solve the world's climate change problem in Chicago," Daley said, "but we can do our part."

Chicago had already drawn praise for its green rooftops program, which boasts plantings on more than two hundred buildings, including city hall and the Target and Apple stores. But not even the cities that have been most ambitious about trying to meet their reduction targets have succeeded. Promises by big-city mayors to plant a million trees each have run into obstacles such as cost and lack of usable land. And New York City mayor Michael Bloomberg's plan to charge cars a

his own benefit."[70] Graham withdrew his support from the bill just before it was introduced because, he said, he was angry about Democratic plans to move immigration legislation onto the Senate floor ahead of it.

This leads straight to a chicken-and-egg question: Are many Republican leaders growing more skeptical about climate change legislation because of concerns raised by their political base? Or are GOP voters following a "congestion pricing" fee for driving into parts of Manhattan was rejected by the state legislature in 2008.

"Every locality is really good about talking about the virtues of their programs, but I don't think we've seen careful analysis and scrutiny about what works and doesn't," Rabe says. "What you have is a lot of self-celebration and claiming of success."

But Rabe notes that many municipal experiments are just getting under way. And Shore says that cities are trying to remake themselves into "green incubators" and engaging in a friendly competition to find the best ways of limiting their local carbon footprints.

"Having hundreds of cities across the country doing a test-run of innovations is a good thing," says Kathleen Casey Ridihalgh, a Sierra Club regional representative in Seattle. "It kind of gives us a huge pilot test of what we need to do at the federal level."

Toward this end, mayors are reducing municipal electricity use, promoting car and bike sharing, and purchasing more environmentally friendly vehicle fleets themselves—and, in New York, requiring cabbies to do the same. Some cities have hired "sustainability directors" who are charged directly with reducing municipal energy consumption.

"People thought I was flaky when I took office and got rid of the city's Crown Victoria that was getting ten miles per gallon and replaced it with a Prius," says Minneapolis mayor R. T. Rybak. "I was not considered as flaky by the time I switched from a Prius to a plug-in."

James Brainard, the mayor of Carmel, Indiana, and a former cochair of a climate change task force for the U.S. Conference of Mayors, says that local officials can have an enormous impact due to their influence over building codes and transportation planning. He points out that since World War II metropolitan areas have been designed around automobile driving. "In some cities, 20 to 25 percent of the total heat load is from engines," Brian Stone Jr., director of the Urban Climate Center at Georgia Tech, told NPR. "Not only are most cities heating up more rapidly than the planet, they tend to be heating up at double the rate."[a]

Cutting down on vehicle miles traveled (VMT) has become a top goal of environmental activists and land-use planners. "Mayors are the ones who decide how planning and zoning are going to take place," Brainard says. "We have to train our planning commissioners and others to insist on good city design where one is not forced to drive from place to place."

Even a prominent advocate of local action such as Seattle's Nickels concedes federal action will be necessary not only to meet the Kyoto standards but also to surpass them. But cities can still have considerable influence over transportation and land-use planning.

Perhaps as important, cities have helped spark and keep alive a dialogue about translating concerns about climate change into tangible action. "Mayor Nickels's getting various mayors to sign off on climate change predates what we did at the state level," says Terry Tamminen, who served as an energy and environment adviser to California governor Schwarzenegger. "It's a great way to stimulate action at the next level of government."

Source: Adapted from Alan Greenblatt, "Confronting Warming," *CQ Researcher*, January 9, 2009, 6.

[a]Richard Harris, "As Temps Rise, Cities Combat Heat Island Effect," NPR, September 4, 2012, www.npr.org/2012/09/04/160393303/as-temps-rise-cities-combat-heat-island-effect.

shift among top officials and the conservative media? "Many ordinary citizens take their cues on complex political issues from leaders of the political party that they identify with," said DiPeso.[71]

But Daniel J. Weiss, senior fellow and director of climate strategy at the Center for American Progress Action Fund, a Democratic-leaning group, thinks that it is public opinion that is leading the leaders in this case. He cites the frequent attacks against global warming legislation efforts launched by Rush Limbaugh and commentators on Fox News Channel. "That has really riled up their highly conservative base," Weiss says.[72]

He also notes that elected officials are well aware of the opposition to congressional climate change legislation led by energy companies and the U.S. Chamber of Commerce. In 2012, fossil-fuel companies devoted more than $150 million to advertising focused on energy issues. "If you're a Republican," Weiss asks, "would you really stand up to them and risk getting on their wrong side when they have so much money to spend?"[73]

International Agreements

Just a couple of weeks after he was elected president in November 2008, Barack Obama offered a videotaped address to state leaders gathered at a climate change policy summit in California. "When I am president, any governor who's willing to promote clean energy will have a partner in the White House," he said.[74] When Obama came into office, he made it clear that climate change was among his highest priorities.

That was welcome news to those assembled, an audience of policymakers who had felt frustrated by the lack of attention that global warming had received under President George W. Bush. Some were openly emotional, believing Obama's remarks signaled a new day. Many state and local leaders had gotten involved in climate change policy only because of the lack of federal action—a state of affairs they felt certain was at its end.

But by the time of Obama's election, it was clear that many states and localities were already too invested in the issue simply to cede the ground to Washington. They became highly vocal lobbyists during deliberations in Congress, as well as in international forums. In contrast to the general run of environmental issues, where policies have largely been set by the federal government even though responsibilities are carried out by the states, climate change had become an issue in which states and localities had already claimed their ground. In large part because its effects are felt differently in different locales, many states and cities had become convinced of the need to formulate their own strategies and plans, even if the logjam in Washington looked like it was ready to be broken.

As it turned out, state leaders who believed greenhouse gas emissions needed to be lowered were still acting on their own. Obama and other world leaders failed to reach any serious agreement at a summit in Copenhagen in December 2009, the purpose of which had been to revamp and update the international treaty on greenhouse gases that had been written in Kyoto a dozen years earlier. A two-week United Nations meeting in Doha at the end of 2012 led to little agreement beyond the idea of extending the old Kyoto Protocol. Climate change was essentially a nonissue in the presidential campaign of 2012. During the presidential debates, Republican candidate Mitt Romney criticized Obama's spending on clean energy companies more than once, while Obama criticized Romney for bragging that as governor of Massachusetts he had shut down coal-fired power plants. They never addressed climate change directly. Candy Crowley of CNN, who moderated one of the debates, said afterward that she had had ready a "question for all of you climate change people. We just, we knew that the economy was still the main thing." All that meant in retrospect that, ultimately, the more significant news out of the California climate change policy summit in 2008 was not Obama's statement but agreements reached between American states and provinces in other countries. At that meeting, governors from thirteen states and regional leaders from four other nations signed a declaration to work together to combat global warming. Under a separate agreement, California, Illinois, and Wisconsin pledged to work with the governors of six provinces within Indonesia and Brazil to help slow tropical deforestation and land degradation through joint projects and incentive programs. "When California passed its global warming law two years ago, we were out there on an island, so we started forming partnerships everywhere we could," Governor Schwarzenegger said.[75] But, as noted earlier, the multistate regional initiatives have had difficulty meeting their own goals.

In 2009, Schwarzenegger and subnational leaders from Canada, Nigeria, France, and Algeria announced that they had formed the Club of 20 Regions, later known as the R20 Regions of Climate Action, to lobby their respective national governments on climate change policies and to implement those policies and any international agreements more quickly. The group, which has received the blessing of the United Nations, launched officially in 2010.

"When Obama got elected, there was a bit of a pause because we thought we'll have federal legislation and an international agreement," said Terry Tamminen, Schwarzenegger's former state EPA secretary. "But the lack of agreement in Copenhagen and, so far, the lack of an agreement in Washington has inspired states to keep going. The frustration level by the states and regions is such that they're going to be launching an alternative to try to get things going internationally."[76]

Conclusion

Climate change has seen considerable policy debate and innovation at the state and local levels over the past decade. In some ways, this is surprising. Global warming, by its name and nature, is an issue that should seek solutions on an international level as opposed to a subnational one.

And states historically have left policy on most environmental issues up to Washington.

But the opposition of the Bush administration to serious curbs on energy use at a time when global warming concerns were at their height led many state and local leaders to chart their own courses. Not all states are convinced that promoting renewable energy sources or curbing carbon emissions is the right or even a necessary course. And there are plenty of critics who charge that most of the policies pursued at the state and local levels have been largely symbolic. It's easy to set targets that won't take effect for several years. And an increasingly loud chorus of voices maintains that even effective measures will not be worth the high cost that they might impose on the economy.

Many states and cities, however, have taken real action to curb their own energy use and to promote conservation and renewable energy sources throughout their economies. They have done this in spite of years of inaction at the national level and in spite of the difficulties in coordinating policy responses that are inherent in the federal system. Despite the challenges, having gotten into this game, many state and local governments clearly intend to stay. They remain frustrated by the inability of Congress to enact legislation in this area. And, even when Washington does act, they will want to be able to pursue policies and programs that by now are pretty well entrenched.

The Latest Research

This chapter has illustrated the ways in which many states have emerged as policy leaders on climate issues. For decades, the federal government was the driver on environmental policy, but lack of anything like consensus in Washington in recent years has allowed states to take various approaches (including none at all) to addressing climate change. Policy innovations among individual states and regional consortiums have provided frameworks not just for the erstwhile efforts of the Obama administration but for efforts at the provincial level in other countries as well.

(Continued)

(Continued)

States have sought ways of addressing climate change only over the past couple of decades, with many important laws passed only in the past few years. Perhaps for that reason, scholarship in this field has emerged relatively slowly, certainly in comparison with other long-standing state and local government concerns, such as budgets, political parties, and crime. This has proven to be a robust field of inquiry nonetheless, as academics can grapple not only with policy innovations and their efficacy but also with a number of questions regarding federalism and intergovernmental relations, since climate is a topic that is inherently cross-jurisdictional in scope.

• • • • • • • • • • • • • • • • • • • •

• **Goulder, Lawrence H., and Robert N. Stavins.** 2011. "Challenges from State-Federal Interactions in US Climate Change Policy." *American Economic Review* 101: 253–257.

Although climate change is an issue that should be addressed at a global level, the politics surrounding it mean there is still plenty of room for subnational governments to create policy in the absence of meaningful federal effort. But problems can arise when there are gaps between policies at the federal and state levels, particularly in the areas of renewable energy and fuel-efficiency standards. Firms that meet more stringent state-level standards on renewable energy production, for instance, will then have excess federal credits to sell to firms in other states that do not need to rely as much on renewable-sourced energy. Goulder and Stavins conclude that this could lead to higher costs but little if any reduction in emissions on a national scale.

• **Krause, Rachel M.** 2012. "Political Decision-Making and the Local Provision of Public Goods: The Case of Municipal Climate Protection in the U.S." *Urban Studies* 49: 2399–2417.

Many examinations of local climate change efforts barely look beyond the question of whether cities participate in networks devoted to the topic. Examining original survey data, Krause looks at what makes a city more likely to engage in specific climate protection efforts. Rather than financial support from other levels of government or the likely local impact of climate change (for instance, because of location alongside a coast), the biggest factors appear to be both the municipal government's own capacity for formulating and implementing policy and the human resources available locally, in terms of both per capita income and, especially, levels of higher education.

• **Rabe, Barry.** 2011. "Contested Federalism and American Climate Policy." *Publius: The Journal of Federalism* 41: 494–521.

Climate change policy has increasingly and perhaps surprisingly taken on an intergovernmental dimension. It originally seemed incumbent upon national governments to craft agreements on a global scale, but the reality in the United States is that lack of action at the federal level has left states free to dominate formulation of climate policy. The Supreme Court decision in *Massachusetts v. EPA* and the election of Barack Obama to the presidency suggested that Washington would take on a leading role, but the failure of major climate legislation and even proposals to preempt state action has left states in a position to continue exerting influence over energy and environmental regulations.

• **Rabe, Barry G., ed.** 2010. *Greenhouse Governance: Addressing Climate Change in America.* Washington, DC: Brookings Institution Press.

The contributions to this volume examine various aspects of policies related to climate change, seeking to address what Rabe calls a "stunning lack" of scholarly engagement with the topic from various social science disciplines. Despite long-standing trends toward greater centralization of authority within the federal government, the states have emerged as central policy innovators on climate. State-level laws put a number of approaches on the national agenda, but the lack of congressional action has meant that states have been the implementers of ideas such as requiring renewable energy standards, regulating carbon emissions, and implementing cap-and-trade systems.

college.cqpress.com/
sites/govstateandlocal

Chapter Review

Key Concepts

- adaptation (p. 521)
- building codes (p. 517)
- cap and trade (p. 509)
- carbon dioxide (p. 506)
- Clean Air Act (p. 506)
- climate change (p. 505)
- fracking (p. 513)
- global warming (p. 505)
- greenhouse gases (p. 506)
- green jobs (p. 518)
- Kyoto Protocol (p. 505)
- mitigation (p. 523)
- New Urbanism (p. 516)
- renewable energy (p. 510)
- smog (p. 506)
- sprawl (p. 513)
- tailpipe emissions (p. 506)
- U.S. Environmental Protection Agency (EPA) (p. 505)
- weatherization (p. 518)
- zoning laws (p. 514)

Suggested Web Sites

- **www.aspanet.org.** Official Web site of the American Society for Public Administration, the largest professional association for those who work for or study public agencies.

- **www.governing.com.** Web version of *Governing* magazine, which is dedicated to covering state and local issues. Includes numerous stories and other resources on agency leaders and performance, e-government, and more.

- **www.pewcenteronthestates.org.** Home to a number of analyses about government effectiveness and efficiency, including the Government Performance Project.

State Stats on Environment and Climate Change

Explore and compare data on the states! Go to college.cqpress.com/sites/govstateandlocal to do these exercises.

1. Which states have the highest per capita energy consumption? Is this surprising? Why or why not?

2. In 2011, which states were responsible for the most pollution? What is it about these states that might explain this?

3. Which state decreased its pollution the most from 1996 to 2000? Which state increased the most? Why is there so much variation?

4. Which state has the most hazardous waste sites? To what extent should cleaning up these sites be a priority?

5. In 1995, which states used the most water? Even though we don't have more recent data, how do you think this might be different now?

Notes

Chapter 1

1. Peter Harkness, "Public Universities Reach a Tipping Point," *Governing,* June 2012, www.governing.com/topics/education/gov-public-universities-reach-tipping-point.html.

2. Alan Greenblatt, "Tuition? UC Riverside Students Say Bill Me Later," *Governing,* April 2012, www.governing.com/topics/education/gov-tuition-uc-riverside-students-say-bill-me-later.html.

3. National Center for Education Statistics, "Total Fall Enrollment in Degree-Granting Institutions, by Control and Type of Institution: 1963 through 2009," *Digest of Education Statistics,* April 2011, http://nces.ed.gov/pubs2011/2011015.pdf.

4. National Center for Education Statistics, "Percentage Distribution of Total Revenue of Public Degree-Granting Institutions, by Source of Funds: 2008–2009," *Digest of Education Statistics,* April 2011, http://nces.ed.gov/pubs2011/2011015.pdf.

5. National Center for Education Statistics, "Fast Facts: Financial Aid," http://nces.ed.gov/fastfacts/display.asp?id=31.

6. National Center for Education Statistics, "Fast Facts: Back to School Statistics," http://nces.ed.gov/fastfacts/display.asp?id=372.

7. Kenneth J. Meier, *Politics and the Bureaucracy* (Pacific Grove, CA: Brooks/Cole, 1993), 2.

8. Christopher Z. Mooney, "Why Do They Tax Dogs in West Virginia? Teaching Political Science through Comparative State Politics," *PS: Political Science & Politics* 31 (June 1998): 199–203.

9. Bridging the Gap, Robert Wood Johnson Foundation, "State Sales Tax on Regular, Sugar-Sweetened Soda (as of July 1, 2011)," www.bridgingthegapresearch.org/_asset/zvh93o/BTG_State_Soda_Sales_Tax_Jul012011_publuse_29Nov11.pdf.

10. Based on a standard ordinary least squares (OLS) regression analysis in which average tuition bills at public four-year universities are the dependent variable and state appropriations as thousands of dollars per enrolled student is the dependent variable. Data taken from National Center for Education Statistics, *Digest of Education Statistics,* http://nces.ed.gov/pubs2011/2011015.pdf.

11. U.S. Bureau of the Census, "State and County Quick-Facts," http://quickfacts.census.gov/qfd/index.html.

12. Richard Morrill, "The Urban US: Growth and Decline," NewGeography, April 11, 2012, www.newgeography.com/content/002769-the-urban-us-growth-and-decline.

13. Associated Press, "Not So Sunny: Florida's Growth Rate Continues to Slide, Census Reports," Naplesnews.com, www.naplesnews.com/news/2010/jun/10/not-so-sunny-floridas-growth-rate-continues-slide-.

14. Daniel J. Elazar, *American Federalism: A View from the States* (New York: Crowell, 1966). This book has gone through three editions, the most recent of which was published in 1984.

15. Ibid., 88.

16. Maureen Moakley, "New Jersey," in *The Political Life of the American States,* ed. Alan Rosenthal and Maureen Moakley (New York: Praeger, 1984), 222.

17. Quoted in Robert D. Putnam, *Bowling Alone: The Collapse and Revival of American Community* (New York: Simon & Schuster, 2000), 293.

18. Russell Hanson, "Political Culture Variations in State Economic Development Policy," *Publius: The Journal of Federalism* 21, no. 2 (Spring 1991): 63–81; Kevin B. Smith, *The Ideology of Education: The Commonwealth, the Market, and America's Schools* (Albany: State University of New York Press, 2003).

19. Bureau of Economic Analysis, "Per Capita Real GDP by State," http://bea.gov/iTable/iTable.cfm?reqid=99&step=1.

20. Phillip W. Roeder, *Public Opinion and Policy Leadership in the American States* (Tuscaloosa: University of Alabama Press, 1994); J. Wolak and C. K. Palus, "The Dynamics of Public Confidence in U.S. State and Local Government," *State Politics & Policy Quarterly* 10 (2010): 421–445.

21. Bruce Wallin, "State and Local Governments Are American Too," *Political Science Teacher* 1 (1988): 1–3.

22. U.S. Bureau of the Census, "Government Employment and Payroll," www.census.gov/govs/apes.

23. U.S. Bureau of the Census, "State and Local Government Finances Summary: 2009," October 11, 2011, www2.census.gov/govs/estimate/09_summary_report.pdf.

24. Evan J. Ringquist and James C. Garand, "Policy Change in the American States," in *State and Local*

Politics, ed. Ronald E. Weber and Paul Brace (New York: Chatham House, 1999).

25. David Osborne and Ted Gaebler, *Reinventing Government: How the Entrepreneurial Spirit Is Transforming the Public Sector* (New York: Plume, 1993).

Chapter 2

1. Cass Sunstein, "The Return of States' Rights," *American Prospect,* November 30, 2002, www.prospect.org/cs/articles?article=the_return_of_states_rights.
2. James Collier and Christopher Collier, *Decision in Philadelphia* (New York: Random House, 1986).
3. Quoted in ibid., 3.
4. Ellen Perlman, "The Preemption Beast: The Gorilla That Swallows State Laws," *Governing* magazine, August 1994, 46–51.
5. Quoted in Harry N. Scheiber, "The Condition of American Federalism: An Historian's View," in *American Intergovernmental Relations,* ed. Laurence J. O'Toole Jr. (Washington, DC: CQ Press, 2000), 71.
6. Ibid.
7. Kala Ladenheim, "History of U.S. Federalism," March 16, 1999, www.cas.sc.edu/poli/courses/scgov/History_of_Federalism.htm.
8. Scheiber, "Condition of American Federalism."
9. Ellis Katz, "American Federalism, Past, Present and Future," *Issues of Democracy* 2, no. 2 (1997), www.doge.us/govecon/AmericanFederalismPast.pdf.
10. Paul L. Posner, *The Politics of Unfunded Mandates: Whither Federalism?* (Washington, DC: Georgetown University Press, 1998), 13.
11. National Conference of State Legislatures, "Mandate Monitor," www.ncsl.org/state-federal-committees/scbudg/mandate-monitor-overview.aspx.
12. Timothy Conlon, "Federalism and Competing Values in the Reagan Administration," *Publius: The Journal of Federalism* 16, no. 4 (1986): 29–47.
13. Thomas J. Anton, "New Federalism and Intergovernmental Fiscal Relationships: The Implications for Health Policy," *Journal of Health Politics, Policy and Law* 22, no. 3 (1997): 691–720.
14. Richard L. Cole and John Kincaid, "Public Opinion and American Federalism: Perspectives on Taxes, Spending, and Trust," *Spectrum: The Journal of State Government* 74, no. 3 (2000): 14–18.
15. "Same-Sex Marriage: Federal and State Authority," *Congressional Digest* 75 (November 1996): 263.
16. Peter Harkness, "Potomac Chronicle: Obama and the States," *Governing,* January 1, 2009, 18.
17. Bardon Aronson, "The Rising Tide of Federalism," CNN.com, February 1, 2001, www.cnn.com/2001/LAW/02/columns/fl.aronson.federalism.02.01.
18. Alan Ehrenhalt, "Devolution in Reverse," *Governing,* December 1, 2008, 8.
19. Michael S. Greve, *Real Federalism: Why It Matters, How It Could Happen* (Washington, DC: AEI Press, 1999), 17.
20. Jeffrey G. Homrig, "*Alden v. Maine*: A New Genre of Federalism Shifts the Balance of Power," *California Law Review* 89, no. 1 (2001): 183–205.
21. David G. Savage, "Justices Rule U.S. Can Ban Medical Pot," *Los Angeles Times,* June 7, 2005.
22. John Dinan, "The State of American Federalism 2007–2008: Resurgent State Influence in the National Policy Process and Continued State Policy Innovation," *Publius: The Journal of Federalism* 38, no. 3 (2008): 381–415.
23. Brady Baybeck and William Lowry, "Federalism Outcomes and Ideological Preferences: The U.S. Supreme Court and Preemption Cases," *Publius: The Journal of Federalism* 30, no. 1 (2000): 73–96.

Chapter 3

1. Referendum A, Colorado, 2004.
2. Shauna Reilly and Sean Richey, "Ballot Question Readability and Roll-Off: The Impact of Language Complexity," *Political Research Quarterly* 64 (2011): 59–67.
3. See chapter 1 for a discussion of Elazar's typology of political cultures.
4. Donald Kettl, "Governor Rehnquist," *Governing,* July 1999.
5. Alan Tarr, *Understanding State Constitutions* (Princeton, NJ: Princeton University Press, 1998), 6–8.
6. Christopher Hammons, "Was James Madison Wrong? Rethinking the American Preference for Short, Framework-Oriented Constitutions," *American Political Science Review* 93, no. 4 (1999): 837.
7. Ibid., 840.
8. Ibid. See also John G. Kester, "Amendment Time," *Washingtonian,* March 1995.
9. Janice C. May, "Trends in State Constitutional Amendment and Revision," in *The Book of the States 2003* (Lexington, KY: Council of State Governments, 2003), 8.
10. Robert J. Taylor, ed., *Massachusetts, Colony to Commonwealth* (New York: Norton, 1961).
11. Quoted in Willi Paul Adams, *The First American Constitutions: Republican Ideology and the Making of the State Constitutions in the Revolutionary Era* (Chapel Hill: University of North Carolina Press, 1980), 53.
12. Quoted in ibid., 61.
13. Quoted in ibid., 207.
14. Tarr, *Understanding State Constitutions,* 121.
15. W. B. Stouffer, Cynthia Opheim, and Susan Bland Day, eds., *State and Local Politics: The Individual and the Governments* (New York: HarperCollins, 1996).
16. Bruce Sundlun, "R.I.'s Martyr for Democracy," *Providence Journal-Bulletin,* August 11, 2002.

17. Delaware is the only state that does not refer constitutional amendments to the electorate as a whole. The legislature may enact constitutional amendments on its own if a measure receives support in two consecutive legislative sessions.

18. *The Book of the States 2001* (Lexington, KY: Council of State Governments, 2001), 5. In South Carolina, a majority of both houses of the legislature must vote to approve a constitutional amendment a second time, after it has passed a popular referendum, before it can go into effect.

19. Initiative and Referendum Institute, www.iandrinstitute .org. The institute's Web site includes detailed time lines of initiative and referendum activity in each state.

20. Juan B. Elizondo Jr., "Ratliff: Time to Rewrite Constitution; Lawmaker Joined by Watchdog," *Austin American-Statesman,* October 28, 1999.

21. *The Book of the States 2003* (Lexington, KY: Council of State Governments, 2003), 3–4.

22. Warren Richey, "Unique Law Lets Florida Voters Make Changes to Constitution," *Christian Science Monitor,* May 8, 1998.

23. Quoted in Alan Ehrenhalt, "Vermont's Judicial Distillery," *Governing,* February 2000, www.governing .com/archive/archive/2000/feb/assess.txt.

24. Hammons, "Was James Madison Wrong?," 839.

25. Joni James, "Voters Hold Key to Big Shake-Up in State Cabinet: The Revision Would Eliminate Three Posts, Give the Governor More Power, and Shift Control of Education Policy," *Orlando Sentinel,* October 20, 1998, D1.

26. Stuart MacCorkle and Dick Smith, *Texas Government* (New York: McGraw-Hill, 1960).

27. Daniel Elazar, *American Federalism: A View from the States,* 3rd ed. (New York: Harper & Row, 1984), 115.

28. Hammons, "Was James Madison Wrong?," 846.

29. See ibid. for a more complete argument along these lines.

30. Melinda Gann Hall, "State Judicial Politics: Rules, Structures, and the Political Game," in *American State and Local Politics,* ed. Ronald Weber and Paul Brace (New York: Chatham House, 1999), 136.

31. National Conference of State Legislatures, "Gubernatorial Veto Authority with Respect to Major Budget Bill(s)," December 2008, www.ncsl.org/Issues Research/BudgetTax/GubernatorialVetoAuthority withRespecttoMajor/tabid/12640/Default.aspx.

32. Andrew Taylor, "Line Item Budget Barely Trims Spending at State Level," *Denver Rocky Mountain News,* January 15, 1995.

33. Scott Milfred, "Some Want to Clip Gubernatorial Wings: A Resolution in the Legislature Would Curtail Wisconsin Governor's Exceptionally Broad Veto Power," *Wisconsin State Journal,* September 23, 2001, A1.

34. Virginia Gray, Herbert Jacob, and Kenneth N. Vines, eds. *Politics in the American States: A Comparative Analysis* (Boston: Little, Brown, 1983).

35. In 2003, the U.S. Supreme Court invalidated laws prohibiting sodomy. Until that time, Alabama, Florida, Idaho, Louisiana, Massachusetts, Mississippi, North Carolina, South Carolina, Utah, and Virginia had laws that explicitly prohibited sodomy. Kansas, Oklahoma, and Texas prohibited same-sex sodomy only. LAMBDA Legal Defense and Education Fund Web site, www.lambda.org.

36. James Madison, *Federalist* No. 10, in Alexander Hamilton, James Madison, and John Jay, *The Federalist Papers,* ed. Charles Kesler and Clinton Rossiter (New York: Penguin Putnam, 1961), 76.

37. Ibid. Hamilton, Madison, and Jay envisioned other safeguards as well. One was the well-known principle of the separation of powers among the three branches of government. The other was the large size of the republic itself. Previous theorists of democracy had worried about republics that became too large to govern. In *Federalist* No. 10, Madison makes the novel claim that a more extensive republic would be less likely to succumb to factionalism than the smaller republics of old.

38. Quoted in David Broder, *Democracy Derailed: Initiative Campaigns and the Power of Money* (New York: Harcourt, 2000), 27.

39. Ibid.

40. Initiative and Referendum Institute, "The History of Initiative and Referendum in the United States," www.iandrinstitute.org.

41. Richard Ellis, *Democratic Delusions: The Initiative Process in America* (Lawrence: University Press of Kansas, 2002).

42. Broder, *Democracy Derailed.*

43. Keon S. Chi, "Emerging Trends Shaping State Governments: 2005 and Beyond," in *The Book of the States 2005* (Lexington, KY: Council of State Governments, 2005).

44. "California Ballot Initiative Petition Signature Costs," Ballotpedia, http://ballotpedia.org/wiki/index.php/ California_ballot_initiative_petition_signature_costs.

45. Broder, *Democracy Derailed,* 1.

46. Lawrence F. Keller, "Municipal Charters," *National Civic Review* 91, no. 1 (2002): 155–161.

Chapter 4

1. Phil Oliff, Chris Mai, and Vincent Palacios, "States Continue to Feel Recession's Impact," Center on Budget and Policy Priorities, www.cbpp.org/cms/index .cfm?fa=view&id=711.

2. Lucy Dadayan and Donald J. Boyd, "Recession or No Recession, State Tax Revenues Remain Negative," Rockefeller Institute of Government, Albany, NY, January 2010, 3.

3. Council of State Governments, "Federal Assistance," 2010, www.staterecovery.org/federal-assistance.

4. Tax Foundation, "State-Local Tax Burdens, All States, 1977–2009," 2011, http://taxfoundation.org/article/state-and-local-tax-burdens-all-states-one-year-1977-2009.

5. These figures and many that follow come from U.S. Department of Commerce, *Statistical Abstract of the United States, 2012* (Washington, DC: U.S. Census Bureau, 2012), www.census.gov/compendia/statab, and refer to the fiscal year that concluded in 2008, one of the most recent years for which such data are available.

6. Ibid.

7. *The Fiscal Survey of States* (Washington, DC: National Governors Association and National Association of State Budget Officers, fall 2009), vii, www.nasbo.org/sites/default/files/fsfall2009.pdf.

8. U.S. Department of Commerce, *Statistical Abstract,* Table 424.

9. Federation of Tax Administrators, "State Cigarette Excise Tax Rates and Rankings," January 1, 2012, www.taxadmin.org/fta/rate/cigarette.pdf.

10. U.S. Department of Commerce, *Statistical Abstract,* Table 435.

11. Estimated sales tax calculated at Minnesota online sales tax calculator for Bloomington, Minnesota, www.taxes.state.mn.us/taxcalc/index.shtml.

12. Tax Foundation, "A Sales Tax Word of Warning in Hawaii, New Mexico, South Dakota, and Wyoming," September 30, 2011, http://taxfoundation.org/blog/sales-tax-word-warning-hawaii-new-mexico-south-dakota-and-wyoming.

13. Katherine Barrett, Richard Greene, Michele Mariani, and Anya Sostek, "The Way We Tax: A 50-State Report," *Governing,* February 2003, www.governing.com/gpp/2003/gp3intro.htm.

14. Donald Bruce, William F. Fox, and LeAnn Luna, "State and Local Sales Tax Revenue Losses from E-Commerce," Center for Business and Economic Research, University of Tennessee, Knoxville, April 13, 2009, http://cber.bus.utk.edu/ecomm/ecom0409.pdf.

15. Cited in Penelope Lemov, "The Untaxables," *Governing,* July 2002.

16. Alan Greenblatt, "The Sales Tax Goes Online," *Governing,* December 2005.

17. "Frequently Asked Questions," Streamlined Sales Tax Governing Board, www.streamlinedsalestax.org/index.php?page=faqs.

18. Saul Hansell, "Court to Amazon: Keep Paying Sales Tax," Bits Blog, January 13, 2009, http://bits.blogs.nytimes.com/2009/01/13/court-to-amazon-keep-collecting-sales-tax-to-new-yorkers.

19. CBS News, "Amazon Is Now Collecting California Sales Tax," September 15, 2012, www.cbsnews.com/8301–18563_162–57513681/amazon-is-now-collecting-california-sales-tax.

20. U.S. Department of Commerce, "State and Local Government Finances Summary: 2009," October 2011, www2.census.gov/govs/estimate/09_summary_report.pdf.

21. U.S. Department of Commerce, *Statistical Abstract,* Table 424.

22. Effective tax rate information for the nation and New Hampshire can be found in ibid., Table 436.

23. Ibid., Table 443.

24. U.S. Department of Commerce, "State and Local Government Finances Summary: 2009."

25. Alan Greenblatt, "The Loathsome Local Levy," *Governing,* October 2001.

26. U.S. Department of Commerce, "State and Local Government Finances Summary: 2009."

27. Fifteen states allow certain localities to impose income taxes as well, but for the most part, income tax receipts are a minor source of funds for cities and counties.

28. U.S. Department of Commerce, *Statistical Abstract,* Table 453.

29. Tax Foundation, "State Individual Income Tax Collections, 2010," February 15, 2012, http://taxfoundation.org/article/facts-figures-handbook-how-does-your-state-compare-0.

30. U.S. Department of Commerce, *Statistical Abstract,* Table 451.

31. Ibid., Table 436.

32. *Fiscal Survey of States,* 18.

33. U.S. Department of Commerce, *Statistical Abstract,* Table 436.

34. National Association of State Budget Officers, "Summary: NASBO State Expenditure Report," December 13, 2011, www.nasbo.org/sites/default/files/Summary%20-%20State%20Expenditure%20Report.pdf.

35. Ibid.

36. U.S. Department of Commerce, *Statistical Abstract,* Table 455.

37. Alan Greenblatt, "Enemies of the State," *Governing,* June 2002.

38. Tax Foundation, "State and Local Tax Burden per Fiscal Year 2009," http://taxfoundation.org/article/facts-figures-handbook-how-does-your-state-compare-0.

39. U.S. Department of Commerce, *Statistical Abstract,* Table 441.

40. "Personal Income per Capita, 2007," *State and Local Sourcebook,* online supplement to *Governing,* 2010, http://sourcebook.governing.com/subtopicresults.jsp?ind=677.

41. Tax Foundation, "State-Local Tax Burdens, All States, 2008."

42. See the Mayflower Compact for further insights into the mind-set of the founders of the Massachusetts Bay Colony, www.pilgrimhall.org/compact.htm.

43. John E. Petersen, "Guide to Municipal Finance: Credit Raters Make Their Mark," *Governing,* June 2005.

44. Penelope Lemov, "The Muni Market in 2012," *Governing*, January 12, 2012, www.governing.com/columns/public-finance/col-municipal-bond-market-2012.html.

45. For a detailed discussion of the state budget process, see National Association of State Budget Officers, "Budget Processes in the States," Washington, DC, January 2002.

46. These states are Connecticut, Hawaii, Indiana, Kentucky, Maine, Minnesota, Montana, Nebraska, Nevada, New Hampshire, North Carolina, North Dakota, Ohio, Oregon, Texas, Virginia, Washington, Wisconsin, and Wyoming. National Conference of State Legislatures, "State Experiences with Annual and Biennial Budgeting," April 2011, www.ncsl.org/issues-research/budget/state-experiences-with-annual-and-biennial-budgeti.aspx.

47. For a detailed discussion of state balanced budget requirements, see National Conference of State Legislatures, "Legislative Budget Procedures: A Guide to Appropriations and Budget Processes in the States, Commonwealths and Territories," November 2008, www.ncsl.org/?TabID=12669, www.ncsl.org/programs/fiscal/balbud2.htm.

48. Robert Zahradnik, "Rainy Day Funds: Opportunities for Reform," Center on Budget and Policy Priorities, March 9, 2005, www.cbpp.org/3-9-05sfp.htm.

49. "United States Federal State and Local Government Spending Fiscal Year 2012 per Capita," usgovernmentspending.com, www.usgovernmentspending.com/US_per_capita_spending.html.

50. U.S. Department of Commerce, *Statistical Abstract*, Table 436; "State and Local Government Employment: Monthly Data," *Governing*, 2012, www.governing.com/gov-data/public-workforce-salaries/monthly-government-employment-changes-totals.html.

51. U.S. Department of Commerce, "State Government Finances," www.census.gov/govs/state/1000usst.html.

52. U.S. Department of Commerce, *Statistical Abstract*, Table 444.

53. "State Fiscal Support for Higher Education, by State, Fiscal Years 2006–07, 2009–10, 2010–11, and 2011–12," Grapevine: An Annual Compilation of Data on State Fiscal Support for Higher Education, http://grapevine.illinoisstate.edu/tables/FY12/Revised_March13/Table%201%20Revised.pdf.

54. National Association of State Budget Officers, "2008 State Expenditure Report," Washington, DC, December 2009, 47.

55. Ibid., 44.

56. Henry J. Kaiser Family Foundation, "Federal and State Share of Medicaid Spending, FY 2010," www.statehealthfacts.org/comparemaptable.jsp?ind=636&cat=4.

57. Georgetown University Health Policy Institute, "Medicaid and CHIP Programs," http://ccf.georgetown.edu/facts-statistics/medicaid-chip-programs.

58. Cynthia Miller, "Leavers, Stayers, and Cyclers: An Analysis of the Welfare Caseload," Manpower Demonstration Research Corporation, New York, November 2002. For a full discussion of the effects of welfare reform, see also Alan Weil, "Ten Things Everyone Should Know about Welfare Reform," no. A-52, Urban Institute, Washington, DC, May 9, 2002.

59. U.S. Department of Health and Human Services. "Federal TANF and State MOE Expenditures Summary by ACF-196 Spending Category, FY 2011," www.acf.hhs.gov/programs/ofa/data/2011fin/table_a1.pdf.

60. U.S. Department of Commerce, *Statistical Abstract*, Table 436.

61. NASBO, "2008 State Expenditure Report," 66.

62. "Total State & Local Highway Spending (in millions), 2006," *State and Local Sourcebook*, online supplement to *Governing*, http://sourcebook.governing.com/subtopicresults.jsp?ind=627.

63. National Association of State Budget Officers, "2009 State Expenditure Report," Washington, DC, 2010, 64.

64. NASBO, "2008 State Expenditure Report," 67.

65. "The Widening Gap Update," Pew Center on the States, Washington, DC, June 2012, www.pewstates.org/uploadedFiles/PCS_Assets/2012/Pew_Pensions_Update.pdf.

66. Greenblatt, "Enemies of the State."

67. Bill Piper, *A Brief Analysis of Voter Behavior Regarding Tax Initiatives: From 1978 to March 2000* (Washington, DC: Citizen Lawmaker Press, n.d.).

68. This section is adapted from the February 2003 *Governing* special issue on state tax systems; see Barrett et al., "The Way We Tax."

Chapter 5

1. John J. Pitney Jr., August 11, 2012, twitter.com/jpitney/status/234476224032956416.

2. Quoted in Alan Greenblatt, "Changing U.S. Electorate," *CQ Researcher*, May 30, 2008, 461.

3. Quoted in Thomas B. Edsall, "Census a Clarion Call for Democrats, GOP," *Washington Post*, July 8, 2001, 1A.

4. Earl Black and Merle Black, *Divided America: The Ferocious Power Struggle in American Politics* (New York: Simon & Schuster, 2007), 10.

5. Chris Evans, "It's the Autonomy, Stupid: Political Data-Mining and Voter Privacy in the Information Age," *Minnesota Journal of Law, Science & Technology* 13 (2012): 868.

6. Steven Hill, *Fixing Elections: The Failure of America's Winner Take All Politics* (New York: Routledge, 2002), 119.

7. Ruy Teixeira, *America's New Swing Region: Changing Politics and Demographics in the Mountain West* (Washington, DC: Brookings Institution Press, 2012), 1.

8. Quoted in Alan Greenblatt, "Blueburbs," *Governing,* October 2008, 22.

9. Ibid.

10. Caroline J. Tolbert, John A. Grummel, and Daniel A. Smith, "The Effects of Ballot Initiatives on Voter Turnout in the American States," *American Politics Research* 29, no. 6 (2001): 625–648.

11. Interview with Rhodes Cook, December 11, 2006.

12. Kevin J. Coleman, Thomas H. Neale, and Joseph E. Cantor, "The Election Process in the United States," Congressional Research Service, Washington, DC, July 6, 1995, 69.

13. National Conference of State Legislatures, "Straight-Ticket Voting," www.ncsl.org/legislatures-elections/elections/straight-ticket-voting-states.aspx.

14. Election Data Services, *The Election Data Book: A Statistical Portrait of Voting in America* (Lanham, MD: Bernan Press, 1992), appendix.

15. Vauhini Vara, "'Instant Runoff' Faces Test," *Wall Street Journal,* October 21, 2011, http://online.wsj .com/article/SB10001424052970204774604576631212229446284.html.

16. Kay Lawson, "How State Laws Undermine Parties," in *Elections American Style,* ed. A. James Reichley (Washington, DC: Brookings Institution, 1987), 241.

17. Cited in William C. Binning, Larry E. Esterly, and Paul A. Sracic, *Encyclopedia of American Parties, Campaigns, and Elections* (Westport, CT: Greenwood Press, 1999), 95.

18. E-mail correspondence with Richard Winger, July 24, 2012.

19. Quoted in Greg Giroux, "Third-Party Push: Hope vs. History," *CQ Weekly,* May 4, 2007.

20. Lawson, "How State Laws Undermine Parties," 246.

21. Quoted in Jesse McKinley, "California Puts Vote Overhaul on the Ballot," *New York Times,* May 27, 2010, A1.

22. Larry Sabato, twitter.com/BuzzFeedBen/statuses/150620246800220162.

23. Binning et al., *Encyclopedia of American Parties,* 95.

24. Quoted in Dan Eggen and Amy Goldstein, "Voter-Fraud Complaints by GOP Drove Dismissals," *Washington Post,* May 14, 2007, A4.

25. Andrew Hacker, "Obama: The Price of Being Black," *New York Review of Books,* September 25, 2008, www .nybooks.com/articles/21771.

26. Megan Reisz, "Register to Vote through Facebook?," *Christian Science Monitor,* July 18, 2012, www.csmonitor .com/Innovation/2012/0718/Register-to-vote-through-Facebook-Washington-reveals-new-app.

27. Phone interview with Curtis Gans, September 4, 2003.

28. Phone interview with Steven Hill, September 11, 2003.

29. Mark Hugo Lopez, "The Latino Electorate in 2010: More Voters, More Non-voters," Pew Hispanic Center, April 26, 2011, www.pewhispanic.org/2011/04/26/the-latino-electorate-in-2010-more-voters-more-non-voters.

30. Interview with Ruy Teixeira, April 2006.

31. Robert D. Putnam, *Bowling Alone: The Collapse and Revival of American Community* (New York: Simon & Schuster, 2000).

32. Barbara G. Salmore and Stephen A. Salmore, *New Jersey Politics and Government,* 2nd ed. (Lincoln: University of Nebraska Press, 1998), 128.

33. See "Texas Politics," Liberal Arts Instructional Technology Services, University of Texas at Austin, http://texaspolitics.lamc.utexas.edu/html/exec/index.html.

34. Associated Press, "The Decatur Daily on Windom Candidacy," October 4, 2001.

35. Quoted in Danielle Todesco, "New Mexico Governor, Attorney General, Battle over Emails," KOB Eyewitness News, July 6, 2012, www.kob.com/article/stories/S2680886.shtml.

36. Quoted in Rob Gurwitt, "The Lone Comptroller," *Governing,* October 2003, 68.

37. Quoted in Alan Greenblatt, "Where Campaign Money Flows," *Governing,* November 2002, 44.

38. Alan Greenblatt, "The Avengers General," *Governing,* May 2003, 54.

39. Zach Patton, "Robe Warriors," *Governing,* March 2006, 34.

40. Initiative and Referendum Institute Web site, www .iandrinstitute.org.

41. John F. Camobreco, "Preferences, Fiscal Policy, and the Initiative Process," *Journal of Politics* 60, no. 3 (August 1998): 822.

42. Presentation at the annual meeting of the National Conference of State Legislatures, Chicago, August 9, 2012.

43. Quoted in James Dao, "Same-Sex Marriage Key to Some G.O.P. Races," *New York Times,* November 4, 2004, P4.

44. Simon Jackman, "Same-Sex Marriage Ballot Initiatives and Conservative Mobilization in the 2004 Election," presentation, http://jackman.stanford.edu/papers/risspresentation.pdf.

45. Quoted in Alan Greenblatt, "Some Presidential Politics Is Local," *New York Times,* October 10, 2004, sec. 4, 5.

46. Ryan Holeywell, "The Rise of the Recall Election," *Governing,* April 2011, www.governing.com/topics/politics/rise-recall-election.html.

47. Alan Greenblatt, "Total Recall," *Governing,* September 2003, 27.

48. Phone interview with Randall Gnant, August 7, 2003.

49. V. O. Key, *Public Opinion and American Democracy* (New York: Knopf, 1964), 7.

50. Interview with Doug Duncan, November 15, 2006.

51. Interview with Mike Haridopolos, August 8, 2012.

52. See especially Robert S. Erikson, Gerald C. Wright, and John D. McIver, *Statehouse Democracy: Public Opinion and Policy in the American States* (New York: Cambridge University Press, 1993).

53. Paul Brace, Kellie Sims-Butler, Kevin Arceneaux, and Martin Johnson, "Public Opinion in the American States: New Perspectives Using National Survey Data," *American Journal of Political Science* 46, no. 1 (January 2002): 173–189.

54. Susan Herbst, "How State-Level Policy Managers 'Read' Public Opinion," in *Navigating Public Opinion: Polls, Policy, and the Future of American Democracy,* ed. Jeff Manza, Fay Lomax Cook, and Benjamin I. Page (New York: Oxford University Press, 2002), 176.

55. Logan Dancey and Paul Goren, "Party Identification, Issue Attitudes, and the Dynamics of Political Debate," *American Journal of Political Science* 54 (July 2010): 686–699.

56. Phone interview with Greg Shaw, September 3, 2003.

57. Phone interview with Paul Brace, September 10, 2003.

Chapter 6

1. Alan Greenblatt, "How a College Kid May Have Helped Pick a Congressman," NPR, May 23, 2012, www.npr.org/blogs/itsallpolitics/2012/05/22/153342541/how-a-college-kid-may-have-helped-pick-a-congressman.

2. Quoted in Alan Greenblatt, "Citizens United's Corporate Candidate," *Governing,* May 2012, www.governing.com/topics/politics/gov-citizen-uniteds-corporate-candidate.html.

3. Ed Kilgore, "Diagnosing Dems," *Blueprint,* May 17, 2006, www.ndol.org/ndol_ci.cfm?kaid=127&subid=171&contentid=253867.

4. Quoted in Mark Leibovich, "The Tea-Party Primary," *New York Times Magazine,* January 10, 2010, 29.

5. Quoted in Alan Greenblatt, "Wired to Win," *Governing,* October 2006, 26.

6. John Celock, "Steve Morris, Kansas Senate President, Blames Moderates' Defeat on Conservative Attack Ads," Huffington Post, August 8, 2012, www.huffingtonpost.com/2012/08/08/steve-morris-kansas-senate-koch-brothers_n_1757928.html.

7. Quoted in Alan Greenblatt, "Politics and Marketing Merge in Parties' Bid for Relevance," *Congressional Quarterly Weekly Report,* August 16, 1997, 1967.

8. Quoted in Jeff Greenfield, "Hayes's Ride," *Washington Monthly,* March 2003.

9. Alvin Kess, *Politics in New York State* (Syracuse, NY: Syracuse University Press, 1965), 29.

10. David R. Mayhew, *Placing Parties in American Politics: Organization, Electoral Settings, and Government Activity in the Twentieth Century* (Princeton, NJ: Princeton University Press, 1986), esp. 24.

11. Quoted in Bertil L. Hanson, "County Commissioners of Oklahoma," *Midwest Journal of Political Science* 9 (1965): 396.

12. Joel H. Sibley, "The Rise and Fall of American Political Parties, 1790–1990," in *The Parties Respond: Changes in the American Party System,* ed. L. Sandy Maisel (Boulder, CO: Westview Press, 1990), 9.

13. Mayhew, *Placing Parties in American Politics,* 105.

14. Ibid., 185.

15. John F. Bibby and Thomas M. Holbrook, "Parties and Elections," in *Politics in the American States: A Comparative Analysis,* 7th ed., ed. Virginia Gray, Russell L. Hanson, and Herbert Jacobs (Washington, DC: CQ Press, 1999), 71.

16. John F. Bibby, "State and Local Parties in a Candidate-Centered Age," in *American State and Local Politics: Directions for the 21st Century,* ed. Ronald E. Weber and Paul Brace (New York: Chatham House, 1999), 198.

17. Rhodes Cook, "Republican Brawls through the Century Helped Define Party for Years to Come," *Congressional Quarterly Weekly Report,* April 6, 1996, 942.

18. John R. Schmidt and Wayne W. Whalen, "Credentials Contests at the 1968—and 1972—Democratic National Conventions," *Harvard Law Review* 82 (May 1969): 1456.

19. Alan Greenblatt, "History: Winds of War Blew through Chicago," *Congressional Quarterly Weekly Report,* August 17, 1996, 23.

20. Bibby, "State and Local Parties," 199.

21. Peter W. Wielhower and Brad Lockerbie, "Party Contacting and Political Participation, 1952–90," *American Journal of Political Science* 38 (February 1994): 213.

22. See John H. Kessel, "Ray Bliss and the Development of the Ohio Republican Party during the 1950s," in *Politics, Professionalism, and Power: Modern Party Organization and the Legacy of Ray C. Bliss,* ed. John C. Green (Lanham, MD: University Press of America, 1994), 49–50.

23. Interview with Lee Herrington, September 2002.

24. Leon D. Epstein, *Political Parties in the American Mold* (Madison: University of Wisconsin Press, 1986), 155.

25. Michael McDonald, "Partisan Voter Registration Totals," Huffington Post, October 13, 2010, www.huffingtonpost.com/michael-p-mcdonald/partisan-voter-registrati_b_761713.html.

26. Malcolm E. Jewell and Sarah M. Morehouse, *Political Parties and Elections in American States,* 4th ed. (Washington, DC: CQ Press, 2001), 76.

27. Bibby, "State and Local Parties," 198.

28. Bibby and Holbrook, "Parties and Elections," 70.

29. Ibid., 71.

30. Quoted in Ruth Marcus, "Party Spending Unleashed; Justices Say Independence from Candidate Is Key," *Washington Post,* June 27, 1996, A1.

31. Alan Greenblatt, "Soft Money: The Root of All Evil or a Party-Building Necessity?," *Congressional Quarterly Weekly Report,* September 26, 1997, 2064.

32. Don Van Natta Jr. and Richard A. Oppel Jr., "Parties Set Up Groups to Elude Soft Money Ban," *New York Times,* November 2, 2002, A1.

33. Agustín Armendariz and Aron Pilhofer, "McCain-Feingold Changes State Party Spending," Center for Public Integrity, May 26, 2005, www.publicintegrity .org/partylines/report.aspx?aid=690.

34. Interview with Larry J. Sabato, May 2002.

35. Tim Storey and Gene Rose, "GOP #1 First Time in 50 Years," *State Legislatures,* December 2002, 12–17.

36. Alan Greenblatt, "Undoing the Split," *Governing,* February 2009.

37. Jewell and Morehouse, *Political Parties and Elections,* 22–23.

38. "Changing Hands," *Governing,* January 2003, 24.

39. Mayhew, *Placing Parties in American Politics,* 291.

40. Ibid., 292–293.

41. Jason Szep, "Youth Turnout in Election Biggest in 20 Years," Reuters, November 8, 2006.

42. Emily Hoban Kirby and Kei Kawashima-Ginsberg, "The Youth Vote in 2008," Center for Information and Research on Civic Learning and Engagement, August 17, 2009, www.civicyouth.org/PopUps/ FactSheets/FS_youth_Voting_2008_updated_6.22 .pdf.

43. Jim Reagen, "Scozzafava: Race Became 'Referendum on Issues Far from Here,'" *Watertown Daily Times,* November 1, 2009, www.watertowndailytimes.com/ article/20091101/NEWS05/311019896.

44. Alan Ehrenhalt, "Political Pawns," *Governing,* July 2000, 20.

45. Greenblatt, "Citizens United's Corporate Candidate."

46. Quoted in Alan Greenblatt, "'Big Tent' Advocates Look Likely to Defeat Abortion Measure," *Congressional Quarterly Weekly Report,* January 10, 1998, 89.

47. Martin P. Wattenberg, *The Decline of American Political Parties, 1952–1992* (Cambridge, MA: Harvard University Press, 1994), x.

48. David B. Magleby, Candice J. Nelson, and Mark C. Westlye, "The Myth of the Independent Voter Revisited," Working Paper 10-01, Center for the Study of Elections and Democracy, Brigham Young University, January 2010, http://csed.byu.edu/Assets/Magleby%20Nelson%20Westlye%202010.pdf.

49. Dana Milbank, "Where Have All the Candidates Gone?," *Washington Post,* May 15, 2012, www .washingtonpost.com/opinions/where-have-all-the-candidates-gone/2012/05/15/gIQA6ZRISU_story.html.

50. Quoted in Cathy Newman and Ben White, "States Left to Pick Reform Ticket," *Washington Post,* August 27, 2000, A5.

51. Quoted in Joel Siegel, "Party's over for Liberals," *Daily News,* February 24, 2003, 20.

52. Greenblatt, "Politics and Marketing," 1967.

53. Pew Research Center for the People & the Press, "Independents Take Center Stage in Obama Era: Trends in Political and Core Attitudes: 1987–2009," May 21, 2009, www.people-press.org/2009/05/21/ independents-take-center-stage-in-obama-era.

54. Larry M. Bartels, "Partisanship and Voting Behavior, 1952–1996," *American Journal of Political Science* 44 (January 2000): 35.

55. Ibid., 36–37.

56. Bruce E. Keith, David B. Magleby, Candice J. Nelson, Elizabeth Orr, Mark C. Westlye, and Raymond E. Wolfinger, *The Myth of the Independent Voter* (Berkeley: University of California Press, 1992).

57. Interview with Jane Jech, August 17, 2012.

58. Quoted in Greenblatt, "Politics and Marketing," 1967.

59. Alan Greenblatt, "The Social Media Shuffle: From Kony to Spooning," NPR, April 19, 2012, www.npr .org/2012/04/19/150964208/young-people-turn-from-kony-to-spooning-record.

60. Ibid.

61. Molly Messick, "Retired Probation Officer Leads (Modest) Fight for Idaho Medicaid Expansion," StateImpact, July 11, 2012, http://stateimpact.npr .org/idaho/2012/07/11/retired-probation-officer-leads-modest-fight-for-idaho-medicaid-expansion.

62. Frank J. Sorauf, *Political Parties in the American System* (Boston: Little, Brown, 1964), 13.

63. Clive S. Thomas and Ronald J. Hrebenar, "Interest Groups in the States," in *Politics in the American States: A Comparative Analysis,* 8th ed., ed. Virginia Gray and Russell L. Hanson (Washington, DC: CQ Press, 2004), 114–115.

64. Leah Rush, "Hired Guns," Center for Public Integrity, December 20, 2007, updated August 19, 2011, www .publicintegrity.org/2007/12/20/5895/influence-booming-business.

65. Virginia Gray and David Lowery, "Interest Representation in the States," in Weber and Brace, *American State and Local Politics,* 267.

66. Quoted in Alan Rosenthal, *The Third House: Lobbyists and Lobbying in the States,* 2nd ed. (Washington, DC: CQ Press, 2001), 17.

67. Quoted in Alan Greenblatt, "Squeezing the Federal Turnip," *Governing,* March 2003, 28.

68. Quoted in Matt Canham, "Utah Cities Are Shelling Out for D.C. Lobbyists," *Salt Lake Tribune,* June 8, 2008.

69. Lee Drutman, "The Complexities of Lobbying: Toward a Deeper Understanding of the Profession," *PS: Political Science & Politics* 43, no. 4 (October 2010): 835.

70. Richard L. Hall and Molly E. Reynolds, "Targeted Issue Advertising and Legislative Strategy: The Inside Ends of Outside Lobbying," *Journal of Politics* 74, no. 3 (July 2012): 888–902.

71. Christopher Swope, "Winning without Steaks and Cigars," *Governing,* November 2000. See also Rob Gurwitt, "Cookie-Jar Clampdown," *Governing,* April 2007.

72. Phone interview with John Weingart, August 18, 2010.

73. Rosenthal, *Third House,* 78.

74. Quoted in Jacob Goldstein, "So You Think You Can Be a Hair Braider?," *New York Times,* June 12, 2012, www.nytimes.com/2012/06/17/magazine/so-you-think-you-can-be-a-hair-braider.html.

75. Rosenthal, *Third House,* 45.

76. Quoted in Alan Greenblatt, "Secondhand Spokesmen," *Governing,* April 2002, www.governing.com/archive/archive/2002/apr/tobacco.txt.

77. Quoted in Rosenthal, *Third House,* 61.

78. Clive S. Thomas and Ronald J. Hrebenar, "Lobby Clout," *State Legislatures,* April 1999.

79. Thomas and Hrebenar, "Interest Groups in the States," 121–122.

80. Alan Greenblatt, "Real Power," *Governing,* June 2006, 46.

81. Phone interview with Alan Rosenthal, February 6, 2007.

Chapter 7

1. Quoted in Philip D. Duncan and Christine C. Lawrence, *Congressional Quarterly's Politics in America 1998* (Washington, DC: CQ Press, 1997), 755.

2. William M. Bulger, *While the Music Lasts: My Life in Politics* (Boston: Houghton Mifflin, 1996), 71.

3. Alexander Hamilton, *Federalist* No. 73, http://thomas.loc.gov/home/fedpapers/fed_73.html.

4. Bob Bergren, presentation at the Council of State Governments western regional meeting, October 7, 2009.

5. Quoted in Nicholas Confessore and Michael Barboro, "New York Allows Same-Sex Marriage, Becoming Largest State to Pass Law," *New York Times,* June 24, 2011, www.nytimes.com/2011/06/25/nyregion/gay-marriage-approved-by-new-york-senate.html?pagewanted=all.

6. Quoted in ibid.

7. Quoted in Rob Gurwitt, "The Riskiest Business," *Governing,* March 2001, 21.

8. "2011 Texas Session Statistics," State Net, September 14, 2011, www.statenet.com/resources/session_statistics.php?state=TX; "2011 Montana Session Statistics," State Net, July 29, 2011, www.statenet.com/resources/session_statistics.php?state=MT&session_id=2011000.

9. Josh Goodman, "A Government Adrift," *Governing,* August 2008, www.governing.com/topics/mgmt/A-Government-Adrift.html.

10. Quoted in Alan Greenblatt, "The Date-Checking Game," *Governing,* October 2006, 17.

11. Tom Loftus, "Optometrists' Kentucky Political Donations Exceed $400,000," *Louisville Courier-Journal,* February 15, 2011, www.courier-journal.com/article/20110215/NEWS01/302150097/Optometrists-Kentucky-political-donations-exceed-400–000?gcheck=1&nclick_check=1.

12. Judith C. Meredith, *Lobbying on a Shoestring,* 2nd ed. (Dover, MA: Auburn House, 1989), 4.

13. "Government Workers Don't Need Even More Protections," *Modesto Bee,* February 17, 2012, www.modbee.com/2012/02/27/2088695/government-workers-dont-need-even.html#storylink=cpy Modesto Bee.

14. Melissa Maynard, "A Bill of Rights for State Workers?," Stateline, April 3, 2012, www.pewstates.org/projects/stateline/headlines/a-bill-of-rights-for-state-workers-85899380541.

15. Greenblatt, "Fit to Be Tied," *Governing,* August 2001, 20.

16. Quoted in Andy Sher, "GOP Claims Strides on Issues," *Chattanooga Times Free Press,* June 21, 2009, A1.

17. Alan Rosenthal, *Engines of Democracy: Politics and Policymaking in State Legislatures* (Washington, DC: CQ Press, 2009), 310.

18. Maggie Clark, "States Find Laws against Sports Head Injuries Tricky to Enact," Stateline, July 19, 2012, www.pewstates.org/projects/stateline/headlines/states-find-laws-against-sports-head-injuries-tricky-to-enact-85899405995.

19. Quoted in Josh Goodman, "Smoked Out," *Governing,* October 2009, 17.

20. Quoted in ibid.

21. Virginia Gray and David Lowery, "Where Do Policy Ideas Come From? A Study of Minnesota Legislators and Staffers," *Journal of Public Administration Research and Theory* 10 (January 2000): 573–597.

22. See Gary F. Moncrief, Joel A. Thompson, and Karl T. Kurtz, "Old Statehouse Ain't What It Used to Be," *Legislative Studies Quarterly* 21, no. 1 (February 1996): 57–72.

23. MSNBC interview with Amy Klobuchar, July 1, 2009.

24. Rosenthal, *Engines of Democracy,* 84.

25. Interview with Rosalind Kurita, October 7, 2002.

26. Alan Rosenthal, *Governors and Legislatures: Contending Powers* (Washington, DC: CQ Press, 1990), 187.

27. Diane D. Blair, *Arkansas Politics and Government* (Lincoln: University of Nebraska Press, 1988), 182, cited in Rosenthal, *Governors and Legislatures.*

28. Katherine Barrett and Richard Greene, "B&G Interview: Questions for John Turcotte," *Governing,* B&G Report column, February 1, 2008, www.governing.com/column/bg-interview-questions-john-turcotte.

29. John Turcotte, presentation at the annual meeting of the National Conference of State Legislatures, July 21, 2009.

30. Alan Rosenthal, Burdett Loomis, John Hibbing, and Karl Kurtz, *Republic on Trial: The Case for*

Representative Democracy (Washington, DC: CQ Press, 2003), 26.

31. Karen Hansen, "Red Tide," *State Legislatures,* December 2010, 14.

32. Wes Clarke, "The Divided Government and Budget Conflict in the U.S. States," *Legislative Studies Quarterly* 23, no. 1 (February 1998): 5.

33. National Conference of State Legislatures, "In Case of a Tie . . . ," www.ncsl.org/legislatures-elections/legislatures/incaseofatie.aspx.

34. Quoted in Alan Greenblatt, "Reformer in Power," *Governing,* January 2009, 20.

35. Meredith, *Lobbying on a Shoestring,* 34.

36. Edmund Burke, "The English Constitutional System," in *Representation,* ed. Hannah Pitkin (New York: Atherton Press, 1969).

37. Quoted in Christopher Swope, "Winning without Steak and Cigars," *Governing,* November 2000, 40.

38. Quoted in Alan Ehrenhalt, "Putting Practice into Theory," *Governing,* November 2000, 6.

39. Quoted in Rosenthal, *Engines of Democracy,* 237.

40. Alan Ehrenhalt, *The United States of Ambition: Politicians, Power, and the Pursuit of Office* (New York: Times Books/Random House, 1991), 158.

41. Foster Church, "Just Like a Woman," *Governing,* September 1990, 26.

42. Virginia Public Access Project, www.vpap.org/committees/profile/money_out_vendors/1696?start_year=2011&end_year=2011&lookup_type=year&filing_period=all&filter_expend=all&order=amount.

43. Virginia Public Access Project, www.vpap.org/committees/profile/money_out_recipients/2936?end_year=2011&start_year=2011&lookup_type=year&filing_period=all.

44. Richard A. Clucas, "Principal-Agent Theory and the Power of State House Speakers," *Legislative Studies Quarterly* 26, no. 2 (May 2001): 319–338.

45. Quoted in Alan Greenblatt, "The Mapmaking Mess," *Governing,* January 2001, 23.

46. Aaron Blake, "Name That District Winner: 'Upside-Down Elephant,'" *Washington Post,* The Fix blog, August 12, 2011, www.washingtonpost.com/blogs/the-fix/post/name-that-district-winner-upside-down-elephant/2011/08/11/gIQABOTABJ_blog.html#pagebreak.

47. Nolan Hicks, "New Congressional Redistricting Maps Very Close to Greg Abbott's Plan," *Houston Chronicle,* Texas on the Potomac blog, February 28, 2012, http://blog.chron.com/txpotomac/2012/02/new-congressional-redistricting-maps-very-close-to-greg-abbotts-plan.

48. Alan Ehrenhalt, "Party Lines," *Governing,* January 2007, 11.

49. Olga Pierce and Jeff Larson, "How Democrats Fooled California's Redistricting Commission,"

ProPublica, December 21, 2011, www.propublica.org/article/how-democrats-fooled-californias-redistricting-commission.

50. Quoted in Josh Goodman, "Why Redistricting Commissions Aren't Immune from Politics," Stateline, January 27, 2012, www.pewstates.org/projects/stateline/headlines/why-redistricting-commissions-arent-immune-from-politics-85899375350.

51. Greenblatt, "The Mapmaking Mess," 22.

52. Josh Goodman, "Farming for Votes," *Governing,* November 2010, 46, www.governing.com/topics/politics/future-redistricting-rural-america.html.

53. Josh Goodman, "Introducing America's Largest State Legislative District," *Governing,* Politics blog, February 11, 2010, www.governing.com/blogs/politics/Introducing-Americas-Largest-State.html.

54. Quoted in Sean Cockerham, "Lawmakers Spar over Adding Seats to Legislature," *Anchorage Daily News,* February 2, 2010, www.adn.com/2010/02/02/1121936/lawmakers-spar-over-adding-districts.html.

55. Rosenthal et al., *Republic on Trial,* 69.

56. Quoted in Howard Troxler, "Choice for Attorney General Not So Easy," *St. Petersburg Times,* October 18, 2002, 1B.

57. Quoted in Alan Greenblatt, "Real Power," *Governing,* June 2006, 46.

58. Otis White, "Making Laws Is No Job for Lawyers These Days," *Governing,* June 1994, 27.

59. Kathleen Dolan and Lynne E. Ford, "Change and Continuity among Women Legislators: Evidence from Three Decades," *Political Research Quarterly* 50 (March 1997): 137–152.

60. Center for American Women and Politics, "Women in State Legislatures 2007," January 2007, www.cawp.rutgers.edu/Facts/Officeholders/stleg.pdf.

61. Renee Loth, "The Matriarchy up North," *Boston Globe,* April 30, 2009, 15.

62. National Conference of State Legislatures, "Percentages of Women in State Legislatures," November 21, 2011, www.ncsl.org/legislatures-elections/wln/women-in-state-legislatures-2011.aspx.

63. Interview with Barbara Lee, October 8, 2002.

64. Thomas H. Little, Dana Dunn, and Rebecca E. Deen, "A View from the Top: Gender Differences in Legislative Priorities among State Legislative Leaders," *Women and Politics* 22, no. 4 (2001): 29–50.

65. Donald E. Whistler and Mark C. Ellickson, "The Incorporation of Women in State Legislatures: A Description," *Women and Politics* 20, no. 2 (1999): 84.

66. Ibid.

67. Michael B. Berkman and Robert E. O'Connor, "Do Women Legislators Matter? Female Legislators and State Abortion Policy," *American Politics Quarterly* 21, no. 1 (January 1993): 105.

68. Kerry L. Haynie, *African American Legislators in the American States* (New York: Columbia University Press, 2001), 19.

69. Ibid., 2.

70. Ibid., 25.

71. Bernard Grofman and Lisa Handley, "Impact of the Voting Rights Act on Black Representation in Southern State Legislatures," *Legislative Studies Quarterly* 16 (1991): 111–128.

72. Malcolm E. Jewell and Samuel C. Patterson, *The Legislative Process in the States* (New York: Random House, 1966), 138.

73. William Pound, "State Legislative Careers: Twenty-Five Years of Reform," in *Changing Patterns in State Legislative Careers,* ed. Gary F. Moncrief and Joel A. Thompson (Ann Arbor: University of Michigan Press, 1992).

74. James D. King, "Changes in Professionalism in U.S. State Legislatures," *Legislative Studies Quarterly* 25, no. 3 (May 2000): 327–343.

75. National Conference of State Legislatures, "Size of State Legislative Staff: 1979, 1988 1996, 2003, 2009," www.ncsl.org/legislatures-elections/legisdata/staff-change-chart-1979-1988-1996-2003-2009.aspx.

76. Josh Goodman, "Pennsylvania Takes Step toward Smaller Legislature," Stateline, April 11, 2012, www.pewstates.org/projects/stateline/headlines/pennsylvania-takes-step-toward-smaller-legislature-85899381094.

77. Wade Rawlins, "Lawmakers Adjourn," *News and Observer* (Raleigh), October 4, 2002.

78. Ellen Perlman, "The 'Gold-Plated' Legislature," *Governing,* February 1998, 37.

79. Editorial, *Clarion Ledger,* April 21, 2008, 6A.

80. Alan Ehrenhalt, "An Embattled Institution," *Governing,* January 1992, 30.

81. Marist Poll, "6/30: NY State Senate Unrest Irks Voters," June 30, 2009, http://maristpoll.marist.edu/630-ny-state-senate-unrest-does-not-sit-well-with-voters.

82. Field Poll, "Brown's Job Rating Remains Favorable. Very Poor Appraisal of the Legislature. Yet, Voters Oppose Having Lawmakers Work Part-Time," February 25, 2012, 6.

83. National Conference of State Legislatures, "Broadcasts and Webcasts of Legislative Floor Proceedings and Committee Hearings," March 2, 2012, www.ncsl.org/issues-research/telecom/legislative-webcasts-and-broadcasts.aspx.

84. Rosenthal, *Engines of Democracy,* 19.

85. Interview with John Hibbing, October 15, 2002.

86. Quoted in Nicholas Confessore, "Perception of Being Slighted Stoked Revolt by Lawmakers," *New York Times,* February 9, 2007, B7.

87. William Powers, "The Saturation Fallacy," *National Journal,* September 7, 2002, 2565.

88. Jonathan Walters, "How to Tame the Press," *Governing,* January 1994, 30.

89. Steve Parker, "Fewer Reporters Are Covering This Year's Super Bowl," *St. Louis Post-Dispatch,* January 27, 2009, www.stltoday.com/news/local/columns/editors-desk/fewer-reporters-are-covering-this-year-s-super-bowl/article_ff4a0baa-1fa5-53e1-9884-77485fdc7294.html.

90. Jennifer Dorroh, "Statehouse Exodus," *American Journalism Review,* April/May 2009, 20.

91. Peverill Squire, "Professionalization and Public Opinion of State Legislatures," *Journal of Politics* 55, no. 2 (1993): 479–491.

92. Interview with Gary Moncrief, October 2, 2002.

93. Quoted in Rob Gurwitt, "Can Nonprofit News Survive?," Stateline, June 9, 2011, www.pewstates.org/projects/stateline/headlines/can-nonprofit-news-survive-85899375041.

94. New Jersey Senate Democrats, "Media Advisory—Senator Whelan to Hold 'Twitter Town Hall' Live on Monday," July 6, 2012, www.njsendems.com/release.asp?rid=4556.

95. Glenn Blain, "Alec Baldwin Engages in Twitter War with State GOP Leader Dean Skelos," *New York Daily News,* October 27, 2011, www.nydailynews.com/news/politics/alec-baldwin-engages-twitter-war-state-gop-leader-dean-skelos-article-1.968221.

96. Jason Linkins, "Jeff Frederick's Twitter Use Foils GOP Virginia Senate Coup," Huffington Post, February 10, 2009, www.huffingtonpost.com/2009/02/10/jeff-fredericks-twitter-u_n_165769.html.

97. Anita Chadha and Robert A. Bernstein, "Why Incumbents Are Treated So Harshly: Term Limits for State Legislators," *American Politics Quarterly* 24 (1996): 363–376.

98. Patricia Lopez, "Coleman's Journey Crosses Typical Divide," *Minneapolis Star Tribune,* October 16, 2002, www.startribune.com/stories/462/3367928.html.

99. Quoted in Rob Gurwitt, "Southern Discomfort," *Governing,* October 2002, 32.

100. Tim Carpenter, "House Member Secretly Tapes Schmidt," *Topeka Capital-Journal,* January 17, 2012, http://cjonline.com/news/2012-01-17/house-member-secretly-tapes-schmidt.

Chapter 8

1. Interview with Dee Richard, September 5, 2012.

2. Quoted in Alan Greenblatt, "When Governors Don't Play Nice," *Governing,* November 2012, 9.

3. Quoted in Larry J. Sabato, *Goodbye to Good-Time Charlie: The American Governorship Transformed,* 2nd ed. (Washington, DC: CQ Press, 1983), 4.

4. Lynn R. Muchmore, "The Governor as Manager," in *Being Governor: The View from the Office,* ed. Thad

Beyle and Lynn R. Muchmore (Durham, NC: Duke University Press, 1983), 83.

5. Terry Sanford, *Storm over the States* (New York: McGraw-Hill, 1967), 185–188, quoted in Eric B. Herzik and Brent W. Brown, "Symposium on Governors and Public Policy," *Policy Studies Journal* 17 (1989): 761.

6. Quoted in Alan Greenblatt, "The Job of a Lifetime," *Governing,* June 2009, 24.

7. E. Lee Bernick, "Gubernatorial Tools: Formal vs. Informal," *Journal of Politics* 42 (1979): 661.

8. Quoted in Alan Rosenthal, *Governors and Legislatures: Contending Powers* (Washington, DC: CQ Press, 1990), 14.

9. Muchmore, "Governor as Manager," 13.

10. Brian Balogh, "Introduction: Directing Democracy," in *A Legacy of Innovation: Governors and Public Policy,* ed. Ethan G. Sribnick (Philadelphia: University of Pennsylvania Press, 2008), 9.

11. Ann O'M. Bowman, Neal D. Woods, and Milton R. Stark II, "Governors Turn Pro: Separation of Powers and the Institutionalization of the American Governorship," *Political Research Quarterly* 63, no. 2 (June 2010): 307.

12. Marjorie Smith, "NH's Executive Branch Needs Reform," *Manchester Union-Leader,* August 1, 2012, 7.

13. Alan Greenblatt, "Steady in a Storm," *Governing,* November 2006, 28.

14. Quoted in Alan Rosenthal, *The Best Job in Politics: Exploring How Governors Succeed as Policy Leaders* (Washington, DC: CQ Press, 2013), 49.

15. Quoted in Jon C. Teaford, "Governors and Economic Development," in Sribnick, *Legacy of Innovation,* 113.

16. Quoted in Alan Greenblatt, "Governing in the Fast Lane," *Governing,* January 2004, 28.

17. Sabato, *Goodbye to Good-Time Charlie,* 4.

18. See Muchmore, "Governor as Manager."

19. Alan Greenblatt, "Tug of War," *Governing,* August 2004, 32.

20. Rob Gurwitt, "The Governor's People," *Governing,* March 1991, 28.

21. Thad Kousser and Justin H. Phillips, *The Power of American Governors* (New York: Cambridge University Press, 2012), 26.

22. Daniel C. Vock, "Govs Enjoy Quirky Veto Power," Stateline, April 24, 2007, www.stateline.org/live/details/story?contentId=201710.

23. Quoted in Alan Greenblatt, "Killing Frankenstein," *Governing,* June 2008, 17.

24. Maggie Clark, "Governors Balance Pardons with Politics," Stateline, February 8, 2013, www.pewstates.org/projects/stateline/headlines/governors-balance-pardons-with-politics-85899449577.

25. Quoted in Alan Greenblatt, "Why Are We Meeting Like This?," *Governing,* August 2002, 40.

26. Quoted in Kim Severson, "South Carolina Supreme Court Rules against Governor in Legislative Feud," *New York Times,* June 7, 2011, 14.

27. Ibid.

28. Quoted in Rosenthal, *Best Job in Politics,* 28.

29. Quoted in Kousser and Phillips, *Power of American Governors,* 40.

30. Laura A. Van Assendelft, *Governors, Agenda Setting, and Divided Government* (Lanham, MD: University Press of America, 1997), 1.

31. Rosenthal, *Best Job in Politics,* 29.

32. Ralph Wright, *Inside the Statehouse: Lessons from the Speaker* (Washington, DC: CQ Press, 2005), 88.

33. Quoted in Alan Greenblatt, "States of Frustration," *Governing,* January 2004, 26.

34. Quoted in Alan Greenblatt, "Rod Reeling," *Governing,* September 2007, 18.

35. Quoted in Lynda Gledhill, "Taxes—or Fees—in New Health Plan Raise Critics' Ire," *San Francisco Chronicle,* January 22, 2007, B1.

36. Quoted in Van Assendelft, *Governors, Agenda Setting, and Divided Government,* 71.

37. Jan Reid, "The Case of Ann Richards: Women in Gubernatorial Office," in *A Legacy of Leadership: Governors and American History,* ed. Clayton McClure Brooks (Philadelphia: University of Pennsylvania Press, 2008), 185.

38. Raphael J. Sonenshein, "Can Black Candidates Win Statewide Elections?," *Political Science Quarterly* 105 (1990): 219.

39. Rosenthal, *Best Job in Politics,* 58.

40. Quoted in Alan Greenblatt, "All Politics Is National," *Governing,* October 2012, 28.

41. Wisconsin Democracy Campaign, "Recall Race for Governor Cost $81 Million," July 25, 2012, www.wisdc.org/pr072512.php.

42. Kousser and Phillips, *Power of American Governors,* 83.

43. Quoted in Thomas Clouse, "Kempthorne at the Helm," *Idaho Statesman,* January 5, 1999, 1A.

44. Quoted in Brian Friel, "For Governors in Congress, No More King of the Hill," *National Journal,* June 27, 2009.

45. Quoted in Clayton McClure Brooks, "Afterword: Governing the Twenty-First Century," in Brooks, *Legacy of Leadership,* 219.

46. Interview with Julia Hurst, January 5, 2004.

47. Quoted in Josh Goodman, "The Second Best Job in the State," *Governing,* April 2009, 34.

48. Quoted in Alan Greenblatt, "Where Campaign Money Flows," *Governing,* November 2002, 44.

49. Megan Verlee, "Secretaries of State at Center of Election Battles," NPR.org, January 18, 2012, www.npr.org/2012/01/18/145351397/secretaries-of-state-at-center-of-election-battles.

50. Quoted in Alan Greenblatt, "Kris Kobach Tackles Illegal Immigration," *Governing,* March 2012, 37.

51. Quoted in Louis Jacobson, "Secretaries of State Still Juggling Politics, Elections," *Governing,* Politics blog, September 21, 2012, www.governing.com/blogs/politics/gov-secretaries-state-juggling-politics-elections.html.

52. Rosenthal, *Best Job in Politics,* 199.

Chapter 9

1. Sandra Day O'Connor, "The Threat to Judicial Independence," *Wall Street Journal,* September 27, 2006, A18.

2. Bill Raftery, "2011 Year in Review: Record Number of Impeachment Attempts against Judges for Their Decisions," Gavel-to-Gavel, December 27, 2011, http://gaveltogavel.us/site/2011/12/27/2011-year-in-review-record-number-of-impeachment-attempts-against-judges-for-their-decisions.

3. Quoted in Scott Shane, "Ideology Serves as a Wild Card on Court Pick," *New York Times,* November 4, 2005, A1.

4. Quoted in "Politics, Intolerance, Fair Courts" (editorial), *New York Times,* August 10, 2012.

5. *Citizens United v. Federal Election Commission,* 558 U.S. (2010) (Stevens, dissenting).

6. O'Connor, "Threat to Judicial Independence," A18.

7. Quoted in Steven M. Puiszis, ed., *Without Fear or Favor in 2011: A New Decade of Challenges to Judicial Independence and Accountability* (Chicago: DRI—The Voice of the Defense Bar, 2011), 5.

8. Ibid., 62.

9. Tom Parker, "Alabama Justices Surrender to Judicial Activism," *Birmingham News,* January 1, 2006, 4B.

10. R. LaFountain, R. Schauffler, R. Strickland, S. Gibson, and A. Mason, *Examining the Work of State Courts: An Analysis of 2009 State Court Caseloads* (Williamsburg, VA: National Center for State Courts, 2011), www.courtstatistics.org/Flashmicrosites/CSP/images/CSP2009.pdf.

11. David Rottman and Shauna M. Strickland, *State Court Organization, 2004* (Washington, DC: Bureau of Justice Statistics, 2004), www.bjs.ojp.usdoj.gov/content/pub/pdf/sco04.pdf.

12. Diana Penner, "Judge: Jurors Antics Harmless," *Indianapolis Star,* November 30, 2006, 1.

13. Court Statistics Project, "Court Structure Charts," National Center for State Courts, www.courtstatistics.org/Other-Pages/State_Court_Structure_Charts.aspx.

14. Sari S. Escovitz, *Judicial Selection and Tenure* 4 (Chicago: American Judicature Society, 1975).

15. Caleb Nelson, "A Re-evaluation of Scholarly Explanations for the Rise of the Elected Judiciary in Antebellum America," *American Journal of Legal History* 37 (April 1993): 190–224.

16. Larry C. Berkson, "Judicial Selection in the United States: A Special Report," *Judicature* 64, no. 4 (1980): 176–193, updated 1999 by Seth Andersen, www.ajs.org/selection/berkson.pdf.

17. G. Alan Tarr, "Rethinking the Selection of State Supreme Court Justices," *Willamette Law Review* 39, no. 4 (2003): 1445.

18. Doug McMurdo, "Voters Reject Changing Judge Selection," *Las Vegas Review-Journal,* November 3, 2010.

19. Pennsylvania Keystone Poll, February 2007, produced by Franklin & Marshall College in Lancaster, Pennsylvania. Polls and other analysis available at http://politics.fandm.edu.

20. Ciara Torres-Spelliscy, Monique Chase, and Emma Greenman, "Improving Judicial Diversity," Brennan Center for Justice, New York University School of Law, 2008, http://brennan.3cdn.net/96d16b62f331bb13ac_kfm6bplue.pdf.

21. American Judicature Society, "Judicial Selection in the States: Diversity of the Bench," www.judicialselection.us/judicial_selection/bench_diversity/index.cfm?state.

22. American Judicature Society, "Judicial Selection in the States" (2012), www.judicialselection.us.

23. Ibid.

24. Frontline, "Justice for Sale: Interview with Justices Stephen Breyer and Anthony Kennedy," www.pbs.org/wgbh/pages/frontline/shows/justice/interviews/supremo.html.

25. Ibid.

26. Paul Brace and Melinda Gann Hall, "Studying Courts Comparatively: The View from the American States," *Political Research Quarterly* 48 (1995): 5. See also Paul Brace and Brent D. Boyea, "State Public Opinion, the Death Penalty, and the Practice of Electing Judges," *American Journal of Political Science* 52, no. 2 (2008): 360–372.

27. Brace and Hall, "Studying Courts Comparatively."

28. Gerald F. Uelmen, "Crocodiles in the Bathtub: Maintaining the Independence of State Supreme Courts in an Era of Judicial Politicization," *Notre Dame Law Review* 72 (1997): 1135–1142.

29. Ibid., 1133, 1137.

30. Stephen J. Ware, "Money, Politics and Judicial Decisions: A Case Study of Arbitration Law in Alabama," *Journal of Law and Politics* 15 (1999): 645.

31. Adam Liptak and Janet Roberts, "Campaign Cash Mirrors a High Court's Rulings," *New York Times,* October 1, 2006.

32. Billy Corriher, *Big Business Taking over State Supreme Courts: How Campaign Contributions to Judges Tip the Scales against Individuals* (Washington, DC: Center for American Progress, August 2012), 2.

33. Ibid., 14.

34. Quoted in Liptak and Roberts, "Campaign Cash," sec. 1, 1.

35. Brennan Center for Justice, New York University School of Law, "Caperton v. Massey," June 8, 2009, www.brennancenter.org/content/resource/caperton_v_massey.

36. Justice at Stake, "Money and Elections," www.justiceatstake.org/issues/state_court_issues/money_elections.cfm.

37. Quoted in Sheila Kaplan, "Justice for Sale," *Common Cause Magazine,* May–June 1987, 29–30.

38. Joan Biskupic, "*Caperton v. AT Massey Coal Co*: Supreme Court Case with the Feel of a Best Seller," *USA Today,* February 16, 2009.

39. Uelmen, "Crocodiles in the Bathtub."

40. Adam Skaggs, Maria da Silva, Linda Casey, and Charles Hall, *The New Politics of Judicial Elections 2009–10: How Special Interest "Super Spenders" Threatened Impartial Justice and Emboldened Unprecedented Legislative Attacks on America's Courts* (Washington, DC: Justice at Stake Campaign, Brennan Center for Justice, and National Institute on Money and State Politics, October 2011), 16.

41. Brennan Center for Justice, "Buying Time—2010," analysis, September 9, 2010, www.brennancenter.org/content/resource/buying-time-2010.

42. David Kidwell, "Attack Ads Target Illinois Supreme Court Justice," *Chicago Tribune,* October 21, 2010.

43. Zach Patton, "Robe Warriors," *Governing,* March 2006.

44. Colorado League of Women Voters, "Colorado Voter Opinions on Judiciary, 2007," Institute for the Advancement of the American Legal System, University of Denver, 4, http://iaals.du.edu/images/wygwam/documents/publications/Nov252008.JudicialWars.pdf.

45. David B. Rottman, Anthony Champagne, and Roy A Schotland, *Call to Action: Statement of the National Summit on Improving Judicial Selection* (Williamsburg, VA: National Center for State Courts, 2002).

46. Quoted in Mark A. Behrens and Cary Silverman, "The Case for Adopting Appointive Judicial Selection Systems for State Court Judges," *Cornell Journal of Law and Public Policy* 11, no. 2 (Spring 2002): 282.

47. American Judicature Society, "Judicial Selection in the States: Appellate and General Jurisdiction Courts," 1986 (updated January 2004), www.ajs.org/js/judicialselectioncharts.pdf.

48. Behrens and Silverman, "Case for Adopting."

49. Berkson, "Judicial Selection in the United States."

50. Ibid.

51. Behrens and Silverman, "Case for Adopting," 303.

52. Ibid.

53. Rottman et al., *Call to Action.*

54. American Judicature Society, "Methods of Judicial Selection," 2012, http://judicialselection.us.

55. Luke Bierman, "Beyond Merit Selection," *Fordham Urban Law Journal* 29 (2002): 851, 864–865.

56. American Bar Association, "An Independent Judiciary: Report of the Commission on Separation of Powers and Judicial Independence" (1997), 48–49; and Henry J. Abraham, *The Judicial Process: An Introductory Analysis of the Courts of the United States, England, and France,* 6th ed. (New York: Oxford University Press, 1993), 42, cited in ibid.

57. American Judicature Society, "Methods of Judicial Selection."

58. Brace and Hall, "Studying Courts Comparatively," 24.

59. MaryAnn Spoto, "Court Sides with Judges in Pension Dispute," *Star-Ledger,* July 25, 2012.

60. Drew Noble Lanier and Roger Handberg, "In the Eye of the Hurricane: Florida Courts, Judicial Independence, and Politics," *Fordham Urban Law Journal* 29 (2002): 1033.

61. National Center for State Courts, "Judicial Compensation FAQs," last modified July 7, 2009, www.ncsconline.org/WC/CourTopics/FAQs.asp?topic=JudCom.

62. Robert L. Misner, "Recasting Prosecutorial Discretion," *Journal of Criminal Law and Criminology* 86 (1996): 741.

63. Steve Weinberg, "Inside an Office: An Elected Prosecutor Explains," Center for Public Integrity, June 26, 2003, www.publicintegrity.org/2003/06/26/5521/inside-office.

64. Daniel S. Medwed, "The Zeal Deal: Prosecutorial Resistance to Post-conviction Claims of Innocence," *Boston University Law Review* 84 (2004): 125–183.

65. Steven W. Perry, *Prosecutors in State Courts 2005,* Bureau of Justice Statistics Bulletin NCJ-213799 (Washington, DC: U.S. Department of Justice, July 2006).

66. Ibid.

67. Misner, "Recasting Prosecutorial Discretion."

68. Carol J. DeFrances, *State Court Prosecutors in Large Districts 2001,* Bureau of Justice Statistics Special Report NCJ-191206 (Washington, DC: U.S. Department of Justice, December 2001).

69. Ibid. "About two-thirds of Part I Uniform Crime Report (UCR) offenses reported to the police in 1998 occurred in the prosecutorial district served by these offices" (2).

70. Los Angeles County District Attorney's Office Web site, http://da.co.la.ca.us.

71. Shelby A. Dickerson Moore, "Questioning the Autonomy of Prosecutorial Charging Decisions: Recognizing the Need to Exercise Discretion—Knowing There Will Be Consequences for Crossing the Line," *Louisiana Law Review* 60 (Winter 2000): 374.

72. Wayne R. LaFave, "The Prosecutor's Discretion in the United States," *American Journal of Comparative Law* 18 (1970): 532, 533.

73. Misner, "Recasting Prosecutorial Discretion."

74. Telephone interview with Kenneth Noto, deputy chief of the narcotics section at the U.S. Attorney's Office for the Southern District of Florida, in William T. Pizzi, "Understanding Prosecutorial Discretion in the United States: The Limits of Comparative Criminal Procedure as an Instrument of Reform," *Ohio State Law Journal* 54 (1993): 1325n88.

75. Perry, *Prosecutors in State Courts 2005.*

76. Moore, "Questioning the Autonomy."

77. Tushar Kansal, "Racial Disparity in Sentencing: A Review of the Literature," Sentencing Project, January 2005, www.sentencingproject.org/doc/publications/rd_sentencing_review.pdf.

78. Steven K. Smith and Carol J. DeFrances, "Indigent Defense," Bureau of Justice Statistics Selected Findings, NCJ-158909, U.S. Department of Justice, Washington, DC, February 1996, http://bjs.ojp.usdoj.gov/content/pub/pdf/id.pdf.

79. Ibid.

80. Lynn Langton and Donald J. Farole Jr., "Public Defender Offices, 2007—Statistical Tables," Bureau of Justice Statistics Selected Findings, NCJ-228538, U.S. Department of Justice, Washington, DC, November 2009 (revised June 17, 2010), http://bjs.ojp.usdoj.gov/content/pub/pdf/pd007st.pdf.

81. Carol J. DeFrances and Marika F. X. Litras, *Indigent Defense Services in Large Counties 1999,* Bureau of Justice Statistics Bulletin NCJ-184932 (Washington, DC: U.S. Department of Justice, November 2000).

82. Criminal Justice Standards Committee, *Standards for Criminal Justice: Providing Defense Services,* 3rd ed. (Chicago: American Bar Association, 1992).

83. Carol Lundberg, "Justice for All," *Michigan Lawyers Weekly,* June 22, 2009.

84. Gene Johnson, "State High Court Limits Public Defender Caseloads," *Seattle Times,* June 15, 2012.

85. Adele Bernhard, "Take Courage: What the Courts Can Do to Improve the Delivery of Criminal Defense Services," *University of Pittsburgh Law Review* 63 (2002): 305.

86. DeFrances and Litras, "Indigent Defense Services in Large Counties."

87. David Cole, *No Equal Justice: Race and Class in the American Justice System* (New York: New Press, 1999), 92.

88. Spangenberg Group, " Rates of Compensation Paid to Court-Appointed Counsel in Non-capital Felony Cases at Trial: A State-by-State Overview," June 2007, http://legis.wisconsin.gov/lc/committees/study/2010/CJFUND/files/oct22spangenberg.pdf. Virginia recently created a fund from which attorneys could petition to exceed the cap, but the fund rarely lasts for the whole year.

89. Andrew Rachlin, "Rights of Defense," *Governing,* January 2007, www.governing.com/archive/archive/2007/jan/defense.txt.

90. Kevin Clermont and Theodore Eisenberg, "Trial by Jury or Judge: Transcending Empiricism," *Cornell Law Review* 77 (1992): 1124.

91. See *Williams v. Florida,* 399 U.S. 78 (1970), approving six-member juries; and *Apodaca v. Oregon,* 406 U.S. 404 (1972), allowing nonunanimous verdicts.

92. Rottman and Strickland, *State Court Organization, 2004.*

93. U.S. Department of Justice, Office of Justice Programs, Office for Victims of Crime, "Executive Summary," in *New Directions from the Field: Victims' Rights and Services for the 21st Century* (Washington, DC: Government Printing Office, 1998).

94. Wayne A. Logan, "Through the Past Darkly: A Survey of the Uses and Abuses of Victim Impact Evidence in Capital Trials," *Arizona Law Review* 41 (1999): 177–178.

95. See *Payne v. Tennessee,* 501 U.S. 808 (1991), which reversed *Booth v. Maryland,* 482 U.S. 496 (1987).

96. "1 in 31: The Long Reach of American Corrections," Pew Center on the States, March 2009.

97. Bureau of Justice Statistics, "U.S. Correctional Population Declined for Second Consecutive Year," December 2011, http://bjs.ojp.usdoj.gov/content/pub/press/p10cpus10pr.cfm.

98. National Association of State Budget Officers, "2010 State Expenditure Report," 52.

99. In *Ring v. Arizona,* 536 U.S. 584 (2002), the Supreme Court invalidated Arizona's capital sentencing procedures, holding that the jury, not the judge, must find the aggravating factors necessary to impose the death penalty. Similar procedures in Colorado, Idaho, Montana, and Nebraska also were ruled unconstitutional.

100. Michael M. O'Hear, "National Uniformity/Local Uniformity: Reconsidering the Use of Departures to Reduce Federal-State Sentencing Disparities," *Iowa Law Review* 87 (2002): 756.

101. Ibid., 749.

102. Robert Mosteller, "New Dimensions in Sentencing Reform in the Twenty-First Century," *Oregon Law Review* 92 (2003): 16–17.

103. Marguerite A. Driessen and W. Cole Durham Jr., "Sentencing Dissonances in the United States: The Shrinking Distance between Punishment Proposed and Sanction Served," *American Journal of Comparative Law* 50 (2002): 635.

104. Bureau of Justice Statistics, National Corrections Reporting Program 2009, Table 9, "First Releases from State Prison," http://bjs.ojp.usdoj.gov/index.cfm?ty=pbdetail&iid=2056.

105. "Sensible Sentences for Nonviolent Offenders" (editorial), *New York Times,* June 14, 2012.

106. Bureau of Justice Assistance, "1996 National Survey of State Sentencing Structures," NCJ-169270, 1998, Exhibit 1–1.

107. Rottman and Strickland, *State Court Organization,* 2004.

108. Driessen and Durham, "Sentencing Dissonances in the United States."

109. Rottman and Strickland, *State Court Organization,* 2004.

110. Ibid.

111. Pew Center on the States, "Time Served: The High Cost, Low of Return of Longer Prison Terms," June 2012, www.pewstates.org/uploadedFiles/PCS_Assets/2012/Prison_Time_Served.pdf.

112. O'Hear, "National Uniformity/Local Uniformity."

113. Ralph Ranalli, "Crack Sentence Debate Reopened: Proof Whites, Blacks Treated Equally Asked," *Boston Globe,* September 26, 1999, B1, cited in ibid., 733n113.

114. Brian Ostrom, Neal Kauder, and Robert LaFountain, *Examining the Work of the State Courts, 1999–2000: A National Perspective from the Court Statistics Project* (Williamsburg, VA: National Center for State Courts, 2000).

115. National Institute of Justice, *Drug Courts: The Second Decade* (Washington, DC: National Institute of Justice, 2006), 32–36, www.ncjrs.gov/pdffiles1/nij/211081.pdf.

116. Judith S. Kaye, "The State of the Judiciary, 2003: Confronting Today's Challenge," annual address, Albany, NY, January 13, 2003, 4.

117. Quoted in Alan Greenblatt, "Docket Science," *Governing,* June 2001, 40, www.governing.com/archive/archive/2001/jun/civil.txt.

118. Ibid.

119. Quoted in ibid. For more on his reforms to the Hennepin County courts, see also the profile of Kevin Burke in "Court Reform," *Governing,* November 2004.

120. Todd Ruger, "Two Minutes, and Home Goes Away," *Sarasota Herald-Tribune,* May 14, 2009, A1; Todd Ruger, "'Rocket Docket' Can Be Slowed," *Sarasota Herald-Tribune,* September 27, 2009, BN1.

121. Greenblatt, "Docket Science."

122. Rebecca A. Koppes Conway, Timothy M. Tymkovich, Troy A. Eid, Britt Weygandt, and Anthony van Westrum, "Report of the Committee on Magistrates in the Civil Justice System," Governor's Task Force on Civil Justice Reform, October 1, 2000, www.state.co.us/cjrtf/report/report2.htm.

123. Rottman et al., *Call to Action.*

124. Carmen Lo, Katie Londenberg, and David Nims, "Spending in Judicial Elections: State Trends in the Wake of *Citizens United,*" report prepared for the California Assembly Judiciary Committee, Spring 2011, http://gov.uchastings.edu/public-law/docs/judicial-elections-report-and-appendices-corrected.pdf.

125. Quoted in Bert Brandenburg, "Protecting Wisconsin's Court from Special Interest Pressure," *Milwaukee Journal Sentinel,* March 27, 2007, www.jsonline.com/news/opinion/29460844.html.

Chapter 10

1. Emily Maltby, "Lemonade Stand Gets Squeezed," *Wall Street Journal,* June 17, 2011, http://blogs.wsj.com/in-charge/2011/06/17/lemonade-stand-gets-squeezed.

2. H. H. Gerth and C. Wright Mills, *Max Weber: Essays in Sociology* (New York: Oxford University Press, 1943).

3. Ronald C. Moe and Robert S. Gilmour, "Rediscovering Principles of Public Administration: The Neglected Foundation of Public Law," *Public Administration Review* 55, no. 2 (March–April 1995): 135–146.

4. John J. Gargan, "Introduction and Overview of State Government Administration," in *Handbook of State Government Administration,* ed. John J. Gargan (New York: Marcel-Dekker, 2000).

5. Jerrell D. Coggburn and Saundra K. Schneider, "The Quality of Management and Government Performance: An Empirical Analysis of the American States," *Public Administration Review* 63, no. 2 (March–April 2003): 206–213.

6. National Center for Education Statistics, "Total Expenditures for Public Elementary and Secondary Education, by Function and Subfunction: Selected Years, 1990–91 through 2008–2009," *Digest of Education Statistics,* http://nces.ed.gov/programs/digest/d11/tables/dt11_188.asp.

7. Charles Barrilleaux, "Statehouse Bureaucracy: Institutional Consistency in a Changing Environment," in *American State and Local Politics,* ed. Ronald E. Weber and Paul Brace (New York: Chatham House, 1999).

8. Michael Lipsky, *Street-Level Bureaucracy* (New York: Russell Sage Foundation, 1980).

9. Cornelius Kerwin, *Rulemaking: How Government Agencies Write Law and Make Policy,* 3rd ed. (Washington, DC: CQ Press, 2003).

10. Deil S. Wright, Chung-Lae Cho, and Yoo-Sun Choi, "Top-Level State Administrators: Changing Characteristics and Qualities," in *The Book of the States 2002* (Lexington, KY: Council of State Governments, 2002).

11. Charles T. Goodsell, *The Case for Bureaucracy: A Public Administration Polemic,* 4th ed. (Washington, DC: CQ Press, 2003).

12. U.S. Department of Commerce, *Statistical Abstract of the United States, 2012* (Washington, DC: U.S. Census Bureau, 2012), Table 461, "Governmental

Employment and Payrolls (1982–2009)," www.census.gov/compendia/statab/2012/tables/12s0461.pdf.

13. Goodsell, *Case for Bureaucracy*.

14. George W. Downs and Patrick D. Larkey, *The Search for Government Efficiency* (Philadelphia: Temple University Press, 1986).

15. Kevin Abourezk, "University Health Privatization a Mixed Bag," *Lincoln Journal-Star,* September 28, 2012, http://journalstar.com/news/local/education/university-health-privatization-a-mixed-bag/article_bd064c84-4524-5581-8f07-37512ebf7ee1.html.

16. Scott Lamothe and Meeyoung Lamothe, "The Dynamics of Local Service Delivery Arrangements and the Role of Nonprofits," *International Journal of Public Administration* 29 (2006): 769–797.

17. J. Norman Baldwin, "Public versus Private Employees: Debunking Stereotypes," *Review of Public Personnel Administration* 12 (Winter 1991): 1–27.

18. Barrilleaux, "Statehouse Bureaucracy," 106–107.

19. John J. DiIulio Jr., Gerald Garvey, and Donald F. Kettl, *Improving Government: An Owner's Manual* (Washington, DC: Brookings Institution, 1993).

20. Pew Center on the States, "The Government Performance Project," www.pewstates.org/projects/government-performance-project-328600.

21. Dennis Cauchon, "Bad Moves, Not Economy behind Busted State Budgets," *USA Today,* June 23, 2003, P1A.

22. Kenneth J. Meier, "Bureaucracy and Democracy: The Case for More Bureaucracy and Less Democracy," *Public Administration Review* 57, no. 3 (May–June 1997): 193–199.

23. Quoted in Katherine Barrett and Richard Greene, "Time for a Check Up," *Governing,* November 2005, www.governing.com/archive/archive/2005/nov/manage.txt.

24. Elizabeth G. Hill, "California Legislative Analyst's Office: An Isle of Independence," *Spectrum: The Journal of State Government* 6, no. 4 (2003): 26–29.

25. Barrett and Greene, "Time for a Check Up."

26. Barbara Romzek and Melvin Dubnick, "Accountability in the Public Sector: Lessons from the Challenger Tragedy," *Public Administration Review* 47, no. 3 (May–June 1987): 227–238.

27. Alfred Steinberg, *The Bosses* (New York: Macmillan, 1972).

28. Dwight Waldo, *The Administrative State* (New York: Holmes and Meier, 1948).

29. "Union Membership Edges Up, but Share Continues to Fall," *Monthly Labor Review,* January 1999, 1–2.

30. WEAC's legislative goals are described on its Web site, at www.weac.org/capitol/2005-06/legagenda/main.htm.

31. Wisconsin Democracy Campaign, "PAC and Corporate Spending: WEAC PAC Fall 2010," www.wisdc.org/index.php?module=wisdc.websiteforms&cmd=pacspending&year=2010&pac=500189.

32. Charles J. Sykes, *Profscam: Professors and the Demise of Higher Education* (New York: St. Martin's Press, 1989).

33. U.S. Department of Commerce, *Statistical Abstract of the United States, 2012,* Table 463, "State and Local Government, Full-Time Employment and Salary by Sex and Race/Ethnic Group: 1980–2009," www.census.gov/compendia/statab/2012/tables/12s0464.pdf.

34. Jennifer 8. Lee, "In Police Class, Blue Comes in Many Colors," *New York Times,* July 8, 2005.

35. C. J. Chivers, "For Black Officers, Diversity Has Its Limits," *New York Times,* April 2, 2001.

36. Sally Selden, *The Promise of Representative Bureaucracy: Diversity and Responsiveness in a Government Agency* (Armonk, NY: M. E. Sharpe, 1997).

37. Adam Liptak, "Supreme Court Finds Bias against White Firefighters," *New York Times,* June 29, 2009; Steven Greenhouse, "Supreme Court Ruling Offers Little Guidance on Hiring," *New York Times,* June 29, 2009.

38. Donald F. Kettl, *The Global Public Management Revolution: A Report on the Transformation of Governance* (Washington, DC: Brookings Institution Press, 2000).

39. H. George Frederickson and Kevin B. Smith, *The Public Administration Theory Primer* (Boulder, CO: Westview Press, 2003), 215.

40. James S. Bowman and Jonathan P. West, "Ending Civil Service Protections in Florida Government: Experiences in State Agencies," in *American Public Service: Radical Reform and the Merit System,* ed. James S. Bowman and Jonathan P. West (Boca Raton, FL: CRC Press, 2007).

41. Christopher Hoene and Jacqueline Bryers, "Local Governments Cutting Jobs and Services," research brief, United States Conference of Mayors, National League of Cities, and National Association of Counties, July 2010.

42. Elizabeth McNichol, "Some Basic Facts on State and Local Government Workers," Center on Budget and Policy Priorities, www.cbpp.org/cms/index.cfm?fa=view&id=3410.

43. Melissa Maynard, "New Governors Drive to Reorganize Agencies," Stateline, June 6, 2011, www.pewstates.org/projects/stateline/headlines/new-governors-drive-to-reorganize-agencies-85899375045.

44. Helisse Levine and Eric Scorsone, "The Great Recession's Institutional Change in the Public Employment Relationship: Implications for State and Local Governments," *State and Local Government Review* 42 (2011): 208–214.

Chapter 11

1. This translation of the oath is available on the National League of Cities Web site, www.nlc.org/about_cities/cities_101/146.cfm.

2. Pew Research Center for the People & the Press, "Growing Gap in Favorable Views of Federal, State Governments: Republicans Like State Government, Especially in GOP-Led States," April 26, 2012, www.people-press.org/2012/04/26/growing-gap-in-favorable-views-of-federal-state-governments/?src=prc-twitter.

3. Richard Cole and John Kincaid, "Public Opinion on U.S. Federal and Intergovernmental Issues in 2006," *Publius: The Journal of Federalism* 36, no. 3 (2006): 443–459.

4. This figure is based on an estimated total population of 300 million.

5. City-Data.com Web site, www.city-data.com/city/Hove-Mobile-Park-North-Dakota.html.

6. David Y. Miller, *The Regional Governing of Metropolitan America* (Boulder, CO: Westview Press, 2002).

7. Quoted in Jonathan Walters, "Cry, the Beleaguered County," *Governing,* August 1996, www.governing.com/archive/archive/1996/aug/counties.txt.

8. See the National Association of Counties Web site, www.naco.org/Template.cfm?Section=About_Counties. See also Roger L. Kemp, ed., *Model Government Charters: A City, County, Regional, State, and Federal Handbook* (Jefferson, NC: McFarland, 2003), 55.

9. Department of Management and Budget, Fairfax County, Virginia, "Fairfax County Adopted Budget 2012," http://testffx.fairfaxcounty.gov/dmb/fy2012/adopted/overview/10_budget_summary.pdf; County Executive Office, Orange County, California, "OC Annual Budget FY 2011–12," http://ocgov.com/gov/ceo/deputy/finance/budget/fy2012/budget.

10. National Association of Counties, "A Brief Overview of County Government," August 2003, www.naco.org/Content/NavigationMenu/About_Counties/County_Government/Default271.htm.

11. Miller, *Regional Governing of Metropolitan America,* 26.

12. U.S. Conference of Mayors Web site, www.usmayors.org.

13. Thomas J. Gradel, Dick Simpson, and Andris Zimelis, with Kirsten Byers and Chris Olson, "Curing Corruption in Illinois: Anti-corruption Report Number 1," February 3, 2009, www.uic.edu/depts/pols/ChicagoPolitics/Anti-corruptionReport.pdf.

14. National League of Cities, "Serving on City Councils," Research Brief on America's Cities, no. 2003–5, Washington, DC, September 2003.

15. Kemp, *Model Government Charters,* 10.

16. These monthly reports are archived and available online at http://phoenix.gov/citygovernment/facts/perfstats/perfreport/index.html.

17. William Hansell, "Evolution and Change Characterize Council-Manager Government," *Public Management* 82 (August 2000): 17–21.

18. Michael Zuckerman, *Peaceable Kingdoms: The New England Towns of the 18th Century* (New York: Knopf, 1970).

19. Miller, *Regional Governing of Metropolitan America,* 41.

20. Quoted in Anwar Syed, *The Political Theory of the American Local Government* (New York: Random House, 1966), 40.

21. Alexis de Tocqueville, *Democracy in America: A New Translation,* trans. George Lawrence, ed. J. P. Mayer (New York: HarperCollins, 2000), 33.

22. Penelope Lemov, "Infrastructure Conference Report: Building It Smarter, Managing It Better," *Governing,* October 1996," 40.

23. Ann O. Bowman, "Urban Government," in *Handbook of Research on Urban Politics and Policy in the United States,* ed. Ronald K. Vogel (Westport, CT: Greenwood Press, 1997), 133.

24. Kemp, *Model Government Charters,* 59.

25. New York State Association of Counties, "State Programs Funded by County Property Taxes," December 2011, www.rensco.com/pdfs/smn/NYSAC%20County%20Mandates%20Report2.pdf.

26. League of Women Voters of California Web site, http://smartvoter.org.

27. Elaine B. Sharpe, "Political Participation in Cities," in *Cities, Politics, and Policy: A Comparative Analysis,* ed. John P. Pelissero (Washington, DC: CQ Press, 2003), 81.

28. Lana Stein, "Mayoral Politics," in Pelissero, *Cities, Politics, and Policy,* 162.

29. Sharpe, "Political Participation in Cities," 71.

30. National League of Cities, "Compensation and Workload for Local Elected Officials," www.nlc.org/About_Cities/cities_101/147.cfm.

31. Ibid.

32. Center for State & Local Government Excellence, *The Great Recession and State and Local Government Work Force* (Washington, DC: Center for State & Local Government Excellence, 2010).

33. Quoted in International City/County Management Association, *How It Plays in Peoria: The Fiscal Crisis on Local Governments* (Washington, DC: ICMA, 2010), 7.

34. Robert O'Neill Jr., "An Opportunity for Creative Destruction," *Governing,* October 2009, www.governing.com/column/opportunity-creative-destruction.

35. Tocqueville, *Democracy in America,* 63.

Chapter 12

1. Rae Archibald and Sally Sleeper, *Government Consolidation and Economic Development in Allegheny County and the City of Pittsburgh* (Santa Monica, CA: RAND Corporation, 2008); Christopher Briem, "A Primer on Local Government Fragmentation and Regionalism in the Pittsburgh Region," www.briem.com/frag/PittsburghIndex.htm.

2. Figures calculated from U.S. Census Bureau data, 2011, http://quickfacts.census.gov/qfd/states/42/42003.html.

3. Advisory Commission on Intergovernmental Relations, "Metropolitan Organization: The Allegheny County Case," February 1992, www.briem.com/files/ACIRAlleghenyCounty.pdf.

4. Allegheny County, Pennsylvania, "Municipality Map," www.alleghenycounty.us/munimap/index.asp.

5. Archibald and Sleeper, Government Consolidation, ix.

6. Anthony Downs, "The Devolution Revolution: Why Congress Is Shifting a Lot of Power to the Wrong Levels," Policy Brief no. 3, Brookings Institution, July 1996, www.brookings.edu/research/papers/1996/07/governance-downs.

7. Office of Management and Budget, "2010 Standards for Delineating Metropolitan and Micropolitan Statistical Areas," www.whitehouse.gov/sites/default/files/omb/assets/fedreg_2010/06282010_metro_standards-Complete.pdf.

8. Office of Management and Budget, OMB Bulletin No. 10–02, www.whitehouse.gov/sites/default/files/omb/assets/bulletins/b10-02.pdf.

9. Bruce Katz, "A Nation in Transition: What the Urban Age Means for the United States," speech presented at the Urban Age Conference, New York, May 3, 2007, www.brookings.edu/speeches/2007/0504communitydevelopment_katz.aspx.

10. David Y. Miller, The Regional Governing of Metropolitan America (Boulder, CO: Westview Press, 2002), 1.

11. David Cieslewits, "The Environmental Impacts of Sprawl," in Urban Sprawl: Causes, Consequences, and Policy Responses, ed. Gregory D. Squires (Washington, DC: Urban Institute Press, 2002).

12. Ibid.

13. See, for example, Myron Orfield, American Metropolitics: The New Suburban Reality (Washington, DC: Brookings Institution Press, 2002).

14. Ibid., 41.

15. Peter Dreier, John Mollenkopf, and Todd Swanstrom, Place Matters: Metropolitics for the Twenty-First Century (Lawrence: University Press of Kansas, 2001).

16. Ibid., 67.

17. Orfield, American Metropolitics, 10.

18. G. Ross Stephens and Nelson Wikstrom, Metropolitan Government and Governance: Theoretical Perspectives, Empirical Analysis, and the Future (New York: Oxford University Press, 1999).

19. "About Metro," www.oregonmetro.gov/index.cfm/go/by.web/id=24201.

20. Heike Mayor and John Provo, "The Portland Edge in Context," in The Portland Edge: Challenges and Successes in Growing Communities, ed. Connie P. Ozawa (Washington, DC: Island Press, 2004).

21. National Association of Regional Councils, "What Is a Regional Council?" http://narc.org/resource-center/cogs-mpos/what-is-a-council-of-government.

22. National Association of Regional Councils, "History" http://narc.org/about-narc/about-the-association/history.

23. Miller, Regional Governing of Metropolitan America, 103.

24. James F. Wolf and Tara Kolar Bryan, "Identifying the Capacities of Regional Councils of Government," State and Local Government Review 41 (2010): 61.

25. Ibid., 67.

26. Simon Andrew, "Recent Development in the Study of Interjurisdictional Agreements: An Overview and Assessment," State and Local Government Review 41 (2010): 133–142.

27. National Association of Counties, "City-County Consolidation Proposals, 1921–Present," www.naco.org/Counties/Documents/City%20County%20Consolidations.01.01.2011.pdf.

28. Quoted in Jeffrey Cohan, "Reports Outline Options in Merging Pittsburgh-Allegheny County Services," Pittsburgh Post-Gazette, April 2, 2004.

29. Lara Brenckle, "City, County Study Merger . . . Again," Pittsburgh Tribune-Review, October 20, 2006, www.pittsburghlive.com/x/pittsburghtrib/news/cityregion/s_475861.htm.

30. National League of Cities, "Serving on City Councils," Research Brief on America's Cities, no. 2003–5, Washington, DC, September 2003.

31. Kate Linebaugh, "Threats to Town Halls Stir Voter Backlash," Wall Street Journal, June 8, 2011.

32. David Rusk, Cities without Suburbs, 2nd ed. (Washington, DC: Woodrow Wilson Center Press, 1995).

33. Ann O. Bowman, "Urban Government," in Handbook of Research on Urban Politics and Policy in the United States, ed. Ronald K. Vogel (Westport, CT: Greenwood Press, 1997), 139.

34. Rob Gurwitt, "Annexation: Not So Smart Growth," Governing, October 2000.

35. Barbara Kelly, Expanding the American Dream: Building and Rebuilding Levittown (Albany: State University of New York Press, 1993).

36. Charles Tiebout, "A Pure Theory of Local Expenditures," Journal of Political Economy 64, no. 5 (October 1956): 422.

37. William Lyons, David Lowery, and Ruth Hoogland DeHoog, The Politics of Dissatisfaction: Citizens, Services, and Urban Institutions (Armonk, NY: M. E. Sharpe, 1992).

38. Paul Teske, Mark Schneider, Michael Mintrom, and Samuel Best, "Establishing the Micro Foundations of a Macro Theory: Information, Movers, and the Competitive Local Market for Public Goods," American Political Science Review 87, no. 3 (September 1993): 702–713.

39. Paul Teske, Mark Schneider, Michael Mintrom, and Samuel Best, "The Empirical Evidence for Citizen Information and a Local Market for Public Goods,"

American Political Science Review 89, no. 3 (September 1995): 707–709.

40. Dante Chinni, "Rural Counties Are Losing Population and Aging, but Are They Really Dying?," PBS NewsHour, March 4, 2011, www.pbs.org/newshour/rundown/2011/03/-as-the-2010-census.html.

41. Nebraska Department of Education, "2011–2012 Number of Districts/Systems," updated November 4, 2011, www.education.ne.gov/dataservices/PDF/11-12_Districts_Nov2011.pdf.

42. Alan Greenblatt, "Little Mergers on the Prairie," *Governing,* July 2006, 49–50.

Chapter 13

1. Quoted in David Tyack and Larry Cuban, *Tinkering toward Utopia: A Century of Public School Reform* (Cambridge, MA: Harvard University Press, 1995), 2.

2. Quoted in Alan Greenblatt, "New Headaches for 'No Child Left Behind,'" *Governing,* November 2011, www.governing.com/topics/education/new-headaches-for-no-child-left-behind.html.

3. Quoted in Michael A. Rebell, "Fiscal Equity Litigation and the Democratic Imperative," *Journal of Education Finance* 24, no. 1 (1998): 23–50.

4. Ibid.

5. Charles Mahtesian, "Too Much Democracy," *Governing,* January 24, 2000, www.governing.com/view/vu01 2400.htm.

6. Jeffrey Barnett and Phillip Vidal, "State and Local Government Finances Summary: 2010," Governments Division Brief, U.S. Census Bureau, September 2012, www2.census.gov/govs/estimate/summary_report.pdf.

7. National Center for Education Statistics, "Public School Revenue Sources," http://nces.ed.gov/programs/coe/pdf/coe_sft.pdf.

8. "Where Does Mega Millions Money Go after the Jackpot?," CBS News, March 30, 2012, www.cbsnews.com/8301-18563_162-57407364/where-does-mega-millions-money-go-after-the-jackpot.

9. Rebell, "Fiscal Equity."

10. Tyack and Cuban, *Tinkering toward Utopia,* 47.

11. William Duncombe, John Ruggiero, and John Yinger, "Alternative Approaches to Measuring the Cost of Education," in *Holding Schools Accountable: Performance-Based Reform in Education,* ed. Helen F. Ladd (Washington, DC: Brookings Institution Press, 1996), 338. See also Christopher B. Swanson, "Ten Questions (and Answers) about Graduates, Dropouts, and NCLB Accountability," Urban Institute, October 21, 2003, www.urban.org/publications/310873.html.

12. Harold Wenglinsky, "School District Expenditures, School Resources, and Student Achievement: Modeling the Production Function," in *Developments in School Finance, 1997: Does Money Matter?,* ed. William J. Fowler Jr. (Washington, DC: National Center for Education Statistics, 1998).

13. Allan Odden, "Equity and Adequacy in School Finance Today," *Phi Delta Kappan* 85 (October 2003): 120–125.

14. Margaret Ritsch, ed., *Money Matters: A Reporter's Guide to School Finance* (Washington, DC: Education Writers Association, 2003), 5.

15. Education Trust, "Funding Gaps 2006," 2006, based on 2003–2004 U.S. Department of Education and U.S. Census Bureau data.

16. Phil Oliff, Chris Mai, and Michael Leachman, "New School Year Brings More Cuts in State Funding for Schools," Center on Budget and Policy Priorities, updated September 4, 2012, www.cbpp.org/files/9-4-12sfp.pdf.

17. "Quality Counts 2003," *Education Week,* January 9, 2003, 22.

18. Richard Rothstein, *The Way We Were: The Myths and Realities of America's Student Achievement* (New York: Century Foundation, 1998), 19.

19. William J. Bushaw and John A. McNee, "Americans Speak Out: Are Educators and Policy Makers Listening?," *Phi Delta Kappan* 91 (September 2009): 8–23.

20. Jennifer McMurrer, "Instructional Time in Elementary Schools: A Closer Look at Changes for Specific Subjects," Center on Education Policy, February 20, 2008, www.arteducators.org/research/Instructional TimeFeb2008.pdf.

21. The latest results in all NAEP subject areas are available at http://nces.ed.gov/nationsreportcard/subject areas.asp.

22. National Center for Education Statistics, "Trends in International Mathematics and Science Study," http://nces.ed.gov/timss/index.asp.

23. College Board, "SAT Participation and Performance: Class of 2012," http://press.collegeboard.org/sat.

24. "The Texas Miracle," CBS News, January 6, 2004, www.cbsnews.com/stories/2004/01/06/60II/main 591676.shtml.

25. Sam Dillon, "U.S. to Require States to Use a Single School Dropout Formula," *New York Times,* April 1, 2008.

26. National Center for Education Statistics, "Dropout Rates," http://nces.ed.gov/fastfacts/display.asp?id=16.

27. Common Core State Standards Initiative, "Mission Statement," www.corestandards.org.

28. Dylan Scott, "States Begin Implementing Common Core Standards," *Governing,* View blog, www.governing.com/blogs/view/States-Begin-Task-of-Implementing-Common-Core-Standards.html.

29. Kevin B. Smith, *The Ideology of Education: The Commonwealth, the Market, and America's Schools* (Albany: State University of New York Press, 2003), 59.

30. Bernard Watson, "Fear, Intimidation Used to Get Teachers to Cheat, Report Says," CBS Atlanta, July 6, 2011, updated August 3, 2011, www.cbsatlanta.com/story/15031243/gov-releases-full-report-on-atlanta-schools-cheating-investigation.

31. Kati Haycock, "Good Teaching Matters: How Well-Qualified Teachers Can Close the Gap," *Thinking K–16* 3, no. 2 (1998).

32. Economists Steven G. Givkin and Eric A. Hanushek, cited (along with researcher William Sanders) in "Quality Counts 2003," 10.

33. U.S. Department of Education, *Teaching Shortage Areas Nationwide Listing: 1990–1991 through 2012–2013* (Washington, DC: U.S. Department of Education, 2012).

34. John Wirt, Susan Choy, Patrick Rooney, Stephen Provasnik, Anindita Sen, and Richard Tobin, *The Condition of Education 2004: Out-of-Field Teacher in Middle and High School Grades* (Washington, DC: National Center for Education Statistics, 2004).

35. Bess Keller, "Most States Pass Federal Review on Highly Qualified Teachers," *Education Week,* August 17, 2006.

36. Diane Stark Rentner, Caitlin Scott, Nancy Kober, Naomi Chudowsky, Victor Chudowsky, Scott Joftus, and Dalia Zabala, "From the Capital to the Classroom: Year 4 of the No Child Left Behind Act," Center on Education Policy, March 2006, www.cep-dc.org/displayDocument.cfm?DocumentID=301.

37. Michael Allen, *Eight Questions on Teacher Preparation: What Does the Research Say?* (Denver, CO: Education Commission of the States, July 2003).

38. Jerry Johnson and Marty Strange, *Why Rural Matters 2009: State and Regional Challenges and Opportunities* (Arlington, VA: Rural School and Community Trust, 2009); Vicki Hobbs, *The Promise and the Power of Distance Learning in Rural Education* (Arlington, VA: Rural School and Community Trust, 2004), www.ruraledu.org/user_uploads/file/Promise_and_the_Power.pdf.

39. Thomas D. Snyder and Sally A. Dillow, *Digest of Education Statistics 2009* (Washington, DC: U.S. Department of Education, 2010), Tables 84 and 86.

40. See studies such as Erin McHenry-Sorber, "School Consolidation in Pennsylvania: An Analysis of Governor Rendell's Policy Proposal," *Beacon,* summer 2009. One study of school consolidation in New York State between 1985 and 1997 by researchers at Syracuse University found substantially reduced operating costs, but only when the smallest districts were consolidated. See William Duncombe and John Yinger, "Does School District Consolidation Cut Costs?," Center for Policy Research, Working Paper no. 33, January 2001, www.maxwell.syr.edu/uploadedFiles/cpr/publications/working_papers2/wp33.pdf.

41. Joe Bard, Clark Gardener, and Regi Wieland, "Rural School Consolidation Report," prepared for the National Rural Education Association Executive Board, University of Oklahoma, Norman, April 1–2, 2005.

42. Melissa Maynard, "Still Too Many Schools?," Stateline, March 22, 2010, www.stateline.org/live/details/story?contentId=470554.

43. Hobbs, *Promise and the Power.*

44. Lowell C. Rose and Alec M. Gallup, "38th Annual Phi Delta Kappa/Gallup Poll," 2006, www.pdkintl.org/kappan/kpoll pdf.htm.

45. Sarah Grady, Stacey Bielick, and Susan Aud, *Trends in the Use of School Choice: 1993 to 2007* (Washington, DC: U.S. Department of Education, 2010).

46. National Center for Education Statistics, *Digest of Education Statistics,* Table 101, http://nces.ed.gov/programs/digest/d11/tables/dt11_101.asp.

47. U.S. Charter Schools, "State Profiles," www.uscharterschools.org/pub/uscs_docs/sp/index.htm.

48. Erika Hayasaki, "Charter Academy Shuts 60 Schools," *Los Angeles Times,* August 16, 2004, http://articles.latimes.com/2004/aug/16/local/me-charter16.

49. Brian P. Gill, P. Michael Timpane, Karen E. Ross, and Dominic J. Brewer, *Rhetoric versus Reality: What We Know and What We Need to Know about Vouchers and Charter Schools* (Santa Monica, CA: RAND Corporation, 2001), xviii; Charles S. Clark, "Charter Schools," *CQ Researcher,* December 20, 2002.

50. U.S. Department of Education, Institute of Education Sciences, National Center for Education Statistics, National Assessment of Educational Progress (NAEP), 2003 Reading Charter School Pilot Study, Washington, DC, December 2004.

51. Dan Keating and Theola Labbé-DeBose, "Charter Schools Make Gains on Tests," *Washington Post,* December 15, 2008. This article and a variety of multimedia resources about the Washington, D.C., charter schools are available at www.washingtonpost.com/wp-srv/metro/specials/charter/index.html.

52. Diana Jean Schemo, "Nation's Charter Schools Lagging Behind, U.S. Test Scores Reveal," *New York Times,* August 17, 2003, www.nytimes.com/2004/08/17/education/17charter.html?hp.

53. Center for Research on Education Outcomes, *Multiple Choice: Charter School Performance in 16 States* (Stanford, CA: Stanford University, Center for Research on Education Outcomes, June 2009), http://credo.stanford.edu/reports/MULTIPLE_CHOICE_CREDO.pdf.

54. Kenneth Jost, "School Vouchers Showdown," *CQ Researcher,* February 15, 2002.

55. See William A. Fischel, "Why Voters Veto Vouchers: Public Schools and Community-Specific Social Capital," *Economics of Governance* 7, no. 2 (2006): 109–132.

56. Josh Hafenbrack, "Update: Florida Supreme Court Strikes Voucher, Property Tax Amendments from the Ballot," *Orlando Sentinel,* Central Florida Political Pulse blog, September 3, 2008, http://blogs.orlandosentinel.com/news_politics/2008/09/florida-supreme.html.

57. Ohio Department of Education, "Ohio EdChoice Scholarship Program Fact Sheet," www.ode.state.oh.us/GD/Templates/Pages/ODE/ODEDetail.aspx?Page=3&TopicRelationID=667&Content=131199.

58. Amanda Paulson, "Milwaukee's Lessons on School Vouchers," *Christian Science Monitor,* May 23, 2006.

59. John Robert Warren, "Graduation Rates for Choice and Public School Students in Milwaukee, 2003–2008," School Choice Wisconsin, February 2010, www.schoolchoicewi.org/data/currdev_links/2010-Grad-Study-1-31-2010.pdf.

60. John F. Witte, Deven Carlson, Joshua M. Cowen, David J. Fleming, and Patrick J. Wolf, *MPCP Longitudinal Educational Growth Study: Fifth Year Report,* Report of the School Choice Demonstration Project (Fayetteville: University of Arkansas, Department of Education Reform, 2012).

61. U.S. General Accounting Office, *School Vouchers: Publicly Funded Programs in Cleveland and Milwaukee,* GAO 01-914 (Washington, DC: U.S. General Accounting Office, 2001), 4; Zachary M. Seward, "Long-Delayed Education Study Casts Doubt on Value of Vouchers," *Wall Street Journal,* July 15–16, 2006.

62. Grady et al., *Trends in the Use of School Choice.*

63. National Center for Education Statistics, *The Condition of Education* (Washington, DC: U.S. Department of Education, 2005).

64. Home School Legal Defense Association, "State Laws," www.hslda.org/laws/default.asp.

65. Matthew H. Boswell, *Courts as Catalysts: State Supreme Courts and Public School Finance Equity* (Albany: State University of New York Press, 2001), 125.

66. See the NEA and AFT Web sites, www.nea.org and www.aft.org.

67. National PTA, "About PTA," www.pta.org/about/?navItemNumber=503.

68. "Jeb Bush: The Once and Future Reformer," StateImpact, NPR, http://stateimpact.npr.org/florida/tag/jeb-bush.

69. Business Coalition for Student Achievement, "Position Statement," 2007, www.biz4achievement.org/about_the_coalition/position_statement.html.

Chapter 14

1. Wendy Ruderman, "414 Homicides a Record Low for New York," *New York Times,* December 29, 2012, A1.

2. Federal Bureau of Investigation, *Uniform Crime Report 2008* (Washington, DC: Federal Bureau of Investigation), Table 1, "Crime in the United States by Volume and Rate per 100,000 Inhabitants, 1989–2009."

3. Daniel B. Wood, "U.S. Crime Rate at Lowest Point in Decades," *Christian Science Monitor,* January 9, 2012, www.csmonitor.com/USA/Justice/2012/0109/US-crime-rate-at-lowest-point-in-decades.-Why-America-is-safer-now.

4. See John J. Donohue III and Steven D. Levitt, "The Impact of Legalized Abortion on Crime," National Bureau of Economic Research working paper, November 2000, www.nber.org/papers/w8004.pdf?new_window=1.

5. Quoted in Jeremy Travis and Michelle Waul, "Reflections on the Crime Decline: Lessons for the Future?," Proceedings from the Urban Institute Crime Decline Forum, Washington, DC, August 2002, 18, www.urban.org/uploadedpdf/410546_crimedecline.pdf.

6. Danielle S. Allen, *The World of Prometheus: The Politics of Punishing in Democratic Athens* (Princeton, NJ: Princeton University Press, 1999), 3.

7. For a brilliant discussion of how this transformation came to pass, see Sir Frederick Pollock and F. W. Maitland, *History of English Law before the Time of Edward I* (Cambridge, UK: Cambridge University Press, 1969).

8. Marc Mauer, "The Crisis of the Young African American Male and the Criminal Justice System," presentation to the U.S. Commission on Civil Rights, Washington, DC, April 15–16, 1999, 6.

9. Kevin Smith, "The Politics of Punishment: Evaluating Political Explanations of Incarceration Rates," *Journal of Politics* 66, no. 3 (2004): 925.

10. Katherine Beckett, *Making Crime Pay: Law and Order in Contemporary Politics* (New York: Oxford University Press, 1997).

11. Smith, "Politics of Punishment."

12. Daniel J. Elazar, *American Federalism: A View from the States,* 2nd ed. (New York: Crowell, 1972), 106–107.

13. For more details on nineteenth-century views of incarceration and on the Quakers' long-standing opposition to corporal punishment, see Norman Johnston, *The Crucible of Good Intentions* (Philadelphia: Philadelphia Museum of Art, 1994).

14. See David Oshinsky's *Worse than Slavery: Parchman Farm and the Ordeal of Jim Crow Justice* (New York: Free Press, 1996). As Oshinsky's title makes clear, he is no fan of Parchman Farm. It is therefore interesting that he concludes in his book's final chapter that the modern penal institution that replaced the farm in the 1970s is in many ways worse.

15. Stephan Thernstrom, remarks made at the Heritage Foundation symposium on the Kerner Commission,

March 13, 1998, www.heritage.org/Research/Political Philosophy/h1619.cfm.

16. "Night of Terror," *Time*, July 25, 1977.

17. This figure—from the Office of National Drug Control Policy—does not include alcohol, which is considered the most popular drug of all.

18. See Robert MacCoun and Peter Reuter, *Drug War Heresies: Learning from Other Vices, Times, and Places* (New York: Cambridge University Press, 2001), 26, 29.

19. Eric Schlosser, *Reefer Madness: Sex, Drugs, and Cheap Labor in the American Black Market* (Boston: Houghton Mifflin, 2003), 26.

20. Kathleen Hunger, "Money Mattering More in Judicial Elections," Stateline, May 12, 2004, www.stateline .org/live/ViewPage.action?siteNodeId=136&languag eId=1&contentId=15646.

21. Pew Center on the States, "One in 100: Behind Bars in America 2008," February 2008, www.pewstates. org/uploadedFiles/PCS_Assets/2008/one%20in%20 100.pdf.

22. National Association of State Budget Officers, *State Expenditure Report, 2008* (Washington, DC: National Association of State Budget Officers, 2009), 58, www .nasbo.org/sites/default/files/FY08%20State%20 Expenditure%20Report.pdf.

23. Pew Center on the States, "One in 100."

24. Allen J. Beck and Thomas P. Bonczar, "Lifetime Likelihood of Going to State or Federal Prison," Bureau of Justice Statistics, Criminal Offenders Statistics, 1997, www.ojp.usdoj.gov/bjs/crimoff.htm.

25. Josh Meyer, "Obama Administration Urges Equal Penalties for Crack, Powder Cocaine Dealers," *Los Angeles Times*, April 30, 2009, http://articles.latimes. com/2009/apr/30/nation/na-crack30; "Bad Science and Bad Policy," *New York Times*, March 2, 2010, www.nytimes.com/2010/03/03/opinion/03wed3 .html.

26. Ryan S. King, "A Decade of Reform: Felony Disenfranchisement Policy in the United States," Sentencing Project, October 2006, www.sentencingproject .org/doc/publications/fd_decade_reform.pdf.

27. Christopher Uggen, Sarah Shannon, and Jeff Manza, "State-Level Estimates of Felon Disenfranchisement in the United States, 2010," Sentencing Project, July 2012, www.sentencingproject.org/doc/publications/ fd_State_Level_Estimates_of_Felon_Disen_2010 .pdf.

28. King, "Decade of Reform."

29. Mauer, "Crisis of the Young African American Male."

30. The first of Peel's nine principles; quoted in Sandra Nazemi, "Sir Robert Peel's Nine Principals [*sic*] of Policing," Los Angeles Community Policing, www .lacp.org/2009-Articles-Main/062609-Peels9Principals-SandyNazemi.htm.

31. For an account of how well-intentioned policies went horribly wrong, see Fred Siegel's *The Future Once Happened Here: New York, D.C., LA, and the Future of America's Big Cities* (New York: Free Press, 1997).

32. James Q. Wilson and George L. Kelling, "Broken Windows: The Police and Neighborhood Safety," *Atlantic Monthly*, March 1982.

33. For an account of the Rodney King beating and the LAPD, see Lou Cannon, *Official Negligence: How Rodney King and the Riots Changed Los Angeles and the LAPD* (New York: Westview Press, 1999).

34. Ibid.

35. For a detailed account of early experiments with community policing and problem-oriented policing, see George L. Kelling and Mary A. Wycoff, *Evolving Strategy of Policing: Case Studies of Strategic Change*, National Criminal Justice Reference Center Document no. 198029 (Washington, DC: National Institute of Justice, May 2001).

36. William Bratton, *Turnaround: How America's Top Cop Reversed the Crime Epidemic* (New York: Random House, 1998), 143, 180.

37. For an account of how CompStat was created and how it is used, see John Buntin, *Assertive Policing, Plummeting Crime: The NYPD Takes on Crime in New York City*, Kennedy School of Government Case Study (Cambridge, MA: Harvard University, August 1999).

38. This section is drawn from the seminar "Reflections on the Crime Decline: Lessons for the Future," Urban Institute, Washington, D.C., August 2002, 12–19.

39. Robert Weisberg and David Mills, "Violence Silence: Why No One Really Cares about Prison Rape," *Slate*, October 1, 2003, www.slate.com/id/2089095. See also Human Rights Watch, "No Escape: Male Rape in U.S. Prisons," 2001, www.hrw.org/reports/2001/prison/ report.html.

40. Doris J. James and Lauren E. Glaze, "Mental Health Problems of Prison and Jail Inmates," Bureau of Justice Statistics Special Report, NCJ 213600, U.S. Department of Justice, September 2006, www.bjs .gov/content/pub/pdf/mhppji.pdf.

41. Human Rights Watch, "Ill-Equipped: U.S. Prisons and Offenders with Mental Illnesses," 2003, www .hrw.org/reports/2003/usa1003.

42. Quoted in Marcia Clemitt, "Prison Health Care," *CQ Researcher*, January 5, 2007.

43. Amnesty International, "Amnesty International Report 2009: State of the World's Human Rights," May 28, 2009, http://thereport.amnesty.org/en/ regions/americas/usa.

44. Death Penalty Information Center, "Facts about the Death Penalty," April 2010, http://deathpenaltyinfo .org/documents/FactSheet.pdf.

45. Amnesty International "United States of America: Rights of Children Must Be Respected" (press release),

April 25, 2003, www.amnesty.org/en/library/asset/AMR51/058/2003/en/327b271c-d6fb-11dd-b0cc-1f0860013475/amr510582003en.pdf.

46. Ibid. Nineteen children were executed in the United States from 1995 through 2003.

47. Quoted in Peter Katel, "Prisoner Reentry," *CQ Researcher,* December 4, 2009.

48. John Buntin, "The Correctionists," *Governing,* November 2010.

49. George Hunter, Mike Williamson, and Holly Fournier, "Police Cuts Loom as Detroit Struggles to Curb Violence," *Detroit News,* June 8, 2012, www.detroitnews.com/article/20120608/METRO01/206080362.

50. "The Most Dangerous Cities in America," 24/7 Wall Street, June 11, 2012, http://247wallst.com/2012/06/11/the-most-dangerous-cities-in-america-2.

51. Brian A. Reaves and Matthew J. Hickman, "Police Departments in Large Cities, 1990–2000," Bureau of Justice Statistics Special Report, NCJ 175703, U.S. Department of Justice, May 2002.

52. U.S. Department of Justice, "COPS Hiring Recovery Program (CHRP)," July 29, 2009, www.cops.usdoj.gov/default.asp?item=2108.

53. Gina Damron, L. L. Brasier, and Christina Hall, "Mergers, Contracts Grow as Michigan Police Shrink 16 Percent," *Detroit Free Press,* December 30, 2012.

54. Federal Bureau of Investigation, *Uniform Crime Report 2011* (Washington, DC: Federal Bureau of Investigation), Table 16, "Rate: Number of Crimes per 100,000 Inhabitants by Population Group, 2011," www.fbi.gov/about-us/cjis/ucr/crime-in-the-u.s/2011/crime-in-the-u.s.-2011/tables/table_16_rate_number_of_crimes_per_100000_inhabitants_by_population_group_2011.xls.

55. National Institute of Justice, "Law Enforcement Technology—Are Small and Rural Agencies Equipped and Trained?," U.S. Department of Justice, Office of Justice Programs, June 2004, www.ncjrs.gov/pdffiles1/nij/204609.pdf.

56. For research and survey findings and other resources, see Meth Action Clearinghouse, National Association of Counties, www.naco.org.

57. John Gramlich, "New Script for Sudafed?," Stateline, March 15, 2010, www.stateline.org/live/printable/story?content Id=468500.

58. Jim Barnett, "Bush Signs Legislation to Fight the Spread of Meth across U.S.," *Oregonian,* March 10, 2006; Chris Casteel, "Meth Imports Rising, Sheriff Says," *Oklahoman,* July 19, 2006.

59. Richard Willing and Gary Fields, "Geography of the Death Penalty," *USA Today,* December 20, 1999, A1.

60. Denny Walsh, "Judge: Rethink Lethal Injection," *Sacramento Bee,* December 16, 2006.

61. John Gramlich, "No End in Sight to Death Penalty Wrangling," Stateline, July 31, 2008, www.stateline.org/live/details/story?contentId=529997.

62. Quoted in Nathan Koppel and Chris Herring, "Lethal Injection Draws Scrutiny in Some States," *Wall Street Journal,* October 15, 2009, A13.

63. Pew Center on the States, "Prison Count 2010," March 2010, www.pewstates.org/uploadedFiles/PCS_Assets/2010/Pew_Prison_Count_2010.pdf.

64. Randal C. Archibold, "Driven to the Financial Brink, a State Opens the Prison Doors," *New York Times,* March 24, 2010, A14.

65. National Institute of Justice, "Correctional Boot Camps: Lessons from a Decade of Research," U.S. Department of Justice, Office of Justice Programs, June 2003, www.ncjrs.gov/pdffiles1/nij/197018.pdf.

66. National Institute of Justice, "Do Drug Courts Work? Findings from Drug Court Research," U.S. Department of Justice, Office of Justice Programs, May 12, 2008, www.ojp.usdoj.gov/nij/topics/courts/drug-courts/work.htm.

Chapter 15

1. John Barry, *The Great Influenza: The Epic Story of the Deadliest Plague in History* (New York: Viking Penguin, 2004).

2. RAND Corporation, "Third Annual Report to the President and Congress of the Advisory Panel to Assess Domestic Response Capabilities for Terrorism Involving Weapons of Mass Destruction," Santa Monica, CA, December 15, 2001, 44.

3. U.S. Centers for Disease Control and Prevention, "Tobacco-Related Mortality," last updated March 21, 2011, www.cdc.gov/tobacco/data_statistics/fact_sheets/health_effects/tobacco_related_mortality.

4. Kaiser Family Foundation, "Establishing Health Insurance Exchanges: An Overview of State Efforts," August 2012, www.kff.org/healthreform/upload/8213-2.pdf.

5. Robert Pear, "Health Care Law Will Let States Tailor Benefits," *New York Times,* December 16, 2011, www.nytimes.com/2011/12/17/health/policy/health-care-law-to-allow-states-to-pick-benefits.html?_r=2&.

6. Gary Bryner, "Welfare Reform in Utah," report no. 14, Nelson A. Rockefeller Institute of Government, Albany, NY, August 2002. See also Deborah A. Orth and Malcolm L. Goggin, "How States and Counties Have Responded to the Family Policy Goals of Welfare Reform," report to the U.S. Department of Health and Human Services, Administration for Children and Families (Grant No. 90XP0028/01),

Nelson A. Rockefeller Institute of Government, Albany, NY, 2003.

7. Kaiser Family Foundation, "The Medicaid Program at a Glance," September 2012, www.kff.org/medicaid/upload/7235-05.pdf. The Kaiser Family Foundation Web site (www.kff.org) provides a host of Medicaid-related facts and statistics.

8. National Association of State Budget Officers, "2010 State Expenditure Report," Washington, DC, 2011, 3, www.nasbo.org/sites/default/files/2010%20State%20Expenditure%20Report.pdf.

9. The preceding three paragraphs are adapted from Josh Goodman, "Dire Warnings in Alabama Budget Vote," Stateline, August 2, 2012, www.pewstates.org/projects/stateline/headlines/dire-warnings-in-alabama-budget-vote-85899408922.

10. Christine Vestal, "States Push to Contain Health Costs," Stateline, June 15, 2012, www.pewstates.org/projects/stateline/headlines/states-push-to-contain-health-costs-85899398539.

11. Christine Vestal, "In California, Adult Day Care Program Is Threatened with Extinction," Stateline, June 10, 2011, www.pewstates.org/projects/stateline/headlines/in-california-adult-day-care-program-is-threatened-with-extinction-85899376889.

12. Christine Vestal, "For Some States, Medicaid Expansion May Be a Tough Fiscal Call," Stateline, July 11, 2012, www.pewstates.org/projects/stateline/headlines/for-some-states-medicaid-expansion-may-be-a-tough-fiscal-call-85899404110.

13. Pew Center on the States, "The Widening Gap Update," June 2012, www.pewstates.org/uploadedFiles/PCS_Assets/2012/Pew_Pensions_Update.pdf.

14. Quoted in Stephen C. Fehr, "West Virginia Tackles Retiree Health Costs," Stateline, March 13, 2012, www.pewstates.org/projects/stateline/headlines/west-virginia-tackles-retiree-health-costs-85899377381.

15. California Legislative Analyst's Office, "Providing Constitutional and Cost-Effective Inmate Medical Care," April 19, 2012, www.lao.ca.gov/reports/2012/crim/inmate-medical-care/inmate-medical-care-041912.pdf.

16. Daniel B. Wood, "Supreme Court Orders California to Slash Prison Population by More than 30,000," Christian Science Monitor, May 23, 2011, www.csmonitor.com/USA/Justice/2011/0523/Supreme-Court-orders-California-to-slash-prison-population-by-more-than-30-000.

17. Paul Starr, The Social Transformation of American Medicine (New York: Basic Books, 1992), 149.

18. Ibid., 72.

19. Ibid.

20. Ibid.

21. NYU Medical Center Web site, www.med.nyu.edu/Bellevue.

22. Samuel Gompers, the head of the AFL, viewed compulsory health insurance as "paternalistic" and worried that it might weaken the labor movement by causing workers to look to employers instead of to unions for benefits. Starr, Social Transformation of American Medicine, 254–255.

23. "Stocks Collapse in 16,410,030-Share Day, but Rally at Close Cheers Brokers," New York Times, October 30, 1929.

24. Scholars such as Theda Skocpol have argued that the federal government's first major foray into safety net programs actually came much earlier, in the form of lavish pensions for Union veterans of the Civil War. Theda Skocpol, "America's First Social Security System: The Expansion of Benefits for Civil War Veterans," Political Science Quarterly 108 (Spring 1993): 85–86.

25. "Social Security," in Columbia Encyclopedia, 6th ed. (New York: Columbia University Press, 2001).

26. Jay Bhattacharya and Darius Lakdawalla, "Does Medicare Benefit the Poor? New Answers to an Old Question," Working Paper w9280, National Bureau of Economic Research, Cambridge, MA, October 2002.

27. Kaiser Commission on Medicaid and the Uninsured, "An Overview of Changes in the Federal Medical Assistance Percentages (FMAPs) for Medicaid," July 2011, www.kff.org/medicaid/upload/8210.pdf.

28. Center for Budget and Policy Priorities, "An Introduction to Medicaid," October 2, 2006, www.cbpp.org/10-2-06health.htm.

29. All Medicaid eligibility figures are calculated from Kaiser Family Foundation, "Where Are States Today? Medicaid and CHIP Eligibility Levels for Children and Non-disabled Adults," July 2012, www.kff.org/medicaid/upload/7993-02.pdf.

30. John Klemm, "Medicaid Spending: A Brief History," Health Care Financing Review 22, no. 1 (2000). For more recent data, see the Kaiser Family Foundation Statehealthfacts Web site, www.statehealthfacts.org.

31. National Association of State Budget Officers, "2010 State Expenditure Report," 44.

32. By 1983, the number of single mothers had fallen back to about 50 percent of AFDC recipients. By 1992, that number had crept back up to 55 percent. National Research Council, Evaluating Welfare Reform in an Era of Transition, ed. Robert A. Moffitt and Michele Ver Ploeg (Washington, DC: National Press, 2001), 17.

33. Steven Roberts, "Food Stamps Program: How It Grew and How Reagan Wants to Cut It Back," New York Times, April 4, 1981.

34. Quoted in Lou Cannon, Governor Reagan: His Rise to Power (New York: Public Affairs, 2003), 349. Of course, Roosevelt made this statement to argue for

government-funded work programs—a measure that Reagan never supported as president.

35. Andy Schneider, *Medicaid Resource Book* (Washington, DC: Kaiser Commission on Medicaid and the Uninsured, July 2002), 97–98.

36. "Public Officials of the Year: Leading in Good Times and in Bad," *Governing,* December 1997.

37. Charles Mahtesian, "Captains of Conservatism," *Governing,* February 1995.

38. National Research Council, *Evaluating Welfare Reform,* 19.

39. Administration for Children and Families, "TANF: Total Number of Recipients, Fiscal Year 2009," U.S. Department of Health and Human Services, Washington, DC, January 28, 2010. Caseload data are available at www.acf.hhs.gov/programs/ofa/data-reports/caseload/caseload_current.htm.

40. Pamela M. Prah, "Why Are Welfare Rolls Flat, While the Food Stamp Program Grows Rapidly?," Stateline, July 2, 2012, www.pewstates.org/projects/stateline/headlines/why-are-welfare-rolls-flat-while-the-food-stamp-program-grows-rapidly-85899402294.

41. For a comprehensive account of this healthcare debate, see Haynes Johnson and David Broder, *The System: The Way of American Politics at the Breaking Point* (Boston: Little, Brown, 1996).

42. Ibid.

43. U.S. Census Bureau, "Income, Poverty and Health Insurance Coverage in the United States: 2011," September 12, 2012, www.census.gov/newsroom/releases/archives/income_wealth/cb12-172.html.

44. Kaiser Commission on Medicaid and the Uninsured, "The Uninsured: A Primer," October 2009, www.kff.org/uninsured/upload/7451-05.pdf.

45. Christopher Swope, "The Medicaid Windfall: Enjoy It While It Lasts," *Governing,* September 1998.

46. Medicaid expenditures grew at an annual rate of 27.1 percent from 1990 to 1992. Kaiser Commission on Medicaid and the Uninsured/Alliance for Health Care Reform, "Medicaid 101 Briefing Charts," Washington, DC, February 28, 2003.

47. Kaiser Commission on Medicaid and the Uninsured, "Enrolling Uninsured Low Income Children In Medicaid and SCHIP," Washington, DC, May 2002.

48. National Conference of State Legislatures, "NCSL Resources—SCHIP General Information," Washington, DC, 2009.

49. Kaiser Family Foundation, "Income Eligibility Limits for Children's Separate CHIP Programs by Annual Incomes and as a Percent of Federal Poverty Level, January 2012," January 2012, www.statehealthfacts.org/comparetable.jsp?ind=204&cat=4&sub=53&yr=257&typ=2&sort=a.

50. National Conference of State Legislatures, "Children's Health Insurance Program Overview," March 2010, http://ncsl.org/default.aspx?tabid=14510.

51. State Health Access Data Assistance Center, "The State of Kids' Coverage," Robert Wood Johnson Foundation, University of Minnesota, Minneapolis, August 9, 2006.

52. Lisa Dubay, Ian Hill, and Genevieve Kenney, "Five Things Everyone Should Know about SCHIP," Urban Institute, Washington, DC, October 2002.

53. Kaiser Family Foundation, "Health Insurance Coverage of Children 0–18," 2011, www.statehealthfacts.org/comparetable.jsp?ind=127&cat=3.

54. Kaiser Family Foundation, "Health Insurance Coverage of Children 0–18 Living in Poverty (under 100% FPL), States (2010–2011), U.S. (2011)," 2011, www.statehealthfacts.org/comparetable.jsp?ind=128&cat=3.

55. Vernon Smith, Dennis Roberts, David Rousseau, and Tanya Schwartz, "CHIP Enrollment: June 2009," Kaiser Commission on Medicaid and the Uninsured, April 2010, www.kff.org/medicaid/upload/7642-04.pdf.

56. John Holahan and Brend Spillman, "A Strong Safety Net Is Not the Same as Insurance," Urban Institute, January 15, 2002, www.urban.org/url.cfm?ID=31041.

57. Benjamin D. Sommers, Katherine Baicker, and Arnold M. Epstein, "Mortality and Access to Care among Adults after State Medicaid Expansions," *New England Journal of Medicine* 367 (2012): 1025–1034, www.nejm.org/doi/full/10.1056/NEJMsa1202099. Also see Amy Finkelstein, Sarah Taubman, Bill Wright, Mira Bernstein, Jonathan Gruber, Joseph P. Newhouse, Heidi Allen, and Katherine Baicker, "The Oregon Health Insurance Experiment: Evidence from the First Year," National Bureau of Economic Research Working Paper, July 2011, www.nber.org/papers/w17190.pdf.

58. Kaiser Family Foundation, "Health Insurance Coverage of Children 0–18."

59. National Association of Community Health Centers, "Health Centers at a Glance: Research Snapshots," 2012, www.nachc.com/Research%20Snapshots.cfm.

60. Bowen Garrett, Matthew Buettgens, Lan Doan, Irene Headen, and John Holahan, *The Cost of Failure to Enact Health Reform: 2010–2020* (Washington, DC: Urban Institute, 2010).

61. Obaid S. Zaman, Linda C. Cummings, and Sari Siegel Spieler, *America's Public Hospitals and Health Systems, 2008* (Washington, DC: National Public Health and Hospital Institute, 2010).

62. Katherine Vogt, "Public Hospitals Seen Slipping Away, Changing into Other Entities," American

Medical News, September 12, 2005, www.ama-assn.org/amednews/2005/09/12/bise0912.htm.

63. Kevin Sack, "Immigrants Cling to Fragile Lifeline at Safety-Net Hospital," *New York Times,* September 24, 2009, A16.

64. Agency for Healthcare Research and Quality, "Rural Health Care," U.S. Department of Health and Human Services, www.ahrq.gov/news/focus/focrural.htm.

65. Brian Heaton, "Will the Affordable Care Act Help Telehealth Flourish?," Government Technology, September 10, 2012, www.govtech.com/health/Will-the-Affordable-Care-Act-Help-Telehealth-Flourish.html.

66. Dylan Scott, "Telehealth's Chance to Revolutionize Health Care," *Governing,* October 2012.

67. Kaiser Family Foundation, "Medicaid Managed Care Enrollees as a Percent of State Medicaid Enrollees," July 1, 2010, www.statehealthfacts.org/comparetable.jsp?ind=217&cat=4&sub=56&yr=138&typ=2&sort=a.

68. Christine Vestal, "Accountable Care Explained: An Experiment in State Health Policy," Stateline, October 11, 2012, www.pewstates.org/projects/stateline/headlines/accountable-care-explained-an-experiment-in-state-health-policy-85899422676.

69. John Buntin (interview with Mike Bonetto, healthcare adviser to Oregon governor John Kitzhaber), "Coordinating More Care in Oregon," *Governing,* August 23, 2011, www.governing.com/topics/health-human-services/coordinating-more-care-oregon.html.

70. Quoted in John Buntin, "What Experts Think of Five Medicaid-Savings Strategies," *Governing,* August 31, 2011, www.governing.com/topics/health-human-services/what-experts-think-five-medicaid-savings-strategies.html.

71. Katherine Barrett, Richard Greene, and Michele Mariani, "Insurance Coverage: Access Denied," *Governing,* February 2004; Penelope Lemov, "Maine's Medical Gamble," *Governing,* November 2004; "Dirigo Agency Reaches Deal with Anthem to Extend DirigoChoice," Associated Press, September 22, 2006.

72. Debra J. Lipson, James M. Verdier, and Lynn Quincy, "Leading the Way? Maine's Initial Experience in Expanding Coverage through Dirigo Health Reforms," Mathematica Policy Research, December 2007, www.commonwealthfund.org/usr_doc/Lipson_leadingthewayMaineexpDirigo_1079.pdf?section=4039.

73. "No Maine Miracle Cure," *Wall Street Journal,* August 21, 2009, http://online.wsj.com/article/SB10001424052970204619004574322401816501182.html.

74. Sharon Anglin Treat, "Competing Lessons from Maine's Health Insurance Plan," *Wall Street Journal,* August 25, 2009, A14.

75. Anna C. Spencer, "Massachusetts Going for Full Coverage," *State Health Notes,* April 17, 2006, www.ncsl.org/programs/health/shn/2006/sn465.htm.

76. Richard Wolf, "Mass. Has Lessons for Health Care Debate," *USA Today,* July 23, 2009.

77. Christine Vestal, "Massachusetts Tackles Health Costs," Stateline, August 16, 2012, www.pewstates.org/projects/stateline/headlines/massachusetts-tackles-health-costs-85899411644.

78. Quoted in Jake Grovum, "Confusion in the Capitols," Stateline, April 8, 2010, www.stateline.org/live/printable/story?contentId=475804.

79. RAND Corporation, "Health Information Technology: Can HIT Lower Costs and Improve Quality?," RAND Health Research Highlights, 2005, www.rand.org/content/dam/rand/pubs/research_briefs/2005/RAND_RB9136.pdf.

80. Ellen Perlman, "Digitally Dazed," *Governing,* June 2007, www.governing.com/archive/archive/2007/jun/healthit.txt.

81. David Blumenthal, "Implementation of the Federal Health Information Technology Initiative," *New England Journal of Medicine* 365 (2011): 2426–2431, www.nejm.org/doi/full/10.1056/NEJMsr1112158.

82. Ellen Perlman, "Finding the Money for Health IT," *Governing,* October 6, 2009, www.governing.com/print/column/finding-money-health-it.

83. Darrell M. West and Allan Friedman, "Health Information Exchanges and Megachange," Brookings Institution, February 8, 2012, www.brookings.edu/~/media/Research/Files/Papers/2012/2/08%20health%20info%20exchange%20friedman%20west/0208_health_info_exchange_west.pdf.

84. Kaiser Family Foundation, "Distribution of Medicaid Enrollees by Enrollment Group, FY2009," 2009, www.statehealthfacts.org/comparetable.jsp?ind=200&cat=4&sub=52&yr=90&typ=2; Kaiser Family Foundation, "Distribution of Medicaid Payments by Enrollment Group, FY2009," 2009, www.statehealthfacts.org/comparetable.jsp?ind=858&cat=4&sub=47&yr=90&typ=4.

85. Molly O'Malley Watts, "The Community Living Assistance Services and Supports (CLASS) Act," Kaiser Commission on Medicaid and the Uninsured, October 2009, available at www.kff.org/healthreform/upload/7996.pdf.

86. Christine Vestal, "Hope for the Long Term," Stateline, April 15, 2010, www.stateline.org/live/details/story?contentId=477299.

87. Ibid.

88. Kaiser Commission on Medicaid and the Uninsured, "Medicaid and Long-Term Care Services and

Supports," June 2012, www.kff.org/medicaid/upload/2186-09.pdf.

89. See, for example, William Galston, "Live Long and Pay for It: America's Real Long-Term Cost Crisis," *The Atlantic,* September 12, 2012, www.theatlantic.com/business/archive/2012/09/live-long-and-pay-for-it-americas-real-long-term-cost-crisis/262247.

90. Vestal, "Hope for the Long Term."

91. Quoted in Aimee Curl, "Bracing for Bird Flu," *Federal Times,* April 10, 2006.

92. Janet Heinrich, "Public Health and Medical Preparedness," testimony before the Subcommittee on Public Health, Committee on Health, Education, Labor, and Pensions, U.S. Senate, Washington, DC, October 9, 2001.

93. Quoted in Robert Roos, "Pandemic Underscored Influenza's Unpredictability," CIDRAP News, April 23, 2010, www.cidrap.umn.edu/cidrap/content/influenza/swineflu/news/apr2310pandemic-jw.html.

94. Nicholas Kristof, "Shaming Young Mothers," *New York Times,* August 23, 2002; Jane Brody, "Abstinence-Only: Does It Work?," *New York Times,* June 1, 2004.

95. Erik W. Robelen, "Program Promoting Sexual Abstinence Gets Resurrected; Instructional Approach Winds Up in Health-Care Law," *Education Week,* April 7, 2010, 6.

96. Faye Flam, "Study Offers Nuanced View of Abstinence Education: Penn's Sex-Education Study," *McClatchy-Tribune Business News,* February 16, 2010.

97. Brady E. Hamilton and Stephanie J. Ventura, "Birth Rates for U.S. Teenagers Reach Historic Lows for All Age and Ethnic Groups," Centers for Disease Control and Prevention, April 2012, www.cdc.gov/nchs/data/databriefs/db89.pdf.

98. National Conference of State Legislatures, "Insurance Coverage for Contraception Laws," February 2012, www.ncsl.org/issues-research/health/insurance-coverage-for-contraception-state-laws.aspx.

99. Helene Cooper and Laurie Goodstein, "Rule Shift on Birth Control Is Concession to Obama Allies," *New York Times,* February 10, 2012, www.nytimes.com/2012/02/11/health/policy/obama-to-offer-accommodation-on-birth-control-rule-officials-say.html?_r=2&pagewanted=all&.

100. Jessica Arons and Elizabeth Rich, "State Efforts to Reject Contraceptive Coverage Laws on Religious Grounds," Center for American Progress, July 30, 2012, www.americanprogress.org/wp-content/uploads/issues/2012/07/pdf/state_contraception.pdf.

101. U.S. Centers for Disease Control and Prevention, "Obesity and Overweight," January 18, 2010, www.cdc.gov/nchs/fastats/overwt.htm; U.S. Centers for Disease Control and Prevention, "Adult Obesity Facts," August 13, 2012, www.cdc.gov/obesity/data/adult.html.

102. Cynthia Ogden and Margaret Carroll, "Prevalence of Obesity among Children and Adolescents: United States, Trends 1963–1965 through 2007–2008," U.S. Centers for Disease Control and Prevention, June 2010, www.cdc.gov/nchs/data/hestat/obesity_child_07_08/obesity_child_07_08.pdf.

103. Todd Zwillich, "CDC: Obesity Is Still an Epidemic," WebMD Health News, June 2, 2005, www.webmd.com/diet/news/20050602/cdc-obesity-is-still-epidemic.

104. Eric A. Finkelstein, Ian C. Fiebelkorn, and Guijing Wang, "National Medical Spending Attributable to Overweight and Obesity: How Much, and Who's Paying?," *Health Affairs,* May 14, 2003.

105. United Health Foundation, American Public Health Association, and Partnership for Prevention, "The Future Costs of Obesity: National and State Estimates of the Impact of Obesity on Direct Health Care Expenses," November 2009, www.fightchronicdisease.org/sites/fightchronicdisease.org/files/docs/CostofObesityReport-FINAL.pdf.

106. Anemona Hartocollis, "Calorie Postings Don't Change Habits, Study Finds," *New York Times,* October 6, 2009, www.nytimes.com/2009/10/06/nyregion/06calories.html?_r=1&.

107. Quoted in Josh Goodman, "Spread of Soda Taxes Fizzles," Stateline, February 14, 2012, www.pewstates.org/projects/stateline/headlines/spread-of-soda-taxes-fizzles-85899375415.

Chapter 16

1. Phone interview with Fran Pavley, October 23, 2009.

2. Joe Romm, "NY Governor Cuomo: 'Anyone Who Thinks That There Is Not a Dramatic Change in Weather Patterns Is Denying Reality,'" ThinkProgress, October 31, 2012, http://thinkprogress.org/climate/2012/10/31/1112301/ny-governor-cuomo-anyone-who-thinks-that-there-is-not-a-dramatic-change-in-weather-patterns-is-denying-reality/

3. Phone interview with Jessica Shipley, November 18, 2009.

4. Phone interview with Barry Rabe, December 8, 2008.

5. Marc Allen Eisner, *Governing the Environment: The Transformation of Environmental Regulation* (Boulder, CO: Lynne Rienner, 2007), 1.

6. Phone interview with John Cahill, December 5, 2008.

7. Barry G. Rabe, *Statehouse and Greenhouse: The Emerging Politics of American Climate Change Policy* (Washington, DC: Brookings Institution Press, 2004), xiv.

8. Quoted in ibid., 77.

9. Alan Greenblatt, "Fran Pavley: Legislative Prodigy," *Governing*, September 2002, 80.

10. Quoted in ibid.

11. Phone interview with Fran Pavley, September 3, 2002.

12. Phone interview with Stanley Young, November 21, 2008.

13. Quoted in Linda Greenhouse, "Justices Say EPA Has Power to Act on Harmful Gases," *New York Times*, April 8, 2007, A1.

14. Quoted in John M. Broder and Felicity Barringer, "EPA Says 17 States Can't Set Greenhouse Gas Rules for Cars," *New York Times*, December 20, 2007, A1.

15. Phone interview with Ron Burke, November 20, 2008.

16. Quoted in Janet Wilson, "EPA Chief Is Said to Have Ignored Staff," *Los Angeles Times*, December 21, 2007, A30.

17. Craig Pittman, "Crist Blasts EPA's Ruling," *St. Petersburg Times*, December 21, 2007, 1A.

18. John M. Broder, "Limits Set on Pollution from Autos," *New York Times*, April 2, 2010, B1.

19. "California Greening," *The Economist*, November 24, 2012, 36.

20. Quoted in Tom Arrandale, "Carbon Goes to Market," *Governing*, September 2008, 26.

21. Phone interview with C. Boyden Gray, April 5, 2010.

22. John M. Broder, "Obama to Open Offshore Areas to Drilling," *New York Times*, March 31, 2010, A1.

23. Quoted in Chelsea Waugaman, "Voltage Charge," *Governing*, November 2005, 76.

24. Quoted in Mannix Porterfield, "Manchin Wants Aggressive Renewable Energy Policy," (Beckley, WV) *Register-Herald*, October 20, 2008.

25. Michael Burnham, "Public Spending Drives Robust Growth in U.S. Geothermal Industry, Report Says," *New York Times*, April 13, 2010, www.nytimes.com/gwire/2010/04/13/13greenwire-public-spending-drives-robust-growth-in-us-geo-72049.html.

26. Phone interview with Margo Thorning, November 13, 2008.

27. Phone interview with Rabe.

28. Phone interview with Terry Tamminen, October 22, 2009.

29. Michael Hawthorne, "How Coal Got a Dirty Name," *Chicago Tribune*, July 9, 2008, 1.

30. Judy Pasternak, "Coal at Heart of Climate Battle," *Los Angeles Times*, April 14, 2008, A1.

31. Phone interview with Bob Eye, May 15, 2008.

32. Quoted in Alan Greenblatt, "Guarding the Greenhouse," *Governing*, July 2008, 21.

33. Steven Mufson, "The Coal Killer," *Washington Post*, November 25, 2012, G1.

34. Quoted in Alan Greenblatt, "Confronting Carbon," *Governing*, December 2008, 14.

35. Quoted in ibid.

36. Quoted in Alan Greenblatt, "Miami's Vision," *Governing*, November 2009, 15.

37. Quoted in ibid.

38. Dirk Johnson, "Chicago Unveils Multifaceted Plan to Curb Emissions of Heat-Trapping Gases," *New York Times*, September 19, 2008, A13.

39. Christopher Swope, "Lofty Goals," *Governing*, March 2009, 22.

40. Phone interview with R. T. Rybak, 2008.

41. Apollo Alliance, "The New Apollo Program: Clean Energy, Good Jobs," September 2008, www.apolloalliance.org/downloads/fullreportfinal.pdf.

42. "Current and Potential Green Jobs in the U.S. Economy," *Global Insight*, October 2008.

43. Phone interview with Pavley, 2009.

44. Phone interview with Eric Crawford, November 20, 2008.

45. Quoted in Anthony DePalma, "New Jersey Dealing with Solar Policy's Success," *New York Times*, June 25, 2008, B1.

46. Phone interview with Myron Ebell, November 19, 2008.

47. Quoted in Rana Foroohar, "The Real Green Revolution," *Newsweek*, April 12, 2010, 25.

48. Al Gore, "The Climate for Change," *New York Times*, November 9, 2008, WK10.

49. Michael Shellenberger and Ted Nordhaus, "A New Inconvenient Truth," *New Republic* Online, November 17, 2008, www.tnr.com/politics/story.html?id=971eed4b-1dc8-4afd-a8fe-193c373286ac.

50. Mireya Navarro and Rachel Nuwer, "Resisted for Blocking the View, Dunes Prove They Blunt Storms," *New York Times*, December 4, 2012, A1.

51. Quoted in Alan Feuer, "Protecting the City, before Next Time," *New York Times*, November 4, 2012, MB1.

52. Quoted in Alan Zarembo and Thomas H. Maugh II, "U.N. Says It's Time to Adapt to Warming," *Los Angeles Times*, November 17, 2007, A1.

53. Phone interview with Tom Adams, November 18, 2008.

54. Roger Pielke Jr., Gwyn Prins, Steve Rayner, and Daniel Sarewitz, "Lifting the Taboo on Adaptation," *Nature*, February 8, 2007, 445.

55. Quoted in Christopher Swope, "Local Warming," *Governing*, December 2007, 25.

56. Quoted in Greenblatt, "Confronting Warming," 10.

57. Anthony Faiola and Juliet Eilperin, "Dutch Defense against Climate Change: Adapt," *Washington Post*, December 6, 2009, A1.

58. Louise Bedsworth and Ellen Hanak, "Preparing California for a Changing Climate," Public Policy Institute of California, San Francisco, November 2008.

59. Chris Bowman, "California Bulks Up Defenses against Tide of Global Warming," *Sacramento Bee*, November 24, 2008, A1.

60. Quoted in Swope, "Local Warming," 25.

61. James Lawrence Powell, "Why Climate Deniers Have No Scientific Credibility," DeSmogBlog, November 15, 2012, www.desmogblog.com/2012/11/15/why-climate-deniers-have-no-credibility-science-one-pie-chart.

62. Frank Newport, "Americans' Worries about Global Warming Up Slightly," Gallup Politics, March 30, 2012, www.gallup.com/poll/153653/Americans-Worries-Global-Warming-Slightly.aspx.

63. Karla Adam and Juliet Eilperin, "Panel Clears 'Climate-Gate' Scientists," *Washington Post,* April 15, 2010, A6.

64. Quoted in Bill McKibben, "Record Snows on a Warming Planet," *Washington Post,* February 14, 2010, B1.

65. Quoted in Rachel Slajda, "Salazar: 'Cap and Trade' Not in the Lexicon Anymore," Talking Points Memo, March 31, 2010, http://tpmdc.talkingpointsmemo.com/2010/03/salazar-cap-and-trade-not-in-the-lexicon-anymore.php.

66. Phone interview with Karlyn Bowman, March 23, 2010.

67. Quoted in Alan Greenblatt, "How Republicans Learned to Reject Climate Change," NPR, March 25, 2010, www.npr.org/templates/story/story.php?storyId=125075282.

68. Phone interview with Jim DiPeso, March 23, 2010.

69. Quoted in William March, "Rubio Questions Climate Change," *Tampa Tribune,* February 13, 2010, 7.

70. Quoted in Andy Barr, "S.C. GOP Castigates Lindsey Graham," Politico, November 13, 2009, www.politico.com/news/stories/1109/29476.html.

71. Phone interview with DiPeso.

72. Phone interview with Daniel J. Weiss, March 19, 2010.

73. Ibid.

74. Quoted in Samantha Young, "Schwarzenegger Opens Climate Summit with Obama," Associated Press, November 19, 2008.

75. Quoted in John M. Broder, "Obama Affirms Climate Change Goals," *New York Times,* November 19, 2008, A4.

76. Phone interview with Terry Tamminen, March 29, 2010.

Glossary

abstinence: Refraining from sexual activity, usually intercourse. (Chapter 15)

accreditation: A certification process in which outside experts visit a school or college to evaluate whether it is meeting minimum quality standards. (Chapter 13)

activist judge: A judge who is said to act as an independent policymaker by creatively interpreting a constitution or statute. (Chapter 9)

adaptation: Taking steps to prepare for and deal with the effects of climate change. (Chapter 16)

ad hoc federalism: The process of choosing a state-centered or nation-centered view of federalism on the basis of political or partisan convenience. (Chapter 2)

affirmative action: A set of policies designed to help organizations recruit and promote employees who are members of disadvantaged groups. (Chapter 10)

Aid to Families with Dependent Children (AFDC): The original federal assistance program for women and their children, started under Roosevelt's New Deal. (Chapter 15)

alternative dispute resolution: A way to end a disagreement by means other than litigation. It usually involves the appointment of a mediator to preside over a meeting between the parties. (Chapter 9)

American Recovery and Reinvestment Act (ARRA): A $787 billion federal government package intended to stimulate economic growth during the recession of 2008–2009. (Chapter 4)

annexation: The legal incorporation of one jurisdiction or territory into another. (Chapter 12)

appeal: A request to have a lower court's decision in a case reviewed by a higher court. (Chapter 9)

appointment powers: A governor's ability to pick individuals to run state government, such as cabinet secretaries. (Chapter 8)

apportionment: The allotting of districts according to population shifts. The number of congressional districts that a state has may be reapportioned every ten years, following the national census. (Chapter 7)

appropriations bills: Laws passed by legislatures authorizing the transfer of money to the executive branch. (Chapter 3)

assigned counsel: Private lawyers selected by the courts to handle particular cases and paid from public funds. (Chapter 9)

at-large election: An election in which city or county voters vote for council or commission members from any part of the jurisdiction. (Chapter 11)

back to basics: A movement against modern education "fads" advocating a return to an emphasis on traditional core subjects such as reading, writing, and arithmetic. (Chapter 13)

balanced budget: A budget in which current expenditures are equal to or less than income. (Chapter 4)

ballot initiative: A process through which voters directly convey instructions to the legislature, approve a law, or amend the constitution. (Chapter 3)

bench trial: A trial in which no jury is present and a judge decides the facts as well as the law. (Chapter 9)

bicameral legislature: A legislature made up of two chambers, typically a house of representatives, or assembly, and a senate. (Chapter 3)

Bill of Rights: The first ten amendments to the Constitution, which set limits on the power of the federal government and set out the rights of individuals and the states. (Chapter 2)

blanket primary: An initial round of voting in which candidates from all parties appear on the same ballot, with the top two vote-getters proceeding on to the general election. (Chapter 5)

block grants: Federal grants-in-aid given for general policy areas that leave states and localities with wide discretion over how to spend the money within the designated policy area. (Chapter 2)

bonds: Certificates that are evidence of debts on which the issuer promises to pay the holders a specified amount of interest for a specified length of time and to repay the loans on their maturity. (Chapter 4)

broken windows policing: Policing that emphasizes maintaining public order, based on the theory that disorder unattended breeds crime. (Chapter 14)

budget deficit, or shortfall: Cash shortage that results when the amount of money coming into the government falls below the the amount being spent. (Chapter 4)

budget process: The procedure by which state and local governments assess revenues and set budgets. (Chapter 4)

building codes: Rules regarding the standards for structures; they mainly have to do with safety issues but sometimes also include requirements for things such as exterior pedestrian walkways. (Chapter 16)

bully pulpit: The platform from which a high-profile public official, such as governor or president, commands considerable public and media attention by virtue of holding office. (Chapter 8)

bureaucracy: Public agencies and the programs and services that they implement and manage. (Chapter 10)

bureaucrats: Employees of public agencies. (Chapter 10)

candidate-centered politics: Politics in which candidates promote themselves and their own campaigns rather than relying on party organizations. (Chapter 6)

cap and trade: A system for limiting pollution by assigning allowances to polluters, which can sell their excess permits if they succeed in reducing their emissions. (Chapter 16)

capital investments: Investments in infrastructure, such as roads. (Chapter 4)

capital outlays: A category of school funding that focuses on long-term improvements to physical assets. (Chapter 13)

carbon dioxide: A naturally occurring gas, the prevalence of which is increased by the burning of fossil fuels. (Chapter 16)

car-dependent living: A situation in which owning a car for transportation is a necessity; an outcome of low-density development. (Chapter 12)

casework: The work undertaken by legislators and their staffs in response to requests for help from constituents. (Chapter 7)

categorical grants: Federal grants-in-aid given for specific programs that leave states and localities with little discretion over how to spend the money. (Chapter 2)

caucus: All the members of a party—Republican or Democrat—within a legislative chamber. Also refers to meetings of members of a political party in a chamber. (Chapter 7)

cause lobbyist: A person who works for an organization that tracks and promotes an issue, for example, environmental issues for the Sierra Club or gun ownership rights for the National Rifle Association. (Chapter 6)

centralized federalism: The notion that the federal government should take the leading role in setting national policy, with state and local governments helping to implement the policies. (Chapter 2)

charter: A document that outlines the powers, organization, and responsibilities of a local government. (Chapter 11)

charter schools: Public schools, often with unique themes, managed by teachers, principals, social workers, or nonprofit groups. The charter school movement was launched in the early 1990s. (Chapter 13)

cities: Incorporated political jurisdictions formed to provide self-governance to particular localities. (Chapter 11)

city commission system: A form of municipal governance in which executive, legislative, and administrative powers are vested in elected city commissioners. (Chapter 11)

city council: A municipality's legislature. (Chapter 11)

city-county consolidation: The merger of separate local governments in an effort to reduce bureaucratic redundancy and service inefficiencies. (Chapter 12)

city manager: An official appointed to be the chief administrator of a municipality. (Chapter 11)

civil case: A legal case that involves a dispute between private parties. (Chapter 9)

Clean Air Act: The law, initially enacted in 1970, that provides authority for federal regulation of air pollution. (Chapter 16)

climate change: A shift in global temperatures. (Chapter 16)

closed primary: A nominating election in which only voters belonging to that party may participate. Only registered Democrats can vote in a closed Democratic primary, for example. (Chapter 6)

coalition building: The assembling of an alliance of groups to pursue a common goal or interest. (Chapter 7)

collective bargaining: A process in which representatives of labor and management meet to negotiate pay and benefits, job responsibilities, and working conditions. (Chapter 10)

colonial charters: Legal documents drawn up by the British Crown that spelled out how the colonies were to be governed. (Chapter 3)

commission-administrator system: A form of county governance in which executive and legislative powers reside with an elected commission, which hires a professional executive to manage the day-to-day operations of government. (Chapter 11)

committee: A group of legislators who have the formal task of considering and writing bills in a particular issue area. (Chapter 7)

common law: Law composed of judges' legal opinions that reflects community practices and evolves over time. (Chapter 14)

common school: In a democratic society, a school in which children of all income levels attend at taxpayer expense. (Chapter 13)

community, or restorative, justice movement: A movement that emphasizes nontraditional punishment, such as community service. (Chapter 14)

community policing: An approach that emphasizes police officers' forming relationships with neighborhood residents and engaging with them in collaborative problem solving. (Chapter 14)

compact theory: The idea that the Constitution represents an agreement among sovereign states to form a common government. (Chapter 2)

comparative method: A learning approach based on studying the differences and similarities among similar units of analysis (such as states). (Chapter 1)

compromise: The result when there is no consensus on a policy change or spending amount but legislators find a central point on which a majority can agree. (Chapter 7)

concurrent powers: Powers that both federal and state governments can exercise. These include the power to tax, borrow, and spend. (Chapter 2)

confederacy: Political system in which power is concentrated in regional governments. (Chapter 2)

constituents: Residents of a district. (Chapter 7)

constituent service: The work done by legislators to help residents in their voting districts. (Chapter 7)

constitutional amendments: Proposals to change a constitution, typically enacted by a supermajority of the legislature or through a statewide referendum. (Chapter 3)

constitutional convention: An assembly convened for the express purpose of amending or replacing a constitution. (Chapter 3)

constitutional revision commission: An expert committee formed to assess a constitution and suggest changes. (Chapter 3)

contract attorney: A private attorney who enters into an agreement with a state, county, or judicial district to work on a fixed-fee basis per case or for a specific length of time. (Chapter 9)

contracting out: Government hiring of private or nonprofit organizations to deliver public goods or services. (Chapter 10)

contract lobbyist: A lobbyist who works for different causes for different clients in the same way that a lawyer represents more than one client. (Chapter 6)

cooperative federalism: The notion that it is impossible for state and national governments to have separate and distinct jurisdictions and that both levels of government must work together. (Chapter 2)

council-executive system: A form of county governance in which legislative powers are vested in a county commission and executive powers are vested in an independently elected executive. (Chapter 11)

council-manager system: A form of municipal governance in which the day-to-day administration of government is carried out by a professional administrator. (Chapter 11)

counties: Geographical subdivisions of state government. (Chapter 11)

county commission system: A form of county governance in which executive, legislative, and administrative powers are vested in elected commissioners. (Chapter 11)

court of first instance: The court in which a case is introduced and nothing has been determined yet. (Chapter 9)

criminal case: A legal case brought by the state intending to punish a violation of the law. (Chapter 9)

criterion-referenced test: A standardized test designed to gauge a student's level of mastery of a given set of materials. (Chapter 13)

crosscutting requirements: Constraints that apply to all federal grants. (Chapter 2)

crossover sanctions: Federal requirements mandating that grant recipients pass and enforce certain laws or regulations as a condition of receiving funds. (Chapter 2)

crossover voting: Members of one party voting in another party's primary. This practice is not allowed in all states. (Chapter 6)

dealignment: The lack of nationwide dominance by any one political party. (Chapter 6)

delegates: Legislators who primarily see their role as voting according to their constituents' beliefs as they understand them. (Chapter 7)

department of education: A state-level agency responsible for overseeing public education. (Chapter 13)

determinate sentencing: The sentencing of an offender, by a judge, to a specific amount of time in prison depending on the crime. (Chapter 9)

deterrence theory: A theory advanced by criminologists that harsh penalties will deter people from committing crimes. (Chapter 14)

devolution: The process of taking power and responsibility away from the federal government and giving it to state and local governments. (Chapter 1)

Dillon's Rule: The legal principle that says local governments can exercise only the powers granted to them by state government. (Chapter 11)

direct democracy: A system in which citizens make laws themselves rather than relying on elected representatives. (Chapter 3)

direct lobbying: A form of lobbying in which lobbyists deal directly with legislators to gain their support. (Chapter 6)

discretionary jurisdiction: The power of a court to decide whether or not to grant review of a case. (Chapter 9)

discretionary spending: Spending controlled in annual appropriations acts. (Chapter 4)

district: The geographical area represented by a member of a legislature. (Chapter 7)

dividend: A payment made to stockholders (or, in Alaska's case, residents) from the interest generated by an investment. (Chapter 4)

drug court: A special tribunal that offers nonviolent drug offenders a chance at reduced or dismissed charges in exchange for their undergoing treatment or other rehabilitation; an alternative forum for sentencing nonviolent drug offenders. (Chapter 14)

dual constitutionalism: A system of government in which people live under two sovereign powers. In the United States, these are the government of their state of residence and the federal government. (Chapter 3)

dual federalism: The idea that state and federal governments have separate and distinct jurisdictions and responsibilities. (Chapter 2)

edgeless cities: Office and retail complexes without clear boundaries. (Chapter 12)

electorate: The population of individuals who can vote. (Chapter 3)

Elementary and Secondary Education Act: Federal law passed in 1965 as part of President Johnson's Great Society

initiative; steered federal funds to improve local schools, particularly those attended primarily by low-income and minority students. (Chapter 13)

en banc: Appeals court sessions in which all the judges hear a case together. (Chapter 9)

entitlement: A service that government must provide, regardless of the cost. (Chapter 4)

entitlement program: A government-run program that guarantees unlimited assistance to those who meet its eligibility requirements, no matter how high the cost. (Chapter 15)

enumerated powers: Grants of authority explicitly given by the Constitution. (Chapter 2)

establishment: The nexus of people holding power over an extended period of time, including top elected officials, lobbyists, and party strategists. (Chapter 6)

estate taxes: Taxes levied on a person's estate or total holdings after that person's death. (Chapter 4)

excise, or sin, taxes: Taxes on alcohol, tobacco, and other similar products that are designed to raise revenues and reduce use. (Chapter 4)

exclusive powers: Powers given by the Constitution solely to the federal government. (Chapter 2)

executive orders: Rules or regulations with the force of law that governors can create directly under the statutory authority given them. (Chapter 8)

expenditures: Money spent by government. (Chapter 4)

exurbs: Municipalities in rural areas that ring suburbs. They typically serve as bedroom communities for the prosperous, providing rural homes with easy access to urban areas. (Chapter 12)

factional splits, or factions: Groups that struggle to control the message within a party; for example, a party may be split into competing regional factions. (Chapter 6)

federalism: Political system in which national and regional governments share powers and are considered independent equals. (Chapter 2)

felony: A serious crime, such as murder or arson. (Chapter 9)

filibuster: A debate that under U.S. Senate rules can drag on, blocking final action on the bill under consideration and preventing other bills from being debated. (Chapter 7)

fiscal federalism: The system by which federal grants are used to fund programs and services provided by state and local governments. (Chapter 4)

fiscal year: The annual accounting period used by a government. (Chapter 4)

focused consumption taxes: Taxes that do not alter spending habits or behavior patterns and therefore do not distort the distribution of resources. (Chapter 4)

for cause challenge: A lawyer's asking the judge to excuse a potential juror because the individual appears to be biased or unable to be fair. (Chapter 9)

formal powers: The powers explicitly granted to a governor according to state law, such as being able to veto legislation and to appoint heads of state agencies. (Chapter 8)

Fourteenth Amendment: Constitutional amendment that prohibits states from depriving individuals of the rights and privileges of citizenship and requires states to provide due process and equal protection guarantees. (Chapter 2)

fracking: A process in which water, sand, and chemicals are pumped into the ground to enable the extraction of natural gas and oil. (Chapter 16)

franchise: The right to vote. (Chapter 3)

full faith and credit clause: Constitutional clause that requires states to recognize each other's public records and acts as valid. (Chapter 2)

general act charter: A charter that grants powers, such as home rule, to all municipal governments within a state. (Chapter 11)

general election: A decisive election in which all registered voters cast ballots for their preferred candidates for a political office. (Chapter 6)

general equivalency diploma (GED) program: A program offering a series of tests that an individual can take to qualify for a high school equivalency certificate or diploma. (Chapter 13)

general jurisdiction trial court: A court that hears any civil or criminal cases that have not been assigned to a special court. (Chapter 9)

general obligation bonds: Investments secured by the taxing power of the jurisdiction that issues them. (Chapter 4)

general revenue sharing grants: Federal grants-in-aid given with few constraints, leaving states and localities almost complete discretion over how to spend the money. (Chapter 2)

general welfare clause: Constitutional clause that gives Congress an implied power through the authority to provide for the "general welfare." (Chapter 2)

gentrification: The physical rehabilitation of urban areas, which attracts investment from developers and drives up property values. (Chapter 12)

gerrymanders: Districts clearly drawn with the intent of pressing partisan advantage at the expense of other considerations. (Chapter 7)

gift taxes: Taxes imposed on money transfers made during an individual's lifetime. (Chapter 4)

global warming: Rising average temperatures worldwide. (Chapter 16)

Goals 2000: The Educate America Act, signed into law in March 1994, which provided resources to states and communities to ensure that all students could reach their full potential. (Chapter 13)

grand jury: A group of between sixteen and twenty-three citizens who decide if a case should go to trial; if the grand jury decides that it should, an indictment is issued. (Chapter 9)

grants-in-aid: Cash appropriations given by the federal government to the states. (Chapter 2)

greenhouse gases: Emissions—primarily carbon dioxide but also other gases such as methane—that are believed to contribute to global warming. (Chapter 16)

green jobs: Occupations that contribute to environmental sustainability. (Chapter 16)

habitual offender laws: Statutes imposing harsher sentences on offenders who previously have been sentenced for crimes. (Chapter 9)

high-stakes standardized testing: Testing of elementary and secondary students in which poor results can mean either that students fail to be promoted or that the school loses its accreditation. (Chapter 13)

home rule: A form of self-governance granted to towns and cities by the state. (Chapter 3) The right of a locality to self-government, usually granted through a charter. (Chapter 11)

homeschooling: The education of children in the home; a movement to grant waivers from state truancy laws to permit parents to teach their own children. (Chapter 13)

impact fees: Fees that municipalities charge builders of new housing or commercial developments to help offset the costs of extending services. (Chapter 12)

impeachment: A process by which the legislature can remove executive branch officials, such as the governor, or judges from offices for corruption or other reasons. (Chapter 8)

implied powers: Broad, but undefined, powers given to the federal government by the Constitution. (Chapter 2)

income taxes: Taxes on wages and interest earned. (Chapter 4)

incumbent: A person holding office. (Chapter 7)

independent expenditures: Funds spent on ad campaigns or other political activities that are run by a party or an outside group without the direct knowledge or approval of a particular candidate for office. (Chapter 6)

indeterminate sentencing: The sentencing of an offender, by a judge, to a minimum and a maximum amount of time in prison, with a parole board deciding how long the offender actually remains in prison. (Chapter 9)

indictment: A formal criminal charge. (Chapter 9)

indirect lobbying: A form of lobbying in which lobbyists build support for their cause through the media, rallies, and other ways of influencing public opinion, with the ultimate goal of swaying legislators to support their cause. (Chapter 6)

individualistic culture: A political culture that views politics and government as just another way to achieve individual goals. (Chapter 1)

informal powers: The things a governor is able to do, such as command media attention and persuade party members, based on personality or position, not on formal authority. (Chapter 8)

insurance trust funds: Money collected from contributions, assessments, insurance premiums, and payroll taxes. (Chapter 4)

interest groups: Individuals, corporations, or associations that seek to influence the actions of elected and appointed public officials on behalf of specific companies or causes. (Chapter 6)

intergovernmental transfers: Funds provided by the federal government to state governments and by state governments to local governments. (Chapter 4)

interjurisdictional agreement (IJA): A formal or informal agreement between two or more local governments to cooperate on a program or policy. (Chapter 12)

intermediate appellate court: A court that reviews court cases to find possible errors in their proceedings. (Chapter 9)

interstate commerce clause: Constitutional clause that gives Congress the right to regulate interstate commerce. This clause has been broadly interpreted to give Congress a number of implied powers. (Chapter 2)

Jim Crow laws: Legislative measures passed in the last decade of the nineteenth century that sought to systematically separate blacks and whites. (Chapter 3)

judicial federalism: The idea that the courts determine the boundaries of state-federal relations. (Chapter 3)

judicial review: The power of courts to assess whether a law is in compliance with the constitution. (Chapter 3)

jury nullification: A jury's returning a verdict of "not guilty" even though jurists believe the defendant is guilty. By doing so, the jury cancels out the effect of a law that the jurors believe is immoral or was wrongly applied to the defendant. (Chapter 9)

Kentucky Education Reform Act: The 1990 law passed in response to court findings of unacceptable disparities among schools in Kentucky; considered the most comprehensive state school reform act to date. (Chapter 13)

Kyoto Protocol: A 1997 international treaty that sought to reduce emissions of greenhouse gases. (Chapter 16)

laboratories of democracy: A metaphor that emphasizes the states' ability to engage in different policy experiments without interference from the federal government. (Chapter 1)

leapfrog development: Development practices in which new developments jump—or leapfrog—over established developments, leaving undeveloped or underdeveloped land between developed areas. (Chapter 12)

legislative overcriminalization: The tendency of government to make a crime out of anything the public does not like. (Chapter 9)

liability: A legal obligation or responsibility. (Chapter 9)

limited, or special jurisdiction, trial court: A court that hears cases that are statutorily limited by either the degree of seriousness or the types of parties involved. (Chapter 9)

line-item veto: The power to reject a portion of a bill while leaving the rest intact. (Chapter 3)

local education agency (LEA): A school district, which may encompass a city, a county, or a subset thereof. (Chapter 13)

logrolling: The practice in which a legislator gives a colleague a vote on a particular bill in return for that colleague's vote on another bill to be considered later. (Chapter 7)

low-density development: Development practices that spread (rather than concentrate) populations across the land. (Chapter 12)

magistrate: A local official or attorney granted limited judicial powers. (Chapter 9)

majority-minority district: A district in which members of a minority group, such as African Americans or Hispanics, make up a majority of the population or electorate. (Chapter 7)

majority rule: The process in which the decision of a numerical majority is made binding on a group. (Chapter 7)

malapportionment: A situation in which the principle of equal representation is violated. (Chapter 7)

managed care: An arrangement for the provision of healthcare whereby an agency acts as an intermediary between consumers and healthcare providers. (Chapter 15)

mandatory jurisdiction: The requirement that a court hear every case presented before it. (Chapter 9)

mandatory minimum sentence: The shortest sentence that an offender may receive upon conviction for a certain offense. The court has no authority to impose a shorter sentence. (Chapter 9)

mayor: The elected chief executive of a municipality. (Chapter 11)

mayor-council system: A form of municipal governance in which there is an elected executive and an elected legislature. (Chapter 11)

Medicaid: A joint state and federal health insurance program that serves low-income mothers and children, the elderly, and people with disabilities. (Chapter 15)

Medicare: The federal health insurance program for elderly citizens. (Chapter 15)

megaregion: An urban area made up of several large cities and their surrounding urban areas that creates an interlocking economic and social system. (Chapter 12)

merit system: A system used in public agencies in which employment and promotion are based on qualifications and demonstrated ability; such a system blends very well with the organizational characteristics of bureaucracy. (Chapter 10)

metropolitan area: A populous region typically comprising a city and surrounding communities that have a high degree of social and economic integration. (Chapter 12)

metropolitan planning organization (MPO): A regional organization that decides how federal transportation funds are allocated within that regional area. (Chapter 12)

metropolitan statistical area (MSA): An area with a city of 50,000 or more people together with adjacent urban communities that have strong ties to the central city. (Chapter 12)

misdemeanor: A less serious crime, such as shoplifting. (Chapter 9)

mitigation: Reduction of emissions of greenhouse gases and other steps taken to curb the forces that cause climate change. (Chapter 16)

model constitution: An expert-approved generic or "ideal" constitution that states sometimes use as a yardstick against which they can measure their existing constitutions. (Chapter 3)

moralistic culture: A political culture that views politics and government as the means to achieve the collective good. (Chapter 1)

municipal bonds: Bonds issued by states, counties, cities, and towns to fund large projects as well as operating budgets. Income from such bonds is exempt from federal taxes and from state and local taxes for the investors who live in the state where they are issued. (Chapter 4)

municipal charter: A document that establishes operating procedures for a local government. (Chapter 3)

municipalities: Political jurisdictions, such as cities, villages, or towns, incorporated under state law to provide governance to defined geographical areas; more compact and more densely populated than counties. (Chapter 11)

National Assessment of Educational Progress (NAEP): The only regularly conducted, independent survey of what a nationally representative sample of students in grades four, eight, and twelve know and can do in various subjects; known as "the nation's report card." (Chapter 13)

National PTA: Umbrella organization founded in 1897 consisting of state-based and school-based parent–teacher associations of volunteers who work to improve and support schools. (Chapter 13)

national supremacy clause: Constitutional clause that states that federal law takes precedence over all other laws. (Chapter 2)

nation-centered federalism: The belief that the nation is the basis of the federal system and that the federal government should take precedence over the states. (Chapter 2)

natural law, or higher law: A set of moral and political rules based on divine law and binding on all people. (Chapter 3)

necessary and proper clause: Constitutional clause that gives Congress an implied power through the right to pass all laws considered "necessary and proper" to carry out the federal government's responsibilities as defined by the Constitution. (Chapter 2)

neutral competence: The idea that public agencies should be the impartial implementers of democratic decisions. (Chapter 10)

New Federalism: The belief that states should receive more power and authority and less money from the federal government. (Chapter 2)

New Urbanism: A design movement that seeks to promote walkable communities through transit-oriented, mixed-use development. (Chapter 16)

No Child Left Behind Act (NCLB): Federal law enacted in January 2002 that introduced new accountability measures for elementary and secondary schools in all states receiving federal education aid. (Chapter 13)

nonpartisan ballot: A ballot that does not list candidates by political party; this type of ballot is still often used in local elections. (Chapter 6)

nonpartisan election: An election in which the candidates do not have to declare party affiliation or receive a party's nomination; local offices and elections are often nonpartisan. (Chapter 5)

norm-referenced test: A standardized test designed to measure how a student's mastery of a set of materials compares with that of a specially designed sampling of students determined to be the national "norm" for that age group. (Chapter 13)

nullification: The process of a state's rejecting a federal law and making it invalid within state borders. (Chapter 2)

obesity: The medical condition of being excessively overweight; defined as having a body mass index (BMI) of more than 25. (Chapter 15)

office group (Massachusetts) ballot: A ballot in which candidates are listed by name under the title of the office they are seeking. (Chapter 5)

open primary: A nominating election that is open to all registered voters regardless of their party affiliations. (Chapter 6)

oversight: The legislature's role in making sure that the governor and executive branch agencies are properly implementing the laws. (Chapter 7)

pandemic: An outbreak of a disease that spreads across a large geographical area and affects a high proportion of the population. (Chapter 15)

panel: A group of (usually) three judges who sit to hear cases in a state court of appeals. (Chapter 9)

parole: Supervised early release from prison. (Chapter 14)

party column (Indiana) ballot: A ballot in which the names of candidates are divided into columns arranged according to political party. (Chapter 5)

party convention: A meeting of party delegates called to nominate candidates for office and establish party agendas. (Chapter 6)

patronage: The practice of elected officials or party leaders handing out jobs to their friends and supporters rather than hiring people based on merit. (Chapter 6) The process of giving government jobs to partisan loyalists. (Chapter 10)

peremptory challenge: A lawyer's dismissal of a potential juror for any reason except race or gender. (Chapter 9)

plea bargain: An agreement in which the accused in a criminal case admits guilt, usually in exchange for a promise that a particular sentence will be imposed. (Chapter 9)

plenary power: Power that is not limited or constrained. (Chapter 3)

plural executive system: A state government system in which the governor is not the dominant figure in the executive branch but, instead, is more of a first among equals, serving alongside numerous other officials who were elected to their offices rather than being appointed by the governor. (Chapter 5)

plurality: The highest number of votes garnered by any of the candidates for a particular office but short of an outright majority. (Chapter 5)

polarization: A split among elected officials or an electorate along strictly partisan lines. (Chapter 6)

policy implementation: The process of translating the express wishes of government into action. (Chapter 10)

political action committee: A group formed for the purpose of raising money to elect or defeat political candidates. PACs traditionally represent business, union, or ideological interests. (Chapter 6)

political culture: The attitudes and beliefs broadly shared in a polity about the role and responsibility of government. (Chapter 1)

political machines: Political organizations controlled by small numbers of people and run for partisan ends. In the nineteenth and twentieth centuries these organizations controlled party nominations for public office and rewarded supporters with government jobs and contracts. (Chapter 6)

political parties: Organizations that nominate and support candidates for elected offices. (Chapter 6)

poverty line, or poverty threshold: An annual income level, set by the federal government, below which families cannot afford basic necessities. (Chapter 15)

precedent: In law, the use of the past to determine current interpretation and decision making. (Chapter 9)

preemption: The process of the federal government overriding areas regulated by state law. (Chapter 2)

prejudicial error: An error that affects the outcome of a case. (Chapter 9)

primary election: An election that determines a party's nominees for offices in a general election against other parties' nominees. Participation in a primary election is sometimes limited to voters registered as members of that particular party. (Chapter 6)

privileges and immunities clause: Constitutional clause that prohibits states from discriminating against citizens of other states. (Chapter 2)

probation: Supervised punishment in the community. (Chapter 14)

professionalization: The process of providing legislators with the resources they need to make politics their main career, such as making their positions full-time or providing them with full-time staff. (Chapter 7) The rewarding of jobs in a bureaucratic agency based on applicants' specific qualifications and merit. (Chapter 10)

professional model of policing: An approach to policing that emphasizes professional relations with citizens, police independence, police in cars, and rapid responses to calls for service. (Chapter 14)

progressive tax system: A system of taxation in which the rate paid reflects ability to pay. (Chapter 4)

prosecutor: A government official and lawyer who conducts criminal cases on behalf of the people. (Chapter 9)

public choice model: A model of politics that views governments and public services in market terms; governments are seen as producers of public services and citizens are seen as consumers. (Chapter 12)

public defender: A government lawyer who provides free legal services to persons accused of crimes who cannot afford to hire lawyers. (Chapter 9)

public health: Area of medicine that addresses the protection and improvement of citizen health and hygiene through the work of government agencies. (Chapter 15)

pure appointive system: A judicial selection system in which the governor appoints judges alone, without preselection of candidates by a nominating commission. (Chapter 9)

rank-and-file members: Legislators who do not hold leadership positions or senior committee posts. (Chapter 7)

ratification: A vote of the entire electorate to approve a constitutional change, referendum, or ballot initiative. (Chapter 3)

realignment: The switching of popular support from one party to another. (Chapter 6)

recall: A way for voters to oust an incumbent politician prior to the next regularly scheduled election; they collect signatures to qualify the recall proposal for the ballot and then vote on the ouster of the politician. (Chapter 5)

recall election: A special election allowing voters to remove an elected official from office before the end of his or her term. (Chapter 8)

recidivism: A return to, or relapse into, criminal behavior. (Chapter 9) The tendency of criminals to relapse into criminal behavior and be returned to prison. (Chapter 14)

Reconstruction: The period following the Civil War when the southern states were governed under the direction of the Union army. (Chapter 3)

recusal: The disqualification of a judge because of an actual or perceived bias or conflict of interest calling the judge's impartiality into question. (Chapter 9)

redistricting: The drawing of new boundaries for congressional and state legislative districts, usually following a decennial census. (Chapters 5 and 7)

reentry program: A program designed to ease released prisoners' return to society and thus prevent recidivism. (Chapter 14)

referendum: A procedure that allows the electorate to either accept or reject a law passed by the legislature. (Chapter 3)

reform perspective: An approach to filling gaps in service and reducing redundancies in local governments that calls for regional-level solutions. (Chapter 12)

regional council: A planning and advisory organization whose members include multiple local governments. Regional councils often are used to administer state and federal programs that target regions. (Chapter 12)

regressive taxes: Taxes levied on all taxpayers, regardless of income or ability to pay; they tend to place proportionately more of a burden on those with lower incomes. (Chapter 4)

renewable energy: Power generated using natural sources that can be replenished, such as wind and solar energy, as opposed to nonrenewable fossil fuels. (Chapter 16)

representation: Individual legislators acting as the voices of their constituencies within the house of representatives or senate. (Chapter 7)

representative bureaucracy: The idea that public agencies that reflect the diversity of the communities they serve will be more effective. (Chapter 10)

representative government: A form of government in which citizens exercise power indirectly by choosing representatives to legislate on their behalf. (Chapter 2)

responsible party model: The theory that political parties offer clear policy choices to voters, try to deliver on those policies when they take office, and are held accountable by voters for the success or failure of those policies. (Chapter 6)

retention election: An election in which a judge runs uncontested and voters are asked to vote yes or no on the question of whether they wish to retain the judge in office for another term. (Chapter 9)

revenue bonds: Investments secured by the revenue generated by a state or municipal project. (Chapter 4)

revenues: The money governments bring in, mainly from taxes. (Chapter 4)

rider: An amendment to a bill that is not central to the bill's intent. (Chapter 7)

rocket docket: Fast-tracked cases that often have limited, specific deadlines for specific court procedures. (Chapter 9)

rulemaking: The process of translating laws into written instructions on what public agencies will or will not do. (Chapter 10)

runoff primary: An election held if no candidate receives a majority of the vote during the regular primary. The two top finishers face off again in a runoff to determine the nominee for the general election. Such elections are held only in some states, primarily in the South. (Chapter 6)

rural flight: The movement of youth and the middle class from rural areas to more urban areas. (Chapter 12)

sales taxes: Taxes levied by state and local governments on purchases. (Chapter 4)

school board: An elected or appointed body that determines major policies and budgets for a school district. (Chapter 13)

school district: A local administrative jurisdiction that hires staff and reports to a school board on the management of area public schools. (Chapter 13)

school voucher movement: Movement dating to the 1950s to allow taxpayer dollars to be given to families to use at whatever public, private, or parochial schools they choose. (Chapter 13)

secession: The process of a government or political jurisdiction withdrawing from a political system or alliance. (Chapter 2)

secret (Australian) ballot: A ballot printed by a state that allows voters to pick and choose among different candidates and party preferences in private. (Chapter 5)

seniority: The length of time a worker has spent in a position. (Chapter 10)

separation of powers: The principle that government should be divided into separate legislative, executive, and judicial branches, each with its own powers and responsibilities. (Chapter 3)

settlement: A mutual agreement between parties to end a civil case before going to trial. (Chapter 9)

severance taxes: Taxes on natural resources removed from a state. (Chapter 4)

site-based management: A movement to increase freedom for building administrators such as school principals to determine how district funds are spent at individual schools. (Chapter 13)

smart growth: Environmentally friendly development practices, particularly those that emphasize more efficient infrastructure and less dependence on automobiles. (Chapter 12)

smog: A type of air pollution; the word comes from the combination of *smoke* and *fog*. (Chapter 16)

sociodemographics: The characteristics of a population, including size, age, and ethnicity. (Chapter 1)

soft money: Money not subject to federal regulation that can be raised and spent by state political parties. A 2002 law banned the use of soft money in federal elections. (Chapter 6)

sovereign immunity: The right of a government to not be sued without its consent. (Chapter 2)

special act charter: A charter that grants powers, such as home rule, to a single municipal government. (Chapter 11)

special district: A local governmental unit created for a single purpose, such as water distribution. (Chapter 11)

spoils system: A system under which an electoral winner has the right to decide who works for public agencies. (Chapter 10)

sprawl: The rapid growth of a metropolitan area, typically as a result of specific types of zoning and development. (Chapters 12 and 16)

standards: In education, fixed criteria for learning that students are expected to reach in specific subjects by specific grade years. (Chapter 13)

standards movement: An effort to create benchmarks of adequate learning in each subject for each grade level so that students and teachers can be evaluated on the mastery of this predetermined material. (Chapter 13)

state board of education: Top policymaking body for education in each of the fifty states, usually consisting of appointees selected by the governor. (Chapter 13)

state-centered federalism: The belief that states are the basis of the federal system and that state governments should take precedence over the federal government. (Chapter 2)

State Children's Health Insurance Program (CHIP): A joint federal-state program designed to expand healthcare coverage to children whose parents earned income above the poverty line but still were too poor to afford insurance. (Chapter 15)

states' rights: The belief that states should be free to make their own decisions with little interference from the federal government. (Chapter 2)

state supreme court: The highest level of appeals court in a state. (Chapter 9)

straight ticket: Originally, a type of ballot that allowed voters to pick all of one party's candidates at once; today,

voting a straight ticket refers to voting for all of one party's candidates for various offices—for instance, voting for all Democrats or all Republicans. (Chapter 5)

street-level bureaucrat: A lower-level public agency employee who actually takes the actions that represent law or policy. (Chapter 10)

strong mayor system: A municipal government in which the mayor has the power to perform the executive functions of government. (Chapter 11)

successful schools model: An education model that uses observed spending levels in the highest-performing schools as the basis from which to calculate necessary spending in other, lower-performing schools. (Chapter 13)

supermajority vote: A legislative vote of much more than a simple majority, for instance, a vote by two-thirds of a legislative chamber to override a governor's veto. (Chapter 8)

supermax security prison: A high-security prison designed to house violent criminals. (Chapter 14)

super PAC: A political action committee that can spend unlimited funds on behalf of a political candidate but cannot directly coordinate its plans with that candidate. (Chapter 6)

superpredators: Ultraviolent youth who experts at one time predicted would further drive up the nation's crime rate. (Chapter 14)

swing voters: Individuals who are not consistently loyal to candidates of any one party. They are true independents whose allegiance is fought for in every election. (Chapter 6)

tailpipe emissions: Greenhouse gases released by cars and other vehicles. (Chapter 16)

tax burden: A measurement of taxes paid as a proportion of income. (Chapter 4)

tax capacity: A measure of the ability to pay taxes. (Chapter 4)

tax effort: A measure of taxes paid relative to the ability to pay taxes. (Chapter 4)

teacher licensure procedures: The processes states use to qualify teacher candidates to work in school districts; requirements for licensing typically include attainment of certain academic degrees, work experience, and adequate performance on adult standardized tests. (Chapter 13)

teachers' unions: Public-sector unions that organize employees at all educational levels to form state and local affiliates. In the United States, the two major teachers' unions are the National Education Association and the American Federation of Teachers, both headquartered in Washington, D.C. (Chapter 13)

Temporary Assistance to Needy Families (TANF): The next-generation welfare program (passed in 1996) that provides federal assistance in the form of block grants to states, which have great flexibility in designing their programs. (Chapter 15)

Tenth Amendment: Constitutional amendment guaranteeing a broad, but undefined, set of powers be reserved for the states and the people. (Chapter 2)

ticket splitting: Voters' or districts' voting for different parties' nominees for different offices—for instance, supporting a Republican for president while supporting a Democrat for Congress. (Chapter 6)

Tiebout model: A model of local government based on market principles wherein a metro area is made up of a series of micropolitical jurisdictions that, on the basis of their services and costs, attract or repel certain citizens. (Chapter 12)

town meeting form of government: A form of governance in which legislative powers are held by the local citizens. (Chapter 11)

townships: Local governments whose powers, governance structure, and legal status vary considerably from state to state. In some states, townships function as general-purpose municipalities; in others, they are geographical subdivisions of counties with few responsibilities and little power. (Chapter 11)

traditionalistic culture: A political culture that views politics and government as the means of maintaining the existing social order. (Chapter 1)

Trends in International Mathematics and Science Study (TIMSS): A regularly updated study launched by the United States in 1995 that compares the performance in science and mathematics of students in forty-six countries. (Chapter 13)

trial court: The first level of the court system. (Chapter 9)

trustees: Legislators who believe they were elected to exercise their own judgment and to approach issues accordingly. (Chapter 7)

truth-in-sentencing laws: Laws that give parole boards less authority to shorten sentences for good behavior by specifying the proportion of a sentence an offender must serve before becoming eligible for parole. (Chapter 9)

unfunded mandates: Federal laws that direct state action but provide no financial support for that action. (Chapter 2)

unicameral legislature: A legislature having only one chamber. Nebraska is currently the only state with a unicameral legislature. (Chapter 3)

unitary system: Political system in which power is concentrated in a central government. (Chapter 2)

urban growth boundary (UGB): A border established around urban areas that is intended to control the density and type of development. (Chapter 12)

U.S. Environmental Protection Agency (EPA). The federal agency charged with protecting the environment. (Chapter 16)

user fees: Charges levied by governments in exchange for services. Such fees constitute a type of hidden tax. (Chapter 4)

variance: The difference between units of analysis on a particular measure. (Chapter 1)

verdict: A jury's finding in a trial. (Chapter 14)

veto: The power to reject a proposed law. (Chapter 8)

voir dire: The interviewing and examination of potential jurors by the attorneys for both sides of a case. (Chapter 9)

voter identification: When a voter identifies strongly with one of the major parties, he or she is considered a Democrat or a Republican; many voters, however, are considered weakly aligned with either major party. (Chapter 6)

voter turnout: The percentage of voting-eligible citizens who register to vote and do vote. (Chapter 5)

ward, or district, election: An election in which voters in a municipal ward vote for a candidate to represent them on a council or commission. (Chapter 11)

wards: Divisions of municipalities, usually representing electoral districts of the city council. (Chapter 11)

weak mayor system: A municipal government in which the mayor lacks true executive powers, such as the ability to veto council decisions or appoint department heads. (Chapter 11)

weatherization: The practice of protecting buildings from the elements (for example, by installing insulation) both to improve their habitability and to cut down on energy use. (Chapter 16)

white flight: A demographic trend in which the middle and upper classes leave central cities for predominantly white suburbs. (Chapter 12)

zoning laws: Regulations that control how land can be used. (Chapters 12 and 16)

Photo Credits

Index

Figures, maps, notes and tables are indicated by *f*, *m*, *n* or *t* following the page number. Alphabetization is letter-by-letter (e.g., "Warner" precedes "War on Drugs").

Health Security Act, 485–486

Heart of Atlanta Motel v. United States (1964), 50–51

Heineman, Dave, 263

Heiney, Joseph, 404

Help America Vote Act (HAVA), 123

Hendrick, Rebecca, 403–404

Henig, Jeffrey, 434

Herbers, John, 49

Herrnson, Paul, 145–146

Hibbing, John, 227

Higher education, 4–6

Higher law, 62

High-stakes standardized testing, 411, 420–422

Highways, as expenditure, 107

Hill, Steven, 126

Hinkle, Robert L., 131

Hispanics, 128, 222–223t. *See also* Minorities

"The Historical Context of Voter Photo-ID Laws" (Davidson), 146

HMOs (health maintenance organizations), 486–487, 489–491

Hodges, Luther, 242

"Holding Mayors Accountable: New York's Executives from Koch to Bloomberg" (Douglas & Carnes), 374–375

Home rule, 82, 108, 367–369

Homeschooling, 430

Hood, M. V., III, 146

Horsford, Steve, 220

Hospitals, 478–479, 488–489

Hotzclaw, Bill, 228

House arrest, 305

Houston, Texas, 422

Hove Mobile Park, North Dakota, 349

Hoxby, Caroline, 417

Hrebenar, Ronald J., 186

Hubbard, Kathy, 371

Hultman, Nathan, 521

Humphrey, Hubert H., 163

Hunstein, Carol, 278

Hunt, Guy, 261

Hunter, Tye, 300

Hurst, Julia, 263

Hynes, Emma, 498–499

Ice, 460–461

Idaho, 106f

"The Ideological Mapping of American Legislatures" (Shor & Nolan), 189

IJA (interjurisdictional agreements), 391

Illinois
- Chicago, 360, 526
- corruption in, 359
- courts in, 281, 282–283f
- local governments, 352
- state constitutions and, 281

Imberman, Scott, 435

Immigration
- Arizona and, 53
- changing attitudes towards, 27–28

literacy threshold for voting and, 125

state-level regulation of, 28, 48

Impact fees, 385

"The Impact of Ballot Type on Voter Errors" (Herrnson et al.), 145–146

Impartial Justice Act, 310

Impeachment, 260–261

Implied powers, 35

Incarceration rates, 444m, 450–451

Income, 128, 136–137

Income taxes, 93–94, 94t

Incumbents, 203

In Defense of Judicial Elections (Bonneau & Hall), 311–312

Independent expenditures, 167

Independents, 175–178

Indeterminate sentencing, 303–304, 450

Indiana, 263

Indiana Ballots, 120–121

Indictments, 296

Indigent defense, 295, 297–299

Indirect lobbying, 183

Individualistic cultures, 11–14, 13m

Informal powers of governors, 243

Initiatives. *See* Ballot initiatives

Inmates. *See* Crime; Reentry programs

Innocence projects, 458, 461

Instant-runoff voting (IRV), 121–122

Insurance trust funds, 95

Integrated family courts, 307

Intensive probation, 305

Interest groups
- cause campaigns, 179
- defined, 117, 152
- incumbents favored by, 183–184
- influence of, 185t
- political parties and, 152–153, 156–157
- public opinion and, 143–144
- school board elections and, 413–414
- types of, 180
- in Wisconsin, 174–175
- *See also* Lobbying

Intergovernmental Panel on Climate Change, 522

Intergovernmental transfers, 95–98

Interjurisdictional agreements (IJA), 391

Intermediate appellate courts, 279, 282–285

Intermodal Surface Transportation Efficiency Act of 1991 (ISTEA), 390

Internet
- Anaheim, California, 398
- media coverage of legislature in, 230
- public opinion and use of, 141
- taxes on sales using, 91
- *See also* Social media

Interstate commerce clause, 36t, 50, 52

Invisible Children, 179

Iowa
- redistricting in, 215
- rural flight and, 401m, 401–402
- same-sex marriage, 276–277

Lorillard Tobacco Co. v. Reilly (2001), 52
Los Angeles Police Department (LAPD), 452–453, 459
Lotteries, 414
Louisiana
    drinking age, 197
    governor power in, 237–238
    Napoleonic Code, 442
    oil spill and, 510
Loveless, Tom, 427–428
Loving v. Virginia (1967), 75
Low-density development, 384–385
Lunsford, Jessica Marie, 198
Lupia, Arthur, 84
Lynch, John, 256
Lynch, Mary Ann, 309

Madison, James, 37, 79
Magistrates, 308
Mah, Ann, 268
Maine, 218, 292, 492
Majority-minority districts, 216–217
Majority rule, 193
Malapportionment, 215
Managed care, 486–487, 489–491
Management by objectives (MBO), 338
Manchin, Joe, 510–511
Mandatory jurisdiction, 284
Mandatory minimum sentences, 304
Mann, Horace, 410–411
Mansell, Al, 217
Manyika, James, 520
Marble cake federalism, 40–42, 41*f*
Marcellus Shale, 514
Maricopa County, Arizona, 300
Marijuana, 448–450
Marriage, 75. *See also* Same-sex marriage
Marshall, John, 50
Martell, Christine, 375
Martin, Trayvon, 182
Martinez, Susana, 256
Maryland, 126, 241, 515, 522
Maryland ex. rel. Washington County v. Baltimore & Ohio Railroad Co. (1845), 352
Masket, Seth, 188–189, 232
Massachusetts
    constituents lawmaking role, 198–199
    county corruption in, 355–357
    environmental protections, 506
    healthcare, 492
    insurance coverage, 488
    judicial budget issues, 309
    property tax limits, 93
    same-sex marriage, 276
Massachusetts Ballots, 120–121
Massachusetts Bay Company, 65
Massachusetts v. EPA (2007), 508, 513
Massie, Thomas, 151–152, 158
Mayor-council systems, 358–359, 360*f*
Mayors, 357, 374–375

MBO (management by objectives), 338
McCain-Feingold campaign financing law, 168
McCarthy, Eugene, 163
McCarty, Nolan, 189
McConnell, Glenn, 249
McConnell, Mitch, 115
McCrory, Pat, 257, 260
McCulloch v. Maryland (1819), 39, 50
McDonald's, 496
McDonough, John, 213
McGehee, Meredith, 169
McGovern, George, 163
McGreevey, Jim, 261
McNulty, John, 146
McWherter, Ned, 252
"Measuring Citizen and Government Ideology in the U.S. States: A Re-appraisal" (Berry et al.), 23
"Measuring Gubernatorial Budgetary Power: A New Approach" (Krupnikov & Shipan), 270
Mecham, Evan, 140, 261
Media
    crime and, 440–441
    governor use of, 252, 255
    judicial candidates and, 291
    legislative coverage by, 197, 202–203, 226–230
    lobbying and, 183
    political advertising, 165, 174–175
    public opinion of legislature and, 227–228
    See also Internet
Mediation, 307
Medicaid
    Affordable Care Act and, 471–472
    creation of, 480
    defined, 471
    eligibility for, 481, 482–483*t*
    growth of, 474–475
    HMOs and, 487
    increasing costs of, 105, 481–483, 558*n*46
    long-term care, 494–495
    waivers about, 483–484
Medicare, creation of, 480
Medinger, John, 207
Megaregions, 382–383. *See also* Metropolitics
Melzer, Scott, 462
Mental illness, 457
Mergers, 391–396, 394*t*, 425
Merit selection, 286–287, 292–293, 310
Merit systems, 332–337, 336
Messner, Marcus, 179
Methamphetamine, 460–461
Metro (Oregon), 388–389
Metropolitan areas, 382. *See also* Metropolitics
Metropolitan planning organizations (MPO), 389–392
Metropolitan statistical areas (MSA), 382, 382*m*, 383*t*. *See also* Metropolitics
Metropolitics
    annexation, 396–397
    benefits of multiple governments, 397–400

Oil production, 510
Oklahoma
    earthquakes, 515
    native groups in, 364
    supreme courts in, 285
    TANF in, 474
O'Laughlin, David, 395
Oliver, Thomas, 498–499
O'Malley, Martin, 241
O'Neill, Robert, Jr., 373
Open primaries, 162–163
Ordinances, 364
Oregon
    income taxes, 93
    long-term care costs, 494
    methamphetamine and, 460
    Metro, 388–389
O'Rourke, P. J., 207
Orton, Josh, 168

PACs, 152. *See also* Super PACs
Palin, Sarah, 525
Pandemics, 472, 495
Panels, 284–285
Pardons, 246–249
Parishes. *See* Counties
Parish jurors, 355
Parker, Annise, 371
Parker, Tom, 280
Parole, 451
Partial vetos, 78
Parties. *See* Political parties
Party column ballots, 120–121
Party conventions, 162
Party machines. *See* Political machines
Pataki, George, 245
Paterson, David A., 256
Patient Protection and Affordable
    Care Act (Obamacare)
    contraception covered by, 495–496
    federalism and, 53
    state expenditures and, 105
    Supreme Court ruling on, 471–472, 493
Patients' bill of rights, 489–491
Patrick, Deval, 256
Patronage, 161, 331
Pavley, Fran, 502–504, 506
Pawlenty, Tim, 525
PBM (performance-based management), 338
Peel, Robert, 452
Pelosi, Nancy, 115
Pence, Stephen, 263
Pendergast, Tom, 286
Pendleton Act (1883), 332
Penitentiaries, 444–445
Penn, William, 446–447
Pennsylvania
    Allegheny County, 379–380
    constitution of, 67

legislature in, 221–223
    voter ID laws, 131
Pensions, budget issues with, 107–108
Peremptory challenges, 301
Performance audits, 327
Performance-based management (PBM), 338
Perot, Ross, 176–177
Perry, Rick, 245
Personal Responsibility and Work Opportunity
    Reconciliation Act (1996), 47, 484
Petrucione, Jennifer, 142
Pfeifer, Paul E., 290
Phillips, Justin H., 245
Phillips, Thomas, 292
Pickerill, J. Mitchell, 54–55
Picket fence federalism, 41*f*, 42–45
Pinchback, P. B. S., 256
Piston, Spencer, 84
Plea bargains, 279, 297
Plenary power, 62–63
Plethysmograph tests, 303–304
Plural executive systems, 132
Plurality, 117
Point sources of pollution, 385
Pokalsky, Kenneth, 509
Polarization of politics, 152
Police
    community policing, 453–456, 459
    crime rate and, 440
    as problem solvers, 452
    professional model of, 452–453, 459
    virtual precincts, 459
    See also Crime
Police protection, as expenditure, 107
Policy implementation by bureaucracies, 319–320
Policymaking, 19–20, 333
Political action committees (PACs), 152.
    See also Super PACs
Political advertising, 165, 174–175
Political candidates, 142–144, 152
Political culture
    defined, 9–10
    effects of, 9–14, 12*t*, 13*m*, 14*t*
    individualistic cultures, 11–14, 13*m*
    moralistic cultures, 10–11, 13*m*, 13–14
    parties effect on, 172–173
    research on, 22–24
    tax variations and, 98–99
    traditionalistic cultures, 13*m*, 13–14
Political data mining, 116
"Political Decision- Making and the Local Provision
    of Public Goods: The Case of Municipal Climate
    Protection in the U.S." (Krause), 530
Political machines
    bureaucracy and, 331
    defined, 160
    lack of expansion of, 173
    local governments and, 359–360
    overview, 160–162

United governments, 212
United States v. Darby Lumber Co. (1941), 50
United States v. Lopez (1995), 52
United States v. Morrison (2000), 52
Units of analysis, 7
Universities and colleges, 4–6
University of Denver, 325
University of North Carolina (UNC), 3–4
University of North Colorado, 324
Unplanned growth, 386
Urban growth boundaries (UGB), 389
Urban sprawl, 384–386, 389, 397, 513–517
U.S. Constitution
    compact theory and, 39–40
    elections and, 120
    enactment of, 30
    federalism and, 34–38, 36*t*, 38*f*
    federal judges and, 286, 294
    judicial federalism, 60
    state constitutions compared, 62–65
    See also Bill of Rights; *Individual amendments*
U.S. Department of Education, 411–412
U.S. Environmental Protection Agency
    (EPA), 505, 508
User fees, 89, 95
U.S. Supreme Court
    Affordable Care Act ruling, 471–472, 493
    cooperative federalism and, 41–42
    dual federalism and, 40
    interpretation of federalism by, 50–53, 51*t*
    on political parties, 167
    state court cases and, 280
Utah, 9, 72

Variances, 7
Vaughan, Robert, 446
VAWA (Violence Against Women Act), 52
Velázquez, Nydia, 371
Ventura, Jesse, 256
"Verbal Style, Gubernatorial Strategies, and Legislative
    Success" (Crew & Lewis), 269–270
Verdicts, 443
Vermont
    debt allowed in, 64
    health information technology, 494
    insurance coverage, 488
    political culture of, 12, 12*t*
    school funding, 416
Vetos
    defined, 240
    governor power in, 244–246, 247–248*t*, 253–254*t*
    line-item vetos, 77–78, 245–246
    partial vetos, 78
    supermajority votes to overcome, 240–241
Victim-impact statements, 302
Victims' rights, 302
Villages. *See* Municipalities
Vilsack, Tom, 249, 402
Violence Against Women Act (VAWA), 52

Virginia
    ballot access in, 122
    bureaucracy in, 328–329*f*
    governor's mansion, 77
    judicial selection, 292
    legislative deadlock in, 196–197
    school board elections and, 414
    vote counting in, 123
    voting restrictions in, 66
Virginia Company of London, 65
Virtual precincts, 459
Voir dire, 301
Volunteers, 340
von Bismarck, Otto, 479
Von Hagen-Jamar, Alexander, 84
Vote counting, 123
Voter fraud, 125, 130–131
Voter identification, 159
Voter ID laws, 130–131, 146
Voter registration, 124–126
Voters
    characteristics of, 116–117
    party identification of, 178
    restrictions on, 124–126, 130–131
    swing voters, 155
    See also Political participation
Voter turnout
    age and, 128, 173
    ballot initiatives and, 119, 139–140
    defined, 126
    overview, 126–129, 127*t*
    polling location and, 146
    voter ID laws and, 146
Votes, popular versus electoral, 117–118
Vote trading, 194, 213
Voting
    ballot types for, 120–121
    felons and, 451–452
    instant-runoff voting, 121–122
    restrictions on, 66–68
    See also Elections
Voting Rights Act (1965), 125
Voting Rights Act (1982), 217
Vouchers, 428–430

Wachtler, Sol, 296
Wade, Tork, 490
Wages, as expenditure, 103
Walker, Scott, 140, 187, 260, 261, 334
Ward elections, 370
Wards, 359
Ware, Stephen, 290
Warner, Mark, 256
War on drugs, 448–450
Washington
    drug sentencing, 448
    environmental adaptation in, 522–523
    local environmental efforts in, 526–527
    primary elections in, 163

⑤SAGE researchmethods

The essential online tool for researchers from the world's leading methods publisher

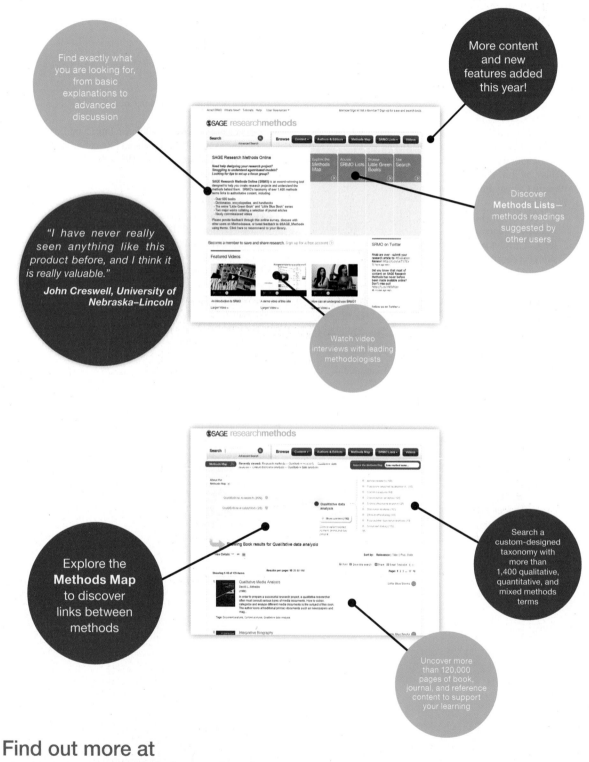

Find exactly what you are looking for, from basic explanations to advanced discussion

More content and new features added this year!

Discover **Methods Lists**— methods readings suggested by other users

"I have never really seen anything like this product before, and I think it is really valuable."

John Creswell, University of Nebraska–Lincoln

Watch video interviews with leading methodologists

Explore the **Methods Map** to discover links between methods

Search a custom-designed taxonomy with more than 1,400 qualitative, quantitative, and mixed methods terms

Uncover more than 120,000 pages of book, journal, and reference content to support your learning

Find out more at
www.sageresearchmethods.com